CONSTITUTIONAL AND ADMINISTRATIVE LAW

PEARSON

We work with leading authors to develop the strongest educational
materials in law, bringing cutting-edge thinking
and best learning practice to a global market.

Under a range of well-known imprints, including Longman,
we craft high quality print and electronic publications which
help readers to understand and apply their content,
whether studying or at work.

To find out more about the complete range of our
publishing, please visit us on the World Wide Web at:
www.pearsoned.co.uk

CONSTITUTIONAL AND ADMINISTRATIVE LAW

Fifteenth Edition

A W Bradley MA LLM, LLD (Hon)

Emeritus Professor of Constitutional Law,
University of Edinburgh;
Barrister, of the Inner Temple;
Institute of European and Comparative Law,
University of Oxford

K D Ewing LLB PhD

Professor of Public Law,
King's College, London

**Longman
is an imprint of**

Harlow, England • London • New York • Boston • San Francisco • Toronto
Sydney • Tokyo • Singapore • Hong Kong • Seoul • Taipei • New Delhi
Cape Town • Madrid • Mexico City • Amsterdam • Munich • Paris • Milan

Pearson Education Limited
Edinburgh Gate
Harlow
Essex CM20 2JE
England

and Associated Companies throughout the world

Visit us on the World Wide Web at:
www.pearsoned.co.uk

First edition 1931 (E C S Wade and G G Phillips)
Second edition 1935 (E C S Wade and G G Phillips)
Third edition 1946 (E C S Wade and G G Phillips)
Fourth edition 1950 (E C S Wade and G G Phillips)
Fifth edition 1955 (E C S Wade)
Sixth edition 1960 (E C S Wade)
Seventh edition 1965 (E C S Wade and A W Bradley)
Eighth edition 1970 (E C S Wade and A W Bradley)
Ninth edition 1977 (A W Bradley)
Tenth edition 1985 (A W Bradley)
Eleventh edition 1993 (A W Bradley and K D Ewing)
Twelfth edition 1997 (A W Bradley and K D Ewing)
Thirteenth edition 2003 (A W Bradley and K D Ewing)
Fourteenth edition 2007 (A W Bradley and K D Ewing)
Fifteenth edition 2011 (A W Bradley and K D Ewing)

© Pearson Education Limited 2011

ISBN: 978-1-4058-7350-5

British Library Cataloguing-in-Publication Data
A catalogue record for this book is available from the British Library

Library of Congress Cataloging-in-Publication Data
Bradley, A. W. (Anthony Wilfred)
Constitutional and administrative law / A.W. Bradley, K.D. Ewing. – 15th ed.
p. cm.
Includes bibliographical references and index.
ISBN 978-1-4058-7350-5
1. Constitutional law – Great Britain. 2. Administrative law – Great Britain.
I. Title.
KD3930.W3 2010
342.41—dc22
2010023415

10 9 8 7 6 5 4 3 2 1
14 13 12 11 10

Typeset in 10.5/11.5pt Dante by 35
Printed and bound by Ashford Colour Press Ltd, Gosport, Hampshire

BRIEF CONTENTS

CONTENTS

PREFACE

In October 2009, the new Supreme Court of the United Kingdom opened for business, in a building at Westminster that had formerly been the Middlesex Guildhall but converted and refurbished to provide a fitting home for the most senior court in the land. This, however, did not mark a dramatic change in the constitutional law of the United Kingdom, the appellate jurisdiction of these twelve senior judges remaining essentially the same as when justice was dispensed by them in the House of Lords.

In May 2010, a keenly fought general election produced an outcome which disappointed each of the three main parties. Labour lost the majority in the House of Commons that it had enjoyed for 13 years, the Conservatives failed to win a controlling majority in the Commons, and the Liberal Democrats secured fewer seats than favourable opinion polls had suggested was possible. The result within a week was the formation of the first peace-time coalition government for eighty years, with the presence of two political parties round the Cabinet table and in the corridors of Whitehall making it necessary to reconsider many traditional practices in the fields of government and politics.

These two events (the creation of the Supreme Court and the formation of a coalition government) provide very different illustrations of constitutional change in the United Kingdom: the former being a significant change in law, but with little direct impact on constitutional practice; the latter being a radical change in constitutional and political practice, but without any necessary change in the law. By contrast with both these events, the cataclysmic affair of parliamentary expenses that occurred in the summer of 2009 had profound effects on the law relating to MPs, with the enactment of the Parliamentary Standards Act 2009 and its early amendment in 2010. The affair also led to many changes in the public's attitude to Parliament, and in the conduct of MPs and the political parties.

In this new edition, we include material dealing with the most significant developments in the United Kingdom's public law since 2006. The period we cover was intended to be until the end of 2009, but in some chapters we have been able to include an indication of later events that occurred before Parliament was dissolved in April 2010. Developments since 2006 have caused every chapter to be revised and in parts rewritten. These include the continuing interplay between the operation of laws against terrorism and the protection of fundamental rights, the clash between official secrecy and the cause of justice in respect of torture and inhuman treatment, the continuing effects within the United Kingdom of EU law and European human rights law, the strain imposed on the electoral system by the extent to which political parties depend on funding from wealthy individuals, the creation for the first time of a system of tribunals affecting potentially the whole of government, the effects of the financial crisis and the government's forced entry into the business of banking, and changes in the law relating to the armed forces with the introduction of a unified code for the armed services.

Our aim, as in previous editions, has been to provide an informed overview of the most significant judicial decisions, new legislation by Parliament, and changing practices in government. We have tried to maintain a balance that reflects the evolution of public law while also bringing recent events into focus. In this edition, we have given some priority to restricting the strong tendency that the book has of growing longer with every new edition. In some areas the text has been reduced a little and the amount of detail pruned, in order to ensure that the central purposes of the book remain clear.

As in previous editions, we have joint responsibility for the whole book, but chapters 1–7, 11, 15, 20 and 27–32 have been revised by AWB and all other chapters by KDE. *Case references* are where possible to the main Law Reports, failing which to WLR or All ER; for cases since 2001, the footnotes include the neutral case citations. We draw attention here to the Case Navigator system, details of which are given in the inside cover, and which it is hoped may encourage readers of the book to go on to read and analyse the leading decisions of the courts on which much of the law is founded. The aim of the *bibliography* is not to provide a comprehensive list of all publications on the public law of the United Kingdom, but simply to provide a convenient list of published books that are cited in the text: it does not include entries for periodicals or official publications, committee reports etc.

We acknowledge the help and guidance that many individuals have given us, including Michael Adler, Sarah Fraser-Butlin, Steven Churches, Cathryn Costello, Peter Davis, Sionaidh Douglas-Scott, Janet Hiebert, Chris Himsworth, David Howarth, Alastair Mowbray, Graeme Orr, Jacob Rowbottom, Caroline Sawyer, and Joo-Cheong Tham, but this acknowledgment is of course subject to the customary disclaimer. We have again been much helped by the Maughan Library at King's College London, the Squire Law Library, Cambridge, the Inner Temple Library, and the Bodleian Law Library, Oxford.

We must express our warm thanks to the team from Pearson Education, notably Zoe Botterill, Philippa Fiszzon, Robert Chaundy, and Sue Gard, who have enabled this edition to appear, despite our inveterate tendency to overrun any deadline that they set us. We also wish to thank the publishers for giving us valuable help with the bibliography and for having prepared the tables (Sarah Beauchamp-Gregory) and index (Kim Harris).

Finally, we are indebted to Kathleen and Gail for (among many other things) giving us a sense of perspective while we have been preparing this edition.

Anthony Bradley
Keith Ewing
June 2010

TABLE OF LEGISLATION

United Kingdom Statutes

United Kingdom Orders and Statutory Instruments

Legislation from other jurisdictions

International conventions

TABLE OF CASES

Cases preceded by an asterisk are Case Navigator cases.
Please see the inside front cover and the Preface for details about Case Navigator.

[Note. In this table, many of the longer entries have been shortened; thus the names of many public authorities and companies are not given in full. The abbreviation 'SSHD' has been used in place of 'Secretary of State for the Home Department' or 'Home Secretary'.]

ABBREVIATIONS

In addition to the standard abbreviations used for the citation of reported cases, the following abbreviations are used for the principal journals and other sources cited.

ACD	*Administrative Court Digest*
AJCL	*American Journal of Comparative Law*
AJIL	*American Journal of International Law*
ALJ	*Australian Law Journal*
APS	*Acts of Parliament of Scotland*
BHRC	*Butterworths Human Rights Cases*
BNIL	*Bulletin of Northern Ireland Law*
BYIL	*British Yearbook of International Law*
CL	*Current Law*
CLJ	*Cambridge Law Journal*
CLP	*Current Legal Problems*
CJQ	*Civil Justice Quarterly*
CMLR	*Common Market Law Reports*
CML Rev	*Common Market Law Review*
COD	*Crown Office Digest*
CPR	Civil Procedure Rules
Crim LR	*Criminal Law Review*
Edin LR	*Edinburgh Law Review*
EHRLR	*European Human Rights Law Review*
EHRR	*European Human Rights Reports*
ELR	*Education Law Reports*
EL Rev	*European Law Review*
Harv L Rev	*Harvard Law Review*
HC	House of Commons Paper
HC Deb	House of Commons Debates (Hansard)
HEL	Sir William Holdsworth, *A History of English Law*
HL	House of Lords Paper
HL Deb	House of Lords Debates (Hansard)
HLE	*Halsbury's Laws of England* (4th edn, 1973 onwards)
HRLR	*Human Rights Law Review*
ICLQ	*International and Comparative Law Quarterly*
ICON	*International Journal of Constitutional Law*
ILJ	*Industrial Law Journal*
J Civ Lib	*Journal of Civil Liberties*
JR	*Judicial Review*
JSSL	*Journal of Social Security Law*
Jur R	*Juridical Review*
Kilbrandon Report	Report of Royal Commission on the Constitution, vol. 1, Cmnd 5460, 1973
LQR	*Law Quarterly Review*
LS	*Legal Studies*
MLR	*Modern Law Review*
MPR	Report of Committee of Ministers' Powers, Cmd 4060, 1932
NIJB	*Northern Ireland Judgment Bulletin*

NILQ	*Northern Ireland Legal Quarterly*
NLJ	*New Law Journal*
OJLS	*Oxford Journal of Legal Studies*
PL	*Public Law*
SI	Statutory Instrument
SLT	*Scots Law Times*
SO	Standing Order
TEU	Treaty on European Union (Maastricht, 1992)
WA	Written Answer
YBEL	*Yearbook of European Law*

Part I

GENERAL PRINCIPLES OF CONSTITUTIONAL LAW

CHAPTER 1

Definition and scope of constitutional law

The starting point for studying constitutional law should ideally be the same starting point as for studying political philosophy or the role of law and government in society. How is individual freedom to be reconciled with the claims of social justice? Is society founded upon a reciprocal network of rights and duties, or is the individual merely a pawn in the hands of state power?

These fundamental questions are often not pursued explicitly in the study of constitutional law. In fact, constitutional law concerns the relationship between the individual and the state, seen from a particular viewpoint, namely the notion of law. As a historian stated: 'It is inherent in the especial character of law, as a body of rules and procedures, that it shall apply logical criteria with reference to standards of universality and equity.'[1] Law is not merely a matter of the rules which govern relations between private individuals (for example between employer and employee or between landlord and tenant). Law also concerns the structure and powers of the state. The constitutional lawyer is always likely to insist that the relations between the individual and the state should be founded upon and governed by law.

But law does not exist in a social and political vacuum. Within a given society, the legal rules that concern relations between employer and employee will reflect that society's attitude to work and employment. So too the rules of constitutional law that govern political relations will, within a given society, reflect a particular distribution of political power. In a stable society, constitutional law expresses what may be a very high degree of consensus about the organs and procedures by which political decisions are taken. But when, within a community, political decisions are taken by recourse to armed force, gang warfare or the might of terrorist violence, the rules of constitutional law are either non-existent or, at best, no more than a transparent cover for a power struggle that is not conducted in accordance with anything deserving the name of law.

Within a stable democracy, constitutional law reflects the value that people attach to orderly human relations, to individual freedom under the law and to institutions such as Parliament, political parties, free elections and a free press. Now the reality is often different from the rhetoric. Laws are the product of human decisions, not the gift of an omniscient deity. As Lord Acton said: 'Power tends to corrupt and absolute power tends to corrupt absolutely.' But the weaknesses and imperfections of human nature are a reason for law, not a reason for discarding law as a means of regulating political conduct. The rules of football are often broken. But if we shoot the referee and tear up the rules, football as an organised activity ceases to exist.

Total disbelief in the value of the individual or in the possibility of public good is therefore a bad starting point for studying constitutional law. But there is no need to go to the other extreme and hold the belief, fiercely savaged by Jeremy Bentham, that in Great Britain we have a 'matchless constitution'.[2] We ought not to be dominated by the lessons which our ancestors learned about constitutional government; nor should we reject those lessons out of hand or from sheer ignorance. A modest claim founded on the past may be made – that constitutional law is one branch of human learning and experience that helps to make life in today's world more tolerable and less brutish than it might otherwise be. But we are unlikely ever to find that any one system of constitutional law has attained a level of perfect effectiveness.

---

[1] Thompson, *Whigs and Hunters*, p 262.
[2] Bentham, *Handbook of Political Fallacies*, pp 154–63.

What is a constitution?

Applied to the system of law and government by which the affairs of a modern state are administered, the word constitution has two main meanings. In its narrower meaning, a constitution means a document having a special legal status which sets out the framework and principal functions of the organs of government within the state and declares the principles or rules by which those organs must operate. In countries in which the constitution has overriding legal force, there is often a high-ranking court which applies and interprets the text of the constitution in disputed cases. Such a court is the Supreme Court in the USA or Canada, or the Federal Constitutional Court in Germany. In these countries, legislative or executive acts may be held by the court to be without legal force where they conflict with the constitution.

In this sense of the word, the United Kingdom of Great Britain and Northern Ireland has no constitution. There is no single document from which is derived the authority of the main organs of government, such as the Crown, the Cabinet, Parliament and the courts of law. No written text lays down the relationship of the primary organs of government one with another or with the people.[3] But the word constitution has a wider meaning. As Bolingbroke stated in 1733:

> By constitution we mean, whenever we speak with propriety and exactness, that assemblage of laws, institutions and customs, derived from certain fixed principles of reason, directed to certain fixed objects of public good, that compose the general system, according to which the community hath agreed to be governed.[4]

In more modern words, constitution in this wider sense refers to 'the whole system of government of a country, the collection of rules which establish and regulate or govern the government'.[5] In this sense, the United Kingdom has a constitution since it has a complex and comprehensive system of government, which has been called 'one of the most successful political structures ever devised'.[6] This system is founded partly on Acts of Parliament and judicial decisions, partly upon political practice and partly upon detailed procedures established by the various organs of government for carrying out their own tasks, for example the law and custom of Parliament or the rules issued by the Prime Minister to regulate the conduct of ministers.[7]

The wider sense of the word constitution necessarily includes a constitution in the narrower sense. In Canada, the USA, India and many other states, the written constitution occupies the primary place among the 'assemblage of laws, institutions and customs' which make up the constitution in the wider sense. But no written document alone can ensure the smooth working of a system of government. Around a written constitution will evolve a wide variety of customary rules and practices which adjust its working to changing conditions.[8] These customary rules and practices may be more easily changed than the constitution itself: their constant evolution will reduce the need for formal amendment of the written text. It has been said of the US constitution that '[the] governing Constitution is a synthesis of legal doctrines, institutional practices,

---

[3] For what such a document might contain, see *The Constitution of the United Kingdom* (Institute for Public Policy Research, 1991). On the notion of a constitution, see King, *Does the United Kingdom still have a Constitution?* and *The British Constitution*; G Marshall, 'The Constitution: its Theory and Interpretation' in Bogdanor (ed.), *The British Constitution in the Twentieth Century*; Tomkins, *Our Republican Constitution*.

[4] From *A Dissertation Upon Parties* (1733), reprinted in Bolingbroke, *Political Writings* (ed. Armitage), p 88.

[5] Wheare, *Modern Constitutions*, p 1. A fuller statement of this kind was adopted by the House of Lords Committee on the Constitution in 2001 as a working guide to its activities: 'the set of laws, rules and practices that create the basic institutions of the state, and its component and related parts, and stipulate the powers of those institutions and the relationship between the different institutions and between those institutions and the individual' (HL Paper 11 (2001–2), ch 2).

[6] Hailsham, *On the Constitution*, p 1.

[7] See *Ministerial Code: A code of conduct and guidance on procedures for Ministers*; chs 7 and 13 B.

[8] For the argument that all constitutions leave important things unsaid, see Foley, *The Silence of Constitutions*; and King, *Does the UK still have a Constitution?*, ch 1.

and political norms.'[9] Professor Mark Tushnet begins his perceptive study of the US constitution by declaring that we can understand how it actually operates 'only by seeing it as a government fundamentally structured around . . . two nationally organized political parties'[10] – yet the existence of those parties is nowhere mentioned in the constitution itself.

In practice, a written constitution does not contain all the rules upon which government depends. Thus the scheme for electing the legislature is usually found not in the constitution but in statutes enacted by the legislature within limits laid down by the constitution. Such statutes can when necessary be amended by ordinary legislation, whereas amendments to the constitution may require a more elaborate process, such as a special majority in the legislature or approval by a referendum. And since the way in which the constitutional text operates may depend upon political practice, the process of constitutional change is not limited to the formal process of textual amendment. At a time when there is some movement towards there being a written constitution for the United Kingdom, we should note Tushnet's iconoclastic comment: 'Typically offered as a paradigm of a nation with a written constitution, the United States actually operates with a constitution that is more similar to than different from the paradigmatic unwritten constitution of the United Kingdom'.[11]

The making of written constitutions

It was in the late 18th century that the word constitution came to be identified with a single document, mainly as a result of the American and French Revolutions. The political significance of the new concept of constitutions was stressed by the radical, Tom Paine:

> A constitution is a thing antecedent to a government, and a government is only the creature of a constitution . . . A constitution is not the act of a government, but of a people constituting a government, and government without a constitution, is power without a right.[12]

In the world today, the making of a constitution normally follows a fundamental political event – the conferment of independence on a subordinate territory; a successful revolution; the creation of a new state by the uniting of states which were formerly separate; or reconstruction of a country's institutions following a war. A documentary constitution normally reflects the beliefs and political aspirations of those who have framed it. During the 1990s, after the collapse of communism, eastern and central Europe saw an era of constitution-making, as revolutions against socialist regimes led to the creation of new structures that embraced liberal and democratic values.

Within the United Kingdom, except between 1653 and 1660 when the country was governed under Cromwell's 'Instrument of Government', political circumstances have never required the enactment of a code of rules covering the whole of government. There have indeed been periods of acute political upheaval culminating in the reform of certain institutions, for example the revolution of 1688, which was the final act of the constitutional conflicts of the 17th century. Later there was the first major reform of the House of Commons in 1832 and the crisis over the Lords which led to the Parliament Act 1911. There have also been the union of England and Scotland in 1707, the union of Great Britain and Ireland in 1800, and the subsequent questions relating to the government of Ireland. There was the abdication crisis affecting the monarchy in 1936. And in 1973 the United Kingdom became a member of what was then the European Communities. But none of these occasions required reconstruction of the whole system of government. Instead, legislation was passed to give effect in law to what the political events made necessary. A pragmatic approach has predominated that avoids the difficult task of stating the

---

[9] Whittington, *Constitutional Construction*, p 3.
[10] Tushnet, *The Constitution of the USA*, p 5.
[11] Tushnet, *The Constitution of the USA*, p 1.
[12] *The Rights of Man* (ed. Kuklick), pp 81 and 174.

shared political beliefs and assumptions on which the system of government depends. In 1973, the Royal Commission on the Constitution reported that its task was to examine the need for devolution of power rather than to make a radical re-examination of the whole constitution.[13] After 1997 the New Labour government of Mr Blair was criticised for making extensive constitutional changes without placing them in an integrated programme of reform. In July 2007, Mr Gordon Brown's government embarked on a new reform initiative,[14] but although this led to the Constitutional Reform and Governance Act 2010, this was a set of discrete measures that fell far short of being a thorough-going and comprehensive programme.

Nevertheless, the Westminster system of government is not incompatible with a written constitution. In the past, numerous constitutions were framed for British territories overseas, whether as colonies or when they attained independence. The earliest constitutions contained no definition of responsible government and did not guarantee human rights. Some of these older constitutions have stood the test of time virtually unchanged, for example the constitution of the Commonwealth of Australia, enacted in 1900. The need for reform has been much discussed by Australians and in 1986 surviving legal links with the United Kingdom Parliament were severed by the Australia Act; but many projected constitutional amendments have failed to win majority support.[15] The Australian position presents a contrast with Canada. In 1982 the Canada Act, the last Act amending the Canadian constitution to be passed at Westminster, gave full powers of constitutional amendment to Canada and enacted the Charter of Rights and Freedoms as part of the Canadian constitution.[16] After 1945, as British colonies acquired their independence, numerous variants of what was often referred to as the 'Westminster model' constitution were created. It became common practice for guarantees of rights and broad political declarations to be included in the constitutions of the newly independent countries, as in 1979 when Rhodesia achieved independence as the republic of Zimbabwe.[17] Within the United Kingdom, interest in the idea of a written constitution continues to be low on the political agenda. In reality, because of devolution to Scotland, Wales and Northern Ireland, the Human Rights Act 1998 and changes in electoral law, as well as the emergence of documents such as the *Ministerial Code* and the *Code of Conduct for MPs*, many areas of government are subject to written rules, some of which have the force of law. The constitution is not as unwritten as it was in the past.[18]

Legal consequences of the unwritten constitution

Where there is a written constitution, the legal structure of government may assume a wide variety of forms. Within a federal constitution, the tasks of government are divided into two classes, those entrusted to the federal (or central) organs of government, and those entrusted to the various states, regions or provinces which make up the federation. Thus in countries such as Germany, Canada, Australia or the USA, constitutional limits bind both levels of government, and these limits are enforceable in law. In many countries it may be desired to place certain rights of the citizen beyond reach of the organs of government; these fundamental rights may be entrenched by requiring a special legislative procedure if they are to be amended or even by rendering them in essence unalterable, as in Germany.[19] Again, many constitutions seek to avoid a concentration of

---

[13] Kilbrandon Report, para 14. And see ch 3 B.

[14] See *The Governance of Britain*, Cm 7170, 2007; and *Constitutional Renewal*, Cm 7342, 2008. The Constitutional Reform and Governance Act 2010 was enacted shortly before the general election.

[15] See H P Lee [1988] PL 535.

[16] See Hogg, *Constitutional Law of Canada*; and app 1 of the 10th edn of this book.

[17] Zimbabwe Constitution Order 1979, SI 1979 No 1600, part III; see de Smith, *The New Commonwealth and its Constitutions*, ch 5 and cf Simpson, *Human Rights and the End of Empire*.

[18] And see Bogdanor, *The New British Constitution*.

[19] Basic Law of the Federal Republic of Germany, arts 19(2) and 79(3).

power in the hands of any one organ of government by adopting a separation of powers, vesting legislative power exclusively in the legislature, executive power in the executive and judicial power in the courts.[20]

Within the United Kingdom, there is no written constitution to secure these objects or serve as the foundation of the legal system. The resulting vacuum is occupied by the doctrines of the legislative supremacy of Parliament and the rule of law, their interrelation being one of the fundamental questions of public law in Britain.[21] These doctrines will be examined later, but one result is that formal restraints upon the exercise of power which exist elsewhere do not exist in the United Kingdom. For example, no truly federal system can exist so long as Parliament's legislative supremacy is maintained. Just as Parliament passed the Government of Ireland Act 1920, devolving powers of self-government upon Northern Ireland, so in 1972 Parliament could suspend operation of the Act of 1920 by re-imposing direct rule upon Northern Ireland.[22] For a formal federal system to be established a written constitution would be necessary, limiting the powers of the Westminster Parliament and preventing it from taking back devolved powers into its own hands. In law, the powers of the Scottish Parliament and the Welsh Assembly may be cut down or revoked by further legislation at Westminster; the safeguards against this happening are political rather than legal.

Many written constitutions contain a chapter of fundamental rights, the enforcement of which is entrusted to the courts. The absence of a written constitution makes it difficult and probably impossible for the courts to be entrusted with the ultimate protection of such rights against legislation by Parliament. In later chapters this subject is examined in depth but, by enacting the Human Rights Act 1998, Parliament has significantly extended the role of the courts in protecting human rights.

What is certain is that the absence of a written constitution means that there is no fixed procedure prescribed for legislation of constitutional importance. Before the Republic of Ireland could join the European Communities, a constitutional amendment had to be approved by referendum of the people. In the United Kingdom, while the European Communities Act 1972 was debated at length in Parliament, the Act was passed by a procedure having the same basic form as applies to ordinary legislation. British membership of the EC was in 1975 confirmed by a consultative referendum; but this was a consequence of divisions in the Labour party. Other referendums have since been held on such matters as the government of Scotland, Wales and Northern Ireland. It was expected at one time that more referendums would be held on European matters, for instance in relation to the European currency or the Lisbon Treaty. These referendums are held because they are desirable or necessary on political grounds, not because of a constitutional obligation. By contrast with written constitutions, which may be described as *rigid* because of the special procedure required if they are to be altered, the United Kingdom has what at least in form is an extremely *flexible* constitution. It would seem that there is no aspect of our constitutional arrangements which could not be altered by an Act of Parliament.[23]

The absence of a written constitution affects the sources of constitutional law. Instead of the constitution being the formal source of all constitutional law, we look both to Acts of Parliament and also to judicial decisions, which settle the law on matters (such as the principles of judicial review) that have never been the subject of comprehensive legislation. Some institutions, like the Cabinet, do not derive their authority from the law; many important constitutional rules are

---

[20] Ch 5.

[21] See Allan, *Law, Liberty and Justice*; and Forsyth (ed.), *Judicial Review and the Constitution*.

[22] Ch 3 A.

[23] In *R (Jackson)* v *A-G* [2005] UKHL 56, [2006] 1 AC 262, Lord Steyn remarked that some fundamentals associated with the rule of law might be beyond the reach of Parliament. See p 65.

not rules of law at all.[24] Accordingly, the absence of a written constitution means that on many matters British government depends less on legal rules and safeguards than upon political and democratic principles.

Constitutionalism[25]

The term 'constitutionalism' often appears in discussion of the relationship between state power, law, democracy and the preservation of liberal values,[26] but it is used with a wide variety of possible meanings. A Norwegian political scientist has said that constitutionalism 'is the political doctrine that claims that political authority should be bound by institutions that restrict the exercise of power'.[27] A Hungarian jurist has written that constitutionalism 'is the set of principles, manners, and institutional arrangements' that have traditionally served to limit government.[28] And for an American commentator, '[the] special virtue of constitutionalism . . . lies not merely in reducing the power of the state, but in effecting that reduction by the advance imposition of rules'.[29]

The idea of constitutionalism is particularly associated with the existence of a written constitution from which the state's authority and legitimacy may be felt to derive, and which may limit the power of the state and help protect the rights of individuals and minorities. The façade of a written constitution may sometimes exist alongside a tyrannical and overbearing state, but the prevailing tradition of western liberalism assumes existence of a written constitution, along with a democratic parliament, a culture of respect for the law by the state's organs, and a system of courts that may protect groups and individuals against the abuse of power.

In the United Kingdom the absence of formal limits upon state power that exist elsewhere has often given rise to demands for a new 'constitutional settlement' including a new Bill of Rights to protect individual liberties.[30] In 1988, a cross-party movement, Charter 88, called for electoral reform and urged that the courts be given new power to protect the individual. In 1991, a research institute published the text of a complete constitution for the United Kingdom.[31] Before the 1997 general election, the Labour and Liberal Democrat parties adopted a common platform of reforms, many of which (in particular, devolution to Scotland and Wales and incorporation of the European Convention on Human Rights) were enacted in 1998. Ten years later, as we have seen, the Brown government's proposals for constitutional reform were less dramatic, and stopped well short of creating a written constitution. In the summer of 2009, the revelation of excessive expenses being paid to MPs,[32] coupled with a belief that the parliamentary process was not protecting the public against abuse of power, caused many to demand a renewed political system, including a written constitution.

---

[24] Ch 2 B.

[25] See Vile, *Constitutionalism and the Separation of Powers*; McIlwain, *Constitutionalism, Ancient and Modern*; and Alexander (ed.), *Constitutionalism: Philosophical Foundations*.

[26] See J E K Murkens (2009) 29 OJLS 1. For discussion of 'common law constitutionalism', see T Poole (2003) 23 OJLS 435. Also King, *The British Constitution*, pp 12–13; and Ziegler, Baranger and Bradley, *Constitutionalism and the Role of Parliaments*, ch 1.

[27] Lane, *Constitutions and Political Theory*, p 19.

[28] Sajó, *Limiting Government: an Introduction to Constitutionalism*, p xiv.

[29] R Kay, in Alexander (ed.), pp 16, 23.

[30] See Scarman, *English Law – The New Dimension* and Hailsham, *The Dilemma of Democracy*. Contrast the sparkling defence of the unwritten constitution as an expression of political culture in Thompson, *Writing by Candlelight*, pp 191–256. Works calling for constitutional reform include Brazier, *Constitutional Reform*; Foley, *The Politics of the British Constitution*; Mount, *The British Constitution*; and Oliver, *Constitutional Reform in the UK*.

[31] Note 3 above.

[32] See ch 11.

What is constitutional law?

There is no hard and fast definition of constitutional law. According to one wide definition, constitutional law is that part of national law which governs the system of public administration and the relationships between the individual and the state.[33] Constitutional law presupposes the existence of the state[34] and includes those laws which regulate the structure and functions of the principal organs of government and their relationship to one another and to the citizen. Where there is a written constitution, emphasis is placed on the rules which it contains and on the way in which they have been interpreted by the highest court with constitutional jurisdiction. One problem of definition in the United Kingdom is that many of the rules and practices under which our system of government operates do not have the force of law.[35] Without knowledge of these rules and practices, knowledge of the legal rules alone is incomplete and sometimes misleading. These rules, principles and practices are essential to an understanding of the relationship between what may be called the 'political constitution' and the 'legal constitution', and give a constitutional meaning to apparently disparate events.[36]

A further problem of definition is that, unlike legal systems in which law is divided up into a series of codes, there is no hard and fast demarcation in Britain between constitutional law and other branches of law. A great legal historian advised students of constitutional law that they should take a wide view of the subject: 'There is hardly any department of law which does not, at one time or another, become of constitutional importance.'[37] For example, in the field of family law, important protection for family life is given by the European Convention on Human Rights[38] and family status is an important basis for many rules of immigration control.[39] In employment law, freedom of association and the law of picketing[40] are of constitutional importance. Numerous civil liberty issues arise out of criminal law and procedure. The way in which the machinery of justice and the courts protect private rights and arbitrate in disputes that involve the public interest is of immense significance. Constitutional law does not comprehend the whole of the legal system, but that the manner in which issues concerning rights, powers and duties are settled is of direct concern to constitutional law.[41]

Constitutional law and administrative law

In the past, constitutional law gave more emphasis to the role of the state in maintaining public order and national security than it did to the individual's right to employment and housing, education and health services and the conservation of the environment. We still look to the courts for protection in the sphere of public order and the criminal law. But in the administration of the social services, and in the exercise of economic regulation, individuals come into contact more often with officials than with judges. When a dispute arises out of these activities, a citizen may wish to go to the courts to assert his or her rights and often the procedure of judicial review enables this to be done.[42] However, the traditional role of members of Parliament in taking forward the grievances of their constituents is still seen as a necessary aspect of representative

---

[33] HLE, vol 8 (2), para 1; and see Marshall, *Constitutional Theory*, ch 1.
[34] For the impact of the changing concept of the state, see N MacCormick (1993) 56 MLR 1, C M G Himsworth [1996] PL 639 and MacCormick, *Questioning Sovereignty*.
[35] Ch 2 B.
[36] Whittington, *Constitutional Construction*, ch 1. See also K D Ewing [2000] PL 405.
[37] Maitland, *Constitutional History*, p 538.
[38] Arts 8 and 12. Ch 19 B.
[39] Ch 20 B.
[40] Ch 24.
[41] Cf the approach to the constitution made in D Feldman [2005] CLJ 329.
[42] Chs 30 and 31.

democracy. Moreover, tribunals and the Parliamentary Ombudsman provide important means of recourse for the citizen against official action or inaction.[43]

There is no precise demarcation between constitutional and administrative law in Britain. Administrative law may be defined as the law which determines the organisation, powers and duties of administrative authorities.[44] Like constitutional law, administrative law deals with the exercise and control of governmental power. A rough distinction is that constitutional law is mainly concerned with the structure of the primary organs of government, whereas administrative law is concerned with the work of official agencies in providing services and in regulating the activities of citizens. Within the vast field of government, questions often arise as to the sources of administrative power, the adjudication of disputes arising out of the public services and, above all, the means of ensuring a system of control over the activities of government which maintains a balance between public needs and the rights and interests of the individual.

Constitutional law and public international law

Public international law (the law of nations) is that system of law whose primary function it is to regulate the relations of states with one another. The system:

> presupposes the state, a territorial unit of great power, possessing within its own sphere the quality of independence of any superior, a quality which we are accustomed to call sovereignty and possessing within that sphere the power and right to make law not only for its own citizens, but also for those of others.[45]

International law thus primarily deals with the *external* relations of a state with other states; constitutional law concerns the *internal* structure of the state and its relations with its citizens and others on its territory or otherwise within its jurisdiction.[46] Both are concerned with regulating by legal process the great power that states wield. The monist tradition seeks to assimilate the national and international legal systems. But in the dualist tradition, which the United Kingdom has generally observed, national and international law operate at two distinct levels. In reality both are concerned with state power. One important branch of constitutional law is the national law relating to a government's power to enter into treaties with other states and thus to create new international obligations.[47] And the procedure of extradition, by which an alleged or convicted criminal who escapes from one state to another may be sent back to the state where the crime was committed, operates in both international and national law.[48] Since 1945, international organisations have established new forms of cooperation between states and have set standards of conduct for the international community, for example, in the creation of the International War Crimes Tribunal. Increasingly, international law has become concerned with protecting the human rights of individuals, national minorities and other groups. For this and other reasons, the interface between constitutional law and public international law is rapidly evolving. Courts in the United Kingdom are increasingly dealing with the effects of what has been called 'the internationalisation of public law'.[49]

---

[43] Ch 29.

[44] Ch 27. Also Maitland, *Constitutional History*, pp 528–35, and Craig, *Public Law and Democracy in the UK and the USA*, pp 1–3.

[45] C Parry, in *Manual of Public International Law* (ed. Sorensen), p 3. And cf note 34 above.

[46] On the meaning of a state's jurisdiction in European human rights law, see *Bancovic v Belgium* (2001) 11 BHRC 435.

[47] Ch 15 B.

[48] Ch 20 C.

[49] See Jowell and Oliver (eds), *The Changing Constitution* (5th edn, 2004), ch 4 (D Feldman). And see note 34 above.

Constitutional law and the law of the European Union

The European Union (EU) was created by the Maastricht Treaty in 1992, entered into by the member states of the European Community. Itself created by means of treaties between the member states, the European Community was from its inception very different from other international organisations, being equipped with legislative, administrative and judicial organs, which exercise their powers with direct effect in the member states. The substantive rules of Community law in the economic and social fields lie outside the scope of this book. But it is now well established that the Community exercises powers of government over the member states, including the United Kingdom, in which the British people participate through elections to the Westminster and European Parliaments: the public law of the United Kingdom has had to adapt to this reality. Accordingly, the main structure of the EU will be outlined and the implications of membership for constitutional law examined, including the relationship between Community law and national law.[50]

Since the EU exercises powers of a governmental nature over its 27 member states, its structure, powers and accountability raise the same questions of public law as can be asked about national governments, although the answers are by no means the same. As a system of government, the EU already has a 'constitution' based on the treaties that have created it but also on the decisions made by the European Court of Justice interpreting the treaties and the complex structure of agreements and practices by which the Union functions.[51] Such a constitution comes within Bolingbroke's use of that term, mentioned earlier in this chapter, as an 'assemblage of laws, institutions and customs' by which states forming the EU have agreed to be governed. In 2005, an ambitious attempt to provide the EU with a 'European Constitution' by that name failed when it was rejected by referendums in the Netherlands and France. One aim behind this attempt was to provide the Union with something closer to a written constitution, at the same time making changes in the EU's system of government, giving greater effect to the EU Charter of Fundamental Rights and rationalising a structure that had evolved untidily since 1957. The deliberate choice of the term 'European Constitution' for the document marking a further stage in European integration probably contributed to the belief that the projected reform of the EU was a direct challenge to the authority of national constitutions. The further attempt at EU reform made by the Lisbon Treaty was approved at the second referendum held in Ireland in October 2009. The treaty itself came into effect on 1 December 2009, the final state to ratify the treaty having been the Czech Republic.

---

[50] Ch 8.
[51] See e.g. S Douglas-Scott, *The Constitutional Law of the European Union.*

CHAPTER 2

Sources and nature of the constitution

If the United Kingdom possessed a written constitution, the main rules of constitutional law would be contained within it. Alterations to these rules would be made by the procedure laid down for amending the constitution. In all probability, Parliament would have power to legislate for such matters as the machinery of elections and the structure of the courts. If a court exercised the function of interpreting and applying the constitution in disputed cases, its decisions would be an authoritative statement of the meaning of the constitution. The sources of constitutional law would comprise: (*a*) the constitution itself and amendments made to it; (*b*) Acts of Parliament dealing with matters of constitutional importance; (*c*) judicial decisions interpreting the constitution. By the word 'source' is meant the formal origin of a rule which confers legal force upon that rule. The word source may also be used in other senses: thus the historical sources of a written constitution include both the immediate circumstances in which it was framed and adopted, and also the long-term factors which influenced its making. So, too, there are broad political principles which influence the content of particular legal rules. Thus a long-standing commitment to democracy underlies the legal right of the people to vote in elections. Such principles are given practical effect in legislation by Parliament and may influence decisions that the courts take on disputed questions of law.

In section A of this chapter, we examine the formal sources of constitutional law, under three headings: (*a*) legislation (*b*) judicial decisions, and (*c*) the law and custom of Parliament. In section B, we consider other types of constitutional rules and principles, in particular those often called 'constitutional conventions' – they do not have the force of law but are of great importance in maintaining constitutional government. We also examine briefly the contribution to constitutional law that is made by the writings of scholars and jurists. Section C deals with some matters relating to the nature of constitutional government in Britain that form a necessary background to the study of the rules and principles of constitutional law.

A. The formal sources of constitutional law

In the absence of a written constitution, the two main sources of constitutional law are the same as those of law in general, namely:

(*a*) *Legislation* (or enacted law) including Acts of Parliament; legislation enacted by ministers and other authorities upon whom Parliament has conferred power to legislate;[1] exceptionally, legislative instruments issued by the Crown under its prerogative powers;[2] and, since 1973, legislation enacted by organs of the European Communities.[3]

(*b*) *Judicial precedent* (or case law), i.e. the decisions of the courts expounding the common law or interpreting legislation. Since 1973, this includes decisions of the European Court of Justice in relation to Community law. The Human Rights Act 1998 requires all courts and tribunals to take account of relevant decisions of the European Court of Human Rights.[4]

---

[1] Ch 28.
[2] Ch 12 D.
[3] Ch 8.
[4] Ch 19 C.

A third branch of constitutional law is found in the 'law and custom of Parliament' (*lex et consuetudo Parliamenti*), which derives from the authority inherent in each House of Parliament to regulate its internal affairs. In general, this is a matter for each House to enforce.[5] As regards customs and practices within government, the courts generally take the view that these matters are outside the law in its strict sense and are not directly enforceable in the absence of legislation giving effect to them. But exceptionally, a well-established governmental practice may give rise to decisions by the courts upholding the practice as lawful[6] or even as creating an obligation to act in a certain way by reason of the principle of legitimate expectations.[7]

Legislation

In the absence of a written constitution, many Acts of Parliament have been enacted which relate to the system of government. There are few topics of constitutional law which are not affected by legislation. Unlike some branches of private law, for example the general law of contract, a study of constitutional law involves frequent recourse to the statute book. Those statutes which deal with matters of constitutional law do not form sections of a complete constitutional code. If a collection were made of all the legislation (from medieval charters to the present day) which deals with the form and functions of government, the result would present a very incomplete description of the constitution.[8] Moreover, these enactments can each be repealed by another Act of Parliament. A few statutes, although in law they are generally considered to be in no different position from other Acts, have special constitutional significance.

1 *Magna Carta*.[9] Magna Carta was granted in 1215 by King John in response to pressure from the nobles at Runnymede, but in various forms the charter was confirmed by later kings with the approval of the English Parliament; it appears on the statute book in the form confirmed by Edward I in 1297. Its importance lies in the fact that it contained a statement of grievances, formulated on behalf of important sections of the community, which the King undertook to redress. The Charter set out the rights of various classes of the medieval community according to their different needs. The Church was to be free; London and other cities were to enjoy their liberties and customs; merchants were not to be subject to unjust taxation. Although both trial by jury and the writ of habeas corpus owe their origins to other sources, chapter 29 declared that no man should be punished except by the judgment of his peers or the law of the land and that to none should justice be denied. These clauses embodied a protest against arbitrary punishment and asserted the right to a fair trial and a just legal system. Today few provisions of Magna Carta remain on the statute book but it has been called 'the nearest approach to an irrepealable "fundamental statute" that England has ever had'.[10]

2 *Petition of Right*. A document enacted by the English Parliament at a much later period of conflict is the Petition of Right 1628, enrolled on the statute book as 3 Car 1 c 1.[11] This contained protests against taxation without consent of Parliament, arbitrary imprisonment, the use of commissions of martial law in time of peace and the billeting of soldiers upon private persons. To these protests the King yielded, though the effect of the concessions was weakened by the view Charles I held that his prerogative powers were not thereby diminished.

---

[5] See p 19 below.

[6] See e.g. *Carltona Ltd* v *Commissioners of Works* [1943] 2 All ER 560; p 115 below.

[7] See ch 30 C.

[8] See the statutes under the title 'Constitutional Law' in *Halsbury's Statutes*, 4th edn, vol 10 (2001 reissue).

[9] For a full historical account, see Holt, *Magna Carta*.

[10] Pollock and Maitland, *History of English Law*, vol I, p 173. See also *R v Home Secretary, ex p Phansopkar* [1976] QB 606; *R v Foreign Secretary, ex p Bancoult* [2001] QB 1067; and A Tomkins [2001] PL 571.

[11] *Halsbury's Statutes*, vol 10, p 26.

3 Bill of Rights and Claim of Right. The 'glorious revolution' of 1688 brought about the downfall of James II of England and James VII of Scotland from his two thrones and the restoration of monarchy in the two kingdoms on terms laid down by the English and Scottish Parliaments respectively. These terms were accepted by the incoming joint monarchs, William and Mary. In England it was the House of Lords and the remnants of Charles II's last Parliament that in 1689 approved the Bill of Rights which was later confirmed by the post-revolution Parliament.[12] This laid the foundations of the modern constitution by disposing of the more extravagant claims of the Stuarts to rule by prerogative right.

Its principal provisions (known as 'articles'), many of which are still in force as part of English law, declared:

(1) That the pretended power of suspending of laws or the execution of laws by regal authority without consent of Parliament is illegal.

(2) That the pretended power of dispensing with laws or the execution of laws by regal authority as it hath been assumed and exercised of late is illegal.

(3) That the commission for erecting the late court of commissioners for ecclesiastical causes and all other commissions and courts of like nature are illegal and pernicious.

(4) That the levying money for or to the use of the crown by pretence of prerogative without grant of Parliament for longer time or in other manner than the same is or shall be granted is illegal.

(5) That it is the right of the subjects to petition the King and all commitments and prosecutions for such petitioning are illegal.

(6) That the raising or keeping of a standing army within the kingdom in time of peace unless it be with consent of Parliament is against the law.

(7) That the subjects which are protestants may have arms for their defence suitable to their conditions and as allowed by law.

(8) That election of members of Parliament ought to be free.

(9) That the freedom of speech and debates or proceedings in Parliament ought not to be impeached or questioned in any court or place out of Parliament.

(10) That excessive bail ought not be required nor excessive fines imposed nor cruel and unusual punishments inflicted.

(11) That jurors ought to be duly impannelled and returned. . . .

(12) That all grants and promises of fines and forfeitures of particular persons before conviction are illegal and void.

(13) And that for redress of all grievances and for the amending, strengthening and preserving of the laws, Parliaments ought to be held frequently.[13]

The Scottish Parliament enacted the Claim of Right in 1689. Its contents followed those of the Bill of Rights with certain modifications; for example, the distinction between the suspending and dispensing powers was not made, but all proclamations asserting an absolute power to 'cass [quash], annul or disable laws' were declared illegal.[14] Many provisions of the Claim of Right are still in force within Scotland.

---

[12] Ibid, p 38.

[13] *Halsbury's Statutes*, vol 10, p 34. See *Congreve v Home Office* [1976] QB 629 (art 4); *Williams v Home Office (No 2)* [1981] 1 All ER 1211 (art 10); and *R v Home Secretary, ex p Herbage (No 2)* [1987] QB 1077 (art 10). Art 7, sometimes cited by the gun lobby, had no effect on the Firearms (Amendment) Act 1997. Art 9 was amended by the Defamation Act 1996, see chs 11 A and 23 F. On the significance of the Bill of Rights, see Wicks, *The Evolution of a Constitution*, ch 1.

[14] APS IX, 38.

4 *The Act of Settlement.* The Act of Settlement 1700, enacted by the English Parliament, not only provided for the succession to the throne, but added important provisions complementary to the Bill of Rights, especially:

> That whosoever shall hereafter come to the possession of this crown shall join in communion with the Church of England as by law established.

> That in case the crown and imperial dignity of this realm shall hereafter come to any person, not being a native of this kingdom of England, this nation be not obliged to engage in any war for the defence of any dominions or territories which do not belong to the crown of England, without consent of Parliament.

> That no person who has an office or place of profit under the King or receives a pension from the crown shall be capable of serving as a member of the House of Commons.

> That . . . judges' commissions be made *quamdiu se bene gesserint* [so long as they are of good behaviour], and their salaries ascertained and established, but upon the address of both Houses of Parliament it may be lawful to remove them.

> That no pardon under the great seal of England be pleadable to an impeachment by the Commons in Parliament.[15]

The Bill of Rights and the Act of Settlement marked the victory of Parliament over the claim of the Stuart kings to govern by the prerogative. There was, however, nothing in these statutes to secure the responsibility of the King's ministers to Parliament. That important principle of parliamentary government developed in the 18th century and later, a product of constitutional practice rather than legislation.[16] This enabled the exercise by ministers of many prerogative powers of the Crown to survive into the 21st century.[17]

5 *Other statutes of constitutional importance.* Other statutes that form part of constitutional law include the Act of Union with Scotland 1707, the Parliament Acts 1911 and 1949, the Crown Proceedings Act 1947, the European Communities Act 1972, the British Nationality Act 1981 and the Public Order Act 1986. Those enacted since 1997 include the Scotland Act 1998, the Human Rights Act 1998, the House of Lords Act 1999, the Terrorism Act 2000 and the Constitutional Reform Act 2005.

If the United Kingdom had a written constitution, this would be likely to require a special procedure to be followed for making textual amendments to the constitution. As it is, in two respects a distinction is sometimes drawn between constitutional and other legislation. First, the House of Commons may refer Bills of constitutional significance for detailed examination to a committee of the whole House rather than to a Public Bill committee,[18] but not all Bills of constitutional significance are treated in this way. Second, by the doctrine of implied repeal, a later Act prevails over an earlier Act which is inconsistent with the later Act; however, in the case of statutes of special significance, the courts are sometimes reluctant to hold that they have been overridden by a later Act. Indeed, in 2002 it was held that 'constitutional' statutes (those that govern the legal relationship between citizen and state 'in some general, overarching manner' or affect the scope of fundamental constitutional rights) are unlike 'ordinary' statutes in that the former may not be impliedly repealed, although they may be repealed when the actual intention of a later Parliament is stated expressly.[19]

---

[15] *Halsbury's Statutes*, vol 10, p 40.

[16] Ch 7.

[17] Ch 12.

[18] See p 187. And R Hazell, [2006] PL 247.

[19] *Thoburn* v *Sunderland City Council* [2002] EWHC 195 (Admin), [2003] QB 151 (the metric measures case, concerning the status of the European Communities Act 1972). On implied repeal, see ch 4 C.

A related question is whether the electorate as a whole should be consulted by means of a national referendum when significant constitutional changes are proposed. The practice of holding such a referendum has developed since 1973, although it is not yet possible to be certain when a referendum will be politically expedient or unavoidable. The Labour government undertook to hold a national referendum on the new European constitution and on entry into the European monetary system; in the event, neither referendum has been needed. It is possible that a referendum would be held to test opinion on a change in the electoral system. But if a future government wished to abolish the Scottish Parliament and the Welsh Assembly, which were established after referendums in those countries, a prior referendum would be inevitable.[20]

Case law

The other main source of rules of law is found in the decisions of the superior courts, stated in authoritative form in the law reports. Under the doctrine of precedent, or *'stare decisis'* (i.e. the duty of courts to observe decided cases), these decisions are binding on inferior courts and may, according to the relative status of the courts in question, bind other superior courts.[21] Judge-made law takes two principal forms.

1 *The common law.* This consists of the laws and customs which have from early times been declared to be law by the judges in deciding cases coming before them. In the reports of these cases are found authoritative expositions of the law relating to the prerogatives of the Crown,[22] the remedies of the subject against illegal acts by public authorities and officials,[23] and the writ of habeas corpus,[24] which in English law protects individuals against unlawful detention. Such decisions established the principle that 'from its very earliest days' the common law 'set its face firmly against the use of torture'.[25]

Examples of judicial decisions are *Entick* v *Carrington*, which held that a Secretary of State had no power to issue general warrants for the arrest and search of those publishing seditious papers;[26] and, in modern times, *Burmah Oil Co* v *Lord Advocate*, which held that the Crown must compensate the owners of property taken in the exercise of prerogative powers,[27] *Conway* v *Rimmer*, which held that the courts had power to order the production of documents in evidence for which Crown privilege had been claimed,[28] and *M* v *Home Office*, holding that the Home Secretary had committed contempt of court in not obeying a judge's order to bring a deported Zairean teacher back to the United Kingdom.[29] Decisions on such matters declare important rules of public law which often would not have been enacted by Parliament. In the absence of a written constitution, such decisions provide what have been called the legal foundations of British constitutionalism.[30] Even so, they are not binding for all time since they may be set aside or amended by Parliament, even retrospectively.[31]

Until September 2009, the final court of appeal took the form of the 'law lords' sitting in the House of Lords, but in October 2009 these judges became Justices of the Supreme Court for the

---

[20] See p 76 below.

[21] See Cross and Harris, *Precedent in English Law*.

[22] Ch 12 D.

[23] Ch 31.

[24] Ch 21 E and ch 31.

[25] *A* v *Home Secretary (No 2)* [2005] UKHL 71, paras [11], [12] (Lord Bingham).

[26] (1765) 19 State Tr 1029.

[27] [1965] AC 75; ch 12 E.

[28] [1968] AC 910; ch 32 C.

[29] *Re M* [1994] 1 AC 377; chs 18 B, 32 C.

[30] See Allan, *Law, Liberty and Justice*, chs 1, 4. Also S Sedley, in Richardson and Genn (eds), *Administrative Law and Government Action*, ch 2 and (1994) 110 LQR 270.

[31] The War Damage Act 1965 reversed the *Burmah Oil* decision above; ch 12 D.

United Kingdom.[32] Sitting as the final court of appeal, the law lords could in exceptional circumstances review and, if necessary, alter the law laid down by their own earlier decisions,[33] and the position of the Supreme Court will be the same. Judicial decisions provide the foundations for such principles as the legislative supremacy of Parliament and judicial review of executive action.[34] But even such fundamental principles are affected by European law. When a case concerns Community law, the decision by a United Kingdom court may be referred to the European Court of Justice at Luxembourg;[35] and in cases concerning rights under the European Convention on Human Rights, the European Court of Human Rights at Strasbourg may hold that the national decision conflicts with the Convention.[36]

2 *Interpretation of statute law.* As a general rule, the courts have no authority to rule on the validity of an Act of Parliament (although they may rule on the validity of subordinate legislation),[37] but they have the task of interpreting enacted law in cases where the correct meaning of an Act is disputed. Important issues of public law may arise out of the interpretation of statutes, as may be seen from many judicial decisions. In a major decision under the Human Rights Act 1998, the House of Lords held that a power conferred by Parliament in 2001 to detain foreigners suspected of involvement with terrorist acts infringed their right to liberty and could not be exercised to bring about their indefinite imprisonment without charge or trial; such imprisonment, said Lord Nicholls, 'is anathema in any country which observes the rule of law'.[38] Another leading decision concerned the power of the Environment Secretary, under an Act of 1985, to make regulations restricting increases in certain residential rents. He used this power to protect tenants against increases resulting from judicial decisions on the assessment of rents; but landlords claimed that the power could be used only as a measure against inflation. In upholding the regulations, the law lords discussed the court's approach to deciding the meaning of the 1985 Act. As Lord Bingham said, 'the overriding aim . . . must always be to give effect to the intention of Parliament as expressed in the words used'.[39] Lord Nicholls said:

> The task of the court is often said to be to ascertain the intention of Parliament expressed in the language under consideration. This is correct and may be helpful, so long as it is remembered that the 'intention of Parliament' is an objective concept, not subjective. The phrase is a shorthand reference to the intention which the court reasonably imputes to Parliament in respect of the language used. It is not the subjective intention of the minister or other persons who promoted the legislation. Nor is it the subjective intention of the draftsman, or of individual members or even of a majority of individual members of either House.[40]

Lord Nicholls explained that in seeking the meaning of the words used by Parliament, the courts employ established principles of interpretation as useful guides and, if necessary, use internal aids (found in the rest of the Act) or external aids (for example, material outside the Act) to identify the mischief that the statute is intended to cure and the purpose of the legislation.

Since most powers of government are derived from statute, the judge-made law which results from the interpretation of statutes is of great importance in administrative law. The principles

---

[32] See ch 18 A.

[33] *Practice Statement (Judicial Precedent)* [1966] 3 All ER 77. For review of a previous decision for due process reasons, see *R v Bow Street Magistrate, ex p Pinochet Ugarte (No 2)* [2000] 1 AC 119.

[34] Ch 4 and chs 30, 31.

[35] For the *Factortame* litigation, ch 8 D.

[36] Ch 19 B.

[37] Ch 28.

[38] *A v Home Secretary* [2004] UKHL 56, [2005] 2 AC 68, [74]. For an equally significant decision, on the legality of control orders, see *Home Secretary v AF (No 3)* [2009] UKHL 28, [2009] 3 All ER 643.

[39] *R v Environment Secretary, ex p Spath Holme Ltd* [2001] 2 AC 349, 388.

[40] Ibid, 396.

(or presumptions) of statutory interpretation are seldom conclusive and sometimes point in opposite directions.[41] The task of the court in discovering the meaning or effect of words used by Parliament always requires analysis of the text of the legislation. But if the policy or purpose of a statute can be determined, it may be possible to give an interpretation consistent with that. There was formerly a rule that the courts may not look at Hansard (the record of debates in Parliament) to discover the meaning of legislation, although limited use might be made of documents such as the reports of royal commissions and parliamentary committees as an aid to identifying the mischief which legislation was intended to remedy.[42] However, Hansard was used to discover the intention of Parliament in approving regulations which gave effect to a decision of the European Court of Justice.[43] In 1992, the House of Lords modified the former rule: a court may use Hansard as an aid to statutory construction where the legislation is ambiguous or obscure and the material relied on consists of clear statements made by a minister or other promoter of the Bill.[44]

Certain presumptions of interpretation are of constitutional importance. Thus many Acts do not in law bind central government, since the Crown is presumed not to be bound by legislation, unless this is expressly stated or necessarily implied.[45] It has often been presumed that Parliament does not intend to take away common law rights by implication, as distinct from express words. Thus the courts have held that Parliament does not intend to take away the property of a subject without compensation[46] or to deprive a subject of access to the courts,[47] and have interpreted penal statutes strictly in favour of the citizen: thus a statute creating a criminal offence will not in the absence of express words be held to be retrospective.[48] In recent decisions, the courts have used these presumptions to develop the idea of common law constitutional rights, such as the right of access to a court, which may be abrogated but only by express words or necessary implication.[49] It has been said that Parliament does not legislate in a vacuum, but against a background of constitutional democracy that includes the 'principle of legality'. According to Lord Hoffmann: 'The principle of legality means that Parliament must squarely confront what it is doing and accept the political cost. Fundamental rights cannot be overridden by general or ambiguous words.'[50]

Most principles of interpretation evolved from judicial decisions, but new rules of interpretation may be imposed on the courts by Parliament. Under the Human Rights Act 1998, all legislation, whenever made, must, 'so far as it is possible to do so', be read and given effect in a way that is compatible with the rights protected by the European Convention. This may lead to an outcome that goes far beyond any interpretation that would have been acceptable in the past, and the effect may be to amend the statute.[51]

British membership of the European Union directly affects our traditional approaches to interpretation, since in most European legal systems the methods of legislative drafting and the rules of statutory interpretation are very different from those in Britain. Where it is necessary for

[41] Marshall, *Constitutional Theory*, ch 4; Cross, *Statutory Interpretation*; Bennion, *Statutory Interpretation*.

[42] *Black-Clawson International Ltd* v *Papierwerke AG* [1975] AC 591; *Davis* v *Johnson* [1979] AC 264.

[43] *Pickstone* v *Freemans plc* [1989] AC 66.

[44] *Pepper* v *Hart* [1993] AC 593. On use of Hansard, see *R* v *Environment Secretary, ex p Spath Holme Ltd* (above); and Lord Steyn (2001) 21 OJLS 59. Also *Wilson* v *First County Trust Ltd (No 2)* [2003] UKHL 40, [2004] 1 AC 816.

[45] *Lord Advocate* v *Dumbarton DC* [1990] 2 AC 580; chs 12 D, 32 C.

[46] *Central Control Board* v *Cannon Brewery Co* [1919] AC 744, 752.

[47] *Chester* v *Bateson* [1920] 1 KB 829.

[48] *Waddington* v *Miah* [1974] 2 All ER 377.

[49] *R* v *Lord Chancellor, ex p Witham* [1998] QB 575. Also *R* v *Home Secretary, ex p Pierson* [1998] AC 539; and *R* v *Home Secretary, ex p Simms* [2000] 2 AC 115.

[50] *R* v *Home Secretary, ex p Simms*, at p 131.

[51] The leading case on interpretation under the Human Rights Act is *Ghaidan* v *Godin-Mendoza* [2004] UKHL 30, [2004] 2 AC 557; and see ch 19 C.

a provision of a European treaty or regulation to be interpreted in a British court, a procedure for seeking a preliminary ruling enables the question of interpretation to be settled by the European Court of Justice.[52] British courts must follow that court's practice by giving a purposive construction to regulations intended to comply with EC directives.[53]

It is an essential principle of the concept of law that enacted laws should be interpreted by judicial bodies independent of the legislature which made the law: statutory provisions authorising the government to define the meaning of terms used in an Act of Parliament endanger this principle. While the courts must be able to act independently of the executive in interpreting legislation, their duty is to decide what Parliament must be taken to have intended and they are not free merely to decide what they believe may be in the public interest.[54]

The law and custom of Parliament

Legislation enacted by Parliament and decisions of the courts are sources of legal rules with which every lawyer is familiar, but the same cannot be said of the law and custom of Parliament. In earlier days, reference was often made to the 'High Court of Parliament'. Although the notion of Parliament as a court has been superseded today, each House has for centuries had certain privileges, including power over its own procedure. A striking illustration of this power is found in the rules of each House that determine how a Bill is considered by the House, setting out the successive stages for debate and possible amendment of the Bill. Other rules of constitutional importance are contained in the standing orders of the two Houses, as well as in resolutions of each House and in rulings by the Speaker of the House of Commons. The inherent authority of each House to control its own affairs is respected by the courts, and in recent times each House adopted a 'Code of Conduct' for its own members. Under the codes, all members had to register their financial and other interests, and compliance with the codes was enforced by each House.[55]

Public anger in the summer of 2009 at media revelations of excessive allowances that many MPs were claiming under the scheme for parliamentary expenses led to the enactment of the Parliamentary Standards Act 2009, that made inroads into the historic authority of the Commons to regulate its own affairs. But the Act did not directly affect the ancient power of the House of Commons to expel or suspend an MP who is in serious breach of the House's rules of conduct.

In addition to the formal rules that govern parliamentary procedure, many informal practices and understandings are observed between the parties in the Commons, and between the front benches and the backbenchers. Such practices are not found in the House's standing orders, but they directly affect parliamentary business. These practices resemble the customary practices and understandings that arise outside Parliament and are examined in the next section of this chapter. For one party to depart unilaterally from these practices could cause other parties to react in kind to the changes. This might lead to the withdrawal of cooperation between government and opposition parties (on such matters as pairing between absent MPs or the timetabling of Bills), at least for the time being, and it might eventually lead to changes in the rules of procedure.

B. Other rules and principles, including constitutional conventions

Many important rules of constitutional behaviour, which are observed by the Queen, ministers, members of Parliament, judges and civil servants, are contained neither in Acts nor in judicial decisions. Disputes which arise out of these rules rarely lead to action in the courts and judicial

---

[52] Ch 8 A.
[53] *Litster* v *Forth Dry Dock and Engineering Co Ltd* [1990] 1 AC 546.
[54] *Duport Steels Ltd* v *Sirs* [1980] 1 All ER 529.
[55] See ch 11 B.

sanctions are not applicable if the rules are broken. A wide variety of names has been given to these rules: the positive morality of the constitution,[56] the unwritten maxims of the constitution,[57] and 'a whole system of political morality, a whole code of precepts for the guidance of public men'.[58] Dicey referred to them as:

> conventions, understandings, habits or practices which, though they may regulate the conduct of the several members of the sovereign power . . . are not in reality laws at all since they are not enforced by the courts.[59]

Under Dicey's influence, the most common name given to this phenomenon is constitutional convention.

This meaning of the word convention is quite different from its meaning in international law, where a convention is a synonym for a treaty, or binding agreement between states. But the notion of conventional conduct does include a strong element of what is customarily expected, in the sense of ordinary or regular behaviour. In common speech behaviour may be described as unconventional if it departs from accepted patterns of social behaviour and opinion. Most discussion of this topic has gone beyond describing a convention as 'a generally accepted political practice, usually with a record of successful applications or precedents'[60] and concludes that conventions give rise to binding rules of conduct.[61] Conventions have thus been described as:

> rules of constitutional behaviour which are considered to be binding by and upon those who operate the Constitution but which are not enforced by the law courts . . . nor by the presiding officers in the Houses of Parliament.[62]

There is indeed an important distinction to be drawn between regarding conventions as (a) merely *descriptive* statements of constitutional practice, based on observation of what actually happens; or as (b) *prescriptive* statements of what should happen, based in part on observation but also on constitutional principle. We return later to the choice between these two approaches;[63] but at present we will assume that conventions are concerned with matters of obligation and will explore the nature of that obligation. First, examples will be given of conventional rules that affect constitutional behaviour and in each case relevant legal rules will be mentioned.

Conventional rules of the constitution: some examples

1 It is a rule of common law that the royal assent must be given before a Bill which has been approved by both Houses of Parliament can become an Act of Parliament.[64] The manner in which the royal assent may be given is now regulated by statute and in certain circumstances the royal assent may be signified by others on behalf of the Queen.[65] These rules deal with a vital matter of legal form. But a more important conventional rule is that the royal assent is granted

---

[56] Austin, *The Province of Jurisprudence Determined*, p 259.

[57] Mill, *Representative Government*, ch 5.

[58] Freeman, *Growth of the English Constitution*, p 109, quoted in Dicey, p 418. Cf O Hood Phillips (1966) 29 MLR 137.

[59] Dicey, *The Law of the Constitution*, p 24.

[60] Mackintosh, *The British Cabinet*, p 13. Brazier, in *Constitutional Practice*, p 3, leaves it open whether the practices that he describes have the status of 'rules'; at (1992) 43 NILQ 262 he distinguishes conventions (which impose duties) from matters of practice.

[61] See e.g. Mitchell, *Constitutional Law*, p 39; Wheare, *The Statute of Westminster and Dominion Status*, p 10; Marshall, *Constitutional Conventions*, chs 1 and 13; Heard, *Canadian Constitutional Conventions*, ch 7.

[62] Marshall and Moodie, *Some Problems of the Constitution*, pp 22–3. Marshall, *Constitutional Conventions*, p 3, refers to conventions as 'non-legal rules of constitutional behaviour'.

[63] Page 28 below.

[64] Chs 4 C, 10 A.

[65] Royal Assent Act 1967, Regency Acts 1937–53.

by the Queen on the advice of her ministers. Where a Bill has been passed by both Houses of Parliament, the royal assent will be given as a matter of course. The monarch's legal power to refuse assent was last exercised by Queen Anne in 1708, when (apparently with the approval of her ministers and without objection by Parliament) the royal assent was refused to the Scottish Militia Bill.[66] In the Irish crisis of 1912–14, the Unionists suggested to George V that he should withhold assent from the Bill to give home rule to Ireland. The Liberal Prime Minister, Asquith, advised the King against this and the royal assent was granted.[67] While the Queen may not of her own initiative refuse the royal assent, the position might be different if ministers themselves advised her to do so, although this advice would have to be defended in Parliament and would be highly controversial.

2 In law the Queen has unlimited power to appoint whom she pleases to be her ministers. Statutes provide for the payment of salaries to ministers and limit the number of appointments which may be made from the House of Commons.[68] There is no rule of law which prevents the monarch appointing to ministerial office a person who is outside Parliament. But all appointments are made by the monarch on the advice of the Prime Minister and the principle of ministerial responsibility[69] requires that a minister should belong to one or other House of Parliament. If a non-member is appointed to ministerial office, he or she will receive a life peerage: the earlier practice of expecting such a person appointed to enter the Commons at an early by-election (last seen in 1965) has lapsed since no government today willingly causes a by-election to be held in one of its own seats.

3 Although the conduct of a general election is governed by detailed statutory rules,[70] no legal rule regulates the conduct of the Prime Minister when the result of the election is known. But by a long-standing conventional rule, the government must have the confidence of a majority in the Commons. Therefore, when it is clear from election results that the Prime Minister on whose advice the election was called has lost the election and another party has been successful, he or she must resign immediately without waiting for the new Parliament to meet.[71] Where the result of the election gives no party an overall majority in the Commons, the Prime Minister may continue in office for so long as is necessary to discover whether he or she is able to form a coalition or to govern with the support of other parties. In February 1974, when this situation arose, three days elapsed before Mr Heath decided to resign, having learned that the Liberal MPs would not support him. In 1979, an Opposition motion of no confidence in the Labour government was carried by one vote (on 28 March 1979) and forced Mr Callaghan to call an election in May 1979. He resigned as Prime Minister as soon as it was clear that the Conservative party had won the election.

4 High Court judges in England and Wales hold their offices by statute during good behaviour, subject to a power of removal by the Queen on an address presented to her by both Houses; by statute they are disqualified from membership of the Commons.[72] Before appointment as a judge, a lawyer may have been active in party politics but a conventional rule requires him or her on appointment to sever links with the party which he or she had formerly supported. In 1968, a Scottish judge, Lord Avonside, agreed to serve on a committee to consider the future constitution of Scotland which Mr Heath, the leader of the Opposition, had established: he

---

[66] Hearn, *The Government of England*, p 61.
[67] Jennings, *Cabinet Government*, pp 395–400; and ch 12 B. Cf Brazier, *Constitutional Practice*, pp 193–6.
[68] Ch 9 G.
[69] Ch 7.
[70] Ch 9 D.
[71] Ch 12 B.
[72] Chs 9 G, 18 C.

resigned from the committee when his membership of the Conservative party's committee became a matter of controversy.[73] This convention is now incorporated in the Guide to Judicial Conduct, which states it to be a specific application of the principle that judges must avoid extra-judicial activities that may give rise to 'a reasonable apprehension of bias'.[74] Until October 2009, the twelve 'law lords' (Lords of Appeal in Ordinary) carried out their judicial functions by sitting as a committee of the House of Lords. While they could take part in the legislative work of the House, they did not belong to a party group and did not speak 'in matters where there is a strong element of party political controversy'.[75] In October 2009, the new Supreme Court for the United Kingdom took over the appellate jurisdiction of the House of Lords; judges on the Court who hold peerages are now disqualified from sitting or voting in the House of Lords.[76]

5 Under the Scotland Act 1998, the Scottish Parliament has, since July 1999, had power to legislate on the subjects devolved to Scotland, but the Westminster Parliament retains full power to legislate for Scotland. By what is known as the 'Sewel convention', now based on an agreement between the government in London and the Scottish Executive, the Westminster Parliament will not legislate for Scotland on devolved matters except with the agreement of the Scottish Parliament.[77]

6 The legal opinions which the Law Officers of the Crown give to the government are in law confidential and are protected by legal privilege from being produced as evidence in court proceedings. They may, however, be published by the government or quoted from in Parliament if (as rarely happens) a minister considers it expedient that the Commons should be told of their contents.[78] During the Westland affair in 1986, the Secretary of State for Trade and Industry (Mr Brittan) authorised civil servants to leak to the press extracts from a confidential letter to him from the Solicitor General, without first seeking the latter's consent. 'Cover' but not approval for the leak was sought from the Prime Minister's office. Under a storm of criticism for these events, Mr Brittan resigned, thus reinforcing the authority of the rule which the Law Officers sought to defend.[79] The code of conduct for ministers now states: 'The fact that the Law Officers have advised or have not advised and the content of their advice must not be disclosed outside Government without their authority'.[80] Much controversy surrounded the government's refusal to publish the text of an opinion given by the Attorney General to the Prime Minister on 7 March 2003 regarding the legality of an invasion of Iraq by American and British forces in the absence of a further resolution from the UN Security Council. The Attorney General published a brief summary of his view a few days later, but the text of his opinion was published two years later only after extensive extracts had been leaked to the press.[81]

Many more examples of conventional rules could be given. They serve a wide variety of purposes and vary widely in importance. Such rules develop under every system of government, whether a written constitution exists or not. Their special importance in Britain today is that it is through such rules and practices that the system of government has developed and continues to evolve. With such a diversity of subject matter, what general characteristics, if any, do these rules possess?

---

[73] See *The Times* and *The Scotsman*, 26 July–6 August 1968.
[74] See *Guide to Judicial Conduct* (revised version, 2008), para 3.3 (www.judiciary.gov.uk).
[75] See statement by the senior Law Lord, Lord Bingham, HL Deb, 22 June 2000, col 419.
[76] Constitutional Reform Act 2005, s 137(3).
[77] See HL Deb, 21 July 1998, col 791; Cm 4444 (1999), para 13. Also ch 3 B.
[78] Edwards, *The Law Officers of the Crown*, pp 256–61.
[79] See e.g. Linklater and Leigh, *Not Without Honour*, ch 11; and G Marshall [1986] PL 184.
[80] *Ministerial Code* (2007), para 2.13; and see chs 7 and 13 C.
[81] The documents are in Sands, *Lawless World*, Apps X, XI; the author analyses them in ch 12.

General characteristics[82]

Although some long-established conventional rules (like the rule that the Queen's speech, read at the opening of each session of Parliament, is prepared by her ministers) have great authority and are universally known, many have developed out of a desire to avoid the formality, explicitness and publicity associated with changes in the law. The development of a regular practice may enable legislation on a point of principle to be avoided. The role of the monarch in the conduct of government has almost disappeared since the 18th century without a series of statutes removing one royal power after another. In the same way, many powers have been acquired by the Prime Minister by the operation of convention rather than as the result of legislation. Conventional rules may be used for discreetly managing the internal relationships of government while the outward legal form is left intact.

The informality of such rules is often accentuated by the fact that the rules themselves are not formulated in writing, but this is not always the case. As we have seen, the rule that judges should not undertake political activities has now a written form. Moreover, the government may give to the Commons an undertaking about the future use of its powers – for example, about the laying of treaties before the House to enable them to be debated[83] – or may convey to the House undertakings regarding future practice in the making of appointments by the Sovereign or Prime Minister. Such undertakings are publicly recorded.[84]

The development of unwritten rules is often an evolutionary process that occurs before clear rules of conduct emerge. In retrospect, we can identify when (for instance) the royal assent was last refused to a Bill (1708) or a member of the House of Lords last held office as Prime Minister (1902). But because such occurrences are impossible today, we cannot conclude that this has always been the case since the last such occasion. At any given time, it may be difficult to tell whether practice on a certain matter has hardened into a rule, particularly when the practice is negative in character. Before the Constitutional Reform Act 2005, one instance concerned whether the Lord Chancellor, as a member of the government, might properly sit as a judge to decide appeals in the House of Lords. Between 1997 and 2003, Lord Chancellor Irvine insisted on retaining the right to sit as a judge,[85] but when Lord Falconer was appointed to the office in June 2003, he declared that he would not do so. This statement could have been sufficient to establish a new convention binding on future Lord Chancellors. In fact, it was a precursor of the Constitutional Reform Act 2005, which took away the judicial role of the Lord Chancellor.

As with all forms of rules, disputes may arise about the meaning and effect of conventional rules, particularly when they have not been formulated in a definitive written form. The enforcement of many conventional rules may depend essentially on the force of public and political opinion. Disputes about the existence and content of legal rules are typically settled by judicial decision. If many legal rules have an 'open texture',[86] how much more 'open' will be the texture of non-legal rules where there is no definite procedure for resolving disputes about existence and content.

In the past, accounts of constitutional conventions often concentrated on the rules by which powers legally vested in the monarch came to be exercised by ministers of the Crown. Dicey considered that conventions were 'rules intended to regulate the exercise of the whole of the

---

[82] A full discussion by the Supreme Court of Canada is in *Reference re Amendment of the Constitution of Canada* (1982) 125 DLR (3d) 1. See also C R Munro (1975) 91 LQR 218, W Maley (1985) 48 MLR 121, R Brazier (1992) 43 NILQ 262 and G Wilson's postscript to Nolan and Sedley, *The Making and Remaking of the British Constitution*, pp 95–133.

[83] The so-called Ponsonby Rule: HC Deb, 1 April 1924, col 2001; ch 15 B.

[84] See HC Deb, 11 December 1962, cols 209–10 (appointment of Serjeant at Arms); and Cmnd 8323, 1981, para 23 (Comptroller and Auditor General).

[85] As he did in *Boddington v British Transport Police* [1999] 2 AC 143.

[86] See Hart, *The Concept of Law*, pp 121–32.

remaining discretionary powers of the Crown'.[87] It is more accurate to say that conventional rules regulate the conduct of those holding public office. Our constitutional system allots different roles to the monarch, ministers, judges, civil servants and so on. Anyone who would play one of these roles must observe the restraints which the system imposes on those who accept that office. Edward VIII was not willing to accept these constraints and was required to abdicate.[88] So, too, a minister who does not observe or does not accept the constraints of his or her office must resign. In January 1986, Mr Michael Heseltine, Secretary of State for Defence, walked out of a Cabinet meeting and resigned his post because he was not prepared to accept a requirement of Cabinet Office clearance for all further ministerial statements on the Westland affair.[89] In 2005, Mr David Blunkett resigned from the Cabinet when it became known that, after leaving a Cabinet post once before, he had breached the clear rule in the *Ministerial Code* that required former ministers to seek advice from an independent committee before they accept business appointments.

Why are conventional rules observed?

Dicey, writing as a lawyer in a period dominated by Austinian jurisprudence according to which laws were observed because they could be enforced against the citizen by the coercive power of the state, said:

> the sanction which constrains the boldest political adventurer to obey the fundamental principles of the constitution and the conventions in which these principles are expressed, is the fact that the breach of these principles and of these conventions will almost immediately bring the offender into conflict with the courts and the law of the land.[90]

To support this view, Dicey argued that Parliament meets at least once a year because the government would be compelled to act unlawfully if this did not happen. This particular argument has been shown to be much weaker than Dicey had supposed.[91] In any event, the rule which the supposed legal sanction supports is antiquated. Today, Parliament is expected not merely to meet once a year but to be in session at Westminster for about 34 weeks in the year, interspersed with holidays and the long summer recess. During these weeks there is a customary pattern of parliamentary work to be done. The Provisional Collection of Taxes Act 1968[92] imposes certain constraints upon the timetable of Parliament, but this in itself does not explain why Parliament meets regularly throughout the year. That Parliament should do so is expected by politicians and citizens alike.

It is nearer the mark to say, as did Sir Ivor Jennings, that conventions are observed because of the political difficulties which arise if they are not.[93] As these rules regulate the conduct of those holding public office, possibly the most acute political difficulty which can arise for such a person is to be forced out of office. It is therefore crucial to know who may exercise the power of removing the holder of public office from his or her position. But an explanation merely in terms of political difficulties is inadequate since not every event which gives rise to political difficulties (for example, an unpopular Bill) is a breach of a conventional rule. The Supreme Court of Canada stated that the main purpose of conventions is to ensure that the legal framework of the constitution is operated

---

[87] Dicey, p 426.
[88] Ch 12 A.
[89] See D Oliver and R Austin (1987) 40 *Parliamentary Affairs* 20; and note 79 above.
[90] Dicey, pp 445–6.
[91] For example, by Jennings, *The Law and the Constitution*, pp 128–9.
[92] Ch 10 C.
[93] *The Law and the Constitution*, p 134. See J Jaconelli (1999) 19 LS 24 and [2005] CLJ 149.

in accordance with the prevailing constitutional values of the period.[94] On this basis, conventions are observed for the positive reason that they express prevailing constitutional values and for the negative reason of avoiding the difficulties that may follow from 'unconstitutional' conduct.

Formulating rules of good government

It has often been said that, as conventional rules derive neither from legislation nor from decisions of the courts, they have an uncertain existence and are not ultimately backed up by any obligation. Indeed, so long as the obligations owed by ministers to Parliament or to the Prime Minister rested on mere understandings of what the political game required, or on values shared by tacit agreement between those concerned, the obligations were not written down and their existence or content could be disputed.

Today, in many areas of government, particularly regarding standards of integrity in public life, written codes of behaviour exist – for the civil service, for ministers, for members of Parliament and for public authorities. These codes may not be authorised by legislation or enforced by the courts, but it would be wrong to claim that observance is not obligatory or that the codes lack legal authority. An important rule in the *Ministerial Code*[95] is that ministers should give accurate and truthful information to Parliament and that ministers who knowingly mislead Parliament will be expected to offer their resignation to the Prime Minister. It is up to each House to ensure that this rule is observed.[96] A minister in breach of the *Ministerial Code* knows that a refusal to resign may lead to a dismissal. Under the same code, ministers must 'ensure that no conflict arises, or appears to rise, between their public duties and their private interests, financial or otherwise'. Enforcement of this principle is primarily for the Prime Minister, acting in the light of public and parliamentary opinion. Yet if a minister's decision breached this principle, and if someone adversely affected sought judicial review of the decision, the Administrative Court could if necessary take provisions of the code into account. Even where a code of rules does not yet exist in an area, clear principles of conduct may have emerged that impose obligations enforceable in public law. Other rules of 'good government' that may have a potentially similar effect are the rules of public accounting,[97] the principles of good administration as applied by the Parliamentary Ombudsman[98] and the principles contained in the Cabinet Office's code of practice on consultation. As regards the judiciary, there is now a statutory basis for the operation of disciplinary rules and procedures affecting various levels of judges.[99] What we can identify here is an evolving regulatory process: the starting point is broad power to lead or direct an organ of government; the need to regulate the conduct of office-holders leads to emergence of principles, best practice and rules, and ultimately a code of rules. The outcome of such a process may be little different in legal terms from a code of practice authorised by statute.[100]

The meaning of 'unconstitutional'

Where a written constitution ranks as fundamental law, acts which conflict with the constitution may be held unconstitutional and thus illegal. In the United Kingdom, the term 'unconstitutional'

---

[94] *Reference re Amendment of the Constitution of Canada* (1982) 125 DLR (3d) 1, 84.

[95] See ch 13 C. NW Barber, (2009) 125 LQR 294, argues persuasively that the *Ministerial Code* is an instance of the process by which conventional rules 'are in the process of crystallization' and acquire greater formality.

[96] The courts may not question the truth of statements in Parliament: Article 9, Bill of Rights; ch 11 A.

[97] See *R v Foreign Secretary, ex p World Development Movement Ltd* [1995] 1 All ER 611; and ch 17 D.

[98] See ch 29 D.

[99] Constitutional Reform Act 2005, ss 108–121.

[100] NW Barber (note 95 above) reaches a similar conclusion regarding the *Ministerial Code*.

has no defined content. The 19th-century jurist, Austin, suggested that the Sovereign was acting unconstitutionally when he infringed the maxims of government which with popular approval he generally observed – but by definition the Austinian Sovereign could not act illegally.[101] For Freeman, unconstitutional conduct was conduct contrary to 'the undoubted principles of the unwritten but universally accepted constitution'.[102] Where conduct breaches a written constitution, 'unconstitutional' is likely to mean 'illegal'; where it breaches unwritten values or principles of government, the term may mean 'wrong'. The two senses of 'unconstitutional' were illustrated in the Canadian constitutional controversy of 1981–82, when the Supreme Court of Canada dealt separately with the issues of whether it would be (a) illegal and (b) in breach of convention for the Federal Parliament to adopt resolutions requesting amendments to the constitution which were opposed by eight of the ten provinces.[103] On the first question, the court held (by seven to two) that such action would not be illegal, but on the second question (by six to three) that it would be in breach of convention.

While conduct may be unconstitutional without being illegal, illegal acts may be unconstitutional. British politicians who instigated or covered up criminal offences for political ends would be in breach of the standards of behaviour recognised by public opinion, as well as in breach of the criminal law. Ministers are restrained from exceeding their powers not only by the likelihood of legal sanctions, but also by the obligation on government to conduct its affairs according to law. When used concerning executive decisions, 'unconstitutional' implies that a decision is not merely incorrect in law but also contrary to fundamental principle, for example where a policy of the Inland Revenue involved 'taxation by self asserted administrative discretion and not by law'.[104] It is in this sense that exemplary damages may in exceptional cases be awarded in the law of tort when public authorities or officials commit wrongful acts that are 'oppressive, arbitrary or unconstitutional'.[105]

However, it may not be easy to determine whether the boundary between constitutional and unconstitutional conduct has been crossed, especially where there is no universally accepted rule of conduct. Different politicians may take opposing views of the constitutional propriety of the acts of a government. Unpopular proposals for new legislation are not for that reason unconstitutional, but a Bill which sought to destroy essential features of the electoral system or to give the Cabinet power to overrule decisions of the courts could rightly be described as unconstitutional.

Another difficulty in determining what is constitutional in a given situation is that there may be no relevant precedent. When in 1932 the Cabinet of the National government agreed to differ on a major issue of economic policy, an attack on the government for unconstitutional conduct was met by the rejoinder:

> Who can say what is constitutional in the conduct of a National Government? It is a precedent, an experiment, a new practice, to meet a new emergency, a new condition of things.[106]

In 1975 the open disagreement of the Labour Cabinet over Britain's continued membership of the EEC was defended in similar terms.

Consequences of a breach of conventional rule

Various consequences may follow the breach of conventional rules. Loss of office or departure from public life is the severest consequence, as when a minister is forced to resign because of an open disagreement with stated government policy. The force of public opinion may compel

[101] Austin, *The Province of Jurisprudence Determined*, pp 257–60.
[102] Freeman, *The Growth of the English Constitution*, p 112.
[103] Note 94 above.
[104] *Vestey v Inland Revenue Commissioners* [1980] AC 1148, 1173.
[105] *Rookes v Barnard* [1964] AC 1129; *Kuddus v Chief Constable of Leicestershire* [2001] UKHL 29, [2002] 2 AC 122.
[106] HC Deb, 8 February 1932, col 535 (Mr Baldwin).

the offender to think again: thus the Scottish judge who in 1968 joined a committee established by the Conservative party resigned rather than prejudice the work of the committee.[107] In these instances, the outcome reinforces the established rule. A less serious consequence would be a reprimand or a reminder not to act similarly in the future, given by someone in a position to enforce the rule. If no adverse consequences follow, the matter becomes more open. It may be expedient that, for instance, the Prime Minister should turn a blind eye to acts of colleagues that breach a rule for ministers: but if such acts are repeatedly condoned, it must be asked whether the rule has been abandoned or modified. Some departures from normal practice do not harm the core elements of government. Between 1997 and 2001 there existed a sub-committee of the Cabinet that included both Labour ministers and Liberal Democrat members. Its function was to provide liaison between the government and Liberal Democrats on reforms which the parties had both supported at the 1997 election. The utility of this device was limited and it was not revived after the election in 2001.

As constitutional rules often give rise to reciprocal obligations, one consequence of a breach may be to release another office-holder from the normal constraints that would apply. When Ian Smith's Cabinet in 1965 unilaterally declared Rhodesia's independence, the immediate response of the UK government, conveyed through the Governor-General of Rhodesia, was to dismiss the entire Cabinet. This dismissal proved purely nominal. More significantly, the Southern Rhodesia Act 1965 was passed at Westminster to give the British government power to legislate for the domestic affairs of Rhodesia, overriding the previous convention that Westminster would not exercise its sovereignty in such matters except with the agreement of the Rhodesian government.[108]

Another consequence may be the passing of legislation to avoid a similar breach in the future. When in 1909 the Lords rejected the Liberal government's Finance Bill, the crisis was resolved only by the Parliament Act 1911, which removed the power of the Lords to veto or delay money Bills. The 1911 Act contained other provisions intended to place the Lords–Commons relationship on a new footing.[109] These provisions led in turn to new conventions regarding the use by the House of Lords of its residual powers. The content of these conventions will be examined in chapter 10 B in relation to reform of the House of Lords. But we will note in the next section what the Joint Committee said about the possibility of 'codifying' the conventions in this area.

Should all conventional rules be enacted as law?

In theory, all conventional rules of the constitution could be enacted by Parliament. Written constitutions in the Commonwealth have adopted various means of incorporating conventions: express enactment of the main rules, wholesale adoption by reference to practice in the United Kingdom and so on.[110]

If a written constitution were to be drafted for the United Kingdom, difficult decisions on these matters would have to be made. It would, for example, be far from easy to provide for every eventuality in which the appointment of a new Prime Minister might be required. Merely to declare that ministers are accountable to Parliament for the decisions that they take would not achieve very much if it was left to Parliament to decide how to enforce that accountability. And to make ministerial responsibility enforceable by the courts would be to change its character entirely.[111]

---

[107] Note 73 above.

[108] Cf *Madzimbamuto v Lardner-Burke* [1969] AC 645, 723.

[109] Ch 10 B.

[110] de Smith, *The New Commonwealth and its Constitutions*, pp 78–87. For an Australian exercise in restating the conventions, see C Sampford and D Wood [1987] PL 231.

[111] In 1996, Sir Richard Scott said that if ministers did not accept the obligations of accountability, a statutory duty requiring them to keep Parliament informed should be enacted and enforced by the courts: [1996] PL 410, 426. And see pp 115 and 276 below.

There is little to be said for attempting to prepare a single document that would include *all* informal constitutional rules: this would be a huge task and it might freeze evolving political practice at an arbitrary moment. But it may be useful to bring together rules on a defined subject matter, like the *Ministerial Code*. And a salutary contribution to promoting the health of democracy was made by the report of the Nolan Committee in 1995,[112] which declared broad standards of integrity and honesty that should be observed in public life and led to more detailed rules of conduct being applied to many areas of government.

The development of new constitutional rules can be achieved without the formality and undue precision associated with legislation. Thus, it is now accepted that Parliament should give its approval before a government under the prerogative commits the armed forces to a new military policy abroad, but the government resisted the argument that this should become a statutory requirement.[113]

In 2006, a joint committee of both Houses examined the conventions relating to the role of the House of Lords in the process of legislation, its remit being to 'consider the practicality of codifying the key conventions' in this highly political area. The committee flatly rejected the idea of codification, declaring that since conventions 'by their very nature, are unenforceable . . . codifying conventions is a contradiction in terms. It would raise issues of definition, reduce flexibility, and inhibit the capacity to evolve. It might create a need for adjudication . . .'[114] This conclusion needs to be read in the context of the committee's inquiry. But, despite rejecting 'codification', the committee stated that it would be useful for the House of Lords to adopt resolutions that would clarify the approach of the House to Bills that the government had promised in its election manifesto and also the need for the House to deal with government business 'in a reasonable time'.

In a democratic state that recognises executive accountability to Parliament, constitutional obligations exist that are based neither on legislation nor on decisions of the courts. Legal rules, whether stemming from the judges or Parliament, may continue in force long after the original reasons for them are forgotten. The relative informality of many constitutional rules makes for greater flexibility as circumstances change.[115] This does not mean that so long as the original circumstances continue, there is no rule or no obligation. The abdication of Edward VIII and the reasons for it have had a continuing influence on later monarchs and their advisers. So, too, the process by which Conservative MPs caused Mrs Thatcher to resign as Prime Minister has implications for later Prime Ministers, however strong their majority in the Commons.

One lesson from previous events is that short-term political expediency may be a temptation that an experienced government ought to resist, and that constitutional principle may provide more reliable guidance. As Freeman wrote in 1872:

> Political men may debate whether such and such a course is or is not constitutional, just as lawyers may debate whether such a course is not legal. But the very form of the debate implies that there is a Constitution to be observed, just as in the other case it implies that there is a law to be observed.[116]

The motives for human conduct are usually mixed. If we seek to understand the conduct of a monarch, a politician or a judge, we may discover both enlightened self-interest and also a strong perception of constitutional obligation. If that perception is shared by others in a similar position, as well as by informed commentators, it is difficult to explain such conduct without reference to the perceived obligation. The fact that conventional rules may change without formal amendment does not mean that they are irrelevant to political behaviour.

---

[112] Cm 2850-I, 1995.

[113] See ch 12 D.

[114] Joint Committee on Conventions, *Conventions of the UK Parliament*, HL Paper 265-1, HC 1212-1, para 279.

[115] For criticism of the distinction between law and convention, see Jennings, *The Law and the Constitution*, p 132 and Mitchell, *Constitutional Law*, pp 34–8; and in reply, Marshall, *Constitutional Theory*, pp 7–12. See also note 82 above.

[116] *The Growth of the English Constitution*, p 112; cf Loughlin, *Public Law and Political Theory*, p 53.

The attitude of the courts

The discussion so far has assumed that conventions are not capable of being enforced through due process of law. If, when a rule has been broken, a remedy is available in the courts for securing relief or penalising the wrongdoer, this indicates that the rule has the quality of law. Where an informal rule has been broken, no direct remedy is available in the courts. Often the citizen's only recourse will be political action – a complaint to an MP, a letter to the press, or a public demonstration. In view of the context of most conventions, the stress on political or parliamentary remedies is appropriate. Moreover, many conventional rules, for example those relating to the Cabinet system, do not affect an individual closely enough for a judicial remedy to be justified.

It may, however, be necessary for a court to take into account the existence of a conventional rule in making its decision on a legal dispute. This is likely to happen in administrative law cases, where the courts have taken judicial notice of the fact that civil servants take decisions in the name of ministers and that ministers may be called to account by Parliament for the decisions. But the courts are also aware that such accountability may not provide an effective remedy for the individual.[117]

The Crossman diaries case, in which the Attorney General tried to prevent a newspaper publishing the diaries of a former Cabinet minister, is an outstanding illustration of the inter-relation of legal and non-legal rules. In this case, an attempt was made by the Attorney General to prevent the breach of a conventional rule and to establish the existence of a legal obligation. The court held that former Cabinet ministers could be restrained by injunction from publishing confidential information which came to them as ministers, since there was a legal duty to respect that confidentiality.[118] But the court was not thereby enforcing the convention of collective responsibility; that convention was no more than one factor taken into account by the judge in establishing the limits of the legal doctrine of confidence. In the different context of the Canadian constitution, by a reference procedure which permits Canadian courts to give wide-ranging advisory opinions, the Supreme Court of Canada in 1981 gave an opinion on the existence of the conventions governing the process of constitutional amendment.[119]

Nonetheless, developments in public law are broadening the scope for judicial decisions about the observance of conventional rules by public authorities. In the GCHQ case, concerning a decision by the Prime Minister that was imposed on the civil servants without prior consultation, evidence showed there to be an invariable practice by government of consulting with civil service unions before changing conditions of employment.[120] If this practice were viewed merely as a constitutional convention, the unions would have no enforceable rights in the matter. But the House of Lords held that, as a matter of public law, the unions had a 'legitimate expectation' of being consulted that would have been protected,[121] had this not been overridden by national security considerations. We have seen that many aspects of ministerial conduct, that formerly rested on unwritten rules, are now contained in the *Ministerial Code*. Should someone be adversely affected by the breach of a minister's duties under the Code, an argument based on legitimate expectations might possibly succeed that would have been certain to fail if phrased in terms of breach of a constitutional convention.

---

[117] *Carltona Ltd* v *Commissioners of Works* [1943] 2 All ER 560; pp 115 and 275 below. And see *R* v *Environment Secretary, ex p Notts CC* [1986] AC 240. For a judicial view of conventions applying to legislation by Westminster for Rhodesia, see *Madzimbamuto* v *Lardner-Burke* [1969] AC 645.

[118] *A-G* v *Jonathan Cape Ltd* [1976] QB 752; ch 13 B.

[119] Note 82 above. Cf *Adegbenro* v *Akintola* [1963] AC 614.

[120] *CCSU* v *Minister for the Civil Service* [1985] AC 374.

[121] See ch 30 C.

Legal and constitutional literature

In English law, no legal textbook has inherent authority as a source of law: the authority of the most eminent text is confined to the extent to which a court considers that it accurately reproduces the law enacted by the legislature or decided by earlier courts. Where a statute has not yet been judicially interpreted or where no court has pronounced authoritatively on a matter of common law, the opinions of textbook writers and academic authors may be of great value when a case arises for decision.[122] Such writing is also of value when questions of principle have to be decided in relation to constitutional issues. Dicey's *Law of the Constitution* has profoundly influenced judicial reasoning; and the development of administrative law owes much to the extensive work of the late Professors de Smith and Sir William Wade.

In Scots law, the position is different as regards the past. A series of eminent legal authors between the mid-17th and early 19th centuries, including Stair, Erskine and Hume, are known as the institutional writers. Their work expounded the private law and criminal law of Scotland in a systematic manner which derived much from the institutional writers of Roman law: in the absence of other authority, a statement in their works may be taken as settling the law.[123] The approach of the Scottish legal system to legal authority was seen in *Burmah Oil Co v Lord Advocate*,[124] relating to the Crown's prerogative: the case having reached the House of Lords on appeal from Scotland, counsel and judges referred extensively to the civilian writers of earlier centuries, in a manner untypical of the English common law.

Legal writers on the constitution are handicapped by the unreality of many of the legal terms which they must sometimes employ.[125] Statements about the prerogative powers of the Crown often seem archaic or to be conferring despotic powers upon the monarch, until it is realised that they concern powers of government exercised by ministers, civil servants and other Crown servants.

In some areas of the constitution, books such as Jennings's *Cabinet Government*, Mackintosh's *The British Cabinet*, Hennessy's *Cabinet* and Brazier's *Constitutional Practice* are a valuable record of practice. Since they are founded both on historical sources and on contemporary political accounts, works on British government are seldom unanimous in their description of controversial events (for example, the differing interpretations of the political crisis in 1931 which led to the formation of the National government).[126] Rules of official secrecy may make it difficult to write about current practice. While most Cabinet papers are publicly available after 30 years, the structure of Cabinet committees and the rules of conduct for ministers were, until 1992, regarded as secret.[127] Another problem is that historical precedents are often of doubtful relevance to present issues. Jennings, whose book was first published in 1936, used constitutional precedents dating from 1841.[128] Today the speed of change in government is such that it may not be useful to look at precedents from before 1979, let alone as far back as 1945.

In the field of parliamentary procedure, a work with special authority is Erskine May's *Parliamentary Practice*. First published in 1844, this is revised regularly under the editorship of the Clerk to the House of Commons and it summarises the collective experience of the Clerks of the House.[129] It is essentially a means of reference to the original sources, which are found in standing orders, in resolutions of the House and in rulings given by the Speaker and recorded in Hansard.

---

[122] For clear recognition of this by the House of Lords, see *Woolwich BS v IRC (No 2)* [1993] AC 70, 163 (Lord Goff).

[123] See *Stair Memorial Encyclopedia, The Laws of Scotland*, vol 22, pp 212–19.

[124] [1965] AC 75; ch 12 D.

[125] Cf Bagehot, *The English Constitution*, pp 99–100. The point is made strongly by Lady Hale in *R (Quark Fishing Ltd) v Foreign Secretary* [2005] UKHL 57, [2006] 1 AC 529, paras [94, 95].

[126] See Bassett, *1931: Political Crisis*.

[127] Ch 13 B.

[128] Jennings, *Cabinet Government*, p 9.

[129] See the 23rd edn by W McKay, 2004.

Finally, there is an unending flow from government and Parliament of reports by such bodies as royal commissions, departmental committees, committees of Parliament and tribunals of inquiry. Many of these reports have concerned important constitutional topics, the most notable in recent years being the first report of the (Nolan) committee on standards in public life, Sir Richard Scott's massive report on the 'arms for Iraq' inquiry[130] and Lord Butler's inquiry into the use of intelligence on weapons of mass destruction in Iraq.[131] There is also the prolific class of reports by select committees of the House of Commons into the activities of government departments.[132] The reports of the Parliamentary Ombudsman give a more detailed insight into the working of central departments than can be obtained from the law reports or Hansard alone. British membership of the European Union gives rise to a flow of official publications from the headquarters of the European Community.

C. Constitutional government in Britain

Evolutionary development

The British system of government is flexible, not in the sense that it is unstable but in that most of its principles and rules can be changed by legislation or by the development of a new conventional rule or practice. Perhaps because of this flexibility, the United Kingdom has, at least since 1688, escaped those revolutionary convulsions which may occur in countries with more rigid constitutions but less stable political or social systems. Since the 17th-century settlement, there have been innumerable changes in the system of government, some freely conceded but many fought for by political action. The result has been a complete change from personal rule by the monarch to the ascendancy of the Prime Minister who, as leader of the majority party in Parliament and head of the executive branch of the state, is able with other ministers in the Cabinet to direct and coordinate the activities of central government.

Many of the older forms of government have survived from earlier times and these (for instance, the Privy Council)[133] are tolerated or respected because they represent historic continuity. Writing in 1867, Walter Bagehot in *The English Constitution* distinguished between the *dignified* parts of the constitution 'which excite and preserve the reverence of the population' and the *efficient* parts, 'by which it, in fact, works and rules'.[134] Bagehot called it the characteristic merit of the constitution, 'that its dignified parts are very complicated and somewhat imposing, very old and rather venerable; while its efficient part, at least when in great and critical action, is decidedly simple and rather modern.'[135] The apparent continuity can be misleading, causing the Royal Commission on the Constitution in 1973 to say: 'The United Kingdom already possesses a constitution which in its essentials has served well for some hundreds of years.'[136] Such a simplistic reflection draws attention away from many significant changes in government and politics that have occurred in the past, are now occurring, and are yet to come. For a full understanding of the constitution, a sense of history is essential.[137]

The evolutionary nature of British government can be illustrated in many ways. While the monarch has lost the role of governing the country since 1688, further changes in the residual functions of

---

[130] Respectively Cm 2850–1, 1995, and HC 115 (1995–6).

[131] HC 898 (2003–4).

[132] Ch 10 D.

[133] Ch 12 C.

[134] *The English Constitution*, p 61.

[135] Ibid, p 65.

[136] Kilbrandon Report, para 395.

[137] For two contrasting studies that reinforce this point, see Wicks, *The Evolution of a Constitution* and Allison, *The English Historical Constitution*.

the monarch may yet occur. Tension remains between the competing claims of Cabinet and Prime Ministerial (or presidential) government. And many questions remain about the accountability of Whitehall to Parliament. The Labour programme of constitutional reform after 1997 proclaimed the need for changes in such matters as the electoral system, the composition of Parliament, the structure of the United Kingdom and the protection of human rights. In 2009, the programme remained to be taken further in respect of such matters as the composition of the House of Lords, control of prerogative powers, the electoral system and the relationship between government and Parliament. And it later became clear that the reforms enacted in the Constitutional Reform and Governance Act 2010 would not deal with the most serious questions affecting the political system.

The party system

Parliamentary government cannot be explained solely in terms of legal and conventional rules. It depends essentially upon the political base which underlies it, in particular the parties around which political life is organised. Under the present electoral system, a basic assumption is that, following a general election, the party with a majority of seats in the House of Commons will form the government. Power to direct national affairs passes to the leadership of the party which, in popular terms, has won the election. Except for February 1974, every general election held between 1935 and 2005 produced an absolute majority in the Commons for one or other of the major parties. Even if that majority is counted in single figures (as it was in 1950–51, 1964–66 and after October 1974) it provides a basis for the government's authority. In terms of ability to govern, it does not matter that the majority of seats in the Commons represents only a minority of votes cast by the electorate – as it did in every election between 1906 and 2005 except in 1931 and 1935. The election in 2005 led to a House of Commons in which there were 355 Labour MPs, 197 Conservative MPs, 62 Liberal Democrats and 31 other MPs. It is remarkable that Labour secured no more than 36 per cent of the total vote, but won 55 per cent of the seats in the Commons. In contrast with the system for electing the Commons, the system used for the Scottish Parliament and the National Assembly for Wales includes additional members elected by region on a proportional basis: this system led to a coalition between Labour and Liberal Democrat parties in Scotland after 1999, and a similar coalition existed in Wales between 2000 and 2003. In Scotland, the election in 2007 led to the formation of a minority government by the Scottish National party.

The tendency of the Westminster electoral system to reward the party with the largest number of votes by conferring on it a majority of seats is often said to provide strong government, on the assumption that the governing party will surely retain the support of its majority in the Commons. However, given the concentration of power in the hands of the executive, the British system is tolerable only because of the restraints on government which exist. One restraint is the certainty of a general election, guaranteed by law to occur at least every five years and likely to occur more frequently. Another restraint is that government policies are subject to debate in Parliament (but generally without the risk of being defeated in the Commons). Another rather uncertain restraint is that no government can wholly ignore the reaction of public opinion and the media to its measures, but a determined government can still hold on to an unpopular policy.

There were times during the 20th century when it was possible to think of the United Kingdom as forming a single political system, dominated by two national parties. This view is no longer tenable. In part, this is because of the electoral advance made, in seats at Westminster, by the third party (now the Liberal Democrats) and also because of representation in the Commons of other parties from Scotland, Wales and Northern Ireland, and also since 1998 because of devolution of power to those countries.

While the Conservative and Labour parties have a common interest in maintaining a two-party system, the constitutional structure of Britain does not rest on that system, even if for many politicians the ideal state of affairs is one in which they hold office with an absolute majority in the Commons, as the Conservatives did between 1979 and 1997 and Labour have done since 1997.

Periods of minority government (for instance between 1976 and 1979), may see developments like the agreement between the Labour government and the Liberal party in 1977–78.[138] There are no constitutional reasons for regretting such developments. Indeed, there will be a democratic bonus if a government's policies can come under more effective scrutiny in the Commons than is possible when the House is dominated by a single-party government. Coalitions, electoral pacts and understandings between the parties are not in themselves unconstitutional.[139] Nor is the occasional decision of an MP to switch allegiance to another party.[140]

There are many features of the political process that determine how the governmental structure operates. The internal procedures of the parties are often of constitutional importance – for example, the election of a leader, the relationship between the parliamentary party and other bodies, and the relationship between the Labour party and the trade unions. It has been the British tradition that the political parties are essentially self-regulating, but that tradition began to change with the Political Parties, Elections and Referendums Act 2000, that sets limits within which the parties operate and maintains a measure of democratic equality between the contesting parties.[141]

We have seen that the 2005 general election produced a House of Commons that was seriously unrepresentative of the electorate. At that election, the turnout of voters (at 61 per cent) was only slightly higher than in 2001, when just under 60 per cent voted. Disenchantment of the electorate with the political system reached its height in the summer of 2009, under the shock of press revelations about the payment of parliamentary expenses under a system which could not survive such exposure. What was most worrying about this dramatic crisis was not the amount of the expenses themselves, and the gulf in expectations that was exposed between the public and elected politicians, but the real possibility that MPs were at the same time failing to perform their constitutional role of calling government to account.

---

[138] See Steel, *A House Divided: the Lib-Lab Pact and the Future of British Politics.*

[139] See Butler (ed.), *Coalitions in British Politics*; Butler, *Governing without a Majority: Dilemmas for Hung Parliaments in Britain*; Bogdanor, *Multi-party Politics and the Constitution.*

[140] On MPs who cross the floor of the Commons between elections, see P Cowley [1996] PL 214.

[141] See ch 9 C–E.

CHAPTER 3

The structure of the United Kingdom

A. The historic structure

While the external identity of a state is a matter for international law, it is constitutional law which regulates the internal relationships of the various territories which make up the state. In the past, writers often used the word 'English' in referring to the constitution, a usage liable to give the false impression that English law prevailed throughout the United Kingdom. Dicey and Bagehot, for example, wrote about the English constitution when they were dealing with the British constitution or, to be completely accurate, with what was then the constitution of the United Kingdom of Great Britain and Ireland. The active political consciousness of Ireland since the 19th century, and that of Scotland and Wales more recently, means that constitutional lawyers must choose their geographical adjectives with care. When in 1969 a royal commission on the constitution was appointed, among its duties was 'to examine the present functions of the central legislature and government in relation to *the several countries, nations and regions* of the United Kingdom'.[1] Some of the deliberate vagueness of the words in italics was dispelled when the commission's report referred to England, Scotland, Wales and Northern Ireland as the four countries which make up the United Kingdom.

Legal definitions

In law, the expression 'United Kingdom' refers to the United Kingdom of Great Britain and Northern Ireland; it does not include the Channel Islands or the Isle of Man.[2] For purposes of international relations, however, the Channel Islands and the Isle of Man are represented by the UK government. So are the remaining overseas territories of the United Kingdom, such as Gibraltar and the Falkland Islands.[3]

The expression 'British Islands' is defined in the Interpretation Act 1978 as meaning the United Kingdom, the Channel Islands and the Isle of Man. The Republic of Ireland is of course outside the United Kingdom.[4] The expression 'Great Britain' refers to England, Scotland and Wales: these first became a single kingdom by virtue of art 1 of the Treaty of Union between England and Scotland in 1707.

The Wales and Berwick Act 1746 provided, curiously to our eyes today, that where the expression 'England' was used in an Act of Parliament, this should be taken to include the dominion of Wales and the town of Berwick-upon-Tweed. But by the Welsh Language Act 1967, s 4, references to England in future Acts do not include Wales. Concerning the boundary between Wales and England, a long-standing controversy was brought to an end by the Local Government Act 1972, which declared Monmouthshire to be within Wales.[5]

The adjective 'British' is used in common speech to refer to matters associated with Great Britain or the United Kingdom. It has no definite legal connotation and one authority has described the

---

[1] See section B in this chapter.
[2] Interpretation Act 1978, Sch 1. By the British Nationality Act 1981, s 50 (1), the United Kingdom includes the Channel Islands and the Isle of Man for purposes of nationality law.
[3] Ch 15 C.
[4] As to which, see Roberts-Wray, *Commonwealth and Colonial Law*, pp 32–5.
[5] Ss 1(12), 20(7) and 269; Interpretation Act 1978, Sch 1.

expression 'British law' as hopelessly ambiguous.[6] In legislation 'British' is sometimes used as an adjective referring to the United Kingdom, particularly in the context of nationality.[7]

Historical development of the United Kingdom

1 Wales.[8] While it is not possible to summarise the lengthy history by which the kingdom of England became a single entity, it is worthwhile briefly to examine the historical formation of the United Kingdom. The military conquest of Wales by the English reached its culmination in 1282, when Prince Llywelyn was killed and his principality passed by conquest to King Edward I of England. Thereafter the principality (which formed only part of what is now Wales) was administered in the name of the Prince, but the rest of Wales was subjected to rule by a variety of local princes and lords; at this period English law was not extended to Wales, where the local customs, laws and language prevailed. From 1471, a Council of Wales and the Marches brought Wales under closer rule from England and the accession of the Tudors did much to complete the process of assimilation. In 1536, an Act of the English Parliament united Wales with England, establishing an administrative system on English lines, requiring the English language to be used, and granting Wales representation in the English Parliament.[9] In 1543, a system of Welsh courts (the Courts of the Great Sessions) was established to apply the common law of England. The Council of Wales and the Marches was granted a statutory jurisdiction which it exercised until its abolition in 1689. In 1830, the Courts of the Great Sessions were abolished and in their place were set up two new circuits to operate as part of the English court system. After the union with England, Acts of Parliament applying exclusively to Wales were rare.[10]

The mid-19th century saw the beginning of a political and educational revival and occasional Acts of Parliament applying only to Wales began again to be passed.[11] In 1906 the Welsh Department of the Board of Education was established, the first central department created specifically to administer Welsh affairs.[12] In 1914 was passed the Welsh Church Act, which disestablished and disendowed the Church of England in Wales. Thereafter, from time to time, the identity of Wales was recognised as new administrative arrangements were made.[13] In 1964, the post of Secretary of State for Wales was established and the Welsh Office emerged as a department of the UK government. Thereafter administration of Wales through the Welsh Office was largely based on the model of the Scottish Office,[14] except that the Welsh Office was never divided into departments and did not maintain a regular legislative programme at Westminster. Wales and England share a common legal system,[15] but some statutes make special provision for Wales. By the Welsh Language Act 1967, the Welsh language may be spoken in any legal proceedings within Wales, by any person who desires to use it; and ministers may prescribe the use of Welsh versions of any official document or form. The Welsh Language Act 1993 created the Welsh Language Board, to further the principle in Wales that public authorities and the courts should treat the English and Welsh languages on a basis of equality.

---

[6] Roberts-Wray, p 69.

[7] British Nationality Act 1981. See ch 20 A.

[8] Kilbrandon Report, ch 5, and Andrews (ed.), *Welsh Studies in Public Law*, specially chs 2 (D Jenkins), 3 (H Carter) and 4 (I L Gowan).

[9] 27 Hen VIII, c 26. The Statute Law Revision Act 1948 called this the Laws in Wales Act 1535, but recent Welsh writers have called it the Act of Union of 1536: *Welsh Studies*, p 28.

[10] See e.g. Welsh Bible and Prayer Book Act 1563: *Welsh Studies*, pp 38–9.

[11] See e.g. Sunday Closing (Wales) Act 1881: *Welsh Studies*, p 48.

[12] *Welsh Studies*, p 49.

[13] E.g. creation of the Welsh Economic Planning Council in 1966.

[14] See *Welsh Studies*, ch 4 (I L Gowan); and HLE, vol 8(2), pp 50–4.

[15] See e.g. Constitutional Reform Act 2005, ss 7–9.

2 Scotland.[16] Unlike Wales, Scotland maintained its national independence against English military and political pressures during the Middle Ages. Scotland retained its own monarchy and only in the 16th century did the two royal lines come closer together with the marriage of Henry VII's daughter, Margaret, to James IV of Scotland. On the death of Elizabeth in 1603, James VI of Scotland, great-great-grandson of Henry VII, became James I of England. This personal union of the two monarchies had the legal consequence that persons born in England and Scotland after the union both owed allegiance to the same King.[17] During the conflicts of the 17th century, there was a brief period under Cromwell when the Commonwealth of England, Scotland and Ireland was subject to a single legislature and executive. But apart from this, and despite the personal union of the monarchies, the constitutions of the two countries were not united and both the English and the Scottish Parliaments maintained separate existences.[18] Following the ousting of James II/VII in 1688, the Scottish Parliament for the first time asserted independence of the royal will. There followed for some 20 years a contest of wills between the English and Scottish Parliaments, marked by religious disputation and by keen rivalry to profit from expanding ventures in world trade, against a deeply insecure European background. In 1704, the Scottish Parliament by the Act of Security went so far as to provide that if Anne died without heirs the Parliament would choose her successor, 'provided always that the same be not successor to the Crown of England', unless in the meantime acceptable conditions of government had been established between the two countries.[19] Following a strong initiative from the English government, the English and Scottish Parliaments authorised negotiations between two groups of commissioners representing each Parliament but appointed by the Queen. The Treaty of Union was drawn up by them and was approved by Act of each Parliament together with an Act to maintain Presbyterian Church government within Scotland.[20]

The Treaty of Union came into effect on 1 May 1707: it united the two kingdoms of England and Scotland into one by the name of Great Britain; the Crown was to descend to the Hanoverian line after Anne's death; there was to be a Parliament of Great Britain including 16 Scottish peers and 45 elected members in the Commons. Extensive financial and economic terms were included in the Treaty. Guarantees were given for the continuance of Scottish private law (art 18) and the Scottish courts (art 19), as well as for the maintenance of the feudal jurisdictions in Scotland and the privileges of the royal burghs in Scotland. The Act to maintain the Presbyterian Church in Scotland was incorporated in the Treaty and it provided for the maintenance of the Scottish universities. The Treaty was described as an incorporating union: it did not establish a federal system and it did not maintain any role for the previous Scottish and English legislatures. But it gave extensive guarantees to Scottish institutions. Guarantees of a similar kind for English institutions were not required as it was obvious that the English would be predominant in the new Parliament of Great Britain.[21]

In the years after 1707, the new unity of Great Britain was challenged by the Jacobite uprisings in 1715 and 1745 but without success. Various expedients were resorted to for governing Scotland from London and, from time to time, new laws were made for Scotland by the Parliament of Great Britain. Some of these, for example the abolition of the Scottish feudal jurisdictions in 1747,

---

[16] Kilbrandon Report, ch 4; Donaldson, *Scotland: James V–James VII*; Ferguson, *Scotland, 1689 to the Present*; HLE, vol 8(2), pp 54–72 and Devine, *The Scottish Nation 1700–2000*, pt 1. Also Wicks, *The Evolution of a Constitution*, ch 2.

[17] *Calvin's* case (1608) 7 Co Rep 1a. And see C Russell [2005] PL 336.

[18] See Donaldson, ch 15, and Terry, *The Scottish Parliament 1603–1707*.

[19] APS XI, 136.

[20] Scottish Act: APS XI, 406, English Act: 6 Anne c 11; *Halsbury's Statutes*, vol 10, p 44. On the making of the union, see Riley, *The Union of England and Scotland* and Devine, ch 1.

[21] On the legal effect of these guarantees, see ch 4 D. Also E Wicks (2001) 117 LQR 109; and (same author), *The Evolution of a Constitution*, ch 2.

were considered in Scotland to be a breach of the Treaty of Union. The Scottish Privy Council having been abolished in 1708, for much of the 18th and 19th centuries the Lord Advocate, the Crown's chief law officer in Scotland, occupied the primary role in politics and government, managing affairs in Scotland on behalf of the Crown. In 1885, a new post of Secretary for Scotland was created and in 1928 the post was raised to Cabinet status with the title of Secretary of State for Scotland. Demands for home rule for Scotland were expressed from the late 19th century onwards: the response of the government was to develop the Scottish Office as the department responsible for Scottish affairs.[22] Political demands for a Scottish legislative assembly were firmly resisted, although greater use was made of committees of Scottish MPs in the Commons. After 1707, Parliament often legislated separately for the English and Scottish legal systems. In particular, the structure of private law, the courts, education and local government in Scotland has always differed from the English pattern.

From 1945 to 1999 the Scottish Office comprised four or five departments of the UK government, located in Edinburgh but headed by a Cabinet minister (the Secretary of State for Scotland).[23] The officials in these departments were members of the British civil service. The functions entrusted to the Scottish Office included agriculture and fisheries, education, the environment, health, housing, local government, police, prisons, roads, social services, transport (except road freight and rail), tourism and town planning. Other functions (such as inland revenue, social security, employment and the control of immigration) were exercised in Scotland by British or UK departments. As well as having direct responsibility for the Scottish Office, the Secretary of State had an indirect interest in all matters affecting Scotland, enabling a Scottish voice to be heard in a wide variety of decisions made in Whitehall.

Although the political direction of government remained centralised in the Cabinet, the Scottish Office system enabled much Scottish business to be handled by civil servants resident in Scotland and, latterly, some financial autonomy was conferred on Scottish ministers. On certain matters, uniform social and economic standards were maintained throughout Great Britain (for example, financing of higher education) but in some services higher levels of expenditure were accepted and Scottish initiatives in administration could be taken. One drawback was that subjects on which separate legislation for Scotland was customary had to compete for time and political support in Westminster's legislative programme. The political legitimacy of the system was brought into question whenever, as from 1970 to 1974 and from 1979 to 1997, the majority of MPs from Scotland were in the Opposition at Westminster. For instance, despite the fact that only ten Conservative MPs (out of 72) were elected from Scotland at the 1987 election, the Conservative government in 1989 abolished domestic rates for financing local government in favour of the notorious poll tax (community charge), one year earlier in Scotland than in England and Wales.[24] Although the Scottish Office system was for a time referred to as 'administrative devolution', it was in essence a form of direct rule of Scotland by the UK government.

3 Northern Ireland.[25] The history of Northern Ireland is inextricably linked with that of Ireland itself. As an entity Northern Ireland dates only from the partition of Ireland in the early 1920s. Ireland itself first came under English influence in the 12th century when Henry II of England

---

[22] See H J Hanham in Wolfe (ed.) *Government and Nationalism in Scotland*, ch 4.

[23] See Drucker (ed.) *Scottish Government Yearbook 1980*, ch 8 (M Macdonald and A Redpath); Keating and Midwinter, *The Government of Scotland*; Milne, *The Scottish Office*. And HLE, vol 8(2), pp 69–71.

[24] See C M G Himsworth and N C Walker [1987] PL 586 and authorities cited below in ch 4, note 167.

[25] For the earlier history, see Donaldson, *Some Comparative Aspects of Irish Law*; for the 1920 Constitution, Calvert, *Constitutional Law in Northern Ireland*, and Kilbrandon Report, ch 6. Also Hadfield, *The Constitution of Northern Ireland*; Hadfield (ed.), *Northern Ireland: Politics and the Constitution*; C McCrudden, in Jowell and Oliver (eds), *The Changing Constitution*, 3rd edn, ch 12; Morison and Livingstone, *Reshaping Public Power*; HLE, vol 8(2), pp 72–93.

became Lord of Ireland. As settlers came from England, courts modelled on those in England were established. While an Irish Parliament began to develop, some English legislation was extended to Ireland by ordinance of the King of England. In 1494, the Irish Parliament passed the statute known as Poyning's Law, which required that all Irish Bills be submitted to the King and his Council in England; only such Bills as the English Council approved were to be returned for the Irish Parliament to pass. In 1541, the title of Lord of Ireland was changed to King of Ireland. During the 17th century, Ireland had its share of religious bitterness and conflict. William of Orange defeated the former King James II at the Battle of the Boyne in 1690. To resolve a dispute over the power of the Irish House of Lords to hear appeals from Irish courts, the British Parliament in 1720 declared by statute that it retained full power to legislate for Ireland and deprived the Irish House of Lords of all its judicial powers. Pressure from Ireland for greater autonomy led in 1782 to the repeal of the Declaratory Act of 1720 and to the recognition by the British Parliament of the Irish Parliament's legislative independence of Britain, although there was no change in the position of the monarchy.[26] But legislative independence was short-lived and after the rising of the United Irishmen in 1798, the British government proceeded to a legislative union with Ireland.

The Union agreement between the two Parliaments was broadly similar to the Union with Scotland, although fewer constitutional guarantees were given to Ireland than had been given to Scotland. Article 1 created the United Kingdom of Great Britain and Ireland and arts 3 and 4 provided for Irish representation in the new Parliament of the United Kingdom. Article 5 provided for the (Protestant) United Church of England and Ireland, whose continuance was stated to be an essential and fundamental part of the Union. Within the enlarged United Kingdom, all trade was to be free; the laws in force in Ireland were to continue, subject to alteration by the UK Parliament from time to time. As with the Scottish Union, the terms of the Union were separately adopted by Act of each of the two Parliaments concerned.[27]

The Irish Union with Britain was less stable than the Anglo-Scottish Union of 1707. For much of the 19th and 20th centuries, the Irish question was one of the most difficult political and constitutional issues within the United Kingdom. Catholic emancipation occurred in 1829, opening the way for demands for further reform, often associated with militant action and violence. The Irish Church was disestablished in 1869 despite the guarantee for its existence contained in the Act of Union.[28] Gladstone's two Home Rule Bills in 1886 and 1893 were both defeated in Parliament, the first in the Commons, the second in the Lords. After the Parliament Act 1911 had taken away the power of the House of Lords to veto legislation,[29] the Government of Ireland Act 1914 became law, but it never came into effect because of the outbreak of world war; its parliamentary history had been marked by the extreme determination of Ulster Protestants not to be separated from Britain.

The Easter rising in Dublin in 1916 was further evidence of the nationalist feeling in Catholic Ireland. In 1919, the Sinn Fein movement established a representative assembly for what was proclaimed to be the Irish Republic. In 1920, the Government of Ireland Act was passed by the UK Parliament, providing for two Parliaments in Ireland, one for six northern counties and one for the remainder of Ireland, with cooperation between the two to be maintained by means of a Council of Ireland. The 1920 Act was ignored by Sinn Fein and, after a period of bitter civil war, an Anglo-Irish Treaty was formally concluded in 1922. This recognised the emergence of the Irish Free State, on which Westminster conferred what was then described as the status of a self-governing dominion within the British Empire.[30] The six northern counties

---

[26] Cf *Re Keenan* [1972] 1 QB 533.
[27] For the Union with Ireland Act 1800, see *Halsbury's Statutes*, vol 31 (2003 reissue), p 628.
[28] *Ex p Canon Selwyn* (1872) 36 JP 54, and see Calvert, pp 20–1.
[29] Ch 10 B.
[30] Ch 15 C.

were excluded from the Irish Free State, acquiring their own government and Parliament under the 1920 Act.

The dominion status of the Irish Free State proved no more than a transitional stage and the Irish Constitution of 1937 declared that Eire was a sovereign independent state. During the Second World War, Eire was neutral. In 1949, the state became the Republic of Ireland and the UK Parliament at last recognised that Eire had ceased to be part of Her Majesty's dominions although it was, perhaps anomalously, also declared that Ireland was not to be regarded as a foreign country.[31]

Under the system of government established under the Act of 1920, Northern Ireland possessed its own executive (Governor, Prime Minister and Cabinet) and a legislature of two houses (Senate and House of Commons) sitting at Stormont.[32] Northern Ireland elected a reduced number of MPs to sit at Westminster and was subject to the legislative supremacy of Westminster. By the 1920 Act, certain matters were reserved for the United Kingdom, including the Crown, treaties and foreign relations, armed forces and defence, postal services and customs and excise. Subject to the reserved matters, the Stormont Parliament had power 'to make laws for the peace, order and good government of Northern Ireland'.[33] Constitutional issues could be referred for decision to the Privy Council, but if an Act of the Stormont Parliament exceeded its competence (for example, by legislating with respect to the armed forces),[34] it could be held invalid by the courts. Stormont was heavily dependent on the United Kingdom for financial support, particularly in maintaining policies that offered the same social benefits as in Great Britain. The courts rarely had to interpret the Act of 1920 and no body of constitutional case law developed.[35] Since the Unionist party representing the Protestant majority was in power throughout the life of Stormont, the Catholic community was in a permanent minority and their accumulated grievances led to civil unrest from 1968 onwards.[36] The UK government had to intervene increasingly in Northern Ireland until, in 1972, direct rule of Northern Ireland was resumed and the 1920 constitution was suspended.[37] In 1973, after a poll of the electorate had shown a clear majority in favour of Northern Ireland remaining part of the United Kingdom, the system of government under the 1920 Act was ended. In its place, an attempt was made to establish a new Assembly and a new form of executive based on the concept of power-sharing.[38] Elections were held by proportional representation, and the Sunningdale agreement (to which the Dublin government was a party) was reached in 1974. This proved to be the first of many constitutional initiatives that failed to achieve sufficient support from both communities, and the Northern Ireland Act 1974 restored direct rule. Later developments included an increase in Northern Ireland's representation at Westminster from 12 to 17 seats,[39] and in 1985 the signing of the Anglo-Irish Agreement by the British and Irish Prime Ministers at Hillsborough.[40] The Agreement gave the assurance that no change in the status of Northern Ireland would occur without consent of the majority of its people, and it sought to increase cooperation between the two governments in relation to

---

[31] Ireland Act 1949, ss 1(1) and 2.

[32] See note 25. Also Birrell and Murie, *Policy and Government in Northern Ireland*; Buckland, *The Factory of Grievances*; Lawrence, *The Government of Northern Ireland*, ch 10.

[33] Government of Ireland Act 1920, s 4(1).

[34] See *R (Hume) v Londonderry Justices* [1972] NILR 91; Northern Ireland Act 1972.

[35] See *Londonderry CC v McGlade* [1925] NI 47; *Gallagher v Lynn* [1937] AC 863; *Belfast Corporation v OD Cars Ltd* [1960] AC 490.

[36] See Cmnd 532, 1969 (the Cameron report).

[37] Northern Ireland (Temporary Provisions) Act 1972.

[38] Cmnd 5259, 1973; Northern Ireland Assembly Act 1973; Northern Ireland Constitution Act 1973.

[39] House of Commons (Redistribution of Seats) Act 1979.

[40] Cmnd 9690. And see Hadden and Boyle, *The Anglo-Irish Agreement*.

security, economic and social matters, thereby causing Unionists to protest at this recognition of the Dublin government's interest in Northern Ireland.[41]

Both direct rule and terrorist activity continued during most of the 1990s. In 1993, the 'Downing Street Declaration' of the two Prime Ministers repeated the earlier assurance that the status of the province could not be changed without majority consent and confirmed that the British government would not oppose a united Ireland for which there was popular consent.[42] Despite a short-lived cessation of terrorist activities, during which further proposals for an Assembly were outlined.[43] no substantial progress towards all-party talks was made and the IRA's bombing of South Quay in London occurred in February 1996.[44] It was the election of the Labour government in 1997 that opened the way for the 'Good Friday Agreement' in 1998, which will be outlined in section B.

Three legal systems

The United Kingdom has often been described as a unitary state, since there is no structure of federalism. But it will be evident that constitutional diversity exists within the United Kingdom alongside many common factors. While the legislative power of Parliament extends to all the United Kingdom, three legal systems exist, each with its own courts and legal profession, namely (a) England and Wales, (b) Scotland and (c) Northern Ireland. A unifying influence is that the Supreme Court for the United Kingdom (replacing in 2009 the House of Lords) is the final court of appeal from all three jurisdictions, except for criminal cases in Scotland. When Parliament legislates, it may legislate for all the United Kingdom (for example, income tax or immigration law), for Great Britain (for example, social security or trade union law), or separately for one or more of the countries within the United Kingdom.

In the next section, we examine aspects of the current devolution legislation applying to Scotland, Wales and Northern Ireland. Emphasis will be given to key structural aspects and it will not be possible in this work to describe how these schemes of devolution are operating.[45]

B. Devolution of government

The Labour government elected in 1997 was committed to securing devolution of government to both Scotland and Wales and to renewing efforts to establish peace and order in Northern Ireland. This commitment caused Westminster in 1998 to legislate separately for Scotland, Wales and Northern Ireland.[46] It is an indication of the asymmetric structure of the United Kingdom that the differences between the three Acts are almost greater than the similarities.

Devolution is not a term of art in constitutional law. Unlike federalism, its nature within the United Kingdom depends not on a written constitution, but on the legislation authorising

---

[41] For an unsuccessful legal challenge, see *Ex p Molyneaux* [1986] 1 WLR 331. And cf *McGimpsey v Ireland* [1990] ILRM 441.

[42] Cm 2442, 1994.

[43] Cm 2964, 1995.

[44] And see Cm 3232, 1996; and Northern Ireland (Entry to Negotiations, etc.) Act 1996.

[45] On the operation of devolution, see the Constitution Unit's series: Hazell (ed.) *The State and the Nations*; Trench (ed.) *The State of the Nations 2001*; Hazell (ed.) *The State of the Nations 2003*; Trench (ed.) *Has Devolution made a Difference?*, *The Dynamics of Devolution* and *The State of the Nations 2008*. Also Hazell and Rawlings, *Devolution, Law Making and the Constitution*.

[46] Scotland Act 1998; Government of Wales Act 1998; and Northern Ireland Act 1998. See Bogdanor, *Devolution in the United Kingdom*; Burrows, *Devolution*; and A J Ward, in Jowell and Oliver (eds), *The Changing Constitution*, 4th edn, ch 5.

devolution and on the practice that develops through new structures for decision-making. In the United Kingdom, devolution has come to mean the vesting of legislative and executive powers in elected bodies in Scotland, Wales and Northern Ireland, who thus have political responsibility for the devolved functions. Legislation to create devolved government includes provision for: (1) an elected assembly for the area in question; (2) a political executive responsible to the assembly; (3) 'machinery of government' matters, including funding; (4) the functions to be devolved; and (5) legal and political control of those powers. Despite the creation of a new level of government, the Parliament and government in London retain authority over all the United Kingdom.

Precursors to devolution

The schemes of devolution created in 1998 were influenced by the abortive attempt in the 1970s to establish devolved government for Scotland and Wales. In 1973, the Royal Commission on the constitution (the Kilbrandon Report)[47] made proposals for devolution that were far from unanimous. For Scotland, eight of the 13 members recommended legislative devolution, with an elected assembly with power to make laws and an executive of ministers drawn from the assembly. But only six members of the Commission favoured a similar scheme for Wales.

The Labour government of 1974–79 undertook to create elected assemblies for Scotland and Wales, but it lacked an absolute majority in the House of Commons for much of this period and it experienced great difficulties with the devolution project. After lengthy debates, the Scotland Act and the Wales Act were enacted in 1978, to come into effect if approved by referendum in each country. In referendums held on 1 March 1979, the scheme for Wales was heavily defeated; in Scotland, a small majority of those voting supported devolution, but they were less than 40 per cent of the whole electorate and did not satisfy the '40 per cent rule' that had been applied to the referendum to guard against a low turnout of voters. Orders repealing the Scotland and Wales Acts were made after the Conservatives were elected into office in May 1979.

Between 1979 and 1997, the Conservative government opposed all proposals for devolution within Great Britain, although in 1995 it supported minor changes in Scottish business at Westminster, extending the functions of the Scottish Grand Committee in the Commons.[48] The Labour and Liberal Democrat parties supported the Scottish Constitutional Convention, a non-governmental body endorsed by many groups and organisations in Scotland. In 1995, the Convention proposed a scheme of devolution which sought to improve upon the Scotland Act 1978.[49] In 1997 the Labour and Liberal Democrat parties agreed that there would be an early referendum in Scotland on the Convention's scheme. For Wales, they favoured an elected assembly to oversee Welsh affairs.

The Referendums (Scotland and Wales) Act 1997 authorised referendums in Scotland and Wales respectively, to gain the approval of electors to the government's schemes for devolution.[50] In 1997, of the 60 per cent who voted in the Scottish referendum, 74 per cent supported the proposed Scottish Parliament and 63.5 per cent agreed that the Parliament should be able to vary the basic rate of income tax for Scottish taxpayers. In Wales, only 50 per cent of the electorate voted, of whom no more than 50.3 per cent supported the proposed Assembly. Thereafter, legislation to implement the schemes was enacted at Westminster and the first elections to the Parliament and the Assembly were held in May 1999.

---

[47] Cmnd 5460, 1973. And see T C Daintith (1974) 37 MLR 544.
[48] See HC S0 94A–94H (1995); HC Deb, 29 November 1995, col 1228, and 19 December 1995, col 1410.
[49] *Scotland's Parliament, Scotland's Right* (1995); J McFadden [1995] PL 215; D Millar (1997) 1 Edin LR 260.
[50] *Scotland's Parliament*, Cm 3658, 1997; and *A Voice for Wales*, Cm 3718, 1997.

The Scotland Act 1998[51]

Part I of the Act created a unicameral Scottish Parliament. Of its 129 members, 73 are elected from single-member constituencies by simple majority vote and 56 are elected by regions under an 'additional member' system of proportional representation. Elections are held every four years (s 2), but exceptionally elections may be held at other times, for example if two-thirds of the members vote for a resolution dissolving the Parliament (s 3). The electoral system is likely to ensure that no single party has an absolute majority. In 2007, the Scottish National Party won the largest number of seats (47) and formed a minority government. Subject to the different electoral system, the electoral rules are similar to those which apply to elections for Westminster.[52] Members of the Scottish Parliament (MSPs) are not prevented by law from being members of the House of Commons or the Lords, or of the European Parliament.

The Scottish Parliament has a broad power to make laws for Scotland, to be known as Acts of the Scottish Parliament (s 28(1)), but this power does not extend to matters reserved to Westminster. 'Reserved matters' include the Crown, the Union, foreign affairs, the civil service, defence of the realm and the armed forces and a long list of domestic matters under 11 headings, including finance and the economy (such as fiscal, economic and monetary policy and financial services), aspects of home affairs (such as the misuse of drugs, data protection, immigration and nationality), trade and industry (such as import and export policy), energy, social security, regulation of the professions, employment, broadcasting and equal opportunities.[53]

If the Scottish Parliament were to go outside its competence by legislating on a 'reserved matter', the provision in question would not be law (s 29(1)). Other limits on the Parliament's competence are that a Scottish Act may not affect the law of any country outside Scotland and may not conflict with Community law or with the European Convention on Human Rights.[54]

By Part II of the Act, the Scottish Executive comprises the First Minister, other ministers and the law officers (the Lord Advocate and the Solicitor-General for Scotland) (s 44). The First Minister is appointed by the Queen after having been nominated by the Parliament (ss 45, 46). The First Minister and other ministers must be MSPs and the nomination of the other ministers must be approved by the Parliament before their formal appointment (s 47). The First Minister, other ministers, and the law officers must resign if the Parliament resolves that the Executive no longer enjoys the confidence of the Parliament (ss 45(2), 47(3)(c), 48(2)). The Executive is thereby accountable to the Parliament, which may scrutinise acts of the Executive and the civil servants who staff the Scottish Administration (s 51). For this purpose, the Parliament has developed a system of committees, dealing with all aspects of the work of the Executive.

The Executive's powers are based on a transfer of functions to Scottish ministers from the UK government. In general, these functions relate to matters within the Parliament's legislative competence, but there are certain matters on which executive power is devolved to the Executive without power to legislate being conferred on the Parliament. Like the Parliament, the Executive may not take decisions that are contrary to European Community law or conflict with Convention rights (s 57).

Parts III and IV of the Act deal with finance. The bulk of the income of the Scottish Administration comes from a block grant made from Westminster. This (together with similar grants for devolved services in Wales and Northern Ireland) is calculated with reference to what is called

---

[51] Himsworth and Munro, *The Scotland Act 1998*; Page, Reid and Ross, *A Guide to the Scotland Act 1998*; N Burrows (1999) 62 MLR 241; Jowell and Oliver (eds), *The Changing Constitution* (6th edn, 2007), ch 9 (B K Winetrobe); Himsworth and O'Neill, *Scotland's Constitution: Law and Practice*, chs 4–6.

[52] See ch 9 D.

[53] Schedule 5 to the Act contains general and specific reservations; detailed provisions modify the effect of the general headings. And see Himsworth and O'Neill, pp 119–40.

[54] S 29(2)(a), (d). And see chs 8 and 19 B, C.

the 'Barnett formula', not found in the Scotland Act itself, which produces a sum that is treated as Scotland's share of public expenditure.[55] Within that total, the Scottish Administration may set its own priorities for expenditure on devolved matters, and it has, for instance, decided to adopt its own policy on university tuition fees and to provide free personal care for the elderly.[56] The Scottish authorities have power (not yet exercised) to increase or reduce the basic rate of income tax paid by Scottish taxpayers[57] on their earned income by 3 pence in the pound, equivalent to an annual power to raise or forgo some £450 million.

While devolution requires that the Executive and Parliament are able to make autonomous decisions (the most controversial one since 1998 being the decision by the Scottish Minister of Justice in 2009 to permit a Libyan prisoner convicted for complicity in the Lockerbie air-disaster to return to Libya), there are safeguards against decisions that would exceed their powers. When a Bill is introduced in the Parliament, the responsible minister must be satisfied that it is within the competence of the Parliament, and the presiding officer must also consider this (s 31). The Supreme Court for the United Kingdom (formerly, the Judicial Committee of the Privy Council) may be asked to decide whether a Bill is within competence (s 33). The Scotland Act also provides for the decision of 'devolution issues'. Such issues arise when an Act of the Scottish Parliament or executive decision is challenged in a court or tribunal on the ground that it is not within devolved powers, including questions as to its compatibility with the European Convention on Human Rights.[58] A devolution issue may be referred by the court or tribunal in which it is raised to a superior court (in Scotland, to the Court of Session or the High Court of Justiciary) and from that court an appeal may lie to the Supreme Court for the UK. Since the Scotland Act is the main written text by which powers are devolved, its interpretation will have constitutional significance.[59] In practice, apart from human rights questions, very few issues arising from the Scotland Act have reached the courts.[60]

The Edinburgh Parliament has been an active legislature, no fewer than 134 Acts being enacted between 1999 and 2008. This does not necessarily mean that a greater volume of legislation is being made for Scotland than before 1999.[61] Moreover, Westminster retains power to legislate for Scotland (s 28(7)) and it has done so frequently. On devolved matters, there is a firm convention, known as the 'Sewel convention', that Westminster should not legislate on a devolved matter or on one that affects the extent of devolved powers without the prior consent of the Scottish Parliament. No less than 42 legislative consent motions were passed in 1999–2003. This extensive use of Westminster's continuing supremacy is controversial[62] but often convenient, though this may depend on whether there is a working relationship between the governments in Edinburgh and London. Scotland's representation in the Commons was in 2005 reduced from

---

[55] The formula, dating from 1979, is used to calculate a population-based proportion for each of Scotland, Wales and Northern Ireland, of changes in planned spending on comparable services in England: see HC 341 (1997–8), HC 619 (1997–8) and HM Treasury, *Funding the Scottish Parliament, National Assembly for Wales and the Northern Ireland Assembly* (2000). Also Trench (ed.), *The Dynamics of Devolution*, ch 8 (D Bell and A Christie) and House of Commons Library Research Paper 07/91, *The Barnett Formula*.

[56] On the latter, see Hazell (ed.), *The State of the Nations 2003*, ch 9 (R Simeon).

[57] For a definition of Scottish taxpayers, see Scotland Act 1998, s 75.

[58] Scotland Act 1998, Sch 6. Significant decisions on devolution issues raising human rights questions include *Anderson v Scottish Ministers* [2001] UKPCD 5, [2003] 2 AC 602 (detention of potentially dangerous psychiatric patients); *Brown v Stott* [2003] 1 AC 681 (car owner's duty to inform police of identity of driver); and *R v Lord Advocate* [2002] UKPC D3, [2004] 1 AC 462 (duty of court to stay delayed prosecution).

[59] See P Craig and M Walters [1999] PL 274 and S Tierney (2001) 5 Edin LR 49.

[60] But see *Whaley v Lord Watson* 2000 SC 340 and *Adams v Scottish Ministers* 2004 SC 665. On the relationship between devolution issues and claims under the Human Rights Act, see *Somerville v Scottish Ministers* [2007] UKHL 44, [2007] 1 WLR 2734.

[61] See Hazell and Rawlings, note 45 above, ch 1 (A Page).

[62] For the 'Sewel convention', see Himsworth and O'Neill, pp 140–3; *Memorandum of Understanding* (Cm 4444, 1999), para 13; A Page and A Batey [2002] PL 501; Hazell and Rawlings, ch 2 (B Winetrobe).

72 seats to 59, through a boundary review of constituencies based on population and on the basis of parity with representation in England. Contrary to the original provision in the Scotland Act, this reduction in seats at Westminster did not mean a reduction in the size of the Scottish Parliament.[63]

The political significance of the Edinburgh Parliament in Scottish public life is immeasurable, enabling as it does the Scottish people to be represented in a forum that has resonances of Scotland's history before 1707. Its existence requires the UK government to take seriously the commitment to 'subsidiarity' that has emerged as a principle of the European Union.[64]

One issue that has arisen after ten years of devolution is whether these constitutional arrangements can be improved while maintaining the principle of devolution, or whether devolution (if successful) must necessarily lead to a demand for independence. In 2009, a cross-party commission chaired by Sir Kenneth Calman (appointed by the London government, at the request of the Labour, Conservative and Liberal Democrat parties in the Scottish Parliament) reported on the need for changes in the present system.[65] The report concluded that devolution had been a 'real success' and that the Scottish Parliament worked well in practice; it was to Scotland's advantage that the UK, despite the asymmetry of its union structure, enjoyed a highly integrated commercial and financial economy. However, the report recommended the enactment of guarantees for the content of common social rights (particularly in health and education) and the formal inclusion of the Sewel convention in the standing orders of both Parliaments. Also recommended were measures for improving the Scottish Executive's financial accountability, included broader devolved powers of taxation, and the creation of a Scottish rate of income tax. In response, the Scottish National Party continued to favour the scheme for a referendum on Scottish independence.

The Government of Wales Act 2006[66]

Although both schemes were created in 1998, devolution to Wales has always differed markedly from devolution to Scotland. Under the remarkably opaque and bureaucratic Government of Wales Act 1998, the National Assembly for Wales had no general power to make laws and was seen as a quasi-executive body, being limited to making secondary (or delegated) legislation by transfer from the Secretary of State for Wales. In composition, the Assembly was and remains a smaller version of the Scottish Parliament: 40 members are elected in single-member constituencies by simple majority, and 20 members by regions under proportional representation. In 2004, a commission appointed by the Assembly, chaired by Lord Richard, recommended that the Assembly should have a broad power to make laws for Wales, that there should be a clear distinction between legislative and executive powers, and that the Assembly should have 80 members, elected by single transferable vote.[67] In response,[68] the government agreed that future legislation at Westminster would give scope for the use of the Assembly's legislative powers, by using 'framework' clauses applying to Wales.[69] The government also agreed to create

---

[63] See the Scottish Parliamentary Constituencies Act 2004 (and HC 77 (2003–04)); ch 9 B.

[64] On the Scottish Parliament, see B K Winetrobe, *Realising the Vision: A Parliament with a Purpose* (Constitution Unit); Trench (ed.) *The Dynamics of Devolution*, chs 2 (J Mitchell), 8 and 12 (A Trench) and 9 (C Jeffery). On devolution generally, Bogdanor, *The New British Constitution*, ch 4.

[65] See *Serving Scotland Better: Scotland and the UK in the 21st Century*, June 2009. For the committee's appointment, see HC Deb, 25 March 2008, col 24.

[66] See Jowell and Oliver (eds), *The Changing Constitution* (6th edn), ch 11 (B Hadfield); A Trench [2006] PL 687. For the position under the Government of Wales Act 1998, see Rawlings, *Delineating Wales: Constitutional, Legal and Administrative Aspects of National Devolution*; and see works cited in note 45 above.

[67] Commission on the Powers and Electoral Arrangements of the National Assembly for Wales, 2004.

[68] *Better Governance for Wales*, Cm 6582, 2005. See R Rawlings [2005] PL 824.

[69] E.g. National Health Service Redress Act 2006, s 17.

a new procedure for devolving legislative powers on a piecemeal basis. However, it rejected both the idea of a larger Assembly and the proposal that the Assembly should have a general power to make laws.

What emerged in 2006 was a new Government of Wales Act, re-enacting much of the 1998 Act but containing new provisions. The following account briefly outlines the current law, as well as changes that may take place in the future.

Assembly elections are held every four years, except that an extraordinary election may be held if at least two-thirds of all members vote for it, or if the Assembly fails to nominate a First Minister within the requisite time (2006 Act, s 5). No person may be nominated on a party's regional list of candidates who has been nominated for election in an Assembly constituency (s 7). The Assembly has a broad power to appoint committees and sub-committees (s 28). Since the Assembly has no general legislative power, it is consulted each year before the UK government draws up its legislative programme for Westminster (s 33), and some laws may be made in this way to meet Welsh needs.[70]

Executive powers are vested in the Welsh Ministers; the 'Welsh Assembly Government' (s 45) comprises the First Minister, the Welsh Ministers, deputy ministers, and the Counsel General to the Welsh Government, a new office created to advise ministers and Assembly on devolution law (s 49). The Government's functions include the promotion of economic, social and environmental well-being (s 60), and the support of culture (including the arts, libraries, sport and the Welsh language) (s 61). There are some 20 fields of government (Schedule 5) in respect of which power to legislate may be devolved under Part 3 of the Act. These include such fields as agriculture and forestry, education, health and social services, local government, tourism, transport and the voluntary sector. As well as exercising powers formerly vested in the Secretary of State for Wales, the Assembly may scrutinise the activities of Welsh public bodies.

The 2006 Act thus brought Wales in some ways closer to the pattern of devolution in Scotland and it provides for two further phases of devolution beyond the powers granted in 1998. Part 3 of the Act empowers the Assembly (in the next phase of devolution) to make laws known as 'Assembly Measures', on matters that may be devolved to the Assembly piecemeal by the making of Orders in Council (s 93), known as Legislative Competence Orders. The matters to be devolved must relate to one or more of the 20 fields already mentioned, subject to various restrictions and exceptions as specified in the order.[71]

Looking further to the future, Part 4 of the Act provides for the granting of more general legislative power to the Assembly, in a manner resembling the power of the Scottish Parliament. Schedule 7 of the Act sets out (with accompanying restrictions) the 20 fields of subjects in which the Assembly would then have power to make laws. But before this part of the Act can come into force, a referendum must be held in Wales, an event that can take place only with the support of two-thirds of all the Assembly members, the Secretary of State for Wales, and both Houses at Westminster. If and when approval is obtained, 'Acts of the Assembly' under Part 4 of the Act will supersede 'Assembly Measures' under Part 3.

However broad the legislative powers of the Assembly may be, the Assembly will remain subject to important restrictions on its competence, for instance to ensure that it does not breach international or European obligations of the United Kingdom, and does not act inconsistently with the Human Rights Act 1998. As with Scotland, the Assembly is primarily funded by an annual block grant from Westminster calculated with reference to the Barnett formula and it can set its own expenditure priorities. But unlike the Scottish Parliament, the Assembly may not vary

---

[70] E.g. Public Services Ombudsman (Wales) Act 2005 and Commissioner for Older People (Wales) Act 2006.

[71] See e.g. the National Assembly for Wales (Legislative Competence) (Environment) Order 2010. The elaborate process for making these orders includes scrutiny by the Welsh Affairs Committee of the Commons. The outcome of this process can be remarkably opaque: see 20th report, House of Lords Constitution Committee, HL Paper 159 (2008–09).

the basic rate of income tax.[72] If devolution issues relating to Wales arise in court proceedings, they will be settled ultimately by the Supreme Court (s 149, schedule 9). In time, the greater devolution of legislative power to Wales may bring into being a distinct Welsh legal system.[73]

The Northern Ireland Act 1998

A major new initiative in Northern Ireland was taken after the general election in 1997. After lengthy talks, the Belfast (or Good Friday) Agreement was reached on 10 April 1998.[74] Strand One of the agreement provided for an elected Assembly in Northern Ireland of 108 members. Strand Two provided for a North/South Ministerial Council, representing the Northern Ireland and Irish governments and with machinery for implementing policies agreed by the Council. Strand Three provided for a British–Irish Council, representing the British and Irish governments, as well as the devolved governments of Northern Ireland, Scotland and Wales, and also a British–Irish Inter-governmental Conference to discuss Northern Ireland matters that were not devolved, such as policing.

The Belfast Agreement was endorsed on 22 May 1998 by separate referendums in both parts of Ireland and elections for the new Assembly were held in June 1998. By the Northern Ireland Act 1998, Northern Ireland is to remain part of the United Kingdom until a majority of the electorate in the province, voting in a poll held for the purpose, decide to the contrary (s 1); in that event, the Secretary of State shall lay proposals to give effect to the majority wish before the Westminster Parliament. The Assembly is, in principle, elected every four years. The electoral system is that of the single transferable vote, with each of the 18 Westminster constituencies returning six members. A complex scheme of power sharing between the main parties provides for key decisions to be taken on a cross-community basis, either by parallel consent of a majority of unionist and nationalist designations or by a weighted majority (60 per cent) of members present and voting, including at least 40 per cent of unionist and nationalist designations. Such key decisions include election of the Assembly chair, the First Minister and the Deputy First Minister.

Certain matters (such as the Crown, defence, immigration, elections and political parties) are *excepted* from devolution (s 4 and Sch 2). Other matters (including civil aviation, criminal law, emergency powers, telecommunications, consumer protection and data protection) are *reserved* from devolution (s 4 and Sch 3). *Transferred* matters, which fall within the scheme of devolution, are neither excepted nor reserved. The Assembly may make laws on transferred matters, but this does not affect the power of Westminster to make laws for Northern Ireland (s 5). The Assembly may not adopt measures that would extend outside Northern Ireland, would be incompatible with the Human Rights Act 1998 or European Community law or would discriminate on grounds of religious belief or political opinion (s 6). As in Scotland, there are safeguards against the Assembly exceeding its competence (ss 11, 14) and provision for the decision of 'devolution issues' (s 79, Sch 10).

The Executive Committee of the Assembly comprises the First Minister, the Deputy First Minister and other ministers appointed by a formula that divides ministries between the main parties on the basis of voting at the previous election. All ministers must take the prescribed pledge of office.[75]

The 1998 Act authorises other aspects of the Belfast Agreement, such as the North/South Ministerial Council and the British–Irish Council and the appointment in Northern Ireland of a

---

[72] See the first report of an independent commission on funding and finance for Wales (the Holtham commission) *Funding devolved government in Wales – Barnett and beyond* (July 2009).

[73] See T H Jones and J M Williams [2004] PL 78.

[74] *The Belfast Agreement: An Agreement Reached at the Multi-Party talks on Northern Ireland*, Cm 3383, 1998. Annexed to the multi-party agreement is an agreement between the British and Irish governments. See B Hadfield [1999] PL 599 and D O'Sullivan [2000] Dublin Univ LJ 112. On subsequent events, see Jowell and Oliver (eds), *The Changing Constitution* (6th edn, 2007), ch 10 (C McCrudden).

[75] See Northern Ireland Act 2000.

Human Rights Commission (ss 68–70) and an Equality Commission (s 73). All public authorities must promote equality of opportunity (s 75) and it is unlawful for a public authority to discriminate on grounds of religious belief or political opinion (s 76).

The progress of devolution was for several years impeded by continuing difficulties in the peace process, in particular as regards decommissioning of arms and other aspects of the security situation. For many months between 2000 and 2007, the Assembly was suspended while Northern Ireland returned to direct rule by the Secretary of State. At elections in 2003 and 2007, the Democratic Unionist Party and Sinn Fein were the leading parties from the two communities. Disagreements between them after 2003 prevented the Assembly from resuming its operations, and UK ministers became responsible for all Northern Ireland departments. In July 2005, the Provisional IRA announced the end of its armed campaign and the independent international commission on decommissioning (that had been formed in 1997) reported that the Provisional IRA had decommissioned all its weapons. On 13 October 2006, the St Andrews Agreement was concluded between the two governments and the major parties in Northern Ireland, and a time-table was set for elections, the formation of a four-party power-sharing government, and the return of devolution.[76] Devolved government under the (amended) Northern Ireland Act 1998 was restored in May 2007, with the Northern Ireland Executive Committee comprising the First Minister, the Deputy First Minister and ten departmental ministers. Debate continued into 2009 over devolving the policing and justice function.[77]

Conclusion

Assuming that devolved government in Northern Ireland will not again be suspended, it might be said that three of the four countries that make up the United Kingdom each now has a written constitution. But each of these 'constitutions' gives no more than a partial account of the government of these countries. For one thing, their operation cannot be understood without reference to the elaborate array of 'Concordats', namely, the agreements reached between Whitehall departments and the devolved executives as to how the two levels of government should relate to each other.[78] And many important functions are still exercised by the Westminster Parliament and by Whitehall. The Secretaries of State for the three countries remain in being, albeit with far fewer functions than before devolution. The positions are sometimes held rather awkwardly with other Cabinet posts,[79] and the activities of each Secretary of State are overseen by a select committee of the Commons.[80] Westminster retains power to alter the present arrangements, but use of that power cannot ignore the politics of devolution.

Devolution within the United Kingdom is indeed asymmetrical. The position in England presents a sharp contrast to Scotland, Wales and Northern Ireland. Except for Greater London, which enjoys a form of regional government in transport, economic and environmental matters,[81] democratic decision-making has not been devolved to a regional level. Yet in 1994 Whitehall divided England outside London into eight regions for official purposes and this structure has been the basis for administrative changes.[82] Until 2004, the government promoted without enthusiasm a scheme for an assembly of 25–35 members elected by proportional representation in any region

---

[76] See Northern Ireland Act 2006, Northern Ireland (Miscellaneous Provisions) Act 2006 and Northern Ireland (St Andrews Agreement) Act 2007.

[77] See Northern Ireland Act 2009. This function was eventually devolved in April 2010.

[78] See *Memorandum of Understanding and Supplementary Agreements*, Cm 4444, 1999. See the treatment of inter-governmental relations in the works cited in note 45 above. Also R Rawlings (2000) 106 LQR 257 and J Poirier [2001] PL 134.

[79] See R Hazell [2003] PL 650 on the short-lived Department of Constitutional Affairs.

[80] See ch 10 D below.

[81] Trench (ed.) *Has Devolution made a Difference?*, ch 6 (M Sandford) and *The Dynamics of Devolution*, ch 5 (M Sandford and P Hetherington).

[82] Regional Development Agencies Act 1998. See ch 17 E.

whose electors voted by referendum for an assembly.[83] In the first (and last) such referendum, held in North-East England in November 2004 by postal ballot, 48 per cent of the electorate voted, of whom 78 per cent rejected the proposed assembly. This decisive defeat halted the scheme for elected regional assemblies in England,[84] but unelected 'regional assemblies' continue in being and have acquired strategic planning functions.[85] In 2008–9, the House of Commons established eight regional affairs committees comprising a few MPs from each region 'to examine regional strategies and the work of the regional bodies!'.[86]

The schemes of devolution established in 1998 have yet to be tested in a situation in which one party is in power in London, and another party has a majority of seats in Edinburgh or Cardiff. Nor has an answer been found to the 'West Lothian question' or, as it is sometimes called, the 'English question'.[87] This question usually takes the form of asking why Scottish MPs may debate and (more importantly) vote at Westminster on, for instance, issues about the NHS, housing policy or education in England, when English MPs are barred from considering these matters in Scotland. Westminster serves both as the Parliament for the United Kingdom and for England. The difficulty would to an extent be eased with a proportional system for electing the Commons, which could lead to a more consensual approach to government, but the underlying lack of balance remains.

While devolution appears not to be leading to the break-up of the United Kingdom, as some of its opponents predicted,[88] it has led to increased complexity in the making of statute law, and in the administrative structure that underlies the political process.[89] One important aspect of devolution is the developing network of governmental relationships, both within the United Kingdom and extending into Europe.[90] Those who would support a return of the United Kingdom to its former simple unitary structure would probably also like to see the United Kingdom withdrawing from the effects of European integration. At one time devolution could be defined as involving 'the delegation of central government powers without the relinquishment of sovereignty'.[91] That conclusion is no longer sustainable except by relying on a simple view of sovereignty that leaves out of account both the new Europe and the new centres of political power in the United Kingdom.[92]

---

[83] See Cm 5511, 2002 and the Regional Assemblies (Preparations) Act 2003.

[84] See Trench (ed.), *The Dynamics of Devolution*, ch 5 (M Sandford and P Hetherington).

[85] Planning and Compulsory Purchase Act 2004, part 1.

[86] H C Standing Order 152F.

[87] B Hadfield [2005] PL 288 and in Jowell and Oliver (note 66 above); Hazell (ed.), *The English Question*.

[88] E.g. Dalyell, *Devolution, the End of Britain?*

[89] See HL Paper 192 (2003–4), App 1 (C M G Himsworth); Hazell and Rawlings, *Devolution, Law Making and the Constitution*. Also A Ross and H Nash [2009] PL 564 (examining the variety of ways by which EU environmental law is implemented within Great Britain).

[90] See HL Committee on the Constitution, *Devolution: Inter-institutional Relations in the United Kingdom*, (HL Paper 28, 2002–3); and Trench (ed.) *The Dynamics of Devolution*, ch 7 (A Trench). For the European dimension, Trench, ch 9 (C Jeffery) and R Rawlings, 'Cymru yn Ewrop: Wales in Europe', in Craig and Rawlings (eds), *Law and Administration in Europe*, ch 13.

[91] Kilbrandon Report, para 543.

[92] MacCormick, *Questioning Sovereignty*, p 74, says in respect of Scotland: 'The unitary sovereignty of the incorporating union agreed in 1707 seems to be at best in its twilight.'

CHAPTER 4

Parliamentary supremacy

It is a fundamental principle of democratic government that there should be an elected assembly representing the people, and that this assembly should have authority to make laws that apply to the entire population. But there is no universal agreement that such an assembly should have an absolute and unlimited power to make laws of whatever kind and subject matter. Indeed, in many national constitutions both the existence of the assembly and the extent of its powers are set out in the constitution itself. Without such a constitutional text, are there limits on legislative authority and, if so, where may they be found? And should measures enacted by Parliament prevail over all other rules of law?

This chapter examines the extent of the formal authority exercised today by the Westminster Parliament. We first consider briefly the stages by which that authority was established, since in the absence of a written constitution, the historical background to the authority of Parliament has great significance.

A. The growth of the legislative authority of Parliament

It is often claimed that the first Parliament was that assembled by Simon de Montfort in 1265 to give counsel to Henry III, which for the first time included representatives of the shires, cities and boroughs of England as well as the feudal barons. But to become a legislature in a modern sense, the enlarged council had to acquire a regular existence as a body with power to legislate and with settled procedure; and the measures which emerged from that procedure had to be accepted as law. By 1485, it was accepted that measures that had been considered by Parliament and enacted by the monarch could change the common law. With the English Reformation, there disappeared the belief that Parliament could not affect the authority of the Roman Church. Henry VIII and Elizabeth I made the Crown of England supreme over all persons and causes and used the English Parliament to attain this end.

Although wide authority was attributed to acts of the 'King in Parliament', two views were held as to the justification for this.[1] The royalist view grounded legislative authority in the King, acting as Sovereign in exercise of divine right, but with the approval of Lords and Commons. By contrast, the parliamentarian view stressed the role of the two Houses, acting on behalf of the nobility and the common people, in exercising supreme authority with the monarch. There continued to be a view that certain natural laws could not be changed, even by the King in Parliament.[2] To set against this view there was much authority in the law reports and in political writing which indicated that the courts had no power to review the validity of Acts of Parliament.[3]

---

[1] For historical attitudes to the authority of Parliament, see Goldsworthy, *The Sovereignty of Parliament*, ch 4. Also P Craig [2000] PL 211.

[2] See *Bonham's case* (1610) 8 Co Rep 114a, quoted below in text at note 66.

[3] Goldsworthy (passim); and Gough, *Fundamental Law in English Constitutional History*.

The struggle for supremacy

Legislative supremacy involves not only the right to change the law but also that no one else should have that right. At the heart of the conflicts of the 17th century that led to the civil war, Charles I's execution, Cromwell's Protectorate and the restoration of the monarchy in 1660, lay the question whether the King could use his prerogative powers to govern without Parliament. In 1603, the King's prerogatives were undefined. Despite the existence of Parliament and the common law courts, the King, through his Council, exercised not only full executive powers but also a residue of legislative and judicial power. Acts of Parliament which sought to take away any of the 'inseparable' prerogatives of the Crown were considered invalid.[4] Four instances of the struggle for authority between Crown and Parliament may be mentioned.

1 *Ordinances and proclamations.* A clear distinction between the statutes of the English Parliament and ordinances of the King in Council was lacking long after the end of the 13th century. The Statute of Proclamations 1539 gave Henry VIII wide powers of legislating by proclamation without reference to Parliament. This statute did not give the King and Council power to legislate, but sought to clarify the obscure position of the authority possessed by proclamations. It safeguarded the common law, existing Acts of Parliament and rights of property, and prohibited the infliction of the death penalty for breach of a proclamation.[5] 'Its chief practical purpose was to create machinery to enforce proclamations.'[6] Despite the repeal of the statute in 1547, Mary and Elizabeth continued to resort to proclamations. The judicial powers of the Council, and in particular of the Court of Star Chamber, were available to enforce proclamations. The scope of the royal prerogative to legislate remained undefined. James I made full use of this power, and in 1611 Chief Justice Coke was consulted by the Council, along with three of his brother judges, about the legality of proclamations. The resulting opinion is to be found in the *Case of Proclamations*:

> (1) The King by his proclamation cannot create any offence which was not one before; for then he might alter the law of the land in a high point; for if he may create an offence where none is, upon that ensues fine and imprisonment.

> (2) The King hath no prerogative but what the law of the land allows him.

> (3) But the King for the prevention of offences may by proclamation admonish his subjects that they keep the laws and do not offend them upon punishment to be inflicted by law; the neglect of such proclamation aggravates the offence.

> (4) If an offence be not punishable in the Star Chamber, the prohibition of it by proclamation cannot make it so.[7]

A definite limit was thus put upon the prerogative, the full force of which was effective only when the Star Chamber and other conciliar tribunals were abolished in 1640. The gist of the *Case of Proclamations* is that the King's prerogative is under the law and that Parliament alone can alter the law which the King is to administer.[8]

---

[4] 'No Act of Parliament can bar a King of his regality': *The Case of Ship Money* (1637) 3 St Tr 825, Finch CJ, at 1235. For the leading 17th-century cases on prerogative, see Keir and Lawson, *Cases in Constitutional Law*, ch II. Also Tomkins, *Our Republican Constitution*, ch 3.

[5] HEL, vol IV, pp 102–3.

[6] G R Elton, in Fryde and Miller, *Historical Studies of the English Parliament*, II, p 206.

[7] (1611) 12 Co Rep 74. This case was applied by the Court of Session in *Grieve v Edinburgh and District Water Trustees* 1918 SC 700.

[8] The Crown retains broad prerogative power to make laws for several overseas territories, but this power is not unlimited: *Campbell v Hall* (1774) 1 Cowp 204; cf *R (Bancoult) v Foreign Secretary (No 2)* [2008] UKHL 61, [2009] 1 AC 453.

2 *Taxation.* If the imposition of taxes is to be lawful, it must be authorised by legislation. But this basic principle was the subject of a long-running dispute between Parliament and the Stuart Kings, who claimed that the Crown had a prerogative right to levy certain forms of taxation without the consent of Parliament. It had been conceded by the time of Edward I that the consent of Parliament was necessary for direct taxation. The history of indirect taxation is more complicated, since the regulation of foreign trade was a part of the royal prerogative relating to foreign affairs. There was no clear distinction between the imposition of taxes in the form of customs duties and the exercise of prerogative powers over foreign trade and defence of the realm:

> In the *Case of Impositions (Bate's Case)*,[9] John Bate refused to pay a duty on imported currants imposed by the Crown on the ground that its imposition was contrary to the statute 45 Edw 3 c 4 which prohibited indirect taxation without the consent of Parliament. The Court of Exchequer unanimously decided in favour of the Crown. The King could impose what duties he pleased for the purpose of regulating trade, and the court could not go behind the King's statement that the duty was in fact imposed for the regulation of trade.

> In the *Case of Ship Money (R v Hampden)*,[10] John Hampden refused to pay ship money, a tax levied by Charles I for the purpose of furnishing ships in time of national danger. Counsel for Hampden accepted that sometimes the existence of danger would justify taking the subject's goods without his consent, but only in actual as opposed to threatened emergency. The Crown conceded that the subject could not be taxed in normal circumstances without the consent of Parliament, but contended that the King was the sole judge of whether an emergency justified the exercise of his prerogative power to raise funds to meet a national danger. A majority of the Court of Exchequer Chamber gave judgment for the King.[11]

The decision was reversed by the Long Parliament,[12] and this aspect of the struggle for supremacy was concluded by the Bill of Rights, art 4, which declared that it was illegal for the Crown to seek to raise money without Parliamentary approval.[13]

3 *Dispensing and suspending powers.* The power of the Crown to dispense with the operation of statutes (for instance, by declaring that a statute need not be applied in a certain situation) may at one time have been necessary because of the form of ancient statutes and the irregular meetings of Parliament. So long, however, as the limits on the dispensing power were not clearly defined, this constituted a potential threat to the legislative authority of Parliament. In *Thomas v Sorrell*,[14] the court took care to define the limits within which the royal power to dispense with laws was acceptable. But in *Godden v Hales*, an unduly compliant court upheld a dispensation from James II to Sir Edward Hales excusing him from taking religious oaths and fulfilling other obligations imposed by the Test Act; it was held that it was an inseparable prerogative of the Kings of England to dispense with penal laws in particular cases and upon necessary reasons of which the King is sole judge.[15]

Thus encouraged, James II proceeded to set aside statutes as he pleased, granting a suspension of the penal laws relating to religion in the Declarations of Indulgence in 1687 and 1688. These acts of James were an immediate cause of the revolution of 1688. The Bill of Rights abolished the Crown's alleged power of suspending laws and prohibited the Crown's power to dispense with

---

[9] (1606) 2 St Tr 371; G D G Hall (1953) 69 LQR 200.

[10] (1637) 3 St Tr 825.

[11] For a full analysis, see D L Keir (1936) 52 LQR 546.

[12] Shipmoney Act 1640.

[13] Page 14 above.

[14] (1674) Vaughan 330.

[15] (1686) 11 St Tr 1165. The judges were hand-picked by James II in advance, and gave cursory reasons for the decision: see A W Bradley [2008] PL 470, 470–2.

the operation of statutes, except where this was authorised by Parliament.[16] Similar provision was made in the Scottish Claim of Right.[17]

4 *The independence of the judiciary.* As was shown by *Godden* v *Hales*, so long as judges could be removed from office at the pleasure of the Crown, there was a continuing risk of their being subservient to the King in cases in which he had a direct interest. To ensure that English judges should not hold office at pleasure of the Crown, the Act of Settlement 1700 provided that they should hold office *quamdiu se bene gesserint* (during good behaviour) but subject to a power of removal upon an address from both Houses of Parliament.[18]

Growth of ministerial responsibility

The Bill of Rights and the Act of Settlement established the legislative authority of the English Parliament vis-à-vis the Crown, while preserving the prerogatives of the Crown in matters which had not been called in question. The settlement reflected the fact that the common lawyers had joined with Parliament to defeat the Crown's claim to rule by prerogative; and it is often said that the common lawyers thereby accepted that legislation by Parliament was of overriding authority as a source of law. However, executive power itself was left in the hands of the monarch and a more democratic base for government was established only by degrees during the two centuries after the Act of Settlement. The changed role of the monarch has been summarised in this way:

> The position of affairs has been reversed since 1714. Then the King or Queen governed through Ministers, now Ministers govern through the instrumentality of the Crown.[19]

The development of Cabinet government and of ministerial responsibility[20] was accompanied by changes in the electoral system, beginning in 1832 with the Reform Act and continuing until universal franchise for adults was achieved in 1928. But we know from our own time that, while the political authority of Parliament may be pre-eminent in relation to the monarch, government ministers exercise many powers for which it is difficult to achieve democratic accountability. As for the composition of Parliament itself, the result of the conflict between Commons and Lords in 1909–11 was to leave the House of Commons in a dominant position within Parliament. Thus it became possible to argue that the legislative authority of Parliament was founded upon the mandate given by the electorate to the party (or parties) holding a majority of seats in the Commons.

B. Meaning of legislative supremacy

In this brief summary, we have examined the rise of Parliament to be at the centre of the constitutional system. We now consider the legal doctrine of the legislative supremacy of Parliament. This doctrine is referred to by many writers, notably by Dicey, as the sovereignty of Parliament. New constitutional developments are often debated in terms of their supposed effect on the sovereignty of Parliament. This was seen in the debate about British membership of the EC; those opposed to British membership proposed, without success, an amendment to the Bill which

---

[16] Articles 1 and 2 of the Bill of Rights, p 14 above. The Bill of Rights did not curtail the prerogative of pardon or the power to enter a nolle prosequi. Cf the present practice of granting extra-statutory concessions in taxation, ch 17 C.
[17] Page 14 above.
[18] See now Supreme Court Act 1981, s 11(3); Constitutional Reform Act 2005, s 33. See also ch 18 A.
[19] Anson, *Law and Custom of the Constitution*, vol II, p 41.
[20] See ch 7.

became the European Communities Act 1972 declaring that British membership would not affect the sovereignty of Parliament.[21] Critics of British membership of the EU complain both at the loss of national sovereignty and at erosion of the sovereignty of Parliament. There is no doubt that Britain's place in Europe affects the role of Parliament, since many laws are now made at a European level. But the same applies to every state that is a member of the EU. Moreover, many states (including the USA) enjoy sovereignty in international law without having a 'sovereign' legislature. In this chapter, the expression legislative supremacy will be used, partly because it is less likely to be confused with the notion of national sovereignty; and to avoid supporting the jurisprudential doctrine of John Austin and his successors that in every legal system there must be a sovereign.[22]

By the legislative supremacy of Parliament is meant that there are no legal limitations on the power of Parliament to legislate. Parliament here does not refer to the two Houses of Parliament individually, for neither House has authority to legislate on its own, but to the constitutional entity known as the Queen in Parliament: namely the process by which a Bill approved by Lords and Commons receives the royal assent and thus becomes an Act of Parliament. Thus defined, Parliament, said Dicey, has 'under the English constitution, the right to make or unmake any law whatever; and further . . . no person or body is recognised by the law of England as having a right to override or set aside the legislation of Parliament'.[23] Dicey was writing at a time when England was often used as a loose synonym for Great Britain or the United Kingdom[24] and today it is necessary to discuss whether the law on this matter is the same throughout the United Kingdom.[25] But the positive and negative aspects of the doctrine emerge clearly from Dicey's formulation, namely that Parliament has power to legislate on any matter whatsoever and that there exists no competing authority with power to legislate for the United Kingdom or to impose limits upon the competence of Parliament.

British membership of the European Union gives rise to the difficult issue of competing supremacies, the supremacy of Parliament on the one hand and the supremacy, or primacy, of Community law, on the other. This question will be considered later,[26] but we first examine the issue in terms of the law of the United Kingdom alone.

Legal nature of legislative supremacy

This doctrine consists essentially of a legal rule which governs the relationship between the courts and the legislature, namely that the courts are under a duty to apply the legislation made by Parliament and may not hold an Act of Parliament to be invalid or unconstitutional. As was at one time justifiably said, 'All that a court of law can do with an Act of Parliament is to apply it.'[27] In *Madzimbamuto* v *Lardner-Burke*, which concerned the effect of the unilateral declaration of independence in 1965 by the Rhodesian government on the Westminster Parliament's power to legislate for Rhodesia, Lord Reid said:

> It is often said that it would be unconstitutional for the United Kingdom Parliament to do certain things, meaning that the moral, political and other reasons against doing them are so strong that

---

[21] HC Deb, 5 July 1972, cols 556–644; HL Deb, 7 August 1972, cols 893–914. And see ch 8.

[22] Austin, *The Province of Jurisprudence Determined*, Lecture 6. See MacCormick, *Questioning Sovereignty* and (same author) (1993) 56 MLR 1; P Eleftheriadis (2009) 22 Canadian Jl of Law & Jurisprudence 367. On sovereignty in Commonwealth law, see Oliver, *The Constitution of Independence*, chs 1, 3, 4, 11, 12.

[23] Dicey, *The Law of the Constitution*, pp 39–40.

[24] Ch 3 A.

[25] Section D in this chapter.

[26] Page 69; and ch 8.

[27] Keir and Lawson, *Cases in Constitutional Law*, p 1. For the position where an Act conflicts with EC law, see p 69 below; and where an Act is incompatible with Convention rights, p 70 below.

most people would regard it as highly improper if Parliament did these things. But that does not mean that it is beyond the power of Parliament to do such things. If Parliament chose to do any of them, the courts could not hold the Act of Parliament invalid.[28]

While the doctrine of legislative supremacy has great political significance, the legal rule defines the outcome of the process of legislation; it does not make a political analysis of whether that process is controlled by the governing party, the Cabinet or the Prime Minister. Certainly, how Parliament exercises its legislative authority is of great importance in the debate about whether its supremacy should be retained or modified. Craig has argued that Dicey's exposition of sovereignty was advanced on the basis of assumptions about representative democracy which (in Craig's view) were flawed even in 1885 and cannot be made today.[29] However, we must distinguish as far as possible between analysing the present law and considering how it should develop in future. Changes in the legislative process do not in themselves alter the legal effect of that process, although they might affect the case for further development of the law.

Only an Act of Parliament is supreme

An Act of Parliament has a legal force which the courts are not willing to ascribe to other instruments which for one reason or another fall short of that pre-eminent status. Thus the following instruments do not enjoy legislative supremacy and the courts will if necessary decide whether or not they have legal effect:

(*a*) a resolution of the House of Commons;[30]

(*b*) a proclamation issued by the Crown under prerogative powers for which the force of law is claimed;[31]

(*c*) a treaty entered into by the government under prerogative powers which seeks to change the law within territory subject to British jurisdiction;[32]

(*d*) subordinate legislation which appears to be issued under the authority of an Act of Parliament by a minister or government department,[33] whether or not this has been approved by resolution of each House of Parliament;[34]

(*e*) an act of a subordinate legislature,[35] such as the Scottish Parliament or the Northern Ireland Assembly;

(*f*) by-laws made by a local authority or other public body;[36]

(*g*) prerogative Orders in Council made for overseas territories, and laws purporting to be made under powers conferred by such Orders.[37]

---

[28] [1969] 1 AC 645, 723. And see *Manuel v A-G* [1983] Ch 77.

[29] In *Public Law and Democracy*, ch 2, Craig argues that Dicey's notion of sovereignty was 'firmly embedded within a conception of self-correcting majoritarian democracy' (p 15) since, in Dicey's words, 'The electors can in the long run always enforce their will'; further, that the British system 'became one dominated by the top, by the executive and the party hierarchy' (p 42) and that the danger has always been one of majoritarian tyranny.

[30] *Stockdale v Hansard* (1839) 9 A & E 1; *Bowles v Bank of England* [1913] 1 Ch 57.

[31] *Case of Proclamations* (p 50 above).

[32] *The Parlement Belge* (1879) 4 PD 129, 154; *A-G for Canada v A-G for Ontario* [1937] AC 326. Cf *Malone v Metropolitan Police Commissioner* [1979] Ch 344. And ch 15 B.

[33] E.g. *Chester v Bateson* [1902] 1 KB 829; ch 28.

[34] *Hoffmann-La Roche v Secretary for Trade & Industry* [1975] AC 295.

[35] *Belfast Corpn v OD Cars Ltd* [1960] AC 490.

[36] E.g. *Kruse v Johnson* [1898] 2 QB 91.

[37] *R v Foreign Secretary, ex p Bancoult (No 2)* (note 8, above); and *R v Foreign Secretary, ex p Bancoult* [2001] QB 1067.

In all these cases, the courts must consider whether the document for which legislative force is claimed is indeed legally binding.[38] So, too, when a litigant relies on an Act of Parliament, the court must if necessary decide whether the provision in question has been brought into force.

The difference between an Act of Parliament and lesser instruments is reflected in a distinction drawn by the Human Rights Act 1998 between 'primary legislation' and 'secondary legislation'. Unfortunately, the line drawn in the 1998 Act does not coincide with the distinctions just drawn. Thus various measures (including prerogative Orders in Council) are treated by the Act as primary legislation.[39]

Position different under written constitution

The doctrine of legislative supremacy distinguishes the United Kingdom from those countries in which a written constitution imposes limits on the legislature and entrusts the ordinary courts or a constitutional court to decide whether acts of the legislature comply with the constitution. In *Marbury* v *Madison*, the US Supreme Court held that the judicial function vested in the court necessarily carried with it the task of deciding whether an Act of Congress was or was not in conformity with the constitution.[40] In a legal system which accepts judicial review of legislation, legislation may be held invalid on a variety of grounds: for example, because it conflicts with the separation of powers where this is a feature of the constitution,[41] infringes human rights guaranteed by the constitution,[42] or has not been passed in accordance with the procedure laid down in the constitution.[43] By contrast, in the United Kingdom the legislative supremacy of Parliament appears to be the fundamental rule of constitutional law and this supremacy includes power to legislate on constitutional matters. In so far as constitutional rules are contained in earlier Acts, there seems to be no Act which Parliament could not repeal or amend by passing a new Act. The Bill of Rights of 1689 could in law be repealed or amended by an ordinary Act of Parliament. This was done in the Defamation Act 1996, section 13 of which amended Article 9 of the Bill of Rights regarding the freedom of speech in Parliament.[44]

Legislative supremacy illustrated

The apparently unlimited powers of Parliament may be illustrated in many ways. The Tudor kings used Parliament to legalise the separation of the English Church from the Church of Rome: Sir Thomas More was executed in 1535 for having denied the authority of Parliament to make Henry VIII supreme head of the Church. In 1715, Parliament passed the Septennial Act to extend the life of Parliament (including its own) from three to seven years, because it was desired to avoid an election so soon after the Hanoverian accession and the 1715 uprising in Scotland. In vain did opponents of the Act argue that the supreme legislature must be restrained 'from subverting the foundation on which it stands'.[45] Less controversially, during the two world wars, Parliament prolonged its own life by amending the rule in the Parliament Act 1911 that a general election must be held at least every five years.

---

[38] This is essentially what was done in *R (Jackson)* v *A-G* [2005] UKHL 56, [2006] 1 AC 262 (p 65 below).

[39] Human Rights Act 1998, s 21(1). See chs 19 C and 28; and P Billings and B Pontin [2001] PL 21.

[40] 1 Cranch 137 (1803).

[41] *Liyanage* v *R* [1967] 1 AC 259; *Hinds* v *R* [1977] AC 195 and see p 83 below.

[42] E.g. *Aptheker* v *Secretary of State* 378 US 500 (1964) (Act of US Congress refusing passports to communists held an unconstitutional restriction on right to travel).

[43] *Harris* v *Minister of Interior* 1952 (2) SA 428. Generally see Brewer-Carias, *Judicial Review in Comparative Law*.

[44] See chs 11 A, 23 F.

[45] Quoted in Marshall, *Parliamentary Sovereignty and Commonwealth*, p 84.

Parliament has altered the succession to the throne (in the Act of Settlement 1700 and His Majesty's Declaration of Abdication Act 1936); reformed the composition of both Houses of Parliament; dispensed with the approval of the House of Lords for certain Bills (the Parliament Acts 1911 and 1949); made possible British membership of the EC (the European Communities Act 1972); given effect to the Scottish and Irish Treaties of Union and later departed from those treaties;[46] and altered the territorial limits of the United Kingdom.[47] Between 1997 and 2005, a flurry of constitutional legislation included the Scotland Act 1998, the Human Rights Act 1998, the House of Lords Act 1999 and the Constitutional Reform Act 2005.

Indemnity Acts and retrospective legislation

Parliament has exercised the power to legalise past illegalities and to alter the law retrospectively. This power has been used by a government with a secure majority in Parliament to reverse inconvenient decisions made by the courts.[48] Retrospective legislation was passed after both world wars, protecting various illegal acts committed in the national interest.[49] Retrospective laws are, however,

> contrary to the general principle that legislation by which the conduct of mankind is to be regulated ought . . . to deal with future acts and ought not to change the character of past transactions carried on upon the faith of the then existing law . . . Accordingly the court will not ascribe retrospective force to new laws affecting rights unless by express words or necessary implication it appears that such was the intention of the legislature.[50]

The rule of interpretation is that a statute will not be read as having a retrospective effect that impairs an existing right or obligation unless this result is unavoidable.[51] The Immigration Act 1971 was held to empower the Home Office to deport Commonwealth citizens who had entered in breach of earlier immigration laws but against whom no such action could have been taken at the time the 1971 Act came into effect:[52] but the Act did not make punishable by criminal sanctions conduct which had occurred before the Act was passed.[53] Although art 7 of the European Convention on Human Rights provides that no one shall be held guilty of a criminal offence for conduct which did not constitute an offence at the time when it was committed,[54] Parliament has power to legislate retrospectively in breach of this. However, 'It is hardly credible that any government department would promote or that Parliament would pass retrospective criminal legislation.'[55] Legislation which authorises payments to be made to individuals in respect of past events is also retrospective,[56] but it may be objectionable if it restricts existing claims or is discriminatory.

---

[46] Ch 3 A, and section D in this chapter.

[47] Island of Rockall Act 1972.

[48] War Damage Act 1965 (*Burmah Oil Co v Lord Advocate* [1965] AC 75); Northern Ireland Act 1972 (*R (Hume* et al.) v *Londonderry Justices* [1972] NILR 91); Education (Scotland) Act 1973 (*Malloch v Aberdeen Corpn* 1974 SLT 253); National Health Service (Invalid Direction) Act 1980 (*Lambeth BC v Secretary of State* (1980) 79 LGR 61).

[49] Indemnity Act 1920 and War Charges Validity Act 1925; Enemy Property Act 1953, ss 1–3.

[50] Per Willes J in *Phillips v Eyre* (1870) LR 6 QB 1, 23. On retrospectivity in general, see Lord Rodger of Earlsferry (2005) 121 LQR 57; and Sampford, *Retrospectivity and the Rule of Law.*

[51] *Yew Bon Tew v Kenderaan Bas Mara* [1983] 1 AC 553, 558. And see *Plewa v Chief Adjudication Officer* [1995] 1 AC 249 (common law presumption applied to recovery of overpaid benefits).

[52] *Azam v Home Secretary* [1974] AC 18.

[53] *Waddington v Miah* [1974] 2 All ER 377, 379 (Lord Reid).

[54] Ch 19 B. On the War Crimes Act 1991, A T Richardson (1992) 55 MLR 73, 76–80; S N McMurtrie (1992) 13 *Statute Law Review* 128. On retrospective penalties, *R v Pora* [2001] 2 NZLR 37; A Butler [2001] PL 586.

[55] [1974] 2 All ER 377, 379; and see *R v Home Secretary, ex p Bhajan Singh* [1976] QB 198.

[56] E.g. Employment Act 1982, s 2 and Sch 1.

Legislative supremacy and international law

There are many reasons why Parliament should take into account the United Kingdom's obligations at international law when it legislates, but the courts may not hold an Act void on the ground that it contravenes general principles of international law.

> The Herring Fishery (Scotland) Act 1889 authorised a fishery board to make by-laws prohibiting certain forms of trawling within the Moray Firth, an area which included much sea that lay beyond British territorial waters. The Danish master of a Norwegian trawler was convicted in a Scottish court for breaking these by-laws. The High Court of Justiciary held that its function was confined to interpreting the Act and the by-laws, and that Parliament had intended to legislate for the conduct of all persons within the Moray Firth, whatever might be the position in international law. 'For us an Act of Parliament duly passed by Lords and Commons and assented to by the King is supreme, and we are bound to give effect to its terms.'[57]

Nor may the courts hold an Act invalid because it conflicts with a treaty to which the United Kingdom is a party.

> An assessment to income tax was challenged on the ground that part of the tax raised was used for the manufacture of nuclear weapons, contrary to the Geneva Convention Act 1957. It was held that the unambiguous provisions of a statute must be followed even if they are contrary to international law. Regarding an argument that tax had been imposed for an improper purpose, the judge said: 'What the statute itself enacts cannot be unlawful, because what the statute says and provides is itself the law, and the highest form of law that is known to this country.'[58]

As far as UK courts are concerned, there are no territorial restrictions on the legislative competence of Parliament. Generally Parliament legislates only in respect of its own territory or in respect of the conduct of its own citizens when they are abroad, but occasionally legislation is intended to operate outside the United Kingdom: thus the Continental Shelf Act 1964 vested in the Queen the rights of exploration and exploitation of the continental shelf; the Act provided for the application of criminal and civil law in respect of installations placed in the surface waters above the continental shelf.[59] A few serious crimes committed abroad by British citizens are justiciable in British courts, such as treason, murder, bigamy and some revenue offences; all torture, wherever it takes place, is a crime in UK law.[60] The courts apply a rule of interpretation that statutes will not be given extraterritorial effect, unless this is expressly provided or necessarily implied.[61] In general, Parliament does not pass laws which would be contrary to the comity of nations. Yet the law in Britain does not always keep pace with Britain's changing international obligations. While the government under the royal prerogative may enter into treaties, treaties must be approved or adopted by Act of Parliament if national law is to be altered.[62] The ratification of a treaty by the government may in some instances create a legitimate expectation that the government will act

---

[57] Lord Dunedin in *Mortensen v Peters* (1906) 8 F(J) 93, 100. The Trawling in Prohibited Areas Prevention Act 1909 later made it an offence to land fish caught in prohibited areas of the sea, thus limiting the extra-territorial effect of the earlier ban.

[58] Ungoed-Thomas J in *Cheney v Conn* [1968] 1 All ER 779, 782; and see *Inland Revenue Commissioners v Collco Dealings Ltd* [1962] AC 1.

[59] See also Antarctic Act 1994. Contrast Sexual Offences (Conspiracy and Incitement) Act 1996 (P Alldridge [1997] Crim LR 30).

[60] Criminal Justice Act 1988, s 134; see *R v Bow Street Magistrate, ex p Pinochet Ugarte (No 3)* [2000] 1 AC 147. On the extra-territorial effect of the Human Rights Act 1998, see *R (Al-Skeini) v Defence Secretary* [2007] UKHL 26, [2008] AC 153.

[61] *Treacy v DPP* [1971] AC 537, 552. And see *R v Kelly* [1982] AC 665; and Bennion, *Statutory Interpretation*, pp 335–8 and 360–84.

[62] Note 32 above.

in accordance with the treaty,[63] but such an expectation does not oblige Parliament to decide to implement the treaty in national law.

British membership of the European Union raises questions as to the relationship between UK law and Community law which cannot be answered by reference to the general principles of international law.[64]

No legal limitations on Parliament

Many illustrations may be given of the use which Parliament has made of its legislative supremacy in legislating on constitutional matters, retrospectively, in breach of international law, and so on. It does not follow from a recital of this kind that the powers of Parliament are unlimited. As Calvert has said:

> No one doubts that the powers of the UK Parliament are extremely wide . . . But that is not what is in issue. What is in issue is whether those powers are unlimited and one no more demonstrates this by pointing to a wide range of legislative objects than one demonstrates the contrary by pointing to matters on which Parliament has not, in fact, ever legislated.[65]

There is much evidence from the law reports that, at least since 1688, judges have been strongly inclined to accept the legislative omnicompetence of Parliament. Yet this has not always been the judicial attitude. In his note on *Dr Bonham's* case, Coke CJ said:

> In many cases, the common law will control Acts of Parliament, and sometimes adjudge them to be utterly void: for when an Act of Parliament is against common right and reason, or repugnant, or impossible to be performed, the common law will control it, and adjudge such Act to be void.[66]

While English judges made similar statements only rarely after 1688,[67] it is not possible from reported cases alone to demonstrate that they have utterly lost the power to 'control' an Act of Parliament – or to show that a judge who is confronted with a statute repugnant to moral principle (for example, a law condemning all of a certain race to be executed) must either apply the statute or resign from office.[68] Support for this has come from New Zealand, where Lord Cooke of Thorndon has urged that within the common law the judges exercise an authority which extends to upholding fundamental values that might be at risk from certain forms of legislation.[69] In 1995, Lord Woolf argued that 'if Parliament did the unthinkable' and legislated without regard for the role of the judiciary in upholding the rule of law, the courts might wish to make it clear that 'ultimately there are even limits on the supremacy of Parliament which it is the courts' inalienable responsibility to identify and uphold'.[70] Lord Steyn has said that the courts might have to revisit the principle of parliamentary supremacy, if Parliament sought 'to abolish judicial review of flagrant abuse of power by a government or even the role of the ordinary courts in standing between the executive and citizens'; in such circumstances, the courts might

---

[63] See ch 15 B.

[64] Page 69 below and ch 8.

[65] *Constitutional Law in Northern Ireland*, p 14.

[66] (1610) 8 Co Rep 113b, 118a. And see S E Thorne (1938) 54 LQR 543; Goldsworthy, *The Sovereignty of Parliament*, pp 111–17; and Gough, *Fundamental Law*, pp 35–40.

[67] E.g. Holt CJ, *City of London v Wood* (1702) 12 Mod 669, 687.

[68] Cf Jennings, *The Law and the Constitution*, pp 159–60. For the attitude that British courts take to foreign legislation which infringes fundamental rights, see *Oppenheimer v Cattermole* [1976] AC 249 and F A Mann (1978) 94 LQR 512.

[69] See *Taylor v New Zealand Poultry Board* [1984] 1 NZLR 394, 398; also J L Caldwell [1984] NZLJ 357 and R Cooke [1988] NZLJ 158.

[70] Lord Woolf [1995] PL 57, 69. See also J Laws [1995] PL 72, 81–93 and cf Lord Irvine [1996] PL 59, 75–8.

have to 'qualify' the supremacy of Parliament, 'a principle established on a different hypothesis of constitutionalism'.[71]

Short of such an extreme situation, it is very unlikely that the courts would of their volition exercise power derived solely from common law to review the validity of Acts of Parliament. Where in modern constitutional systems judicial review of legislation takes place, this is generally derived from a written constitution.[72] But in the United Kingdom, Parliament enjoys an unlimited power to legislate on constitutional matters. Is it therefore possible that, *on the initiative of Parliament itself*, the courts could begin to exercise a power of judicial review derived from constitutional legislation passed by Parliament? This possibility has often been dismissed out of hand by invocation of the principle that no Parliament may bind its successors. It has been said that the rule that the courts enforce without question all Acts of Parliament is the one rule of the common law which Parliament may not change.[73] But, it has been asked, 'Why cannot Parliament change that rule; since all other rules of the common law are subject to its sovereignty?'[74] It is to this difficult and fundamental question that we now turn.

C. The continuing nature of parliamentary supremacy

Within a modern legal system, enacted laws remain in force until they are repealed or amended, unless they are declared when enacted to have a limited life.[75] It is inherent in the nature of a legislature that it should be free to make new laws. The fact that legislation about, say, divorce or consumer protection was enacted five or 50 years ago is no reason why fresh legislation on the same subject should not be enacted today: even if social conditions have not changed, the legislature may wish to adopt a new approach. When Parliament does so, it is convenient if the new Act expressly repeals the old law or states the extent to which the old law is amended. Suppose that this is not done and a new Act is passed which conflicts with an older Act but does not expressly repeal it. There now appear to be two inconsistent statutes on the statute book. How is the apparent conflict to be resolved?

The doctrine of implied repeal

It is for the courts to resolve this conflict because they must decide the law which applies to a given situation. Where two Acts conflict with each other, and the conflict cannot be resolved in another way, the courts apply the Act which is later in time; the earlier Act is taken to have been repealed by implication to the extent of the inconsistency.

> If two inconsistent Acts be passed at different times, the last must be obeyed . . . Every Act is made either for the purpose of making a change in the law, or for the purpose of better declaring the law, and its operation is not to be impeded by the mere fact that it is inconsistent with some previous enactment.[76]

---

[71] *R (Jackson)* v *A-G*, [102], note 118 below.

[72] Israel is an apparent exception: I Zamir [1991] PL 523, 529–30, C Klein (1996) 2 *European Public Law* 225. Also Navot, *The Constitutional Law of Israel*, pp 57–63, 156–67.

[73] H W R Wade [1955] CLJ 172, 187–9; and (1996) 112 LQR 568.

[74] E C S Wade, Introduction to Dicey, p lv.

[75] This has always been the position in English law (Greenberg, *Craies on Legislation*, p 382). But Scottish Acts passed before 1707 may by the doctrine of desuetude cease to be law through non-use and change of circumstances: *M'Ara* v *Magistrates of Edinburgh* 1913 SC 1059; Mitchell, *Constitutional Law*, pp 21–2.

[76] Lord Langdale, in *Dean of Ely* v *Bliss* (1842) 5 Beav 574, 582. See also *Thoburn* v *Sunderland Council* [2002] EWHC 195 (Admin), [2003] QB 151 and ch 8 D; Bennion, *Statutory Interpretation*, pp 315–20; and Young, *Parliamentary Sovereignty and the Human Rights Act*, ch 2.

This doctrine is found in many legal systems, but in Britain the operation of the doctrine is sometimes considered to have special constitutional significance.

> Before 1919, many public and private Acts of Parliament empowered public authorities to acquire land compulsorily and laid down many differing rules of compensation. In 1919, the Acquisition of Land (Assessment of Compensation) Act was passed to provide a uniform code of rules for assessing the compensation to be paid in future. Section 7(1) provided: 'The provisions of the Act or order by which the land is authorised to be acquired, or of any Act incorporated therewith, shall, in relation to the matters dealt with in this Act, have effect subject to this Act, and so far as inconsistent with this Act those provisions shall cease to have or shall not have effect.' The Housing Act 1925 sought to alter the 1919 rules of compensation by reducing the compensation payable in respect of slum-housing. In *Vauxhall Estates Ltd* v *Liverpool Corporation*,[77] it was held that the provisions of the 1925 Act must prevail over the 1919 Act so far as they were inconsistent with it. The court rejected the ingenious argument of counsel for the slum-owners that s 7(1) (and especially the words 'or shall not have effect') had tied the hands of future Parliaments so that the later Parliament could not (short of express repeal) legislate inconsistently with the 1919 Act. In a similar case, *Ellen Street Estates Ltd* v *Minister of Health*, Maugham LJ said: 'The Legislature cannot, according to our constitution, bind itself as to the form of subsequent legislation, and it is impossible for Parliament to enact that in a subsequent statute dealing with the same subject matter there can be no implied repeal. If in a subsequent Act Parliament chooses to make it plain that the earlier statute is being to some extent repealed, effect must be given to that intention just because it is the will of Parliament.'[78]

The correctness of these two decisions is not in doubt, for there were very weak grounds for suggesting that in 1919 Parliament had been attempting to bind its successors. But Maugham LJ went far beyond the actual situation in saying that Parliament could not bind itself as to the *form* of subsequent legislation. He would have been closer to the facts of the case had he said that Parliament could not bind itself as to the *contents* of subsequent legislation.[79] However, these cases, which illustrate the doctrine of repeal by implication, have been used to support a broad constitutional argument that Parliament may never bind its successors.[80]

Can Parliament bind its successors?

The rule that Parliament may not bind its successors (and that no Parliament is bound by Acts of its predecessors) is often cited both as a limitation on legislative supremacy and as an example of it. To adopt for a moment the language of sovereignty: if it is an essential attribute of a legal sovereign that there should be no legal restraints upon him or her, then, by definition, the rules laid down by a predecessor cannot bind the present sovereign, for otherwise the present holder of the post would not be sovereign. Dicey, outstanding exponent of the sovereignty of Parliament, accepted this point:

> The logical reason why Parliament has failed in its endeavours to enact unchangeable enactments is that a sovereign power cannot, *while retaining its sovereign character*, restrict its own powers by any parliamentary enactment.[81] (italics supplied)

Thus to state that no Parliament may bind its successors is to assume that all future Parliaments must have the same attribute of sovereignty as the present Parliament. But why must this be so? The problem is less intractable than the comparable conundrum of whether an omnipotent deity

---

[77] [1932] 1 KB 733.
[78] [1934] 1 KB 590, 597.
[79] H R Gray (1953) 10 Univ of Toronto LJ 54, 67.
[80] Cf H W R Wade [1955] CLJ 172, 187.
[81] Dicey, p 68.

can bind itself,[82] for even sovereign Parliaments are human institutions; and there is nothing inherently impossible in the idea of a supreme Parliament having power to make fresh constitutional arrangements for the future. Merely to state that Parliament may not bind its successors leaves unclear both the nature of the obligation which a present Parliament is unable to impose on its successors and also the meaning of 'successors'.[83] Indeed, the doctrine that Parliament may not 'bind' its successors is an oversimplification.

(*a*) Some matters authorised by legislation are of such a kind that, once done, they cannot be undone by a later Act. Thus, over 60 years after Parliament approved the cession of Heligoland to Germany in 1890, Parliament repealed the statute by which cession was approved.[84] But in so doing, Parliament did not expect that this would recover the territory for the United Kingdom. On the many occasions after 1960 when independence was conferred on an overseas territory, it was the practice after 1960 for Parliament to provide that no future Act of the UK Parliament 'shall extend or be deemed to extend' to the independent country as part of its law; and that the UK government should thereafter have no responsibility for the government of the country in question.[85] Earlier Independence Acts were less categorical, since it was thought that it might sometimes be convenient for the Westminster Parliament to continue to legislate at the request of the territory concerned.[86] At one time it was suggested that provisions conferring independence could be revoked by the Westminster Parliament.[87] The true position is that conferment of independence is an irreversible process: 'freedom once conferred cannot be revoked'.[88] Thus, by ceding territory or conferring independence, Parliament may restrict the geographical area over which future Parliaments may legislate effectively. In the Canada Act 1982, which conferred full power of constitutional amendment on Canada, it was provided that no subsequent Act of the UK Parliament 'shall extend to Canada as part of its law'. If Westminster in future should seek to reverse the historical clock by attempting to legislate for Canada, Canadian courts would ignore any such attempt, unless the Canadian Parliament had authorised them to give effect to the legislation from Westminster. But British courts would be bound to give effect to the Westminster legislation so far as it lay within their jurisdiction to do so.[89]

(*b*) In a different way, Parliament may bind future Parliaments by altering the composition of the two Houses or the succession to the throne. Thus in 1832, when Parliament reformed the House of Commons to secure more democratic representation, later Parliaments were bound by that legislation inasmuch as the only lawful House of Commons was one elected in accordance with the 1832 Act. The pre-1832 House had ceased to exist. The present House of Commons was elected under election laws that are different from what they were in 1900 or in 1945. As for the House of Lords, in 1958 authority was given for creating life peerages and in 1999 all but 92 hereditary peers were removed from the House. Every change in the composition of the Lords must either be approved by that House (as constituted for the time being), or in the absence of such approval be enacted under the Parliament Acts 1911 and 1949.[90] In 1936, His Majesty's Declaration of Abdication Act altered the line of succession to the throne laid down by the Act of Settlement 1700, by removing Edward VIII from the throne: if a later Parliament had wished the throne to revert to Edward VIII, the assent of the Sovereign (George VI or his descendant)

---

[82] Cf Hart, *The Concept of Law*, p 146; Marshall, *Parliamentary Sovereignty and the Commonwealth*, p 13; and H R Gray, note 79 above.

[83] R Stone (1966) 26 Louisiana LR 753, 755.

[84] Anglo-German Agreement Act 1890, repealed by Statute Law Revision Act 1953, s 1.

[85] E.g. Kenya Independence Act 1963, s 1; and see Roberts-Wray, *Commonwealth and Colonial Law*, p 261.

[86] Statute of Westminster 1931, s 4 and e.g. Ceylon Independence Act 1947, s 1; ch 15 C.

[87] *British Coal Corpn v R* [1935] AC 500, 520.

[88] *Ndlwana v Hofmeyr* 1937 AD 229, 237; *Ibralebbe v R* [1964] AC 900, 923; *Blackburn v A-G* [1971] 2 All ER 1380.

[89] *Manuel v A-G* [1983] Ch 77, 88.

[90] Ch 10 B.

would have been required, just as Edward VIII's assent was needed for the Abdication Act itself. Thus, the supreme Parliament may alter the rules that determine who the successors of the component parts of Parliament are to be (and, it might be added, may abolish one of these component parts, e.g. the House of Lords, though this issue receives separate discussion below).

By contrast, when Westminster creates an assembly or parliament with devolved power to make law for part of the United Kingdom, it takes care to ensure that this does not limit its own power to legislate for the whole United Kingdom. The Scotland Act 1998, s 28, empowered the Scottish Parliament to make laws on devolved matters; but the Act stated that conferment of that power to make laws 'does not affect the power' of the UK Parliament to make laws for Scotland (s 28(7)). A similar provision is found in the Northern Ireland Act 1998 (s 5(6)). The same declaration in grander language was in the Government of Ireland Act 1920, which established a parliament for Northern Ireland and by s 75 provided that the 'supreme authority' of the UK Parliament 'shall remain unaffected and undiminished over all persons, matters and things' in Northern Ireland. The power retained by Westminster includes in law the power to repeal the entire scheme of devolution. Thus in 1972 Westminster abolished the Stormont Parliament. On the Diceyan view of supremacy, it is not necessary in law to include express provision in a devolution Act to preserve Westminster's legislative powers. But such provision serves a deeper political purpose, as the existence of the Scottish Parliament presents a definite challenge to Westminster's continuing legislative authority over Scotland.[91]

The rule that Parliament may not bind its successors presents difficulties for certain constitutional reforms (for example, the creation of an entrenched Bill of Rights, discussed below). But it presents no obstacle to the adoption of a new constitutional structure for the United Kingdom. As was said about Gladstone's first Home Rule Bill for Ireland, 'if the Irish Government Bill had become law the Parliament of 1885 would have had no successors'.[92] The object of securing that no subsequent Parliament enjoyed the attribute of legislative supremacy could be achieved in a variety of ways, for example by creating a federal system in the United Kingdom under which England, Scotland, Wales and Northern Ireland would each have its own legislature and executive; these bodies, together with a federal legislature and executive, would all be subject to the constitution as interpreted by a federal court. The creation of such a system would be inconsistent with the continuing supremacy of the present Parliament. The legislative ground for the new constitution would be laid by the supreme Parliament before it ceased to exist.

With the possible exception of the Union between Scotland and England in 1707 and the Union between Ireland and Great Britain in 1800,[93] no actual reforms have been intended to go as far as this. However, as with British accession to the European Community,[94] problems have arisen where the clear intention of Parliament to divest itself of legislative supremacy has not been manifested and where it may be argued that the overriding rule of supremacy has not been affected. The question is not, 'May a supreme Parliament bind its successors?' but 'What must a supreme Parliament do (a) to express the definite intention that future Parliaments should not be supreme and (b) to ensure (whether by positive direction or structural changes) that the courts will give effect to that intention?' The second part of the question is important: for if the matter were to rest merely on the stated intention of the present Parliament, it is likely (in the absence of significant structural changes) that the courts would hold that a later Parliament would be free to depart from that intention. Moreover, it would only be by subsequent judicial decisions, taken in the light of relevant political events, that it would be known whether or not the (supreme) Parliament had successfully achieved its stated objective.

---

[91] And see ch 3 B.
[92] W R Anson (1886) 2 LQR 427, 436.
[93] Ch 3 A and section D in this chapter.
[94] Ch 8.

We must at this point examine more fully a question which has already been mentioned,[95] namely the need for legal rules identifying the measures which are to be accepted as Acts of Parliament.

What is an Act of Parliament?[96]

In an extremely simple community, where all powers within the human group are exercised by one person recognised as sovereign, no legal problems of identifying acts of the sovereign arise. But, as R T E Latham said:

> Where the purported sovereign is anyone but a single actual person, the designation of him must include the statement of rules for the ascertainment of his will, and these rules, since their observance is a condition of the validity of his legislation, are rules of law logically prior to him.[97]

Latham pointed out that Parliament, regarded only as an assembly of human beings, was not sovereign. 'It can only be sovereign when acting in a certain way prescribed by law. At least some rudimentary "manner and form" is demanded of it: the simultaneous incoherent cry of a rabble, small or large, cannot be law, for it is unintelligible.'[98]

In the absence of a written constitution to guide the courts in identifying an Act of Parliament, the definition of an Act of Parliament is primarily a matter of common law.[99] The rule of English common law is that for a Bill to become law, it must have been approved by Lords and Commons and have received the royal assent. In the ordinary case, this simple test will be satisfied by a rapid inspection of the Queen's Printer's copy of an Act of Parliament which will bear at its head formal words of enactment.[100] When Acts of Parliament have been challenged on the ground of procedural defects during their passage through Parliament, the judges have laid down the 'enrolled Act' rule.

> In *Edinburgh & Dalkeith Railway* v *Wauchope*, a private Act which adversely affected Wauchope's rights against a railway company was challenged by him on the ground that notice of its introduction as a Bill into Parliament had not been given to him, as required by standing orders of the Commons. The court rejected this challenge. Lord Campbell said: 'All that a court of justice can do is to look to the Parliament roll: if from that it should appear that a Bill has passed both Houses and received the Royal Assent, no court of justice can inquire into the mode in which it was introduced into Parliament, or into what was done previous to its introduction, or what passed in Parliament during its progress in its various stages through both Houses.'[101] And in *Lee* v *Bude & Torrington Railway Co* it was said: 'If an Act of Parliament has been obtained improperly, it is for the legislature to correct it by repealing it; but, so long as it exists as law, the courts are bound to obey it.'[102]

This principle was reaffirmed in 1974, when the House of Lords in *Pickin* v *British Railways Board* held that a local or private Act of Parliament was binding whether or not the standing orders of each House had been complied with.

---

[95] Pages 54–5 above.

[96] R T E Latham (1939) *King's Counsel* 152 and G Marshall (1954) 2 *Political Studies* 193.

[97] *The Law and the Commonwealth*, p 523; compare Hart's 'rule of recognition', *The Concept of Law* (pp 75, 245 and ch 6). And see on Latham, P Oliver (2002) 2 *King's College Law Journal* 153.

[98] (1939) *King's Counsel*, 153, quoted in Heuston, *Essays in Constitutional Law*, pp 7–8.

[99] Sir Owen Dixon (1957) 31 ALJ 240. And see *Prince's Case* (1606) 8 Co Rep 1, 20b. Also *R (Jackson)* v *A-G*, discussed below.

[100] Interpretation Act 1978, s 3. And see *Manuel* v *A-G* [1983] Ch 77, 87.

[101] (1842) 8 Cl and F 710, 725.

[102] (1871) LR 6 CP 577, 582 (Willes J).

Private Acts of 1836 and 1845 authorised the taking of land for a railway and provided that, if the line were ever abandoned, the land should vest in the owners of the adjoining land. In 1968, another private Act was passed, promoted by the British Railways Board, which abolished this rule. In 1969, Pickin bought a small piece of adjoining land and, when the railway was discontinued, claimed a declaration that under the 1836 and 1845 Acts he was entitled to a strip of the old line. He alleged that the board had fraudulently misled Parliament when promoting the 1968 Act, and had not complied with the standing orders of each House requiring individual notice to be given to owners affected by private legislation. Although the Court of Appeal held that these allegations raised a triable issue,[103] the House of Lords held that the courts had no power to disregard an Act of Parliament, whether public or private, nor had they any power to examine proceedings in Parliament to determine whether an Act had been obtained by irregularity or fraud.[104]

There are several reasons for this reluctance of the courts to inquire into the internal procedures of Parliament. One important reason is the privilege of each House to regulate its own proceedings.[105] For officers of Parliament to be summoned before a court to give evidence about the internal proceedings of Parliament would create a danger of the courts infringing art 9 of the Bill of Rights.[106] On many matters of parliamentary procedure, the courts have declined to intervene whether or not alleged breaches of statute were involved.[107] The rule that a Bill must be read three times in each House is not a requirement of the common law but is part of the 'law and custom of Parliament' and on this the standing orders of each House are based. If one House wished to alter the requirement, say by abolishing the third reading, this change would not affect the duty of the courts to apply the 'enrolled Act' rule.

But some comments must be made on the 'enrolled Act' rule. First, there is today no Parliament roll: in case of necessity, all that a court could inspect is the two vellum prints of an Act which since 1849 have been signed by the Clerk of Parliaments and preserved in the National Archives and the House of Lords Record Office.[108] Second, the rule is reinforced by the provision in the Interpretation Act 1978 that every Act passed after 1850 shall be a public Act and judicially noticed as such, unless the contrary is expressly provided by the Act.[109] Third, if it should appear that a measure has not been approved by one House, then (unless the Parliament Acts 1911–49 apply) the measure is not an Act.[110] Fourth, where there is a written constitution, this may lay down the procedures which must be followed before a Bill can become an Act. Thus in South Africa, the former constitution provided that certain entrenched rights could be revoked only by legislation adopted at a joint sitting of both Houses of the South African Parliament, voting by a two-thirds majority: when this procedure was not followed, the result was not a valid Act of Parliament.[111]

Could the 'enrolled Act' rule be changed by Act of Parliament? To an extent this has already occurred. Thus the Regency Acts 1937–53 make permanent provision for the infancy, incapacity

---

[103] [1973] QB 219.

[104] [1974] AC 765.

[105] Ch 11 A. The Scottish Parliament does not enjoy this privilege (*Whaley v Lord Watson of Invergowrie* 2000 SC 125) but by the Scotland Act 1998, s 28(5), the validity of an Act of that Parliament is not affected by any invalidity in proceedings leading to its enactment.

[106] Page 14 above.

[107] *Bradlaugh v Gossett* (1884) 12 QBD 271; *Bilston v Wolverhampton Corpn* [1942] Ch 391; *Harper v Home Secretary* [1955] Ch 238; *Rediffusion (Hong Kong) Ltd v A-G of Hong Kong* [1970] AC 1136 (O Hood Phillips (1971) 87 LQR 321). And see B Beinart [1954] SALR 135.

[108] Heuston, *Essays in Constitutional Law*, p 18; and Erskine May, *Parliamentary Practice*, p 661.

[109] For an explanation of this rule, see *Craies on Statute Law*, pp 23–4.

[110] *The Prince's Case* (1606) 8 Co Rep 1a.

[111] *Harris v Minister of Interior* 1952 (2) SA 428. See Marshall, *Parliamentary Sovereignty and the Commonwealth*, part 3; Loveland, *By Due Process of Law*, chs 7 and 8.

or temporary absence abroad of the monarch.[112] A regent appointed under these Acts may exercise all royal functions, including assenting to Bills, except that he or she may not assent to a Bill for changing the order of succession to the Crown or for repealing or altering the Act of 1707 securing Presbyterian Church Government in Scotland. If, which is unlikely, a regent did assent to a Bill for one of these purposes, the courts ought not to regard the resulting measure as an Act of Parliament.

Similarly, the Parliament Acts 1911–49[113] provide that in certain circumstances a Bill may become an Act without having been approved by the Lords. The 1911 Act provides special words of enactment which refer to the Parliament Acts (s 4(1)) and also provides that the Speaker's certificate that the requirements of the Acts have been complied with shall be conclusive for all purposes (s 3). But this procedure does not apply either to a Bill to extend the life of Parliament or to private or local Bills. If it were attempted to extend the life of Parliament by a measure which had not been approved by the Lords, a court should decline to regard the result as an Act of Parliament: the 'conclusiveness' of the Speaker's certificate would not bar such a decision by the court.[114]

In respect of the Regency Acts and the Parliament Acts, it has been argued that measures which become law thereunder are Acts of a subordinate legislature to which the supreme Parliament has made a limited delegation of its powers; such measures must therefore be regarded as delegated legislation.[115] In other contexts, courts have been reluctant to apply to a legislature the principle that delegated power may not be sub-delegated (*delegatus non potest delegare*)[116] and a contrasting view is that, except for the excluded purposes, Parliament has provided a procedure for legislation which is alternative to the procedure of legislation by the supreme Parliament.[117] This question came up for decision in the unusual case of *R (Jackson)* v *Attorney-General*.[118]

> The Hunting Act 2004, which made fox hunting with dogs unlawful and had been strongly opposed in the Lords, had been enacted under the Parliament Act 1911, as amended by the Parliament Act 1949. Supporters of hunting claimed that the Hunting Act was invalid; they argued that the Parliament Act 1949 was invalid as it had not been passed by the supreme Parliament, yet it had amended the conditions on which power to legislate without the approval of the Lords had been created in 1911 (by reducing the delaying power of the Lords from two years to one). The Court of Appeal had held that 'major constitutional changes' could not be made under the Parliament Act 1911, but that the reduction in the period of delay was not a major change. The nine Law Lords who heard the appeal *held*, unanimously, that both the 1949 Act and the Hunting Act were valid. The broad consensus that emerged from eight separate judgments was that in 1911 Parliament had intended to restrict the powers of the Lords by enabling the Commons and monarch to legislate without the Lords' approval. The procedure was an alternative to the usual process of legislation, and a measure passed under the Parliament Acts was primary (not delegated) legislation. The power to enact legislation in this way was not subject to implied exceptions but, as expressly stated in the 1911 Act, the life of Parliament could not be extended without consent of the Lords. A majority of the judges held obiter that the Parliament Act procedure could not be used to remove this exception from the 1911 Act.

---

[112] See R Brazier [2005] CLJ 352.

[113] Ch 10 B.

[114] Section 3 of the 1911 Act requires that the Speaker's certificate shall be given 'under this Act'; in interpreting this section, a court could hold that the test of ultra vires had not been ousted: cf *Minister of Health* v *R* [1931] AC 494 and *Anisminic Ltd* v *Foreign Compensation Commission* [1969] 2 AC 147; ch 31.

[115] H W R Wade [1955] CLJ 172, 193–4 and *Constitutional Fundamentals*, pp 27–8.

[116] *R* v *Burah* (1878) 3 App Cas 889 and *Hodge* v *R* (1883) 9 App Cas 117.

[117] P Mirfield (1979) 95 LQR 36, 47–50.

[118] [2005] UKHL 56, [2006] 1 AC 262. See A Young [2006] PL 187, A McHarg, [2006] PL 539, Lord Cooke of Thorndon (2006) 122 LQR 224, M Plaxton (2006) 69 MLR 249, R Ekins (2007) 123 LQR 91. Also Report of House of Lords Committee on the Constitution, HL Paper 141 (2005–06), App 3 (A W Bradley).

The judgment of Lord Steyn included some obiter remarks that questioned whether Dicey's account of the 'pure and absolute' nature of parliamentary supremacy was 'out of place in the modern United Kingdom'. Taken with similar comments by Lord Hope and Lady Hale, this raised the possibility of circumstances in which a court might refuse to apply an Act of Parliament that breached a fundamental constitutional principle, for instance by seeking to abolish judicial review of executive decisions.[119] For present purposes, *Jackson* decided that the definition of an Act of Parliament differs according to whether it has been enacted with the consent of both Commons and Lords, or with consent of the Commons alone. Moreover, the judges accepted that legislation by means of the Parliament Acts may include matters of constitutional importance (for instance, changes in the composition and functions of the House of Lords), although there was disagreement about the extent of this power. Further, despite hesitation by some of the judges, on an issue that was not contested by the Attorney General in this case, *Jackson* confirms that the courts have jurisdiction to decide whether an instrument relied on in litigation is or is not an Act of Parliament, at least where the issue turns on a matter of statutory interpretation. In 1974, a different view was expressed by Lord Morris in *Pickin's* case:

> It must surely be for Parliament to lay down the procedures which are to be followed before a Bill can become an Act. It must be for Parliament to decide whether its decreed procedures have been followed.[120]

That was said in the context of an alleged departure from the standing orders of the Commons, where the issue was rightly held to be a matter of internal procedure, not one for the courts to decide. But *Jackson* may be said to confirm that, in the rare situation where there is an issue as to the status of a legislative instrument, the court must decide whether that document satisfies the 'enrolled Act' rule at common law, or any other rule that a statute may have laid down for the enactment of legislation.

In the light of *Jackson*, we may consider a question that has been much discussed,[121] namely whether a parliament with supreme legislative authority may bind itself by laying down rules that determine the 'manner and form' of future legislation. Although the case concerned a subordinate legislature, *A-G for New South Wales v Trethowan*[122] illustrates issues that may arise when a legislature departs from rules governing the process of legislation which it had itself enacted.

> Under the Colonial Laws Validity Act 1865, the legislature of New South Wales had power to make laws respecting its own constitution and procedure, provided that these laws were passed 'in such manner and form' as might be required by a law for the time being in force in the state. In 1929, an Act provided that the upper House of the legislature should not be abolished until a Bill approved by both Houses had been approved by a referendum of the electorate; the requirement of a referendum applied also to amendments of the 1929 Act. Following a change of government, a Bill passed through both Houses which sought to abolish both the upper House and the requirement of a referendum. The government did not intend to submit the Bill to a referendum. An injunction was granted by the New South Wales court to restrain the government from presenting the Bill for the royal assent unless a majority of the electors had approved it. On appeal, the Privy Council held that the requirement of a referendum was binding on the legislature until

---

[119] On what Lord Steyn might have meant by 'a different hypothesis of constitutionalism', see J Jowell [2006] PL 562.

[120] [1974] AC 765, 790. There is an ambiguity here: does 'Parliament' refer to an Act of Parliament, or to a decision made by resolution of one of the two Houses?

[121] The work of Jennings, Latham, Marshall and others is examined in Oliver, *The Constitution of Independence*, ch 4. See also M Gordon [2009] PL 519 (Jennings' understanding of Parliament's power to alter the 'manner and form' of legislation is contrasted with the 'increasingly antiquated' orthodoxy associated with Dicey and Wade).

[122] [1932] AC 526. And see Marshall, *Parliamentary Sovereignty and the Commonwealth*, ch 8; Loveland, *Constitutional Law*, pp 35–40; Oliver, *The Constitution of Independence*, pp 72–5.

it had been abolished by a law passed in the 'manner and form' required by law for the time being, i.e. with the approval of a referendum.

One view of *Trethowan's* case is that it depended solely on the fact that the legislature was a subordinate legislature, subject to the rule in the Colonial Laws Validity Act that a constitutional amendment had to be enacted 'in such manner and form' as the law required from time to time. On this view, *Trethowan* is not relevant to the Westminster Parliament.[123] Another view is that there is a rule at common law that legislation may be enacted only in such manner and form as is laid down, that this rule applies to the UK Parliament, and that the 1865 Act put into statutory form a rule that is fundamental to the court's task of deciding whether a measure has the force of law.[124] The judgments in the Hunting Act case certainly give support to the view that identifying an Act of Parliament depends on the rules as to 'manner and form' currently required of legislation. But they are not conclusive of how a future court would resolve a dispute concerning the Westminster Parliament on facts resembling those in *Trethowan*.[125]

The Human Rights Act 1998 provides an example of a change in procedure that might give rise to a 'manner and form' argument. By s 19, a minister who is in charge of a Bill in Parliament must, before it is debated on second reading, state either that the Bill is compatible with the rights protected by the 1998 Act or, if it is not so compatible, that the government wishes the Bill to proceed. Would failure by a minister to make such a statement affect the validity of the resulting Act? For several reasons, the answer to this question is no. The requirement of a ministerial statement would be seen as a parliamentary procedure, enforceable only by Parliament. And a court would be unlikely to hold that in enacting s 19, Parliament was intending to alter the 'enrolled Act' rule.[126]

We have seen that the doctrine of implied repeal has been used in support of the argument that Parliament may not bind its successors. Has Parliament the power to modify the doctrine of implied repeal itself? Two recent developments suggest that it can. The first, the 'metric measures' case,[127] concerned the relation between Community law and English law. The court held that Parliament could not abandon its sovereignty by stipulating that a statute may not be repealed. However, it also held that where (as with the European Communities Act 1972) Parliament legislates on a subject with 'overarching' constitutional importance, such an Act (unlike an 'ordinary' statute) is not subject to implied repeal; it may be repealed only where a later Parliament declared expressly that this is its intention.[128] Second, the scheme of the Human Rights Act 1998 in effect excludes the ordinary operation of implied repeal: if Parliament wishes in future to legislate in breach of the Convention rights protected by that Act, it will succeed in doing so only if it uses express words or in some other way makes absolutely clear its intention to legislate with that effect.[129]

Summary

The argument in this chapter may be summarised as follows. In principle, a legislature must remain free to enact new laws on matters within its competence: if a conflict occurs between the laws enacted at different times, the courts apply the later of the two laws. The authority of

---

[123] H W R Wade [1955] CLJ 172, 183; E C S Wade, Introduction to Dicey, *The Law of the Constitution*, pp lxxiii–v.

[124] E.g. Jennings, *The Law and the Constitution*, p 153; R T E Latham (1939) King's Counsel 152, 161; O Dixon (1935) 51 LQR 590, 603.

[125] See in particular in *R (Jackson) v A-G*, Lady Hale's observations at [160]–[163].

[126] See N Bamforth [1998] PL 572, 575–82, citing *Mangawaro Enterprises v Attorney-General* [1994] 2 NZLR 451.

[127] *Thoburn v Sunderland Council* [2002] EWHC 195 Admin, [2003] QB 151. And see below ch 8 D.

[128] *Thoburn v Sunderland Council* at [63].

[129] This effect arises from the novel duty of interpretation imposed by the Human Rights Act 1998, s 3; and see ch 19 C. For a different view, see Young, *Parliamentary Sovereignty and the Human Rights Act*, ch 2.

Parliament includes power to legislate on constitutional matters, including both the composition of Parliament and the 'manner and form' by which new legislation may be made. While the courts may not of their own accord review the internal proceedings of Parliament, the scope for judicial decision could be extended if, by statute, Parliament altered the common law rules according to which the courts recognise or identify an Act of Parliament. The doctrine of parliamentary supremacy is no bar to the adoption of a written constitution for the United Kingdom which imposes judicially enforceable limits upon a future legislature, at least if such structural changes are made that the new legislative process is materially different from the present process involving Lords, Commons and royal assent. However, if changes were *not* made in the structure of the legislature but an attempt were made to limit or restrict the powers of Parliament, the courts would be unlikely to regard the purported limits or restrictions as ousting the continuing legislative supremacy of Parliament. It is not possible to predict the outcome of changes made by Parliament to the 'manner and form' of the legislative process since, depending on the nature and reasons for such changes, the courts might still be influenced by a deep-seated belief in the Diceyan proposition that Parliament cannot bind itself.

These general principles will now be discussed briefly in relation to some specific constitutional issues.

1 *Constitutional guarantees for Northern Ireland*.[130] An account is given elsewhere of the events by which the Irish Republic broke from the United Kingdom.[131] In the Ireland Act 1949, the UK Parliament recognised the independence of the Republic. The Act also declared that 'in no event' would Northern Ireland 'or any part thereof' cease to be part of the United Kingdom 'without consent of the Parliament of Northern Ireland'.[132]

However, the 1949 Act did not guarantee the continued existence of the Parliament of Northern Ireland. When that Parliament was abolished in 1973 by Westminster, a new guarantee was given that Northern Ireland would not cease to be part of the United Kingdom without the consent of the majority of the people.[133] Today the Northern Ireland Act 1998, s 1, declares that Northern Ireland 'in its entirety remains part of the United Kingdom and shall not cease to be so without the consent of a majority of the people of Northern Ireland' voting in a poll held for the purpose. The guarantee is of great political significance. But has Parliament fettered itself from, say, ceding Londonderry to the Republic without first obtaining the consent of the majority of the people of Northern Ireland? Or could Parliament at a future date repeal the 1998 Act and provide nothing in its place? The strongest legal argument for the proposition that Parliament could not breach the guarantee takes the form that for the purposes of legislating for the future status of Northern Ireland, Parliament has redefined itself so that an additional stage, namely approval by a border poll, is mandatory. But would the courts hold that this intention had been so clearly expressed that a subsequent Parliament had lost the legal capacity to repeal the 1998 Act, expressly or by implication? At one time, a court might have been reluctant to recognise an individual's standing to challenge action by Parliament,[134] and reluctant to grant injunctive relief. However, standing to sue has presented few difficulties in recent public law cases and a declaratory judgment would be an appropriate remedy.[135] It has been suggested that the Northern Ireland guarantee is an example of a limitation which Parliament may impose on itself but which does

---

[130] Calvert, *Constitutional Law in Northern Ireland*, pp 23–33; Heuston, *Essays in Constitutional Law*, ch 1; Hadfield, *The Constitution of Northern Ireland*, pp 104–5.

[131] Ch 3 A.

[132] For an analogous provision in Gladstone's first Home Rule Bill, see Marshall, *Parliamentary Sovereignty and the Commonwealth*, pp 63–6.

[133] Northern Ireland Constitution Act 1973, s 1.

[134] Ch 31.

[135] See e.g. *R v Employment Secretary, ex p EOC* [1995] 1 AC 1.

not incapacitate Parliament from acting.[136] In reality, the political constraints against breach of the guarantee provide a greater safeguard for the Ulster Unionists than reliance on litigation to establish that in 1998 Parliament had limited the powers of future Parliaments.

2 *British membership of the European Union.* A later chapter will outline the structure of the European Union and will discuss the relationship between national law and Community law. Community law has been held by the European Court of Justice to prevail over any inconsistent provisions of the national law of the member states:

> the law stemming from the Treaty, an independent source of law, cannot because of its very nature be overridden by rules of national law, however framed . . . without the legal basis of the Community itself being called into question.[137]

The European Communities Act 1972 gave effect within the United Kingdom to those provisions of Community law which were, according to the European treaties, intended to have direct effect within member states. This applied both to existing and future treaties and regulations. The Community organs therefore may legislate for the United Kingdom, as they do for all member states. While Britain remains a member of the EU Community, the Westminster Parliament is not the sole body with power to make new law for the United Kingdom. Nor can Community law appropriately be described as delegated legislation.[138]

The extent to which Community law overrides inconsistent national law was seen in *R v Transport Secretary, ex p Factortame Ltd*:[139]

> Spanish fishing interests that had formed companies registered in the United Kingdom challenged as contrary to Community law the Merchant Shipping Act 1988. This Act, by defining the term 'British fishing vessels' in a restrictive way, sought to prevent non-British interests from having access to the British fishing quota. In interim proceedings to protect Spanish interests pending decision of the substantive case, the European Court of Justice held that a national court must set aside a rule of national law if this was the sole obstacle to the granting of temporary relief to protect Community rights. Thus the British courts must disregard s 21 of the Crown Proceedings Act 1947 (no injunctions to be granted against the Crown)[140] and must also not apply the Merchant Shipping Act 1988. In the House of Lords, Lord Bridge challenged the view that 'this was a novel and dangerous invasion by a Community institution of the sovereignty of the United Kingdom Parliament'. He stated that long before the United Kingdom joined the Community, the supremacy of Community law over the laws of member states was well established. 'Thus whatever limitation of its sovereignty Parliament accepted when it enacted the European Communities Act 1972 was entirely voluntary.'[141]

In *R v Employment Secretary, ex p EOC*,[142] the House of Lords declared that provisions in the Employment Protection (Consolidation) Act 1978, making protection for part-time workers (who were mainly female) subject to conditions that did not apply to full-time workers (who were mainly male), were incompatible with the right of female workers under Community law to equal treatment with male workers.

---

[136] Mitchell, *Constitutional Law*, p 81.

[137] *Case 11/70, Internationale Handelsgesellschaft* case [1970] ECR 1125, 1134. And see ch 8 B.

[138] Cf Cmnd 3301, 1967, para 22.

[139] [1990] 2 AC 85 and (the same) (*No 2*) [1991] 1 AC 603. See also N Gravells [1989] PL 568 and [1991] PL 180; and ch 8 D.

[140] See ch 32 C.

[141] [1991] 1 AC at 659. And see *Thoburn v Sunderland Council* [2002] EWHC 195 Admin, [2003] QB 151 (upholding the sovereignty of Parliament but giving broad effect to the European Communities Act 1972).

[142] [1995] 1 AC 1. Cf *Case C 9/91, R v Social Security Secretary* [1992] 3 All ER 577 (upholding differential age in state pensions scheme).

These decisions establish that the British courts must not apply national legislation, whether enacted before or after the European Communities Act 1972, if to do so would conflict with Community law. In the late Sir William Wade's view, decisions such as *Factortame* effected a 'constitutional revolution', by holding that Parliament in 1972 did bind its successors.[143] A narrower explanation is that the 1972 Act created a rule of construction requiring the courts to apply UK legislation consistently with Community law, except where an Act expressly overrides Community law.[144] Whichever explanation is preferred, the primacy of Community law is an inescapable consequence of membership of the European Union.

3 *The Human Rights Act 1998.* The doctrine that Parliament may not bind its successors is a major obstacle to enactment of a Bill of Rights intended to protect human rights against legislation by later Parliaments. In outlining its scheme for the Human Rights Act, the government denied that it was trying to transfer power from future Parliaments to the courts:

> To make provision in the Bill for the courts to set aside Acts of Parliament would confer on the judiciary a general power over the decisions of Parliament which under our present constitutional arrangements they do not possess, and would be likely on occasions to draw the judiciary into serious conflict with Parliament. There is no evidence to suggest that they desire this power, nor that the public wish them to have it. Certainly this Government has no mandate for any such change.[145]

This stance applied to both existing and future Acts of Parliament, although Parliament in 1998 undoubtedly could have provided that the rights protected by the Human Rights Act should prevail over all *existing* statutes. On whether those rights should be entrenched against *subsequent* legislation, the government mentioned the procedure for amending the US constitution and stated:

> an arrangement of this kind could not be reconciled with our own constitutional traditions, which allow any Act of Parliament to be amended or repealed by a subsequent Act of Parliament. We do not believe that it is necessary or would be desirable *to attempt to devise such a special arrangement* for this Bill.[146]

Certainly, if a wholly new constitution for the United Kingdom were to be created, it could include entrenched fundamental rights. Short of that, are there ways in which fundamental rights could be protected against infringement by a future Parliament? In 1979, a select committee of the House of Lords, considering the desirability of a Bill of Rights for the United Kingdom, said:

> there is no way in which a Bill of Rights could protect itself from encroachment, whether express or implied, by later Acts. The most that such a Bill could do would be to include an interpretation provision which ensured that the Bill of Rights was always taken into account in the construction of later Acts and that, so far as a later Act could be construed in a way that was compatible with a Bill of Rights, such a construction would be preferred to one that was not.[147]

As will be seen later, the Human Rights Act 1998 did not attempt to bind future Parliaments from legislating in breach of rights protected by the Act. Instead, the Act (s 3) imposed a new duty on the courts to interpret all legislation, whatever its date, consistently with the Convention, *if such an interpretation is possible.*[148] If such an interpretation is not possible, the conflicting provision remains in effect, but it may be declared by a superior court to be incompatible with

---

[143] (1996) 112 LQR 568.

[144] P Craig (1991) 11 YBEL 221, 251. And see ch 8 D.

[145] *Rights Brought Home*, Cm 3872 (1997), para 2.13. And see ch 19 C.

[146] Ibid, para 2.16 (emphasis supplied). Note the use of the word 'attempt' in the italicised phrase.

[147] HL 176 (1977–8), para 23. Contrast the view of the Northern Ireland Standing Advisory Committee on Human Rights in 1977: Cmnd 7009, 1977.

[148] As to which see *Ghaidan v Godin-Mendoza* [2004] UKHL 30, [2004] 2 AC 557.

Convention rights, in which case the government may make a 'remedial order' removing the incompatibility from the statute.[149] This scheme preserves the formal authority of an Act of Parliament, while extending the powers of the judiciary to subject Parliament's work to detailed scrutiny. As Judge LJ said in 2001, 'The Act is carefully drafted to ensure that the court cannot and must not strike down or dispense with any single item of primary legislation.'[150] Yet under the scheme of the Act, all other Acts of Parliament (regardless of their date) are subject to judicial scrutiny to determine whether they are compatible with the Convention rights.

4 *Abolition of the House of Lords.* In chapter 10 B we examine the role of the House of Lords under the Parliament Acts 1911 and 1949. Here we deal only with the issue of whether, as one of the component parts of the supreme legislature, the House of Lords can be abolished.[151] It would indeed be a fundamental change if 'whatever the Queen, Lords and Commons enact is law' were to become 'whatever the Queen and Commons enact is law'. If, as argued earlier, the former proposition is founded upon decisions of the courts, the latter proposition would be authoritatively established only when the courts accepted the legislative supremacy of the Queen and Commons in place of the former supreme legislature. Arguably this change could be regarded as a legal revolution or a breach in legal continuity,[152] but would use of this language be accurate if the courts had given direct effect to a change expressly authorised by the former legislature?

Two issues of practical significance might arise. First, if the Act abolishing the House of Lords included a Bill of Rights which was declared to be incapable of amendment by the new legislature (Queen and Commons), the courts would then have a choice between whether (a) to give effect to the stated intention of the former legislature, by holding that the Bill of Rights must prevail over any Acts passed by the new legislature or (b) to hold that the new legislature was as legislatively supreme as its predecessor. Since the courts might not wish to create a legislative vacuum (i.e. a situation in which certain legislation is totally impossible), the outcome might depend on whether any procedure was available if it became necessary in an emergency to encroach upon the Bill of Rights.

Second, could the House of Lords be lawfully abolished against the wishes of the House, by use of the Parliament Acts 1911 and 1949? In *Jackson* v *A-G*,[153] it was held that the Parliament Acts could be used to achieve major constitutional changes without the consent of the upper House.[154] The rejection of the 'delegated legislation' argument in that case strengthens the view that these major changes include abolishing the House of Lords. But the question did not arise for decision, and most of the judgments do not deal with it.[155]

D. The Treaty of Union between England and Scotland

In section C, we discussed whether the Westminster Parliament may impose legal limitations upon its successors. The Anglo-Scottish Union of 1707 raises the different question, 'Was the

---

[149] Human Rights Act 1998, ss 4, 5 and 10.

[150] *Re K (a child)* [2001] Fam 377, para 121.

[151] For the main arguments, see P Mirfield (1979) 95 LQR 36 and G Winterton (1979) 95 LQR 386. And Dicey, *The Law of the Constitution*, pp 64–70.

[152] Mirfield, pp 42–5.

[153] Above, p 65.

[154] In 2000, the royal commission on reform of the House of Lords recommended that the Parliament Acts be amended to exclude the possibility of their being further amended by use of Parliament Act procedures: Cm 4534, para 5.15.

[155] But note, at para [101], Lord Steyn's observations (obiter) on this point.

United Kingdom Parliament born unfree?'[156] The main features of the Treaty of Union have already been outlined.[157] Now it is necessary to examine more closely provisions of the Treaty concerning the power to legislate after the Union.

The Treaty contemplated that the new Parliament of Great Britain would legislate both for England and Scotland; but no grant of general legislative competence to Parliament was made in the Treaty. Article 18 provided that the laws concerning regulation of trade, as well as customs and excise duties, should be uniform throughout Britain; subject to this, all other laws within Scotland were to remain in force,

> but alterable by the Parliament of Great Britain, with this difference betwixt the laws concerning public right, policy, and civil government, and those which concern private right; that the laws which concern public right, policy and civil government may be made the same throughout the whole United Kingdom, but that no alteration be made in laws which concern private right except for evident utility of the subjects within Scotland.

By art 19, the Court of Session and the Court of Justiciary were to remain 'in all time coming' within Scotland as then constituted and with the same authority and privileges as before the Union, 'subject nevertheless to such regulations for the better administration of justice as shall be made by the Parliament of Great Britain'. Other courts were to be subject to regulation and alteration by Parliament. No causes in Scotland were to be capable of being heard by the Courts of Chancery, Queen's Bench, Common Pleas (or any other court in Westminster Hall). An Act for securing the Protestant religion and Presbyterian Church government in Scotland was passed at the same time by the English and Scottish Parliaments and was declared to be a fundamental and essential condition of the Treaty of Union 'in all time coming'.

There is substantial evidence that, while the framers of the Union intended the new Parliament to be the sole legislature, they sought to distinguish between matters on which Parliament would be free to legislate, matters on which it would have a limited authority to legislate, and matters which were declared fundamental and unalterable. The Treaty made no provision for future amendment of itself or for future renegotiation of the terms of the Union. The former English and Scottish Parliaments ceased to exist. No machinery was provided for applying the distinction drawn in art 18 between the laws concerning 'public right, policy and civil government' and the laws concerning 'private right' or, in the latter case, for discovering what changes in those laws might be for 'evident utility' of the Scottish people.

The argument that the Union imposed limitations upon the new Parliament can be summarised as follows: the new Parliament entered into its life by virtue of the Union; its powers were limited by the guarantees in the Treaty, which had been enacted by the separate Parliaments before the united Parliament was born. The assertion that a sovereign Parliament may not bind its successors may be countered by the view that even if both the English and Scottish Parliaments were supreme before 1707,[158] each committed suicide in favour of a common heir with limited powers. The Treaty of Union, concludes the argument, is a fundamental constitutional text which prevents the British Parliament from itself enjoying the attribute of legislative supremacy. When, as in *Cheney v Conn*, an English judge remarks, 'what the statute says and provides is the highest form of law that is known to this country',[159] a Scots lawyer might reply: 'Not so: the Treaty of Union is a higher form of law and may prevail over inconsistent Acts of Parliament.'

---

[156] Mitchell, *Constitutional Law*, pp 69–74; T B Smith [1957] PL 99; D N MacCormick (1978) 29 NILQ 1. See also Munro, *Studies in Constitutional Law*, pp 137–42; M Upton (1989) 105 LQR 79; *Stair Memorial Encyclopedia: The Laws of Scotland*, vol 5, pp 137–62 (T B Smith) and 2002 reissue, pp 29–83 (N Walker); HLE, vol 8(2), pp 54–8; MacCormick, *Questioning Sovereignty*, ch 4.

[157] Ch 3 A.

[158] On whether the Scottish Parliament was supreme before 1707, see Donaldson, *Scotland: James V–James VII*, ch 15; Dicey and Rait, *Thoughts on the Union between England and Scotland*, pp 19–22, 242–4.

[159] Page 57 above.

This viewpoint is subject to both theoretical and historical difficulties. First, no legislature other than the British Parliament was created. If circumstances changed, and amendments to the Union became desirable, how could they be made except by Act of Parliament? Thus in 1748, the heritable jurisdictions were abolished and, when Scottish local government was reformed in 1975, the royal burghs were abolished.[160] In 1853, the Universities (Scotland) Act abolished the requirement that the professors of the ancient Scottish universities should be confessing members of the Church of Scotland, thus repealing an 'unalterable' provision of the Act for securing the Presbyterian Church. Second, the distinction between laws concerning 'public right, policy and civil government' and laws concerning 'private right' is a very difficult one. For example, power to tax private property or to acquire land compulsorily for public purposes concerns both public and private right; and is the law of education or industrial relations a matter of public or private right? Third, the test of 'evident utility' for changes in the law affecting private right is obscure: who is to decide – Scottish MPs, the Scottish Parliament, the Scottish Ministers, the courts or other bodies in Scotland?[161] Fourth, after the Union the Westminster Parliament continued to conduct its affairs exactly as before, subject only to its enlargement by members from Scotland.[162] As dominant partners in the Union, the English assumed that continuity from pre-Union days was unbroken. On a matter left silent by the Treaty of Union, the House of Lords in its judicial capacity heard appeals from Scotland in civil cases for 200 years following the case of *Greenshields* in 1709 (the House of Lords was not a court within Westminster Hall within the meaning of art 19 of the Union) but it had no jurisdiction in Scottish criminal cases, a position that is maintained in the jurisdiction of the new Supreme Court.[163] Fifth, even if the framers of the Union intended there to be limitations on the British Parliament, this might not be sufficient to vest jurisdiction in the courts to hold Acts of Parliament invalid on the ground that they conflicted with the Treaty. In Dicey's view, the subsequent history of the Union 'affords the strongest proof of the futility inherent in every attempt of one sovereign legislature to restrain the action of another equally sovereign body'.[164]

These matters have been debated in several important Scottish cases.

In *MacCormick* v *Lord Advocate*,[165] the Rector of Glasgow University challenged the Queen's title as 'Elizabeth the Second', on the grounds that this was contrary to historical fact and contravened art 1 of the Treaty of Union. At first instance, Lord Guthrie dismissed the challenge for the reason, among others, that an Act of Parliament could not be challenged in any court as being in breach of the Treaty of Union or on any other ground. In the Inner House of the Court of Session, the First Division dismissed the appeal against Lord Guthrie's decision, but on narrower grounds. After holding that MacCormick had no legal title or interest to sue, that the royal numeral was not contrary to the Treaty, and that the Royal Titles Act 1953 was irrelevant, Lord President Cooper said: 'The principle of the unlimited sovereignty of Parliament is a distinctively English principle which has no counterpart in Scottish constitutional law.' He had difficulty in seeing why it should have been supposed that the Parliament of Great Britain must have inherited all the peculiar characteristics of the English Parliament but none of the Scottish Parliament. He could find in the Union legislation no provision that the Parliament of Great Britain should be 'absolutely sovereign' in the sense that it should be free to alter the Treaty at will. He reserved opinion on whether breach of such fundamental law as is contained in the Treaty of Union would raise an issue justiciable in the courts; in his view there was no precedent that the courts of Scotland or England had authority to determine 'whether a

---

[160] Cf arts 20 and 21 of the Treaty of Union.

[161] The court was prepared to find a statute to be of 'evident utility' in *Laughland* v *Wansborough Paper Co* 1921 1 SLT 341, but cf *Gibson* v *Lord Advocate* (p 74 below).

[162] Hence the comment by Bryce, *Studies in History and Jurisprudence*, vol 1, p 194, that in 1707 England altered the constitution of the enlarged state no further than by admitting additional members to Parliament and suppressing certain offices in Scotland.

[163] Constitutional Reform Act 2005, s 40(3).

[164] Dicey, *The Law of the Constitution*, p 65; and cf Dicey and Rait, p 252.

[165] 1953 SC 396.

governmental act of the type here in controversy is or is not conform to the provisions of a Treaty, least of all when that Treaty is one under which both Scotland and England ceased to be independent States and merged their identity in an incorporating union'. Lord Russell, who concurred, stressed the limited functions of the courts in political matters, suggesting that a political remedy would be more suitable for MacCormick than a judicial remedy.

Lord Cooper's judgment went beyond what was necessary for decision of the case and much uncertainty remained on fundamental issues. In particular, the denial that the courts have jurisdiction to decide whether 'a governmental act of the type here in controversy' conformed to the Treaty must be read in relation to the disputed royal title. If the Westminster Parliament were to pass an Act which sought to deprive persons in Scotland of access to the Scottish courts in matters of private right, the courts would be bound to decide whether to give effect to that Act.

In 1975, a Scottish fisherman unsuccessfully claimed in the Court of Session that British membership of the European Community was incompatible with the Treaty of Union.

In *Gibson* v *Lord Advocate*, Gibson claimed that an EC regulation granting EC nationals the right to fish in Scottish waters and the European Communities Act 1972, which gave this legal effect in Britain, were contrary to art 18 of the Union, since this was a change in the law concerning a private right which was not for the 'evident utility' of the Scottish people. Lord Keith held that the control of fishing in territorial waters was a branch of public law, which might be made the same throughout the United Kingdom and was not protected by art 18. Obiter, Lord Keith said that the question whether an Act of Parliament altering Scots private law was for the 'evident utility' of the Scottish people was not a justiciable issue. 'The making of decisions upon what must essentially be a political matter is no part of the function of the court.'[166]

Both in *MacCormick* and in *Gibson* the question was held open of the validity of legislation seeking to abolish the Court of Session or the Church of Scotland, both being institutions safeguarded by the Union. Short of such an extreme situation, the Scottish courts are reluctant to claim a power to review the validity of Acts of Parliament. This attitude was maintained when the Court of Session declined to hold that the community charge (or poll tax) legislation, which applied to Scotland a year earlier than in England and Wales, was contrary to art 4 of the Treaty of Union.[167]

The Scotland Act 1998 conferred on the courts a new jurisdiction to decide 'devolution issues', namely questions as to the extent of the powers of the Scottish Parliament and Executive.[168] But this new jurisdiction would not cause the Scottish courts to review the validity of Acts of the Westminster Parliament. A related question is whether the Scotland Act affected the historical jurisdiction of the Scottish courts on matters relating to government and the people. Section 37 of the 1998 Act declares that the Union with Scotland Act 1706 and the Union with England Act 1707 shall 'have effect subject to this Act'. This provision aims 'to ensure that neither the Scotland Act 1998 nor legislation or actions authorised under its terms should be vulnerable to challenge on the ground of their inconsistency with the Acts of Union'.[169]

In 1999, the Committee of Privileges in the House of Lords considered whether the proposal to remove Scottish hereditary peers from the House along with other hereditary peers would breach the Treaty of Union, art 22 of which entitled 16 peers of Scotland to sit in the House. In fact, the Peerage Act 1963 had removed the limit of 16 and entitled all surviving Scottish peers

---

[166] 1975 SLT 134.

[167] *Pringle, Petitioner* 1991 SLT 330 and *Murray* v *Rogers* 1992 SLT 221. See N C Walker and C M G Himsworth [1991] JR 45; D J Edwards (1992) 12 LS 34; and *R (Jackson)* v *A-G*, note 118 above at para [106] (Lord Hope).

[168] See ch 3 B.

[169] Himsworth and Munro, *The Scotland Act 1998*, p 52.

to sit; and art 22 had later been repealed. The Committee of Privileges unanimously held that removal of the Scottish peers would not breach the Treaty of Union.[170] Lord Hope left open, without deciding, whether the courts have jurisdiction to decide whether some provisions of the Treaty of Union might have binding force. Even if the exclusion of the Scottish peers had been considered to breach the Union, it is not at all likely that the validity of the House of Lords Act 1999 would have been affected.

E. Conclusions

This chapter has examined whether there are legal limits on the legislative supremacy of Parliament, in particular whether there are, or could be, any limits capable of being enforced judicially. While British tradition has been strongly against judicial review of primary legislation, the courts must if necessary decide whether a document for which legislative authority is claimed is indeed an Act of Parliament.[171] While the basic rule of legislative supremacy is a matter of common law that has political significance, it cannot be demonstrated from existing precedents that under no circumstances could this rule be qualified by judicial decision – still less that the rule could not be changed by Act of Parliament. It is therefore not possible to assert dogmatically that the legislative supremacy of Parliament will continue to be the primary rule of constitutional law in the United Kingdom. According to Lord Hope in *R (Jackson)* v *Attorney-General*, 'Our constitution is dominated by the sovereignty of Parliament. But parliamentary sovereignty is no longer, if it ever was, absolute.'[172] Indeed, the advancing pace of European integration has already made extensive inroads into Dicey's doctrine of legislative supremacy; the Human Rights Act 1998 stops short of enabling the courts to set aside an Act of Parliament but authorises them to review legislation for compliance with the European Convention on Human Rights; and the advent of devolution means that Westminster is not the only legislature in the United Kingdom.

Political significance of legislative supremacy

There are difficulties in assessing the political significance of the legislative supremacy of Parliament. For one thing, constitutional and legal rules tend to reflect political facts, but sometimes only with a considerable time lag. Moreover, the doctrine has always been affected by a tinge of unreality since it would empower Parliament to do many unlikely, immoral or undesirable things which no one wishes it to do. Does Parliament really need power to condemn all red-haired males to death or to make attendance at public worship illegal? Or to create criminal offences retrospectively?

Yet it would be wrong to ignore the strong political argument for retaining supremacy, particularly when the wishes of a newly elected House of Commons can be identified with the will of the majority. Legislative supremacy is well suited to a centralised, unitary system of government in which the needs of the executive are closely linked with the dominant political voice in Parliament, and in which the judiciary exercise an important but subordinate role. Even in such a system, there are many factors that limit the use to which the executive can put Parliament's legislative powers. Dicey suggested that political sovereignty, as opposed to legislative sovereignty, lay in the electorate and that ultimately the will of the electorate would prevail on all subjects determined by the British government.[173] Certainly, the electoral system influences the

---

[170] *Lord Gray's Motion* [2000] 1 AC 124.
[171] This function was performed in *R (Jackson)* v *A-G*, note 118 above.
[172] See A W Bradley, in Jowell and Oliver (eds), *The Changing Constitution*, 6h edn, ch 2.
[173] Dicey, *The Law of the Constitution*, p 73. And see p 54 above.

use of legislative powers, but this influence is very generalised and sporadic in effect: and depends in turn on the political parties, on the media, on economic and social groups and on other means by which public opinion is formed and expressed. Moreover, the electoral system produces a House of Commons which does not accurately reproduce the distribution of views among the electorate[174] and provides only weak protection for unpopular minorities.

Parliament and the electorate

Under the British system, the electorate takes no direct part in legislative decision-making, save by electing the House of Commons. In some constitutions, for example in Ireland and Australia, constitutional amendments take effect only if they are approved by referendum. In other constitutions (for example, Denmark and Switzerland) legislative proposals may be subject to referendum. Until 1975, the United Kingdom found no place for direct democracy, save in the case of the border poll in Northern Ireland.[175] Where major political issues are concerned, the outcome of a general election may indicate the degree of popular support for key changes. In 1910, two elections were held because of the legislative veto of the Lords and the need to gain support for the changes involved in overcoming that veto. In general, however, it is difficult to decide from the result of a general election the state of opinion on particular issues. Since the party which wins an election can claim to have a mandate to implement its manifesto, a government cannot be criticised for carrying out its election programme. Conversely, a government may be criticised for proposing major reforms which have not been put to the electorate. The Conservative government elected in 1970 was criticised by those opposed to British membership of the European Communities for having signed the Treaty of Accession and secured the European Communities Act 1972 without allowing the electorate the opportunity to vote on this issue.

For these reasons, but mainly because of the division of opinion within the Labour party, a referendum on Britain's membership of the Communities was held in 1975. In 1979, and again in 1997, referendums were held in Scotland and Wales on schemes for a Scottish Parliament and a Welsh Assembly.[176] There is increasing support for use of the referendum on other constitutional issues, such as changing the electoral system or approving a new European Constitution. While advisory referendums do not directly affect the authority of Parliament, it would affect the position of Parliament if referendums were to become mandatory for certain purposes. It has been argued that referendums should be used 'as an extra check against government, an additional protection to that given by Parliament'.[177] This would entrench certain matters against action by the elected majority in the Commons.

What aspects of the constitution should be protected in this way? There is a case to be made for requiring a referendum whenever it is proposed to transfer the powers of Parliament; as John Locke said, 'it being but a delegated power from the People, they who have it cannot pass it to others'.[178] Recent use of referendums has been on an ad hoc basis, with the ground rules being laid down afresh for each referendum. The Political Parties, Elections and Referendums Act 2000 introduced rules on public funding for campaign groups, and broke new ground with rules on spending limits during a referendum campaign, and a supervisory role for the Electoral Commission.[179]

---

[174] Ch 9 F.
[175] Page 68 above.
[176] Ch 3 B.
[177] Bogdanor, *The People and the Party System*, p 69.
[178] *Second Treatise on Civil Government*, quoted in Bogdanor, p 77.
[179] See K D Ewing [2001] PL 542, 562–5; and ch 9 E.

Summary

The view taken in this chapter has been that Parliament's legislative authority includes power to make new arrangements under which future Parliaments would not necessarily be supreme. The argument for retaining legislative supremacy is strengthened if it can be shown that the political system provides safeguards against legislation which would be contrary to fundamental constitutional principle or basic human rights. It is, however, doubtful whether the political system does adequately protect individuals or minority groups who may be vulnerable to oppressive action by the state. In reality, Parliament's role within British government depends less on exercising absolute legislative power than on its effectiveness as a forum in expressing public opinion and in exercising control over government. As for the consequences of European development, the United Kingdom's place in the EU has necessarily caused cherished constitutional tenets to be revised, in order to gain the benefits of a more closely integrated Europe.

CHAPTER 5

The relationship between legislature, executive and judiciary

Emphasis on the legislative supremacy of Parliament as the basic doctrine of constitutional law may cause principles of constitutionalism to be undervalued. The 'separation of powers' is one of these principles that is found, in one form or another, in most modern constitutions. The need for some separation of powers within the state is essential both to the maintenance of democracy but also for the legal system, where an independent judiciary is essential if the rule of law is to have any substance.[1]

Many observers of British government have minimised the significance of the separation of powers as a feature of that system. Dicey referred in passing to the doctrine as being 'the offspring of a double misconception'[2] and Sir Ivor Jennings sought at length to show that it was of little significance.[3] Today, with the growing recognition of the judicial role in public law, the legal significance of the separation of powers is more often recognised. Lord Mustill has said:

> It is a feature of the peculiarly British conception of the separation of powers that Parliament, the executive and the courts have each their distinct and largely exclusive domain. Parliament has a legally unchallengeable right to make whatever laws it thinks right. The executive carries on the administration of the country in accordance with the powers conferred on it by law. The courts interpret the laws, and see that they are obeyed.[4]

This model for the exercise of legislative, executive and judicial powers may be seen in the law of taxation: to authorise the levying of a new tax is a legislative function; to assess and collect the tax payable by individuals is an executive (or administrative) function; to settle disputes between the tax official and a taxpayer as to the tax due in a particular case is a judicial function, involving interpretation of the law and applying it to the facts. So, too, in criminal law: the creation of a new offence is a matter for legislation, enforcement of the law is an executive function, and the trial of alleged offenders is a judicial function. The same three-sided model is seen in the judicial review of executive decisions, when typically the court decides at the request of an individual claimant whether an official decision was properly taken under powers granted by Parliament.[5]

This chapter seeks to deal briefly with two questions:

(a) to what extent are the three functions (legislative, executive and judicial) distinguishable?

(b) to what extent are these functions exercised separately by Parliament, the executive and the courts?

The legislative function

The legislative function involves the enactment of general rules determining the structure and powers of public authorities and regulating the conduct of citizens and private organisations. In

---

[1] Vile, *Constitutionalism and the Separation of Powers*; Allan, *Law, Liberty and Justice*, chs 1, 3, 8 and Allan, *Constitutional Justice*, ch 2. Also Mount, *The British Constitution Now*, pp 81–92; E Barendt [1995] PL 599; N W Barber [2001] CLJ 59.
[2] Dicey, *Law of the Constitution*, p 338.
[3] Jennings, *Law and the Constitution*, pp 18–28 and App 1.
[4] *R v Home Secretary, ex p Fire Brigades Union* [1995] 2 AC 513, 567.
[5] Chs 30 and 31.

the United Kingdom, new law is enacted when, usually on the proposal of the government, a Bill has been approved by Commons and Lords and has received the royal assent. Exceptionally, under the Parliament Acts of 1911 and 1949, legislation may be enacted without the approval of the House of Lords.[6]

While primary legislative authority is vested in the Queen in Parliament, not all new legislation is made directly by Parliament.

(*a*) Parliament itself frequently confers legislative powers on executive bodies such as ministers, government departments and local authorities. Subordinate legislation of this kind is made under the authority of an Act, but it is not directly made by Parliament.[7] Another form of secondary legislation is that, within limits stated by Parliament, laws may be made by the Scottish Parliament and the Assemblies in Wales and Northern Ireland.[8]

(*b*) By the European Communities Act 1972, it was accepted that the organs of the European Communities (the European Parliament, the Council and the Commission) could legislate for the United Kingdom on Community matters.[9]

(*c*) While one result of the 17th-century constitutional conflict was to impose severe limits on the authority of the Crown to make new law without the approval of Parliament, a few legislative powers of the Crown have survived.[10] It was the exercise of such a power that lay behind a decision of the House of Lords in 1995 on separation of powers.[11]

(*d*) While full legislative authority is vested in Parliament, the two Houses have other functions that do not involve legislating. In the Commons, the legislative programme occupies about half the time available, and the House gives much attention to debating government policies and to scrutinising the work of Whitehall.[12]

(*e*) Although a few Acts of Parliament each year come from the initiative of backbench MPs, most Bills are proposed and drafted by the government, with ministers being responsible for supervising their passage through each House. The executive therefore plays what is often a decisive role in the legislative process, especially when the government has a large majority in the Commons.

(*f*) When a new law has been enacted by Parliament, the interpretation of that law is a matter for the courts. The interpretation of statutes is in one sense a vital part of the law-making process, as only at that stage will it be known whether the intentions of those who framed the law have been fulfilled. In this task, the judges do not challenge the political authority of the legislature to decide what new laws should be made.[13] They must decide disputed questions by applying principles of interpretation which are derived from the common law, and have been modified by statute.[14]

The executive function

It is more difficult to give a simple account of the executive function than of the legislative function. The executive function broadly comprises the whole corpus of authority to govern, other than that which is involved in the legislative functions of Parliament and the judicial functions of the courts. The general direction of policy includes initiating and implementing legislation,

---

[6] Ch 10 B.

[7] Ch 28.

[8] See ch 3 B.

[9] Ch 8.

[10] Ch 12 D.

[11] *R v Home Secretary, ex p Fire Brigades Union* [1995] 2 AC 513 (E Barendt [1995] PL 357). Cf *R v HM Treasury, ex p Smedley* [1985] QB 657, 666 (Donaldson MR).

[12] Ch 10 C and D; and see Griffith and Ryle, *Parliament*, p 403.

[13] *Stock v Frank Jones (Tipton) Ltd* [1978] 1 All ER 948; *Duport Steels Ltd v Sirs* [1980] 1 All ER 529.

[14] See ch 2 A and (for the Human Rights Act 1998, s 3) ch 19 C.

maintaining order and security, promoting social and economic welfare, administering public services and conducting the external relations of the state. The executive function has therefore a residual character, its techniques ranging from the formation of broad policy to the detailed management of routine services. Historically, the executive was identified with the monarch, in whose name many acts are still performed by the Prime Minister and other ministers. Today, in a broad sense, the executive comprises all officials and public authorities by which functions of government are exercised, including the civil service and armed forces. Executive functions are also performed by the police, local authorities and many statutory bodies, as well as by the executives with devolved powers in Scotland, Wales and Northern Ireland. British membership of the European Union has meant that the Council and the Commission exercise executive functions in relation to the United Kingdom.[15]

The judicial function

The primary judicial function is to determine disputed questions of fact and law in accordance with the laws made by Parliament and declared by the superior courts. This function is exercised mainly by professional judges. Civil jurisdiction covers both issues of private law and public law. Criminal jurisdiction includes the conduct of trials, as well as the granting of bail[16] and sentencing those convicted. Lay magistrates exercise criminal justice in the lower courts and ordinary citizens serve on juries at criminal trials. The courts do not have a monopoly of the judicial function, and many disputes arising in areas of government are entrusted to tribunals. Today these tribunals are a recognised part of the machinery of justice, and they operate under the supervision of the superior civil courts.[17] In matters of Community law, judicial functions are exercised for the United Kingdom by the European Court of Justice and the Court of First Instance. Under the Human Rights Act 1998, all UK courts and tribunals must take account of decisions made by the European Court of Human Rights.

The doctrine of the separation of powers

Within a system of government based on law, there are legislative, executive and judicial functions to be performed; and the primary organs for discharging these functions are respectively the legislature, the executive and the courts. A legal historian has remarked:

> This threefold division of labour, between a legislator, an administrative official, and an independent judge, is a necessary condition for the rule of law in modern society and therefore for democratic government itself.[18]

As a matter of history, Parliament, the courts and central government in Britain all owe their origin to the monarchy. Before these institutions developed as distinct entities, the King governed through his Council, dealing variously with legislative, executive and judicial work. Today these tasks are all performed in the name of the Crown, but with a differentiation of process and personnel. Lord Rodger has said, 'it is a hallmark of the modern idea of a democratic state that there should be a separation of powers between the legislature and the executive, on the one hand, and the judiciary, on the other'.[19] It is indeed important that judges are independent both of Parliament and government. While there are reasons why Parliament should not be merely a rubber stamp for the Cabinet, the Parliament–government relationship is one of

---

[15] Ch 8.

[16] See *The State* v *Khoyratty* [2006] UKPC 59.

[17] Ch 29 A.

[18] Henderson, *Foundations of English Administrative Law*, p 5.

[19] *The State* v *Khoyratty* (note 16 above), [29].

mutual dependence, rather than independence. However, it may be argued that essential values of law, liberty and democracy are best protected if the three primary functions of a law-based government are discharged by distinct institutions. Robson described the separation of powers as 'that antique and rickety chariot . . . , so long the favourite vehicle of writers on political science and constitutional law for the conveyance of fallacious ideas'.[20] But this does not do justice to the constitutional values that aspects of separation have made to democratic government and the continuing need to restrain abuse of governmental power.[21] The rest of this chapter will examine the doctrine and how far it applies in Britain today.

Locke and Montesquieu

In 1690, John Locke wrote in his *Second Treatise of Civil Government* that:

> it may be too great a temptation to humane frailty apt to grasp at Power, for the same Persons who have the Power of making Laws, to have also in their hands the power to execute them, whereby they may exempt themselves from Obedience to the Laws they make, and suit the Law, both in its making and execution, to their own private advantage.[22]

For this reason, Locke urged that there should exist a legislature to act in the public good when necessary and a separate executive with a continuing existence.

The doctrine of separation of powers was developed further by the French jurist, Montesquieu, who based his exposition on the English constitution of the early 18th century as he understood it. His division of power did not correspond except in name with the classification which has become traditional: although he followed the usual meaning of legislative and judicial powers, by executive power he meant only 'the power of executing matters falling within the law of nations', i.e. making war and peace, sending and receiving ambassadors, establishing order, and preventing invasion.[23] He stated the essence of the doctrine thus:

> When legislative power is united with executive power in a single person or in a single body of the magistracy, there is no liberty . . . Nor is there liberty if the power of judging is not separate from legislative power and from executive power. If it were joined to legislative power, the power over the life and liberty of the citizens would be arbitrary, for the judge would be the legislator. If it were joined to executive power, the judge could have the force of an oppressor.
>
> All would be lost if the same man or the same body of principal men, either of nobles, or of the people, exercised these three powers: that of making the laws, that of executing public resolutions, and that of judging the crimes or the disputes of individuals.[24]

This statement emphasises that the judicial function should be exercised by a body separate from legislature and executive. Montesquieu did not mean that legislature and executive ought to have no influence or control over the acts of each other, but only that neither should exercise the whole power of the other.[25]

In observing the English constitution in the 18th century, Montesquieu saw that Parliament had achieved legislative dominance over the King by means of the Bill of Rights and that the independence of the judiciary had been declared, but that the King still exercised executive power. By 1800, however, there had been established in Britain the Cabinet system, under which the King governed only through ministers who were members of Parliament and responsible to it.

---

[20] Robson, *Justice and Administrative Law*, p 14.
[21] See Vile, *Constitutionalism and the Separation of Powers*, for reassessment of the link between legal values and separation of powers; also Marshall, *Constitutional Theory*, ch 5, and Munro, *Studies in Constitutional Law*, ch 9.
[22] Locke, *Two Treatises of Government* (ed. Laslett), ch XII, para 143.
[23] But cf Vile, p 87.
[24] Montesquieu, *The Spirit of the Laws* (ed. Cohler, Miller and Stone), book XI, ch 6.
[25] Jennings, *The Law and the Constitution*, app 1.

This system, with its emphatic link between Parliament and the executive, in a major respect ran contrary to Montesquieu's doctrine. It is in the US constitution that his influence can best be seen.

Separation of powers in the US constitution

In the US constitution of 1787 the separation of powers formed one pillar of the new edifice.[26] The framers of the constitution intended that a balance of powers should be attained by vesting each primary function in a distinct organ. Possibly they were imitating the British constitution, but by that time in Britain executive power was passing from the Crown to the Cabinet. The US constitution vests legislative powers in Congress, consisting of a Senate and a House of Representatives (art 1), executive power in the President (art 2) and judicial power in the Supreme Court and such other federal courts as might be established by Congress (art 3). The President holds office for a fixed term of four years and is separately elected: he may therefore be of a different party from that which has a majority in either or both Houses of Congress. His powers, like those of Congress, are declared by the constitution. While the heads of the chief departments of state are known as the Cabinet, they are individually responsible to the President and not to Congress.

Neither the President nor members of his Cabinet sit or vote in Congress; they have no direct power of initiating Bills or securing their passage through Congress. The President may recommend legislation in his messages to Congress, but he cannot compel it to carry out his recommendations. While he has a power to veto legislation passed by Congress, this veto may be overridden by a two-thirds vote in each House of Congress. Treaties may be negotiated by the President, but must be approved by a two-thirds majority of the Senate. The President may nominate to key offices, including the justices of the Supreme Court, but the Senate must confirm these appointments and may refuse to do so. The President himself is not directly responsible to Congress for his conduct of affairs: in normal circumstances he is irremovable, but the constitution authorises the President to be removed from office by the process of impeachment at the hands of the Senate, 'for treason, bribery, or other high crimes and misdemeanours' (art 2(4)). The prospect of impeachment was the immediate cause of President Nixon's resignation in 1974 following his complicity in the Watergate affair; 25 years later, President Clinton successfully defended the impeachment proceedings that were brought against him.[27] Once appointed, the judges of the Supreme Court are independent both of Congress and the President, although they too may be removed by impeachment. Early in its history, the Supreme Court assumed the power, expressed in the historic judgment of Chief Justice Marshall in *Marbury v Madison*,[28] to declare acts of the legislature and the President to be unconstitutional should they conflict with the constitution.

Even in the US constitution, there is not a complete separation of powers between the executive, legislative and judicial functions, if by this is meant that each power can be exercised in isolation from the others. Having established the threefold allocation of functions as a basis, the constitution constructed an elaborate system of checks and balances to enable control and influence to be exercised by each branch upon the others. The Watergate affair showed not only the strong position of a President elected into office by popular vote: it also showed how a combination of powers exercised by Congress and the Supreme Court, as well as such forces as public opinion and the press, could combine to remove even the President from office.[29]

---

[26] For a classic defence of the US approach to separation, see *The Federalist*, XLVII (Madison).

[27] See Gerhardt, *The Federal Impeachment Process*.

[28] 1 Cranch 137 (1803).

[29] See *US v Nixon* 418 US 683 (1974). For separation of powers issues under the US constitution, see Tribe, *Constitutional Choices*, part II. For reassessment of US-style separation of powers as a constitutional model, see B Ackerman (2000) 113 Harv LR 634.

Separation of powers in other constitutions

Many other constitutions have been influenced by the separation of powers. Written constitutions often contain distinct chapters dealing with legislative, judicial and executive powers, but display no uniformity in the extent to which these functions are separate. In France, the doctrine is important but it has manifested itself very differently from the American version. It is considered to flow from the separation of powers that the ordinary courts should have no jurisdiction to review the legality of acts of the legislature or executive. In place of the courts the Conseil d'Etat, structurally part of the executive, has developed a jurisdiction over administrative agencies and officials which is exercised independently of the political arm of the executive; a more recent creation, the Conseil Constitutionnel, may review the constitutionality of new laws.[30]

The constitutions of countries in the Commonwealth have been influenced by the separation of powers in a variety of ways. Under the Australian constitution, for example, delegation of legislative powers to executive agencies has been accepted more readily than the delegation to them of judicial powers.[31] In Canada, the Constitution Act 1867 did not provide for a general separation of powers; legislative powers may be delegated by both the federal Parliament and the provincial legislatures, but the latter are subject to restrictions in seeking to confer judicial powers on tribunals that ought to be vested in the courts.[32] The former constitution of Sri Lanka was held to be based on an implied separation of powers; legislation to provide special machinery for convicting and punishing the leaders of an unsuccessful coup infringed the fundamental principle that judicial power was vested only in the courts.[33] Where the constitution is based on an express or implied separation of powers, the courts may have to decide whether a particular statutory power should be classified as legislative, executive or judicial.[34] British courts do not have this task but have sometimes classified powers for such purposes as applying the law of contempt of court and the rules of natural justice.[35]

Meaning of separation of powers

As the contrast between the United States and France shows, the doctrine of separation of powers has a variety of meanings, and the complete separation of powers is possible neither in theory or in practice. The concept of 'separation' may mean at least three different things:

(a) that the same persons should not form part of more than one of the three branches of the state, for example, that ministers (being members of the executive) should not sit in Parliament;

(b) that one branch of the state should not control or intervene in the work of another, for example, that the executive should not interfere in judicial decisions;

(c) that one branch should not exercise the functions of another, for example, that ministers should not have judicial powers.

---

[30] See Bell, *French Constitutional Law*. The power of the Conseil Constitutionnel to review legislation was extended when the French Constitution was amended in July 2008.

[31] Lumb and Moens, *The Constitution of the Commonwealth of Australia*, pp 23–27.

[32] See Hogg, *Constitutional Law of Canada*, section 7.3(a).

[33] *Liyanage* v R [1967] 1 AC 259.

[34] *Hinds* v R [1977] AC 195 (Jamaica). And see *DPP of Jamaica* v *Mollinson* [2003] UKPC 6, [2003] 2 AC 411, para [13].

[35] Chs 18 D and 27.

1 *Legislature and executive.* Writing in 1867, Bagehot described the 'efficient secret' of the British constitution as 'the close union, the nearly complete fusion, of the legislative and executive powers'.[36] Bagehot's critics have rejected the concept of fusion, arguing that the close relationship between executive and legislature does not negate the constitutional distinction between the two. As one senior politician wrote over 50 years ago:

> Government and Parliament, however closely intertwined and harmonized, are still separate and independent entities, fulfilling the two distinct functions of leadership, direction and command on the one hand, and of critical discussion and examination on the other. They start from separate historical origins, and each is perpetuated in accordance with its own methods and has its own continuity.[37]

This comment still has some formal significance, but it reflects the theory of an earlier age rather than the reality of the Westminster–Whitehall relationship today.

The three meanings of separation mentioned above will be applied to the relationship between executive and legislature:

(*a*) Do the same persons form part of both the legislature and executive? Leaving aside the formal position of the Queen, there is a strong convention that ministers are members of one or other House of Parliament. Their membership of Parliament goes along with responsibility to Parliament for their acts as ministers. However, there is a statutory limit on the number of ministers who may be members of the Commons.[38] Apart from these ministers, most persons who hold positions within the executive (including the civil service, the armed forces, the police and the holders of many public offices) are disqualified from the Commons. Only ministers are key figures in both Parliament and the executive.

(*b*) Does the legislature control the executive or the executive the legislature? This question goes to the heart of parliamentary government in Britain and no brief answer is possible. In one sense, the Commons ultimately controls the executive since the House can oust a government which is no longer able to command a majority on an issue of confidence. The Commons did this to Mr Callaghan's minority government in March 1979. But so long as the Cabinet has the support of the Commons, it exercises far-reaching control over the work of the House. In 1978, the Select Committee on Procedure concluded (in words which still resonate today) that

> the balance of advantage between Parliament and Government in the day to day working of the Constitution is now weighted in favour of the Government to a degree which arouses widespread anxiety and is inimical to the proper working of our parliamentary democracy.[39]

In fact, the 1970s saw a limited willingness by MPs to use their voting power in the Commons to indicate their disapproval of particular government measures. This trend was at its height during periods of minority government in 1974 and in 1976–79.[40] From 1979 to 1997, during Conservative rule, and thereafter under Labour, the government could virtually always rely on a clear majority in the Commons. The effects of this are not limited to facilitating legislation but also weaken the government's accountability to Parliament. The existence of an assured majority in the Commons is not incompatible with there being some MPs who are vigilant in

---

[36] Bagehot, *The English Constitution*, p 65.

[37] Amery, *Thoughts on the Constitution*, p 28: also Vile, *Constitutionalism and the Separation of Powers*, pp 224–30, and Mount, *The British Constitution Now*, pp 39–47.

[38] Ch 9 G.

[39] HC 588–1 (1977–78), p viii.

[40] See works by Norton: *Dissension in the House of Commons, 1945–74*; (same title) *1974–79*; *The Commons in Perspective*; and [1978] PL 360.

scrutinising the executive, and since 1979 the system of select committees has encouraged such scrutiny, but this does not ensure that accountable government is achieved.[41]

(c) Do the legislature and the executive exercise each other's functions? The most extensive area in which the executive exercises legislative functions is in respect of secondary legislation. There is no legal limit on the power of Parliament to delegate legislative powers to the government, and it often is convenient to ministers and departments that they should be able to supplement or even amend primary legislation by making regulations. Parliamentary procedures exist to oversee the use made of delegated power, but they are unable to curb the current expansion in the delegation of legislative power.[42]

2 *Executive and judiciary.* We now examine the relationship between the judiciary and the other two organs of government. Again the three questions may be asked:

(a) Do the same persons form part of the judiciary and the executive? The courts are the Queen's courts, but it is the judges who sit in them. The Judicial Committee of the Privy Council was historically an executive organ, but it has long functioned as a court of law.[43] The Lord Chancellor, a senior member of the Cabinet, was formerly also head of the judiciary and could preside over the House of Lords in its role as the final court of appeal. This departure from the separation of powers came to be seen as incompatible with independence of the judiciary.[44] Under the Constitutional Reform Act 2005, the Lord Chancellor (whose much modified office is held with that of Secretary of State for Justice) remains a Cabinet minister, but has lost his judicial functions.

The law officers of the Crown (in particular the Attorney General in England and the Lord Advocate in Scotland) have duties of enforcing the criminal law which are sometimes described as 'quasi-judicial'; nonetheless, the law officers are not judges and like all ministers they hold office at the pleasure of the Prime Minister.[45]

(b) Does the executive control the judiciary or the judiciary control the executive? The independence of the judges from the executive is secured by law, by constitutional custom, and by professional and public opinion.[46] Since the Act of Settlement 1700, judges of the superior English courts have held office during good behaviour, not at pleasure of the executive. Inferior judges and members of tribunals have statutory protection against arbitrary dismissal by the government.[47] In 2005, Parliament declared that all ministers of the Crown 'and all with responsibility for matters relating to the judiciary . . . must uphold the continued independence of the judiciary'.[48]

One judicial function is to protect the citizen against unlawful acts of public agencies and officials.[49] It is manifestly necessary that judges who decide claims of judicial review brought by individuals should be wholly independent of the departments and other public authorities whose decisions are challenged. In a somewhat similar way within the EU, the Court of Justice and the Court of First Instance ensure that the acts of Community organs comply with the treaties on which the Community system is based.

---

[41] Ch 7.
[42] Ch 28.
[43] Ch 18 E.
[44] Under the Human Rights Act 1998 and art 6(1) ECHR, there was concern as to whether a court including the Lord Chancellor would be an 'independent' tribunal. See ch 19 C and cf *Starrs v Ruxton* 2000 JC 208. See also Feldman (ed.) *English Public Law*, ch 6 (A W Bradley) and A W Bradley [2008] PL 470.
[45] Ch 18 E.
[46] Ch 18 C.
[47] Ch 29 A.
[48] Constitutional Reform Act 2005, s 3(1).
[49] Chs 30–32.

(c) Do the executive and judiciary exercise each other's functions? The value of an independent judiciary would be reduced if essential judicial functions, for example the conduct of civil and criminal trials, were removed from the courts and entrusted to administrative authorities. The European Convention on Human Rights, art 6(1), requires that many decisions affecting the individual should be made by 'independent and impartial' judges. In fact, many disputes which arise out of public services today are decided not in the ordinary courts, but by tribunals that also form part of the machinery of justice and must observe the same standards as the courts. Thus tribunals dealing with such matters as tax assessments and social security benefits carry out their work independently of the departments concerned.[50] Some matters are entrusted not to tribunals but to government departments and ministers. Procedures such as the public inquiry have been developed to maintain standards of fairness and openness in leading to a decision by the department concerned in which full account may be taken of departmental policy, rather than a decision based solely on the application of legal rules.[51]

There is no sharp distinction between decisions which should be entrusted to courts and tribunals on the one hand, and those which should be entrusted to administrative authorities on the other. When a new statutory scheme is created, there is often a wide choice to be made between different procedures for deciding disputes likely to arise under the scheme. The separation of powers affords little direct guidance as to how particular categories of dispute should be settled, except as regards the need for judicial independence: decisions which are best made independently of political influence should be entrusted to courts or tribunals, and decisions for which ministers should be responsible to Parliament must be entrusted to executive departments or agencies.

The importance of the judiciary being independent of the executive was reinforced in *M v Home Office*, when it was held that ministers and civil servants were subject to the contempt jurisdiction of the courts, and that the Home Secretary was in contempt of court when he disobeyed a judge's order to return to London a Zairean teacher who had sought asylum in England.[52] A perceptive summary of the position was given by Nolan LJ:

> The proper constitutional relationship of the executive with the courts is that the courts will respect all acts of the executive within its lawful province, and that the executive will respect all decisions of the courts as to what its lawful province is.[53]

This is a subtle statement of a sensitive relationship. But it does not prevent tension arising in areas of the law, notably the criminal justice system, when the courts make decisions which are unpopular in the media (for instance in sentencing offenders, or as regards the detention of serious offenders serving life imprisonment),[54] and which are not welcomed by ministers.[55]

3 Judiciary and legislature. Finally, the relationship between the judiciary and the legislature:

(a) Do the same persons exercise legislative and judicial functions? All full-time judicial appointments disqualify for membership of the Commons. As regards the House of Lords, it was for well over a century accepted that the Law Lords (Lords of Appeal in Ordinary) should receive life peerages enabling them to sit in the House of Lords, although in recent times they took only a limited part in legislative business. The Constitutional Reform Act 2005 ended this mixture of legislative and judicial functions by creating a Supreme Court for the United Kingdom, separate

---

[50] Ch 29 A.

[51] Ch 29 B. And see *R (Alconbury Developments Ltd) v Environment Secretary* [2001] UKHL 23, [2003] 2 AC 295.

[52] [1994] 1 AC 377; see G Marshall [1992] PL 7, M Gould [1993] PL 568.

[53] *M v Home Office* [1992] QB 270, 314.

[54] See *R v Home Secretary, ex p Hindley* [2001] 1 AC 410.

[55] See 6th Report of the House of Lords Committee on the Constitution, *Relations between the executive, the judiciary and Parliament* (HL Paper 151, 2006–07) ch 2. And A W Bradley [2008] PL 470.

from the House of Lords.[56] Supreme Court justices will not receive life peerages, and any serving judge who is a member of the House of Lords is disqualified from sitting or voting in the House or a committee of the House.[57]

(b) Is there any control by the legislature over the judiciary or by the judiciary over the legislature? By statute judges of the superior courts may be removed by the Crown on an address from both Houses, but only once since the Act of Settlement has Parliament exercised the power of removal.[58] The rules of debate in the Commons protect judges from certain forms of criticism.

While the courts may examine executive decisions to ensure that they conform with the law, the doctrine of legislative supremacy denies the courts power to review the validity of legislation. The judges must apply and interpret the laws enacted by Parliament. The effect of their decisions may be altered by Parliament, both prospectively and also if necessary retrospectively. In one sense, therefore, the courts are ultimately subordinate to Parliament, but the courts are bound only by Acts of Parliament and not by resolutions of each House, which have no legal force unless they relate to the internal affairs of the House.[59] The European Communities Act 1972 provides an outstanding example of the control which the legislature may exercise over the judiciary: by s 3, the courts are required to follow the case law of the European Court of Justice in matters of Community law and to take full account of the reception of Community law into the United Kingdom. This duty may require the courts to 'disapply' an Act of Parliament which clashes with rights in Community law.[60] Under the Human Rights Act 1998, the superior courts may declare an Act of Parliament to be inconsistent with European Convention rights, but may not refuse to apply it.[61]

(c) Do the legislature and judiciary exercise each other's functions? What were formerly the judicial functions of the House of Lords have been transferred to the Supreme Court. Each House of Parliament has power to enforce its own privileges and to punish those who offend against them. This power might in some circumstances lead to a direct conflict with the courts.[62]

Because of the doctrine of precedent, the judicial function of declaring and applying the law enables the superior courts to make law by their decisions. But this power is narrower than the ability of Parliament to legislate, since Parliament is free to change established rules of law. There continues to be much scope for judicial law-making in relation to the principles of public law and the protection of human rights. Decisions in these areas may be welcomed as bringing old law up to date (for example, by reversing the rule that a married man cannot, in law, rape his wife or by broadening the meaning of 'family' to include a long-standing homosexual relationship)[63] or may be criticised for failing to do so.[64] The rules of precedent themselves are judge-made, except where, as in the European Communities Act 1972 and the Human Rights Act 1998, statute has intervened. In 1966, the House of Lords announced that it would in future be prepared to depart from a former decision by the House when it appeared right to do so.[65] The first important instance of this occurred when in *Conway v Rimmer*[66] the House held that the courts might overrule a minister's claim on grounds of public interest immunity to withhold evidence in civil litigation.

---

[56] Ch 18 A.

[57] Constitutional Reform Act 2005, s 137(3).

[58] Ch 18 C.

[59] E.g. *Stockdale v Hansard* (1839) 9 Ad & El 1; ch 11 A. *Bowles v Bank of England* [1913] 1 Ch 57; ch 4 B.

[60] See the *Factortame* litigation, p 69 above and *R v Employment Secretary, ex p EOC* [1995] 1 AC 1.

[61] Ch 19 C.

[62] Ch 11 A.

[63] See, respectively, *R v R (Rape: marital exemption)* [1992] 1 AC 599; *Fitzpatrick v Sterling Housing Association Ltd* [2001] 1 AC 27.

[64] *R v Lemon* [1979] AC 617 (offence of blasphemy), ch 23 D; *R v Brown* [1994] AC 212 (criminal nature of consensual sado-masochistic acts).

[65] [1966] 3 All ER 77. Between 1898 and 1966, a contrary rule prevailed: *London Street Tramways Co v LCC* [1898] AC 375.

[66] [1968] AC 910; ch 32 C.

As *Conway* v *Rimmer* illustrates, judicial decisions are important as a source of law in matters on which the government is unwilling to propose legislation – for instance, measures that would expose itself to more effective judicial control. Some judicial decisions directly affect the formal relationship between the courts and Parliament, and these too may be on matters that Parliament itself would be slow to address.[67]

Summary

In the absence of a written constitution, there is no formal separation of powers in the United Kingdom. No Act of Parliament may be held unconstitutional on the ground that it seeks to confer powers in breach of the doctrine. The functions of legislature and executive are closely inter-related and ministers are members of both. Yet '[it] is a feature of the peculiarly British conception of the separation of powers that Parliament, the executive and the courts each have their distinct and largely exclusive domain'.[68]

The formal process of legislation is different from the day-to-day conduct of government, just as the legal effect of an Act of Parliament differs from that of an executive decision.[69] In practice, Parliament frequently delegates power to legislate upon the executive, but at least in theory it retains oversight of such delegated powers. However close the relationship between Parliament and the executive may be in the British system of government, a separation of powers between the legislature and the executive, on one hand, and the judiciary on the other, is a constitutional fundamental.[70]

The effect of British membership of the EU is that European organs now exercise legislative, executive and judicial powers in respect of the United Kingdom. While judicial powers are exercised by the European Court of Justice, whose independence is guaranteed, legislative authority is vested in the Council, representing the governments of the member states.[71] The Human Rights Act 1998 brought to UK courts a need to consider aspects of the separation of powers (such as the independence of courts and tribunals) that are central to rights protected by the European Convention on Human Rights, such as the right to a fair trial.

While the classification of the powers of the state into legislative, executive and judicial powers involves some conceptual difficulties, in a system of government based on law it remains important to distinguish in constitutional structure between the primary functions of law-making, law-executing and law-adjudicating. If these distinctions are abandoned, the concept of law itself can scarcely survive.[72]

---

[67] E.g. *R* v *Home Secretary, ex p Fire Brigades Union* [1995] 2 AC 513; and *Pepper* v *Hart* [1993] AC 593.

[68] *R* v *Home Secretary, ex p Fire Brigades Union* [1995] 2 AC at 567 (Lord Mustill). The case concerned the 'separation' of legislative functions between Parliament and the Home Secretary.

[69] It was the government's failure to observe this distinction which gave rise to the *Fire Brigades Union* case.

[70] See notes 18, 19 above.

[71] Ch 8 A.

[72] And see Allan, *Constitutional Justice*, ch 2 of which begins: 'When the idea of the rule of law is interpreted as a principle of constitutionalism, it assumes a division of governmental powers or functions that inhibits the exercise of arbitrary state power.' (p 31).

CHAPTER 6

The rule of law

During 1971, at what we now know was an early stage of open strife between the communities in Northern Ireland, the IRA increased the ferocity of its campaign of violence in Northern Ireland, shooting soldiers and police and blowing up buildings. Early in August, the government of Northern Ireland, after consulting with the UK government, decided to exercise the power of internment available to it under the Civil Authorities (Special Powers) Act (Northern Ireland) 1922.[1] This power could be used against persons suspected of having acted or being about to act in a manner prejudicial to the preservation of peace or the maintenance of order. On 9 August, 342 men were arrested. By November 1971, when the total arrested had risen to 980, 299 of those arrested were being interned indefinitely; the remainder were held under temporary detention orders or had already been released.

The security forces saw in internment an opportunity of obtaining fresh intelligence about the IRA. Fourteen detainees were interrogated in depth. The procedures of interrogation included keeping the detainees' heads covered with black hoods; subjecting them to continuous and monotonous noise; depriving them of sleep; depriving them of food and water, except for one slice of bread and one pint of water at six-hourly intervals; making them stand facing a wall with legs apart and hands raised. It was later held by a committee of inquiry that these procedures constituted physical ill-treatment.[2]

In November 1971, after these facts had been established, three Privy Councillors were asked to consider whether the procedures 'currently authorised' for interrogating persons suspected of terrorism needed to be changed. They produced two reports.[3] Two members, a former Lord Chief Justice and a former Conservative Cabinet minister, recommended that the procedures could continue to be used subject to certain safeguards, including the express authority of a UK minister for their use, the presence of a doctor with psychiatric training at the interrogation centre, and a complaints procedure. This report did not express any view on the legality of the interrogation procedures, but stated that valuable information about the IRA had been discovered through the interrogation.

The minority report, by Lord Gardiner, a former Labour Lord Chancellor, held that the interrogation procedures had never been authorised:

> If any document or minister had purported to authorise them, it would have been invalid because the procedures were and are illegal by the domestic law and may also have been illegal by international law.

Should legislation be introduced enabling a minister in time of emergency to fix in secret the limits of permissible ill-treatment to be used in interrogating suspects? Lord Gardiner viewed with abhorrence any proposal that a minister should be empowered to make secret law. Nor could he agree that a minister should fix secret limits without the authority of Parliament, 'that is to say illegally', and then if found out ask Parliament for an Act of Indemnity: that, he said, would be a flagrant breach of the whole basis of the rule of law and of the principles of democratic government.

---

[1] The power did not survive into the Terrorism Act 2000; see ch 26 E. On the internments in 1971–6, see R J Spjut (1986) 49 MLR 712.

[2] Cmnd 4823, 1971 (Compton Report).

[3] Cmnd 4901, 1972 (Parker Report).

The government accepted Lord Gardiner's report and abandoned the interrogation procedures. When those who had been interrogated sued the government for damages for their unlawful treatment, liability was not contested and substantial awards of damages were made. The European Commission on Human Rights held that the interrogation procedures amounted to inhuman and degrading treatment and also torture, contrary to art 3 of the European Convention on Human Rights. When the Irish government referred the case to the European Court of Human Rights, the court held that the procedures were inhuman and degrading treatment but did not amount to torture.[4]

No clearer illustration could be given of the need to adhere to the rule of law if citizens are to be protected against arbitrary and harsh acts of government. However lawless may have been the acts of the IRA, and however seriously those acts infringed life and liberty, government must not retaliate with measures which are not only unlawful but are of such a nature that it would be impossible on moral and political grounds to make them lawful. Controversial as the power of internment was, it was authorised by the legislature and its use was a matter of public knowledge and admitted political responsibility. But in law the power to intern does not include power to interrogate or to administer physical ill-treatment or torture.[5]

By similar reasoning, while use of reasonable force is permitted in self-defence or in the prevention of crime or the arrest of offenders, and in some situations the use of firearms may be justified,[6] the adoption of a 'shoot to kill' policy by the police or armed forces would be seriously objectionable. This was alleged to have occurred in 1988 when three IRA members were shot dead by British forces in Gibraltar while organising a terrorist attack. The European Court of Human Rights held that force resulting in the taking of life could be used only in 'absolute necessity' for purposes stated in the European Convention on Human Rights (art 2). Claims that the three deaths were premeditated were not upheld; but the Court held (by 10−9) that, on what was known of the arrest operation, the killings were not justified by 'absolute necessity'.[7] The British government was angered by this decision, but reluctantly complied with the Court's order to reimburse the dead terrorists' families for their legal costs.

The above events occurred before Northern Ireland had entered a more peaceful stage in its history. Since the 9/11 atrocities in the USA, many urgent questions have been raised as to the legality (in national and international law) of measures taken in the 'war against terrorism'. One aim of the Bush administration in establishing a detention centre at the Guantanomo Bay naval base on Cuba was to place detainees outside the protection of any legal system, but in 2004 the US Supreme Court held that this had not been achieved.[8] There can now be no doubt that procedures amounting to torture were authorised by the Bush administration.

In the United Kingdom, two particularly significant decisions have arisen from the 'war against terror': (1) indefinite detention without trial under the Anti-Terrorism, Crime and Security Act 2001 was held to breach the European Convention on Human Rights;[9] and (2) evidence obtained or likely to have been obtained by torture committed abroad by a foreign state's agents was held

---

[4] *Ireland v UK* (1978) 2 EHRR 25; and see ch 19 B. In 2004, Lord Hope wrote: 'It seems likely that the mixture of physical and psychological pressures that were used in the case of the IRA suspects would now be regarded as torture . . .': (2004) 53 ICLQ 807, 826. The UN Convention against Torture (UNCAT) was signed by the UK in 1984 and ratified in 1988 after enactment of the Criminal Justice Act 1988, s 134.

[5] For the report of the Bennett inquiry into police interrogation procedures in Northern Ireland in 1975–78, see Cmnd 7497, 1979.

[6] See ch 26 A, B.

[7] *McCann v UK* (1995) 21 EHRR 97. And see Windlesham and Rampton, *Report on 'Death on the Rock'.*

[8] *Rasul v Bush* 124 S Ct 2686 (2004); *Hamdi v Rumsfeld* 124 S Ct 2633 (2004); *Boumediene v Bush* 128 S Ct 2229 (2008). For commentary, see D Golove (2005) 3 *Int Jl of Const Law* 128; S Hannett [2008] PL 636. And see Lord Steyn (2004) 53 ICLQ 1; Sands, *Lawless World* and (same author) *Torture Team.*

[9] *A v Home Secretary* [2004] UKHL 56, [2005] 2 AC 68; *A v Home Secretary (No 2)* [2005] UKHL 71, [2006] 2 AC 221.

to be inadmissible in proceedings before the Special Immigration Appeals Commission.[10] The decisions underline the continuing relevance of values associated with the 'rule of law'. In the first case, Lord Nicholls said that 'indefinite imprisonment without charge or trial is anathema in any country which observes the rule of law';[11] Lord Hoffmann said that there was 'nothing more antithetical to the instincts and traditions of the people of the United Kingdom'.[12] A Court of Appeal judge has written of this decision: 'It is a powerful statement by the highest court in the land of what it means to live in a society where the executive is subject to the rule of law.'[13]

A. Historical development

In a review of the history of political philosophy, Anthony Quinton has written: 'In all its historical variations the state has sought to discharge two connected functions: the maintenance of order within its domain by the promulgation and enforcement of law and the defence of the nation against external enemies'.[14] To perform these functions, the state possesses coercive powers that may be used to oppress the people as well as confer benefits upon them.[15] Law is an instrument for exercising state power that in some circumstances is also a means of protecting the people against arbitrary or abusive government. Aristotle argued that government by laws was superior to government by men.[16] But one dominant theme in the story of western civilisation in the last 500 years has been the struggle for liberty and rights against absolutism in its several forms, including the absolutism of the state and its use of law.[17]

Of the idea of law in the middle ages, Gierke wrote: 'Medieval doctrine, while it was truly medieval, never surrendered the thought that law is by its origin of equal rank with the state and does not depend on the state for its existence.'[18] Bracton, in the 13th century, maintained that rulers were subject to law: 'The King shall not be subject to men, but to God and the law: since law makes the King.'[19] Magna Carta and its later confirmations expressed the principle that justice according to law was due both to the ruler and to the other classes of the feudal hierarchy. When renaissance and reformation in the 16th century weakened the idea of a universal natural law, emphasis shifted to the function of law as an aspect of the sovereignty of the state.[20] In Britain,

---

[10] *A v Home Secretary (No 2)* (above). At [101], Lord Hope said: '[In times of emergency] where the rule of law is absent, or is reduced to a mere form of words to which those in authority pay no more than lip service, the temptation to use torture is unrestrained.'

[11] *A v Home Secretary* (above) at [74].

[12] Ibid, at [86].

[13] Dame M Arden (2005) 121 LQR 604, 622. The account given above of the unlawful methods of interrogating IRA suspects first appeared in this book in 1977. It should by 2009 have been possible to relegate this to the pages of history, since a government assurance was given in 1972 (repeated by the Attorney General in 1977) that the unlawful techniques had been prohibited. Sadly, recent events involving the brutal death of an Iraqi citizen while in the custody of British troops in Basra have caused the Joint Committee on Human Rights at Westminster serious concern regarding 'discrepancies' in the evidence from military sources on use of the techniques. See Joint Committee on Human Rights, 28th report (2007–08), HL Paper 157, HC 527; also 19th report (2005–06), HL Paper 185, HC 701; and 23rd report (2008–09), HL Paper 153, HC 553. And see *R (Al-Skeini) v Defence Secretary* [2007] UKHL 26, [2008] AC 153 (below, p 316).

[14] Kenny (ed.) *The Oxford History of Western Philosophy*, ch 6 (A Quinton), p 296.

[15] See d'Entrèves, *The Notion of the State*.

[16] d'Entrèves, p 71.

[17] See Grayling, *Towards the Light*.

[18] Quoted in d'Entrèves, p 83.

[19] d'Entrèves, p 86; Maitland, *Constitutional History*, pp 100–4; McIlwain, *Constitutionalism Ancient and Modern*, ch 4.

[20] For the rule of law in 16th-century England, see Elton, *Studies in Tudor and Stuart Politics and Government*, vol 1, p 260.

the 17th-century constitutional settlement rejected the claims of absolute monarchy based on the divine right of kings, in favour of a mixed system of government that relied on the authority of the Houses of Parliament and the common law courts.

The Bill of Rights in 1689 affirmed that the monarchy was subject to the law. Not only did it force the Crown to govern through Parliament, but it also established the right of individuals to challenge unlawful interference in respect of their life, liberty and property.

> In *Entick v Carrington*, two King's Messengers were sued for having unlawfully broken into the plaintiff's house and seized his papers: the defendants relied on a warrant issued by one of the Secretaries of State ordering them to search for Entick and bring him with his books and papers before the Secretary of State for examination. The Secretary of State claimed that the power to issue such warrants was essential to government, 'the only means of quieting clamours and sedition'. The court *held* that, in the absence of a statute or judicial precedent upholding the legality of such a warrant, the practice was illegal. Lord Camden CJ said: 'What would the Parliament say if the judges should take upon themselves to mould an unlawful power into a convenient authority, by new restrictions? That would be, not judgment, but legislation . . . And with respect to the argument of State necessity, or a distinction that has been aimed at between State offences and others, the common law does not understand that kind of reasoning, nor do our books take notice of any such distinction.'[21]

The 'general warrant' cases sought to protect rights to liberty and property, but such rights were not absolute. In 1772 Lord Mansfield, reversing earlier decisions, held that the common law did not recognise the right of a slave-owner to enforce his ownership of a slave brought from Jamaica to England.[22] The procedure by which individual liberty was protected was that of habeas corpus, a common law writ which had been rendered more effective by statute.[23] Formal adherence to the law was thus one of the public values of 18th-century Britain, although not all the people gained equally from it.[24] Economic and social developments since 1765 have qualified the forthright declaration of Lord Camden that in the absence of precedent no common law powers of search and seizure will be recognised,[25] but *Entick v Carrington* still exercises influence on judicial attitudes to the claims of government.

Dicey's exposition of the rule of law

One reason for this is found in the work of A V Dicey, whose lectures at Oxford were first published in 1885 under the title, *Introduction to the Study of the Law of the Constitution*.[26] Dicey's aim was to introduce students to 'two or three guiding principles' of the constitution, foremost among these being the rule of law. The spirit of *Entick v Carrington* seems to run through Dicey's arguments, but he expressed the general doctrine of the rule of law in the form of several statements describing the English constitution, some of them derived from authors who immediately preceded him.[27] Dicey gave to the rule of law three meanings:

---

[21] (1765) 19 St Tr 1030, 1067, 1073. And see *Wilkes v Wood* (1763) Lofft 1.

[22] *Somersett v Steuart* (1772) 20 St Tr 1. The comparable decision in Scotland was *Knight v Wedderburn* (1778) Mor 14545.

[23] See chs 21 E and 31.

[24] Thompson, *Whigs and Hunters*, pp 258–69. And see Tomkins, *Our Republican Constitution*. In the age of colonialism, British rule was not always characterised by adherence to law: see Kostal, *A Jurisprudence of Power*, examining the impact on opinion in London of atrocities during the Jamaica uprising in 1865.

[25] Ch 21 D. And see *Malone v Metropolitan Police Commissioner* [1979] Ch 344.

[26] The main text was settled by Dicey in 1908; it appears in the 10th edn (with introduction by E C S Wade). See also Cosgrove, *The Rule of Law: Albert Venn Dicey, Victorian Jurist*, and the symposium of articles at [1985] PL 587.

[27] H W Arndt (1957) 31 ALJ 117.

It means, in the first place, the absolute supremacy or predominance of regular law as opposed to the influence of arbitrary power, and excludes the existence of arbitrariness, of prerogative, or even of wide discretionary authority on the part of the government . . . ; a man may with us be punished for a breach of law, but he can be punished for nothing else.

Thus none could be made to suffer penalties except for a distinct breach of law established before the ordinary courts. In this sense Dicey contrasted the rule of law with systems of government based on the exercise by those in authority of wide or arbitrary powers of constraint, such as a power of detention without trial.

Second, the rule of law meant

equality before the law, or the equal subjection of all classes to the ordinary law of the land administered by the ordinary law courts.

In Dicey's view, this implied that no one was above the law; that officials like private citizens were under a duty to obey the same law; and that there were no 'administrative courts' to decide claims by citizens against the state or its officials.

Third, the rule of law meant

that with us the law of the constitution, the rules which in foreign countries naturally form part of a constitutional code, are not the source but the consequence of the rights of individuals, as defined and enforced by the courts; that, in short, the principles of private law have with us been by the action of the courts and Parliament so extended as to determine the position of the Crown and of its servants; thus the constitution is the result of the ordinary law of the land.[28]

Thus the rights of the individual were secured not by guarantees set down in a formal document but by the ordinary remedies of private law available against those who unlawfully interfered with someone's liberty, whether they were private citizens or officials.

Assessment of Dicey's views[29]

These three statements about the rule of law raise many questions. In the first, what is meant by 'regular law'? Does this include, for example, social security law, anti-discrimination law or the Terrorism Act 2000? Does 'arbitrary power' refer to powers of government that are so broad they could be used for a wide variety of different purposes; powers that are capable of abuse if they are not properly controlled; or powers that directly infringe individual liberty (for example, power to detain a citizen without trial)? If 'arbitrary power' and 'wide discretionary authority' alike are unacceptable, how may the limits of acceptable discretionary authority be settled? If it is contrary to the rule of law that discretionary authority should be given to government departments or public officers, then the rule of law applies to no modern constitution. Today the state regulates national life in multifarious ways. Discretionary authority in most spheres of government is inevitable. While there are still certain powers which we are unwilling to trust to the executive (for example, the power to detain individuals without trial) except when national emergencies dictate otherwise,[30] attention has to be given not so much to attacking the existence of discretionary powers as to establishing legal and political safeguards by which the use of such

---

[28] Dicey, pp 202–3.
[29] See Jennings, *The Law and the Constitution*, ch 2 and app 2; F H Lawson (1959) 7 *Political Studies* 109, 207; H W Arthurs (1979) Osgoode Hall LJ 1; Lord Bingham [2002] PL 39; Craig, *Public Law and Democracy*, ch 2; Loughlin, *Public Law and Political Theory*, ch 7. For endorsement of Dicey's approach, see Allan, *Law, Liberty and Justice*, ch 2, and *Constitutional Justice*, ch 1. A devastating dissection of Dicey's methodology is in Allison, *The English Historical Constitution*, ch 7.
[30] Chs 21 C and 25. And see *A v Home Secretary* (note 9 above).

powers may be controlled.[31] Doubtless Dicey would have regarded as arbitrary many powers of government on which social welfare and economic regulation now depend.

Dicey's second meaning stresses the equal subjection of all persons to the 'ordinary law'. The 14th Amendment to the US Constitution provides that no state shall 'deny to any person within its jurisdiction the equal protection of the law', a provision which has been a fertile source of constitutional challenges to discriminatory state legislation. Similar provisions are in the constitutions of India, Germany and Canada.[32] In fact, the legislature must frequently distinguish between categories of person by reference to economic or social considerations or legal status. Landlords and tenants, employers and employees, company directors and shareholders, British citizens and aliens – these and innumerable other categories are subject to differing legal rules. What a constitutional guarantee of equality may achieve is to enable legislation to be invalidated which distinguishes between citizens on grounds which appear irrelevant, unacceptable or offensive (for example, discrimination between persons on grounds of sex, race, origin or colour).[33] Dicey had in mind no such jurisdiction. The specific meaning he attached to equality before the law was that all citizens (including officials) were subject to the ordinary courts should they transgress the law which applied to them, and that there should be no separate administrative courts, as in France, to deal with unlawful conduct by officials.[34] He believed that *droit administratif* in France favoured the officials and that English law through decisions such as *Entick v Carrington* gave better protection to the people.

These views of Dicey long impeded the proper understanding of administrative law. Today the need for such law cannot be denied. Administrative courts in most European countries, including France, protect the individual against unlawful acts by public bodies. Britain has no administrative courts on the French model, but in 2000 a section of the High Court in London was renamed the Administrative Court. This change of name was justified by the vast expansion in public law litigation in the last three decades.[35]

Dicey's third meaning of the rule of law expressed the view that the principles of common law declared by the judges were the basis of the citizen's rights and liberties. Dicey had in mind the fundamental political freedoms – freedom of the person, freedom of speech, freedom of association. Someone whose freedoms were infringed could seek a remedy in the courts and did not need to rely on constitutional guarantees. Dicey believed that the common law gave better protection to the citizen than a written constitution. The Habeas Corpus Acts, which made effective the remedy by which persons unlawfully detained might be set free, were 'for practical purposes worth a hundred constitutional articles guaranteeing individual liberty'.[36] Today, we cannot share Dicey's faith in the common law as the primary means of protecting our liberties against the state. First, fundamental liberties at common law may be eroded by Parliament and thus they have a residual character (namely, what is left after all statutory restrictions have taken effect). Second, the common law does not assure the economic or social well-being of the people. Third, the belief that there is value in a formal declaration of basic rights has led to the Human Rights Act 1998 and the creation of new procedures for protecting those rights.[37]

Dicey's view of the rule of law, like his view of parliamentary sovereignty, is based on many assumptions about the British system of government that no longer apply. Although he did not satisfactorily resolve the potential conflict between the two notions of the rule of law and

---

[31] Davis, *Discretionary Justice*.

[32] India, 1949 Constitution, art 14; Federal Republic of Germany, Basic Law, art 3; Canadian Charter of Rights and Freedoms, s 15.

[33] Ch 19 A; and Feldman, *Civil Liberties and Human Rights*, ch 3.

[34] See Brown and Bell, *French Administrative Law*; and ch 27.

[35] See chs 30 and 31.

[36] Dicey, p 199. And see ch 31.

[37] Ch 19 B.

the supremacy of Parliament,[38] a recent formulation of the relationship implies the need for equilibrium and balance rather than conflict:

> The maintenance of the rule of law is in every way as important in a free society as the democratic franchise. In our society the rule of law rests upon twin foundations: the sovereignty of the Queen in Parliament in making the law and the sovereignty of the Queen's courts in interpreting and applying the law.[39]

We have already seen that Dicey's views on the sovereignty of Parliament remain influential today. The same cannot be said of his treatment of the rule of law. But we cannot avoid considering the meaning of the rule of law today, since in the Constitutional Reform Act 2005 (s 1), Parliament declared (without attempting a definition) that the Act 'does not adversely effect . . . the existing constitutional principle of the rule of law'. What follows in this chapter seeks to explore the main aspects of the rule of law today, in a discussion which is not cast in the Diceyan mould.

B. The rule of law and its implications today

Emphasis will be placed on three related ideas. First, statements of the rule of law embody a preference for orderly life within an organised community, rather than a situation of anarchy or strife in which there is no security for persons, their well-being or their possessions. Some stability in society is a precondition for the existence of a legal system. Second, the rule of law expresses the fundamental principle that government must be conducted according to law and that in disputed cases what the law requires is declared by judicial decision. This principle is manifest in innumerable decisions of the courts, and represents existing law. Third, the rule of law refers to a rich body of opinion on matters such as the powers that the state should or should not have (for example, whether ministers should have power to detain without trial), the procedures to be followed when action is taken by the state (for example, the right to a fair hearing in criminal trials), and the values inherent in a system of justice. This third idea is relevant to debates about what the law should be, particularly when our lives are challenged by events such as unrest on the streets or international terrorism, whether these debates occur in Parliament or in a court when new issues are confronted by the judges.

The relation between the second and third ideas may be put in this way. The requirement that government be conducted according to law (the principle of legality) is a necessary condition for the rule of law; but insistence on legality alone does not ensure that the state's powers are consistent with values such as liberty and due process. This emphasis is found in case-law of the European Court of Human Rights.[40]

These three aspects of the rule of law are now examined in more depth.

Three aspects of the rule of law

1 *Law and order better than anarchy.* In the limited sense of law and order, the rule of law may appear to be preserved by a dictatorship or a military occupation as well as by a democratic form of government. Under a government which is not freely elected, courts of law may function, settling disputes between private citizens and such disputes between citizens and government officials as the regime permits to be so decided. However, constitutionalism and the rule of law will not thrive unless legal restraints apply to the government. The maintenance of law and

---

[38] Dicey, ch 13. For an approach that sees no such conflict, see Allan, *Law, Liberty and Justice*, chs 3, 11; and (same author) *Constitutional Justice*, ch 7.

[39] *X v Morgan-Grampian Ltd* [1991] AC 1, 48 (Lord Bridge).

[40] See p 99 below and ch 19 B.

order and the existence of political liberty are not mutually exclusive, but interdependent. As the Supreme Court of Canada has said, 'democracy in any real sense of the word cannot exist without the rule of law.'[41] The Universal Declaration of Human Rights states: 'It is essential if man is not to be compelled to have recourse, as a last resort, to rebellion against tyranny and oppression, that human rights should be protected by the rule of law.'[42] In a democracy, it must be possible by political means to change a government without threatening the existence of the state. Unless this possibility exists, the state becomes identified with coercive might and the role of law within the state is emptied of moral content, for 'the State cannot be conceived in terms of force alone'.[43]

2 *Government according to law.* The principle of legality requires that the organs of the state operate through law. If the police need to detain a citizen or if taxes are levied, the officials concerned must be able to show legal authority for their actions. In Britain, their authority may be challenged before a court of law, as was done in *Entick* v *Carrington*. Acts of public authorities which are beyond their legal powers may be declared ultra vires and quashed by the courts.[44] In a striking instance, the High Court held (30 years after the event) that the enforced removal of some 1,000 British citizens from the Chagos islands in the Indian Ocean to make way for the US base on Diego Garcia had lacked any legal authority.[45] It is because of the principle of legality that legislation must be passed through Parliament if (for instance) the police are to have additional powers to combat terrorism. The rule of law serves as a buttress for democracy, since new powers of government may be conferred only by Parliament.[46]

In the British tradition of government according to law, it is from the ordinary courts that a remedy for unlawful acts of government is to be obtained: the Human Rights Act 1998 extended to all courts a duty where possible to interpret legislation consistently with the European Convention on Human Rights.[47] In many European legal systems, jurisdiction in public law is assigned not to the ordinary civil courts but to administrative courts. Such courts vary greatly in structure and procedure, but they share much in common as regards the aims of judicial review of executive acts and the standards of legality that public bodies must observe.

Public authorities and officials must be subject to effective sanctions if they depart from the law. Often the sanction is that their acts are declared invalid by the courts. Another sanction is the duty to compensate citizens whose rights have been infringed. Today it is unlikely that the British Prime Minister would be sued for damages, not because he or she is immune from such action but because his or her decisions do not normally have direct legal effect; but in 1959 the Premier of Quebec was held liable in damages for having maliciously and unlawfully directed a licensing authority to cancel the licence of a restaurant proprietor who had repeatedly provided bail for Jehovah's Witnesses accused of police offences.[48] In Britain, government departments became liable to be sued for their wrongful acts under the Crown Proceedings Act 1947.[49] That Act

---

[41] *Reference Concerning Certain Questions Relating to the Secession of Quebec* (1998) 161 DLR (4th) 385, 416–17.

[42] Preamble, 3rd para.

[43] d'Entrèves, *The Notion of the State*, p 69.

[44] Ch 30.

[45] *R* v *Foreign Secretary, ex p Bancoult* [2001] QB 1067; A Tomkins [2001] PL 571. According to Ewing and Gearty, *The Struggle for Civil Liberties*, ch 1, the principle of legality is the essence of the rule of law. And see *R* v *Home Secretary, ex p Pierson* [1998] AC 539, 587–9 (Lord Steyn).

[46] On the relevance of the rule of law to government, see Jowell and Oliver (eds), *The Changing Constitution*, 6th edn, ch 1 (J Jowell). In the case of the Chagos islands (see previous note) further 'powers of government' were in 2004 conferred not by Parliament, but by the wholly undemocratic procedure of a prerogative Order in Council: see *R* v *Foreign Secretary, ex p Bancoult (No 2)* [2008] UKHL 61, [2009] 1 AC 453.

[47] Ch 19 C.

[48] *Roncarelli* v *Duplessis* (1959) 16 DLR (2d) 689.

[49] Ch 32.

preserved the personal immunity of the Sovereign, an immunity which in other legal systems is enjoyed by the head of state. Thus in the USA, the President in office is immune from liability for his unlawful acts and he is irremovable except on a successful impeachment. If the President is removed, he can then be sued or prosecuted for unlawful acts which he may have committed. Even a President while in office may not disregard the law.

> In the course of criminal investigations into the Watergate affair, the special prosecutor appointed by the Attorney-General requested President Nixon to produce tape-recordings of discussions which the President had had with his advisers. When presidential privilege was claimed for the tapes, the US Supreme Court held that this claim had to be considered 'in the light of our historic commitment to the rule of law'. The court rejected the claim and ordered the tapes to be produced, since 'the generalised assertion of privilege must yield to the demonstrated, specific need for evidence in a pending criminal trial'.[50]

Nixon thereafter resigned rather than face impeachment proceedings before a hostile Congress. In 1998–99, when President Clinton was impeached, he was acquitted by the Senate on charges that included one of giving false testimony to a federal grand jury in the Lewinsky affair.[51] In 1999, presidential immunity of a different kind came before the House of Lords: General Pinochet, former President of Chile, was held liable to be extradited to Spain to stand trial on charges of conspiring to commit torture contrary to international law, relating to events while he was in office.[52] In 1993, the House of Lords held that the Home Secretary was liable for contempt of court, in that he decided not to order the return to the United Kingdom of a Zairean teacher who was claiming refugee status, despite an order by a High Court judge that this should be done.[53] Lord Templeman said: 'For the purpose of enforcing the law against all persons and institutions, . . . the courts are armed with coercive powers exercisable in proceedings for contempt of court.' The Home Secretary's argument that the courts had no such powers against ministers 'would, if upheld, establish the proposition that the executive obey the law as a matter of grace and not as a matter of necessity, a proposition which would reverse the result of the Civil War'.[54]

The doctrine of legality stresses the importance of there being legal authority for the acts of government. In a system in which Parliament is supreme, and so long as the Cabinet has a majority in the Commons, legal authority may not be difficult for the government to obtain. In the absence of constitutional guarantees for fundamental rights, these rights are not protected against legislative invasion. The supreme Parliament may grant the executive powers which drastically affect individual liberty, as it did in 2001 when it authorised the indefinite detention without trial of foreign nationals suspected of terrorist involvement.[55] If all that the rule of law means is that official acts must be clothed with legality, this gives no guarantee that other fundamental values are not infringed.

3 *The rule of law as a broad doctrine affecting the making of new law.* If law is not to be merely a means of achieving whatever ends a particular government may favour, the rule of law must go beyond the principle of legality. The experience and values of the legal system are relevant not only to the question, 'What legal authority *does* the government have for its acts?' but also to the questions, 'What powers *ought* the government to have? And how *ought* those powers to be exercised?' If, for example, the government wishes to introduce criminal sanctions for conduct contrary to its economic or social policies, the new legislation ought to respect principles of fair criminal procedure. If a Bill departs from these principles, arguments invoking the rule of law will be used in debate on the Bill. Such arguments are reinforced by the Human Rights Act 1998 and

---

[50] *US v Nixon* 418 US 683 (1974); for public interest immunity in Britain, see ch 32 C.
[51] Gerhardt, *The Federal Impeachment Process*, ch 14. And see Berger, *Impeachment*.
[52] *R v Bow Street Magistrate, ex p Pinochet Ugarte (No 3)* [2000] 1 AC 147.
[53] *M v Home Office* [1994] 1 AC 377.
[54] Ibid at 395.
[55] See *A v Home Secretary (No 2)* (note 9 above) and ch 26 E.

the right to a fair trial under the European Convention on Human Rights, art 6. So, too, will 'rule of law' arguments be relevant when a court is considering a new situation that is not governed by existing precedents.

As a broad principle influencing development of the law, the content of the 'rule of law' has been much debated. What *are* the essential values which have emerged from centuries of legal experience? Are they absolute values, or are there circumstances in which political necessity justifies the legislature in departing from them? To revert to the example of interrogation in depth with which this chapter began, could it ever be justified to use such methods to compel those suspected of terrorist activities to reveal information? Could there be legislation to authorise this that would not also permit measures amounting to torture or degrading treatment in breach of article 3, ECHR?

Since 2001, there have been many claims that measures amounting to torture have been used by states against suspected terrorists. In 2005, as we have seen, the Law Lords held that evidence that might have been obtained by means of torture committed abroad is inadmissible in special immigration proceedings. Having surveyed national and international rules against torture, Lord Bingham said:

> it would of course be within the power of a sovereign Parliament (in breach of international law) to confer power on [a tribunal] to receive third party torture evidence. But the English common law has regarded torture and its fruits with abhorrence for over 500 years, and that abhorrence is now shared by over 140 countries which have acceded to the Torture Convention.[56]

For legislation to connive at the use of torture would indeed be to erode the rule of law.

The 'rule of law' implications are not always clear-cut. In 2008, the Divisional Court relied on the court's responsibility to secure the rule of law in holding that the Director of the Serious Fraud Office had acted unlawfully in deciding to drop an investigation into charges of bribery against BAE Systems plc, following threats from Saudi Arabia to take action that, if the criminal process continued, would damage the United Kingdom's security. The House of Lords disagreed, holding that the Director's decision had been properly made and that the ordinary principles of judicial review gave effect to the rule of law. [57]

Is the rule of law then in this broad sense too subjective and uncertain to be of any value? Would discussion of developing law be clearer if the 'rule of law' were excluded from the vocabulary of debate? One attempt to ascertain the values inherent in law was made by Lon Fuller, who argued that the enactment of secret laws would be contrary to the essential nature of a legal system, as would heavy reliance on retrospective legislation or on legislation imposing criminal sanctions for conduct which is not defined but may be deemed undesirable by an official.[58]

Joseph Raz argues that the term 'rule of law' should be limited to formal values associated with the legal system. Thus, laws should be prospective, open, certain and capable of guiding human conduct; judges should be independent and the courts accessible; and litigants should receive a fair hearing. While these standards may ensure formal conformity to the rule of law, Raz emphasises that they do not ensure that the substance of the law meets the needs of the people; and that conformity to legal values is a matter of degree, to be balanced against competing claims.[59]

---

[56] *A v Home Secretary* (No 2) (note 9 above), [51].

[57] *R (Corner House Research) v Director of SFO* [2008] UKHL 60, [2008] 4 All ER 927. For criticism of the decision on appeal, see J Jowell [2008] JR 273 and Lord Steyn [2009] PL 338.

[58] Fuller, *The Morality of Law.* For endorsement of Fuller's approach, see Allan, *Constitutional Justice.* For a vivid illustration of the perversion of legal process, see Lord Steyn's quotation from Kafka's *The Trial* in *R (Roberts) v Parole Board* [2005] UKHL 45, [2005] 2 AC 738, [95]. See also the decision of nine judges on the use of 'special advocates' in *A v Home Secretary (No 3)* [2009] UKHL 28, [2009] 3 All ER 643.

[59] J Raz (1977) 93 LQR 195. See also Raz, *Ethics in the Public Domain,* ch 16.

While Raz regards the rule of law as dealing with matters of form, other jurists favour a more substantive concept.[60] But the distinction between form and substance is not always clear-cut (is the case against 'arbitrary power' based on matters of form or substance or both?). Raz accepted that the rule of law is 'compatible with gross violations of human rights', but also argued that 'deliberate disregard for the rule of law violates human dignity'.[61] Raz rightly warns against identifying the rule of law with utopia. But is the rule of law observed under a dictatorship in which the judges diligently apply the dictator's decrees, including one that permits indefinite detention without trial for those suspected of subversive activity? Many would conclude that the rule of law in a strong sense thrives only alongside values of human dignity, liberty and democracy.[62]

Among British judges there is an important vein of belief in the values to be upheld in a legal system. The nature of these values can be discovered from judicial decisions[63] and from a growing body of articles and lectures by judges.[64] Today these values include those inherent in the European Convention on Human Rights.

International aspects of the rule of law

Since 1945, there have been constant efforts within the international community to further the rule of law in international relations and to secure respect for human rights. The Universal Declaration of Human Rights, adopted in 1948, was followed by the European Convention on Human Rights, signed at Rome in 1950.[65] The Convention recognised that European countries have 'a common heritage of political traditions, ideals, freedom and the rule of law' and created machinery for protecting certain human rights. In *Golder*'s case, upholding the right of a convicted prisoner in the United Kingdom to have access to legal advice regarding a civil action against the prison authorities, the European Court of Human Rights said, 'in civil matters one can scarcely conceive of the rule of law without there being a possibility of having access to the courts'.[66]

Both the Convention and the case-law of the Strasbourg Court support the analysis of the rule of law made in this chapter. The Convention seeks to protect individuals against the arbitrary or unlawful exercise of state power, and it requires national legal systems to bear the primary burden of protecting Convention rights. In respect of those Convention rights that (unlike the right not to be tortured) are not absolute, any restrictions in the public interest must (among other things) satisfy the test of being 'prescribed by law'. This test means (in outline) that (1) the restriction must be authorised in national law and (2) the 'quality' of the national law must be compatible with the Convention.[67] In English law, it was formerly held that public authorities might do anything which did not interfere with the rights of individuals, even if they had no express authority for such action.[68] This approach is not acceptable where Convention rights are concerned.

The European Convention, established through the Council of Europe, to which 47 European states belong, is one of many multilateral treaties that encourage states to provide protection

---

[60] See P Craig [1997] PL 467 and (the same) in Feldman (ed.), *English Public Law*, ch 13 B.

[61] J Raz (1977) 93 LQR 195, 204 and 205.

[62] See Lord Bingham's analysis of the rule of law at [2007] CLJ 67 and his book, *The Rule of Law*.

[63] See D Feldman (1990) 106 LQR 246. On the power of the court to stay proceedings which 'have only been made possible by acts which offend the court's conscience as being contrary to the rule of law', see *R v Horseferry Road Magistrates, ex p Bennett* [1994] 1 AC 42, 76 (Lord Lowry).

[64] In addition to Lord Bingham (note 62 above), articles by other judges include: J Laws (1994) 57 MLR 213, [1995] PL 72, [1996] PL 622, [1997] PL 455, [1998] PL 221; R Scott [1996] PL 410 and 427; S Sedley (1994) 110 LQR 260; Lord Steyn [1997] PL 84, (2004) 53 ICLQ 1; Lord Woolf [1995] PL 57, [2004] CLJ 317.

[65] Ch 19 B. For the background, see Simpson, *Human Rights and the End of Empire*.

[66] *Golder v UK* (1975) 1 EHRR 524.

[67] See *Sunday Times v UK* (1979) 2 EHRR 245; *Malone v UK* (1984) 7 EHRR 14. Harris, O'Boyle and Warbrick, *Law of the European Convention on Human Rights*, pp 344–8.

[68] *Malone v Metropolitan Police Commissioner* [1979] Ch 344; cf *R v Somerset CC, ex p Fewings* [1995] 3 All ER 20.

for human rights. Multilateral treaties adopted under the United Nations include the International Covenant on Civil and Political Rights, the International Convention on the Elimination of all Forms of Racial Discrimination and the Convention against Torture.[69]

Within the Commonwealth, the heads of government at their biennial meetings regularly express support for the rule of law. In 1991 at Harare they linked the rule of law, the independence of the judiciary and the protection of human rights, with 'democratic processes and institutions which reflect national circumstances' and 'just and honest government' as being among the fundamental values of the Commonwealth association.[70]

Social and economic aspects of the rule of law

The rule of law movement has broadened to include social and economic goals which lie far beyond the typical values associated with the courts, legal process and the legal profession. Such a broadening of the 'rule of law' raises difficult issues, since it is directly related to policies for government action in relation to the economy and social welfare. It has been argued that individual autonomy and the ability to plan one's affairs will be prejudiced if governments retain powers to intervene in social and economic affairs.[71] Now certainty and predictability are values often associated with law. In a different context, Lord Diplock said in 1975: 'The acceptance of the rule of law as a constitutional principle requires that a citizen, before committing himself to any course of action, should be able to know what are the legal consequences that will flow from it.'[72] But however desirable it may be that discretionary powers of government should be controlled by rules,[73] this principle is difficult to apply to the state's responsibilities for the economic and social well-being of its people.

A related question is whether legal protection for the classic civil and political rights (such as personal liberty and freedom of expression) can or should be extended to economic and social rights (such as rights to employment or housing).[74] Constitutional protection for these rights is possible, although in the case of some social rights there are problems of definition and enforcement. But in any event, individuals ought to have enforceable rights to the delivery of some public goods, such as education or medical care. In South Africa, constitutionally-protected social rights (including rights to housing, health care, food and shelter) are enforceable by the Constitutional Court.[75] Within the Council of Europe, there has since 1995 been a collective complaints procedure to enable cases to be taken to the Social Rights Committee by organisations claiming that a member state is in breach of an obligation under the European Social Charter. The United Kingdom has not ratified the collective complaints protocol, but this is included in the Revised Social Charter of 1996.[76] In the United Kingdom, much detailed legislation has long existed in these areas, and individuals may typically enforce rights under that legislation by appealing to the appropriate tribunal (where one exists) or, where there is no right of appeal, by recourse to judicial review.[77]

---

[69] For the texts of these conventions, see Brownlie and Goodwin-Gill, *Basic Documents on Human Rights*.

[70] Harare Communiqué, 1991. And see e.g. Communiqué of the Commonwealth Heads of Government Meeting in Uganda, 2007. Also ch 15 C.

[71] Hayek, *The Constitution of Liberty*, makes a profound analysis of rule of law concepts; for a critique, see Loughlin, *Public Law and Political Theory*, pp 84–101.

[72] *Black-Clawson International Ltd v Papierwerke AG* [1975] AC 591, 638.

[73] Davis, *Discretionary Justice*, ch 3.

[74] For a review of the issues, see S Fredman and M Wesson in Feldman (ed.), *English Public Law*, ch 10. Also K D Ewing (2001) 5 Edin LR 297; G van Beuren [2002] PL 456.

[75] See *Government of Republic of South Africa v Grootboom* 2001 (1) SA 46 (CC); and M Wesson [2007] PL 748.

[76] See Harris and Darcy, *The European Social Charter*. The EU Charter of Fundamental Rights (2000) includes both civil and political rights, and social and economic rights, and it seeks to break down the traditional distinction between the two: Fredman and Wesson (above) pp 473–8. See also ch 8 B.

[77] Ch 29 A.

Conclusion

It is not possible to formulate a simple and clear-cut statement of the rule of law as a broad political doctrine. As the needs of national and international communities change, so we need to restate the received values of law in response to those changes. A government's changing programme must not lead it to suppose that new areas of public action (such as regulation of the public utilities)[78] can be isolated from the scope of law and subjected only to administrative or political controls. Through the European Union, the United Kingdom is part of a supranational system which exercises control in legal form over important areas of economic activity. Indeed, the powers granted to European organs are capable of enlarging the effective scope of the rule of law, for example by granting to the individual rights of legal protection against the governments of member states.[79]

Challenges to the orderly working of law and society are presented by phenomena such as hijacking, urban terrorism, direct action by militant groups, campaigns of civil disobedience, and violent protests and demonstrations. All these are sometimes described indiscriminately as a threat to the rule of law (by which may simply be meant the authority and stability of established institutions). There are many important distinctions to be drawn between these different forms of political or criminal action. But, if we leave aside acts of criminal violence at one end of the scale and law-abiding political expression at the other end, do acts of non-violent civil disobedience endanger the legal system? In particular, does the rule of law require complete obedience to the law from all citizens and organisations?[80] It may be argued both that, in a democratic society, there are important reasons for obeying the law which do not exist in other forms of government, and also that there are forms of principled disobedience that do not run counter to the customary reasons for obedience, particularly those which are designed to improve the working of democratic procedures for political decisions.[81] While individuals may be driven by their consciences to resist a particular law that they regard as unjust or immoral, there is a danger that decisions to disobey particular laws taken by organised groups (whether public authorities, private bodies or business corporations) may cumulatively suggest that there is no general obligation to obey the law, but only the law of which one approves. In fact, the maintenance of life in modern society requires a willingness from most people for most of the time to observe the laws, even when individually they may not agree with them. It deserves to be remembered that law, like the democratic process, may protect the weaker, underprivileged sections of society against those who can exercise physical or economic force.

---

[78] See ch 14.

[79] See Case 11/70, *Internationale Handelsgesellschaft* [1970] ECR 1125; Case 5/88, *Wachauf* v *Germany* [1989] ECR 2609. See further, ch 8 B.

[80] Marshall, *Constitutional Theory*, ch 9; Dworkin, *Taking Rights Seriously*, ch 8; Allan, *Law, Liberty, and Justice*, ch 5.

[81] Singer, *Democracy and Disobedience*. The Strasbourg Court has recognised that direct action may involve Convention rights to freedom of expression and association: *Steel* v *UK* (1998) 28 EHRR 603. See H Fenwick and G Phillipson [2000] PL 627 and (2001) 21 LS 535.

CHAPTER 7

Responsible and accountable government

Within a democracy, those who govern must be accountable, or responsible, to those whom they govern. The power to govern derives directly from the votes of the electors, as well as from their continuing willingness to be governed by the elected government. Between general elections, one continuing function of the elected representatives is to call the government to account for its acts and policies. This both requires government to justify its decisions by giving the reasons for them and enables decisions that appear unjustified or mistaken to be criticised. The process enables electors at their next opportunity to vote to make an informed appraisal of the government's record; until then it influences the formation of public opinion regarding the government.

In ordinary speech, the words 'responsible' and 'accountable' have several meanings; and the concept of responsible government takes several forms.[1] During the 1990s, because of some serious failures of accountability, attempts were made to clarify the essential meaning of accountable government. In 1996, the Scott report on the 'arms for Iraq' affair contained penetrating criticism of numerous incomplete and misleading answers given in Parliament by ministers to questions about the government's policy.[2] In the same year, an influential report by the Public Service Committee of the House of Commons, while affirming that ministerial responsibility 'is a central principle of the British Constitution', examined the difficulties inherent in the principle.[3] In 2001, an independent committee urged that Parliament must be at the apex of the system of scrutiny of the executive and must develop both a culture of scrutiny and more effective methods of securing accountability.[4] In 2007, the Public Administration committee of the Commons referred to the 'robust system of political accountability' in the United Kingdom, but urged that the relationship between ministers and the civil service should ensure the 'ultimate accountability of the government' to the electorate.[5]

This chapter examines the political responsibility of government to Parliament, including both collective and individual responsibility. Another form of responsibility is the legal responsibility of ministers and officials for their acts. Whereas legal responsibility may be enforced in the courts, political responsibility is enforced primarily through Parliament. A government's relationship with Parliament is too complex to be summarised in a code of precise rules, but the essential features of responsibility to Parliament give rise to obligations which ought to be observed in the regular practice of government. A summary of these obligations may now be found in two related documents, the Ministerial Code and the Civil Service Code,[6] as well as in resolutions of each House at Westminster.

---

[1] Related principles include popular control of decision-making and political equality: see Weir and Beetham, *Political Power and Democratic Control in Britain*, ch 1. Tomkins, *Our Republican Constitution*, p 1, emphasises that the government is responsible *to Parliament*.

[2] HC 115 (1995–6), vol IV, section K.8, pp 1799–806; and see R Scott [1996] PL 410.

[3] HC 313–I (1995–6). For the government's response, see HC 67 (1996–7).

[4] Hansard Society, *The Challenge for Parliament: Making Government Accountable* (the Newton report). See also HC 300 and 748 (1999–2000), Cm 4737, 2000, HC 321 (2000–01) and D Oliver [2001] PL 666.

[5] HC 122 (2006–07). For the government's response, see HC 1057 (2007–08).

[6] See respectively ch 13 A and ch 13 E. And see ch 2 B.

Early origins of responsible government

So long as government was carried on by the King, the nature of monarchy made it difficult to establish any responsibility for acts of government. In medieval times, the practice developed by which the royal will was signified in documents bearing a royal seal, and applied by one of the King's ministers. In this practice lay 'the foundation for our modern doctrine of ministerial responsibility – that for every exercise of the royal power some minister is answerable'.[7] With the responsibility of ministers came a specific understanding of the rule that 'the King can do no wrong'. This meant not that everything done on behalf of the King was lawful, but that the King's advisers and ministers were punishable for illegal measures that occurred in the course of government.[8] Today legal and political responsibility for an order made by the Queen in Council is borne by the Cabinet minister whose department decided that the order should be made.[9]

This responsibility was at one time enforced by the English Parliament through impeachment. Officers of state were liable to be impeached by the Commons at the bar of the House of Lords for the treason, high crimes and misdemeanours they were alleged to have committed. In the 17th century, impeachment became a political weapon wielded by Parliament for striking at unpopular royal policies.[10] Following the granting of a royal pardon to Danby in 1679 to forestall his impeachment, the Act of Settlement provided that a royal pardon could not be pleaded in bar of an impeachment. The last instance of a purely political impeachment came when the Tory ministers who in 1713 negotiated the Peace of Utrecht were later impeached by a Whig House of Commons. Thereafter, only two impeachments occurred, of Warren Hastings between 1788 and 1795 for misgovernment in India and of Lord Melville in 1806 for alleged corruption. The power of impeachment is still available to Parliament: but more modern means of achieving ministerial responsibility have rendered it an obsolete weapon in the United Kingdom.[11]

The legal responsibility of government

The principle that government must be conducted according to law has already been discussed.[12] The Queen may not personally be sued or prosecuted in the courts. But servants or officers of the Crown who commit crimes or civil wrongs are, and always have been, subject to the jurisdiction of the courts. This jurisdiction extends to contempt of court.[13] Superior orders or the interest of the state are no defence to such proceedings.[14] Public authorities other than the Crown are at common law liable for the wrongful acts of their officials or servants.[15] The departments of central government became liable to be sued under the Crown Proceedings Act 1947 and their decisions are subject to control by means of judicial review.[16] It is with political responsibility that this chapter is concerned.

---

[7] Maitland, *Constitutional History*, p 203. Cf art 106 of the Belgian Constitution (1994).

[8] Chitty, *Prerogatives of the Crown*, p 5. For rules on the use of seals and recording of decisions, see Anson, *Law and Custom of the Constitution*, vol II, part I, pp 62–72; HLE, vol 8(2), pp 233, 518–19.

[9] See *R (Bancoult) v Foreign Secretary* [2008] UKHL 61, [2009] 1 AC 453.

[10] Maitland, *Constitutional History*, pp 317–18; Taswell-Langmead, *English Constitutional History*, pp 164–5, 353–4, 529–38; Clayton Roberts, *The Growth of Responsible Government in Stuart England*; Berger, *Impeachment*, ch 1.

[11] See Carnall and Nicholson (eds), *The Impeachment of Warren Hastings*, ch 7 (A W Bradley). Cf Dicey, *The Law of the Constitution*, p 499.

[12] Ch 6.

[13] *M v Home Office* [1994] 1 AC 377.

[14] Smith and Hogan, *Criminal Law*, pp 357–8; Dicey, pp 302–6; *Entick v Carrington*, p 92 above.

[15] *Mersey Docks and Harbour Board Trustees v Gibbs* (1866) LR 1 HL 93.

[16] Chs 30–2.

Development of responsibility to Parliament

After 1688 the doctrine of collective responsibility developed in fits and starts as the Cabinet system came into being.[17] For much of the 18th century the Cabinet was a body of holders of high office whose relationship with one another was ill-defined; the body as a whole was not responsible to Parliament. Although the King rarely attended Cabinet meetings after 1717, it was the King's government in fact as well as in name, and the King could act on the advice of individual ministers. Under Walpole, the first 'Prime Minister', ministries were relatively homogeneous. Other Cabinets in the century were less united. Parliament could force the dismissal of individual ministers who were not approved, but could not dictate appointments to the King. The King sometimes consulted those who were out of office without the prior approval of his ministers. There was no clear dividing line between matters dealt with by individual ministers and matters dealt with in the Cabinet. As late as 1806, it was debated in the Commons whether ministers must accept collective responsibility for the general affairs of government or whether only those ministers who carried policies into execution were individually responsible.[18]

By the early 19th century, as the scope for personal government by the Sovereign sharply declined, the tendencies towards the collective responsibility of the Cabinet became more marked. After 1832, it became evident that the Cabinet must retain the support of the majority in the House of Commons if it wished to continue in office. Just as it had earlier been recognised that a single minister could not retain office against the will of Parliament, so it was realised that all ministers must stand or fall together in Parliament, if the Cabinet were to function effectively.

By the mid-19th century, ministerial responsibility was the accepted basis of parliamentary government in Britain.[19] Critics of the rule of Cabinet unity were reminded that 'the various departments of the Administration are but parts of a single machine . . . and that the various branches of the Government have a close connection and mutual dependence upon each other'.[20]

The development of collective responsibility was accompanied by an expansion in government, not least in the period after 1832 when new central agencies were created to oversee areas of social administration, such as the reformed poor law and public health. After some experimenting with appointed public boards that were not directly responsible to Parliament and had no one in Parliament to defend them against their critics,[21] a strong political preference was expressed for vesting the new powers in a minister who sat in Parliament and could account to Parliament for what was done. The development of parliamentary procedures for financial scrutiny and for obtaining information through questions addressed to ministers enabled members to influence matters within the minister's responsibility.[22] The corollary of this, as the civil service itself was reformed following the Northcote-Trevelyan report of 1854, was the anonymity and permanence of the civil servants who administered the new departments under the control or oversight of ministers.[23]

The meaning of collective responsibility

The doctrine of collective responsibility was stated in absolute terms by Lord Salisbury in 1878:

> For all that passes in Cabinet every member of it who does not resign is absolutely and irretrievably responsible and has no right afterwards to say that he agreed in one case to a compromise, while in another he was persuaded by his colleagues . . . It is only on the principle that absolute

---

[17] Mackintosh, *British Cabinet*, ch 2.
[18] Williams, *The 18th Century Constitution*, pp 123–5.
[19] For a notable summary, see Grey, *Parliamentary Government*, p 4.
[20] Grey, p 57.
[21] F M G Willson (1955) 33 *Public Administration* 43, 44.
[22] Chester and Bowring, *Questions in Parliament*, ch 2.
[23] Parris, *Constitutional Bureaucracy*, ch 3.

responsibility is undertaken by every member of the Cabinet, who, after a decision is arrived at, remains a member of it, that the joint responsibility of Ministers to Parliament can be upheld and one of the most essential principles of parliamentary responsibility established.[24]

In 2007, the Prime Minister's statement of the doctrine took this form:

Collective responsibility requires that Ministers should be able to express their views frankly in the expectation that they can argue freely in private while maintaining a united front when decisions have been reached. This in turn requires that the privacy of opinions expressed in Cabinet and Ministerial Committees, including in correspondence, should be maintained.[25]

Yet it is difficult to control political behaviour in absolute terms. In the 19th century, the degree of political cohesion was variable. Cabinet unity could not always be achieved when ministers held deeply divided opinions. Some subjects were regarded as 'open questions', for example women's suffrage between 1906 and 1914 and more recently capital punishment.[26] But it was a sign of political weakness if many issues were accepted as open questions. Except for open questions, ministers who did not wish to be publicly identified with Cabinet policies were expected to resign.

Today, collective responsibility embodies a number of related aspects. Like other principles of government, it is neither static nor unchangeable and may give way before more pressing political forces.

(1) The Prime Minister and other ministers are collectively responsible to Parliament, and to the Commons in particular, for the conduct of national affairs. In practice, so long as the governing party retains its majority in the House, the Prime Minister is unlikely to be forced to resign (although this was Mrs Thatcher's fate in 1990, after over 11 years in office) or to seek a dissolution of Parliament.

(2) When a Prime Minister dies or resigns office, then even if the same party continues in power, all ministerial offices are at the disposal of the new Prime Minister.

(3) Although ministers are individually responsible to Parliament for the conduct of their departments, if members of the Commons seek to censure an individual minister, the government generally will rally to his or her defence: collective responsibility is a means of defending an incompetent or unpopular minister. However, this may not succeed when there is a sustained media campaign to pillory and remove a particular minister.

(4) Ministers while in office share in the collective responsibility of all ministers. As the Ministerial Code states bluntly: 'Decisions reached by the Cabinet or Ministerial Committees are binding on all members of the Government.'[27] A Cabinet minister could at one time ask for dissent from a decision to be recorded in the private minutes of Cabinet.[28] All ministers are expected to support the government by voting in Parliament. Cabinet ministers who were also members of the National Executive Committee of the Labour party were in 1974 told by the Prime Minister that they must observe the conventions of collective responsibility at Executive meetings.[29]

(5) As a former Cabinet minister said, an element of concealment is inherent in the concept of collective responsibility. 'Ministers must in the nature of things have differences, but they must outwardly appear to have none.'[30] In principle, secrecy attaches to Cabinet proceedings, but it is common for one or more subjects considered in a Cabinet meeting to be mentioned to the media. At this level of government, the Freedom of Information Act has made little difference, since the Cabinet Office view is that to release Cabinet papers would put at risk the public

---

[24] *Life of Robert, Marquis of Salisbury*, vol II, pp 219–20.

[25] *Ministerial Code* (Cabinet Office, 2007), para 2.1.

[26] Jennings, *Cabinet Government*, pp 277–9; Hanham, *The Nineteenth Century Constitution*, pp 79, 84–94; Grey, p 116.

[27] *Ministerial Code*, para 2.3. And see ch 13 C.

[28] Mackintosh, *British Cabinet*, p 534. The current Ministerial Code does not provide for this.

[29] Wilson, *The Governance of Britain*, pp 74–5, 191–3; and see D L Ellis [1980] PL 367, 379–83.

[30] Gordon Walker, *The Cabinet*, pp 27–8.

interest in collective responsibility.[31] Exceptionally, a minister who has resigned may explain in detail the reasons for the resignation, both in Parliament and the press.[32] Today leakages about controversial matters frequently occur and the principle of secrecy continues to be under pressure to give way to a more open system of government.

(6) Similarly, in principle secrecy attaches to dealings between departments. Decisions reached by the Cabinet or ministerial committees are 'normally announced and explained as the decision of the Minister concerned'.[33] Thus collective responsibility reinforces the principle of the indivisibility of the executive.[34] Again, an element of concealment is evident: departments are expected to agree with each other because their ministers are members of the same Cabinet. In real life, serious disputes between departments occur, and the ministers concerned may not always wish the nature of the disagreement to be kept from the public.

(7) Where necessary, decisions of the Cabinet are communicated to the monarch by the Prime Minister. One exception exists to the principle of collective responsibility for advice to the monarch: in advising the monarch on the prerogative of mercy, the Home Secretary acts on his or her own responsibility.[35]

Collective responsibility serves a variety of political uses. As most governments are drawn from one party, it reinforces party unity and prevents backbench MPs from inquiring too far into the processes of government. It helps to maintain government control over legislation and public expenditure and to contain public disagreement between departments. It supports the authority of the Prime Minister.[36]

Some purposes served by the doctrine are controversial, in particular over the degree of protection which should be given to the secrecy of decision-making, the authority of the Prime Minister and the need for external unanimity. In some open processes of government, especially public inquiries, the separate views of government departments are regularly made public.[37] But there is an obvious political advantage in at least an outward appearance of unity. For this reason, some aspects of collective responsibility apply also to the 'shadow Cabinet' of the main opposition party. The political authority of the Labour 'shadow Cabinet' was weakened when, in a Commons debate about denationalisation, two inconsistent policies were advocated by the leading speakers for the Opposition.[38]

As is clear from the current *Ministerial Code*, many important decisions of national policy are not taken in full Cabinet. In the past, the decision to manufacture the British atomic bomb,[39] to mount the Suez operation in 1956, to raise the bank rate in 1957[40] and to devalue the pound in 1967[41] were taken by a few ministers meeting with the Prime Minister. So were the decisions to ban trade union membership for staff at Government Communications Headquarters,[42] and to give the Bank of England responsibility for setting interest rates in 1997. In such cases, other members of the Cabinet are in no better position than ministers outside the Cabinet to influence the decision before it is taken. While Mr Blair was Prime Minister, he appears to have made little use of meetings of the Cabinet for collective decision-making. The late Robin Cook, a former

---

[31] See *Guide to Cabinet and Cabinet Committee Business* (2008, Cabinet Office); ch 13 F.

[32] See R Brazier [1990] PL 300.

[33] *Ministerial Code*, para 2.3.

[34] Heclo and Wildavsky, *The Private Government of Public Money*, p 116.

[35] Ch 12 D.

[36] See ch 13 A. Crossman commented that collective responsibility had come to mean collective obedience to the Prime Minister (Introduction to Bagehot, *The English Constitution*, p 53).

[37] Ch 29 B.

[38] HC Deb, 10 November 1981, cols 438, 499.

[39] Crossman, Introduction to Bagehot, pp 54–5. This was not an isolated event: Hennessy, *Cabinet*, ch 4.

[40] Cmnd 350, 1957; and R A Chapman (1965) 43 *Public Administration* 199.

[41] Wilson, *The Labour Government 1964–70*, ch 23.

[42] See *CCSU v Minister for the Civil Service* [1985] AC 374.

senior Cabinet minister before his resignation in 2003, wrote, 'Tony does not regard the Cabinet as a place for decisions. Normally he avoids discussions in Cabinet until decisions are taken and announced to it.'[43] Although Cook said that policy in relation to Iraq was often discussed in Cabinet during 2002,[44] the Butler review of intelligence on weapons of mass destruction in Iraq criticised the informality with which Cabinet discussion took place on difficult questions of policy without circulation of relevant papers.[45]

Whether decisions are taken by the Cabinet or are merely reported to it, a minister may at any time resign in protest against decisions with which he or she disagrees. Such resignations may indicate a deep disagreement over the way in which the Prime Minister is conducting government. Sir Geoffrey Howe's resignation in November 1990 after a series of other Cabinet resignations set in train the events leading to Mrs Thatcher's own resignation on 23 November 1990. Resignations over particular policy issues do not affect decisions that have already been taken.[46]

Agreements to differ

In exceptional circumstances, it may be politically impossible for the Cabinet to maintain a united front. In 1932, the coalition or 'National' government, formed in 1931 to deal with the economic crisis, adopted an 'agreement to differ'. The majority of the Cabinet favoured the adoption of a general tariff of 10 per cent, against the strong opposition of three Liberal ministers and one National Labour minister. It was announced that the dissenting ministers would be free to oppose the proposals of the majority by speech and vote, both in Parliament and outside. When the Labour opposition criticised the government for violating 'the long-established constitutional principle of Cabinet responsibility', the motion of censure was defeated by an overwhelming majority.[47] Eight months later the dissenting ministers resigned on the related issue of imperial preference. This short-lived departure from the principle of unanimity took place in the special circumstances of a coalition government formed to deal with a serious national crisis.

In 1975, the Labour Cabinet agreed to differ over Britain's continued membership of the European Communities, an issue on which the Labour party was divided. Party unity was maintained in the two general elections in 1974 by an undertaking from Prime Minister Wilson to renegotiate the terms of British membership and to submit the outcome to the people for decision, either at a general election or by referendum. When in April 1975 the renegotiation of terms was completed, the Cabinet by 16–7 decided to recommend continued membership to the electorate. It was agreed that ministers who opposed this policy should be free to speak and campaign against it, but only outside Parliament.[48] In fact, majorities against Cabinet policy were recorded in the Parliamentary Labour Party, in the National Executive Committee and at a special party conference. When a junior minister, Eric Heffer, insisted on opposing Britain's membership in the Commons,[49] he had to resign from office. Other difficulties arose over the answering of parliamentary questions on European subjects by ministers opposed to British membership.[50]

Such agreements to differ give rise to many political difficulties, but neither in 1932 nor in 1975 did they lead to the downfall of the government. It is difficult to describe these rather desperate expedients as 'unconstitutional'. If conventions are observed because of the political difficulties

---

[43] Cook, *The Point of Departure*, p 115. And see Foster, *British Government in Crisis*, p 291: 'Power has drained from Parliament, Cabinet and civil service into the PM and those around him.'

[44] *The Point of Departure*, p 116.

[45] HC 898 (2003–04), paras 610–611. According to the *Ministerial Code*, para 2.4, 'No definitive criteria can be given for issues which engage collective responsibility'. And see ch 13 B.

[46] Cf Alderman and Cross, *The Tactics of Resignation*.

[47] Jennings, *Cabinet Government*, pp 279–81.

[48] See Cmnd 6003, 1975; HC Deb, 23 January 1975, col 1745; HC Deb, 7 April 1975, col 351 (WA). And Wilson, *The Governance of Britain*, pp 194–7.

[49] HC Deb, 9 April 1975, cols 1325–32.

[50] E.g. HC Deb, 5 May 1975, cols 989–1015.

which follow if they are not,[51] both in 1932 and 1975 it was less difficult to depart from Cabinet unanimity than to seek to enforce it. During a period of minority government, a free vote was allowed to the Labour party (including ministers) on the second reading of the European Assembly Elections Bill.[52] Agreements to differ in respect of such contentious political issues are, of course, distinct from other questions, notably capital punishment, on which ministers like other MPs are free to vote according to their conscience.[53]

Other aspects of collective responsibility

In any government there are more ministers outside the Cabinet than within it. Some have heavy departmental duties; others are concerned only with a specific range of subjects.[54] These ministers are bound by Cabinet decisions and must refrain from criticising them in public. The *Ministerial Code* accepts that on certain constituency matters a minister may wish to make his or her views clearly known to the responsible minister, but on all other matters the principle of collective responsibility requires ministers to ensure that their public statements are consistent with government policy.[55] The policy content and timing of all major speeches by ministers 'must be cleared in good time with the No 10 Press Office'.[56]

A somewhat similar restraint is that ministers 'may not, while in office, write and publish a book on their ministerial experience'.[57] In 1969, a parliamentary secretary resigned to publish a book on the economy and the machinery of government. Refusing him permission to publish the book and remain a minister, the Prime Minister stated that he had no alternative 'but to uphold the principles which every Prime Minister must maintain in relation to the collective responsibility of the Administration'.[58] Collective responsibility can thus be invoked by the Prime Minister to control the behaviour of ministers. The consequences of collective responsibility are to a large extent what the Prime Minister of the day chooses to make them. The obligation to support government policy on important issues extends to the backbench MPs who act as unpaid parliamentary secretaries to ministers, and may be dismissed for stepping too far out of line.[59]

Operation of individual responsibility today[60]

Ministerial responsibility remains important, but structural changes in government have affected the application of the concept. During the 20th century, as the tasks of the state expanded and vast Whitehall departments were created, officials continued to act in their minister's name, but the ability of ministers to oversee their work declined. The state's economic and social functions led to the creation of non-departmental bodies, public corporations and other agencies. Many of these (especially the boards of the nationalised industries after 1945) were intended to operate beyond the reach of ministerial responsibility, at least for day-to-day decisions. By contrast, the executive agencies created since 1988 under the 'Next Steps' initiative were intended to achieve effective delegation of managerial power, without necessarily reducing overall ministerial control.[61]

---

[51] Page 24 above.
[52] HC Deb, 23 March 1977, col 1307; and see D L Ellis [1980] PL 367, 388.
[53] E.g. HC Deb, 13 July 1983, col 972.
[54] *Ministerial Code*, paras 4.6, 4.7.
[55] *Ministerial Code*, para 8.3.
[56] *Ministerial Code*, para 8.2.
[57] *Ministerial Code*, para 8.9.
[58] *The Times*, 26 and 29 September 1969.
[59] *Ministerial Code*, paras 3.8, 3.9. And see P Norton [1989] PL 232.
[60] Marshall, *Constitutional Conventions*, ch 4; Brazier, *Ministers of the Crown*, ch 15; Woodhouse, *Ministers and Parliament*; and D Woodhouse (2004) 82 *Public Administration* 1.
[61] See chs 13 D and 14.

In the tradition of parliamentary government, a minister answers to Parliament for his or her department; praise and blame are addressed to the minister, not to civil servants. An aspect of this tradition is that as a general rule ministers may not excuse the failure of policies by turning on their expert advisers and administrators. Attempts to do so may seriously damage the minister's reputation, as the Home Secretary (Michael Howard) discovered in 1995; after intervening repeatedly in the operation of the Prison Service, Howard denied responsibility for defects in prison security and dismissed the Service's director, saying that the defects had been an operational matter entrusted to the director.[62] The corollary of the minister's responsibility is that civil servants are not directly responsible to Parliament for government policies or decisions, although they are responsible *to ministers* for their own actions and conduct. In 1996 the government defended 'the fundamental principle that civil servants are servants of the Crown, accountable to the duly constituted government of the day, and not servants of the House'.[63]

Much of the work of Parliament rests on this basis. Government Bills are drafted on the instructions of ministers, who are responsible for the proposals they contain. Question time emphasises the responsibility of ministers.[64] Although civil servants have no voice in most parliamentary proceedings, they appear before select committees to give evidence on departmental policies and decisions. In giving such evidence, they 'do so on behalf of their Ministers and under their directions' and their purpose 'is to contribute to the central process of Ministerial accountability, not to offer personal views or judgments on matters of political controversy, . . . or to become involved in what would amount to disciplinary investigations . . . '.[65]

The sanctions for individual responsibility

What are the sanctions which underlie this general practice of Parliament? The system assumes that ministers fulfil their parliamentary duties, such as introducing legislation and answering questions. By a rota system, departments are assigned days for answering questions and a minister could not refuse to appear on the assigned day. Ministers may refuse to answer a question if they consider that it does not fall within their responsibility, that it would be contrary to the public interest to answer the question or that the expense of obtaining the information requested would be excessive.[66] These grounds are similar to the grounds that exempt from disclosure under the Freedom of Information Act 2000.[67] If a minister persistently refused to answer questions that were properly asked, political pressure could build up against such refusals. But if the Opposition were then to table a motion of censure on the minister, the motion would stand little chance of succeeding in view of the government majority in the House. Situations may occur in which a Prime Minister is unable to protect a minister from pressure to resign exerted in other ways. In 1986, the Westland affair caused the Trade and Industry Secretary (Mr Brittan) to resign for

---

[62] See HC Deb, 16 October 1995, col 30 and 19 October 1995, col 502, and ch 13 D. Also A Barker (1998) 76 *Public Administration* 21 and, for later events, C Polidano (2000) 71 *Political Quarterly* 177.

[63] HC 67 (1996–7), app, para 10. And see ch 13 D.

[64] Ch 10 D. Chester and Bowring, pp 251–68, and app II; Franklin and Norton (eds), *Parliamentary Questions*.

[65] *Departmental Evidence and Response to Select Committees (the 'Osmotherly Rules')* (Cabinet Office, 2005), paras 40, 41. The rules apply to departments and their agencies, but not to members of non-departmental public bodies (paras 1, 2). See *Guidance on Code of Practice for Board Members of Public Bodies* (2004), app 2; and HC 447, 1055 (2003–4).

[66] And see Erskine May, *Parliamentary Practice*, pp 339–54. Since 1993, the House of Commons Table Office has rejected questions only when a minister has refused to answer them in the same session: HC 313–I (1995–6), para 39; and R Scott [1996] PL 410, 416–17. On ministerial accountability and parliamentary questions, see HC 820 (1997–8), HC 821 (1998–9), HC 61 (2000–1), HC 1086 (2001–2), HC 355 (2003–4), HC 449 (2004–5) and HC 853 (2005–06) (reports by the Public Administration Committee).

[67] See ch 13 F; and HC 449 (2004–5). In HC 853 (2005–06), the government explained why Freedom of Information Act grounds for refusing disclosure in the public interest could not be applied to parliamentary questions.

having improperly released to the press a confidential letter from the Solicitor General. Mr Brittan refused to answer questions from the Commons Defence Committee about his role in the matter.[68] In more normal situations, the Commons select committees may question the conduct of ministers who appear to be avoiding their responsibility to Parliament, and their inquiries may today relate directly to the duties of ministers under the Ministerial Code.[69]

Ministerial responsibility for departmental maladministration

Ministers are, or ought to be, responsible to Parliament for their own decisions and policies and for the administration of their departments. The position in respect of the errors of civil servants is less clear. Two questions arise: (a) to what extent is a minister responsible for acts of maladministration in the department? (b) if serious maladministration occurs, does such responsibility involve a duty to resign? The Crichel Down affair has long been the starting point for discussion of these questions.

> Farmland in Dorset known as Crichel Down had been acquired under compulsory powers from several owners by the Air Ministry in 1937. After the war, the land was transferred to the Ministry of Agriculture, for whom it was administered by a commission set up under the Agriculture Act 1947. While the future of the land was being considered, Lieutenant-Commander Marten, whose wife's family had previously owned much of the land, asked that it be sold back to the family. Misleading replies and false assurances were given when this and similar requests were refused, and a seriously inaccurate report was prepared by a junior civil servant which led the ministry to adhere to a scheme which it had prepared for letting all the land to a single tenant. Inadequate financial information was supplied to the headquarters of the ministry. When Conservative MPs took up Marten's case with the Minister of Agriculture, Sir Andrew Clark QC was appointed to hold an inquiry. His report established that there had been muddle, inefficiency, bias and bad faith on the part of some officials named in the report.[70] A subsequent inquiry to consider disciplinary action against the civil servants reported that some of the deficiencies were due as much to weak organisation within the ministry as to the faults of individuals.[71]

During a Commons debate on these reports, the Minister of Agriculture, Sir Thomas Dugdale, resigned. Speaking in the debate, the Home Secretary, Sir David Maxwell Fyfe, reaffirmed that a civil servant is wholly and directly responsible to his minister and can be dismissed at any time by the minister – a 'power none the less real because it is seldom used'. He outlined a number of categories where differing considerations apply.

(1) A minister must protect a civil servant who has carried out his explicit order.

(2) Equally a minister must defend a civil servant who acts properly in accordance with the policy laid down by the minister.

(3) Where an official makes a mistake or causes some delay, but not on an important issue of policy and not where a claim to individual rights is seriously involved, the Minister acknowledges the mistake and he accepts the responsibility although he is not personally involved. He states that he will take corrective action in the Department.

(4) Where action has been taken by a civil servant of which the minister disapproves and has no previous knowledge, and the conduct of the official is reprehensible, there is no obligation on a minister to endorse what he believes to be wrong or to defend what are clearly shown to be errors of his officers. He remains however, 'constitutionally responsible to Parliament for the fact that something has gone wrong', but this does not affect his power to control and discipline his staff.[72]

---

[68] HC (1985–6) 519; and see HC Deb, 29 October 1986, col 339; also A Tomkins (1996) 16 LS 63, 76–7.
[69] See below, ch 13 C.
[70] Cmd 9176, 1954.
[71] Cmd 9220, 1954.
[72] HC Deb, 20 July 1954, cols 1286–7.

This statement and the implications of the Crichel Down affair have been much discussed.[73] Was the resignation due to the part which the minister had played, to the unpopularity of the department's policy among Conservative MPs, or was he accepting vicarious responsibility for the civil servants? Maxwell Fyfe's analysis sought to identify situations in which a minister must 'accept responsibility' for the acts of civil servants. The analysis did not state that a minister's duty to accept responsibility carried with it a duty to resign.[74]

Subsequent events have confirmed that there is no 'duty' on a minister to resign because of misconduct by officials within his or her department, and today there is no expectation that this will occur.[75] Different considerations apply where the personal conduct of a minister is an issue: the Chancellor of the Exchequer's inadvertent disclosure of a Budget secret caused him to resign in 1947;[76] and in 1963 the Secretary of State for War resigned for having lied to the Commons in a personal statement.[77] Other resignations because of personal misconduct occurred in 1973 and on other occasions.[78] Resignations are unavoidable if a minister's own conduct makes it too difficult for the individual to perform his or her duties in the face of continuing criticism in the media[79] (a convenient formula that is often used to explain a forced resignation). In some situations, it may be that events in a department call into question the manner in which a minister has been heading the department: thus in 2002, two Cabinet ministers resigned essentially because of perceived shortcomings in their conduct of departmental affairs.[80] Publicity given to serious departmental errors (such as the discovery in April 2006 that the Home Office had released over 1000 foreign prisoners at the end of their prison sentences for serious crimes rather than considering them for deportation)[81] may force the Prime Minister to make an immediate Cabinet reshuffle in which the minister leaves the government.

Before we look briefly at some key instances of practice in this area, we must remember that, 40 years ago, the British system of government was marked by a degree of secrecy that would not be accepted today. The only information allowed to be known about decision-making in Whitehall was that given by ministers; unauthorised disclosures ran the risk of prosecution under the draconian Official Secrets Act 1911. This level of secrecy protected the government machine from external scrutiny. The Crichel Down affair was unusual in that a public inquiry exposed the acts of officials to the light of day. In 1968, the first major investigation by the newly created Parliamentary Ombudsman found that there had been maladministration by the Foreign Office in the Sachsenhausen affair.[82] The Foreign Secretary (George Brown) 'assumed personal responsibility' for decisions made in the Foreign Office, while reluctantly agreeing to provide compensation for the claimants. But he also said: 'We will breach a very serious constitutional position if we start holding officials responsible for things that are done wrong . . . If things are wrongly done, then they are wrongly done by ministers.'[83] This statement failed to recognise that an investigation by the Ombudsman into a complaint of maladministration must inevitably probe behind statements by the minister.

However, the creation of the Ombudsman did not mean an overnight change in the relationship between ministers and the civil service; ministers continued to insist that it followed 'from

---

[73] See e.g. J A G Griffith (1955) 8 MLR 557; (1954) 32 *Public Administration* 385 (C J Hamson) and 389 (D N Chester). For a reinterpretation, see Nicolson, *The Mystery of Crichel Down.*

[74] And see Sir R Scott [1996] PL 410 at 412–13.

[75] S E Finer (1956) 34 *Public Administration* 377, analyses the range of political factors that may be in play.

[76] HC 20 (1947–8).

[77] HC Deb, 22 March 1963, col 809; 17 June 1963, cols 34–170; and Cmnd 2152, 1963.

[78] Cmnd 5367, 1973. In June 2009, several ministers, including the Home Secretary, Jacqui Smith, left the government in a reshuffle caused in part by concern about their claims for parliamentary expenses.

[79] See D Woodhouse, *Ministers and Parliament,* and (1993) 46 *Parliamentary Affairs* 277; and R Brazier [1994] PL 431.

[80] D Woodhouse (2004) 82 *Public Administration* 1.

[81] See HC Deb, 26 April 2006, col 573 and 3 May 2006, col 969 (statements by Charles Clarke MP).

[82] Ch 29 D, and see G K Fry [1970] PL 336.

[83] HC Deb, 5 February 1968, col 112.

the principle that the minister alone has responsibility for the actions of his department' that individual civil servants should remain anonymous.[84]

In fact, the Ombudsman's method of reporting has never included the 'naming and shaming' of individual civil servants. By contrast, a senior civil servant was exposed to public criticism when a tribunal of inquiry investigated the affairs of the Vehicle and General Insurance company in 1971. The company had collapsed, leaving a million policyholders uninsured. It was alleged that the Department of Trade and Industry had failed to use its regulatory powers over the company in time to minimise the losses of the policyholders. The inquiry found that the department's regulatory functions had (by a scheme of delegation) been left entirely in the hands of a named under-secretary (Mr Jardine), whose conduct had fallen below a proper standard and must be regarded as being negligent.[85] The findings in the report, made after a public inquiry, appeared to leave no scope for the principle that a minister takes the praise for a department's successes and the blame for its failures.[86] Possibly that principle might still apply if the only information about a matter comes from what the minister tells Parliament, but today we are slow to accept a minister's statement as conclusive, and often insist that there should be a means of verifying what she or he has said. Significant progress has been made towards a more open system of government, to which the Parliamentary Ombudsman, public inquiries, select committees of the House of Commons and the Freedom of Information Act have all contributed. By one or more of such means, it is often possible to form a judgement about disputed events that is far more objective and persuasive than the minister's explanation.

In April 1982, the Argentine invasion of the Falkland Islands caused the Foreign Secretary, Lord Carrington, and two Foreign Office ministers to resign. They 'accepted responsibility' for the conduct of policy on the Falkland Islands, and insisted on resigning, against the express wishes of the Prime Minister. A committee of privy counsellors later reviewed the way in which government responsibilities had been discharged before the invasion, found that there had been a misjudgement of the situation within the Foreign Office and recommended changes in the intelligence organisation. But no blame was attached to any individual, nor did the committee consider that criticism for the events leading to the invasion could be attached to the government.[87]

In 1996, the report by the judge, Sir Richard Scott, on the 'arms for Iraq' affair found there to have been numerous occasions on which ministers failed to inform Parliament adequately about their policy on exporting arms and machine tools to Iraq and did not reveal changes they had made in the policy. Their answers to repeated questions had been misleading,[88] but ministers persuaded the inquiry that they had not intentionally misled Parliament. However, as Scott observed, without the provision of full information it is not possible for Parliament

> to assess what consequences, in the form of attribution or blame, ought to follow . . . A failure by Ministers to meet the obligations of Ministerial accountability by providing information about the activities of their departments undermines . . . the democratic process.[89]

When the report was debated in the Commons, the government survived by one vote. No ministers resigned.[90]

---

[84] HC 350 (1967–8), para 24 (the Attorney General, Sir Elwyn Jones).

[85] HL 80, HC 133 (1971–2), para 344.

[86] See HC Deb, 1 May 1972, col 34; and R J S Baker (1972) 43 *Political Quarterly* 340. The collapse of the Barlow Clowes investment business in 1988 led to a detailed investigation by the Ombudsman of the role of the civil service in the affair: no ministers were implicated and no civil servants were named, although serious faults were found. See R Gregory and G Drewry [1991] PL 192, 408 and ch 29 D.

[87] Cmnd 8787, 1983.

[88] See e.g. the summary at HC 115 (1995–6), vol IV, pp 1799–1800.

[89] HC 115 (1995–6), vol IV, p 1801.

[90] HC Deb, 26 February 1996, col 589. On the Scott report, see articles at [1996] PL 357–507; Thompson and Ridley (eds), *Under the Scott-light* and Tomkins, *The Constitution after Scott*.

Failings in a different context were revealed by the massive inquiry conducted by another judge (Lord Phillips) and two scientists into the response of five government departments to the problems for health and agriculture posed by BSE and variant CJD.[91] The Phillips report examined in detail the actions of ministers, civil servants and scientific advisers from 1986 to 1996. It was much less critical in tone than the Scott report, and no question of resignations had arisen. What is certain is that a fact-finding judicial inquiry, with access to relevant material in Whitehall, enables informed conclusions to be drawn that will not easily emerge from the political process in Parliament. When an inquiry into a departmental affair is made by a Commons committee, this is likely to be less effective than an independent inquiry.[92] But even a judicial inquiry will not settle the political verdict on a controversial affair.

In 2003, a senior judge, Lord Hutton, conducted an inquiry into the tragic suicide of the scientist, Dr David Kelly, under the pressure of events relating to the government's 'dodgy dossier' on Iraq. The inquiry itself was notable for the mass of evidence that came from Whitehall and was placed on the internet. But the Hutton report itself did not persuade informed opinion that the judge had reached well-founded conclusions in the dispute between the BBC and the government.[93] The report of the Butler inquiry in 2004 by a committee of privy counsellors into what was known about weapons of mass destruction before Britain went to war in Iraq was more widely accepted,[94] and Butler made serious criticism of the approach to collective decision-making while Mr Blair was Prime Minister.

Responsibility and accountability restated

A central theme in this area is the tension between government power and democratic accountability. In 1986, responding to a parliamentary inquiry into the Westland affair, the head of the civil service restated the duties of ministers towards Parliament;[95] in a revised form, the statement was later given to other Commons committees and the Scott inquiry.[96] The statement contrasted 'accountability' (in its non-financial sense) with 'responsibility'. A minister is *accountable* to Parliament for everything which occurs in a department: the duty, which may not be delegated, is to *inform* Parliament about policies and decisions of the department, except in rare cases where secrecy is an overriding necessity (as with sensitive questions of defence secrets). If something goes wrong, the minister owes it to Parliament to find out what has happened, ensure necessary disciplinary action and take steps to avoid a recurrence.

By contrast, a minister is said to be '*responsible*' only for broad policies, the framework of administration and issues in which he or she has been involved, not for all departmental affairs. The emphasis is on matters for which the minister may be personally praised or blamed. Since decision-making may be delegated, the minister is *not* responsible for what is done or decided by civil servants (for example, by the chief officer of an executive agency) within the authority assigned to them.[97]

This distinction between accountability and responsibility requires close scrutiny, since it provides a means by which a minister may avoid liability for unpopular or mistaken decisions; and

---

[91] HC 887–1 (1999–2000).

[92] See C Polidano (2001) 79 *Public Administration* 249, discussing inquiries into the Sandline affair: HC 1016 (1997–8), HC 116–I (1998–9). See also ch 29 C.

[93] See HC 247 (2003–4). See R P Kaye (2005) *Parliamentary Affairs* 171, 172–6; Rogers (ed.), *The Hutton Inquiry and its Impact*. For defence of his report, see Lord Hutton [2006] PL 807.

[94] The Butler report is at HC 898 (2003–4). And see Runciman (ed.), *Hutton and Butler: lifting the lid on the workings of power*.

[95] HC 92–II (1985–6). And Cmnd 9916, 1986, para 40.

[96] E.g. HC 390 (1992–3), para 25; HC 27 (1993–4), paras 118–20; Cm 2748, 1995, para 16; HC 313–I (1995–6), paras 15–18. See also the Scott report, HC 115 (1995–6), vol IV, pp 1805–6.

[97] On executive agencies, see ch 13 D.

it opens up potential areas of government for which no one is 'responsible' to Parliament, even though a minister remains 'accountable'. In 1996, the Public Service Committee of the Commons insisted that no clear dividing line can be drawn between accountability and responsibility, and that the two main aspects of ministerial responsibility are (i) the duty to give an account and (ii) the liability to be held to account.[98]

One outcome of the Scott inquiry and other events was that in 1997 both Houses adopted a resolution stating the principles that must govern the conduct of ministers in relation to Parliament. These principles are now included in the *Ministerial Code* issued by the Prime Minister, in the following form:

(*a*) Ministers must uphold the principle of collective responsibility;

(*b*) Ministers have a duty to Parliament to account, and be held to account, for the policies, decisions and actions of their departments and agencies;

(*c*) it is of paramount importance that Ministers give accurate and truthful information to Parliament, correcting any inadvertent error at the earliest opportunity. Ministers who knowingly mislead Parliament will be expected to offer their resignation to the Prime Minister;

(*d*) Ministers should be as open as possible with Parliament, refusing to provide information only when disclosure would not be in the public interest, which should be decided in accordance with the relevant statutes and the Freedom of Information Act 2000;

(*e*) Ministers should similarly require civil servants who give evidence before Parliamentary Committees on their behalf and under their direction to be as helpful as possible in providing accurate, truthful and full information in accordance with the duties and responsibilities of civil servants as set out in the Civil Service Code.[99]

These principles are not enacted as legislation but, having been endorsed by both Houses and the Prime Minister, they have great weight as rules that are today fundamental to the relationship between executive and Parliament.[100]

The pre-eminent duty of ministers is indeed to keep Parliament informed, without misleading Parliament by providing inaccurate or incomplete information, and correcting errors 'at the earliest opportunity'. For a minister knowingly to mislead Parliament is a contempt of Parliament,[101] and civil servants must not draft ministerial answers to parliamentary questions that would be misleading.[102]

Inevitably, difficulties remain in the way of achieving a more open system of governance. One is the government's restrictive approach to the giving of evidence by civil servants to select committees:[103] should ministers be able to censor evidence as to matters of fact which civil servants give at Westminster? Another is the power of the executive to control the timing and manner in which reports critical of government policies and decisions are published, so as to minimise the impact of those reports in the Commons and the media.[104]

The concept of accountability has been described as 'a generic term', since in practice there are multiple forms of accountability.[105] In 2007, the Public Administration committee of the Commons urged that the discharge of responsibilities by ministers and civil servants should reflect the way in which decisions are in fact taken, and that the civil service's responsibilities should include

---

[98] HC 313 (1995–6), paras 21 and 32. For the BSE inquiry's views on ministerial accountability, see HC 887 (1999–2000), vol 15, paras 8.7, 8.8.

[99] HC Deb, 19 March 1997, col 1046. Also HL Deb, 20 March 1997, col 1055. And see ch 13 D.

[100] On their status and enforceability, see ch 2 B.

[101] Ch 11 A.

[102] See *Guidance to Officials on Drafting Answers to Parliamentary Questions* (2005).

[103] See *Departmental Evidence and Response to Select Committees*, note 65 above, paras 40–66. And ch 13 D.

[104] For a clear abuse of this power, see the manner in which the Scott report was published in 1996.

[105] See HL Committee on the Constitution, HL Paper 68, 2003–04, para 48.

'responsibility to Parliament and the constitution'. In the committee's view, greater transparency in government need not prejudice the political accountability of ministers to Parliament.[106] In its reply, the government sought to justify a more traditional framework:

> Civil servants are accountable to Ministers, who in turn are accountable to Parliament. It is this line of accountability which makes clear that ultimately Ministers are accountable to the electorate.[107]

This difference is evidence of continuing tension between the actual operations of government and the traditional emphasis on retaining ministers as the link between executive and Parliament. It now seems remarkable that the doctrine of ministerial responsibility was used as an argument *against* creating the Parliamentary Ombudsman in 1967,[108] and *against* adoption of the present select committees of the Commons in 1979 – fortunately on each occasion without success. The principle of accountable government is ultimately more important than ministerial responsibility. If there is any conflict between the two, the former principle ought to apply.

Ministerial responsibility and the courts

The courts play no part in determining the accountability of ministers to Parliament, and the desire to keep the courts well away from the internal affairs of the two Houses is sometimes seen as a reason why good constitutional practice should not be embodied in legislation.[109] Legislative practice today is to vest new executive powers in 'the Secretary of State'. This means that the power may if necessary be exercised by any one of the many Cabinet ministers who, by a constitutional fiction, are regarded as holders of a single office. In the past, powers were sometimes conferred on a named ministerial post. Whether a power is conferred on the Secretary of State or another minister, does this mean that only a Secretary of State or the minister may exercise the power?

> In *Carltona Ltd* v *Commissioners of Works*, an order to requisition a factory was issued under defence regulations by an assistant secretary in the Ministry of Works; it was challenged on the ground that the minister had not personally considered the matter. The challenge failed. It was held that government could not be carried on unless civil servants could take decisions on behalf of the minister. 'Constitutionally, the decision of such an official [the assistant secretary] is, of course, the decision of the minister. The minister is responsible. It is he who must answer before Parliament for anything that his officials have done under his authority.'[110]

On this basis, the powers of ministers may in law be exercised by civil servants, and it is not necessary to establish a formal delegation of authority to them (except where a statutory provision requires such delegation).[111] Likewise, in an early 20th-century case regarding a public inquiry into the compulsory purchase of unfit housing, it was held that the owner was entitled to be heard at the inquiry by an inspector appointed by the minister, but he had no right to a hearing in person before the minister himself.[112] However, there are cases where, from the nature of the power or because of express statutory provision, the general principle does not

---

[106] See *Politics and Administration: Ministers and Civil Servants*, HC 122, 2006–07. Annexed to the report is a 'Compact between Ministers and the Home Office Board' (January 2007) which states that officials who head Home Office services (i.e. the executive agencies) have the function of 'increasingly answering *externally* for operational matters for which they are responsible' (emphasis supplied).

[107] Government Response, HC 1057, 2007–08.

[108] Ch 29 D.

[109] See *Conventions of the UK Parliament*, HL Paper 265, HC 1212 (2004–05), paras 279, 285.

[110] [1943] 2 All ER 560, 563. Also *Lewisham MB* v *Roberts* [1949] 2 KB 608; *R* v *Skinner* [1968] 2 QB 700; and *Re Golden Chemical Products Ltd* [1976] Ch 300. See ch 13 D.

[111] *Commissioners of Customs and Excise* v *Cure & Deeley Ltd* [1962] 1 QB 340.

[112] *Local Government Board* v *Arlidge* [1915] AC 120; ch 30 B. See also *Liversidge* v *Anderson* [1942] AC 206.

apply and powers must be exercised personally by the minister.[113] Where a statutory function is vested in one minister, he or she may not adopt a policy whereby decisions are made by another minister.[114]

When executive decisions are challenged in the courts by judicial review today, what the courts must decide is whether any legal grounds have been shown which make the decision vulnerable to judicial review; the judges are not concerned to adjudicate on the merits of executive policies and individual decisions.[115] For much of the 20th century, before the emergence of judicial review in its present form, the evolution of administrative law was impeded by the fact that some courts relied on ministerial responsibility as a reason for not reviewing the legality of ministers' decisions.[116] It is arguable that the rapid evolution of administrative law after 1980 was influenced by the failure of Parliament to take adequate steps to enforce the accountability of ministers.[117] Today, it is accepted that judicial review and ministerial responsibility serve different purposes and are not mutually exclusive.[118] But the scope and intensity of judicial review have been extended by the Human Rights Act 1998, and the courts must now form judgments about executive decisions on grounds that in the past would undoubtedly have been regarded in law as falling within the area of ministerial responsibility to Parliament.[119]

Devolution and ministerial responsibility

This chapter has dealt with current practice relating to the responsibility of UK ministers at Westminster. What has been described here does not necessarily apply to the Scottish Parliament or the Assemblies in Wales and Northern Ireland. As we have seen, the three forms of devolution differ both from each other and from the Westminster model.[120] In Scotland, where the structure is closest to that at Westminster, the Scottish ministers may not continue in office if Parliament resolves that it has lost confidence in the Executive;[121] and Parliament has its own procedures for calling the ministers to account for their departmental functions. The original position in Wales was very different, when executive powers were vested in the Assembly itself, but the Government of Wales Act 2006 has created a ministerial structure that comes closer to that in Scotland.[122] In Northern Ireland, government is based on an elaborate scheme of power-sharing and this necessarily affects the accountability of the ministers to the Assembly.

---

[113] E.g. Immigration and Asylum Act 1999, s 70(1)(a), s 570(3)(b), s 570(6)(b). And see *R v Home Secretary, ex p Oladehinde* [1991] 1 AC 254.

[114] *Lavender and Son Ltd v Minister of Housing* [1970] 3 All ER 871. In practice, much consultation between ministers and departments takes place before decisions are announced, and this 'internal process' is not disclosed: *Ministerial Code*, para 2.3.

[115] See chs 30, 31.

[116] See J D B Mitchell [1965] PL 95; and Dicey, *Law of the Constitution*, app 2.

[117] See e.g. *R v Home Secretary, ex p Fire Brigades Union* [1995] 2 AC 513, 572–3, 575 (Lord Mustill).

[118] See e.g. *R v IRC, ex p National Federation of Self-Employed* [1982] AC 617, 644.

[119] See chs 19 C and 30; and, as a leading example, *A v SSHD* [2004] UKHL 56, [2005] 2 AC 68.

[120] Ch 3 B.

[121] Scotland Act 1998, s 45(2). See the *Scottish Ministerial Code* and *Guide to Collective Decision Making* (2003). Also B Winetrobe, in Jowell and Oliver (eds), *The Changing Constitution* (6th edn), pp 213–16 and (same author) [2003] PL 24.

[122] See ch 3 B.

CHAPTER 8

The United Kingdom and the European Union

The European Economic Community was created in 1957, the original six member states being West Germany, France, Italy, Belgium, the Netherlands and Luxembourg. It was not until 1973 that Britain became a member, following the enactment of the European Communities Act 1972. There are now 27 member states of the EU, the number likely to be increased still further as several other candidate countries complete the process of entry.[1] From the earliest days membership has caused great constitutional anxiety for some in Britain, despite the fact that the United Kingdom is claimed to have the most flexible and the only unwritten constitution among the member states. Nevertheless, attempts to challenge entry were made on the ground that it constituted an abuse of the prerogative treaty-making power to the extent that it would undermine the sovereignty of Parliament,[2] and on the ground also that the Treaty would breach art 18 of the Treaty of Union of 1707.[3] More recently the renegotiation of the EC Treaty at Maastricht in 1992 led to further challenges in the British courts, an unsuccessful attempt being made to prevent the government from ratifying it.[4] But if British membership has caused constitutional concerns, these are overshadowed by the political controversies it has generated. Political parties have been divided, constitutional conventions have been formally and informally suspended, and the only national referendum in the twentieth century was held in 1975 on continued membership of what was then the EEC.[5]

There is no sign of the controversy abating, with contemporary politics having been dominated by the question whether another referendum should have been held before the United Kingdom ratified the Treaty of Lisbon in 2007.[6] The latter is the latest stage in the evolution of the European Union,[7] with a number of treaty amendments along the way (for example the Single European Act of 1986, the Maastricht Treaty in 1992, and the Nice Treaty in 2001) having expanded the powers of what were then the 'Community' institutions and enabling an expanding volume of what was then 'Community' law to be made on the basis of qualified majority voting rather than the agreement of all member states. The Lisbon Treaty arose from the ashes of ambitious plans for a European Constitution, as designed by the Convention on the Future of Europe in 2003, under the chairmanship of a former French President (Giscard d'Estaing).[8] Although signed by all the member states,[9] the Constitution could only be introduced once formally ratified by each of them. In some cases ratification would require a referendum, and in June 2005 the peoples of

---

[1] On legal issues arising from the 2005 accessions, see *Case C-273/04, Poland v Council* [2007] ECR I-8925; *Case 413/04, Parliament v Council* [2006] ECR I-11221.

[2] *Blackburn v A-G* [1971] 1 WLR 1037. See ch 12 D.

[3] *Gibson v Lord Advocate* 1975 SLT 134. See ch 4 D.

[4] *R v Foreign Secretary, ex p Rees-Mogg* [1994] QB 552. See G Marshall [1993] PL 402, and also R Rawlings [1994] PL 254, 367.

[5] Referendum Act 1975. See also Cmnd 5925, 1975 and 6251, 1975.

[6] See *R (Wheeler) v Office of Prime Minister* [2008] EWHC 1409 (Admin) – no legal obligation to hold a referendum on the treaty.

[7] For a full analysis of the Lisbon Treaty, see HL Paper 62-I (2007–08).

[8] For commentary, see (2005) 11 *European Public Law* 1–164; (2005) 1 *European Constitutional Law Review* 1–147; and (2005) 3 *International Journal of Constitutional Law* 173–515.

[9] A legal challenge to the British government signing the draft Constitution was predictably unsuccessful: *R v Foreign Secretary, ex p Southall* [2003] 3 CMLR 562.

France and the Netherlands voted to reject the proposals.[10] In rescuing much (though not all) of the substance of the draft Constitution, the Lisbon Treaty significantly amended and substantially re-wrote (and re-numbered) the two treaties which provide the legal base on which the EU now stands.[11] One (created at Maastricht in 1992) is the Treaty on European Union (TEU), and the other (created originally in Rome in 1957) is the Treaty on the Functioning of the European Union (TFEU), as the EC Treaty (TEC) was renamed at Lisbon. The European Community and EC law thus no longer exist.

These changes were duly ratified by the British government,[12] and it is with the domestic implications of EU membership that we are principally concerned in this chapter. In the meantime, it is to be noted that guiding principles of the EU are set out in the TEU. This provides by article 2 that the Union 'is founded on the values of respect for human dignity, freedom, democracy, equality, the rule of law and respect for human rights'.[13] These values are said to be 'common to the Member States in a society in which pluralism, non-discrimination, tolerance, justice, solidarity and equality between men and women prevail'. Many constitutional texts and international treaties contain sententious phrases of this kind, though in this case there is a political procedure for holding to account a member state thought to breach these 'values'.[14] Otherwise, the ambitions of the Union include the removal of internal frontiers (in which the United Kingdom is a reluctant party), the establishment of an internal market based on balanced economic growth and a highly competitive social market economy, and the establishment of economic and monetary union with the euro as its currency (in which the United Kingdom does not participate).[15] However, the Union can act only in accordance with the competences granted to it by the member states (the principle of 'conferral'); but even then – by virtue of the principle of subsidiarity – the Union can exercise power in areas where it does not have exclusive competence only if and so far as the objectives of the proposed action cannot be sufficiently achieved by the member states.[16]

A. European Union institutions

The TFEU now makes provision for seven different EU institutions: the European Council, the Commission, the Council, the European Parliament, the Court of Justice, the European Central Bank, and the Court of Auditors (though not presented in that order by the Treaty).[17] The difference between the European Council and the Council calls for an explanation. Thus, the European Council consists of heads of state or government and meets at least twice a year to 'provide the Union with the necessary impetus for its development', and define the general political directions and priorities of the Union.[18] The Council in contrast consists of ministerial representatives from each member state and has policy-making, legislative and budgetary functions, which in the latter cases are exercised jointly with the European Parliament. An important feature of the Lisbon reforms has been the creation of the office of President of the European Council, elected by the European Council for a renewable term of two-and-a-half years.[19] It is the responsibility of the

---

[10] The British government gave an undertaking that the Constitution would not be ratified without there first being a referendum. The results in the Netherlands and France relieved the government of the need to hold such a referendum, which some commentators believed would not provide sufficient support for the Constitution.

[11] P P Craig (2008) 33 EL Rev 137.

[12] Implemented by the European Union (Amendment) Act 2008.

[13] On the rule of law and EU law, see K Lenaerts (2007) 44 CMLR 1625.

[14] TEU, art 7.

[15] TEU, art 3.

[16] Ibid, art 5.

[17] Ibid, art 13.

[18] Ibid, art 15.

[19] Ibid, art 15(5).

President to chair and drive forward the work of the European Council and to represent the foreign and security policies of the Union in relations with countries outside the Union.[20] In the last case, this is without prejudice to the powers of the EU's High Representative for Foreign Affairs and Security Policy, another creation of the Lisbon amendments. This is a position characterised popularly as corresponding to the position of the US Secretary of State (an office with responsibilities for foreign affairs).

The Commission

1 Composition. The Commission consists of one member for each member state, though its numbers are to be reduced in November 2014.[21] Before the recent enlargements in 2005 and 2007, the Commission had a membership of 20, the largest of the member states having two Commissioners each. The practice in the United Kingdom (where nominations are made by the Prime Minister) has been for Commissioners to be senior political figures, and the convention was that one should have a record of service in the Labour party and the other in the Conservative party. Now that Britain has only one Commissioner, new practices have been established to determine who should be nominated when vacancies arise: recent Labour governments have nominated members of the Labour party based in the House of Lords for this role. Each Commissioner has responsibility for a specific area of the Commission's activity, with the British-nominated Commissioner at the time of writing (Baroness Ashton) previously having responsibility for trade, before being appointed as the inaugural High Representative for Foreign Affairs and Security Policy (which also has a seat on the Commission). The President of the Commission (not to be confused with the President of the European Council referred to above) is nominated by the European Council, acting by qualified majority with the approval of the European Parliament.[22] Once nominated, both the President and the other members of the Commission are then 'subject as a body to a vote of consent by the European Parliament', following which they are appointed by the European Council acting by a qualified majority.[23] Although the Commission 'shall be responsible to the Parliament', the latter has no power to veto an individual nomination, and no power to remove an individual Commissioner.[24] Complaints about a breach of duty by a Commissioner may be made by the Council (acting by a majority) or the Commission to the ECJ, which may require the Commissioner to be compulsorily retired or to be deprived of his or her pension or other benefits.[25] They may also be compulsorily retired by the ECJ on a reference by the Council (again acting by a majority) or the Commission if they no longer fulfil the conditions required for the performance of their duties, or if guilty of serious misconduct.[26]

2 Functions. The Commission – which works under the political guidance of its President – has two principal functions.[27] The first is to initiate proposals for legislation, to be considered by the Council and the Parliament. In this way the Commission plays a central role in the development of EU policy in the different areas of its competence and in initiating legislative proposals to give effect to that policy. However, Commission initiatives are not always endorsed by the Council,

---

[20] Ibid, art 15(6).

[21] Ibid, art 17(5).

[22] Ibid, art 17(7).

[23] Ibid.

[24] Ibid.

[25] TFEU, art 245 (ex TEC, art 213). See *Case C-432-4, Commission v Edith Cresson* [2006] ECR 1-6387.

[26] TFEU, art 247 (ex TEC, art 216).

[27] For the main functions of the Commission, see TEU, art 17(1); other powers are found elsewhere in the Treaty, e.g. TFEU, art 45 (ex TEC, art 39).

particularly where the unanimity of the Council is required.[28] The Commission's second main function is to ensure that the provisions of the Treaties, as well as EU law generally, are implemented and applied. This may mean initiating enforcement proceedings in the Court of Justice against another EU institution,[29] or against any member state which is in breach of the treaties or which has failed to implement directives or regulations.[30] So in case *C-382/92, Re Business Transfers: EC Commission v UK*,[31] enforcement proceedings were initiated in respect of a failure to implement directives protecting workers in the event of business restructuring; and in *Case C-222/94, EC Commission v UK*,[32] proceedings were initiated in respect of a failure to implement correctly a directive on television broadcasting.[33] The Commission must be 'completely independent' in carrying out their responsibilities,[34] which means that commissioners must 'neither seek nor take instructions from any government or other institution, body, office or entity'.[35]

The Council

1 *Composition and functions*. The Council consists of political representatives of the member states, each being represented by a minister who is 'authorised to commit the government of [that] member state' and 'cast its vote'.[36] The Council meets in nine different 'configurations', based on a decision as to the nature of these configurations taken by a qualified majority of Council members.[37] The representative at any particular session will depend on the subject of the meeting, so that – for example – on transport matters the United Kingdom representative will be a minister with responsibility for transport. The Presidency of the Council configurations rotates between member states,[38] in accordance with a Council decision adopted by qualified majority.[39] Under the treaties, the Council has policy-making and 'coordinating' functions,[40] as well as a pivotal role in the legislative process, in the sense that it must approve Commission initiatives. Indeed, the Council is in a real sense the principal legislative authority within the Union,[41] albeit that this legislative authority must now be shared with the Parliament. Unusually for a 'legislative' body, however, the Council's deliberations were not conducted in public, until changes made recently by the Lisbon Treaty. Council business is now divided into two parts, the first dealing with legislative business to which the public have access, and the second dealing with non-legislative business which continues to be conducted in private.[42]

---

[28] On voting procedures in the Council, see p 121 in this chapter.

[29] As in *Case C-110/02, European Commission v Council* [2004] ECR 1-6333.

[30] TFEU, art 258 (ex TEC, art 226). See p 123 below.

[31] [1994] ECR I-2435. For the sequel, see SI 1995 No 2587. See also *R v Trade and Industry Secretary, ex p UNISON* [1997] 1 CMLR 459. See further M Radford and A Kerr (1997) 60 MLR 23.

[32] [1996] ECR I-4025.

[33] See also *Case C-246/89, Commission v UK* [1991] ECR 1-4585.

[34] TEU, art 17.

[35] Ibid.

[36] Ibid, art 16.

[37] Ibid, art 16(6); TFEU, art 236. At the time of writing (March 2010) the configurations were general affairs and external relations; economic and financial affairs; justice and home affairs; employment, social policy, health and consumer affairs; competitiveness; transport, telecommunications and energy; agriculture and fisheries; environment; and education, youth and culture: Council Decision of 22 March 2004 adopting the Council's Rules of Procedure (2004/338/EC, Euratom) – Annex I. List of Council configurations, in *Official Journal of the European Communities* (OJEC), 28 August 2002, No L 230, p 37.

[38] TEU, art 16(6), TFEU, art 236.

[39] TFEU, art 236.

[40] TEU, art 16.

[41] D Curtin (1993) 30 CML Rev 17.

[42] TEU, art 16(8).

2 *Procedure*. In performing its functions, the Council is required to act by a qualified majority vote unless the treaties provide otherwise.[43] There are as we have seen circumstances where the Council may act by simple majority, and as we shall see circumstances where unanimity is still required.[44] The formula for determining the votes to be secured for the purposes of QMV will change in 2014.[45] In the meantime, the votes of each country are weighted broadly by population, with France, Germany, Italy and the United Kingdom each having 29 out of a total of 345 votes, the weightings having changed since the enlargement of the EC in 2005 and again in 2007. Where QMV is required, acts of the Council need the support of at least a majority of the member states and a minimum of 255 votes which represents just under three-quarters of the whole. One of the many protocols to the treaties now also provides that when a decision is to be adopted by the Council by a qualified majority, a member of the Council may request that a check is made to ensure that 'the Member States constituting the qualified majority represent at least 62 per cent of the total population of the [European] Union'.[46] Although there has been an extension of the areas in which the Council can act by QMV, as already suggested there remain important areas where unanimity is still required and where one country does have a power of veto; this problem has arisen in the approximation of laws affecting social policy, where the unanimity of the Council continues to be required for measures on matters such as the social protection of workers and the protection of workers where their contracts of employment are terminated, as well as arrangements relating to the representation and the collective defence of the interests of workers.[47] As the EU continues to grow, the likelihood of unanimity being secured for such controversial issues seems remote.

European Parliament

1 *Composition*. The status and powers of the European Parliament have greatly increased since its inception. Now it is elected for periods of five years by direct universal suffrage,[48] with the number of representatives elected in each state varying according to the population of the state in question. There are 736 seats in the unicameral Parliament, with the larger member states predictably having more seats than the smaller member states. Thus Germany has 99 seats, with France, Italy and the United Kingdom each having 72. Elections in Great Britain are conducted on the basis of a regional list system, by which the country is divided into 11 electoral regions (the number of members returned varying according to the size of the region), with votes being cast for registered parties rather than candidates. Seats are then allocated to individuals on the party lists (in the order in which they appear on the list) to reflect the votes cast in favour of each party in the region in question. So the more votes cast for a party, the larger the number of seats it will be allocated.[49] Although the TEU declares that 'political parties at European level contribute to forming European political awareness and to expressing the will of citizens of the Union',[50] there are no European political parties as such. After each election, however, MEPs participate in different political rather than national groupings. Labour party members belong to the Party of European Socialists (PES) along with other socialist and social democratic parties;

---

[43] Ibid, art 16(3).

[44] See p 117 above.

[45] TEU, art 16(5).

[46] Protocol No 36.

[47] TFEU, art 153 (ex TEC, art 137).

[48] See European Parliamentary Elections Act 1978, amended by the European Parliamentary Elections Act 1999, and European Parliament (Representation) Act 2003.

[49] Three members are elected from Northern Ireland by single transferable vote. One of the English regions now includes Gibraltar (European Parliament (Representation) Act 2003, Pt 2), following a decision of the European Court of Human Rights that the lack of representation of Gibraltar in the European Parliament was a breach of the ECHR (First Protocol, art 3) (*Matthews v UK* (1998) 28 EHRR 361).

[50] TEU, art 10(4).

the Liberal Democrats are part of the Alliance of Liberals and Democrats for Europe; and the Conservative party is now associated with the European Conservatives and Reformists, having been previously aligned with the more mainstream European People's Party.[51] Once elected, MEPs enjoy an immunity from liability in damages for opinions expressed in the course of their parliamentary duties, as well as other privileges.[52]

2 _Functions_. The European Parliament has been said to represent 'the principal form of democratic, political accountability in the Community system'.[53] Its most important functions relate to its role in the legislative process on the one hand, and its powers in relation to the Union's budget on the other. So far as the former is concerned, the Council has been the principal legislative body of the Union, though the focus in recent years has been not to substitute the Parliament for the Council but to develop a system which would enable the Parliament to play a fuller part in the law-making process.[54] Initially the Parliament enjoyed only a consultative status, but the TEU now provides that legislative functions are to be exercised by the Council and the Parliament jointly.[55] Under the 'ordinary' legislative procedure in the TFEU (which does not apply in all cases), legislative instruments (regulations, directives and decisions) require the approval of both the Council and the Parliament,[56] and provision is made in the TFEU for resolving disputes between the two by conciliation.[57] If conciliation fails, so does the instrument concerned.[58] So far as the budget is concerned, this will be prepared annually by the Commission on the basis of estimates submitted by each of the EU's institutions. The draft budget is then presented for approval to the Council and the Parliament, with the Council submitting its position on the budget to the Parliament, which then has 42 days to approve or propose amendments to the Council's position. If the latter, a Conciliation Committee must be convened to resolve the differences between the Council and the Parliament (with equal representation of each), in which the Commission also participates. If this process is unable to secure an agreed outcome, a new draft budget must be submitted by the Commission, and the process will begin again.

The European Court of Justice[59]

1 _Composition and jurisdiction_. The function of the Court (ECJ) is to 'ensure that in the interpretation and application of the Treaties the law is observed'.[60] It consists of one judge for each member state and may sit in chambers (normally of 5 judges) or in a Grand Chamber (of 13 judges),[61] as provided by its own statute, which is annexed as a protocol to the treaties. The Court is assisted by eight Advocates General, an office without parallel in the United Kingdom.[62] Under TFEU, art 252 (ex TEC, art 222) the duty of the Advocates General is to make reasoned submissions on cases brought before the Court in order to assist the Court in the performance

---

[51] See Shaw, _The Transformation of Citizenship in the European Union_.

[52] See _Cases C-200/07_ and _201/07, Marra v De Gregorio_ [2008] ECR I-07929. See also _Case T-345/05, Mote v European Parliament_ [2009] 1 CMLR 15.

[53] _Matthews v UK_, above.

[54] D Curtin (1993) 30 CML Rev 17.

[55] TEU, arts 14 and 16.

[56] TFEU, art 289.

[57] Ibid, art 294 (ex TEC, art 251).

[58] Ibid, art 294(12).

[59] For the work of the ECJ, see D Edward (1995) 20 EL Rev 539. And see generally, Arnull, _The European Union and its Court of Justice_, and Brown and Kennedy, _The Court of Justice of the European Communities_.

[60] TEU, art 19.

[61] TFEU, art 251 (ex TEC, art 221).

[62] See A Dashwood (1982) 2 LS 202.

of its tasks. These submissions will include an assessment of the legal position in the matter referred for determination, an assessment which will often be endorsed by the Court. The submissions of the Advocates General are reported along with the judgment of the Court. Both judges and Advocates General are appointed from among people who are eligible for the highest judicial offices in their respective countries and appointments are made 'by common accord of the Governments of the member states for a term of six years'.[63] Every three years there is a partial replacement of both the judges and the Advocates General, although retiring judges and Advocates General are eligible for reappointment. The judges elect the President of the Court from among their number for a period of three years, a retiring President being eligible for re-election.[64] In addition to the Court of Justice, there is a General Court (known previously as the Court of First Instance) which hears and determines a defined class of cases, the aim being to reduce the pressure of work on the ECJ itself, but to which there is a right of appeal on a point of law.[65]

Under TFEU, art 263 (ex TEC, art 230), cases may be brought before the ECJ in a number of ways.[66] First, as already suggested, proceedings may be brought by the Commission against a member state where it considers that the state has failed to comply with a Treaty obligation.[67] If the Commission considers that a member state has failed to fulfil a Treaty obligation, it must first deliver a reasoned opinion on the matter after giving the state concerned an opportunity to submit its observations. It is only if the state does not comply with the opinion that the Commission may bring the matter before the Court.[68] Second, one state may initiate proceedings against another where the former considers that the latter has failed to comply with a Treaty obligation.[69] Before this is done the matter must first be referred to the Commission, which will deliver a reasoned opinion in this situation too. Where the ECJ finds that a state has failed to comply with a Treaty obligation, 'the state shall be required to take the necessary measures to comply with the judgment of the Court',[70] and failure to do so could lead to subsequent proceedings before the Court initiated by the Commission with a view to imposing a financial penalty on the state.[71] Third, it may also be possible for one member state to challenge the legality of a legal instrument in proceedings against an EU institution, as in *Case C-84/94, UK v EU Council*[72] where the British government unsuccessfully contested the legal basis of the Working Time Directive (93/104/EC), as exceeding powers under what was then TEC, art 118a.[73] In addition to proceedings against states and against EU institutions, a natural or legal person in some circumstances may also challenge decisions which are either addressed to them personally or are of 'direct and individual

---

[63] TFEU, art 253 (ex TEC, art 223).

[64] Ibid.

[65] Ibid, art 256 (ex TEC, art 225).

[66] TEU, art 19(3).

[67] TFEU, art 258 (ex TEC, art 226). Liability under TFEU, art 258 (ex TEC, art 226) arises whatever the agency of the state whose action or inaction is the cause of the failure to fulfil its obligations, even in the case of a constitutionally independent institution: *Case 77/69, EC Commission v Belgium* [1970] ECR 237 (difficulty in securing parliamentary approval because Parliament had been dissolved).

[68] TFEU, art 258 (ex TEC, art 226). See *Case 293/85, EC Commission v Belgium* [1988] ECR 305, and *Case 74/82, EC Commission v Ireland* [1984] ECR 317.

[69] TFEU, art 259. See *Case 141/78, France v UK* [1979] ECR 2923.

[70] Ibid, art 260(1). In the *Factortame* affair (pp 128–9, 139–41 below), secondary legislation was introduced to remove the discriminatory effect of the vessel registration scheme set out in the Merchant Shipping Act 1988. See note 105 below.

[71] TFEU, art 260(2) (ex TEC, art 228).

[72] [1996] 3 CMLR 671.

[73] It was subsequently held that key provisions of the Directive were insufficiently precise for the Directive to have direct effect, thereby preventing workers from recovering holiday pay for the period in which the United Kingdom failed to implement the Directive: *Gibson v East Riding Council* [2000] ICR 890.

concern' to him or her where addressed to another.[74] If such an action is well-founded, the Court shall declare the act concerned to be void.[75] These latter cases are almost always commenced in the General Court.

2 TFEU, Article 267 (ex TEC, Article 234). Apart from the foregoing, the Court also has jurisdiction under art 267 (previously TEC, art 234 and before that EC Treaty, art 177) to give preliminary rulings concerning the interpretation of the Treaties, as well as the validity and interpretation of acts of the institutions, bodies, offices or agencies of the Union.[76] A preliminary ruling may be sought by a national court or tribunal where the court or tribunal 'considers that a decision on the question is necessary to enable it to give judgment'.[77] In the case of a court or tribunal 'against whose decisions there is no judicial remedy under national law', the court or tribunal must bring before the ECJ for a ruling any question on a matter which is necessary for it to give judgment.[78] According to the ECJ, a reference is not required where the question of EU law is irrelevant, or the matter has already been decided by the ECJ, or the position is 'so obvious as to leave no scope for any reasonable doubt'.[79] A national court or tribunal is not empowered to refer a matter unless it is pending before the court,[80] though a reference may be made at any time during the domestic proceedings at the discretion of the national court.[81] Where a reference is made, the court will request an answer to specific questions by the ECJ;[82] the latter is not empowered to resolve the dispute between the parties, it being for the national court to apply the ruling to the facts of the case before it.[83] The ECJ generally considers itself bound to give a ruling, and will decline to do so only in exceptional circumstances.[84]

In *Bulmer Ltd v Bollinger SA*,[85] Lord Denning gave detailed guidance first on when 'a decision on the question is necessary to enable [a court] to give judgment' and, second, when in such a case the Court should exercise its discretion to make a reference. As to the former, (i) the point must be conclusive of the case; while (ii) substantially the same point must not have already been decided by the ECJ, unless (iii) there are reasons to believe that an earlier decision of the ECJ is wrong. Moreover, the Court may decline to make a reference where the point is reasonably clear

---

[74] TFEU, art 263 (ex TEC, art 230). In some cases the requirement for individual concern may be dispensed with where the challenge is to a regulatory act (not defined) which is of 'direct concern' and does not entail 'implementing measures' (not defined) (TFEU, art 263(4)). For significant recent challenges by individuals or organisations (not all of which succeeded), see *Joined Cases C-402/05P and 415/05P, Kadi v Council and Commission*, 3 September 2008 (below, p 127); *Case T-345/05, Mote v European Parliament*, above; *Case C-345/06, Heinrich* [2009] 3 CMLR 7; *Case T-284/08, People's Mojahedin Organization of Iran v Council of the European Union* [2009] 1 CMLR 44; and *Case C-355/08 P, WWF-UK v Council and Commission*, 5 May 2009.

[75] TFEU, art 264 (ex TEC, art 231). See *Case C-345/06, Heinrich*, above.

[76] TFEU, art 267 (ex TEC, art 234). This has been said to be 'the ideal instrument to define and develop the law of the [Union]' (Mathijsen, above, p 130), but also 'an instrument of cooperation between the Court of Justice and national courts' (*Case C-313/07, Kirtuna SL v Red Elite de Electrodomesticos SA* [2009] 1 CMLR 14, at para 25).

[77] TFEU, art 267 (ex TEC, art 234). On the meaning of a court or tribunal for this purpose, see *Case C-416/96, El-Yassini v Home Secretary* [1999] ECR 1-1209 (immigration adjudicator a court or tribunal).

[78] TFEU, art 267 (ex TEC, art 234). This would apply to the House of Lords and now the Supreme Court of the United Kingdom (but see *R v Employment Secretary, ex p EOC* [1995] 1 AC 1), and possibly also to bodies whose decisions are protected by a privative clause.

[79] *Case 283/81, CILFIT v Ministry of Health* [1982] ECR 3415.

[80] *Cases C-422-424/93, Zabala Erasun v Instituto Nacional de Empleo* [1995] ECR I-1567.

[81] *Case C-303/06, Coleman v Attridge Law* [2008] IRLR 722.

[82] The questions will normally be agreed with the parties in advance: see *Marks and Spencer plc v Customs and Excise Commissioners* [2005] UKHL 53.

[83] The ECJ 'has consistently held that under [TFEU, art 267, ex TEC art 234] it has no jurisdiction to rule on the compatibility of national measures with Community law': *Case C-458/93, Saddik* [1995] ECR I-511.

[84] *Joined Cases C 261/07 and 299/07, VTB-UAB NV v Total Belgium NV* [2009] 3 CMLR 697, and *Case C-460/07, Puffer v Unabhangiger Finanzsenat* [2009] 3 CMLR 783, para 38.

[85] [1974] 1 Ch 401. See J D B Mitchell (1974) 11 CMLR 351.

or free from doubt (*acte claire*). As to the latter, however, even if a point of EU law is necessary to dispose of the case, there is no obligation to make a reference: 'The English court has a discretion either to decide the point itself or to refer it to the European court, with a number of prescribed factors to be taken into account in the exercise of that discretion, including the time it will take to get a ruling, the expense in doing so, and the wishes of the parties.[86] Although they have been very influential,[87] these guidelines have been replaced in practice by a new formulation by Lord Bingham, who before referring to *Bulmer* said:

> . . . if the facts have been found and the Community law issue is critical to the court's final decision, the appropriate course is ordinarily to refer the issue to the Court of Justice unless the national court can with complete confidence resolve the issue itself. In considering whether it can with complete confidence resolve the issue itself the national court must be fully mindful of the differences between national and Community legislation, of the pitfalls which face a national court venturing into what may be an unfamiliar field, of the need for uniform interpretation throughout the Community and of the great advantages enjoyed by the Court of Justice in construing Community instruments. If the national court has any real doubt, it should ordinarily refer.[88]

In *McCall* v *Poulton*,[89] the Court of Appeal upheld a reference made by a county court (despite an earlier decision of the House of Lords on the same issue), on the ground that the position had been rendered unclear by an intervening decision of the ECJ in a TEC, art 234 (now TFEU, art 267) reference from another country.[90] In *OFT* v *Abbey National plc*,[91] in contrast, the Supreme Court of the United Kingdom declined to make a reference in a controversial case where neither party 'showed any enthusiasm' for it, and where there was 'a strong public interest in resolving the matter without further delay'.[92]

B. European Union Law

As we shall see, there is a distinctive EU constitutional law, the fundamentals of which were in place before Britain's accession in 1973, and the bold claims of which are not easy for the British public lawyer, schooled in the traditions of Dicey and others, to embrace. These claims relate particularly to claims about the supremacy of EU law in its expanding field of competence, as established by the ECJ in several ground-breaking early decisions. While as a practical matter any potential conflict between national constitutional law and the constitutional law of the EU is unlikely to be an issue of day-to-day concern, the possibility of serious disagreement between the British government and the EU institutions at some time in the future ought not to be discounted. It is at this point that unresolved issues of principle may become important, and it is at this point a national government will be faced with the strong claims of the ECJ in *Case 26/62, Van Gend en*

---

[86] *Bulmer Ltd* v *Bollinger SA* [1974] 1 Ch 401, at p 423.

[87] See e.g. *Customs and Excise Commissioners* v *ApS Samex* [1983] 1 All ER 1042; *R* v *Pharmaceutical Society of Great Britain, ex p Association of Pharmaceutical Importers* [1987] 3 CMLR 951; *BLP Group* v *Customs and Excise Commissioners* [1994] STC 41; *Feehan* v *Commissioners of Customs and Excise* [1995] 1 CMLR 193. For Scotland, see *Prince* v *Secretary of State for Scotland* 1985 SLT 74; *Wither* v *Cowie* 1990 SCCR 741.

[88] *R* v *International Stock Exchange, ex p Else* [1993] QB 534, at p 545. Also *R* v *Secretary of State for Defence, ex p Perkins* [1997] 3 CMLR 310, *Booker Aquaculture Ltd* v *Secretary of State for Scotland* 2000 SC 9, *Trinity Mirror plc* v *Commissioners of Customs and Excise* [2001] 2 CMLR 759, and *RBS plc* v *HM Revenue and Customs* [2007] CSIH 15. See Weatherill and Beaumont, pp 334–40.

[89] [2008] EWCA Civ 1313; [2009] 1 CMLR 1239.

[90] See below, pp 142–3.

[91] [2009] UKSC 6, paras 48 and 50 (Lord Walker).

[92] See also *Johnson* v *Medical Defence Union* [2007] EWCA Civ 262; [2008] Bus Law Rev 503. Where a matter is referred, the decision of the ECJ is binding only to the extent that it is based on the facts established by the domestic court that made the TFEU, art 267 (ex TEC, art 234) reference: *Arsenal FC* v *Reed* [2003] EWCA Civ 96; [2003] 3 All ER 865.

Loos v *Nederlandse Administratie der Belastingen*,[93] in which it was noted that what was then the EEC Treaty 'is more than an agreement which merely creates mutual obligations between the contracting states', and in which the Court asserted:

> By contrast with ordinary international treaties, the EEC Treaty has created its own legal system which, on the entry into force of the Treaty, became an integral part of the legal systems of the member states and which their courts are bound to apply. By creating a Community of unlimited duration, having its own institutions, its own personality, its own legal capacity and capacity of representation on the international plane and, more particularly, real powers stemming from a limitation of sovereignty or a transfer of powers from the states to the Community, the member states have limited their sovereign rights, albeit within limited fields, and have thus created a body of law which binds both their nationals and themselves.

The point was reinforced forcefully in *Case 6/64, Costa* v *ENEL* (considered below),[94] and reflected in the Declaration concerning primacy annexed to the Lisbon Treaty (Declaration 17). This provides:

> In accordance with well settled case law of the Court of Justice of the European Union, the Treaties and the law adopted by the Union on the basis of the Treaties have primacy over the law of Member States, under the conditions laid down by the said case law.[95]

The supremacy of EU law

1 *The general principle*. Within the Community legal order, the ECJ thus claims that EU law takes priority over national law. In the landmark *Costa* case referred to above, Mr Costa claimed that he was not obliged to pay for electricity supplied to him by ENEL on the ground that the supplier was an entity which had been nationalised in 1962 in breach of provisions of what was then the EEC Treaty. The Italian court (the Giudice Conciliatore of Milan) referred to the ECJ for consideration whether Italian law violated the Treaty in the manner suggested, only to be faced with the argument by the Italian government that the reference was 'absolutely inadmissible' inasmuch as 'a national court which is obliged to apply a national law cannot avail itself of art 177 [now TFEU, art 267]'. In rejecting this argument, the ECJ held:

> The integration into the laws of each member state of provisions which derive from the Community, and more generally the terms and the spirit of the Treaty, make it impossible for the states, as a corollary, to accord precedence to a unilateral and subsequent measure over a legal system accepted by them on a basis of reciprocity. Such a measure cannot therefore be inconsistent with that legal system. The executive force of Community law cannot vary from one state to another in deference to subsequent domestic laws, without jeopardising the attainment of the objectives of the Treaty.[96]

The ECJ further asserted that 'the laws stemming from the Treaty, an independent source of law, could not, because of its special and original nature, be overridden by domestic legal provisions, however framed, without being deprived of its character as Community law, and without the legal basis of the Community itself being called into question'.[97]

This case thus unequivocally declared the supremacy of Community – and now EU – law over inconsistent domestic law, including in particular domestic law introduced after

---

[93] [1963] ECR 1.

[94] [1964] ECR 585.

[95] Ibid, p 593. Attached to the Declaration is an Opinion of the Council Legal Service of 22 June 2007 pointing out that this principle of 'primacy' is a result of the case law of the Court of Justice (referring specifically to the *Costa* case), and is not mentioned in the Treaty.

[96] Ibid, pp 593–4.

[97] Ibid, p 594.

accession.[98] EU law also takes priority over inconsistent provisions of national constitutional law. The leading case, *Case 11/70, Internationale Handelsgesellschaft v Einfuhrund Vorratsstelle für Getreide und Futtermittel,*[99] was concerned with regulations which required applicants for export and import licences to pay a deposit which was forfeited if terms of the licence were violated. The German authorities were of the view that the system of licences violated certain principles of German constitutional law 'which must be protected within the framework of the German Basic Law'. But the ECJ disagreed and held:

> Recourse to the legal rules or concepts of national law in order to judge the validity of measures adopted by the institutions of the Community would have an adverse effect on the uniformity and efficacy of Community law. The validity of such measures can only be judged in the light of Community law. In fact, the law stemming from the Treaty, an independent source of law, cannot because of its very nature be overridden by rules of national law, however framed, without being deprived of its character as Community law and without the legal basis of the Community itself being called into question.[100]

Further, 'the validity of a Community measure or its effect within a member state cannot be affected by allegations that it runs counter to either fundamental rights as formulated by the constitution of that state or the principles of a national constitutional structure'.[101] Although Community law thus prevails over even fundamental rights guaranteed by national constitutions, the ECJ did, nevertheless, hold that 'respect for fundamental rights forms an integral part of the general principles of law protected by the Court of Justice' and that 'protection of such rights, whilst inspired by the constitutional traditions common to the member states, must be ensured within the framework of the structure and objectives of the Community'.[102] On the facts it was held that the system of licences in question did not violate any such rights.

> The respect for fundamental rights has meant that the ECHR has a special status in EU law. Otherwise, however, EU law takes priority over the international law obligations of the EU and its member states, as in *Joined Cases C-402/05P and 415/05P, Kadi v Council and Commission*[103] which concerned a regulation authorising the freezing of the assets of the applicant to comply with UN resolutions. It was held by the ECJ that the regulation in question was ultra vires and it was annulled. This was partly because there was no power in the EC Treaty to make a regulation of this kind, and partly because it was not consistent with respect for fundamental rights drawn 'from the constitutional traditions common to the Member States and from the guidelines supplied by international instruments for the protection of human rights on which the Member States have collaborated or to which they are signatories'. Here the rights in question related to respect for private property and the right to effective judicial protection (the right to be heard). In the view of the ECJ, 'an international agreement cannot affect the allocation of powers fixed by the Treaties or, consequently, the autonomy of the Community legal system'. Although a welcome decision, the subordination of international law to EU law may be less attractive where economic freedoms in the TFEU are accorded priority over fundamental social rights in international and regional treaties to which Member States are party.[104]

---

[98] See also *Case 106/77, Amministrazione delle Finanze dello Stato v Simmenthal SpA* [1978] ECR 629.

[99] [1970] ECR 1125.

[100] Ibid, p 1134.

[101] See also *Case 44/79, Hauer v Land Rheinland-Pfalz* [1979] ECR 3727, and more recently *Case C-438/05, International Transport Workers' Federation and Finnish Seamen's Union v Viking Line ABP* [2007] ECR I-10779.

[102] [1970] ECR 1125, 1134. See now TEU, art 6(3). See below, pp 132–3.

[103] 3 September 2008. On the supremacy of EU law over international law, see also *Case C-308/06, R (International Association of Independent Tanker Owners) v Transport Secretary*, 3 June 2008, and *Case C-122/95, Germany v Council* [1998] ECR I-973.

[104] *Case 438-05, International Transport Workers' Federation and Finnish Seamen's Union v Viking Line ABP*, above; *Case 341/05, Laval un Partneri Ltd v Svenska Byggnadsarbetareförbundet and Others* [2007] ECR I-11767.

2 *EU law and the United Kingdom.* The implications of the supremacy of EU law for the United Kingdom were revealed by the *Factortame* series of cases in which the company challenged the Merchant Shipping Act 1988 and regulations made thereunder on the ground that they violated provisions of the EEC Treaty, including arts 7 and 52 (now TFEU, arts 26 and 46 respectively).[105] The Act had been introduced to prevent what was called 'quota hopping' and amended the rules relating to the licensing of fishing vessels by providing that only British-owned vessels could be registered, a requirement which excluded the Spanish-owned vessels of the applicants. In judicial review proceedings in *Factortame (No 1)* the Divisional Court made a reference under EEC Treaty, art 177 (now TFEU, art 267) for a preliminary ruling on the issues of Community law raised by the proceedings and ordered by way of interim relief that the application of the 1988 Act should be suspended as regards the applicants. This latter order was set aside by the Court of Appeal on the ground that the court had no power to suspend the application of an Act, since 'it is fundamental to our (unwritten) constitution that it is for Parliament to legislate and for the judiciary to interpret and apply the fruits of Parliament's labours'.[106] By the time the case reached the House of Lords, however, the question of parliamentary sovereignty had been diluted, although not completely displaced. Lord Bridge said:

> If the applicants fail to establish the rights they claim before the ECJ, the effect of the interim relief granted would be to have conferred upon them rights directly contrary to Parliament's sovereign will and correspondingly to have deprived British fishing vessels, as defined by Parliament, of the enjoyment of a substantial proportion of the United Kingdom quota of stocks of fish protected by the common fisheries policy. I am clearly of the opinion that, as a matter of English law, the court has no power to make an order which has these consequences.[107]

It was also held that under English law it was not possible (at that time) to grant an interlocutory injunction against the Crown.

In the view of the ECJ, however, 'the full effectiveness' of Community law (as it then was) would be impaired 'if a rule of national law could prevent a court seised of a dispute governed by Community law from granting interim relief in order to ensure the full effectiveness of the judgment to be given on the existence of the rights claimed under community law'. It therefore followed that 'a court which in those circumstances would grant interim relief, if it were not for a rule of national law, is obliged to set aside that rule'. As a result EC law (now EU law) must take priority over domestic legislation, even if this means that the British courts are required to set aside a fundamental constitutional principle. However, there is nothing novel about such a conclusion, the ECJ holding on a number of occasions that the supremacy of Community law (now EU law) applies even in respect of provisions of national constitutional law. The position was reinforced by *Factortame (No 4)* which was concerned with whether the government was liable to the plaintiffs in damages for loss suffered as a result of the legislation.[108] It had already been held that failure to implement a directive could in some circumstances give rise to liability

---

[105] For the *Factortame* litigation, see *R v Transport Secretary, ex p Factortame Ltd (No 1)* [1989] 2 CMLR 353 (CA), [1990] 2 AC 85 (HL); *Case C-213/89, R v Transport Secretary, ex p Factortame Ltd (No 2)* [1991] AC 603 (ECJ and HL); *Case C-221/89, R v Transport Secretary, ex p Factortame Ltd (No 3)* [1992] QB 680 (ECJ); *Case C-48/93, R v Transport Secretary, ex p Factortame Ltd (No 4)* [1996] QB 404 (ECJ); *R v Secretary of State for Transport, ex p Factortame (No 5)* [2000] 1 AC 524. For proceedings by the Commission under art 169 (now 226) see *Case C-246/89, Commission v UK* [1991] ECR I-4585. For the sequel, see Merchant Shipping Act 1988 (Amendment) Order 1989, SI 1989 No 2006. For an account of the costs of the *Factortame* case, see HL Deb, 4 July 2000, WA 132.

[106] [1989] 2 CMLR 353, 397 (Lord Donaldson MR).

[107] [1990] 2 AC 85, 143.

[108] [1996] QB 404. Although the government moved quickly to repair the legislation, losses were sustained from the time the 1988 Act came into force (31 March 1989) until the offending discrimination was removed (2 November 1989).

in damages on the part of a state to a citizen who suffered loss as a result.[109] In *Factortame (No 4)*, the ECJ held:

> The fact that, according to national rules, the breach complained of is attributable to the legislature cannot affect the requirements inherent in the protection of the rights of individuals who rely on Community law and, in this instance, the right to obtain redress in the national courts for damage caused by the breach.[110]

So not only may an Act of Parliament be 'disapplied'; the courts may also be called on to make an award of damages for losses suffered as a result of its terms where the conditions for state liability are met. In *Factortame (No 5)*, the House of Lords held that the 'deliberate adoption of legislation which was clearly discriminatory on the ground of nationality and which inevitably violated [what was then] article 52 of the Treaty' was a sufficiently serious breach to give rise under Community law to a right to compensatory damages.[111]

The sources of EU law

1 *EU Treaty*. EU law takes a number of different forms. The highest form of law are the Treaties (TEU, TFEU) themselves, which not only set out the constitution of the EU, but also deal with substantive matters, some of which give rise to rights which are directly effective in national courts. *Case 26/62, Van Gend en Loos* v *Nederlandse Administratie der Belastingen*[112] was concerned with the interpretation of what was then art 12 of the EEC Treaty, this requiring member states to refrain from introducing between themselves new customs duties, or increasing those already in force, in trade with each other. The question referred by the Dutch tribunal to the ECJ was whether the then art 12 of the EEC Treaty had direct effect in the domestic courts 'in the sense that nationals of member states may on the basis of [the] article lay claim to rights which the national court must protect'. The ECJ held:

> Independently of the legislation of member states, Community law . . . not only imposes obligations on individuals but is also intended to confer upon them rights which become part of their legal heritage. These rights arise not only where they are expressly granted by the Treaty, but also by reason of obligations which the Treaty imposes in a clearly defined way upon individuals as well as upon the member states and upon the institutions of the Community.[113]

But not all terms of the Treaties have direct effect in the sense that they will be enforceable by individuals in their own national courts.[114] Much will depend on the nature of the treaty provision in question, it being stated in *Van Gend en Loos* that the then art 12 contained 'a clear and unconditional prohibition' which was unqualified 'by any reservation on the part of states which would make its implementation conditional upon a positive legislative measure enacted under national law'.[115] This made it 'ideally adapted to produce direct effects in the legal relationship between member states and their subjects'.

Where a treaty provision does have direct effect, in some cases it may be relied on by one private party against another, in which case it is said to have 'horizontal' direct effect. A provision which can be relied upon only against the state is said in contrast to have 'vertical' direct effect.

---

[109] See below, p 141.

[110] [1996] QB 404, 497.

[111] *R v Secretary of State for Transport, ex p Factortame Ltd (No 5)* [2000] 1 AC 524, at p 545 (Lord Slynn). See A Cygan (2000) 25 EL Rev 452. Article 52 is now TFEU, art 43.

[112] [1963] ECR 1.

[113] Ibid, p 12.

[114] See e.g. *R v Home Secretary, ex p Flynn* [1995] 3 CMLR 397 (EC Treaty, art 7a (now TFEU 26) held not to have direct effect).

[115] [1963] ECR 1, p 13.

Among the cases in which the ECJ has held that treaty provisions have horizontal direct effect, *Case 43/75, Defrenne v Sabena*,[116] was concerned with the then art 119 (then art 141, now TFEU, art 257), which provides that 'each member state shall during the first stage ensure and subsequently maintain the application of the principle that men and women should receive equal pay for equal work'. The article was said to promote a double aim, one economic and the other social, the former seeking to eliminate unfair competition and the latter furthering social objectives of the Community 'which is not merely an economic union, but is at the same time intended, by common action, to ensure social progress and seek the constant improvement of living and working conditions'.[117] The principle of equal pay formed part of 'the foundations of the Community', and art 119 was held to have direct effect even though its complete implementation 'may in certain cases involve the elaboration of criteria whose implementation necessitates the taking of appropriate measures at Community and national level'. The ECJ held that direct effect would apply in particular to 'those types of discrimination arising directly from legislative provisions or collective labour agreements, as well as in cases where men and women receive unequal pay for equal work which is carried out in the same establishment or service, whether private or public'.[118]

2 EU legislation. As we have seen, the Treaties also confer law-making powers on the EU institutions, these taking a number of different forms. By TFEU, art 288 (ex TEC, art 249) the institutions are empowered to 'adopt regulations, directives, decisions, recommendations and opinions'. These different measures have different legal consequences. **Regulations** have 'general application' in the sense that they are binding in their entirety and directly applicable in all member states.[119]

> *Case 93/71, Leonesio v Italian Ministry of Agriculture*[120] was concerned with an EEC regulation of 1969 providing a subsidy for those who slaughtered milk cows. The question for the ECJ was whether the regulation conferred on farmers a right to payment of the subsidy enforceable in national courts. In holding that it did, the Court held that, as a general principle, 'because of its nature and its purpose within the system of sources of Community law', a regulation 'has direct effect and is, as such, capable of creating individual rights which national courts must protect'. It was no excuse in this case that the national Parliament had not allocated the necessary funds to meet the costs of the subsidy, for to hold otherwise would have the effect of placing Italian farmers in a less favourable position than their counterparts elsewhere 'in disregard of the fundamental rule requiring the uniform application of regulations throughout the Community'.[121]

Like some provisions of the Treaty, regulations may have horizontal as well as vertical direct effect.[122] It would also be possible in English law for the Attorney General – in his or her capacity as guardian of the public interest – to seek an injunction to restrain a private party from acting in breach of a regulation.[123]

---

[116] [1976] ECR 455.

[117] Ibid, p 472.

[118] *Defrenne* was relied upon by the ECJ in the controversial decision in *Case C-438/05, International Transport Workers' Federation and Finnish Seamen's Union v Viking Line*, above, in holding that a company can proceed against a trade union where the right to freedom of establishment of the former is impeded by industrial action of the latter. See K Apps (2009) 34 E L Rev 141 for some of the important remedial implications of this decision.

[119] TFEU, art 288 (ex TEC, art 249).

[120] [1972] ECR 287.

[121] See also *Case 128/78, Re Tachographs: Commission v UK* [1979] ECR 419.

[122] *Case C-253/00, Antonio Muñoz y Cia SA v Frumar Ltd* [2003] Ch 328.

[123] *DEFRA v ASDA Stores* [2003] UKHL 71; [2004] 4 All ER 268.

Directives generally require implementing legislation by a member state before they give rise to enforceable obligations in the member state in question, the TFEU providing that directives are binding 'as to the result to be achieved', the national authorities being left 'the choice of form and methods'.[124] So 'where different options are available for and effective to achieve the objects of the Directive it is for Member States to choose between them'.[125] This gives member states 'considerable flexibility' in implementation.[126] But directives also may have vertical direct effect,[127] the point having been established in *Case 41/74, Van Duyn v Home Office* where the ECJ said that it would be 'incompatible with the binding effect attributed to a directive by art 249 [now TFEU, art 288] to exclude, in principle, the possibility that the obligation which it imposes may be invoked by those concerned'.[128] According to one line of authority, 'wherever the provisions of a directive appear, as far as their subject matter is concerned, to be unconditional and sufficiently precise, those provisions may be relied upon by an individual against the state where that state fails to implement the directive in national law by the end of the prescribed period or where it fails to implement the directive correctly'.[129] As a general rule, however, Directives do not have horizontal direct effect (though they may sometimes have what has been termed 'incidental effect').[130]

In *Case 152/84, Marshall v Southampton and South West Hampshire AHA,*[131] it was held that art 5(1) of the Equal Treatment Directive (76/207/EEC) was directly effective, thereby allowing a woman (who had been dismissed at the age of 62 in circumstances where men would not have been dismissed until the age of 65) to bring proceedings in domestic law for sex discrimination on an issue to which domestic legislation did not then apply. It was held that although directives have only 'vertical' rather than 'horizontal' direct effect, a directive nevertheless may be relied on against the state 'regardless of the capacity in which the latter is acting, whether employer or public authority'.[132]

Decisions are binding in their entirety on those to whom they are addressed, while **recommendations** and **opinions** have no binding force.[133]

---

[124] TFEU, art 288 (ex TEC, art 249). For a full account, see S Prechal, *Directives in EC Law*.

[125] *Wilson v St Helens Borough Council* [1999] 2 AC 52, per Lord Slynn.

[126] *R (Amicus–MSF) v Secretary of State for Trade and Industry* [2004] IRLR 430, per Richards J. See also *Wilson v St Helens Borough Council* [1999] 2 AC 52, per Lord Slynn.

[127] On which, see P P Craig (2009) 34 EL Rev 349 on the complex position now emerging on the legal status of directives.

[128] [1974] ECR 1337.

[129] *Case 8/81, Becker v Finanzamt Münster-Innenstadt* [1982] ECR 53.

[130] *Case C-194/94, CIA Security International SA v Signalson SA* [1996] ECR I-2201; *Case C-443/98, Unilever Italia v Central Food* [2000] ECR I-7535; *Case C-201/02, Wells v Secretary of State for Transport, Local Government and the Regions* [2004] ECR I-723; *Joined Cases C-152/07 to 154/07, Arcor AG* [2008] ECR I-05959.

[131] [1986] ECR 723. See A Arnull [1987] PL 383.

[132] *Marshall,* at p 749. The Area Health Authority was a public authority (or emanation of the state) for this purpose. See further *Case C-222/84, Johnston v Chief Constable of the RUC* [1987] QB 129 (police authority); *Case 188/89, Foster v British Gas* [1991] 2 AC 306 (nationalised industry); and *Griffin v South West Water* [1995] IRLR 15 (privatised water company). It has also been said that a directive may be 'relied on against organisations or bodies which are subject to the authority or control of the State or have special powers beyond those which result from the normal rules applicable to relations between individuals, such as local or regional authorities or other bodies which, irrespective of their legal form, have been given responsibility by the public authorities and under their supervision, for providing a public service': *Joined Cases C-253/96 to C-258/96, Kampelmann v Landschaftsverband Westfalen-Lippe* [1997] ECR 6907. However, a private company (the Motor Insurance Bureau) was held not to be an emanation of the state for the purposes of direct effect, even though it was the party to an agreement with the government by which a directive was to be implemented: *Byrne v MIB* [2008] 2 WLR 234. But see now *McCall v Poulton* [2008] EWCA Civ 1313; [2009] 1 CMLR 1239 (below, pp 142–3).

[133] TFEU, art 288 (ex TEC, art 249). On decisions, see R Greaves (1996) 21 EL Rev 3.

The EU, the ECHR and fundamental rights

An issue of growing interest is the extent to which fundamental rights play a part in the developing law of the EU.[134] It is, of course, the case that many national constitutions include protection for fundamental rights, the nature of the protection varying from state to state. All member states have ratified the European Convention on Human Rights as well as the Council of Europe's Social Charter of 18 October 1961 or its Revised Social Charter of 3 May 1996. Fundamental rights (as guaranteed by the ECHR) are deemed to 'constitute general principles of the Union's law', the TEU, Art 6(3) now giving effect expressly to an initiative to this end by the ECJ.[135] In this way the Court has been willing in a developing line of jurisprudence (i) to construe Community legal instruments in a manner which is consistent with fundamental rights;[136] and (ii) to set aside or annul decisions by Community institutions which are in breach of fundamental rights.[137] National courts have also been called upon to deal with fundamental rights when deciding matters of what is now EU law.[138] But the EU is not yet a party to the ECHR and so complaints cannot be taken to the Strasbourg court claiming that the Union is in breach of the ECHR,[139] though it would be possible for a complaint to be made to the Strasbourg court from a member state where it is claimed that the implementation of EU law in the state in question constitutes a breach of Convention rights.[140] Following the Lisbon amendments, the TEU now requires the EU to accede to the ECHR,[141] with the caveat that any accession 'shall make provision for preserving the specific characteristics of the Union and Union law'.[142] But this has yet to take place, and despite the mandatory provisions of TEU, art 6, any decision concluding accession will first need the agreement of the Council (acting unanimously) as well as the consent of the Parliament,[143] before being approved by all member states 'in accordance with their respective constitutional requirements'.[144]

An important initiative in reinforcing the role of fundamental rights in EU law was the EU Charter of Fundamental Rights, adopted at Nice in December 2000.[145] This is a wide-ranging document which is particularly important for its commitment to 'the indivisible, universal values of human dignity, freedom, equality and solidarity'. A document of 54 articles, it is divided into seven chapters, entitled respectively dignity (articles 1–5); freedoms (articles 6–19); equality

---

[134] See Betten and Grief, *EU Law and Human Rights*.

[135] *Internationale Handelsgesellschaft* [1970] ECR 1125. For a full treatment, see Craig and De Burca, ch 7; and Tridimas, ch 6.

[136] See *Case-13/94, P v S and Cornwall County Council* [1996] ECR I-02143; *Case C-60/00, Mary Carpenter* [2002] ECR I-6279; *Case C-112/00, Eugen Schmidberger v Austria* [2003] ECR I-5659 (F Agerbeek (2004) 29 EL Rev 255; A Biondi [2004] EHRLR 37); and *Case 438-05, International Transport Workers' Federation and Finnish Seamen's Union v Viking Line ABP*, above.

[137] *Case C-185/95, Baustahlgewerbe GmbH v Commission* [1998] ECR I-8417.

[138] See *Booker Aquaculture Ltd v Secretary of State for Scotland* 2000 SC 9.

[139] Indeed, prior to the Lisbon amendments, the EU had no power under the treaties then in force to accede to the ECHR (*Opinion 2/94, Re the Accession of the Community to the European Human Rights Convention* [1996] ECR I-1759), as some had proposed (House of Lords, Select Committee on European Union, 8th Report (1999–2000), for discussion of this issue).

[140] See K D Ewing and J Hendy (2010) 39 ILJ 2.

[141] TEU, art 6(2), where it is stated that the Union 'shall' accede.

[142] Protocol No 8. It is also provided that the 'accession of the Union shall not affect the competences of the Union or the powers of its institutions', nor is it to affect the right of member states to derogate from the ECHR or to accept certain provisions with reservations.

[143] TFEU, art 218.

[144] Ibid, art 218(8). It is unclear what this now means in the context of the United Kingdom.

[145] See A Arnull [2003] PL 774, S Douglas-Scott [2004] EHRLR 37, and Peers and Ward (eds), *The EU Charter of Fundamental Rights*. The Charter had been seen as 'a prelude to a European constitution' (F Jacobs (2001) 26 EL Rev 331).

(articles 20–26); solidarity (articles 27–38); citizens' rights (articles 39–46); justice (articles 47–50); and general provisions (articles 51–54). The Charter draws freely on other texts for its contents, including the ECHR and the Council of Europe's Social Charter, as well as the Community's Charter of the Fundamental Social Rights of Workers of 1989. The Nice Charter is addressed to the institutions and bodies of the Union and to the member states only when they are implementing Union law. Where the Charter includes rights which are also to be found in the ECHR, 'the meaning and scope of those rights shall be the same as those laid down' by the Convention, minimising the possibility of conflicting interpretations of Convention rights by the two highest courts in the European legal order.[146] The legal status of the Charter was transformed by the Lisbon Treaty, with the TEU, art 6 now also providing that the Charter 'shall have the same legal value as the Treaties', albeit not integrated into the treaties. In the case of the United Kingdom (and Poland) however, Protocol No 30 provides that the Charter does not extend the ability of the ECJ (or of any domestic court) to find that any provision of domestic law is inconsistent with its terms; the Protocol also provides for 'for the avoidance of doubt' that nothing in title IV of the Charter (dealing with certain trade union freedoms and employment rights) creates justiciable rights applicable to the United Kingdom.[147]

C. EU law and British constitutional law[148]

We have seen so far that the EU treaties have created a new legal order, that the ECJ has asserted the supremacy of EU law over national law and that EU law may have direct effect in national legal systems. In each of these respects EU law presents a challenge to traditional English (but perhaps not Scottish) constitutional law, in so far as this is deeply rooted in parliamentary supremacy and in the obligation of the courts to give effect to legislation passed by Parliament. Britain is not alone in experiencing difficulties in reconciling EU law with the principles of national constitutional law.[149] But the question of legislative supremacy is not the only potential flashpoint, with the courts being presented with difficulties of a more practical nature which some see as a challenge to their authority. Apart from the differences of style in the drafting of English and EU law,[150] there is the more serious point that British judges must determine questions of EU law in accordance with the principles laid down by and in accordance with any relevant decisions of the European Court of Justice.[151] Before considering the response of the courts, it is necessary to consider in some detail the constitutional issues presented by EU membership.

The constitutional implications of UK membership of the EC/EU

The constitutional implications of what was then EC membership were canvassed in a white paper published by the Labour government in 1967, which formed an important basis for the European Communities Act 1972.[152] It was pointed out that complex legislation would need to

---

[146] On the relationship between the two courts, see *Bosphorus Hava Yollari Turizm v Ireland* (2005) 42 EHRR 1. See generally, S Douglas-Scott (2006) 43 CML Rev 629; G Harpaz [2009] CMLR 105.

[147] For a full discussion, see HL Paper 62-I (2007–08), paras 5.84–5.111.

[148] See Jowell and Oliver (eds), *The Changing Constitution*, ch 2 (A W Bradley), and ch 4 (P Craig), and Nicol, *EC Membership and Judicialization of British Politics*.

[149] See Craig and De Burca, ch 10, Weatherill and Beaumont, pp 443–53, and A Albi and P van Elsuwege (2004) 29 EIL Rev 741.

[150] See *Bulmer v Bollinger SA* [1974] Ch 401, 425.

[151] European Communities Act 1972, s 3.

[152] Cmnd 3301, 1967.

be introduced to implement measures which did not have direct effect and that further legislation would be needed to give effect to subsequent Community instruments. Legislation would also be required in the case of those provisions of Community law which are 'intended to take direct internal effect within the member states':

> This legislation would be needed, because, under our constitutional law, adherence to a treaty does not of itself have the effect of changing our internal law even where provisions of the treaty are intended to have direct internal effect as law within the participating states.[153]

The white paper further pointed out that 'the legislation would have to cover both provisions in force when we joined and those coming into force subsequently as a result of instruments issued by the Community institutions'. Although 'no new problem would be created by the provisions which were in force at the time we became a member of the Communities', a constitutional innovation would lie 'in the acceptance in advance as part of the law of the United Kingdom of provisions to be made in the future by instruments issued by the Community institutions – a situation for which there is no precedent in this country'. These instruments were said like ordinary delegated legislation to 'derive their force under the law of the United Kingdom from the original enactment passed by Parliament'.[154]

Quite whether this constitutional innovation could be successfully implemented is a question which was not resolved before the introduction of the 1972 Act. The 1967 white paper noted:

> The Community law having direct internal effect is designed to take precedence over the domestic law of the member states. From this it follows that the legislation of the Parliament of the United Kingdom giving effect to that law would have to do so in such a way as to override existing national law so far as inconsistent with it.[155]

But this merely rehearses rather than resolves the question: what happens if Parliament should legislate in a manner inconsistent with the directly effective terms of the Treaty? The answer it seemed was that 'within the fields occupied by Community law Parliament would have to refrain from passing fresh legislation inconsistent with that law as for the time being in force', although this 'would not however involve any constitutional innovation', for 'many of our treaty obligations already impose such restraints – for example, the Charter of the United Nations, the European Convention on Human Rights and GATT'.[156] But this did not provide an answer either: what would be the position of a post-accession statute which is incompatible with a subsequently introduced regulation having direct effect or a statute introduced to comply with the Treaty, the terms of which are expanded in a novel and unpredictable way by the ECJ? In this context, the examples of the UN Charter or the ECHR are beside the point, for unlike what was then the EC Treaty these provisions do not seek to create directly effective obligations, but rely instead on implementing legislation for any obligations they generate.

The European Communities Act 1972

Britain's application for membership was made in 1967. The Treaty of Accession was signed on 22 January 1972 and was implemented by the European Communities Act 1972.[157] This deals

---

[153] Para 22.

[154] Ibid. Today this analogy is seen to be badly misconceived. Delegated legislation (see ch 28) does not give rise to an autonomous body of law claiming supremacy over the source of its legal authority in domestic law.

[155] Para 23.

[156] Ibid.

[157] As amended by the European Communities (Amendment) Acts 1986, 1993, 1998 and 2001, the European Union (Accessions) Act 2003, and the European Union (Amendment) Act 2008. Also important is the European Parliamentary Elections Act 1978, esp s 6. On the interaction of some of these measures, see *R v Foreign Secretary, ex p Rees-Mogg* [1994] QB 552.

with two central questions which were said to be 'fundamental to the structure and contents' of the Act,[158] the first being those provisions intended to embody in domestic law the provisions of Community (now EU) law designed to have direct effect and the second being the provisions which did not have direct effect but where action was necessary for their implementation. So far as the former is concerned, s 2(1) of the 1972 Act, said to be 'at the heart of the Bill',[159] provides:

> All such rights, powers, liabilities, obligations and restrictions from time to time created or arising by or under the Treaties, and all such remedies and procedures from time to time provided for by or under the Treaties, as in accordance with the Treaties are without further enactment to be given legal effect or used in the United Kingdom shall be recognised and available in law, and be enforced, allowed and followed accordingly.

What this does is to provide that in so far as EEC/EU law has direct effect, it shall be enforceable in the UK courts. It is also designed to ensure that directly effective EEC/EC/EU obligations take precedence over national law. But it does not address the question of what should happen where there is a statute which is inconsistent with directly effective EEC/EC/EU obligations. This, however, is addressed by s 2(4) which provides (inter alia):

> any enactment passed or to be passed [i.e. by the Westminster Parliament], other than one contained in this part of this Act, shall be construed and have effect subject to the foregoing provisions of this section.

Together with s 2(1), this is expressly designed to mean that 'the directly applicable provisions ought to prevail over future Acts of Parliament in so far as they might be inconsistent with them'.[160] As such, s 2 is an attempt by one Parliament to fetter the continuing supremacy of another by providing that, while future Parliaments may legislate in breach of Community (now EU) law, the courts must (to the extent of any inconsistency) deny it any effect.[161]

The provisions of Community (now EU) law which do not have direct effect were addressed in two ways by the 1972 Act. The first was by making a number of amendments to existing legislation to bring it into line with Community (now EU) law; and the second was by introducing a general power to make subordinate legislation to cover future as well as some existing Community instruments. Although there was concern about the new power to make subordinate legislation, the government did not expect the power to be frequently used,[162] an expectation which was clearly unfulfilled. By s 2(2) of the 1972 Act, regulations may be introduced by a designated minister for the purpose of implementing any Community (now EU) obligation. This is subject to Sched 2 which provides that regulations may not be used for a number of purposes, these being (i) an imposition of or increase in taxation; (ii) a provision having retrospective effect; (iii) a power delegating legislative authority; and (iv) a measure creating a new criminal offence punishable with imprisonment for more than two years, or punishable on summary conviction with imprisonment for more than three months or with a fine of more than level 5 on the standard scale. The power to make regulations under these provisions is exercisable by statutory instrument which, if not made following a draft being approved by resolution of each House of Parliament, is subject to annulment by either House.[163] Fresh obligations under Community (now EU) law continue to be implemented by both primary and secondary legislation.[164] Although

---

[158] HC Deb, 15 February 1972, col 271.

[159] Ibid, col 650.

[160] Ibid, col 278.

[161] See S A de Smith (1971) 34 MLR 597, H W R Wade (1972) 88 LQR 1, J D B Mitchell et al. (1972) 9 CML Rev 134, F A Trindade (1972) 35 MLR 375, G Winterton (1976) 92 LQR 591.

[162] HC Deb, 15 February 1972, col 282.

[163] For parliamentary scrutiny of delegated legislation, see ch 28.

[164] See e.g. Trade Union Reform and Employment Rights Act 1993 and SI 1995 No 2587.

the power to make subordinate legislation has been widely construed,[165] the government must indicate in clear terms what (if any) primary legislation is being repealed or amended when this procedure is invoked.[166]

Parliamentary scrutiny of EU legislation

In addition to the need to give effect to Community (now EU) law, there was also a need to put in place procedures for ensuring the accountability of ministers who were engaged in the making of new Community (now EU) law, in particular where the Community (now EU) instruments would have direct effect without the need for implementing legislation or other intervention by Parliament. The government expressed the view that 'Parliament should be informed about and have an opportunity to consider at the formative stage those Community instruments which, when made by the Council, will be binding in this country'.[167] Traditional parliamentary procedures, such as questions, adjournment debates and (the now discontinued) supply days, would continue to apply and an undertaking was given that 'No Government would proceed on a matter of major policy in the Council unless they knew that they had the approval of the House.'[168] Nevertheless, the government expressed the view that the traditional means of parliamentary accountability needed to be strengthened and that 'special arrangements' should be made under which the House would be 'apprised of draft regulations and directives before they go to the Council of Ministers for decision'.[169] In 1974 special committees were set up by both Houses of Parliament, now the European Scrutiny Committee in the case of the Commons, and the European Union Committee in the case of the Lords. The Commons committee (which may appoint sub-committees) is empowered to examine European Community documents (a term defined to include proposed legislation), to report its opinion on the legal and political importance of each and to consider any issue arising on any such document.[170] There are now over 1,100 documents considered by the Committee each year. The revised terms of reference of the highly respected Lords committee enable it to 'consider European Union documents and other matters relating to the European Union'. The Lords committee also has the power to appoint sub-committees, of which there are in fact seven, and it is mainly through the medium of these seven sub-committees that business is conducted.[171] Debates on matters identified by the Commons Scrutiny Committee now take place in one of three European Standing Committees where ministers may make a statement and be questioned.[172]

In recent years steps have been taken at both EU and national level to help overcome some of the formidable political obstacles to effective scrutiny of EU legislation.[173] Attempts to enhance the role of national Parliaments are to be found in the TEU which provides that

---

[165] See *R v Trade and Industry Secretary, ex p UNISON* [1997] 1 CMLR 459.

[166] *R (Orange Personal Communications Ltd) v Trade and Industry Secretary* [2001] 3 CMLR 36.

[167] HC Deb, 15 February 1972, col 274.

[168] Ibid.

[169] Ibid, col 275.

[170] HC SO 143. The committee has 16 members.

[171] The sub-committees deal with Economic and Financial Affairs, and International Trade (A), Internal Market (B), Foreign Affairs, Defence and Development Policy (C), Environment and Agriculture (D), Law and Institutions (E), Home Affairs (F), and Social Policy and Consumer Affairs (G).

[172] HC SO 119. See generally, Cygan, *The United Kingdom Parliament and European Union Legislation*. A valuable guide to the Commons procedure is also produced by the Department of the Clerk of the House, *The European Scrutiny System in the House of Commons* (June 2005). There is also now a European and External Relations Committee of the Scottish Parliament with wide-ranging scrutiny functions.

[173] HC 588-I (1977–8), para 4.1. It was also said that 'the nature of the Community is such that it is inherently difficult to make Community decision makers accountable to any Parliament, national or European' (D Marquand (1981) 19 *Journal of Common Market Studies* 223). For proposals to improve scrutiny, see HC 465 (2004–05).

national Parliaments should be better informed and be sent draft legislation in good time so that they may consider it properly.[174] By Protocol 1, legislative proposals from the Commission should be sent to national Parliaments at the same time as they are sent to the Council and the European Parliament, while a period of eight weeks must elapse between the sending of a legislative proposal to national Parliaments and the date when it is placed on the provisional agenda of the Council for consideration as a legislative instrument, unless the matter is urgent.[175] Moreover, by a Commons resolution of 17 November 1998 (the 'scrutiny reserve resolution'), no Minister of the Crown should give 'agreement' to any 'proposal for European Community legislation', '(a) which is still subject to scrutiny (that is, on which the European Scrutiny Committee has not completed its scrutiny) or (b) which is awaiting consideration by the House (that is, which has been recommended by the European Scrutiny Committee for consideration)'.[176] However, these obligations may be waived in the case of a proposal which is confidential, routine, or trivial, or is substantially the same as a proposal on which scrutiny has been completed. The minister may also give agreement before scrutiny is complete with the consent of the Committee or if there are 'special reasons', although the minister should explain the reasons to the Scrutiny Committee and in some cases the House itself. It is uncertain to what extent a minister is bound by a resolution of one of the European Standing Committees and views predictably differ between government and Parliament. But while ministers are unlikely to accept any formal constraint, departure from a Committee resolution is a decision that is unlikely to be taken lightly without the involvement of other ministers, thereby raising the possibility that the matter would become one of collective rather than individual responsibility.[177]

D. Response of the courts

As we have seen, the questions of parliamentary supremacy presented by Britain's membership were identified but not resolved in the pre-accession era. It would clearly be possible in principle for the United Kingdom to leave the EU,[178] and to that extent the supremacy of Parliament is preserved. But this is a theoretical point which bears no relationship to contemporary reality, any more than do claims in another context that Parliament could legislate to regain sovereignty over former colonies.[179] The real problem is whether Parliament can legislate in a manner which is expressly in defiance of EU law. Should that happen, how should the United Kingdom courts respond? It is on this question that the politicians abdicated all responsibility in the pre-accession debates. The point was made by the Lord Chancellor in 1967:

> There is in theory no constitutional means available to us to make it certain that no future Parliament would enact legislation in conflict with Community law. It would, however, be unprofitable to speculate on the academic possibility of a future Parliament enacting legislation expressly designed to have that effect. Some risk of inadvertent contradiction between United Kingdom legislation and Community law could not be ruled out.[180]

---

[174] TFEU, art 12(a).

[175] Under Art 3 of this Protocol, national Parliaments may send to the Parliament, the Council and the Commission a reasoned opinion on whether a draft legislative act is consistent with the principle of subsidiarity.

[176] HC Deb, 17 November 1998, col 778. Also HL Deb, 6 December 1999, col 1019. The European and External Relations Committee of the Scottish Parliament considers and reports on proposed European Communities legislation and EU issues.

[177] For further discussion, see Cygan (note 172 above).

[178] See TEU, art 50: 'Any Member State may decide to withdraw from the Union in accordance with its own constitutional requirements'.

[179] See ch 4 above.

[180] HL Deb, 8 May 1967, col 1203.

EU law and parliamentary supremacy

For the first decade after the passing of the 1972 Act, the courts vacillated between mutually conflicting positions. In *Felixstowe Dock and Railway Co v British Transport Docks Board*,[181] Lord Denning commented that once a Bill 'is passed by Parliament and becomes a statute, that will dispose of all discussion about the Treaty. These courts will then have to abide by the statute without regard to the Treaty at all'.[182] Only three years later, Lord Denning appeared to change his mind. In *Macarthys Ltd v Smith*,[183] the question was whether the Equal Pay Act 1970 permitted a woman to claim equal pay only with men currently in the employment of the employer or whether she could use as a comparator her male predecessor. The Court of Appeal was divided on the question: the majority (Lawton and Cumming Bruce LJJ) were of the view that domestic law did not permit such claims, but that EC law (now EU law) was unclear. They were therefore minded to make a reference under art 177 (now TFEU, art 267) to determine whether equal pay for equal work under art 119 (now TFEU, art 157) was 'confined to situations in which men and women are contemporaneously doing equal work for their employer'. Lord Denning was of the view that EC law (now EU law) permitted the woman's claim and that domestic law should be construed accordingly, saying:

> In construing our statute, we are entitled to look at the Treaty as an aid to its construction: and even more, not only as an aid but as an overriding force. If on close investigation it should appear that our legislation is deficient – or is inconsistent with Community law – by some oversight of our draftsmen – then it is our bounden duty to give priority to Community law. Such is the result of section 2(1) and (4) of the European Communities Act 1972.[184]

The ECJ confirmed the interpretation of art 119 (now TFEU, art 157) which had been suggested by Lord Denning[185] following which the Court of Appeal sought to make it plain that the provisions of the Treaty 'take priority over anything in our English statute on equal pay which is inconsistent with art 119 (now TFEU, art 157)', this priority having been 'given by our own law'. According to Lord Denning:

> Community law is now part of our law: and, whenever there is any inconsistency, Community law has priority. It is not supplanting English law. It is part of our law which overrides any other part which is inconsistent with it.[186]

Although Lord Denning appeared thus to have changed his mind, he also observed:

> Thus far I have assumed that our Parliament, whenever it passes legislation, intends to fulfil its obligations under the Treaty. If the time should come when our Parliament deliberately passes an Act – with the intention of repudiating the Treaty or any provision in it – or intentionally of acting inconsistently with it – and says so in express terms – then I should have thought that it would be the duty of our courts to follow the statute of our Parliament.[187]

On this basis the European Communities Act 1972, s 2, effected only a limited form of entrenchment: it would have the effect that Community law (now EU law) will apply in preference to any post-1972 statute and to that extent Parliament would have bound its successors. In these cases the courts would assume that Parliament had not intended to depart from Community (now EU) obligations. But Lord Denning left open the possibility that Parliament might wish to assert its

---

[181] [1976] 2 Ll L Rep 656.
[182] Ibid, p 663.
[183] [1979] ICR 785. See T R S Allan (1983) 3 OJLS 22.
[184] Ibid, p 789.
[185] *Case 129/79, Macarthys Ltd v Smith* [1981] 1 QB 180.
[186] [1981] 1 QB 180, 200. See also Cumming Bruce LJ, at p 201.
[187] [1979] ICR 785, 789.

supremacy by stating clearly that a domestic statute is to apply notwithstanding Community law (now EU law). In this case the domestic statute would displace to that extent s 2 of the 1972 Act. Further support in the early cases for the view that s 2 of the 1972 Act had only qualified the supremacy of Parliament was provided by *Case 12/81, Garland v British Rail Engineering Ltd.*[188] In an important passage which potentially goes further than Lord Denning in preserving the priority to be given to domestic legislation, Lord Diplock raised the question whether:

> having regard to the express direction as to the construction of enactments 'to be passed' . . . contained in section 2(4), anything short of an express positive statement in an Act of Parliament passed after January 1, 1973, that a particular provision is intended to be made in breach of an obligation assumed by the United Kingdom under a Community treaty, would justify an English court in construing that provision in a manner inconsistent with a Community treaty obligation of the United Kingdom.[189]

'Factortame'

The most recent and authoritative view is that expressed in the *Factortame* series of cases.[190] In *Factortame (No 1)* it was said by Lord Bridge (in upholding the Court of Appeal's refusal to grant interim relief to restrain the operation of the Merchant Shipping Act 1988 pending the outcome of the art 177 (now TFEU, art 267) reference) that s 2(4) was to be regarded as having

> precisely the same effect as if a section were incorporated in Part II of the Act of 1988 which in terms enacted that the provisions with respect to registration of British fishing vessels were to be without prejudice to the directly enforceable Community rights of nationals of any member state of the EEC.[191]

As we have seen, however, the House of Lords held that they had no jurisdiction to grant the interim relief sought; on a reference under art 177 (now TFEU, art 267), the ECJ ruled that a national court must set aside a rule of national law which precludes it from granting interim relief in a case concerning Community law (now EU law). When the matter returned to the House of Lords, relief was granted, thereby restraining the operation of the Merchant Shipping Act 1988 in relation to the plaintiffs pending the final resolution of the case.[192] In a much quoted passage in *Factortame (No 2)*, Lord Bridge said:

> Some public comments on the decision of the European Court of Justice, affirming the jurisdiction of the courts of member states to override national legislation if necessary to enable interim relief to be granted in protection of rights under Community law, have suggested that this was a novel and dangerous invasion by a Community institution of the sovereignty of the UK Parliament. But such comments are based on a misconception. If the supremacy . . . of Community law over the national law of member states was not always inherent in the EEC Treaty it was certainly well established in the jurisprudence of the European Court of Justice long before the UK joined the Community. . . . Thus, whatever limitation of its sovereignty Parliament accepted when it enacted the European Communities Act 1972 was entirely voluntary. Under the terms of the Act of 1972 it has always been clear that it was the duty of a UK court, when delivering final judgment, to override any rule of national law found to be in conflict with any directly enforceable rule of Community law. Similarly, when decisions of the European Court of Justice have exposed areas of UK statute law which failed to implement Council directives, Parliament has always loyally

[188] [1983] 2 AC 751.
[189] Ibid, p 771.
[190] See note 105 above. On the question of parliamentary sovereignty, see P P Craig (1991) 11 YBEL 221; N Gravells [1989] PL 568, [1991] PL 180; and H W R Wade (1991) 107 LQR 1, (1996) 112 LQR 568.
[191] [1990] 2 AC 85, 140.
[192] [1991] 1 AC 603.

accepted the obligation to make appropriate and prompt amendments. Thus there is nothing in any way novel in according supremacy to rules of Community law in those areas to which they apply and to insist that, in the protection of rights under Community law, national courts must not be inhibited by rules of national law from granting interim relief in appropriate cases is no more than a logical recognition of that supremacy.[193]

In this way, the House of Lords appears to have effected a form of entrenchment of s 2(4) of the 1972 Act which thereby does what no statute has done before, namely fetter the continuing supremacy of Parliament.[194] The late Sir William Wade referred to this as a constitutional revolution: 'The Parliament of 1972 had succeeded in binding the Parliament of 1988 and restricting its sovereignty, something that was supposed to be constitutionally impossible.'[195] But although this may be necessary as a matter of European integration, it is unclear whether the House of Lords in *Factortame (Nos 1 and 2)* satisfactorily dealt with the issue as a matter of domestic constitutional law; nor is it clear that the decision answers all the questions which arise. Indeed, it is open to question whether the decisions advance the matter much beyond the Court of Appeal decision in *Macarthys Ltd* v *Smith*.[196] It is unfortunate that in a case of such constitutional significance, the full range of constitutional authorities was not addressed in the course of argument, even if it would have been difficult for the defendants to have mounted a full frontal attack on the constitutional implications of s 2(4). But in terms of unanswered questions, what would be the position in the (admittedly unlikely) event that Parliament should say expressly (or by clear implication) that a statutory provision should apply notwithstanding any EU obligation to the contrary? Wade argued that: 'If there had been any such provision in the Act of 1988 we can be sure that the European Court of Justice would hold that it was contrary to Community law to which by the Act of 1972 the Act of 1988 is held to be subject.'[197] But does it follow that in such a case national courts would be required to give effect to the 1972 Act rather than the 1988 Act? As a matter of British constitutional law (and regardless of what the ECJ might say), it would appear in such an eventuality that Parliament had repudiated the 'voluntary' 'limitation of its sovereignty' which it accepted when it enacted the 1972 Act (at least insofar as the 1988 Act is concerned).[198]

Some of these matters were considered in *Thoburn* v *Sunderland City Council*[199] (the so-called 'Metric Martyrs' case) where the appellant had been convicted for breaching the Weights and Measures Act 1985 by selling fruit in imperial rather than metric measurements. As originally enacted the 1985 Act had permitted fruit to be sold in either measure, but the Act had been amended by regulations and now required fruit to be sold in metric measures only. These regulations, made partially under the authority of the European Communities Act 1972, s 2(2), had been introduced in order to comply with the EC Metrication Directive. The appeal failed, with the Administrative Court rejecting on a number of grounds the argument that the Weights and Measures Act 1985 impliedly repealed the European Communities Act 1972, s 2(2), to the extent of any inconsistency. But in the course of his judgment Laws LJ made a number of important observations about the relationship between British and EC law.

---

[193] Ibid, pp 658–9.

[194] See also *R* v *Employment Secretary, ex p EOC* [1995] 1 AC 1 where declarations were made that provisions of the Employment Protection (Consolidation) Act 1978 were incompatible with art 119 (now art 141) of the EEC Treaty and Council Directive 75/117/EEC and that other provisions of the Act were incompatible with the latter. For subsequent developments see D Nicol [1996] PL 579.

[195] (1996) 112 LQR 568.

[196] [1979] ICR 785.

[197] (1996) 112 LQR 568, p 570.

[198] This is not to deny that such a decision would give rise to serious political and constitutional problems at EU level. But it would be for the Commission to take appropriate action by way of enforcement proceedings or otherwise, and it is perhaps in that way that any problems should be resolved rather than in the British courts.

[199] [2002] EWHC 195 (Admin), [2003] QB 151 (D Marshall and J Young [2002] PL 399, G Marshall (2002) 118 LQR 493, and A Perreau-Saussine [2002] CLJ 528).

According to Laws LJ, the House of Lords in *Factortame (No 1)* (above) had effectively accepted that s 2(4) of the 1972 Act could not be impliedly repealed ('albeit the point was not argued'). In this way the common law had created an exception to the doctrine of implied repeal (an exception which in the view of Laws LJ should be extended to all 'constitutional statutes', of which the European Communities Act 1972 was an example).[200] This did not mean that the 1972 Act could not be repealed or modified. But it did mean that repeal or modification could be achieved only by 'express words in the later statute, or by words so specific that the inference of an actual determination to effect the result contended for was irresistible'. By these means the courts were said to 'have found their way through the *impasse* seemingly created by two supremacies, the supremacy of European law and the supremacy of Parliament'.

Parliamentary supremacy and the principle of indirect effect

Questions about parliamentary supremacy also arise, although rather less acutely, in the context of the interpretation of domestic legislation where questions are raised about its compatibility with directives. This presents problems of what is sometimes referred to as the indirect effect of directives, a matter which has given rise to a degree of inconsistency on the part of the ECJ. In one case (*Von Colson*),[201] a question arose about the relationship between German national law and the Equal Treatment Directive (76/207/EEC). According to the ECJ, 'in applying the national law and in particular the provisions of a national law specifically introduced in order to implement [a directive], national courts are required to interpret their national law in the light of the wording and the purpose of the directive'. In a more recent case (*Marleasing*),[202] the ECJ took a wider view of the application of directives, concluding now that 'in applying national law, whether the provisions in question were adopted before or after the directive, the national court called upon to interpret it is required to do so, as far as possible, in the light of the wording and the purpose of the directive in order to achieve the result pursued by the latter'. Domestic courts are thus required to construe domestic law in line with the requirements of a directive, regardless of whether the legislation pre-dates or post-dates the directive. But there is no overriding obligation to construe legislation in this way, so that – for example – where a directive is implemented at national level after its prescribed commencement date, domestic courts are not required to construe the implementing legislation retrospectively to cover the period of the delay.[203] Any such obligation would conflict with 'general principles of law, particularly those of legal certainty and non retroactivity'.[204] Under the *Francovich* principle, however, it may be possible in appropriate cases to bring an action against a national government for damages where an individual has suffered loss as a result of a failure properly to implement a directive which neither has direct nor indirect effect.[205] Any such action would be brought in the national courts.[206]

---

[200] See ch 4 C above on this aspect of the case.

[201] *Case 14/83, Von Colson and Kamann v Land Nordrhein-Westfalen* [1984] ECR 1891.

[202] *Case 106/89, Marleasing SA v La Comercial Internacional de Alimentación SA* [1990] ECR I-4135. See now *Cases C-397-403/01, Pfeiffer v Deutches Roles Kreuz, Kreisverband Waldshut eV* [2004] ECR I-8835 (S Prechal (2005) 42 CMLR 1445), *Case C-212/04, Adeneler v Ellinikos Organismos Galaktos* [2006] ECR I-6057, and *Case C-268/06, IMPACT v Minister for Agriculture and Food* [2008] ECR I-02483.

[203] *Case C-268/06, IMPACT v Minister for Agriculture and Food*, above.

[204] Ibid, para 100.

[205] *Cases C-6&9/90, Francovich and Bonifaci v Italy* [1991] ECR I-5357 (R Caranta [1993] 52 CLJ 272). Also *Case C-91/92, Faccini Dori v Recreb Srl* [1994] ECR I-3325; *Case C-261/95, Palmisani v INPS* [1997] ECR I-4025; *Case C-224/01, Gerhard Köbler* [2003] ECR I-10239. For a valuable account of the application of *Francovich* in different member states, see M-P F Granger (2007) 32 EL Rev 157.

[206] See *Spencer v Secretary of State for Work and Pensions* [2008] IRLR 911.

So far as the response of domestic courts to these questions is concerned, the issue first arose for consideration by the House of Lords in *Duke v Reliance Systems Ltd*,[207] concerned with the differential retirement ages for men and women which were permitted by UK law but which were in breach of the Equal Treatment Directive. As we have seen, however, the directive does not have horizontal direct effect and so could not be enforced in the domestic courts by someone who was not employed by a public authority. It was argued, nevertheless, that the Sex Discrimination Act 1975 should be construed so as to conform to the directive, a contention which drew the following response from Lord Templeman:

> a British court will always be willing and anxious to conclude that United Kingdom law is consistent with Community law. Where an Act is passed for the purpose of giving effect to an obligation imposed by a directive or other instrument a British court will seldom encounter difficulty in concluding that the language of the Act is effective for the intended purpose.[208]

In the *Duke* case, however, the Act in question was not passed to give effect to the directive. Indeed, it was expressly intended to preserve discriminatory retirement ages and was not reasonably capable of bearing any construction to the contrary. In these circumstances, it was held that s 2(4) of the 1972 Act does not 'enable or constrain a British court to distort the meaning of a British statute in order to enforce against an individual a Community directive which has no direct effect between individuals'. In more recent decisions, however, the House of Lords adopted a radically different approach in cases where statutory instruments had been introduced quite clearly to give effect to a directive. Indeed, in two cases the House was prepared to take the extraordinary step of implying words into the legislation quite consciously to change its literal meaning,[209] for fear that the measures would otherwise have 'failed their object and the United Kingdom would have been in breach of its treaty obligations to give effect to directives'.[210] The courts now freely refer to directives to discover 'the correct application' of domestic law,[211] and in the course of doing so accept that 'as between [a] directive and the domestic implementing regulations, the former is the dominant text'.[212] But what about legislation (primary and secondary) which covers the field occupied by a directive but which was not passed necessarily in order to implement it? The approach in *Duke* no longer appears to be followed, it now being accepted in *Webb v EMO Air Cargo (UK) Ltd*[213] (following *Marleasing*) that an English court should construe a statute to comply with a directive regardless of whether the statute was passed before or after the directive was made. However, the following case reveals that there may be other obstacles to indirect effect:

> *White v Motor Insurers' Bureau*[214] was concerned with the implementation of the Motor Insurance Directive, which requires each member state to set up a body to provide compensation for the victims of uninsured drivers. Rather than establish a statutory body, the government made an agreement with the MIB, a company limited by guarantee whose members are motor insurance companies for compensation to be administered by the Bureau. The House of Lords held that the *Marleasing* principle cannot be stretched to

---

[207] [1988] AC 618.

[208] Ibid, p 638.

[209] *Pickstone v Freemans plc* [1989] AC 66 (see A W Bradley [1988] PL 485) and *Litster v Forth Dry Dock & Engineering Co Ltd* [1990] 1 AC 546. This is a process that becomes less remarkable by usage in the lower courts: see *Leicestershire City Council v UNISON* [2005] IRLR 920, and *UK Coal Mining v NUM* [2008] IRLR 5.

[210] *Litster*, ibid, at p 558.

[211] *Whitehouse v Chas A Blatchford & Sons Ltd* [2000] ICR 542. See also *A v National Blood Authority* [2001] 3 All ER 289 (A Arnull (2001) 26 EL Rev 213); and *Director General of Fair Trading v First National Bank* [2002] 1 AC 481.

[212] *Director General of Fair Trading v First National Bank*, above, per Lord Steyn.

[213] [1992] 4 All ER 929. See N Gravells [1993] PL 44.

[214] [2001] UKHL 9; [2001] 2 CMLR 1.

require contracts of this kind to be interpreted in a manner which would impose obligations which the contract did not impose. This was so even though the government was one of the parties to the contract, and the contract was the chosen means for implementing the Directive. Although on the facts the agreement was found to be consistent with the requirements of the directive, this is nevertheless a highly unsatisfactory decision, which means that the rights under domestic law of the insured third party in this case are left to depend on the manner by which the government elects to implement a directive, the *Marleasing* principle being held to apply only to legislation (primary and secondary).

However, this latter restriction was called into question as a result of the *Pfeiffer* decision,[215] where the ECJ said that 'a national court is required, when applying the provisions of domestic law adopted for the purpose of transposing obligations laid down by a directive, *to consider the whole body of rules of national law* and to interpret them, so far as possible, in the light of the wording and purpose of the directive in order to achieve an outcome consistent with the objective pursued by the directive'. In the light of these remarks, the Court of Appeal dismissed an appeal from a county court decision in which a TEC, art 234 (now TFEU, art 267) reference was made, effectively to clarify whether the restriction in *White* was consistent with EU law.[216] At the time of writing the decision had not been made. Although previously accepting that directives may be implemented by agreements of this kind, the ECJ had also emphasised that any such agreement should be capable of interpretation and applied so that bodies such as the MIB are required to meet the full requirements of the directive.[217]

E. Conclusion

Whether or not the late Sir William Wade was correct in his assertion that a revolution has taken place,[218] British membership of the European Union continues to generate political controversy and legal uncertainty. At least three issues of constitutional law continue to be of interest. The first is the impact of ever closer political union in Europe and with it an enhancement of the role of the EU institutions.[219] Constitutional law has a role to play in this process, as political demands for more popular involvement as a prelude to closer union have so far been largely ignored. Although the government was committed to holding a referendum before ratifying the draft European Constitution that was concluded in 2003, this commitment was avoided with the collapse of the Constitution and its reconstruction in a different guise in the form of the Lisbon Treaty. Second, there is the concern about what some refer to as the democratic deficit in the EU, which takes a number of forms. But at its heart is a legislative process in which the dominant part (the Council) is at best only indirectly elected and whose activities have been in need of greater transparency. Although it has been said that 'neither the Council nor Parliament is capable, on its own, of assuring a satisfactory level of democratic accountability, in the complex political nexus of a constitutional order of States',[220] it remains to be seen how far the important Lisbon reforms will in practice extend the principles of liberal democracy into this important arena, while at the same time ensuring a greater degree of parliamentary accountability on the part of those who represent the United Kingdom in the process. Third, there is the matter of the constitutional

---

[215] *Cases C-397–403/01, Pfeiffer v Deutches Roles Kreuz, Kreisverband Waldshut eV*, above.

[216] *McCall v Poulton* [2008] EWCA Civ 1313; [2009] 1 CMLR 1239.

[217] *Case C-63/01, Evans v Secretary of State for Environment, Transport and the Regions* [2003] ECR I-4447. See S Drake (2005) 30 EL Rev 329.

[218] Cf J Eekelaar (1997) 113 LQR 185 and T R S Allan (1997) LQR 443.

[219] On some of the wider implications of this, see S Douglas-Scott (2001) 12 KCLJ 75, MacCormick, *Questioning Sovereignty*, and Weiler, *The Constitution of Europe*. Also J C Piris (1999) 24 EL Rev 557.

[220] A Dashwood (2001) 26 EL Rev 215, 220.

base on which the whole enterprise is constructed. Although constitutional dogma has been shaken,[221] the problem of sovereignty has not been adequately resolved; it is, however, unlikely that everyone would agree now with the view expressed in 1972 that 'the ultimate supremacy of Parliament will not be affected, and it will not be affected because it cannot be affected'.[222] The problem has been fudged rather than resolved, though it has yet to be established whether these are problems of any practical significance and, if so, whether closer European union can continue to be built on such foundations.

---

[221] See *Thoburn v Sunderland City Council*, pp 140–41 above.
[222] HC Deb, 5 July 1972, col 627. See also HL Deb, 7 August 1972, col 911.

Part II

THE INSTITUTIONS OF GOVERNMENT

CHAPTER 9

Composition and meeting of Parliament

In this and the next two chapters, we examine the structure of Parliament, the functions of the two Houses and their privileges. Although both the House of Commons and the House of Lords meet in the palace of Westminster, they sit separately and are constituted on entirely different principles. The process of legislation is a matter in which both Houses take part and the two-chamber structure is an integral feature of the parliamentary system. Within Parliament the House of Commons is the dominant House, as it is on the ability to command a majority in the Commons that a government depends for holding office. Under the Parliament Acts of 1911 and 1949, the formal power of the Lords in legislation is limited to imposing a temporary veto on public Bills, a power which may sometimes be an effective check on controversial legislation. The role of the Lords as a revising chamber is important, especially for securing amendments to Bills which have been subjected to timetabling in the Commons,[1] and the House serves other constitutional purposes. The Queen is formally also part of Parliament: she opens each session of Parliament and the royal assent is necessary for primary legislation. These functions are performed on the advice of the government, but in very rare circumstances the Queen may have a personal discretion to exercise in relation to Parliament.

A. The electoral system

Before 1918 the right to vote was largely dependent on the ownership or occupation of property. It was also affected by the ancient distinction between counties and boroughs. For more than five centuries after Simon de Montfort's Parliament of 1265, the English people were represented in the Commons by two knights from every county and by two burgesses from every borough. Before the Reform Act of 1832 the franchise was exercisable in the counties by those men who owned freehold land worth 40 shillings per year. In the boroughs, the franchise varied according to the charter of the borough and to local custom. In fact, many seats in the House before 1832 were controlled by members of the landowning aristocracy who had sufficient influence by purchasing votes or other means to nominate the successful candidates. In Scotland 'the principle of representation', according to 'ancient rules', was said to depend on 'the payment of direct taxes; and those who were excluded from voting for representatives, or from the privilege of being elected, were such persons only as, while they shared in the benefits and protection afforded by the government, contributed nothing directly towards the expense of upholding it'.[2] Such people could nevertheless be expected to share in other obligations of the state, such as military service in war. Acts for widening the franchise were passed in 1832, 1867, 1884, 1918, 1928, 1948 and 1969, until today the total electorate is over 44 million. The details of the earlier Acts have passed into history. In 1918 a uniform franchise based on residence was established for county and borough constituencies.[3] Votes for women over 30 were introduced in 1918 and in 1928 for women over 21. The voting age for men and women is now 18, and it is sometimes suggested that

---

[1] Ch 10 A.

[2] More, *Lectures on the Law of Scotland*, vol II, pp 214–15.

[3] See Butler, *The Electoral System in Britain since 1918* and, for the law and practice today, Price, De Silva and Clayton (eds), *Parker's Law and Conduct of Elections*; also Blackburn, *The Electoral System in Britain*, Rawlings, *Law and the Electoral Process*, and Watt, *UK Election Law*.

it should be lowered still further to 16. After 1918 various categories of person had the right to vote more than once either by reason of occupying land for business purposes or because of the right of graduates to vote in separate constituencies representing the universities. These elements of plural voting were abolished in 1948.

The franchise

The law is now contained in Part I of the Representation of the People Act 1983,[4] which consolidated earlier legislation and which has itself been amended, notably in 1985 when the right to vote was extended to certain British citizens resident outside the United Kingdom.[5] As amended in 2000, s 1 of the 1983 Act provides that the right to vote at parliamentary elections is exercisable by all Commonwealth citizens (which in law includes all British citizens and British subjects),[6] and citizens of the Republic of Ireland who are (a) registered in the register of electors for the constituency in which they wish to vote; (b) not subject to any legal incapacity to vote (on which see below); and (c) of voting age (now 18 years or over).[7] Under the 1983 Act a person is entitled to be registered in a constituency if he or she is resident there and is otherwise entitled to vote.[8] There is not now a qualifying period of residence before an elector may register in a particular constituency (except in Northern Ireland where the elector must be resident in the Province – not necessarily a particular constituency – for at least three months);[9] and it is no longer necessary to be resident in the constituency on a particular date (which until the 2000 amendments used to be 10 October, which was referred to as the qualifying date).

The meaning of residence for electoral purposes is governed by the 1983 Act, s 5 (as amended). This provides rather enigmatically that in determining whether someone is resident in a particular constituency, 'regard shall be had, in particular, to the purpose and other circumstances, as well as to the fact, of his presence at, or absence from, the address on that date'. A person who is staying at one place otherwise than on a permanent basis may be taken to be resident there if he or she has no home elsewhere, or not resident there if he or she does have a home elsewhere.[10] Residence is not to be taken as interrupted by reason of an absence 'in the performance of any duty arising from or incidental to any office, service or employment'; and for this purpose a temporary absence for educational purposes may be treated in the same way as a temporary absence for the performance of an aforementioned duty.[11] This means that students living away from home may register in their home constituencies or in the constituency where they are studying.[12] Specific provision is made for the registration of patients in mental hospitals, remand

---

[4] The Act has been heavily amended since enactment, notably by the Representation of the People Act 2000, the Political Parties, Elections and Referendums Act 2000, the Electoral Administration Act 2006, and the Political Parties and Elections Act 2009. Although the amendments are taken in below, the specific sources of the amendments are not identified.

[5] Representation of the People Act 1985, s 1; amended by the Political Parties, Elections and Referendums Act 2000 (PPERA), s 141, reducing from 20 to 15 years the period during which British citizens formerly resident in this country may continue to be registered to vote.

[6] See British Nationality Act 1981, s 37; see ch 20 A below.

[7] Representation of the People Act 1983 (RPA), s 1.

[8] Ibid, s 4 (as amended).

[9] Ibid.

[10] RPA, s 5(2) (as amended). See *Scott v Phillips* 1974 SLT 32 (ownership of a country cottage as a second home is not enough to make the owner resident there if, on the facts, the owner's use of it is incidental to the owner's main home); and *Hipperson v Newbury Registration Officer* [1985] QB 1060 (Greenham Common women resident in peace camp for electoral purposes).

[11] RPA, s 5(3), (5).

[12] See (on the law as it was before the Representation of the People Act 2000), *Fox v Stirk* [1970] 2 QB 463.

prisoners and homeless people.[13] In the case of the last, a homeless person may make a 'declaration of local connection' which enables him or her to be registered in the constituency where he or she 'commonly spends a substantial part' of his or her time. A person may be resident at more than one address and may be entered on the register for more than one constituency. But no one may vote more than once as an elector at a parliamentary election.[14]

The parliamentary franchise may not be exercised by:

(a) persons who are subject to legal incapacity (such as those who because of mental illness, drunkenness or infirmity lack the capacity at the moment of voting to understand what they are about to do);[15]

(b) persons who are neither Commonwealth citizens nor citizens of the Republic of Ireland;[16]

(c) persons who have not attained the age of 18 by the date of the poll;[17]

(d) persons convicted of a criminal offence and detained in a penal institution in pursuance of a sentence.[18] Remand prisoners may vote if they are on the register, and at the general election in 2005 prisoners who were part of an intermittent custody scheme were also permitted to vote;[19]

(e) persons detained in mental hospitals under statutory authority, including the Mental Health Act 1983 and the Criminal Procedure (Insanity) Act 1964;[20]

(f) persons who are members of the House of Lords. Hereditary peers were previously disqualified; but they may now vote in a parliamentary election unless they have retained a place in the Lords by virtue of the House of Lords Act 1999;[21]

(g) persons convicted of corrupt or illegal practices at elections, the extent of disqualification depending on the nature of the offence.[22]

The most controversial of these disqualifications is (d): it is not clear why convicted prisoners should be denied the right to vote.[23] Although the domestic courts held that the restriction did not breach the Human Rights Act,[24] in *Hirst v United Kingdom (No 2)*[25] the Strasbourg court found that the blanket disqualification of convicted prisoners breached art 3 of the First Protocol to the Convention, noting that it applied automatically irrespective of the length of the prisoner's sentence, and irrespective of the nature and gravity of the offence.[26] But the government has been extremely slow to implement this decision, and at the time of writing the disqualification of prisoners remains in force.

---

[13] RPA, ss 7, 7A and 7B (as amended).

[14] RPA, s 1(2) (as amended).

[15] RPA, s 1(1)(b) (as amended). Nor may anyone vote on behalf of someone disqualified for lack of capacity: Mental Capacity Act 2005, s 29.

[16] RPA, s 1(1)(c) (as amended). Citizens of the European Union resident in the UK may vote and stand in local government elections and in elections to the European Parliament: see SI 1995 No 1948 and SI 1994 No 342.

[17] RPA Act, s 1(1)(d) (as amended).

[18] Ibid, s 3.

[19] On which see RPA, s 7A (as amended).

[20] Ibid, s 3A (as amended).

[21] House of Lords Act 1999, s 3.

[22] RPA, ss 160, 173.

[23] For the position in Canada, see *Sauve v Canada (No 1)* [1992] 2 SCR 438, and *Sauve v Canada (No 2)* [2002] SCR 519.

[24] *R (Pearson) v Home Secretary*, The Times, 17 April 2001.

[25] Application No 74025/01.

[26] *Hirst v United Kingdom (No 2)* (2005) BHRR 441. See also *Smith v Scott* 2007 SLT 137 (declaration of incompatibility re RPA, s 3).

The register of electors

As already pointed out, it is a condition precedent to exercising the vote that the elector should be entered in the register of electors. The register is prepared by the registration officer of each constituency, who in England and Wales is appointed by each district council or London borough.[27] Each registration officer is required to conduct an annual canvass of the area to determine who is entitled to be on the register, and is required to take all necessary steps to maintain the register in what continues to be a system of household voter registration.[28] The canvass for any year is to be conducted by reference to residence on 15 October and a revised version of the register must then be published after the annual canvass by 1 December each year.[29] But it is also possible for an elector to be added to the register between annual canvasses. The amendments to the Representation of the People Act 1983 in 2000 introduced the principle of the 'rolling register', designed to remove obstacles to registration and voting. We have thus moved from what was referred to as a 'fixed register' (amended annually) to a 'rolling register' (amended constantly): the former may be said to be more sensitive to the needs of the administration responsible for maintaining the register; and the latter more responsive to the interests of electors.

Under the arrangements now in place, an elector may apply to be registered at any time and the registration officer must issue alterations to the register at regular intervals.[30] So if someone moves house, for example, it is now possible to register immediately in a new constituency without the need to wait for the annual canvass. But in order to be effective for an election, a new registration must normally take effect at a prescribed time before the poll, a measure which can be justified as a device to prevent electoral fraud and for administrative convenience.[31] Detailed arrangements for registration are made by regulations.[32] If the registration officer's decision including or excluding someone from the register is disputed, an appeal lies to the county court (in Scotland to the sheriff court) and thence on a point of law to the Court of Appeal (in Scotland to the Electoral Registration Court of three judges).[33] The decision of the county court may also be reviewed on jurisdictional grounds.[34] It is the practice for electoral registers to be made available by registration officers to third parties, such as political parties for canvassing and other electoral purposes and companies which engage in direct mailing and telesales.[35] The 2000 amendments permit regulations to be made requiring registration officers to compile a full and an edited register,[36] and electors are permitted to have their names and addresses withheld from the latter.[37]

---

[27] RPA, s 8.

[28] Ibid, ss 9, 9A, 10 (as amended). Powers to move gradually to a system of individual voter registration (thought to be superior for dealing with fraud) are to be found in the Political Parties and Elections Act 2009, ss 30–33.

[29] Ibid, s 13 (as amended).

[30] Ibid, s 13A (as amended).

[31] Ibid, s 13B (as amended).

[32] See SI 2001 No 341, regs 23–49.

[33] RPA, ss 56–8. Additions or alterations to the register may be ordered by the High Court: R v Hammond, ex parte Nottingham Council, The Times, 10 October 1974. For Scotland, see John Ferguson 1965 SC 16.

[34] R v Hurst, ex p Smith [1960] 2 QB 133.

[35] It was held in R (Robertson) v Wakefield DC [2001] EWHC 915 (Admin), [2002] QB 1052 that the disclosure of this information containing personal details of electors is contrary to EC Directive 95/46/EC, as well as the Human Rights Act 1998 (ECHR, art 8 and First Protocol, art 3).

[36] RPA, Sch 2(10)–(11) (as amended).

[37] SI 2002 No 1871.

Conduct of elections

Normally voting takes place in person at a convenient polling station allotted by the returning officer.[38] But there are circumstances in which absent voting may take place, the term absent voting meaning voting by proxy or by post. The Representation of the People Act 2000 relaxed the rules with the aim of enabling more people to vote by post if they so wish. Under the existing rules, the registration officer must grant an application to vote by post if satisfied that the elector is registered,[39] and otherwise meets prescribed statutory requirements.[40] The registration officer must also grant an application to vote by proxy where the applicant is a registered service voter, blind or suffers another physical disability; is unable to attend the polling station because of work or educational commitments; or unable to go to the polling station in person without making a journey by sea or air (as in the case of overseas voters).[41] In order to increase voter turnout,[42] pilot schemes for voting by postal ballot only were introduced at the European and local government elections in 2004.[43] But the increased use of postal voting has been controversial. Apart from the failures of the postal system,[44] it has given rise to concerns about irregularity and fraud.[45] Nevertheless, at the election in 2005, some 27.1 million votes were cast, including 3.9 million postal votes which were accepted. The proceedings at parliamentary elections are to be conducted in accordance with the Parliamentary Elections Rules in Schedule 1 of the 1983 Act. These detailed rules deal with the nomination of candidates, as well as the procedure to be followed at the polling station and in particular help to ensure the secrecy of the ballot.[46]

Responsibility for the official conduct of an election in each constituency rests with the returning officer, who in England and Wales in the case of a county constituency wholly contained within the area of a county council is the sheriff, and in the case of a borough constituency wholly contained within a local government district is the chairman of the district council.[47] Most functions of the returning officer are, however, discharged by the registration officer or by an appointed deputy. Certain matters, for example the declaration of the poll, may be reserved for the returning officer. The official costs of an election, as distinct from the expenses of the candidates, are paid out of public funds in accordance with a scale prescribed by the Treasury. In the past, office-holders who conducted elections did not always exercise their functions impartially. In the great case of *Ashby* v *White*, the Mayor of Aylesbury as returning officer wrongfully refused to allow Ashby to vote and Ashby sued him for damages. The House of Lords upheld the view of Chief Justice Holt (dissenting in the Queen's Bench) that the remedy of damages should be given. In Holt's words: 'To allow this action will make public officers more careful to observe the constitution of cities and boroughs, and not to be so partial as they commonly are in all elections.'[48] Today, officials concerned with the conduct of elections are required to carry out their duties impartially and are subject to criminal penalties if they do not, but they cannot be sued for damages if breach of official duty is alleged.[49]

---

[38] RPA, Sch 1(25).

[39] Representation of the People Act 2000, Sch 4(3).

[40] SI 2001 No 341, Part IV.

[41] Representation of the People Act 2000, Sch 4(3).

[42] At the general election in 2005, only 61% of those eligible to vote did so, compared with 59% in 2001.

[43] European Parliamentary and Local Elections (Pilots) Act 2004. For previous pilots see H Lardy [2003] PL 6.

[44] *Knight* v *Nicholls* [2004] EWCA Civ 68, [2004] 1 WLR 1653 (election not invalidated by late arrival of voting papers).

[45] See *R (Afzal)* v *Election Court* [2005] EWCA (Civ) 647. A number of anti-fraud measures were introduced by the Electoral Administration Act 2006, s 14.

[46] Also RPA, s 66.

[47] Ibid, s 24(1).

[48] (1703) 2 Ld Raym 938, 956.

[49] RPA, s 63.

B. Distribution of constituencies

Before 1832, the unreformed House of Commons was composed on the general principle that every county and borough in England and Wales was entitled to be represented by two members. A similar principle applied to Scottish representation at Westminster, subject to the limit of numbers imposed in the Treaty of Union, which led to the grouping of certain shires and royal burghs for this purpose. Representation thus depended on the status of the unit of local government and bore no regard to population. Counties such as Cornwall, which contained many tiny boroughs, were grossly over-represented by comparison with areas of rapidly growing industrial population. From the Reform Act 1832 onwards, successive measures of redistributing constituencies to remove glaring differences were undertaken, usually at the same time as reforms in the franchise were made.[50] Only since 1917 has there been general acceptance of the principle of broad mathematical equality in the size of constituencies,[51] and only since 1945 has there been permanent machinery to enable boundaries to be adjusted from time to time to take account of the shifting population and to avoid excessive disparities developing between constituencies. The legislation has sought to establish impartial machinery, but in practice the system has not operated without controversy. The system does not try to achieve strict arithmetical equality between constituencies, but lays emphasis also on the territorial aspect of representation, on the link between the elected member and his or her constituency, and on the desirability of parliamentary boundaries not clashing with local government boundaries. The degree of discretion built into the system of electoral apportionment makes it particularly necessary to ensure that the machinery is impartial and charges of gerrymandering are avoided. As the late Aneurin Bevan once said, there was 'nothing that could undermine the authority of Parliament more than that people outside should feel that the constitutional mechanism by which the House of Commons is elected has been framed so as to favour one party in the State'.[52]

Boundary review

By the Parliamentary Constituencies Act 1986, which consolidated the former House of Commons (Redistribution of Seats) Acts 1949 and 1958, there are four permanent boundary commissions, for England, Wales, Scotland and Northern Ireland. These commissions are 'independent, non-political, and impartial' bodies which 'emphasise that the results of previous elections do not, and should not, enter into [their] considerations'.[53] The Speaker is the chairman of each commission, but in practice does not sit, and a judge from the appropriate High Court (in Scotland, from the Court of Session) is appointed deputy chairman of each commission. Each commission includes two other members, those for England being appointed by ministers, as well as two official assessors, those for England being the Registrar General and the Director General of Ordnance Survey. The commissions must undertake a general review of constituencies in that part of the United Kingdom assigned to them, at intervals of not less than ten or more than 15 years (reduced in 1992 to an interval of from eight to 12 years);[54] changes in particular constituencies may be proposed from time to time when necessary. Notice must be given to the constituencies affected by any provisional recommendations. If objections are received from an interested local authority or from a body of at least 100 electors, a local inquiry must be held into the recommendations. Having received a report on the inquiries, a commission must submit its report to the Secretary of State. The 1986 Act, by s 3(5), imposes a duty on the Secretary of

---

[50] Butler note 3 above, app II.
[51] Report of Speaker's Conference, Cd 8463, 1917; Report of Committee on Electoral Machinery, Cmd 6408, 1943.
[52] HC Deb, 15 December 1954, col 1872.
[53] Boundary Commission for England, *Annual Report 2008/2009* (2009), p 4.
[54] Boundary Commissions Act 1992.

State, 'as soon as may be after a Boundary Commission has submitted a report', to lay the report before Parliament together with a draft Order in Council for giving effect, with or without modifications, to the recommendations in the report (reasons must be given to Parliament for any modifications). The draft Order must be approved by resolution of each House before the final Order can be made by the Queen in Council. The validity of any Order in Council which purports to be made under the 1986 Act and recites that approval was given by each House is not to be called into question in any legal proceedings.[55]

The 1986 Act contains the rules which the commissions must observe in redistributing seats. Wales must be represented by not fewer than 35 seats, Northern Ireland by between 16 and 18 seats, and Great Britain by 'not substantially greater or less than 613'.[56] Following devolution, it is no longer the case that Scotland must be represented by at least 71 seats,[57] and in 2005 Scottish representation at Westminster was reduced from 72 to 59,[58] in the process reducing the number of seats in the House of Commons from 659 to 646. The legislation provides for the calculation of a separate electoral quota for each of England, Scotland, Wales and Northern Ireland, the quota to be determined by dividing the total electorate by the number of constituencies at the time the review begins. Each commission must secure that the electorate of a constituency shall be as near the relevant electoral quota as is practicable, having regard to certain other rules, for example, that parliamentary constituencies shall as far as practicable not cross certain local government boundaries. Strict application of these principles may be departed from if special geographical considerations make it desirable; and account must be taken of inconveniences that may follow the alteration of constituencies and of local ties that might be broken by alteration. The commissions thus have a broad discretion to decide how much priority should be given to achieving arithmetical equality between constituencies.[59]

Boundary review in practice

General reviews were completed by the four boundary commissions in 1954, 1969, 1982, 1994 and 2006. In 1954 the review resulted in the abolition of six constituencies and the creation of 11 new ones, all in England, to bring membership of the House up to 630. As well as other difficulties experienced by the English commission,[60] the method of calculating the electoral quota for England under the 1949 Act resulted in the draft Orders in Council being challenged in the courts. In *Harper* v *Home Secretary*,[61] however, the Court of Appeal expressed reluctance to interfere in these matters, though such intervention was not ruled out where the commissions had made recommendations manifestly in complete disregard of the Act, which was not the position in this case. In 1954 the government gave effect without modification to the recommendations of the four commissions. But events took a different turn in 1969 when the next general review was completed. The commission for England proposed major changes to 271 constituencies and five new constituencies for England. At the time the commissions submitted their reports, a radical reorganisation of local government in England (outside Greater London) and in Wales was in train and the Labour government decided that revision of parliamentary boundaries should wait until local government had been reorganised. The government therefore delayed laying the commissions' reports in Parliament and instead introduced a Bill which gave effect

---

[55] 1986 Act, s 4(7).
[56] Ibid, Sch 2.
[57] Scotland Act 1998, s 86.
[58] SI 2005 No 250 (S1).
[59] *R v Boundary Commission for England, ex p Foot* [1983] QB 600.
[60] D E Butler (1955) 33 *Public Administration* 125.
[61] [1955] Ch 238, 251. See also Marshall and Moodie, *Some Problems of the Constitution*, ch 5; and S A de Smith (1955) 18 MLR 281.

only to the changes affecting Greater London and a few abnormally large constituencies elsewhere. The government thus sought by legislation to depart from its obligations under the Acts of 1949 and 1958.

The Bill passed the Commons against severe criticism but was drastically amended by the Lords and was abandoned by the government when in October 1969 that House refused to give way to the Commons. An elector for the borough of Enfield then sought an order of mandamus from the High Court requiring the Home Secretary to perform his statutory duty of laying before Parliament the commission reports together with draft Orders in Council.[62] Thereupon the Home Secretary laid before Parliament the reports and the draft Orders in Council, but invited the Commons to reject them, using the government majority for this purpose. By this tangled course of events, the Labour government succeeded in postponing the much needed adjustments of constituency boundaries until after the 1970 general election, following which the new Conservative government promptly secured parliamentary approval to the changes recommended in 1969. Some MPs complained that Parliament had fettered its hands by setting up the boundary commissions and argued that Parliament must retain the right to make the final decisions. But the Conservative Home Secretary considered it 'enormously important' that Parliament comply with the impartial recommendations of the four commissions.[63] In 1983 the general review again led to extensive changes in constituencies, with seats in Great Britain being increased by ten and the total in the House rising to 650. The Labour party leader challenged the English changes in the High Court, but with no success.[64] The review which was completed in 1994 increased the number of seats in England from 524 to 529 and the total in the Commons to 659.[65]

The evolving framework

The review of the Scottish constituencies completed in 2004 led to a reduction in the number of Scottish seats in the House of Commons, and a reduction of the total number of seats to 646. In terms of population, Scotland had been heavily over-represented at Westminster before devolution. Although the impact of the change was felt most keenly by the Labour party, the changes enjoyed a cross-party consensus, and were implemented in full (and without modification) in time for the general election in 2005.[66] Despite the impact of the changes on safe Labour seats, the government (which was the author of the need for change in the Scotland Act 1998) was able to take a principled stand on the independence of the commission coupled with the latter's 'considerable thoroughness' and 'systematic analysis'.[67] The changes did, however, have implications for the Scottish Parliament with its 73 constituencies based on the Westminster constituencies which existed at the time of devolution.[68] Although it was anticipated at the time of devolution that the size of the Scottish Parliament might be reduced in line with the reduced number of Westminster seats, there were second thoughts in Scotland about this, and a desire to retain the existing composition of the Scottish Parliament with 73 constituency and 56 regional members. As a result the Scottish Parliament (Constituencies) Act 2004 provides that the constituencies for the Scottish Parliament should continue to be based on the Westminster constituencies in force

---

[62] *R v Home Secretary, ex p McWhirter, The Times*, 21 October 1969. The application was dismissed in view of the Home Secretary's action in October 1969 in laying the reports and draft Orders in Parliament.

[63] HC Deb, 28 October 1970, col 241 ff.

[64] *R v Boundary Commission for England, ex p Foot* [1983] QB 600.

[65] The boundary commission reports for England (HC 433–i (1994–95)), Scotland and Wales were implemented by SI 1995 Nos 1626, 1037 and 1036, and took effect at the 1997 election.

[66] SI 2005 No 250 (S1).

[67] First Standing Committee on Delegated Legislation, 24 January 2005 (Ms Anne McGuire). Also HL Deb, 1 February 2005, col 179.

[68] Scotland Act 1998, Sch 1.

in 1998,[69] with separate representation for Orkney and Shetland. This means that the constituency boundaries for the Scottish Parliament are now different from the constituency boundaries for the Westminster Parliament.

The fifth boundary reviews for England and Wales (started in 2000 and completed in 2006) were also given effect without modification.[70] As a result of the recommendations of the Boundary Commission for England,[71] four additional seats have been created, increasing the size of the House of Commons to 650 after the general election in 2010. It had been expected that the fifth review would have been the last to be conducted by the Boundary Commissions, with the Political Parties, Elections and Referendums Act 2000 providing for the transfer of this function to the Electoral Commission.[72] Under these proposed arrangements, only an Electoral Commissioner or a deputy Electoral Commissioner would have been able to participate, thereby removing the judicial role in the process of boundary review. In an examination of the Electoral Commission by the Committee on Standards in Public Life in 2007, it was recommended that this plan be aborted and that the legislation providing for the transfer of functions be repealed, proposals duly implemented by the Local Democracy, Economic Development and Construction Act 2009. According to the Committee on Standards in Public Life, the existing system was 'demonstrably impartial and independent',[73] and appeared to work well, at a time when there was concern about the effectiveness of the Electoral Commission.[74] There is much to be said for retaining the status quo, not least because it has also managed to avoid the problem of persistent judicial review of Boundary Commission recommendations. Unlike in the United States where electoral redistricting is much more contentious,[75] the process of boundary review in the United Kingdom is more likely to be blocked in the House of Commons than to be set aside by the courts, though the fifth review was largely uncontroversial.

C. Political parties

Central to the role of modern democracy are political parties: they provide the policies and personnel of government (and opposition) and have other important functions as well.[76] Although electors vote for individuals to represent them in Parliament, the candidates will typically be chosen by a political party. It is unusual for a candidate who is not representing one of the established parties to be elected to Parliament,[77] or for an independent to be elected.[78] The parties also dominate appointments to the House of Lords. Yet political parties remain voluntary associations in the eyes of the law: bodies exercising a public function but governed by private law.[79] The

---

[69] These are to be found in SI 1995 No 1037.

[70] See Cm 7032, 2007 (England) and HC 743-1 (2005–06) (Wales); SI 2007 No 1681 (England), and SI 2006 No 1041; SI 2008 No 1791 (Wales).

[71] Cm 7032, 2007, para 6.1.

[72] Political Parties, Elections and Referendums Act 2000, ss 14–20, Sch 3 (now repealed, see below).

[73] Cm 7006, 2007, para 2.108.

[74] See Sir Hayden Phillips, *Strengthening Democracy: Fair and Sustainable Funding of Political Parties* (2007).

[75] *Baker v Carr*, 369 US 186 (1962), *Reynolds v Sims*, 377 US 533 (1964). On the contemporary position in the United States, see S Issacharoff (2002) 116 Harv L Rev 593, and S Issacharoff and P S Karlen (2004) 153 *University of Pennsylvania Law Review* 541.

[76] See Fisher, *British Political Parties*, pp 194–9, and Webb, *The Modern British Party System*.

[77] In 2001 and again in 2005 a seat was won by a party registered as the Independent Hospital and Health Concern, while in 2005 a seat was won by a new party called Respect.

[78] In 1997 the broadcaster Martin Bell was famously elected as an independent for Tatton, while in 2005 Peter Law was elected as an independent for Blaenau Gwent.

[79] But see on the special and complex position of the Conservative party, *Conservative and Unionist Central Office* v *Burrell* [1982] 2 All ER 1.

relationship between a political party and its members is one based on contract and the contract may be enforced in the courts by an aggrieved member. Cases arise from time to time from individuals who claim to have been expelled from a party in breach of the rules, and from individuals challenging the procedures for the selection of a party's candidate for election to public office.[80] In one case it was held that all-women shortlists for the selection of parliamentary candidates were contrary to the Sex Discrimination Act 1975.[81] These shortlists had been introduced by the Labour party for the selection of some candidates in order to increase the number of women MPs, and the practice was restored following the Sex Discrimination (Election Candidates) Act 2002. Otherwise, however, discrimination by political parties in the selection of candidates is likely to be unlawful under both the Sex Discrimination Act 1975 and the Race Relations Act 1976.[82]

Registration of political parties

Provision for the registration of political parties was first made in 1998[83] and is now to be found in the Political Parties, Elections and Referendums Act 2000.[84] Registration was first introduced in anticipation of the elections to the European Parliament for which a new electoral system was introduced by the European Elections Act 1999. This was known as a party list system whereby members are elected from large regional constituencies in proportion to the votes cast in favour of the different parties in the region in question. For this system to work effectively it was thought that only registered political parties should take part. Registration is now important for other reasons. Only candidates representing a registered party may be nominated for election; other candidates must be nominated as independents or without description.[85] This overcomes an irritant of British elections whereby individuals would present themselves in a manner which was calculated to confuse electors, as in one case where a candidate stood as a Literal Democrat.[86] The other principal reason why registration is important relates to party political broadcasts which broadcasters may carry only if made by registered parties.[87]

It is important to stress that registration of political parties is not compulsory, but that it is necessary in order to enjoy a number of prescribed benefits. There is no definition of a political party for this purpose, with registration being open to any party that declares that it intends to contest one or more 'relevant elections' in Great Britain or Northern Ireland.[88] There are separate registers for Great Britain and Northern Ireland. A party seeking registration must register its principal office-holders (including its leader and treasurer) and its financial structure.[89] The latter obligation is in pursuance of a requirement that the parties adopt a scheme approved by the Electoral Commission which 'sets out the arrangements for regulating the financial affairs of the party'.[90] An application must be made to the Electoral Commission and must be granted unless the proposed name (i) is the same (or sufficiently similar to cause confusion) as that of a party already registered; (ii) comprises more than six words; (iii) is obscene or offensive; (iv) includes

---

[80] *Lewis v Heffer* [1978] 1 WLR 1061; *Weir v Hermon* [2001] NIJB 260; *Mortimer v Labour Party, The Independent*, 28 February 2000; and *Donaldson v Empey* [2004] NIJB 1.

[81] *Jepson v Labour Party* [1996] IRLR 116.

[82] *Ahsan v Watt* [2007] UKHL 51; [2008] AC 696.

[83] Registration of Political Parties Act 1998; for comment, see O Gay [2001] PL 245.

[84] For a fuller account of the Act (hereafter PPERA), see K D Ewing [2001] PL 542.

[85] PPERA, ss 22 and 28.

[86] *Sanders v Chichester* (1994) SJ 225.

[87] PPERA, s 37.

[88] Ibid, ss 22 and 28.

[89] Ibid, ss 24–7.

[90] Ibid, s 26(2). Where the party is composed of a number of separate 'accounting units' (such as the headquarters and each constituency party or association, as is the practice with the main parties), the treasurer of each accounting unit must also be registered (s 27).

words which if published would be likely to amount to the commission of an offence; (v) includes any script other than Roman; or (vi) includes any words or expression prohibited by order made by the Secretary of State.[91] A registered party may also register three emblems to be used on ballot papers.[92] At the general election in 2005, no fewer than 113 registered parties fielded a total of 3,550 candidates.[93]

Funding of political parties

The funding of political parties has been a constant source of controversy.[94] The obligations of parties are such that it is not possible for them to rely on the subscriptions of members alone. Concern is frequently expressed about large private donations to political parties, which are sometimes associated with allegations of corruption.[95] The Political Parties, Elections and Referendums Act 2000 imposes obligations of transparency on political party funding and restricts the sources of party funding. The Act was passed to implement the recommendations of the Committee on Standards in Public Life,[96] the terms of reference of which were extended in 1997 to enable it to investigate party funding following a number of incidents involving both the Conservative party and the Labour party. All donations to a political party in excess of £7,500 nationally, and £1,500 locally must be reported to the Electoral Commission on a quarterly basis,[97] with the names of donors and the amount of donation published by the Electoral Commission.[98] Donations may only be received from a permissible donor, defined to mean individuals who are on the electoral register in this country or organisations (such as companies and trade unions) that are based here and conduct business and activity here.[99] The aim is to stop the foreign funding of British political parties, although as we have seen it is possible to be resident overseas and yet be on the electoral register, while it is also possible to be a resident in the UK and yet not be on the electoral register.[100]

A major political storm broke early in 2006 relating to the funding of political parties, when the Labour and Conservative parties were forced to reveal that they had accepted secret loans to finance their general election campaigns in 2005. In the case of the Labour party, 12 wealthy businessmen had loaned just under £14 million, while the Conservatives revealed loans of just under £16 million from 12 individuals and one company, and repaid another £5 million to anonymous lenders who did not wish publicly to be identified. The Liberal Democrats also admitted to having received loans, though on a much smaller scale. Apart from the secrecy of the loans, allegations were made that loans to the Labour party in particular had been made in

---

[91] Ibid, s 28(4).

[92] Ibid, s 29.

[93] But of these 62 fielded candidates in only one constituency. See www.psr.keele.ac.uk.

[94] See Ewing, *The Funding of Political Parties in Britain*, Ewing, *The Cost of Democracy*, and Pinto-Duschinsky, *British Political Finance 1830–1980*.

[95] Under the Honours (Prevention of Abuses) Act 1925 it is an offence to make or receive a donation in return for an honour. But the problems of proof are overwhelming.

[96] Cm 4057, 1998. See L Klein (1999) 31 *Case Western Reserve Journal of International Law* 1.

[97] PPERA, ss 62, 63. Before the changes made by the Political Parties and Elections Act 2009, the reporting thresholds were £5,000 and £1,000 respectively.

[98] Ibid, ss 69, 149. The information is made available by the Electoral Commission on its website: www.electoralcommission.org.uk. It is possible to track the main donors to the parties. The information is also reported in the press on a quarterly basis.

[99] PPERA, s 54. Additional restrictions were introduced by the Political Parties and Elections Act 2009 (ss 10, 11) prohibiting donations (and loans) from persons not resident in the United Kingdom for income tax purposes (so-called 'non-doms').

[100] *R (Electoral Commission)* v *City of Westminster Magistrates' Court and UKIP* [2009] EWCA Civ 1078, where it was also held that the forfeiture of impermissible donations under PPERA, s 58 does not constitute a breach of convention rights.

return for the promise of a peerage; indeed, four of the lenders were nominated for peerages without the House of Lords Appointments Commission being informed of the loans. Three of the nominees were vetoed by the Commission on other grounds; a fourth was rejected when the Commission was made aware of the undisclosed loan. The 'cash for honours' affair sparked a highly controversial police investigation into whether there had been a breach of the Honours (Prevention of Abuses) Act 1925 or the Political Parties, Elections and Referendums Act 2000. Although there were no prosecutions under either Act, the affair did, however, lead to (i) a change in the law, so that political parties must (under the Electoral Administration Act 2006) now report loans as well as donations to the Electoral Commission, and perhaps to (ii) a more active approach by the Commission in its supervision of the political parties.

State support for political parties

In many countries, political parties receive annual subventions of public funds to enable them more effectively to perform their functions without the need for excessive reliance on wealthy private donors.[101] In other countries the parties are assisted by the provision of income tax relief for donations to political parties, designed to encourage more people to make small donations. A scheme for public funding of political parties was proposed by the Houghton committee in 1976 but never implemented;[102] and proposals by the Committee on Standards in Public Life (Neill committee) in 1998 for income tax relief for small contributions to political parties were rejected by the government.[103] Media disquiet about large donations to the parties has revived interest in public funding, to relieve the parties of the need to rely on such donations. But the case for public funding of political parties was rejected by the Electoral Commission in 2004, mainly for lack of public support and because of opposition from the two main parties.[104] Nevertheless, fresh proposals for public funding of political parties were made several years later by Sir Hayden Phillips, a retired civil servant who had been appointed by the then Prime Minister to look at the matter again in the light of the 'cash for honours' crisis. But although producing a well thought out scheme,[105] like others before him Sir Hayden was unable to secure all-party agreement for his proposals. At a time of public funding cuts, financial support for political parties is unlikely to be a popular priority for any government in the near future.

This is not to say that there is no state support for political parties in Britain, although it is limited when compared to some other countries. Parliamentary candidates are provided with free postage for one election communication and are permitted to use school halls for election meetings free of charge.[106] Free time is made available to the political parties for party political broadcasts and party election broadcasts by both the BBC and the independent broadcasters, a facility which in the latter case exists as a matter of legal obligation.[107] The amount of time made available for the parties is determined by the broadcasters in consultation with the parties.[108] Finally, public money is made available to the opposition parties in Parliament to assist them in the performance of their parliamentary activities;[109] and a relatively small sum of money (£2m)

---

[101] Ewing (ed.), *The Funding of Political Parties: Europe and Beyond* (chapters on France, Spain, Italy and Japan), and Ewing and Issacharoff (eds) *Party Funding and Campaign Financing in International Perspective* (chapters on New Zealand, Australia, Canada, United States and Japan).

[102] Cmnd 6601, 1976.

[103] HC Deb, 10 January 2000, col 114 (Mr Mike O'Brien).

[104] Electoral Commission, *The Funding of Political Parties* (2004).

[105] Sir Hayden Phillips, above. See also HC 163 (2006–07).

[106] Representation of the People Act 1983, ss 91, 95.

[107] Communications Act 2003, s 333. See pp 161–2 in this chapter.

[108] For an account of the arrangements, see L Klein at note 96 above.

[109] These are the so-called Short and Cranborne monies for the House of Commons and House of Lords respectively. See Cm 4057, 1998, ch 9.

is now available for distribution to eligible parties (those with parliamentary representation) to assist with policy development.[110] In the case of the former the amounts involved are not inconsiderable, the principal opposition party now receiving in excess of £4.7m,[111] with correspondingly smaller sums being made available to the other opposition parties in Parliament.[112] Concern has been expressed by the Public Administration Committee of the House of Commons about the lack of effective scrutiny to ensure that the money is spent only for parliamentary purposes,[113] and the audit and accounting procedures have been tightened up as a result.[114] There is also provision for the public funding of campaign groups (up to £600,000 for each side) in the event of a national referendum.[115]

D. The conduct of elections

There is now a substantial body of law which has developed to regulate both local and national election campaigns. There are a number of objectives which legislation must promote, with the overriding objective being the need to maintain public confidence in the fairness and integrity of the electoral process. So it is necessary to ensure that neither electors nor candidates are subject to improper influences or pressures, and necessary also to ensure that there is a measure of equality of arms between candidates representing major strands of opinion. It has been acknowledged judicially that there is a need

> to achieve a level financial playing field between competing candidates, so as to prevent perversion of the voters' democratic choice between competing candidates within constituencies by significant disparities of local expenditure. At the constituency level it is the voters' perception of the personality and policies of the candidates, and the parties which they represent, which is intended to be reflected in the voting, not the weight of the parties' expenditure on local electioneering.[116]

It is important also that no party is able to secure an electoral advantage because of its greater financial resources or because it has better access to radio and television. British law has now developed detailed, sophisticated and in some respects uncompromising rules to help promote electoral fairness between the main parties and to reduce the influence of money in electoral politics. But because campaigning is expensive (yet of contestable effect), money cannot be removed completely from the scene; there will thus inevitably be disagreements about the content of some of the regulatory means which have been chosen to control its influence.

Local spending limits

Under Part II of the Representation of the People Act 1983 every candidate must appoint an election agent, but a candidate may appoint himself or herself to act in that capacity. There are now restrictions on who may donate to candidates,[117] but the most important control is the limit on candidates' election expenses in s 76 of the 1983 Act, knowingly to breach which is an illegal practice. First introduced in 1883, the amount which a candidate may spend 'on account of or in

---

[110] PPERA, s 12.

[111] This includes an allowance of £652,936 for the Leader of the Opposition.

[112] A similar scheme operates in the Scottish Parliament: SI 1999 No 1745.

[113] HC 238 (1999–2000); HC 293 (2000–1). There is also uncertainty about what is covered by the term parliamentary purposes.

[114] HC Deb, 27 June 2005, col 1336 W.

[115] PPERA, s 110. Provision is also made for referendum campaign broadcasts (ibid). Cf on the latter, *Wilson v IBA* 1979 SC 351.

[116] *R v Jones* [1999] 2 Cr App R 253, at p 255.

[117] RPA, s 71A, as inserted by PPERA, s 130 and Sch 16.

respect of the conduct or management of the election' depends on the number of electors in the constituency and on whether it is a borough or county constituency. But at the time of writing a maximum sum of £10,000–£12,000 would not be atypical.[118] The limit applies principally during the election period itself, which means that there were no limits on candidates' spending before then. Steps to address this problem were taken by the Political Parties and Elections Act 2009, though the measures adopted seem unlikely to deal fully with the concerns that have been raised about unregulated expenditure. In addition to this limit on the amount of permitted expenditure, certain forms of expenditure are forbidden. These include the payment to an elector for the display of election posters unless payment is made in the ordinary course of the elector's business as an advertising agent; and payments to canvassers.[119] Corrupt practices include bribery, treating and undue influence, such as the making of threats and attempts to intimidate an elector.[120] Election agents must submit a return of their candidate's election expenses to the returning officer within 35 days of the result being declared.[121]

Also important is s 75 which contains a measure first introduced in 1918 imposing a limit on the election expenses which may be incurred by third parties promoting or opposing a candidate. These third parties may be local businesses, trade unions or local interest groups who believe that their cause would be well served by the election of one particular candidate or poorly served by the election of another. They may wish as a result to campaign in the election and in the absence of controls could, in theory, exceed the permitted expenditure of the candidates themselves. It is thus a corrupt practice under the widely construed s 75 to (i) incur an election expenditure with a view to promoting or procuring the election of a candidate, (ii) on account of holding public meetings, issuing advertisements or circulars or otherwise presenting the candidate or his views to the electorate, (iii) except with the authority of the candidate (in which case the authorised expenditure falls to be treated as part of the candidate's expenses).[122] This is subject to an exception for the media to ensure that press and broadcasting activity is not inadvertently caught, and another to a limit which permitted a third party to spend up to £5. That latter limit was found to be too low by the European Court of Human Rights, and a violation of art 10 of the ECHR.[123] Following an amendment introduced by the Political Parties, Elections and Referendums Act 2000,[124] the limit is now £500, which means that individuals and campaign groups may spend up to £500 promoting or attacking candidates without any candidate having to account for the expense.

National spending limits

Since 2001, the spending limits on candidates have been accompanied by spending limits on the national election spending incurred by political parties and others during a general election campaign. It was for a long time the case that, although the expenditure of candidates was subject to limits, there was no corresponding limit on the national election campaigns of the parties.[125]

---

[118] See SI 2005 No 269. A much higher level of expenditure is permitted at by-elections. In 2001, this was set at £100,000.

[119] RPA, ss 109 and 111.

[120] Ibid, s 115. See *R v Rowe, ex p Mainwaring* [1992] 4 All ER 821.

[121] Ibid, s 81 (as amended). The return, which must now also include a statement of donations to the candidate (Sch 2A), must be accompanied by a declaration made by the agent and the candidate that the return is a true record of expenses incurred. For a high-profile but unsuccessful prosecution of a candidate for allegedly making a false declaration, see *R v Jones* [1999] 2 Cr App R 253.

[122] In *DPP v Luft* [1977] AC 962 it was held that expenditure on negative publicity aimed at preventing the election of a candidate was covered by this provision, as well as expenditure on positive promotional material aimed at procuring the election of a candidate.

[123] *Bowman v UK* (1998) 26 EHRR 1.

[124] PPERA, s 131.

[125] *R v Tronoh Mines Ltd* [1952] 1 All ER 697.

These campaigns were becoming more sophisticated and more expensive: at the general election in 1997 the Conservative and Labour parties were thought to have spent £28 and £26.5m respectively, which in each case was more than double the amount spent at the general election in 1992. The Committee on Standards in Public Life (the Neill Committee as it then was) recommended that national spending should be limited,[126] and this recommendation forms the basis of Part V of the Political Parties, Elections and Referendums Act 2000 (with corresponding limits on national referendum expenditure in Part VII). This imposes a limit on the campaign expenditure of political parties,[127] the limit depending on the number of constituencies which are contested by party candidates.[128] But a national party which puts up a candidate in every constituency would be able to spend up to about £20m to promote the electoral success of the party. This is in addition to the £10,000 or so which may be spent by each candidate under the Representation of the People Act 1983 on the conduct or management of his or her campaign. There are also statutory spending limits on political parties for referendum campaigns (£5m for each of the largest in a national referendum).[129]

It is not only the national campaigns of political parties that are subject to restrictions. Spending limits are also imposed on the campaigns of so-called third parties, such as trade unions, companies and pressure groups (such as the Countryside Alliance). These bodies may take part in an election by incurring expensive national advertising to promote particular issues that may tend to benefit one party at the expense of the others. Under Part VI of the 2000 Act, third parties may incur 'controlled expenditure' of up to £10,000 in England and £5,000 in each of Scotland, Wales and Northern Ireland without restraint. 'Controlled expenditure' is defined to mean expenses incurred in connection with the production or publication of election material that is made available to the public at large or any section of the public (s 85). A third party wishing to spend more must register with the Electoral Commission to become a 'recognised third party'. A recognised third party may incur controlled expenditure of up to just under £1m, though within this overall limit there are separate limits for England (£793,500), Scotland (£108,000), Wales (£60,000) and Northern Ireland (£27,000). A recognised third party must also submit an election return after the election, giving details of income received and controlled expenditure incurred. At the general election in 2005, there were 22 third party registrations, compared with only seven in 2001:[130] they included a number of trade unions and interest groups associated with a wide range of causes, from the countryside and animal welfare to abortion.

Broadcasting and elections

Political broadcasting at election times has also given rise to difficulties. It is an illegal practice for any person to procure the use of transmitting stations outside the United Kingdom with intent to influence voters at an election.[131] The Office of Communications (OFCOM) is under a statutory duty to review and revise standards designed to ensure that news programmes are accurate and impartial and that due impartiality is preserved in political programmes.[132] Political advertising is banned on ITV and on commercial radio stations,[133] a measure justified

---

[126] Cm 4057, 1998, ch 10.

[127] For the definition of campaign expenditure, see PPERA, s 72 and Sch 8.

[128] Ibid, s 79 and Sch 9.

[129] PPERA, Part VII. There are also limits on campaign groups and others. See Ewing, *Cost of Democracy*, note 94 above, ch 7 for fuller treatment of this issue.

[130] Electoral Commission, *Election 2001*, p 53.

[131] RPA, s 92.

[132] Communications Act 2003, s 319. The BBC, which exists under royal charter, seeks to maintain due impartiality but it is not subject to statutory restrictions.

[133] Communications Act 2003, ss 319–21. A Geddis [2002] PL 615.

judicially as being necessary to prevent elections from becoming 'auctions' and to stop wealthy interests dominating a scarce medium of communication.[134] But as already pointed out, free time is provided to the parties by the broadcasters for party election broadcasts. These broadcasts must comply with the various obligations of the broadcasters relating to matters such as taste and decency,[135] or harm and offence.[136] The allocation of time presents particular problems for the small parties and has given rise to a number of unsuccessful challenges in the courts on different grounds by parties which have been denied a broadcast or allocated an amount of time which they consider to be unfair.[137] At the general election in 2005, the Labour party and the Conservative party were allocated five broadcasts each and the Liberal Democrats four broadcasts in England; whereas in Scotland each of these parties was allocated four broadcasts, as was the Scottish National Party. An equal four-way distribution was adopted in Wales where Plaid Cymru was the fourth party. Time was also provided for one broadcast for eight of the smaller parties which had candidates standing in the election.[138] These other parties had to contest at least one-sixth of the parliamentary seats to qualify: for a party contesting seats in England it would have to stand in 88 constituencies to qualify for an election broadcast.[139]

The other major issue relating to broadcasting concerns the ability of the broadcasters to report about activities in particular constituencies. The curious effect of the Representation of the People Act 1983, s 93, was that if a candidate took part in an item about a constituency election, the item could not be broadcast without his or her consent; and it was an offence for a candidate to take part in such an item for the purpose of promoting his or her election unless the broadcast had the consent of every other candidate for the constituency.[140] To 'take part' in a constituency item meant to participate actively, for example in an interview or discussion; a candidate could not prevent the BBC from filming while he or she was campaigning in streets.[141] These measures – which effectively gave individual candidates a veto over what might be broadcast – were widely criticised and they were replaced by the Political Parties, Elections and Referendums Act 2000. Section 93 now provides that each broadcasting authority must adopt a code of practice to deal with 'the participation of candidates at a parliamentary or local government election in items about the constituency'. Before drawing up the code, the broadcasters must 'have regard' to any views expressed by the Electoral Commission. The broadcasters thus now have a free hand, perhaps inevitably after the Human Rights Act 1998. The OFCOM Broadcasting Code (which on this matter does not apply to the BBC)[142] provides that a candidate may take part in a broadcast about his or her constituency only if the candidates of each of the other major parties are also offered an opportunity to take part.[143] If, however, another candidate is unable or refuses to take part, the broadcast may nevertheless go ahead.

---

[134] R (Animal Defenders International) v Secretary of State for Culture, Media and Sport [2008] UKHL 15, paras [28], [29] (Lord Bingham). For a robust academic defence of these measures, see J Rowbottam, in Ewing and Issacharoff, note 101 above, ch 5.

[135] Pro-Life Alliance v Pro-Life Alliance BBC [2003] UKHL 23, [2004] 1 AC 185.

[136] OFCOM, Broadcasting Code, p 26.

[137] See Grieve v Douglas-Home 1965 SLT 186, R v Broadcasting Complaints Commission, ex p Owen [1985] QB 1153 and R v BBC and ITC, ex p Referendum Party [1997] COD 459. Also R (Pro-Life Alliance) v BBC [2003] UKHL 23, [2004] 1 AC 185. Cf Wilson v IBA 1979 SC 351 (restraints on referendum broadcasts; see now PPERA, s 110).

[138] This does not include the arrangements in Northern Ireland where a number of parties had broadcasts.

[139] The rules are set out in Ofcom Rules on Party Political and Referendum Broadcasts (2004).

[140] RPA, s 93(1).

[141] Marshall v BBC [1979] 3 All ER 80. And see McAliskey v BBC [1980] NI 44.

[142] The BBC Trust agrees a fresh code before each election.

[143] OFCOM, Broadcasting Code, para 6.9.

E. Supervision of elections

If elections are to be conducted according to law there must be effective machinery for invest-igating alleged breaches of the law and for imposing appropriate sanctions. Since the House of Commons has a direct interest in its own composition, it formerly claimed as a matter of privilege the right to determine questions of disputed elections. The Commons exercised the right to determine such questions from 1604 to 1868; and objected, not always with success, to breaches of election law being raised in the ordinary courts.[144] From 1672 election disputes were decided by the whole House, but the growth of party government resulted in disputes being settled by purely party voting. In 1868, Parliament entrusted the duty of deciding disputed elections to the courts. The matter is now regulated by the Representation of the People Act 1983, which provides a procedure for contesting elections and for these contests to be dealt with in the courts. Also important, however, is the Electoral Commission established under the Political Parties, Elections and Referendums Act 2000.[145] Apart from supervising the new regulatory regime intro-duced by the Act, the Commission has wide-ranging responsibilities for the conduct of elections.

Election petitions

The principal way of challenging an election is by way of an election petition.[146] This can be done only to challenge the election of a candidate: there is no way by which a general election result can be challenged. Within 21 days of the official return of the result of an election, an election petition complaining of an undue election may be presented by a registered elector for the con-stituency in question, by a person who claims the right to have been elected at the election, or by any person claiming to have been validly nominated as a candidate.[147] The petition may raise a wide variety of issues, including the improper conduct of the election by officials,[148] the legal qualification of the successful candidate to be a member of the Commons,[149] and the commis-sion of election offences such as unauthorised election expenditure.[150] The petition is heard by an Election Court consisting of two judges of the Queen's Bench Division in England or of the Court of Session in Scotland. The Election Court, which 'has the authority of the High Court and is a court of record,'[151] has a wide range of powers, including the power to order a recount or a scrutiny of the votes. The court determines whether the person whose election is complained of was duly elected and whether any alleged corrupt or illegal practices at the election were proved.

   If the court finds the candidate to have been disqualified from membership of the House, the court may, if satisfied that the cause of the disqualification was known to the electorate, deem the votes cast for him or her to be void and declare the runner-up to have been elected.[152] If the election has not been conducted substantially in accordance with the law or if there have been irregularities which have affected the result, the court must declare the election void and require a fresh election to be held.[153] The decision of the court – from which there is no appeal – is notified

---

[144] *Ashby* v *White* (1703) 2 Ld Raym 938; *R* v *Paty* (1704) 2 Ld Raym 1105. And ch 11 A.

[145] For the Commission, see www.electoralcommission.org.uk.

[146] For less formal ways of correcting any mistakes in the conduct of elections, see *Gough* v *Local Sunday Newspapers (North) Ltd* [2003] EWCA Civ 297, [2003] 1 WLR 1836.

[147] See *Ahmed* v *Kennedy* [2002] EWCA Civ 1793, [2003] 1 WLR 1820.

[148] *Re Kensington North Parliamentary Election* [1960] 2 All ER 150.

[149] *Re Parliamentary Election for Bristol South East* [1964] 2 QB 257.

[150] *Grieve* v *Douglas-Home* 1965 SC 186.

[151] *Attorney-General* v *Jones* [2000] QB 66, at p 69.

[152] As in the *Bristol South East* case.

[153] *Morgan* v *Simpson* [1975] QB 151; *Ruffle* v *Rogers* [1982] QB 1220 (local election cases).

to the Speaker and is entered in the journals of the House of Commons. The House must then give the necessary directions for confirming or altering the return or for issuing a writ for a new election, as the case may be.[154] In recent years there have been very few petitions in respect of parliamentary elections. The last instance of a successful candidate being unseated for election practices arose after the general election in December 1923.[155] Election petitions are more frequent in respect of local elections, where the procedure for challenging an irregular election is broadly the same,[156] though local government cases are heard by barristers who are appointed as Commissioners for this purpose. The decisions of Commissioners are subject to judicial review.[157]

Election offences

The other way by which election law can be enforced is by a criminal prosecution.[158] A person convicted on indictment of a corrupt practice is liable normally to imprisonment of up to one year and a fine; summary conviction carries a lesser penalty which may still lead to six months' imprisonment.[159] Conviction for an illegal practice carries a penalty of a fine not exceeding level 5 on the standard scale.[160] Equally important, conviction brings certain political disabilities, in the sense that a person found guilty of a corrupt or illegal practice is disqualified from being registered as an elector 'or voting at any parliamentary election in the United Kingdom or at any local government election in Great Britain'.[161] A person found guilty of a corrupt or illegal practice is also incapable of being elected to the House of Commons and of holding 'any elective office' for five years. Anyone elected to the House of Commons who is subsequently found to have committed a corrupt or illegal practice, is required to vacate his or her seat.[162] In the case of a conviction for a corrupt practice the disqualification is for five years and three years in the case of an illegal practice. Similar disqualifications may face anyone found to have committed a corrupt or illegal practice by an election court following an election petition. Prosecutions must be brought within a year of the alleged offence being committed.[163]

> In *Attorney-General* v *Jones*,[164] the defendant – the Labour member for Newark – had been convicted of the corrupt practice of knowingly making a false declaration of her election expenses. As a result her seat became vacant by the operation of s 160(4) of the 1983 Act. The conviction was reversed on appeal, at which point it was held that the seat ceased to be vacant, and that the existing member was entitled to resume her seat. Following this case the law was changed so that where a sitting member is convicted of a corrupt or illegal practice, the seat does not become vacant until the end of the period within which an appeal may be lodged against the conviction. If notice of appeal is given, the seat becomes vacant three months after the conviction, unless the appeal is withdrawn or is unsuccessful (in which case it is vacated immediately), or unless the appeal is heard and succeeds (in which case the seat is not vacated). Where a seat is vacated and the appeal ultimately succeeds, this will not entitle the member to resume his or her seat.[165]

Failure to comply with the provisions of the Political Parties, Elections and Referendums Act 2000 has altogether much less dramatic consequences, although these are not to be underestimated.

---

[154] RPA, s 144(7).
[155] Butler, *Electoral System*, note 3 above, p 57.
[156] See *R (Afzal)* v *Election Court* [2005] EWCA Civ 647.
[157] Ibid. See also *R* v *Cripps, ex p Muldoon* [1984] QB 686.
[158] See *Attorney-General* v *Jones* [2000] QB 66, at p 69.
[159] RPA, s 168.
[160] Ibid, s 169.
[161] Ibid, s 173.
[162] Ibid, s 173(1)(b).
[163] Ibid, s 176.
[164] [2000] QB 66.
[165] 1983 Act, s 173 (as amended above).

The main provisions here are the national spending limits. Although it recommended that there should be such a limit, the Committee on Standards in Public Life thought it 'wholly unrealistic' to suppose that a general election could be set aside and 'the runner-up party to be declared the winner' where the winning party exceeded the national limit.[166] The 'only realistic sanction' was thought to be the imposition of a 'heavy financial penalty' on the defaulting party.[167] It is the criminal law which must thus bear the greater part of the burden of enforcing the limits in the 2000 Act, although financial penalties are combined with the possibility of imprisonment of party officials in the event of a breach. So in the event of expenditure in excess of the statutory maximum, an offence is committed by both the party and the treasurer who authorised the expenditure, in this case the penalty on the party being an unlimited fine.[168] But it is the treasurer who must accept responsibility for any failure to deliver a return of campaign expenditure to the Commission or for making a false declaration about its contents.[169] In both the 2001 and 2005 elections over-spending was not a problem as all the parties reported spending some way below the permitted limits, which the Electoral Commission has recommended should be reduced.[170]

The Electoral Commission

One of the other major innovations of the Political Parties, Elections and Referendums Act 2000 was the creation of the Electoral Commission, with a wide range of functions. It must publish a report on the conduct of elections and referendums, and keep under review a number of electoral matters (including political party income and expenditure and political advertising in the broadcast media).[171] The Commission must also be consulted about any changes to electoral law,[172] and is empowered to give advice and assistance (but not financial assistance) to registration officers, returning officers, political parties and others.[173] This advice may be sought during election campaigns about election law.[174] Independent broadcasters must take into account the views of the Commission before making rules relating to party political broadcasts and the £2m made available to the parties for policy development is to be distributed in accordance with a scheme drawn up by the Commission and approved by the Ministry of Justice, which is the government department responsible for elections.[175] As we have also seen, the Commission plays a crucial part in the administration of the law relating to donations to political parties and electoral expenditure. Under s 145 of the 2000 Act the Commission has a general duty to monitor compliance not only with the provisions of the Political Parties, Elections and Referendums Act, but also 'the restrictions and other requirements imposed by other enactments' relating to 'election expenses incurred by or on behalf of candidates at elections', which extends obviously to the Representation of the People Act 1983.[176] But although the Commission has wide powers of investigation, it bears no responsibility for the prosecution of offenders.

The Political Parties and Elections Act 2009 introduces a number of important changes to the Electoral Commission, including its powers to monitor, investigate and enforce the law. The main

---

[166] Cm 4057, 1998, para 10.25.

[167] Ibid, para 10.26.

[168] PPERA, s 79(2).

[169] Ibid, ss 80–3.

[170] Electoral Commission, *The Funding of Political Parties* (2004).

[171] PPERA, ss 5 and 6. See Electoral Commission, *Election 2001*.

[172] Ibid, s 7.

[173] Ibid, s 9.

[174] See Electoral Commission, *Election 2001*, for details of the range of advice sought.

[175] PPERA, ss 11 and 12. The Commission also has an important educational function regarding the electoral systems (s 13).

[176] With the exception of Scottish local government elections, unless the Scottish ministers so provide (s 145(2)).

impact of the changes is to introduce a more flexible enforcement regime, including a greater power to use civil sanctions.[177] There are also changes to its composition, with provision being made for the political parties to nominate four (out of 9 or 10) Commissioners. The three largest parliamentary parties will each be entitled to nominate a Commissioner, with the fourth place to be allocated to one of the other parliamentary parties, provided it has at least two MPs.[178] This is a change which had been recommended by Sir Hayden Phillips in the wake of the cash for honours affair, when it was felt that the Commission was not sufficiently aware of how political parties operate.[179] It is unclear, however, whether political commissioners are a desirable or a necessary response to that crisis (especially as the performance of the Electoral Commission appears greatly to have improved): the new provisions challenge the political independence of the Commission, they favour the established national political parties at the expense of the others (notably the nationalist parties which compete in elections in different parts of the country), and there is already provision in the Political Parties, Elections and Referendums Act 2000 for the parliamentary parties panel to be an effective channel of communication between the Electoral Commission and the political parties. Apart from the foregoing, the 2009 Act relaxes the political restrictions on Electoral Commission staff: the old rule whereby staff had to be free of political activity for 10 years preceding their appointment has been replaced by a restriction of 5 years.[180]

F. Electoral systems and electoral reform

Under the present electoral system in the United Kingdom, each constituency returns a single member. Each elector can vote for only one candidate and the successful candidate is the one who receives the highest number of valid votes. This system of 'first past the post' is known as the relative majority system since whenever there are more than two candidates in a constituency, the successful candidate may not have an absolute majority of votes but merely a majority relative to the vote of the runner-up. This system is simple, but as a means of providing representation in Parliament it is very crude. It makes no provision for the representation of minority interests, nor does it ensure that the distribution of seats in the Commons is at all proportionate to the national distribution of votes. In Britain, the general tendency of the system has been to exaggerate the representation of the two largest parties and to reduce that of the smaller parties; but even for the larger parties there is no consistent relation between the votes and the seats they obtain. The distortion felt by some is illustrated by the general election of 2005 which saw the Labour party win 355 of the 646 seats (with a majority of 65) with only 36 per cent of the vote (and with the support of only 22 per cent of those eligible to vote).[181] The advantages claimed for the system include the simplicity of the voting method, the close links which develop between the member and his or her constituency, and its tendency to produce an absolute majority of seats in the House of Commons out of a large minority of votes. In defence of the system it is claimed that the function of a general election is to elect a government as well as a Parliament, and that the system produces strong government. This last claim needs to be examined with care, since a relatively small change of political support in a few constituencies may be exaggerated into an

---

[177] 2009 Act, ss 1–3.

[178] Ibid, s 5.

[179] Sir Hayden Phillips, above, p 21.

[180] 2009 Act, s 7.

[181] In 2001 the Labour party won 412 of the 659 seats (with a majority of 165) with only 41% of the vote. It works the other way too. In 1983 the Conservatives won 42% of the votes and 61% of the seats and in 1992 they won 42% of the votes and 52% of the seats. The main losers have been the Liberal Democrats, whose parliamentary representation regularly falls far short of votes cast nationally. In 2001 the Liberal Democrats polled 18% of the vote for 8% of seats. (The Conservatives polled 32% of the vote for 25% of the seats.)

apparent change of mind from one party to the other by a majority of the electorate. The system also distorts the influence on electoral outcomes of a relatively few marginal constituencies.

Other voting systems

Other electoral systems have long been devised with a view to securing better representation of minorities and a distribution of seats which bears a less haphazard relation to the votes cast. Many different systems are used in other countries.[182] One method, the alternative vote system which operates in Australia (where it is known as preferential voting), retains single-member constituencies but allows the elector to express a choice of candidates in order of preference. If no candidate has an absolute majority of first preferences, the lowest on the list is eliminated and his or her votes are distributed according to the second preference shown on the voting papers. The procedure continues until one candidate obtains an absolute majority. This system eliminates the return of a candidate on a minority vote when account is taken of second and later preferences, but it would not necessarily secure representation in the Commons proportional to the first preferences of the electorate on a national basis. Other systems have been designed to secure representation in Parliament directly proportional to the national voting strengths of the parties. Thus by the list system, as used in Israel and South Africa, voting for party lists of candidates takes place in a national constituency, with each party receiving that number of seats which comes closest to its national votes; this system does not provide for any directly accountable local links between voters and their representatives. In Germany, a mixed system is used by which each elector has two votes, one to elect a candidate in a single-member constituency, the other to vote for a party list; the list seats are assigned to parties to compensate for disproportionate representation arising from the constituency elections, but a party must record 5 per cent of the national vote or win three constituencies to gain any list seats. A similar system to replace first past the post was introduced in New Zealand in 1993 where it is known as mixed member proportional.[183]

The system which is likely to produce a reasonably close relationship between votes and seats while maintaining a local basis for representation is that of the single transferable vote. This method has been used within the United Kingdom for several purposes.[184] It would require the country to be divided into multi-member constituencies, each returning between three and, say, seven members. Each elector would have a single vote but would vote for candidates in order of preference. Any candidate obtaining the quota of first preferences necessary to guarantee election would be immediately elected, the quota being calculated by a simple formula: in a five-member constituency, this quota would be one vote more than one-sixth of the total votes cast.[185] The surplus votes of a successful candidate would be distributed to other candidates proportionately according to the second preference expressed; any candidate then obtaining the quota would be elected and a similar distribution of the surplus would follow. If at any count no candidate obtained the quota figure, the candidate with the lowest number of votes would be eliminated and all his or her preferences distributed among the others. Under this scheme, parties would both nationally and locally be likely to secure representation according to their true strength; minority parties and independent candidates would stand a better chance of election; and the number of ineffective votes would be reduced. Within the constituency, electors could in their order of

---

[182] Bogdanor, *The People and the Party System*, parts III–V; and Blackburn, above, ch 8.

[183] On the New Zealand experience, see A Geddis and C Morris (2004) 32 *Federal Law Review* 451.

[184] E.g. for university constituencies between 1918 and 1948; in Northern Ireland for elections to Stormont in 1922–28, to the Assembly in 1973 and 1982, to the Constitutional Convention in 1975 and to the European Parliament. Its use for electing assemblies in Scotland and Wales was proposed by the Royal Commission on the Constitution in 1973 (Cmnd 5460, 1973, paras 779–88), but this proposal was not adopted either in 1978 or in 1998.

[185] See the formula in SSI 2007 No 42, Sched 1, paras 46–55 (STV for Scottish local government elections).

preference choose between candidates from the same party and could base their choice of candidates on non-party considerations. Unless voting habits were to change, one party would be less likely to secure an absolute majority of seats in the Commons than at present; and Britain would become used to periods of minority or coalition government.[186]

Electoral reform

The case for electoral reform has been examined many times and a number of different electoral systems have been introduced in Britain since 1997. Under the Scotland Act 1998, a form of the additional member system has been adopted for elections to the Scottish Parliament, which contains 73 constituency members and 56 regional members.[187] Registered parties may submit lists of candidates to be regional members for a particular region, with up to 12 names on each party list, although only seven may be elected.[188] Electors have two votes: one for a constituency member; and the other for regional members to be exercised by voting for a political party which has submitted a regional list.[189] Constituency members are to be elected by first past the post as is currently the case for Westminster elections, and a measure of proportionality is secured by the regional member seats; these are allocated to the parties on the basis of a complex formula which allocates seats according to votes cast for the party in the region.[190] The regional member constituencies are the same constituencies which existed for the purposes of the European Parliament, before the European Parliamentary Elections Act 1999. The new electoral system for European Parliament elections is very different (based on closed party lists in much larger regional constituencies) and is considered in chapter 8. A system similar to the Scottish system is in place for the National Assembly for Wales.[191] In the case of both Scotland and Wales the electoral system tends to ensure that no one party has a majority of seats in the devolved legislatures; and in the case of Scotland, after the election in 2007 the SNP assumed office with only 47 of the 129 seats, the defeated Labour administration securing 46 seats.

Different systems have been adopted for the Northern Ireland Assembly and the Greater London Authority. In the case of the former, the single transferable vote is used to elect six candidates from each of the parliamentary constituencies for Northern Ireland.[192] The single transferable vote is defined in the Act as a vote (a) 'capable of being given so as to indicate the voter's order of preference for the candidates for election as members for the constituency', and (b) 'capable of being transferred to the next choice when the vote is not needed to give a prior choice the necessary quota of votes or when a prior choice is eliminated from the list of candidates because of a deficiency in the number of votes given for him'.[193] In the case of London, the system is different again. An elector has three votes: one for a mayoral candidate; one (a constituency vote) for an Assembly candidate; and one (a London vote) for a registered party or an individual candidate standing for election as London member.[194] Mayoral candidates are elected by simple majority unless there are more than two in which case the supplementary vote system is used: this means that where none of the candidates has a majority of the votes cast, all but the first two are eliminated with the second preference votes of the eliminated candidates then distributed

---

[186] Ch 2 D.

[187] Scotland Act 1998, s 1. This contrasts with the first past the post system which had been proposed in the Scotland Act 1978. See Cmnd 6348, 1975, p 9.

[188] Scotland Act 1998, s 5(6).

[189] Ibid, s 6.

[190] Ibid, s 1; Sch 1.

[191] Government of Wales Act 1998, Part 1. This contrasts with the first past the post system which had been proposed in the Wales Act 1978.

[192] Northern Ireland Act 1998, s 34.

[193] Ibid, s 34(3).

[194] Greater London Authority Act 1999, s 4(1).

to the candidates still in the contest.[195] The Assembly is elected on the basis of a variation of the additional member system used in Scotland and Wales.[196] There are thus three or four electoral systems operating in different parts of the country for the purposes of different elections, with still more variety introduced when STV was adopted for Scottish local authority elections in 2007.[197] This gave rise to considerable confusion when the new system was introduced for local authority elections held on the same day as the Scottish Parliament elections with a different electoral system.[198]

The Jenkins Commission

There are thus new electoral systems for the European Parliament, the devolved bodies and local government (in some parts of the country). But what about Westminster? There have been many proposals for reforming the Westminster system, one of the earliest being a recommendation by a royal commission in 1910 for the introduction of the alternative vote.[199] This was followed in 1917 by the recommendations of a Speaker's Conference on electoral reform for the adoption of the single transferable vote.[200] But after some vacillation Parliament refused to accept either this or the alternative vote. The matter was revived by the second Labour government in 1929,[201] and a Bill which sought to introduce the alternative vote was passed by the Commons but abandoned when the government fell in 1931. The Speaker's Conference on electoral reform in 1944 rejected by a large majority proposals for change, as did a similar conference in 1967.[202] Electoral reform nevertheless continued to have its strong advocates, with few countries electing their legislatures on the basis of first past the post and with all the new electoral regimes adopted in Britain in recent years rejecting it in favour of a system which is perceived to be fairer in terms of producing a more representative outcome. Before the general election in 1997, the Labour and Liberal Democratic parties agreed that an early referendum should be held on electoral reform and a commitment to this effect was included in the Labour party's general election manifesto of that year.

In acknowledgement of the manifesto commitment, in December 1997 the Prime Minister appointed the Independent Commission on the Voting System under the chairmanship of Lord Jenkins to consider and recommend alternatives to the voting system for Westminster elections. By its terms of reference the Commission was required to 'observe the requirement for broad proportionality, the need for stable Government, an extension of voter choice and the maintenance of a link between MPs and geographical constituencies'. The Commission recommended the introduction of 'a two-vote mixed system which can be described as either limited AMS or AV top-up'. The majority of MPs (80–85 per cent) would continue to be elected from single-member constituencies, but by alternative vote; and the remainder 'elected on a corrective top-up basis which would significantly reduce the disproportionality and the geographical divisiveness' which were said to be inherent in first past the post.[203] Although the report and its proposals were

---

[195] The candidate with the largest number of first preference votes and distributed second preferences from the other candidates is the winner. See Greater London Authority Act 1999, s 4(3).

[196] Ibid, s 4(4) (Assembly members elected under simple majority system) and s 4(5) (London members elected from party lists in a single London-wide constituency). It is in this latter respect (one rather than several additional member constituencies) that London differs from Scotland and Wales.

[197] SSI 2007 No 42.

[198] See Electoral Commission, *Independent Review of the Scottish Parliamentary and Local Government Elections, 3 May 2007* (2007) – a stinging review by Ron Gould, a senior Canadian election administrator. For comment, see N Ghaleigh (2008) 12 Edin LR.142, and H Lardy [2008] PL 214.

[199] Cd 5163, 1910.

[200] Cd 8463, 1917 and Representation of the People Act 1918, s 20. See Butler, above, part 1.

[201] Cmd 3636, 1930.

[202] Cmd 6534, 1944; Cmnd 3202, 1967.

[203] *The Report of the Independent Commission on the Voting System* (1998), p 50.

widely praised for their elegance and subtlety, at the time of writing no referendum on these or other proposals has been held. There was, however, renewed interest in electoral reform following the problems in 2009 relating to MPs expenses,[204] which gave rise to a number of proposals designed to repair the reputation of Parliament. But the matter remains controversial and does not enjoy all-party support. Nevertheless, it is possible that some form of proportional representation could be introduced for the House of Lords should further reform of the Lords lead to a wholly or partially elected chamber.[205]

G. Membership of the House of Commons

The following are the main categories of persons who are disqualified from sitting and voting in the House of Commons.[206]

(*a*) Both by common law and by statute, aliens are disqualified; [207] 'qualifying' Commonwealth citizens and citizens of the Republic of Ireland are not disqualified.[208]

(*b*) Persons under 18 on the day they are nominated as candidates.[209]

(*c*) Mental patients. Under the Mental Health Act 1983, s 141, when a member is ordered to be detained on grounds of mental illness, the detention must be reported to the Speaker. The Speaker obtains a medical report from two medical specialists, followed by a second report after six months. If the member is still detained and suffering from mental illness, his or her seat is vacated.

(*d*) Peers and peeresses. But following the House of Lords Act 1999, hereditary peers are no longer disqualified unless they are one of the 92 hereditary peers (on which see below) who has retained his or her membership of the House under s 2 of the Act.

(*e*) Bankrupts. Under the Insolvency Act 1986, s 426A, a person who is subject to a bankruptcy restriction order is disqualified from membership of the Commons. Where a sitting member is adjudged bankrupt, his or her seat becomes vacant and if he or she stands for re-election, his or her return shall be void should he or she be re-elected. Where a court makes a bankruptcy restriction order on a sitting MP, it must inform the Speaker.[210]

(*f*) Persons guilty of corrupt or illegal practices, under the Representation of the People Act 1983. A person found to have committed a corrupt practice is disqualified from being elected to the Commons for five years; and anyone found to have committed an illegal practice is disqualified for three years.[211]

(*g*) Under the Forfeiture Act 1870, a person convicted of treason is disqualified from membership until expiry of the sentence or receipt of a pardon. The effect of the Criminal Law Act 1967 was that other criminal convictions, even where a substantial prison sentence was imposed, did not disqualify from membership of the House. Since 1981, a person convicted of an offence and sentenced to prison for more than a year by a court in the United Kingdom or elsewhere is, while detained in the British Isles or in the Republic of Ireland or unlawfully at large, disqualified from being nominated and from being a member. If he or she is already a member, the seat is vacated.[212]

---

[204] See ch 11 B below.

[205] Cd 5291, 2001, paras 48–53. And see pp 179–80 below.

[206] For greater detail, see Erskine May, *Parliamentary Practice*, ch 3.

[207] See for example, Act of Settlement 1700, s 3.

[208] British Nationality Act 1981, Sch 7; Electoral Administration Act 2006, s 18.

[209] Electoral Administration Act 2006, s 17.

[210] Insolvency Act 1986, s 426A(5).

[211] RPA, ss 160, 173.

[212] Representation of the People Act 1981; and see C P Walker [1982] PL 389.

It is within the disciplinary powers of the House to expel a member, but expulsion does not prevent him or her from being re-elected.[213] Formerly a person who held contracts with the Crown for the public service was disqualified from membership. But this disqualification was abolished in 1975 along with the disqualification of those who held pensions from the Crown. It was also the case that ordained clergy and ministers of the Church of Scotland were disqualified from membership of the House of Commons.[214] But these disqualifications were removed in 2001,[215] although it is still provided that a person is disqualified from being or being elected as a member of the House of Commons if he is a Lord Spiritual (that is to say, one of the Bishops of the Church of England who is a member of the House of Lords).

Disqualification of office-holders

In addition to the above, there are a number of office-holders who are also disqualified. Until 1957 the law governing the disqualification which arose from the holding of public offices was 'archaic, confused and unsatisfactory'.[216] That law had grown out of ancient conflicts between Crown and Commons. During the early seventeenth century, the House secured recognition of the right to control its own composition. In particular, the House asserted the principle that a member could not continue to serve when appointed by the Crown to a position the duties of which entailed prolonged absence from Westminster. After 1660, the House feared that the Crown would exercise excessive influence over it by the use of patronage and sought to avert a situation in which members held positions of profit at pleasure of the Crown. This fear led in 1700 to a provision in the Act of Settlement to the effect that no one who held an office or place of profit under the Crown should be capable of serving as a member of the House. This provision, which would have excluded ministers from the Commons, was repealed before it took effect. In its place, the Succession to the Crown Act 1707 enabled certain ministers to retain their seats in the House, subject to re-election after appointment, but excluded those who held office of a non-political character, for example in what today would be regarded as the civil service. But much legislation was necessary to establish the distinction between ministerial, or political, office-holders, who were eligible for membership and non-political office-holders, who were excluded. Moreover, it was necessary to restrict the number appointed to ministerial office from the Commons, to avoid a situation in which the executive (now in the form of the Prime Minister) exercised excessive control by patronage over the House.

The House of Commons Disqualification Act 1957 (re-enacted in 1975) replaced disqualification for holding 'an office or place of profit under the Crown' by disqualification attached to the holding of specified offices. There are three broad reasons for disqualification: (1) the physical impossibility for certain office-holders of attendance at Westminster, (2) the risk of patronage and (3) the conflict of constitutional duties. Under s 1 of the 1975 Act, the disqualifying offices fall into the following categories:

(a) Lords spiritual (that is to say the 26 bishops who are also members of the House of Lords);

(b) A great variety of judicial offices, listed in Sch 1 of the Act, including judges of the Supreme Court of the United Kingdom; judges of the Court of Appeal, High Court and circuit judges in England and Wales; and judges of the Court of Session and sheriffs in Scotland, as well as the

---

[213] Ch 11 A below.

[214] House of Commons (Clergy Disqualification) Act 1801, Roman Catholic Relief Act 1829, s 9. There was no similar disqualification from membership of the European Parliament, the Scottish Parliament, the National Assembly for Wales or the Northern Ireland Assembly.

[215] House of Commons (Removal of Clergy Disqualification) Act 2001. The Act implements a recommendation of the Home Affairs Committee (HC 768-I (1997–8), para 127). See Blackburn, note 3 above, ch 5.

[216] HC 120 (1940–41) and HC 349 (1955–6).

holders of less senior judicial office. The principle is that no person may hold full-time judicial office and be a practising politician. Lay magistrates are not affected.

(*c*) Employment in the civil service of the Crown, whether in an established or temporary capacity, whole time or part time. The disqualification extends to members of the civil service of Northern Ireland and the diplomatic service. Civil servants who wish to stand for election to Parliament are required by civil service rules to resign before becoming candidates.[217]

(*d*) Membership of the regular armed forces of the Crown. Members of the reserve and auxiliary forces are not disqualified if recalled for active service. Members of the armed forces, like civil servants, must resign before becoming candidates for election to Parliament and they may apply for release to contest an election. A spate of such applications in 1962 led to the appointment of an advisory committee of seven members to examine the credentials of applicants and to test the sincerity of their desire to enter Parliament.[218]

(*e*) Membership of any police force maintained by a police authority.

(*f*) Membership of the legislature of any country or territory outside the Commonwealth, except – following the Disqualifications Act 2000 – in the case of the Republic of Ireland. It is likely that members of a legislature other than that of the Irish Republic would be debarred by their status as aliens from membership of the Commons.

(*g*) A great variety of disqualifying offices arising from chairmanship or membership of commissions, boards, agencies, administrative tribunals, public authorities and undertakings; in a few cases the disqualification attaches only to particular constituencies (Sch 1, Parts 2–4). As these offices cover such a wide range, each office is specified by name. The Schedule may be amended by Order in Council made following a resolution approved by the House of Commons (s 5). This power – which is frequently used – avoids the need for amendment by statute as and when new offices are created.

For one purpose alone acceptance of an office of profit continues to disqualify. From early times a member of the House was in law unable to resign his seat and acceptance of an office of profit under the Crown was the only legal method of release from membership. The offices commonly used for the purpose were the office of Steward or Bailiff of the Chiltern Hundreds or of the Manor of Northstead. Under the Act of 1975 these offices are disqualifying offices (s 4). Appointment to them is made by the Chancellor of the Exchequer on the request of the member concerned.

Other matters

1 *Ministers in the House of Commons.* British practice requires that the holders of ministerial office should be members of either the Commons or the Lords and that the great majority should be drawn from the Commons. But it has long been necessary for limits to be imposed on the number of ministers who may sit in the Commons, lest excessive powers of patronage be exercised by the Prime Minister over the House. The present law is found partly in the House of Commons Disqualification Act 1975 and partly in the Ministerial and Other Salaries Act 1975. Section 2 of the former allows no more than 95 holders of ministerial office (whether paid or unpaid, it would seem) to sit and vote in the Commons; this limit had been raised from 70 to 91 in 1964,[219] and to 95 in 1974.[220] If more members of the Commons are appointed to ministerial office than are allowed by law, those appointed in excess must not sit or vote in the House until

---

[217] Servants of the Crown (Parliamentary, European Assembly and Northern Ireland Assembly) Order 1987, *Civil Service Management Code*, paras 4.4.20–4.4.21. See also ch 13 D.

[218] HC 111 and 262 (1962–3); HC Deb, 18 February 1963, col 163.

[219] Ministers of the Crown Act 1964, noted by A E W Park (1965) 28 MLR 338.

[220] Ministers of the Crown Act 1974.

the number has been reduced to the permitted figure (s 2(2)). The Ministerial and Other Salaries Act (as amended) sets out the salaries payable to various categories of ministerial office, these salaries being subject to revision.[221] Schedule 1 to the Act imposes limits on the total number of such salaries payable at any one time to the various categories. Thus, in category 1 (holders of posts in the Cabinet apart from the Lord Chancellor) not more than 21 salaries are payable. Not more than 50 salaries are payable to posts in category 1 taken together with category 2 (ministers of state and departmental ministers outside the Cabinet). Not more than 83 salaries are payable to posts in categories 1, 2 and 4 (parliamentary secretaries) taken together. In addition, salaries are paid to the law officers of the Crown (category 3), to five Junior Lords to the Treasury (government whips in the Commons) and to seven assistant whips in the Commons, as well as to various political posts in the royal household, some of which may be held only by members of the Lords. Provision is also made for the payment of salaries to the Leader of the Opposition and to the Opposition whips (s 2).

2 Effects of disqualification. If any person is elected to the House while disqualified by the 1975 Act, the election is void (s 6(1)) and this could be so determined on an election petition. If a member becomes disqualified after election, his or her seat is vacated and the House may so resolve. Before 1957, Parliament might pass an Act of Indemnity in favour of members who had unwittingly become subject to disqualification. Today, the House may direct by order that a disqualification under the 1975 Act which existed at the material time be disregarded if it has already been removed (for example, by the member's resignation from the office in question) (s 6(2)). Thus a new election is unnecessary where the House itself has dispensed with the consequences of the disqualification, but no such order can affect the proceedings on an election petition (s 6(3)). Disputed cases of disqualification are in general determined by the House after consideration by a select committee. Thus in 1961 the Committee of Privileges reported that Mr Tony Benn was disqualified because he had succeeded to his father's peerage while a member of the Commons.[222] While disputes under the 1975 Act as to disqualifying offices arise rarely, the Judicial Committee of the Privy Council has jurisdiction to declare whether a person has incurred a disqualification under that Act (s 7). Any person may apply to the Judicial Committee for a declaration of disqualification but must give security for costs. Issues of fact may on the direction of the Judicial Committee be tried by the High Court in England, the Court of Session in Scotland or the High Court in Northern Ireland (s 7(4)). A declaration may not be made if an election petition is pending, if one has been tried in which disqualification on the same grounds was in issue, nor where the House has given relief by order (s 7(5)). This procedure has yet to be used.[223] Another procedure open where there is a dispute over disqualification is for the Commons to petition the Crown to refer the matter to the Judicial Committee of the Privy Council for an advisory opinion on the law.[224]

H. The House of Lords

Historically, membership of the House of Lords was confined to hereditary peers and the bishops of the Church of England.[225] The former inherited their status and a considerable body

---

221 See Ministerial and Other Salaries Act 1997.
222 HC 142 (1960–61).
223 Erskine May, above, p 59.
224 Under the Judicial Committee Act 1833, s 4; and see *Re MacManaway* [1951] AC 161.
225 A good history is provided by Lowell, *The Government of England*, ch 21. See also Maitland, *The Constitutional History of England*, pp 166–72.

of law has developed to regulate title to the peerage.[226] The latter held their position ex officio and ceased to occupy a seat in the Lords on resignation or retirement. In 1876, provision was made for the appointment of Lords of Appeal in Ordinary to conduct the judicial business of the House;[227] and in 1958 the Life Peerages Act allowed for the appointment of others to the peerage for life, without the conferring of a title which would pass to succeeding generations. Membership of the House of Lords was thus confined to those who inherited their position or who were appointed by the Crown (in the case of the bishops, the law lords and the life peers). The House of Lords Act 1999 broke the link between the hereditary peerage and membership of the House of Lords:[228] until then all hereditary peers were entitled to a seat in the Lords. There continue to be four categories of members of the House of Lords, although the effect of the House of Lords Act 1999 has been greatly to alter the balance between the different categories, with hereditary peers displaced by the life peers as the largest group. The four categories of membership are as follows:

(a) Life peers created under the Life Peerages Act 1958.

(b) Law Lords appointed under the Appellate Jurisdiction Act 1876.

(c) Lords Spiritual, being 26 senior clergy of the Church of England.

(d) Hereditary peers, of whom there are 92.

Life peers

It was decided in 1856 that the Crown, although able to create a life peerage, could not create such a peerage carrying with it the right to a seat in the House of Lords.[229] If life peers were to be created to sit in the Lords, legislation was thus necessary. The Life Peerages Act 1958 both strengthened the Lords and weakened the hereditary principle. The Act enabled the Queen by letters patent to confer a peerage for life with a seat in Parliament on a man or woman. It did not restrict the power of the Crown to confer hereditary peerages, although it made it unnecessary for new hereditary peerages to be created. In fact very few hereditary peerages have since been created, although Mrs Thatcher revived the practice of making such appointments when she nominated Viscount Whitelaw and Speaker Thomas in 1983.[230] An appointment under the 1958 Act is irrevocable: unlike a hereditary peerage a life peerage cannot be disclaimed,[231] though in 2009 government proposals were made to allow life peers to resign from the House of Lords and alternatively to disclaim their peerage.[232] In March 2009, there were 601 life peers, of whom 145 were women. Life peers may not vote in House of Commons elections and they may not stand as parliamentary candidates.[233] But they may vote and stand for election to the devolved parliament and assemblies.[234]

There is a great deal of criticism that the system of appointment on the recommendation of the Prime Minister is an inappropriate way to recruit a legislative chamber and that it allows too much patronage on the part of the Prime Minister. In order to address such criticism, Mr Blair

---

[226] HLE, vol 35. See also 12th edition of this work, pp 164–6.

[227] Appellate Jurisdiction Act 1876.

[228] House of Lords Act 1999, s 1: 'No one shall be a member of the House of Lords by virtue of a hereditary peerage.' This is subject to s 2, on which see below.

[229] *Wensleydale Peerage case* (1856) 5 HLC 958.

[230] See Brazier, *Constitutional Practice*, p 241.

[231] See pp 176–7 below.

[232] Constitutional Reform and Governance Bill 2009, cl 32, 33. However, these measures were dropped and not included in the Constitutional Reform and Governance Act 2010.

[233] See p 170 above.

[234] See Scotland Act 1998, s 16; Government of Wales Act 1998, s 13; and Northern Ireland Act 1998, s 36(6).

established the House of Lords Appointments Commission which is a non-statutory, non-departmental public body, attached to the Cabinet Office.[235] It is chaired by a peer and its members include nominees of the three main national political parties and three independent members. The role of the Commission is to make recommendations for non-political peers and to vet all nominations for peerages by the political parties on grounds of propriety. Prior to the creation of the Commission in 2000,[236] this latter role was performed by the Political Honours Scrutiny Committee which still operated to scrutinise political honours other than peerages (such as knighthoods) until it was abolished in 2005.[237] But it remains the case that although Canada also has a nominated second chamber (the Senate), nomination is nevertheless an uncommon method of composition when compared to other countries, where second chambers are typically elected, either directly (as in Australia or the USA) or indirectly (as in France and Germany).[238]

Law Lords and Lords Spiritual

The peers appointed under the Appellate Jurisdication Act 1876 to perform the judicial functions of the House of Lords were styled Lords of Appeal in Ordinary. They could sit and vote for life, notwithstanding resignation or retirement from their judicial appointment. In March 2009, 22 members of the House of Lords had been appointed under the 1876 Act. Since the creation of the Supreme Court, however, the House of Lords ceases to have a judicial function, and the Appellate Jurisdiction Act 1876 has been repealed. Supreme Court judges are ineligible to sit in the House of Lords, and while the Lords of Appeal in Ordinary at the time of the creation of the Supreme Court were by statute to become the first justices of the Supreme Court,[239] they will no longer sit and vote in the House of Lords or its committees. Existing Supreme Court judges appointed under the 1876 Act will be able to resume their parliamentary activities following their retirement from judicial office, but otherwise the need for legal expertise to carry out the scrutiny work of the House of Lords will now have to be met by the appointment as life peers under the Life Peerages Act 1958 of lawyers who do not hold judicial office. The judicial members of the House had in the past taken a particular interest in debates about the reform of the legal profession on the one hand,[240] and human rights on the other.[241]

The Lords Spiritual are 26 bishops of the Church of England; they hold their seats in the Lords until they resign from their episcopal office. The Archbishops of Canterbury and York and the Bishops of London, Durham and Winchester have the right to a seat. The remaining Lords Spiritual are the 21 other diocesan bishops having seniority of date of appointment, with the exception of the Bishop of Sodor and Man who may not take a seat. When a bishop with a seat in the Lords resigns or retires, his place in the Lords is taken by the next senior diocesan bishop.[242] In 1847, it was enacted that the number of bishops sitting in Parliament should not be increased whenever a new diocesan bishopric is created.[243] This right of representation is nevertheless not

---

[235] For details of its work, see www.houseoflordsappointmentscommission.gov.uk. For proposals to enhance the status and role of the Commission, see HC 153 (2007–08); HC 137 (2008–09) (Public Administration Committee).

[236] See Cm 4183, 1999.

[237] For an account of the work of the Committee, see Cm 4057, 1998, ch 14.

[238] For a full account, see Russell, *Reforming the House of Lords*.

[239] Constitutional Reform Act 2005, s 24.

[240] See HL Deb, 7 April 1999, cols 1307–1480.

[241] Particularly on the proceedings relating to the Human Rights Bill: see K D Ewing (1999) 62 MLR 79.

[242] Under the Ecclesiastical Offices (Age Limit) Measure 1975, bishops retire from their sees, and therefore from membership of the House, at age 70. Retired bishops are entitled to use the facilities of the House available to members of the House outside the Chamber.

[243] Ecclesiastical Commissioners Act 1847, s 2; Bishoprics Act 1878, s 5.

extended to other faiths or churches and its continued existence reflects the special constitutional position of the Church of England. Although justified historically, such representation is bound to be closely questioned in an age which is simultaneously both more multicultural and more secular. It is possible for members and clergy of other churches and faiths to be appointed under the Life Peerages Act 1958, in the case of those churches and faiths which do not prohibit their senior clergy from accepting positions of political authority.[244] But this is not the same as an entitlement to a guaranteed number of places.

Hereditary peers

It was previously the case that a hereditary peerage carried with it the right to a seat in the House of Lords. The House of Lords Act 1999 now provides that hereditary peers are no longer entitled to membership of the Lords. But hereditary peers have not been excluded altogether. In order to expedite the passing of the House of Lords Act 1999, the government accepted an arrangement whereby 90 hereditary peers (plus the Earl Marshal and the Lord Great Chamberlain)[245] would remain in the Lords until the process of reform was completed.[246] These 90 are elected in accordance with the standing orders of the House. In 2000, the House of Lords was thus still graced by two dukes, one marquess, 28 earls and countesses and 17 viscounts. The removal of the hereditary peers was nevertheless challenged as breaching the Treaty of Union, which provides a guarantee that 16 Scottish peers would be accepted into membership of the House of Lords. But this was rejected by the House of Lords Committee of Privileges, which concluded that the Treaty of Union did not provide an unalterable restraint on the power of Parliament.[247] Hereditary peers are now eligible to vote and to stand for election to Parliament, unless they are members of the House of Lords.[248]

Under the standing orders of the House governing the election of hereditary peers,[249] 15 of the 90 places were set aside for those hereditary peers who were office-holders in the House: deputy speakers and deputy chairmen of committees. They were elected by the whole House. The remaining 75 places were elected by the hereditary peers to reflect the strength of the different parties from among their number. So 42 places were allocated to the Conservatives; three to the Liberal Democrats; two to Labour; and 28 to the cross-benchers. These members were elected from constituencies of their own party or group (so that, for example, only Conservative hereditary peers elected the 42 Conservatives).[250] A peerage cannot be alienated or surrendered,

---

[244] For a valuable account of religious representation in the House of Lords, see C Smith [2002] PL 674, and A Harlow, F Cranmer and N Doe [2008] PL 490.

[245] The Earl Marshal has responsibility for ceremonial matters, while previous editions of the *Companion to the Standing Orders and Guide to the Proceedings of the House of Lords* referred to the Lord Chamberlain as 'the hereditary officer of state to whom the sovereign entrusts the custody and control of those parts of the Palace of Westminster not assigned to the two Houses' (such as the Queen's Robing Room).

[246] House of Lords Act 1999, s 2. For an account of how these figures were arrived at, see R Brazier, House of Lords Act 1999, *Current Law Statutes 1999*. In addition to the places reserved to hereditary peers by the House of Lords Act 1999, another ten were made life peers to enable them to remain. These were mainly hereditary peers of first creation. Another two hereditary peers reverted to sitting under the authority of life peerages which they already had.

[247] *Lord Gray's Motion* 2000 SC (HL) 46.

[248] House of Lords Act 1999, s 3.

[249] HL Standing Order 9.

[250] Should a vacancy arise, provision is made in Standing Order 10 for a by-election, at which only those hereditary peers who remain in membership of the House may vote. So only the 41 remaining Conservative hereditary peers could vote in a by-election for a new Conservative hereditary peer to become a member of the House. See A Murphy (2003) 71 *The Table* 11.

although under the Peerages Act 1963 a hereditary peer may disclaim his or her title for life.[251] The primary purpose of granting this right was to enable hereditary peers to sit in the Commons, following an unsuccessful action by Tony Benn, then Viscount Stansgate by succession, who challenged the existing law which disqualified members of the Lords from standing for election to Parliament.[252] In addition, the government's Constitutional Reform and Governance Bill 2009 proposed that excepted hereditary peers (that is to say those hereditary peers who survived the 1999 cull) should be entitled to resign from membership of the House of Lords, in the same way as life peers. More importantly, the Bill also proposed an end to the by-elections to replace hereditary peers who die or resign. But these proposals were not included in the Constitutional Reform and Governance Act 2010.

I. Membership of the House of Lords

Although there are thus a number of different routes to membership of the House of Lords, a member may not take his or her seat until he or she has obtained a writ of summons, which is issued by direction of the Lord Chancellor, from the office of the Clerk of the Crown in Chancery (a senior officer of the House). New writs are issued before the meeting of each Parliament to all Lords – temporal and Spiritual – who are entitled to receive them.[253] Writs are also issued to peers newly created during the life of a Parliament. But no writs are issued to any peer who is known to be disqualified from sitting and there are currently four categories of disqualification:[254] aliens;[255] those under the age of 21;[256] those in respect of whom a bankruptcy restriction order has been made;[257] and those convicted of treason (until they have served their sentence or been pardoned).[258] Convicted persons may resume their seats after serving a prison sentence,[259] though the government's Constitutional Reform and Governance Bill 2009 proposed that members should be removed from the Lords on conviction of a criminal offence with a prison sentence of more than a year. It is also necessary for a new peer to be formally introduced into the House. A day for this purpose is fixed by the Speaker and by custom not more than two introductions may take place on any one day. Lords are normally introduced by two peers 'of the same degree in the House'.[260] It is not to be overlooked that despite the manner of its composition and the formality of its proceedings, the House of Lords exists principally to transact political

---

[251] Under the 1963 Act existing peers were given 12 months from royal assent to disclaim and new peers were given 12 months from the date of their succession (s 1). This still applies unless the peer is excepted from s 1 of the 1999 Act by s 2 of the same Act. A sitting member of the Commons was given one month from the death of his predecessor in which to disclaim (1963 Act, s 2); but this has been repealed by the 1999 Act. Where a peer disclaims his title, it could not be restored to him, although the title would pass to the next generation following the death of the person who disclaimed. A person who disclaimed could be restored to the House of Lords by a life peerage under the 1958 Act. It would presumably be possible – if unlikely – for a new hereditary peerage to be conferred on the person who disclaimed.

[252] *Re Parliamentary Election for Bristol South East* [1964] 2 QB 257. It was under the 1963 Act that the Earl of Home disclaimed his title on being appointed Prime Minister in 1964 in succession to Mr Harold Macmillan.

[253] House of Lords, *Companion to the Standing Orders and Guide to the Proceedings of the House of Lords*, para 1.09.

[254] The Peerage Act 1963, s 6 removed the disqualification on peeresses in their own right to receive a writ of summons. See *Viscountess Rhondda's Claim* [1922] 2 AC 339.

[255] Act of Settlement 1700, s 3 (as amended by the British Nationality Act 1981, Sch 7).

[256] HL SO 2.

[257] Insolvency Act 1986, s 426A.

[258] Forfeiture Act 1870.

[259] This is a matter which gave rise to some concern following the imprisonment of Lord Archer of Weston-super-Mare in 2001.

[260] House of Lords, *Companion to the Standing Orders and Guide to the Proceedings of the House of Lords*, para 1.13.

business. This gives rise to questions about the political balance of the chamber and the obligations of its members.

The political composition of the House of Lords

The effect of the House of Lords Act 1999 was significantly to reduce the size of the House of Lords: in 1999, there were 1,295 members who were culled to 695 by October in the following year. This still makes the House of Lords the largest second chamber in Europe. Of these 695, 549 were life peers; 28 law lords; 26 bishops and archbishops; and 92 hereditary peers. A common refrain about the unreformed House was that it had an inbuilt Conservative bias. This is because most of the hereditary peers (who were the largest category of peers) were supporters of the Conservative party. Conservative governments thus always had a majority in the Lords, while governments of other parties were always in a minority.[261] But although the House has been reformed by the 1999 Act and although a large number of Labour peers have been created since 1997, it was not until 2005 that Labour became the largest party. By 2009, 215 of the 730 members were declared as Labour; 197 Conservative; 72 Liberal Democrat; and 204 as cross-benchers (non-party political or independent members), there being 16 'other' peers and 26 bishops. The government consequently does not have a majority in the House of Lords, which is distinguished from the House of Commons also by its strong independent element, with neither the cross-benchers nor the bishops taking a party whip.

The legislative role of the House of Lords makes it inevitable that the government should have some presence in the chamber, to ensure that business is conducted efficiently and that an account is given of government proposals. In recent years the practice has been for only two or three Cabinet ministers to be drawn from the House of Lords, though these do not now necessarily include the Lord Chancellor. By convention the Prime Minister must be a member of the House of Commons and the same is true of other senior Cabinet posts: it is inconceivable in particular that the Chancellor of the Exchequer could be a member of the House of Lords.[262] But there is no reason in principle why other ministers should not be based in the Lords and the life peerage provides an opportunity for the Prime Minister to bring into his or her government an individual who may not be a member of Parliament (as in the case of Lord Mandelson by Mr Brown). It also provides an opportunity for the Prime Minister to retain the services of a minister who may have lost his or her Commons seat in a general election (as in the case of Mrs Lynda Chalker who lost her seat in 1992 but who was elevated to the peerage, retaining her position as minister for overseas development in Mr Major's government). In 2009 there were in fact several ministers who held seats in the Lords. Apart from the Leader of the House, the Secretary of State for Business, Innovation and Skills, and the Secretary of State for Transport, these included the Attorney General, the Advocate General for Scotland, nine whips, four ministers of state and 10 parliamentary secretaries.

Obligations of membership

Unlike the House of Commons, many members of the House of Lords are not engaged full time in the business of the House or activities incidental thereto. Indeed it is one of the strengths of the House that its many part-time members are occupied in other pursuits, on the experience of which they may draw in their work in the upper chamber. But there must be some obligation of attendance and participation, particularly on the part of the life peers who

---

[261] On this, see Miliband, *Capitalist Democracy in Britain*, p 125.

[262] Lord Carrington was Foreign Secretary in the House of Lords in Mrs Thatcher's government until he resigned in 1982 following the invasion of the Falkland Islands.

have voluntarily assumed the benefits of office. House of Lords Standing Order 23 – introduced on 16 June 1958 – provides that 'Lords are to attend the sittings of the House or, if they cannot do so, obtain leave of absence, which the House may grant at pleasure.' It is also provided, however, that this particular standing order 'shall not be understood as requiring a Lord who is unable to attend regularly to apply for leave of absence if he proposes to attend as often as he reasonably can'.[263] At any time during a Parliament, a Lord may obtain leave of absence for the rest of the Parliament by applying in writing to the Clerk of the Parliaments.[264] Before the beginning of every new Parliament, the Clerk of the Parliaments (a senior officer of the House) writes to each member who was on leave in the previous Parliament asking whether he or she wishes to apply for leave in the forthcoming Parliament.[265]

A peer who has been granted leave of absence is expected not to attend sittings of the House during the period of leave, although provision is made for a peer who wishes to terminate his or her leave of absence to give a month's notice.[266] The House has no power to expel a member but it does have the power to suspend members for breach of the rules governing conduct.[267] This power was exercised in 2009 in relation to two Labour peers who had been reported by the *Sunday Times* as being willing to use their position to promote commercial interests for financial advantage.[268] Since 1957 a daily attendance allowance has been paid and travel costs are met; attending peers also receive allowances for overnight stays away from home, as well as for secretarial and research assistance. There is a sense, however, that membership of a part-time legislative chamber on an unpaid basis is difficult for people from outside London and the south-east. The average daily attendance in the House is said to have more than trebled since the introduction of life peers: from 136 in 1959/60 to 446 in 1998/99. It has also been said that the introduction of life peers has broadened the areas of expertise of the Lords, 'beyond the traditional fields of agriculture, the armed forces and the law'.[269]

Further reform

The House of Lords Act 1999 was designed to be only the first step in the process of reform. But as was discovered by the Royal Commission on the Reform of the House of Lords which reported in 2000, it is difficult to produce a solution for a reformed House which commands agreement across the political spectrum.[270] Democratic instinct suggests that the only credible solution is a wholly or largely elected (directly or indirectly) Upper House (perhaps one renamed as a Senate).[271] But the difficulty with this is that it could end up with a House wholly dominated by the political parties and, depending on election results, with the same party in control of both the Commons and the Lords. In that case, there would be little prospect of effective scrutiny

---

[263] HL SO 23(1).

[264] Ibid, 23(2).

[265] Ibid, 23(3).

[266] Ibid, 23(4). It was hoped in this way to diminish the influence of backwoodsmen – mainly hereditary peers who played little part in the work of the House but who might be summoned by their party leaders to vote on crucial and contentious divisions. After the culling of the hereditary peers, this ought to be much less of a problem today.

[267] HL 87 (2008–09). Powers of expulsion were included in the government's Constitutional Reform and Governance Bill 2009. But they were not enacted.

[268] HL 88 (2008–09). And see ch 11 C.

[269] Cm 4534, 2000, paras 2.8–2.10.

[270] For good accounts of the difficulties, see Bogdanor, *Politics and the Constitution*, ch 14; Brazier, *Constitutional Reform*, ch 11; and Shell, *The House of Lords*.

[271] See Richard and Welfare, *Unfinished Business*. See also R Blackburn, in Blackburn and Plant, *Constitutional Reform*, ch 1 and Billy Bragg, *A Genuine Expression of the Will of the People*.

or revision of government business. Conversely, election could lead to a House with a majority different from that of the Commons, leading to the alternative result of stalemate or gridlock in the legislative process, with both Houses claiming a mandate for their actions and each claiming a superior mandate to the other. It is thus a curious paradox that a nominated House without an electoral mandate is able to produce a revising chamber which simultaneously provides a greater measure of independent scrutiny of government than the House of Commons, without at the same time undermining the political supremacy of the House of Commons, or unduly impeding or frustrating the implementation of the government's programme.[272]

Any proposal for the reform of the composition of the House of Lords ought logically to begin by asking what it is we expect the House of Lords to do and to tailor composition to function. If the purpose is to act as a restraint on government, the case for an elected chamber would be irresistible (provided election were guaranteed to produce a House with a different political majority from the Commons). If, however, the purpose is (as currently) that of revision and scrutiny, there may be a case for other methods of composition. It has, however, proved to be impossible to build a consensus around the next stage of reform, perhaps because there is no consensus on the role of a second chamber in the British constitution. Deep divisions were on display in 2007 when the Commons voted for a wholly or largely (80 per cent) elected House of Lords, to be followed only a few days later by the House of Lords voting for a wholly nominated chamber.[273] It is, of course, the case that fundamental reform is unlikely to take place without the agreement of the Lords itself, though it is not to be overlooked that the 1999 Act was passed with their consent. Although the Labour government in 2008 was committed publicly to an elected second chamber,[274] its Constitutional Reform and Governance Bill of the following year had the much more modest aims to which we have referred above. Lords reform thus continues to be as intractable in 2010 as it was in 1918, 1945 and 1968,[275] and it may be that only a clear electoral mandate for a clearly expressed proposal will be enough to break the log-jam.

J. Meeting of Parliament

In law, a new Parliament is summoned by means of a royal proclamation. It is by the Queen that Parliament is prorogued, which occurs when a session of Parliament is terminated; and dissolved, when the life of one Parliament is brought to an end. These powers of the Queen are prerogative powers, derived from the common law powers of the Crown, not from statutes.[276] They were used as political weapons by the Stuart kings during their struggles with Parliament in the seventeenth century; since then they have been subjected to both legal and political controls, originally to ensure that the King could not govern without Parliament. In 1689, art 13 of the Bill of Rights provided that 'for redress of all grievances, and for the amending, strengthening and preserving of the laws, Parliament ought to be held frequently'.[277] In 1694, the Meeting of Parliament Act (formerly the Triennial Act) supplemented this rather vague demand by requiring that Parliament should meet at least once every three years, a requirement which still forms part of the law.

---

[272] The elected option was rejected by the Royal Commission on the Reform of the House of Lords which had been appointed in 1999, although it did recommend that there should be an elected element: Cm 4534, 2000.

[273] HC Deb, 6 March 2007, col 1389, 7 March 2007, col 1524; HL Deb, 12 March 2007, col 451, 13 March 2007, col 626.

[274] Cm 7027, 2007; Cm 7170, 2007; Cm 7438, 2008.

[275] Cd 9038, 1918; Cmd 7380, 1948; and Cmnd 3799, 1968. See G Phillipson [2004] PL 352.

[276] Ch 12 D. And see Blackburn, *The Meeting of Parliament*.

[277] Ch 2 A.

Frequency and duration of Parliament

Parliament has met annually ever since 1689, though this is not a matter of legal obligation. It has been the practice since then for some essential legislation, including authority for certain forms of taxation and expenditure, to be passed only for a year at a time; the legislation in question must therefore be renewed annually if lawful government is to be maintained.[278] Today the many pressures on government to maintain a flow of legislation through Parliament and the expectation of all politicians that Parliament should meet regularly ensure that, subject to customary periods of holiday, Parliament is in almost constant session. The Meeting of Parliament Act 1694 also regulated the life of a Parliament: no Parliament was to last for more than three years and, unless sooner dissolved, was then to expire by lapse of time. The Septennial Act 1715 extended the life of Parliament to seven years but the Parliament Act 1911 reduced the period to five years; the five-year period runs from the day appointed by writ of summons for Parliament to meet after a general election.[279] In practice, apart from the two world wars, when the life of Parliament was extended annually to avoid the holding of a general election during wartime, all modern Parliaments have been dissolved by the Queen, rather than expiring by lapse of time. The length of recent Parliaments has varied: that elected in February 1974 lasted only until October 1974; by contrast, the Parliaments elected in 1987, 1992 and 2005 lasted for almost the full five years, whereas those elected in 1997 and 2001 each lasted for four years.

Parliament continues for five years unless it is dissolved sooner by the Queen on the advice of the Prime Minister. Save in exceptional circumstances, the Queen must give effect to the Prime Minister's request. The opportunity to choose the timing of a general election is an important power at the disposal of the Prime Minister, who may choose a time when there is a revival in the economy or when the government's popularity is rising.[280] It is sometimes said that the right to request a dissolution is a powerful weapon in the hands of a Prime Minister to compel recalcitrant supporters in the Commons to conform. Where government policies are challenged by major national interests, the Prime Minister may take the dispute to the electorate in the hope of getting renewed support, as happened in February 1974 when Mr Heath called an election because the miners' strike challenged his economic policy. But dissolution is too ultimate a deterrent to be a convenient means of bringing pressure to bear on government members of the Commons, since an election at an unfavourable time may mean that the party goes out of office sooner than it otherwise would have done.[281] Nevertheless, the possibility of a dissolution before the statutory life of a Parliament has run its course leaves the executive with a means of controlling Parliament which would not be available if the law required an election of a new Parliament at prescribed intervals (for example, once every four years).[282] Since the Representation of the People Act 1867, the duration of Parliament has been independent of the life of the monarch.[283]

---

[278] So too authority for the maintenance of the army has been continued in force annually, although this is now done by resolution of Parliament and not by Act. Ch 16.

[279] Septennial Act 1715 and Parliament Act 1911, s 5.

[280] See Ch 12 B.

[281] See Ch 13 A.

[282] See Ch 12 B.

[283] If Parliament should be prorogued or adjourned when the monarch dies, Parliament must reassemble at once without a summons (Succession to the Crown Act 1707, s 5). Should the monarch die after a dissolution, but before the date fixed for the election, the former Parliament must meet immediately and polling day is postponed for 2 weeks (Representation of the People Act 1985, s 20, repealing the Meeting of Parliament Act 1797, ss 3–5).

Summoning of Parliament

Modern practice is that the same proclamation both dissolves Parliament and summons a new one. Formerly Parliament would be dissolved only after it had first been prorogued, but dissolution may now occur while the two Houses are adjourned.[284] After the summoning of Parliament by proclamation, individual writs are issued to the members of the Lords and writs are issued to returning officers commanding an election of members of the Commons to be held. Between general elections, a session of Parliament usually runs from late October or early November for about one year. After the long summer adjournment of both Houses, there is usually a short resumption of the two Houses to complete necessary legislative business. Parliament is then prorogued and a new session opens a few days later. When a vacancy occurs in the House during a Parliament, for example by the death of a member, the Speaker may by warrant authorise the issue of a writ for the holding of a by-election. When the House is sitting, the Speaker issues the warrant upon the order of the House.[285] By long-established custom of the House, the motion for the issue of a writ is moved by the Chief Whip of the party which held the seat before the vacancy occurred. There is no time limit for filling the vacancy. In 1973 the Speaker's Conference on electoral law recommended that the writ for a by-election should normally be moved within three months of the vacancy occurring.[286]

Prorogation brings to an end a session of Parliament. Parliament is prorogued not by the Queen in person but by a royal commission, through whom the prorogation speech reviewing the work of the session is delivered to Parliament. Parliament may be recalled by proclamation at one day's notice during a prorogation, if this should be necessary.[287] Prorogation previously terminated all business pending in Parliament so that any public Bills which had not passed through all stages in both Houses would lapse. The Standing Orders now make provision for carry-over Bills which means that a Bill may begin life in one session of Parliament and be completed in another.[288] At the beginning of every session, the first business is the debate on the speech from the throne. This speech announces in outline the government's plans for the principal business of the session. It is delivered in the House of Lords, to which the Commons are summoned to hear the speech read by the Queen or by the Lord Chancellor, as the senior Lord Commissioner (despite being a member of the House of Commons), or the Lord President of the Council in his or her place. In each House an address is moved in answer to the speech and a general debate of national affairs takes place, lasting some four or five days.

Election of the Speaker

After a dissolution or a prorogation, Parliament is opened by the Queen in person or by royal commissioners. When a new Parliament meets, the House of Commons first elects a Speaker, for which purpose the MP who has the longest continuous period of membership and is not a minister of the Crown presides over the proceedings.[289] After this the House adjourns until the election of the Speaker has been announced by the Lord Chancellor (even though he or she may no longer be a member of the House of Lords) in the House of Lords.[290] The Lords take the oath of allegiance as soon as Parliament has been opened and the Commons as soon as the Speaker

---

[284] See R Blackburn [1987] PL 533.
[285] By the Recess Elections Act 1975, which re-enacted an Act of 1784, the Speaker may order the issue of a writ during a recess caused by prorogation or adjournment.
[286] Cmnd 5500, 1973.
[287] Parliament (Elections and Meetings) Act 1943, s 34.
[288] HC SO 80A.
[289] Ibid, SO 1(1) and see HC 111 (1971–72).
[290] On the Lord Chancellor, see ch 18 below.

has taken the oath.[291] The chief officer of the House of Commons is the Speaker. Except when the House is in committee, he or she is its chair and is responsible for the orderly conduct of debate. It is through the Speaker that the House communicates with the Queen. Today, the Speaker is expected to act with complete impartiality between the parties and to preserve the rights of minorities in the House.[292] A member of the House is elected to be Speaker at the beginning of each new Parliament and whenever a vacancy otherwise occurs. It is customary for the party with a majority in the House to select a candidate from among its own number, but that person will not necessarily be elected. When Michael Martin from the Labour backbenches was elected to succeed Betty Boothroyd in 2000, it was the first time in recent years that a retiring Speaker had been succeeded by someone from the same side of the House. The election of Speaker Martin proved controversial for a number of reasons and led to the introduction of formal rules for dealing with contested elections for Speaker in new standing orders of the House.[293]

If the Speaker in the previous Parliament is re-elected as an MP at the general election, it is customary for him or her to be re-elected as Speaker when the new Parliament meets. In such a case, he or she will have fought the election as Speaker, not as a member of his or her former party. While the Speaker is unable to represent his or her constituency's interests in debate, he or she is able to take up the grievances of constituents privately with the departments concerned. It is very unusual for a Speaker to be removed from office or to be forced to resign. In 2009, however, Speaker Martin became the first Speaker in living memory to resign when it appeared that he had lost the confidence of the House. Following an election under the procedures referred to above, he was succeeded by a Conservative backbencher, John Bercow. The Speaker's salary is payable out of the Consolidated Fund. A retired Speaker receives a peerage by convention (as did Speaker Martin), and a statutory pension. If a Speaker dies in office, all business of the House comes to a halt until a successor is appointed. The Lord Speaker in the House of Lords is in contrast a much more recently created position, and has come into being as a result of the constitutional changes which led to a transformation in the role of the Lord Chancellor. The latter was in effect the Speaker of the House of Lords, a role which was combined (anomalously in the view of some) with governmental and judicial responsibilities. House of Lords Standing Orders now provide for the election of a Lord Speaker to hold office for renewable periods of up to five years.[294] The Lord Speaker – whose appointment must be approved by the Queen – may be removed by the House.[295]

---

[291] Under the Oaths Act 1978, s 5, members may make a solemn affirmation in lieu of the oath.
[292] See Laundy, *The Office of Speaker*.
[293] HC SO 1A and 1B.
[294] HL SO 19.
[295] Ibid.

CHAPTER 10

Functions of Parliament

We have already examined the relationship between Parliament, the executive and the judiciary and the principle of responsible government. In looking more closely at the functions of Parliament, we will focus attention on the House of Commons, since it is the composition of this House that determines which party will form the government, it is from the Commons that most ministers are drawn and it is the House of Commons that by withdrawing its support can cause the Prime Minister to resign or to seek a dissolution. But the work of the House of Commons must not be exaggerated beyond its context. First, the role of the House of Lords in Parliament, especially in legislation, is significant, although the political role of the House is secondary to that of the Commons. Second, the political authority of the House of Commons does not extend to its undertaking the work of government itself. Most members of the Commons are not members of the government. Nor could an elected assembly of 650 members itself take on the executive role in national affairs.

A classic statement of both the importance of parliamentary control of government and its limitations was made by the political philosopher, John Stuart Mill:

> There is a radical distinction between controlling the business of government, and actually doing it. The same person or body may be able to control everything, but cannot possibly do everything; and in many cases its control over everything will be more perfect, the less it personally attempts to do . . . It is one question, therefore, what a popular assembly should control, another what it should itself do . . . Instead of the function of governing, for which it is radically unfit, the proper office of a representative assembly is to watch and control the government; to throw the light of publicity on its acts; to compel a full exposition and justification of all of them which anyone considers questionable; to censure them if found condemnable, and, if the men who compose the government abuse their trust, or fulfil it in a manner which conflicts with the deliberate sense of the nation, to expel them from office, and either expressly or virtually appoint their successors.[1]

Mill stressed that an important function of the Commons was also to be a sounding board for the nation's grievances and opinions, 'an arena in which not only the general opinion of the nation, but that of every section of it . . . can produce itself in full light and challenge discussion'.[2]

This high-principled analysis is still of value, even though the strength of the executive power today, the present electoral and party system, and the fact that economic power is located outside the House of Commons, together present a formidable challenge to the political authority of the House. If it is a duty of the House to find out about, scrutinise and influence the many acts of government agencies, two consequences follow: first, the House needs procedures and resources that match the scale of the task; second, the members of the House who do not hold ministerial office need the political will to do more than simply sustain the government in office while voting through the measures laid before it. The creation by the Commons in 1979 of a system of specialist committees to scrutinise the main departments of government was a notable reform,[3] but the committees operate within a House which for many tasks still adopts an adversarial approach to politics in its proceedings. And although parliamentary procedure has undergone a process of modernisation since 1997, the reformer's scalpel has been less keenly felt in this area

---

[1] Mill, *Representative Government*, ch 5.
[2] Ibid.
[3] Section D in this chapter.

than in others. Indeed it has been suggested – perhaps with only some exaggeration – that the government's approach to legislative modernisation 'always owed more to its desire to secure the passage of its business than a desire to improve the effectiveness of parliamentary scrutiny'.[4]

Many writers have sought to list the principal functions of Parliament, a task complicated by the fact that the House must supply the personnel of the government which it is expected to hold to account. Bagehot in *The English Constitution* included within the functions of the House of Commons the expressive function (expressing the opinion of the people), the teaching function and the informing function ('it makes us hear what otherwise we should not'),[5] as well as the functions of legislation and finance. In 1978, the House's Select Committee on Procedure, whose report led to the reform of the committee system in 1979, considered that the major tasks of the Commons fell into four main categories: legislation, the scrutiny of the activities of the executive, the control of finance and the redress of grievances.[6] Inevitably these categories overlap and the list does not include the broader political functions of the House that underlie its more detailed tasks. Here the work of Parliament will be examined under five headings: (*a*) legislation; (*b*) conflict between the two Houses; (*c*) financial procedure; (*d*) scrutiny of administration; and (*e*) its role as constitutional watchdog.[7] The redress of collective grievances is related to all these headings; the redress of individual grievances is an aspect of the scrutiny of administration and also relevant is the Parliamentary Ombudsman, whose work will be considered in chapter 29 D.

A. Legislation

In chapter 4, we saw that the legislative supremacy of Parliament does not mean that the whole work of legislating is carried on within Parliament or that the parliamentary stage is the most formative stage in the process of legislation. Many government policies can be achieved within the framework of existing legislation: for example, by the provision of more money for certain purposes or by the use of existing powers to direct local authorities. But other policies require legislation and most legislation is initiated by the government. The scope for legislative initiatives by individual MPs is severely limited, both because of restricted parliamentary time, and the tight hold the government maintains over departmental action. The process by which government policies are turned into law falls into three broad stages:

(*a*) before publication of the Bill;

(*b*) the passage of the Bill through Parliament;

(*c*) after the Bill has received the royal assent.

In this section, emphasis is placed on the second of these stages. But stages (*a*) and (*c*) are both important to an understanding of the legislative process.[8] The process of legislation, like most aspects of parliamentary procedure, is complicated.[9] A distinction must be drawn between

---

[4] P Cowley and M Stuart (2001) *Parliamentary Affairs* 238.

[5] Bagehot, p 153. And see Norton, *Parliament in British Politics*.

[6] HC 588-1 (1977–8), p viii.

[7] See also Ryle and Richards (eds), *The Commons Under Scrutiny*; Walkland (ed.), *The House of Commons in the Twentieth Century*; Norton, *The Commons in Perspective*; Norton, *Parliament in British Politics*; Griffith and Ryle, *Parliament*. For a valuable historical account dealing with the House of Commons in particular, see P Seaward and P Silk, in Bogdanor (ed.), *The British Constitution in the Twentieth Century*. A Kelso, in Flinders et al. (eds), *The Oxford Handbook of British Politics*, ch 13 is a good contemporary overview.

[8] Cf the analysis in Hansard Society, *Making the Law*.

[9] See HC 538 (1970–71); HC 1097 (2005–6); Griffith, *Parliamentary Scrutiny of Government Bills*; Erskine May *Parliamentary Practice* (esp ch 22); Griffith and Ryle, *Parliament*, ch 6; and Hansard Society (note 8).

public and private Bills. A public Bill seeks to alter the general law and is introduced into Parliament under the standing orders of the two Houses relating to public business. A private Bill is a Bill relating to a matter of individual, corporate or local interest and is subject to separate standing orders relating to private business.[10] A private Bill must not be confused with a public Bill introduced by a private member, which is known as a private member's Bill.[11]

The pre-Bill stage

A Bill will typically be included in a government's legislative programme, which since 2007 has been announced before the Queen's Speech. The Draft Legislative Programme will set out the details of each proposed bill: 'its purpose, main elements, key benefits (as viewed by the government) and territorial extent'. According to the House of Commons Modernisation Committee, the government's stated aim in producing the Draft Legislative Programme was 'to provide advance information about its legislative intentions and to conduct a wider consultation so that, if necessary, the programme could be altered before its announcement in the Queen's Speech'.[12] The life history of a Bill will, however, usually have begun long before this, originating perhaps in a party's election manifesto or in the efforts of a pressure group to get the law changed. Public authorities may have experienced difficulties in administering the existing law and may seek wider powers. A royal commission, the Law Commissions or bodies such as the Committee on Standards in Public Life may have published reports recommending law reform. Economic problems or the action of terrorists may have made it necessary for government to take preventive measures. A decision of the courts, including the European Court of Human Rights and the European Court of Justice, may have shown the need for legislation. The government may have entered into a treaty which imposes an obligation to change the law of the United Kingdom.

Once it is decided to proceed with a Bill, it is for the department primarily concerned to determine precisely what it should contain, and these instructions are conveyed to Parliamentary Counsel who are responsible for drafting all government Bills. While a Bill is being drafted, extensive consultation may take place with other departments affected and successive revisions of the draft Bill will be circulated confidentially within government. There may also be consultation with organisations outside government representing the interests primarily affected, but until recently it was uncommon for a draft Bill to be disclosed. These consultations will normally cover both the general principles of the Bill as well as some of its more detailed provisions, especially where they are contentious. In recent years the government has adopted the practice of publishing a number of Bills in draft form, a practice welcomed by the House of Commons Modernisation Committee in 2002 as providing a 'real chance for the House to exercise its powers of pre-legislative scrutiny in an effective way'.[13] In an important report on the *Legislative Process*, the Modernisation Committee returned to the theme in 2006 and announced that pre-legislative scrutiny of draft Bills was 'one of the most successful Parliamentary innovations of the last ten years', and 'should become more widespread, giving outside bodies and individuals a chance to have their say before a bill is introduced and improving the quality of the bills that are presented to Parliament'.[14] The government has acknowledged the valuable role of departmental select committees in scrutinising draft Bills, and is committed to publishing more Bills in draft 'to improve the quality of legislation'.[15]

---

[10] Page 192.
[11] Page 189.
[12] HC 81 (2007–8), para 1.
[13] HC 1168 (2001–2). For an account of scrutiny of draft Bills, see A Kennon [2004] PL 477.
[14] HC 1097 (2005–6).
[15] Ibid, p 3.

Public Bill procedure

1 *From first reading to committee.* In the case of government Bills, the sponsoring minister presents the Bill to the Commons; it receives a formal first reading and is then printed and published. There follows the second reading of the Bill, when the House may debate its general proposals. If the second reading is opposed, a division may take place on an opposition amendment to postpone the second reading for three or six months or (more usually) on a reasoned amendment opposing the Bill. For a government Bill to be lost on second reading would be a serious political defeat. This setback has been avoided by most modern governments, but not by the government in 1986 when the Shops Bill, to reform the law on Sunday opening of shops, was defeated on second reading in the Commons by 296 votes to 282.[16] The amount of time devoted to the second reading of a Bill will vary, though modern practice has been to schedule all second reading debates to last for no more than a day, with a maximum of $6^{1}/_{2}$ hours for debate.[17] Where a Bill involves new public expenditure or new taxation, the Commons must approve a financial resolution on the proposal of a minister before the clauses concerned may be considered in committee; the financial resolution is approved immediately after a Bill's second reading.[18] In some cases the second reading may take place in the Scottish Grand Committee,[19] the Welsh Grand Committee,[20] or in a second reading committee.[21] An expedited procedure exists for Consolidation Bills.[22]

After second reading, a Bill is normally referred for detailed consideration to a public bill committee, consisting of between 16 and 50 members nominated by the Committee of Selection.[23] The Committee of Selection must have regard to the qualifications of the members and to the composition of the House, which means in practice that the parties are represented as nearly as possible in proportion to their representation in the House. If the government came into office with an overall majority over other parties and later lost that majority, questions would arise about its continuing majorities on public bill committees.[24] Following the Modernisation Committee's report on the *Legislative Process*, public bill committees may now receive both written and oral evidence from interested parties as part of their examination of a Bill. Instead of referring a Bill to a public bill committee, the House may commit the Bill to a committee of the whole House,[25] for which purpose the Speaker's place is taken by the Chairman of Ways and Means or one of the deputy chairmen. In practice this happens only on the proposal of the government, whether for minor Bills on which the committee stage is purely formal, for Bills of outstanding political or constitutional importance, or for Bills which the government wishes to see become law as soon as possible.[26] Occasionally the committee stages of parts of a Bill will be dealt with in a committee of the whole House, with the other parts being dealt with in a public bill committee.

---

[16] HC Deb, 14 April 1986, cols 584–702. See Brazier, *Constitutional Practice*, pp 219–20. On the willingness of MPs to rebel, see Cowley, *The Rebels*.

[17] HC 1096 (2005–06), paras 41–45. It has been suggested that this is too long for some bills and too short for others, and that more flexibility is required by the business managers in the House (ibid).

[18] Page 200 below; Erskine May, ch 31; Griffith and Ryle, p 324.

[19] HC Standing Orders (HC SO(s)) 92–99. See C M G Himsworth (1996) 1 Edin LR 79.

[20] HC SOs 102–108.

[21] HC SO 90; Griffith and Ryle, p 323.

[22] HC SO 140. See Lord Simon of Glaisdale and J V D Webb [1975] PL 285.

[23] HC SOs 84, 86; Griffith and Ryle, pp 325–30.

[24] See Erskine May, p 799.

[25] HC SO 63, 66.

[26] It is a 'long-standing convention of the House' that 'bills of first class constitutional importance' should 'have all their stages on the floor of the House'. This is said to derive from a memorandum submitted by the Labour government to the Procedure Committee in 1945. See HC 190 (1997–8), paras 74–5. Major Bills taken in committee of the whole House have included the Bills for the European Communities Act 1972, the Scotland Act 1998, the Government of Wales Act 1998, the Northern Ireland Act 1998, the Human Rights Act 1998, the House of Lords Act 1999, the Representation of the People Act 2000, and parts of the Political Parties, Elections and Referendums Act 2000, and the Political Parties and Elections Act 2009.

2 *From committee to third reading.* Whether a Bill is considered in a public bill committee or in a committee of the whole House, the object of the committee stage is to consider the individual clauses of the Bill and to enable amendments to be made. While general approval has been given to the Bill on second reading, members opposed to the Bill may use the committee stage to propose amendments narrowing its scope or in other ways rendering it more acceptable to them. Members may be able to persuade the minister in charge of the Bill to reconsider a specific point, but the government expects to maintain its majority in committee and an amendment is not often made against the wishes of the government. On one notable occasion, however, a committee of the whole House inflicted the first Commons defeat on the post-1997 Labour government when it accepted an amendment to reject proposals for the detention without charge of terrorist suspects for up to 90 days.[27] After the amendments to a clause have been considered, there may take place a further debate on the motion that the clause, or the clause as amended, should stand part of the Bill. Occasionally Bills will formally be referred to a select committee, though this procedure is now used mainly for the quinquennial armed forces Bills.[28]

When a Bill has completed its committee stage, it is reported as amended to the whole House. On the report stage, further amendments may be made to the Bill on the proposal of ministers, sometimes to give effect to undertakings which they have given in committee, sometimes to remove amendments made in committee but not accepted by the government. The Opposition may use the report stage to urge further amendments upon the government, although it is rare for these amendments to succeed and the Speaker has the discretion to select the amendments which will be debated.[29] A Bill committed to the whole House and not amended in committee is not considered by the House on report. Bills which were considered by a second reading committee or the Scottish Grand Committee (but not the Welsh or Northern Ireland Grand Committees) may be referred to a committee to consider Bills on report or to the Scottish Grand Committee for the report stage, but there has been reluctance to deprive the whole House of its opportunity to consider Bills at this stage,[30] and any such referral can be blocked by the objection of at least 20 members. After a Bill has been considered on report, it receives its third reading; only verbal amendments may be made to a Bill at this stage.[31] Such debates as there are tend to be brief and formal, although with a controversial Bill the Opposition may wish once more to vote against it.

Government business and the role of backbenchers

1 *Allocation of time.* In the legislative work of the Commons, the time factor is always of importance both to the government, which wishes to see its Bills pass through Parliament without delay, and to the Opposition and backbench MPs, who may seek to prolong proceedings as a means of persuading the government to make concessions. As well as the power of the Speaker or chairman to require a member to discontinue speaking who persists in irrelevance or tedious repetition,[32] various methods of curtailing debates have been adopted by the House, of which allocation of time orders are now the most important. In practice the most common are now programme orders, whereby a fixed amount of time is allocated in advance to each stage of a Bill in the House of Commons.[33] A programme motion may be moved only by a minister

---

[27] HC Deb, 9 November 2005, col 386.

[28] See HC 828, 2005–06. On Bills other than the armed forces Bills, see Railway Bill 1999 and Health (Wales) Bill 2003.

[29] HC SO 32(1).

[30] HC SO 92; Griffith and Ryle, pp 394–5.

[31] HC SO 77.

[32] HC SO 42.

[33] HC SO 83A–83I. See Griffith and Ryle, p 416.

before second reading, with the vote on the motion taking place immediately after second reading. Although this seems a rather obvious way to conduct legislative business, it is a fairly recent innovation, being first used in 1998 following a recommendation of the Modernisation Committee.[34] It also remains a mildly controversial innovation, with the Modernisation Committee addressing concerns that a good idea had been corrupted in practice and that programming was undermining the rights of backbenchers by squeezing them out of debates. Acknowledging these concerns, the Committee nevertheless noted that programming 'has become much less prescriptive and is used to ensure full debate', while the government 'works hard to make programming consensual' and that 'opposition to programming has decreased'.[35]

A second and longer established method of curtailing debates by means of an allocation of time order is the 'guillotine', which may also be moved by a minister with a view to alloting a specified number of days or portions of days to the consideration of a Bill in committee of the whole House or on report. The difference between this and a programme order is that the latter is moved after the second reading as we have seen, while the guillotine motion will be moved at a later stage if the government believes that a Bill is being held up deliberately. The guillotine motion may be debated for no more than three hours, and if it is carried, it is the duty of the Business Committee, which consists of the Chairman of Ways and Means and up to eight other members nominated by the Speaker, to divide the Bill into parts and to allot to each part a specified period of time.[36] A similar procedure exists by which the House may allocate time for the proceedings of a public bill committee on any Bill; the detailed allocation of time is then made by a business sub-committee.[37] The effect of a guillotine motion is that at the end of each allotted period, the portion of the Bill in question is voted on without further discussion. Compulsory timetabling of this latter kind is unusual, though it has been more common in some years than in others, with the heaviest use of the guillotine since 1945 occurring in 1998–1999 and 1999–2000. The increase in the use of programme orders (which have much the same effect) should make the use of the guillotine much less frequent, and indeed a total of only eight guillotine orders were made between 2000–2001 and 2006–2007.

2 _Private members' Bills._ Although the bulk of the legislative programme is taken up by government Bills, a small but significant part consists of Bills introduced by backbench MPs. There are three ways by which Bills may be introduced by backbenchers in the House of Commons. First and most importantly, although standing orders generally give precedence to government business, they set aside 13 Fridays in each session on which private members' Bills have priority. On the first seven of these Fridays, precedence is given to the second reading of Bills presented by members who have secured the best places in the ballot for private members' Bills held at the beginning of each session. On the remaining Fridays, precedence is given to the later stages of those Bills which received their second readings earlier in the session.[38] As in the case of government Bills, private members' Bills are referred to a public bill committee, and as a general rule only one public bill committee should sit at any one time to consider private member's Bills. The composition of a public bill committee on a private member's Bill usually reflects the voting of the House on second reading, so that the supporters of the Bill form a majority. Otherwise, a member may seek leave under Standing Order 23 to introduce a Bill under the 'ten-minute rule' procedure (on Tuesdays and Wednesdays only), and may speak briefly in support of the Bill,

---

[34] See HC 190 (1997–98). See also HC 589 (1999–2000), HC 382 (2000–1), HC 1222 (2002–3), and HC 1097 (2005–6).

[35] HC 337 (2006–07), paras 120–2.

[36] HC SOs 82, 83. For the history, see Jennings, _Parliament_, pp 241–6; for more recent practice, Griffith and Ryle, pp 413–18.

[37] HC SO 120.

[38] HC SO 14(4), (5).

while an opponent may reply, and the House may then divide on the issue.[39] There may also be an opportunity under Standing Order 57 for a private member simply to present a Bill for its first reading, after giving notice, but without previously obtaining the leave of the House.[40] Under each of these latter procedures the chances of a Bill proceeding further depend on whether it is completely unopposed or on whether some time can be found for a second reading debate and later stages, either by the government or on a Friday devoted to private members' business.

In the 25-year period between 1983 and 2008, some 230 private members' Bills have been enacted. Most of these (179) originated under Standing Order 14, which means that a not insignificant number originated under the Standing Order 23 and 57 procedures. Private members' Bills are used for a variety of purposes including matters of social reform (for example, abortion and divorce law reform) on which public opinion may be too sharply divided for the government to wish to take the initiative, matters of special interest to minority groups (for example, rights of disabled persons) and topics of law reform which may be useful but have too low a priority to find a place in the government's programme.[41] A private member may not, however, propose a Bill the main object of which is the creation of a charge on the public revenue,[42] and where a Bill proposes charges on the revenue which are incidental to its main object, a financial resolution moved by a minister is needed before the financial clauses can be considered in committee. It is not the practice for the government to use its majority to defeat a private member's Bill by applying the whips.[43] The government has undertaken 'to make available the resources of parliamentary counsel whenever it appears that a Bill is likely to pass, for the purpose of ensuring that its terms give effect to its supporters' intentions'. This assistance is provided whether or not the government supports the Bill.[44] Not all private members' Bills become law: many are talked out by their opponents. Allocation of time orders are not applicable (whether in the form of programme motions or the guillotine), and the closure of debate needs the support of 100 members, which may not be easy to achieve on a Friday. A Bill which has not become law by the end of the session lapses. While less than 10% of private members' Bills are enacted, these initiatives form a small but valuable part of the whole legislative work of Parliament.

The House of Lords and the royal assent

1 *Procedure in the House of Lords*.[45] Except under the Parliament Acts 1911 and 1949, which are considered later, a Bill may be presented for the royal assent only when it has been approved by both Houses. After a public Bill has had its third reading in the Commons, it will be introduced into the Lords. The various stages in the Lords are broadly similar to those in the Commons, although they are governed by separate standing orders. The main difference has been that the committee stage of Bills is usually taken in committee of the whole House. In 1995 for the first time the 'committee of the whole House' sat in a separate room at Westminster to consider the Children (Scotland) Bill, enabling the House itself to deal with other business.[46] Bills not considered in a 'committee of the whole House' may be considered instead by a Grand Committee which is a committee unlimited in number and which all members of the House are entitled to attend.[47]

---

[39] HC SO 23.

[40] HC SO 57(1).

[41] See Richards, *Parliament and Conscience*, and (same author) in Walkland (ed.), *The House of Commons in the Twentieth Century*, ch 6; Bromhead, *Private Members' Bills in the British Parliament*; Griffith and Ryle, pp 539–58; and Cowley (ed.), *Conscience and Parliament*.

[42] HC SO 48.

[43] Richards, *Parliament and Conscience*, p 27, describes this as a 'strong convention'.

[44] HC 610 (2003–04), para 20. Also HC Deb, 23 June 2008, col 10w.

[45] Griffith and Ryle, ch 12; Shell, *The House of Lords*, chs 5 and 6.

[46] HL Deb, 6 June 1995, col CWH 1.

[47] Erskine May, pp 555–6.

In committee, there is no provision for the selection of amendments so that any amendments tabled may be moved. Even if no amendments are made in committee, there may be a report stage; although there is no limitation on the amendments which may be moved at the third reading, the House agreed normally to resolve major points of difference by the end of the Report stage, and to use Third Reading for tidying up the Bill. It is generally accepted that the House must consider government business within a reasonable time, but whether in fact this occurs often gives rise to disagreement. Exceptionally, a Bill may be referred to a select committee after second reading as in the case of the controversial Constitutional Reform Bill in 2004, which was so referred against the wishes of the government.[48]

The distinctive procedures of the House, in contrast with those of the Commons, facilitate the submission and consideration of amendments.[49] While some Bills coming from the Commons are approved by the Lords unchanged and with little debate, it is more usual for Bills to be considered in detail by the Lords and amendments made. This is particularly valuable when the effect of timetabling has been that only part of a Bill has been considered in detail by the Commons. The government itself tables many amendments in the Lords, some in response to undertakings given in the Commons. The passage of a Bill through the Lords thus enables the drafting of Bills to be improved as well as substantial amendments to be made and new material introduced. While the foregoing account has assumed that Bills are always introduced in the Commons, in principle Bills may originate in either House. The major exception is that by ancient privilege of the Commons, Bills of 'aids and supplies', i.e. those which relate to national taxation and expenditure or to local revenues and charges upon them, must begin in the Commons.[50] Moreover, the democratic character of the Commons and the fact that most ministers are MPs mean that Bills of major political importance start there. These factors often mean that early in a session the Lords have too little legislative work and have too much later in the session when a load of Bills approved by the Commons reaches them. In 1972 a standing order was adopted by the Commons which relaxed the extent of the Commons' financial privilege in the case of government Bills and made it easier for Bills with financial provisions to begin in the Lords.[51]

2 The royal assent. Parliament cannot legislate without the concurrence of all its parts and therefore the assent of the Queen is required after a Bill has passed through both Houses. The Queen does not attend Parliament to assent in person, since an Act of 1541 authorised the giving of the assent by commissioners in the presence of Lords and Commons and this became the invariable practice. Formerly the business of the Commons was interrupted to enable the Commons to attend the Lords for the purpose. But by the Royal Assent Act 1967, the assent, having been signified by letters patent under the Great Seal signed by the Sovereign, is notified separately to each House by its Speaker.[52] The traditional procedure has not, however, been abolished. In giving the royal assent ancient forms are used.[53] A public Bill, unless dealing with finance, as also a private Bill other than one of a personal nature, is accepted by the words '*La Reyne le veult*'. A financial Bill is assented to with the words '*La Reyne remercie ses bons sujets, accepte leur benevolence et ainsi le veult*'. The formula for the veto was '*La Reyne s'avisera*'. The right of veto has not been exercised since the reign of Queen Anne. The veto could now only be exercised on ministerial advice and no government would wish to veto Bills for which it was responsible or for

---

[48] See HL 125 (2003–04). For an account, see R Walters (2005) 73 *The Table* 87.

[49] See D N Clarke and D Shell [1994] PL 409, 412.

[50] Erskine May, ch 33; HC 538 (1970–71), paras 19–21. And see M Ryle, in Walkland (ed.), *The House of Commons in the Twentieth Century*, pp 355–9.

[51] HC Deb, 8 August 1972, col 1656; Erskine May, pp 921–2.

[52] See HL Deb, 2 March 1967, col 1181.

[53] Erskine May, p 565.

the passage of which it had afforded facilities through Parliament.[54] The consent of the Queen is requested before legislation which affects any matter relating to the royal prerogative is debated. Although the seeking of such consent may today be no more than an act of courtesy so far as government Bills are concerned, the need for this consent presents a potential obstacle for a private member's Bill which seeks to abolish one of the Queen's prerogatives, since it enables the government to prevent the House considering any such proposals.[55]

While the royal assent concludes the formal process by which Bills become law, it would be wrong to assume that the assent also marks the end of the legislative process. The royal assent may bring the Act into force immediately,[56] but the operation of all or part of an Act is often suspended by provisions in the Act itself. Thus the Act may specify a later date on which it is to come into force or may give power to the government by Order in Council or to a minister by statutory instrument to specify when the Act, or different parts of it, will operate.[57] Moreover, many Acts confer powers on the government to regulate in detail topics which are indicated only in outline in the Acts. Exercise of these powers is primarily a matter for the executive, subject to scrutiny by Parliament.[58] Parliamentary interest in what happens after a Bill becomes law is not confined to delegated legislation, but traditional procedures are not designed for enabling MPs to monitor the operation of legislation. In 1971 the Select Committee on Procedure recommended that use should be made of 'post-legislation' committees. These committees would examine the working of a statute within a short period of its enactment and would consider whether there was a need for early amending legislation to deal with difficulties arising in the administration of the Act.[59] Support for such scrutiny was subsequently expressed by other select committees of both Houses as well as by the Law Commission,[60] and in 2008 the Leader of the House issued a cautious statement of government support, with post-legislative scrutiny to be conducted in appropriate cases not implausibly by the existing select committees, rather than by a new committee dedicated to this task as the Law Commission had proposed.[61]

Private Bills

A private Bill is a Bill to alter the law relating to a particular locality or to confer rights on or relieve from liability a particular person or body of persons (including local authorities and statutory undertakers, providing public utilities). The procedure is regulated by the standing orders of each House relating to private business.[62] When the objects of the Bill have been advertised and plans and other documents have been displayed in the locality concerned, a petition for the Bill together with the Bill itself must be deposited in Parliament by 27 November each year. Landowners and

---

[54] See ch 2 B. On the question whether the royal assent could be refused by a monarch in the exercise of his or her human rights (such as the right to freedom of conscience in art 9 of the ECHR), see R Blackburn [2003] PL 205.

[55] Erskine May, 22nd edn, pp 603–5. It has been said, however, that the government's 'usual practice' is to advise the granting of consent even to Bills of which it disapproves (Erskine May, p 710).

[56] Acts of Parliament (Commencement) Act 1793 and Interpretation Act 1978, s 4: Acts deemed in force at beginning of day on which royal assent given, if no other provision made.

[57] Even if power to bring an Act into force has not been exercised, existence of the power may prevent the minister from acting under the prerogative to make provision inconsistent with the Act: *R v Home Secretary, ex p Fire Brigades Union* [1995] 2 AC 513; and E Barendt [1995] PL 357.

[58] Ch 28.

[59] HC 538 (1970–71), pp vii–ix; and HC 588–1 (1977–8), p xxvii.

[60] See respectively HC 190 (1997–98) and HC 1097 (2005–06) (Modernisation Committee); HC 558 (2002–03) (Liaison Committee); HL 173 (2003–04) (Constitution Committee); and Law Commission, Cm 7170, (2007), (Law Commission, which had been asked by the government to undertake this inquiry).

[61] Cm 7320, 2008 (Response to the Law Commission, above).

[62] See Williams, *History of Private Bill Procedure*, vol I; and Erskine May, chs 37–41.

others whose interests are directly affected are separately notified by the promoters and they may petition against the Bill. The practice in recent years has been for the second reading debate on private Bills to be wide ranging debates on the merits of the Bill. If read a second time, the Bill is committed to a committee of four members in the Commons or of five members in the Lords. The committee stage is usually the most important stage in the passage of a private Bill, particularly if there are many petitions of objection to it, and committee members are obliged to attend the meetings. The promoters and opponents of the Bill are usually represented by counsel and call evidence in support of their arguments. For its part, the committee first considers whether or not the facts stated in the preamble, which sets out the special reasons for the Bill, have been proved. If the preamble is accepted, the clauses are taken in order and may be amended. If the preamble is rejected, the Bill is dead. After the committee stage the Bill is reported to the House and its subsequent stages are similar to those of a public Bill.

This method of obtaining special statutory powers is useful to local authorities who seek wider powers than are generally conferred or who have special needs for which the general law does not provide. One reason for the elaborate procedure is to ensure that Parliament does not inadvertently take away an individual's private rights.[63] But this curious process – as much quasi-judicial as it is legislative – is elaborate, expensive and lengthy. Nowadays, there are other means of obtaining statutory authority for the exercise of special powers, notably under the Transport and Works Act 1992. This applies principally to schemes for the construction of railways, waterways and guided transport systems so that the need to use the private Bill procedure in these cases has been displaced. Where the Act applies, the proposed developer (public authority or private body) may make an application to the appropriate minister in England or the National Assembly in Wales, with applications being made typically in the past by bodies like Railtrack, London Underground and local authorities.[64] If an order is made under the Act by the minister or the National Assembly (after a local inquiry where objectors will have an opportunity to be heard), it may authorise the construction of the project, the compulsory purchase of land, and the power to make by-laws. It is now only in the case of projects which in the opinion of the Secretary of State are of 'national significance' that any parliamentary approval is required, in this case in the form of a motion approved by both Houses before an order is made by the minister.[65] Other schemes for the taking of land without the need for a private Act of Parliament are to be found in the Statutory Orders (Special Procedure) Acts 1945 and 1965.

A hybrid Bill has been defined as 'a public Bill which affects a particular private interest in a manner different from the private interest of other persons or bodies of the same category or class'.[66] Thus a Bill to confer a general power on the Secretary of State to acquire land for the construction of railway tunnels is not a hybrid Bill since all landowners are potentially affected: but the Bill which became the Channel Tunnel Act 1987, after a protracted parliamentary battle, was a hybrid Bill since it sought to confer power to acquire specific land and construct specific works. After its second reading, a hybrid Bill is referred to a select committee and those whose rights are adversely affected by the Bill may petition against it and bring evidence in support of their objections. The Bill may then pass through committee and later stages as if it were an ordinary Bill. Whether a public Bill is hybrid and therefore subject to the standing orders for private business is a matter decided initially by the Examiners of Petitions for Private Bills, usually before the second reading. This is a procedure that governments may seek to avoid being

---

[63] Cf *Pickin* v *British Railways Board* [1974] AC 765; ch 4 C.

[64] A separate and infrequently used procedure operates for Scotland under the Private Legislation Procedure (Scotland) Act 1936. But this does not apply where the public authority or persons are seeking powers wholly within the competence of the Scottish Parliament: Scotland Act 1998, Sch 8. See Erskine May, p 979, where it is thought as a result that these powers will now be used only rarely.

[65] Transport and Works Act 1992, s 9.

[66] Erskine May, pp 640–7.

drawn into, and it is notable that when the Labour government intervened to rescue Northern Rock in 2008 it did so by enacting legislation of a general nature, purporting to authorise the acquisition of other financial institutions should the relevant provisions of the Act have been met. Although these powers did need to be used in other cases, it was acknowledged that one reason why the Banking (Special Provisions) Act 2008 was not confined to Northern Rock was the belief that a Bill with such an effect would have to be treated as a hybrid bill, giving rise to time-consuming procedures which would have frustrated the urgent response the government believed to be necessary.[67]

B. Conflict between the two Houses

Before it can be presented for the royal assent, a Bill must be approved by both Houses of Parliament. In practice, however, the two Houses do not have the same political composition, so that it cannot today be assumed that the Lords will always acquiesce with the wishes of the Commons. Historically this was not a problem for the Conservative Party, as traditionally it enjoyed a large in-built majority as most of the hereditary peers tended to be Conservatives. But it was a problem for Labour governments, even after the Life Peerages Act 1958 allowed for life peers to be appointed. Since the House of Lords Act 1999 the hereditary peers have all but gone, and no one party has a majority in the House of Lords, which is now a problem for all governments. The formal position is that the House of Lords has the power to reject any Bill which is presented to it, regardless of whether it is a government Bill, and regardless of whether it has been approved by the House of Commons. The House of Lords also has the power to make whatever amendments it likes to Bills and to insist that these amendments are included in the Bill as a condition of its acceptance. In practice, however, the relationship between the two Houses is regulated by law (the Parliament Acts 1911–1949) and by convention (the so-called Salisbury Convention), both designed to affirm the supremacy of the House of Commons as the democratically elected chamber. But although subordinated to the Commons in these ways, it would be a very grave mistake to underestimate the very real political power retained by the House of Lords, and a mistake also to underestimate its willingness to use that power.[68] In 2002–3, for example, the government was defeated 88 times on 14 separate Bills. This was 'more than in any one session since 1975–76'.[69] Although this figure has not been repeated in any session since, the government was nevertheless defeated no fewer than 237 times in the five sessions beginning in 2003–04.

The Parliament Acts 1911–49

The immediate origin of the Parliament Act 1911 was the crisis caused when the House of Lords rejected Lloyd George's 'People's Budget' in 1909. However, conflict between the two houses had been simmering for some time,[70] and it was unsurprising that the matter would reach boiling point as a Liberal government with a popular mandate from an ever-widening franchise confronted a second chamber with a permanent majority of Conservative hereditary peers. The budget crisis of 1909 was resolved only when, after two general elections in 1910, the Liberal government made known George V's willingness on the Prime Minister's advice to create over

---

[67] HC Deb, 19 Feb 2008, col 173 (Chancellor of the Exchequer).

[68] Between 1970 and 1995, there were 603 government defeats in the Lords: HL Deb, 16 October 1995, col 90 (WA) and 27 November 1995, col 23 (WA), an average of 24 per session.

[69] P Cowley and M Stuart (2004) 57 *Parliamentary Affairs* 301, at p 304. See also P Cowley and M Stuart (2005) 58 *Parliamentary Affairs* 301.

[70] See Lowell, *The Government of England*, ch 22.

400 new Liberal peers to coerce the Lords to accept formal restraints on its powers.[71] The 1911 Act, which did not alter the composition of the upper House, made three main changes: (*a*) it reduced the life of Parliament from seven to five years; (*b*) it removed the power of the Lords to veto or delay money Bills; and (*c*) in the case of other public Bills, apart from a Bill to prolong the life of Parliament, the veto of the Lords was abolished and there was substituted a power to delay legislation for two years. But the period of delay which the Lords could impose meant that in the fourth and fifth years of a Parliament the Lords could hold up a Bill knowing that it could not become law until after a general election. After 1945, faced with a massive programme of nationalisation which it wished to get through Parliament, the Labour government proposed to reduce the period of delay from two years to one year. After extensive discussions on the reform of the House of Lords, which broke down on the period of delay, the Parliament Act 1949 became law under the 1911 Act procedure.

Under the Parliament Acts 1911–49, Bills may in certain circumstances receive the royal assent after having been approved only by the Commons. This may happen (*a*) if the Lords fail within one month to pass a Bill which, having passed the Commons, is sent up at least one month before the end of the session and is endorsed by the Speaker as a money Bill;[72] or (*b*) if the Lords refuse in two successive sessions, whether of the same Parliament or not, to pass a public Bill (other than a Bill certified as a money Bill or a Bill to extend the maximum duration of Parliament beyond five years) which has been passed by the Commons in those two sessions, provided that one year has elapsed between the date of the Bill's second reading in the Commons in the first of those sessions and the date of its third reading in that House in the second of those sessions.[73] A money Bill is a public Bill which, in the opinion of the Speaker, contains only provisions dealing with: the imposition, repeal, remission, alteration or regulation of taxation; the imposition of charges on the Consolidated Fund or the National Loans Fund or on money provided by Parliament for the payment of debt or other financial purposes or the variation or repeal of such charges; supply; the appropriation, receipt, custody, issue or audit of public accounts; or the raising or guarantee or repayment of loans. Bills dealing with taxation, money or loans raised by local authorities or bodies for local purposes are not certifiable as money Bills.[74] The statutory definition has been so strictly interpreted that many annual Finance Bills have not been endorsed with the Speaker's certificate.[75] However, Consolidated Fund and Appropriation Bills are invariably certified as money Bills.[76]

Where a Bill is presented for the royal assent under s 2 of the 1911 Act, it must be endorsed with the Speaker's certificate that s 2 has been complied with. As the Speaker must certify that it is the same Bill which has been rejected in two successive sessions, there are strict limits on the alterations which may be made to a Bill between the first and second sessions. But the Bill in the second session may include amendments which have already been approved by the Lords and, in sending up the Bill in the second session, the Commons may accompany it with further suggested amendments without inserting them into the Bill.[77] Any certificate of the Speaker given under the 1911 Act 'shall be conclusive for all purposes, and shall not be questioned in any

---

[71] See Jenkins, *Mr Balfour's Poodle*; Nicolson, *King George V*, chs 9 and 10; Jennings, *Cabinet Government*, pp 428–48. For an account of why the 1911 Act took the form it did, see J Jaconelli (1991) 10 *Parliamentary History* 277. See also *R (Jackson) v A-G* (see note 87 below).

[72] 1911 Act, s 1.

[73] Ibid, s 2 (as amended by the 1949 Act).

[74] Ibid, s 1 (as amended by the National Loans Act 1968). See D Morris (2001) 22 Statute LR 211.

[75] Erskine May, pp 929–30; and Jennings, *Parliament*, pp 416–19. Before giving the certificate, the Speaker must, if practicable, consult two members appointed from the chairmen's panel each session by the Committee of Selection of the House of Commons.

[76] Erskine May, p 880.

[77] 1911 Act, s 2(4). The procedure was used in relation to the Bill which became the Trade Union and Labour Relations (Amendment) Act 1976.

court of law',[78] a formula which seeks to exclude any challenge to the validity of an Act passed under the Parliament Acts based on alleged defects in procedure. Apart from not applying to Bills which seek to extend the maximum duration of Parliament beyond five years, the Parliament Acts do not apply to local and private legislation or to public Bills which confirm provisional orders. Nor do they apply to delegated legislation: here the formal powers of the Lords will depend on whether the parent Act expressly empowers the Lords to approve or disapprove of the delegated legislation in question.[79]

The Parliament Acts in operation

Apart from the Welsh Church Act 1914 and the Government of Ireland Act 1914, only the Parliament Act 1949 became law under the Parliament Act procedure before the War Crimes Act 1991. The War Crimes Bill proposed retrospectively to authorise prosecutions in Britain in respect of war crimes in Germany between 1939 and 1945 by persons who had become British citizens. It had not been part of the Conservative programme at the 1987 election and was carried on free votes in the Commons. It was, however, twice defeated on second reading in the Lords: following the second such defeat, the royal assent was given to it. The debates in the Lords were confused on the constitutional issues,[80] but those peers who voted against the Bill on the second occasion knew that their action would not prevent the Bill from becoming law. Although the Parliament Acts applied in a clear way to the War Crimes Bill, the procedure under the Acts has potential difficulties (for example, at what stage has a Bill 'not been passed' by the Lords subsequently, once it has been given a second reading?). The statutory method of calculating the one year's delay means that the effective delay may be considerably less than 12 months.

The willingness on the part of the House of Lords more readily to challenge the Commons led to the Parliament Acts being used on several occasions since 1997: on one occasion following the defeat of the European Parliamentary Election Bill, and on another following the defeat of the Sexual Offences (Amendment) Bill. Most controversially the Parliament Acts were used to secure the enactment of the Hunting Bill in 2004. Recent events have also revealed some of the limitations of the Parliament Acts: they do not apply to Bills which begin in the Lords (and so could not be invoked when the Lords voted down the Criminal Justice (Mode of Trial) Bill);[81] or – as we have seen – to secondary legislation (and so could not be invoked when the Lords rejected the Greater London Authority (Election Expenses) Order 2000 – the first time an affirmative order had been rejected by the Lords since 1968).[82] These features of the Parliament Acts were acknowledged by the (Wakeham) Royal Commission on House of Lords Reform, as were others: it had been argued that it should be possible for the Commons to amend a Bill before presenting it to the Lords on the second occasion without the Bill losing the protection of the Parliament Acts; at present the Commons may only 'suggest' amendments. But such technical questions were not thought to have given rise to any 'real difficulty in practice'[83] and no amendment to the Act was proposed, although it was proposed that the House of Lords should lose its power to veto secondary legislation, a recommendation accepted by the government.[84]

---

[78] 1911 Act, s 3.

[79] Ch 28.

[80] G Ganz (1992) 55 MLR 87.

[81] One practical effect of this is that the House of Lords has an absolute veto over Commons amendments to Lords Bills.

[82] HL Deb, 22 February 2000, cols 134–82. On the same day the Lords also, for the first time, rejected an instrument subject to an annulment (Greater London Authority Election Rules 2000). See HL Deb, 22 February, cols 182–5.

[83] Cm 4534, (2000), p 36.

[84] Ibid, pp 77–8. See p 198 below.

The Wakeham Commission had also broadly endorsed the present statutory procedures and conventional practices relating to the distribution of powers between the two Houses. But the Commission apparently felt it unnecessary to address the argument that the Parliament Act 1949 is invalid since the Parliament Act procedure was never intended to be used for amending the 1911 Act itself, and since a delegate may not use delegated authority to increase the scope of his or her power.[85] While there are indeed limits on the Bills which may become law under the Parliament Act procedure, the argument that the 1949 Act is invalid depended on the view that measures passed by the Commons and the Crown alone should be regarded as delegated legislation: yet the interpretation of Commonwealth constitutions suggests that a legislature is not subject to the limitations implied by the maxim *delegatus non potest delegare*.[86] The issue was considered in *R (Jackson)* v *Attorney General*[87] where it was argued that the Hunting Act 2004 was invalid because it had been passed by using the Parliament Acts 1911–49, the contention being that the 1949 Act was invalid. But in a unanimous decision, this was rejected as implausible by the House of Lords. According to Lord Bingham, for 'the past half century, it has been generally, if not universally, believed that the 1949 Act has been validly enacted, as evidenced by the use made of it by governments of different political persuasions'. In his opinion that belief was 'well-founded'.

The Salisbury–Addison and other conventions

The supremacy of the House of Commons is not based on legislation alone, and indeed it would be impractical if all Bills had to go through the lengthy process to be found in the Parliament Acts before being enacted. For much of the interwar period the problem of conflict between the two houses was contained by the fact that the Conservative party was in government for much of the period. In 1945, however, the Labour party won a landslide victory at the general election, standing on a platform of radical reform, including the nationalisation of many industries and the creation of a national health service. Although the government was poorly represented in the House of Lords, the Conservative leader in the Lords (Lord Salisbury) nevertheless announced that Bills anticipated by the Labour party election manifesto would be accepted by the Lords as having been approved by the people; but that the Conservative peers 'reserved full liberty of action' as to measures that had not been in the election manifesto.[88] This became known as the Salisbury convention, more recently referred to as the Salisbury–Addison convention,[89] and was designed to avoid direct confrontation between the Lords and the Commons, the general practice of the Lords being to allow a second reading to Bills coming from the Commons. This important convention reflects 'the status of the House of Commons as the United Kingdom's pre-eminent political forum', and the 'fact that general elections are the most significant expression of the political will of the electorate'.[90]

This convention was reviewed along with others by a joint committee of both Houses in 2006, which had been established at the invitation of the government to 'consider the practicality of codifying the key conventions on the relationship between the two Houses . . . which affect the consideration of legislation'. The committee saw its main task as being 'to seek consensus on

---

[85] Hood Phillips and Jackson, *Constitutional and Administrative Law*, pp 79–81; Hood Phillips, *Reform of the Constitution*, pp 18–19, 91–3.

[86] *R* v *Burah* (1878) 3 App Cas 889; *Hodge* v *R* (1883) 9 App Cas 117.

[87] [2005] UKHL 56; [2006] 1 AC 262.

[88] HL Deb, 4 November 1964, col 66; Griffith and Ryle, pp 708–11; and see HL Deb, 19 May 1993, col 1780.

[89] See Cm 4534, 2000, pp 39–40 for a discussion of the origins and purpose of the Convention. It is sometimes referred to as the Salisbury–Addison convention, as it is based on an understanding between Viscount Cranborne (the fifth Marquess of Salisbury) and Viscount Addison (the Leader of the Lords): HL Paper 265, HC 1212 (2005–06), para 63.

[90] Para 4.21.

the conventions applicable [to the legislative process], and to consider the practicality of codifying them'.[91] The key question was whether the formal position of the Lords as a legislative body had been moderated by conventions reflecting the primacy of the Commons. The evidence showed that, particularly since the exclusion of most hereditary peers in 1999, the House has become more assertive of its authority. While this was acceptable to opposition parties, the government was not so happy, arguing that the Lords had recently moved too far beyond the limited role of the House under the Salisbury–Addison convention. Although the government wished the convention to be re-stated in terms supporting this view, the committee found that the Salisbury–Addison convention had changed since 1945, and particularly since 1999. In its current form, the convention required that every 'manifesto Bill' should receive a second reading in the Lords; such Bills should not be subject to 'wrecking amendments' that departed from the government's manifesto intention; and they should be passed and sent to the Commons in time for that House to consider the Bill with amendments proposed by the Lords.

In its unanimous report, the committee found that there would be value in the upper House adopting resolutions concerning manifesto Bills and the need to consider government business in reasonable time, on the understanding 'that conventions as such are flexible and unenforceable, particularly in the self-regulating environment of the House of Lords'. In making these recommendations, the joint committee stated its complete opposition to legislation on such matters. It did not wish conventions to be turned into rules, nor for there to be any scope for judicial review of parliamentary procedures: 'The courts have no role in adjudicating on possible breaches of parliamentary conventions. Parliament is accountable to the electorate, not to the judiciary.'[92] The government's response to this report insisted that the Commons must maintain its primacy in Parliament, and that the Lords must not exercise its power as a revising chamber in a way that undermines the Commons.[93] The government supported further reform in composition of the Lords, but emphasised that the current conventions on the legislative process should apply whatever the future composition of the upper house. There the matter rests concerning the legislative process, though it seems quite implausible to insist that an elected House of Lords should be subordinate to the House of Commons in the manner provided by existing arrangements, with the government acknowledging in another white paper on Lords reform that an elected chamber would be expected to be even more assertive than the House it replaced.[94] The authority that an elected House of Lords would draw from a mandate may also render implausible the proposal that the relationship between the two Houses can continue to operate without clear rules (whether statutory or otherwise), particularly if support for more formal constitutional arrangements were to gather strength.

C. Financial procedure[95]

No government can exist without raising and spending money. In the Bill of Rights 1689, art 4, the levying of money for the use of the Crown without grant of Parliament was declared illegal. Relying on the principle that the redress of grievances preceded supply, the Commons could after 1689 insist that the Crown pursued acceptable policies before granting the taxes or other revenue which the Crown needed. It has been said of the financial procedure of Parliament that the

---

[91] HL Paper 189, HC 1151 (2005–06).

[92] *Ibid*, p 75.

[93] Cm 6997, 2006.

[94] Cm 7438, 2008.

[95] See also ch 17, with which this section should be read and J F McEldowney, in Jowell and Oliver (eds), *The Changing Constitution* (6th edn), ch 15.

Crown demands money, the Commons grants it, and the Lords assents to the grant.[96] Today, the assent of the Lords is only nominal and it is generally regarded as vital to a government's existence that its financial proposals be accepted by the Commons. It is unlikely that a government would accept that the Commons should modify its expenditure proposals. A government which failed to ensure supply would have to resign or to seek a general election.[97] The requirement of statutory authority before a government can impose charges on the citizen is a fundamental principle which gives the citizen protection in the courts against unauthorised charges.[98] Another principle is that no payment out of the national Exchequer may be made without the authority of an Act, and then only for the purposes for which the statute has authorised the expenditure.[99] By contrast with the rule on taxation, this is less likely to give rise to litigation in the courts since the rights of individuals are not in issue if it is broken. Yet taxpayers and certain interest groups may have a sufficient interest in an expenditure decision to seek judicial review of its legality.[100] The elaborate system of controlling expenditure which exists today still owes much to reforms linked with Gladstone's tenure of office as Chancellor of the Exchequer in the 1860s, though they have been overhauled by the Government Resources and Accounts Act 2000.[101]

Basic principles and rules of financial procedure

The basic principles of financial control by, and accountability to, Parliament form part of a broader public expenditure process, which has helpfully been described as having four stages: (i) expenditure planning by the executive; (ii) parliamentary debate and approval of the executive's request for supply; (iii) spending by the executive of the money voted by Parliament; and (iv) accounting for the money spent.[102] Our concern in this chapter is principally with the second of these steps in the process, with the other three being considered more fully in chapter 17. But although the 'power of the purse' is 'central to the ability of Parliament to call government to account',[103] it ought not to be assumed that Parliament has developed adequate methods for this purpose. For, as has been pointed out, in reality 'little substantial scrutiny is involved' in these procedures, for 'the policy objectives on which the money is spent are not determined by the Commons but by the government of the day'.[104] Indeed, one prominent backbencher referred to the 'charade' of the House of Commons 'rubber stamping tablets of stone handed down by the executive of the day'.[105] This is perhaps inevitable in a parliamentary democracy which operates on the basis of a mandate claimed by government for a range of actions: the government can normally expect that its promises will not be frustrated by the Commons. Yet although government can properly claim the opportunity to implement its mandate, this ought not to be at the expense of rigorous and effective financial scrutiny of how money is to be spent, as well as of how money has been spent. But as the Clerk of Supply has pointed out, it is for the members

---

[96] Erskine May, p 848.

[97] Hence the necessity for a general election after the Lords had rejected the Liberal government's Finance Bill in 1909. In 1975, the failure of the Prime Minister of Australia to ensure supply (because of opposition from the Australian Senate to two Appropriation Bills) was the reason given by the Governor General for dismissing him; ch 12 B.

[98] Ch 17. And see *Congreve v Home Office* [1976] QB 629; *Woolwich Building Society v IRC (No 2)* [1993] AC 70.

[99] *Auckland Harbour Board v R* [1924] AC 318.

[100] *R v Foreign Secretary, ex p World Development Movement* [1995] 1 All ER 611: decision to finance Pergau Dam in Malaysia declared to be ultra vires the Overseas Development and Cooperation Act 1980. The government made up the money from other public funds: HC Deb, 13 December 1994, col 773.

[101] See ch 17; HC 841 (1999–2000), Annex A; and HC 426 (2007–8), paras 15–22.

[102] White and Hollingsworth, *Audit, Accountability and Government*, p 1.

[103] Ibid.

[104] J F McEldowney, in Jowell and Oliver (5th edn), p 381.

[105] HC Deb, 3 December 2002, col 871 (Andrew Mackinley).

of Parliament themselves to determine 'the extent to which the process of authorising public expenditure constitutes a rubber stamp'.[106]

The financial procedures of the Commons are intricate and can only be outlined here. According to Erskine May, three key rules govern present procedure.[107] For the purpose of these rules, the word 'charge' includes both charges upon the public revenue, i.e. expenditure, and charges upon the people, i.e. taxation:

(1) A charge 'whether upon public funds or upon the people' must be authorised by legislation;[108] it must generally originate in the Commons, and money to meet authorised expenditure must be appropriated in the same session of Parliament as that in which the relevant estimate is laid before Parliament.

(2) A charge may not be considered by the Commons unless it is proposed or recommended by the Crown. The financial initiative of the Crown is expressed in a standing order of the Commons which in part dates from 1713: 'This House will receive no petition for any sum relating to public service or proceed upon any motion for a grant or charge upon the public revenue . . . unless recommended from the Crown.'[109] This rule gives the government formal control over almost all financial business in the Commons, and severely restricts the ability of Opposition and back-benchers to propose additional expenditure or taxation.

(3) A charge must first be considered in the form of a resolution which, when agreed to by the House, forms an essential preliminary to the Bill or clause by which the charge is authorised. Before 1967, these resolutions had to be passed by the whole House sitting as the Committee of Supply, in the case of expenditure, or as the Committee of Ways and Means, in the case of taxation.[110] These committees no longer exist and the resolutions are now passed by the House itself. Certain financial Bills must be preceded by a Commons resolution before they can be read a second time. But for most Bills, whether the main object or an incidental object is the creation of a public charge, the financial resolution normally follows the second reading and must be proposed by a minister.[111]

The work of the Commons is conducted on a sessional basis, each session usually running for a year from early November. However, the government's financial year runs from April, thereby crossing two parliamentary sessions. The result is a complex annual financial cycle, which will now be described – first in relation to the authorisation of expenditure (supply), and second in relation to taxation.

The system of supply: government estimates

Funds are requested by the government by means of estimates. These are prepared in government departments and examined by the Treasury to ensure that they are consistent with the government's overall spending plans. After scrutiny by and debate in Parliament, the estimates are approved by a resolution of the House of Commons. Scrutiny of individual departmental estimates is now mainly undertaken as a 'core task' of select committees,[112] which may take

---

[106] C Lee (2004) 72 *The Table* 14.

[107] Erskine May, ch 29. For discussion of earlier forms of the rules, see Reid, *The Politics of Financial Control* and M Ryle, in Walkland (ed.), ch 7.

[108] Erskine May, p 850.

[109] HC SO 48. For background, see Reid, pp 35–45.

[110] See HC 122 (1965–66).

[111] HC SO 50.

[112] HC 514 (2008–9).

evidence from ministers and officials (, but there is no suggestion that the estimates should be 'cleared' by the select committees before being put to the House for approval).[113] Although select committees may receive advance copies of the estimates in draft, it is claimed that they may have only between two and four weeks at most to consider them.[114] However, there is also an opportunity for the House as a whole to debate and vote on individual estimates on three estimates' days set aside for this purpose under the Commons standing orders.[115] These debates in principle are informed by the reports of the select committees, with the time allocated on the basis of advice given by the chairman of the Liaison Committee (the committee of select committee chairmen).[116] Under Standing Order 55, 14 days must elapse between the presentation of the estimates and the vote to authorise spending. Nevertheless, serious questions have been raised about the adequacy of the procedures, having regard to the sums of money involved, the resources at the disposal of the House, and the time available to it.[117] According to one leading opposition backbencher:

> Select committees need to exercise more oversight of departments' spending. Most now look at annual reports and spending plans. But few get into the detail of their department's budget, and there's no real link between the government's estimates and the committee responsible, other than the nomination by the liaison committee of a handful of reports for debate on the floor of the house.[118]

While at times difficult to comprehend, the financial procedure of the House remains crucially important: the scrutiny of government spending (and the attendant authorisation for the raising of taxes) is one of the most important functions of Parliament. The current procedure provides that once the House of Commons has agreed the grants set out in the estimates, the Consolidated Fund (Appropriation) Bill is introduced and passed through all stages before the summer recess. The Act (known as the Appropriation Act) will do the following:

(a) authorise the issue from the Consolidated Fund of the balance of the grant of the estimates for the current financial year.[119] To add to the complexity of the procedures, some money will already have been voted on account to meet departmental expenditure. This is because – as already indicated – the Appropriation Act will not normally be passed until after the financial year has started, which means that unless some other method were available to supply money to the departments, they would be unable to carry out their business. So in the Consolidated Fund Act passed in the previous session, money will be provided by a vote on account to fund activities pending the enactment of the Appropriation Act. The vote on account is typically 45 per cent of the amount voted to the service or activity in the year in which the vote is made (that is the year previous to the year for which it is to be applied);[120]

(b) specify in a table in the Appropriation Act the total receipts that may be applied as appropriations in aid to each department or service to be funded. These appropriations in aid appear beside the amount of grant authorised to be made from the Consolidated Fund to the department or service in question. So there will be three columns next to each department or

---

[113] HC 426 (2007–8), para 68. See also HC 321 (2000–1), para 5.

[114] *The Guardian*, 9 December 2009 (Michael Fallon).

[115] HC SOs 54, 55. It is proposed that this should be extended to five days. See HC 426 (2007–8) and HC 1117 (2008–9).

[116] HC 514 (2008–09).

[117] HC 426 (2007–8).

[118] *The Guardian*, 9 November 2009 (Michael Fallon). For proposals that answer such concerns, see HC 426 (2007–08) (pp 204–5 below).

[119] On the Consolidated Fund, see ch 17 C.

[120] See HC 1235 (2004–5), para 3.

service. One will specify the total resources that may be used; a second will specify the amount to be issued from the Consolidated Fund for spending by the department or service; and a third will specify the amount of the appropriations in aid, which will be much smaller in amount than the second column. Appropriations in aid represent income received by departments (usually in return for services provided) and retained to meet departmental expenditure. Any additional income received by a department beyond the appropriation in aid must be paid into the Consolidated Fund.

(c) The Appropriation Act will authorise the bulk of expenditure for the current year. However, there are two additional wrinkles. First, a department may exceed its estimated expenditure during the current financial year – because of unforeseen circumstances or a new policy initiative; in that case supplementary estimates will have to be approved, usually towards the end of the financial year in question (though midway through the parliamentary session). Secondly, there is also the possibility that a department may spend more than provided for in the annual estimate, but has been unable to cure the excess before the end of the financial year. This will have to be authorised after the event by what is referred to as an excess vote (usually in an Act of Parliament in the next financial year, though sometimes later still). These matters are usually addressed in a separate Appropriation Act, which will also begin life as a Consolidated Fund (Appropriation) Bill.

There will not normally be a debate on the Consolidated Fund (Appropriation) Bills.

The system of supply: statutory authorisation

The three principal statutes in a typical parliamentary session for the grant of supply are thus the Consolidated Fund Act (passed in December); the Appropriation Act (passed in March) to deal with supplementary estimates in the financial year about to end, and excess spending in the previous financial year; and the Appropriation (No 2) Act (passed in July) to deal with the main estimates for the current financial year. By means of votes on account, the Consolidated Fund Act provides interim funding for departmental expenditure, with the Appropriation (No 2) Act authorising further supply to departments or programmes. By way of illustration, between December 2008 and July 2009, the three pieces of financial legislation crossing the boundaries of two financial years provided as follows:

(1) The Consolidated Fund Act 2008 received the royal assent on 18 December 2008. This authorised the use of additional resources in the current financial year (ending 31 March 2009) of £7.4 billion (for unspecified purposes), and authorised £32 billion to be issued from the Consolidated Fund (also for unspecified purposes). For the purposes of our illustration, however, the same measure also authorised on account the use of resources for the service of the following financial year (ending on 31 March 2010) and the issuing of money from the Consolidated Fund for these purposes. The sums involved were £202 billion and £194 billion respectively.

(2) The Appropriation Act 2009 received the royal assent on 12 March 2009, just before the end of the financial year. This provided not only for supplementary estimates for 2008–09, but also for an excess vote for 2007–08. An additional £37 billion in terms of resources was authorised for use, of which an additional £12 billion was authorised for payment from the Consolidated Fund, by way of supplementary estimates. These supplementary estimates were for the benefit of several departments.

(3) The Appropriation (No 2) Act 2009 received the royal assent on 21 July 2009. This authorised the use of additional resources of £281.8 billion for the service of the year ending 31 March 2010. It also authorised the Consolidated Fund to pay out up to £291.5 billion, the sums being appropriated under 57 separate headings. Together with the Consolidated Fund Act 2008, the Appropriation (No 2) Act 2009 thus authorised a total of £484.2 billion by way of resources to

be used during the financial year 2009–10, and up to £486 billion to be paid from the Consolidated Fund.[121]

This, however, will not be the whole of it; supplementary resources and an excess vote would be appropriated in the following financial cycles, and so it will go on. Moreover, other government expenditure is authorised by what are referred to as Consolidated Fund standing services: these charges have separate statutory authority and do not need annual approval. This form of public spending is used for matters such as the Civil List, judicial salaries, and payments to the European Union,[122] and accounts for in excess of another £20 billion.[123] An additional standing charge was introduced by the Banking Act 2009 in the wake of the global banking crisis. If the Treasury is satisfied that the need for the expenditure is too urgent for arrangements to be made for the provision of money by Parliament, it may be met by payments from the Consolidated Fund.[124] Where money is paid in reliance of this remarkable power, 'the Treasury shall as soon as is reasonably practicable lay a report before Parliament specifying the amount paid (but not the identity of the institution to or in respect of which it is paid)'. But even this obligation can be dispensed with on public interest grounds.[125] And this still is not the whole of it, for there is also a Contingencies Fund which may be used to meet unforeseen government expenditure,[126] the fund being of an amount equal to 2 per cent of the net cash requirement for the previous year.[127] Although the fund may not be drawn upon for any purpose for which legislation is necessary until a second reading has been given to the Bill in question, the existence of the Fund is a striking exception to the principle that parliamentary authority should be obtained before expenditure is incurred; effective scrutiny of the Fund depends on the Treasury, backed up by the Comptroller and Auditor General's powers of audit. The legality of payments from the Fund appears uncertain, but is not likely to arise for decision in the courts.[128] Indeed, decisions of the courts that certain government expenditure is unlawful may lead to the Fund being used to underwrite the contested expenditure.[129]

The raising of money: taxation and the budget

Government expenditure must be paid for from taxation, which must in turn be authorised by Parliament.[130] While many forms of revenue, such as customs and excise duties, are raised under Acts which continue in force from year to year, some taxes, notably income tax and corporation tax, are authorised from year to year. The machinery for the collection of these taxes is permanent but Parliament must approve each year the rates of tax. The Labour government has reverted to the traditional practice of presenting its budget in the spring, though it also presents its *Pre-budget Report* in the previous November or December. This provides an assessment of the economic position and gives an account of the government's proposed tax and spending plans.

---

[121] As might be expected the largest appropriations were to the large spending departments, such as Health (£82 billion), Work and Pensions (£78 billion), Defence (£39.7 billion), and Local Government (£38.7 billion).

[122] See ch 17 C below. See also HC 929 (2008–09) (Consolidated Fund Account).

[123] See HC 484 (2004–05). This contributes to what has been said to be 'more than a third of government spending included in budgets' which is not voted in Estimates: HC 426 (2007–08), para 28.

[124] Banking Act 2009, s 228(5).

[125] Ibid, s 228(6), (7) respectively.

[126] See J F McEldowney [1988] PL 232.

[127] Miscellaneous Financial Provisions Act 1946; Contingencies Fund Act 1974.

[128] HC 118–1 (1980–81) p xiv; HC 137 (1981–2), app 20; HC 24–1 (1982–3), p xliii. And see J F McEldowney, in Jowell and Oliver, pp 367–8.

[129] See McEldowney, ibid, pp 367, 370 citing *R v Foreign Secretary, ex parte World Development Movement* [1995] 1 All ER 611 (Pergau Dam).

[130] See *Congreve v Home Office* [1976] QB 629.

The contents of the budget are kept secret until the speech is delivered. While the government is collectively responsible for the budget speech and the Chancellor prepares it in close consultation with the Prime Minister, the contents are traditionally made known to the Cabinet only on the previous day or even on the morning of the speech. 'The budget is seen, not as a simple balancing of tax receipts against expenditure, but as a sophisticated process in which the instruments of taxation and expenditure are used to influence the course of the economy.'[131] The Chancellor may find it necessary to announce changes in indirect taxation and expenditure decisions at other times in the year.

As soon as the Chancellor's speech is completed, the House passes formal resolutions which enable immediate changes to be made in the rates of existing taxes and duties and give renewed authority for the collection of the annual taxes. These resolutions are confirmed by the House at the end of the budget debate. The taxing resolutions are later embodied in the annual Finance Act. The effect of any changes made by the Finance Act may be made retrospective to the date of the budget or any selected date. It was for long the practice to begin at once to collect taxes under the authority of the budget resolutions alone. But in *Bowles v Bank of England*,[132] Bowles successfully sued the Bank for a declaration that it was not entitled to deduct any sum by way of income tax from dividends, until such tax had been imposed by Act of Parliament. This decision illustrates the principle in *Stockdale v Hansard*[133] that no resolution of the House of Commons can alter the law of the land. The decision made it necessary to pass a law which has now been re-enacted in the Provisional Collection of Taxes Act 1968.

This Act gives statutory force for a limited period to resolutions of the House varying an existing tax or renewing a tax imposed during the preceding year. Under the Act (as amended),[134] the Finance Bill which embodies the resolution must be read a second time within 30 sitting days of the resolution having been approved by the House; and an Act confirming the resolutions must become law within four months from the date of the resolution, or by 5 May in the next calendar year if voted in November or December. As now amended the Act applies to income tax and corporation tax, as well as a range of other taxes and duties.[135] Because the Finance Bill must become law by a set date, the government must ensure that it is passed by the Commons and sent to the Lords as quickly as possible. Although the House of Lords generally debates the Finance Bill on its second reading, its passage through the Lords is unopposed. Even if the Finance Bill is not certified as a 'money Bill' for the purposes of the Parliament Act 1911, it would be a serious breach of the financial privileges of the Commons for the Lords to seek to amend it as it comes within the hallowed class of 'Bills of Aids and Supplies'.[136] However, no such breach occurs if the Lords amend a Bill concerning the revenue-raising powers of local government.[137]

Improving financial scrutiny

As pointed out above, it is expected that Parliament should play a key role in scrutinising government spending. But as also pointed out, there are serious concerns about the way in which that role is currently being performed, concerns which were reinforced by a powerful report by the Liaison Committee (the committee of Select Committee chairmen) entitled *Recreating Financial*

---

[131] Plowden Report, Cmnd 1432, 1961, para 10.
[132] [1913] 1 Ch 57.
[133] (1839) 9 A & E 1; ch 11 A.
[134] For example, Finance Act 1993, s 205, Finance Act 2000, s 30.
[135] For details, see Erskine May, pp 910–12.
[136] Erskine May, ch 33.
[137] Ibid; and R Brazier (1988) 17 *Anglo-American LR* 131.

Scrutiny.[138] The purpose of this latter report was to propose steps to enhance parliamentary control of government spending, in view of the Committee's concern that for 'far too long the House has shirked the task of providing itself with the means to carry out financial scrutiny effectively, and it is time that the House was more assertive in this area'.[139] The first problem identified by the Committee was the complexity of government finances, in which three different financial frameworks are used for budgeting by departments: government Spending Reviews (which do not require parliamentary authority); estimates (for which parliamentary authority is required for anticipated government spending); and resource accounts (in which departments account for their expenditure).[140] In what is referred to as the Alignment Project, however, the Treasury has proposed a radical revision of government finances,[141] which aims 'to create a single, coherent financial regime, that is effective, efficient and transparent, enhances accountability to Parliament and the public, and underpins the Government's fiscal framework'. This 'highly ambitious' initiative was warmly welcomed by the Liaison Committee, which also recognised that in 'revising the basis of Parliament's financial control and the system of reporting to Parliament, [the project] is potentially a historic development in the long story of Parliament's scrutiny of government finances'.[142] The phased implementation of the project is due to begin in April 2010;[143] it will have major implications for the procedure discussed above and will require new Standing Orders.[144]

Simplification of government finances and better quality information for Parliament address only part of the problem: the others are the opportunities for and the willingness of the House to take its responsibilities more seriously. Apart from a 'sensible division of tasks' between select committees and the House itself, the Liaison Committee also identified a number of other needs if these responsibilities are more effectively to be discharged, notably (a) the ability to engage with financial issues under discussion within government before decisions are made; (b) adequate opportunities to debate and vote on financial decisions, including specific spending proposals, after the government has made them; and (c) expert assistance for members on financial matters.[145] So far as (a) is concerned, the committee thought it 'absurd that the outcome of the Comprehensive Spending Review was discussed for only an hour and a half in the Chamber', this making 'a mockery of the House's right to scrutinise government expenditure'. It recommended that 'the results of Spending Reviews be the subject of a day's debate on the floor of the House', and that 'the timing be such that select committees can report on the outcome in order to inform that debate'.[146] So far as (b) is concerned, a number of steps were proposed to enhance the work of the committees (some of which it was proposed could be done at staff level), while growing cooperation between the Public Accounts Committee (responsible for monitoring government expenditure) and the other select committees (responsible for scrutinising government estimates) was welcomed.[147] And so far as (c) was concerned, the need here was for increased expertise in scrutiny of budgets and budget management, a need that could be met in part by increased resources for the Committee Office Scrutiny Unit and the better training of MPs.[148] The implementation of the Alignment project will allow some of these concerns to be met, and to address some of the problems relating to select committees identified in the following section.

---

[138] HC 426 (2007–08).

[139] Ibid, para 89.

[140] See ch 17 below.

[141] See Cm 7170, 2007; 7567, 2009; HC 804 (2008–09); HC 1074 (2008–09).

[142] HC 426 (2007–08), para 38.

[143] HC 1074 (2008–09).

[144] HC 804 (2008–09).

[145] Ibid, para 62.

[146] Ibid, para 66.

[147] Ibid, paras 69–71.

[148] Ibid, paras 85–87.

D. Scrutiny of administration

In chapter 7, the principle of responsible government was discussed. We are now concerned with the procedures within the Commons by which the conduct of the administration may be scrutinised by the House. The legislative and financial procedures of Parliament have strongly influenced the means by which Parliament finds out about the work of government. But certain procedures have an importance which is related neither to legislation nor to finance.

Parliamentary questions[149]

According to Erskine May, parliamentary questions 'should relate to the public affairs with which [ministers] are officially connected, to proceedings pending in Parliament or to matters of administration for which they are responsible'.[150] The regular questioning of the Prime Minister receives much attention in the media and the use of 'open' questions to the Prime Minister (for example, asking him to list his engagements for the day) is permitted as a device for enabling a wide range of supplementary questions to be asked. In May 1997, the allocation for questions to the Prime Minister was changed from 15 minutes every Tuesday and Thursday to 30 minutes every Wednesday. So far as other ministers are concerned, 45 to 55 minutes are set aside each day the House is sitting (except Fridays) to enable members to question ministers. Departmental ministers attend for questioning by rota, in what has been said to be pre-eminently a device for emphasising the 'individual responsibility of ministers'.[151] However, many more questions are tabled than can possibly be answered in the time available, so questions are chosen by the Speaker on a random (or 'shuffle') basis. In order to ensure that they can be printed and circulated, and to give the relevant department an opportunity to prepare a response, questions must be tabled at least three days before the question is to be answered. Longer notice is required in the case of oral questions to the Secretaries of State for Northern Ireland, Scotland and Wales.[152]

Members may ask questions for written answer at any time, and questions tabled for oral answer which are not taken will also receive a written answer. Written answers are published in Hansard. While ministers customarily answer questions which have been accepted as being in order by the clerks of the House, acting under the Speaker's direction, it is for the minister to decide whether and how to reply to questions: 'An answer to a question cannot be insisted upon, if the answer be refused by a minister.'[153] As might be anticipated, there are a number of grounds on which information sought may be withheld: for example, if the cost of obtaining the information would be excessive or if it would be contrary to the public interest for the information to be given (for example, matters relating to Cabinet proceedings or to the security and intelligence services). Because of the existence of question time, however, matters concerning their constituencies may be raised by members in correspondence with ministers, who know that an unsatisfactory reply may lead to the tabling of a question. Partly for this reason, questions are used more for concentrating public attention on topics of current concern than for securing the redress of individual grievances. Questions may be ruled out of order or refused an answer if they relate to matters for which the ministers are not responsible, including decisions by local authorities, the BBC, courts and tribunals, the universities, trade unions and so on.

---

[149] Chester and Bowring, *Questions in Parliament*; Franklin and Norton (eds), *Parliamentary Questions*; Griffith and Ryle, pp 519–29; HC 393 (1971–72); HC 379 (1989–90); HC 178 (1990–91); HC 859 (2008–09); HC 129 (2009–10); Erskine May, pp 339–58.

[150] Erskine May, pp 344–5.

[151] Chester and Bowring, p 287.

[152] HC SO 22–22B.

[153] Erskine May, p 352.

In 1996, the Scott report on 'arms for Iraq' extensively criticised attitudes within government to the answering of questions.[154] Civil servants are now instructed that in preparing answers they must be as open as possible with Parliament, although ministers are entitled to present government actions in a positive light; information should not be omitted merely because disclosure could lead to political embarrassment; and answers should be avoided 'which are literally true but likely to give rise to misleading inferences'.[155] When a question to a minister concerns a matter which has been assigned to an executive agency set up under the 'next steps' initiative,[156] it is generally answered by a letter to the MP from the agency's chief executive (the minister may be consulted on what is said). MPs may require a ministerial response if they are dissatisfied with the chief executive's reply. The answers from chief executives to MPs have, since 1992, been printed in Hansard.[157] The marked increase in the number of questions asked for written answer in recent years, which is linked with the use by some MPs of research assistants, is not considered to make necessary any limit on the number of questions which MPs may ask.[158] However, the effectiveness of parliamentary questions as a means of securing information which the government does not wish to make available has often been doubted.[159] In addition to oral and written questions, Standing Orders also make provision for urgent questions (known previously as Private Notice Questions).[160] MPs may also use the Freedom of Information Act 2000 to obtain information from government departments, though this ought not to be necessary.[161]

Debates

At the end of every day's public business, when the adjournment of the House is formally moved, half an hour is available for a private member to raise a particular issue and for a ministerial reply. Members periodically ballot for the right to initiate an adjournment debate and advance notice of the subject is given so that the relevant minister may reply. While this gives more time for discussion of an issue than is possible in question time, the minister's reply, which often consists of a reasoned defence of the department's decision, may not advance the matter very far. During the debate, incidental reference to the need for legislation may be permitted by the Speaker. These brief debates are not followed by a vote of the House.[162] More substantial debates may be held at short notice under Standing Order 24 for the purpose of discussing a specific and important matter that should have urgent consideration (so-called emergency debates). The Speaker must be satisfied that the matter is proper to be discussed under the urgency procedure and either the request must be supported by at least 40 members or leave for the debate must be given by the House, if necessary upon a division. In deciding whether the matter should be debated, the Speaker considers the extent to which it concerns the administrative responsibilities of ministers or could come within the scope of ministerial action,

---

[154] HC 115 (1995–6), esp vol IV, section K.8.

[155] See HC 671 (1996–7), annex C. See also *Civil Service Code*, para 8. See further ch 13 E.

[156] Ch 13 D.

[157] See P Evans, in Giddings (ed.), *Parliamentary Accountability*, ch 7. Also HC 178 (1990–91) and HC 14 (1996–7).

[158] HC 859 (2008–09). According to the Modernisation Committee, 'The average number of questions appearing on the notice paper each day increased from 414 in 2007 to 434 in 2008, and had reached 514 by March 2009. This is a significant rise from the average figure of about 350 WPQs per day that persisted between 2002 and 2005' (ibid, para 5).

[159] See B Hough [2003] PL 211. But see HC 859 (2008–09), where it is said by the Procedure Committee that 'WPQs are highly valued by Members as a means of scrutinising government and obtaining information' (para 6).

[160] HC SO 21(2). These must relate to matters of public importance.

[161] See *Office of Government Commerce* v *Information Commissioner* [2008] EWHC 737 (Admin).

[162] See HC SO 9(7); Erskine May, pp 378–80.

but he or she does not give reasons for his or her decision. In recent years, 'such applications have only rarely been successful'.[163]

In recent times a number of other opportunities have been provided for backbenchers wishing to raise matters in debate. Some of these follow the reform of financial procedures, described elsewhere in this chapter. Before 1982, 29 'supply days' were assigned for debate on topics chosen by the Opposition, taken during the session at times when the estimates were formally approved. In 1982, the House severed the connection between debates initiated by the Opposition and formal consideration of the estimates.[164] In each session 20 days in the whole House are allotted for Opposition business,[165] 17 at the disposal of the Leader of the Opposition and three at the disposal of the leader of the second largest opposition party. The existence of Opposition days is thought to be one of the reasons why the emergency debate procedure is not now used more frequently. But although very important, it is also the case that the Opposition days do not necessarily satisfy the needs of backbenchers who are looking for 'effective ways of bringing a constituency problem or some other topic to the personal attention of Ministers and putting to them a case to which they have both an opportunity and an obligation to make a full reply'.[166]

The foregoing needs were addressed to some extent by reforms introduced in 1995 whereby every Wednesday morning was given over to a motion for the adjournment of the House. But in November 2000 this arrangement was superseded by adjournment debates in Westminster Hall where a parallel chamber has been established to help meet backbench demand. These Westminster Hall debates last between three and four-and-a-half hours in total, with debates on several topics in each session.[167] According to Erskine May, the debates are initiated by backbenchers and allocated by the Speaker by ballot.[168] The Westminster Hall initiative has – in the government's view – 'greatly widened the opportunities for members to raise matters of concern to them', though it is also the case that there is now 'a significant surplus of applications over the slots available'.[169] But despite these and other opportunities for members to debate the administration of government departments (including debates on the Queen's Speech), all such debates are limited by the adversary framework in which they are often held, and individual members may have no means of probing behind the statements made by ministers.

These limitations have given rise to demands for other procedures by which the House may inform itself more directly of the work of government. Where it is alleged that maladministration by a department has caused injustice to individual citizens, a member may refer the citizen's complaint for investigation to the Parliamentary Ombudsman.[170] Another method of investigating an issue is for the matter to be examined by a select committee.

Select committees

Select committees were much used to investigate social and administrative problems in the nineteenth century. A group of MPs would examine a topic of current concern, with power on behalf of the House to take evidence from witnesses with first-hand knowledge of the issues.

---

[163] Erskine May, p 327. See also Griffith and Ryle, p 378, who claim that the procedure has 'almost fallen into extinction' (p 497). For an outstanding example of such a debate, see that on the Westland affair on 27 January 1986. But only nine such debates took place between then and August 2009. See generally HC 337 (2006–07), paras 65–71.

[164] See HC 118 (1980–81) and HC Deb, 19 July 1982, col 117.

[165] HC SO 14(2).

[166] HC 194 (1998–9), para 24.

[167] HC SO 10; Erskine May, p 319.

[168] Ibid.

[169] HC 440 (2001–02) (Memorandum by the Leader of the House), para 8, and HC 337 (2006–07), para 124 respectively.

[170] Ch 29 D.

Their report, published with the supporting evidence, might convince the House of the need for legislative reforms. The use of select committees declined as departments grew in strength and resources, as the primary initiative for legislation moved to the government, and as the party system established stricter control over backbench MPs. The experience of the select committee on the Marconi scandal, when Liberal ministers were accused of reaping financial rewards through their prior knowledge of a government contract, showed that a select committee was not appropriate for investigations directly involving the reputation of Cabinet ministers.[171] However, the Public Accounts Committee has since 1861 had the task of reporting to the House on the financial and accounting practices of departments.[172] In the period after 1945, little use was made of committees for scrutinising the administration, apart from specialist committees dealing with government finance, the technical scrutiny of delegated legislation by the committee on statutory instruments,[173] and (from 1956 to 1979) the work of the select committee on nationalised industries.

One obstacle to the development of such committees was the fear that their investigations would interfere with the running of departments and conflict with ministerial responsibility. In 1959 the Select Committee on Procedure rejected a proposal for a committee on colonial affairs, on the ground that this was 'a radical constitutional innovation': 'there is little doubt that the activities of such a committee would be aimed at controlling rather than criticising the policy and actions of the department concerned. It would be usurping a function which the House itself has never attempted to exercise.'[174] By the mid-1960s the mood of the Commons had changed. In 1965, the Committee on Procedure declared that lack of knowledge of how the executive worked was the main weakness of the House.[175] Some limited reforms were made in 1966–8 while Richard Crossman MP was Leader of the House. Two specialised committees were created in 1966, one to consider the activities of a department (the Ministry of Agriculture, Fisheries and Food), the other to consider the subject of science and technology. The latter committee was regularly reappointed, but the Committee on the Ministry of Agriculture survived only for two sessions. Other committees established piecemeal at this time included committees to examine the activities of two departments (Education and Science, and Overseas Development), race relations and immigration and Scottish affairs. During the 1970s, such committees existed alongside the Expenditure Committee and its sub-committees.[176]

In 1978, an influential report by the Select Committee on Procedure recommended a complete reorganisation of the select committees to produce a more rational structure and to provide means by which MPs could regularly scrutinise the activities of the main departments.[177] The incoming Conservative government moved with notable speed to adopt these recommendations.[178] Now embodied in the House's standing orders,[179] the system of select committees is directly related to the principal government departments. Select committees are appointed for the life of a Parliament to examine the 'expenditure, administration and policy' of the main departments, with the Standing Orders in 2009 providing for 19 such Committees. The number is, however, growing, with the creation most recently of eight committees to cover each of the administrative

---

[171] Donaldson, *The Marconi Scandal*; and ch 13 C.

[172] Ch 17.

[173] Ch 28.

[174] HC 92–1 (1958–9), para 47; Crick, *The Reform of Parliament*, ch 7.

[175] HC 303 (1964–5).

[176] See Morris (ed.), *The Growth of Parliamentary Scrutiny by Committee*; and Mackintosh, *Specialist Committees in the House of Commons – Have they Failed?*

[177] HC 588–1 (1977–8), chs 5–7; and see HC Deb, 19 and 20 February 1979, cols 44, 276.

[178] HC Deb, 25 June 1979, col 33. The literature on the select committees includes Drewry (ed.), *The New Select Committees*; Englefield (ed.), *Commons Select Committees*; Griffith and Ryle, ch 11; and N Johnson, in Ryle and Richards (eds), *The Commons under Scrutiny*, ch 9. Also A Kelso, in Flinders *et al.* (eds), *The Oxford Handbook of British Politics*, ch 13.

[179] HC SOs 121–152C.

regions in England. Proposed by the government in 2007,[180] and endorsed by the Modernisation Committee,[181] this is a step taken in order to address what was seen as an 'accountability gap at regional level'.[182] Each committee typically has 11 or 14 members, and each may appoint a sub-committee. As well as examining the work of the principal department specified for the committee, each committee has power to look at 'associated public bodies', that is, executive agencies, public corporations, boards and advisory bodies in the relevant field. There are also a number of joint select committees composed of members drawn from both Houses. These committees include the Joint Committee on Human Rights with a remit which includes the examination of proposed legislation.

The work of the select committees

The committees are chaired by senior backbenchers, with positions allocated by the Committee of Selection, which is dominated by the party whips. This can give rise to difficulty if it appears that the government is seeking to control appointments to these key positions, as seems to have occurred in 2001. After the general election the chairs of the Transport Committee (Gwyneth Dunwoody) and the Foreign Affairs Committee (Donald Anderson) in the previous Parliament were not renominated. In the row which followed, the government allowed a free vote when nominations of committee chairs came forward for approval and both Dunwoody and Anderson were reinstated. This affair caused some bitterness and led the House of Commons Modernisation Committee to conclude that the existing method of filling these positions by the Committee of Selection 'no longer enjoys the confidence of the House'.[183] Only backbench MPs serve on the committees. Each committee has a majority of members from the government side of the House, but some committee chairs are Opposition members. The committees are serviced by House of Commons clerks and they may appoint specialist advisers. Within its subject area, each committee may choose the topics for investigation, subject only to the avoidance of duplication with other committees. The topics investigated by select committees vary widely, ranging from major subjects that may take a year or longer to complete, to the latest departmental estimates and issues of topical concern which a committee may seek to influence by holding public hearings and publishing the evidence with a report and recommendations. This freedom for a committee to decide for itself what to investigate is very important and no government approval is needed.

The reports of select committees would be valueless if they merely reproduced the government's justification of its policies. The committees are aware that, even though they do not often change government decisions, as all-party committees they exercise an important critical function. Voting on party lines can occur when a committee is deciding the contents of its report, but this is exceptional and not the rule. For criticism of the government to be made, it must have been supported in the committee by one or more MPs from the government side of the House. The committee's report contains only the majority view; but the extent of unity or division is revealed in the minutes of proceedings that are published with the report. In 1979, some MPs believed that such committees might detract from the adversary quality of parliamentary procedure, might develop consensus politics, might develop too close a relationship with the departments concerned and so on. These fears have not been borne out. But the 1979 reform of committees did not transform the power relationship between government and Parliament. The government

---

[180] Cm 7170, 2006–07, para 119.

[181] HC 282, 2007–08.

[182] Ibid, para 14.

[183] HC 224 (2001–02), para 6. It was said that the Committee of Selection had 'come to interpret its role as limited to confirming the proposals put to it by the front benches on both sides' (ibid, para 9). See D Oliver [2001] PL 666. The Committee of Selection is still responsible for appointments, but see pp 211–12 below for proposals for reform.

undertook at an early stage to cooperate fully with the committees,[184] but it lays down the rules by which civil servants may give evidence; these rules seek to protect from investigation the process of decision making within government.[185] Some committees have occasionally encountered difficulties in securing evidence, whether from ministers who refused to attend;[186] individuals prohibited by government from attending; or departments that refused to release documents.[187] But these difficulties are not commonplace, and it has been said by the House of Commons Liaison Committee in a comprehensive review of the select committee system that 20 years after it had been established, the system was now:

> widely acknowledged to be a success. Select Committees had become a vital source of scrutiny, analysis and ideas; they had made the political process more accessible; and they had provided a much-needed climate of Parliamentary accountability. In so doing, they became more visible and widely known, and an entrenched part of our constitutional arrangements.[188]

This is not to say that the system does not need to be improved and in an important report – *Shifting the Balance: Select Committees and the Executive*[189] – the Liaison Committee made a number of recommendations for the committees to be more effective and independent. Concern was expressed about the system for the nomination of members, which was 'too much under the control of the Whips', with members kept off or removed 'on account of their views'. The committee also recommended that more time should be spent on the floor of the House considering select committee reports. Although an opportunity for greater consideration has arisen by the use of Westminster Hall (where debates on committee reports do take place), this was thought not to be a substitute for 'debating time on the floor of the House, on substantive motions'. The committee also proposed a 'select committee half hour once a week on a Tuesday', in which a minister would respond to a recently published report followed by contributions from committee members, and other members of the House. Other recommendations related to better scrutiny of government expenditure; more pre-legislative scrutiny of legislation by select committees;[190] and more joint work by committees: 'Joined-up government must be scrutinised by joined-up committees.' There was also a need to address the 'insufficient knowledge of select committees and of Parliament generally, among departmental officials'. Further proposals for reform were made by the Modernisation Committee in 2002, the Committee having expressed concern that the select committees generally were 'much poorer in the resources they can command than in other parliaments and they have a weak record of stability of membership. They also have a much more marginal role in scrutinising legislation, which is the principal function of the parallel committees in some other parliaments.'[191]

E. Reform of Parliament

Although this account has focused on three principal functions of Parliament, as already indicated there are other functions as well. Not the least is Parliament's role as a constitutional watchdog, a role that has been enhanced in recent years by the establishment of the Joint Committee on

---

[184] HC Deb, 25 June 1979, col 45; and 16 January 1981, col 1697.

[185] See ch 13 D where this matter is more fully explored.

[186] See HL 152, HC 230 (2008–09), esp para 51 where the JCHR reported repeated attempts to request oral evidence from ministers on the question of British government complicity in the torture of terrorist suspects. It is clear from the Committee's reports that such a refusal was rare to the point of being unique, leading the committee to reflect that 'the constitutional significance of the ministers' refusal should not be underestimated' (ibid).

[187] HC 321 (2000–01), paras 118–26. Difficulties have also arisen in relation to a witness who refused to answer questions put to him by a Committee: see HC 1044 (2002–03).

[188] HC 321 (2000–01), para 2. See also HC 224 (2001–02), para 2.

[189] HC 300 (1999–2000); also HC 748 (2000–01); and HC 321 (2000–01). See Oliver, *Constitutional Reform in the UK*, ch 9.

[190] On which see above, p 186.

[191] HC 224 (2001–02), para 4.

Human Rights in 2001,[192] along with the Constitutional Committee of the House of Lords.[193] Some notable work has been done by both committees, with the Joint Committee on Human Rights in its scrutiny of the Anti-terrorism, Crime and Security Bill 2001 being a good example, even if its conclusions about the disproportionate nature of the British government's response to the terrorist events in the United States on 11 September 2001 appeared to fall on deaf ears.[194] The working practices of the JCHR have evolved gradually, and it now considers both the implications of proposed legislation for human rights, as well as the human rights aspects of a wider range of policy questions. But while important, this is nevertheless but a small part of a process of parliamentary reform that has been undertaken in recent years, which is now an ongoing and continuing activity, even if there remains a concern about the nature and speed of reform. While governments appear responsive to calls to improve the legislative process, they need to be equally responsive to proposals – from within Parliament and beyond – to enhance parliamentary scrutiny of other executive action.[195]

Important changes have been proposed which would increase the role of backbenchers in the House of Commons, enhance the quality of parliamentary scrutiny of government spending (including an expanded role for select committees), and increase the independence of the select committees. These proposals are included in two significant select committee reports – *Recreating Financial Scrutiny*, (a report of the Liaison Committee which is considered at some length above),[196] and *Rebuilding the House* (a report of the select committee on Reform of the House of Commons which was appointed in July 2009). The latter made a number of well-received proposals, which complement the earlier proposals of the Liaison Committee, including the suggestion that select committees should be elected by the House (with members voting in a secret ballot), and not selected by the party whips. It was also said to be time for members of the House, through a committee of their elected colleagues, to take some responsibility for what the House debates, when and for how long; and also for what it does not wish to debate, either at all or at its current length.[197] But the problem remains one of government control, likely to continue so long as the electoral system delivers large parliamentary majorities to well-disciplined parties, and so long as the Standing Orders of the House of Commons unequivocally give the government priority over any other business.[198]

---

[192] HC SO 152B. See Ewing, *Bonfire of the Liberties*, ch 8 on the work of the JCHR. See further, ch 19 C below.

[193] The responsibility of the latter is to examine the constitutional implications of all Bills brought before the House; and to keep under review the operation of the Constitution. For background, see Cm 4534, 2000, Ch 5, and HL 11 (2000–01).

[194] This matter is considered more fully in ch 19.

[195] See especially Hansard Society, *The Challenge for Parliament: Making Government Accountable* (D Oliver [2001] PL 666), and Hansard Society, *The Fiscal Maze: Parliament, Government and Public Money* (2006).

[196] HC 426 (2007–08).

[197] HC 1117 (2008–09), para 178. To this end a new Backbench Business Committee was proposed to look after the interests of the House and to deal with government on the allocation of time.

[198] HC SO 14.

CHAPTER 11

Privileges of Parliament

Parliamentary privilege consists of the rights and immunities which the two Houses of Parliament and their members and officers possess to enable them to carry out their parliamentary functions effectively. Without this protection members would be handicapped in performing their parliamentary duties, and the authority of Parliament itself in confronting the executive and as a forum for expressing the anxieties of citizens would be correspondingly diminished.[1]

These words, opening the report of a committee of both Houses at Westminster in 1999, emphasise that parliamentary privilege is part of the framework which enables each House and its members to fulfil their duties. The privileges of each House have both external and internal aspects: they protect it against attempts from outside to interfere in its proceedings; and they require its members to refrain from abusing their privileged position.

As an important part of the law and custom of Parliament, privilege has been developed over centuries by the response of Parliament, especially the Commons, to changing circumstances and also, since privilege affects those outside Parliament, by decisions of the courts. Neither House can by its own resolution create new privileges. When a matter of privilege is disputed, 'it is for the courts to decide whether a privilege exists and for the House to decide whether such privilege has been infringed.'[2] The joint report in 1999 recommended a Parliamentary Privileges Act that would declare the law in a clear manner, make essential changes and abolish obsolete aspects of privilege. But ten years later, this had still not been done and the need for legislation was reinforced when controversial issues of parliamentary privilege arose in 2009.

This chapter does not discuss the application of privilege to the Scottish Parliament and the Assemblies for Wales and Northern Ireland. These bodies enjoy certain rights and immunities enacted by legislation,[3] but beyond this they do not share in Westminster's privileges.[4] Emphasis in this chapter is placed on the House of Commons, but questions of privilege also arise in relation to the Lords.

A. House of Commons

For centuries certain privileges and immunities have been attached to the House and its members. At the opening of each Parliament, the Speaker formally claims for the Commons 'their ancient and undoubted rights and privileges' and, in particular, 'freedom of speech in debate, freedom from arrest, freedom of access to Her Majesty whenever occasion shall require; and that the most favourable construction should be placed upon all their proceedings.' What is the substantive importance today of the first two of these freedoms?

---

[1] Report of joint committee on parliamentary privilege (HL 43-I, HC 214-I, 1998–9), para 3 (cited here as the 'Nicholls report'). And see P M Leopold [1999] PL 604. Also Erskine May, chs 5–11; Griffith and Ryle, *Parliament*, ch 3; Oliver and Drewry (eds), *The Law and Parliament*, chs 1, 2, 4, 5, 7.

[2] *Pepper v Hart* [1993] AC 595, 645 (Lord Browne-Wilkinson).

[3] See e.g. Scotland Act 1998, ss 22 and Sch 3 (standing orders), ss 23–26 (witnesses and documents), 39 (members' interests), 41 (defamatory statements), 42 (contempt of court), and 43 (corrupt practices).

[4] See *Whaley v Lord Watson of Invergowrie* 2000 SLT 475. And C R Munro [2000] PL 347. On the European Parliament, see Protocol on the Privileges and Immunities of the European Union (16 December 2004), arts 7–9; and C-200/07 *Marra v De Gregorio* [2009] 1 CMLR 15.

Freedom from arrest[5]

The ancient privilege of freedom from *civil* arrest developed to enable members to attend the House at a time when imprisonment was a common means of enforcing payment of debts. Its archaic nature is illustrated by the fact that members may not be arrested in connection with civil proceedings for a period that runs from 40 days before to 40 days after a session of Parliament. Today, an MP is protected against committal for contempt of court where this is sought to compel performance of a civil obligation.[6] Members have no immunity from having civil actions brought against them,[7] but they retain minor privileges in regard to such litigation. Thus it is a contempt of the House to serve a writ on a member within the precincts of the House.[8] Members are not protected against bankruptcy proceedings, and are no longer exempt from jury service.[9] In 1967 and in 1999, it was recommended that any surviving freedom from civil arrest should be abolished.[10]

As regards criminal law, members have no immunity from arrest. This was seen when Damian Green MP, then the Conservative shadow Home Secretary, was arrested at his home in November 2008 while police were investigating a series of leaks from the Home Office to the press that had led the Cabinet Office to call in the police. The affair raised many questions as it was not obvious that the leaks constituted criminal offences at all.[11] The police also made an unprecedented search of Mr Green's office at Westminster, seizing documents, computer and other materials, on the basis of a consent-form that the police had caused the Serjeant at Arms to sign, which she did without getting the approval of more senior House authorities. The Speaker (Michael Martin MP) responded by instructing that no future search of an MP's office could take place without a warrant, but this itself raised difficult questions about the impact of parliamentary privilege on police powers and the right of the House to resist intrusive police action.[12]

Members may be required to give surety to keep the peace or security for good behaviour, and could be committed for contempt of court where the contempt has a criminal character.[13] An MP was held in preventive detention under defence regulations during the Second World War.[14] The House insists on receiving immediate information of the imprisonment of a member, with reasons for the detention. While a member awaiting trial may carry out many duties as a constituency representative, a member who is imprisoned after conviction may do so only if granted exceptional concessions under prison rules.[15] A term of imprisonment for more than a year causes the seat to be vacated.[16]

Freedom of speech[17]

Freedom of speech is the most substantial privilege of the House. Its essence is that no penal or coercive action should be taken against members for what is said or done in Parliament. Claims

---

[5] Erskine May, ch 7; and Nicholls report, paras 325–8.
[6] As in *Stourton v Stourton* [1963] P 302. Erskine May, pp 121–3.
[7] *Re Parliamentary Privilege Act 1770* [1958] AC 331.
[8] HC 221 (1969–70) and HC 144 (1972–3).
[9] Insolvency Act 1986, s 427. And see Criminal Justice Act 2003, s 9 and Sch 1, pt 3.
[10] Nicholls report, para 327.
[11] In view of the Official Secrets Act 1989; ch 25.
[12] On the police investigation itself, see HC 157 and HC 1026 (2008–09); and Sir Denis O'Connor, *Review of lessons learned from the Metropolitan Police Service's investigation* (October 2009). For a full account of the events, see report of the select committee chaired by Sir Menzies Campbell QC (HC 62, 2009–10).
[13] Ch 18 D. And see note 6 above.
[14] HC 164 (1939–40) (Captain Ramsay's case).
[15] HC 185 (1970–1). And see G J Zellick [1977] PL 29.
[16] See Representation of the People Act 1981; and ch 9 G.
[17] Erskine May, ch 6; Nicholls report, paras 36–134, 189–228. And P M Leopold [1981] PL 30.

for the privilege were regularly made by the Speaker from the end of the sixteenth century. The right of the Commons to criticise the King's government was called in question in 1629 when Eliot, Holles and Valentine were convicted by the Court of King's Bench for seditious words spoken in the Commons and for tumult in the House.[18] This judgment was reversed in 1668 by the House of Lords on the ground that words spoken in Parliament could be judged only in Parliament. In art 9 of the Bill of Rights 1689, it was declared 'that the freedom of speech and debates or proceedings in Parliament ought not to be impeached or questioned in any court or place out of Parliament'.[19]

The most important consequence of this declaration (but not the only one) is that no member may be made liable in the courts for what is said or written in course of parliamentary proceedings. Thus members who speak in the House are immune from the law of defamation.[20] Nor can what is said in Parliament be examined by a court for the purpose of deciding whether it supports a cause of action in defamation which has arisen outside Parliament: 'a member must have a complete right of free speech in the House without any fear that his motives or intentions or reasoning will be questioned or held against him thereafter'.[21] The courts may not receive in any proceedings 'evidence, questioning or submissions designed to show that a witness in parliamentary proceedings deliberately misled Parliament'.[22]

Since 1818, leave of the House has been required before officers of the House may give evidence in court of proceedings in the Commons. In 1980, the House relaxed its practice by giving general permission for reference to be made in court to Hansard and to the published evidence and reports of committees.[23] This change did not diminish the effect of art 9 of the Bill of Rights, nor did it alter the rule that Hansard could not be used in court as an aid to statutory interpretation. In 1993, the Law Lords changed the latter rule, holding that courts may use ministerial statements in Hansard to resolve ambiguities in legislation; such use does not 'impeach or question' freedom of speech in the Commons.[24]

Moreover, ministerial statements in Parliament announcing new policies or executive decisions are frequently used as evidence in judicial review proceedings.[25] Such statements may be relied on for the explanation they may give of the motivation for executive action outside the House, even if they go to show that the executive action involved the improper exercise of power.[26] When a court has to decide whether a statute is compatible with rights under the Human Rights Act 1998, it may read Hansard to find out the background to the legislation, the problem at which it was aimed and its likely effect, but the speeches may not be used to determine such matters as the proportionality of the provision.[27]

---

[18] *Eliot's case* (1629) 3 St Tr 294.

[19] And see *Re Parliamentary Privilege Act 1770*, note 7 above.

[20] *Lake v King* (1667) 1 Saunders 131; *Dillon v Balfour* (1887) 20 LR Ir 600. And see *A v UK* (2003) 36 EHRR 917 (MP's immunity from defamation compatible with arts 6(1) and 8, ECHR).

[21] *Church of Scientology of California v Johnson-Smith* [1972] 1 QB 522, 530 (Browne J).

[22] *Hamilton v Al Fayed* [2001] 1 AC 395, 403 (Lord Browne-Wilkinson).

[23] HC Deb, 3 December 1979, col 167, and 31 October 1980, col 879; HC 102 (1978–9); and P M Leopold [1981] PL 316.

[24] *Pepper v Hart* [1993] AC 593; and ch 2 A.

[25] Ibid, 639 (Lord Browne-Wilkinson); Nicholls report, paras 46–59. The Nicholls committee considered that such statements could be used even to question the minister's good faith: cf *Prebble v Television New Zealand Ltd* [1995] 1 AC 321, 333.

[26] *Toussaint v A-G of St Vincent* [2007] UKPC 48, [2008] 1 All ER 1. Cf *Office of Government Commerce v Information Commissioner* [2008] EWHC 774 (Admin) (Information Tribunal not entitled to rely on interpretation placed on Act by minister or committee in Parliament).

[27] *Wilson v First County Trust Ltd* [2003] UKHL 40; [2004] 1 AC 816. And see *R (Age UK) v Business, Innovation and Skills Secretary* [2009] EWHC 2336 (Admin) (court taking into account parliamentary material as background to interpretation of regulations).

The protection of members for words spoken extends to criminal as well as civil liability. Disclosures to Parliament may not be made the subject of prosecution under the Official Secrets Acts,[28] although the MP concerned may be liable to the disciplinary jurisdiction of the House. Speeches or questions in Parliament may be in breach of the House's *sub judice* rule if they concern pending judicial proceedings, but they may not be held to be in contempt of court.[29]

In protecting MPs from liability for speaking in Parliament, one indirect effect of the Bill of Rights was to restrict the ability of MPs to sue in defamation. The reason for this was that if an MP sued a newspaper for a defamatory report about his or her conduct, art 9 of the Bill of Rights prevented the newspaper from showing that the report was true by bringing evidence of what had been said or done in Parliament: in the interests of justice, the court would require the case to be stayed.[30] In 1996, concern at 'cash for questions' allegations led Parliament hastily to amend the Bill of Rights to enable Neil Hamilton MP to sue *The Guardian*: by s 13 of the Defamation Act 1996, any individual (whether an MP or not) may waive parliamentary privilege so that an action can proceed.[31] This was an unsatisfactory change in the law. In 1999, the Nicholls committee recommended that s 13 of the 1996 Act be repealed; in its place, each House (but not individuals) should have power to waive privilege in court proceedings, subject to safeguards to maintain protection of the Bill of Rights for individuals.[32]

The meaning of 'proceedings in Parliament'

Protection for members is not confined to debates in the House. It covers asking questions, giving written notice of questions and 'everything said or done by a member in the exercise of his functions as a member in a committee in either House, as well as everything said or done in either House in the transaction of parliamentary business'.[33] Protection extends to officials of the House acting in course of their duties, as well as to witnesses giving evidence to committees of the House. It may be that privilege is not confined to words spoken or acts done within the precincts of the House, and includes words spoken outside Parliament, for example, a conversation between a minister of the Crown and a member on parliamentary business in a minister's office. Conversely, it may not extend to a casual conversation within the House on private affairs. The posting of alleged libels to members in the House on matters unconnected with proceedings in the House is not protected.[34]

The question of whether a member's letter to a minister concerning a publicly owned industry was a 'proceeding in Parliament' arose in 1957.

> G R Strauss MP had written to the minister responsible for the electricity industry, complaining of the methods of disposal of scrap cable followed by the London Electricity Board. The minister referred the letter to the board, who protested to Mr Strauss at its contents. The solicitors to the board told him that they were instructed to sue for libel unless he withdrew and apologised. This threat was referred by the House to the Committee of Privileges. The crucial question was whether the original letter from the member to the minister was a 'proceeding in Parliament' within the meaning of the Bill of Rights. The committee concluded that Mr Strauss was engaged in a proceeding in Parliament, that the threat to sue him for libel was a threat to impeach or question his freedom of speech in Parliament, and that the board and their solicitors had acted in breach of privilege. But on 8 July 1958, the House decided by a narrow margin (218 to 213) to disagree

---

[28] *Duncan Sandys* case, HC 101 (1938–9). On liability for criminal conspiracy, see *Ex p Wason* (1869) LR 4 QB 573.

[29] E.g. the disclosure of Colonel B's identity on 20 April 1978; HC 667 (1977–8) and 222 (1978–9); and p 381 below.

[30] *Prebble* v *Television New Zealand Ltd*; see ch 23 F below and P M Leopold (1995) 15 LS 204.

[31] By using s 13, Mr Hamilton later sued Mr Al Fayed over allegations already examined by a Commons committee: *Hamilton* v *Al Fayed* [2001] 1 AC 395 (and see A W Bradley [2000] PL 556). See also ch 23 F.

[32] Nicholls report, paras 60–82.

[33] HC 101 (1938–9).

[34] *Rivlin* v *Bilainkin* [1953] 1 QB 485.

with the committee, and resolved that (a) the original letter was not a proceeding in Parliament and (b) nothing in the subsequent correspondence was a breach of privilege.[35]

In support of the majority view, it was argued that members should not widen the scope of absolute parliamentary privilege and should rely on the defence of qualified privilege in the law of defamation. Certainly, a complaint addressed by an MP to a minister on an issue of public concern in which the minister has an interest is protected by qualified privilege.[36] But qualified privilege may be rebutted by proof of express malice, and it might be held to constitute malice if a member forwarded to a minister without making any inquiry a letter from a constituent containing defamatory allegations. If a member uses the letter as the basis of a parliamentary question to a minister, at what stage does the letter itself become a 'proceeding in Parliament'? Many matters are raised in correspondence by MPs with ministers that do not, but could, become the subject of questions.

The Commons resolution in 1957 does not have the effect of an Act of Parliament. The House could change its mind, and it may fall to a court to decide whether a particular matter constitutes a 'proceeding in Parliament'. In 1990, a judge held that the register of MPs' financial interests was not itself a 'proceeding in Parliament'.[37] By contrast, it was held that a decision by the Speaker to withhold certain facilities from Sinn Fein members who refused to take their seats at Westminster was probably a 'proceeding in Parliament', but that in any event the decision was within the 'exclusive cognizance' of the Commons, and was not subject to judicial review.[38] In 1999, the Nicholls committee accepted the argument that 'proceedings in Parliament' should be defined by legislation,[39] but the committee did not agree that the absolute protection given by the Bill of Rights should be extended to letters between MPs and ministers.[40]

An issue not addressed in the Strauss case was whether for someone to sue an MP for defamation in respect of a proceeding in Parliament is itself a breach of privilege. One view is that MPs should leave it to the courts to reject such an action as being bound to fail, and that the House should not treat the action itself as a breach of privilege,[41] but this view would not be shared by many MPs.

Publication of parliamentary proceedings outside Parliament

Although such a claim could not be made today, the House formerly maintained the right to control publication of its debates outside Parliament. By resolution of 3 March 1762, any publication in the press of speeches by members was declared a breach of privilege. In modern times this resolution bore no relation to reality. On 16 July 1971, the House resolved that in future it would entertain no complaint of contempt or breach of privilege regarding the publication of debates in the House or its committees, except when the House or a committee sat in private session. The House thus retains the power to protect committees and sub-committees that wish to meet in private.[42] While select committees generally take evidence in public, their deliberations,

---

[35] HC 305 (1956–7); *Re Parliamentary Privilege Act 1770* [1958] AC 331; HC 227 (1957–8). Also S A de Smith (1958) 21 MLR 465; D Thompson [1959] PL 10.

[36] *Beach v Freeson* [1972] 1 QB 14 (MP forwarding complaint about solicitors to the Law Society and Lord Chancellor); and ch 23 F.

[37] *Rost v Edwards* [1990] 2 QB 460: this decision was doubted in *Prebble's* case [1995] 1 AC 321, 337. See also P M Leopold [1990] PL 475; and Nicholls report, paras 122–3.

[38] *Re McGuinness's application* [1997] NI 359.

[39] Nicholls report, paras 127–9. And see HC 261 (1969–70), pp 8–12; Cmnd 5909, 1975, p 51; HC 417 (1976–7), p v.

[40] Nicholls report, paras 103–112.

[41] S A de Smith (1958) 21 MLR 465, 468–75. Lord Denning's unpublished dissent in *Re Parliamentary Privilege Act 1770* (above) is at [1985] PL 80.

[42] HC 34 (1966–7), paras 116–29.

especially when a draft report is being considered, are in private. Premature reporting of these proceedings may be regarded as a serious breach of privilege,[43] but the reporting of evidence taken at public sittings of committees is not restricted.[44]

The public interest in reports of parliamentary proceedings is recognised in the law of defamation: unless a defamed person can prove malice, a fair and accurate unofficial report of proceedings in Parliament is privileged, as is an article founded upon such proceedings, provided it is an honest and fair comment upon the facts.[45] The defence of qualified privilege applies to a 'parliamentary sketch' (an impressionistic and selective account of a debate),[46] but not to reports of detached parts of speeches published with intent to injure individuals. A member who repeats or confirms outside Parliament what he or she has said in Parliament is liable if the speech contains defamatory material.[47] It is doubtful if qualified privilege attaches to the publication of a member's speech for the information of constituents.[48]

Sound broadcasting of proceedings in both Houses began in 1978.[49] Debates in the Lords were first televised in 1985 and in the Commons in 1989. The broadcasting authorities have full editorial control to select what is broadcast, but the use of extracts for light entertainment or political satire is excluded. It is likely that those who broadcast Parliament are protected against liability for defamation by the common law defence of qualified privilege and by the Parliamentary Papers Act 1840 (considered below), s 3 of which was extended to radio broad-casting in 1952 and to television in 1990.[50]

Parliamentary papers

A difficult question at common law concerned the authority of the House to publish accounts of debates and reports of committees outside Parliament. In 1839, after a protracted dispute between the House and the courts, it was established that at common law the authority of the House was no defence when defamatory material was published outside the House and, more fundamentally, that the House could not create a new privilege by its own resolution.

> In *Stockdale* v *Hansard*,[51] Hansard had by order of the Commons printed and sold to the public a report by the inspectors of prisons which stated that an indecent book published by Stockdale was circulating in Newgate Prison. The first action in defamation raised by Stockdale against Hansard was decided for Hansard on the ground that the statement in the report was true. When Stockdale brought a second action, after the report had been republished, Hansard was ordered by the House to plead that he had acted under an order of the Commons, a court superior to any court of law; that the House had declared that the case was one of privilege; that each House was the sole judge of its own privileges; and that a resolution of the House declaring its privileges could not be questioned in any court. The court rejected this defence, holding that only the Queen and both Houses of Parliament could make or unmake laws; that no resolution of a single House could place anyone beyond control of the law; and that, when it was necessary to decide the rights of persons outside Parliament, the courts should determine the nature and existence of privileges of the Commons. It was also held that the House had no privilege to permit publication of defamatory matter outside the House.

---

[43] E.g. HC 357 (1967–8), debated on 24 July 1968; HC 185 (1969–70); HC 180 (1971–2); and HC 22 (1975–6), debated on 16 December 1975.

[44] HC Deb, 31 October 1980, col 917; and HC SO 136.

[45] *Wason* v *Walter* (1868) LR 4 QB 73. And see ch 23 F.

[46] *Cook* v *Alexander* [1974] QB 279.

[47] *Buchanan* v *Jennings* [2004] UKPC 36, [2005] 1 AC 115.

[48] Cf *Davison* v *Duncan* (1857) 7 E & B 229.

[49] See HC 376 (1981–2) for the history, and the Nicholls report (paras 358–61) for the present position.

[50] Nicholls report, paras 355–75. See P M Leopold [1987] PL 524, (1989) 9 LS 53 and [1999] PL 604, 614.

[51] (1839) 9 A & E 1. For the background, see P and G Ford (eds), *Luke Graves Hansard's Diary 1814–1841*. And E Stockdale [1990] PL 30.

One sequel to *Stockdale v Hansard* was the *Case of the Sheriff of Middlesex*, which will be considered later. The other sequel was the Parliamentary Papers Act 1840. By s 1, any civil or criminal proceedings arising out of the publication of papers, reports etc. made by the authority of either House must be stayed on the production of a certificate of such authority from an officer of the House. Thus the Act gave the protection of absolute privilege to parliamentary papers. The official report of debates in the House (Hansard) has absolute privilege under the 1840 Act and so do documents (such as committee reports) that are published as *House of Commons papers*. But *Command papers* (published by the government) are not protected in this way: if the report of an inquiry may contain defamatory material, a minister will move an order calling for the report to be produced to Parliament, so bringing it within the 1840 Act.[52] Section 3 of the 1840 Act protects (in the absence of malice) the publication of fair and accurate extracts from papers published under the authority of Parliament: thus press reports of parliamentary papers are protected by qualified privilege, and the same now applies to broadcast reports.[53] But the 1840 Act does not apply to press reports of debates which are based not on Hansard but on the reporter's own notes.

Right to control internal proceedings

The House has the right to control its proceedings and to regulate its internal affairs without interference by the courts. This right to 'exclusive cognizance' of its own proceedings is one reason why the courts refuse to investigate alleged defects of procedure when the validity of an Act of Parliament is challenged on this ground.[54] For the same reason, the court refused to enforce a contract between two local authorities by which one council had promised not to oppose in Parliament a Bill promoted by the other council;[55] and the courts will not consider whether the report of a Commons committee is invalid because of procedural defects.[56]

The House is also considered to have the right 'to provide for its own constitution as established by law'.[57] This no longer includes the right to decide disputed elections (these are now decided by the courts).[58] But the House retains the right (*a*) to regulate the filling of vacant seats by ordering the issue of a warrant by the Speaker for a writ for a by-election;[59] (*b*) to determine whether a member is qualified to sit in the House and to declare a seat vacant if she is not so qualified;[60] and (*c*) to expel a member whom it considers unfit to continue as a member. Expulsion does not disqualify a member from being re-elected. Subject to this, expulsion is the ultimate disciplinary sanction which the House can exercise over its members. It was exercised in 1947 when Mr Allighan MP published an article that accused MPs of disclosing when drunk or for payment the proceedings of confidential party meetings held in the precincts of the House. Mr Allighan failed to substantiate these allegations and his conduct was considered to be a gross contempt of the House justifying expulsion.[61]

By contrast with the position in the United States,[62] no court in Britain may review the legality of a resolution of the House to exclude or expel a member. One safeguard against abuse of the power of expulsion is that a constituency may re-elect an expelled member, as in the case of John

---

[52] Cmnd 5909, 1975, p 55; P M Leopold [1990] PL 183; Nicholls report, paras 343–54.
[53] Defamation Act 1952, s 9(1); Broadcasting Act 1990, s 203(1) and Sch 20, para 1.
[54] *Pickin v British Railways Board* [1974] AC 765.
[55] *Bilston Corpn v Wolverhampton Corpn* [1942] ch 391.
[56] *Dingle v Associated Newspapers Ltd* [1961] 2 QB 162.
[57] Erskine May, pp 90–1.
[58] Ch 9 E.
[59] Page 182 above.
[60] Cf *A-G v Jones* [2000] QB 66 (Speaker asking court to decide whether MP's seat, vacated on her conviction for an election offence, reverted to her when she won her appeal against conviction.) And see ch 9 E.
[61] HC 138 (1946–7).
[62] *Powell v McCormack* 395 US 486 (1970).

Wilkes in the eighteenth century. Today, a member who commits severe misconduct is more likely to resign or undertake not to stand at the next general election than to be expelled.[63]

This right of the House to regulate its proceedings includes the right to maintain order and discipline during debates. A member guilty of disorderly conduct who refuses to withdraw may, on being named by the Speaker, be suspended from the service of the House either for a specified time or for the remainder of the session.[64] In *Eliot's* case[65] the question of whether the courts could deal with an assault on the Speaker committed in the House was left open when the judgment was declared illegal by resolutions of both Houses. In principle criminal acts in the precincts of Parliament may be dealt with in the ordinary courts, even when (as in the case of an assault on the Speaker) they also constitute a contempt of the House. For this reason, the police in 2009 investigated claims of fraud and/for theft against some MPs who appeared to have made dishonest claims for parliamentary allowances (see below). In the case of a statutory offence, the prosecutor must be able to show that the statute applies to the Palace of Westminster: in 1935, an attempt to convict members of the Kitchen Committee of the House for breaches of licensing law failed, primarily because of the right of the House to regulate its internal affairs.[66]

Breaches of privilege and contempt of the House

The House has inherent power to protect its privileges and to punish those who violate its privileges or commit contempt of the House. The penal powers of the House include power to order the offender to be reprimanded by the Speaker. Members may be suspended or expelled; officers of the House may be dismissed; and non-members such as lobby correspondents, who are granted certain facilities in the Palace of Westminster, may have those facilities withdrawn.[67] Although the House has no power to impose a fine, it has power to commit a person to the custody of its own officers. Today, arrests for criminal conduct are likely to be made by police officers who are always on duty in the House, and it would be very surprising if the House were to commit someone to prison for contempt of the House until the end of the session.

The term 'breach of privilege' is not synonymous with contempt of the House, and someone could be guilty of contempt who had not infringed any privilege of the House.[68] Contempt of the House, like contempt of court, is a very wide concept. In Erskine May's words:

any act or omission which obstructs or impedes either House of Parliament in the performance of its functions, or which obstructs or impedes any member or officer of such House in the discharge of his duty, or which has a tendency, directly or indirectly, to produce such results may be treated as a contempt even though there is no precedent of the offence.[69]

Contempt has been held to include: disorderly conduct by those within the precincts of the House;[70] refusal without reasonable excuse to give evidence to a committee of the House;[71] interference with the giving of evidence by others to a committee;[72] obstruction of a member

---

[63] For the case of the disappearing MP, John Stonehouse, who was eventually convicted of fraud and resigned, see HC 273, 357, 373, 414 (1974–5), and HC Deb, 11 June 1975, col 408.

[64] HC SOs 42–45A.

[65] Page 215 above.

[66] *R v Graham-Campbell, ex p Herbert* [1935] 1 KB 594. Cf Nicholls report, paras 240–51.

[67] Cf HC 22 (1975–6).

[68] In *Allighan's* case, above, the false reports about party meetings at Westminster involved an affront to the House but not a breach of privilege as such.

[69] Erskine May, p 128; see HC 34 (1967–8), pp xi–xviii and 95–101; Nicholls report, paras 262–70.

[70] For the precedents and full references, see Erskine May, chs 8 and 9.

[71] On the power to compel evidence to be given to a select committee, see P M Leopold [1992] PL 516.

[72] The House resolved in 1688 that all witnesses summoned to the House should have the privilege of the House 'in coming, staying and returning'; and see the Witnesses (Public Inquiries) Protection Act 1892.

in coming to and from the House;[73] uttering lies in a personal statement to the House; bribery and corruption, or attempts thereat, in relation to members;[74] molesting a member on account of conduct in the House (for example, when a newspaper invited readers to telephone a member at his home to express their views about a question which he had tabled);[75] publishing material which is derogatory of the House (for example, an allegation of drunkenness);[76] premature disclosure of the proceedings of a committee of the House;[77] and the secret recording by a journalist of his conversations with MPs at Westminster while trying to persuade them to accept cash for asking questions.[78] Action by the police or prison officers intended to prevent a constituent communicating with her MP could be a contempt, even if the communication would not itself have been a 'proceeding in Parliament'. But it was held not to be a contempt for some pressure to be exercised on a person to withdraw a complaint which he had asked his MP to raise in Parliament.[79]

The fact that certain action may be a contempt does not mean that the House will take action against the offender. In 1978, it was agreed that the House should use its penal jurisdiction as sparingly as possible and only when the House

> is satisfied that to do so is essential to provide reasonable protection for the House, its members or its officers, from such improper obstruction or attempt at or threat of obstruction as is causing or is liable to cause, substantial interference with the performance of their respective functions.[80]

Civil servants are subject to direction by ministers in giving evidence to select committees,[81] but this controversial rule does not apply to members of non-departmental public bodies: when a member of one such body (CAFCASS) gave evidence to a Commons committee about its poor administration, other members of CAFCASS and the Lord Chancellor were held to have acted in contempt of the House in taking action against her because she had given that evidence.[82]

The courts and contempt of the House

While the courts assert jurisdiction to decide the existence and extent of privileges of the House, what constitutes a contempt is a matter for the House to decide. This principle was decided in the past in relation to the ancient power of the House to detain persons for contempt. Could the courts review the House's decision to detain an individual? What eventually emerged from the decisions turned on the procedure of habeas corpus. If the return to the writ of habeas corpus stated the events which had caused the individual to be detained, the court could decide whether that was a sufficient reason for the detention; but if the bald statement was that the detainee had committed contempt of the House, the court would make no inquiry into the reasons.[83] This principle was applied in the *Case of the Sheriff of Middlesex*. This was the sequel to *Stockdale v Hansard*, in which we have seen that the Commons ordered Hansard to plead a defence in law that was rejected by the court. When Stockdale attempted to recover the damages from Hansard that he had been awarded, the House committed for contempt the sheriffs who

---

[73] Cf *Papworth v Coventry* [1967] 2 All ER 41.

[74] And see section B of this chapter.

[75] The *Daily Graphic* case, HC 27 (1956–7).

[76] *Duffy's* case, HC 129 (1964–5) and see HC 302 (1974–5).

[77] See notes 43 above and 96 below.

[78] HC 351-I (1994–5).

[79] *Stevenson's* case, HC 112 (1954–5).

[80] HC 34 (1967–8), para 15; HC Deb, 6 February 1978, cols 1155–98.

[81] See the so-called *Osmotherly Rules* (p 109 above). And see ch 13 D.

[82] See HC 210, 447 and 1055 (2003–4).

[83] *Paty's* case (1704) 2 Lord Raymond 1105; *Burdett v Abbot* (1811) 14 East 1.

attempted to carry out the judgment of the court. The House's return to the writ of habeas corpus stated merely that the sheriffs had been committed for contempt, and this statement was accepted by the court.[84] The ultimate outcome of the dispute came with enactment of the Parliamentary Papers Act 1840, as we have already seen.

It remains possible that a disagreement between the courts and the Commons could arise today over an issue of privilege (for instance, as to the meaning of 'proceedings in Parliament'), but if it did the dispute would be unlikely to lead to a head-on conflict between the two institutions. On the specific issue of power to detain for contempt, the House does not need powers of detention today, except for power to detain briefly anyone who tries to disrupt a sitting of the House. In 1999, the Nicholls committee concluded that the High Court should be granted power to punish non-members of the House for contempt, but only by imposing a fine.[85] Such a solution would be more likely to be compatible with the European Convention on Human Rights (articles 5, the right to liberty, and 6, the right to a fair hearing by a court) than the exercise of penal jurisdiction by the Commons against someone who is not an MP.[86]

The courts and parliamentary privilege[87]

As we have seen, questions of privilege used to be a potential source of conflict between the Commons and the courts. The House claimed to be the sole judge of its own privileges, a claim that conflicted with the right of the courts, asserted in *Stockdale* v *Hansard*, to determine the limits of parliamentary privilege in adjudicating on the rights of individuals outside the House. Another illustration of the relationship between courts and Parliament is provided by complex events in the 1880s relating to the radical Charles Bradlaugh, an atheist who was elected MP for Northampton but was prevented by the House from taking the oath as required by the existing legislation. In outline, the court first held Bradlaugh subject to penalties payable to a member of the public (common informer) who was seeking to enforce the Parliamentary Oaths Act 1866.[88] Later, following his re-election to Parliament, the dispute continued and the House resolved that the Serjeant at Arms should exclude Bradlaugh from the House. Bradlaugh challenged this resolution by seeking an injunction against the Serjeant at Arms. In *Bradlaugh* v *Gossett*, it was held that, since this was a matter relating to the internal management of the House, the court had no power to interfere. Lord Coleridge CJ said, 'If injustice has been done, it is injustice for which the courts of law afford no remedy.'[89] And Stephen J held that the court could not interfere with a resolution of the House concerning internal management of the House. However, 'as regarded rights to be exercised out of and independently of the House, such as a right of suing for a penalty for having sat and voted, the statute must be interpreted by this court independently of the House'.[90]

It has been said that, 'there may be at any given moment two doctrines of privilege, the one held by the courts, the other by either House, the one to be found in the Law Reports, the other in Hansard'.[91] But this dualism must not be exaggerated. On the one hand, new privileges, for example, the absolute privilege which an MP has in forwarding a citizen's complaint to the Parliamentary Ombudsman,[92] must be created by statute and not by resolution of the House. On

---

[84] (1840) 11 A & E 273. And see E Stockdale [1990] PL 30.
[85] Nicholls report, paras 271–314.
[86] And see *Demicoli* v *Malta* (1992) 14 EHRR 47.
[87] Erskine May, ch 11.
[88] *Clarke* v *Bradlaugh* (1881) 7 QBD 38. And see Arnstein, *The Bradlaugh Case*.
[89] (1884) 12 QBD 271, 277.
[90] Ibid, 282.
[91] Keir and Lawson, *Cases in Constitutional Law*, p 255.
[92] Parliamentary Commissioner Act 1967, s 10(5); ch 29 D.

the other hand, the courts recognise the control which the House has over its own proceedings. Today it is not conceivable that the House would use its power to commit for contempt so as indirectly to create a new privilege when it was not willing to do this by legislation.[93]

In 1999, the Nicholls committee examined potential problems for privilege arising from the increased use of judicial review, but it concluded that privilege was not a reason for restricting judicial review of executive decisions.[94] In 1993, a warning was given by Speaker Boothroyd that the parties to an application for judicial review of the government's decision to ratify the Treaty on European Union should respect art 9 of the Bill of Rights; in the event, the court proceedings dealt solely with issues affecting the legality of the decision.[95]

The House today makes a restrained use of its powers, especially when a minor breach of privilege or contempt is committed by a non-member. However, MPs still protect the right of a select committee to deliberate in private: it has repeatedly been emphasised that disclosure of a draft committee report and its unauthorised use or retention are contempts of the House.[96]

Procedure

How does the House exercise its power when a complaint of breach of privilege or contempt is raised? Before 1978, members had to bring a privilege complaint to the notice of the whole House at the earliest opportunity. Today, the procedure operates under less pressure and trivial complaints receive less publicity.[97] A member must give written notice of a privilege complaint to the Speaker as soon as is reasonably practicable. If the Speaker decides that the complaint should not have precedence over other Commons business, the MP is told this by letter, and it is then up to the member (if he or she can) to find another way of bringing the matter to the House. If the Speaker decides that the complaint should have priority over other business, this decision is announced to the House, and the member may table a motion for the next day proposing that the matter be referred to the Committee on Standards and Privileges. The motion is then debated and voted on by the House. The committee, which has 11 members, was created in 1995 in place of the former Committee of Privileges. The committee decides on the procedure for investigating the complaint. It is not the practice of the House to permit the person complained against to be represented by counsel. After examining witnesses and being advised by the Clerk of the House on relevant precedents, and if necessary by the Attorney General on matters of law, the committee reports to the House and may recommend action by the House. The House need accept neither the conclusions nor the recommendations. The party whips are not applied on privilege issues,[98] but this does not mean that voting is not affected by party political considerations.

This procedure has been criticised, in particular because the individual complained against has inadequate procedural safeguards. In 1999, the Nicholls committee set out what procedural fairness requires, referred to the right to a fair hearing under art 6 ECHR, and urged that the Committee on Standards and Privileges should devise an appropriate procedure.[99] One solution

---

[93] Cf G F Lock [1985] PL 64 and (same author) in Oliver and Drewry (eds), *The Law and Parliament*, ch 4.

[94] Nicholls report, paras 46–55.

[95] See HC Deb, 21 July 1993, col 353; R Rawlings [1994] PL 367, 377–81; and *R v Foreign Secretary, ex p Rees-Mogg* [1994] QB 552.

[96] HC 607 (1998–9) (draft report of foreign affairs committee); HC 747 (1998–9) (social security committee). Also HC 376 (1985–6) and HC Deb, 20 May 1986, cols 293–332. And see Griffith and Ryle, *Parliament*, pp 148–50. See also note 43 above.

[97] HC 417 (1976–7); HC Deb, 6 February 1978, col 1155; and HC Deb, 29 April 1981, col 789.

[98] In 1996, a junior whip resigned after seeking to exercise improper pressure on the former Committee on Members' Interests: HC 88 (1996–7).

[99] Nicholls report, paras 280–92, citing *Demicoli v Malta* (see note 86 above). See HC 403 (2002–3) for response of the Committee on Standards and Privileges to the Committee on Standards in Public Life (Cm 5663) urging procedural reforms. For earlier recommendations of reform, see HC 34 (1967–8) and HC 417 (1976–7).

to the need for fair procedure would be for the House to vest power to decide questions of privilege in an independent and impartial body outside the House, but the House would be unlikely to accept this. Nicholls advised against such a solution, but stated that the role of the House should be limited to endorsing the report of the Privileges and Standards Committee or reducing a proposed penalty.[100]

B. Financial interests and payment of members

It is one thing to assert the principle that MPs should have complete freedom of speech in Parliament, but another to ensure that they are, in fact, free of undue influence from financial and business interests outside the House and do not abuse their public office for private gain. In this section we will examine (a) the system that existed before 2009 of regulation by the House of MPs' external financial interests; (b) the dramatic issues exposed by the media in 2009 relating to the payment of MPs' expenses; and (c) the hurried legislative response to those issues in 2009.

Two preliminary points may be made. First, it was only in 1911 that MPs who did not hold ministerial office received a salary. Payment of salaries became essential once the Law Lords had held that the use of trade union funds for political purposes was ultra vires and illegal,[101] thus preventing unions from paying salaries to the Labour MPs whom they supported. Today, it is accepted that the payment of salaries to MPs is essential, but difficulties arise as to how much they should be paid (since 1987, the salaries have been linked by means of a formula to civil service pay scales)[102] and as to any other allowances that may be needed to enable members to perform their duties.[103] Secondly, MPs have never been required to give up their existing business or professional interests when they are elected to the House, although for practical reasons many must cut down the time they give to such interests and others must resign from their previous jobs.

Payments and rewards to members of Parliament from external sources

Every MP is expected to take an active interest in questions that directly affect their constituency and their constituents. At the national level, numerous interest groups (trade unions, professional associations, companies and voluntary organisations) seek for a variety of reasons to influence the government and to win support in Parliament. Many groups consider it worthwhile to obtain advice from MPs and to ensure that opportunities of promoting their cause in Parliament are taken. Where an MP gives time and effort to helping a constituent, no question of additional remuneration arises. But where an MP takes an interest in other matters, may he or she expect to be rewarded for this? And how is a line to be drawn between payments and rewards that are acceptable, and those that are not?

As long ago as 1695, the House resolved that 'the offer of any money, or other advantage, to any member of Parliament for the promoting of any matter whatsoever depending or to be transacted in Parliament is a high crime and misdemeanour'. In 1858, the House resolved that it was improper for a member to promote or advocate in the House any proceeding or measure in which he was acting for pecuniary reward. In 1945, it was considered that, in accordance with the resolution of 1695, it would be a breach of privilege for money or other advantage to be

---

[100] Nicholls report, para 294. See also text at pp 227–8 below.

[101] *Amalgamated Society of Railway Servants v Osborne* [1910] AC 87. Under the Trade Union and Labour Relations (Consolidation) Act 1992, unions may contribute to the expenses of parliamentary candidates from separate political funds.

[102] See HC Deb, 3 November 1993, col 455; 13 July 1994, col 1105; and 26 October 1995, col 1191.

[103] For the history of members' salaries, see Erskine May, ch 1.

offered to a member, or to a local party or a charity, to induce him or her to take up a question with a minister.[104]

Moreover, by an old rule of the House, no member who has a direct pecuniary interest in a question may vote upon it. But this rule was narrowly interpreted: Speaker Abbot declared in 1811 that the rule applied only where the interest was a 'direct pecuniary interest and separately belonging to the persons . . . and not in common with the rest of His Majesty's subjects, or on a matter of state policy'. The rule was applied only to private legislation and a vote on a public Bill has never been disallowed.[105] By custom of the House, members had to declare their direct pecuniary interest when speaking in a debate, but this did not apply to question time or to letters sent by a member to a minister.[106] The duty to disclose private interests became a rule of the House on 25 May 1974, when the House resolved:

> That in any debate or proceedings of the House or its committees or transactions or communications which a member may have with other members or with Ministers or servants of the Crown, he shall disclose any relevant pecuniary interest or benefit of whatever nature, whether direct or indirect, that he may have had, may have or may be expecting to have.

This resolution governs all parliamentary proceedings, but not in terms to dealings which MPs have with local councils, public corporations or foreign governments.

One reason why this resolution was adopted by the House in 1974 was that in 1972 the business network associated with the architect John Poulson collapsed. Bankruptcy proceedings revealed that the network had largely been founded on bribing officials in central and local government, police committees and health authorities. Three MPs, including a senior member of the shadow Cabinet, had used their position as MPs to promote Poulson's business without disclosing benefits which they were receiving from him. The conduct of one of these MPs, who had raised matters in the House for reward, was held to be a contempt of the House.[107]

Apart from public offices which disqualify from membership,[108] members may take paid employment outside the House or act as advisers or consultants to commercial or other organizations. Problems are bound to arise when payments from outside sources relate to actions of the member in Parliament.[109]

Such difficulties arose as long ago as 1947, when W J Brown, the general secretary of a civil service union who had been elected to the House, by a new contract agreed to be the union's 'parliamentary general secretary'. In this specially created position, he was required to deal with all questions relating to the union that needed parliamentary action, but at the same time the contract said that he was entitled to engage in his political activities with complete freedom. When the union wished to bring the contract to an end, the issues were considered by the Commons Committee of Privileges.[110] Thereafter the House resolved that it was improper for an MP

> to enter into any contractual agreement with any outside body, controlling or limiting the Member's complete independence and freedom of action in Parliament or stipulating that he shall act in any way as the representative of such outside body in regard to any matters to be transacted in Parliament; the duty of a Member being to his constituents and to the country as a whole, rather than to any particular section thereof.[111]

---

[104] *Henderson's* case, HC 63 (1944–5). See also *Robinson's* case HC 85 (1943–4).

[105] HC 57 (1969–70), p xii; Erskine May, pp 491–3.

[106] See *Boothby's* case, HC 5 (1940–1).

[107] See HC 490 (1976–7); HC Deb, 26 July 1977, col 332; and G J Zellick [1978] PL 133.

[108] Ch 9 G.

[109] See generally HC 57 (1969–70); First Report of the (Nolan) Committee on Standards in Public Life, Cm 2850-I (1995); and HC 637 (1994–5).

[110] HC 118 (1846–7).

[111] HC Deb, 15 July 1947, col 284.

This was an important statement of principle, but why was it not breached by Brown's contract, which in return for payment envisaged action in Parliament? The view taken was that the contract did not *require* Brown to take any specific action in Parliament – so that (in one sense) he was free to decide what issues to raise. This left the door wide open for the growth of what came to be called 'parliamentary consultancies,' a door which in 1995 the Nolan committee said must be closed.[112]

Today the relationship between trade unions and Labour MPs in the House bears no resemblance at all to the ambiguous contract in the *Brown* case. Since 1995, no money has been paid directly to an MP but to constituency funds under a constituency development plan agreement.[113] In the past, there were instances of questions of privilege being raised when branches of a union became dissatisfied with the political work of MPs whom they were sponsoring.[114]

Register of members' interests

MPs were slow to accept the need for a systematic method of making members' interests more transparent, but the Poulson affair caused the House in 1975 to establish a compulsory register of their interests.[115] The aim was to publish information of any pecuniary interest or benefit which might affect the conduct of members, or influence their actions, speeches or vote in Parliament. The register was maintained by a senior clerk of the House and supervised by a select committee. In 1990 an MP who failed to register his financial interests was suspended from the House for 20 days.[116]

In 1995, two MPs were found to have been prepared to accept £1,000 from a *Sunday Times* reporter posing as a businessman, in return for asking a parliamentary question. Although the reporter was found to have committed a contempt of the House by secretly recording his conversations at Westminster with the MPs, the two MPs were suspended from the House, for 10 and 20 days respectively.[117]

This 'cash for questions' affair was one reason for the government's decision to appoint the Nolan Committee on Standards in Public Life. In its first report,[118] the committee restated seven key principles of conduct in public life (summarising these qualities as selflessness, integrity, objectivity, accountability, openness, honesty and leadership) and examined their application to MPs. MPs, said the Nolan committee, should be barred from selling their services to firms engaged in lobbying on behalf of clients. The committee was against placing the rules of conduct for MPs on a statutory basis, and proposed new arrangements to enable the House to enforce the rules.

To give effect to these recommendations, the House in 1995 adopted a number of measures.[119] These included appointment of a new officer of the House, the Parliamentary Commissioner for Standards, to maintain the Register of Members' Interests, and to investigate complaints about registration and MPs' conduct.[120] The Committee on Standards and Privileges was created to oversee the work of the new Commissioner, to consider matters relating to the conduct of

---

[112] Cm 2850-I (1995), pp 24–32.

[113] Ewing, *The Funding of Political Parties in Britain*, p 56. And see HC 57 (1969–70), app III.

[114] See e.g. HC 50 (1971–2), HC 634 (1974–75) and HC 512 (1976–7).

[115] See HC 57 (1969–70); and HC 102 (1974–5).

[116] See HC 135 (1989–90) and HC Deb, 7 March 1990, col 889. Also M Ryle [1990] PL 313; Griffith and Ryle, *Parliament*, pp 98–102.

[117] HC 351-I (1994–5) and HC Deb, 20 April 1995, col 350.

[118] Cm 2850-I, 1995. And see ch 14 B.

[119] HC 637 and 816 (1994–5); HC Deb, 18 May 1995, col 481.

[120] See HC SO 150.

members referred to it by the Commissioner, and to consider issues of privilege referred to it by the House.[121] Stricter rules were adopted as to the categories of interests to be registered. These included company directorships, employment, profession and vocation; services to clients arising from the member's position as MP; financial sponsorships, whether as a candidate for election or as a member; gifts and hospitality relating in any way to membership; overseas visits; land and property of substantial value; shareholdings; and a residual category of any interest or benefit received which might reasonably be thought by others to influence the member's actions in Parliament.[122] Where an MP entered into an agreement to provide services as a member, the full agreement had to be registered with the Commissioner.[123] A code of conduct for members was adopted.[124]

The 1947 resolution[125] was restated by the House, with the addition of the following:

in particular, no Members . . . shall, in consideration of any remuneration, fee, payment, or reward or benefit in kind, direct or indirect . . .

(a) advocate or initiate any cause or matter on behalf of any outside body or individual, or

(b) urge any other Member of either House . . . including Ministers, to do so, by means of any speech, Question, Motion, introduction of a Bill or amendment to a Motion or Bill.[126]

Between 1997 and 2005, the Committee on Standards and Privileges issued almost 100 reports, many of which concerned failure by MPs to register relevant interests. When a serious failure was shown to have occurred, the Committee recommended that the MPs in question be suspended from the House for stated periods.[127] The most substantial inquiry made by the first Commissioner, Sir Gordon Downey, upheld allegations that Neil Hamilton MP had received undisclosed cash payments from Mr Al Fayed for lobbying services and undisclosed hospitality, including a stay at the Ritz Hotel in Paris.[128] In such serious cases of misconduct, an adverse report could cause the MP to resign or to leave Parliament at the next election. The Committee's scrutiny included the accuracy of a personal statement made to the House by a former Cabinet minister and the breach by a committee chairman of the rule against paid advocacy.[129] In the light of the events of 2009, we may note that the Committee's reports in this period often concerned alleged mistakes or abuse arising from allowances or expenses payable to MPs.[130]

Complaints about the Code of Conduct and the Register of Interests were made to the Parliamentary Commissioner for Standards, who could decide whether to investigate them,[131] and if so the form of the investigation. In 2003, after the Committee on Standards in Public Life had made proposals to strengthen these procedures, changes were made to the House's standing orders. The Commissioner was authorised not to report to the Committee a minor failure to register an interest where the matter had been rectified. To deal with difficult factual disputes, an

---

[121] See HC SO 149.

[122] The register is regularly updated and may be read on the Commons website, as may the latest version of *The Code of Conduct together with the Rules Relating to the Conduct of Members.*

[123] Ibid, paras 35–6.

[124] HC 688 (1995–6); and HC Deb, 24 July 1996, col 392.

[125] See text at note 111 above.

[126] HC Deb, 6 November 1995, cols 604, 661.

[127] See HC 260 (1999–2000) (untruthful denial of connections with offshore companies, intended to deceive Committee); and HC 297 (2001–2) (inadequate replies to questions from Commissioner and Committee).

[128] See HC 30, 261 (1997–8); and HC Deb, 17 November 1997, cols 81–121. Mr Hamilton later sued Mr Al Fayed for libel without success (see note 31 above).

[129] See respectively HC 854 and HC 421 (2005–6).

[130] See e.g. HC 435, 946, 947 (2002–3), HC 71, 189, 233 (2004–5) and HC 419 (2005–6).

[131] HC SO 150(2)(e). The Commissioner's findings were not subject to judicial review: *R v Parliamentary Commissioner for Standards, ex p Al Fayed* [1998] 1 All ER 93.

investigatory panel might be appointed consisting of the Commissioner, a legal assessor, and an MP assessor appointed by the Speaker. Another change in 2003 was to protect the Commissioner from being removed from office, except for unfitness or inability to act; and future appointments were to be made for a single period of five years, not renewable.[132]

MPs and the criminal law of corruption[133]

We have seen that MPs have no general immunity from criminal law, but the application to them of criminal law must take account of the law of parliamentary privilege, in particular the protection afforded by art 9 of the Bill of Rights. The law relating to an MP who corruptly provides services in Parliament in return for payment is uncertain. In 1976, a royal commission considered that neither statute law nor the common law on corruption applied where an MP was involved and recommended legislation to strengthen the criminal law.[134] Another view is that the existing law does apply to MPs, except that the court may not rely on what has been said in Parliament to prove commission of an offence.[135] However, there should be no uncertainty in this area of the law, nor should the Bill of Rights be a shield for corrupt conduct. By 2009, legislation to remove the uncertainty had still not been enacted. As with MPs' expenses and allowances, to which we now turn, reliance on self-regulation for maintaining acceptable standards of conduct is no longer enough. To enable the ordinary process of criminal law to apply, legislation to clarify the position is needed.[136]

MPs' expenses and allowances

As well as their salaries, MPs have long been able to claim allowances for costs they incur in respect of such matters as travel, constituency expenses, and staff to do research and handle dealings with constituents. In 1971, MPs from constituencies outside London became able to claim an additional costs allowance (ACA) to compensate them for '*expenses wholly, exclusively and necessarily incurred when staying overnight away from their main UK residence . . . for the purposes of performing Parliamentary duties*'. Thereafter the scope and interpretation of the italicised words widened until in effect the ACA was seen by many MPs as an entitlement. By 2007–8, a maximum tax-free payment of £23,083 per year could be charged for such items as interest on a second mortgage, rent, furnishings, home maintenance and a food allowance (£400 per month).[137] The system was overseen by the Members' Estimate Committee and the Committee on Members' Allowances, the former being chaired by the Speaker and having the same membership as the House of Commons Commission.[138]

---

[132] See Nicholls report, pp 77–8; Cm 5663 (8th report, Committee on Standards in Public Life); HC 403 (2002–3); HC Deb, cols 1239–58 (26 June 2003); and HC SO 149, 150. The change in the rules of appointment was made to prevent a repeat of the unfortunate manner in which the appointment of the second Commissioner (Ms Elizabeth Filkin) had not been renewed in 2001.

[133] See P M Leopold, in Oliver and Drewry (eds), *The Law and Parliament*, ch 5; D Oliver (1997) 45 *Political Studies* 539.

[134] Cmnd 6524, 1976 (the Salmon report).

[135] G J Zellick [1979] PL 31. The common law of corruption applies to MPs in Canada (*R v Bunting* (1885) 7 OR 524) and Australia (*R v Boston* (1923) 33 CLR 386). See also *A-G of Ceylon v de Livera* [1963] AC 103, *US v Johnson* 383 US 169 (1966) and (in English law) *R v Greenway* (1992), reported at [1998] PL 356.

[136] Nicholls report, paras 135–42. See the Draft Bribery Bill (2008–9) and report of the joint committee at HL paper 115, HC 430 (2008–9), ch 13. Also the earlier Draft Corruption Bill (Cm 5777, 2003) and HL paper 157, HC 705 (2002–3), ch 4.

[137] For details of the scheme, see the *Green Book* that was issued from time to time to MPs.

[138] See House of Commons (Administration) Act 1978.

The publication of MPs' claims and expenses. When in 2005 the Freedom of Information Act 2000 came into effect, some individuals sought to discover details of expenses claimed by leading MPs, but this was resisted by the House of Commons authorities. In 2008, the Divisional Court, upholding a decision by the Information Tribunal, held that there was a direct public interest in knowledge of the scheme being available: the court referred to 'the absence of a coherent system for the exercise of control' over a 'deeply flawed' scheme.[139] An attempt thereafter in Parliament to exempt the Commons from the Freedom of Information Act did not succeed. In May 2009, in a journalistic coup, the *Daily Telegraph* began publishing details of claims by and payments to every MP.[140] These revelations were based on material leaked to the newspaper before the House authorities published information about allowances they had been required to make public under the Act of 2000, but the newspaper's reports were much more informative than the redacted version published in July 2009 by the House.

It was clear from these reports that MPs' claims spanned a very wide range, extending from a few apparently fraudulent claims for non-existent second mortgages, the opportunist 'flipping' of allowances between two homes to get maximum financial advantage, and the avoidance of capital gains tax on selling a second home, to a wide variety of claims only some of which were within the stated aims of the scheme. Many MPs had forgotten the scheme's reminder that 'the requirement of ensuring value for money is central in claiming for accommodation, goods or services – Members should avoid purchases which could be seen as extravagant or luxurious'. Knowledge of how the scheme operated caused widespread public anger. Some ministers resigned over claims they had made, other MPs were disciplined by their parties or decided to retire at the next general election, and the Speaker (Michael Martin MP) had to resign, mainly because of a failure to give leadership in the complex wrangling over publication of the expenses. The government decided that self-regulation of MPs' expenses must end, and asked the Committee of Standards in Public Life to make an urgent review of these matters.[141] Legislation was hastily enacted to provide a new structure for salaries and allowances in place of self-regulation by the House. Some obvious abuses in the scheme were removed when a revised 'Green Book' containing the rules of the scheme was issued in July 2009.

The Parliamentary Standards Act 2009. This Act (as amended in 2010) provides a wholly new legal structure for salaries and allowances. The aim of the Act, which does not apply to the House of Lords (s 2(1)), was to end self-regulation of these matters by the Commons and to create a new regulatory body, the Independent Parliamentary Standards Authority (IPSA) (s 3, and sched 1). The five members of IPSA must include a retired senior judge, an auditor and a member who was formerly an MP, but no serving MPs may be appointed. Members are formally appointed by the Queen on an address from the Commons, having been selected 'on merit on the basis of fair and open competition' by a committee of eight MPs and three other persons chaired by the Speaker (sched 1, para 2; sched 3, as amended). IPSA will report annually to each House of Parliament, but its independent status means that it is not directly accountable for its decisions to the Commons. IPSA is charged with paying salaries and allowances to MPs in accordance with schemes of salaries and allowances that will be adopted by IPSA itself after consultation with interested persons, including all MPs, the Committee on Standards in Public Life and the Review Body on Senior Salaries (ss 4, 5, as amended). Allowances may be paid only when they have been claimed by an MP, and MPs have a right to appeal against decisions made by IPSA, first to the Compliance Officer and then to a tribunal (s 6A).

---

[139] *Corporate Officer of the House of Commons* v *Information Commissioner* [2008] EWHC 1084 (Admin); [2009] 3 All ER 403.

[140] See the *Daily Telegraph*'s booklet, *The Complete Expenses File* (20 June 2009) and P Leyland [2009] PL 675.

[141] For the committee's report (the Kelly report), see Cm 7274 (November 2009). Sir Thomas Legg, a retired civil servant, was at the same time reviewing MPs' claims for expenses made since 2004.

To ensure that the scheme of MPs' allowances is properly administered, there is a new post of Compliance Officer (s 3(3) and sched 2, as amended) who is to be appointed by IPSA. The Officer serves for one term of not more than five years, may not be re-appointed, and may be removed from office only for unfitness or inability to carry out his duties. If an investigation by the Compliance Officer establishes that an MP was wrongly paid an allowance, the over-payment may be recovered from a serving MP by deduction from any payments due to the MP, and from a former MP by county court proceedings (sched 4). A civil penalty may be imposed on an MP who fails to comply with the Compliance Officer's requirements. It is a criminal offence for an MP knowingly to provide false or misleading information when making a claim for an allowance (s 10). The new measures exist alongside the disciplinary powers of the House's Committee on Standards and Privileges. IPSA and the Compliance Officer must prepare a scheme for co-operating with the Parliamentary Commissioner for Standards, the Director of Public Prosecutions and the police (s 10A).

The 2009 Act includes a declaration (s 1) that the Act shall not affect the protection for proceedings in Parliament given by the Bill of Rights, art 9. Despite its constitutional significance, the Act was enacted by an accelerated procedure that made it impossible for the proposals in the Bill to be fully considered.[142] Many provisions of the Act were amended by Part 3 of the Constitutional Reform and Governance Act 2010, which restored power to the House to determine the code of conduct on MPs' financial interests, but removed from the House the power to determine MPs' salaries by resolution of the House. Some critics of the 2009 Act feared that it would lead to judicial review of decisions made in the House of Commons. However, it is not the first time that Parliament has conferred one of its historic functions on an independent body.[143] And the effect of the 2009 and 2010 Acts will be a vastly more acceptable and open regime for MPs' expenses than the scheme that brought the House into such low repute in 2009.[144]

C. House of Lords

By comparison with the Commons, questions of privilege seldom arise in the Lords, but events in 2009 showed that the House needs disciplinary powers equivalent to those of the Commons, and that the payment of allowances to members for attending at Westminster needed to be revised.

Privileges of the House and of peers

1 *Freedom from civil arrest.* In *Stourton v Stourton*[145] a peer was held to be privileged from a writ of attachment for civil contempt following his failure to send his wife her property under a court order. The judge found that arrest was being sought to compel performance of a civil obligation. This privilege may be claimed by an individual peer at any time, but the House claims privilege

---

[142] For criticism of the time available to consider this legislation, see HL Committee on the Constitution: HL Papers 130 and 134 (2008–9). For criticism of high-speed legislation in general, see the same Committee's report, *Fast-track Legislation: Constitutional Implications and Safeguards* (HL Paper 116, 2008–9).

[143] Disputes over election results used to be decided by the Commons, but since 1868 they have been decided by the Election Court (see ch 9 E).

[144] The Scottish Parliament and the National Assembly for Wales had already adopted more open schemes for members' expenses: see for Scotland, A Langlands et al., *Independent Review of Parliamentary Allowances* (2008) and for Wales, R L Jones et al., *Getting it right for Wales* (2009).

[145] [1963] P 302.

only 'within the usual times of privilege of Parliament'.[146] Freedom from civil arrest should be abolished for members of the Lords as well as for MPs.[147]

2 *Freedom of speech*. Article 9 of the Bill of Rights applies to the Lords as it does to the Commons; a speech made in the House is not privileged if published separately from the rest of the debate.[148]

3 *The right to exclude disqualified persons from the proceedings of the House*. The House itself decides, through the Committee for Privileges, the right of newly created peers to sit and vote. Claims to disputed hereditary peerages were formerly decided by the Committee for Privileges,[149] but such questions are likely to be of little practical importance today.

4 *The right to deal with contempt*. The House has a power that has not been exercised in modern times to commit a person for a definite term and in the past claimed a power to impose fines. In 2009, the question arose as to what sanctions the House had over misconduct by its members. It was alleged by the *Sunday Times* that four peers had told journalists that parliamentary services to commercial interests could be provided by peers in return for payment. An investigation by a sub-committee of the Committee for Privileges found that two peers had breached the House's code of conduct, and the conduct of the two other peers was criticised.[150] The Committee reported that the House has always had power to discipline its members: although the House may not expel a member, the House has an inherent power to suspend a member for a period not exceeding the life of the current Parliament.[151] This was considered an appropriate sanction to be exercised today, unlike the power of the House to detain or to fine someone who had breached privileges of the House. Two peers were suspended for the rest of the session for their misconduct, and two apologised to the House. In 2009–10, the Constitutional Reform and Governance Bill included provision enabling peers to resign, and giving power to the House to suspend and expel members, but these clauses were not enacted.

Financial interests of peers

The House of Lords has not always been under the same pressure as the Commons concerning disclosure of interests. At one time the view was held that peers ought not to have to account publicly for their interests in the same manner as elected MPs. Yet peers take an influential part in the legislative process and many have access to government; they cannot expect to observe lower standards of conduct than MPs. In 1995, the House resolved that its members should act always on their personal honour and should never accept a financial benefit in return for exercising parliamentary influence; peers who had a direct interest in lobbying ought not to speak, vote or otherwise use their office on behalf of clients. The House created a register of peers' consultancies and similar interests in lobbying for clients, but this register was of much narrower scope than the Commons register.[152] In 2000, the Committee on Standards in Public

---

[146] HL SO 78. Regarding the Mental Health Act 1983, see HL 254 (1983–4). Also P M Leopold [1985] PL 9 (on the 1983 Act) and [1989] PL 398 (on peers' freedom from arrest); and Nicholls report, para 336.

[147] Nicholls report, paras 325–8.

[148] *R v Lord Abingdon* (1795) 1 Esp 226.

[149] See e.g. *The Ampthill Peerage* [1977] AC 547.

[150] HL Committee for Privileges, *The Conduct of Lord Moonie, Lord Snape, Lord Truscott and Lord Taylor of Blackburn* (2nd report, HL Paper 88, 2008–9).

[151] See HL Committee for Privileges, *The Powers of the House of Lords in respect of its Members* (1st report, HL Paper 87, 2008–9).

[152] See HL 90 and 98 (1994–5); HL Deb, 1 November 1995, col 1428, and 7 November 1995, col 1631.

Life recommended that the House should adopt a Code of Conduct, extending the register of interests, requiring declaration of a wider range of interests and continuing to restrict members in parliamentary lobbying. That Code came into effect on 31 March 2002, when it replaced the rules on financial interests adopted in 1995.[153] Complaints of failure to register an interest were heard by a sub-committee on registration of interests, with a right of appeal to the House's Committee for Privileges. Events in 2009 caused the House to return to the matter and in November 2009 a new Code of Conduct was adopted: this provides for the appointment of a House of Lords Commissioner for Standards and bars peers from undertaking 'parliamentary consultancies' and receiving payment for advice on lobbying.[154]

Although peers do not receive a salary for their services, they are entitled to an allowance for each day on which they attend the House, and they may claim travelling and overnight expenses and for secretarial assistance. The increased openness in the publication of MPs' allowances and expenses led in 2009 to publication of the payments made to every peer. Although the Parliamentary Standards Act 2009 does not apply to the Lords, the House decided in December 2009 to approve the outline of a new scheme for providing its members with financial support that would ensure greater accountability and openness.[155]

---

[153] Cm 4903, 2000; HL 68 (2000–01); HL Deb, 2 July 2001, col 630 and 24 July 2001, col 1849.

[154] See report of the Leader's Group on the Code of Conduct (the Eames report), HL Paper 171 (2008–09); for its adoption, see HL Deb, 30 November 2009, col 590 ff.

[155] See report of HL House Committee (HL paper 12, 2009–10) and Senior Salaries Review Body, *Review of Financial Support for Members of the House of Lords*. Also HL Deb (14 Dec 2009), col 1317 ff.

CHAPTER 12

The Crown and the royal prerogative

We have already seen that the functions of the executive are more diverse than those of the legislature and judiciary, having acquired a residual character after the legislature and judiciary had become separated from the main work of governing.[1] The functions of the executive have been said to include 'the execution of law and policy, the maintenance of public order, the management of Crown property . . . the direction of foreign policy, the conduct of military operations, and the provision, regulation, financing, or supervision of such services as education, public health, transport and national insurance'.[2] Today such a catalogue is far from complete. To perform all the tasks of government the executive must comprise a wide array of officials and agencies. These include the Prime Minister and other ministers, government departments, the civil service, the armed forces and also the police, who are being drawn more into the direct hierarchy of central government and exercise a vital executive function. Outside central government, but closely linked to it, are local authorities and many public bodies and regulatory agencies, which may be considered to perform executive functions, albeit confined to one locality or one activity.

It is still formally the case that executive power in the United Kingdom is vested in the Crown, however little this may reflect the reality of modern government. The Queen may reign, but it is the Prime Minister and other ministers who rule. Yet within the executive in Britain, it is not possible to dismiss the position of the monarch as an anachronism since the monarch as head of state performs some essential functions. The fact that central government is carried on in the name of the Crown has left its mark on the law. Our law has never developed a notion of 'the state': the judges have been opposed to the idea of allowing interests of the state to override common law rights.[3] Although it is common to speak of state schools, state regulation and so on, legislation rarely refers to the state as such.[4] Instead, the Crown has developed as 'a convenient symbol for the State',[5] though it is unclear whether the two terms can always be used as synonyms.[6] One distinction refers to 'the Sovereign' in matters concerning the personal conduct or decisions of the monarch (though that too is misleading in a country where legal sovereignty is acknowledged to rest with Parliament),[7] and to 'the Crown' as the collective entity which in law may stand for central government.

---

[1] Ch 5.

[2] HLE, vol 8(2), para 9.

[3] *Entick* v *Carrington* (1765)19 State Tr 1029. But cf *Council of Civil Service Unions* v *Minister of State for Civil Service* [1985] AC 374. See p 257 below.

[4] Cf *Chandler* v *DPP* [1964] AC 763; and Constitutional Reform and Governance Act 2010, part 1.

[5] G Sawer's phrase, quoted in Hogg, *Liability of the Crown* (1st edn), p 10; and see Marshall, *Constitutional Theory*, ch 2.

[6] See Commissioners for Revenue and Customs Act 2005, which provides for the appointment of Commissioners to act on behalf of the Crown (s 1(4)) but to serve in the civil service of the State (s 1(5)).

[7] See ch 4 above.

A. The monarchy[8]

Most advanced liberal democracies have moved to a republican system of government, sometimes with an elected president as head of state, the best known examples being France and the United States. But Britain is by no means alone in having a hereditary monarch as head of state, an institution which is to be found in other G8 countries (notably Canada, which shares the same monarch) as well as other European Union countries (notably Sweden and Spain). If there was a written constitution for the United Kingdom, the role and functions of the monarch as head of state would be set down, as they are in Spain. There the constitution provides by art 54 that the King's role is largely symbolic and representative – he is the symbol of unity and permanence, and assumes the highest representation of the state in international relations. In the United Kingdom the role of the monarchy has evolved over many years, and we can say that it has a number of symbolic and ceremonial duties which bring dignity and solemnity to constitutional government. But the monarchy also has representative and practical duties to perform which in the latter case may be necessary for the continuity and stability of constitutional government. As the experience of other countries demonstrates, these different roles need not be performed by a hereditary monarch, with those other countries relying on other symbols or institutions.

Title to the Crown

In 1689, the Convention Parliament (summoned by Prince William of Orange at the request of an improvised assembly of notables) filled the constitutional vacuum which arose on the departure of James II by declaring the throne vacant and inviting William of Orange and his wife Mary jointly to accept the throne.[9] These events finally confirmed the power of Parliament to regulate the succession to the Crown as it should think fit.[10] Today title to the Crown is derived from the Act of Settlement 1700, subsequently extended to Scotland in 1707 and to Ireland in 1800 by the Acts of Union. By the Act of Settlement, the Crown shall 'be remain and continue to the said most excellent Princess Sophia' (the Electress of Hanover, granddaughter of James I) 'and the heirs of her body being Protestant'.[11] The limitation to the heirs of the body, which has been described as a parliamentary entail, means that the Crown descends in principle as did real property under the law of inheritance before 1926.[12] That law inter alia gave preference to males over females and recognised the right of primogeniture. The major exception to the common law rules of inheritance is that for practical reasons the right of two or more sisters to succeed to real property as co-parceners does not apply: as between sisters, the Crown passes to the firstborn.[13]

The Act of Settlement disqualifies from the succession Roman Catholics and those who marry Roman Catholics; the Sovereign must swear to maintain the Churches of England and Scotland and must join in communion with the former Church. This is a restriction that has been questioned in recent years as being not easily justifiable in an increasingly multicultural and secular society. Since 1714, when the Hanoverian succession took effect under the Act of Settlement, the line of hereditary succession has been altered only once: it was provided by His Majesty's

---

[8] For a fuller account of the law relating to the monarchy (dealing with styles and titles, royal marriages, accession and coronation, minority and incapacity and illness and incapacity), see the 12th edn of this work, pp 255–8. On regency, see J Jaconelli [2002] PL 449.

[9] Maitland, *Constitutional History*, pp 283–5; Taswell-Langmead, *English Constitutional History*, pp 443–8.

[10] Taswell-Langmead, p 504.

[11] See *A-G v Prince Ernest Augustus of Hanover* [1957] AC 436, for construction of Princess Sophia Naturalization Act 1705 (repealed by British Nationality Act 1948) which entitled to British nationality all non-Catholic lineal descendants of Princess Sophia.

[12] On which, see C d'O Farran (1953) 16 MLR 140, and HLE, vol 8(2), paras 34–40.

[13] Blackstone, *Commentaries*, I, p 193; Chitty, *Prerogatives of the Crown*, p 10.

Declaration of Abdication Act 1936 that the declaration of abdication by Edward VIII should have effect; that the member of the royal family then next in succession to the throne should succeed (thus Edward VIII's brother became King George VI); and that Edward VIII, his issue, if any, and the descendants of that issue should not thereafter have any right to the succession. The eldest son of a reigning monarch is the heir apparent to the throne; he is Duke of Cornwall by inheritance and is invariably created Prince of Wales.[14]

Financing the monarchy[15]

In the seventeenth century, when the Sovereign personally carried out the functions of government, the revenue from the taxes which Parliament authorised was paid over to the Sovereign and merged with the hereditary revenues already available to him. Today a separation is made between the expenses of government and the expenses of maintaining the monarchy. Since the time of George III, it has been customary at the beginning of each reign for the monarch to surrender to Parliament for his or her life the ancient hereditary revenues of the Crown, including the income from Crown lands.[16] Provision is then made by Parliament for meeting the salaries and other expenses of the royal household. This provision, known as the Civil List, was granted to the Queen for her reign and six months after, by the Civil List Act 1952. In 1952, the total annual amount paid was £475,000 but following an inquiry into the financial position of the monarchy by a select committee of the House of Commons,[17] the amount was raised to £980,000 by the Civil List Act 1972. The 1972 Act also provided that the annual sum might be increased by means of a Treasury Order subject to annulment by the House of Commons.[18]

The Civil List, which is used 'to meet official expenditure necessarily incurred through [the monarch's] duties as head of state',[19] 'accounts for only a small percentage of government expenditure on the monarchy'.[20] Thus certain expenses in connection with the maintenance of the royal palaces and royal travel are now met by separate grants in aid voted annually by Parliament. The total head of state expenditure from public funds for 2009 was £41.5 million, which included the Queen's Civil List payment. Civil List accounts are now published annually in the interests of transparency. The Prince of Wales enjoys separate provision out of the Duchy of Cornwall to meet official and personal expenses, although he receives no parliamentary annuity. The Act of 1952, as amended in 1972, also makes provision for the Duke of Edinburgh, the Queen's younger children and other members of the royal family. Since 1975, however, the Queen has reimbursed the Treasury for the annuities paid to three members of her extended family, and since 1993 she has reimbursed all but those paid to herself, the Duke of Edinburgh and the late Queen Mother.[21]

The monarch also holds property in a personal capacity and derives income from this. In 1971 the Commons select committee was assured that suggestions that the Queen owned private funds in the region of £50 million were 'wildly exaggerated' but no estimate of their actual value was given to the committee. In 1996 the Press Complaints Commission upheld a complaint from the Press Secretary to the Queen about an article in *Business Age* magazine which claimed that the

---

[14] On the constitutional role of the Prince of Wales, see R Brazier [1995] PL 401. See also Blackburn, *King and Country: Monarchy and the Future King Charles III*.

[15] For a good account, see Bogdanor, *The Monarchy and the Constitution*, ch 7.

[16] Under the Crown Estate Act 1961, the Crown Estate Commissioners are responsible for administering the Crown Estate: for the history, see HC 29 (1971–2), app 18. The Commissioners have wide powers under the Act. See *Walford v Crown Estate Commissioners* 1988 SLT 377.

[17] HC 29 (1971–2).

[18] SI 1990 No 2018.

[19] Bogdanor, p 186.

[20] Ibid, p 187.

[21] HC 29 (1971–2), para 31.

Queen was the wealthiest person in Britain with an estimated wealth of £2.2 billion. In the view of the Commission 'the article presented speculation as established fact', 'failed adequately to check its facts' and 'made a number of errors which were not properly addressed'.[22] One matter of concern was the failure to distinguish private wealth from that held in trust by the Queen as Sovereign and Head of State and not as an individual. Unlike other members of the royal family, the Queen benefits from the principle that the Crown is not liable to pay taxes unless Parliament says so either expressly or by necessary implication.[23] In 1992, however, it was announced that the Queen had undertaken to pay tax on her private income with effect from 1993,[24] but this does not extend to inheritance tax. The Prince of Wales has also agreed on a voluntary basis to pay tax on income derived from the Duchy of Cornwall.[25]

Duties of the monarch

No attempt can be made to list the full duties which fall to the Queen to perform in person.[26] Many formal acts of government require her participation. Many state documents require her signature, and she receives copies of all major government papers, including reports from ambassadors abroad and their instructions from the Foreign Office, as well as minutes of Cabinet meetings and other Cabinet papers. 'There is therefore a continuing burden of unseen work involving some hours reading of papers each day in addition to Her Majesty's more public duties.'[27] She gives frequent audiences to the Prime Minister and visiting ministers from the Commonwealth, receives foreign diplomatic representatives, holds investitures and personally confers honours and decorations. She receives visits to this country by the heads of foreign states and makes state visits overseas. She attends numerous state occasions, for example to deliver the Queen's Speech at the opening of each session of Parliament. Her formal consent is needed for appointments made by the Crown on the advice of the Prime Minister, the Lord Chancellor and other ministers.

A catalogue of official duties does not reveal what influence, if any, the monarch has on the political direction of the country's affairs. In general, the monarch is bound to act on the advice of the Prime Minister or other appropriate minister, for example, the Home Secretary in respect of the prerogative of mercy. The monarch cannot reject the final advice that ministers offer to her without the probable consequence of bringing about their resignation and their replacement by other ministers, thereby bringing the future of the monarchy into controversy. But to what extent may the Queen offer them guidance from her own fund of experience in public affairs? Bagehot described the monarch's rights as being the right to be consulted, the right to encourage and the right to warn.[28] While this may entitle the monarch to express personal views on political events to the Prime Minister, these views may have little influence over the whole range of the government's work.[29] However, both Mr Major and Mr Blair have each paid tribute to the advice received from the Queen during their time as Prime Minister.[30]

Much light was thrown upon the role of the monarch in the twentieth century by Sir Harold Nicolson's biography of George V and by Sir John Wheeler-Bennett's biography of George VI.

---

[22] Press Complaints Commission, Report No 34 (1996), pp 5–8.

[23] HC 29 (1971–2), app 12; and ch 12 D.

[24] HC Deb, 26 November 1992, col 982.

[25] HC 464 (1992–3). See also HC 313 (2004–5).

[26] See HC 29 (1971–2), paras 16–17 and evidence by the Queen's Private Secretary, pp 30–41 and app 13. See also generally Pimlott, *The Queen: A Biography of Elizabeth II*.

[27] HC 29 (1971–2), para 17.

[28] *The English Constitution*, p 111. See also Brazier, *Constitutional Practice*, p 185.

[29] Although it has been said as a result that 'the Sovereign may have a marginal but beneficial influence on governmental decisions' (Brazier, ibid, p 185).

[30] R Blackburn [2004] PL 546, at p 558, note 40.

Thus it appears that the monarch, even before the days when Cabinet conclusions were regularly recorded by the Cabinet secretariat, could insist on the advice of the Cabinet being given in written form, if he felt that it was dangerous or opposed to the wishes of the people. This was so that the King could record in writing the misgivings and reluctance with which he followed the advice of his Cabinet.[31] The clear impression is given in these two biographies that the monarch is far from being a mere mouthpiece of his constitutional advisers. In more recent times, the advice of Queen Elizabeth II was said to be particularly valuable in relation to Commonwealth affairs where she was considered by Mr Major to have an 'encyclopaedic knowledge'.[32] But it would be wrong to suppose that the right to be consulted, to encourage and to warn applies to all areas of policy making, in many of which the monarch will have had no relevant experience.

The Private Secretary to the Queen plays a significant role in conducting communications between the monarch and her ministers and, in exceptional circumstances where this is constitutionally proper, between the monarch and other political leaders. Occasionally, the Queen's Private Secretary may be drawn into public controversies. In 1986, Sir William Heseltine, the Queen's Private Secretary, wrote to *The Times* following alleged disagreements between the Prime Minister (Mrs Thatcher) and the Queen on policy matters. Sir William made three points which he considered axiomatic:

(1) The Queen has the right – indeed the duty – to counsel, encourage and warn her government. She is thus entitled to have opinions on government policy and to express them to her chief minister.

(2) Whatever personal opinions the Queen may hold or may have expressed to her government, she is bound to accept and act on the advice of her ministers.

(3) The Queen is obliged to treat her communications with the Prime Minister as entirely confidential between the two of them.[33]

Sir William asserted that it was preposterous to suggest that the Queen would suddenly depart from these principles.

Reform of the monarchy

Unlike many of the other parts of the constitution, the monarchy has survived the reforming and modernising zeal of the 1990s. Indeed, in its election manifesto of 1997, which was the basis of much of the contemporary constitutional reform, the Labour party announced: 'We have no plans to replace the monarchy.'[34] Although this 'fell considerably short of a ringing endorsement of the institution of monarchy',[35] it remains the case that there has been little serious debate about the desirability of retaining a hereditary monarch as head of state in a modern democracy. In the 1990s, the monarchy weathered a lot of unwanted publicity about the private lives and business activities of some of its senior figures, and was subject to public criticism following the premature death of the Princess of Wales in 1997.[36] But greater public exposure and a less deferential media have at most ignited concerns for a more responsive monarchy, not its replacement. The difficulties of reform of the latter kind were highlighted by the referendum in Australia in 1999 where the people voted to retain the monarchy when given

---

[31] Nicolson, *George V*, p 115.
[32] Major, *The Autobiography*, p 508.
[33] *The Times*, 29 July 1986. See G Marshall [1986] PL 505.
[34] Labour Party, *New Labour: Because Britain Deserves Better* (1997), p 33.
[35] Blackburn and Plant (eds), *Constitutional Reform*, p 139.
[36] On which see Barnett, *This Time: Our Constitutional Revolution*.

the option of a republic instead. So the Queen remains the Head of State in Australia and indeed in a number of other prominent Commonwealth countries. One of the problems facing the republican campaigners in Australia was the division among the anti-monarchists about how the head of state in a republic should be chosen. Those who favoured a directly elected president (on the Irish model) were unhappy with the choice in the referendum between retaining the monarchy or moving to a president elected by Parliament.[37]

B. Personal prerogatives of the monarch

It is commonplace to distinguish between prerogative powers that are exercised by the monarch, and those that are exercised by ministers in her name. The former are referred to as personal prerogatives, and the latter as the 'prerogative powers of ministers'.[38] The existence of personal prerogatives – as they were referred to by Jennings – implies an element of personal discretion on the part of the monarch in the exercise of these powers. This, however, has been disputed as being contrary to political reality and constitutional sense. It has been claimed that these prerogatives should be understood 'not as personal discretionary powers of the monarch, nor as matters over which the monarch has any independent personal rights', but as 'clearly circum-scribed constitutional duties to be carried out on the advice of the Prime Minister'. The removal of the residue of personal and unaccountable power from a hereditary head of state is thought by some to be important to maintain the political neutrality of the monarchy, which in turn must be the 'golden rule' for its continuity.[39]

The appointment of a Prime Minister[40]

In appointing a Prime Minister the monarch must appoint that person who is in the best position to command the support of the majority in the House of Commons. This does not involve the monarch in making a personal assessment of leading politicians, since no major party could fight a general election without a recognised leader. Where an election produces an absolute majority in the Commons for one party, the leader of that party will be invited to become Prime Minister or, if already Prime Minister, he or she will continue in office. In these circumstances, the Queen 'has no choice whom he or she should appoint as Prime Minister, and it is obvious who should be called to the Palace'.[41] By modern practice, a defeated Prime Minister resigns from office as soon as a decisive result of the election is known. Where after an election no one party has an absolute majority in the House (as in 1923, 1929 and February 1974), the Prime Minister in office may decide to wait until Parliament resumes to see whether he or she can obtain a majority in the new House with support from another party (as Baldwin did after the 1923 election, only to find that he could not) or he may resign without waiting for Parliament to meet (as Baldwin did in 1929 and Heath in 1974). When he or she has resigned, the Queen will send for the leader of the party with the largest number of seats (as in 1929 and 1974) or with the next largest number of seats (as in January 1924 after Baldwin had been defeated by combined Labour and Liberal votes).[42] Thus, where the election produces a clear majority for one party, the Queen has no

---

[37] See C Munro [2000] PL 3. Also J Uhr [2000] 11 *Public Law Review* 7.
[38] HC 422 (2003–4), para 1.
[39] R Blackburn [2004] PL 546; also (in reply) R Brazier [2005] PL 45.
[40] See Jennings, *Cabinet Government*, ch 2; Brazier, chs 2, 3; and Bogdanor, ch 6.
[41] Bogdanor, p 84.
[42] The precedents thus show a preference for 'minority government' rather than 'majority coalition' (Bogdanor, p 253).

discretion to exercise. Where an election does not produce a conclusive result, the Queen has no discretion except where the procedure described still fails to establish a government in office; in this case, the Queen would have to initiate discussions with and between the parties to discover, for example, whether a government could be formed by a politician who was not a party leader or whether a coalition government could be formed.[43]

Where a Prime Minister resigns because of ill-health or old age or dies while in office, a new leader of the governing party must be found and a new Prime Minister appointed. Formerly, in the case of the Liberal and Conservative parties, this was a situation in which the monarch was required to exercise a discretion, namely to invite a person to be Prime Minister who would command general support within the governing party, as happened in 1957 and 1963. The parties now choose their own leader in accordance with their own rules. It was initially the case that the leader of the Conservative party was chosen by the party's MPs. It was under these rules that Mr Major replaced Mrs Thatcher as leader of the party in 1990,[44] following which Mrs Thatcher resigned as Prime Minister and 'arrangements' were made for Mr Major 'to see the Queen the next morning'.[45] The current leadership rules of the Conservative party provide for the leader to be elected by the members of the party in a postal ballot.[46] The rules provide, however, that the candidates for election are to be chosen by the 1922 Committee, which is a committee of Conservative MPs. It is also provided that 'the procedure by which the 1922 Committee selects candidates for submission for election shall be determined by the Executive Committee of the 1922 Committee'. It was under these procedures that Mr David Cameron was elected party leader in 2005. Conservative MPs took part in several votes that reduced the number of candidates to two – Mr Cameron and Mr Davis – before party members were able to vote.

In the case of the Labour party, the right to vote in the election of leader was formerly confined to Labour MPs, but in 1981 the party changed its constitution and standing orders to provide for the leader and deputy leader to be elected at a party conference.[47] The electoral college is in three sections, Labour MPs and constituency parties each having one-third of the votes and affiliated organisations also having one-third. Successive ballots are held until one candidate has more than half the votes so apportioned. When Labour is in opposition, an election shall be held at each annual conference. When Labour is in government and the party leader is Prime Minister, an election takes place only if required by a majority of the conference on a card vote. While both parties have used their own procedures to elect leaders when in opposition, new ground was broken in 1976, again in 1990, and yet again in 1995. In 1976, when Harold Wilson announced his intention of resigning as Prime Minister, he remained in office until (under the party's former rules) Labour MPs elected their new leader, Mr Callaghan. Mr Wilson then resigned and Mr Callaghan became Prime Minister. In 1990, the Conservative party removed Mrs Thatcher as party leader against her wishes while she was also Prime Minister. Although Mrs Thatcher's leadership had previously been challenged by using the leadership procedures, her replacement by Mr Major in 1990 represents the first occasion in modern times that a serving peacetime Prime Minister has been forcibly removed from office. And in 1995, Mr Major resigned as leader of the Conservative party, thereby forcing an election for party leader, in which he was a candidate. He did not resign as Prime Minister, though presumably he would have done so had he not succeeded in being re-elected as party leader.

---

[43] See Brazier, ch 3; Butler, *Governing without a Majority*, ch 5; and Bogdanor, *Multi-party Politics and the Constitution*, chs 5, 6.

[44] See R K Alderman [1992] PL 30.

[45] Major, *The Autobiography*, p 199.

[46] For background, see K Alderman (1999) 52 *Parliamentary Affairs* 260.

[47] The rules were revised again in 1993: see R K Alderman [1994] PL 24.

While therefore under stable political conditions the Queen will not need to exercise a personal discretion in selecting a Prime Minister (as again when Mr Brown succeeded Mr Blair in 2007), circumstances could arise in which it might become necessary for her to do so.[48] First, since the election of a new leader may take some weeks, the appointment of an acting Prime Minister might well be needed if, unlike the position in 1976, the outgoing Prime Minister had died or was too ill to continue in office. Presumably a senior member of the Cabinet would be so appointed.[49] Moreover, there could well be circumstances in which reliance on normal party procedures would not produce an immediate solution: for example, where a party holding office broke up after serious internal dissensions; or where no party had a majority in the House and there was a deadlock between the parties as to who should form a government; or where a coalition agreement had broken down.[50] In such situations, the Queen could not avoid taking initiatives to enable a new government to be formed, for example by initiating inter-party discussions. In 1931, when Ramsay MacDonald and the Labour Cabinet resigned because of serious disagreement within the Cabinet over the steps that should be taken to deal with the financial crisis, George V, after consulting with Conservative and Liberal leaders, invited MacDonald to form a 'National Government' with Liberal and Conservative support. The extreme bitterness which MacDonald's defection caused in the Labour party led to criticism of George V's conduct as unconstitutional, but such criticism seems unjustified.[51]

Dissolution of Parliament[52]

In the absence of a regular term for the life of Parliament fixed by statute, in principle the Queen may by the prerogative dissolve Parliament and cause a general election to be held at any time. In practice, however, the Queen normally accepts the advice of the Prime Minister and grants a dissolution when this is requested. Since 1918, it has become established practice that a Cabinet decision is not necessary before the Prime Minister may seek a dissolution, although members of the Cabinet may be consulted before the Prime Minister makes a decision.[53] The refusal of a dissolution when the Prime Minister had requested it would probably be treated by him or her as tantamount to a dismissal. It is doubtful whether there can be grounds for the refusal of a dissolution to a Prime Minister who commands a clear majority in the Commons.[54] Political practice accepts that a Prime Minister may choose the time for a general election within the five-year life of Parliament prescribed by the Parliament Act 1911. Are there circumstances in which the Sovereign would be justified in refusing a dissolution, or is it automatic that the Sovereign should grant a dissolution when requested?

---

[48] Cf R Blackburn [2004] PL 546, at p 552. The position is very different in Scotland in relation to the First Minister under the Scotland Act 1998, s 45. See Himsworth and O'Neill, *Scotland's Constitution: Law and Practice* where it is said that the Queen has 'only the formal role of accepting the recommendations made to her. It would be unconstitutional for her to do otherwise' (p 166).

[49] Cf Brazier, p 17. Under the Labour party rules, when the party is in government and the leader becomes 'permanently unavailable', 'the Cabinet shall in consultation with the National Executive Committee appoint one of its members to serve as party leader until a ballot . . . can be carried out'.

[50] See R Brazier [1986] PL 387.

[51] A full account is in Bassett, *1931: Political Crisis*. See also Mackintosh, *British Cabinet*, pp 419–20 and Middlemas and Barnes, *Baldwin*, ch 23.

[52] Forsey, *The Royal Power of Dissolution in the British Commonwealth*; Markesinis, *The Theory and Practice of Dissolution of Parliament*; Marshall, *Constitutional Conventions*, ch 3; R Blackburn [2009] PL 760.

[53] Jennings, pp 417–19; Mackintosh, pp 453–5; Markesinis, ch 5 A.

[54] Markesinis, pp 84–6; Forsey, p 269. If an opportunist Prime Minister decided to take advantage of the death of the Leader of the Opposition to seek an immediate dissolution, knowing that the rules of the opposition party required the election of a new leader to take a month, could the Queen insist on delaying the election so that the parties could campaign on more equal terms?

If the Queen did refuse dissolution to a Prime Minister who commanded a majority in the House and the Prime Minister then resigned from office with the other ministers, any other politician invited to be Prime Minister (for example, the Leader of the Opposition) would presumably have no prospect of a majority at Westminster until an election had been held. The Queen would therefore be faced with an early request for a dissolution from the new Prime Minister and with inevitable criticism of political bias if the request were granted. Where a minority government holds office, the position is more complicated but here again it is essential for the Prime Minister to choose the time for an election. Much would depend on the circumstances in which the minority government had come about and on how recently a general election had been held. Thus a Prime Minister who had been granted one dissolution and failed to get a majority at the ensuing election could not necessarily insist on a second dissolution immediately. Indeed, it might be argued that there would be a duty to resign and to give the leader of another party the opportunity of forming a government. Where a Prime Minister had been in office for a considerable period (for example, some months) since the previous election and was then defeated on an issue of confidence in the House, he or she would then have a choice between resigning or, as MacDonald did in 1924, seeking a dissolution.

The issue arose in 1950, during discussion of the problems caused by the Labour government's small majority after the election of that year. Sir Alan Lascelles, Private Secretary to George VI, wrote to *The Times*, under a pseudonym, to outline the circumstances in which he believed the monarch could properly refuse a dissolution when requested by the Prime Minister. According to Sir Alan, the monarch could properly refuse a dissolution if he were satisfied that (*a*) the existing Parliament was still 'vital, viable, and capable of doing its job', (*b*) a general election would be detrimental to the national economy, and (*c*) he could rely on finding another Prime Minister who could carry on his government for a reasonable period with a working majority.[55] It will be seldom that all these conditions can be satisfied and it might even be argued that these are eminently matters for the Prime Minister in office to decide. It might be particularly difficult for the monarch to be reasonably certain that another Prime Minister could command a working majority in the House. Again the monarch would be strongly criticised if, having refused a dissolution to one Prime Minister, he or she were faced with an early request from the new Prime Minister for dissolution.

In the last 100 years there are no instances of the monarch having refused a dissolution in the United Kingdom. However, the controversy between the 'automatic' and 'discretionary' views of the prerogative of dissolution arose afresh in 1974. After the election in February of that year, when no party had an absolute majority, it was asked whether Mr Wilson as Prime Minister was entitled to a dissolution if his government were defeated in the Commons by a combined opposition vote. Certain Labour MPs, who feared that a Liberal–Conservative coalition might be formed to govern the country, urged that the Queen was both constitutionally and morally bound to grant a dissolution whenever the Prime Minister requested it. In reply, the Lord President of the Council, Mr Edward Short, told them: 'Constitutional lawyers of the highest authority are of the clear opinion that the Sovereign is not in all circumstances bound to grant a Prime Minister's request for dissolution'; it was impossible to define in advance the circumstances in which the Queen's discretion to refuse a request for a dissolution might be exercised.[56] The government refused to allow the matter to be debated in the Commons. In the event, when Mr Wilson sought a dissolution in September 1974, this was granted without question by the Queen. That the monarch should not refuse a Prime Minister's request for dissolution except for very strong reasons is obvious. In practice, the political significance of the Prime Minister's power to decide when Parliament should be dissolved is much greater than the possibility of the

---

[55] For this pseudonymous letter to *The Times*, see Markesinis, pp 87–8 and app 4.
[56] *The Times*, 11 May 1974.

Queen's refusal of a dissolution. But the view that the monarch's reserve power may serve to restrain a Prime Minister who otherwise might be tempted to abuse his or her position is an argument for maintaining the reserve power as a potential weapon, not for abolishing it.[57]

Dismissal of ministers

The account so far has been concerned principally with whether the monarch may refuse a request for a dissolution of Parliament made by the Prime Minister. But what about the other side of the coin? Are there circumstances in which the monarch can insist on a general election against the wishes of a Prime Minister? There are few precedents from recent British practice to help inform answers to such questions, but the experiences of other Commonwealth jurisdictions where similar powers and principles apply are sometimes illuminating. The last known example of a British monarch requiring a general election is in 1910, when George V insisted that a general election be held on the Liberal proposal to remove the veto of the House of Lords, before he would create enough new Liberal peers to pass the Parliament Bill through the Lords against Conservative opposition; this decision was accepted by the Prime Minister, Asquith. But in other situations a refusal by the monarch to accept advice could be seen as a direct challenge to the authority of the Prime Minister and might lead to his or her immediate resignation. The underlying question is whether the monarch is merely part of the formal apparatus of government and thus incapable of taking an independent position on a point of constitutional principle, or whether the monarchy provides some kind of safeguard against potential abuses of power by the Prime Minister and Cabinet.[58]

The last occasion on which it was seriously urged that the monarch should intervene to ensure that a general election should be held against the wishes of the government was during the crisis over Home Rule for Ireland between 1912 and 1914.[59] After the Parliament Act 1911 had become law, the Liberal government intended that the Government of Ireland Bill should be passed under the Parliament Act procedure. Opposition leaders regarded the relationship between the Liberal party and the Irish Nationalists as 'a corrupt parliamentary bargain'. They urged George V to insist that an election be held before the Bill became law or to withhold the royal assent. Asquith, the Prime Minister, reminded George V of the constitutional limitations on the monarch, of the principle of ministerial responsibility, and of the value for the monarch of having no personal responsibility for the acts of executive and Parliament. The King concluded that he should not adopt the extreme course of withholding the royal assent from the Bill 'unless there is convincing evidence that it would avert a national disaster, or at least have a tranquillizing effect on the distracting conditions of the time'.[60]

Where the question is that of assent to a Bill which has passed through Parliament, it would not be prudent for the monarch to challenge the wishes of a majority in the House of Commons. Yet the relationship between monarch and Prime Minister is bilateral in the sense that both persons hold office subject to some principles of constitutional behaviour, however vague these principles often appear to be. If the Prime Minister steps outside those principles (as, for example, Ian Smith, Prime Minister of Rhodesia, did in 1965 when with his Cabinet he unilaterally declared Rhodesia independent of the United Kingdom), the monarch may respond by dismissing his or her ministers and by seeking to ensure the maintenance of constitutional government. In 1975, the Labor government of Australia was failing to get essential financial legislation through the Canberra Parliament because of opposition from the Senate, whose approval to the legislation

---

[57] For a robust defence of the reserve power, see G Marshall [2002] PL 4.

[58] See R Brazier, in Bogdanor (ed.), *The British Constitution in the Twentieth Century*: 'the only insurance of constitutional propriety in a dire emergency is the Sovereign' (p 83).

[59] See Nicolson, ch 14; Jennings, ch 13.

[60] Draft letter by George V, 31 July 1914.

was required. When Sir John Kerr, the Governor General, had satisfied himself that Prime Minister Whitlam was not willing to hold a general election to resolve the deadlock, he dismissed Whitlam and invited the Opposition leader, Malcolm Fraser, to form an interim government and hold an election. The election was won by Fraser, but the acts of the Governor General gave rise to controversy of a kind which would be more damaging to a hereditary monarchy than to a Governor General with a limited tenure of office.[61]

British government depends to a large extent on implicit agreement between the parties and their leaders about the rules and understandings of the political contest. If, in a particular situation, it were clear that one party or its leader had seriously departed from the accepted rules, personal intervention by the monarch could be justified on constitutional grounds. But a plain instance of flagrant abuse is less likely than a situation which is not covered by existing rules and understandings and in which it may be difficult to determine what are the constitutional requirements. Perhaps falling into the category of flagrant abuse are the circumstances that led in March 2009 to the removal from office of the Prime Minister and government of the Turks and Caicos Islands (along with parts of the constitution) by Order in Council.[62] This step was taken in the light of allegations of corruption in the British Overseas Territory. Although it may indicate the type of situation in which the prerogative power may be used, nevertheless care should be taken about treating this as a relevant precedent for constitutional government in the United Kingdom, if only because this was an act of government under statutory authority not an act of the monarch acting in her personal capacity under prerogative power. Care should also be taken not to underestimate the very real practical problems facing a monarch who sought to force a general election against the wishes of an incumbent Prime Minister who enjoys the support of his or her party, not least because the monarch needs the cooperation of ministers even for the purpose of dissolving Parliament and causing a new general election to be held.[63]

> The lack of real power available to the monarch is perhaps revealed by events in Canada where the general election in 2008 returned a minority Conservative government led by Stephen Harper. Six weeks after the election the new government was faced with a motion of no confidence as the opposition parties lined up against the new government's financial proposals. Faced with likely defeat, the Prime Minister asked the Governor General of Canada to prorogue Parliament for two months.[64] It was open to the Governor General to (i) agree, (ii) refuse and appoint the leader of the opposition Liberal Party to be Prime Minister, or (iii) require a fresh election. It is not known why the Governor General agreed to accept the Prime Minister's advice (the reasons are not published), and her decision was inevitably controversial.

> The decision nevertheless could be defended on a number of grounds (the Liberals had recently been defeated at the polls, the country was gripped by a global financial crisis, and time would allow negotiations to take place between the parties). During the period of prorogation, the Liberals changed both their leader and their strategy, the government modified its plans to meet some of the objections they had faced, and the Governor General was arguably vindicated by the outcome. Quite unprecedented in modern times, the decision does, however, emphasise the extent to which the exercise of the monarch's personal prerogatives is based on the advice of her Prime Minister,[65] though as the parallel events in the Turks and Caicos Islands indicate, accepting such advice cannot always be unconditional.

---

[61] The literature includes Evans (ed.), *Labor and the Constitution 1972–75*; Kerr, *Matters for Judgment*; Sawer, *Federation under Strain*; and Whitlam, *The Truth of the Matter*. For a retrospective account, see M Coper [2000] 11 *Public Law Review* 251.

[62] SI 2009 No 701 (made under the West Indies Act 1962). See also HC Deb, 16 March 2009, col 39.

[63] Jennings, pp 412–17; Markesinis, p 56.

[64] Ch 2 B.

[65] *Globe and Mail*, 3–5 December 2008.

C. The Queen in Council

The Tudor monarchs governed mainly through the Privy Council, a select group of royal officials and advisers, having recourse to Parliament only when legislative authority was considered necessary for matters of taxation or to give effect to royal policies. The Privy Council survived the seventeenth-century conflicts, although its judicial arm, the Court of Star Chamber, was abolished in 1641. But in the 50 years after the restoration of the monarchy in 1660, the Privy Council lost its position as the main political executive and its numbers grew, many becoming members because of other offices which they held. As the Cabinet system developed, so did the English Privy Council lose its policy-making and deliberative role.[66] Soon after the union of England and Scotland in 1707, the Scottish Privy Council was abolished and its functions were assumed by the Privy Council for Great Britain.[67] In a formal sense the Council remained at the centre of the administrative machinery of government, but despite an attempt by Parliament in the Act of Settlement to insist that the Privy Council should exercise its former functions, the Council had lost its political authority. Significantly, politicians began to remain members of the Council after they had ceased to be ministers, a practice which has continued until today.

Privy Counsellors and Orders in Council

Membership of the Privy Council is now a titular honour. Appointments are made by the Queen on ministerial advice. By convention all Cabinet ministers become Privy Counsellors. Members of the royal family and holders of certain high offices of a non-political character, such as archbishops and Lord Justices of Appeal, are appointed members of the Council. So in recent years have the leaders of the opposition parties 'so that they can be given classified information on "Privy Counsellor terms" should the need arise on a matter affecting national security'. In the 1970s, Len Murray, general secretary of the TUC, was made a Privy Counsellor to facilitate consultation on government policy.[68] The office is a recognised reward for public and political service and appointments to it figure in the honours lists. The Council now numbers over 500 members. Members are entitled to the prefix, 'Right Honourable'. They take an oath on appointment which binds them not to disclose anything said or done 'in Council' without the consent of the Sovereign. As all members of the Cabinet are also Privy Counsellors, it has been considered that it is this oath which, in addition to their obligations under the Official Secrets Acts 1911–89, binds to secrecy all present and past Cabinet ministers, who may disclose Cabinet proceedings and other confidential discussions only if so authorised by the Sovereign; but little reliance was placed on this oath in the *Crossman Diaries* case[69] and its wording does not seem apt to include Cabinet proceedings. Aliens are disqualified, but on naturalisation an alien becomes qualified for membership.[70]

Despite the many powers conferred by statutes on individual ministers, the Order in Council remains an important method of giving the force of law to acts of the government, especially the more significant executive orders. A royal proclamation is issued when it is desired to give wide publicity to the action of the Queen in Council, as for the purpose of dissolving a Parliament and summoning its successor. Orders in Council are approved by the Queen at a meeting of the Council to which only four members are normally summoned. No discussion of substance on the merits of an instrument takes place at these meetings, and the acts of the Council are mainly formal. Orders are made either under the prerogative, as for the dissolution of Parliament, or under an Act of Parliament, for example, orders which make regulations under the Civil Contingencies

---

[66] For the history of this period, see Mackintosh, ch 2.
[67] See Devine, *The Scottish Nation*, pp 18, 21.
[68] Hennessy, *Whitehall*, pp 350–1.
[69] *A-G v Jonathan Cape Ltd* [1976] QB 752; for the oath, see HLE, vol 8(2), p 523.
[70] *R v Speyer* [1916] 2 KB 858.

Act 2004.[71] Prerogative orders are treated as equivalent to primary legislation and are regarded as such for the purposes of the Human Rights Act 1998, while statutory Orders in Council are generally subject to the Statutory Instruments Act 1946.[72] Legislation made in the Channel Islands must be sanctioned by Order in Council before it comes into force.

Judicial and other functions

In 1833, the Judicial Committee of the Privy Council was set up by statute to exercise the jurisdiction of the Council in deciding appeals from colonial, ecclesiastical and admiralty courts.[73] In the heyday of the British Empire, the Judicial Committee was indeed an imperial court exercising what was potentially a vast jurisdiction over much of the globe. Today, its role as an appeal court within the Commonwealth has much declined, as leading members, such as Australia, Canada, India, Pakistan and South Africa, no longer – or do not – permit appeals to the Privy Council. Nevertheless, a steady flow of cases continues to be heard from other Commonwealth countries,[74] while the Privy Council remains the final court of appeal from British Overseas Territories (such as Gibraltar) and Crown dependencies (such as the Channel Islands and the Isle of Man). A matter may also be referred to the Privy Council by the Crown for an advisory opinion, an interesting but infrequently used procedure established by s 4 of the 1833 Act,[75] which has survived the creation of the Supreme Court of the United Kingdom. The devolution legislation extended the Privy Council's jurisdiction by providing initially for it to be the final court of appeal on the powers of the devolved Parliament and assemblies. But this was short-lived, with jurisdiction being transferred to the Supreme Court of the United Kingdom when it was established in 2009. The composition of the Judicial Committee is governed by the 1833 Act: cases are usually heard by three or five Supreme Court justices or other senior judges in what is a 'strictly judicial proceeding'.[76]

So far as other functions are concerned, issues of constitutional importance are sometimes referred to ad hoc committees of the Privy Council, as, for example, the legal basis of the practice of telephone tapping and matters affecting state security.[77] A committee of six Privy Counsellors reviewed British policy towards the Falkland Islands leading up to Argentina's invasion in 1982; after the Prime Minister had consulted with five former Prime Ministers to secure their consent, the committee had access to the papers of previous governments and secret intelligence assessments.[78] More recently, a committee of five Privy Counsellors was appointed to review the collection, assessment and use of intelligence prior to the invasion of Iraq in 2003.[79] The functions of the Privy Council are quite distinct from those of the Cabinet. The first gives legal form to certain decisions of the government; the second exercises the policy-making function of the executive in major matters. There is, however, an overlap between the Cabinet and the Privy Council: decisions of the latter are normally taken by ministerial members, while the Lord President of the Council is usually a senior member of the Cabinet. He or she in the past has acted as chairman of Cabinet committees and the position may be held with the office of Leader of the House of Commons or Leader of the House of Lords. Much of the work of the Privy Council today is

---

[71] Ch 26.

[72] Ch 28.

[73] Judicial Committee Act 1833.

[74] Chs 15 C, 18 A. For the background, see L P Beth [1975] PL 219. See also Swinfen, *Imperial Appeal*.

[75] See *Re MacManaway* [1951] AC 161; *Re Parliamentary Privilege Act 1770* [1958] AC 331. For a rare recent example, see *Hearing on the Report of the Chief Justice of Gibraltar* [2009] UKPC 43.

[76] *Hull v McKenna* [1926] IR 402.

[77] Ch 25.

[78] HC Deb, 1 July 1982, col 1039, and 8 July 1982, col 469; Cmnd 8787, 1983; and ch 13 B.

[79] HC 898, 2003–04.

spent dealing with institutions and companies established by Royal Charter. The Privy Council must, for example, approve any changes to university statutes.

D. The royal prerogative

Both the monarch, as head of state, and the government, as personified for many purposes by the Crown, need powers to be able to perform their constitutional functions. The rule of law requires that these powers are grounded in law and are not outside or above the system of law which the courts administer. In Britain, the powers of the monarch and the Crown must either be derived from Act of Parliament or must be recognised as a matter of common law, for there is no written constitution to confer powers on the executive. In the seventeenth-century constitutional settlement, it was established that the powers of the Crown were subject to law and that there were no powers of the Crown which could not be taken away or controlled by statute. Once that position had been achieved against the claims of the Stuarts, the courts thereafter accepted that the monarch and the Crown enjoyed certain powers, rights, immunities and privileges which were necessary to the maintenance of government and which were not shared with private citizens. Acknowledged to be 'a notoriously difficult concept to define adequately',[80] the term prerogative is used as a collective description of these matters. Blackstone referred to prerogative as 'that special pre-eminence which the King hath, over and above all other persons, and out of the ordinary course of the common law, in right of his royal dignity'.[81] A modern definition would stress that the prerogative has been maintained not for the benefit of the monarch but to enable the government to function, and that prerogative is a matter of common law and does not derive from statute. Thus Parliament may not create a new prerogative, although it may confer on the Crown new rights or powers which may be very similar in character to prerogative power, for example, the statutory power to deport aliens from the United Kingdom whose further presence is considered undesirable,[82] or the statutory power to create life peerages.

History of the prerogative[83]

The medieval King was both feudal lord and head of the kingdom. He thus had all the rights of a feudal lord and certain exceptional rights above those of other lords. Like other lords, the King could not be sued in his own courts; as there was no lord superior to the King, there was no court in which the King could be sued. In addition, the King had powers accounted for by the need to preserve the realm against external foes and an 'undefined residue of power which he might use for the public good'.[84] We have already seen that medieval lawyers did not regard the King as being above the law.[85] Moreover certain royal functions could be exercised only in certain ways. The common law courts were the King's courts and only through them could the King decide questions of title to land and punish felonies. Yet the King possessed a residual power of doing justice through his Council where the courts of common law were inadequate. In the seventeenth century, the main disputes arose over the undefined residue of prerogative power claimed by the Stuart kings.[86] Those common lawyers who allied with Parliament in

---

[80] HC 422 (2003–4), para 3.
[81] Blackstone, *Commentaries*, I, p 239. Cf Wade, *Constitutional Fundamentals*, pp 45–53.
[82] Ch 20 B.
[83] A valuable account is in Keir and Lawson, *Cases in Constitutional Law*, part II. See also Heuston, *Essays*, ch 3, and more recently, Tomkins, *Our Republican Constitution*, ch 3.
[84] Keir and Lawson, p 70.
[85] Ch 6.
[86] Ch 4 A.

resisting the Stuart claims asserted that there was a fundamental distinction between what was called the ordinary as opposed to the absolute prerogative. The ordinary prerogative meant those royal functions which could only be exercised in defined ways and involved no element of royal discretion. Thus the King could not himself act as a judge; he must dispense justice through his judges. In 1607 James, who had by then also become King James I of England, claimed the right in England to determine judicially a dispute between the common law courts and the ecclesiastical courts. In the case of *Prohibitions del Roy*, it was decided by all the common law judges, headed by Coke, that the right of the King to administer justice no longer existed.[87] In a famous passage, Coke declared:

> that the King in his own person cannot adjudge any case, either criminal, as treason, felony, etc., or betwixt a party and party, concerning his inheritance, chattels or goods, etc., but this ought to be determined and adjudged in some Court of Justice, according to the law and custom of England; . . . true it was, that God had endowed His Majesty with excellent science, and great endowments of nature; but His Majesty was not learned in the laws of his realm of England, and causes which concern the life, or inheritance, or goods, or fortunes of his subjects, are not to be decided by natural reason, but by the artificial reason and judgment of law, which law is an act which requires long study and experience, before that a man can attain to the cognizance of it: that the law was the golden metwand and measure to try the causes of the subjects; and which protected His Majesty in safety and peace.

This declaration may not have been supported by all Coke's precedents,[88] but it served to establish a fundamental constitutional principle. At the same time, it was established that the King could make laws only through Parliament.[89]

By contrast, the absolute or extraordinary prerogative meant those powers which the King could exercise in his discretion. They included not only such powers as the right to pardon a criminal or grant a peerage, but also the King's undoubted powers to exercise discretion in the interest of the realm, especially in times of emergency. It was these powers on which Charles I relied in seeking to govern without Parliament. The conflict was resolved only after the execution of one King and the expulsion of another. But the particular disputes often gave rise to cases in the courts, in which the rival political theories were expressed in legal argument. Where the judges accepted the Crown's more extreme claims, their decisions had subsequently to be reversed by Parliament. As well as the cases on taxation and the dispensing power,[90] another outstanding case was *Darnel's* or *The Five Knights* case,[91] where it was held that it was a sufficient answer to a writ of habeas corpus to state that a prisoner was detained *per speciale mandatum regis* (by special order of the King). Thus the King was entrusted with a power of preventive arrest which could not be questioned by the courts and which in *Darnel's* case was used to enforce taxation levied without the consent of Parliament. This arbitrary power of committal was declared illegal by the Petition of Right 1628 and in 1640 the subject's right to habeas corpus against the King and his Council was guaranteed by statute.[92] The problem of the prerogative was confronted in two stages. The first was that of the seventeenth-century struggle culminating in the Bill of Rights 1689, which declared illegal certain specific uses and abuses of the prerogative.[93] The second stage was the growth of responsible government and the establishment of a constitutional monarchy.[94] It

---

[87] (1607) 12 Co Rep 63.
[88] Cf Dicey, *The Law of the Constitution*, p 18.
[89] *The Case of Proclamations* (1611) 12 Co Rep 74; ch 4 A.
[90] Ch 4 A.
[91] (1627) 3 St Tr 1.
[92] Habeas Corpus Act 1640. And see ch 31.
[93] Ch 2 A.
[94] Ch 7.

became established that prerogative powers could be exercised only through and on the advice of ministers responsible to Parliament. Nonetheless, the ability of ministers to rely on prerogative powers gives rise to continuing problems of accountability.

The prerogative today

Today the greater part of government depends on statute. But certain powers, rights, immunities and privileges of the monarch and of the Crown, which vary widely in importance, continue to have their legal source in the common law. Where these powers or rights are common to all persons, including the Crown (for example, the power to own property or enter into contracts), they are not described as matters of prerogative;[95] but the term royal prerogative is properly applied to those legal attributes of the Crown which the common law recognises as differing significantly from those of private persons. Thus the legal relationship between the Crown and Crown servants is an aspect of the prerogative since it still differs markedly from the normal contractual relationship between employer and employee; the same applies to the power of the Crown in certain circumstances to override contracts to which it is a party.[96] Although Crown servants are now typically employed under contracts of employment, the Crown nevertheless retains a prerogative power to terminate them at pleasure.[97] Except in those special instances where prerogative powers involve the personal discretion of the Queen, prerogative powers are exercised by or on behalf of the government of the day. For their exercise, just as for the use of statutory powers, ministers are responsible to Parliament.

Thus questions may be asked of ministers about the exercise of prerogative power. Where a matter does not fall within the province of a departmental minister, questions may be addressed to the Prime Minister. To this rule there are certain exceptions: for example, the Prime Minister may not be questioned in the Commons as to the advice that may have been given to the Queen regarding the grant of honours or the ecclesiastical patronage of the Crown.[98] Although an Act of Parliament may abolish or curtail the prerogative, the prior authority of Parliament has traditionally not been required for the exercise of a prerogative power. Parliament may criticise ministers for their action and for the consequences; but Parliament has no right to be consulted in advance, except to the extent that a conventional practice has developed of assuring the opportunity for such consultation.[99] Certain prerogatives could be exercised only if the government were assured of subsequent support from Parliament. The Crown may declare war, but Parliament alone may vote the supplies which enable war to be waged. Again, where a treaty envisages changes in our domestic law, Parliament could frustrate the treaty made by the Crown if it subsequently refused to pass the necessary legislation.[100] Proposals for better parliamentary scrutiny of the exercise of prerogative powers have been made from time to time. But there is little prospect of the prerogative being abolished, as was proposed by one senior Cabinet minister before he joined the government.[101]

---

[95] And see B V Harris (1992) 108 LQR 626.

[96] Ch 32 B.

[97] See ch 13 D.

[98] Erskine May, *Parliamentary Practice*, p 347.

[99] For the 'Ponsonby rule' in relation to treaties, see ch 15 B, and for a proposed new convention on parliamentary approval in relation to the war power, see p 251 below.

[100] And see now Constitutional Reform and Governance Act 2010, s 20 (treaties to be laid before Parliament before ratification).

[101] Jack Straw, MP, 'Abolish the Royal Prerogative' in A. Barnett (ed.), *Power and the Throne: The Monarchy Debate* (1994): '[t]he royal prerogative has no place in a modern western democracy . . . [The prerogative] has been used as a smoke-screen by Ministers to obfuscate the use of power for which they are insufficiently accountable' (p 129).

The extent of the prerogative today

Because of the diverse subjects covered by prerogative and because of the uncertainty of the law in many instances where an ancient power has not been used in modern times, it is not possible to give a comprehensive catalogue of prerogative powers.[102] Instead the main areas in which the prerogative is used today will be mentioned briefly; most of these are discussed more fully in other chapters.

1 *Powers relating to the legislature.* By virtue of the prerogative the Queen summons, pro- rogues and dissolves Parliament. The prerogative power to create hereditary peers has been diminished in practice, first by the Life Peerages Act 1958 and then by the House of Lords Act 1999. But it is presumably possible in principle for the Queen to confer hereditary titles on her subjects (presumably also on the advice of her Prime Minister), who would not as a result be entitled to membership of the House of Lords,[103] though this is a power that seems likely to fall into abeyance as inappropriate in modern times. It is under the prerogative that the Queen assents to Bills. The Crown retains certain powers to legislate under the prerogative by Order in Council or by letters patent. Described as an 'anachronistic survival',[104] this power remains in use for the surviving overseas territories,[105] and in respect of the civil service.[106] While the Crown may not create new criminal offences or impose new obligations upon citizens,[107] it may under the prerogative create schemes for conferring benefits upon citizens provided that Parliament appropriates the necessary money to pay for these benefits; thus concerning the Criminal Injuries Compensation scheme, set up by means of a non-statutory document noticed to Parliament, Diplock LJ said:

> It may be a novel development in constitutional practice to govern by public statement of inten- tion made by the executive government instead of by legislation. This is no more, however, than a reversion to the ancient practice of government by royal proclamation, although it is now sub- ject to the limitations imposed on that practice by the development of constitutional law in the 17th century.[108]

2 *Powers relating to the judicial system.*[109] The Crown can no longer by the prerogative create courts to administer any system of law other than the common law.[110] This restriction had its roots in the common lawyers' distrust of the prerogative courts of the Star Chamber and the High Commission. Its effect today is that new courts and tribunals may be created only by Act of Parliament, but this does not prevent the Crown under prerogative from establishing a body to administer a scheme for conferring financial benefits on individuals.[111] The Crown also exercises many functions in relation to criminal justice. Thus in England prosecutions on indictment may be stopped by the Attorney General entering a *nolle prosequi*,[112] a power exercisable even in the case of those prosecutions over which he or she has no power of superintendence, as in the case of

---

[102] For a review of the scope of the prerogative, see HC Deb, 21 April 1993, col 490. See also HC 422 (2003–4) (Memorandum by Treasury Solicitor's Department).

[103] House of Lords Act 1999, s 1.

[104] *R (Bancoult) v Foreign Secretary* [2008] UKHL 61, at [69] (Lord Bingham).

[105] Roberts-Wray, *Commonwealth and Colonial Law*, ch 5. And see *R (Bancoult) v Foreign Secretary*, above.

[106] E.g. Civil Service Order in Council 1995. See ch 13 D.

[107] *The Case of Proclamations* (1611) 12 Co Rep 74.

[108] *R v Criminal Injuries Compensation Board, ex p Lain* [1967] 2 QB 864, 886; cf Wade, pp 47–8. See also *R v Home Secretary, ex p Harrison* [1988] 3 All ER 86, and *R v Home Secretary, ex p Fire Brigades Union* [1995] 2 AC 513.

[109] Ch 18.

[110] *Re Lord Bishop of Natal* (1864) 3 Moo PC (NS) 115.

[111] *R v Criminal Injuries Compensation Board, ex p Lain* [1967] 2 QB 864; ch 12 E.

[112] On which see *Allen* (1862) 1 B&S 850.

prosecutions by HM Revenue and Customs.[113] It has been explained that 'a *nolle prosequi* acts as a stay upon the proceedings', and 'puts an end to a prosecution but does not operate as a bar or discharge or acquittal on the merits', which means in principle that the accused could be re-indicted.

A *nolle prosequi* application will normally be made to the Attorney General by the defendant, and the power is most commonly used 'when the defendant cannot attend court for plea or attend trial because of physical or mental incapacity, which is expected to be permanent'.[114] The Crown may pardon convicted offenders,[115] though under the Criminal Appeal Act 1995 the Home Secretary may seek the advice of the Criminal Cases Review Commission.[116] Pardons may take three forms – as a special remission granted after a prisoner has been released early by mistake, as a conditional pardon to commute a sentence (such as the death penalty to life imprisonment), or as a free pardon to address a miscarriage of justice.[117] In civil matters the Attorney General represents the Crown as *parens patriae* to enforce matters of public right.[118] In this capacity he or she has the power to seek an injunction to restrain a breach of the criminal law, but cannot be required to exercise the power if he or she chooses not to do so.[119] In 1991, the Court of Appeal held that the Crown, unlike ministers and servants of the Crown, was not subject to the contempt jurisdiction vested in the courts.[120]

3 *Powers relating to foreign affairs*.[121] The conduct of foreign affairs by the government is carried on mainly by reliance on the prerogative. The prerogative includes power to acquire additional territory; thus by royal warrant in 1955, the Crown took possession of the island of Rockall, subsequently incorporated into the United Kingdom as part of Scotland by the Island of Rockall Act 1972. It is doubtful whether the Crown may by treaty cede British territory without the authority of Parliament and modern practice is to secure parliamentary approval,[122] but it seems that the prerogative includes power to declare or to alter the limits of British territorial waters.[123] The phrase 'act of state' is often used to refer to acts of the Crown in foreign affairs: while these acts would often fall within the scope of the prerogative, the concept of the prerogative is best confined to powers of the Crown exercised in relation to its own subjects, and 'act of state' should apply only to a limited plea to the jurisdiction of the British courts, in respect of acts of the Crown performed in foreign territory in relation to aliens.[124]

There is no prerogative power to expel British subjects or forcibly to remove them to another part of the country for the purposes of internal exile, though the position may be different under the prerogative in relation to an overseas territory.[125] By means of the writ *ne exeat regno*, the

---

[113] HC 115 (1995–6) (Scott Report), para C 3.10. For proposals to abolish this power, see p 389 below.

[114] HC Deb, 5 March 2004, col 1202 W.

[115] *R v Home Secretary, ex p Bentley* [1994] QB 349; *R (Shields) v Secretary of State for Justice* [2008] EWHC 3102 (Admin).

[116] 1995 Act, s 16.

[117] For a good discussion, see Ministry of Justice, *Review of the Executive Royal Prerogative Powers – Final Report* (2009), pp 15–18.

[118] *Gouriet v Union of Post Office Workers* [1978] AC 435.

[119] Criminal Appeal Act 1995, s 16.

[120] *M v Home Office* [1992] QB 270. The House of Lords held the same, for other reasons: [1994] 1 AC 377.

[121] Ch 15.

[122] Anson, *Law and Custom of the Constitution*, II, ii, pp 137–42; and Roberts-Wray, ch 4. The Hong Kong Act 1985 provides that 'As from 1st July 1997 Her Majesty shall no longer have sovereignty or jurisdiction over any part of Hong Kong' (s 1(1)).

[123] *R v Kent JJ, ex p Lye* [1967] 2 QB 153; cf W R Edeson (1973) 89 LQR 364.

[124] See the varying opinions on the application of prerogative abroad in *Nissan v A-G* [1970] AC 179; and ch 15 A. There may now also be issues under the Human Rights Act – see ch 16.

[125] See *Bancoult*, note 104 above. See also Sibley and Jeffries, *The Shameful Deportation of a Trade Union Leader* (on the removal of trade union leader Albert Fava from Gibraltar to England after the second world war).

Crown could restrain a person from leaving the realm when the interests of state so demanded, but it is doubtful whether the power would today be exercised. In time of war the Crown may possibly under the prerogative restrain a British subject from leaving the realm or recall him or her from abroad, but during modern wars entry and exit have been controlled by statutory powers. Although the Crown has power under the prerogative to restrain aliens from entering the United Kingdom, it is uncertain whether it has a prerogative power to expel aliens who have been permitted to reside here. Today, powers over aliens are exercised under the Immigration Act 1971, although that Act expressly reserves such prerogative powers as the Crown may have (s 33(5)). The issue of passports to citizens is based on the prerogative.[126]

4 *Powers relating to war and the armed forces.*[127] It is under the prerogative that the government may declare war, said by some to be 'the most significant of the prerogative powers'.[128] In modern times, however, it has not been the practice to make a formal declaration of war before commencing military activity, as in the case of the invasion of Iraq in 2003, or the military operations in Afghanistan. Such military activity is also authorised by the prerogative. Both by prerogative and by statute the Queen is commander-in-chief of the armed forces of the Crown. The Bill of Rights 1689 prohibited the keeping of a standing army within the realm in time of peace without the consent of Parliament; thus the authority of Parliament is required for the maintenance of the army, the Royal Air Force and other forces serving on land. It has been pointed out that while the army and the RAF are now governed by statute 'the Royal Navy is still maintained by virtue of the prerogative'.[129]

Although many matters regarding the armed forces are thus regulated by statute, their control, organisation and disposition are within the prerogative and cannot be questioned in a court.[130] In 2006 the House of Lords Committee on the Constitution proposed a new convention to determine the role of Parliament before British troops were deployed for the purposes of armed conflict outside the United Kingdom.[131] The government made a similar proposal in 2008 in the White Paper *Constitutional Renewal*, where it was suggested that the matter could best be addressed by a House of Commons resolution. It was also suggested, however, that a high degree of flexibility would be required, to take account of the very different circumstances in which the troops may need to be deployed. At the time of writing these proposals had not been implemented, though it is to be noted that a parliamentary debate was held before the invasion of Iraq in 2003.[132]

5 *Patronage, appointments and honours.*[133] On the advice of the Prime Minister or other ministers, the Queen appoints ministers, judges and many other holders of public office, including the members of royal commissions to inquire into matters of controversy.[134] Appointments to the civil service are appointments to the service of the Crown. The Queen is the sole fountain of honour and alone can create peers, confer honours and decorations,[135] grant arms and regulate

---

[126] Ch 20 A.

[127] Ch 16 A.

[128] HC 422 (2003–4), para 18.

[129] Ibid, para 9. See now Armed Forces Act 2006; ch 16 below.

[130] *China Navigation Co Ltd* v *A-G* [1932] 2 KB 197; *Chandler* v *DPP* [1964] AC 763; Crown Proceedings Act 1947, s 11.

[131] HL Paper 35, 2005–06.

[132] HC Deb, 18 March 2003, cols 760–911. The House of Commons voted by 412 to 149 to support a detailed government motion that authorised the 'use of all means necessary' to ensure that disarmament of Iraq's weapons of mass destruction. No such weapons have been found.

[133] Jennings, ch 14; Richards, *Patronage in British Government*, ch 10; Walker, *The Queen has been Pleased*.

[134] On judicial appointments, see ch 18 B.

[135] On which see Cm 1627, 1991 (the Gulf Medal); and Cm 6936, 2006 (Iraq medal).

matters of precedence.[136] Honours are generally conferred by the Queen on the advice of the Prime Minister. In the case of peerages, the formal position is that the House of Lords Appointments Commission advises the Prime Minister about the non-political nominations and the Prime Minister passes these on to the Queen.[137] The Commission also advises the Prime Minister about party political nominees, performing a task which was previously performed by the Political Honours Scrutiny Committee which is to vet all nominations to ensure the highest levels of propriety. The Political Honours Scrutiny Committee (a committee of three Privy Counsellors) which also advised on the suitability of those who are recommended for other political honours (such as knighthoods and the like) has been abolished.[138] Certain honours, namely the Order of the Garter, the Order of the Thistle, the Royal Victoria Order (for personal services to the Queen) and the Order of Merit are in the personal gift of the Queen.

6 *Immunities and privileges*. It is a principle of interpretation that statutes do not bind the Crown except by express statement or necessary implication.

> In *Lord Advocate* v *Dumbarton Council*, the Ministry of Defence decided to erect an improved security fence at its submarine base at Faslane, Dunbartonshire. Part of the fence ran alongside the A814 road and when the roads authority (Strathclyde Council) discovered that the Ministry intended to place temporary works on part of the road, they notified the Ministry that it would require their consent under the Roads (Scotland) Act 1984. The Ministry replied that these provisions did not bind the Crown and contractors took possession of a one-mile stretch of part of the road by erecting a temporary fence. Thereupon the roads authority (Strathclyde) and the planning authority (Dumbarton) gave various notices under statutes to stop the work. The Lord Advocate sought judicial review of the councils' conduct, alleging that the statutes in question did not bind the Crown. Although the Crown's immunity was restricted by the Inner House of the Court of Session, the wider immunity was restored by the House of Lords. In the view of Lord Keith, 'the Crown is not bound by any statutory provision unless there can somehow be gathered from the terms of the relevant Act an intention to that effect. The Crown can be bound only by express words or necessary implication.' At the same time, Lord Keith rejected as no longer tenable the view that 'the Crown is in terms bound by general words in a statute but that the prerogative enables it to override the statute'.[139]

Tax is not payable on income received by the monarch as such, neither in respect of Crown property, nor on income received on behalf of the Crown by a servant of the Crown in the course of official duties.[140] But as we have seen, the Queen has undertaken to pay tax on her private income since 1993 and it is claimed on the official royal website that her private income is taxable 'as for any taxpayer'.[141] Many of the immunities of the Crown in civil litigation were removed by the Crown Proceedings Act 1947, but the Crown and government departments still have certain privileges. The 1947 Act preserved the personal immunity of the Sovereign from being sued.[142] The question has arisen whether the Crown enjoys immunity from criminal liability. During the Spycatcher affair in the mid-1980s, a retired MI5 officer, Mr Peter Wright, alleged that members of the Security Service had been engaged in surveillance operations which included burgling premises in London. The Home Secretary announced that the government

---

[136] A Wagner and G D Squibb (1973) 80 LQR 352.

[137] See ch 9.

[138] See Cmd 1789, 1922; and Cm 4057-1, 1998. It is an offence to trade in honours: Honours (Prevention of Abuses) Act 1925.

[139] [1990] 2 AC 580; and ch 32 C.

[140] *Bank voor Handel en Scheepvaart NV* v *Administrator of Hungarian Property* [1954] AC 584.

[141] www.royal.gov.uk/today/finance. See also on royal finances, pp 235–6 above.

[142] Ch 32 C.

had never asserted that actions 'could lawfully be done under the prerogative when they would otherwise be criminal offences'.[143]

7 *The prerogative in time of emergency.* The extent of the prerogative in times of grave emergency cannot be precisely stated. That prerogative powers were wide was admitted by Hampden's counsel in the *Case of Ship Money*. Save in regard to taxation, they were not abridged by the Bill of Rights. In 1964, Lord Reid said: 'The prerogative certainly covers doing all those things in an emergency which are necessary for the conduct of war'; but he added that there was difficulty in relating the prerogative to modern conditions since no modern war had been waged without statutory powers:

> The mobilisation of the industrial and financial resources of the country could not be done without statutory emergency powers. The prerogative is really a relic of a past age, not lost by disuse but only available for a case not covered by statute.[144]

According to the old law, in time of sudden invasion or insurrection, the King might demand personal service within the realm.[145] Either the Crown or a subject might invade the land of another to erect fortifications for the defence of the realm.[146] But it is not certain whether this should be regarded as an aspect of the prerogative since it was a duty shared by the Crown with all its subjects. Extensive emergency powers have now been granted by Parliament, and these confer authority on ministers to make regulations that provide for the confiscation of private property, with or without compensation.[147] But if, for example, an emergency arose in which it was necessary for the armed forces to take immediate steps against terrorist action within the United Kingdom, it is possible both that private property needed for this purpose could be occupied under prerogative, and (as will be considered below) that compensation would at common law be payable to the owners.

8 *Miscellaneous prerogatives.* Other historic prerogative powers concerning matters which are today largely regulated by statute relate to: the creation of corporations by royal charter;[148] the right to mine precious metals; coinage; the grant of franchises, for example, markets, ferries and fisheries;[149] the right to treasure trove;[150] the sole right of printing or licensing others to print the Authorised Version of the Bible,[151] the Book of Common Prayer and state papers;[152] and the guardianship of infants (a prerogative jurisdiction of the Crown said to be delegated to the courts).[153] The courts may interfere 'for the protection of infants, qua infants, by virtue of the

---

[143] HC Deb, 29 January 1988, col 397 (WA). Cf *A-G v Guardian Newspapers Ltd (No 2)* [1990] 1 AC 109, 190. See now Intelligence Services Act 1994, s 7.

[144] *Burmah Oil Co Ltd v Lord Advocate* [1965] AC 75, 101; and see ch 26.

[145] Chitty, p 49.

[146] *The Case of the King's Prerogative in Saltpetre* (1607) 12 Co Rep 12.

[147] Civil Contingencies Act 2004, ss 18–22.

[148] On the BBC, see Ministry of Justice, *Review of the Executive Royal Prerogative Powers – Final Report*, above, p 23, and ch 23 below.

[149] Cf *Spook Erection Ltd v Environment Secretary* [1989] QB 300 (beneficiary of market franchise not entitled to Crown's exemption from planning control).

[150] Treasure trove, i.e. gold or silver objects that have been hidden and of which no owner can be traced, is the property of the Crown: *A-G of Duchy of Lancaster v G E Overton (Farms) Ltd* [1982] Ch 277. See now Treasure Act 1996.

[151] *Universities of Oxford and Cambridge v Eyre & Spottiswoode Ltd* [1964] Ch 736 (royal prerogative did not extend to New English Bible).

[152] Copyright, Designs and Patents Act 1988, s 163.

[153] *Butler v Freeman* (1756) Amb 302; and *Wellesley v Duke of Beaufort* (1827) 2 Russ 1.

prerogative which belongs to the Crown as *parens patriae*,[154] though 'jurisdiction is carefully and cautiously applied by judges in circumstances in which the welfare of those to whom the inherent jurisdiction applies positively require its exercise for their protection'.[155] When a court is exercising this paternal jurisdiction it is empowered to exclude the public where it is necessary to do so.[156] In R v *Central Television plc*,[157] however, it was held that the power could not be invoked to obscure the pictures of a man in a television programme imprisoned for indecency with young boys, on the ground that his identification would cause harm to his child: the programme had nothing to do with the care or upbringing of the child.

E. The royal prerogative and the courts

Some prerogative acts are unlikely to give rise to the possibility of challenge in the courts, for example the conferment of an honour or the dissolution of Parliament. But where an act purporting to be done under the prerogative directly affects the rights of an individual, the courts may be asked to determine a number of issues.

The existence and extent of a prerogative power

In principle the courts will not recognise the existence of new prerogative powers. In *Entick* v *Carrington*, in which the court held that the mere plea of state necessity would not protect anyone accused of an unlawful act, Lord Camden CJ said, 'If it is law, it will be found in our books. If it is not to be found there, it is not law.'[158] And in 1964 Diplock LJ said,

> It is 350 years and a civil war too late for the Queen's courts to broaden the prerogative. The limits within which the executive government may impose obligations or restraints on citizens of the United Kingdom without any statutory authority are now well settled and incapable of extension.[159]

But some prerogative powers are very wide and difficulties arise when the courts are asked to decide whether an ancient power applies in a new situation; for example, whether the Crown's power to act in situations of grave national emergency justifies action to deal with a wholly new form of terrorist activity which threatens the nation or whether the prerogative right to intercept postal communications justifies the tapping of telephones.[160] In these situations, it may be difficult to distinguish between creating a new prerogative and applying an old prerogative to new circumstances.

> In R v *Home Secretary, ex p Northumbria Police Authority*,[161] the Home Secretary made available CS gas and baton rounds to the police to deal with situations of serious public disorder, notwithstanding the objections of the local police authority. The police authority sought a declaration that the Home Secretary had no power to provide the equipment without their consent, save in a situation of grave emergency. The Court of

---

[154] *In re Spence* (1847) 2 Ph 247 (Lord Cottenham, LC), cited with approval by Lord Denning (*In re L (An Infant)* [1968] P 119), cited with approval in turn by Dame Elizabeth Butler-Sloss (*In re a Local Authority* [2003] EWHC 2746 (Fam); [2004] Fam 96).

[155] *In re a Local Authority*, ibid, para 61. And see *Re T* [2001] NI Fam 4.

[156] *Scott* v *Scott* [1913] AC 417.

[157] [1994] Fam 192.

[158] (1765) 19 State Tr 1029, 1066: ch 6 A. *Entick*'s case was distinguished in *Malone* v *Metropolitan Police Commissioner* [1979] Ch 344 (no evidence of unlawful act in tapping telephones); ch 22.

[159] *BBC* v *Johns* [1965] ch 32, 79.

[160] Cf Cmd 283, 1957. In *Malone*'s case, no claim of prerogative power was made.

[161] [1989] QB 26, criticised by A W Bradley [1988] PL 297.

Appeal held that the provision of the equipment was authorised by the Police Act 1964, but also by the royal prerogative. In so concluding, the court had first to determine that there did in fact exist a 'prerogative to enforce the keeping of what is popularly called the Queen's peace within the realm'. Although the court had difficulty in finding authority for such a power, Croom-Johnson LJ nevertheless concluded that such a general power is bound up with the Crown's 'undoubted right to see that crime is prevented and justice administered'. The supply of baton rounds and CS gas was held to fall within the scope of the prerogative, since it is open to the Home Secretary 'to supply equipment reasonably required by police forces to discharge their functions'.

A related question is whether the courts have power to rule that an ancient prerogative has become so unsuited to modern conditions that it can no longer be relied on by the Crown. In general, rules of common law do not lapse through desuetude.[162] But it is difficult to see why a court should be required to give new life to an archaic power which offends modern constitutional principles, merely because its existence had been recognised several centuries ago.

The difficulty of applying the old common law in contemporary circumstances was evident in *Burmah Oil Company v Lord Advocate*.[163]

In 1942 extensive oil installations were destroyed by British troops in Rangoon, not accidentally as a result of fighting but deliberately so as to prevent the installations falling into enemy hands. One day later, the Japanese army entered Rangoon. After receiving some £4 million from the British government as an ex gratia payment, the company sued the Lord Advocate representing the Crown in Scotland for over £31 million. It was agreed that the destruction had not been ordered under statutory authority and the company claimed compensation for the lawful exercise of prerogative power. The House of Lords held (a) that, as a general rule, compensation was payable by the Crown to the subject who was deprived of property for the benefit of the state, by prerogative act in relation to war, and (b) that the destruction of the refineries did not fall within the 'battle damage' exception to the general rule. But the House left open the basis on which compensation should be assessed.

This decision established that where private property was taken under the prerogative, the owner was entitled at common law to compensation from the Crown; but the War Damage Act 1965 retrospectively provided that no person should be entitled at common law to receive compensation in respect of damage to or destruction of property caused by lawful acts of the Crown 'during, or in contemplation of the outbreak of, a war in which the Sovereign is or was engaged'. This Act prevented the Burmah Oil Company's claim from succeeding but its effect was limited to acts of the Crown which destroyed property during or in contemplation of a war; the principle that the Crown is obliged to pay compensation for property taken under the prerogative for use of the armed forces still seems to apply.[164] Thus the Crown may under prerogative requisition British ships in time of urgent national necessity, but compensation is payable, as it was in 1982 when British ships were requisitioned for use in the recapture of the Falkland Islands.[165] By the right of angary, the Crown may in time of war appropriate the property of a neutral which is within the realm where necessity requires, but compensation must be paid.[166] In both world wars, statutory powers of requisitioning property have been conferred on the Crown and compensation has been paid.

---

[162] Maitland, *Constitutional History*, p 418; cf *Nyali Ltd v A-G* [1956] 1 QB 1, and *McKendrick v Sinclair* 1972 SC (HL) 25, 60–1.

[163] [1965] AC 75, discussed by A L Goodhart (1966) 82 LQR 97; T C Daintith (1965) 14 ICLQ 1000; and (1966) 79 Harv LR 614.

[164] E.g. *Nissan v A-G* [1970] AC 179, 229 (Lord Pearce).

[165] Requisitioning of Ships Order 1982. And see *Crown of Leon v Admiralty Commissioners* [1921] 1 KB 595; W S Holdsworth (1919) 35 LQR 12.

[166] *Commercial and Estates Co of Egypt v Board of Trade* [1925] 1 KB 271. And see W I Jennings (1927) 3 CLJ 1.

The effect of statutes upon prerogative powers

Parliament may abolish or restrict prerogative powers expressly or by necessary implication, whether or not coupling this with the grant of statutory powers in the same area of government. But often Parliament has not expressly abolished prerogative powers and has merely created a statutory scheme dealing with the same subject. Where this is the case, as a general principle must the Crown proceed under the statutory powers or may it rely instead upon the prerogative?

In *Attorney-General v De Keyser's Royal Hotel*[167] a hotel was required for housing the administrative staff of the Royal Flying Corps during the First World War. The Army Council offered to hire the hotel at a rent but, negotiations having broken down, a letter was sent on the instruction of the Army Council stating that possession was being taken under the Defence of the Realm Acts and Regulations. A petition of right was later brought against the Crown claiming compensation as of right for the use of the hotel by the authorities.

It was argued for the Crown that there was a prerogative power to take the land of the subject in case of emergency in time of war; that no compensation was payable as of right for land so taken; and that this power could be exercised, notwithstanding provisions of the Defence Act 1842 which had been incorporated into the Defence of the Realm Acts and provided for statutory compensation as of right to the owners. The argument for the owners of the hotel was that the Crown had taken possession under the statutes and so could not fall back on the prerogative.

The House of Lords rejected the argument of the Crown, holding that on the facts the Crown had taken possession under statutory powers. The House also held that the prerogative had been superseded for the time being by the statute. The Crown could not revert to prerogative powers when the legislature had given to the Crown statutory powers which covered all that could be necessary for the defence of the nation, and which were accompanied by important safeguards to the individual. Thus for the duration of the statutory powers, the prerogative was in abeyance. The House therefore did not have to decide whether the Crown had a prerogative power to requisition land in time of war without paying compensation, but serious doubts were expressed about this claim.[168]

The principle in this case, that the 'executive cannot exercise the prerogative in a way which would derogate from the due fulfilment of a statutory duty',[169] is subject to a number of refinements. First, it applies only when Parliament has not given an express indication of its intention. Thus the Immigration Act 1971 provided that the powers which it conferred should be additional to any prerogative powers (s 33(5)), as did the Emergency Powers (Defence) Act 1939.[170] Second, there are suggestions that it may apply only where the statute confers rights or benefits on the citizen which would be undermined were the Crown to retain the right to use the prerogative power. In the *Northumbria Police* case, the Court of Appeal held that the supply of baton rounds and CS gas was authorised by the Police Act 1964, s 41, but also by the prerogative power to maintain the peace. Was the prerogative power displaced by the statute or could both exist and operate simultaneously? In opting for the latter position, Purchas LJ said:

It is well established that the courts will intervene to prevent executive action under prerogative powers in violation of property or other rights of the individual where this is inconsistent with statutory provisions providing for the same executive action. Where the executive action is directed towards the benefit or protection of the individual, it is unlikely that its use will attract the intervention of the courts . . . [B]efore the courts will hold that such executive action is contrary to legislation, express

---

[167] [1920] AC 508.

[168] See subsequently the *Burmah Oil* case, p 255 above. See also *C O Williams Construction Ltd v Blackman* [1995] 1 WLR 102, 108; *R v Home Secretary, ex p Fire Brigades Union* [1995] 2 AC 513; and *Attorney-General v Blake* [2001] AC 268.

[169] *R v Home Secretary, ex p Fire Brigades Union* [1995] 2 AC 513.

[170] Ch 26 D.

and unequivocal terms must be found in the statute which deprive the individual from receiving the benefit or protection intended by the exercise of prerogative power.[171]

In the *Northumbria Police* case, even if the statute had not provided the necessary authority, the court was unable to find 'an express and unequivocal inhibition sufficient to abridge the prerogative powers, otherwise available to the Secretary of State, to do all that is reasonably necessary to preserve the peace of the realm'. Third, where the statute restricting the prerogative is repealed, 'the prerogative power would apparently re-emerge as it existed before the statute'.[172] This is subject to 'words in the repealing statute which make it clear that the prerogative power is not intended by Parliament to be revived or again brought into use'.[173]

The manner of exercise of a prerogative power

Although the courts have long had the power to determine the existence and extent of a prerogative power, traditionally they have had no power to regulate the manner of its exercise. This contrasts with statutory powers of the executive, which the courts have held must generally be exercised in accordance with the rules of natural justice and in accordance with the so-called *Wednesbury* principles.[174] Thus, the courts have held that the courts cannot question whether the Crown has wisely exercised its discretionary power regarding the disposition of the armed forces;[175] nor could the courts say whether the government should enter into a particular treaty;[176] nor whether the Home Secretary had properly advised the Queen regarding the prerogative of mercy.[177] In *Gouriet v Union of Post Office Workers*[178] the House of Lords held that the exercise of the Attorney General's discretion in giving consent to the bringing of relator actions could not be reviewed by the courts. But when this decision was given, there were already some indications of a more flexible approach by the courts.[179] Although it may not have been fully appreciated at the time,[180] *R v Criminal Injuries Compensation Board, ex p Lain*[181] was to prove an important breakthrough, where it was held that the High Court had the power to review the activities of the board, a body set up under the royal prerogative to administer benefits for the victims of criminal injury. Lord Parker CJ could see no reason why a body set up by prerogative rather than by statute should be any less amenable to judicial review for that reason alone.[182] The position is now governed by the landmark decision of the House of Lords in *Council of Civil Service Unions v Minister of State for Civil Service*.[183]

> In January 1984, the Foreign Secretary announced the government's decision to exclude trade unions from Government Communications' Headquarters (GCHQ). This would be done under an Order in Council of 1982 authorising the Minister for the Civil Service to give instructions regulating the terms and conditions of civil service employment. The instructions given directed that staff at GCHQ would no longer be permitted to be

---

[171] [1989] QB 26, 53.

[172] *Burmah Oil Co Ltd v Lord Advocate* [1965] AC 75, Lord Pearce at 143.

[173] *R v Foreign Secretary, ex p CCSU* [1984] IRLR 309, at 321 (Glidewell J).

[174] See ch 30 A.

[175] *China Navigation Co Ltd v A-G* [1932] 2 KB 197; *Chandler v DPP* [1964] AC 763; Crown Proceedings Act 1947, s 11.

[176] *Blackburn v A-G* [1971] 2 All ER 1380. Also *R v Foreign Secretary, ex p Rees-Mogg* [1994] QB 552.

[177] *Hanratty v Lord Butler* (1971) 115 SJ 386, discussed by A T H Smith [1983] PL 398, 432. Cf B V Harris [1991] PL 386. But see *R v Home Secretary, ex p Bentley* (note 186 below).

[178] [1978] AC 435.

[179] See *Chandler v DPP* [1964] AC 763, 810 (Lord Devlin).

[180] See C P Walker [1987] PL 62.

[181] [1967] 2 QB 864.

[182] See also *Laker Airways Ltd v Department of Trade and Industry* [1977] QB 643 (Lord Denning).

[183] [1985] AC 374. See H W R Wade (1985) 101 LQR 180.

members of the civil service unions, but only to join an officially approved staff association. These steps had been taken because of earlier industrial action at GCHQ.

In deciding whether the government's decision was reviewable by the courts, a majority in the House of Lords held that the courts could review the manner of exercise of discretionary powers conferred by the prerogative just as they could review the manner of exercise of discretionary powers conferred by statute. Lord Diplock could 'see no reason why simply because a decision-making power is derived from a common law and not a statutory source, it should for that reason only be immune from judicial review'. It does not follow, however, that all prerogative powers would be subject to review in this way. According to the House of Lords, it depends on the nature of the power, and in particular whether the power in question is justiciable, i.e. whether it gives rise to questions which are capable of adjudication in a court of law. It is not clear which powers are justiciable, though Lord Roskill gave many examples of those which are not, including the making of treaties, the disposition of the armed forces, the granting of honours and the dissolution of Parliament.

It may be presumed that the prerogative power to regulate terms of employment in the civil service is subject to review, although the impact of this is to some extent reduced by the willingness of the courts to accept that civil servants are employed under contract, with an expectation that they should seek a remedy in private law.[184] However, it was quickly accepted that the power to issue a passport is subject to judicial review,[185] and also that 'some aspects of the exercise of the Royal Prerogative [of mercy] are amenable to the judicial process'.[186] In *R v Home Secretary, ex p Fire Brigades Union*,[187] it was held to be an 'abuse of the prerogative' when the Home Secretary failed to implement a statutory scheme to compensate the victims of crime and chose instead to reintroduce a less favourable scheme by relying on common law powers.[188] It does not follow, however, that because a power is subject to judicial process the courts will be willing to intervene. In *R (Bancoult) v Foreign Secretary (No 2)* the House of Lords went further than in *CCSU* by holding that the making of an Order in Council could be reviewed, as well as the manner of exercise of the power it conferred (the *CCSU* case being concerned only with the latter).[189] Nevertheless, in *Bancoult* an Order in Council preventing displaced Chagos Islanders from returning home was upheld, the House of Lords (by a majority) accepting government arguments based on cost and security. Moreover, litigation arising from the events in Iraq in 2003 was a sobering reminder that by no means all decisions under the prerogative are subject to judicial review in this way. An attempt was made to challenge the legality of British involvement in the hostilities on the ground that they did not have a clear UN mandate. But this was unsuccessful, with the Divisional Court (of three members) applying the *CCSU* decision to hold that such matters were not justiciable.[190]

The prerogative and the Human Rights Act

The growing willingness of the courts to review the exercise of prerogative powers is reinforced by the Human Rights Act 1998 which gives the courts even greater powers of review. Under the Human Rights Act, Orders in Council made under the authority of the royal prerogative are deemed to be primary legislation[191] and must be read and given effect to in a way which is

---

[184] See chs 13 D and 32 B.

[185] *R v Foreign Secretary, ex p Everett* [1989] QB 811.

[186] *R v Home Secretary, ex p Bentley* [1994] QB 349. See subsequently, *R v Bentley* (2001) 1 Cr App Rep 307. Compare *Hanratty* v *Lord Butler* (1971) 115 SJ 386, and *de Freitas* v *Benny* [1976] AC 239.

[187] [1995] 2 AC 513; T R S Allan [1995] CLJ 489.

[188] The case was thought not to involve an application of the *De Keyser* principle (above, p 256), because the statutory provisions (Criminal Justice Act 1988) had not been brought into force and thus had 'no legal significance of any kind'.

[189] [2008] UKHL 61, [2009] 1 AC 453.

[190] *CND v Prime Minister* [2002] EWHC 2759 (QB); *The Times*, 27 December 2002.

[191] On which see P Billings and B Pontin [2001] PL 21.

compatible with Convention rights (s 3).[192] Where the terms of such an Order in Council breach Convention rights, the courts are empowered to declare the Order in Council incompatible with Convention rights, although they are bound to continue to apply it until it is revoked or revised (s 4). A more likely source of challenge to the exercise of prerogative powers arises as a result of s 6 of the Human Rights Act 1998, which provides that it is unlawful for a public authority to act in a way that is incompatible with Convention rights. The right to enforce Convention rights against an exercise of prerogative power does not formally depend on the power in question being justiciable. But in view of the fact that many prerogative powers deal with issues such as defence of the realm and national security, it may be expected that the courts would exercise caution in response to any claim under the Act.

So much is confirmed by *R (Abbasi) v Foreign Secretary*[193] which was concerned with the detention of British citizens by the US government in Guantanamo Bay in circumstances described by Lord Steyn extra-judicially as being a 'legal black hole'.[194] Arguing that the detention violated their Convention rights, the claimants sought to require the British government to take all reasonable steps to require the US government to release them. But the action failed, with the Court of Appeal holding that the British government is not under a duty to take positive action to prevent violations of human rights that occur outside the jurisdiction and for which it has no responsibility. Similarly, in *R (Gentle) v Prime Minister*[195] it was held that the mothers of two soldiers killed in Iraq had no right under article 2 of the ECHR (which protects the right to life) to require the government to establish a public inquiry to consider whether the decision to go to war in 2003 was consistent with international law. The House of Lords concluded that article 2 imposes no duty to ensure that the country does not go to war contrary to international law. It could not therefore be said that there was 'an independent duty to use reasonable care to ascertain whether the war would be contrary to [international law] or not'.[196]

---

[192] For a full account of the Act, see ch 19 below.
[193] [2002] EWCA Civ 1598. Also *R(al Rawi) v Foreign Secretary* [2006] EWCA Civ 1279; [2007] 2 WLR 1219.
[194] Lord Steyn (2004) 53 ICLQ 1. See also *Abbasi*, ibid, at para 66.
[195] [2008] UKHL 20.
[196] Ibid, para 16 (Lord Hoffmann).

CHAPTER 13

The Cabinet, government departments and the civil service

As organs of government, the Cabinet and the office of Prime Minister have evolved together since the eighteenth century. Their existence is recognised in occasional statutes (for example, the Ministerial and other Salaries Act 1975) but their powers of government derive neither from statute nor from common law administered in the courts. Parliament could confer powers directly on the Prime Minister or on the Cabinet. In practice this does not often happen, statutory powers being conferred either on named ministers or on the Queen in Council. Yet the Prime Minister and the Cabinet occupy key places at the heart of the political and governmental system.[1] As the Prime Minister provides the individual leadership of the majority party in the House of Commons, so the Cabinet provides the collective leadership of that party.[2] If national affairs are to be directed in any systematic way, if deliberate choices in government between competing political priorities are to be made, these decisions can be made only by the Prime Minister and the Cabinet. In the past, descriptions of the British system of government often labelled it Cabinet government. As L S Amery wrote:

> The central directing instrument of government, in legislation as well as in administration, is the Cabinet. It is in Cabinet that administrative action is co-ordinated and that legislative proposals are sanctioned. It is the Cabinet which controls Parliament and governs the country.[3]

Recently, more emphasis has been placed on the role of the Prime Minister and less on the Cabinet itself. In 1963, when he had not yet served as a Cabinet minister, Richard Crossman wrote: 'The post-war epoch has seen the final transformation of Cabinet government into Prime Ministerial government', arguing that the Cabinet had joined the Crown and the House of Lords as one of the 'dignified' elements in the constitution.[4] This judgment appears to have been reinforced in the 1980s when it is claimed that 'members of Mrs Thatcher's Cabinets had allowed the usual forms of Cabinet government to be displaced by imperious prime ministerial rule'.[5] A 'presidential' style of government is also associated with Mr Blair,[6] it being suggested that the role of Cabinet as a forum for the discussion of policy had been significantly reduced: meetings were shortened and major decisions were taken by the Prime Minister in consultation with a small

---

[1] Bagehot's celebrated description of the Cabinet in *The English Constitution*, pp 65–9, must still be read, though his definition of the Cabinet as 'a committee of the legislative body selected to be the executive body' is misleading. For general accounts, see Jennings, *Cabinet Government*; Mackintosh, *The British Cabinet*; Gordon Walker, *The Cabinet*; Wilson, *The Governance of Britain*; Hennessy, *Cabinet*; Hennessy, *The Prime Minister*; and James, *British Cabinet Government*.

[2] Gordon Walker, p 56.

[3] *Thoughts on the Constitution*, p 70. This orthodoxy is reproduced today in the *Ministerial Code*, which provides that the business of the Cabinet consists in the main of (a) 'questions which significantly engage the collective responsibility of the government because they raise major issues of policy or because they are of critical importance to the public', and (b) 'questions on which there is an unresolved argument between departments' (*Ministerial Code* (2007 edn), para 2.2).

[4] Introduction to Bagehot, pp 51, 54. See also Berkeley, *The Power of the Prime Minister* and Mackintosh, ch 24; cf A H Brown [1968] PL 28, 96.

[5] R Brazier (1991) 54 MLR 471, 476.

[6] See Foley, *The Rise of the British Presidency*.

group of senior colleagues.[7] There seems little doubt that the grip of the Prime Minister tightened after 1997,[8] but it is also the case that Mr Blair was blessed with a very large parliamentary majority, a well-disciplined government and a relatively united party. Gordon Brown was not so fortunate. Although sometimes credited with having restored the formality of Cabinet government, Mr Brown's authority as Prime Minister was diminished from the start by a series of personal miscalculations and political crises.

A. The Prime Minister[9]

The nature of the office

Like the Cabinet, the office of Prime Minister has evolved as a matter of political expediency and constitutional practice rather than of law. Although he did not recognise the title, Robert Walpole is now regarded as having been the first Prime Minister when he was First Lord of the Treasury, from 1721 to 1742. William Pitt the Younger did much to create the modern office of Prime Minister in the years after 1784. In fact the post acquired its present form only with the advent of the modern party system and the creation of the present machinery of government. For most of its history, the office of Prime Minister has been held together with a recognised post, usually that of First Lord of the Treasury. Between 1895 and 1900 Lord Salisbury was both Prime Minister and Foreign Secretary, and between 1900 and 1902 he was Prime Minister and Lord Privy Seal; during these years A J Balfour was First Lord of the Treasury and Leader of the Commons. Since 1902, the offices of Prime Minister and First Lord of the Treasury have always been held together by a member of the Commons.

In 1905, by act of the prerogative, the Prime Minister was given precedence next after the Archbishop of York,[10] and as already mentioned the existence of the office is recognised increasingly by statute.[11] Since 1937 statutory provision of a salary and a pension has assumed that the Prime Minister is also First Lord of the Treasury. In the latter capacity, the Prime Minister is one of the Treasury ministers, although the financial and economic duties of the Treasury are borne primarily by the Chancellor of the Exchequer. Exceptionally, the Prime Minister may decide also to hold another office: Ramsay MacDonald was both Prime Minister and Foreign Secretary in the first Labour government in 1924. During the Second World War, Churchill assumed the title of Minister of Defence, although without a separate ministry and without his duties being defined. The Prime Minister is also minister for the civil service,[12] though there is now also a Minister for the Cabinet Office (of Cabinet rank) who has day-to-day responsibility for civil service matters.

The Prime Minister is responsible for the appointment of commissioners to oversee the interception of communications and the work of the intelligence services.[13] The approval of the Prime Minister is also required for appointment of the most senior civil servants. Important Crown appointments are filled on his or her nomination, for example, the senior judges, the bishops, the chairman of the BBC and the Parliamentary Ombudsman. The Prime Minister also still advises

---

[7] See Lord Butler (Chair), Review of Intelligence on Weapons of Mass Destruction: Report of a Committee of Privy Counsellors (HC 898, 2004), paras 606–11.

[8] See Foster, *British Government in Crisis*, esp Part 4.

[9] For a good account of the office and recent incumbents, see Hennessy, *The Prime Minister*.

[10] *London Gazette*, 5 December 1905.

[11] E.g. Chequers Estate Act 1917; Chevening Estate Act 1959; Ministerial and other Pensions and Salaries Act 1991; Regulation of Investigatory Powers Act 2000; Political Parties, Elections and Referendums Act 2000; and Constitutional Reform Act 2005.

[12] See *CCSU v Minister for the Civil Service* [1985] AC 374.

[13] Regulation of Investigatory Powers Act 2000, ss 57, 59. For details, see ch 25.

the Queen on new peerages,[14] on appointments to the Privy Council and the grant of honours[15] and the filling of those university chairs which are in the gift of the Crown. In these appointments, the Prime Minister's freedom of action may to a greater or lesser extent be restricted by conventions requiring prior consultation with the interests affected, or by the Public Appointments Order in Council 2002.[16] In the case of peerages, some nominations are now made by the House of Lords Appointments Commission, which also considers the Prime Minister's nominations;[17] in the case of judges, appointments to the new Supreme Court of the United Kingdom will be determined largely by ad hoc Supreme Court Selection Commissions.[18] Nonetheless, the Prime Minister's extensive patronage continues to give rise at least to the possibility that non-political appointments could be used for political purposes.[19]

Powers of the Prime Minister in relation to the Cabinet

Although each Prime Minister must adopt his or her own style of leadership, the Prime Minister is in a position to exercise a dominant influence over the Cabinet, having powers that other ministers do not have, however senior and experienced they may be. But the point should not be exaggerated. As one commentator wrote following the removal of Mrs Thatcher, 'a Prime Minister's main political strength comes from the Cabinet and . . . from the parliamentary party'.[20] A Prime Minister who loses the confidence of both will be in a very vulnerable position, even though he or she may be the choice of the electorate. On the other hand, for the following reasons we should not underestimate the political power of the Prime Minister where such confidence does exist:

1 The Prime Minister effectively makes all appointments to ministerial office, whether within or outside the Cabinet. He or she may ask ministers to resign, recommend the Queen to dismiss them or, with their consent, move them to other offices. The Prime Minister settles the order of precedence in the Cabinet, and may name one of the Cabinet to be Deputy Prime Minister,[21] or First Secretary of State. In forming his or her first Cabinet, a new Prime Minister will be expected to appoint from the senior members of the party; and a leading politician may be able to stipulate the Cabinet post which he or she is prepared to accept. In the case of the Labour party, the standing orders of the parliamentary party provide that on taking office as Prime Minister, the leader must appoint as members of his or her Cabinet those who were elected members of the Shadow Cabinet before the general election, provided that they have retained their seats in the new Parliament. Although there are no similar constraints on Conservative leaders, they too will normally rely on an established team when assuming the responsibilities of office.[22] But as the tenure of the Prime Minister extends, constraints of this kind will begin to wane: only nine members of Mr Blair's first Cabinet (including Mr Blair himself) were still Cabinet ministers in 2001; by 2005 that had fallen to seven.

---

[14] See ch 9 H.

[15] Some honours are granted on the advice of other ministers, e.g. the Foreign Secretary and the Defence Secretary. Some appointments are made on the recommendation of other bodies such as the House of Lords Appointments Commission (some life peers).

[16] See ch 14 below. The OCPA Code of Practice may apply in cases where the Order in Council does not. See HC 165 (2002–3), paras 26–8.

[17] Ch 9 above.

[18] Ch 18 below.

[19] Cf T Benn (1980) 33 *Parliamentary Affairs* 7.

[20] R Brazier (1991) 54 MLR 471, 477. For an assessment of the relationship between Prime Ministers and their Cabinets, see S James (1994) 47 *Parliamentary Affairs* 613, and Hennessy, *The Prime Minister*.

[21] In 1951, George VI refused to appoint Eden to this 'non-existent' office: Wheeler-Bennett, *King George VI*, p 797. But see Brazier *Constitutional Practice*, pp 78–81.

[22] See Brazier, ibid, pp 61–7.

2   The Prime Minister controls the machinery of central government in that he or she decides how the tasks of government should be allocated to departments and whether departments should be created, amalgamated or abolished. In 2009 further reorganisation consolidated changes Mr Brown had made in 2007 on assuming office, when the large Department for Business, Innovation and Skills was created, with 10 ministers, three of whom may attend Cabinet. The Prime Minister may take an interest in different areas of government from time to time and may indeed carry out policy in close cooperation with a minister whom he or she has appointed. Most Prime Ministers must take a special interest in foreign affairs, the economy and defence. He or she is also likely to take the lead on major issues such as the national and international response to the global economic crisis in 2008 and 2009. In consultation with individual ministers, he or she may take decisions or authorise them to be taken without waiting for a Cabinet meeting. According to a Committee of Privy Counsellors in 2004, in the period before the invasion of Iraq in 2003 it was a 'small number of key Ministers, officials and military officers most closely involved' who 'provided the framework of discussion and decision-making within Government'.[23]

3   By presiding at Cabinet meetings, the Prime Minister is able to control Cabinet discussions and the process of decision-making by settling the order of business, deciding which items are to be discussed,[24] and by taking the sense of the meeting rather than by counting the votes of Cabinet members. While the Cabinet Secretariat provides services for the whole Cabinet, it owes a special responsibility to the Prime Minister, who, if necessary, settles disputes over the minutes. Lord Wilson said after having served as Prime Minister that 'the writing of the Conclusions is a unique responsibility of the Secretary of the Cabinet . . . The Conclusions are circulated very promptly after Cabinet, and up to that time, no minister, certainly not the Prime Minister, asks to see them or conditions them in any way.'[25] By way of contrast, Mr Michael Heseltine was concerned about the minutes of a Cabinet meeting before his resignation in 1986, in particular the failure to record his protest about the Prime Minister's refusal to allow discussion on competing plans to rescue Westland, a helicopter manufacturing company.

4   The doctrine of collective responsibility helps to reinforce the powers of the Prime Minister. The effect of the doctrine is that ministers must not criticise government policy in public and if necessary must be prepared to defend it. This means that if the firm hand of the Prime Minister is guiding that policy, there will be no public criticism from the most influential and informed people in the government. The importance of the doctrine for silencing potential criticism is underlined by the fact that – as we have seen – many decisions of government are not taken by the Cabinet as a whole, but by the Prime Minister in consultation with a few key colleagues. This was true, for example, of an important decision such as transferring to the Bank of England in 1997 the responsibility for the setting of interest rates.[26] On one interpretation of the events, it was the attempt to control Cabinet colleagues by the doctrine of collective responsibility for decisions which had not been taken by the Cabinet which led to Mr Heseltine's resignation as Secretary of State for Defence in January 1986.

5   Compared to other ministers, the Prime Minister has a more regular opportunity to present and defend the government's policies in Parliament and elsewhere.[27] He or she is available for

---

[23] Lord Butler (Chair), Review of Intelligence on Weapons of Mass Destruction: Report of a Committee of Privy Counsellors, above, para 610.

[24] Mackintosh, p 449, asserts that the Prime Minister can keep any item off the agenda indefinitely but the examples he gives do not support this. Cf Wilson, p 47.

[25] Wilson, p 56.

[26] See Hennessy, *The Prime Minister*, pp 480–1.

[27] But see P Dunleavy, G W Jones et al. (1993) 23 *British Journal of Political Science* 267 on the declining accountability of the Prime Minister to Parliament. This is a process which has continued since 1997.

questioning in the Commons on Wednesdays (admittedly not always an unmixed blessing for a Prime Minister whose political authority is waning), and he or she may choose when to intervene in debates.[28] The Prime Minister is also in a position to dominate if not control the government's communications to the press, and to disclose information about government decisions and Cabinet business.[29] Alone among Cabinet ministers, he or she has regular meetings with the Queen and is responsible for keeping the Queen informed of the Cabinet's handling of affairs. In particular, he or she may recommend to the Queen that a general election be held and in doing so is not required to discuss this first with the Cabinet.[30] It is sometimes argued that the threat of a dissolution is a device whereby a Prime Minister may exercise authority over colleagues in government and Parliament. But this may not always be an option. Why would a Prime Minister wish to recommend that a general election be called if his or her party was weakened by internal dissension, particularly when the dissidents may not be among those most likely to lose their seats?

B. The Cabinet

Composition of the Cabinet

A modern Cabinet usually consists of 22 or 23 members (including the Prime Minister). No statute regulates the composition of the Cabinet, but there are both administrative and political constraints on the Prime Minister's freedom of choice. Thus in peacetime it is impossible to exclude certain offices, such as the Home Secretary, the Foreign Secretary, the Lord Chancellor and the Chancellor of the Exchequer. In addition to the Secretaries of State and ministers in charge of the major departments, every Cabinet includes two or three members with few if any departmental responsibilities, for example, the Lord President of the Council, also Leader of the House of Lords; and the Chancellor of the Duchy of Lancaster, also Leader of the House of Commons.[31] Since 1951 the government chief whip in the Commons, whose formal title is Parliamentary Secretary to the Treasury, has regularly attended Cabinet. The Law Officers of the Crown[32] are not appointed to the Cabinet but, like other ministers outside the Cabinet, the Attorney General may attend Cabinet meetings for particular matters.

In addition to political considerations of these kinds, the number of salaried Cabinet posts is limited by statute: apart from the Prime Minister and the Lord Chancellor, not more than 20 salaries may be paid to Cabinet ministers at one time.[33] Political necessity requires that all members of the Cabinet are members of the Commons or the Lords, unless a minister is actively seeking election to the Commons at a by-election or is to be created a life peer.[34] It is no longer necessary for the Lord Chancellor to be a member of the House of Lords, but it is normal for at least some ministers to be drawn from the upper House, though it would be undesirable for many senior positions to be held by peers. In all modern governments there have been some ministers with departmental responsibilities who are outside the Cabinet. They may serve on Cabinet committees, will see Cabinet papers relating to their departments, and may be asked to attend Cabinet meetings. The amalgamation of departments to form larger departments which took place during the 1960s[35] meant that all major departments were placed under the supervision of a

---

[28] On Prime Minister's question time, see R K Alderman (1992) 45 *Parliamentary Affairs* 66.

[29] See Margach, *The Abuse of Power*.

[30] Ch 12 B.

[31] Some Prime Ministers have also appointed a Minister without Portfolio with responsibility for party rather than government affairs. There is no such minister in Mr Brown's Cabinet at the time of writing.

[32] Ch 18 E.

[33] Ministerial and other Salaries Act 1975. See ch 9 G.

[34] Ch 2 B.

[35] Section C below.

Cabinet minister and this continues to be the case. In wartime the normal Cabinet may be superseded by a small War Cabinet to take charge of the conduct of the war. In 1916 the War Cabinet consisted of five, later six, senior ministers, of whom only the Chancellor of the Exchequer had departmental duties. The War Cabinet of 1939–45 was larger, varying between seven and ten, including several senior departmental ministers.[36]

Cabinet committees[37]

The increase in the scale of government since 1900 has not been matched by a corresponding increase in the size of the Cabinet. Few problems of government can be solved by a single department acting on its own, if only because most policy decisions have expenditure and personnel implications (hence the interest of the Treasury in all new policies). The Cabinet could not have kept abreast of its work had there not developed under its umbrella a complicated structure of committees. Cabinet committees are said by the Cabinet Office to have two key purposes. The first is to relieve the burden on the Cabinet by dealing with business that does not need to be discussed at full Cabinet; and the second is to 'support the principle of collective responsibility by ensuring that, even though a question may never reach the Cabinet itself, it will be fully considered [and] the final judgment [will be] sufficiently authoritative [to ensure] that the Government as a whole can be expected to accept responsibility for it'.[38] As explained in a previous edition of the *Ministerial Code*, decisions reached by Cabinet committees are 'binding on all members of the Government', although they are 'normally announced and explained as the decision of the Minister concerned'. Because of the doctrine of collective responsibility, 'the privacy of opinions' expressed in Cabinet committee, as in the Cabinet itself, should be maintained.[39]

The 45 Cabinet committees and sub-committees in 2009 included major strategic committees such as the newly created National Economic Council (of 22 ministers chaired by the Prime Minister), the Democratic Renewal Council (17 ministers chaired by the Prime Minister), and the Domestic Policy Council (18 ministers chaired by the Prime Minister). There is a concern, however, that the formality of decision-making by Cabinet committees (itself controversial in its day) is being gradually displaced by the informality of decision-making by the Prime Minister in conjunction with ministers either individually or in small groups (also controversial in the present day). This development – associated principally with Mr Blair's tenure as Prime Minister – reflects a view of government in which the role of Cabinet ministers has changed: they are no longer responsible as being engaged in a process of collective decision-making so much as being responsible for the implementation of policy determined in No 10 Downing Street. Lord Butler has revealed, for example, that in the run up to the invasion of Iraq, the Cabinet Committee on Defence and Overseas Policy did not meet, with key decisions taken – as already indicated – by a small group of ministers and advisers. Although Lord Butler's Committee did not suggest that the evolving procedures 'are in aggregate any less effective now than in earlier times', it did express concern that the effect was

> to limit wider collective discussion and consideration by the Cabinet to the frequent but unscripted occasions when the Prime Minister, Foreign Secretary and Defence Secretary briefed the Cabinet orally. Excellent quality papers were written by officials, but these were not discussed in Cabinet or in Cabinet Committee. Without papers circulated in advance, it remains possible but is obviously

---

[36] For the War Cabinet, see 8th edn of this book, 1970, pp 201, 203–7; Jennings, ch 10; and Mackintosh, ch 14 and pp 490–9.

[37] Jennings, pp 255–61; Mackintosh, pp 521–9; Gordon Walker, pp 38–47; Wilson, pp 62–8; Hennessy, *The Prime Minister*, pp 482–3.

[38] Cabinet Office, *A Guide to Cabinet and Cabinet Committee Business* (2008).

[39] *Ministerial Code* (2005 edn), paras 6.16–6.17.

much more difficult for members of the Cabinet outside the small circle directly involved to bring their political judgement and experience to bear on the major decisions for which the Cabinet as a whole must carry responsibility.[40]

The Cabinet Office[41]

In 1917, to enable the War Cabinet and its system of committees to function efficiently, a Secretary to the Cabinet was appointed to be present at meetings of the Cabinet and its committees, to circulate minutes of the conclusions reached, to communicate decisions rapidly to those who had to act on them and also to circulate papers before meetings. The conclusions prepared by the Secretary to the Cabinet and circulated to the Queen and Cabinet ministers continue to be the only official record of Cabinet meetings. This account is designed to record agreement and not controversy. Differences of opinion in discussion are not attributed to individuals, although the arguments for and against a decision may be summarised: 'behind many of the decisions lay tensions and influences which are not reflected in the official records'.[42] However, if a minister expressly wishes his or her dissent to be recorded, then this will be done.[43] Today, the Cabinet Secretary is based in the Cabinet Office which plays a key role at the heart of government. The primary responsibility of the Cabinet Office is to support the Prime Minister by defining and implementing the government's objectives; to support the Cabinet in terms of the coherence and quality of government activity; and to ensure that the civil service is organised and capable to implement the government's objectives. Day-to-day direction of the department is led by the Minister for the Cabinet Office, but the Cabinet Office reports to the Prime Minister as head of the government and Minister for the Civil Service.

There are several different secretariats within the Cabinet Office, each with different areas of responsibility (such as economic policy, European policy, and foreign and defence policy, as well as more trivial matters such as honours and appointments), all designed 'to ensure that the business of Government is conducted in a timely and efficient way and that proper collective consideration takes place when it is needed before policy decisions are taken'.[44] The secretariats work closely with the Prime Minister's Private Office and the No 10 Policy Unit, and seek 'to ensure that the Prime Minister's views are taken into account, particularly where business will not come before Cabinet or a Cabinet Committee which he chairs'.[45] The secretariats also work closely with a number of units based in the Cabinet Office, notably the Strategy Unit which is designed to provide strategy and policy advice to the Prime Minister and government departments. Notable too is the Propriety and Ethics Team which has responsibility for advising the Cabinet Secretary about issues arising under the *Ministerial Code*,[46] the *Civil Service Code*, and the *Code of Conduct for Special Advisers*. The Cabinet Office – which deals additionally with the programme of civil service reform as well as civil contingencies and security and intelligence matters – thus continues to grow and strengthen, and is thought to be the Prime Minister's Department 'in all but

---

[40] Lord Butler (Chair), Review of Intelligence on Weapons of Mass Destruction: Report of a Committee of Privy Counsellors, above, para 610.

[41] Jennings, pp 242–5; Gordon Walker, pp 47–55; Mosley, *The Story of the Cabinet Office*; Wilson, *The Cabinet Office to 1945*.

[42] Wilson, *The Cabinet Office to 1945*, p 4. At p 142 are printed instructions on minute-taking current in 1936. Crossman's comment 30 years later was that the minutes 'do not pretend to be an account of what actually takes place in the Cabinet' (p 198).

[43] It was the alleged failure to follow this convention which added to the drama surrounding the resignation of Mr Michael Heseltine in the so-called Westland affair in 1986.

[44] http://www.cabinetoffice.gov.uk/secretariats/about.aspx.

[45] Ibid.

[46] This is despite the fact that the current version of the *Ministerial Code* states expressly that 'it is not the role of the Cabinet Secretary or other officials to enforce the code': para 1.3.

name'. But although expanding the Cabinet Office, Mr Blair resisted formally setting up such a department 'in order to avoid charges of presidentialism'.[47]

Cabinet secrecy

The operation of the Cabinet system is surrounded by considerable secrecy.[48] It is the 'working assumption' of government that most Cabinet papers are protected from disclosure under the Freedom of Information Act 2000,[49] only to be made available as historical records for public inspection in the National Archives after 30 years.[50] Many Cabinet decisions are notified to Parliament or otherwise made public, but the doctrine of collective responsibility throws a heavy veil over decision-making in Cabinet. That veil is only rarely pierced, as when Lord Hutton laid bare the internal workings of the Cabinet in his report on the circumstances surrounding the death of Dr David Kelly, a senior civil servant who took his own life in 2003.[51] One justification for Cabinet secrecy commonly supported by those with experience of the system is the view that anything which damages the collective unity and integrity of the Cabinet damages the good government of the country.[52] Certainly the public interest in national security requires that some information about defence and external relations must be kept secret by those in government. But the 'good government' argument goes very much further than national security since it seeks to preserve the process of decision-making within government from scrutiny by those outside. Some critics argue, on the contrary, that 'good government' in a democracy requires that more light be thrown on political decision-making and that government be more open. In fact the media frequently contains speculation about the Cabinet's deliberations, some of which may be based on unauthorised disclosures of Cabinet proceedings by ministers who wish to make their points of view known.

One important practice is that the ministers in one government do not have access to the papers of an earlier government of a different political party. On a change of government, the outgoing Prime Minister issues special instructions about the disposal of the Cabinet papers of his or her administration. The practice applies to papers of the Cabinet and ministerial committees, as well as departmental papers that contain the private views of ministers and advice given by officials. The main reason for the practice is to prevent a minister from one party having access to 'matters that the previous administration had been most anxious to keep quiet'.[53] Former ministers retain the right of access to documents that they saw in office. Before access to Cabinet papers or other ministerial documents of a former government can be given to third persons, the present Prime Minister must seek the agreement of the former Prime Minister concerned or the current leader of his or her party. Thus, when a committee of privy counsellors was appointed to review British policy towards the Falkland Islands before the Argentine invasion, five former Prime Ministers agreed to the relevant documents being seen by the committee.[54] Ministers relinquishing office without a change of government 'should hand back to their department any Cabinet documents and/or other departmental papers in their possession'.[55]

---

[47] *The Times*, 13 June 2001.

[48] Williams, *Not in the Public Interest*, ch 2; Gordon Walker, pp 26–33, 164–8; Report on Section 2 of Official Secrets Act 1911, Cmnd 5104, 1972, ch 11; Report on Ministerial Memoirs, Cmnd 6386, 1976.

[49] See Part F below.

[50] See Freedom of Information Act 2000, ss 35, 36, 63–7; and Public Records Act 1958, s 5 (amended by the Freedom of Information Act 2000, s 67). See http://www.foi.gov.uk/guidance/exguide/sec35/annex-b.pdf.

[51] Lord Hutton, Report of the Inquiry into the Circumstances Surrounding the Death of Dr David Kelly C.M.G. (2004). See also Butler Report, above, and the evidence given in public by Cabinet ministers and senior civil servants to the Chilcott inquiry of 2010 into the events leading up to the invasion of Iraq in 2003.

[52] Cmnd 5104, 1972, p 68.

[53] HC Deb, 8 July 1982, col 474 (Mr M Foot).

[54] HC Deb, 1 July 1982, col 1039; 8 July 1982, col 469. See Lord Hunt [1982] PL 514.

[55] *Ministerial Code*, para 2.7. And see R Brazier [1996] CLJ 65, on the sale of the Churchill papers in 1995.

Cabinet secrecy and the courts

In law, Cabinet documents are protected to some extent from (*a*) production as evidence in litigation by public interest immunity which authorises non-disclosure of documents which it would be injurious to the public interest to disclose,[56] and (*b*) examination by the Parliamentary Ombudsman;[57] they may also be protected by the Official Secrets Acts[58] and be exempt from disclosure under the Freedom of Information Act 2000.[59] Political sanctions also operate: a serving Cabinet minister would be liable to lose office if he or she could be shown improperly to have revealed the details of Cabinet discussions. But is a former Cabinet minister, who may be subject to no political sanction, under a legal obligation not to reveal such secrets? The question arose for decision in *Attorney-General* v *Jonathan Cape Ltd.*[60]

> Richard Crossman kept a political diary between 1964 and 1970 while a Labour Cabinet minister. After his death in 1974, his diary for 1964–66 was edited for publication and, as was customary, submitted to the Secretary to the Cabinet. He refused to consent to publication, since the diary contained detailed accounts of Cabinet discussions, reports of the advice given to ministers by civil servants and comments about the suitability of senior civil servants for promotion. When Crossman's literary executors decided to publish the diary, the Attorney General sought an injunction to stop them. Lord Widgery CJ held that the court had power to restrain the improper publication of information which had been received by a Cabinet minister in confidence, and that the doctrine of collective responsibility justified the court in restraining the disclosures of Cabinet discussions; but that the court should act only where continuing confidentiality of the material could clearly be shown. On the facts, he held that publication in 1975 of Cabinet discussions during the period 1964–66 should not be restrained. In this decision, no reliance was placed either upon the Privy Counsellor's oath of secrecy or upon the Official Secrets Acts.

This decision established the power of the court to restrain publication of Cabinet secrets but gave no clear guidance as to when the power should be exercised. The problems of memoirs of ex-Cabinet ministers were subsequently considered by a Committee of Privy Counsellors.[61] The committee distinguished between secret information relating to national security and international relations, on which an ex-minister must accept the decision of the Cabinet Secretary, and other confidential material about relationships between ministers or between ministers and civil servants. In the latter case there should be no publication within 15 years, except with clearance from the Cabinet Secretary, but in the event of a dispute it must in the last resort be for ex-ministers themselves to decide what to publish. Advice given by a civil servant to a minister should not be revealed while the adviser is still a civil servant. The committee recommended against legislation, preferring to suggest a clear working procedure which would be brought to the attention of every minister on assuming office. The committee's recommendations were accepted by the government in 1976 and have been maintained by subsequent governments. There has since been a spate of ministerial memoirs,[62] though the government believes that the existing procedures generally work well in practice.[63]

---

[56] Ch 32 C. On the relationship between the Cabinet and the courts, see M C Harris [1989] PL 251.

[57] Parliamentary Commissioner Act 1967, s 8(4); ch 29 D.

[58] Ch 25.

[59] Ch 13 F.

[60] [1976] QB 752; Young, *The Crossman Affair*.

[61] Cmnd 6386, 1976 (Radcliffe Report). For more recent considerations of this issue, see HC 689 (2005–06); HC 664 (2007–08); HC 428 (2008–09).

[62] The *Ministerial Code* requires former ministers to submit their manuscript to the Cabinet Secretary and to conform to the principles set out in the Radcliffe Report (para 8.10).

[63] HC 428 (2008–09).

C. Ministers and departments

Ministerial offices

Some ministerial offices have a much longer history than the office of Prime Minister, others have been created more recently. The office of Lord Chancellor goes back to the reign of Edward the Confessor and was of great political and judicial significance for several centuries after the Norman conquest. The office of Lord Privy Seal dates from the fourteenth century and in a later period was often held by leading statesmen; but the historic duties in respect of the Privy Seal were abolished in 1884 and the office now carries no departmental responsibilities. The office of Lord President of the Council was created in 1497 and became important during the period of government through the Council under the Stuarts. The office of Secretary of State has almost as long a history, acquiring its political significance in the Tudor period, particularly during the tenure of the Cecils under Elizabeth I. It came to be recognised as the means by which communications could take place between citizen and monarch.[64] From the seventeenth century, two and sometimes three Secretaries of State were appointed who divided national and foreign affairs between them.

In 1782 a different division of functions vested in one Secretary of State responsibility for domestic affairs, and the colonies and in the other Secretary responsibility for foreign affairs. Thus were created the offices of Home Secretary and Foreign Secretary. In 1794 a Secretary of State for War was appointed and thereafter, from time to time, additional Secretaryships (for example, for the colonies, for India, for Scotland) were created and abolished as need arose. Appointments are now made on the advice of the Prime Minister who decides what offices are needed, and what departments should be created to support the office holders.[65] In 2009 there were 17 Secretaries of State, who between them headed nearly all the major departments. When statutory powers are conferred on a Secretary of State, it is usual for the statute to designate him or her as 'the Secretary of State' but it will be obvious from the context which Secretary of State is intended to exercise the new functions.[66] In law the duties of Secretaries of State are interchangeable, but in practice each Secretary's functions are limited to those related to his or her own department. One Secretary of State may be named by the Prime Minister as First Secretary; while this makes no legal difference to the office, it determines precedence in the Cabinet and the First Secretary may deputise for the Prime Minister in the latter's absence. The position as First Secretary of State may be combined with the office of Deputy Prime Minister.

Government departments

While the term 'government department' has no precise meaning in law, it usually refers to those branches of the central administration which are staffed by civil servants, paid for out of exchequer funds and headed by a minister responsible to Parliament. A single minister may be responsible for more than one department: thus the Chancellor of the Exchequer is responsible for the Treasury as well as HM Revenue and Customs. Moreover, one person may hold two offices: in 2005, the Secretary of State for Transport was also the Secretary of State for Scotland, while the Secretary of State for Northern Ireland was also the Secretary of State for Wales. These were not seen universally to have been successful precedents. Exceptionally, there are departments which for constitutional reasons do not have a ministerial head: thus the National Audit Office is headed

---

[64] For the history of the Secretaries of State, see Anson, *The Law and Custom of the Constitution*, vol II, i, pp 172–84.
[65] HC 540 (2008–09).
[66] By the Interpretation Act 1978, unless the contrary intention appears, 'Secretary of State' means 'one of Her Majesty's Principal Secretaries of State'. See *Agee v Lord Advocate* 1977 SLT (Notes) 54.

by the Comptroller and Auditor General.[67] For the purposes of legal proceedings against the Crown, a list of departments is maintained under the Crown Proceedings Act 1947.[68] For the purposes of investigation by the Parliamentary Ombudsman, a statutory list of departments is maintained and this is revised as new departments are established.[69] There are many public bodies with governmental functions which are not regarded as government departments. They include local authorities; regulatory bodies such as the Equality and Human Rights Commission; grant-giving bodies such as the Arts Councils and the Higher Education Funding Council; and other bodies which may report to ministers but are not directly controlled by them (for example, the English and Scottish Law Commissions).[70] Often such bodies are financed from central government funds.[71]

To enable changes in the structure of government to be carried out quickly, there have been statutory powers since 1946 by which new needs can be met without recourse to Acts of Parliament. The Ministers of the Crown Act 1975 now authorises the Crown, by Order in Council, to transfer to any minister functions previously exercised by another minister; to provide for the dissolution of a government department and for the transfer to other departments of the functions previously exercised by that department; and to direct that functions shall be exercised concurrently by two ministers. Consequential steps may also be authorised, such as the transfer of property from one department to another and changes in the title of ministers. Orders in Council under the 1975 Act are subject to parliamentary scrutiny. The extensively used powers conferred by the 1975 Act are in addition to the Crown's prerogative powers which may still be exercised to make some governmental changes,[72] and are without prejudice to the government's ability to seek parliamentary approval for the creation of a new department by introducing a Bill.[73] Although the Foreign and Commonwealth Office, the Home Office and the Ministry of Defence have remained intact since 1970, there are many changes elsewhere. Most recently new departments have been created for Justice; Culture, Media and Sport; and Energy and Climate Change. There are also now separate departments for Health on the one hand and Work and Pensions on the other. While it is important that the structure of government should not be ossified, it is equally important that the capacity to engineer radical structural change is subject to meaningful parliamentary scrutiny,[74] though recommendations to this effect have not been met with great enthusiasm.[75]

Ministers of the Crown[76]

According to one statutory definition, minister of the Crown means 'the holder of any office in Her Majesty's Government in the United Kingdom, and includes the Treasury . . . and the Defence Council'.[77] In a less technical sense, ministers are those members or supporters of the party in power who hold political office in the government. They are all appointed by the Crown on the advice of the Prime Minister and their offices are at the disposal of an incoming Prime Minister. They do not include members of the civil service or the armed forces, who continue in

---

[67] Ch 17 D.

[68] Ch 32 C.

[69] Ch 29 D.

[70] See Ch 14 B.

[71] See also the peculiar position of the public utility regulators: ch 14 C.

[72] 1975 Act, s 5; see above, p 263.

[73] See Defence (Transfer of Functions) Act 1964. The now defunct Ministry of Labour was also created by statute – see New Ministries and Secretaries Act 1916.

[74] HC 672 (2006–7); HC 160 (2007–08) (House of Commons Public Administration Committee).

[75] HC 514 (2007–08); HC 540 (2008–09) (government response).

[76] See Brazier, *Ministers of the Crown*, for a full account.

[77] Ministers of the Crown Act 1975, s 8(1).

office despite a change of government; or special advisers to ministers, who may be paid salaries and are temporarily attached to departments but who lose their position when a minister leaves office; or members of public boards, regulatory bodies and so on. Unlike many of these other office-holders, ministers are not disqualified from membership of the House of Commons. Indeed, it is a convention that ministerial office-holders should be members of one or other House of Parliament. There is, however, no law that a minister must be in Parliament and the possibility of recruiting ministers from outside is sometimes discussed. This could only take place if the individuals in question could be made responsible to Parliament other than by membership, and it is not clear that it would be a good practice. If a Prime Minister wishes to appoint to ministerial office someone who is not already in Parliament, the current practice is to confer a life peerage on the individual in question so that he or she may take a seat in the Lords, and this not infrequently happens.

There are various grades of ministerial appointment today, but they may be grouped into three broad categories: (*a*) Cabinet ministers, who may or may not have departmental responsibilities; (*b*) departmental ministers and ministers of state who are outside the Cabinet, the duty of a minister of state being to share in the administration of a department headed by a Cabinet minister; and (*c*) parliamentary secretaries, whose duty it is to assist in the parliamentary work of a department and who may also have some administrative responsibility. The two Law Officers of the Crown for England and Wales are within category (*b*) but the government whips, who have no departmental responsibilities, may be allotted among the categories according to their status and seniority. By exercise of the prerogative, new posts in the Crown's service can be created, for example, extra Secretaries of State. But when a new ministry is formed, there is often secondary legislation to create the minister a corporation sole, thus giving him or her legal capacity, and providing in broad terms for his or her functions.[78] There are no legal limits on the number of ministers which the Crown may appoint, assuming that they are not to receive a salary and do not sit in the House of Commons. However, as already pointed out, there are statutory limits on the number of ministers who may be members of the Commons and on the number of salaries payable to holders of ministerial office.[79] Ministerial salaries are now governed by a formula set out in the Ministerial and Other Salaries Act 1975, as amended by the Ministerial and Other Salaries Act 1997.[80]

The *Ministerial Code*

The conduct of ministers is governed by the *Ministerial Code*, now 'an integral part of the new constitutional architecture'.[81] The Code – which is not legally binding – was first compiled by Attlee in 1945, although some of its provisions go back further.[82] It deals with a range of matters relating to the relationship between ministers and the government, Parliament and the civil service. It also deals with ministers' private interests. Previously known as *Questions of Procedure for Ministers* (QPM), the Code was first made public by Mr Major in 1992 and was revised following the recommendations of the Committee on Standards in Public Life,[83] before being reissued by each of his successors.[84] The current code was issued in 2007, with a revised style, concentrating

---

[78] Important examples include SI 2001 No 2568; SI 2007 No 3224; and SI 2009 No 2478.

[79] Ch 9 G.

[80] The salary of the Lord Chancellor is governed by the Ministerial and other Pensions and Salaries Act 1991, by which his salary is '£2,500 a year more than the salary for the time being payable to the Lord Chief Justice' (s 3). But in 2005 the Lord Chancellor took a Cabinet minister's salary rather than a Lord Chancellor's salary.

[81] HC 235 (2000–01), para 15.

[82] Ibid.

[83] Cm 2850-I, 1995.

[84] The Code is set out in full at www.cabinetoffice.gov.uk

more on principles and less on procedures.[85] Section 1 reminds ministers that they are 'expected to behave in a way that upholds the highest standards of propriety'. In particular, they are required to observe the ten principles of ministerial conduct that are set out in the Code. These include a duty to uphold the principle of collective responsibility; a requirement to account for the activities of their departments and executive agencies; and an obligation to 'give accurate and truthful information to Parliament, correcting any inadvertent error at the earliest opportunity'. Ministers who 'knowingly mislead Parliament will be expected to offer their resignation to the Prime Minister'. There are those who feel that the word 'knowingly' should be removed from the text.[86]

In addition to the duty not to mislead Parliament, the Code also advises ministers of the need to be 'as open as possible with Parliament and the public, refusing to provide information only when disclosure would not be in the public interest'. This should be determined in accordance with relevant statutes (which are not specified) and the Freedom of Information Act 2000.[87] One of the other key principles provides that ministers should require civil servants who give evidence before select committees 'on their behalf and under their direction', to be as 'helpful as possible in providing accurate, truthful and full information in accordance with the duties and responsibilities of civil servants as set out in the Civil Service Code'. Otherwise, the Code deals with ministerial conflicts of interest (on which see below) and a prohibition on using government resources for party political purposes. Ministers are also required to uphold the political impartiality of the civil service, and they are reminded of their responsibility 'for justifying their actions and conduct to Parliament', and that they can 'remain in office [only] for so long as they retain the confidence of the Prime Minister', who is 'the ultimate judge of the standards of behaviour expected of a Minister and the appropriate consequences of a breach of those standards'. Where a breach of the Code is alleged, the Prime Minister may refer the matter for independent investigation.[88]

Financial interests of ministers

Because of their office, many ministers take decisions which have a direct financial effect on particular businesses, sections of industry and land values. They also have access to confidential information about future decisions which could be put to financial profit. The Marconi affair of 1912 involved three leading members of the Liberal government who were alleged to have made use of secret information about an impending government contract to make an investment in Marconi shares: an inquiry by a parliamentary committee established that they had bought shares not in the company to which the contract was about to be awarded, but in a sister company.[89] In 1948 the Lynskey Tribunal of Inquiry reported on allegations that ministers and other public servants had been bribed in connection with the grant of licences by the Board of Trade; a junior minister, who later resigned from Parliament, was found to have received presents of wine and spirits and other gifts, knowing that they had been made to secure favourable treatment by the department of applications for licences.[90] While such conduct could give rise to criminal proceedings, additional safeguards are required if ministers are to avoid suspicion.

In 1952 the rules then in force were published in a parliamentary written answer.[91] They still remain in operation, although they have been amended and are now to be found in the *Ministerial*

---

[85] See HC 381,1056 (2007–08).
[86] See A Tomkins [1996] PL 484. Cf HC 115 (1995–6), para K8.5.
[87] See Ch 13 F below.
[88] For background, see HC 1457 (2005–06); HC 381, 1056 (2007–08).
[89] See Donaldson, *The Marconi Scandal*.
[90] Cmd 7616, 1949.
[91] HC Deb, 25 February 1952, col 701; and 20 March 1980, col 293 (WA).

Code. The overriding principle is that ministers must ensure that no conflict arises, or appears to arise, between their private interests and their public duties. This conflict could arise if a minister took any active part or had a financial interest in any undertaking which had contractual or other relations (for example, receiving a licence or a subsidy) with his or her department. Under the current rules, ministers should, on assuming office, provide their Permanent Secretary with a full list of interests that might be thought to give rise to a conflict. Where necessary, a minister will be advised by the Permanent Secretary and the independent adviser on ministers' interests about which interests need to be disposed of.[92] Ministers are no longer reminded by the *Ministerial Code* of legal obligations relating to conflicts of interest, but the Code does still provide that ministers should seek advice from the Advisory Committee on Business Appointments about any appointments they wish to take up within two years of leaving office, and that they are expected to abide by the advice of the Committee.[93]

D. Civil service: organisation and accountability

Who is a civil servant?

The departments of central government are staffed by administrative, professional, technical and other officials who constitute the civil service. Civil servants perform many functions, from the development to the implementation of government policy. It has been said to be 'common ground that the civil service defies an easy universally applicable definition' and that 'a civil servant has no specific legal status'. A civil servant has been defined as 'a servant of the Crown working in a civil capacity who is not: the holder of a political (or judicial) office; the holder of certain other offices in respect of whose tenure of office special provision has been made; a servant of the Crown in a personal capacity paid from the Civil List'.[94] This definition excludes ministers of the Crown, members of the armed forces (who are Crown servants but are not employed in a civil capacity), the police and those employed in local government and the National Health Service, even though they are all engaged in public services. A somewhat similar definition is contained in s 2(6) of the Crown Proceedings Act 1947, which limits proceedings against the Crown in tort (or in Scots law, delict) to the act, neglect or default of an officer who 'has been directly or indirectly appointed by the Crown and was at the material time paid in respect of his duties as an officer of the Crown' wholly out of the national exchequer.[95] More recently the government has suggested when publishing a Draft Civil Service Bill in 2004 that 'there is no satisfactory, authoritative and comprehensive definition of the term "Civil Service"'. Consequently it was proposed that 'in order to achieve the necessary clarity and certainty about coverage', there would be provided 'a comprehensive listing of every part of the Civil Service to which the Bill is to apply'.[96] The government subsequently showed greater confidence (though not necessarily greater clarity) in the Constitutional Reform and Governance Act 2010 (which succeeded in placing the civil service on a statutory footing), in which the civil service is defined to mean 'the civil service of the State', with some exceptions.[97]

There are now about 500,000 civil servants. As far as their employment position is concerned, there is a sharp contrast between legal doctrine and practical reality. It is true that although civil servants traditionally have been regarded as appointed under the royal prerogative, the courts

---

[92] See HC 381, 1056 (2007–08).

[93] See HC 651, 1087 (2006–07).

[94] HC 390–II (1992–3), p 261.

[95] Ch 32 A.

[96] Cm 6373, 2004, pp 8–9.

[97] The exceptions included the secret intelligence service, the security service and GCHQ, leading to the conclusion that they are regarded by government as part of the civil service but separately regulated.

nevertheless have gradually recognised that they may have terms of service 'which are contractually enforceable'.[98] But although recognising the existence of a contract, the courts seem unwilling to challenge the traditional rule that civil servants are employed at the pleasure of the Crown,[99] which means that they may be dismissed with no common law remedy for wrongful dismissal.[100] So if civil servants are to be regarded as being employed under a contract, its terms will be limited by the prerogative power of the Crown to dismiss without notice for any reason. But although civil servants have no right to notice on termination, the *Civil Service Management Code* provides minimum notice periods which 'in practice' departments and agencies 'will normally apply'.[101] More importantly it is also the case that civil servants are deemed by statute to be employed under contracts of service for some employment protection purposes and will normally be able to bring an action for unfair dismissal.[102] There are also internal procedures which apply in the event of dismissal, with a final appeal to the Civil Service Appeals Board which is independent of the departments concerned. The decisions of the Board are subject to judicial review.[103] Other employment protection rights typically also apply now to civil servants, reflecting what has been a trend towards providing civil servants with the same formal protections as their counterparts in the private sector. But whatever the precise legal nature of the civil servant's relationship with the Crown, it is an important constitutional principle that those concerned with the administration of government departments should, in fact, enjoy a tenure of office by which they may serve successive ministers of different political parties. Particularly since 1979, the size, expense and organisation of the civil service have become matters of political controversy. But without the service, the achievements of modern government would have been impossible.

Civil service structure

The structure of the civil service has undergone a great deal of change since the 1980s, reflecting growing Treasury concerns about cost and efficiency.[104] The starting point is the publication in 1988 of a report to the Prime Minister drawn up by Sir Robin Ibbs, entitled *Improving Management in Government: The Next Steps*.[105] This was the most far-reaching and fundamental review of the civil service since 1968 and led to the most radical changes since 1854.[106] The report expressed concern that the civil service (then with over 600,000 staff) was too big and too diverse to be managed as a single organisation, and recommended that attempts should be made to establish a different way of conducting the business of government. It was suggested that the central civil service should consist of a relatively small core engaged in the function of servicing ministers and managing departments, which would be the main sponsors of particular government policies and services. Responding to these departments would be a range of agencies employing their own staff, concentrating on the delivery of their particular service with responsibilities clearly defined between the Secretary of State and the Permanent Secretary, on the one hand, and the chairman

---

[98] *McLaren v Home Office* [1990] IRLR 338, 341; *R v Lord Chancellor's Department, ex p Nangle* [1992] 1 All ER 897. And see S Fredman and G Morris [1991] PL 485; and ch 32 B.

[99] See *Civil Service Management Code*, s 11.1.1. Compare *Wells v Newfoundland* [1993] 3 SCC 199.

[100] *Dunn v R* [1896] 1 QB 116; *Riordan v War Office* [1959] 1 WLR 1046. And see ch 32 B.

[101] *Civil Service Management Code*, s 11.1.

[102] Employment Rights Act 1996, s 191.

[103] See *R v Civil Service Appeal Board, ex p Bruce* [1988] 3 All ER 686; *R v Civil Service Appeal Board, ex p Cunningham* [1991] 4 All ER 310.

[104] For a full account, see HL 55 (1998). See also G Drewry, in Jowell and Oliver (eds), *The Changing Constitution* (6th edn), ch 8.

[105] The report had been commissioned in 1986. For the reaction to it, see Hennessy, *Whitehall*, pp 620–1, and Lawson, *The View from No 11*, pp 391–3. See also Woodhouse, *Ministers and Parliament*, chs 11, 12.

[106] See respectively Cmnd 3638, 1968 (Fulton Committee) and Northcote–Trevelyan Report (reprinted in app B of the Fulton Report).

and chief executive of the agency, on the other.[107] These proposals reflected a perceived need to give greater priority to organising government so that its service delivery functions operated effectively.

The proposals were largely accepted by the government and by 2000 137 agencies had been created (accounting for some 80 per cent of the civil service), though the number of such agencies has declined in more recent years. Spanning a wide range and diversity of functions, they varied enormously in size, from 45 to 45,000 staff. Each agency has a defined task, or range of tasks, which are set out in its published framework document. In addition, 'key performance targets – covering financial performance, efficiency and service to the customer – are set out by ministers annually. Each agency has a chief executive, normally directly accountable to ministers and with personal responsibility for the success of the agency in meeting its targets.'[108] Like other government bodies, executive agencies may be subject to judicial review.[109] Alongside the delegation of tasks to the agencies has been the delegation to the agencies and departments of responsibility for the pay and working conditions of staff. The process of delegation in the setting of working conditions (with an emphasis on performance-related incentives) was facilitated by the Civil Service (Management of Functions) Act 1992. In 1996 the long-established central pay bargaining arrangements were entirely replaced by a system which delegated to the departments and agencies the authority to make their own pay arrangements, 'albeit within the overall Treasury limits on running costs'.[110] According to the *Civil Service Management Code*, departments and agencies must develop arrangements for the remuneration of their staff which are 'appropriate to their business needs, are consistent with the Government's policies on the Civil Service and public sector pay, and observe public spending controls'.[111]

The civil servant within the department

The senior civil servant within a department is the Permanent Secretary.[112] Beneath the Permanent Secretary, the affairs of the department will be handled by a number of divisions or branches, controlled (in descending order of seniority) by deputy secretaries, under-secretaries and assistant secretaries. These posts together form what is known as the 'Senior Civil Service', an entity created in 1996.[113] A key role is also played by special advisers to ministers, a position which has grown in numbers since 1997.[114] Where schemes of delegation exist within a department, they do not generally affect the legal position of the department or of outsiders dealing with it. Where the power to make a discretionary decision affecting an individual is vested in a minister, an official within the department may in general take that decision on behalf of the minister (the *Carltona* principle),[115] unless there are express or implied limitations in the statute conferring the power.[116] In a criminal case in which it was claimed that the Home Secretary had never approved a breathalyser device as required by the Road Safety Act 1973, Widgery LJ said: 'The minister is not expected personally to take every decision entrusted to him by Parliament. If

---

[107] For the previous consideration of this option with reference particularly to Sweden, see Cmnd 3638, 1968, paras 188–91.

[108] Cm 2750, 1994, p ii.

[109] See *R (Denfleet International Ltd) v NHS Purchasing and Supply Agency* [2005] EWHC 55 (Admin); and *R (Botswana Meat Commission) v Rural Rights Agency* [2005] EWHC 1163 (Admin).

[110] HL 55 (1997–8), para 94. See also Cm 4310, 1999, p 58.

[111] *Civil Service Management Code*, s 7.1.2.

[112] For a study of permanent secretaries, see K Theakston and G K Fry (1989) 67 *Public Administration* 129.

[113] HL 55 (1997–8). On the continuing influence of the civil service in the legislative process, see E C Page (2003) 81 *Public Administration* 651.

[114] See HC 238 (1999–2000); and HC 423-I (2003–4), Q 63. On special advisers, see T Daintith [2002] PL 13.

[115] *Carltona Ltd v Commissioners of Works* [1943] 2 All ER 560. See ch 7.

[116] *R v Home Secretary, ex p Oladehinde* [1991] 1 AC 254, at p 282.

a decision is made on his behalf by one of his officials, then that constitutionally is the minister's decision.'[117] In regard to the Secretary of State's powers under the Immigration Act 1971, it was held that immigration officers (in whom certain functions are expressly vested by the Act) were also entitled by virtue of the *Carltona* principle to exercise decision-making powers in regard to deportation on behalf of the Secretary of State.[118]

New questions about departmental delegation arise following the introduction of the executive agencies. But despite initial doubts to the contrary,[119] it seems likely that the *Carltona* principle is sufficiently flexible to accommodate these new developments. It is important to stress that the framework documents establishing the agencies typically make clear that it is the minister who has ultimate responsibility for determining the policy and financial framework within which the agency operates, and that it is the minister who is accountable to Parliament for all matters concerning the agency, even though he or she is not normally involved in the day-to-day running of the agency. The framework documents also provide that the agency chief executive will represent the minister at parliamentary committees and answer questions on his or her behalf, an arrangement reinforced by the Cabinet Office rules relating to evidence to select committees. The latter make clear that chief executives give evidence 'on behalf of the minister to whom they are accountable and are subject to that minister's instruction'.[120] In terms of the adaptability of the *Carltona* principle, it is perhaps instructive that its alleged shortcomings were not raised in *Quinland v Governor of Swaleside Prison*[121] where the claimant brought an action for false imprisonment against two prison governors and the Lord Chancellor's Department. As a result of an administrative error by an official in the Court Service (then an executive agency of the Lord Chancellor's Department), the claimant had served a longer sentence than was required. The claim failed, not because there was no departmental responsibility for officials employed by the agency (a point which was never raised by the defence), but because the agency was covered by the immunity from liability in the Crown Proceedings Act 1947, s 2(5) for those performing a judicial function (a point vigorously contested by the defence).

Civil servants and ministerial responsibility

The principle of responsibility through ministers to Parliament is one of the most essential characteristics of the civil service. In a memorandum to the House of Commons Treasury and Civil Service Committee in the early 1990s, the Cabinet Office asserted that,

> The Minister in charge of a department is the only person who may be said to be ultimately accountable for the work of his department. It is usually on the Secretary of State as minister that Parliament has conferred powers, and Parliament calls on ministers to be accountable for the policy, actions and resources of their departments and the use of those powers. While ministers may delegate much of the day to day work of their departments, often now to agencies, they remain ultimately accountable to Parliament for all that is done under their power. Civil servants, except in those particular cases where statute confers powers on them directly, cannot take decisions or actions except insofar as they act on behalf of ministers. Civil servants are accountable to ministers, ministers are accountable to Parliament.[122]

---

[117] *R v Skinner* [1968] 2 QB 700, 707. See also *Copeland v H M Advocate* 1988 SLT 249, and *R v Home Secretary, ex p Doody* [1994] 1 AC 531, at p 566. And see ch 7.

[118] *R v Home Secretary, ex p Oladehinde* [1991] 1 AC 254.

[119] See M R Freedland [1996] PL 19. Also M R Freedland, in Sunkin and Payne (eds), *The Nature of the Crown*, ch 5.

[120] Cabinet Office, *Departmental Evidence and Response to Select Committees* (2009), para 50.

[121] [2002] EWCA Civ 174; [2003] QB 306. Hale LJ pointed out: 'The Court Service may be an agency of the executive but it exists in part, if not in whole, to facilitate and implement the workings of the judiciary.'

[122] HC 27-II (1993–4), p 188.

According to the Cabinet Office, ministerial responsibility has often been used to describe this process. In recent years, however, there has been a significant refinement of the principle, the government taking the view that ministers are 'accountable' to Parliament for the work of their department, but are not 'responsible' for all the actions of civil servants in the sense of being blameworthy. There appears as a result to be a greater willingness to attribute responsibility for operational matters to individual civil servants. Although the distinction has been strenuously defended, there are those who remain sceptical, yet it remains unclear how far the distinction expresses anything which is qualitatively different from what was expressed by Sir David Maxwell-Fyfe in the aftermath of the Crichel Down affair in the 1950s.[123]

This is a question which has been brought sharply into focus as a result of the creation of the executive agencies. Although ministers are formally accountable for the work of the agencies, there is nevertheless concern that there is now a responsibility gap, as ministers are able to deflect blame onto the shoulders of chief executives.[124] These concerns were highlighted following difficulties in the Prison Service which led to the dismissal in October 1995 of its chief executive, Mr Derek Lewis, by the Home Secretary, Mr Michael Howard. Mr Lewis is not the only chief executive to lose office because of failure within an agency,[125] but his departure has been the most controversial. It followed the report of a review of security procedures in prisons by General Sir John Learmont, conducted after the escape of three prisoners from Parkhurst Jail on the Isle of Wight. The report made a number of criticisms of Parkhurst and its security, but also claimed that some of the problems could be 'traced along the lines of communication to Prison Service headquarters'.[126] In the words of the Home Secretary, Learmont did not find that 'any policy decision of [his], directly or indirectly, caused the escape'.[127] Mr Lewis was dismissed, although not without complaining of ministerial interference in operational matters and not without a substantial settlement being made in his favour for the premature termination of his appointment.[128] In the controversy that followed this dismissal, the Home Secretary declined to accept responsibility for the agency failures. In his view there was a distinction between policy and operations, a distinction said to be 'reflected in the framework document that established the Prison Service as an Executive Agency'.[129]

Civil servants and select committees

Select committees are now an important channel for ministerial accountability. Although it is the departmental minister who is responsible to Parliament, the select committees nevertheless may wish to take evidence from civil servants within the minister's department, sometimes for a more informed and detailed account of the issues which the department may be dealing with. A question which has arisen is whether select committees can summon and require the attendance of named officials,[130] or whether a minister can instruct the official not to attend and thereby potentially frustrate a select committee's investigation. During the Westland affair in 1985–86, the House of Commons Defence Committee wished to examine five named officials, three from the Department of Trade and Industry and two from the Prime Minister's Office. The government took the view, however, that because these officials had participated in an internal departmental inquiry, it would be neither fair nor reasonable to expect them to submit to a second round of

---

[123] HC Deb, 20 July 1954, cols 1285–7. And see ch 7.

[124] HC 27-II (1993–4), p 189.

[125] See *The Guardian*, 17 November 2004 (resignation of Chief Executive of the Child Support Agency).

[126] HC Deb, 16 October 1995, col 31.

[127] Ibid.

[128] *The Times*, 17 October 1995.

[129] HC Deb, 19 October 1995, col 519.

[130] See also p 211 above.

detailed questioning. The Defence Committee nevertheless asserted that 'its power to secure the attendance of an individual *named* civil servant is unqualified',[131] and that it was unacceptable for the government to prevent these officials from attending, a power which the same committee reasserted in 1994.[132] Although such instances are rare, Westland is not unique: in 1992, the Ministry of Defence frustrated efforts by the Trade and Industry Committee's inquiry into arms to Iraq (following allegations that British companies had sold arms to Iraq), the Committee having wished to take evidence from recently retired officials.[133] In a decision which was subsequently criticised by Sir Richard Scott (a Lord Justice of Appeal who had been appointed by the government to investigate the allegations of arms for Iraq), the Ministry refused to help contact the officials in question on the ground that 'retired officials are not normally given access to departmental papers'.[134]

Sir Richard, in fact, proposed that in the interests of full and effective accountability, select committees should not be hindered by the government in summoning named officials to appear before them, as did the Public Service Committee in 1996 which proposed that 'there should be a presumption that Ministers accept requests by Committees that named individual civil servants give evidence to them'.[135] The government agreed that 'where a Select Committee indicates that it wishes to hear evidence from named civil servants, Ministers should normally accept such a request',[136] and the rules have been amended accordingly.[137] But these rules – sometimes known as the Osmotherly Rules – also provide that ministers retain the right to suggest an alternative official to that named by the committee if they feel that the former is better placed to represent them.[138] The rules further provide that it is not the role of a select committee to act as a disciplinary tribunal and that a minister may wish to suggest someone else where the named official is likely to be exposed 'to questioning about their personal responsibility or the allocation of blame as between them and others'.[139] But as the amended rules also make clear: 'If a Committee nonetheless insists on a particular official appearing before them, contrary to the Minister's wishes, the formal position remains that it could issue an order for attendance, and request the House to enforce it.'[140]

> In 2003, the Foreign Affairs Committee summoned Dr David Kelly, a distinguished weapons inspector seconded to the Defence Science and Technology Laboratory (a trading fund of the Ministry of Defence). There had been much political controversy arising from a claim by a BBC journalist that the government had exaggerated Saddam Hussain's military capabilities in the run-up to the war in Iraq. Dr Kelly had been disclosed as the source of the journalist's claim, and the Defence Secretary agreed to the Foreign Affairs Committee's request to take evidence from him in the light of an inquiry they had recently concluded on the war in Iraq. Despite the provisions of the Osmotherly Rules (and para 46 in particular), Dr Kelly was questioned not about government policy but about his own role in the preparation of the dossier and his relationship with journalists. It was felt by at least one member of the committee that Dr Kelly had been 'thrown to the

---

[131] HC 519 (1985–6).

[132] HC 27-I (1993–4). But this was contested by the government, which pointed out that it was ministers who were ultimately accountable to Parliament 'for the whole range of a department's business', even though this did not mean that 'Ministers must be expected to be personally responsible, in the sense of being creditworthy or blameworthy, for every act of their department' (Cm 2627, 1994, p 28).

[133] HC 86 (1991–2).

[134] HC 115 (1995–6), para F4.64.

[135] HC 313-I (1995–6), para 83.

[136] HC 67 (1996–7), p x.

[137] Cabinet Office, *Departmental Evidence and Response to Select Committees* (2009). The rules now provide that 'Where a Select Committee indicates that it wishes to take evidence from a particular named official, including special advisers, the presumption should be that the minister will agree to meet such a request' (para 44).

[138] Ibid, para 44.

[139] Ibid, para 46.

[140] Ibid, para 47.

wolves'. Dr Kelly took his own life two days later. The Defence Secretary had agreed to the Committee's request that Dr Kelly appear as a witness despite the fact that he was 'a relatively junior official', unaccustomed 'to being thrust into the public eye'. In the subsequent inquiry into the circumstances surrounding Dr Kelly's death, Lord Hutton concluded that 'there would have been a serious political storm' if the Defence Secretary had refused to permit Dr Kelly to appear before the Committee. The decision to agree to the request that Dr Kelly should appear was not one that could be 'subject to valid criticism'.[141]

E. Civil service: ethics and standards

The Civil Service Code

A statement of the ethical standards by which the civil service should be bound is to be found in the *Civil Service Code* which was brought into operation in 1996 and revised in 2006. The Code states explicitly that it forms part of the contractual relationship between the civil servant and his or her employer, and that it creates an expectation of 'high standards of behaviour'.[142] A slight and insubstantial document of 'core values', the Code is by no means exhaustive of the obligations of civil servants, with individual departments imposing additional requirements. The Code declares that civil servants are expected to carry out their role 'with dedication and a commitment to the Civil Service and its core values: integrity, honesty, objectivity and impartiality'. This means that civil servants are expected to put the obligations of public service above their own personal interests, to be truthful and open, to base their advice and decisions on rigorous analysis of the evidence, and to 'act solely according to the merits of the case', serving equally well 'Governments of different political persuasions'. Apart from laying out the various duties of the civil servant, the *Civil Service Code* includes a procedure for civil servants to raise concerns where they believe that they are being required to act in a way that contradicts the Code, or if they believe that others are acting contrary to the Code. The final stage in the procedure involves the Civil Service Commissioners for those who remain unsatisfied by a response given at a lower level.[143] Criminal or other unlawful activity may be reported to the police or other appropriate authorities. But there is no right, far less any duty, to bring wrongdoing to public notice.[144]

Significant provisions of the Code under the rubric of *integrity* require the civil servant to make sure that public money is used 'properly and efficiently', deal with the public fairly and promptly, and comply with the law and uphold the administration of justice. Under the rubric of *honesty*, civil servants are required to set out facts and issues truthfully, use resources only for the public purposes for which they are provided, and refrain from deceiving or knowingly misleading ministers, Parliament or others. So far as *objectivity* is concerned, this is stated to mean that the civil servant must provide accurate and evidence-based advice to ministers and others, take due account of expert and professional advice, and must not frustrate the implementation of policies once decisions have been taken. *Impartiality* means that the civil servant must carry out his or her responsibilities in a way that is fair, just and equitable and does not unjustifiably favour or discriminate against particular individuals or interests. The Code also addresses specifically the question of political impartiality, and provides that civil servants must serve governments of whatever political persuasion to the best of their ability, regardless of their own political beliefs, acting in a

---

[141] See HC 390-I (2003–04) (Foreign Affairs Committee Report) and Lord Hutton, Report of the Inquiry into the Circumstances Surrounding the Death of Dr David Kelly, C.M.G., above.

[142] The Code also states that it applies to all Home civil servants, and that those working for the Scottish Executive and the Welsh Assembly will have their own versions of the Code, as will the Executive Agencies.

[143] The Civil Service Commissioners were set up in 1870 with the rather different task of promoting competitive entry into the civil service on the principle of intellectual merit. There is no provision in the Code addressing the powers of the Commissioners in these circumstances.

[144] The issue was considered inconclusively by the Public Service Committee in HC 313-I (1995–6).

way that retains the confidence of ministers while ensuring that they will be able to establish a similar relationship with the members of a future government. It is specifically provided that civil servants must not act in a way that is determined by party political considerations, use official resources for party political purposes, or allow personal views to determine advice or actions.

Financial interests of civil servants

We have seen that ministers are subject to rules enforced by the Prime Minister that are intended inter alia to ensure that they do not profit improperly from their public position.[145] The *Civil Service Code* informs civil servants that they should not 'misuse [their] official position, for example by using information acquired in the course of [their] official duties to further [their] private interests or those of others'. Nor should they place themselves in a position which 'might reasonably be seen to compromise their personal judgment or integrity'. The separate and much larger *Civil Service Management Code* provides further that civil servants must have departmental permission before engaging in any occupation which might affect their work; they must also disclose any directorships or shareholdings that could be advanced by their official position and accept any instruction as to their retention, disposal or management. There are strict rules about civil servants entering into business relationships with government departments (such as letting property or buying surplus stock), as well as about the acceptance of gifts or hospitality which might compromise the civil servant's judgement or integrity. Breach of the *Civil Service Management Code* could give rise to contractual sanctions (including dismissal in appropriate cases), though in some cases, a failure of duty could also give rise to prosecution. The Prevention of Corruption Acts 1906 and 1916 apply to civil servants, and the *Civil Service Management Code* requires their provisions to be brought to the attention of staff.[146]

The public interest in integrity needs also to address the positions held by officials after they leave the civil service. Suspicions may be aroused – for example – where a civil servant with responsibility for defence procurement is employed by a weapons' manufacturer following retirement from the service. How can we be sure that the official was not moved by considerations of personal interest when making major decisions before retirement? The Business Appointment Rules provide for the scrutiny of appointments which former civil servants propose to accept in the first two years after they leave the service. The aim of the rules is to 'avoid any suspicion that the advice and decisions of a serving officer might be influenced by the hope or expectation of future employment with a particular firm or organisation'; and 'to avoid the risk that a particular firm might gain an improper advantage over its competitors by employing someone who, in the course of their official duties, has had access to technical or other information which those competitors might legitimately regard as their own trade secrets or to information relating to proposed developments in government policy which may affect that firm or its competitors'. Applications submitted under the rules may be approved without condition, and in some cases a waiting period or other conditions may be imposed. The process is supervised by the Advisory Committee on Business Appointments, an independent body appointed by the Prime Minister whose members have experience of the relationship between the civil service and the private sector. There have been calls in the past for the rules to be strengthened.[147]

---

[145] Section C in this chapter.

[146] The foregoing provisions are drawn from *Civil Service Management Code*, Section 4. See also pp 281–2 below, on links with lobbyists.

[147] See HC 651 (2006–07), and the government's response (HC 1087 (2006–07)), The current rules from which the foregoing is drawn are to be found in the *Civil Service Management Code*, Section 4.3, Annex A. They are also to be found in the Annual Reports of the Advisory Committee on Business Committees, which helpfully gives an account of the advice it has given in individual cases. See http://acoba.independent.gov.uk.

Political activities of civil servants

Servants of the Crown are prohibited from parliamentary candidature and disqualified from membership of the Commons.[148] But should civil servants be subject to additional limitations, to secure the political impartiality of the civil service as a whole? The *Civil Service Management Code* points out that 'from the nature of the work which a civil servant is required to do and the context in which he has to do it, there must be certain restrictions on the type of political activities in which a civil servant is allowed to participate and the extent to which he may do so will, of course, depend on his position and seniority'.[149] The present scheme, first brought into force in 1954,[150] recognises that the political neutrality of the civil service is fundamental, but that the rules need not be the same for all members of the service. The scheme was fully reviewed by the Armitage Committee in 1978, in response to requests from the civil service unions for greater political freedom for civil servants. The committee reasserted the constitutional importance of the political neutrality of the civil service. It recommended that the scheme then in force should continue subject to substantial changes in its operation, the effect of which would be to reduce the number of civil servants in the 'restricted' category.[151] In 1984 these recommendations were adopted after extensive discussion between government and the civil service unions.[152]

Participation in national political activities (for example, holding office in a political party; expressing public views on matters of national political controversy) is barred to the Senior Civil Service and other senior grades. This 'politically restricted' category must seek permission to take part in local political activities and must comply with any conditions laid down by their department or agency. A second 'intermediate' category may, with the leave of their departments, take part in national or local activities, although some grades have a mandate to take part in such activities without the need for permission. In cases where there is no mandate, permission will normally be refused only where civil servants are employed in sensitive areas where the impartiality of the civil service is most at risk. A post is regarded as sensitive if it is closely engaged in policy assistance to ministers; it is in the private office of a minister; it requires the post-holder to speak regularly for the government; the post-holder represents the government in dealing with overseas governments; or the post-holder is involved in regular face-to-face contact with the public. The third 'politically free' category combines industrial and non-office grades: they are free to engage in all political activities, national and local, except when on duty or on official premises or while wearing their uniform. These procedures are reinforced by the *Civil Service Code* which provides that civil servants must comply with political restrictions that apply to them.[153]

Civil servants and lobbyists

In 1998 new guidelines about contacts with lobbyists were issued to civil servants. These followed a press report that a journalist posing as an American businessman had been introduced by a lobbyist to a senior Downing Street official. In a disputed remark the official is reported to have said

---

[148] For comparable provisions in local government which were found not to violate Convention rights, see *Ahmed v United Kingdom* (2000) 29 EHRR 1.

[149] *R v Civil Service Appeal Board, ex p Bruce* [1988] 3 All ER 686, at p 690 (May LJ). The arrangements are dealt with in *Civil Service Management Code*, Section 4.4.

[150] See Cmd 7718, 1949, and Cmd 8783, 1953.

[151] Cmnd 7057, 1978.

[152] HC Deb, 26 March 1981, col 1186; 4 March 1982, col 503; 19 July 1984, col 272 (WA).

[153] Ch 25. Apart from personal involvement in political activities, civil servants may wish to participate in political action through their trade unions. Civil service unions may establish political funds under what is now the Trade Union and Labour Relations (Consolidation) Act 1992 to enable them more effectively to represent their members by campaigning politically. None is affiliated to any political party (although there are no legal restrictions on such affiliation), but several are affiliated to the TUC. See further ch 24 A.

to the putative businessman: 'Just tell me what you want, who you want to meet and . . . I will make the call for you.'[154] As we have seen in chapter 11 B, the Cash for Questions affair in the 1990s led to the creation of the Committee on Standards in Public Life and tight rules to regulate the relationship between MPs and lobbyists. But at the time of 'Lobbygate', as this incident was known, there was no regulation of civil service contact with lobbyists. The new rules adopt what might best be referred to as a minimalist approach and reflect the view in the first report of the Committee on Standards in Public Life that 'it is the right of everyone to lobby Parliament and ministers, and it is for public institutions to develop ways of controlling the reaction to approaches from professional lobbyists in such a way as to give due weight to their case while always taking care to consider the public interest'.[155] The government's approach in the guidelines then is not to ban contacts between civil servants and lobbyists, but 'to insist that wherever and whenever they take place they should be conducted in accordance with the *Civil Service Code*, and the principles of public life set out by the Nolan Committee' which are considered in chapter 14 E. Indeed, the guidelines acknowledge that lobbyists are 'a feature of our democratic system'.

The guidelines are drawn from the principle in the *Civil Service Code* that civil servants should conduct themselves with honesty and integrity. Some activities are said to be 'completely un-acceptable' and to be serious disciplinary offences which could lead to dismissal. These are the leaking of confidential or sensitive material, especially market-sensitive material, to a lobbyist and deliberately helping a lobbyist to attract business by arranging for clients to have privileged access to a minister or undue influence over policy. Other situations are to be handled with care, although again any misjudgement could lead to disciplinary action. Ten basic rules are set out. These provide that the civil servants should not: grant a lobbyist preferential or premature access to information; meet one group making representations on a particular issue without offering other groups a similar opportunity; accept gifts from a lobbyist; do anything which might breach parliamentary privilege (for example, by revealing the contents of a report not yet published); use knowledge of the workings of government to impress a lobbyist; help a lobbyist to obtain a benefit to which he or she is not entitled; or give the impression of offering a lobbyist preferential access to ministers. Civil servants should also declare to their department any family or business interests which may create a conflict of interest with departmental work; and take care in accepting hospitality from a lobbyist. Although meetings between civil servants and lobbyists are now recorded,[156] the government rejected proposals that these records should be published.[157]

A statutory framework for the civil service

The large-scale changes to the civil service since 1988 have given rise to a great deal of analysis and assessment. In a major report in 1998, the House of Lords Select Committee on Public Service concluded that the changes represented a 'radical' and 'fundamental revolution' in public administration. But the committee accepted that there had been 'little open or public debate about the extent of the structural changes being made to the Civil Service', and expressed itself as being not satisfied that 'the constitutional implications of the changes were fully thought through' before they were introduced. There was a tension between the (economic) justification for change based on efficiency, effectiveness and value for money, on the one hand, and traditional (political) concerns based on responsibility and accountability, on the other. The creation of the executive agencies was not thought, in a constitutional sense, to 'recast the architecture of the state', 'but only so long as accountability of Ministers to Parliament for the work of executive agencies remains the same as their accountability for any other aspect of their Department's work'.

---

[154] *The Observer*, 5 July 1998. The allegations were strongly denied: HC Deb, 8 July 1998, col 1065.
[155] Cm 280-I, 1995, para 72.
[156] See Cm 4557-I, 2000, R 28; and HC 1058 (2008–09).
[157] See HC 36 (2008–09), and the government's response HC 1058 (2008–09).

The committee was concerned that 'the devolution to executive agencies was contributing to a sense of disunity in the Civil Service' although not yet to fragmentation. There was a need to determine how far this process of reducing the role of the core civil service should go and a need for 'open and public debate' about the irreducible nucleus of functions which must be carried out by the core civil service: this is as much 'a matter for the governed as for the governors'.

The process of civil service reform continued under the Labour government elected in 1997 and has taken on a new dimension.[158] In the white paper, *Modernising Government*, it was announced in 1999 that permanent secretaries and heads of department would have performance targets 'for taking forward the government's modernisation agenda and ensuring delivery of the government's key targets'.[159] There is now great emphasis not only on the public service values of impartiality, objectivity and integrity, but also on the need for 'greater creativity, radical thinking, and collaborative working', as well as efficiency in the delivery of public services.[160] This 'rapid, fundamental and often controversial change in Whitehall'[161] has reinforced calls for a Civil Service Act to replace the current regulation of the civil service by royal prerogative which enables changes to be made to the organisation, structure and composition of the civil service without any parliamentary or public debate. Many proposals to this effect have been made by parliamentary committees, and by the Committee on Standards in Public Life,[162] the government has indicated a commitment to such a measure,[163] and a draft Civil Service Bill was published in late 2004.[164] Although this made little progress, as we have seen a new statutory framework for the civil service was finally introduced by the Constitutional Reform and Governance Act 2010.

F. Open government and freedom of information

Background

Discussion of the structure of the civil service and its proposed regulation by statute leads directly to a consideration of open government and the public right of access to official information. Historically there was no such right in the United Kingdom, in contrast to the position in other parliamentary democracies (notably Australia, Canada and New Zealand) where the right of access to information was introduced much earlier than in Britain.[165] Such access is important for a number of reasons, not least because of the insights it provides into the conduct of government and the enhanced opportunities it provides for politicians, the press and the public more effectively to hold government to account. In 1979 a green paper on open government was published by the then Labour government, offering modestly a non-binding code of practice on access to official information.[166] But electoral defeat meant that these proposals were never implemented. Although campaigners for open government were thus disappointed, important initiatives in the

---

[158] On the implementation of these reforms, see C D Foster (2001) 79 *Public Administration* 725. For further analysis, see Hennessy, *The Prime Minister*, ch 18. For a full account of civil service reform, see Bogdanor (ed.), *The British Constitution in the Twentieth Century*, ch 7.

[159] See Cm 4310, 1999.

[160] Cabinet Office, *Civil Service Reform – Delivery and Values* (2004).

[161] HC 128 (2003–04), para 4.

[162] Cm 4557-I, 2000.

[163] Cm 6373, 2004.

[164] Ibid.

[165] Open government was actively discouraged by the Official Secrets Act 1911, esp s 2 by which it was an offence for a civil servant to communicate any information to a member of the public without authorisation. There was no right to information and no right to disclose it. Section 2 of the 1911 Act was repealed by the Official Secrets Act 1989. See ch 25.

[166] Cmnd 7520, 1979.

direction of reform were nevertheless taken in the 1980s and 1990s. Apart from a number of specific statutory provisions,[167] these included the *Citizen's Charter* introduced in 1991, providing that every citizen is entitled to expect openness and stating unequivocally that there should be no secrecy about how public services are run, how much they cost, who is in charge and whether or not they are meeting their standards.[168] This was followed in 1993 by the white paper, *Open Government*, which revived the idea of a non-binding code of practice. Such a code was, in fact, introduced in 1994 and revised in 1997,[169] allowing for complaints to be made to the Ombudsman (through the medium of a member of Parliament) that information had been unreasonably withheld.[170]

It was the Labour government's turn to publish a white paper ('with green edges') on freedom of information in 1997.[171] The original plan was to replace existing open government initiatives (including the Code of Practice) 'with clear and consistent requirements which would apply across government'.[172] The white paper proposed the introduction of 'a right, exercisable by any individual, company or other body to records or information of any date held by the public authority concerned in connection with its public functions'.[173] The presumption would be that information should be released unless disclosure would cause harm to one or more specified interests or would be contrary to the public interest. But these original proposals were abandoned and responsibility for open government transferred from the Cabinet Office to the Home Office (said to be 'one of the most overworked and accident-prone departments of government').[174] A diluted measure was subsequently introduced, this forming the basis of what is now the Freedom of Information Act 2000,[175] which was not brought fully into force until 1 January 2005, along with a separate regime for access to environmental information held by public authorities.[176] Although the Act gives a legal right of access to official information, it was nevertheless criticised for being too restrictive in a number of key respects, these criticisms being voiced on two occasions by the Public Administration Committee of the House of Commons.[177] The government openly acknowledged some of these criticisms,[178] and responded by having 'some of that diluting removed'.[179] A similar regime was introduced in Scotland by the Freedom of Information (Scotland) Act 2002, and the Environmental Information (Scotland) Regulations 2004.[180]

Scope of the Act

The Freedom of Information Act 'creates a general right of access to information upon written request made to a public authority'.[181] Any person making a request for information is entitled

---

[167] Access to Personal Files Act 1987, Access to Medical Reports Act 1988, Access to Health Records Act 1990, Environmental Information Regulations 1992, SI 1992 No 3240. Also important was the Data Protection Act 1984 (now Data Protection Act 1998). See ch 22.

[168] Cm 1588, 1991. See C Scott [1999] PL 595; G Drewry [2002] PL 12.

[169] Cm 2290, 1993.

[170] See Birkinshaw, *Freedom of Information*, pp 238–50.

[171] *Your Right to Know: Freedom of Information*, Cm 3818, 1997. For comment, see P Birkinshaw [1998] PL 176.

[172] Cm 3818, 1997, para 1.6.

[173] Ibid, para 2.6.

[174] HL Deb, 20 April 2000, col 836.

[175] For a valuable account, see S Palmer, in Beatson and Cripps (eds), *Freedom of Expression and Freedom of Information*, ch 15.

[176] SI 2004 No 3391, implementing EC Directive 2003/4/EC. These regulations revoked the earlier SI 1992 No 3240.

[177] HC 570-I (1998–9); HC 78 (1999–2000).

[178] HL Deb, 20 April 2000, col 824.

[179] Ibid, col 831.

[180] SSI 2004 No 520.

[181] *R(Ofcom) v Information Commissioner* [2008] EWHC 1445 (Admin), para 5.

(*a*) to be told in writing by the authority whether it holds information of the type specified in the request, and if so (*b*) to have that information communicated to him or her (s 1). A public authority's duty to comply with (*a*) is referred to as 'the duty to confirm or deny'. The public authorities to which the Act applies are listed in Schedule 1: there are over 400 such bodies,[182] a list which may be added to by order of the Secretary of State for Justice (now the minister responsible for freedom of information) (s 4).[183] The list – which inevitably is amended as new legislation creates new public authorities – includes central government departments, local authorities, national health service bodies, schools and educational institutions, and the police. A few of the bodies in question are listed only in relation to some information they hold: for example, the BBC is listed 'in respect of information held for purposes other than those of journalism, art or literature'. In this respect the Act contrasts sharply with the Human Rights Act 1998, which also applies to public authorities. There is no definition of a public authority in the Human Rights Act (save to make clear that a court is a public authority), the scope of the Act being left to the courts to determine.[184] Although there ought thus to be less room for uncertainty about the application of the Freedom of Information Act 2000, tortuous difficulties have arisen about the nature of its application to bodies like the BBC.[185]

A request for information is to be made in writing to the relevant public authority (s 8), which may (but need not) charge a fee for the information in accordance with regulations (s 9).[186] The fee may be not insignificant, and may be charged at a rate of up to £25 an hour.[187] Requests are to be dealt with promptly and within 20 working days of receipt (s 10). There is a right only to have access to information: there is no right to have access to documents,[188] though in practice documents will often be produced.[189] The authority may refuse to comply with a request for information where the cost would be excessive (s 12), or where the application is vexatious (s 14). The public authorities to which the Act applies must provide advice and assistance to persons who propose to make or who have made requests under the Act (s 16). Where an application for information is refused, the public authority must issue the applicant with a notice explaining the grounds for the refusal (s 17). Publication schemes must be approved by the Information Commissioner (s 19), who is also required to produce model publication schemes (s 20). The publication scheme should specify the classes of information which the authority in question publishes or intends to publish, specifying the manner in which information of each class is to be published, indicating whether a charge is made. It has been said that 'the requirement for all public authorities to apply a scheme for publication – in effect to say what, when and how information will be published – is probably the most powerful push to openness in the [Act]'.[190]

---

[182] Although there are over 400 bodies listed in the Act, some of these are listed collectively (such as NHS bodies, universities and local authorities). As a result there are over 100,000 individual bodies to which the Act applies.

[183] The Act also allows an order to be made bringing in private bodies exercising public functions, such as companies running prisons and the British Board of Film Classification: HL Deb, 20 April 2000, col 825.

[184] See ch 19 C.

[185] *BBC* v *Information Commissioner* [2009] UKHL 9. See subsequently *BBC* v *Information Commissioner* [2009] EWHC 2348 (Admin).

[186] The regulations provide a limit of £600 or £450 depending on the nature of the public authority: SI 2004 No 3244.

[187] See SI 2004 No 3244.

[188] Compare TFEU, art 15: any citizen of the Union, and any natural or legal person residing or based in the Union, has a 'right of access' to documents of the Union institutions. See Regulation 1049/2001/EC. For fuller treatment, see Douglas-Scott, *The Constitutional Law of the European Union*, ch 3.

[189] *Home Office* v *Information Commissioner* [2009] EWHC 1611 (Admin), para 8.

[190] HL Deb, 20 April 2000, col 826 (Lord Falconer).

Exemptions

It is almost certainly the case that 'no legislation which any responsible government could introduce would completely satisfy [the more ardent advocates of freedom of information]'.[191] Nevertheless it is a striking feature of the FOI regime that there are so many categories of exempted information. Many of the 24 sections of exempt information (ss 21–44) are wholly predictable, with the exemptions falling into two groups: those which carry absolute exemption and those which do not (s 2). In the latter case, the exemption applies only where the public interest in maintaining the exclusion of the duty to confirm or deny (s 1(1)(a)), or in withholding the information (s 1(1)(b)) outweighs the public interest in disclosing whether the public authority holds the information or in communicating it to the person seeking access, as the case may be (s 2(1),(2)).[192] Information which will be absolutely exempt includes that which is reasonably accessible to the public by other means (s 21), information which relates to bodies dealing with security matters (s 23), information relating to court records (s 32), information which consists of personal data the release of which would violate the data protection principles (s 40),[193] information obtained in confidence (s 41) and information the disclosure of which is prohibited by statute, incompatible with an EU obligation or would constitute a contempt of court (s 44).

The larger category of information to which an absolute exemption does not apply includes information which is held by the authority with a view to its future publication (s 22), information required for the purpose of safeguarding national security (s 24), information relating to defence (s 26), information the disclosure of which would prejudice international relations (s 27), information the disclosure of which would prejudice relations between Whitehall and the devolved administrations or between the devolved administrations (s 28), and so on at some length. Among the other noteworthy exemptions in this context are information which if disclosed would or would be likely to prejudice the economic interests of the United Kingdom or any part thereof or any administration in the United Kingdom (s 29);[194] information which relates to criminal investigations conducted by a wide range of statutory agencies (s 30) or law enforcement (s 31); information which relates to the formulation or development of government policy (s 35); as well as an exemption for information held by a government department which if disclosed could prejudice the effective conduct of public affairs (s 36). It will be noted that many of these exemptions apply on the low threshold that publication would cause 'prejudice'. It was felt by some that the higher standard of 'substantial prejudice' or 'necessity' would be more appropriate.

Public interest considerations

Since the Act was introduced, there have been several notable decisions of the High Court in which government departments have challenged rulings that they release information. Many of these have been contested on public interest grounds, which on some occasions concerned important constitutional principles and practices not always consistent with freedom of information. In *HM Treasury v Information Commissioner*,[195] it was held that the convention that the law officers' advice to ministers (in this case the Attorney General's advice on the compatibility of the Financial Services and Markets Act 2000 with the Human Rights Act 1998) had not been given sufficient weight by the Information Tribunal in ordering its release. This convention had been

---

[191] HL Deb, 20 April 2000, col 863.

[192] See *Home Office v Information Commissioner*, above: a broad judgment is required to determine where the public interest lies (para 25), citing *Office of Communications v Information Commissioner* [2009] EWCA Civ 90.

[193] These principles are set out in the Data Protection Act 1998 (see ch 22 below). On how personal data protected by the 1998 Act might be rendered suitable for release under the FOI Act 2000, see *Common Services Agency v Scottish Information Commissioner* [2008] UKHL 47.

[194] On the purpose of this exemption, see HL Deb, 19 October 2000, col 1287.

[195] [2009] EWHC 1811 (Admin).

breached on only five occasions since 1968, and in the view of Blake J, it had not been modified by the 2000 Act. It had rather been preserved but rendered 'amenable to being out-weighed by greater considerations of the public interest requiring disclosure of information in either limb of the Convention'. Section 35(1)(c) of the 2000 Act specifically refers to 'the provision of advice by any of the Law Officers or any request for the provision of such advice' as information exempt from disclosure, and the tribunal was found to have erred by 'failing to conclude that Parliament intended real weight should continue to be afforded to [the] Law Officers' Convention'.

On the other hand, in *House of Commons v Information Commissioner*,[196] there was no question of parliamentary privilege standing in the way of a request for information about MPs' allowances,[197] which had been required by the Information Commissioner and the Information Tribunal. In a strong judgment it was held by a three-member Administrative Court that the 'legitimate public interest engaged by these applications [was] obvious', with questions relating to MPs' allowances having 'a wide resonance throughout the body politic', and to 'bear on public confidence in the operation of our democratic system at its very pinnacle'. Also, in *Home Office v Information Commissioner*[198] it was held that the public interest in knowing that civil servants conduct themselves properly was a factor legitimately taken into account in what was referred to as a 'meta application', whereby the applicant sought the disclosure of information about the way in which earlier FOI applications by him to the Home Office had been handled. The applicant suspected that his claims had been treated in a discriminatory way. Here, constitutional principle favoured rather than militated against disclosure, the Commissioner having resisted arguments from the Home Office that 'disclosure in this case would make officials responsible for providing advice and recording information less likely to perform their duties properly'.

Enforcement and remedies

Enforcement of the Act is the initial responsibility of the Information Commissioner (s 18). A complaint may be made to the Commissioner that a public authority has failed to comply with the requirements of Part I of the Act and if the complaint is upheld the Commissioner may issue a decision notice specifying steps to be taken to comply with the Act (s 50). These notices are published on the Commission's website, and there is now a significant volume of them that – along with the other enforcement responsibilities of the Commissioner – still awaits full academic analysis. The Commissioner is also empowered to issue an enforcement notice (s 52), failure to comply with which may lead to the matter being referred to the High Court or Court of Session to be punished as a contempt of court (s 54). The right of appeal to the Information Tribunal against a decision of the Commissioner (s 57) has been transferred to the unified tribunal system,[199] with a further appeal on a point of law to the High Court or the Court of Session (s 59). Under s 60, the Tribunal (which in some cases will be the First-tier Tribunal but in others the Upper Tribunal) has been given powers to quash a ministerial certificate protecting national security information from disclosure. As an expert body, the tribunal 'is not required to defer to the views of Ministers or civil servants' when exercising its powers under the Act,[200] though as already indicated the courts have emphasised on several occasions the need to take seriously government claims that information must be withheld in particular cases on public interest

---

[196] [2008] EWHC 1084 (Admin). See P Leyland [2009] PL 675.

[197] But compare *Office of Government Commerce v Information Commissioner* [2008] EWHC 737 (Admin). See chapter 11 above.

[198] [2009] EWHC 1611 (Admin).

[199] Tribunals, Courts and Enforcement Act 2007; see ch 29 below. Under the new appeal system, it is intended that the judicial and non-judicial members of the Tribunal will transfer across and continue to hear information rights appeals.

[200] *Home Office v Information Commissioner* [2009] EWHC 1611 (Admin), at para 29.

grounds.[201] It is an offence to destroy or tamper with information, but only if this is done after a request for disclosure has been made (s 77).

Although he has wide powers under the Act, the government has nevertheless been reluctant to leave the last word to the Commissioner (or the tribunals or courts), taking the remarkable view that it would be 'profoundly undemocratic' to permit the Commissioner to have the final say on what should be disclosed. Section 53 thus contains a so-called 'executive override', a 'kind of nuclear option for the Government',[202] allowing a minister in some limited circumstances to override a decision notice (under s 50) or an enforcement notice (under s 52) of the Commissioner which has been served on a government department.[203] This power – to be exercised by means of a ministerial certificate which must be laid before Parliament – reflects the government's belief that 'there will be certain cases dealing with the most sensitive issues where a senior member of the Government, able to seek advice from his Cabinet colleagues, should decide on the final question of public interest in relation to disclosure'.[204] The power was used in 2007 to prevent publication of minutes of two Cabinet meetings in March 2003 (relating to the Iraq war), and again in 2009 to prevent the publication of minutes of Cabinet sub-committee meetings in 1997 (relating to devolution). On this latter occasion, the Justice Secretary claimed that 'disclosure of the information in this case would put the convention [of collective responsibility] at serious risk of harm'.[205] The consistent use of the over-ride in relation to Cabinet minutes (suggesting the existence of a policy) seems calculated to be tested in judicial review proceedings at some point.

---

[201] See also *Common Services Agency* v *Scottish Information Commissioner,* above, para [4].
[202] HL Deb, 22 November 2000, col 843.
[203] The power applies only to decisions taken in relation to exempt information.
[204] HL Deb, 14 November 2000, col 258.
[205] *BBC News*, 10 December 2009.

CHAPTER 14

Public bodies and regulatory agencies

We have already considered the constitutional position of government departments and have seen that they are staffed by civil servants and headed by ministers who are responsible to Parliament for their activities. When functions are entrusted to local authorities, the administrative structure is very different from that in central government and political responsibility for the policies and decisions of local councils is borne by the elected councillors. Today many public tasks are entrusted not to central or local government, but to a wide variety of official boards, commissions and other agencies. Some are well known, such as the BBC, the Equality and Human Rights Commission, and ACAS; but many of them operate in obscurity, known only to a few civil servants and specialists in the area concerned. Apart from the rich variety of fields in which they operate, it is also the case that these bodies perform many different functions, some being purely advisory, others having responsibility to administer public services, while others perform a regulatory or supervisory role, sometimes empowered to impose penalties. It is difficult to generalise about such diversity, but these bodies have one feature in common, namely that the members of the boards and agencies are not publicly elected. Instead, these members have all been appointed to their posts, in the vast majority of cases by central government (that is, by the minister of the department concerned with the activity in question).

It is perhaps because these bodies appear in such a variety of shapes and sizes that they have no common appellation, no common framework, and no common regulatory structure. 'Public bodies' is an official term used by government, but this applies only to what are referred to as Non Departmental Public Bodies (NDPBs), though the term in the past also included public corporations (of which there are now very few). Public bodies do not include regulatory agencies, such as those established when the different public utilities were privatised in the 1980s and 1990s. Nor do they include the less formal government advisory bodies which have multiplied in recent years, operating beyond some of the more formal controls to which public bodies and regulatory agencies may be subject. These include task forces, ad hoc advisory groups and reviews appointed by ministers or departments to give advice on specific issues, though sometimes they develop into something more elaborate. But whatever their nature or form, the evolution of such bodies is not something about which constitutional lawyers can be sanguine: this is a 'major, if under-explored', feature of the modern constitution,[1] giving rise to questions about the system of appointment to the bodies in question and the amount of patronage vested in ministers, as well as the accountability of the bodies for the decisions which they make and the activities which they pursue.

A. Origins and purpose

History

The creation of specialised public agencies that are not government departments is not new. In the eighteenth century, there were innumerable bodies of commissioners created by private Acts, which exercised limited powers for such purposes as police, paving, lighting, turnpikes and local improvements. Through the curtailment of the powers of the Privy Council in the previous

---

[1] P Norton (2004) 57 *Parliamentary Affairs* 785.

century, they were free from administrative control by central government, but in England they were subject to legal control by means of the prerogative writs issued by the Court of King's Bench. These bodies were essentially local in character. In the period of social and administrative reform that followed the reform of Parliament in 1832, experiments were made in setting up national agencies with powers covering the whole country. One of the most notable experiments occurred in 1834 when the English Poor Law was reformed. The Poor Law Commissioners enforced strict central control on the local administration of poor relief, by means of rules, orders and inspection. Yet no minister answered for the commissioners in Parliament, to defend them against political attack or to control their decisions. In 1847, the experiment gave way to a system based on a minister responsible to Parliament but similar experiments occurred, such as the General Board of Health in 1848. Administration by the board system was much used in Scotland and in Ireland. By the late nineteenth century, it was accepted that the vesting of public powers in departments of central government had the great constitutional advantage of securing political control through ministerial responsibility.[2] As Chester remarked, the House of Commons has never found a way of making anybody other than ministers accountable to it.[3]

In the twentieth century, new public bodies were created as the state took wide-ranging powers to intervene more extensively in social and economic affairs. Steps were taken to regulate working conditions (and to create trade boards and wages councils for this purpose); new national insurance and social security systems were created (with different boards and commissions established to manage the various schemes); and a national health service was set up (along with various bodies to administer its operation). In addition, the Labour governments from 1945 onwards adopted a programme of nationalisation of many key areas of the economy, leading to the creation of public corporations like the National Coal Board and British Rail to administer the industries taken into public ownership. It is true that since 1979 a major programme of privatisation has seen the dismantling of public corporations and the transfer to the private sector of many of the activities which had previously been the responsibility of the state. Yet this has not led to a decline in the need for public bodies, but rather the emergence of different kinds of bodies to regulate rather than manage the public utilities. These include the Gas and Electricity Markets Authority established under the Utilities Act 2000, with similar bodies having been created by the legislation privatising telecommunications, water, and the railways.[4] Regulatory agencies have also been established in a number of other fields as the role of the state evolves from one of direct provider of public services to one of regulator of public service providers.

Reasons for the creation of public corporations and non-governmental bodies[5]

In theory, the tasks entrusted to public boards and agencies could be undertaken directly by civil servants working in government departments, although this would mean a vast increase in the civil service and the adoption by it of new methods. Indeed, before the Post Office was established in 1969 as a public corporation, postal and telephone services had been for very many years provided by the Post Office as a government department.[6] But the existence of public corporations affords strong evidence for the view that departmental administration of major industries is likely to be less efficient and less flexible than management by a public board. The post-war

---

[2] See also ch 7 above and, for rise and fall of the board system, F M G Willson (1955) 33 *Public Administration* 43, and Parris, *Constitutional Bureaucracy*, ch 3.

[3] D N Chester (1979) 57 *Public Administration* 51, 54.

[4] See section D below.

[5] The extensive literature includes: Chester, *The Nationalization of British Industry 1945–51*; Robson, *Nationalised Industries and Public Ownership*; Friedmann and Garner (eds), *Government Enterprise*; Prosser, *Nationalised Industries and Public Control*.

[6] See now Postal Services Act 2000.

nationalisation legislation sought to apply the concept of the public corporation associated with the late Herbert Morrison.[7] This aimed at a combination of vigorous and efficient business management with an appropriate measure of public control and accountability. Civil service methods, Treasury control and complete accountability to Parliament were considered unsuited to the successful running of a large industry. In the 1945–51 period, when major public utilities, transport and energy undertakings were acquired by the state, they were thus entrusted not to departments but to new statutory boards. The relevant ministers were given important powers relating to the boards but were not expected to become concerned with day-to-day management of the industries. Similar reasoning led to the creation of public corporations to take over certain activities formerly performed by departments, for example the Atomic Energy Authority (1954) and the British Airports Authority (1965).

Another reason for establishing public corporations is to entrust an activity to an autonomous body and thereby reduce the scope for direct political control or interference. The existence of the BBC separate from the government is necessary if ministers are not to be responsible for every programme broadcast. The same reason explains why many grant-giving bodies have been established to distribute funds provided by Parliament. The government is responsible for the total grants made to such bodies as research councils, arts councils and the Higher Education Funding Councils, but not for the detailed allocation of these funds. The aim of enabling discretionary decisions to be made by an agency without regard to short-term political considerations explains also the existence of bodies such as the Equality and Human Rights Commission and the Competition Commission. However, ministers may not absolve themselves of broad responsibility for the existence, activities, funding and composition of such agencies. Nor have all attempts to take a sensitive area of administration 'out of politics' by entrusting it to an appointed board been successful.[8]

Privatisation

As we have seen, Conservative governments after 1979 operated a policy of privatisation of public corporations, whereby the ownership of many state-controlled enterprises was transferred to the private sector. In an important report by the Public Accounts Committee published in 1998, it was stated that:

> During that time over 150 United Kingdom businesses have been privatised, ranging from major undertakings with billions of pounds to small loss-making enterprises. In the process, the proportion of Gross Domestic Product accounted for by state-owned businesses has fallen from 11 per cent to 2 per cent. These privatisations have shared a number of overall objectives, including improving the efficiency of the business concerned, promoting the development of a market economy, reducing state debt and increasing state revenues.[9]

The privatisation programme took several forms, including the denationalisation and break up of state corporations such as British Gas, British Telecom, British Airways, British Coal and British Rail;[10] the disposal of shares in companies previously owned by the government (such as Jaguar, Rolls-Royce, Amersham International, British Nuclear Fuels Ltd, and Cable and Wireless);[11] and

---

[7] See his book, *Government and Parliament*, ch 12.

[8] As with financial relief for the unemployed in 1934: see Millett, *The Unemployment Assistance Board*.

[9] HC 992 (1997–8).

[10] See Gas Act 1986, Civil Aviation Act 1980, Telecommunications Act 1984, Railways Act 1993 and Coal Industry Act 1994. Other major privatisations included water (Water Act 1989) and electricity (Electricity Act 1989).

[11] See Atomic Energy (Miscellaneous Provisions) Act 1981 (Amersham, BNFL); British Telecommunications Act 1981, s 79 (Cable and Wireless). See also Atomic Energy Authority Act 1995. For the developments in the motor industry, see A A McLaughlin and W A Maloney (1996) 74 *Public Administration* 435.

the sale of government holdings in companies such as British Petroleum.[12] Two hotly contested privatisations, for different reasons, were of the water supply industry in England and Wales and the Trustee Savings Bank,[13] while two highly symbolic privatisations were those of the coal industry and the railways, both of which had been nationalised by the post-war Labour government.

For a number of reasons, this programme of privatisation was likely to be irreversible. Indeed, it is not to be overlooked that the process of off-loading state enterprises continues under Labour governments elected since 1997;[14] nor that when the government intervened to rescue the banking industry during the global financial crisis in 2009, it did not do so by creating an elaborate public corporation. Rather, the government became a major shareholder in a number of banks, with a company wholly owned by the Treasury – United Kingdom Financial Investments – being established (without the inconvenience of primary legislation) to manage the government's shareholdings on behalf of the taxpayer. It is expected that the banks in question – RBS, Lloyd's Banking Group, Northern Rock, and Bradford and Bingley – will be returned fully to private ownership as soon as economic conditions are such as to ensure an adequate return for the Treasury.[15] And while it is true that the Post Office remains in public ownership for the time being, this is not necessarily a reflection of a strong political commitment to an exclusively public postal service, with the government's several attempts in the past to secure private funding for the Post Office having foundered in the face of stiff political opposition.[16]

B. Classification, status and composition of public bodies

Classification

The wide range of activities exercised by public bodies makes it difficult to classify them. The approach adopted by the government, is helpful, but limited, with the Cabinet Office until recently dividing public bodies into three groups, excluding the Bank of England which is now classified as a 'central bank'. These three categories were said to reflect different functions and funding arrangements and included:

1 Public corporations, previously a term that covered a number of nationally significant bodies, such as the National Coal Board, the British Railways Board, the British Gas Corporation, and the British Steel Corporation. It is now greatly diminished in significance, but would still include bodies such as the Royal Mail, the BBC and the Channel 4 Television Corporation, though not much else besides.

2 National Health Service bodies which manage an organisation which employs c 1.5 million people, and which is frequently re-organised. NHS bodies currently include special health authorities (such as the National Blood Authority) and the 10 strategic health authorities, as well as NHS trusts (such as primary care trusts, ambulance trusts, and acute trusts), foundation trusts, and mental health trusts.

3 Non-departmental public bodies, a huge collection of 790 bodies in 2008 which is in turn classified to include as follows:

(a) Executive NDPBs (of which there were 198) are statutory bodies which carry out administrative, regulatory and executive functions. Examples of such bodies include the Advisory Conciliation

---

[12] On this form of state intervention (the mixed enterprise), see pp 309–10 of the 10th edn of this book.
[13] See *Ross v Lord Advocate* [1986] 1 WLR 1077; and M Percival (1987) 50 MLR 231.
[14] See for example Commonwealth Development Corporation Act 1999 and Transport Act 2000 (National Air Traffic Services).
[15] See www.ukfi.gov.uk.
[16] See most recently HC 172 (2008–09).

and Arbitration Service (ACAS), the Equality and Human Rights Commission, the Competition Commission, the Higher Education Funding Council, the Local Better Regulation Office, and the Independent Police Complaints Commission.

(*b*) Advisory NDPBs (of which there were 410) set up to 'provide independent and expert advice to ministers on particular topics of interest'. Included in this category are the Advisory Committee on Pesticides, the Commission on Human Medicines, the Low Pay Commission, the Fuel Poverty Advisory Group, the Administrative Justice and Tribunals Council, and the Risk and Regulation Advisory Council.

(*c*) Tribunal NDPBs (of which there were 33 species) with jurisdiction in specialist fields of law. They include both standing tribunals (with a permanent membership) and those covered from panels so that the actual number of tribunals sitting varies. Examples include the Central Arbitration Committee, the Competition Appeal Tribunal, the Insolvency Practitioners Tribunal, and the Horserace Betting Levy Appeal Tribunal.[17]

The category of 790 NDPBs also includes other bodies, most notably 149 independent monitoring boards of prison, immigration removal centres and immigration holding rooms. But it excludes a large number of other bodies, including local authorities and the civil and criminal courts (although it does include bodies like the Investigatory Powers Tribunal established by the Regulation of Investigatory Powers Act 2000 whose membership includes senior members of the judiciary). More controversially, however, it also excludes what are referred to as non-ministerial government departments, on the one hand, and the next steps agencies, on the other.[18] The former includes utility regulators, such as, the Gas and Electricity Markets Authority and the Water Services Regulation Authority (OFWAT),[19] as well as agencies like the Food Standards Agency. Although the regulators are not treated as 'public bodies', to confuse matters further for these purposes, bodies representing the interests of public utility consumers (such as the National Consumer Council) are included.

Legal status

Except where statutes provide otherwise, departments of central government share in the legal status of the Crown and may benefit from certain privileges and immunities which are peculiar to the Crown.[20] But local authorities, statutory bodies set up for local commercial purposes and privately owned companies do not benefit from Crown status.[21] Into which category do other public bodies fall?

> In *Tamlin* v *Hannaford*, it had to be decided whether, after nationalisation of the railways, a dwelling-house owned by the British Transport Commission was subject to the Rent Restriction Acts or was exempted from them by virtue of being Crown property. After examining the Transport Act 1947, the Court of Appeal rejected the view that the Commission was the servant or agent of the Crown, even though the Ministry of Transport had wide statutory powers of control over the Commission. 'In the eye of the law, the corporation is its own master and is answerable as fully as any other person or corporation. It is not the Crown and has none of the immunities or privileges of the Crown. Its servants are not civil servants and its property is not Crown property . . . It is, of course, a public authority and its purposes, no doubt, are public purposes, but it is not a government department nor do its powers fall within the province of government.'[22]

---

[17] Ch 29 A.

[18] Ch 13 D.

[19] See p 298 below.

[20] Chs 12 D and 32 C.

[21] *Mersey Docks and Harbour Trustees* v *Gibbs* (1866) LR 1 HL 93; ch 32 A.

[22] [1950] 1 KB 18, 24 (Denning LJ).

It would seem that this decision governs the status of other public corporations, unless they are expressly made to act by and on behalf of the Crown or are directly placed under a minister of the Crown. In *Pfizer Corpn* v *Ministry of Health*, it was held that, since a hospital board was acting on behalf of the then Minister of Health, the treatment of patients in NHS hospitals was a government function and thus the use of drugs was use 'for the services of the Crown'; the Crown could therefore make use of its special rights under patent law for importing drugs.[23] By contrast, in *BBC* v *Johns*, the BBC were held not to be entitled to benefit from the Crown's immunity from taxation since broadcasting had not become a function of the central government.[24] It was strange that financial considerations led the BBC in this case to argue its close dependence upon the Crown and central government, whereas usually the BBC is anxious to stress its independence. The immunities of many NHS bodies were later removed by the National Health Service and Community Care Act 1990.

It is today common for the statute which creates a new public body to make express provision for its status. Thus the Health and Safety Commission and the Health and Safety Executive, created in 1974 to exercise functions previously exercised by departments, are stated to perform their functions on behalf of the Crown.[25] The National Audit Act 1983 provides that the staff of the National Audit Office are not to be regarded as holding office under Her Majesty or as discharging any functions on behalf of the Crown. More recently, legislation has tended to provide that an agency created by statute shall not be regarded as a servant or agent of the Crown or as enjoying any status, immunity or privilege of the Crown. This is a form of words used, for example, in the case of bodies as diverse as the Personal Accounts Delivery Authority, the Committee on Climate Change, and the Young People's Learning Agency for England.[26] However, this form of words is not used in the case of utility regulators such as the Gas and Electricity Markets Authority. The Utilities Act 2000 is silent as to the status of the latter, though the Act does provide that the Authority is to be treated as if it were a minister of the crown for some purposes, and that it needs the approval of ministers for other purposes (such as the recruitment of staff).[27]

Appointments to public bodies

NDPBs are bodies which exercise a government function, but which are appointed rather than elected, whether directly or indirectly. Not surprisingly, ministerial patronage of this kind has given rise to concern and was fully addressed by the Committee on Standards in Public Life.[28] In its first report the committee found no evidence of political bias in public appointments and rejected calls for an impartial and independent body to be given the responsibility for making appointments, recommending that 'ultimate responsibility for appointments should remain with ministers'. But it did not follow that ministers 'should act with unfettered discretion', and it was proposed that existing procedures should be 'substantially improved' in order to ensure that they were 'sufficiently robust'. The two safeguards proposed were first 'the establishment of clear published principles governing selections for appointment', and secondly more effective external scrutiny of appointments. So far as the former is concerned, this was to include the principle of appointment on merit; the principle that 'selection on merit should take account of the need to

---

[23] [1965] AC 512. Cf *BMA* v *Greater Glasgow Health Board* [1989] AC 1211 and, from a different point of view, *Norweb plc* v *Dixon* [1995] 3 All ER 952.

[24] [1965] Ch 32.

[25] Health and Safety at Work etc. Act 1974, s 10(7).

[26] See Pensions Act 2007, Climate Change Act 2008, and Apprenticeships, Skills, Children and Learning Act 2009. See also Regulatory Enforcement and Sanctions Act 2008, Sch 1.

[27] Utilities Act 2000, Sch 1.

[28] Cm 2850-I, 1995. One complaint was that public bodies were ceasing to be representative and were increasingly dominated by business people. On developments in the health service, see L Ashburner and L Cairncross (1993) 71 *Public Administration* 357.

appoint boards which include a balance of skills and backgrounds'; and that appointments should be made only after advice from a panel or committee which includes independent members, who should normally account for at least one-third of the membership. So far as external scrutiny is concerned, this was to be achieved principally by the appointment of a Commissioner for Public Appointments to 'monitor, regulate and approve departmental appointments procedures' and to draw up a Code of Practice for public appointments procedures.

These recommendations were accepted by the government and a Commissioner for Public Appointments was appointed by Order in Council in November 1995 to oversee the way public appointments are made to the executive departmental bodies, a term defined then to include only 274 NDPBs and executive NHS bodies. The jurisdiction of the Commissioner has since been extended and now covers NDPBs, health bodies, public corporations, public broadcasting authorities and some utility regulators. Although there are still a number of exempt posts,[29] it is thought that about 10,000 positions are currently covered by the OPCA process.[30] In performing her role under what is now the Public Appointments Order in Council 2002, the Commissioner must maintain 'the principle of selection on merit in relation to public appointments', though she is to do so in a way that will promote 'economy, efficiency, effectiveness, diversity, and equality of opportunity in the procedures for making public appointments'.[31] The Commissioner is also required to 'prescribe and publish a code of practice on the interpretation and application' of the principle of appointment on merit and is expressly empowered to adopt and publish from time to time such additional guidance to appointing authorities as she thinks fit.[32] In order to ensure that any procedures are duly followed, the Commissioner must 'audit appointment policies and practices pursued by appointing authorities to establish whether the code of practice is being observed',[33] and OPCA currently engages as many as 148 independent public appointment assessors, in an exercise that invites questions about its proportionality.[34]

The Code of Practice is based on seven principles.[35] While recognising that 'the ultimate responsibility for appointment rests with ministers', the Code emphasises that 'all public appointments should be governed by the overriding principle of selection based on merit'. Provision is made for independent scrutiny in all appointments to which the Code applies, as well as the need to promote equal opportunities. There is also a recognition of the need for openness and transparency to be applied to the appointments process, as well as proportionality in the appointments procedures. This means that these procedures should be 'appropriate for the nature of the post and the size and weight of its responsibilities' and there is a concern that some of the procedures are too elaborate.[36] The Code of Practice is accompanied by the Commissioner's more detailed guidance on appointments to public bodies, which now requires candidates for public appointment to indicate involvement in political activities in the immediately preceding five years (which includes disclosing any donations to political parties).[37] Although political activity is not generally a bar for appointment to public bodies, this is a useful way of controlling the making of public

---

[29] HC 122 (2006–07), paras 101–2.

[30] HC 152 (2007–08), para 5.

[31] Public Appointments Order in Council 2002, art 2(1) (as amended in 2008). On the issue of diversity in public appointments, see L Barmes [2002] PL 606.

[32] Ibid, art 2(2).

[33] Ibid, art 2(3).

[34] See HC 122 (2006–07), paras 92–93.

[35] The code can be found at http://www.publicappointmentscommssioner.org.

[36] See Sixth Report of the Committee on Standards in Public Life, *Reinforcing Standards*, Cm 4557-I, 2000, ch 9.

[37] For background to this, see HC 327 (1997–8), paras 36–43; Commissioner for Public Appointments, Third Report 1997–1998 (1998). See also Commissioner for Public Appointments, Fourth Report 1998–1999 (1999); and Cm 4557-I, 2000, pp 118–120. There has been a decline in the number of people declaring a political activity in recent years – from 19 per cent of appointees in 2000–01 to 10.2 per cent in 2008: see Commissioner for Public Appointments, Fourteenth Report 2008–2009 (2009), p 29.

appointments for reason of party advantage. Complaints about public appointments may be made to the Commissioner,[38] who is subject to scrutiny by the Public Administration Committee of the House of Commons,[39] as well as the Committee on Standards in Public Life.[40] By a separate initiative, some senior appointments to public bodies may now be subject to scrutiny by select committees.[41]

C. Public utilities: the general framework

From public to private ownership

There was no uniform legislative framework for the nationalised industries. The structure of the British Gas Corporation was, however, typical. The corporation was established after a reorgan-isation of the industry by the Gas Act 1972, replacing the Gas Council established by the Gas Act 1948. It 'provided a public service, the supply of gas, to citizens of the state generally under the control of the state which could dictate its policies and retain its surplus revenue'.[42] The chairman and between 10 and 20 other members of the corporation were appointed by the Secretary of State (s 1(2)), and were paid salaries and allowances determined by the Secretary of State with the consent of the Minister for the Civil Service. It was the duty of the corporation, which had a 'spe-cial monopoly power for the supply of gas',[43] to develop and maintain an efficient, coordinated and economical system of gas supply and to satisfy so far as economical to do so all reasonable demands for gas (s 2). The minister was authorised to give to the corporation such directions as he considered appropriate for securing that it was managed efficiently (s 4), and was empowered to give 'directions of a general character as to the exercise and performance by the Corporation of their functions . . . in relation to matters which appear to him to affect the national interest' (s 7).[44] Certain broad financial duties were laid upon the corporation (including a duty to ensure that revenues were 'not less than sufficient' to meet outgoings) (s 14), but many of its financial powers (for example to borrow money) required the consent of the minister given with the approval of the Treasury (s 17). The corporation was required to keep proper accounts which had to be audited by a person approved by the Secretary of State, to whom a copy of the accounts had to be sent (s 23). The corporation was also required to give such information to the Secretary of State about its activities as he might require and to report annually to the minister, the report being laid before Parliament.

The difficulty in privatising nationalised industries with this structure was that the corpor-ations had no share capital which could be sold to private investors.[45] Although privatisation has been secured by a number of different techniques,[46] the difficulty was overcome in some cases by

---

[38] See Commissioner for Public Appointments, Ninth Report 2003–2004 (2004), p 3: four departments routinely showed shortlists privately to ministers during the appointment process. The Commissioner expressed concern that the unrecorded involvement of a minister at such a late stage in the appointments process could be con-strued as 'political interference or personal preference'.

[39] HC 165-I (2002–3); HC 122 (2006–07); HC 152 (2007–08).

[40] See Cm 6704, 2005; and Cm 6723, 2005 (government's response). For the Committee on Standards in Public Life, see pp 307–8 below.

[41] Cm 7170, 2007, pp 28–9; HC 152 (2007–08); also HC 119 (2008–09) (pre-appointment hearing by Business Innovation and Skills, and Culture. Media and Sport committees sitting jointly, relating to chairman of OFCOM).

[42] *Foster v British Gas plc* [1991] 2 AC 306, 316.

[43] Ibid. On the monopoly, see Gas Act 1972, s 29.

[44] See SI 1981 No 1459.

[45] For a full account of the issues raised in this paragraph, see C Graham and T Prosser (1987) 50 MLR 16.

[46] See e.g. Coal Industry Act 1994, Atomic Energy Authority Act 1995 and, in the case of HMSO, see HC Deb, 18 December 1995, col 1272.

providing that on a day appointed by the Secretary of State all the property, rights and liabilities of the corporation would be transferred to a company nominated by the minister, the company in question being limited by shares wholly owned by the Crown. The government was then empowered to retain a holding in this successor company, with the proceeds of the sale of the rest being paid into the Consolidated Fund. The Secretary of State could by order dissolve the old corporation as soon as he was satisfied that its affairs had wound up and nothing remained to be done. This technique was used in the case of British Aerospace, the British Transport Docks Board, British Airways, British Telecom, British Gas and the water and electricity companies.[47] Each statute was 'very much a skeleton' with little provision being made with regard to the design of the privatised company.[48] These were matters dealt with in the articles of association of the companies, which are now governed by the Companies Act 2006 in terms of their legal structure, although the public utilities in particular are subject to extensive regulation of their activities on a number of grounds discussed below. The nature of that regulation continues to evolve, with the focus in the early years post-privatisation being on the creation of a viable regulatory framework. The concern in more recent years, however, has been with regulatory methods and with initiatives designed (a) to lighten the regulatory burdens on service-providers, and (b) to shift from criminal to civil law the means of enforcing regulatory obligations. This is not necessarily consistent with the function of the regulator in protecting the consumer.

The legal structure of the privatised utility

A study by the Comptroller and Auditor General in 1996 of the four main public utilities (water, gas, electricity and telecommunications) pointed out that they are 'large and economically significant' and together served some 25 million customers, in the process employing assets with a value of some £240 billion. Their total annual turnover of £51 billion represented roughly 8 per cent of annual GDP of the UK.[49] These considerations alone make it inevitable that they should be subject to some form of regulation, as does the fact that each of the industries contains an important element of monopoly or dominance by a small number of firms. An example of the statutory model of regulation is found in the Gas Act 1986, which abolished the statutory monopoly of British Gas.[50] Since heavily amended in crucial respects (by the Gas Act 1995, the Competition Act 1998, the Utilities Act 2000, and the Energy Acts 2004 and 2008), the Gas Act 1986 provides that the principal objective of both the Secretary of State and the regulator (now the Gas and Electricity Markets Authority) is to protect the interests of consumers 'by promoting effective competition between persons engaged in, or in commercial activities connected with, the shipping, transportation or supply of gas'.[51] But although this is the principal objective, both the minister and the regulator are required generally to carry out their functions in a manner which will ensure that 'all reasonable demands' for gas are met, and that licence holders are able to finance their activities; as well as contribute to the achievement of sustainable development.[52] Both the minister and the regulator are also directed generally to have regard to the interests of individuals who are disabled or chronically sick, as well as those who are of pensionable age, who have low incomes or who live in rural areas.[53] In addition, when carrying out their functions both

[47] See British Aerospace Act 1980, Transport Act 1984, Civil Aviation Act 1980, Telecommunications Act 1984, Gas Act 1986, Water Act 1989 and Electricity Act 1989. For an earlier approach, see Iron and Steel Act 1953.
[48] C Graham and T Prosser, above, p 22.
[49] HC 645 (1995–6), p 2.
[50] Gas Act 1986, s 3. It is important to emphasise that this model has variations of more or less significance when applied to other areas of regulatory activity: T Prosser, in Feldman (ed.), *English Public Law*, ch 5.
[51] Gas Act 1986, s 4AA (as substituted by the Utilities Act 2000, s 9).
[52] Ibid, as amended by the Energy Act 2008, s 83.
[53] Ibid, s 4AA(3).

the minister and the regulator must have regard to principles whereby 'regulatory activities should be transparent, accountable, proportionate, consistent and targeted only at cases in which action is needed', as well as best regulatory practice.[54]

Licences for the supply of gas were issued originally by the Secretary of State in consultation with the regulator, but as a result of amendments in the Gas Act 1995 are now issued by the regulator alone. Under the Gas Act 1986, licences – which include a formula for prices – were issued for periods of 25 years. The terms of the licence could be varied only with the consent of the licence holder (s 23), failing which a reference could be made by the regulator to the Monopolies and Mergers Commission (now the Competition Commission) to investigate and report on whether any matter relating to the supply of gas by a public gas supplier to tariff customers operated against the public interest (s 24); if the Commission reached adverse conclusions about the public interest, the regulator was required to make the necessary modifications to the licence conditions.[55] It was under these procedures that references were made to the Monopolies and Mergers Commission about the gas industry in the early 1990s. After a major review, the Commission concluded that British Gas should be required to separate its transportation and storage business from its trading business and that the tariff formula in the licence should be modified to permit a lower price increase.[56] It is true that the need for licence holders to agree to a licence change gave the utility companies a veto over any such changes without the intervention of the Commission. But the threat of a reference by the regulator was usually enough to encourage companies to accept a proposed change in order to avoid the great inconvenience of such a reference.[57] Nevertheless, amendments in 1995 and 2000 allow licence modifications to be made in some circumstances without consent and without the need for a reference to the Competition Commission.[58] Although it was expected that the role of the regulator in the fixing of prices would become much less important with the introduction of full competition for gas supply under the Gas Act 1995, it has been necessary to give the Gas and Electricity Markets Authority additional powers to deal with anti-competitive practices.[59] But although there is thus little immediate prospect of the Authority being made redundant by the operation of the market,[60] as already suggested the extension of the regulator's powers are to some extent contradicted by even more recent requirements that they do not impose unnecessary burdens on the regulated community.[61]

The role of the regulator

The regulation of public utilities has generated a large body of academic and non-academic literature.[62] The key to the regulatory model initially adopted is based on the idea of 'a single independent regulator for each industry, operating without undue bureaucracy and supported by a small staff', the government rejecting regulatory systems found overseas, particularly the

---

[54] Ibid, s 4AA(5A)(b) (as inserted by the Energy Act 2004, s 178).

[55] On the requirements of the regulator following a Competition Commission report, see *Re Northern Ireland Electricity plc's Application for Judicial Review* [1998] NI 300. See now Utilities Act 2000, s 83, amending Gas Act 1986.

[56] Cm 2315, 1993.

[57] T Prosser, in Jowell and Oliver (eds), *The Changing Constitution* (6th edn), p 352.

[58] See Utilities Act 2000, s 82 (amending Gas Act 1986, s 23).

[59] Sch 10, para 3. On the changing role of the regulators, see McCrudden (ed.), *Regulation and Deregulation*, ch 13.

[60] See T Prosser, in Feldman (ed.) above.

[61] Regulatory Enforcement and Sanctions Act 2008, ss 72–74. For background, see Department for Business, Enterprise and Regulatory Reform, *Next Steps on Regulatory Reform* (2007), pp 19–20.

[62] Important contributions are Graham, *Regulating Public Utilities*; McCrudden (ed.), above; Prosser, *Laws and the Regulators*; and T Prosser, in Jowell and Oliver (eds), note 57 above, ch 14, which give a good insight into the sheer scale and scope of regulatory activity in contemporary Britain.

United States, 'in favour of a quicker and less bureaucratic system of regulation'.[63] But this model was strongly criticised by the Comptroller and Auditor General, who raised questions about 'the over-concentration of power in one pair of hands', leading him to consider whether there might be a case for 'possible alternatives to the current system of industry-specific regulation by single regulators'. The gas and electricity regulators – OFGAS and OFFER – were merged in 1999, to become OFGEM (the Office of Gas and Electricity Markets) which operates under the direction of the Gas and Electricity Markets Authority following the introduction of the Utilities Act 2000.[64] In making this move, the government explained that the task of regulation was becoming increasingly complex, with the interests of what are now hundreds of licensees to be considered and balanced. It is thus accepted that regulatory responsibilities can best be undertaken by a regulatory authority, to ensure that regulatory decisions are 'less dependent on the personality of a single regulator', thereby ensuring in turn greater continuity and consistency in decision making.[65]

The regulators are a constitutional curiosity, bodies sui generis, sometimes described as 'a non-ministerial government department',[66] a phrase which contrasts with other descriptions of regulators as being 'independent of government', albeit with 'strong powers'.[67] Interesting questions arise not only about their accountability,[68] but also about their functions, the regulators exercising a blend of legislative, executive and judicial powers. In the case of the gas industry, the Gas and Electricity Markets Authority has the power to make statutory instruments (a legislative power), to issue licences, vary the terms of licences and regulate the activities of licence holders (an executive power), and deal with complaints from consumers (a quasi-judicial power). Under the Utilities Act 2000, the regulator also has the power to impose financial penalties on licence holders who have breached a licence condition, a power which has given rise to questions about compliance with art 6 of the ECHR (which guarantees the right to a fair trial in the determination of civil rights and obligations):

> How can the regulator, who determines the penalty, be an independent and impartial tribunal? The regulator decides whether he will pursue the licensee. He assesses whether the licensee has broken the terms of his licence. He then decides what the penalty is. He is an individual appointed by the executive . . . he is legislator, prosecutor and judge, all rolled into one.[69]

There is, however, a right of appeal against the imposition of a penalty and against the amount of the penalty. The appeal is to the High Court in England and Wales or the Court of Session in Scotland, the court having the power to quash the penalty or substitute a lesser penalty.[70]

D. The accountability of public utilities and public utility regulators[71]

Accountability to government

1 *Public corporations.* Public ownership of an industry usually came about because of the need for greater public control than could be obtained by means of legal restrictions imposed on privately owned undertakings. Where there was public control of a corporation, this was achieved

---

[63] A Carlsberg (1992) 37 *New York Law School Law Rev* 285.
[64] For background see Cm 3898, 1998; T Prosser (1999) 62 MLR 196.
[65] HL Deb, 4 May 2000, col 1141.
[66] HL Deb, 5 July 1989, col 1201 (Baroness Hooper).
[67] HC Deb, 18 July 1983, col 36 (Mr Cecil Parkinson).
[68] See T Prosser, in Jowell and Oliver, p 350.
[69] HL Deb, 4 May 2000, col 1171 (Lord Kingsland).
[70] Gas Act 1986, s 30E, as inserted by Utilities Act 2000, s 95. See also Energy Act 2004, s 173.
[71] See generally HL Paper 68 (2003–04).

primarily through the relevant minister, who appointed the chair and members of the board, who had power to call for information and give directions to the board, who approved the board's external financing limits, and who received the board's accounts and annual report. This did not mean that ministers should be responsible for every act of day-to-day administration, but they did at least have power to intervene on strategic matters which by the legislation were subject to their approval. In turn, ministerial responsibility to Parliament required that ministers should account to Parliament for the use that they made of their statutory powers.

Whatever the framers of the nationalisation Acts in 1945–50 may have intended, ministers, in fact, exercised very considerable control over the industries and often intervened in their affairs. One reason for this was that while for some periods some nationalised industries were financially profitable, many went through periods when they made heavy losses and needed financial support from the government. Another reason was that the industries played a substantial part in the national economy, as employers, as providers of basic means of communication and energy, and in their investment programmes: management of the industries became an aspect of the management of the economy. Many of the industries' decisions had widespread social and economic repercussions, for example the level of prices charged to the consumer, wage rates for their employees, purchasing decisions (for example, whether British Airways should buy British aeroplanes) and the closure of unprofitable activities (for example, railway lines and coalmines). It was impossible to insulate such decisions from the political process, but it was extremely difficult to strike the right balance. A Commons select committee in 1968 advocated an 'arm's length' relationship between boards and ministers, with political intervention being confined to a few key points.[72]

2 Privatised utilities. Privatisation has not removed the scope for ministerial intervention in the activities of the former nationalised industries. As the Comptroller and Auditor General pointed out: 'The Government determined the initial position in which the industries would begin their life following privatisation. In particular they laid down the licences issued to companies, determined the capital structure of those companies that were formerly public owned, and set initial price controls for those which were monopolies or had a dominant position'.[73] The government also has a role in promoting competition, where the industry in question contains what is a 'natural monopoly' and for this purpose legislation may be necessary, as for example in the case of the Gas Act 1995 which extended competition in gas supply. On the other hand, the government has a role to play in protecting consumers from the unfair practices of the utility companies and to this end the legislation makes provision for the appointment by ministers of a regulator in each of the industries in question, with responsibilities determined by the government and Parliament. In some cases the legislation will address specific abuses, such as the provisions of the Utilities Act 2000 which deal with concerns about the large salaries which the directors of some of the utility companies were paying themselves. The companies must report annually to the Gas and Electricity Markets Authority whether there is in force an arrangement linking directors' remuneration to levels of performance regarding service standards. Where such an arrangement is in force, the report must also describe the arrangements and the remuneration, and the details must be published by the company in a manner which will 'secure adequate publicity for it'. The report may also be published by the Authority.

Together with the regulator, ministers generally have prescribed statutory duties, as we have seen. Ministers are also empowered in some cases to give directions to the regulator in determining the allocation of priorities in the performance of his or her duties. Under the Gas Act 1986, the Secretary of State is required to issue guidance to the regulator about social and

---

[72] HC 371-I (1967–8), p 3.
[73] HC 645 (1995–6), p 7.

environmental policies.[74] Otherwise, the legislation empowers the minister to make regulations, although in the case of the gas industry the effect of the Gas Act 1995 has been to transfer much of this power to the regulator. Nevertheless, the power to make regulations can generally be exercised only with the consent of the minister, who in any event retains some powers, for example in the case of public safety.[75] Thus the Secretary of State may make regulations empowering an officer to (i) enter premises in which there is a gas service pipe for the purpose of inspecting gas fittings on the premises; (ii) examine and test any such fittings or other related equipment; and (iii) disconnect or seal off any gas system on the premises, where 'in his opinion it is necessary to do so for the purpose of averting danger to life or property'. Powers under the Utilities Act 2000 give the Secretary of State the authority to introduce regulations requiring the adjustment of charges where he or she considers that any group of customers of authorised suppliers are treated less favourably than other customers. The Energy Act 2008 introduced additional powers to make regulations relating to the storage of gas.

Select committees and accountability

1 *Public corporations.* The difficulties encountered by MPs in obtaining information about the nationalised industries, together with the lack of adequate procedures for dealing with the reports and accounts laid annually before Parliament, led in the early 1950s to various attempts to use committees of the Commons to establish greater parliamentary control. In 1954–5, the House appointed a committee to inform Parliament about the current policy and practice of the industries, but excluded from its remit matters which involved a minister's responsibility to Parliament or were matters of day-to-day administration.[76] In 1956, there was set up a select committee with the duty of examining the reports and accounts of the nationalised industries.[77] The committee was regularly reappointed until 1979. By then its terms of reference had been widened to include powers in respect of other public undertakings, such as the Independent Broadcasting Authority and the Bank of England, except for certain of the Bank's activities which were reserved from inquiry. Between 1956 and 1979 this all-party committee made a series of searching and sometimes highly critical inquiries into the industries and their relationships with the government. The inquiries started from the published reports and accounts of the industry under review, but evidence was taken from the industry, the department concerned and other interested parties.

The committee sought to discover how far the industries were subject to informal ministerial control and to ensure that ministers were responsible to Parliament for the influence which they in fact exercised, especially when ministerial pressure had prevailed against the commercial judgement of the boards. The committee's reports on topics of general concern, for example, ministerial control of the industries (in 1968), contributed much to the development of policies relating to the nationalised industries. The success of the committee on a non-partisan basis also contributed to the spread of specialised parliamentary committees into other areas of governmental activity.[78] When in 1979 the present scheme of select committees was set up, each committee was empowered to examine the expenditure, administration and policy of the principal departments and their 'associated public bodies'.[79] This was considered to leave no place for the nationalised industries committee. Certain industries have been reviewed by the resulting

---

[74] Gas Act 1986, s 4 AB (as inserted by the Utilities Act 2000, s 10).

[75] As part of the process of regulatory reform, the Regulatory Enforcement and Sanctions Act 2008 provides that regulations authorising the introduction of criminal sanctions under the Gas Act 1986 may now include civil penalties instead (s 62–71).

[76] HC 120 (1955–6).

[77] Coombes, *The Member of Parliament and the Administration.*

[78] Ch 10 D.

[79] HC SO 152(1); ch 10 D.

committees such as the Treasury Committee, the Trade and Industry Committee (as it then was) and the Transport Committee.[80] Some aspects of the industries' finances have been considered by the Public Accounts Committee, but although the accounts of the industries were laid annually in Parliament, the Comptroller and Auditor General had no power to inspect the books of the industries themselves.[81] The National Audit Act 1983 extended the Auditor General's power to examine the economy, efficiency and effectiveness of government departments and related bodies, but the nationalised industries and other public authorities, such as the BBC, were expressly excluded from the scope of the Act.[82]

2 *Privatisation.* Although privatisation has reduced the scope for scrutiny of the former nationalised industries by the select committees, it has by no means disappeared. Investigations of different kinds have been conducted mainly by the Public Accounts Committee and the Trade and Industry Committee (a predecessor of the Business, Innovation and Skills Committee), though others have also played a part. The Public Accounts Committee has been concerned mainly to investigate the process by which state enterprises have been sold, with a view to establishing whether value for money has been secured for the taxpayer.[83] Although it has highlighted good practice where it exists,[84] many PAC reports have included stinging criticism of government failure to raise more money from the sales or for paying too large a subsidy to purchasers.[85] The Stationery Office was sold for less than 'the most pessimistic pre-sale valuation',[86] the (Railway) Rolling Stock Leasing Companies were sold for £1.5 billion and then sold on for £2.7 billion,[87] and the share prices of AEA Technology, British Energy plc and Railtrack respectively rose sharply after the sales.[88] Both of the last two failures were said to demonstrate 'the merits of selling only part of the government's shareholding in a company on initial flotation'.[89] Other criticisms have related to the consequences of the sales, with the privatisation of the Rolling Stock Leasing Companies being condemned for having been conducted in a way which 'enabled a small number of former British Rail managers to become millionaires, with windfall gains ranging from £15 million to £33 million'. 'Such large payments', complained the Committee, 'risk discrediting privatisation as a whole.'[90]

Both the Public Accounts Committee and the Trade and Industry Committee have conducted a number of enquiries into the work of the regulators, who have been 'fairly regular witnesses' before select committees.[91] The Public Accounts Committee has been concerned to ensure that OFGEM maintained pressure on the gas companies to reduce their prices,[92] while the Trade and Industry Committee has in the past examined the annual reports of OFGAS (the former gas regulator)[93] and investigated the work of OFGAS and more recently OFGEM.[94] These investigations have dealt with a range of issues, although a constant refrain has been the role of the regulator

---

[80] See e.g. HC 597 (1988–9), HC 141 (1990–1).

[81] HC 115 (1980–1).

[82] National Audit Act 1983, s 7(4) and Sch 4; ch 17 D.

[83] See generally HC 992 (1997–8).

[84] HC 151 (2007–08) (privatisation of QinetiQ).

[85] For an example of the latter, see HC 601 (1998–9).

[86] HC 599 (1997–8).

[87] HC 782 (1997–8).

[88] HC 749 (1997–8); HC 242 (1998–9); HC 256 (1998–9).

[89] HC 242 (1998–9), p vii.

[90] HC 782 (1997–8).

[91] HC 193-i (1999–2000), p i.

[92] HC 171 (1999–2000).

[93] HC 646 (1994–5).

[94] HC 185 (1993–4); HC 193-i, ii (1999–2000).

in promoting price competition, on the one hand, and protecting the 'fuel poor', on the other.[95] The select committees have also examined the work of other regulators, including OFCOM, OFWAT and the Rail Regulator,[96] while the investigation by the Culture, Media and Sport Committee into the National Lottery included an examination of the work of the National Lottery Commission.[97] A number of important reforms to the regulatory framework have been proposed by the select committees,[98] and reforms have also been proposed by both witnesses and the committees in relation to the structure and powers of the select committees.[99] Many of the former (regulatory framework reforms) have been implemented by the Utilities Act 2000.[100] Otherwise the select committees have examined the utility companies themselves, and their practices, as well as the problems of fuel debt and the practice of disconnection by the gas and electricity companies.[101] But proposals by the House of Lords Constitution Committee to enhance scrutiny by establishing a joint committee of both Houses to scrutinise 'the regulatory state' failed to secure government support.[102]

Judicial review

1 *Public corporations.* As public corporations do not generally benefit from immunities of the Crown, in carrying out their operations they are fully subject to the law as are industrial enterprises in private ownership. In fact, many corporations provide public utility services which were subject to statutory control long before the era of nationalisation. So far as the principal powers and duties of the nationalised corporations were concerned, these were usually expressed in such general terms in the parent Acts that it was doubtful whether they could be enforced by legal process:

> In *Charles Roberts and Co Ltd* v *British Railways Board*[103] a company which manufactured railway tank wagons sought a declaration that the board were not authorised to manufacture such wagons for sale to an oil company for use on railways in Britain. *Held* that the court should not interfere with the board's bona fide decision that such manufacture was an efficient way of carrying out the board's business within its statutory powers and duties; the judge declined to consider the economic effect which the board's policies might have on private manufacturers.

It would similarly be difficult by action in the courts to enforce the general duties of a board, as this seems to be left by the statutes to the minister concerned.[104] But public corporations were subject to the jurisdiction of the courts if they committed a tort or a breach of contract, if they exceeded their powers or if they failed to observe statutory procedures or to perform specific

---

[95] HC 174 (1998–9); HC 171 (1999–2000); HC 193-ii (1999–2000); HC 206 (2003–04); HC 297 (2004–05); and HC 422 (2004–05).

[96] See HC 407 (2004–05); HC 463 (2003–04); and HC 205 (2003–04).

[97] HC 56, 57 (2000–2001). The committee lamented the lack of 'relevant skills or experience on the part of the Commission' and questioned whether the body selecting the licence holder should also be the regulator. See also HC 196 (2003–04).

[98] HC 481 (1994–5).

[99] HC 646 (1994–5) (calls from gas regulator for separate select committee for the 'regulation and regulators'); HC 536 (1999–2000) (need for committee to take evidence from previous regulators where incumbent unable to explain decisions of predecessor).

[100] Notably the duty of the Gas and Electricity Markets Authority to give reasons for decisions: Utilities Act 2000, s 87.

[101] HC 297-I (2004–05).

[102] HL Paper 68 (2003–04), and for the government's response see HL Paper 150 (2003–04). It was also proposed that 'select committees consider expanding their terms of reference to include a requirement routinely to consider and react to regulators' annual reports, and monitor the use of resources. These activities would be in addition to the *ad hoc* inquiries they undertake from time to time'.

[103] [1964] 3 All ER 651. See also *NUM* v *National Coal Board* [1986] ICR 736.

[104] Cf *British Oxygen Co Ltd* v *South West Scotland Electricity Board* 1956 SC (HL) 112, 1959 SC (HL) 17.

statutory duties.[105] Questions have arisen as to the extent to which the BBC is subject to judicial review. Although it has been held that the corporation's duty of political impartiality is not enforceable in the courts,[106] it is not now possible to argue that judicial review does not apply at all on the ground that the BBC is a creature of prerogative.[107] The Corporation is a public authority for the purposes of the Human Rights Act.[108] Judicial review casts a long shadow and even regulatory bodies that do not exercise statutory functions may be subject to judicial review.[109]

2 *Privatisation*. So far as the privatised utilities are concerned, it is unclear whether the companies themselves would be subject to judicial review. Although it has been held that a privatised water and sewerage undertaker is a public body for the purposes of the Human Rights Act,[110] the courts appear unwilling to entertain claims against utility companies where the regulator can provide a remedy to an aggrieved party, even though it may not be the same remedy as any the courts could provide.[111] Privatised utilities may also be regarded as authorities of the state for the purposes of the direct effect of EU directives, as were the nationalised industries after the House of Lords decision in *Foster v British Gas plc*.[112] In *Griffin v South West Water Services Ltd*,[113] it was held that a privatised water company satisfied the test laid down in the *Foster* case for the purposes of direct effect to the extent that it was a body which (i) provided a public service, (ii) under the control of the state, for the purposes of which (iii) it had special powers. It was the second of these three conditions which gave rise to most difficulty, but the fact that the court was prepared to acknowledge such a degree of state control is an interesting reflection on the public nature of the activities of the privatised companies. Indeed, Blackburne J went so far as to say that the extent of control by the state under legislation and licence was 'at least as great' as that exercised in relation to the nationalised industries, although this alone is not enough to make these companies subject to judicial review. The fact that the water company operated in what was described as 'a business environment in compliance with legislation but driven by economic criteria' did not detract from the conclusion of the court, although on the facts the point was academic for it was also held that the directive in question (75/129/EC) was not sufficiently precise and unconditional to give rise to obligations which could be enforced directly in the domestic courts.

Different considerations apply in the case of the minister (exercising powers under the relevant regulatory legislation) and the regulators. There is perhaps more scope for review of the regulator than of anyone else in the process, either because of a failure to comply with ministerial directions, or because of a mis-reading of statutory powers.[114] But because judicial review may be available in principle, it does not follow that it is 'always appropriate' or 'a substitute for proper political supervision and well thought-out decision-making procedures'.[115] Indeed, it has been suggested that judicial review offers no meaningful protection to a party that feels it has been wronged by a regulator's decision, on the ground that the courts are unprepared 'to question the quality of

---

[105] *Warwickshire CC v British Railways Board* [1969] 3 All ER 631; *Booth & Co (International) Ltd v National Enterprise Board* [1978] 3 All ER 624; *Grunwick Processing Laboratories Ltd v ACAS* [1978] AC 655; *Home Office v Commission for Racial Equality* [1982] QB 385; *R v Radio Authority, ex p Bull* [1997] 2 All ER 561.

[106] *Lynch v BBC* [1983] NILR 193.

[107] Cf *R v BBC, ex p Lavelle* [1983] ICR 99. See also *CCSU v Minister of State for the Civil Service* [1985] AC 374.

[108] *R (Pro-Life Alliance) v BBC* [2003] UKHL 23; [2003] 1 AC 185.

[109] *R v Panel on Take-Overs and Mergers, ex p Datafin plc* [1987] QB 815; ch 31.

[110] *Marcic v Thames Water Utilities Ltd* [2002] EWCA Civ 64, [2002] QB 929. On the implications of the Human Rights Act, see Graham, *Regulating Public Utilities*, pp 136–42.

[111] See *Marcic v Thames Water Utilities Ltd* [2003] UKHL 66; [2004] 2 AC 42.

[112] [1991] 2 AC 306.

[113] [1995] IRLR 15.

[114] *R v Director of Passenger Rail Franchising, ex p Save our Railways, The Times*, 18 December 1995; *Re Northern Ireland Electricity plc's Application for Judicial Review* [1998] NI 300.

[115] A McHarg [1995] PL 539, at p 550.

the regulator's decision or require that the evidence underpinning the decision be examined'.[116] By way of contrast, however, there is evidence that at least one regulator (OFGAS) went to considerable lengths to avoid judicial review by adopting a 'deliberate policy' of refusing to give reasons for decisions and by failing to keep adequate records of reasons for decisions (in this case relating to the adoption of a particular price control). This was strongly deprecated by the Public Accounts Committee, which considered it 'essential that public bodies keep adequate records of the reasons for their decisions, to help ensure the proper conduct of public business and accountability'.[117] The Utilities Act 2000 now requires reasons to be given for a wide range of decisions taken by both the Gas and Electricity Markets Authority and the Secretary of State.[118] There is also now a right to appeal some decisions of the Gas and Electricity Markets Authority to the Competition Commission,[119] though different appeal procedures apply in the case of other regulators.[120]

Consumer consultation

The legislation establishing public corporations often provided formal machinery for consultation between the industries themselves and the consumers and users of their services. Consumer councils and consultative committees were created at different times for electricity, gas, coal, rail and air transport and the Post Office. Such consultative committees provided a means for the expression of the views of consumers, including opinions on the quality of services. They also provided a channel by which dissatisfied consumers might seek redress for grievances regarding the services they had received. But the existence of these consultative bodies was not widely known and in 1976 it was suggested that an Ombudsman be established for the industries to be an impartial investigator of consumer complaints.[121] Privatisation saw the abolition of the existing consultative committees and consumer councils, although somewhat similar bodies have been established in the newly privatised utilities. Under the Utilities Act 2000, for example, the Gas and Electricity Consumer Council appointed by the Secretary of State had a number of wide-ranging responsibilities. These included providing advice and information and the investigation of consumer complaints. The Council was empowered to direct both the regulator and any licence holder to supply it with information which it needed to carry out its functions.[122] Despite being designed to act as a 'powerful consumer champion, operating independently of the regulator,'[123] the Council was abolished by the Consumers, Estate Agents and Redress Act 2007, which established a new National Consumer Council with a power to represent the views of consumers to regulatory bodies generally.

E. Advisory bodies

While public boards may provide services or manage undertakings themselves, subject to a degree of control by ministers and departments, where a department wishes to retain all decision-making and management in its own hands, it may seek through advisory bodies to receive expert

---

[116] HC 481-iii (1994–5), p 77 (memorandum submitted by National Power plc). For fuller treatment of judicial review in this context, see McCrudden (ed.), ch 7; and Graham, pp 68–75.

[117] HC 37 (1996–7).

[118] Utilities Act 2000, s 87, amending Gas Act 1986, s 38A.

[119] Energy Act 2004, s 173. This is a right which is additional to the right to appeal to the High Court or the Court of Session against the imposition of penalties for breach of licence conditions.

[120] See T Prosser, in Feldman (ed.), *English Public Law*, ch 5.

[121] Report by Justice, *The Citizen and Public Agencies: Remedying Grievances*. See also Robson, ch 10; HC 514 (1970–1) and Cmnd 5067, 1972; and HC 334 (1978–9).

[122] See Utilities Act 2000, Part III.

[123] HL Deb, 4 May 2000, col 1134.

advice and assistance from persons outside government. Such advisory bodies take many different forms. Some are primarily concerned with considering the need for fresh legislation; others are concerned with the choice of policies under existing laws. Some are appointed because an Act of Parliament says that they must be; others are appointed simply because the government wishes to seek information and advice from wherever it can find it. Some are appointed for a particular purpose and have a temporary existence. We now consider briefly some of the main kinds of advisory body.

Royal commissions and departmental committees

The appointment of a royal commission or a departmental committee is an act of the executive which requires no specific parliamentary approval, although often it may be a response to political demands. When an issue of public policy or a possible change in the law requires thorough examination and the government is not already politically committed to a definite policy, the task may be entrusted to an invited group of persons from outside the relevant departments. A departmental committee is appointed by one minister or by several ministers acting jointly. For substantial matters where greater formality is considered appropriate and where time is not of the essence, a royal commission may be appointed instead. This requires a royal warrant to be issued to the commissioners by the Queen on the advice of a Secretary of State. Apart from the formality and greater prestige of a royal commission, both commissions and departmental committees carry out their inquiries in a similar manner. The commission or committee will usually call for evidence from individuals and organisations outside government as well as from public authorities and it may undertake its own programme of research. Usually a royal commission hears the main evidence in public and copies of the oral and written evidence received are published; the commission's report is invariably published and laid before Parliament. A departmental committee is more likely to receive evidence in private and it is less common for its evidence to be published. But both the Committee on Ministers' Powers (1929–32) and the Committee on Administrative Tribunals and Inquiries (1955–57) took evidence in public and this was later published.[124] The reports of departmental committees are usually but not always published.[125]

Neither royal commissions nor departmental committees have power to compel the attendance of witnesses, unlike inquiries appointed by ministers under the Inquiries Act 2005.[126] The choice of the chairperson to a commission or committee is important since he or she must ensure that the commission or committee carries through its work efficiently and will seek to achieve a unanimous report where possible.[127] Usually the commission or committee disbands when it has reported but committees or commissions may be appointed on a more permanent basis and will produce a series of reports (for example, the Committee on Standards in Public Life, first appointed in 1994). When the investigating body has delivered its report, it is for the minister or the government to decide how far its recommendations are acceptable and if so in what form they should be carried out, for example by the preparation of a Bill to amend the law. Royal commissions and departmental committees have been much less conspicuous in recent times than in the past, with a a number of seminal reports being published (on matters such as official secrecy, obscenity and film censorship, and financial aid to political parties) in the 1970s in particular.[128]

---

[124] Ch 27.

[125] For the use of commissions and committees in 1945–69, see Cartwright, *Royal Commissions and Departmental Committees in Britain.*

[126] Ch 29 C; cf Cartwright, pp 142–5.

[127] Report of Balfour Committee on Procedure of Royal Commissions, Cd 5235, 1910; and see Lords Benson and Rothschild (1982) 60 *Public Administration* 339.

[128] Cmnd 5104, 1972; Cmnd 7772, 1979; Cmnd 6601, 1976.

However, these forms of advisory body are far from dead. A royal commission under the chairmanship of Lord Wakeham was appointed in 1999 to consider the reform of the House of Lords.[129] Some of the work which in the past might have been undertaken by such bodies is now conducted by bodies such as the Committee on Standards in Public Life and by task forces, the latter having been described by one commentator as 'a surrogate for old Royal Commissions or departmental committees'.[130]

The Committee on Standards in Public Life

A particularly important and effective advisory committee in recent years has been the Committee on Standards in Public Life, though its best work has perhaps already been done. The Committee was established initially in 1994 by Mr John Major when he was Prime Minister, following allegations that some members of Parliament had accepted payments from a businessman for asking questions in Parliament on his behalf.[131] Chaired initially by Lord Nolan, the Committee included members who had political experience and those who were independent of party. Whatever the original intention of Mr Major, the Committee has become a standing body and as such is regarded as a genuinely independent body. Its members are appointed by the Prime Minister and formally it is an advisory NDPB sponsored by the Cabinet Office. Lord Nolan was replaced as the Committee's chairman by Lord Neill of Bladen in 1997 and in turn by Sir Nigel Wicks in 2001, Sir Alistair Graham in 2004, and Sir Christopher Kelly in 2008. In its first report the Committee developed a series of seven principles for the conduct of public life (selflessness, integrity, objectivity, accountability, openness, honesty and leadership). The first report is important also for applying these principles to guide the behaviour of MPs, ministers and civil servants, as well as appointments to public bodies.[132]

Many of the recommendations of the first report have been dealt with at different points in this book: these include the new rules relating to the conduct of MPs; the revision of the rules relating to the conduct of ministers and civil servants; and the creation of a Public Appointments Commissioner.[133] Other reports have dealt with the government of local funding bodies, standards of conduct in local government, NDPBs and NHS trusts, the funding of political parties, the standards of conduct in Parliament, and the relationship between ministers' special advisers and the civil service.[134] In its sixth report the Committee also undertook a review of the implementation of the first report, and in the course of doing so made a number of additional recommendations.[135] For the purposes of the inquiry into the funding of political parties, the terms of reference of the Committee had formally to be extended by the Prime Minister. The Committee's far-reaching recommendations led to the Political Parties, Elections and Referendums Act 2000, which requires the disclosure of contributions to political parties; restricts the foreign funding of political parties; and introduces expenditure limits for political parties and others during general elections.[136] The Act also imposes spending limits in referendums, contrary to the recommendations of the Committee. The Committee most recently completed an inquiry into MPs' expenses.[137]

---

[129] Cm 4534, 2000. See chs 9 I and 10 B.
[130] Peter Hennessy, as quoted in Cm 4557-1, 2000, para 10.1.
[131] See Major, *The Autobiography*, pp 567, 572–7. For the terms of reference, see HC Deb, 25 October 1994, col 758.
[132] Cm 2850, 1995.
[133] See chs 11, 13 D, 13 E and 14 B respectively.
[134] Cm 3557, 1996; Cm 3702, 1997; Cm 4057, 1998; Cm 4903, 2000; Cm 5563, 2002; and Cm 5573, 2003.
[135] Cm 4557, 2000.
[136] See ch 9 C, E.
[137] Cm 7724, 2009.

Consultative committees

The practice of consultation between government departments and organisations outside government is a widespread phenomenon of British government even today. Consultation serves to meet the needs of the administrator for expert information and advice on scientific, technical or industrial matters. It also is an important means by which those in government seek to maintain the continuing consent of the governed and it thus serves important political purposes. Where consultative committees and advisory councils exist, they enable the practice of consultation to be placed on a regular and structured footing. Consultative committees are used over the whole range of government. They have proved particularly useful in the process by which new delegated legislation is prepared, but their use is not confined to projected legislation. In some cases there is a statutory obligation on a minister to consult a standing committee or named association, although the advisory body may be unable to take the initiative in discussing a subject without the matter being referred to it by the minister. Many advisory bodies are appointed and consulted at the discretion of the minister or department concerned and their discussions are often regarded as confidential, even where a more open approach to government would promote administrative fairness.[138]

An illustration of a statutory body which ministers must consult is the Police Negotiating Board. Regulations relating to the government, administration and conditions of service in police forces can be made under the Police Act 1996 and the equivalent Acts for Scotland and Northern Ireland only after the Secretary of State has consulted the Board, on which sit representatives of local police authorities and of all ranks of the police.[139] The Social Security Advisory Committee gives advice and reports to the Secretary of State for Work and Pensions on his or her functions under the Social Security Acts. In particular, where the Secretary of State proposes to make regulations about social security benefits the proposal must be referred to the committee; when the regulations are laid before Parliament, the Secretary of State must inform Parliament of the committee's views and, if effect is not to be given to the committee's recommendations, of the reasons for this.[140] The Administrative Justice and Tribunals Council, appointed to keep under review the administrative justice system as well as the constitution and working of statutory inquiries,[141] is essentially a body which advises and is consulted by government departments; like most advisory bodies it has no executive functions, but its watchdog role includes scrutinising and commenting on proposed legislation relating to tribunals.[142]

---

[138] *R v Secretary of State for Health, ex p US Tobacco Inc* [1992] QB 353.
[139] Police Act 1996, s 61.
[140] See now Social Security Administration Act 1992, Part XIII.
[141] Tribunals, Courts and Enforcement Act 2007, s 44. The Act abolished the Council on Tribunals, which performed a similar role in the past (s 45).
[142] Ch 29 A.

CHAPTER 15

Foreign affairs and the Commonwealth

International law has the primary function of regulating the relations of independent, sovereign states with one another,[1] and this is still the position despite current trends in relation to human rights, the global environment, and international criminal law that bring more closely together international and national public law.[2] In international law, the United Kingdom of Great Britain and Northern Ireland is a state, with authority to act for its dependent possessions, such as the Channel Islands, the Isle of Man and its surviving overseas territories, such as Gibraltar, none of which is a state at international law. But political groupings and national boundaries seldom last for all time. The British Empire gave way to the Commonwealth, whose members are all independent states. And organs of the European Union now have capacity on behalf of the member states to conduct relations on economic and commercial matters between the Union and non-member states.[3]

This chapter considers (*a*) the executive's power to conduct foreign affairs; (*b*) aspects of the making of treaties; and (*c*) in outline, the development and nature of the Commonwealth. It does not, however, deal with the whole of what can be called foreign relations law.[4]

A. The foreign affairs prerogative, international law and the courts

In 1820, Chitty believed it essential for the conduct of foreign affairs that 'the exclusive power of managing and executing state measures' should be vested in one individual, as it was not practical for an assembly of people to decide what action should be taken by the state. The constitution, said Chitty, had vested in the King the supreme and exclusive power of managing the country's foreign affairs.[5] At common law, this power, like control of the armed forces,[6] is still vested in the Crown, although many aspects of foreign relations law are the subject of legislation (for example, the State Immunity Act 1978).[7] As a prerogative power, the foreign affairs power is exercised on the authority of the Cabinet or of ministers, in particular the Prime Minister and the Secretary of State for Foreign and Commonwealth Affairs. While parliamentary approval is not generally needed before action is taken, ministers are responsible to Parliament for their policies and decisions.[8]

The Foreign Secretary is responsible for the Foreign and Commonwealth Office, which includes the diplomatic and consular service that represents British interests abroad. Other ministers and departments deal as required with international aspects of their work. These include the Department for International Development, the Ministry of Defence, the Home Office (especially immigration

---

[1] Page 10 above. See Brownlie, *Principles of Public International Law*, Jennings and Watts, *Oppenheim's International Law: the Law of Peace* and Shaw, *International Law*.

[2] See D Feldman's perceptive study of the internationalisation of public law in Jowell and Oliver (eds), *The Changing Constitution* (6th edn), ch 5.

[3] Ch 8 A and p 319 below.

[4] See HLE, vol 18(2), title *Foreign Relations Law* (4th edn, reissue, 2000).

[5] Chitty, *Prerogatives of the Crown*, ch 4.

[6] Ch 16.

[7] Page 311 below.

[8] HLE, vol 8(2), pp 310–15.

control), and the departments of Revenue and Customs, and Work and Pensions, concerned with British citizens who work abroad and foreigners who work in the United Kingdom.

The prerogative extends to the 'whole catalogue of relations with foreign nations',[9] such as making treaties, declaring war and making peace, instituting hostilities that fall short of war (as with the Gulf campaign, Afghanistan and Iraq), the recognition of foreign states, sending and receiving ambassadors, issuing passports[10] and granting diplomatic protection to British citizens abroad.[11]

But Crown prerogative does not include everything that is needed to carry out the government's foreign policies. Except in wartime, the prerogative does not extend to controlling trade between the United Kingdom and foreign countries. Thus import and export controls are authorised by statute.[12] Although some prerogative power exists to control the movement of aliens to and from the United Kingdom, immigration control is essentially derived from statute.[13] The prerogative does not include power to impose taxes for regulating foreign trade,[14] and the power to make treaties does not include power to change the law of the United Kingdom.[15]

Although the government may in general take action in foreign affairs without first getting the consent of Parliament, this does not allow it to dispense with political support. Foreign affairs are often the subject of debate and questions in Parliament; and the Foreign Affairs Committee of the Commons examines 'the expenditure, administration and policy of the Foreign and Commonwealth Office and of associated public bodies'.[16] Since 1979 the committee has reviewed many areas of foreign policy, sometimes in very critical terms.[17] In 2010, the law was changed to create a formal requirement for parliamentary involvement in the ratification of new treaties.[18]

The relationship between national and international law[19]

The relationship between national and international law raises difficult questions in both theory and practice. By art 25 of the German Constitution, the general rules of public international law are declared to be an integral part of German law; they take precedence over other German laws and create rights and duties for the people. By contrast with this instance of 'monism', English law in general favours 'dualism', that is, a position in which the two systems of law (national and international) coexist, but function separately: each has distinct purposes and the subjects of international law are typically sovereign states, not individual persons. This coexistence does not guarantee harmony between the two systems. Thus an executive act in foreign affairs which is lawful in national law – under the prerogative or by statute – may be a breach of international law for which the United Kingdom is responsible.[20] Conversely, an executive act which seeks to perform an international obligation may be unlawful in national law.[21] This dualism is best seen in respect of treaties.

---

[9] Mann, *Foreign Affairs in English Courts*, p 4.

[10] *R v Foreign Secretary, ex p Everett* [1989] QB 811; p 314 below.

[11] Cf *Mutasa v A-G* [1980] QB 114; *R v Foreign Secretary, ex p Abbasi* [2002] EWCA Civ 1598, (2003) UKHRR 76.

[12] See Import and Export Control Act 1990: and (Scott Report) HC 115 (1995–6), vol I, pp 49–105; vol IV, pp 1759–66.

[13] Ch 20 B; cf Immigration Act 1971, s 33(5).

[14] Bill of Rights, art 4 (p 14 above; and ch 12 D).

[15] See section B.

[16] And see ch 10 D.

[17] C Y Carstairs, in Drewry (ed.), *The New Select Committees*, ch 9.

[18] Constitutional Reform and Governance Act 2010, part 2, ss 20–25. The case for greater parliamentary control of the prerogative was made by the Public Administration Committee in *Taming the Prerogative*, HC 422 (2003–04).

[19] Mann, chs 6–8; Brownlie, ch 2; Jennings and Watts, pp 56–63; Shaw, ch 4. Also P Sales and J Clement (2008) 124 LQR 388 (stressing need to maintain constitutional safeguards in this relationship).

[20] E.g. *Mortensen v Peters* (1908) 8 F(J) 93; p 57 above.

[21] E.g. *Walker v Baird* [1892] AC 491; p 315 below.

It is axiomatic that municipal courts have not . . . the competence to adjudicate upon or to enforce the rights arising out of transactions entered into by independent sovereign states between themselves on the plane of international law.[22]

When new obligations are created by treaty, legislation is needed for them to become rules of national law.[23]

In respect of customary international law (the 'common law' of inter-state relations), English courts at one time stated that international law was part of the common law of England. Blackstone declared: 'the law of nations (wherever any question arises which is properly the object of its jurisdiction) is here adopted to its full extent by the common law, and is held to be a part of the law of the land'.[24] On this approach, by which international law may be said to be 'incorporated' in national law,[25] no specific act of 'transformation' is needed: a national court may directly apply the rule of customary international law, if this would not be contrary to statute or a prior decision binding on the court.[26]

For the courts to apply such a rule of international law, it must have 'attained the position of general acceptance by civilised nations as a rule of international conduct, evidenced by international treaties and conventions, authoritative textbooks, practice and judicial decision'.[27] The difficulties in the process of deciding whether such a rule exists include the task of deciding whether a new rule of international law has emerged or whether an established international rule has changed. They are illustrated by the two following decisions.

In *R v Home Secretary, ex p Thakrar*,[28] arising from the expulsion of Asians from Uganda in 1972, the applicant, Thakrar (born in Uganda), claimed to be entitled to enter the United Kingdom on the basis of a rule of customary international law to the effect that a British protected person expelled from the country in which he was resident (here, Uganda) was entitled to enter British territory. The Court of Appeal held that no such rule of international law existed, nor (if it did) could it prevail against the Immigration Act 1971; in any event such a rule could not be enforced against the United Kingdom by a private individual, only by other states.

By contrast, in *Trendtex Trading Corporation* v *Central Bank of Nigeria*[29] a majority in the Court of Appeal held that because of changing practice in international law restricting sovereign immunity, the Central Bank of Nigeria was not immune from the jurisdiction of British courts. Since the rules of international law were changing to a narrower view of sovereign immunity, the court did not follow an earlier decision on the basis of which the bank would have been immune from being sued in British courts.

In reality, the adoption of customary international law by national courts in this manner is limited. One reason for this is that many matters such as state and diplomatic immunity are now subject to legislation enacted in response to multilateral agreements.[30] The State Immunity Act 1978, enacted in part to give effect to the European Convention on State Immunity,[31] takes a narrower view of sovereign immunity than did the common law. Immunity from the jurisdiction of UK courts is enjoyed only by foreign states, governments and other entities exercising sovereign

---

[22] *Rayner (Mincing Lane) Ltd* v *Dept of Trade* [1990] 2 AC 418, at 499 (Lord Oliver).

[23] Section B.

[24] *Commentaries*, iv, 67. And see e.g. *Triquet* v *Bath* (1764) 3 Burr 1478.

[25] See Brownlie, pp 41–5; Shaw, pp 138–57.

[26] *Chung Chi Cheung* v *R* [1939] AC 160, at 168 (Lord Atkin).

[27] *The Christina* [1938] AC 485, at 497 (Lord Macmillan). On the creation of norms of customary international law, see *R (European Roma Rights Centre)* v *Immigration Officer at Prague Airport* [2004] UKHL 55, [2005] 2 AC 1, [24] (Lord Bingham).

[28] [1974] QB 684, criticised by M B Akehurst (1975) 38 MLR 72.

[29] [1977] QB 529, criticised by Mann, pp 124–5. See now State Immunity Act 1978, s 3.

[30] See e.g. Consular Relations Act 1968 and International Organisations Act 1968.

[31] Cmnd 5081, 1972.

authority.[32] Exceptions from immunity arise in relation to commercial transactions, contracts to be performed in the United Kingdom, the ownership or possession of land in the United Kingdom and death or personal injury arising from acts in the United Kingdom (ss 3–5). Similarly, immunity from legal process for diplomatic staff is now governed by the Diplomatic Privileges Act 1964.[33] This legislation has effect against a background in which '[it] is a basic principle of international law that one sovereign state (the forum state) does not adjudicate on the conduct of a foreign state. The foreign state is entitled to procedural immunity from the processes of the forum state. The immunity extends to both criminal and civil liability.'[34]

But international law is not static, and difficult questions arise from the developing international criminal law, involving in particular genocide, crimes against humanity and torture.[35] Under the State Immunity Act 1978, both the state as an entity and its officials are immune from civil liability for torture.[36] Issues of criminal liability are also subject to the 1978 Act: it was an obscure provision of this Act that the Law Lords had to interpret in deciding that Pinochet, the former military dictator of Chile, was liable to be extradited to Spain because of crimes of torture committed while he was in office.[37] Questions of justiciability, rather than immunity, arose from the claim that conduct alleged to involve the international crime of aggression (for instance, sending British forces into Iraq in 2003) would also give rise to criminal liability in national law.[38] The response of the courts has been that they will not determine the meaning of international instruments that operate on the plane of international law alone,[39] and that it must be for Parliament to create new criminal offences. Both the courts and Parliament provide what have been called 'constitutional filters' that come into play in regulating the assimilation of international and national law.[40]

Executive evidence and 'facts of state'[41]

One problem for the courts in dealing with disputes relating to international events is that these are often the subject of conflicting opinions and are particularly within the experience and knowledge of the executive; it has been considered expedient that the judiciary and the executive should speak with one voice on these matters.[42] Rather than calling for proof of the relevant issues by evidence, the courts have evolved a practice by which certain matters are proved by a certificate from the Foreign Secretary or by a statement of the Attorney General. These matters

---

[32] See e.g. *Kuwait Airways Corpn v Iraqi Airways Co* [1995] 3 All ER 694. The 1978 Act does not apply to visiting forces in the UK, but common law immunity may apply: *Holland v Lampen-Wolfe* [2000] 3 All ER 833 (and p 339 below). See generally Fox, *Law of State Immunity.*

[33] Giving effect to the Vienna Convention on Diplomatic Relations (Cmnd 1368, 1964).

[34] *R v Bow Street Magistrate, ex p Pinochet Ugarte (No 3)* [2000] 1 AC 147, 201 (Lord Browne-Wilkinson). On the protection in respect of civil litigation given to a foreign head of state by the State Immunity Act 1978, see *Aziz v Aziz (Sultan of Brunei intervening)* [2007] EWCA (Civ) 712, [2008] 2 All ER 501.

[35] See UN Convention against Torture 1984; Criminal Justice Act 1988, s 134(1); *R v Bow Street Magistrate, ex p Pinochet Ugarte (No 3)* (above). Also *Al-Adsani v UK* (2001) 34 EHRR 11 (state immunity serves legitimate aim for ECHR purposes).

[36] *Jones v Ministry of the Interior, Saudi Arabia* [2006] UKHL 26, [2007] 1 AC 270.

[37] *R v Bow Street Magistrate, ex p Pinochet Ugarte (No 3)* [2000] 1 AC 147.

[38] *R v Jones (Margaret)* [2006] UKHL 16, [2007] 1 AC 136. And *R (Gentle) v Prime Minister* [2008] UKHL 20, [2008] AC 1356.

[39] See e.g. *R (Corner House Research) v Director, Serious Fraud Office* [2008] UKHL 60, [2009] AC 756 [43–46] (Lord Bingham), [59–68] (Lord Brown).

[40] See Feldman, note 2 above and Sales and Clement, note 19 above.

[41] Mann, ch 2.

[42] E.g. *The Arantzazu Mendi* [1939] AC 256, 264 (Lord Atkin); *Carl Zeiss Stiftung v Rayner & Keeler Ltd (No 2)* [1967] 1 AC 853, 961 (Lord Wilberforce).

include such questions as whether the United Kingdom is at war with another state,[43] the extent of British territorial jurisdiction,[44] whether the status of a person gives rise to immunity from jurisdiction[45] and whether the existence of a state has been recognised.[46] An example of the last kind arose in *Carl Zeiss Stiftung v Rayner & Keeler Ltd*,[47] where the Foreign Office certificate stated that what was then East Germany was not an independent state but was subordinate to, and governed by, the Soviet Union. The court had therefore to determine the legal effect of decrees in East Germany on this basis. Such certificates state what the Foreign Office recognises, not necessarily what other states or persons would accept.[48]

Before 1980, these certificates might state whether the United Kingdom had recognised the new government of a state (after a coup or other such change of government). In 1980, the Foreign Office abandoned its practice of recognising governments where a new regime came to power unconstitutionally.[49] If necessary, the courts must now decide whether a foreign entity exists as a government. The following criteria are applied: (*a*) whether it is the constitutional government of the state; (*b*) the degree, nature and stability of the administrative control, if any, that it exercises over the territory; (*c*) whether the British government has had relations with it and, if so, their nature; and (*d*) in marginal cases, the extent of international recognition that it has as government of the state.[50] Criterion (*c*) requires evidence in the form of a Foreign Office certificate as to the dealings, if any, that Britain has had with the entity in question.

By judicial practice, the statement of facts in such a certificate is conclusive.[51] Several statutes now provide for certificates to be given on particular matters within the knowledge of the executive.[52] Thus a certificate issued under the State Immunity Act 1978 provides conclusive evidence of the facts that it states.[53] Despite the conclusive effect of such a certificate in national law, a litigant might be able to show that the certificate is in breach of an overriding rule of Community law.[54]

Moreover, a certificate stating the facts (as perceived by the Foreign Office) is not conclusive as to the legal inferences that may be drawn. It is for the court to decide the legal consequences of a certificate declaring that a state has been recognised.[55] The court should not seek an executive certificate as a means of obtaining guidance as to the principles of international law to be applied.[56]

Judicial review of decisions under the prerogative

As we have seen,[57] the House of Lords in *CCSU v Minister for the Civil Service* held that decisions under the prerogative are in principle subject to judicial review. As Lord Scarman said, 'the controlling factor in deciding whether the exercise of prerogative power is subject to judicial review

---

[43] *R v Bottrill, ex p Kuechenmeister* [1947] KB 41. Cf *Sadiqa Ahmed Amin v Brown* [2005] EWHC 1670 (Ch) (government statements showing that UK not at war with Iraq).

[44] *The Fagernes* [1927] P 311, approved in *Post Office v Estuary Radio Ltd* [1968] 2 QB 740.

[45] *Mighell v Sultan of Johore* [1894] 1 QB 149. Even without a certificate, material before a court may establish sovereign immunity: e.g. *Mellenger v New Brunswick Development Corpn* [1971] 2 All ER 593.

[46] For such a certificate, see *Buttes Gas & Oil Co v Hammer* [1982] AC 888, 927–8.

[47] [1967] 1 AC 853.

[48] Mann, p 24.

[49] HLE, vol 18(2), pp 461–7; Brownlie, pp 101–2. Also C R Symmons [1981] PL 249.

[50] See *Republic of Somalia v Woodhouse Drake & Carey (Suisse) SA* [1993] 1 QB 54; *Sierra Leone Telecommunications Co Ltd v Barclays Bank plc* [1998] 2 All ER 821.

[51] *Carl Zeiss Stiftung*, note 42 above, at 901.

[52] E.g. Foreign Jurisdiction Act 1890, s 4 (extent of British jurisdiction in foreign country); Crown Proceedings Act 1947, s 40(3) (and see *Trawnik v Lennox* [1985] 2 All ER 368); Diplomatic Privileges Act 1964, s 4.

[53] Section 21. And see *R (Alamieyeseigha) v Crown Prosecution Service* [2005] EWHC 2704 Admin.

[54] By analogy with *Johnston v Chief Constable, RUC* [1987] QB 129.

[55] *Carl Zeiss Stiftung*, note 42 above, at 950 (Lord Upjohn).

[56] Cf *The Philippine Admiral* [1977] AC 373, 399.

[57] Ch 12 E.

is not its source but its subject matter'.[58] However, in *CCSU* it was envisaged that many prerogative powers would not be justiciable, including the making of treaties.[59] More generally, it has been stated that 'the conduct of foreign affairs cannot attract judicial review'.[60] Whether the government should make a treaty with state A,[61] or take proceedings in an international court against state B,[62] are essentially not matters for the judiciary to decide. But not all powers relating to foreign affairs are of the same kind. Even before *CCSU*, the Court of Appeal reviewed the legality of action taken by the government under a treaty with the United States concerning airline routes.[63] After *CCSU*, a Foreign Office decision as to the issue of a passport was held subject to review, on the basis that it 'is a matter of administrative decision, affecting the rights of individuals and their freedom of travel. It raises issues which are just as justiciable as the issues arising in immigration cases'.[64] The courts may also rule on the legality of action taken in the course of foreign policy. In 1993, an application for judicial review of the government's decision to ratify the Treaty on European Union was rejected on the merits of the issues. The court held that by entering the Union's common security and foreign policy the government was exercising prerogative power, not relinquishing it.[65] By contrast, the court declared unlawful a government decision to fund the Pergau Dam project, since the statutory conditions for granting foreign aid had not been met.[66] The criteria applied in such cases derive from the principles of administrative law, not directly from public international law.[67]

Acts of state[68]

The Crown's prerogative in foreign affairs does not include power to change the law. But the Crown's actions may nonetheless have legal effects for individuals; for example, a government decision to take action against another state (for instance, the use of the armed forces against Argentina to regain the Falkland Islands in 1982) may adversely affect British citizens or the citizens of third countries who reside in that state, or may prevent companies from doing business there. Those affected by such action may seek compensation for any loss that they have suffered. For two reasons, the British courts are unlikely to afford this relief. First, the acts of the Crown are likely to be within the prerogative; lawful acts in general do not give rise to a duty to compensate. (In exceptional cases there may be a duty to compensate if the prerogative act amounts to a taking of private property for public use.)[69] Second, the international element in a dispute may lead the court to conclude that, whether or not a claim is well founded in international law, it is outside the jurisdiction of national courts: if so, the court turns the claimant away without deciding the legal merits of the claim.

---

[58] [1985] AC 374, 407 (Lord Scarman).

[59] Ibid, 418 (Lord Roskill). See also cases in note 38 above.

[60] Mann, p 50. And see *R (Bancoult) v Foreign Secretary (No 2)* [2008] UKHL 61, [2009] 1 AC 453 (prerogative order in council subject to judicial review, but policy as to 'security and diplomatic interests of the Crown' is 'peculiarly within the competence of the executive': Lord Hoffmann, para [58]). The majority decision in *Bancoult (No 2)* is criticised by M Elliott and A Perreau-Saussine [2009] PL 697.

[61] *Rustomjee v R* (1876) 2 QBD 69; *Blackburn v A-G* [1971] 2 All ER 1380.

[62] *R v Foreign Secretary, ex p Pirbai*, *The Times*, 17 October 1985; cf *R v Foreign Secretary, ex p Abbasi* [2002] EWCA Civ 1598 (note 11 above).

[63] *Laker Airways v Department of Trade* [1977] QB 643.

[64] *R v Foreign Secretary, ex p Everett* [1989] QB 811, 820 (Taylor LJ).

[65] *R v Foreign Secretary, ex p Rees-Mogg* [1994] QB 552; see G Marshall [1993] PL 402; R Rawlings [1994] PL 254, 367.

[66] *R v Foreign Secretary, ex p World Development Movement* [1995] 1 All ER 611. Also *R v Foreign Secretary, ex p Bancoult* [2001] QB 1067 (unlawful removal of population).

[67] Cf Sales and Clement (n 19, above), 404–7.

[68] See Harrison Moore, *Act of State in English Law*; J G Collier [1968] CLJ 102; Mann, note 9 above, chs 9, 10; P Wesley-Smith (1986) 6 LS 325; HLE, vol 18(2), pp 452–9.

[69] *Burmah Oil Co v Lord Advocate* [1965] AC 75; ch 12 D.

Although it is applied confusingly to different situations,[70] the term 'act of state' is used in this context. One definition of act of state is that it is 'an act of the Executive as a matter of policy performed in the course of its relations with another state, including its relations with subjects of that state, unless they are temporarily within the allegiance of the Crown'.[71] This is not a wholly satisfactory definition,[72] and different legal inferences may be drawn from it. But some propositions may be stated briefly:

1 In general, a plea of state necessity is not a justification for acts of the executive that are otherwise unlawful.[73]

2 The fact that the Crown has acquired territory or concluded a treaty does not in itself give rise to rights enforceable against the Crown.[74]

3 In limited circumstances, a plea of act of state is a reason why a claim for damages in tort or for compensation brought may be held by British courts to be outside their jurisdiction. Such a plea is available to the Crown or an agent of the Crown when a foreign citizen who is resident abroad sues in respect of acts committed abroad.[75] 'Act of state' is here a plea to the jurisdiction of the courts and is not to be confused with the defence that the Crown was acting lawfully under the prerogative. Whether such a defence is valid needs to be decided by the courts only if the claim is within their jurisdiction. It is, however, for the court to decide whether the acts in question are 'acts of state' for this purpose.

> In *Nissan v Attorney-General*, a United Kingdom citizen who owned a hotel in Cyprus claimed compensation from the Crown for the occupation of the hotel by British troops; they had first entered Cyprus by agreement with the Cyprus government, and later remained there as part of a United Nations peace-keeping force. The House of Lords held that the Crown could not rely on the plea of 'act of state' as a bar to Nissan's claim. The House took the view that, while the agreement between the British and Cyprus governments might well have been an 'act of state', acts of the British forces in occupying the hotel did not constitute such an act of state: the claim was accordingly justiciable in the British courts.[76]

Among the points of law left open by the House of Lords in *Nissan* was whether the plea of act of state can ever be raised to bar a claim brought against the Crown by a British citizen. Nor did the House resolve the question of whether prerogative power is being exercised by the Crown when its agents are carrying out its policy abroad.[77]

4 In the event of war being declared against a foreign state,[78] citizens of that state who are in the United Kingdom are liable to be detained as enemy aliens and if they seek their release in the British courts, they may be met by a plea of act of state (or, as seems more satisfactory, by the defence of lawful action under the prerogative).[79] However, where war has not been declared by the United Kingdom against a foreign state, but military action is undertaken, as it was during the Gulf hostilities involving Iraq in 1991, nationals of that state resident in the United Kingdom are

---

[70] *Buttes Gas & Oil Co v Hammer* [1982] AC 888, 930 (Lord Wilberforce).

[71] E C S Wade (1934) 15 BYIL 98, 103.

[72] *Nissan v A-G* [1970] AC 179, 212 (Lord Reid); cf P J Allott [1977] CLJ 255, 270.

[73] *Entick v Carrington* (1765) 19 State Tr 1029; ch 6 A.

[74] *Civilian War Claimants Association v R* [1932] AC 14.

[75] *Buron v Denman* (1848) 2 Ex 167; *Walker v Baird* [1892] AC 491. Cf *Johnstone v Pedlar* [1921] 2 AC 262 (no act of state when US citizen arrested in United Kingdom).

[76] *Nissan v A-G* [1970] AC 179.

[77] Ibid, 213 (Lord Reid), 236 (Lord Wilberforce) and cf 227 (Lord Pearce).

[78] As to why a formal declaration of war is unlikely today, see C J Greenwood (1987) 36 ICLQ 283. Also *Sadiqa Ahmed Amin v Brown* (note 43 above).

[79] *R v Vine Street Police Station, ex p Liebmann* [1916] 1 KB 268; *Netz v Ede* [1946] Ch 224.

entitled to be protected by the courts against unlawful detention,[80] just as other friendly aliens within the jurisdiction are entitled to be protected against unlawful action.[81]

5 The plea of a 'foreign act of state' may arise where an action is brought in a British court in respect of the executive acts of foreign states; in this situation, the court declines jurisdiction and will hold the matter to be non-justiciable: 'the courts will not adjudicate on the transactions of foreign sovereign states'.[82] Thus British courts have no jurisdiction to rule on the validity of the constitution of a foreign state,[83] nor on the interpretation of a UN Security Council resolution when this did not affect rights or duties under domestic law.[84]

It will be evident from this discussion that the term 'act of state' is not a universal bar to legal claims arising from government action with a foreign element. The term came into use in a period when the doctrine of national sovereignty was at its most absolute and when judicial review of executive action was much narrower in scope than it is today. However, the concept of 'act of state' does not require courts to recognise foreign legislation that is contrary to British public policy.[85] Today its use has diminished since, as we have seen, some of the barriers between international and national law are being eroded. The claim that acts of 'foreign policy' affecting individuals are thereby beyond judicial scrutiny will not readily be accepted today. A vivid illustration of this is given by the claims brought in England on behalf of Iraqi citizens who died in the course of military action during the occupation of Iraq, including one who died as the result of abuse or torture while in British custody. The Ministry of Defence did not plead act of state, presumably because the combined effect of the European Convention on Human Rights and the Human Rights Act 1998 excluded that plea to the jurisdiction of the court. The main issues to be decided were whether the Human Rights Act applied to all or some of the aspects of British military action in Iraq and, if so, whether the Iraqis in question had been within the 'jurisdiction' of the United Kingdom for the purposes of art 1, ECHR at the time when they were killed.[86]

B. Treaties[87]

By the Vienna Convention on the Law of Treaties, a treaty is defined as an international agreement concluded between states in written form and governed by international law, whether embodied in a single instrument or in two or more related instruments and whatever its particular designation.[88] Whatever name may be given to it (convention, covenant, protocol, charter, exchange of notes etc.), a treaty is an agreement between two or more sovereign states which creates rights and obligations for the parties. A country's constitutional law determines who can exercise the treaty-making power. By the US Constitution, this power is vested in the President,

---

[80] See e.g. *R v Home Secretary, ex p Cheblak* [1991] 2 All ER 319; also I Leigh [1991] PL 331, F Hampson [1991] PL 507.

[81] *Johnstone v Pedlar* [1921] 2 AC 262. Also *Sadiqa Ahmed Amin v Brown* (above).

[82] See *Buttes Gas & Oil v Hammer* [1982] AC 888, 931–4. And see *R v Bow Street Magistrate, ex p Pinochet Ugarte (No 3)* [2000] 1 AC 147, 201.

[83] *Buck v A-G* [1965] Ch 745; *Fitzgibbon v A-G* [2005] EWHC 114 (Ch).

[84] *Campaign for Nuclear Disarmament v Prime Minister* [2002] EWHC 2759 QB. Cf *R (Al-Jedda) v Defence Secretary* [2007] UKHL 58, [2008] AC 332 (UK forces in Iraq authorised by UN Security Council Resolution 1546 to detain claimant with dual UK and Iraqi citizenship).

[85] *Kuwait Airways Corporation v Iraqi Airways Co* [2002] UKHL 19, [2002] 2 AC 883 (government decree expropriating civilian aircraft).

[86] *R (Al-Skeini) v Defence Secretary* [2007] UKHL 26, [2008] AC 153. On art 1 ECHR, see *Bancovic v Belgium* (2001) 11 BHRC 435. Consider also *R (Al-Jedda) v Defence Secretary* (note 84, above).

[87] See McNair, *Law of Treaties*; Brownlie, note 1 above, ch 26; Jennings and Watts, note 1 above, ch 14; Aust, *Modern Treaty Law and Practice*.

[88] Cmnd 4848, 1969, art 2, para 1.

'by and with the advice of the Senate', provided that two-thirds of the Senate concur; treaties so approved have a status equal to that of legislation by Congress.[89]

By contrast, in the United Kingdom there is no direct parliamentary involvement in the making of treaties. To this, three qualifications must be made. First, under the so-called Ponsonby rule, which applies to treaties that have been negotiated and signed but have not come into effect because they have not (in international law) been ratified by the parties, the government notifies Parliament of the treaty and must not ratify it (save in cases of urgency) until 21 parliamentary days have elapsed.[90] This both informs Parliament of the treaty and enables it to be debated. Second, Parliament may restrict the ability of the executive to conclude or ratify treaties by imposing an express requirement of parliamentary consent.[91] Third, a treaty which is entered into by the government does not alter the law in the United Kingdom: 'the making of a treaty is an executive act, while the performance of its obligations, if they entail alteration of the existing domestic law, requires legislative action'.[92] Further, '[except] to the extent that a treaty becomes incorporated into the laws of the United Kingdom by statute, the courts . . . have no power to enforce treaty rights and obligations at the behest of a sovereign government or at the behest of a private individual.'[93] If the objects of a treaty require national law to be changed, this must be done by legislation. Often an Act of Parliament is necessary, but a minister may be able to make the required changes in national law by exercising existing powers of delegated legislation.[94] To avoid a situation in which a treaty has become binding but the necessary changes in national law have not been made, the implementing legislation may need to be enacted before the government ratifies the treaty. In general, a state cannot rely on defects in its own law as a defence to a claim in international law.[95]

Where a treaty has not been incorporated in national law by legislation, the courts may not directly enforce the treaty. Thus in 1991 the House of Lords held that the European Convention on Human Rights, ratified in 1951 but not the subject of legislation, could not be a source of rights and obligations.[96] In 1995, the High Court of Australia held that an unincorporated treaty could give rise to a 'legitimate expectation' that executive decision makers would act in accordance with the treaty.[97] The Australian government took prompt steps to prevent such an expectation arising, and there are conflicting decisions of the Court of Appeal on whether the principle that an unincorporated treaty may give rise to an expectation of executive compliance is recognised in English law.[98]

The courts will generally regard the interpretation of a treaty that has not been incorporated as non-justiciable.[99]

---

[89] US Constitution, art II(2), art IV; *Whitney v Robertson* 124 US 190 (1888).

[90] HC Deb, 1 April 1924, cols 2001–4; Erskine May, *Parliamentary Practice*, pp 264–5; HLE, vol 8(2), pp 465–9. The procedure is now governed by the Constitutional Reform and Governance Act 2010, part 2.

[91] See European Parliamentary Elections Act 1978, s 6(1) (no treaty increasing powers of European Parliament to be ratified unless approved by Act); *R v Foreign Secretary, ex p Rees-Mogg* [1994] QB 552.

[92] *A-G for Canada v A-G for Ontario* [1937] AC 326, 347 (Lord Atkin).

[93] *Rayner (Mincing Lane) Ltd v Department of Trade* [1990] 2 AC 418, 477 (Lord Templeman); *Littrell v USA (No 2)* [1994] 4 All ER 203.

[94] See ch 28.

[95] Vienna Convention on Law of Treaties, art 27; and Brownlie, p 34.

[96] *R v Home Secretary, ex p Brind* [1991] 1 AC 696. See ch 19 B. For ways in which, apart from incorporation, the courts could take account of the ECHR, see Hunt, *Using Human Rights Law in English Courts*.

[97] *Minister of State for Immigration v Teoh* (1995) 128 ALR 353. See R Piotrowicz [1996] PL 190 and Lord Lester [1996] PL 187. Also ch 30 C.

[98] *R v Home Secretary, ex p Ahmed* [1998] INLR 570. *Behluli v Home Secretary* [1998] Imm AR 407. Cf *Tavita v Minister for Immigration* [1994] NZLR 257.

[99] E.g. the *Campaign for Nuclear Disarmament* case (above). For an exceptional case, see *Ecuador v Occidental Exploration Co* [2005] EWCA Civ 1116, [2006] QB 432.

Even where a treaty seeks to benefit a definite class of persons (for example, where a foreign government provides funds to compensate British citizens who have suffered at that government's hands), such persons do not acquire rights of enforcing the treaty against the British government.[100] The money received under such treaties may be distributed in accordance with a statutory scheme by the Foreign Compensation Commission, whose decisions are subject to an appeal to the courts.[101] In the Sachsenhausen case, which went to the Parliamentary Ombudsman,[102] this procedure was not followed: a shortcut taken by the Foreign Office proved unsatisfactory, because of an erroneous view that the Office had formed of the so-called Butler rules. Were this to occur today, someone who claimed that the Foreign Office was not correctly applying the rules of distribution could seek judicial review.[103] Such an application might be strengthened if the treaty in question declared that the government was acting as agent or trustee for its subjects.[104] But this would not necessarily be decisive, since not all governmental obligations in the nature of a trust are justiciable.[105]

Interpretation of legislation giving effect to treaties

The methods by which Parliament may give effect in national law to obligations arising under a treaty include the following.[106] First, the statute may enact the substance of the treaty in its own words without referring to the treaty.[107] Second, the statute may name the treaty (for example, in the title of the Act) and then either enact all or part of the substance of the treaty in its own words.[108] Third, the statute may set out the text of the treaty in a schedule, while giving legal effect either to part of the treaty[109] or to the whole text.[110]

Where a problem of interpretation arises, for example from a discrepancy between statutory words and the treaty, the courts' approach to the problem does not turn on the precise manner of incorporation in a particular case, provided it appears, if necessary from extrinsic evidence, that a statute was enacted in pursuance of an international obligation. If Parliament uses express and unambiguous language, this must be given effect by the courts even if the result of so doing departs from what was intended by the treaty.[111] However,

> it is a principle of construction of United Kingdom statutes, now too well established to call for citation of authority, that the words of a statute passed after the treaty has been signed and dealing with the subject matter of the international obligation of the United Kingdom, are to be construed, if they are reasonably capable of bearing such a meaning, as intended to carry out the obligation and not to be inconsistent with it.[112]

The law may be developing even beyond this so that, whether the court is construing statutory words or resolving a disputed question of common law in an area where the United Kingdom has

---

[100] *Civilian War Claimants Association v R* [1932] AC 14; *Lonrho Exports Ltd v Export Credits Guarantee Dept* [1999] Ch 158, 178–9. Also p 315 above.

[101] Foreign Compensation Act 1969, s 3 (enacted after *Anisminic Ltd v Foreign Compensation Commission* [1969] 2 AC 147; and see ch 30 A).

[102] Ch 29 D.

[103] *R v Criminal Injuries Compensation Board, ex p Lain* [1967] 2 QB 864; see ch 12 D, E.

[104] *Civilian War Claimants Association* (note 100) at 26–7 (Lord Atkin).

[105] *Tito v Waddell (No 2)* [1977] Ch 106; cf *Mutasa v A-G* [1980] QB 114.

[106] Mann, 97–102.

[107] E.g. Evidence (Proceedings in other Jurisdictions) Act 1975, considered in *Re Westinghouse* [1978] AC 547.

[108] E.g. Arbitration Act 1975.

[109] E.g. Geneva Conventions Act 1957 (F Hampson [1991] PL 507); and Diplomatic Privileges Act 1964.

[110] E.g. Carriage of Goods by Road Act 1965; and *Buchanan & Co v Babco Ltd* [1978] AC 141.

[111] *Salomon v Commissioners of Customs & Excise* [1967] 2 QB 116.

[112] *Garland v British Rail Engineering Ltd* [1983] 2 AC 751, 771 (Lord Diplock).

international obligations, the court may have regard to the treaty 'as part of the full content or background of the law'.[113] Before the Human Rights Act 1998, this doctrine enabled the courts to take some account of the European Convention on Human Rights. Under the Human Rights Act, the courts must take into account decisions by the European Court of Human Rights and must if possible interpret legislation so that it is in conformity with the Convention rights.[114]

When a court needs to consider a treaty,[115] further questions may arise as to how that text should be interpreted. According to Lord Wilberforce, the approach 'must be appropriate for the interpretation of an international convention, unconstrained by technical rules of English law, or by English legal precedent, but on broad principles of general acceptance'.[116] In a case on political asylum where a UK statute excluded the removal of any person in breach of the Geneva Convention on the Status of Refugees, the House of Lords held that British courts must determine and apply the true meaning of the Convention, 'approached as an international instrument created by the agreement of contracting states as opposed to regulatory regimes established by national institutions', even if a different meaning were applied by French and German courts.[117]

The European Union and the law on treaties

The current legal order in Europe has consequences that go far beyond the general law of treaties. The European Union (EU) is now governed by the Treaty on European Union (TEU) and the Treaty on the Functioning of the European Union (TFEU).[118] The EU replaces what was previously the European Community, which in turn was a consolidation of what at one time had been a number of European Communities. In giving effect to EU law (or EEC law as it then was), the European Communities Act 1972 provided a further variant to the methods of treaty implementation described earlier. The European Treaties in force in 1972 were listed in a schedule to the Act, but their texts were not set out. Those rights, obligations and other matters arising from the treaties that were to have legal effect without further enactment within the United Kingdom were declared to have that effect (s 2(1)).[119] Under the 1972 Act (as now amended to take account of the creation of the European Union), future European Treaties may be designated by Order in Council and thus brought within its scope (s 1(3)). While such an Order in Council is delegated legislation, and could be challenged as *ultra vires* if the treaty named could not properly be regarded as a European Treaty,[120] such a challenge would be unlikely to succeed. In fact, major European treaties have generally been designated by primary legislation, as most recently in the case of the TEU and the TFEU.[121] It is a unique feature of EU law (and EC law before it) that many of these treaty provisions have direct effect in national law and may be enforced in national courts, without any implementing measures.[122]

The TEU makes extensive provision for EU external affairs and the development of a common foreign and security policy.[123] The EU is obliged to develop relations with third countries and international organisations, and may conclude agreements with states or international organisations in areas covered by the TEU.[124] Provisions of the TFEU envisage that agreements will be

---

[113] *Pan-American World Airways v Department of Trade* [1976] 1 Lloyd's Rep 257.
[114] Ch 19 C.
[115] See e.g. *Derbyshire CC v Times Newspapers Ltd* [1993] AC 534.
[116] *Buchanan & Co v Babco Ltd* (note 110), 152 (Lord Wilberforce).
[117] *R v Home Secretary, ex p Adan* [2001] 2 AC 474, 515 (Lord Steyn). And see ch 20 B.
[118] Ch 8 A.
[119] Ch 8 C.
[120] *R v HM Treasury, ex p Smedley* [1985] QB 657.
[121] European Union (Amendment) Act 2008, and see e.g. European Union (Accessions) Act 2003.
[122] Ch 8 B.
[123] TEU, arts 21–45.
[124] Ibid, art 21.

made with third countries or international organisations for other purposes:[125] such agreements concluded by the Union 'are binding upon the institutions of the Union and on its member states' (art 218). Under the TFEU, such agreements must be authorised by the Council following a recommendation by the Commission (or in some cases the High Representative for Foreign Affairs and Security Policy). The negotiated agreement must be approved by the Council and, depending on its subject-matter, there may be a duty either to consult with or secure the consent of the European Parliament. There is no need for such consultation or consent in the case of agreements relating exclusively to the common foreign and security policy, though in these cases the Parliament must be kept informed.[126] It has been held by the European Court of Justice that 'each time the [Union], with a view to implementing a common policy envisaged by the Treaty, adopts provisions laying down common rules . . . the Member States no longer have the right, acting individually or even collectively, to undertake obligations with third countries which affect those rules'.[127] Thus in these areas there is a transfer of treaty-making power from member states to the Union.

C. The United Kingdom and the Commonwealth[128]

In the heyday of empire, the imperial Crown, government and Parliament were at the apex of an impressive network of power that extended to many countries. Authority was exercised through laws and executive decisions made in London; and the Judicial Committee of the Privy Council heard appeals from courts across the world.[129] Imperial rule was often indirect rule, since many territories in the sovereignty or protection of the Crown developed their own forms of government; other territories retained rulers that were in power before they came within British influence.[130] The form of government for a territory might be laid down in a constitution, enacted by the imperial Parliament or issued by the Crown, whether under prerogative powers (in the case of conquered or ceded colonies)[131] or under powers granted by statute (for example, the Foreign Jurisdiction Acts 1890 and 1913). For some countries that were settled from Britain, democratic forms of government developed during the eighteenth and nineteenth centuries: the need for responsible government in Canada was recognised in 1838.[132] While a territory might have its own constitution, the imperial authorities could override this, whether by executive action or by recourse to the legislative authority of the Crown or the Westminster Parliament.[133]

Today, the constitutional law of the colonies and the Empire is primarily of historic interest, but a few overseas possessions of the United Kingdom remain.[134] In most of those territories, there is now legislative protection for human rights, although this was not the former colonial

---

[125] See arts 207 (commercial affairs), 209 (development cooperation), 212 (economic cooperation). Also TEU, art 6 (accession to the ECHR).

[126] TFEU, arts 216–219.

[127] *Case 22/70*, the ERTA case [1971] ECR 263, 274.

[128] See Roberts-Wray, *Commonwealth and Colonial Law*, and Dale, *The Modern Commonwealth*. Also Wheare, *The Constitutional Structure of the Commonwealth*, and de Smith, *The New Commonwealth and its Constitutions*.

[129] Page 326 below and ch 12 A.

[130] Morris and Read, *Indirect Rule and the Search for Justice*.

[131] See *R (Bancoult) v Foreign Secretary (No 2)*, note 60 above.

[132] See the Earl of Durham's *Report on the Affairs of British North America*.

[133] The leading case on colonial law, *Campbell v Hall* (1774) 1 Cowp 204, concerned the power of the Crown to legislate, not the authority of the British Parliament.

[134] In 2009 the overseas territories included Anguilla, Bermuda, British Antarctic Territory, British Indian Ocean Territory, British Virgin Islands, Cayman Islands, Falkland Islands, Gibraltar, Montserrat, Pitcairn Islands, Turks and Caicos Islands. See Cm 4264, 1999 and the British Overseas Territories Act 2002. See also report on the overseas territories by the Foreign Affairs Committee, HC 147 (2007–08).

tradition.[135] By making declarations under the European Convention on Human Rights, art 56, the UK government has extended the Convention to most but not all of the territories, and this is sometimes accompanied by local legislation corresponding to the Human Rights Act 1998.[136]

By contrast with the emphasis on law and legality in the European Union, the structure of the Commonwealth is scarcely a matter of law at all. For the Commonwealth, there is no written constitution nor, unlike most international organisations, was it created by treaty; it is 'a community of states in which the absence of a rigid legal basis of association is compensated by the bonds of common origin, history and legal tradition'.[137]

Dependence and independence[138]

The Commonwealth evolved from a protracted process in which the United Kingdom's dependent territories first received some kind of representative legislature; then acquired responsible self-government in domestic affairs while subject to imperial control in matters of defence and external relations; and eventually achieved independence. By this last step, the territory became a separate state in international law, having its own organs of government and power to determine its own policies. The English common law was often received into the legal system; and there developed a body of law relating to the powers and duties of colonial authorities. The Colonial Laws Validity Act 1865 was a statute of wide significance.[139] Its main aim was to confirm that, subject to certain limits, laws made by a colonial legislature were valid even if they differed from the English common law or from statutes enacted at Westminster.[140] The Act also authorised a colonial legislature at least half of whose members were democratically elected in the colony, to make laws respecting its own constitution, powers and procedure, provided that these laws were passed in such manner and form as required by any Act of Parliament or other law applying to the colony.[141] This Act strengthened the ability of colonial legislatures to act within their powers, but confirmed that these powers were limited and subject to imperial control.

What became known as Dominion status developed in the late nineteenth century as certain colonies (particularly those in Australia, Canada, New Zealand and South Africa) moved towards full statehood.[142] By the mid-1920s, the Dominions had full internal autonomy in accordance with their constitutions (that were contained in Acts of the imperial Parliament: for example, the British North America Act 1867, and the Commonwealth of Australia Act 1900) and had acquired the right to conduct foreign relations. The imperial conference in 1926 declared that Great Britain and the Dominions were:

> autonomous Communities within the British Empire, equal in status, in no way subordinate to another in any aspect of their domestic or external status, though united by a common allegiance to the Crown, and freely associated as members of the British Commonwealth of Nations.[143]

---

[135] Simpson, *Human Rights and the End of Empire*.

[136] Whether or not equivalent local legislation has been enacted, it is doubtful whether these territories are within the scope of the Human Rights Act 1998: *R (Quark Fishing Ltd) v Foreign Secretary* [2005] UKHL 57, [2006] 1 AC 529.

[137] Jennings and Watts, 266.

[138] See Roberts-Wray, chs 5, 6. Oliver, *The Constitution of Independence*, makes a perceptive analysis of the emergence of sovereignty and independence in Australia, Canada and New Zealand.

[139] Roberts-Wray, 396–409. For the background to the Act, see O'Connell and Riordan, *Opinions on Imperial Constitutional Law*, pp 60–74; and Swinfen, *Imperial Control of Colonial Legislation 1813–1865*.

[140] For the difficulty caused by the Act's inclusion of Orders in Council in the category of 'colonial laws', see *R (Bancoult) v Foreign Secretary (No 2)*, note 60 above; and A Twomey (2009) 9 *Ox Univ Commonwealth Law Jl* 47.

[141] This was the background to *A-G for New South Wales v Trethowan* [1932] AC 526; p 66 above.

[142] The older meaning of 'dominion' in the phrase 'Her Majesty's dominions', denotes all territories belonging to the Crown: Roberts-Wray, 23–9.

[143] Cmd 2768, 1926, 14; Dale, 21.

This statement of equality reflected the changing conventional relationship between the United Kingdom and the Dominions, but in law the Dominions were still colonies and subject to the Colonial Laws Validity Act. Even in 1926 the Canadian Parliament had no power to abolish certain criminal appeals from Canadian courts to the Privy Council.[144]

To deal with these limitations on Dominion authority, and to implement resolutions of three imperial conferences,[145] the Statute of Westminster was enacted by Parliament in 1931.[146] Its preamble described the Crown as the symbol of the free association of the members of the British Commonwealth of Nations, united by a common allegiance to the Crown; and referred to the 'established constitutional position' that changes in the law relating to the succession to the throne and the royal style and titles should receive the assent of the Dominion parliaments as well as of the United Kingdom Parliament.[147] The Statute broadened the powers of the Dominion legislatures by authorising them to amend or repeal Acts of the United Kingdom Parliament applying to the Dominion (s 2). However, this did not enable a legislature to ignore limits on its powers laid down in the Act containing the country's constitution.[148]

Section 4 of the Statute stated that no future Act of the British Parliament would extend to the Dominion as part of its law 'unless it is expressly declared in that Act that that Dominion has requested, and consented, to the enactment thereof'. The effect of this on the sovereignty of the Westminster Parliament was considered in the *British Coal Corporation* case, when Lord Sankey said that the power of the imperial Parliament to legislate for Canada on its own initiative remained unimpaired, adding: 'But that is theory and has no relation to realities.'[149] A more decisive note was struck by the Supreme Court of South Africa: 'freedom once conferred cannot be revoked'.[150]

The ability of Westminster to legislate for Canada remained important long after 1931. This was because the British North America Act 1867, which contained Canada's federal constitution, included no amendment power, so that legislation at Westminster was required to amend the Canadian constitution. This anomaly was removed when the Canada Act 1982 was enacted at Westminster to bring about the 'patriation' of the constitution to Canada. The 1982 Act had gone through a controversial process in Canada before being transmitted to Westminster for enactment.[151] The outcome was a Constitution Act which provided for its own future amendment; and it was declared that no future Act of the United Kingdom Parliament should extend to Canada as part of its law.[152] When the validity of the 1982 Act was challenged by indigenous peoples in Canada who claimed that their consent was needed to the legislation, the English Court of Appeal held that it was sufficient compliance with the Statute of Westminster that the 1982 Act declared that 'Canada' had requested and consented to its enactment; the court could not go behind this declaration.[153]

A less controversial change took place in 1986 with the passing of the Australia Act at Westminster, together with related legislation by parliaments of the Commonwealth of Australia

---

[144] *Nadan v R* [1926] AC 482; and see p 326 below.

[145] Cmd 2768, 1926; Cmd 3479, 1930; Cmd 3717, 1930.

[146] Wheare, *The Statute of Westminster and Dominion Status*; Marshall, *Parliamentary Sovereignty and the Commonwealth*; Dale, part 1.

[147] On the accession of Elizabeth II, see Wheare, *Constitutional Structure of the Commonwealth*, pp 164–8.

[148] See s 7(1) (Canada) and ss 8, 9(1) (Australia). For South Africa, see *Harris v Minister of the Interior* 1952 (2) SA 428 and D V Cowan (1952) 15 MLR 282, (1953) 16 MLR 273.

[149] *British Coal Corporation v R* [1935] AC 500, 520.

[150] *Ndlwana v Hofmeyr* 1937 AD 229, 237. And see *Blackburn v A-G* [1971] 2 All ER 1380.

[151] See *Re Amendment of the Constitution of Canada* (1981) 125 DLR (3d) 1; Marshall, *Constitutional Conventions*, ch 11; and Oliver, note 138 above, ch 7.

[152] Canada Act 1982, s 2.

[153] *Manuel v A-G* [1983] Ch 77 (and Marshall, *Constitutional Conventions*, ch 12); also *R v Foreign Secretary, ex p Indian Association of Alberta* [1982] QB 892.

and the Australian states. This severed the remaining legislative links between the United Kingdom and Australia, and it also terminated appeals to the Privy Council from any Australian court.[154] In New Zealand, the Constitution Act 1986 consolidated the main elements of the country's constitution and revoked the application of the Statute of Westminster.[155]

In 1931, as we have seen, it was envisaged that there might be subjects on which the United Kingdom would still legislate for the Dominions. When in the years after 1945 independence was granted to India, Pakistan, Ceylon, Ghana and many other countries, it was accepted that Westminster should not retain any power to legislate for independent states, even with their consent. Accordingly, the independence legislation usually provided that the United Kingdom government should have no responsibility for the country's government, and that no future Act of the Westminster Parliament should extend to the country as part of its law.[156]

Although the political campaign for independence in many territories was often stormy, in most cases independence was conferred by due legislative process. One exception to this occurred in 1965 when Ian Smith and other Cabinet ministers of the self-governing colony of Rhodesia, impatient for independence, unilaterally declared Rhodesia to be independent. This unlawful declaration had complex consequences[157] until in 1979 a constitutional conference in London laid the basis for a return to legality. In 1980, under the authority of the Westminster Parliament, independence was conferred on the new state of Zimbabwe.[158]

The divisibility of the Crown

At one time the British Crown was considered in law to be a single, ubiquitous entity in the many territories under British sovereignty. Thus in 1919 the Privy Council referred to the Crown as 'one and indivisible throughout the Empire'.[159] But this unity could not be maintained given the growth of responsible government in many colonies, the creation of federal constitutions in Canada and Australia and (later) the conferment of independence. As separate governments came into being (except of course where a country chose to be a republic on becoming independent), the legal concept of the Crown inevitably began to fragment. Moreover, when independence was conferred, obligations of the British government in relation to a territory passed by succession to that country's government.[160] Thus, the Crown 'in right of the United Kingdom' (i.e. the British government) was held to have no continuing liability in respect of a royal proclamation of 1763 that reserved certain land in Canada for the Indian peoples; any liability under that proclamation was enforceable, if at all, against the Crown in right of Canada (i.e. the Canadian government).[161]

While the transfer of such responsibilities is an inevitable consequence of a country's independence, the divisibility of the Crown could arise at an earlier stage of development.[162] In 1968, it was held that passports issued to citizens of Mauritius by the governor of the colony were not United Kingdom passports, even though their holders were 'citizens of the United Kingdom and Colonies'.[163] The consequences of this approach to distinguishing between different levels of government have not all been beneficial. The proposition that the Crown is 'divisible' (that is,

---

[154] See J Goldring [1986] PL 192.

[155] Joseph, *Constitutional and Administrative Law in New Zealand*, pp 164–170; Oliver, ch 8.

[156] See e.g. Nigeria Independence Act 1960, s 1(2) and Sch 1.

[157] They included the Southern Rhodesia Act 1965 and, in the Privy Council, *Madzimbamuto v Lardner-Burke* [1969] 1 AC 645. (And see the 10th edn of this work, pp 430–2.)

[158] See the Southern Rhodesia Act 1979, the Zimbabwe Act 1979 and SI 1979 No 1600.

[159] *Theodore v Duncan* [1919] AC 696, 706 (Lord Haldane).

[160] Cf *A-G v Great Southern and Western Rly* [1925] AC 754.

[161] *R v Foreign Secretary, ex p Indian Association of Alberta* [1982] QB 892.

[162] The judgments in *Ex p Indian Association* offer three different explanations of the date of the 'division' of the Crown.

[163] *R v Home Secretary, ex p Bhurosah* [1968] 1 QB 266.

capable of being divided) should not have led, as it has done, to a situation in which judges disregard the factors that (*a*) the UK government is responsible for an overseas territory's international relations; (*b*) the UK government has absolute control over action taken in relation to a territory like South Georgia and the South Sandwich Islands; and (*c*) the only democratic accountability owed by the decision-maker (the Secretary of State) is to the Westminster Parliament.[164] Since such a territory is not a state in international law, it is remarkable that it has been said to have its own head of state.[165] As it is, the current approach of the courts unduly favours the strategic interests of the UK government, since the powers of government in an overseas territory are very broad, and operate subject to democratic and legal controls that are either non-existent or are much weaker than would be acceptable in Britain.

Membership of the Commonwealth

Independence of the United Kingdom and membership of the Commonwealth are not the same. The granting of independence to a dependent territory is a matter for the British government and the territory concerned. But the admission of a new member to the Commonwealth requires the agreement of existing members. In 1971, it was declared by the heads of Commonwealth governments meeting at Singapore that the Commonwealth

> is a voluntary association of independent sovereign states, each responsible for its own policies, consulting and co-operating in the common interests of their peoples and in the promotion of international understanding and world peace.[166]

There are no written rules of membership.[167] Before 1949, all members owed common allegiance to the Crown. But in that year India announced its intention of becoming a republic. The response of other Commonwealth governments was to note India's desire to continue its full membership of the Commonwealth and its acceptance of the British Sovereign 'as the symbol of the free association of its independent member nations and as such the Head of the Commonwealth'. Thereafter, some states adopted republican status after becoming independent, others became republics upon independence or became monarchies with their own royal head of state. In 2009, under a third of the 54 Commonwealth states owed allegiance to the Crown, but all of them recognised the Queen in the figurehead role of Head of the Commonwealth, a role that carries with it no specific governmental functions.

In 1961, in the era of apartheid, when South Africa decided to become a republic, the government withdrew its application to remain in membership rather than have it rejected: with the ending of apartheid 30 years later, South Africa was welcomed back to membership.[168] A member state may leave the Commonwealth at any time and it is likely that a member could be expelled against its wishes. In 1995, because of the lack of democracy and disregard for human rights, the membership of Nigeria was suspended. In 2003, after Zimbabwe had been suspended because of an unfair presidential election in 2002, its government resigned from the Commonwealth rather than face continued suspension. A category of Special Member exists for certain very small territories (including Nauru and Tuvalu) which have the right to participate in

---

[164] Cf *R (Quark Fishing Ltd) v Foreign Secretary* [2005] UKHL 57, [2006] 1 AC 529. Earlier case law includes *Tito v Waddell (No 2)* [1977] Ch 106, 254 and *Trawnik v Lennox* [1985] 2 All ER 368, 357. The soundness of the majority decision in *Quark* was doubted by Lord Hoffmann in *R (Bancoult) v Foreign Secretary (No 2)*, note 60 above at [48].

[165] By Lord Hope in *Quark Fishing*, [71], [73]. Cf Lady Hale's comment: 'There is an air of complete unreality about this case' [94].

[166] Commonwealth Declaration, 22 January 1971 (Dale, 41).

[167] For the practice, see Dale, ch 3.

[168] And see the South Africa Act 1995.

activities of the Commonwealth but not to attend meetings of heads of Commonwealth governments.[169] Membership is reserved for independent states. In 1995 Mozambique was admitted to membership, as was Rwanda in 2009, although neither had ever been a dependency of the United Kingdom.

Meetings of heads of Commonwealth governments

After 1944, meetings of Commonwealth Prime Ministers were held in London and were always presided over by the British Prime Minister. There are now biennial meetings of heads of Commonwealth governments, over which the head of government of the host country presides. In 1965, the Commonwealth Secretariat was established, headed by a Secretary General.[170] The headquarters are in London, but the Secretariat is responsible for servicing Commonwealth conferences wherever they are held and for overseeing many forms of Commonwealth cooperation. The Secretary General has an important diplomatic role on international issues that directly affect the Commonwealth.

Today, while the biennial heads of government meetings provide an umbrella for many forms of practical cooperation, the meetings are mainly concerned with contentious issues of world politics, such as economic development and the global environment. In 1971, the Singapore meeting produced the Commonwealth Declaration, which defined the nature of the Commonwealth, stressed the diversity of its membership and stated the principles which were held in common by the members. This declaration was reaffirmed in 1991 at the Harare meeting, which renewed support for the 'fundamental political values' of the Commonwealth and for the promotion of sustainable economic development within a framework of respect for human rights and protection of the global environment.[171] In 1995 the Commonwealth Ministerial Action Group on the Harare Declaration was created to assess and respond to serious departures from the Harare principles in Commonwealth countries.

Other aspects of Commonwealth membership

As independent sovereign states, members of the Commonwealth observe no uniform pattern in their systems of government. While most of them gained independence with constitutions drafted under the influence of Westminster and Whitehall, few of these constitutions have survived without being overturned, replaced or radically altered. In the case of states which are monarchies and owe allegiance to the Queen, a Governor General is appointed by the Queen, on the advice of the government of the state in question, to act as head of state. As long ago as 1926, an imperial conference declared that the Governor General in a Dominion held the same position in relation to affairs of the Dominion as the Sovereign did in the United Kingdom and that he was not the representative or agent of the United Kingdom government.[172] Indeed, depending on the constitution of the country concerned, the Governor General may have to consider exercising a personal discretion which could not arise in the same form in Britain.[173] Moreover, where issues arise as to the conduct of the Governor General, advice to the Queen on the action that she should take comes from the Prime Minister of the country in question, not from the British Prime Minister.[174]

---

[169] Dale, 62.

[170] Under the Commonwealth Secretariat Act 1966, the secretariat enjoy diplomatic immunities and privileges.

[171] And see A W Bradley [1991] PL 477.

[172] Cmd 2768, 1926, p 7. And see Evatt, *The King and his Dominion Governors*.

[173] As in Australia in 1975, when the Governor General, Sir John Kerr, amid fierce controversy, dismissed the Labor Prime Minister; ch 12 B.

[174] V Bogdanor and G Marshall [1996] PL 205.

The United Kingdom's relations with other Commonwealth members are carried on by the Secretary of State for Foreign and Commonwealth Affairs. For historical reasons, members are represented in other member states by high commissioners, who are members of the diplomatic service of their own state and are equal in status to ambassadors. By contrast with the European Union, which is an entity in international law, the position of the Commonwealth in international law is uncertain.[175]

Appeals to the Privy Council

In deciding appeals from the remaining overseas territories of the United Kingdom, the Judicial Committee of the Privy Council exercises the ancient jurisdiction of the King in Council to hear appeals from the overseas dependencies of the Crown.[176] This jurisdiction was based on 'the inherent prerogative right . . . of the King in Council to exercise an appellate jurisdiction, with a view not only to ensure . . . the due administration of justice in the individual case, but also to preserve the due course of procedure generally'.[177] This jurisdiction was given statutory form by the Judicial Committee Acts of 1833 and 1844.[178] In criminal cases, the Judicial Committee does not act as a court of appeal in the usual sense of the term: it may allow an appeal with special leave only where there has been a clear departure from the requirements of justice and, whether by a disregard of due legal process or by some violation of principles of natural justice, or otherwise, substantial and grave injustice has been done.[179]

When a territory becomes independent of the United Kingdom, it acquires the power to abolish or restrict appeals to the Privy Council,[180] though this power must be exercised in accordance with the national constitution. Most Commonwealth states have abolished appeals to the Privy Council; states that had not done so by 2009 include Antigua, the Bahamas, Belize, Dominica, Jamaica, Mauritius, Saint Lucia, and Trinidad and Tobago. In 2005, the creation of the Caribbean Court of Justice to be a court of first instance for treaty questions relating to Caricom (the Caribbean Community), had also the aim of replacing appeals to the Privy Council from several Caribbean countries. The latter aim ran into difficulty in Jamaica, where the proposed rights of appeal could be created only by legislation passed with a two-thirds majority in the legislature.[181]

At one time, the Judicial Committee played an important but controversial role as a constitutional court, especially in regard to Canada; it has helped to develop the common law in jurisdictions outside the United Kingdom,[182] and it still seeks to uphold fundamentals of criminal justice.[183] Occasional proposals made for turning the Judicial Committee into a travelling Commonwealth court were never supported.[184] The Committee has a key role in interpreting those national constitutions that include protection for fundamental human rights, but its decisions

---

[175] Fawcett, *The British Commonwealth in International Law*; Dale, note 128 above, ch 6; Jennings and Watts, note 1 above, 263–5.

[176] Roberts-Wray, note 128 above, 433–63.

[177] *R v Bertrand* (1867) LR 1 PC 520, 530.

[178] As amended by the Constitutional Reform Act 2005, s 138. On how this jurisdiction is exercised, see Judicial Committee (Appellate Jurisdiction) Rules 2009, SI No 224, and associated Practice Directions (at www.privy-council.org.uk). Also 14th edn of this work, 340–2.

[179] *Ibrahim v R* [1914] AC 599. For an instance of serious injustice occurring in New Zealand, see *Taito and Bennett v R* [2002] UK PC 15.

[180] *Moore v A-G of Irish Free State* [1935] AC 484; *British Coal Corporation v R* [1935] AC 500; *A-G for Ontario v A-G for Canada* [1947] AC 127.

[181] *Independent Jamaica Council for Human Rights (1998) Ltd v Marshall-Burnett* [2005] UKPC 3, [2005] 2 AC 356.

[182] This did not mean that it imposed uniformity: see e.g. *Invercargill City Council v Hamlin* [1996] 1 All ER 756.

[183] E.g. *Dunkley v R* [1995] 1 AC 419 (withdrawal of counsel during murder trial); *Burut v Public Prosecutor* [1995] 2 AC 579 (confession obtained by oppression).

[184] Roberts-Wray, 461–3. See Swinfen, *Imperial Appeal*, for an excellent historical account; and Stevens, *The Independence of the Judiciary*, chs 4 and 8.

have fluctuated between adopting an unduly legalistic approach to fundamental rights provisions and a broader, more purposive approach that recognises the constitution as a living instrument.[185] Decisions by the Committee in death penalty cases have done much to temper the harshness and injustice of 'death row' conditions in the Caribbean, but they are marked by many differences of judicial opinion.[186] Notable decisions have been made regarding freedom of expression.[187]

The judges who sit on the Judicial Committee are usually the Justices of the Supreme Court for the United Kingdom (replacing the former Law Lords), but privy counsellors under the age of 75 who hold or have held high judicial office may also sit.[188] In 2009, the decision of devolution questions relating to Scotland, Wales and Northern Ireland was transferred from the Committee to the Supreme Court.[189] The Judicial Committee is likely to continue in being as long as is necessary to hear appeals from overseas territories and from Commonwealth jurisdictions; it now sits in the Supreme Court building, rather than in its historic accommodation in Downing Street.[190] Around 60 decisions are made each year, and these often include difficult issues of constitutional significance.[191]

---

[185] K D Ewing, in Finnie, Himsworth and Walker (eds), *Edinburgh Essays in Public Law*, 231. For the broader approach, see e.g. *Minister of Home Affairs v Fisher* [1980] AC 319; and *A-G of Trinidad and Tobago v Whiteman* [1991] 2 AC 240. For the least liberal decision, see *Ong Ah Chuan v Public Prosecutor* [1981] AC 648 (criticised in Pannick, *Judicial Review of the Death Penalty*). On the revival of flogging in the Bahamas, see *Pinder v R* [2002] UKPC 46, [2003] 1 AC 620.

[186] The leading decision is *Pratt and Morgan v A-G of Jamaica* [1994] 2 AC 1. Other death row cases include *Henfield v A-G of Bahamas* [1997] AC 413; *Fisher v Minister of Public Safety* [1998] AC 673; *Thomas v Baptiste* [2000] 2 AC 1; *Roodal v State of Trinidad and Tobago* [2003] UKPC 78, [2005] 1 AC 328; *Matthew v State of Trinidad and Tobago* [2004] UKPC 33, [2005] 1 AC 433.

[187] See e.g. *De Freitas v Permanent Secretary of Ministry of Agriculture* [1999] 1 AC 69; *Benjamin v Minister of Information and Broadcasting* (2001) 10 BHRC 237; *Observer Publications Ltd v Matthew* (2001) 10 BHRC 252.

[188] Constitutional Reform Act 2005, s 138 and sch 16.

[189] Ibid, s 40(4) and sch 9.

[190] In 2008 the Committee sat in Mauritius to hear appeals from Mauritian courts.

[191] E.g. *Hearing on the Report on the Chief Justice of Gibraltar* [2009] UKPC 43 (Committee deciding by 4–3 under the Constitution of Gibraltar that the Chief Justice be dismissed).

CHAPTER 16

The armed forces

It has been said that 'the defence of the state against the threats and depredations of external enemies has been recognised as one of the cardinal features of government'.[1] In the interests of constitutional government and the rule of law, however, the exercise of the physical might of the modern state must be subject to democratic control. Experience of government at the hands of Cromwell's army led after the restoration of the monarchy in 1660 to a declaration by Parliament in the Militia Act 1661 that:

> the sole supreme government, command and disposition of the militia and of all forces by sea and land is, and by the laws of England ever was, the undoubted right of the Crown.

Subsequent attempts by Charles II and James II against parliamentary opposition to maintain their own armies led to the declaration in the Bill of Rights that:

> the raising or keeping of a standing army within the Kingdom in time of peace, unless it be with consent of Parliament, is against law.

This declaration remains important not because there is now any possibility that Parliament would withdraw authority for the continued maintenance of an army but because it asserts that the armed forces are constitutionally subordinate to Parliament.

From the earliest times the armed forces have thus raised important constitutional issues and that legacy continues to determine the constitutional position of the army, navy and air force today. In this chapter we concentrate on three such issues, with a full account of service law being beyond the scope of a work such as this. The first issue relates to the constitutional structure within which the armed forces operate: the nature of legislative authority and parliamentary scrutiny. The second issue concerns aspects of service law and, in particular, the rights and duties of service personnel, as well as the special procedures for dealing with military discipline. Here we find that a number of important changes have taken place in recent years, partly as a result of decisions of the European Court of Human Rights, which have been welcomed as leading to improvements in the system of military justice.[2] The third issue raises questions about the rule of law and the extent to which the military authorities are subject to the ordinary law of the land. The need for military effectiveness in the defence of the realm does not mean that the armed forces should be immune from criminal or civil liability in appropriate cases, though it does not follow that military values will always be consistent with the requirements of civilian justice.[3]

---

[1] *R v Spear* [2002] UKHL 31; [2003] 1 AC 734, para 3 (Lord Bingham).

[2] HC 828-1 (2005–06).

[3] See G R Rubin (2007) 26 *University of Queensland L J* 353.

A. The constitutional structure

Legislative authority for the armed forces[4]

After the Bill of Rights, it became the custom of Parliament each year to pass a Mutiny Act, giving authority for one year to the Crown to maintain armed forces up to the limit of manpower stated in the Act, and to enforce rules of discipline. Eventually what had become a lengthy and detailed collection of rules of military law was codified in the Army Act 1881. This code was until 1955 continued in force from year to year by the passing of an Act known after 1917 as the Army and Air Force (Annual) Act. Amendments to the 1881 Act were made when necessary by the annual Act. When a separate Air Force was constituted in 1917, its discipline was governed by the Army Act 1881 with modifications. By 1955, it had come to be accepted that approval of the size of the armed forces was granted through parliamentary consideration of the defence estimates and the formal procedure for appropriating supply to the armed forces. Following a series of reports from select committees of the Commons,[5] there was enacted the Army Act 1955 and the Air Force Act 1955. Each Act was in the first instance limited to a duration of 12 months,[6] but for a period of five years it could be continued in force from year to year by resolution of each House of Parliament. At the end of the five years, further primary legislation was needed to keep it in force, setting in train a process of quinquennial armed forces bills.[7]

One consequence of this process of five-yearly renewal with amendments was the creation of a very complex body of law, as amendment was piled upon amendment to the different service statutes. The nature and scale of these amendments grew significantly every five years, often to give effect to decisions of the European Court of Human Rights on matters relating to military discipline. The Armed Force Act 2006 was thus a welcome measure, not only consolidating service law in a single statute, but also simplifying matters greatly by bringing all three services under the same body of law in a unified tri-service framework. Following the example of the 1955 Acts, however, the continuation in force of the 2006 Act must also be approved annually by parliamentary resolution, and it will lapse after five years unless kept in force by an Act of Parliament. So we can expect the process of renewal and amendment to begin again. Like the other quinquennial Acts since 1955, the Armed Forces Act 2006 was passed by adopting the unusual parliamentary procedure whereby the Bill was, after second reading, referred to an ad hoc select committee of the Commons, where it was examined in detail. The Committee was empowered to take written and oral evidence and to make visits to locations at home and abroad,[8] and in accordance with normal practice this was done in public.[9]

As well as the full-time regular forces of the Crown, reserve forces are also maintained under statutory authority. The legislation makes provision for the recall of the reserve forces, in some circumstances by notice from the Secretary of State for Defence, but in the case of imminent

---

[4] For the history of the legal position of the armed forces, see Maitland, *Constitutional History*, pp 275–80, 324–9, 447–62; Anson, *Law and Custom of the Constitution*, vol II (2), ch 10. For the current position, see Rowe, *Defence: The Legal Implications*; and Rowe, *The Gulf War 1990–91*.

[5] HC 244 and 331 (1951–2), 289 (1952–3) and 223 (1953–4).

[6] On the importance of annual renewal, see HC 747 (2005–6).

[7] See Army and Air Force Act 1961; Armed Forces Act 2001, s 1. Although a 'relatively short maximum period' compared to other countries (P Rowe, in Sunkin and Payne (eds), *The Nature of the Crown*, p 270), it has been argued that these arrangements do not overcome the Bill of Rights prohibition on a standing army: see (1981) 4 *State Research* 149.

[8] See e.g. HC 170 (1985–6), HC 179 (1990–1), HC 143 (1995–6), HC 828 (2005–06).

[9] On this occasion, however, the government agreed for the first time that the clause-by-clause consideration of the Bill could also take place in public: HC 828 (2005–06).

national danger or great emergency by an order of the Queen, signified by the Secretary of State and notified to Parliament; if Parliament is not sitting at the time, it must meet within five days.[10] Although this is an unusual requirement in connexion with the exercise of such powers, it is not unique.[11] It is an offence for a member of the reserve forces to fail to respond to a call out, unless he or she has leave or reasonable excuse. The power to recall was used (selectively) during the Gulf hostilities when those with 'medical qualifications were called out to supplement volunteers with relevant military and medical experience';[12] again in 2001 during the hostilities in Afghanistan; and yet again in 2003, when over 7,000 reservists (including members of the Territorial Army) were mobilised for events in Iraq. Reservists – who continue to support military operations in Iraq, Afghanistan and the Balkans – enjoy some protection under the Reserve Forces (Safeguarding of Employment) Act 1985 (as amended), in the sense that an employer must reinstate a reservist at the end of his or her period of service.[13]

Central organisation for defence

Like other branches of central government, the armed forces are placed under the control of ministers of the Crown, who are in turn responsible to Parliament. Formerly each of the main services had its own ministerial head. Today the responsibility for a unified defence policy rests on the Secretary of State for Defence, whose office has undergone several changes since the post of Minister of Defence was created and occupied by Winston Churchill in the Second World War. In 1964, the Ministry of Defence became a unified ministry for the three services and absorbed the Admiralty, the War Office and the Air Ministry.[14] The present ministerial structure dates from May 1981, when the junior minister for the navy was dismissed after publicly criticising proposed reductions in Britain's naval strength. The Prime Minister promptly abolished the separate junior ministerial posts for the three services. The Ministry was in 2010 headed by the Secretary of State for Defence, supported by two ministers of state (dealing with 'strategic defence acquisition reform', and the armed forces respectively), and two under secretaries of state (dealing with defence equipment, and veterans' affairs respectively), as well as a Minister for International Defence and Security.

All statutory powers for the defence of the realm which formerly were vested in the separate service ministers were in 1964 vested in the Secretary of State.[15] The creation of a unified Ministry of Defence was necessary because it had been found inadequate for a Minister of Defence to seek to control defence policy by coordinating the policies of three departments responsible to separate ministers. A unified ministry was also essential if the defence budget were to strike a proper balance between the commitments, resources and roles of the three services. Within the Ministry of Defence, there is a Defence Council, whose members include the defence ministers, the Chief of the Defence Staff, the three service chiefs of staff and the Vice-Chief of the Defence Staff. Non-ministerial members of the Defence Council sit on the Defence Board, along with other military personnel and civil servants, together with people appointed from business, to provide leadership and strategic management to defence. The chiefs of staff are the professional heads of the armed forces; they give professional advice to the government on strategy and military operations, and on the military implications of defence policy.

---

[10] Reserve Forces Act 1996, ss 52–4.
[11] Civil Contingencies Act 2004, s 28 (Parliament to be recalled in the event of emergency regulations being made).
[12] P Rowe [1991] PL 170, 173.
[13] See *Slaven v Thermo Engineers Ltd* [1992] ICR 295. But see HC 57 (2003–4) for difficulties faced by some reservists.
[14] Cmnd 2097, 1963.
[15] Defence (Transfer of Functions) Act 1964.

The collective responsibility of the government for defence in 2010 was exercised primarily through the Cabinet Sub-Committee on Overseas and Defence under the chairmanship of the Prime Minister. Its terms of reference require it 'to consider issues relating to conflict, and defence, foreign and development policy; and report as necessary to the Committee on National Security, International Relations and Development'. It is the responsibility of the latter 'to consider issues relating to national security, and the Government's international, European and international development policies'. Apart from senior ministers, meetings of the Overseas and Defence Sub-Committee may be attended by the heads of the intelligence agencies, the chairman of the Joint Intelligence Committee, and the Chief of Defence Staff. However, major questions of defence policy cannot be decided in purely military and strategic terms without reference to the government's financial and economic policies, which affect the size, disposition and equipment of the armed forces, as well as the capacity of the country to support long military campaigns.

Parliamentary scrutiny of the armed forces

As we shall see in chapter 21, the chain of command within the police stops with the chief constable, and neither local police authorities nor central government may give him or her instructions on the operational use of the police. This is not the case with the armed forces. In the case of the army, for example, the line of command runs upwards from the private soldier, through his or her commanding officer and higher levels of command to the Chief of the Defence Staff and the Secretary of State for Defence. During active operations many immediate decisions have to be taken by soldiers in the field. But the tasks which are undertaken by the armed forces, the objectives which they are set and the manner in which they carry out these tasks are matters for which the government is accountable to Parliament – whether it be the making of a controversial public speech by a high-ranking army officer, the sinking of the Argentinian ship *General Belgrano* during the Falklands conflict in 1982, the role of the army while performing peace-keeping duties in what was once Yugoslavia, the use of troops during a national strike by firefighters (as in 2002–3), or the conduct of troops during the invasion of Iraq or occupation of Afghanistan. The full range of parliamentary procedures which are available in respect of other branches of central government may be used in respect of defence and the armed forces. Thus the Public Accounts Committee has often investigated cases of spending by the services.

Since 1979 the Defence Committee of the House of Commons has conducted major inquiries into a wide range of defence and military matters. The committee played an important part in the Westland affair in 1985 and in the process did much to raise the profile and highlight the value of select committees generally.[16] The committee has subsequently delivered a strong rebuke to the Ministry of Defence for its response to allegations of a 'Gulf War syndrome' afflicting those who had served in the conflict, as well as their families. The ministry was said to have been 'reactive rather than proactive' and to have behaved with 'scepticism, defensiveness and general torpor'.[17] More recently, the committee has reported difficulties in obtaining information from the Ministry of Defence. In its report in 2004 on *Lessons of Iraq*, the Committee drew attention to a number of documents to which it was denied access, including 'the directives issued by the Chief of Defence Staff to the commanding officers in theatre'. They also included the rules of engagement under which British forces fought. In both cases the requests were made after the conclusion of combat operations, and in both cases the Committee 'would have been prepared to receive them as a classified document'. It was pointed out that the American rules of engagement had been published, and concern was expressed that the Committee had been denied access to other information that had been provided to the National Audit Office.[18]

---

[16] See HC 518 and 519 (1985–6). Also ch 10 D.

[17] HC 197 (1994–5), para 60. See also HC 125, 753 (1999–2000); 517-1 (2001–2).

[18] HC 57 (2003–4). For the government's response, see HC 635 (2003–4).

Defence policies and expenditure are often matters of keen political debate in the House. As mentioned earlier, military law has received close scrutiny from select committees appointed to consider the Armed Forces Bills. Members of the forces are entitled under service regulations to communicate with MPs on all matters,[19] including service matters, so long as they do not disclose secret information, but it is the policy of the Ministry of Defence that wherever possible service-men and women should pursue the normal channels of complaint open to them through super-ior officers.[20] While allegations of maladministration on the part of the Ministry of Defence may be referred by MPs for investigation by the Parliamentary Ombudsman, it is outside his or her jurisdiction to investigate action relating to appointments, pay, discipline, pensions, or other per-sonnel matters affecting service in the armed forces; nor may he or she investigate complaints relating to the conduct of judicial proceedings under service law.[21] A proposal for a Military Ombudsman was revived in the light of concerns about serious bullying in the armed forces,[22] and although it was rejected again by the Select Committee on the Armed Forces Bill,[23] provision has been made in the Act for a Service Complaints Commissioner as an important first step in this direction.[24]

B. The military covenant, military service and military discipline

The military covenant and service law[25]

Service law is the internal law of the armed forces, administered by officers with appropriate authority, by courts-martial and on appeal by the Courts-Martial Appeal Court. It is made by Parliament and, under the authority of Parliament, by the defence authorities by means of Queen's Regulations. The sometimes unique features of service law (not to be confused with martial law) reflect the unique features of military service, which are highlighted in the so-called 'military covenant'.[26] The latter is rooted in the idea that members of the armed forces are expected 'to put the needs of the Nation and the Army before their own, and to forego some of the rights enjoyed by those outside the Armed Forces'. In return, it is said that 'soldiers must always be able to expect fair treatment, to be valued and respected as individuals, and that they (and their families) will be sustained and rewarded by commensurate terms and conditions of service'. The 'military covenant' has no legal status, but it has become a powerful rhetorical tool in public debates about the treatment of the armed forces and their families, particularly in recent years when resources have been stretched by campaigns in Iraq and Afghanistan. It may, however, be underpinned by law to the extent that the common law recognises that the Crown owes a duty of care to members of the armed forces.[27]

So far as the military covenant is concerned, the legal framework tilts perhaps more towards the duties rather than the compensating rights of the soldier (and his or her family). Thus, the consolidating Armed Forces Act 2006 re-introduces a number of offences contained previously in

---

[19] HC Debs, 9 May 1956, col 1382 (a right said to be 'jealously safeguarded'). Cf the Stevenson case, HC 112 (1954–5).

[20] Armed Forces Act 2006, ss 334–339.

[21] Parliamentary Commissioner Act 1967, Sch 3, paras 6, 10.

[22] HC 63 (2005–06); N Blake QC, *The Deepcut Review*, HC 795 (2005–06), p 403 (R 26).

[23] HC 828-1 (2005–06), paras 122–9.

[24] See HC 277 (2008–09) and HC 985 (2008–09) (government response).

[25] See Rant, *Court Martial and Service Law* (3rd edn by J Blackett), for a complete account, and J Stuart-Smith (1969) 85 LQR 478 for a lucid introduction. For a full account of recent developments, see G R Rubin (2002) 65 MLR 36.

[26] See www.army.mod.uk.

[27] *R (Smith) v Defence Secretary* [2009] EWCA Civ 441. See for example, *Wilson v Ministry of Defence* [2007] EWCA Civ 485.

the separate service legislation, such as the Army Act 1955. These include mutiny, insubordination, disobedience to orders, desertion, absence without leave, malingering, and a residual offence of any act or omission that is 'prejudicial to good order and service discipline'.[28] It is also an offence for any person subject to service law to commit a civil offence, i.e. an offence punishable by English criminal law or which, if committed in England, would be so punishable.[29] Moreover, British armed forces serving abroad 'are triable for genocide, crimes against humanity and war crimes under the International Criminal Court Act 2001'.[30] As well as civilian employees of the Ministry of Defence who accompany the armed forces when they are on active service, it is a long established practice that service law also applies (albeit with modifications) to (i) civilians who are employed outside the United Kingdom within the limits of the command of any officer commanding a body of the regular forces, and (ii) the families of members of the armed forces who are residing with them outside the United Kingdom.[31] This particularly affects civilians accompanying the armed forces in Cyprus and Germany.[32]

So far as the other side of the bargain is concerned, a range of issues have been raised and addressed in recent years. So far as conditions of service are concerned, the problem of bullying and harassment has been exposed as a serious issue, particularly in the light of the suicides of a number of young recruits. It is unclear whether this problem will be met by the new procedures introduced by the Armed Forces Act 2006, these creating a new service complaints procedures, with the introduction of an independent element in some cases, subject to the overall supervision of the Service Complaints Commissioner, to which we have already referred. So far as military equipment and resources are concerned, concerns have been expressed periodically about on the one hand the adequacy of the equipment supplied to the troops to deal with the conditions in Iraq, and on the other the inadequacy of the equipment necessary to protect the troops from enemy activity in Afghanistan, notably improvised explosive devices. And so far as the welfare of those injured on duty is concerned, concern has been expressed about the adequacy of the no-fault Armed Forces Compensation Scheme, for those who suffer injury on active service.[33] While the Defence Select Committee has paid tribute to the army medical services, it also had reservations about the facilities made available to deal with the mental health problems of soldiers returning from armed conflict.[34]

Military service and service law

Because of the loss of freedom involved in military service, it is important that enlistment into the forces is voluntary. It is true that in both world wars conscription was authorised by Parliament, and that it was continued after the Second World War under the National Service Act 1948. But conscription was brought to an end in 1960, and there is no reason to believe that it will be reintroduced. The formal process of enlistment is now governed by the Armed Forces Act 2006, with the terms of engagement on which members of the forces are enlisted being governed

---

[28] Armed Forces Act 2006, s 19; see *R v Dodman* [1998] 2 Cr App R 338.

[29] Ibid, s 42. On the compatibility of these arrangements with the ECHR, see *R v Spear* [2002] UKHL 31; [2003] 1 AC 734.

[30] *R (Al Skeini) v Defence Secretary* [2007] UKHL 26, [2008] AC 153, at para [26] (Lord Bingham).

[31] Now Armed Forces Act 2006, s 42; Sch 15. Offences in these cases may be tried by the Service Civilian Court established by s 51 of the 2006 Act, replacing the Standing Civilian Court. See *Cox v Army Council* [1963] AC 48 (careless driving on a public road in Germany).

[32] HC 828-I (2005–06), para 107.

[33] SI 2005 No 439. The government announced a number of improvements to the scheme in February 2010. See further *Ratcliffe v Defence Secretary* [2009] EWCA Civ 39; *Defence Secretary v Duncan* [2009] EWCA Civ 1043; and *Viggers v Defence Secretary* [2009] EWCA Civ 1321. Questions have also been raised from time to time about the poor condition of housing made available for the families of service personnel.

[34] HC 327 (2007–08).

by regulations made by the Defence Council, to which reference has already been made. Apart from dealing with the conditions of eligibility for enlisting, these regulations may also specify the periods of fixed-term service (initially for a period of four years), and the circumstances in which a recruit may be discharged from military service. The Queen's Regulations offer various protections for pay and benefits, while as we have seen the Armed Forces Act 2006 includes detailed provisions for the raising and redress of grievances.[35] But members of the armed forces do not have the right to form and join trade unions, or to take part in trade union activities.[36]

The military covenant notwithstanding, it nevertheless does not follow that those who join the armed forces should be required to surrender the right to be treated fairly or that they should be expected to waive their human rights.[37] In 1994 (as a result of the requirements of what was then EC law), the Sex Discrimination Act 1975 was extended to members of the forces[38] and there have been many cases, some highly controversial, involving service women who were discharged because of their pregnancy and who were able successfully to seek compensation as a result.[39] The regulations extending the 1975 Act provide that nothing is to render unlawful an act done for the purpose of ensuring the combat effectiveness of the naval, military or air forces of the Crown.[40] The Race Relations Act 1976 applied to the armed forces from the time of enactment,[41] although initially enforcement was by way of a complaint to the Defence Council under the Army Act 1955.[42] Following the Armed Forces Act 1996, complaints relating to race discrimination, sex discrimination and equal pay may now be made to employment tribunals, although in all cases complainants are required to submit their case for consideration under the services' internal grievance procedures, a requirement which at least in sex discrimination complaints involves a qualification rather than an extension of an existing right.

Particularly controversial has been the policy of the armed forces towards homosexual men and women. Although it was not unlawful for members of the armed forces to take part in homosexual acts,[43] homosexual activity or orientation was an absolute bar to recruitment. The European Court of Human Rights held the ban to breach art 8 of the ECHR,[44] and in 2000 the government announced that it had been lifted. No primary or secondary legislation was necessary for this purpose, and a new Code of Social Conduct was introduced at the same time to deal with the personal relationships of those serving in the armed forces. The code – which is still applicable – is designed to apply across the forces, regardless of service, 'gender or sexual orientation, rank or status' and to 'complement existing policies' such as those dealing with bullying, harassment and discrimination. At the heart of the code is what is referred to as the service test, whereby people are judged not on the basis of their sexuality but on whether their 'actions or behaviour' have 'adversely impacted' or are 'likely to impact on the efficiency or operational effectiveness of the service'.[45] More recently, the Employment Equality (Sexual Orientation)

---

[35] Armed Forces Act 2008, ss 328–339.

[36] Trade Union and Labour Relations (Consolidation) Act 1992, s 274.

[37] See *Smith* v *Assistant Deputy Coroner for Oxfordshire* [2008] EWHC (Admin) 694; *R (Smith)* v *Defence Secretary* [2009] EWCA Civ 441, below, p 340.

[38] SI 1994 No 3276.

[39] For background to this issue, see *Ministry of Defence* v *Cannock* [1994] ICR 918.

[40] See *Sidar* v *Defence Secretary* [1999] All ER (EC) 928. Following a Ministry of Defence Review in 2002 it was decided to continue to exclude women from close combat roles: HL Deb, 22 May 2002, WA 97. This appears still to be the case, though many of the 17,670 women in the armed forces now operate on the front line (*The Times*, 19 June 2008).

[41] But for serious allegations of racism in the armed forces, see J Mackenzie, NLJ, 14 June 1996. Also HC 143 (1995–6), pp 209–15.

[42] *R* v *Army Board, ex p Anderson* [1992] QB 169.

[43] Criminal Justice and Public Order Act 1994, s 146.

[44] *Lustig-Prean* v *UK* (1999) 29 EHRR 548.

[45] HC Deb, 12 January 2000, cols 287 et seq. For the code, see www.mod.uk.

Regulations 2003 apply to render discrimination on the grounds of sexual orientation unlawful in the armed forces, as elsewhere.[46]

Military offences and service law

There are a number of different police forces in the armed forces: known collectively as the service police,[47] these are the Royal Navy Police, the Royal Military Police and the RAF Police. These bodies come to public prominence from time to time and are not to be confused with the Ministry of Defence Police.[48] New powers of the service police (which do not apply to the MOD Police) were introduced by the Armed Forces Act 2001, and were retained by the Armed Forces Act 2006. These powers are very similar to the powers contained in the Police and Criminal Evidence Act 1984 and relate to powers of stop and search,[49] the arrest and search of persons following arrest,[50] as well as powers of entry, search and seizure of property.[51] There is a power to stop and search service personnel (or anyone 'who is, or whom the service policeman has reasonable grounds for believing to be, a person subject to service law or a civilian subject to service discipline') for stolen or prohibited articles, drugs or Her Majesty's stores.[52] The power may only be exercised on reasonable suspicion and may be exercised in a public place or on property occupied or controlled by the armed forces;[53] but not in a dwelling or service living accommodation.[54] In some cases these powers may also be exercised by the commanding officer of a member of the armed forces.[55] Provision is also made for the searching of residential premises, which normally requires a warrant from a judge advocate (see below) on application by the service police, though exceptionally a Commanding Officer may authorise a search.[56]

The prosecution of offences against service law is now dealt with by the procedures in the Armed Forces Act 2006, which embraces a number of changes that had been introduced in recent years following several complaints that procedures previously in operation violated the ECHR, and in particular articles 5 and 6.[57] These major revisions, which include the creation of a Director of Service Prosecutions, have been designed to enhance the independence of the disciplinary procedure and to bring it more into line with the standards expected in civilian life. Less serious offences may be dealt with by the accused's Commanding Officer,[58] subject to the right of the accused to elect trial by court-martial.[59] Where a case is dealt with by the Commanding Officer, there is a right of appeal to the Summary Appeal Court, consisting of a judge advocate and two other officers.[60] Other cases are dealt with by court-martial, now a standing court which is chaired by a judge advocate (equivalent in status to a crown court judge). The court-martial, which will normally sit in public, will also include five to seven 'lay' members, of whom several must be

---

[46] SI 2003 No 1661, reg 36. The Employment Equality (Religion and Belief) Regulations, SI 2003 No 1660 also apply to service in the armed forces.

[47] Armed Forces Act 2006, s 375.

[48] This is a civilian force dedicated to meeting the policing requirements of the Ministry of Defence.

[49] Armed Forces Act 2006, ss 75–82.

[50] Ibid, ss 67–74.

[51] Ibid, ss 83–93.

[52] Ibid, s 75.

[53] Ibid, s 78.

[54] Ibid, s 78(b).

[55] Ibid, s 76.

[56] Ibid, ss 83–89.

[57] See *Hood v UK* (1999) 29 EHRR 365; *Grieves v UK* (2004) 39 EHRR 51; *Cooper v UK* (2004) 39 EHRR 171; *Thompson v UK* (2005) 40 EHRR 245. And see *Findlay v UK* (1997) 24 EHRR 221.

[58] Armed Forces Act 2006, ss 52, 53.

[59] Ibid, s 129.

[60] Ibid, ss 140–151.

officers or warrant officers.[61] The findings and sentence of the court-martial are those of a majority of its members (with the judge advocate not having a vote on the findings, but having a casting vote on sentence).[62] The court-martial has wide sentencing powers, from imprisonment, to dismissal with disgrace from the service, to dismissal from the service.[63]

A key actor in the court-martial procedure is the Judge Advocate General, who appoints the judge advocates of courts-martial.[64] The Judge Advocate General's office, which has been in continuous existence since 1666, is not governed by statute but by letters patent. The incumbent, who has an overall responsibility to monitor the criminal justice system in the services, in order to ensure that it works properly and efficiently, is appointed by the Crown on the advice of the Lord Chancellor, and must have a ten-year qualification within the meaning of the Courts and Legal Services Act 1990. The office is a civilian one (though this does not prevent the appointment of someone who has previous military experience).[65] The Courts-Martial Appeal Court is another important link with the civil justice system, served by the Lord Chief Justice, the judges of the Court of Appeal and such of the judges of the Queen's Bench Division of the High Court and corresponding judges for Scotland and Northern Ireland as may be nominated, together with such other persons of legal experience as the Lord Chancellor may appoint.[66] A person convicted by a court-martial may appeal to the court against both conviction and sentence, which means that all court-martial decisions are subject to scrutiny by a civilian court. A further appeal lies to the House of Lords by leave of the court or of the House on a point of law of general public importance.[67]

C. The armed forces and the ordinary law

Dual jurisdiction

To what extent are the military subject to the ordinary law? We have already seen that steps have been taken to bring service law closer to the standards of procedure that would normally be expected to apply in civilian law to the investigation of crime and the prosecution of offenders. We have also seen that the system of service law is subject to civilian oversight. It does not follow, however, that those who are subject to service law are not also subject to the ordinary criminal law and to the jurisdiction of the criminal courts in the United Kingdom. For except so far as Parliament provides otherwise, the soldier's obligations under service law are in addition to his or her duties as a citizen. Indeed, the Armed Forces Act 2006, s 42 provides that an offence under the ordinary law committed by a person subject to service law may be dealt with as an offence against service law; but if committed in the United Kingdom certain serious crimes (including treason, murder, manslaughter and rape) will be tried by the competent civil court.

Does the dual jurisdiction of the service and civilian courts lead to a possible conflict of duty for the soldier? In theory there is no conflict since service law is part of the law of the land and a soldier is only required to obey orders which are lawful.[68] If an order involves a breach of the

---

[61] Ibid, s 155.

[62] Ibid, s 160(2).

[63] Ibid, s 164.

[64] Ibid, s 155(5).

[65] The incumbent in 2010 was also a circuit judge who had previously served in the Royal Navy.

[66] A judge is not disqualified because he or she may previously have acted for the Ministry of Defence before elevation to the Bench: *R v Spear* [2001] QB 804. See subsequently [2002] UKHL 31; [2003] 1 AC 734.

[67] E.g. *Cox v Army Council* [1963] AC 48, *R v Warn* [1970] AC 394, *R v Martin* [1998] AC 917, and *R v Spear* [2002] UKHL 31; [2003] 1 AC 734.

[68] Armed Forces Act 2006, s 12.

general law, a soldier is not only under no obligation to obey it but is under an obligation not to obey it. In practice, particularly when troops are operating in a peace-keeping role within the United Kingdom at a time when the civil courts are functioning, as was recently the case in Northern Ireland, soldiers may be placed in an awkward position. On the one hand, if the soldier obeys an order which was unlawful, he or she may be liable to an action for damages or to a criminal prosecution if injury is inflicted on a third party as a result. On the other hand, if a soldier disobeys an order claiming that it is unlawful, a court-martial may hold that it was lawful, and the soldier may face criminal charges as a result for disobeying the lawful command. The practical difficulty for the soldier is only partially eased by the possibility of an appeal to the Courts-Martial Appeal Court, whose judges are in a position to ensure that service law and the ordinary law do not conflict; indeed, their duty is to use their powers 'so far as they think it necessary or expedient in the interests of justice'.[69]

There is little direct authority on this matter. In *Keighley* v *Bell*, Willes J expressed the opinion that if a prosecution results from obedience to an order, the soldier who obeys it is not criminally liable unless the order was necessarily or manifestly illegal.[70] This opinion was followed during the Boer War by a special court in South Africa which acquitted of murder a soldier who had shot a civilian in obedience to an unlawful order given to him by his officer,[71] a decision which today seems an alarming one in view of the facts. It would seem that for the defence to succeed the mistaken belief in the legality of the order must be reasonable and this would be a matter for the jury to decide. In a Scottish case, *Her Majesty's Advocate* v *Hawton and Parker*, when a naval officer and a marine were charged with killing a fisherman on a trawler which was being intercepted by a naval vessel, Lord Justice General McNeill said: 'It was the duty of the subordinate to obey his superior officer, unless the order given by his superior was so flagrantly and violently wrong that no citizen could be expected to obey it.'[72] This test is materially different from that proposed by Willes J but there was in the Scottish case no order to kill. In the circumstances in which British troops have been used in Northern Ireland, the question of criminal liability for the death or injury of a civilian would normally depend not on the legality of army orders but on whether a soldier's use of firearms was reasonably justifiable in the immediate circumstances.[73] It was held in *R* v *Clegg* that a soldier who killed a person by discharging a firearm in self-defence was guilty of murder rather than manslaughter where the force used was excessive and unreasonable.[74]

Criminal offences and civil liability

In practice, most criminal offences committed by members of the armed forces in the United Kingdom are dealt with in peacetime by the civil courts. The decision rests with the civil prosecutor: but offences affecting the person or property of a civilian will usually be prosecuted in the civil courts.[75] Even alleged breaches of the Official Secrets Acts may be dealt with in civil rather than military courts, as with the prosecution of eight signals personnel based in Cyprus who were prosecuted unsuccessfully in 1986 under the 1911 Act for allegedly passing intelligence information

[69] Courts-Martial (Appeals) Act 1968, s 1(3).

[70] (1866) 4 F & F 763, 790.

[71] *R* v *Smith* (1900) 17 *Cape of Good Hope SCR* 561.

[72] (1861) 4 Irvine 58, 69.

[73] The case of Marine Bek, *The Times*, 31 March 1971; *A–G for Northern Ireland's Reference (No 1 of 1975)* [1977] AC 105; *Farrell* v *Defence Secretary* [1980] 1 All ER 166; *R* v *Thain* (1985) 11 NIJB 31. And see ch 26.

[74] [1995] 1 AC 482. See Cm 2706, 1995, p 52.

[75] Stuart-Smith, note 25 above, p 492.

to enemy agents in return for sexual favours.[76] Where a person subject to military law has been tried for an offence by court-martial or has been dealt with summarily by his or her commanding officer, a civil court may not try him or her subsequently for the same or substantially the same offence.[77] Apart from this there is no restriction on a civil court trying a member of the armed forces for an offence under criminal law. A person tried by a civil court in the United Kingdom or elsewhere is similarly not liable to be tried again under service law in respect of the same or substantially the same offence.[78] In general, a person who is no longer subject to service law is liable to be tried under service law for offences committed while he or she was so subject, but only for a period of six months after he or she ceased to be subject to service law.[79]

Apart from its duty of care owed to British soldiers,[80] questions also arise as to whether the Crown can be vicariously liable in tort or delict for the acts or omissions of members of the armed forces. The problem could arise in the event of a member of the armed forces negligently causing damage to another member of the services or to a third party; and such a case could arise either in wartime or in peace. Before the Crown Proceedings Act 1947 difficulties would have been faced by some claimants (particularly those who were themselves members of the armed forces) by virtue of the Crown's immunity from liability. But even with the passing of the Act difficulties would still be encountered by a member of the armed forces who was injured by the negligence of another, if the Secretary of State issued a certificate under s 10 of the 1947 Act that the (death or) injury of the applicant was attributable to service for the purposes of a war pension. However, s 10 was repealed in 1987[81] though the 1987 Act does not apply to injuries caused by events before 1987.[82] Complex provision is made for the revival of s 10 of the 1947 Act in response to any 'imminent national danger or of any great emergency' or 'for the purposes of any warlike operations in any part of the world outside the United Kingdom'. The order must be made by the Secretary of State, the power being exercisable by statutory instrument which is subject to annulment by Parliament. As a result of the 1987 Act, it is thus possible for a member of the armed forces to sue the Ministry of Defence, not only in respect of injuries sustained by the negligence of another as a result of military operations in peacetime (as in Northern Ireland), but also in times of war or other hostilities (as in the case of the campaign in Afghanistan, and the invasion and occupation of Iraq).

For reasons explained this is a matter about which there is not a great deal of authority.[83] There is, however, authority for the view that the Crown could be vicariously liable for injuries sustained by a member of the armed forces as a result of the negligence of another in peacetime[84] and by third parties as a result of negligence by a member of the armed forces who was not engaged at the time in operations against the enemy.[85] But there is also authority for the view that there is

---

[76] A subsequent inquiry found the pre-trial detention and questioning of the suspects to be unlawful, in the sense that the 'procedures in RAF and military law intended to protect individuals against oppressive treatment and arbitrary detention had been honoured more in the breach than in the observance'. The government undertook to make ex gratia payments to those involved. See Cmnd 9781, 1986 (Calcutt Report); A W Bradley [1986] PL 363.

[77] Armed Forces Act 2006, s 64.

[78] Ibid, s 66.

[79] Ibid, s 55. The time limit may be over-ridden in some cases with the consent of the Attorney General (s 61).

[80] *R (Smith) v Defence Secretary* [2009] EWCA Civ 441.

[81] See Crown Proceedings (Armed Forces) Act 1987; and ch 32 A.

[82] On the compatibility of these measures with the ECHR, see *Matthews v Ministry of Defence* [2003] UKHL 4; [2003] 1 AC 1163.

[83] For an account of some of the issues, see Z Cowan (1950) 66 LQR 478.

[84] *Groves v Commonwealth of Australia* (1982) 150 CLR 113. See also *Barrett v Ministry of Defence* [1995] 3 All ER 87; *Jebson v Ministry of Defence* [2000] 1 WLR 2055 (scope of liability where a soldier off duty dies or is injured because of over-indulgence in alcohol); and *Ministry of Defence v Radclyffe* [2009] EWCA Civ 635.

[85] *Shaw, Savill and Albion Co Ltd v The Commonwealth* (1940) 66 CLR 344.

no liability to a third party where the injury is sustained by the negligence of a member of the armed forces while in the course of an actual engagement with the enemy.[86]

In *Mulcahy* v *Ministry of Defence*[87] a soldier deployed in Saudi Arabia during the Gulf conflict was injured as a result of a fellow soldier negligently causing a howitzer to fire while the plaintiff was fetching water from the front of the gun. An action for damages for negligence, claiming that the Ministry was vicariously liable, was struck out by the Court of Appeal on the ground that it disclosed no cause of action. Although no order had been made under s 2 of the 1987 Act to revive s 10 of the Crown Proceedings Act 1947, it was nevertheless held that (adopting a dictum of the High Court of Australia)[88] there is no civil liability for injury caused by the negligence of persons in the course of an actual engagement with the enemy, in accordance with 'common sense and sound policy'. In the view of Sir Iain Glidewell, 'it could be highly detrimental to the conduct of military operations if each soldier had to be conscious that, even in the heat of battle, he owed [a duty of care] to his comrade'.

This immunity (sometimes referred to as 'combat immunity') does not, however, apply to negligence causing loss or damage to individuals during policing and peacekeeping operations, such as those in Kosovo.[89] Possible liabilities under the Human Rights Act 1998 are considered below.

Visiting Forces Act 1952

Just as it is necessary for British military jurisdiction to be exercised when British forces are stationed abroad, so it is necessary that foreign troops stationed in the United Kingdom should be able to enforce their own military law. This would be unlawful without the authority of Parliament. The Visiting Forces Act 1952 gave effect to an agreement reached between parties to the North Atlantic Treaty on the legal status of the armed forces of one state when stationed in the territory of another.[90] It also applies to forces from member states of the Commonwealth which are stationed in the United Kingdom and it may be extended to forces from other countries by Order in Council. The Act was extended by the Armed Forces Act 1996 to apply also to countries with which this country has 'arrangements for defence cooperation', to accommodate the possibility of military personnel from the countries of central and eastern Europe exercising in the UK.

Under Part I of the Act, the service courts and service authorities of visiting forces may exercise in the United Kingdom all the jurisdiction given to them by their own national law over all persons (including civilians accompanying the visiting forces) who may be subject to their jurisdiction; the death penalty may not, however, be carried out in the United Kingdom unless under United Kingdom law the death sentence could have been passed (s 2). The Act excludes the jurisdiction of criminal courts in the United Kingdom over members of visiting forces only if the alleged offence (*a*) arises out of and in the course of military duty; or (*b*) is one against the person or a member of the same or another visiting force, for example, murder or assault; or (*c*) is committed against property of the visiting force or of a member thereof (s 3). The service authorities of the visiting force may, however, waive jurisdiction over such an offence. A member of a visiting force who has been tried by his or her own service court cannot be put on trial in a United Kingdom court for the same offence (s 4). Police powers of arrest and search in respect of offences against United Kingdom law may still be exercised notwithstanding the jurisdiction of the visiting service authorities, but the police may deliver an arrested member of a visiting force into the custody of that force (s 5). The 1952 Act also makes provision for the settlement by the

---

[86] *Shaw, Savill and Albion*, ibid.
[87] [1996] QB 732.
[88] *Groves* v *Commonwealth of Australia*, in note 84.
[89] *Bici* v *Ministry of Defence* [2004] EWHC 786 (QB).
[90] Cmd 8279, 1951.

Secretary of State for Defence of certain civil claims in respect of acts or omissions of members of visiting forces (s 9).

In Part II of the 1952 Act, s 13 confers important powers on the police and on United Kingdom courts to arrest and hand over into the custody of the appropriate visiting force persons who are deserters or absentees without leave from the forces of any country to which the Act applies. In *R v Thames Justices, ex p Brindle*,[91] the Court of Appeal held that this power could be exercised in respect of any person who had deserted from any of the forces of a country to which the Act applied and was not restricted to persons who had deserted from visiting forces while they were serving in the United Kingdom; thus a United States citizen who deserted from a unit of the US army in Germany and came to England could be handed over to the US authorities in England, who might then return him in custody to the United States. A British civilian, or a member of the British armed forces, may be required to appear before a service court of visiting forces in order to give evidence. In such cases the summons must be issued by 'an officer of any of the home forces'.[92] Difficulties of a different kind arose in relation to the community charge; although visiting forces were exempt, British wives of US service personnel were not.[93]

D. Conclusion

The striking feature of service law is the extent to which it has been transformed by Convention rights. This was acknowledged by the Select Committee on the Armed Forces Bill in 2006, which also anticipated that there would be further challenges to service procedure in what is an evolving process.[94] But as the debates about equality for women and discrimination on the grounds of homosexuality reveal, human rights affect not only military procedures but also the rights and duties of service personnel.[95] In the highly publicised *Smith v Assistant Deputy Coroner for Oxfordshire*[96] it was said by Collins J that 'the soldier does not lose all protection simply because he is in hostile territory carrying out dangerous operations. Thus, for example, to send a soldier out on patrol or, indeed, into battle with defective equipment could constitute a breach of Article 2' of the ECHR (which protects the right to life).[97] It was also said, however, that 'the lives of members of the armed forces when sent to fight or to keep order abroad cannot receive absolute protection'. Illustrating the point historically, Collins J said that: 'the failures of the commissariat and the failures to provide any adequate medical attention in the Crimean War would, whereas the Charge of the Light Brigade would not, be regarded as a possible breach of Article 2.'

Although it is now accepted that 'the protection of Article 2 is capable of extending to a member of the armed forces wherever he or she may be', whether it does so or not 'will depend on the circumstances of the particular case'.[98] On the other hand, the question of liability to foreign nationals for the conduct of British soldiers in Iraq was raised in *R (Al Skeini) v Secretary of State for Defence*,[99] where it was held that the Act did not apply to the case of five men killed on the street or in their home by British troops in Basra because it could not be said that Basra was under

---

[91] [1975] 3 All ER 941. And see *R v Tottenham Magistrates' Court, ex p Williams* [1982] 2 All ER 705.

[92] Visiting Forces and International Headquarters (Application of Law) Order 1999, SI 1999 No 1736, reg 16 and Sch 7. The Order also confers other immunities and privileges on visiting forces, similar to those enjoyed by UK forces. For background, see HC 521 (1998–9). For amendments, see SI 2009 No 705.

[93] *Tatum v Cherwell DC* [1992] 1 WLR 1261 and *Earl v Huntingdonshire DC* [1994] CLYB 2936.

[94] HC 828-I (2005–06), paras 31–33.

[95] For a full account, see Rowe, *The Impact of Human Rights Law on Armed Forces*.

[96] [2008] EWHC (Admin) 694.

[97] See ch 19.

[98] This decision was upheld by the Court of Appeal: [2009] EWCA Civ 441.

[99] [2005] EWCA Civ 1609.

British control at the time. Different considerations applied in the case of a sixth man – Baha Mousa – killed while in the custody of the British army,[100] This latter incident led to court-martial proceedings, with one soldier pleading guilty of inhuman treatment, said to be the first ever conviction of a British soldier for a war crime under the International Criminal Court Act 2001.[101] The Ministry of Defence made a substantial award of compensation to Mr Mousa's family, and a public inquiry was announced into the circumstances of his death, with immunity from prosecution being offered to soldiers who gave evidence, some of which proved to be shocking.

---

[100] *R (Al Skeini)* v *Defence Secretary*, note 30 above. See also *R (B)* v *Foreign Secretary* [2004] EWCA Civ 1344; [2005] QB 643.

[101] War crimes are punishable under English law by virtue of s 51 of the 2001 Act. War crimes are defined in Sch 8 of the Act, which is based on arts 6–9 of the Statute of the International Criminal Court signed at Rome on 17 July 1998.

CHAPTER 17

The Treasury, public expenditure and the economy

Government policies for taxation and public expenditure have long been liable to give rise to legal and constitutional disputes. In the twentieth century, the responsibilities of central government widened to include not just raising and spending the proceeds of taxation to meet the costs of government, but also the task of managing the national economy. These responsibilities will continue long into the twenty-first century, but in the meantime our concern in this chapter is to provide an outline of the main financial procedures of government, with chapter 10 C having already provided an account of the financial procedures of Parliament. These matters are mostly the responsibility of the Treasury, which – with the Cabinet Office – is at the centre of government. We also deal in this chapter with some of the institutional structures which have evolved for the purpose of managing the economy, now principally a Treasury responsibility. These structures are, however, constantly evolving as the adoption of new economic orthodoxies and new economic circumstances suggest the need for different arrangements for economic management.

A. The Treasury[1]

Since 1714 the ancient office of Lord High Treasurer has been in commission; that is, its duties have been entrusted to a board of commissioners. Today the commissioners are the First Lord of the Treasury, an office held by the Prime Minister; the Chancellor of the Exchequer; and the Junior Lords of the Treasury, who are the assistant government whips in the House of Commons. The Treasury Board never meets, individual ministers being responsible for the Treasury's business. The Chancellor of the Exchequer's responsibilities cover the whole range of Treasury business, including the control of public expenditure and the direction of economic and financial policy. The other Treasury ministers include the Chief Secretary to the Treasury, who is often a member of the Cabinet and deals with public expenditure planning and control, public sector pay, and the public services. Other ministers in 2010 included the Financial Secretary, with responsibility for the tax system and tax credits; the Economic Secretary, with responsibility for a wide range of economic issues (such as growth, enterprise and productivity); the Exchequer Secretary, with responsibility for excise duties, personal savings and pensions policy; and the Financial Services Secretary with responsiblity for financial services, banking support, and foreign exchange reserves. These portfolios are not fixed or permanent, and there is no guarantee that all of these offices will continue in the future or that if they do they will be responsible for the duties currently assigned to them.

Functions of the Treasury

The Treasury's functions were formerly concerned primarily with financial matters, including the imposition and regulation of taxation, the control of expenditure and the management of the government's funds and accounts. But in the twentieth century, except for two periods when a

---

[1] See Beer, *Treasury Control*; Bridges, *The Treasury*; Heclo and Wildavsky, *The Private Government of Public Money*; Roseveare, *The Treasury*; and Thain and Wright, *The Treasury and Whitehall*. For the views of insiders, see Barnett, *Inside the Treasury*; Healey, *The Time of My Life*, chs 18–22; and Lawson, *The View from No 11*. For a detailed textbook-style description of some of the matters raised in this chapter, see Daintith and Page, *The Executive in the Constitution*, chs 4–6.

separate department for economic affairs was established (for some months in 1947 and between 1964 and 1969), the Treasury also became an economic policy department. Indeed, the role of the Treasury as 'the United Kingdom's finance and economics ministry' was made clear in the *Departmental Strategic Objectives* published in 2007, which were based on the need to maintain sound public finances, and ensure 'high and sustainable levels of economic growth, well being and prosperity for all'. To these ends the Treasury has a role to play in raising the productivity of the British economy, providing the conditions for business success in the United Kingdom, improving economic performance in the English regions, maximising employment opportunities, and reducing the number of children in poverty (with a view to eradicating child poverty by 2020).[2]

The economic functions of the Treasury, together with its control over government spending (through initiatives such as public service agreements), give the Treasury a uniquely powerful position in government. Although responsibility for monetary policy was recently transferred to the Bank of England, it is nevertheless sometimes suggested not only that the strategic influence of the Treasury has grown, but also that it now exercises too much influence on the policy-making of government.[3] Indeed, the suggestion has been made that the Treasury should show 'greater humility and inclusiveness', a view endorsed by the House of Commons Treasury Committee.[4] It may be significant, however, that the National Economic Council established in 2008 is chaired by the Prime Minister rather than the Chancellor of the Exchequer. This is designed to be an important Cabinet committee for the co-ordination of economic policy, and as such it replaces the Economic Development Committee which had been chaired by the Chancellor. But although the establishment of the Council may allow for greater supervision of the Treasury by No 10, it is not clear whether this will reinforce the power of the Prime Minister at the Chancellor's expense, and it is also unclear whether other government departments will notice any significant reduction in Treasury power or influence over policy or its implementation.

Statutory duties and powers

It is a measure of the importance of the Treasury in modern government that it now has a number of significant statutory duties and powers. The former include the provisions of the Fiscal Responsibility Act 2010 which imposes a duty on the Treasury to reduce government borrowing. This is considered in more detail below. So far as the statutory powers of the Treasury are concerned, these deal with two major preoccupations of government, namely the global financial crisis on the one hand and international terrorism on the other. Powers to deal with the first of these were taken initially in the Banking (Special Provisions) Act 2008, designed to enable the Treasury to intervene to safeguard the Northern Rock bank – by allowing it to be transferred into public ownership, though the wide terms in which the Act was drafted allowed it to be used to rescue a number of other financial institutions as well.[5] The position is now governed by the Banking Act 2009, which, in a comprehensive framework for the banking industry, provides permanent powers for intervention to safeguard financial institutions, the Treasury exercising these powers together with the Bank of England and the Financial Services Authority (the 'relevant authorities'). The three so-called stabilisation options available under the 2009 Act to deal with a failing bank include the power to transfer the bank in question to a private sector purchaser (as in the case of the Dunfermline Building Society in 2009),[6] or into temporary public sector ownership.

Important powers of a very different nature have been conferred on the Treasury to deal with the funding of terrorist organisations. Although there are clumsy powers to freeze the assets of

---

[2] HM Treasury Group, *Departmental Strategic Objectives 2008–2011* (2009).
[3] See Hennessy, *The Prime Minister*, pp 513–14. See also HC 73 (2000–01), para 25.
[4] HC 57 (2007–08), para 48.
[5] See SI 2008 Nos 432, 2546, 2644, 2666, 2674.
[6] SI 2009 No 814.

terrorist suspects in the Anti-terrorism, Crime and Security Act 2001,[7] the Treasury has generally preferred to use other sources of legal authority for this purpose. Regulations made under the United Nations Act 1946,[8] to give effect to UN Security Council Resolutions 1373 and 1390 respectively allow the Treasury to freeze the assets of people reasonably suspected to be involved in terrorist activity, with the definition of terrorism being drawn directly from the Terrorism Act 2000.[9] These measures are thought to be more advantageous than the powers in the 2001 Act, not least because they are not limited to foreign nationals. Unlike the 2001 Act, the 2001 Order provides for an appeal to the High Court or the Court of Session by individuals and others who are the subject of a freezing order. The regulations were, however, found to be ultra vires by the Supreme Court of the United Kingdom,[10] and the Court refused to postpone the operation of its decision to give the government time to respond.[10a] This led to the enactment of temporary legislation which passed through both Houses of Parliament at great speed to declare that the regulations in question were deemed to have been validly made, that anything done under the regulations was lawful, and that the 'prohibitions and obligations imposed by those Orders have legal force and criminal liability may be incurred by a person who fails to comply'.[11]

B. The Bank of England

The Bank of England was first established in 1694, mainly to provide loans to meet the needs of the Crown; it eventually became the government's bankers for all purposes. It was taken into public ownership under the Bank of England Act 1946, although the Treasury had for many years been able to control its policies. Under the 1946 Act, the Bank of England remains a separate institution from the Treasury and it is not a government department, although the governor and directors of the Bank are appointed by the Crown,[12] and the Treasury may issue formal directions to the Bank;[13] not now, however, in relation to monetary policy.[14] It also enjoys certain legal immunities of a kind associated with the Crown.[15] But it has been pointed out that 'unlike the detailed constitutions of some of the other central banks', the 1946 Act 'did not accord the Bank stated duties and responsibilities'.[16] Instead, it was an 'apparently simple Act by which the Treasury merely acquired stock from the Bank's proprietors, made arrangements for the Crown to appoint the Governors and directors, and gave legal support firstly to the ultimate authority of the Treasury over the Bank in matters of policy and secondly to the authority of the Bank over the banks'.[17]

Constitution and functions

The constitution of the Bank of England is now governed by the Bank of England Act 1998 (as amended by the Banking Act 2009), which made a number of radical changes to the functions

---

[7] 2001 Act, s 4. The powers allow for the freezing of funds for reasons other than those related to terrorism: see SI 2008 No 2668 (Icelandic bank; see HC 402, 656 (2008–09)).

[8] Terrorism (United Nations Measures) Order 2006, SI 2006 No 2657 and the al-Qaeda and Taliban (United Nations Measures) Order 2006, SI 2006 No 2952.

[9] See ch 26.

[10] *HM Treasury* v *Ahmed* [2010] UKSC 2.

[10a] *HM Treasury* v *Ahmed (No 2)* [2010] UKSC 5.

[11] Terrorist Asset-Freezing (Temporary Provisions) Act 2010.

[12] The Governor, Deputy Governor and directors are known as the Court of Directors: Bank of England Act 1998, s 1.

[13] Bank of England Act 1964, s 4.

[14] Bank of England Act 1998, s 10. But see 1998 Act, s 19 (Treasury reserve powers), discussed below.

[15] Banking Act 2009, s 244; see below, p 346.

[16] HC 98-I (1993–4), para 13.

[17] Fforde, *The Bank of England and Public Policy 1941–1958*, p 5.

performed by the Bank. The Bank continues to be governed by a court of directors, which consists of the governor, two deputy governors and up to nine directors, all appointed by the Crown. It was the optimistic intention of the government that the directors would be representative of the nation as a whole.[18] The governor and deputy governors are appointed for renewable periods of five years; and the directors for three.[19] Members of the court may be removed from office by the Bank for a number of prescribed reasons, with the consent of the Chancellor of the Exchequer (Sch 1). The functions of the court of directors as set out in the 1998 Act are to 'manage the Bank's affairs, other than the formulation of monetary policy' (which is the responsibility of the Monetary Policy Committee) (s 2(1)). These functions include in particular 'determining the Bank's objectives (including objectives for its financial management) and strategy' (s 2(2)). Following an amendment to the 1998 Act (by the Banking Act 2009), it is now an objective of the Bank to help protect and enhance financial stability in the United Kingdom (s 2A), and to this end provision is made for a Financial Stability Committee of the Bank's court of directors (s 2B).[20] However, concern was expressed before the Treasury Select Committee that the Bank was unclear about what just it is expected to do to promote this latter objective.[21]

In addition to the foregoing, the Bank has a number of responsibilities which have evolved over its long history: these include acting as banker to the government and to the clearing banks; the implementation of monetary policy; and the issue of currency.[22] A major initiative introduced in 1997 was to give the Bank operational responsibility to set interest rates.[23] This step was taken by the Prime Minister and the Chancellor of the Exchequer, without consulting the Cabinet, in order 'to ensure that decision-making on monetary policy was more effective, open, accountable, and free from short-term political manipulation'.[24] Under the 1998 Act the Bank is responsible for monetary policy within the objectives set out in the Act: these are to maintain price stability and to support the economic policy of the government, 'including its objectives for growth and employment' (s 11). Provision is also made for the government to set the inflation target for the Bank, which is reviewed annually and announced in the Budget; it is the operational responsibility of the Bank to achieve that target (s 12).[25] It is the specific responsibility of the Monetary Policy Committee of the Bank of England to formulate monetary policy. The committee consists of the governor and the deputy governors, two senior Bank officials with responsibility for monetary policy and market operations, but also 'four other expert members appointed from outside the Bank by the government'.[26] The Treasury has reserve powers to give the Bank directions relating to monetary policy in 'extreme economic circumstances' (s 19).[27]

Transparency and accountability

A great deal of secrecy has traditionally surrounded matters of national finance and it remains the case that there are still restrictions on access to banking and financial information. Public

---

[18] HC Deb, 20 May 1997, col 509.

[19] The Banking Act 2009 amends the 1998 Act so that neither the Governor nor the deputy governors may be appointed for more than two terms.

[20] A Treasury representative may attend meetings of the Fiscal Stability Committee (but may not vote).

[21] HC 767 (2008–09).

[22] Responsibilities for the management of government debt were transferred to the Treasury (HC Deb, 20 May 1997, col 509) and for the supervision of other banks and financial institutions to the Financial Services Authority (Bank of England Act 1998, s 21).

[23] HC Deb, 6 May 1997, col 509; also HC Deb, 20 May 1997, col 507 et seq.

[24] HC Deb, 20 May 1997, col 508 (Mr Gordon Brown).

[25] Ibid.

[26] Ibid.

[27] The government expects this power to be used 'rarely, if at all' (HC Deb, 20 May 1997, col 509).

interest immunity applies to documents 'which cover discussions and communications between the Bank and the government', as well as to financial information communicated to the government and to the Bank by major businesses.[28] It is also the case that the Freedom of Information Act 2000 has an exemption for information the disclosure of which would or would be likely to prejudice the financial interests of any administration in the United Kingdom (s 29).[29] Nevertheless, important steps in the direction of greater transparency were taken in 1997 and contained in the Bank of England Act 1998. These include a requirement that the Bank must report annually to the Chancellor, who must lay the report before Parliament (s 4). Perhaps more importantly, the interest rate decisions of the Monetary Policy Committee must be published immediately (s 14), and minutes of the meetings of the Committee must be published within six weeks (s 15). The Bank must (now by statute) also prepare a quarterly inflation report, which must be published (subject to the approval of the Monetary Policy Committee) (s 18).

Transparency of decisions and decision-making of this kind will help to enhance the scrutiny which Parliament can provide. Between 1969 and 1979 the Bank was, in some of its activities, subject to investigation by the select committee on the nationalised industries.[30] Since 1979, the Bank has come within the sphere of the Treasury and Civil Service Committee and now the Treasury Committee, as one of the 'associated public bodies' related to the Treasury.[31] A major study of the Bank was conducted by the Treasury and Civil Service Committee in 1993,[32] which is said to have influenced the reforms introduced in 1997.[33] Several times a year, senior officials of the Bank appear before the Treasury Committee to answer questions on the Bank's inflation reports. The Committee has also shown considerable interest in the work of the Monetary Policy Committee: in addition to examining the work of the MPC,[34] the Treasury Committee also holds confirmation hearings to see whether those nominated to the MPC are adequately qualified, though the views of the Committee are not binding on the Treasury. Valuable scrutiny work is also undertaken by what is now the House of Lords Economic Affairs Committee.[35] In terms of accountability through the courts, it is to be noted that the Bank enjoys a statutory immunity from liability in damages in respect of its role as a central bank on the one hand, and its work on financial stability on the other.[36]

C. Public finance

The annual cycle of revenue and expenditure that was established in the nineteenth century depended on a highly centralised system of financial procedure built up by a combination of statutory and parliamentary rules, Cabinet conventions and administrative practices. In chapter 10 C we saw that without the formal authority of Parliament the Crown could neither raise money by taxation nor incur expenditure. While permanent authority was given by statute for some forms of expenditure and revenue, authority for much expenditure and taxation was given by Parliament strictly on an annual basis. This led to the system by which each year the Treasury coordinated the expenditure needs of the departments. While the annual cycle ensured that Parliament should regularly approve the government's financial proposals, the government in

---

[28] *Burmah Oil Co v Bank of England* [1980] AC 1090. See ch 32 C below.

[29] Also Bank of England Act 1998, Sch 7.

[30] Ch 14 D. See HC 258 (1969–70).

[31] Ch 10 D.

[32] HC 98-I (1993–4).

[33] HC Deb, 20 May 1997, col 508.

[34] HC 42 (2000–01).

[35] See HL Paper 110 (2008–09) (Banking Supervision and Regulation).

[36] Banking Act 2009, s 244. The immunity does not apply to action or inaction in bad faith, or in breach of the Human Rights Act 1998, s 6(1).

fact retained a firm control over the House; thus by a standing order of the House dating from 1713, the House could not consider new charges on the public revenue or new taxes except on the recommendation of the Crown signified by a minister.[37] This emphasised that the government bore responsibility for all taxation and expenditure. In this section we consider three issues which relate to that responsibility: the legal authority for the raising of money by taxation; the funds into which tax and other revenues are paid and from which expenditure is made; and the procedures for accounting for government finance.[38]

Authority for taxation

Permanent authority for tax collection is contained in such Acts as the Taxes Management Act 1970 which makes provision for the collection and management of income tax, corporation tax and capital gains tax. Under the direction of HM Revenue and Customs, a citizen's liability to tax is assessed by inspectors of taxes who are also civil servants.[39] In performing their duties, HM Revenue and Customs are subject to the authority, direction and control of the Treasury.[40] Where a taxpayer does not accept that he or she has been correctly assessed for income tax, he or she has a right of appeal to what is now the Tax Chamber of the First-Tier Tribunal established under the Tribunals, Courts and Enforcement Act 2007, with a further appeal to the Upper Tribunal (Tax and Chancery). The principal forms of indirect taxation, such as value added tax and customs and excise duties, are also administered now by HM Revenue and Customs. As with income tax, VAT and customs and excise duties must be collected in accordance with the law and assessments are also subject to an appeal to the Tax Chamber of the First-Tier Tribunal. The detailed rules of these forms of taxation are contained in continuing Acts of Parliament, but the rates of duty may be subject to variation by the Treasury or by a Secretary of State under statutory authority.[41] Many duties administered by HM Revenue and Customs are directly affected by obligations which arise from British membership of the EU.

In dealing with tax disputes, the courts may take into account the ancient principle in the Bill of Rights that the authority of Parliament must be shown to exist if any charge on the citizen is to be lawful.[42] Thus a tax may not be imposed in reliance on a resolution of the House of Commons alone, in the absence of a statute giving legal effect to the resolution.[43] Subordinate legislation which infringes the Bill of Rights principle may be declared invalid by the courts;[44] when in 1975 the television licence fee was increased, it was held unlawful for the Home Office to use a discretionary power to revoke licences so as to prevent viewers from receiving the benefit of an overlapping licence bought at the lower rate just before the increased fee became operative.[45] Money which has been paid to a public authority under tax regulations which are ultra vires is recoverable by the taxpayer as of right and with interest.[46] The implications of the Human Rights Act 1998 for taxation (and for other areas of the Treasury's work) have yet to be fully tested,[47] but arts 6 (right to a fair trial), 8 (right to private life) and 14 (prohibition of discrimination)

---

[37] Ch 10 C.

[38] For the comparable arrangements relating to Scotland, see Public Finance and Accountability (Scotland) Act 2000.

[39] See Johnston, *The Inland Revenue*.

[40] Commissioners for Revenue and Customs Act 2005, s 11. Cf *IRC v Nuttal* [1990] 1 WLR 631.

[41] E.g. Excise Duties (Surcharges or Rebates) Act 1979.

[42] Ch 2 A.

[43] *Bowles v Bank of England* [1913] 1 Ch 57; ch 10 C.

[44] *Commissioners of Customs and Excise v Cure and Deeley Ltd* [1962] 1 QB 340.

[45] *Congreve v Home Office* [1976] QB 629.

[46] *Woolwich Building Society v IRC (No 2)* [1993] AC 70. See J Beatson (1993) 109 LQR 401; and ch 32 A.

[47] See Tiley, *Revenue Law*: 'human rights doctrines are clearly having an influence on the Revenue' (p 47).

of the ECHR are clearly relevant.[48] So too is art 1 of the First Protocol which the government accepted had been breached by a bereavement tax allowance made available to widows but not widowers.[49] Awareness of Convention rights is revealed in the Banking Act 2009: stabilisation powers must be exercised in a way that does not violate the First Protocol, while as we have seen the Bank of England's immunity from liability in suit is subject to an exception for Convention rights generally.[50] However, the European Court of Human Rights has emphasised 'a Contracting State's margin of appreciation in the tax field'.[51]

Although the assessment of tax is governed by law, some areas of tax administration tend to escape judicial control. Thus the revenue authorities may exercise their discretion not to enforce payment against an individual taxpayer or a class of taxpayers; only in very exceptional circumstances could another taxpayer complain of such a decision to the courts.[52] Although they have been criticised for doing so, the revenue authorities may also issue extra-statutory concessions by which they announce that tax due will be waived in certain circumstances,[53] and in other cases may agree a settlement which is not a true estimate of liability, a feature of the investigation of wealthy tax avoiders carried out by the Inland Revenue (now HM Revenue and Customs) which was exposed by the prosecution of a senior tax inspector for corruption in 1997.[54] But this power to grant concessions is necessarily a limited one, and in one case could not be used to grant a bereavement allowance to widowers when the legislation made provision only for widows, even though such discrimination was conceded by the government to violate Convention rights.[55] While it would not normally be proper for the tax authorities to absolve a taxpayer from an undisclosed tax liability of which the authorities were unaware, in principle it may be possible successfully to challenge a decision by HM Revenue and Customs assessing liability to pay tax if it is unfair to the taxpayer on the grounds that the later conduct of the Revenue is similar to a breach of contract or a breach of a representation in view of earlier events.[56] This principle does not enable a taxpayer to avoid payment of tax where a full disclosure of the facts has not been made to the tax authorities.[57]

Consolidated Fund and other funds

With certain exceptions, all revenue derived from taxation is paid into the Consolidated Fund.[58] In the case of receipts which arise in the course of a department's business (for example, sales or

---

[48] See *Georgiou v United Kingdom* [2001] STC 80, *Han and Yau v Commissioners of Customs and Excise* [2001] STC 1188, and *King v Walden* [2001] STC 822 (art 6); *R (Morgan Grenfell) v Special Commissioner* [2002] STC 786 (art 8); and *Hobbs v United Kingdom* [2008] STC 1469, and *Burden v United Kingdom* [2008] STC 1305 (art 14). The Human Rights Act 1998 presented a number of difficulties during the passage of the Financial Services and Markets Act 2000. See Financial Services and Markets Bill. Memorandum from HM Treasury to the Joint Committee on Parts V, VI and XII of the Bill in relation to the ECHR, www.treasury.gov.uk/docs/1999/fsmbmemo175.

[49] *R (Wilkinson) v IRC* [2005] UKHL 30; [2005] 1 WLR 1718. But in a claim brought under the Human Rights Act the claimant was unable to succeed because of s 6(2) of the Act, which provides a defence to a public authority that it is bound by legislation to do as it did. In this case the legislation applied only to widows and could not be read to apply also to widowers. See subsequently *Hobbs v United Kingdom*, above.

[50] Banking Act 2009, ss 4, 244.

[51] *National and Provincial Building Society v UK* (1997) 25 EHRR 127, at p 169. See also *Burden v United Kingdom* [2008] STC 1305, and *Jussila v Finland* [2009] STC 29; but compare *Bulves AD v Bulgaria* [2009] STC 1193.

[52] *R v IRC, ex p National Federation of Self-Employed* [1982] AC 617; and ch 31.

[53] *Vestey v IRC* [1980] AC 1148; ch 28.

[54] *Guardian*, 19, 20 February 1997.

[55] *R (Wilkinson) v IRC* above.

[56] *R v IRC, ex p Preston* [1985] AC 835; and ch 30 C.

[57] *R v IRC, ex p Matrix-Securities Ltd* [1994] 1 All ER 769.

[58] Consolidated Fund Act 1816 and Exchequer and Audit Departments Act 1866, s 10. Certain payments are made to special funds, e.g. the National Insurance Fund in the case of social security contributions (Social Security Administration Act 1992, s 162).

fees for services provided), these may be appropriated in aid of the department's estimate of the resources which it will need, thereby reducing the provision which would otherwise have to be made by Parliament. Formerly, all money lent by the government came from the Consolidated Fund; but in 1968 a separate account with the Bank of England was established, named the National Loans Fund, through which all borrowing by central government and most domestic lending transactions now pass. The operations of the two funds are very closely linked: thus sums needed to meet charges on the National Loans Fund must be paid into it from the Consolidated Fund and a process of daily balancing takes place between the funds.[59]

The annual cycle of financial provision by Parliament proved unsuitable as a means of financing activities of government which were in the nature of trading or business undertakings. In 1973, it was provided that certain services (for example, the Royal Mint and Her Majesty's Stationery Office) could be financed by means of a trading fund established with public money, instead of by means of annual votes and appropriations from Parliament.[60] The enabling powers in the Act were extended in the Government Trading Act 1990 as part of civil service management changes. The 1990 Act 'somewhat elaborated the 1973 regime, but did not change its general principles'.[61] If it appears to a minister that any operations of a department are suitable to be financed by a trading fund and that such a fund would be in the interests of improved efficiency and effectiveness of the management of these operations, he or she may by order, with Treasury concurrence, establish such a fund. The order may designate a person other than the minister to control and manage the fund, but a main objective of establishing a trading fund is that the business activities of the fund should finance all or most of its activities,[62] and indeed 'some trading funds move on to become wholly owned companies within the public sector'.[63]

These initiatives were designed to encourage the civil service to take a more business-like approach to the efficiency and quality of government services, by introducing greater financial discipline akin to that under which private sector organisations operate.[64] A trading fund is 'either part of a department or a department in its own right'.[65] As such, the funds are sometimes referred to as non-ministerial departments, and therefore not directly accountable to Parliament. Most trading funds are likely to be established in agencies created under the 'next steps' programme (which is considered more fully in chapter 13 D), although agencies which are not trading funds can now be required by the Treasury to produce commercial-style accounts to be audited by the Comptroller and Auditor General and laid before Parliament.[66] By 2003, 19 funds had been established,[67] some of which have had their scope and borrowing powers extended subsequently. One example is the Land Registry Trading Fund, established in 1993 under the control and management of the Chief Land Registrar with designated assets, liabilities and public dividend capital. Assets include freehold and leasehold land used or allocated for use in the funded operations as well as plant and equipment and computer hardware and software. The fund is empowered to borrow up to a statutory limit, with the National Loans Fund being designated as the authorised lender.[68]

---

[59] National Loans Act 1968, s 18.

[60] Government Trading Funds Act 1973.

[61] Daintith and Page, note 1 above, p 136. The 1990 Act was amended by the Finance Acts 1991, 1993 and 2003.

[62] HM Treasury, *Managing Public Money*, para 7.5.1.

[63] Ibid, para 7.5.6.

[64] See HC Deb, 8 January 1990, cols 726–9.

[65] HM Treasury, *Managing Public Money*, para 5.1.1.

[66] Government Resources and Accounts Act 2000, s 7: this enables the Treasury to direct a government department to prepare for each financial year accounts in relation to any specified matter.

[67] HM Treasury, *Government Accounting*, para 7.1.9.

[68] SI 1993 No 938, amended by SI 2003 No 2094.

Consolidated Fund and supply services

The expenditure of central departments may be classified under two heads, namely Consolidated Fund services and supply services. The Consolidated Fund services are payments under statutes which provide continuing authority for the payments in question: the customary statutory phrase is that such payments 'shall be charged on and paid out of the Consolidated Fund'. As this authority continues from year to year, it is not necessary for the payments to be voted each year by the Commons. A principal expenditure under this heading has been the provision which is made via the National Loans Fund for paying the interest on the national debt. There are also charged on the Consolidated Fund other payments which for constitutional reasons are considered inappropriate for annual authorisation by Parliament. These include the Civil List,[69] and the salaries of the judiciary, the Comptroller and Auditor General, the Parliamentary Ombudsman, and the members of the Electoral Commission. This means that there is no regular annual opportunity of discussing in Parliament the work of these officers. This practice tends purposely to preserve their independence, but the justification for it loses some of its force during rapid inflation when the Civil List and public salaries may need to be increased or supplemented annually.

A different example of a charge on the Consolidated Fund was created by the European Communities Act 1972: s 2(3) gives continuing authority for payment from the Consolidated Fund or National Loans Fund of any amounts required to meet EU obligations.[70] While it was argued by the government in 1972 that such continuing authority was an essential feature of British membership of the EEC,[71] it is politically convenient for the government to have continuing authority to pay over the sums concerned, without seeking fresh approval from Parliament each year. By contrast, supply services involve charges for purposes stated by the statutes which authorise them to be payable 'out of money to be provided by Parliament'. Following the introduction of new accounting arrangements by the Government Resources and Accounts Act 2000, the form in which the appropriation is presented in the Appropriation Acts has changed: the Appropriation Acts (which indicate the purposes for which supply may be spent by each department) now indicate the resources as well as the cash which is to be made available for these purposes. The great bulk of departmental expenditure is voted annually on this basis, through the procedure of supply already described.[72]

Questions arise, however, about how far the annual Appropriation Act can be regarded as sufficient authority for the exercise of functions by a government department in cases where no other statutory authority exists. In a Treasury–Public Accounts Committee Concordat of 1932, it was accepted that there should be both (i) statutory authority for the expenditure and (ii) a vote of supply to meet it. This followed criticism of the then Ministry of Labour in 1932 for relying on the Appropriation Act to finance schemes for unemployed workers without having other statutory authority.[73] Nevertheless, the Treasury takes the view that in 'certain limited circumstances' departments may (with Treasury approval) rely on the Appropriation Act alone for small items of expenditure, or for expenditure not likely to last more than two years.[74] Current practice also permits ministers to make a start on a new activity in anticipation of parliamentary approval not yet given. Here again, the Treasury may approve the expenditure on the authority of the Appropriation Act alone for reasons of genuine urgency in the public interest, provided the Bill authorising the activity has already been introduced and given a second reading in the Commons, and the planned legislation is 'certain, or virtually certain' to pass into law 'in the near future'.[75]

---

[69] Ch 12 A.

[70] See *Monckton v Lord Advocate* 1995 SLT 1201.

[71] HC Deb, 22 February 1972, col 1137, and 8 June 1972, col 813. Cf *R v HM Treasury, ex p Smedley* [1985] QB 657.

[72] Ch 10 C.

[73] HM Treasury, *Managing Public Money*, Annex 2.1.

[74] Ibid, para 2.3.3.

[75] Ibid, para 2.4.3.

Government accounting practices

The Government Resources and Accounts Act 2000 introduced important changes to the way in which government accounts are managed and presented.[76] The Act was said to go 'to the heart of Parliament's role in holding government to account' and to mark 'a milestone on the way to full implementation of the biggest reform and modernisation of the country's public finances since the time of Gladstone'.[77] As such it was the first major piece of legislation since 1921 to deal with government accounting and the main purpose of the Act attracted all-party support. Indeed, the preparatory work for what was to become the 2000 Act had been undertaken in the Treasury when the Conservatives were in government. This is not to say that the 2000 Act was wholly uncontroversial, with a number of criticisms being made by the House of Commons Public Accounts Committee in particular,[78] as well as by a number of prominent parliamentarians experienced in the field of government accounting.[79] But these criticisms were of a practical nature, concerned more with a failure fully to consult with the Public Accounts Committee in good time about the legislation and about the difficulties encountered in the move to a new accounting system than by the principles embraced by the Act.

The main purpose of the Act was to replace the existing cash-based system of accounting and budgeting with what accountants refer to as resource accounting and resource-based supply. This is secured by s 5(1), which requires government departments for which an estimate is approved by the House of Commons to prepare accounts detailing (*a*) resources acquired, held or disposed of by the department during the year; and (*b*) the use by the department of resources during the year. The accounts are to be prepared in accordance with directions issued by the Treasury (s 5(2)), although these should seek to ensure that the resource accounts conform to 'generally accepted accounting practice' (s 5(3)). Resource accounting was explained by the Public Accounts Committee as a 'commercial-style accrual accounting for central Government departments'.[80] It was also explained that accounts 'will include for the first time a balance sheet to show a department's assets and liabilities'; that departments will 'provide an analysis of expenditure by aims and objectives'; and that 'Parliament will authorise the resources, rather than the cash, that departments can use'.[81] The Public Accounts Committee endorsed the introduction of resource accounting on the ground that 'it should lead to greater clarity and improved financial information to Parliament'.[82] The new resource-based financial management system was fully implemented in April 2001.[83]

The other major accounting initiative introduced by the Government Resources and Accounts Act 2000 dealt with 'whole of government accounts', said by one leading Opposition member in the Lords to be 'accounts which are broadly in line with the private sector, both with regard to the profit and loss account and with regard to balance sheets'.[84] This is dealt with in s 9 of the Act,

---

[76] See F White and K Hollingsworth [2001] PL 50; also White and Hollingsworth, *Audit, Accountability and Government*, esp ch 2, and Daintith and Page, note 1 above, pp 164–8.

[77] HL Deb, 10 April 2000, col 11.

[78] HC 127 (1999–2000) (4th Report), and HC 159 (1999–2000) (9th Report).

[79] As is so often the case, the most effective contributions were made in the House of Lords: see HL Deb, 10 April 2000, col 16 et seq.

[80] HC 159 (1999–2000) (9th Report), para 7. The difference between cash and accrual accounting was explained by the Treasury in 1995: 'Cash accounts record payments and income as they are actually made and received, regardless of when the obligation to pay arises and of the period over which it may extend, whereas accruals accounts record current expenditure and income in the year to which that obligation relates, even if the cash was not paid or received in that year, also recording the difference between the accruals measure and the actual cash paid or received, usually as a creditor or debtor' (Cm 2929, 1995, p 5).

[81] 9th Report, ibid.

[82] Ibid, para 11.

[83] HM Treasury, *Managing Resources: Full Implementation of Resource Accounting and Budgeting*, p 2.

[84] HL Deb, 10 April 2000, col 19 (Lord Higgins).

which requires the Treasury to prepare annual accounts to cover bodies which exercise functions of a public nature or which are entirely or substantially funded from public money. Bodies that are designated by order of the Treasury to fall within the scope of the Act must provide financial information to the Treasury as requested, in the form directed by the Treasury (s 10). This initiative was said by ministers to have three overlapping aims. First, it was designed to improve the information available to support the conduct and monitoring of fiscal policy; second, to improve the accountability of the government to Parliament; and third, to provide greater transparency to taxpayers.[85] It was realised, however, that 'full audited whole of government accounts' will need 'greater conformity of accounting policies, systems and procedures' and that as a result it would be necessary to develop this initiative on a staged basis.[86]

D. Public expenditure control and accountability

The raising of income and authorising its use are only one part of the Treasury's responsibilities for public finance. Also of critical importance is the role of the Treasury in controlling public expenditure. The context within which public expenditure is now incurred is determined by the government's fiscal rules and its Code for Fiscal Stability which was introduced in 1998. So far as the former are concerned, the first is the so-called Golden Rule by which the government will borrow only to invest but not to fund current spending; and the second is the Sustainable Investment Rule by which borrowing to fund investment will be set at a stable and prudent level (no more than 40 per cent of GDP). As far as the Code for Fiscal Stability is concerned, this is based on the 'key principles of transparency, stability, responsibility, fairness and efficiency' in fiscal policy and national debt management policy.[87] These measures were qualified (some would say abandoned) by what was referred to as the 'temporary operating rule' to deal with the global financial crisis beginning in 2008. However, a commitment to maintain sound public finances is to be seen in the Fiscal Responsibility Act 2010, to which reference has already been made. The obligation to reduce the public debt which this Act imposes on the Treasury is not legally enforceable, nor does it give rise to legal proceedings. But it will almost inevitably have an impact on public spending, for economic growth alone is unlikely to cause the deficit to decline.

Public expenditure limits

In 1961 the Plowden report recommended that regular surveys should be made of public expenditure as a whole, over a period of years ahead and in relation to prospective resources; and that decisions involving substantial future expenditure should be taken in the light of those surveys.[88] This influential report led to the creation of a new system of public expenditure control,[89] but changes in that system became necessary in the 1970s as economic growth declined and the control of expenditure broke down during the period of rapid inflation in 1973–75. Further changes were made in the 1980s to accommodate the new policy of government to reduce

---

[85] Ibid, cols 13–14 (Lord McIntosh).

[86] It was intended initially to concentrate on central government, executive agencies and non-departmental public bodies, before making any decisions about extending the coverage to the rest of the public sector: ibid, col 14.

[87] Finance Act 1998, s 155. Also Daintith and Page, p 166. On the effectiveness of transparency, see D Heald (2003) 81 *Public Administration* 723.

[88] Cmnd 1432, 1961.

[89] For early accounts of PESC, see Cmnd 4071, 1969, and HC 549 (1970–1); Clarke, *New Trends in Government*, ch 2; and Heclo and Wildavsky, ch 5.

public expenditure in real terms.[90] Under current arrangements (which have no statutory authority) there has evolved a practice of regular review of government spending, known previously as the Public Expenditure Survey and now referred to as the spending review (see below). The effect of this process is to plan government spending as far as possible on the basis of three-year cycles.

The most significant change made during the 1970s was probably the introduction of cash limits in 1976.[91] Before then, public expenditure was essentially planned in 'volume terms'; that is, it was based on the volume of approved programmes (for example, so many new miles of motorway). As wages and prices of material increased with inflation, the programmes were not themselves affected and the cash requirement was automatically increased. In 1976, cash limits were applied by the Labour government to counter this automatic increase in cash provision. The method was extended by the Conservative government after 1979 as a primary means of restraining public expenditure and of managing the economy. Cash limits are applied to as many spending programmes as possible, including the revenue support grant paid to local authorities, but they do not apply to programmes which are 'demand determined', such as social security payments, which must be paid to every person who becomes entitled to them (although from 1988 cash limits were imposed on payments from the Social Fund).[92] Since 1979, cash limits have been related directly to the supply estimates and as such are approved by Parliament.

In 1992, new arrangements were introduced for the distribution of public expenditure. Concern had been expressed about earlier procedures and the dominant role played by bilateral discussions between the Chief Secretary and individual ministers, it being argued that this arrangement left insufficient room for consideration of priorities in the government's overall spending plans.[93] Limits were set on each department rather than particular programmes being considered on their merits. The drawbacks of this arrangement led to reforms and in particular to 'a more explicitly top-down approach'[94] to the distribution of public expenditure, with the government agreeing to what was referred to as the new control total (NCT) for each of the three planning years. Under these arrangements expenditure was measured against a new spending aggregate, which was to be constrained to a rate that ensured that total public spending grew by less than the economy as a whole over the economic cycle.[95] A new Cabinet committee prepared options for particular programmes for the Cabinet to consider. This was followed by the bilateral discussions between the Chief Secretary and the individual ministers in which the Chief Secretary's role was similar to that in the past, except that there was now no need for him or her to reach an agreement with the ministers in question. Rather, he or she reported back to the Cabinet committee which was able to make an informed decision on the basis of the Chief Secretary's discussions.

The spending review and public service agreements

Yet further changes for the planning and control of public expenditure were introduced with effect from 1999–2000. Under the new arrangements, the former annual Public Expenditure Survey has been replaced by biennial reviews which set firm plans for three years ahead in 'spending

---

[90] See generally, Harrison, *The Control of Public Expenditure 1979–89*. See *Autumn Statement 1992*, Cm 2096, 1992, paras 2.01–02. It was also announced that new ways would be found to mobilise 'the private sector to meet needs which have traditionally been met only by the public sector'. See also HC 508 (1992–3).

[91] Cmnd 6440, 1976; HC 274 (1977–8); M Elliott (1977) 49 MLR 569; and Likierman, *Cash Limits and External Financing Limits*.

[92] See Social Security Contributions and Benefits Act 1992, s 168, and e.g. *R v Social Fund Inspector, ex p Stitt* [1990] COD 288.

[93] HC 20 (1989–90).

[94] HC 201 (1992–3), para 174.

[95] *Autumn Statement 1992*, Cm 2096, 1992, para 2.02.

reviews'. In the course of a spending review,[96] all departments are set departmental spending limits, and all must meet objectives set out in public service agreements concluded between departments and the Treasury.[97] The process was supervised by a Cabinet committee chaired by the Chancellor of the Exchequer (the Public Services and Public Expenditure Committee, replacing similar committees of previous administrations), though it was emphasised that the Treasury was the key source of decision making about the allocation of resources rather than the committee, which principally had an oversight function.[98] But not all expenditure can be subject to firm limits extending over three years. These cases were referred to as annually managed expenditure and fall outside departmental expenditure limits for which the three-year plans are made. This category is subject to annual review in the Budget process. In the current Treasury jargon, departmental expenditure limits together with annually managed expenditure constitute total managed expenditure, said to be the broadest measure of total public spending.[99] TME is projected to reach over £700 billion in 2010–2011.[100]

Public service agreements between the Treasury and individual departments were said to be 'essentially a contract with the Treasury for the renewal of public services',[101] a contract which sets down departmental objectives and targets to be met over a three-year period, the stages by which these objectives and targets will be met, the ways in which departments intend to allocate resources to achieve the objectives and targets, and the process that will monitor results. PSAs are now fully embedded as a Treasury instrument for controlling public spending, with 30 new agreements being announced as part of the *Comprehensive Spending Review* in 2007. The form of these agreements continues to evolve, with the most recent batch being linked to the government's priority outcomes, and being subject to a number of over-arching objectives in response to the global economic 'downturn', as the global financial crisis is referred to by government. The agreements not only embrace performance indicators, but are underpinned by 'delivery agreements', which include some extraordinary illustrations of detailed micro-management. It is also a feature of this process that 'PSAs will typically be delivered across many departments', though 'in order to ensure robust accountability, one Secretary of State will be in the lead'.[102] But although it is the stated purpose of the government that PSAs should improve public services,[103] the use of the language of contract in this context has been said to be a 'remarkable tribute to the current dominance of market-based thought and discourse in public administration'.[104]

The current arrangements provide for an enhanced but unclear role for the National Economic Council which makes 'commitments' which it seems are to be delivered in part through PSAs. Supervision of the agreements is the responsibility of Cabinet Committees, which in Treasury jargon 'drive performance by regularly monitoring progress, holding departments and programmes to account and resolving inter-departmental issues where they arise'.[105] There is also a Senior Responsible Officer for each PSA who reports to the relevant Cabinet Committee. The House of Commons Treasury Committee has been critical in the past about the fact that the Treasury both 'set the framework within which departments should operate, using the Spending Review and PSA process', and also acted as 'the sole assessor of whether or not departments are

---

[96] On which see HM Treasury, *Spending Review 2004*, Cm 6237, 2004; HM Treasury, *2007 Pre-Budget Report and Comprehensive Spending Review*, Cm 7227, 2007.

[97] On which see Cm 7227, 2007, Annex C.

[98] Daintith and Page, note 1 above, p 150.

[99] See HM Treasury, *Managing Public Money*, para 5.1.1.

[100] Cm 7630, 2009, p 26.

[101] HC Deb, 14 July 1998, col 188 (statement by the Chancellor of the Exchequer on the Comprehensive Spending Review).

[102] Cm 7227, 2007, Annex C, para 3.

[103] HM Treasury, *Spending Review 2004*, Cm 6237, 2004.

[104] Daintith and Page, p 192.

[105] Ibid.

achieving their objectives'.[106] Under the Cabinet Committee structure established in 2008, the Committee on Public Services and Public Expenditure (chaired by the Chancellor) has an ill-defined responsibility to consider public expenditure, including PSAs; while it is the role of a Domestic Affairs sub-committee (chaired by the Lord Chancellor) to 'consider issues relating to the delivery of public services across all Public Service Agreements – including inspection, service transformation and citizen and community engagement in public services; and report as necessary to the Committee on Domestic Affairs and the Committee on Public Services and Public Expenditure'. But there is no question of direct parliamentary monitoring.

Departmental accountability for public expenditure

For each government department the Treasury appoints an accounting officer (AO) who, by long-standing practice approved by the Public Accounts Committee, is the permanent secretary of the department, although in the case of the executive agencies the chief executive may be designated the AO. According to the Treasury, the AO has the personal duty of signing the resource accounts described in his or her letter of appointment, and may be 'called to account in Parliament for the stewardship of the resources within the organisation's control'.[107] The AO is then expected to appoint the permanent heads of the department's executive agencies as Agency AOs, and the permanent heads of departmental NDPBs as AO for each of these bodies.[108] Apart from those already referred to, AOs have a number of personal responsibilities in relation to the management of departmental resources: these include upholding standards of propriety, which means that they must seek Treasury approval for any unusual expenditure; ensuring value for money, which means that the department's 'procurement, projects and processes' are systematically evaluated and assessed; and accounting accurately for the government's financial position, to ensure that 'the government's financial information is transparent and up to date'.[109] In a nutshell, the AO must ensure that 'the organisation, and any subsidiary to it or organisation sponsored by it, operates effectively and to a high standard of probity', while 'acting within the authority of the minister(s) to whom he or she is responsible'.[110]

But what happens where a minister's instructions conflict with an AO's duties? One such case arose in 1991 when the Foreign Secretary overruled the AO in the Overseas Development Administration about expenditure of £234 million on the Pergau Dam project in Malaysia.[111] Treasury guidance states that there is 'no set form' for dealing with this, though the AO should raise the matter with the minister and be 'specific about the nature of his or her objections'.[112] This should be confirmed in writing, and has been said to arise in the past in relation to conduct which is (i) irregular, as being 'outside legal powers', parliamentary consent, or Treasury delegation; (ii) improper, as being in breach of parliamentary control procedures; and (iii) poor value for money, where an alternative proposal or 'doing nothing' would deliver better value. Problems of this kind are said to arise 'rarely', though it has also been said that they are on the increase.[113] But where they do arise, the AO should contact the Comptroller and Auditor General, who 'will normally draw the matter to the attention of the PAC, who will attach no blame to the AO'.[114]

---

[106] HC 73 (2000–01), para 32.

[107] HM Treasury, *Managing Public Money*, para 3.1.2.

[108] Ibid, para 3.2.3.

[109] Ibid, para 3.3.3.

[110] Ibid, Box 3.1.

[111] See HC 271 (1993–4), Cm 2602, 1993–4. See also F White, I Harden and K Donnelly [1994] PL 526. See further *R v Foreign Secretary, ex p World Development Movement* [1995] 1 All ER 611.

[112] HM Treasury, *Managing Public Money*, para 3.4.2.

[113] White, Harden and Donnelly, where 15 such instances since 1979 are noted.

[114] HM Treasury, *Managing Public Money*, para 3.4.4.

The AO should follow the minister's instruction 'without further ado',[115] it now being a matter for which the minister rather than the AO will have to account to Parliament. This process – in which the 'ultimate judgment must lie with the AO' – is said to balance the 'rights' of ministers to frank advice, with the need to protect 'the quality of internal debate'.[116]

In the case of non-departmental public bodies, the responsibilities of the AO are much the same as above, though the latter must also have regard to special responsibilities arising from the legislation establishing the body, as well as the framework document agreed with the sponsoring department.[117] In addition, the AO of a sponsoring department is expected to exercise some oversight, and ensure that the AO of the NDPB is carrying out his or her duties appropriately, the Treasury guidelines making clear that it is not acceptable to establish NDPBs or executive agencies 'in order to avoid or weaken parliamentary scrutiny'.[118] Oversight arrangements will normally be included in the framework document setting up those bodies which operate at arm's length. Issues arise here too where the AO of the NDPB is instructed by the chair or board of the body in question to carry out a course of action which is inconsistent with the standards of propriety and financial management the AO is expected to uphold. If despite the AO's reservations, the body decides to proceed with a course of action, the AO should ask the AO of the sponsoring department to intervene to resolve any difference. If the decision of the body is confirmed, its AO should then ask for a written direction to carry it out, ask the sponsoring department to inform the Treasury, implement the decision without delay, but also inform the Comptroller and Auditor General of what has happened.[119]

Comptroller and Auditor General[120]

An essential aspect of parliamentary control of expenditure is that the House of Commons should be able to ensure that public money is used for the purposes for which it has been voted. The Comptroller and Auditor General is head of the National Audit Office, known before 1984 as the Exchequer and Audit Department.[121] Like senior judges, he holds office during good behaviour, subject to a power of removal by the Crown on an address from both Houses of Parliament. His duties are twofold. First, as Comptroller, he ensures that all revenue is duly paid into the Consolidated Fund and the National Loans Fund, and his authority to the Bank of England is required before the Treasury may withdraw money from the Funds; in this capacity, he must see that the total limits of expenditure authorised by Parliament are not exceeded. Second, as Auditor General, he is responsible for examining the resource accounts of departments annually, to ensure that money had been spent only for the purpose intended by Parliament.[122] In practice, from the nineteenth century the audit also sought to discover instances of waste and extravagance. Express authority for 'value for money' and 'efficiency' auditing was given by the National Audit Act 1983.[123] The Comptroller and Auditor General may under that Act carry out examinations into the economy, efficiency and effectiveness with which a department has used its resources in discharging its functions; but he may not question the merits of the policy objectives set for a department. His powers extend not only to central departments but also to the National Health Service, and to other bodies or institutions (such as the universities) which are wholly or

---

[115] Ibid.

[116] Ibid.

[117] Ibid, para 3.8.1.

[118] Ibid, para 3.8.2.

[119] Ibid, paras 3.8.1–3.8.6.

[120] Normanton, *The Accountability and Audit of Governments*; White and Hollingsworth, esp chs 3–6.

[121] Exchequer and Audit Departments Act 1866.

[122] Exchequer and Audit Departments Act 1921, s 1, now Government Resources and Accounts Act 2000, s 6.

[123] For the background, see Cmnd 7845, 1980; HC 115 (1980–1), discussed by G Drewry [1981] PL 304; and Cmnd 8323, 1981. See White and Hollingsworth, ch 3.

mainly supported from public funds and to whose records and accounts he has access for inspection purposes.[124] Since 1994, the Comptroller and Auditor General may examine records relating to expenditure by the Security Service under the intelligence vote. The Public Accounts Commission examines the annual accounts of the National Audit Office.[125]

The Comptroller and Auditor General reports on his investigations to the Public Accounts Committee of the Commons,[126] said to be the 'doyen' of select committees,[127] with no other select committee having the 'same authority, clarity of remit and breadth and depth of advice available to it'.[128] This committee has 15 members and its chairman by tradition is always a senior Opposition MP.[129] According to the Committee, its main work is to examine reports produced by the Comptroller and Auditor General on his value for money studies of the economy, efficiency and effectiveness with which public funds are used. The Committee may also conduct examinations of bodies which fall outside his jurisdiction, such as the Duchy of Cornwall.[130] In exceptional circumstances, as described earlier, a minister may have to account to the Committee for a particular item of expenditure.

In session 2009–10, matters and programmes examined by the Committee included the way in which HM Revenue and Customs dealt with the tax obligations of older people; services for people with rheumatoid arthritis; financial stability in the British banking industry; the procurement of legal aid by the Legal Services Commission; the National Chlamydia Screening Programme; International Aid for Malawi; and procedures for developing the skills of the workforce.

The reports made to the Commons by the Public Accounts Committee – of which there are typically about 50 a session – are debated twice a year by the House.[131] The government is expected to reply to criticisms and to act on them. The published rulings made by the Committee and the related Treasury Minutes are an authoritative guide to the main rules of financial accountability.

Important changes in the status of the Comptroller and Auditor General were made by the National Audit Act 1983. Appointments to the office are no longer made by the Crown on the advice of the Prime Minister, but by the Crown on a resolution of the House of Commons, moved by the Prime Minister with the approval of the chairman of the Public Accounts Committee (s 1(1)). The Comptroller and Auditor General is declared to be an officer of the House of Commons (s 1(2)), a statutory change which confirmed the assumption made since 1866 that he exercises his powers on behalf of the House. While he has complete discretion in exercising his functions, the Comptroller must take into account proposals regarding his investigations that may be made by the Public Accounts Committee (s 1(3)). The staff of the Comptroller are no longer civil servants: they are appointed by and are answerable to him.[132] The aim behind these reforms was to strengthen still further the authority and independence of the audit system and to improve the ability of the Commons to ensure the proper use of public funds. Independently of these

---

[124] National Audit Act 1983, ss 6–8.

[125] National Audit Act 1983, s 2. The Commission consists of the chair of the Commons Public Accounts Committee, the Leader of the House and seven other MPs appointed by the House, none of whom is a minister. See Public Accounts Commission, Thirteenth Report (HC 915 (2006–07)).

[126] The Committee is appointed to examine 'the accounts showing the appropriation of the sums granted by Parliament to meet the public expenditure, and of such other accounts laid before Parliament as the committee may think fit' (HC SO 148).

[127] J F McEldowney, in Jowell and Oliver (eds), *The Changing Constitution* (3rd edn), ch 7. The same author's contribution to the 6th edition of *The Changing Constitution* (ch 15) contains a valuable account of the issues discussed in this chapter.

[128] A Robinson, in Drewry (ed.), *The New Select Committees*.

[129] Erskine May, *Parliamentary Practice*, p 785. On the Public Accounts Committee, see also Griffith and Ryle, *Parliament*, ch 11; and White and Hollingsworth, pp 122–5.

[130] HC 313 (2005–06).

[131] HM Treasury, *Guide to Scrutiny of Public Expenditure*, p 43.

[132] See I Harden (1993) 13 LS 16, at p 23.

arrangements, there is now also an Office of Government Commerce based in the Treasury with responsibility to ensure that the government gets best value for its money. The Office plays an important role in relation to public procurement and other matters.

E. Management of the economy

The raising of money by taxation and the expenditure of public finance conceal the many ways by which governments seek to manage the economy,[133] and the objectives that they seek to promote when undertaking such management. The interest of the constitutional lawyer is engaged by the fact that economic management may also encourage the development of different institutional arrangements to promote the policy objectives, arrangements which will reflect the nature of the problems facing government at any particular time, the prevailing economic orthodoxy, and the government's preferred solutions for reconciling political need with economic thinking. Here we give two examples of how different economic circumstances and different government priorities can produce different forms of government to deal with them. The first is now perhaps of rather historic interest and reflects forms that were adopted at a time when Keynesian economic policy was dominant, and wage inflation a major concern of government. With a new economic orthodoxy having become embedded since 1979, however, governments have different concerns and these latter forms of economic management have largely disappeared. The second example is more contemporary and is concerned with active steps taken by government to promote economic growth in the regions. This has seen the creation by statute of new institutional structures at regional level, with the strong guiding hand of central government.

Tripartism and the 'social contract'[134]

So far as the former is concerned, perhaps the most significant development in the post-war period was the emergence of systematic consultation between government and the leaders of the trade union and business communities. Important symbols of this phenomenon (which is common practice in other European countries and which was not confined to Labour governments) were the wage restraint bargain of 1948, the creation of the National Economic Development Council in 1962 and the 'social contract' of 1974–76. The first two initiatives were tripartite, and in terms of institutional innovation the creation of the NEDC is perhaps the most significant. Designed to be a national planning body which 'established a permanent niche for itself in the machinery of economic policy making', it did not, however, have any executive power and hardly evolved beyond being 'a useful framework for the exchange of different views'.[135] It was chaired by the Chancellor of the Exchequer and included senior trade and industry ministers as well as senior representatives of the trade union and business communities.[136] Yet despite its symbolic and practical importance, the NEDC was not the creature of statute, but a product of the relative informality of much of the British administrative state, which could easily be sidelined and eventually abolished (in 1992) when it no longer suited government strategy in terms of the content or method of economic policy making.[137]

The special powers which economic difficulties during the 1970s forced governments to take to deal with inflation were usually limited in duration; they enabled governments to intervene

---

[133] On which, see H Thompson, in Flinders *et al.* (eds), *The Oxford Handbook of British Politics*, ch 48.
[134] See K D Ewing [2000] PL 405.
[135] Grant and Marsh, *The Confederation of British Industry*, p 141.
[136] See National Economic Development Council, Annual Report 1978–79, for an account of membership and terms of reference, as well as the activities of the NEDC.
[137] See Davies and Freedland, *Labour Legislation and Public Policy*, p 439.

more extensively in private economic transactions than had previously been possible in peacetime. This legislation (long since repealed) had a number of novel aspects. Thus the Price Commission, a regulatory body set up under the Counter-inflation Act 1973, could issue orders or notices to employers and businesses. Breach of these could create criminal liability, yet the orders or notices themselves might define expressions used in the Act under which they were issued.[138] The Remuneration, Charges and Grants Act 1975 was notable for the manner in which the 'social contract' approved by the trade unions as a basis for voluntary wage restraint was given a measure of statutory effect and provision made for a new policy document to take its place.[139] One consequence of the need to continue an incomes policy after the 1975 'social contract' expired came in the Chancellor of the Exchequer's 1976 Budget: certain increases in personal tax allowances were made conditional on the agreement of the trade unions being obtained to an incomes policy. This agreement was duly obtained and the allowances were included in the Finance Act 1976, but some considered that this development diminished the authority of both government and Parliament.[140]

Between 1979 and 1997, Conservative governments adopted a wholly different approach to economic management, emphasising the importance of a market economy and the need to remove perceived barriers to the free functioning of the market. Financial and economic policy was directed mainly at the control of inflation, the restraining of public expenditure and the lifting of bureaucratic controls on pay, prices, dividends, credit and foreign exchange. Industrial policy was directed mainly at the encouragement of small firms, the break-up of monopolies, the fostering of competition and the releasing of business from public sector constraints. In the labour market, policy was directed at encouraging flexibility, a goal reflected in the spate of legislation since 1980 designed to limit the power of trade unions and reduce the scope of employment protection legislation.[141] One consequence of viewing trade unions as an obstacle to the free functioning of the market was to deny them any role in economic policy making.[142] While in the 1970s trade unions reached the zenith of their power in a quasi-corporatist state, by 1997 they had little if any political influence on a government which repudiated the very idea that they had a role to play in the formulation of economic policy.

Trade unions which had been drawn into the process of economic management were now pushed to the margins of government, there being no doubt that until 1979 trade unions had an important constitutional role. It is true that, as already indicated, this did not crystallise in any formal legal sense, but this did not make it any less real: as Beer has pointed out in relation to the wage restraint bargain of 1948 (which was not embodied in any legislative instrument), it 'achieved a regulation of an important aspect of the British economy that no such legislative instrument by itself could have done. Indeed, one may think of it as a kind of extra-governmental legislation.'[143] With the abolition of the NEDC and the retreat of dialogue between government and the social partners, it is seriously open to question how much of the 'constitutional architecture of the Keynesian State', built with 'no formal constitutional changes', remains intact, as has been suggested.[144] Although regulatory informality has not been removed altogether with the reshuffling of the pack of constitutional players, there is a sense in which it is in retreat having been displaced to some extent by a greater emphasis on regulatory instruments, including contracts and licences.

---

[138] Counter-inflation Act 1973, Sch 3, para 1(1).

[139] Remuneration, Charges and Grants Act 1975, s 1.

[140] E.g. *The Times*, 7 April 1976 (editorial). See also the Labour government's efforts to enforce non-statutory guidelines on pay by means that included the boycotting of companies which breached the guidelines. See R B Ferguson and A C Page (1978) 128 NLJ 515; G Ganz [1978] PL 333; HC Deb, 13 December 1978, col 673, and 14 December 1978, col 920.

[141] See Cmnd 9474, 1985.

[142] See K D Ewing, in Graham and Prosser (eds), *Waiving the Rules: The Constitution under Thatcherism*, ch 8.

[143] Beer, *Modern British Politics*, p 205.

[144] I Harden [1994] PL 609, at p 616.

Regional development agencies

One of the government's over-arching priorities as outlined in the 2007 *Comprehensive Spending Review* (and in the Public Service Agreements) is the improvement of the economic performance of the regions, with a view to reducing the gap in economic growth between different parts of the country. Specific policies devoted to regional economic development have been a feature of most governments at least since the 1960s if not before, though a number of important innovations have taken place since 1997. Foremost among these is the establishment of regional development agencies to 'provide for effective and properly coordinated regional economic development', and to 'enable the English regions to improve their competitiveness'.[145] The Regional Development Agencies Act 1998 divides England into nine regions, with a development agency appointed for each (s 1). Some saw the agencies not only as instruments of economic regeneration, but also as a scheme for English devolution in embryo, along with the projected regional assemblies. But there appears to be little appetite for such devolution, for however strong may be the arguments in favour of democratically elected regional assemblies, the government was forced to abandon plans for such assemblies (as set out in the Regional Assemblies (Preparations) Act 2003) when in a referendum held in 2004 the people of the North-East voted by 78 per cent to 22 per cent on a 48 per cent turnout to reject such a body.

The regional development agencies, established as non-departmental public bodies,[146] have from 8 to 15 members, all appointed by the Secretary of State.[147] Members should have some experience which is relative to the functions of the agency; and the minister must consult representatives of local authorities, businesses, trade unions and the rural economy, as well as others, before making an appointment (s 2). The functions of an agency are set out in s 4 of the 1998 Act: to further the economic development and the regeneration of its area; to promote business efficiency and competitiveness; to promote employment; to enhance the development and application of skills relevant to employment in its area; and to contribute to the achievement of sustainable development in the United Kingdom. To perform these functions, powers set out in s 5 enable the agencies to provide financial assistance, dispose of land at below market value and form or acquire an interest in a body corporate, although in all cases the consent of the minister is required. Ministers may delegate additional functions to the agencies (although not functions of a legislative character or functions which involve the fixing of fees or charges) (s 6), while each RDA is now under a duty (introduced by the Local Democracy, Economic Development and Construction Act 2009) to have regard to the regional strategy for its region when exercising its functions (s 7).

The regional development agencies – described as 'the most powerful quangos ever seen in this country'[148] – are thus subject to a great deal of ministerial control, in terms of their membership and in the exercise of their functions. The lack of democratic accountability to the communities they serve was seen by many as a key weakness of the agencies, criticised as being 'constitutionally objectionable' not only because none of the board members would be directly elected,[149] but also because of the 'enormous increase in ministerial power bestowed by [the Act]'.[150] That power is to be seen in the arrangements for the financing of RDAs, with the Act providing that the minister is to 'determine the financial duties of the agency', albeit after consultation with the agency and with the approval of the Treasury (s 9). Moreover, it is for the minister – again with

---

[145] HC Deb, 14 January 1998, col 372. Also Cm 3814, 1997.

[146] See ch 14.

[147] The government anticipated that there would be 12 members on each board, which would be 'business-led', but which would also include people with experience in education, the trade unions, rural interests and the voluntary sector (HC Deb, 14 January 1998, col 378).

[148] H C Deb, 14 January 1998, col 385.

[149] Ibid.

[150] Ibid, col 381.

the approval of the Treasury – to make 'to a regional development agency grants of such amount, and on such terms, as he thinks fit' (s 10). The power of the agencies also depends on the consent of the minister, who in turn must have the approval of the Treasury (s 11). Ministerial control can be detected in s 16 which imposes a duty on an agency to provide the minister with 'such information, advice and assistance as he may require', and in s 17, which requires the agencies to report to the minister on an annual basis; the reports must be laid before Parliament and are published. Other ministerial powers include an authority to alter regional boundaries (s 25), and to issue guidance or directions to an agency (s 27).

Following a major review in 2007, a stronger role has been found for local authorities in regional policy,[151] though parliamentary concern was expressed about whether under these arrangements 'business interests [will] be presumed to take precedence over the democratically expressed wishes of local communities'.[152] The local authority role under the Local Democracy, Economic Development and Construction Act 2009 is to be performed through bodies called Leaders' Boards. These bodies are to be established for each region, for the purposes of which the participating authorities (county councils and district councils) are to develop a scheme to be approved by the Secretary of State (s 71). Together with Regional Development Agencies, the Leaders' Boards are referred to as 'responsible regional authorities' and as such have duties in relation to regional strategy inherited at the time the 2009 Act was passed. The responsible regional authorities may review and revise their regional policy on giving notice to the Secretary of State (s 74), and any such revision must take into account national government strategies as well as the regional strategy of neighbouring authorities (s 77); it must also be approved by the Secretary of State (s 78). The latter has power to initiate a review and revision of a regional strategy (s 74), and a reserve power to impose revisions where the regional authorities fail to carry out their duties under the Act (s 79).

---

[151] HM Treasury, *Review of Sub-national Economic Development and Regeneration* (2007).

[152] HC 89 (2008–09), para 117. According to the government, 'the new regional strategies need to take account of both community and business views wherever possible', but in response to parliamentary concerns 'it will be up to the new Leaders' Board and the RDA to decide between them how the various elements of the strategy and its delivery are brought together' (HC 7643 (2008–09), para 12).

CHAPTER 18

The courts and the machinery of justice

In this chapter we address a number of constitutional questions relating to the judiciary and the machinery of justice. After the barest outline of the structure of the courts, we consider first, the manner of appointment of the judges, and the measures designed to protect their independence; secondly, the steps taken to ensure that litigants have a right to a fair trial, and the circumstances in which that right may collide with the rights of others; and thirdly, the role of the executive in the administration of justice, concentrating on the position of the Lord Chancellor and the Ministry of Justice, together with the procedures for the prosecution of offenders. These are all areas where in recent years extensive changes have been made, the most important of these being introduced by the Constitutional Reform Act 2005.[1] Designed to reinforce both the rule of law and the independence of the judiciary, the Act proved to be highly controversial and many of its provisions were hotly contested. An important driving force behind the Act was a belief in the principle that the judicial function should be institutionally distinct from the legislative function, and that the highest court should not be based in the legislature.[2]

A. The courts

There are in the United Kingdom three court systems: in England and Wales, in Scotland, and in Northern Ireland.[3] Each system is separate from the others, though judges and senior practitioners from all three are eligible for appointment to the Supreme Court of the United Kingdom. They are also eligible for appointment to the Court of Justice of the European Union,[4] and to the European Court of Human Rights.[5] In addition to the ordinary civil and criminal courts, Parliament has from time to time created specialised courts or tribunals; some of these are composed solely of judges of the superior courts (for example, the Election Court,[6] or the Patents Court), and some of these include both judges and lay members (for example, the Employment Appeal Tribunal, established in 1975 to hear appeals on points of law from employment tribunals, for example on claims by employees against employers for unfair dismissal).[7] There is also now a wide range of tribunals set up to resolve disputes of various kinds, in whose proceedings judges of the civil and criminal courts do not play a prominent part. The tribunals system has been radically reformed and greatly streamlined by the Tribunals, Courts and Enforcement Act 2007, in circumstances examined in chapter 29 A.

---

[1] For a summary of the 2005 Act and the issues raised by it, see A W Bradley, HL 83, 2005–6 (Appendix 1). See also Lord Windlesham [2005] PL 806; [2006] PL 35.

[2] See ch 5 above.

[3] For accounts of the English legal system, see Ingman, *The English Legal Process*; Partington, *Introduction to the English Legal System*; Spencer, *Jackson's Machinery of Justice*; and Zander, *Cases and Materials on the English Legal System*. For Scotland, see White and Willock, *The Scottish Legal System*.

[4] See ch 8.

[5] Human Rights Act 1998, s 18.

[6] Ch 9 E.

[7] Employment Tribunals Act 1996.

Courts of civil and criminal jurisdiction

In England and Wales, civil jurisdiction is exercised by the High Court, the judges of which sit in three divisions (Queen's Bench, Chancery and Family) and, on appeal, by the Court of Appeal, Civil Division. Together the High Court, the Court of Appeal and the Crown Court form the Senior Courts of England and Wales (having been previously known as the Supreme Court of England and Wales until the creation of the Supreme Court of the United Kingdom in 2009).[8] The High Court in England and Wales deals with applications for judicial review, the procedure normally followed for actions against public bodies. These cases are now considered by specially assigned judges in what is now called the Administrative Court, which in turn is part of the Queen's Bench Division. From the Court of Appeal, and in some cases direct from the High Court, appeals lie with leave to the Supreme Court of the United Kingdom. A broad civil jurisdiction is exercised by the county courts, and on some subjects by the magistrates' courts, though the jurisdiction of the former may be extended by powers contained in the Courts and Legal Services Act 1990, which authorises the transfer of business from the High Court to the county courts.[9] Criminal jurisdiction is exercised at first instance in summary trials by the magistrates' courts and in jury trials by the Crown Court, created by the Courts Act 1971, which sits in London and in a number of provincial centres. In the Crown Court the judge may be a High Court judge, a circuit judge or a recorder. Criminal appeals lie to the Court of Appeal, Criminal Division, and a further appeal on a question of law may lie, with leave, to the Supreme Court of the United Kingdom.

In Scotland, civil jurisdiction is exercised by the ancient Court of Session.[10] Single judges sit in the Outer House for trials at first instance; ten senior judges form the Inner House, sitting in two divisions for mainly appellate purposes.[11] A wide civil jurisdiction is exercised by the sheriff court, from which appeals may lie to the Inner House of the Court of Session. Criminal jurisdiction, for jury trials and appeals, is exercised by the High Court of Justiciary, which comprises the same judges as sit in the Court of Session; and also by the sheriff court, both for summary trials and jury trials. The district courts, established by the District Courts (Scotland) Act 1975, have a summary criminal jurisdiction. Appeals from Scotland in civil cases, but not in criminal cases, lie to the Supreme Court of the United Kingdom, as do appeals on devolution issues (which had previously been dealt with by the Privy Council).[12] In Northern Ireland, jurisdiction is exercised by the High Court, the Crown Court, and the Court of Appeal, forming the Court of Judicature of Northern Ireland (previously the Supreme Court of Judicature). Civil jurisdiction in Northern Ireland is exercised by the High Court (with Queen's Bench, Chancery and Family divisions) and the Court of Appeal. At an intermediate level, civil jurisdiction is exercised by the county courts. At a local level, civil and criminal jurisdiction is exercised by magistrates' courts, presided over by district judges.[13] Civil and criminal appeals from the Court of Appeal and, in specified cases, from the High Court lie to the Supreme Court of the United Kingdom.

---

[8] Constitutional Reform Act 2005, s 59, Sch 11.

[9] SI 1991 No 724.

[10] The constitution and administration of the Court of Session are now governed by the Court of Session Act 1988, as amended by the Judiciary and Courts (Scotland) Act 2008, ss 44–46.

[11] An Extra Division of three judges often sits because of the pressure of work.

[12] The procedure governing the lower courts in Scotland has given rise to a number of challenges under the Scotland Act 1998 on the ground that it violated Convention rights: see *S v Millar* 2001 SLT 531, *S v Millar (No 2)* 2001 SLT 1304, and *Clark* v *Kelly* 2003 SLT 308.

[13] The fact that these magistrates are legally qualified is not a sufficient guarantee against 'outrageous conduct' on their part: *In re McFarland* [2004] UKHL 17; [2004] 1 WLR 1289, at para 31 (Lord Steyn).

The House of Lords

Until 1 October 2009, the House of Lords was the court of final appeal in the United Kingdom.[14] Although the members of that court were members of the House of Lords in its legislative capacity as well,[15] for practical purposes judicial and legislative business was quite separate. By long established convention, no lay peer took part in appellate work of the Lords, which was conducted not on the floor of the House, but by appellate committees consisting exclusively of members with suitable legal qualifications. A shortage of peers with such qualifications led to the Appellate Jurisdiction Act 1876, this providing for the appointment of two Lords of Appeal in Ordinary, for whom the statutory qualification was to have held high judicial office in the United Kingdom or to have been a practising barrister (or advocate in Scotland) for 15 years. The Act declared that appeals should not be heard unless there were present at least three from the following: the Lord Chancellor, the Lords of Appeal in Ordinary, and such peers as held or had previously held high judicial office (i.e. in a superior court in the United Kingdom). The increase in the volume of work led to an increase in the number of appointments under the 1876 Act (which has now been repealed), and by the time the appellate jurisdiction of the House was abolished in 2009, up to 12 Lords of Appeal in Ordinary could hold office at any one time.[16] Usually appeals were heard by a committee of five judges but in exceptional cases seven – or even nine – judges might sit.[17]

Being at the apex of the hierarchy of courts in the United Kingdom, except that it had no jurisdiction in Scottish criminal cases, the House of Lords had great authority in influencing the development of the law through the system of precedent.[18] For many years the House regarded itself as bound by its own previous decisions,[19] but in 1966 the Lords of Appeal in Ordinary made through the Lord Chancellor a statement modifying that doctrine and accepting that too rigid adherence to precedent might lead to injustice in a particular case and unduly restrict the proper development of the law.[20] The House of Lords subsequently regarded its former decisions as normally binding but was prepared to depart from a previous decision when it appeared right to do so.[21] Although the House of Lords no longer has a judicial function in the sense considered here, the body of case law built up over many years is still authoritative, and it is likely that the Supreme Court of the United Kingdom will consider these decisions as being normally binding and of the highest authority. The likelihood is reinforced by the fact that the first members of the Supreme Court of the United Kingdom were Law Lords who had been appointed to the latter position under the 1876 Act (with the then senior Law Lord becoming the first President of the Supreme Court).[22]

---

[14] For an account of its work in some fields between 1876–2009, see Blom-Cooper, Dickson and Drewry (eds), *The Judicial House of Lords*.

[15] See ch 9 H above.

[16] Maximum Number of Judges Order 1994, SI 1994 No 3217.

[17] E.g. *Murphy v Brentwood DC* [1991] 1 AC 398; *Pepper v Hart* [1993] AC 593; *R v Bow Street Metropolitan Stipendiary Magistrate, ex p Pinochet Ugarte (No 3)* [2000] 1 AC 147; *A v Home Secretary* [2004] UKHL 56, [2005] 2 AC 68; and *A v Home Secretary (No 2)* [2005] UKHL 71; [2006] 2 AC 221.

[18] For studies of its work, see Blom-Cooper and Drewry, *Final Appeal*; Paterson, *The Law Lords*; Stevens, *Law and Politics*; and B Dickson, in Carmichael and Dickson, *The House of Lords*, ch 7.

[19] *London Street Tramways Co v LCC* [1898] AC 375.

[20] Practice Statement [1966] 3 All ER 77; and see Paterson, ch 6. But see *R v Kansal* [2001] UKHL 62, [2002] 2 AC 69.

[21] For use made of this freedom in public law cases, see e.g. *Conway v Rimmer* [1968] AC 910, *Knuller Ltd v DPP* [1973] AC 435, *R v Home Secretary, ex p Khawaja* [1984] AC 74, and *Murphy v Brentwood DC* [1991] 1 AC 398. For exercise of the power in criminal law, see *R v Shivpuri* [1987] AC 1 and *R v G* [2003] UKHL50; [2004] 1 AC 1034. For a fuller account, see Ingman, pp 226–35.

[22] Constitutional Reform Act 2005, s 24.

The Supreme Court of the United Kingdom

On 1 October 2009, the new Supreme Court of the United Kingdom acquired the existing appellate jurisdiction of the House of Lords, as well as the devolution jurisdiction of the Privy Council.[23] The Constitutional Reform Act 2005 provides that the court is to consist of twelve judges, who (with the exception of the President and Deputy President) are to be styled Justices of the Supreme Court. As we have seen, the founding members of the Court were the Law Lords in post at the time the Court was created. These members retained their titles as Lords of Appeal in Ordinary (which under the 1876 Act cannot be revoked); but as discussed below, serving justices of the Supreme Court are prohibited from taking an active part in the work of the legislature, from which they had in any event largely withdrawn even before the Supreme Court was established. Subsequent appointments to the Supreme Court are governed by the Constitutional Reform Act 2005, with the qualifications for appointment being similar to those under the (repealed) Appellate Jurisdiction Act 1876.[24] Appointment to the Supreme Court will not, however, bring a peerage (and hence not the style 'Lord' or 'Lady'), though there is no reason why retired justices of the Supreme Court could not be made life peers under the Life Peerages Act 1958, so long as the House of Lords remains a wholly or partially nominated body.

When a vacancy arises on the Supreme Court, the 2005 Act requires an ad hoc Supreme Court Selection Commission to be appointed, the Commission to consist of the President and Deputy President of the Court, together with a member of each of the Judicial Appointments Commission and its Scottish and Northern Irish equivalents (at least one of whom must be a non-lawyer). The Selection Commission determines the selection procedure to be applied, but in doing so it is required to consult the Lord Chancellor and senior judges, as well as senior ministers in Scotland, Wales and Northern Ireland. Selection is to be made on merit, though the Selection Commission will be required to take into account guidance on relevant matters given by the Lord Chancellor. Once the selection has been made, the Selection Commission must report to the Lord Chancellor, who must then consult senior judges as well as the senior ministers already referred to. Thereafter the Lord Chancellor will have a number of options: to notify the selection to the Prime Minister, to reject the selection, or to require the Commission to reconsider the selection. Accordingly, although the Lord Chancellor no longer makes the selection of candidates for presentation to the Prime Minister, he or she will retain a veto on who may be appointed. However, a candidate may only be rejected on the ground that 'in the Lord Chancellor's opinion', the person selected is not suitable for the office concerned, and written reasons will have to be given to the Commission by the Lord Chancellor.[25]

B. The judiciary and judicial appointments

Judicial appointments in the United Kingdom are a matter for the executive, the Queen's judges being appointed on the advice of the Queen's ministers. Appointments to the Supreme Court, and to the most senior judicial posts in England (including Lord Justice of Appeal, Master of the Rolls, President of the Family Division and Lord Chief Justice) are made by the Queen on the advice of the Prime Minister. High Court judges, circuit judges, recorders and district judges are appointed by the Queen on the advice of the Lord Chancellor.[26] Magistrates are appointed to the commission of the peace by the Lord Chancellor. Judges of the Court of Session (as well as

---

[23] Ibid, s 40.

[24] Ibid, s 25.

[25] The procedure is set out in the 2005 Act, ss 26–31; provisions for the Selection Commission are to be found in Sch 8.

[26] Supreme Court Act 1981 (sometimes now referred to as the Senior Courts Act 1981), s 10; Justices of the Peace Act 1997, s 10A, inserted by the Access to Justice Act 1999.

sheriffs principal and sheriffs) are now appointed by the Queen on the recommendation of the First Minister, who must consult the Lord President before making a recommendation. The Lord President of the Court of Session and the Lord Justice Clerk (also in the Court of Session) are appointed by the Queen on the recommendation of the Prime Minister, who in turn must recommend the persons nominated by the First Minister. The First Minister must consult the Lord President and the Lord Justice Clerk (unless in either case the office is vacant) before making a nomination.[27] Unlike in the United States, there is no requirement anywhere in the United Kingdom that executive nominees should be subject to scrutiny and confirmation by Parliament, and no such procedure was introduced by the Constitutional Reform Act 2005.[28]

Qualifications for appointment

By statute, minimum qualifications for appointments must be observed. Before the Courts and Legal Services Act 1990, judges of the High Court had to be of at least ten years' standing as a barrister. Since the 1990 Act, however, it is now possible for solicitors with rights of audience in the High Court and for circuit judges of at least two years' standing to be appointed.[29] As far as the Court of Appeal is concerned, candidates for appointment as a Lord Justice of Appeal had previously to be of at least 15 years' standing as a barrister or already to have been a High Court judge.[30] Since the 1990 Act, this has been reduced to ten years and extended to include solicitors with rights of audience in the High Court, as well as anyone who is already a member of the High Court[31] (which in principle would allow someone appointed to the circuit bench to move quickly through the system). In Scotland, membership of the Court of Session is regulated by a rule of five years' standing as a member of the Faculty of Advocates.[32] In 1990, however, the rules were relaxed, with eligibility being extended to sheriffs principal and sheriffs (who must have held office for at least five years) and solicitors, who must have had a right of audience in the Court of Session for at least five years.[33] There are also rules of standing for members of the lower judiciary.

A major innovation in recent years has been the advertisement of some vacancies up to the level of the High Court. In general, however, appointments to the superior courts are made only from successful legal practitioners and the average experience of those appointed is well above the legal minimum. Appointment to the more senior positions (Court of Appeal and Supreme Court) is normally by way of promotion, and it remains very difficult for someone to be appointed to senior judicial position without coming through the traditional channels. Although there have been a few appointments of academics to judicial office in recent years, those appointed from such a background must also satisfy the standard requirements of office, which emphasise the need for many years of practical experience. In other countries experience as a legal practitioner is not the only route to a career on the Bench, with civil law countries in particular providing opportunities for recruitment at a young age into a career judiciary, with opportunities to progress through the various layers in the court structure. Without removing the scope for appointment of legal professionals, arrangements of this kind would help to ensure

---

[27] Scotland Act 1998, s 95. In making his nomination, the First Minister must have regard to the recommendations of a panel established under the Judiciary and Courts (Scotland) Act 2008, s 19 and Sch 2.

[28] For discussion of this issue, see K D Ewing, in Flinders et al. (eds), *The Oxford Handbook of British Politics*, pp 275–7.

[29] Courts and Legal Services Act 1990, s 71.

[30] Supreme Court Act 1981, s 10(3).

[31] Courts and Legal Services Act 1990, s 71.

[32] Treaty of Union 1706, art 19.

[33] Law Reform (Miscellaneous Provisions) (Scotland) Act 1990, s 35.

that there is no single route to appointment, nor a monopoly of the appointment process by one particular interest group, and may help also to overcome some of the problems of diversity addressed below.[34]

Judicial Appointments Commission

In the Constitutional Reform Act 2005, the government yielded to growing concern about the process of judicial appointment, widely criticised for its secrecy and lack of transparency. The creation of a Judicial Appointments Commission, which was formally launched in April 2006, follows the formation of a Judicial Appointments Board in Scotland in 2001,[35] albeit on a non-statutory basis, and the creation of a Commission for Judicial Appointments for England and Wales in the same year. Established by Order in Council, the latter was empowered only to review rather than recommend appointments, though even in this limited capacity it did cause some discomfort by reporting on the role of the Lord Chancellor in some judicial appointments.[36] The Commission established for England and Wales under the 2005 Act has a much wider remit than the non-statutory body which preceded it, and consists of a lay chairman,[37] as well as 14 other Commissioners appointed by the Queen on the recommendation of the Lord Chancellor. Detailed provision is made for appointing people from mixed backgrounds: judges, legal practitioners, lay justices and non-lawyers. In the case of legal practitioners there must be consultation with their professional bodies (the Bar Council and the Law Society). Under the Act anyone selected by the Commission for appointment must be of good character, and selection must be solely on merit,[38] having regard to advice on selection issued by the Lord Chancellor.[39]

Different procedures apply for different appointments. Under that applying to the senior posts of Lord Chief Justice, Master of the Rolls, President of the Queen's Bench Division, President of the Family Division and Chancellor of the High Court, in the event of any such vacancy arising the Lord Chancellor may ask the Commission to make a recommendation. This must be done by a selection panel of four members, in this case to include the Lord Chief Justice, together with the Chairman of the Commission and another lay member chosen by him or her. As with the procedure for appointments to the Supreme Court already described, the Lord Chancellor may accept or reject the selection made by the panel, or may require the selection panel to reconsider the selection. The procedures for the selection of judges to the Court of Appeal and the High Court follow a similar pattern, though the composition of the selection panels is different. In the case of the Court of Appeal, the panel is to consist of the Lord Chief Justice, a Head of Division, the Chairman of the Commission and a lay member appointed by the Chairman.[40] In the case of the High Court, there is no mandatory composition for a selection panel. Where the Lord Chancellor accepts a recommendation under these procedures, he or she must then make the relevant appointment or recommendation for appointment.[41] Complaints about judicial appointments may be made to the Judicial Appointments and Conduct Ombudsman, a new office established by the Constitutional Reform Act 2005.

---

[34] See K D Ewing (2000) 38 *Alta Law Rev* 708.

[35] There is now a statutory Judicial Appointments Board for Scotland: Judiciary and Courts (Scotland) Act 2008, Part 2.

[36] See Commission for Judicial Appointments, *Annual Report 2005*, para 2.44; Commission for Judicial Appointments, *Review of the Recorder 2004/05 Competition (Midland Circuit)* (2005), pp 89–90.

[37] On which see K Malleson [2004] PL 102.

[38] Constitutional Reform Act 2005, s 63.

[39] Ibid, s 65.

[40] Ibid, s 80.

[41] Ibid, s 96.

Composition of the judiciary

Should the judiciary be 'representative' and, if so, what does this mean? The idea that the judiciary should be 'representative of the community' was repudiated by the Home Affairs Committee and by the Lord Chancellor's Department, on behalf of which it was asserted in 1996 that:

> It is not the function of the judiciary to reflect particular sections of the community, as it is of the democratically elected legislature. The judges' role is to administer justice in accordance with the laws of England and Wales. This requires above all professional legal knowledge and competence. Any litigant or defendant will usually appear before a single judge and it is of paramount importance that the judge is fully qualified for the office he or she holds, and is able to discharge his or her functions to the highest standards. Social or other considerations are not relevant for this purpose; the Lord Chancellor accordingly seeks to appoint, or recommend for appointment, those who are the best qualified candidates available and willing to serve at the time.[42]

On the other hand, there is recognition of the principle that the judiciary should 'more closely' reflect the make-up of society as a whole, which should tend over time to emerge by 'ensuring the fullest possible equality of opportunity for persons in all sections of society who wish to enter the legal profession and who aspire to sit judicially'. But as was pointed out, this will require 'equality of opportunity at all levels of the educational system and the legal system as well as in the appointments system itself', a sentiment that it is perhaps easier to express than implement.[43]

The Constitutional Reform Act 2005 requires the Judicial Appointments Commission to have regard to 'the need to encourage diversity in the range of persons available for selection for appointments' (s 64). But although there has been some improvement in recent years, women and members of the ethnic minority communities remain poorly represented on the Bench, particularly at its highest levels. On 31 December 2009 only one member of the Supreme Court was female, all the heads of division were men, only three of 43 Court of Appeal judges were female, and all but eight of the 106 High Court judges were men. Apart from the chronic under-representation of women, it is thought that ethnic minorities continue to be even more poorly represented. As the Judicial Appointments Commission has pointed out, however, the judiciary 'will always be dependent on the diversity of the legal profession' (at least so long as judges continue to be recruited from experienced legal practitioners), where there is an issue about the lack of diversity at the more senior levels. The Commission points out, for example, that only 20–25 per cent of partners in solicitors' firms are women, though women make up a majority of those entering the profession; and that only 10 per cent of QCs are women, though women account for 49 per cent of pupils. Only 4 per cent of QCs are from black and ethic minority backgrounds.[44] Diversity cannot be separated from methods of recruitment and barriers – formal and informal – to career progression.

C. Independence of the judiciary

The principle of judicial independence is now formally recognised in legislation, with the Constitutional Reform Act 2005 introducing a legal duty to 'uphold' the continued independence of the judiciary.[45] This duty is addressed to the Lord Chancellor, other government ministers, and

---

[42] HC 52-II (1995–6), p 130.

[43] Contrast the policy as to the representativeness of the magistracy, which should 'broadly [reflect] the communities which they serve' (HC 52-II (1995–6)) and the view that 'the aim of balancing the bench to take account of the age, employment background and political leanings of magistrates has not, as yet, been achieved' (HC 52-I (1995–6)). See also *Arthur v Attorney-General* [1999] ICR 631.

[44] Judicial Appointments Commission, *Annual Report 2008/09*, p 38.

[45] For comparable provisions in Scotland, see Judiciary and Courts (Scotland) Act 2008, s 1.

anyone else 'with responsibility for matters relating to the judiciary or otherwise to the administration of justice'.[46] In addition, the Lord Chancellor must have regard to (i) the need to defend that independence, (ii) the need for the judiciary to have the support necessary to carry out its functions, and (iii) 'the need for the public interest in regard to matters relating to the judiciary or otherwise to the administration of justice to be properly represented in decisions affecting those matters' (s 3(6)). As might be expected, there is no definition of judicial independence in the 2005 Act, though the principle has been re-invigorated also by the Human Rights Act 1998, with art 6 of the ECHR guaranteeing a right to a fair and public hearing 'by an independent and impartial tribunal'. It has been said that the Lord Chancellor's duty requires him to draw to the attention of the Cabinet any proposed legislation that would undermine the independence of the judiciary, and that it obliges him to deal with any ministers who indulge in personal attacks on judges.[47]

Judicial immunity from civil action

Just as the public interest in free debate in Parliament justifies the rule of absolute privilege for things said in the course of parliamentary debates, so the public interest in the administration of justice justifies similar protection for judicial proceedings. At common law no action will lie against a judge for any acts done or words spoken in his or her judicial capacity in a court of justice:

> It is essential in all courts that the judges who are appointed to administer the law should be permitted to administer it under the protection of the law independently and freely, without favour and without fear. This provision of the law is not for the protection or benefit of a malicious or corrupt judge, but for the benefit of the public, whose interest it is that the judges should be at liberty to exercise their functions with independence and without fear of consequences.[48]

The judge of a superior court is not liable for anything done or said in the exercise of judicial functions, however malicious, corrupt or oppressive are the acts or words complained of.[49] A similar immunity attaches to the verdict of juries[50] and to words spoken by parties, counsel and witnesses in the course of judicial proceedings.[51] But barristers no longer enjoy immunity for the negligent conduct of a client's case in court.[52]

The immunity of judges is reinforced by the Crown Proceedings Act 1947, s 2(5), which absolves the Crown from liability for any person 'while discharging or purporting to discharge any responsibilities of a judicial nature vested in him' or in the execution of judicial process. But immunity does not extend to the acts or words of a judge in his or her private capacity. Judicial immunity also applies to the work of lower courts, for example county courts and magistrates' courts, though the immunity is narrower than in the case of the superior courts. In *Sirros* v *Moore*,[53] the Court of Appeal appeared to assimilate the position of judges in lower courts to that of judges in superior courts when it held that a circuit judge was immune from liability for damages after he had by a wholly erroneous procedure ordered a Turkish citizen to be detained by the police. The Court of Appeal considered that no distinction should be drawn in principle between the protection given to superior court judges and that given to lower courts. According

---

[46] Constitutional Reform Act 2005, s 3. See HL Paper 151 (2006–07), para 39.

[47] HL Paper 151 (2006–07), paras 38–40. The Act expressly provides that the Lord Chancellor and other ministers must not seek to influence particular judicial decisions through any special access to the judiciary (s 3(5)).

[48] *Scott* v *Stansfield* (1868) LR 3 Ex 220, 223 (Kelly CB).

[49] *Anderson* v *Gorrie* [1895] 1 QB 668. And see generally Olowofoyeku, *Suing Judges*.

[50] *Bushell's case* (1670) 6 St Tr 999.

[51] *Munster* v *Lamb* (1883) 11 QBD 588.

[52] *Hall (Arthur JS) & Co* v *Simons* [2002] 1 AC 615.

[53] [1975] QB 118, discussed by M Brazier [1976] PL 397.

to Lord Denning and Ormrod LJ, every judge, including a justice of the peace, was entitled to be protected from liability in respect of what he did while acting judicially and in the honest belief that his acts were within jurisdiction. But the scope of this decision was doubted, at least as far as justices of the peace are concerned. They are now protected by legislation for acts done within their jurisdiction and for acts outside their jurisdiction unless, in the latter case, the claimant can show bad faith.[54] There is also immunity for the members of government appointed inquiries.[55]

Political criticism of the judiciary

Judicial independence requires that judges should be protected from political pressure to reach decisions which suit the government or other powerful interests. In recent years, however, there has been an erosion of the long-standing convention that ministers do not criticise the judiciary or judicial decisions. For example, in 2003 the sentence imposed on a convicted paedophile by the Recorder of Cardiff attracted criticism from the then Home Secretary (and a junior minister), which in turn fanned a hostile press response addressed to the courts. Concern was compounded by a feeling that the Lord Chancellor had been too slow to defend the judge (against whose decision there was no appeal by the Attorney General).[56] This latter affair led to calls for the *Ministerial Code* to be amended to include 'strongly worded guidelines setting out the principles governing public comment by ministers on individual judges'.[57] No less contentious were comments made by the Prime Minister in 2005 which were seen as being designed to put pressure on the courts generally in cases about the extradition of foreign terrorist suspects. After noting that each tightening of the terrorism laws had met 'fierce opposition in the courts', and that the 'rules of the game are changing', the Prime Minister continued by saying that should legal obstacles arise in the future, the government 'will legislate further including, if necessary, amending the Human Rights Act in respect of the interpretation of the European Convention on Human Rights'.[58] Although the Prime Minister's comments were not seen to impugn an individual judge, it is nevertheless difficult to recall circumstances in which a Prime Minister has informed the judiciary in advance of any litigation that the law will be changed if the government is unhappy with the result.

Members of Parliament are also subject to restraints in their criticism of judges. There is a long-standing rule of the House that unless the discussion is based on a substantive motion, reflections must not be cast on the conduct of judges or upon judges generally.[59] Another parliamentary rule seeks to protect the principle of a fair trial rather than the status of the judges: by the *sub judice* rule, matters awaiting the adjudication of a court may not be raised in debate. The rule – which was codified for the first time in 1963 and updated in 1972 and again in 2001[60] – is designed to ensure that there is no interference with the right to a fair trial. In this sense the rule complements (though it does not overlap precisely with) the Contempt of Court Act 1981, which does not apply to parliamentary proceedings. The rule is also designed to acknowledge the respective roles of judiciary and Parliament: if the role of the former is to be discharged effectively the judges 'should not only be, but also be seen to be, the only constitutional body

---

[54] Courts Act 2003, ss 31, 32. The immunity applies also to justices' clerks. See also Human Rights Act 1998, s 9.
[55] Inquiries Act 2005, s 37.
[56] HL Paper 151 (2006–07), paras 45–49. The Lord Chancellor would now have a duty under the Constitutional Reform Act 2005 to intervene.
[57] Ibid, para 49.
[58] www.number-10.gov.uk/output/Page8041.asp (2 November 2005).
[59] Erskine May, *Parliamentary Practice*, pp 386–7 and 438–9.
[60] See HC Deb, 23 July 1963, col 1417 and HC Deb, 28 June 1972, col 1589. For the text of the current rule, see HC Deb, 15 November 2001, col 1012. Also HL Deb, 11 May 2000, cols 1725–6. For the report of the Joint Committee on Parliamentary Privilege, see HC 214-I–III (1998–9) and HL 43-I–III (1998–9).

for determining issues which come before the courts'.[61] Under the terms of the rule, matters which are the subject of legal proceedings may not be referred to in any motion, debate or question. This is subject to a discretion on the part of the Speaker to permit such a reference 'where a ministerial decision is in question', or where the case 'concerns issues of national importance such as the economy, public order or the essential services'. The reason for this relaxation is to permit some parliamentary discussion of ministerial decisions or other major issues of public concern, notwithstanding the fact that legal action may have been instituted.[62] Nevertheless, the operation of the rule continues to give rise to frustration on the part of MPs.[63]

Security of tenure

At the apex of the principle of judicial independence is security of tenure: judges cannot be dismissed because they are unpopular with the government. Judges of the High Court and Court of Appeal hold office during good behaviour, subject to a power of removal by the Queen on an address presented by both Houses of Parliament,[64] with a similar provision applying to the Justices of the Supreme Court.[65] These statutory rules clearly prevent a judge from being removed at the pleasure of the Crown, but their meaning is not wholly certain. The wording of the provision in the Act of Settlement from which these rules derived,[66] suggests that the intention of Parliament was that, while a judge should hold office during good behaviour, Parliament itself should enjoy an unqualified power of removal. Assuming that there was no intention to alter the effect of the Act of Settlement by the revised wording now contained in modern legislation, it is thus theoretically possible for a judge to be dismissed not only for misconduct but for any other reason which might induce both Houses to pass the necessary address to the Crown. This appears to be the understanding of the Ministry of Justice, which appoints judges on the condition that they may be removed from office for misbehaviour or inability by the Lord Chancellor, with the concurrence of the Lord Chief Justice.[67] At the same time, the Constitutional Reform Act 2005 continues to recognise that judges may be removed by an Address, presumably for reasons other than misbehaviour or inability (s 109).

But whatever the theoretical position, there are a number of reasons which help to ensure that these latter powers are unlikely ever to be used, with the security of judicial tenure relying not so much on legal rules as on a shared constitutional understanding which these rules reflect. In Scotland, these understandings are reinforced by legislation that gives the Scottish judge greater security then his or her English counterpart. The historic tenure on which Scottish judges hold office is *ad vitam aut culpam*, which means that they cannot be removed except on grounds of misconduct.[68] Judges of the Court of Session now hold office until retirement, and may be removed by Her Majesty following a recommendation by the First Minister, who may make a recommendation only with the authority of the Scottish Parliament.[69] Provision is to be made for a tribunal (to be chaired by a judicial member of the Privy Council) to be established by the First Minister to investigate whether a Court of Session judge is unfit for office by reason of 'inability, neglect of duty or misbehaviour'.[70] This must be done before the First Minister seeks parliamentary

---

[61] HC 125 (2004–5), para 13, citing evidence of Lord Nicholls.

[62] See e.g. debate on the thalidomide cases, HC Deb, 29 November 1972, col 432.

[63] HC 125 (2004–5). The rule does not affect the power of Parliament to legislate: the War Damage Act 1965 altered the law retrospectively while litigation against the government was in process.

[64] Supreme Court Act 1981, s 11(3).

[65] Constitutional Reform Act 2005, s 33.

[66] Ch 2 A.

[67] http://www.judicialappointments.gov.uk/static/documents/00351_otcs.pdf.

[68] Claim of Right 1689, art 13; *Mackay and Esslemont* v *Lord Advocate* 1937 SC 860.

[69] Scotland Act 1998, s 95.

[70] Ibid, s 95(8). See now Judiciary and Courts (Scotland) Act 2008, ss 35–39.

approval to recommend the removal of a judge. A sheriff may be removed from office only after a tribunal constituted by the First Minister (to include senior judicial as well as lay representation) has established unfitness for office due to inability, neglect of duty or misbehaviour. The sheriff may be removed by the First Minister by statutory instrument, after the tribunal's report has been laid before the Scottish Parliament.[71] Judges lower down the pecking order in England and Wales may be removed from office by the Lord Chancellor for incapacity or misbehaviour.[72]

Use of judges for extra-judicial purposes

Judges have often been called on by the government to preside over royal commissions, departmental committees and inquiries conducted under the Tribunals of Inquiry (Evidence) Act 1921 (now replaced by the Inquiries Act 2005). It has been claimed that there were 366 major commissions and inquiries throughout the twentieth century, as well as another 1,000 or so departmental inquiries. Thirty per cent of these major commissions and inquiries are said to have been conducted by a judge.[73] These have included matters as diverse as safety at sports grounds, prison riots, the collapse of an international bank, the so-called Arms for Iraq affair, the future of legislation against terrorism, BSE and the Bloody Sunday killings in 1972. An emerging theme of some significance has been the appointment of senior judges as commissioners to oversee and to report annually to the Prime Minister about the operation of surveillance powers created by legislation such as the Regulation of Investigatory Powers Act 2000,[74] though the practice has changed in recent years in the sense that these roles are now generally performed by retired judges. Also important was the appointment of Lord Nolan in 1994 to examine concerns about standards of conduct in public life.[75] Many judges are well suited to this work but there are potential dangers to judicial independence, especially when matters of acute political controversy are referred to a judge for an impartial opinion.[76]

Particularly controversial references in the past were the investigations conducted by Lord Denning on the request of the Prime Minister into the security aspects arising out of the resignation of a minister (J Profumo) in 1963; by the Lord Chief Justice, Lord Widgery, in 1972 into deaths in Londonderry; and by Lord Bridge in 1985 into allegations of improper telephone tapping of trade unionists and peace activists by members of the security service.[77] Such references may give rise to allegations that the government is using the judiciary for its own ends; and they may expose the judge in question, particularly if he or she is the sole member of the inquiry, to political or personal criticism by those who disagree with his or her report. The report by Lord Hutton in 2004 about the circumstances surrounding the death of a government scientist (Dr David Kelly) attracted a great deal of media criticism and led some to question the wisdom of this form of judicial activity.[78] Before a judge is appointed to an inquiry, ministers would normally consult with senior judges about the appointment, a practice which is now sometimes mandatory.[79] It needs to be stressed that such work is not the primary task of the judges and that

---

[71] Sheriff Courts (Scotland) Act 1971, s 12A–12F (as inserted by the Judiciary and Courts (Scotland) Act 2008, s 40).

[72] Courts Act 1971, s 17(4). Lay magistrates may be removed from office for incapacity, misbehaviour, incompetence or neglect of duty: Courts Act 2003, s 11. District judges (magistrates' courts) may be removed for incapacity or misbehaviour (s 22(5)). On the procedure to be followed, see Constitutional Reform Act 2005, s 108.

[73] J Beatson (2005) 121 LQR 221.

[74] See ch 22 D.

[75] HC Deb, 25 October 1994, col 757. Lord Nolan was also a commissioner under the Interception of Communications Act 1985. And see ch 22 D.

[76] See also Beatson, above.

[77] See respectively Cmnd 2152, 1963; HC 220 (1971–2); and The Times, 7 March 1985.

[78] I Steele [2004] PL 738.

[79] Inquiries Act 2005, s 10.

the government cannot assume that the services of a judge will be available whenever an awkward political situation might be eased by an impartial inquiry. There may also be concerns about judges being too intimately involved with the operation and needs of government, particularly in cases where they are drawn on to give advice on a matter about which they are subsequently called upon to adjudicate, albeit in a different context. Nor is it to be overlooked that drawing some judges away from their core task will increase the burdens on those left behind.

Judges in the political process

The role of judges acting at the behest of the executive in the manner described above is increasingly anomalous in a constitution which now embraces a stronger formal commitment to judicial independence, and to a greater separation of powers. In such arrangements, the less the two branches of government have to do with each other, the better. That such activity should continue is all the more anomalous for the fact that judicial involvement in the political process generally has greatly receded in recent years. It is true that by a strong convention considered in Chapter 5 the judges must not be seen to be engaged in party political activity, a convention now set down in the outline terms and conditions of service which provides that judges 'must expect to forgo any kind of political activity and be on their guard against circumstances arising in which their involvement in any outside activity might be seen to cast doubt on their judicial impartiality'. It is true that this convention did not in the past prevent Law Lords from taking part in the political work of the House, when they felt inclined to do so. Judicial members of the House of Lords took part in a number of debates on a number of bills affecting the legal profession, and were responsible for a number of amendments which improved measures such as the Contempt of Court Act 1981 (s 10 was an amendment tabled by Lord Scarman), and the Police and Criminal Evidence Act 1984 (s 78 was also a Scarman amendment). It is also the case that the Law Lords (serving and retired) played a prominent part in the debates relating to the Human Rights Bill.[80] But that is in the past.

As explained above, these opportunities for parliamentary participation have been brought to an end by the Constitutional Reform Act 2005, with Supreme Court justices being prohibited from sitting in the House of Lords. Members of the House of Lords who are appointed as Supreme Court justices (notably the Law Lords in post at the time the Supreme Court was created) will be entitled to receive a writ of summons at the beginning of each session (and presumably to attend the House), but not to sit or vote in its proceedings or those of its committees.[81] Despite the removal of the platform provided by the House of Lords, it is implausible to believe that the senior judges will cease to be engaged in public affairs. As they are subjected to demands for greater accountability and more public scrutiny and media attention in the wake of the Human Rights Act and the creation of the new Supreme Court, the senior judges may feel obliged to defend and explain their role in various forums.[82] Apart possibly from exceptional provisions in the Constitutional Reform Act 2005,[83] there are no formal channels for this to be done, but judges

---

[80] See K D Ewing (1999) 62 MLR 79.

[81] Constitutional Reform Act 2005, s 137. By the same token, it will be possible for (a) a serving Justice of the Supreme Court to be made a life peer, or (b) an existing life peer (suitably qualified) to be made a justice of the Supreme Court, but subject to provisions of the CRA, s 137 by which they would be unable to sit or vote until retirement from the bench.

[82] See HL Deb, 12 February 2004 (Lord Hoffmann responding to the 'unconstitutional, inexcusable behaviour' of Mr Blunkett, then Home Secretary).

[83] Section 5 of the 2005 Act provides that 'The chief justice of any part of the United Kingdom may lay before Parliament written representations on matters that appear to him to be matters of importance relating to the judiciary, or otherwise to the administration of justice, in that part of the United Kingdom.' But this seems designed as a 'nuclear option' signalling a serious breakdown in relations between the government and the judiciary collectively.

are increasingly responding to events by way of unattributed interviews in the press, by way of speeches reported in the press and elsewhere,[84] and in the case of retired judges by way of media interviews. Select committees provide another important forum for senior judges to make their views known, though there are sensitive constitutional issues to be considered when judges appear before such bodies.[85] But if these problems can be overcome, the select committees provide an opportunity for structured dialogue between legislature and judiciary which may be of benefit to both.[86]

D. Contempt of court and safeguards for the administration of justice

As we have seen, article 6 of the ECHR provides that the individual has the right to a fair and public hearing within a reasonable time by an independent and impartial tribunal. There are a number of legal rules which are designed to maintain the quality of justice in the courts. In principle all trials are conducted in open court,[87] although, exceptionally, cases may be heard ex parte or in camera;[88] witnesses may be permitted to give evidence anonymously;[89] and restrictions may be imposed on reporting legal proceedings,[90] where authorised by statute.[91] The written rules of court procedure as well as the unwritten rules of natural justice seek to ensure for each litigant a fair and orderly hearing.[92] The rules of evidence, particularly in criminal trials before a jury,[93] exclude material which might be unfairly prejudicial to an accused. To the extent that legal representation contributes to the quality of justice, there are also schemes to enable people with limited means to be defended by a lawyer in criminal proceedings and to seek redress through the civil courts. In some circumstances, the interests of the accused or the respondent may be represented by a special advocate appointed by the court, especially (though not only) in national security cases.[94] Nevertheless, the right to a fair and public hearing has to be balanced against other Convention rights, most notably the right to freedom of expression in art 10 of the ECHR. There is a difficult tension between the right to a fair trial and the right to freedom of expression when newspapers publish material which might prejudice the position of an accused person by

---

[84] See for example Lord Woolf [2004] CLJ 317. See also *Guardian*, 15 September 2005 (Lord Bingham responding robustly to criticism of the judiciary).

[85] HL 66-iii, HC 332-iii (2000–01), Q 77.

[86] The Senior Law Lord, the Lord Chief Justice and the Master of the Rolls appeared together before the Joint Committee on Human Rights in 2000–01: HL 66, HC 133 (2000–01). See also HC 51 (2004–05) (Beatson J before the Public Administration Committee), HC 754-i (2005–06) (Lord Phillips before the Constitutional Affairs Committee), and HL 165-ii/HC 150-ii (2007–08) (Baroness Hale before the JCHR). See further K D Ewing, in Flinders *et al.* (eds), *The Oxford Handbook of British Politics*, pp 275–7.

[87] See *Scott* v *Scott* [1913] AC 417. Also *Clibbery* v *Allan* [2002] EWCA Civ 45; [2002] Fam 261 for a review of the issues; and *BBC, Petitioners* 2002 SLT 2.

[88] Official Secrets Act 1911, s 8(4); Children and Young Persons Act 1933, s 37. See also *R* v *H* [2004] UKHL 3; [2004] 2 AC 134.

[89] *R* v *Murphy* [1990] NI 306; *R* v *Lord Saville of Newdigate ex p A* [1999] 4 All ER 860 (B Hadfield [1999] PL 633); *R (Al-Fawwaz)* v *Governor of Brixton Prison* [2001] UKHL 69; [2002] 1 AC 666; and *In re Times Newspapers Ltd* [2008] EWCA Crim 2396, [2009] 1 WLR 1015.

[90] For example, Judicial Proceedings (Regulation of Reports) Act 1926, on which see *Gilchrist* v *Scott* 2000 SCCR 28; Children and Young Persons Act 1933, s 39, on which see *In re S (A Child)* [2004] UKHL 47; [2004] 4 All ER 683. See also *A G's Reference No 3 of 1999: Reporting Restriction Order* [2009] UKHL 34.

[91] There is no common law power authorising a court to make an order to restrain the publication of proceedings (though publication could amount to contempt if designed to interfere with the administration of justice: *Independent Publishing Co Ltd* v *AG of Trinidad and Tobago* [2004] UKPC 26; [2005] AC 190).

[92] Ch 30 B.

[93] On which, see ch 21 E.

[94] For a consideration of this issue see *R (Roberts)* v *Parole Board* [2005] UKHL 45; [2005] 2 AC 738.

influencing a jury.[95] One of the functions of the law of contempt of court is to manage this tension,[96] although it also has other functions; these include protecting the dignity of the court and generally safeguarding the administration of justice.

The nature of contempt

Contempt of court, broadly speaking, takes two forms. Civil contempt is the failure to obey the order of a superior court of record which prescribes certain conduct upon a party to a civil action. A civil judge may commit to prison anyone who disregards an order addressed to him or her. In this way, decrees of specific performance and injunctions, as well as the writ of habeas corpus and other judicial orders, may be enforced by the High Court. The power of courts to enforce their orders against litigants is not available against the Crown, but ministers of the Crown and civil servants are liable to be proceeded against for contempt of court in respect of acts or omissions by them personally, and it is no defence that what would otherwise constitute a contempt of court was committed in the discharge or purported discharge of official duties.[97] Although a civil contempt is not a criminal offence or a misdemeanor,[98] the court may nevertheless commit a wrongdoer to prison for a fixed period,[99] may fine him or her or may order his or her property to be sequestrated. The Official Solicitor to the Senior Courts (a public official appointed by the Lord Chancellor) is required to review all cases of persons committed to prison for contempt and may intervene to secure their release.[100] The Crown may not grant a pardon in cases of civil contempt since this would be to intervene in litigation between parties.

Conduct which is calculated to interfere with the due administration of justice or to bring the courts into disrepute gives rise to proceedings which are in the nature of criminal proceedings, and both civil and criminal courts may exercise the jurisdiction. Although criminal contempt takes various forms and although it is necessary to protect the workings of the courts, nevertheless judges should seek to ensure, in the words of Lord President Normand,

> that the greatest restraint and discrimination should be used by the court in dealing with contempt of court, lest a process, the purpose of which is to prevent interference with the administration of justice, should degenerate into an oppressive or vindictive abuse of the court's powers.[101]

The need for restraint is all the greater since one of the consequences of contempt of court is to restrict freedom of expression. But not all judges are so sanguine, with concern being expressed in one case that the Contempt of Court Act 1981 may have tilted the balance too much in favour of freedom of expression: 'Parliament may have redrawn the boundary at a point which would not have been chosen by those people looking at the matter primarily from the standpoint of the administration of justice.'[102] Higher levels of tolerance have also seen judges being much less willing to challenge those who impute unfairness, partiality or stupidity to them in the discharge of their duties.[103]

---

[95] See *Miami Herald* v *Tornillo* 418 US 241 (1974).

[96] See *Attorney-General* v *BBC* [2007] EWCA Civ 280.

[97] *M* v *Home Office* [1994] 1 AC 377. And see *R* v *City of London Magistrates' Court, ex p Green* [1997] 3 All ER 551.

[98] *Cobra Golf Ltd* v *Rata* [1998] Ch 109.

[99] On which see *Nicholls* v *Nicholls* [1997] 2 All ER 97; and *Taylor* v *Ribby Hall Leisure Ltd* [1997] 4 All ER 760.

[100] *Churchman* v *Joint Shop Stewards' Committee* [1972] 3 All ER 603; *Enfield BC* v *Mahoney* [1983] 2 All ER 901.

[101] *Milburn, Petitioner* 1946 SC 301, 315.

[102] *Cox and Griffiths, Petitioners* 1998 SCCR 561.

[103] See *R* v *Metropolitan Police Commissioner, ex p Blackburn (No 2)* [1968] 2 QB 150. Compare *R* v *New Statesman, ex p DPP* (1928) 44 TLR 301. See also *Ambard* v *A-G for Trinidad and Tobago* [1936] AC 322, 335 (Lord Atkin). And see now *Anwar, Respondent* 2008 SLT 710.

Contempt in the face of the court

All superior courts have power to punish summarily by fine or imprisonment violence committed or threats uttered in face of the court. Thus the judge may punish an attack on anyone in court or restrain the use of threatening words or scurrilous abuse. The issue whether an act constitutes a contempt is for the judge alone. If the act is committed in court, the judge is in a sense prosecutor, chief witness, judge and jury.

> In *Morris v Crown Office*,[104] a group of students demonstrated in support of the Welsh language by interrupting a sitting of the High Court in London, where they sang, shouted slogans and scattered pamphlets. After order was restored, the trial judge sentenced some of the students to prison for three months and fined others £50 each. On appeal, the Court of Appeal, Civil Division, held that a High Court judge still had power at common law to commit instantly to prison for criminal contempt; and that the requirement under the Criminal Justice Act 1967 that prison sentences under six months be suspended did not apply to committal for contempt. The court did not consider the prison sentences to be excessive, but, having regard to all the circumstances, allowed the appeal against sentence and bound over the appellants to be of good behaviour for one year.

Contempt in the face of the court includes insulting behaviour,[105] disregard of a judge's ruling, and refusal by a witness to give evidence or to answer questions which he or she is required to answer.[106]

> In *Attorney-General v Mulholland and Foster*,[107] two journalists refused to disclose their sources of information to a tribunal of inquiry appointed after an Admiralty clerk, Vassall, had been convicted of espionage. The tribunal had by statute the powers of the High Court in examining witnesses.[108] On appeal against a prison sentence imposed by the High Court, to which the tribunal had reported the journalists, it was held that journalists had no legal privilege to refuse to disclose sources of information given to them in confidence, where the information was relevant and necessary to the trial or inquiry.

So too, in *British Steel Corporation v Granada Television Ltd*,[109] the House of Lords ordered the Granada company to reveal the name of an employee of the corporation who had passed secret documents to Granada that were then used in a programme about the corporation. Although failure by Granada to comply with this order would have constituted contempt, the matter was resolved when the employee concerned made his identity known. In the Contempt of Court Act 1981, the power of the court to demand information was limited by s 10. The court may not now request a person to disclose the source of information contained in a publication for which he or she is responsible, unless the court is satisfied that disclosure is necessary in the interests of justice or national security or for the prevention of disorder or crime.[110] If cases such as *Mulholland* and *British Steel Corporation* were to occur today, the statutory test of necessity would have to be applied before the court decided to require disclosure, but the outcome might still be the same.

> In *Secretary of State for Defence v Guardian Newspapers Ltd*[111] a junior civil servant delivered anonymously to the *Guardian* newspaper confidential documents addressed to Cabinet ministers by the Secretary of State for Defence. The documents related to the arrival of US cruise missiles at Greenham Common airbase. The Ministry of Defence sought to recover the documents to help them to identify the person responsible for the

---

[104] [1970] 2 QB 114.
[105] See *R v Powell* (1994) 98 Cr App R 224.
[106] *R v Montgomery* [1995] 2 Cr App R 23.
[107] [1963] 2 QB 477. And see *Senior v Holdsworth* [1976] QB 23.
[108] Ch 29 C.
[109] [1981] AC 1096.
[110] Contempt of Court Act 1981, s 10.
[111] [1985] AC 339.

leak. The House of Lords held that s 10 of the 1981 Act was a valid defence not only where a journalist was asked a direct question in court, but also in an action for recovery of property where the property once recovered would help to reveal the newspaper's source. But the House also held (Lords Fraser and Scarman dissenting) that it was necessary to recover the documents and identify the source of the leak in the interests of national security. The minister had expressed concern that a significant document relating to the defence of Britain had found its way to a national newspaper. This was of grave importance for national security, since Britain's allies could not be expected to continue to entrust the government with secret information if it was liable to unauthorised disclosure.

Guardian Newspapers is only one of a number of cases in which the courts at the highest levels have been willing to order the disclosure of journalists' sources by applying a low threshold which applicants need cross.[112] The more robust view of the European Court of Human Rights on this issue has led to conflict between that body and the House of Lords.[113] The domestic courts nevertheless appear willing to require the disclosure of sources where this will help an employer to identify an employee within an organisation who has leaked commercial information, or confidential medical information about a patient.[114] But the courts may refuse to order the disclosure of sources where the applicant's interests will be adequately protected by an injunction[115] or where in the circumstances the applicant has not tried to find the source of the disclosure by other means first.[116]

The strict liability rule

Until the Contempt of Court Act 1981, it was on the basis of the common law that penalties were imposed on those whose publications were prejudicial to a fair trial or to civil proceedings.[117] The law was reformed in 1981, following recommendations of the Phillimore committee,[118] and the decision of the European Court of Human Rights in the *Sunday Times* case.

> Nearly 400 claims against Distillers Ltd, the manufacturers of thalidomide, were pending when the *Sunday Times* published an article which inter alia urged the company to make a generous settlement. Later it proposed to publish an article examining the precautions taken by the company before the drug was sold. On the Attorney General's request, the Divisional Court granted an injunction to restrain publication of the article, holding that it would create a serious risk of interference with the company's freedom of action in the litigation. The Court of Appeal discharged the injunction, on the grounds that the article commented in good faith on matters of outstanding public importance and did not prejudice pending litigation since the litigation had been dormant for some years.
>
> The House of Lords restored the injunction, holding that it was a contempt to publish an article prejudging the merits of an issue before the court where this created a real risk that a fair trial of the action would be prejudiced; the thalidomide actions were not dormant, since active negotiations for a settlement were

---

[112] *Maxwell v Pressdram Ltd* [1987] 1 All ER 656, *Re an Inquiry under the Company Securities (Insider Dealing) Act 1985* [1988] AC 660, and *X v Morgan Grampian (Publishers) Ltd* [1991] 1 AC 1. See T R S Allan [1991] CLJ 131; S Palmer [1992] PL 61.

[113] *Goodwin v UK* (1996) 22 EHRR 123, concluding that the decision in *Morgan Grampian* contravened art 10 of the ECHR.

[114] See *Camelot Group v Centaur Ltd* [1999] QB 124, and *Ashworth Hospital Authority v MGN* [2002] UKHL 29; [2002] 1 WLR 2033.

[115] See *Saunders v Punch Ltd* [1998] 1 WLR 986.

[116] *John v Express Newspapers* [2000] 1 WLR 1931, and *Broadmoor Hospital v Hyde*, *The Independent*, 4 March 1994.

[117] Leading cases arising out of criminal litigation before 1981 include *R v Bolam, ex p Haigh* (1949) 93 SJ 220; *R v Evening Standard Co Ltd* [1954] 1 QB 578; *R v Thomson Newspapers Ltd, ex p A-G* [1968] 1 All ER 268; and *Stirling v Associated Newspapers Ltd* 1960 JC 5. And in relation to civil litigation, see *Vine Products Ltd v Green* [1966] Ch 484.

[118] Cmnd 5794, 1974.

going on. It was a contempt to use improper pressure to induce a litigant to settle a case on terms to which he or she did not wish to agree, or to hold a litigant up to public obloquy for exercising his or her rights in the courts.[119] Thereafter the *Sunday Times* claimed that the decision of the House of Lords infringed the freedom of expression protected by art 10 of the European Convention on Human Rights. Before the European Court of Human Rights, the main issue was whether, under art 10, the ban on publication was 'necessary in a democratic society . . . for maintaining the authority and impartiality of the judiciary'. By 11 to 9 votes, the court held that the ban had not been shown to be necessary for this purpose.[120]

The Contempt of Court Act 1981 was designed to bring British law into line with the requirements of the *Sunday Times* decision, although there is much scope for argument about whether it does so fully.[121]

Liability for contempt under the 1981 Act is based on the strict liability rule, defined to mean 'the rule of law whereby conduct may be treated as a contempt of court as tending to interfere with the course of justice in particular legal proceedings regardless of intent to do so' (s 1). By s 2, the strict liability rule applies to any publication which creates 'a substantial risk that the course of justice in the proceedings in question will be seriously impeded or prejudiced'. This applies to both civil and criminal proceedings. The other requirement of s 2 is that the proceedings in question must be 'active', governed by Sch 1, which lays down in detail when civil or criminal proceedings begin to be active. Criminal proceedings become active when an individual is arrested or orally charged or when an arrest warrant is issued (whereas at common law liability for contempt could arise where legal proceedings were imminent).[122] Civil proceedings become active not when the writ is served but when the action is set down for trial. In some cases, proceedings may be instituted at common law to deal with publications which are likely to prejudice the outcome of proceedings not yet active within the statutory definition.[123] Proceedings remain active in criminal cases until concluded by acquittal, sentence or discontinuance, and in other cases until the proceedings are disposed of, discontinued or withdrawn.[124] Apart for criminal liability, it may be possible to restrain a publication in breach of the strict liability rule by injunction, though this will be difficult if the information is already in the public domain.[125]

Application of the strict liability rule

The question whether there is a substantial risk that the course of justice in particular legal proceedings will be seriously impeded or prejudiced is ultimately one of fact; this will depend primarily on whether the publication will bring influence to bear which is likely to direct the proceedings in some way from the course which they would otherwise have followed.[126] Many of the cases on contempt of court, both before and after 1981, are concerned with pre-trial publicity which may influence the jury, though questions such as the impact of publication on an ongoing police investigation are also relevant.[127] Thus *Attorney-General v Times Newspapers Ltd* concerned reports carried by newspapers about a man who had intruded into the Queen's bedroom at

---

[119] *A-G v Times Newspapers Ltd* [1974] AC 273.

[120] *Sunday Times v UK* (1979) 2 EHRR 245.

[121] See S Bailey (1982) 45 MLR 301.

[122] *R v Savundranayagan* [1968] 3 All ER 439; *R v Beaverbrook Newspapers Ltd* [1962] NI 15.

[123] *A-G v News Group Newspapers* [1989] QB 110. Cf *A-G v Sport Newspapers Ltd* [1991] 1 WLR 1194.

[124] On the question of appeals against sentence and 'misguided' press campaigns, see *R v Vano*, *The Times*, 29 December 1994.

[125] *Attorney-General v BBC* [2007] EWCA Civ 280.

[126] *Re Lonrho* [1990] 2 AC 154.

[127] *Attorney-General v BBC* [2007] EWCA Civ 280.

Buckingham Palace.[128] The man in question was awaiting trial on a number of counts, including the theft of a bottle of wine. It was held that a newspaper report that he had admitted the theft was a contempt, since it was difficult to see how an assertion that an accused person had admitted the very fact that was in issue could do otherwise than cause a very substantial risk that the trial might be prejudiced. The leading case on s 2(2), however, is *Re Lonrho plc*,[129] an extraordinary case which arose out of a battle for control of the London department store, Harrods.

In 1987 the Secretary of State for Trade and Industry appointed inspectors to investigate the affairs of the company which owned the store. The inspectors submitted their report in 1988, but the Secretary of State refused to publish it and he also refused to refer the matter to the Monopolies and Mergers Commission. Lonrho instituted two applications for judicial review, designed to compel the minister to publish the inspectors' report and to refer the matter to the Commission. While appeals on both applications were pending before the House of Lords, Lonrho acquired a copy of the inspectors' report, which the *Observer* agreed to publish in a special issue of the newspaper. Some copies of the issue were sent to persons on a mailing list to whom Lonrho had been regularly sending propaganda literature. These people included four of the five Lords of Appeal in Ordinary who were to hear the appeals. These circumstances were referred to three other members of the House of Lords. They held that the special issue (which contained extensive extracts from the inspectors' report as well as editorial comment accusing the Secretary of State of bad faith) did not create a substantial risk that the course of justice in Lonrho's appeals would be seriously impeded or prejudiced. 'So far as the appellate tribunal is concerned, it is difficult to visualise circumstances in which any court in the United Kingdom exercising appellate jurisdiction would be in the least likely to be influenced by public discussion of the merits of a decision appealed against or of the parties' conduct in the proceedings.'

A number of defences are provided in the 1981 Act. The first of these is the defence of innocent publication (s 3), where the person responsible for the publication can prove that, having taken all reasonable care, he or she did not know that relevant legal proceedings were active.[130] The second is the contemporary reporting of legal proceedings in respect of 'a fair and accurate report of legal proceedings held in public, published contemporaneously and in good faith' (s 4(1)). However, a court may order that publication of reports be delayed – but not prevented indefinitely[131] – where necessary to avoid a substantial risk of prejudice to the administration of justice (s 4(2)).[132] 'In forming a view whether it is necessary to make an order for avoiding such a risk a court will inevitably have regard to the competing public interest considerations of ensuring a fair trial and of open justice.'[133] The power was used at the trial of Clive Ponting under the Official Secrets Act 1911 to prevent a television company from recreating the court proceedings as a drama documentary at the end of each day.[134] Before granting an order under s 4(2), the magistrates are entitled to hear representations from the press that the order should not be granted.[135] The third

---

[128] *The Times*, 12 February 1983. See also *A-G v News Group Newspapers Ltd* [1986] 2 All ER 833; *A-G v ITN Ltd* [1995] 2 All ER 370; *A-G v BBC* [1997] EMLR 76; *A-G v MGN Ltd* [1997] 1 All ER 456 (no contempt where trial would not take place for several months and where already saturation coverage); *A-G v Birmingham Post and Mail Ltd* [1999] 1 WLR 361. For Scotland, see *HM Advocate v Caledonian Newspapers Ltd* 1995 SCCR 330; *Cox and Griffiths, Petitioners* 1998 SCCR 561; *Al Megrahi v Times Newspapers Ltd* 1999 SCCR 824; *HM Advocate v The Scotsman Publications* 1999 SLT 466; *Scottish Daily Record v Thompson* 2009 SLT 363.

[129] [1990] 2 AC 154.

[130] See also *HM Advocate v Express Newspapers plc* 1998 SCCR 471.

[131] *BBC, Petitioners* 2002 SLT 2; *In re Times Newspapers Ltd v R* [2007] EWCA Crim 1925; [2008] 1 WLR 234.

[132] For the approach which the courts should adopt in such cases, see *MGN Pension Trustees Ltd v Bank of America* [1995] 2 All ER 355. On the right of appeal against an order issued under s 4(2), see Criminal Justice Act 1988, s 159. For Scotland, see *The Scottish Daily Record, Petitioner* 1998 SCCR 626; *Galbraith v HM Advocate* 2001 SLT 465; and *BBC, Petitioners* 2002 SLT 2.

[133] *Ex p The Telegraph plc* [1993] 2 All ER 971, at 975. See *R v Horsham Justices, ex p Farquharson* [1982] QB 762; M J Beloff [1992] PL 92.

[134] Ewing and Gearty, *Freedom under Thatcher*, p 145.

[135] *R v Clerkenwell Metropolitan Magistrate, ex p The Telegraph plc* [1993] QB 462.

defence is where the publication contains a good faith discussion of public affairs if the risk of prejudice to particular legal proceedings is merely incidental to the discussion (s 5). In *Attorney-General v English* Lord Diplock noted that s 5 does not take the form of an exception to s 2, but stands on an equal footing with it: 'It does not set out exculpatory matter. Like s 2(2) it states what publications shall *not* amount to contempt of court despite their tendency to interfere with the course of justice in particular legal proceedings.'[136]

> In *Attorney-General v English* the *Daily Mail* published an article in support of a woman standing for election to Parliament as an independent pro-life candidate, one of her aims being to stop the alleged practice in hospitals whereby newly born disabled babies were allowed to die. At the time the article was published a well-known paediatrician was standing trial, accused of murdering a three-day-old boy with Down's syndrome, by allowing him to die of starvation. The House of Lords held that this did not amount to a contempt of court; although the publication of the article on the third day of the trial was capable of prejudicing the jury, the publication was a discussion in good faith on a matter of wide public interest and the risk of prejudice was incidental to the discussion. To hold otherwise 'would have prevented [the candidate] from . . . obtaining publicity for what was a main plank in her election programme and would have stifled all discussion in the press . . . about mercy killing from the time that [the doctor] was charged in the magistrates' court in February 1981 until the date of his acquittal [in] November of that year.'[137]

The strict liability rule does not apply to the good faith reporting of proceedings of the Scottish Parliament or Welsh Assembly.[138] Nor does it apply to tribunals which do not exercise the 'judicial power of the state'.[139]

Other acts interfering with the course of justice

Nothing in the Contempt of Court Act 1981 is designed to restrict liability for contempt of court in respect of conduct intended to impede or prejudice the administration of justice (s 6(2)). Many other acts are punishable as contempts, some of them also being criminal offences in their own right, for example attempts to pervert the course of justice or interference with witnesses.[140] A prison governor who, acting under prison rules, obstructed a prisoner's communication with the High Court was held to be in contempt.[141] It is a contempt to punish or victimise a witness for evidence which has already been given, even in proceedings which have concluded, since this might deter potential witnesses in future cases.[142] It may be a contempt of court for a solicitor to disclose to a journalist documents relating to litigation.

> A prisoner challenged the legality of a Home Office decision to set up a 'control unit' for prisoners considered to be troublemakers. An order for discovery of documents being made against the Home Office, a large number of official documents were made available to the prisoner's solicitor. She undertook that the documents would be used only for the case in hand, but she later allowed a journalist to see documents which had been read out in open court. The journalist published an article based on these documents. The House of Lords held (by three to two) that although the documents had been read in court, and could have been reported by journalists present, the solicitor was guilty of contempt since she had used the documents

---

[136] [1983] 1 AC 116, 141.
[137] [1983] 1 AC 116, at 144 (Lord Diplock).
[138] Scotland Act 1998, s 42; and Government of Wales Act 2006, s 43.
[139] Contempt of Court Act 1981, s 19. See *Pickering v Liverpool Daily Post plc* [1991] 2 AC 370 and *General Medical Council v BBC* [1998] 1 WLR 1573. For background, see *AG v BBC* [1981] AC 303.
[140] See *Peach Grey & Co v Sommers* [1995] 2 All ER 513.
[141] *Raymond v Honey* [1983] AC 1.
[142] *A-G v Butterworth* [1963] 1 QB 696; *Moore v Clerk of Assize, Bristol* [1973] 1 All ER 58.

for a purpose which was not necessary for the conduct of her client's case, and had broken her implied under-taking to the court that had ordered discovery.[143]

Interference with the work of a jury may constitute contempt, whether before, during or after a trial. By s 8 of the Contempt of Court Act 1981, it is a contempt of court to solicit, obtain or disclose details of any statements made or votes cast by jurors during their deliberations in any legal proceedings. This reversed a decision in 1980 that a magazine article disclosing aspects of the jury's deliberations during the trial of Mr Jeremy Thorpe was not a contempt of court.[144] It is an offence under s 8 for a newspaper to publish information disclosed to it by a jury member, but the section applies only to 'what passes among the jurors while they are considering their verdict after the judge has directed them to retire to do so'.[145] It is an offence for a jury member to write to a relative of a convicted person to expose unfairness by jurors,[146] but it is not an offence to raise such concerns with the court.[147]

The dynamic nature of the law of contempt has been well demonstrated by decisions arising out of important disputes between the courts and the press. It is a contempt for a newspaper to disregard a judge's directions that the names of prosecution witnesses in blackmail cases should not be published.[148] But the power to issue such directions is not limited to blackmail cases.

> In *Attorney-General* v *Leveller Magazine Ltd* a magazine published the name of a prosecution witness at an official secrets trial, who had been described in court as Colonel B. The House of Lords held that it was contempt of court to publish a witness's name if this interfered with the administration of justice. But on the facts no contempt had occurred, since inter alia, no clear direction against publication had been given by the magistrates; and Colonel B's identity could have been discovered from evidence given in open court.[149]

The uncertainties left by this decision were lessened by the Contempt of Court Act 1981. By s 11, where a court has the power to withhold evidence from the public (although the court is sitting in public) and allows the name of a witness or other matter to be withheld, it may restrict publication accordingly.[150] Although the courts should be careful about exercising this power (which should not be used to protect privacy or avoid embarrassment),[151] nevertheless it would be a contempt of court to publish information, even though the identity of the witness could be discovered from evidence given in open court, as in the *Leveller Magazine* case. However, a court cannot prohibit the press from reporting names which are mentioned in court unless there has first been a direction that these names should be withheld from the public.[152] Nor can an order

---

[143] *Home Office* v *Harman* [1983] AC 280. Subsequent proceedings under the European Convention on Human Rights were the subject of a friendly settlement. In 1987 the decision was largely reversed by an amendment to the Rules of the Supreme Court, which released parties from any undertaking once the material has been read in open court. See *Apple Corp* v *Apple Computer Inc, The Times,* 10 April 1991, and *Lilly Icos Ltd* v *Pfizer Ltd* (No 2) [2002] EWCA Civ 2; [2002] 1 All ER 842.

[144] *A-G* v *New Statesman Publishing Co* [1981] QB 1.

[145] *Scottish Criminal Cases Review Commission, Petitioners* 2001 SLT 1198, at p 1200, and *A-G* v *Associated Newspapers* [1994] 2 AC 238 respectively.

[146] *A-G* v *Scotcher* [2004] UKHL 36; [2005] 1 WLR 1867.

[147] *R* v *Mirza* [2004] UKHL 2; [2004] 1 AC 1118.

[148] *R* v *Socialist Worker Ltd, ex p A-G* [1975] QB 637. But magistrates cannot withhold their identity from the public or the press: *R* v *Felixstowe JJ, ex p Leigh* [1987] QB 582.

[149] [1979] AC 440.

[150] On the circumstances in which a court has the power to withhold evidence from the public, see *In re Times Newspapers Ltd* [2008] EWCA Crim 2396, [2009] 1 WLR 1015.

[151] *R* v *Westminster City Council, ex p Castelli, The Times,* 14 August 1995. Also *Trustor AB* v *Smallbone* [2000] 1 All ER 811. This applies particularly where anonymity is sought by one of the parties to litigation rather than by a witness: *R* v *Legal Aid Board, ex p Kaim Todner* [1999] QB 966.

[152] *R* v *Arundel Justices, ex p Westminster Press* [1985] 2 All ER 390.

be issued under section 11 to prevent *speculation* about what may have been said in camera, with section 11 applying only to prohibit the publication of a *name or matter*. The Court of Appeal has warned, however, that such speculation might constitute a contempt of court at common law, which is expressly preserved by the 1981 Act (s 6(C)).[153]

It may also be contempt to publish material which has been the subject of an injunction against another party.[154] A third party who knowingly acts in breach of the terms of the injunction may be in contempt even though he or she is not a party to the proceedings and indeed may not have had an opportunity to make representations in these proceedings:

> In 1986 interlocutory injunctions were granted against two newspapers, the *Guardian* and the *Observer*, restraining them from publishing material from the book *Spycatcher*, by Mr Peter Wright, pending a full trial of the action in which the Attorney General sought permanent injunctions on the ground that the information was confidential. While interlocutory injunctions were still in force, extensive extracts from the book were published in other newspapers, including the *Sunday Times*. The House of Lords held that these publications amounted to a contempt of court, even though the injunctions had not been issued against these newspapers in the first place. In the view of the House, where a party (C) knowingly does something which would if done by B be a breach of an injunction obtained by A against B, C is guilty of contempt of court if this conduct interferes with the administration of justice between A and B. In this case the publication by C (the *Sunday Times*) did interfere with proceedings between A (the Attorney General) and B (the *Guardian* and the *Observer*). The consequence of the publication by the *Sunday Times* before the main *Spycatcher* trial was to nullify, in part at least, the purpose of such trial, because it put into the public domain part of the material which the Attorney General claimed should remain confidential.

The principle in this case is sometimes referred to as the 'Spycatcher principle', for obvious reasons. The Court of Appeal has since been unwilling to accept that 'conduct by a third party which is inconsistent with a court order in only a trivial or technical way should expose a party to conviction for contempt'.[155] However, the importance of the principle is not to be underestimated, nor is the willingness of the courts to enforce it.

> In *AG v Punch Ltd*[156] an interlocutory injunction was granted to restrain Associated Newspapers Ltd (proprietors of the *Mail on Sunday*) from publishing any information obtained from Mr David Shayler which was obtained by him in the course of or as a result of his employment in the security service. Mr Shayler subsequently started to write a weekly column for *Punch*, the aim of the column being to criticise the performance of the security service. Following the publication of an article about an IRA bombing in London, the Attorney General brought contempt proceedings against *Punch*. The Court of Appeal overturned the first instance decision that there had been a contempt, the court accepting that the editor 'thought that the purpose of the [injunction] was to restrain material dangerous to national security' which it was not his intention to publish. But on an appeal by the Attorney General, the original decision was restored. According to Lord Nicholls, the editor of *Punch* knew that the action against Shayler raised confidentiality issues relating to national security: 'He must, inevitably, have appreciated that by publishing the article he was doing precisely what the order was intended to prevent, namely, pre-empting the court's decision on these confidentiality issues. That is knowing interference with the administration of justice.'[157]

---

[153] *Times Newspapers Ltd v R* [2007] EWCA Crim 1925, [2008] 1 WLR 234. For full consideration of this case, see Ewing, *Bonfire of the Liberties*, ch 5.

[154] *A-G v Times Newspapers Ltd* [1992] 1 AC 191. See also *A-G v Observer* [1988] 1 All ER 385.

[155] *A-G v Newspaper Publishing plc* [1997] 1 WLR 926 (Lord Bingham CJ). Also *Harrow LBC v Johnstone* [1997] 1 WLR 459.

[156] [2002] UKHL 50; [2003] 1 AC 1046.

[157] Ibid at para 52.

E. The executive and the machinery of justice[158]

Questions about the court structure, the buildings in which the courts should be housed, and how the courts should be funded, are questions for the government that cannot be decided by the judges and lawyers (though they may be consulted about such decisions). Before 2007, the Lord Chancellor's Department (latterly the Department for Constitutional Affairs) and the Home Office were the government departments principally responsible for such matters. They are now the responsibility of the Ministry of Justice, which as one of the biggest departments in government inherited the duties of the Department for Constitutional Affairs as well as duties performed hitherto by the Home Office.[159] The birth of the Ministry of Justice proved to be controversial, mainly because of the way in which the new Ministry was established, drawing criticism of the government from the House of Lords Constitution Committee (and from the House of Commons Constitutional Affairs Committee).[160] It was a particular concern that the government had failed to consult the judiciary in good time about its plans, the Lords Committee advising that the government must learn to treat the judges as a constitutional partner rather than merely the subjects of change. The Lord Chancellor and Secretary of State for Justice is the ministerial head of the Ministry of Justice. The position is different in Scotland, where there is a Department of Justice in the Scottish Executive.

Lord Chancellor

The office of Lord Chancellor was regarded as one of the great offices of state with an unbroken pedigree stretching back to 1068, the position having been held in that time by some notable historical figures, including Thomas Becket, Thomas Wolsey and Sir Thomas More. Apart from being a member of the Cabinet as political head of an important government department, the Lord Chancellor was also the Speaker of the House of Lords, for which a portion of his salary was paid by the House of Lords. On appointment, moreover, the Lord Chancellor took the judicial oath and was entitled to preside over the House of Lords in its judicial work and the Judicial Committee of the Privy Council. Lord Mackay sat on 67 occasions (House of Lords and Privy Council) between 1987 and 1994, while Lord Hailsham sat 68 times as Lord Chancellor between 1979 and 1987.[161] Lord Irvine also took part in a number of cases,[162] though he was the last to do so. The role of the Lord Chancellor has been radically redefined since 2003, with the Constitutional Reform Act 2005 giving effect to a series of changes that were under way before the Act was passed. The Lord Chancellor has ceased to be a judge and no longer takes the judicial oath,[163] with a new oath for the Lord Chancellor being introduced by the Constitutional Reform Act 2005.[164] Also, the Lord Chancellor is no longer the Speaker of the House of Lords, which now elects its own presiding officer.[165]

Unusually for a government minister, there are statutory provisions relating to eligibility for appointment of the Lord Chancellor. The Constitutional Reform Act 2005 provides that a person may not be recommended for appointment as Lord Chancellor unless 'qualified by experience', which includes experience as a minister, a member of either House of Parliament, a legal practitioner,

---

[158] See Brazier, *Constitutional Practice*, ch 12.

[159] The creation of a Ministry of Justice had been proposed by the Haldane committee on The Machinery of Government as long ago as 1918: Cd 9230, 1918.

[160] See HL Paper 151 (2006–07), and HC 466 (2006–07). See further A W Bradley [2008] PL 470.

[161] HL Deb, 24 October 1994, col 395 (WA). Also HL Deb, 20 October 1992, col 82 (WA).

[162] See for example *DPP v Jones* [1999] 2 AC 240 (ch 24); and *National Power plc v Carmichael* [1999] ICR 1227.

[163] 2005 Act, s 17.

[164] Ibid, amending the Promissory Oaths Act 1868.

[165] 2005 Act, s 18.

a university law teacher, and anything else the Prime Minister 'considers relevant'.[166] None of these factors is a requirement or condition of appointment, and in particular the Lord Chancellor need no longer be a member of the House of Lords, nor need he or she be legally qualified. Indeed the first incumbent under the new regime (Jack Straw) was a member of the House of Commons. Some of the responsibilities previously discharged by the Lord Chancellor have been reassigned by the Constitutional Reform Act 2005, many going to the Lord Chief Justice, whose administrative role as Head of the Judiciary in England and Wales has been greatly enhanced by that Act.[167] The Lord Chancellor nevertheless still remains concerned with virtually all judicial appointments. Despite the reform to the system of judicial appointments, the Lord Chancellor appoints to the lay magistracy, and makes recommendations to the Queen about the appointment of district judges (magistrates' courts), and district judges.[168] Although senior appointments now fall within the scope of the Judicial Appointments Commission, the formal position remains that the Lord Chancellor either makes or recommends the appointment.[169]

Ministry of Justice

Despite the apparent diminution in the role and status of the Lord Chancellor, he remains head of what is claimed to be one of the largest government departments, with a wide range of responsibilities. These relate principally to the administration of justice in its widest sense (including the courts, prisons and probation services), as well as constitutional matters (including human rights). Some of these responsibilities are underpinned by statute in the sense that the Lord Chancellor has a statutory duty to ensure that there is an efficient and effective system to support the carrying on of the business of the courts.[170] This includes the appointment of staff and the provision of accommodation,[171] and the appointment of court security officers with powers of search, as well as powers of exclusion, removal and restraint.[172] Otherwise, there are several important executive agencies within the Ministry of Justice, including the National Offender Management Service (NOMS) (administering the prisons and probation services), Her Majesty's Courts Service (administering the civil, family and criminal courts), and the Tribunals Service (providing administration for the tribunals throughout the United Kingdom). As we have seen however, the creation of the Ministry of Justice with such a wide remit provoked a great deal of controversy, and led to a souring of relations between government and judiciary. One concern expressed by the judges was that funding for the courts, tribunals and legal aid might be put at risk by having to compete in the Ministry of Justice with expenditure needed for prisons. The impasse was resolved when the Lord Chancellor (Jack Straw) and Lord Chief Justice Phillips agreed to establish an executive agency, Her Majesty's Courts Service, which unlike other executive agencies was to be based on a 'partnership model', an approach adopted because the courts 'are by their nature a shared endeavour between the judiciary, who are responsible for the judicial function to deliver justice independently, and the government, which has overall responsibility for the justice system within the framework and resources set by Parliament'.

In April 2008, details of the agreement were laid before Parliament in the form of Her Majesty's Courts Service Framework Document.[173] In outline, the Lord Chancellor and the Lord

---

[166] Ibid, s 2.

[167] 2005 Act, ss 12, 13; Sch 1, 2.

[168] Courts Act 2003, ss 10, 22; County Courts 1984, s 6 (as amended).

[169] 2005 Act, s 96. And see above, section B.

[170] Courts Act 2003, s 1.

[171] Ibid, s 3. Although employed as civil servants, court service staff may be regarded by the courts as part of the judicial arm of the state, as in *Quinland v Governor of Swaleside Prison* [2002] EWCA Civ 174; [2003] QB 306.

[172] Courts Act 2003, ss 51–7.

[173] Cm 7350, 2008.

Chief Justice will jointly agree the aims and objectives for the Courts Service, and the priorities for funding within the Service. The Document recognises that all citizens, 'according to their different needs, are entitled to timely access to justice, whether as victims of crime, defendants accused of crimes, consumers in debt, children at risk of harm or business people involved in commercial disputes'.[174] A new board of 11 members will give leadership to the Courts Service, to be chaired by an independent non-executive chair (who is neither a judge nor a civil servant). The board will include three judges, four executive directors, a representative of the Ministry of Justice, and two non-executive directors. The staff of the Service will owe a joint duty both to the Lord Chancellor and the Lord Chief Justice for the 'effective and efficient operation of the courts'.[175] The financing of the Courts Service is a matter of particular concern to the judges, and the Framework Document provides for greater judicial engagement through the Courts Service Board in the financing of the courts. Moreover, the Lord Chief Justice will have a clear role in representing the views of the judiciary on provision and allocation of resources. The partnership model for the Courts Service differs in many respects from the usual agency framework found in Whitehall today.[176] If for any reason the partnership is terminated, 'the governance of the [Courts Service] will revert to a conventional agency model reporting directly to the Lord Chancellor, unless and until a new model is agreed between the Lord Chancellor and Lord Chief Justice or a different legislative framework is put in place'.[177]

The Law Officers of the Crown[178]

The Attorney General and Solicitor General are the law officers of the Crown, ministerial positions to which the incumbents are appointed by the Prime Minister. Their historic role is to represent the Crown in the courts, and they now act as legal advisers to the government on important matters, though ministers may also receive legal advice from within their own departments. Serviced by the Attorney General's office, the Law Officers operate independently of the Ministry of Justice and have a number of responsibilities. These include leading for the Crown in major prosecutions (especially in trials involving state security or official secrecy) or in major civil actions to which the Crown is a party; in other cases (the great bulk) recruiting and appointing counsel who appear on behalf of the government in legal proceedings; appointing a special advocate to represent the interests of a party who cannot for security or other reasons be fully informed of all the material relied on against him or her;[179] and lodging an appeal against sentences which are considered to be unduly lenient. The Attorney General's consent is also needed for relator actions, with decisions granting or refusing such consent not yet subject to review by the courts.[180] Otherwise, the Law Officers have parliamentary responsibilities, helping to see legal and fiscal Bills through the Commons and giving advice to parliamentary committees (notably the Standards and Privileges Committee).

It has been said that in the exercise of these many different functions, 'the Attorney General acts not as a minister of the Crown (although he is of course such) and not as the public officer with overall responsibility for the conduct of prosecutions, but as independent, unpartisan guardian of the public interest in the administration of justice'.[181] It had been the practice since the reign of George III for the Attorney General to be an MP, but since 1999 the office has been

---

[174] Ibid, para 2.2.
[175] Ibid, para 7.1.
[176] Ibid, para 15.6.
[177] Ibid, para 15.7.
[178] Edwards, *The Law Officers of the Crown*, and *The Attorney General, Politics and the Public Interest*.
[179] See *R v H* [2004] UKHL 3; [2004] 2 AC 134.
[180] *Gouriet v Union of Post Office Workers* [1978] AC 435; chs 12 E and 31.
[181] *R v H*, above, per Lord Bingham, at para 46.

held by life peers (Lords Williams and Goldsmith and Baroness Scotland respectively).[182] In view of his or her duties in connection with prosecutions, it is regarded as preferable that the Attorney General should remain outside the Cabinet as the government's chief legal adviser, attending particular Cabinet meetings only when summoned. After a detailed examination of the role of the Law Officers carried out in 2007–2008, the government concluded that the Attorney General should continue as the law officer and as a minister responsible to Parliament, rejecting a suggestion that the work of the Attorney should be carried out by an official outside party political life. The government did, however, propose that the independence of the office should be strengthened by a new oath, committing the incumbent to uphold the rule of law, while the government also seemed open to the possibility of greater parliamentary scrutiny of the office.[183]

The Law Officers' advice

The invasion of Iraq in 2003 gave rise to a number of political concerns, not the least of which was the legal basis for the government's action, it being widely believed in this country that the action did not have the necessary authority under international law. Related to this was the advice which the government received from the Attorney General, the extent to which that advice was made fully available to the Cabinet as a whole, and the circumstances – if any – in which it might be made available to Parliament and the public, either at the time it was given, or after the event when questions were raised about the legality of the government's conduct. Erskine May refers to a 'long-standing convention, observed by successive governments', that 'the fact of, and substance of advice from, the law officers of the Crown is not disclosed outside government', explaining that 'the purpose of this convention is to enable the government to obtain full and frank legal advice in confidence'.[184] This is not to say that the advice may not be disclosed, but it does mean that it will not be laid before Parliament or quoted from in debate, unless a minister considers it expedient to do so,[185] though even then it may be appropriate to make disclosure only with the consent of the law officer concerned. According to the *Ministerial Code*, 'the fact that the Law Officers have advised or have not advised and the content of their advice must not be disclosed outside government without their authority'.[186] Breach of this principle may lead to the resignation of a minister, as during the Westland affair in 1985–86 when a Cabinet minister resigned following the leak to the media of a confidential letter of advice from the Solicitor General to other ministers.

The disclosure of the advice given by the Law Officers thus takes place very infrequently, despite the highly charged circumstances in which advice may sometimes have to be given. It has been said by one authority that there is 'an impregnable moat around the Law Officer's opinions',[187] and acknowledged judicially that

> there are only five occasions in the 40 years before 2008 when the government of the day decided that the public interest favoured disclosure of such advice. These were: 1971, when the substance of the advice but not the actual advice relating to the United Kingdom's obligations to supply arms to South Africa under the Simonstown Agreement; 1986: the disclosure of a letter of advice in respect of issues arising under the so-called Westland Affair, there having been an unauthorised partial leak of advice; 1992: the advice of the Law Officers regarding the legal regime governing arms sales to Iraq was disclosed to the Scott Enquiry following the collapse of the Matrix Churchill trial;

[182] For a critique of this departure from long established practice, see *The Guardian*, 21 November 2005 (editorial), and for a defence see Lord Goodhart, *The Guardian*, 22 November 2005 (letter to the editor).
[183] Cm 7342, 2008, paras 91–98. Compare HC 306 (2006–07); HL Paper 93 (2007–08).
[184] Erskine May, p 443.
[185] See HC Deb, 17 March 2003, col 515 (WA).
[186] *Ministerial Code* (2007 edn), para 2.13.
[187] Edwards, *The Attorney General, Politics and the Public Interest*, p 226.

1997: the advice of the Law Officers was disclosed in connection with the government's liabilities for breaching community law in the Factortame litigation; 2003 and 2006: the advice of the Attorney General on the legality of the use of force against Iraq was disclosed in March 2003 in part and subsequently in May 2006 in whole.[188]

The government's review of the office of Attorney General in 2007–2008 did not lead it to recommend that the current arrangements should be changed, taking the view (in accordance with a majority of respondents to its consultation exercise) that 'the benefits, which would come from regular disclosure (transparency and accountability)', would be 'vastly outweighed by the downsides (adverse impact on the openness of communications between client and lawyer)'.[189] The government would continue to provide Parliament and the public with an explanation of why a particular course of action is lawful, acknowledging that any such explanation must be consistent with the advice received, and 'must not dishonestly represent that advice'.[190]

The machinery of justice in Scotland

The procedures relating to the machinery of justice in Scotland were transformed by the Scotland Act 1998. The Scottish Parliament now has responsibility for such matters, and within government they are currently administered by the Cabinet secretary and justice minister. As such, he deals with a range of issues, including criminal law and procedure; police, prisons and sentencing policy; legal aid, the legal profession; the courts and law reform; victim support; and civil law, as well as miscellaneous issues such as human rights, liquor licensing and charity law. A major innovation has seen changes to the Scottish Courts Service, previously an executive agency of the Justice department. Now a statutory body with the same name, the Service is said to be part of the Scottish Administration but not part of the Scottish government. As such, it continues to be responsible for providing and maintaining the court houses, for ensuring the supply of staff and other services for the courts, and for supporting the judges, including sheriffs.[191] The new statutory body – which has a duty to advise ministers – consists of both judicial members (including the most senior Scottish judges) and non-judicial members (who are appointed by the Lord President of the Court of Session). MPs, MEPs and MSPs are disqualified from membership.

The Law Officers for Scotland are the Lord Advocate and the Solicitor General for Scotland. They represent the Crown's interests before the Scottish courts, advise the Scottish Executive on legal matters, and control public prosecutions in Scotland. Before devolution both the Lord Advocate and the Solicitor General were ministers in the United Kingdom government and as such the Lord Advocate at least would normally be a member of the Westminster Parliament (if necessary by means of a peerage).[192] Under the Scotland Act 1998, however, the Scottish Law Officers are now members of the Scottish Executive and as such are appointed and may be removed by the Queen on the recommendation of the First Minister, whose recommendation must have the prior agreement of the Scottish Parliament.[193] The Lord Advocate at the time of writing is not a member of the Scottish Parliament. The Scotland Act 1998 created a new position in the United Kingdom government to fill some of the space left by the transfer of the Lord Advocate and the Solicitor General for Scotland. The function of the Advocate General for Scotland is to advise the United Kingdom government on questions of Scots law. There are no statutory qualifications for appointment to the office and although the first holder of the office

---

[188] *HM Treasury* v *Information Commissioner* [2009] EWHC 1811 (Admin), at para [9].

[189] Cm 7342, 2008, para 66.

[190] Ibid, para 68.

[191] Judiciary and Courts (Scotland) Act 2008, s 61.

[192] For difficulties of the first Labour government, see J P Casey (1975) 26 NILQ 18.

[193] Scotland Act 1998, s 48. On the Lord Advocate's obligations and the Human Rights Act, see *Montgomery* v *HM Advocate* 2001 SC (PC) 1.

was a Member of Parliament this is not required by law.[194] Scottish Law Officers often become judges, and in *Davidson v Scottish Ministers (No 2)*[195] it was held that a Court of Session judge could not sit in a case which raised matters in which he had previously been engaged in a ministerial capacity.

F. Prosecution of offenders and miscarriages of justice

In practice, the great majority of criminal prosecutions are initiated by the police; others are instituted by government departments (for example, HM Revenue and Customs for evasion of tax) or local authorities (for example, for breach of by-laws). The position regarding criminal prosecutions in England and Wales was overhauled by the Prosecution of Offences Act 1985, which introduced the Crown Prosecution Service.[196] The philosophy of the Act was 'to separate the functions of the investigation of crime, that being the responsibility of the police, and the prosecution of offences, that being the responsibility of a single national prosecution service'.[197] It has been emphasised that prosecution is a quasi-judicial act which requires 'the evaluation of the strength of the evidence and also a judgment about whether an investigation and/or prosecution is needed in the public interest'.[198] Prosecutors are thus expected to take decisions in 'a fair and impartial way, acting at all times in accordance with the highest ethical standards and in the best interests of justice'.[199] In principle, private persons may institute prosecutions in English law for any criminal offence unless by statute this has been excluded,[200] a potentially important safeguard against abuse on the part of the prosecuting authorities. The position has traditionally been very different in Scotland where prosecutions are under the control of the Lord Advocate and where private prosecutions are extremely rare.[201]

The Crown Prosecution Service

The Crown Prosecution Service, 'an autonomous and independent agency' though 'not a body corporate but a collection of individuals with statutory functions to perform',[202] is under the central direction of the Director of Public Prosecutions, an office created in 1879. A barrister or solicitor of not fewer than ten years' standing, the DPP is appointed by the Attorney General to work under his or her general supervision. Apart from the DPP, other key personnel in the Crown Prosecution Service are the Chief Crown Prosecutors (appointed by the DPP to supervise the work of the CPS in geographical areas), and Crown Prosecutors (barristers or solicitors who conduct proceedings under the direction of the DPP).[203] The CPS reviews cases submitted by the police for prosecution and conducts prosecutions on behalf of the Crown. The Service also institutes proceedings in difficult or important cases and gives advice to the police on all matters relating to criminal offences. Although the CPS is under a duty to take over all legal proceedings instituted by the police, it is not required to but may take over proceedings begun by others (such

---

[194] See generally Convery, pp 301–3; and Scotland Act 1998, s 87.

[195] 2002 SLT 1231.

[196] See Report of Royal Commission on Criminal Procedure, Cmnd 8092, 1981, part II.

[197] *Elguzouli-Daf* v *Metropolitan Police Commissioner* [1995] QB 335, at p 346.

[198] Protocol between the Attorney General and the Prosecuting Departments (2010), para 4.1.

[199] Ibid.

[200] For the procedural rights of a private prosecutor, see *R v George Maxwell (Developments) Ltd* [1980] 2 All ER 99; *R v DPP, ex p Hallas* (1988) 87 Cr App Rep 340.

[201] See Renton and Brown, *Criminal Procedure in Scotland*, paras 3.09–3.15.

[202] *Elguzouli-Daf*, above, at pp 346, 351.

[203] Perhaps surprisingly, the dismissal of a Crown Prosecutor from his or her employment is not normally subject to judicial review: *R v Crown Prosecution Service, ex p Hogg*, The Times, 14 April 1994.

as private prosecutions). Having taken over such proceedings the CPS may discontinue them if the evidence is insufficient, if the proceedings would be contrary to the public interest, to avoid duplication, or for any other good reason.[204] If it is too late to discontinue, the prosecutor may offer no evidence, so that an acquittal automatically follows. The Attorney General has a separate prerogative power to stop a prosecution on indictment by issuing a nolle prosequi. This power is rarely used today,[205] and the government has proposed that it should be abolished.[206]

The Prosecution of Offences Act 1985 requires the DPP to issue a Code for Crown Prosecutors,[207] an initiative acknowledged judicially as being important to ensure consistency in prosecuting decisions.[208] In setting out the principles governing prosecutions, the Code for Crown Prosecutors makes it clear that there is no duty to bring criminal proceedings against a person suspected of having committed an offence.[209] The general rule is that proceedings will be brought only when (*a*) there is enough evidence to provide a realistic prospect of conviction, and (*b*) it is in the public interest to prosecute; the Code gives guidance on the factors to be weighed in making this judgment.[210] As a document issued under statutory authority, the Code has been said by the House of Lords to constitute 'law' for the purposes of the ECHR, which means that it must meet Convention standards of accessibility and forseeability. Although the Code appears generally to meet these standards, it was held in one case attracting great media interest to have given insufficient information about prosecution decisions in the case of assisted suicide. As a result, the DPP was instructed by the House of Lords to issue a policy to identify the facts and circumstances he would take into account in deciding whether to consent to a prosecution for assisting a suicide.[211] While there is no duty to prosecute in every case, equally the DPP does not have the power to grant an immunity from prosecution: 'The power to dispense with and suspend laws and the execution of laws without the consent of Parliament was denied to the Crown and its servants by the Bill of Rights 1688.'[212] A decision not to prosecute is subject to judicial review,[213] although the power is 'sparingly exercised'.[214]

The role of the Attorney General in prosecutions

What opportunities are there for political considerations to be brought to bear in the prosecution of offenders? The question arises because (i) prosecution policy generally is under the superintendence of a government minister (the Attorney General) and therefore liable in principle to interference; (ii) some prosecution decisions require the consent of the Attorney General, for example under the Official Secrets Act 1911, the Theatres Act 1968, and the Public Order Act

---

[204] See *R v DPP, ex p Duckenfield* [2000] 1 WLR 55.

[205] For examples of its use in relation to customs prosecutions (where the Attorney General had no duty of superintendence), see HC 115 (1995–6) (Scott Report), para C 3.10.

[206] Cm 7342, 2008, paras 93–94.

[207] www.cps.gov.uk/code. The DPP may also have the power to make a public statement on his or her prosecuting policy other than in the Code for Crown Prosecutors: *R (Pretty) v DPP* [2001] UKHL 61; [2002] 1 AC 800, at para 39; *R (Purdy) v DPP* [2009] UKHL 45, at para 54. The Lord Advocate exercises such a power in Scotland: *Pretty*, above, esp Lord Hope at paras 79–82.

[208] *Purdy*, above.

[209] As explained by Sir Hartley Shawcross QC when Attorney General: 'It has never been the rule in this country – I hope it never will be – that suspected criminal offences must automatically be the subject of prosecution' (HC Deb, 29 January 1951, col 681). See *Smedleys Ltd v Breed* [1974] AC 839.

[210] Code for Crown Prosecutors (2010 edn), paras 4.16–4.17.

[211] *R (Purdy) v DPP*, above.

[212] *R (Pretty) v DPP*, above, at para 39 (Lord Bingham).

[213] *R v DPP, ex p C* [1995] 1 Cr App R 136. But the decision to prosecute is not, 'absent dishonesty, mala fides or an exceptional circumstance': *R (Pretty) v DPP* above, at para 67, applying *R v DPP, ex p Kebeline* [2000] 2 AC 326. See also *Pretty v United Kingdom* (2002) 35 EHRR 1.

[214] *R v DPP, ex p Manning* [2001] QB 330, at p 343.

1986; and (iii) the Attorney General has the power to intervene to discontinue prosecutions. Concern about the appearance of possible opportunities for political interference is compounded by the fact that in recent years some very high profile investigations of a highly political nature have not been followed through to the stage of prosecution, these including the cash for honours affair in 2005–06 and the investigation of alleged corruption by a British company in 2007. In the first case, prosecutions under the Honours (Prevention of Abuses) Act 1925 did not require the consent of the Attorney General, and in any event the CPS had been unable to find sufficient evidence on which to base a prosecution. It would, however, have been a matter of acute embarrassment for the Attorney General if those for whom he was accountable were in a position of having to decide whether or not it was in the public interest to prosecute members or supporters of the governing political party, including the Prime Minister.[215] In the second case, an investigation by the Serious Fraud Office into allegations of corruption by a British company was brought to an end, following intervention by the Prime Minister who advised that the proceedings would damage national security, and could lead to a refusal of the Saudi government to provide sensitive information needed for counter-terrorism purposes. The investigation was discontinued, the House of Lords holding that the SFO was entitled to bring it to an end in such circumstances.[216] Although the decision was that of the Director General, the Attorney General was also actively involved.

It is perhaps unsurprising that proposals should be made from time to time to remove ministerial involvement in prosecution decisions. However, although it has been suggested that the Attorney General's consent should no longer be required for prosecutions, it has also been proposed that it should be retained for cases involving national security.[217] The current guidelines emphasise that 'it is a constitutional principle' that the Attorney General 'acts independently of government' when taking decisions about prosecutions, but that unless expressly required to do so by statute he or she should not normally be consulted about decisions which are politically sensitive (because they relate to MPs, political parties, or the conduct of elections). They also make it clear that the Attorney may exceptionally direct that a prosecution is not started or discontinued where such intervention is necessary 'for the purpose of safeguarding national security'.[218] The procedures adopted in such circumstances were fully canvassed in *R (Corner) House Research) v Director of the Serious Fraud Office*,[219] where it was pointed out that before intervening to prevent or discontinue a prosecution, the Attorney may engage in what is called a 'Shawcross exercise', so called because it is based on a statement made to the House of Commons in 1951 by the then Attorney General (Sir Hartley Shawcross).[220] The essence of the statement is that 'when deciding whether or not it is in the public interest to prosecute in a case where there is sufficient evidence to do so the Attorney General may, if he chooses, sound opinion among his ministerial colleagues, but that the ultimate decision rests with him alone and he is not to be put under pressure in the matter by his colleagues'.[221] Where the Attorney General intervenes in this way, a statement will be made to Parliament giving reasons for his or her action. It is in order for

---

[215] See CPS Decision: 'Cash for Honours' Case – Explanatory Document (2007) – http://www.cps.gov.uk/news/press_releases/146_07_document. The Attorney had previously intervened under the Contempt of Court Act 1981 to restrain the publication of evidence relating to the case that had been leaked to the BBC: *Attorney-General v BBC* [2007] EWCA Civ 280.

[216] See *R (Corner House Research) v Director of the Serious Fraud Office* [2008] UKHL 60, [2009] 1 AC 756.

[217] Cm 7342 (2008), paras 85–89.

[218] Protocol between the Attorney General and the Prosecuting Departments (2010), para 4(b)1.

[219] Above, note 216.

[220] HC Deb, 29 January 1951, col 681. See *R (Corner) House Research) v Director of the Serious Fraud Office*, above, para 6.

[221] *Corner House*, ibid, para 6.

questions to be asked in Parliament about particular decisions made by the Attorney General: how much information the Attorney General gives in reply is a matter for his or her own discretion.[222]

Accountability of the Crown Prosecution Service

The creation of the Crown Prosecution Service in 1988 brought into prominence both the scope for central influence over the criminal justice system, which had previously been exercised without publicity, and the question of accountability for the abuse of power by public prosecutors. It has been acknowledged judicially that 'by convention the Attorney General is answerable to Parliament for general prosecution policy and for specific cases where the Attorney General and the Director of Public Prosecutions intervenes'.[223] But because both the Attorney and the DPP should be free from extraneous political interference in their work, there is inevitably a limit to what Parliament can do,[224] and it may not, for example, give directions to the Law Officers about the conduct of particular cases. Nevertheless, parliamentary accountability is not to be underestimated: it was an alleged political interference in a prosecution decision in 1924 that led to the defeat of the first Labour government on an opposition vote of no confidence.[225] In brief, the Attorney General, Sir Patrick Hastings, who was experienced in advocacy but not in ministerial work, authorised the prosecution of J R Campbell, acting editor of the *Workers' Weekly*, for having published an article which apparently sought to seduce members of the armed forces from their allegiance to the Crown. A few days later, the prosecution was withdrawn in circumstances suggesting that political pressure had been brought to bear on the Attorney General. The true facts are not easy to establish, but the Cabinet appears thereafter to have courted further controversy by requiring the Attorney to seek its prior approval before initiating prosecutions of a political character, a requirement that was of doubtful constitutional propriety.

Apart from parliamentary accountability, there are other ways of holding the prosecuting authorities to account. For example, the role of the Attorney General in the Matrix Churchill affair in the 1990s was closely reviewed and sharply criticised by Sir Richard Scott's inquiry into the export of arms for Iraq. Sir Richard found in his report that the decision to prosecute three executives of the company was taken by the Commissioners of Customs and Excise (now HM Revenue and Customs) following the advice of Treasury counsel. In this decision the Attorney General was not consulted and indeed he was not necessarily or usually kept informed of important Customs prosecutions, having no duty of superintendence of such prosecutions, although he did have 'an overall purview of prosecutions brought by the Crown by any authority'. His position was called into question nevertheless, as a result of his conduct in relation to public interest immunity (PII) certificates dealing with the development of government policies over exports to Iraq, the granting of export licences to Matrix Churchill and other companies, and certain security operations. Although a number of ministers had signed such certificates, the President of the Board of Trade (Mr Heseltine) refused to do so, on the ground that the interests of justice required the disclosure of many of the documents in question. Yet although he had not read them, the Attorney General informed Mr Heseltine that he was under a duty to sign the certificates (as a result of the case law),[226] but that his reservations could be put to the judge. In the event Mr Heseltine's reservations were not even disclosed to the prosecution legal team,

---

[222] Cf Edwards, *Law Officers of the Crown*, p 261.

[223] *Elguzouli-Daf v Metropolitan Police Commissioner* [1995] QB 335, at p 346.

[224] 'Parliament can usually only call the Attorney General to account after a prosecution has run its course' (ibid).

[225] Edwards, *Law Officers of the Crown*, chs 10 and 11; Edwards, *The Attorney General, Politics and the Public Interest*, pp 310–17; F H Newark (1969) 20 NILQ 19; Ewing and Gearty, *The Struggle for Civil Liberties*, ch 3. For the censure debate, see HC Deb, 8 October 1924, col 581.

[226] *Makanjuola v Metropolitan Police Commissioner* [1992] 3 All ER 617. On the law of public interest immunity, see ch 32 C and especially *R v Chief Constable of the West Midlands Police, ex p Wiley* [1995] 1 AC 274, where the House of Lords overruled *Makanjuola*. Compare HC 115 (1995–6) (Scott Report), para G 59.

despite the fact that Mr Heseltine's position was well known in government, an omission which drew a strong rebuke from Sir Richard Scott. Sir Richard also repudiated the belief of the Attorney General that he was personally, as opposed to constitutionally, blameless for the inadequacy of the instructions sent to prosecuting counsel, in relation particularly to the position of Mr Heseltine.[227]

Miscarriages of justice

One of the most regrettable features of the criminal justice system in the 1970s and 1980s was the number of miscarriages of justice, particularly the number of people who were wrongly convicted for offences which they did not commit.[228] Some of these cases arose out of terrorist incidents, most notably the pub bombings at Guildford and Birmingham in 1974,[229] although there were many other cases unrelated to acts of terrorism, including that of the so-called 'Bridgewater Three'.[230] A number of different factors were responsible for these events, not the least significant of which were the serious shortcomings of the police and the prosecuting authorities.[231] The matter was reviewed by the Royal Commission on Criminal Justice appointed in 1991, with terms of reference which included 'whether changes were needed in the arrangements for considering and investigating allegations of miscarriages of justice when appeal rights have been exhausted'.[232] The procedures then in force were governed by the Criminal Appeal Act 1968, s 17, which authorised a reference to the Court of Appeal by the Home Secretary. Although this provided 'the mechanism for unlocking the door back to the criminal justice system',[233] the royal commission pointed out that the Home Secretary and the civil servants advising him operated within 'strict self-imposed limits', which rested 'both upon constitutional considerations and upon the approach of the Court of Appeal itself to its own powers'. The Home Secretary would not refer cases to the Court of Appeal merely to enable it to reconsider matters that it had already considered, but would 'normally only refer a conviction if there is new evidence or some other consideration of substance which was not before the trial court'. The Home Office adopted this approach 'not only because they have thought that it would be wrong for ministers to suggest to the Court of Appeal that a different decision should have been reached by the courts on the same facts', but also because there was 'no purpose' in referring a case where there was 'no real possibility of the Court of Appeal taking a different view than it did on the original appeal because of the lack of fresh evidence or some other new consideration of substance'.[234]

These arrangements were criticised both by Sir John May (who had been asked to inquire into the cases of the Guildford Four and the Maguire Seven)[235] and by the Royal Commission on Criminal Justice,[236] and a new procedure was proposed for the referral of cases. This would require the creation of a new body, independent of both the government and the courts, for

---

[227] See further A W Bradley [1996] PL 373.

[228] For a wider definition of the term, see HC 419 (1993–4). For a detailed examination of miscarriages of justice, see Nobles and Schiff, *Understanding Miscarriages of Justice*. See also Whitty et al., *Civil Liberties Law*, ch 3.

[229] See *R v Richardson*, The Times, 20 October 1989; *R v McIlkenny* [1992] 2 All ER 417; *R v Maguire* [1992] QB 936. And note *R v Ward* [1993] 1 WLR 619.

[230] See *The Times*, 21–22 February 1997.

[231] See on specific aspects, I H Dennis [1993] PL 291.

[232] Cm 2263, 1993.

[233] *R v Home Secretary, ex p Hickey (No 2)* [1995] 1 All ER 490, at p 494.

[234] Cm 2263, 1993, pp 181–2. The propriety of this approach was called into question in *R v Home Secretary, ex p Hickey (No 2)* [1995] 1 All ER 490 where it was suggested that the Secretary of State should ask another question: could the new material reasonably cause the Court of Appeal to regard the verdict as unsafe? If it could, the matter should then have been referred without more ado.

[235] HC 296 (1992), pp 93–4.

[236] Cm 2263, 1993, pp 181–2.

dealing with allegations that a miscarriage of justice had occurred, reflecting concern that the Home Secretary should not be 'directly responsible for the consideration and investigation of alleged miscarriages of justice as well as being responsible for law and order and for the police'.[237] The Criminal Appeal Act 1995 addresses the incompatibility of these procedures 'with the constitutional separation of powers as between the courts and the executive',[238] and makes provision for the appointment by the Queen (on the advice of the Prime Minister) of a Criminal Cases Review Commission (s 9). The Commission is empowered to refer to the Court of Appeal (following the conviction of an offence on indictment) any conviction or sentence where it considers that 'there is a real possibility that the conviction, verdict, finding or sentence would not be upheld were the reference to be made' (s 13): this is a 'judgment entrusted to the Commission and to no one else'.[239] The Act also introduces for the first time a power (on the part of the Commission) to refer convictions or sentences arising from cases tried summarily (s 11), in this case to the Crown Court, subject to the same conditions as apply in the case of references to the Court of Appeal following a conviction on indictment. The Commission has wide powers to obtain documents and to appoint investigating officers to carry out inquiries in relation to a case under review, although these will generally be carried out by the police rather than by the Commission's own officers (ss 17–20).[240]

The prerogative of pardon

The royal prerogative of pardon is exercised by the Crown on the advice of the Home Secretary in cases from England and Wales and, in cases from Scotland, by the Scottish ministers. Each minister acts on his or her individual responsibility in giving his or her advice to the Crown. A royal pardon could in law be used as a bar to criminal prosecution being brought (as was the effect of the blanket pardon given by President Ford to ex-President Nixon in 1974). But in British practice, a pardon is granted only after conviction when there is some special reason why a sentence should not be carried out or why the effects of a conviction should be expunged. Pardons under the prerogative are of three kinds: (*a*) an absolute or free pardon, which sets aside the sentence but not the conviction;[241] (*b*) a conditional pardon, which substitutes one form of punishment for another (for example, the substitution of life imprisonment for the death penalty, which occurred when the prerogative of mercy was exercised in the days of capital punishment);[242] and (*c*) a remission, which reduces the amount of a sentence without changing its character, and has been used to enable a convicted spy to be exchanged for a British subject imprisoned abroad, or to reward prisoners who have given exceptional assistance to prison staff, the police or the prosecuting authorities. It is to be noted, however, that governments may intervene by means other than a pardon to free a prisoner who may be the victim of an injustice.[243]

---

[237] Ibid, p 182.

[238] Ibid. And see HC Deb, 6 March 1995, col 32.

[239] *R v Criminal Cases Review Commission, ex p Pearson* [1999] 3 All ER 498, at p 505. For concerns that the Commission may be applying the test too strictly, see HC 106 (1998–9), para 30. For clarification of the powers of the Commission, see Criminal Cases Review (Insanity) Act 1999.

[240] Leading cases include *R v Bentley* [2001] 1 Cr App R 307; *R v Johnson* [2001] 1 Cr App R 408; and *R v Kansal* [2001] UKHL 62; [2002] 2 AC 69. For an inside account of the work of the Commission, see G Zellick (2005) *Amicus Curiae*, May/June, p 2; and [2005] Crim LR 937. For an account of the work of its Scottish counterpart, see P Duff (2009) 72 MLR 693. See also R Nobles and D Schiff (2008) 71 MLR 464.

[241] *R v Foster* [1985] QB 115.

[242] P Brett (1957) 20 MLR 131.

[243] The convicted Lockerbie bomber Abdel Baset al-Megrahi (who many believed to be the victim of a miscarriage of justice) was released on licence in 2009 by the Justice Secretary in the Scottish government on 'compassionate' grounds under the Prisoners and Criminal Proceedings (Scotland) Act 1993, s 3, in controversial circumstances. See http://www.scotland.gov.uk/News/This-Week/Speeches/Safer-and-stronger/lockerbiedecision.

The prerogative power of pardon may not be used to vary the judgment of the court in matters of civil dispute between citizens. Under the Act of Settlement 1700, a pardon may not be pleaded in bar of an impeachment by the Commons, nor under the Habeas Corpus Act 1679 may the unlawful committal of any person to prison outside the realm be pardoned. The power has most recently been used, however, in the case of an individual who was returned to this country to serve his sentence following a conviction in Bulgaria which the Home Secretary believed to have been unsafe.[244] Extensive use of the power of pardon could come close to being an attempt to exercise the royal power to dispense with laws which was declared illegal in the Bill of Rights 1689. The Home Secretary is answerable to Parliament for the advice which he or she gives to the Queen. Before the abolition of the death penalty, questions could not be raised in the House of Commons regarding a case while it was still pending.[245] The question arises whether the power of pardon is now needed following the reforms introduced by the Criminal Appeal Act 1995. In the view of the government, however, it is thought still to be necessary but only for 'the very exceptional case' where there is new evidence which for some reason is inadmissible.[246] In these cases the Home Secretary may refer to the Criminal Cases Review Commission 'any matter which arises in the consideration of whether to recommend the exercise of Her Majesty's prerogative of mercy in relation to the conviction' (s 16). The Commission is required to give reasons where it is of the opinion that the minister should recommend the exercise of the prerogative, but strangely is not required to do so where it makes no such recommendation, even though it is in the latter type of case that the need for judicial review is likely to be greater.[247]

---

[244] For background, see *R (Shields) v Justice Secretary* [2008] EWHC 3102 (Admin).
[245] G Marshall [1961] PL 8.
[246] HC Deb, 6 March 1995, col 26.
[247] See *R v Home Secretary, ex p Bentley* [1994] QB 349. See, further, ch 12 E.

Part III

THE CITIZEN AND THE STATE

CHAPTER 19

The nature and protection of human rights

This chapter is concerned with the protection of human rights. The first task is to determine what is meant by human rights: there is a great deal of terminological inconsistency in this area, with a number of terms frequently used – human rights, civil liberties, fundamental rights – often referring to the same thing. For our purposes, human rights take two forms. On the one hand, there are the classical civil and political rights – the right to liberty of the person, the right to form political parties and to participate in elections, and the rights to freedom of conscience, religion and expression. On the other hand, there are social and economic rights – the right to employment, health care, housing and income maintenance during periods of ill health, unemployment or old age. Human rights lawyers have traditionally confined their concerns to the former category, to the exclusion of the latter even though social and economic security is indispensable to effective participation in the civil and political life of the community.

Yet although there are several international treaties promoting social and economic security,[1] the boldness of their aspirations is generally matched only by the difficulties in their enforcement, and few democracies in the common law tradition take them seriously as fundamental rights. The position is different with regard to so-called civil and political rights. One international treaty in particular – the European Convention on Human Rights[2] – has had a significant influence on British law and practice, with the British government having been held in violation of its terms on numerous occasions and having been required more than once to introduce legislation to give effect to specific rulings of the European Court of Human Rights.[3] Many countries give constitutional protection to civil and political rights, often in a Bill of Rights with which in some cases both executive and legislative measures must comply, failing which they may be struck down by the courts. Legal protection of human rights in Britain is now to be found in the Human Rights Act 1998, which enables the Convention rights to be enforced in the British courts.[4]

A. The classical approach

The traditional British approach to the protection of civil liberties and human rights has been greatly influenced by Dicey.[5] For him there was no need for any statement of fundamental principles operating as a kind of higher law, because political freedom was adequately protected by the common law and by an independent Parliament acting as a watchdog against any excess of

---

[1] These include the Conventions of the International Labour Organization, a United Nations agency based in Geneva, set up to promote the interests of working people. Also important is the Council of Europe's Social Charter of 1961 and the Revised Social Charter of 1996, while the EC Charter of the Fundamental Social Rights of Workers of 1989 has contributed to the development of social law. There is also the EU Charter of Fundamental Rights, adopted at Nice in December 2000. On the Council of Europe's Social Charter, see Harris and Darcy, *The European Social Charter*. On the EC Charter, see Bercusson, *European Labour Law*, and on the EU Charter, see chapter 8 B above.

[2] Cmd 8969, 1953.

[3] See A W Bradley, 'The United Kingdom before the Strasbourg Court 1975–1990', in Finnie, Himsworth and Walker (eds), *Edinburgh Essays in Public Law*.

[4] See section B.

[5] Dicey, *The Law of the Constitution*. And see ch 6.

zeal by the executive.[6] Under the common law, a wide measure of individual liberty was guaranteed by the principle that citizens are free to do as they like unless expressly prohibited by law. So people already enjoy the freedom of religion, the freedom of expression and the freedom of assembly, and may be restrained from exercising these freedoms only if there are clear common law or statutory restrictions. This approach is illustrated by a number of classical decisions, the first of which is *Entick v Carrington*[7] where the Secretary of State issued a warrant to search the premises of John Entick and to seize any seditious literature. When the legality of the conduct was challenged, the minister claimed that the existence and exercise of such a power were necessary in the interests of the state. But the court upheld the challenge on the ground that there was no authority in the common law or in statute for warrants to be issued in this way. A second example is *Beatty v Gillbanks*,[8] where members of the Salvation Army in Weston-super-Mare were forbidden to march on Sundays because their presence attracted a large hostile crowd of people, thereby causing a breach of the peace. When the Salvationists ignored the order not to assemble, they were bound over to keep the peace for having committed the crime of unlawful assembly. The order binding them over was set aside on appeal because they had done nothing wrong. In the view of the court, they could not be prohibited from assembling merely because their lawful conduct might induce others to act unlawfully.

> A more recent example of liberty being protected by the common law is *A v Home Secretary (No 2)*[9] where the issue was whether evidence obtained by torture could be admitted by the Special Immigration Appeal Commission. In a case said by Lord Hoffmann to be of 'great importance' to the 'reputation of English law', the House of Lords held unanimously that such evidence could not be admitted, with Lord Bingham saying that common law principles 'compel the exclusion of third party torture evidence as unreliable, unfair, offensive to ordinary standards of humanity and decency and incompatible with the principles which should animate a tribunal seeking to administer justice'. However, the House divided on the standard of proof required before such evidence should be excluded. The majority took the view that evidence should not be admitted if it is concluded on a balance of probabilities that it was obtained by torture. The minority – in contrast – would have gone further and excluded any evidence unless satisfied that there was no real risk that it had been obtained by torture. According to Lord Nicholls, the approach of the majority 'would place on the detainee a burden of proof which, for reasons beyond his control, he can seldom discharge. In practice that would largely nullify the principle, vigorously supported on all sides, that courts will not admit evidence procured by torture.' It was also accepted as lawful for the police to act on a tip-off from an official foreign source to take steps to prevent a terrorist incident, even though the tip-off might be based on evidence obtained by torture.

Although there are thus important illustrations of the principle, it is open to question whether this approach is an adequate basis for the protection of liberty. In the first place, the common law rule that people are free to do anything which is not prohibited by law applied (it would seem) equally to the government. As a result, the government could violate individual freedom even though it was not formally empowered to do so, on the ground that it was doing nothing which was prohibited by law. So in *Malone v Metropolitan Police Commissioner*[10] the practice of telephone tapping was exposed as being done by the executive without any clear lawful authority. But when Mr Malone sought a declaration that the tapping of his telephone was unlawful, he failed because he could not point to any legal right of his which it was the duty of the government not to invade. There was no violation of his property rights, no breach of confidence and no invasion of any

---

[6] For a vivid expression of this view, see *Wheeler v Leicester City Council* [1985] AC 1054, at 1065 (Browne-Wilkinson LJ). For a powerful critique, see Craig, *Public Law and Democracy*.

[7] (1765) 19 St Tr 1030; ch 6.

[8] (1882) 9 QBD 308.

[9] [2005] UKHL 71; [2006] 1 All ER 575.

[10] [1979] Ch 344.

right to privacy recognised by the law at the time. A second difficulty with the British approach is that liberty is particularly vulnerable to erosion. The common law merely recognises that people are free to do anything which is not unlawful, but is powerless to prevent new restrictions from being enacted by the legislature. Paradoxically, many restrictions on liberty are imposed by the common law, for it is sometimes convenient for the executive to avoid seeking new powers from Parliament.[11] In this way the authorities may seek a decision of the courts which will develop the law restrictively and create a precedent of general application. As a source of restraint of individual liberty, rules of this kind can be as effective as legislation by Parliament. Thus in *Moss v McLachlan*[12] the Divisional Court created, from the common law powers of the police to control and regulate public assemblies, an extended right to prevent people from assembling in the first place. And in the *Spycatcher* and other cases, it was held that injunctions could be granted to the Attorney General to restrain the publication of confidential government secrets.[13]

B. European Convention on Human Rights[14]

The protection of human rights, which is primarily a matter for the state in whose territory the rights may be enjoyed, cannot today be confined within national boundaries. The European Convention on Human Rights was signed at Rome in 1950, was ratified by the United Kingdom in 1951, and came into force among those states which had ratified it in 1953. The Convention is a treaty under international law and its authority derives solely from the consent of those states who have become parties to it. Now one of a number of human rights treaties, which include the International Covenant on Civil and Political Rights of 1966,[15] the making of the ECHR was a direct result of the movement for cooperation in Western Europe which in 1949 created the Council of Europe. Inspiration for the Convention came from the wide principles declared in the United Nations Universal Declaration of Human Rights in 1948. The Convention declares certain human rights which are or should be protected by law in each state. It also provides political and judicial procedures by which alleged infringements of these rights may be examined at an international level. In particular, the acts of public authorities may be challenged even though they are in accordance with national law. The Convention thus provides a constraint on the legislative authority of national parliaments, including that at Westminster.[16]

The scope of the Convention

The Convention does not cover the whole field of human rights. It omits economic and social rights and is confined to certain basic rights and liberties which the framers of the Convention considered would be generally accepted in the liberal democracies of Western Europe. These rights and liberties include:

---

[11] Cf Lord Browne-Wilkinson [1992] PL 397, and Sir J Laws [1993] PL 59.

[12] [1985] IRLR 76, and now *Austin v Metropolitan Police Commissioner* [2009] UKHL 5; [2009] 1 AC 564. See ch 24 below.

[13] *A-G v Guardian Newspapers Ltd* [1987] 1 WLR 1248; [1990] 1 AC 109.

[14] The extensive literature includes Amos, *Human Rights Law*; Harris, O'Boyle and Warbrick, *Law of the European Convention on Human Rights*; Jacobs and White, *The European Convention on Human Rights*; Janis, Kay and Bradley, *European Human Rights Law: Text and Materials*; Mowbray, *Cases and Materials on the European Convention on Human Rights*. For valuable comparative studies of the operation of the Convention in a number of jurisdictions, see Blackburn and Polakiewicz (eds), *Fundamental Rights in Europe*; and Gearty (ed.), *European Civil Liberties*. Also important is Simpson, *Human Rights and the End of Empire*.

[15] On the ICCPR, see D Fottrell [2002] PL 485.

[16] Ch 4 C.

the right to life (art 2);

freedom from torture, or inhuman or degrading treatment or punishment (art 3);

freedom from slavery or forced labour (art 4);

the right to liberty and security of the person (art 5), including the right of one who is arrested to be informed promptly of the reasons for his or her arrest, and of any charge against him or her;

the right to a fair trial by an impartial tribunal of a person's civil rights and obligations and of criminal charges against him or her (art 6), including the right to be presumed innocent of a criminal charge until proved guilty, and the right to be defended by a lawyer and to have free legal assistance 'when the interests of justice so require';

the prohibition of retroactive criminal laws (art 7);

the right to respect for a person's private and family life, his or her home and correspondence (art 8);

freedom of thought, conscience and religion (art 9) and freedom of expression (art 10);

freedom of peaceful assembly and of association with others, including the right to form and join trade unions (art 11);

the right to marry and found a family (art 12).

By art 14, the rights declared in the Convention are to be enjoyed

without discrimination on any ground such as sex, race, colour, language, religion, political or other opinion, national or social origin, association with a national minority, property, birth or other status.

All persons within the jurisdiction of the member states benefit from the Convention regardless of citizenship, although a state may restrict the political activities of aliens.

Many of these rights are subject to exceptions or qualifications. Thus art 5 sets out the grounds on which a person may lawfully be deprived of his or her liberty; these include the lawful arrest of a person to prevent his or her entering the country without authority and the lawful detention 'of persons of unsound mind, alcoholics or drug addicts or vagrants' (art 5(1)(f)). So too the right to respect for private and family life under art 8 is protected from interference by a public authority

except such interference as is in accordance with the law and is necessary in a democratic society in the interests of national security, public safety or the economic well-being of the country, for the prevention of disorder or crime, for the protection of health or morals, or for the protection of the rights and freedoms of others.

Clearly, it is essential that such restrictions should not be interpreted so widely that the protected right becomes illusory. Member states may derogate from most but not all of their obligations under the Convention in time of war or other public emergency (and the United Kingdom has on occasion done so in respect of Northern Ireland and other anti-terrorist legislation), but they must inform the Secretary General of the Council of Europe of the measures taken and the reasons (art 15).[17]

The scope of the Convention was extended by the First Protocol concluded as an addendum to the Convention in 1952 and ratified by the United Kingdom. By this protocol, every person is entitled to the peaceful enjoyment of his or her possessions (art 1); the right to education is protected and states must respect the right of parents to ensure education of their children in conformity with their own religious and philosophical convictions (art 2);[18] and the right to take part

---

[17] See *Lawless v Ireland* (1961) 1 EHRR 15; *Brannigan v UK* (1993) 17 EHRR 539; *Aksoy v Turkey* (1996) 23 EHRR 553; and *Marshall v UK* (10 July 2001, Application No 41571/98). And more recently, see *A v Home Secretary* [2004] UKHL 56; [2005] 2 AC 68 (esp per Lord Bingham), and *A v United Kingdom* [2009] ECHR 301.

[18] The United Kingdom accepted the latter principle 'only so far as is compatible with provision of efficient instruction and training, and the avoidance of unreasonable public expenditure'; see *Campbell and Cosans v UK* (1982) 4 EHRR 293.

in free elections by secret ballot is declared (art 3).[19] The Fourth Protocol to the Convention, concluded in 1963, guarantees freedom of movement within a state and freedom to leave any country; it also precludes a state from expelling or refusing to admit its own nationals. This protocol has not been ratified by the United Kingdom.[20] The Sixth Protocol provides for the abolition of the death penalty, thereby qualifying the terms of art 2 of the Convention itself. Under the terms of the protocol, which is now ratified by the United Kingdom, no one is to be condemned to death or executed, with the only exception being made for times of war when the penalty could be imposed only 'in the instances laid down in the law and in accordance with its provisions'. The Seventh Protocol (not ratified by the UK) deals mainly with appeals procedures in criminal cases, although it also provides (in art 5) for 'equality of rights and responsibilities of a private law character' between spouses. Of the remaining protocols, the Eleventh and Twelfth are among the most significant. The former is dealt with below and the latter (which has not been ratified by the United Kingdom) contains a general prohibition against discrimination.[21] The Thirteenth Protocol makes further provision for the abolition of the death penalty, and has been ratified by the United Kingdom, as has the Fourteenth, also dealt with below.

Institutions and procedure

One novel feature of the Convention was the right which it gave to individuals to complain of breaches of the Convention by the states party to it. The enforcement procedure initially made use both of the Committee of Ministers of the Council of Europe (a committee of political representatives of the member states) and of two institutions created by the Convention: (*a*) the European Commission of Human Rights, which comprised individual members, elected by the Committee of Ministers but in office acting independently; and (*b*) the European Court of Human Rights, comprising judges elected by the Consultative Assembly of the Council of Europe. No two members of the Commission or the Court respectively could be citizens of the same state. The function of the Commission was to receive and inquire into alleged breaches of the Convention either (*a*) at the request of any state party to the Convention which alleged that another state had breached the Convention (known as inter-state cases); or (*b*) where a state had recognised the competence of the Commission to receive such petitions, on the receipt of a petition from an individual or a non-governmental organisation alleging a violation of rights by the state in question.

Although not all states recognised the right of individuals to petition to the Commission, very many more individual petitions came to the Commission than inter-state cases. When an individual petition was received, the Commission had first to decide whether it was admissible under the Convention. If a petition cleared the hurdle of admissibility, the Commission had then to investigate the facts fully and offer its services to the parties with a view to securing a friendly settlement of the dispute. If such a settlement was not arranged, a report on the dispute was sent by the Commission to the state or states concerned and to the Committee of Ministers. Thereafter the matter might be dealt with finally by the Committee of Ministers, deciding by a two-thirds majority, or it could be brought within three months before the European Court of Human Rights. A case could be at that time brought before the Court only where the states concerned had accepted the compulsory jurisdiction of the Court or expressly consented to the case coming to the Court. Only the Commission or a state concerned could refer a case to the Court: the individual applicant had only a limited right to do so.[22]

---

[19] See *Liberal Party* v *UK* (1982) 4 EHRR 106 (simple majority electoral system not a breach of Convention), and *Matthews* v *UK* (1998) 28 EHRR 361.

[20] For British citizenship and immigration law, see ch 20.

[21] See U Khaliq [2001] PL 457 on the Twelfth Protocol.

[22] See A R Mowbray [1991] PL 353.

New procedures for dealing with complaints were introduced by the Eleventh Protocol, which abolished the Commission and created a new full-time court. Although it has the same title as the old court which it replaced, 'it is an entirely different body with new functions, powers and composition'.[23] Under the new arrangements, the court – which has made an important contribution to the development of the Convention[24] – consists of a number of judges equal to the number of states which are party to the Convention (art 20), with a judge from each country (art 22). The judges serve for renewable periods of six years (to be changed by the Fourteenth Protocol to non-renewable periods of nine years). The main effect of the Eleventh Protocol was to enable applicants complaining of a breach of the Convention to apply directly to the Court, and for this purpose the Court operates in a number of forms, the judges sitting in committees, chambers and the Grand Chamber (art 27). Because of a massive increase in the workload of the Court as the Council of Europe has expanded, further streamlining of the Court's procedures is to be found in the Fourteenth Protocol (agreed in 2004), which was expected to come into force in 2010.[25]

Applications may continue to be made by one state against another (art 33) or by 'any person, non-governmental organisation or group of individuals claiming to be the victim of a violation' (art 34). There is still a requirement that an applicant should have exhausted all domestic remedies and have brought the complaint within six months of the final decision of the domestic authorities. The Court is required to declare inadmissible any application submitted under art 34 considered to be incompatible with the terms of the Convention, manifestly ill-founded or an abuse of the right of individual application (art 35). Under the Fourteenth Protocol, it will be possible for cases to be struck out also because the applicant has not suffered a significant disadvantage. Cases are dealt with initially by a committee of three judges who determine whether the complaint is admissible, and under the Fourteenth Protocol the committee may also dispose of the matter on the merits if the issues raised are already the subject of the well-established case law of the Court (art 28). Otherwise, the merits will be considered by a chamber of seven judges (art 29), which also has power to deal with admissibility questions in some cases. On matters of particular importance, the chamber may relinquish jurisdiction in favour of a Grand Chamber of 17 judges (art 30).[26]

Cases involving the United Kingdom

Under the original scheme of the Convention, enforcement depended essentially on a state recognising both the right of individuals to apply to Strasbourg and the compulsory jurisdiction of the Court. In 1966, the British government first made the two optional declarations for which the Convention provided[27] and these declarations were renewed at intervals.[28] One result of the changes in 1998 is that member states today have no choice in these fundamental matters and must accept the right of individuals to apply to the Court. Since 1966 a wide variety of individual petitions have been brought against the UK government and there have also been inter-state references to the Commission by the Republic of Ireland. Although individuals may now enforce Convention claims before the domestic courts,[29] a significant number of cases continue to be referred to Strasbourg from the United Kingdom. In the three years from 2002 to 2004, no fewer

---

[23] A R Mowbray [1994] PL 540 (and [1993] PL 419).
[24] For valuable accounts of the role of the Court, see C A Gearty [1993] 45 CLJ 89, and A R Mowbray [2005] 5 HRLR 57. Also important is Mowbray, *The Development of Positive Obligations under the European Convention on Human Rights by the European Court of Human Rights.*
[25] See A R Mowbray [2002] PL 252; (2004) 4 HRLR 331.
[26] See A Mowbray [2007] PL 507 for an account of the work of the Grand Chamber.
[27] For the making of the decisions involved, see A Lester [1984] PL 46 and [1998] PL 237.
[28] See HC Deb, 13 December 1995, col 647.
[29] Ch 19 C below.

than 4,287 applications were lodged, of which 179 were declared admissible.[30] In the same period the European Court of Human Rights held in 69 cases that the United Kingdom had violated at least one provision of the treaty, holding in only six cases that there had not been any violation, with a friendly settlement being reached in another 13 cases.[31] These figures are all the more remarkable when contrasted with the statistics of an earlier era. Thus in the period from 1975 to 1990, the Court decided only 30 cases involving the United Kingdom, in which at least one breach of the Convention was found in 21 cases.[32] By 2000 (when the Human Rights Act came into force), there had been only 64 decisions of the Court in which a violation of the Convention had been found against the United Kingdom.[33] In other words, the United Kingdom was found in breach of the Convention in the three years between 2002 and 2004 more often than in the 25 years between 1975 and 2000.

The British cases before the Court have spanned a wide range of subjects. In *McCann* v *United Kingdom*[34] it was held that art 2 (protecting the right to life) had been violated following the use of lethal force by members of the security forces in Gibraltar. In *Jordan* v *United Kingdom*[35] a breach of art 2 was found where there had been no effective investigation into the circumstances surrounding the death of the claimant's son, who had been killed by the police.[36] But in *Pretty* v *United Kingdom*[37] it was held that the right to life does not include the right to die, in a case where a terminally ill applicant sought an undertaking that her husband would not be prosecuted if he assisted her suicide. Questions concerning the interpretation of art 3 (protection against torture and inhuman or degrading treatment or punishment) arose in *Republic of Ireland* v *United Kingdom*[38] in relation to the interrogation of IRA suspects, in *Tyrer* v *United Kingdom*[39] in relation to the corporal punishment of juveniles in the Isle of Man, and in *Soering* v *United Kingdom*[40] in relation to the request for the extradition of a German citizen to the USA to stand trial for murder with the risk of being sentenced to capital punishment and being kept on Death Row. In *X* v *United Kingdom*[41] the Court held certain procedures for the compulsory detention of mental patients to infringe art 5, a similar conclusion being reached in *Brogan* v *United Kingdom*[42] in relation to the provisions of the Prevention of Terrorism (Temporary Provisions) Act 1984 authorising the detention of suspects for up to seven days without judicial authority. The automatic denial of bail for certain offences in the Criminal Justice and Public Order Act 1994 was found to breach art 5 in *Caballero* v *United Kingdom*.[43] Article 6 has been found to have been violated in a number of cases, including *Murray* v *United Kingdom*[44] where the applicant was denied access to a solicitor for 48 hours while in police detention. Similarly in *Benham* v *United Kingdom*[45] a complaint was upheld

---

[30] Council of Europe, *European Court of Human Rights – Survey of Activities 2002–04*. See now M Amos [2007] PL 655.

[31] Ibid.

[32] See Bradley, note 3 above.

[33] See Blackburn and Polakiewicz, note 14 above, pp 972–3.

[34] (1995) 21 EHRR 97.

[35] (2003) 37 EHRR 52.

[36] See also *McShane* v *UK* (2002) 35 EHRR 593, and *Edwards* v *UK* (2002) 35 EHRR 487.

[37] (2002) 35 EHRR 1.

[38] (1978) 2 EHRR 25.

[39] (1978) 2 EHRR 1. See also *Costello-Roberts* v *UK* (1995) 19 EHRR 112, and *A* v *UK* (1998) 27 EHRR 611 (child severely beaten by stepfather).

[40] (1989) 11 EHRR 439. See also *D* v *UK* (1997) 24 EHRR 423 (proposed removal of drug smuggler to St Kitts under the Immigration Act 1971. Applicant had AIDS and proposed removal found to be in breach of art 3).

[41] (1981) 4 EHRR 188.

[42] (1988) 11 EHRR 117; and see ch 26.

[43] (2000) 30 EHRR 643.

[44] (1996) 22 EHRR 29.

[45] (1996) 22 EHRR 293. See also *Perks* v *UK* (2000) 30 EHRR 33 (applicant imprisoned by magistrates for non-payment of the community charge, without the benefit of legal representation at her trial).

in a case brought by a person denied legal aid and imprisoned for failure to pay the community charge (poll tax) without the benefit of legal representation. Article 6 was also found to have been breached in *V v United Kingdom*[46] following the conviction of two minors (for a notorious murder of a child) after a trial conducted in the full glare of highly charged media publicity. More recently, a breach of art 6 was found to have occurred where two environmental activists were denied legal aid to defend themselves in an action for libel brought against them by a large multinational company (McDonald's) which had the benefit of an experienced team of lawyers.[47]

In *Dudgeon v United Kingdom*,[48] legislation in Northern Ireland making homosexual conduct between adult males a crime was held to infringe the individual's right to respect for his private life under art 8. The practice of telephone tapping was held to infringe art 8 in *Malone v United Kingdom*[49] and in *Halford v United Kingdom*.[50] The law of contempt of court was held to infringe freedom of expression under art 10 in *Sunday Times Ltd v United Kingdom*,[51] but the English law on obscene publications survived scrutiny in *Handyside v United Kingdom*.[52] In three other important cases it was held that art 10 had been violated by (i) restraints on the publication by newspapers (the *Observer*, *Guardian* and *Sunday Times*) of the contents of a book (*Spycatcher*) by a retired security service officer;[53] (ii) a requirement imposed by a court that a journalist should disclose the confidential sources of an article he had written, publication of which had been restrained by the courts;[54] and (iii) the award of £1.5m damages to Lord Aldington for defamatory remarks contained in a pamphlet written by a historian.[55] Cases under art 10 have also called into question restrictions in electoral law[56] and on the freedom of peaceful protest.[57] In *Young, James and Webster v United Kingdom*[58] three former employees of British Railways, dismissed for refusing to join a trade union, established that their freedom of association had been infringed as a result of legislation on the closed shop initiated by a Labour government in 1974 and 1976: they were awarded substantial compensation.[59] Conversely, in *Wilson v United Kingdom*[60] a former employee of the *Daily Mail* successfully claimed that art 11 had been breached in a case where he suffered discrimination because he refused to agree to new working practices whereby pay would be determined by individual rather than collective negotiation. In *Air Canada v United Kingdom* it was held that there was no breach of art 1 of the First Protocol where an aeroplane was seized by customs officers after it was found to be carrying cannabis.[61] And in *Nerva v United Kingdom*[62] it was held that there was no breach of art 1 of the First Protocol in circumstances where an employer was entitled to treat as wages the tips left by customers to waiters.

These decisions have often led to changes in the law intended to prevent future infringements of the Convention. Such legislative changes include the Contempt of Court Act 1981 (regulating

---

[46] (2000) 30 EHRR 121.

[47] *Steel and Morris v UK* (2005) 41 EHRR 403. Cf *McVicar v UK* (2002) 35 EHRR 566.

[48] (1981) 4 EHRR 149. See also *Smith v UK* (2000) 29 EHRR 493 (discharge of military personnel because they were homosexual found to be a breach of art 8). But cf *Laskey v UK* (1997) 24 EHRR 39 (conviction of homosexual men for sado-masochistic practices conducted in private not a breach of art 8).

[49] (1984) 7 EHRR 14.

[50] (1997) 24 EHRR 523.

[51] (1979) 2 EHRR 245; and see ch 18 D.

[52] (1976) 1 EHRR 737. See also *Wingrove v UK* (1996) 24 EHRR 1.

[53] (1991) 14 EHRR 153, 229.

[54] *Goodwin v UK* (1996) 22 EHRR 123.

[55] *Tolstoy Miloslavsky v UK* (1995) 20 EHRR 442.

[56] *Bowman v UK* (1998) 28 EHRR 1; C Gearty (2000) 51 NILQ 381.

[57] *Steel v UK* (1999) 28 EHRR 603; and *Hashman v UK* (1999) 30 EHRR 241.

[58] (1981) 4 EHRR 38.

[59] See K D Ewing and W M Rees (1983) 12 ILJ 148.

[60] (2002) 35 EHRR 523 (K D Ewing (2003) 32 ILJ 1).

[61] (1995) 20 EHRR 150.

[62] (2003) 36 EHRR 31.

the circumstances in which pre-trial publicity is unlawful), the Interception of Communications Act 1985 and the Regulation of Investigatory Powers Act 2000 (regulating the circumstances in which telephone tapping may take place and giving individuals a right of redress against improper use) and the Homosexual Offences (Northern Ireland) Order 1982 (changing the law on homosexual conduct in Northern Ireland). Other significant consequences of Court decisions include the introduction of amendments to the procedures for detention and release of mental patients following the decision in *X v United Kingdom*,[63] the issuing of new prison rules and changing practices in prisons following decisions on prisoners' correspondence, and the amending of employment legislation to protect employees from anti-union discrimination by employers. In at least two cases, however, the government has been unwilling to give effect to decisions of the European Court and has taken steps to avoid doing so. In *Abdulaziz v United Kingdom*[64] the Court held that British immigration rules discriminated against women permanently settled in the United Kingdom because their husbands and fiancés were not entitled to enter, whereas the wives and fiancées of men settled here were entitled to enter. The government responded to this decision by amending the Immigration Rules to remove the entitlement of wives and fiancées to enter, thereby removing the source of discrimination. More recently, in *Brogan v United Kingdom*[65] the government responded to the Court's decision, that the detention powers of the Prevention of Terrorism (Temporary Provisions) Act 1984 violated art 5, by declaring that the power was necessary on security grounds and by depositing at Strasbourg a limited derogation from the Convention to the extent that the legislation violated art 5. Government resistance to Strasbourg rulings is emerging as a more persistent problem, with the Court issuing a number of high profile decisions against the government in recent years. There is a marked phenomenon of government delay in implementing decisions, in governments seeking to have Chamber decisions reconsidered by the Grand Chamber, and of minimalist implementation by legislation.[66]

The continuing importance of the Strasbourg process

As already pointed out, the Human Rights Act means that it is now possible to enforce Convention rights in the domestic courts without having to travel to Strasbourg. It is thus possible that many of the cases that went to the Strasbourg court in the past would now be resolved at 'home'. It is not the case, however, that the Strasbourg process has been rendered redundant by the Human Rights Act. A recent study has revealed that there has been a significant surge in the number of complaints to Strasbourg since the Human Rights Act came into force,[67] though because of the long delays in the Strasbourg system it may be some time before a confident judgment can be made about the true extent to which the filtering of complaints by the Human Rights Act leads to a long-term decline in (i) the number of complaints found to be admissible, and (ii) the number of admissible complaints found to yield at least one breach of the Convention by the European Court of Human Rights.

There are a number of reasons why applications will still have to be made to Strasbourg, the first being that the Human Rights Act does not always provide a remedy for the applicant whose rights have been violated. One such example is *ASLEF v United Kingdom*[68] where the trade union alleged that its art 11 rights had been breached by legislation that prohibited it from excluding or expelling from membership individuals who were members of the British National Party, in

---

[63] (1981) 4 EHRR 188.
[64] (1985) 7 EHRR 471.
[65] (1988) 11 EHRR 117. See now ch 26.
[66] For consideration of the implementation of Strasbourg jurisprudence, see HL 112/HC 555 (2006–7); HL 173/HC 1078 (2007–08); and HL 85/HC 455 (2009–10).
[67] M Amos [2007] PL 655.
[68] [2002] IRLR 568 (see K D Ewing (2007) 36 ILJ 245).

accordance with the policy of the union. The complaint was upheld, and the law changed.[69] It is a striking feature of that case that the Strasbourg application was made following a decision of an employment tribunal (this being a sufficient exhaustion of domestic remedies). Secondly, a related reason may be that where the violation of Convention rights has arisen as a result of legislation, it will be necessary to proceed to Strasbourg to seek a remedy, with the domestic courts in such circumstances being empowered only to declare the statutory provisions in question to be incompatible with Convention rights. For example, in the landmark *A v Home Secretary*,[70] the House of Lords made a declaration of incompatibility in relation to the provisions of the Anti-terrorism, Crime and Security Act 2001 which provided for the indefinite detention without trial of suspected international terrorists. It was held that these powers violated art 5 together with art 14, a conclusion with which the Strasbourg court agreed, which for good measure addressed a number of other related matters as well. The applicants were awarded compensation and costs.[71]

A third reason why an application may have to be made to Strasbourg is because the domestic courts have found that the action complained of did not violate the applicant's (or appellant's) Convention rights. Indeed, in a study of the jurisprudence of the House of Lords, it has been calculated that only one in three human rights cases lead to a finding that Convention rights have been violated.[72] Although it does not follow that the Strasbourg court will take a different view, it is understandable that disappointed litigants will want to take their case a step further. A good example is *S v United Kingdom*[73] where two applicants had been arrested by the police in unrelated incidents, after which they each had samples taken and entered on the DNA database, though neither was convicted of any offence. In one case the charges were dropped, and in the other the child was found not guilty. The House of Lords held that the operation of the database did not violate Convention rights and that there was no breach, even in the case of people who had not been convicted.[74] The Strasbourg court took a different view, the Grand Chamber holding unanimously that there had been a breach of art 8.

Finally, the Strasbourg applications will continue to be important in dynamic areas where the domestic courts appear reluctant to follow the lead of the Strasbourg court, or want more guidance or certainty before doing so. This has arisen in relation to art 11 (freedom of association) where the Strasbourg court has most recently repudiated an established line of authority in which it had been held that the right to freedom of association did not include the right to bargain collectively or the right to strike. In a decisive rejection of that view, the Grand Chamber of the Strasbourg Court unanimously changed its mind in 2008, holding that the right to freedom of association includes the right to bargain collectively in line with international labour standards.[75] In subsequent decisions, other chambers of the Court have extended protection to the right to strike under the umbrella of freedom of association, though they did not unequivocally state that the right to strike was protected.[76] When these developments were put to the Court of Appeal, it expressed some unease, especially in relation to the argument that art 11 now includes the right to strike, in view of what it regarded as a 'summary discussion of the point' in the case law.[77] It will thus require a Strasbourg application by a British trade union to make the domestic courts feel confident that art 11 should be construed in the manner they contend.

---

[69] Employment Act 2008, s 19 (see K D Ewing (2009) 38 ILJ 50).

[70] *A v Home Secretary* [2004] UKHL 56; [2005] 2 AC 68.

[71] *A v United Kingdom* [2009] ECHR 301. For other examples see M Amos, above.

[72] T Poole and S Shah [2009] PL 347.

[73] [2008] ECHR 1581.

[74] *R v South Yorkshire Chief Constable* [2004] UKHL 39, [2004] 1 WLR 2196. See ch 22.

[75] *Demir and Baykara v Turkey* [2008] ECHR 1345.

[76] See K D Ewing and J Hendy QC (2010) 39 ILJ 2 for full details.

[77] *Metrobus Ltd v Unite the Union* [2009] EWCA Civ 829, [2009] IRLR 851.

C. The Human Rights Act 1998[78]

The Human Rights Act 1998 provides that Convention rights may now be enforced in the domestic courts. For the purposes of the Act, Convention rights are defined to mean arts 2–12 and 14 of the ECHR, arts 1–3 of the First Protocol and arts 1 and 2 of the Sixth Protocol (s 1(1)). These are to be read with arts 16 and 17 of the Convention: the former permits the imposition of restrictions on the political activities of aliens; while the latter deals with the abuse of rights by providing that no state, group or person has any right to engage in any activity or perform any act aimed at the destruction of any of the Convention rights. The main exclusions are thus arts 1 and 13. Article 1 imposes a duty on the 'High Contracting Parties' to 'secure to everyone within their jurisdiction' the rights and freedoms set out in the Convention, an obligation which the government considers to have been met by the enactment of the Human Rights Act. The exclusion of art 13 in contrast is more controversial, this providing that everyone whose Convention rights and freedoms are violated 'shall have an effective remedy before a national court'. Not everyone is prepared to accept that the contents of the Act fully satisfy this requirement, as the government also claimed.[79]

Convention rights and the Strasbourg case law

The incorporation of Convention rights raises questions about the substance of these rights, which are brought to life and given meaning by the case law of the European Court of Human Rights. Section 2 of the Human Rights Act requires a domestic court or tribunal when considering Convention rights to 'take into account' judgments, decisions, declarations or advisory opinions of the European Court of Human Rights. They must also take into account any opinion or decision of the now defunct European Commission of Human Rights as well as any decision of the Committee of Ministers (a political body). It is important to note that unlike decisions of the ECJ, which are binding on British courts on matters of EC law,[80] decisions of the Strasbourg bodies are only to be taken into account. This would clearly allow the courts to set off on a journey of their own in the interpretation of what one judge referred to as 'our Bill of Rights'.[81] Although it would be difficult for the domestic courts to set standards below those required by Strasbourg, the Strasbourg court could not object to the domestic courts raising these standards. Yet while it is true that the House of Lords has unusually refused to follow the Strasbourg jurisprudence,[82] it is nevertheless surprising just how much weight is given not only to the decisions of the Strasbourg court, but also to the jurisprudence of the Commission.[83]

The leading case in relation to section 2 is *R (Ullah) v Special Adjudicator*[84] where Lord Bingham said that while 'not strictly binding' on the domestic courts, the courts should, 'in the absence of some special circumstances, follow any clear and constant jurisprudence of the Strasbourg court'.[85]

---

[78] There is a very full literature on the Act. The leading practioners' work is Clayton and Tomlinson, *The Law of Human Rights*. Academic studies include Fenwick, Phillipson and Masterman (eds), *Judicial Reasoning under the UK Human Rights Act*; Gearty, *Principles of Human Rights Adjudication*; Kavanagh, *Constitutional Review under the UK Human Rights Act 1998*; and Leigh and Masterman, *Making Rights Real*.

[79] See HL Deb, 18 November 1997, cols 475–7. For a fuller discussion of points raised during the passing of the Act, see K D Ewing (1999) 62 MLR 79.

[80] Ch 8 above.

[81] *Brown v Stott*, note 152 below, at 708 (Lord Steyn).

[82] *R v Spear* [2002] UKHL 31; [2003] 1 AC 734.

[83] Compare J Wright [2009] PL 595 who fails to make good her claim that the courts have developed an indigenous meaning of Convention rights.

[84] [2004] UKHL 26; [2004] 2 AC 323 (R Masterman [2004] PL 725; J Lewis [2007] PL 720).

[85] Citing *R (Alconbury Developments Ltd) v Secretary of State for the Environment, Transport and the Regions* [2003] 2 AC 295, para 26.

According to Lord Bingham, this was said to reflect the fact that the Convention is an international instrument, 'the correct interpretation of which can be authoritatively expounded only by the Strasbourg court', with the result that 'a national court subject to a duty such as that imposed by section 2 should not without strong reason dilute or weaken the effect of the Strasbourg case law'. Although it is open to member states to provide for rights more generous than those guaranteed by the Convention, according to Lord Bingham any such provision 'should not be the product of interpretation of the Convention by national courts, since the meaning of the Convention should be uniform throughout the states party to it'. In his view (and in the view of other judges) '[t]he duty of national courts is to keep pace with the Strasbourg jurisprudence as it evolves over time: no more, but certainly no less'. To the same effect, Baroness Hale said subsequently that 'we must interpret the Convention rights in a way which keeps pace with rather than leaps ahead of the Strasbourg jurisprudence as it evolves over time'.[86]

A case which takes this to considerable lengths is N v Home Secretary[87] where the claimant had entered the country illegally and had claimed asylum. Her application was refused and she was to be deported, despite the fact that she had AIDS for which she was being treated in the United Kingdom. The effect of her deportation to a country where she would not have had access to appropriate drugs would have been dramatically to shorten her life. Following a close textual analysis of the Strasbourg jurisprudence, it was found that there was no breach of the claimant's art 3 rights. The harshness of the decision was compounded by the concession by Lord Nicholls that the Strasbourg jurisprudence 'lacks its customary clarity'.[88] Perhaps less dramatically, in M v Work and Pensions Secretary,[89] the House of Lords upheld discriminatory arrangements under the Child Support Act 1991 which required a parent who had entered into a homosexual relationship with a third party to pay more by way of child maintenance than a parent who had entered into a heterosexual relationship with a third party. This was done on the basis that it was permitted on a close reading of the Strasbourg jurisprudence, which at the time did not require such discriminatory practices to be ended.

The effect of section 2 was looked at again by Lord Hoffmann in In Re P,[90] a case about the eligibility of unmarried couples to adopt children, the House of Lords holding by a majority that the restrictions in Northern Irish law were a breach of the Convention rights of prospective adopters. In an important speech, Lord Hoffmann provided a timely reminder that within the meaning of the 1998 Act, Convention rights are 'domestic and not international rights'. Although the domestic courts are bound only to take into account the Strasbourg jurisprudence, they are not bound by it if there are good reasons why it should be followed. He continued:

> The best reason is the old rule of construction that when legislation is based upon an international treaty, the courts will try to construe the legislation in a way which does not put the United Kingdom in breach of its international obligations. If Strasbourg has decided that the international Convention confers a right, it would be unusual for a United Kingdom court to come to the conclusion that domestic Convention rights did not. Unless the Strasbourg court could be persuaded that it had been wrong (which has occasionally happened) the effect would be to result in a finding that the United Kingdom would be in breach of the Convention.[91]

---

[86] R(S) v South Yorkshire Chief Constable [2004] UKHL 39; [2004] 1 WLR 2196, at para 78. Also R (Al Skeini) v Defence Secretary [2007] UKHL 26, [2008] 1 AC 153; R (Gentle) v Prime Minister [2008] UKHL 20, [2008] 1 AC 1356, at para [56]; R (RJM) v War Pensions Secretary [2008] UKHL 63, [2009] 1 AC 311; and R (Black) v Justice Secretary [2009] UKHL 1, [2009] 1 AC 949.

[87] [2005] UKHL 31; [2005] 2 AC 296. Compare EM (Lebanon) v Home Secretary [2008] UKHL 64, [2009] 1 AC 1198.

[88] Ibid, at para 14.

[89] [2006] UKHL 11, [2006] 2 AC 91.

[90] [2008] UKHL 38, [2008] WLR (D) 198 (A Kavanagh (2009) 72 MLR 828).

[91] Ibid, para 35.

Lord Hoffmann also pointed out, however, that where the Strasbourg court had held that a matter fell within the margin of appreciation, it would be for each member state to decide how it wanted to proceed. In determining what was possible within the margin of appreciation, it would be for the domestic courts to decide on the basis of Convention rights, and these would be given a principled and rational meaning under the Human Rights Act, in accordance with their status as rights under domestic law.

The Human Rights Act and parliamentary sovereignty

The structure of the Human Rights Act reflects the government's desire that 'courts should not have the power to set aside primary legislation, past or future, on the ground of incompatibility with the Convention'. This reflects the importance 'which the government attaches to parliamentary sovereignty'.[92] In practice this is not always a relevant factor, given that many of the cases which have gone to Strasbourg in the past have not been concerned with legislative action, so much as with executive or administrative action, and in some cases judicial action (relating to the operation of the common law). But it does not follow from this that the courts have no powers in relation to legislation. In the first place, they are required to interpret legislation (primary and secondary) where possible in a manner consistent with the Convention (s 3(1)).[93] This is in effect 'a new rule of construction',[94] which applies if the Court has decided that there would otherwise be a breach of Convention rights.[95] It has been said judicially that s 3 is a 'strong adjuration',[96] and that it is 'a powerful tool whose use is obligatory'.[97] Thus, 'it is not an optional canon of construction. Nor is its use dependent on the existence of ambiguity'.[98] As a result, s 3 has been said by some to be a 'radical tool';[99] but by others to contain a power which is a significant limitation of Parliament's sovereign will.[100]

Section 3 has been considered by the House of Lords on a number of occasions, and has given rise to a vigorous debate about its meaning.[101] After some hesitancy about its proper scope, the views of Lord Nicholls in *Ghaidan v Godin-Mendoza*[102] appear to capture the essence of the mainstream position. In the first place, the courts may be required to construe legislation consistently with Convention rights even where there is no ambiguity in the legislation. That is to say, to give the statute a construction which is contrary to its clearly expressed meaning, and the 'unambiguous meaning the legislation would otherwise bear'.[103] Second, this may mean that the courts must depart from the intention of Parliament in interpreting any contentious legislation, though this will only be permissible to the extent that in doing so the courts give effect to the intention 'reasonably to be attributed to Parliament' in enacting s 3 of the Human Rights Act. But third, in determining what interpretation of legislation is possible notwithstanding its clear and

---

[92] Cm 3782, 1997, para 2.13. See A W Bradley, in Jowell and Oliver (eds), *The Changing Constitution*, ch 2; and Young, *Parliamentary Sovereignty and the Human Rights Act*.

[93] See A Lester [1998] EHRLR 520 and F Bennion [2000] PL 77.

[94] *R (Wardle) v Leeds Crown Court* [2001] UKHL 12; [2002] 1 AC 754.

[95] See A Lester [1998] EHRLR 665.

[96] *R v DPP, ex p Kebeline* [2000] 2 AC 326, at 373 (Lord Cooke of Thorndon).

[97] *Re S (FC)* [2002] UKHL 10; [2002] AC 291, at para [37].

[98] Ibid, Lord Nicholls, para [37]. See also *R v A* [2001] UKHL 25; [2002] 1 AC 45, para [44] (Lord Steyn).

[99] F Klug and K Starmer [2001] PL 654, at p 664.

[100] T Campbell, in Campbell, Ewing and Tomkins (eds), *Sceptical Essays on Human Rights*, ch 2.

[101] See especially *R v A*, above; *R v Lambert* [2001] UKHL 37; [2002] 2 AC 545; *Re S (FC)*, above; *R (Anderson) v Home Secretary* [2002] UKHL 46; [2003] 1 AC 837; *Ghaidan v Godin-Mendoza* [2004] UKHL 30; [2004] 2 AC 557.

[102] [2004] UKHL 30; [2004] 2 AC 557.

[103] Ibid, at para 31. See *R v A*, note 98 above; and *R (Baiai) v Home Secretary* [2008] UKHL 53, [2009] 1 AC 287 (reading words into the Youth Justice and Criminal Evidence Act 1999, s 41, and the Asylum and Immigration (Treatment of Claimants etc.) Act 1994, s 19. Compare *R v Briggs-Price* [2009] UKHL 19, [2009] 1 AC 1026.

unequivocal terms, Parliament is not to be taken to have empowered the courts to adopt a meaning which is inconsistent with a fundamental feature of the legislation. In seeking to do what is possible, the courts are thus not empowered to construe legislation compatibly with the Convention at all costs. In an important passage, Lord Nicholls reminds the reader that Parliament has retained the right to enact legislation which is not Convention compliant. In *Re S (FC)*,[104] Lord Nicholls had earlier warned against using s 3 to amend rather than construe legislation.[105]

Where it is not possible to construe legislation in a manner which is consistent with Convention rights, the High Court and superior courts (but not tribunals or inferior courts), after giving the Crown an opportunity to take part in the proceedings (s 5),[106] may make a declaration of incompatibility (s 4(2)). Such a declaration is stated not to be binding on the parties and does not affect the validity or operation of primary legislation (s 4(6)). By 11 July 2007, 17 statutory provisions had been declared incompatible, and another six declarations had been overturned on appeal.[107] It is a striking feature of these declarations of incompatibility that very few of them were made in relation to legislation passed after the Human Rights Act was introduced,[108] and striking too that the House of Lords will go to considerable lengths to avoid making such a declaration.[109] According to Lord Steyn in *Ghaidan* v *Godin-Mendoza*, 'resort to s 4 must always be an exceptional course',[110] though it has been emphasised subsequently that the making of a declaration of incompatibility is for the discretion of the court.[111] If such a declaration is made, it is for the government and Parliament to decide how to proceed – whether to amend the legislation or not. Such a device goes as far as possible without undermining Parliament's sovereignty and, in introducing the Human Rights Bill, the Home Secretary indicated that there were circumstances where the government would be unwilling to bring forward amending legislation, citing the area of abortion as an example.[112] Nevertheless, an Act of Parliament which carries a declaration of incompatibility is likely to be badly wounded and some confusion may arise as a result.

It may be very difficult for any public authority to apply a provision that has been declared incompatible with Convention rights, since both the individual who obtained the declaration of incompatibility and the others affected by the incompatible provision will be encouraged by the declaration to apply to Strasbourg for a ruling on the matter. But a public authority may be bound to apply the law until it is repealed and may be challenged for not doing so. If a declaration of incompatibility is made, the government will normally be expected to respond by introducing primary legislation to remove the incompatibility, as in the case of the Prevention of Terrorism Act 2005, which repealed the provisions of the Anti-terrorism, Crime and Security Act 2001 ruled incompatible by the House of Lords.[113] Where the minister considers that there are 'compelling reasons' for doing so, the Human Rights Act empowers the government to make a 'remedial

---

[104] See note 97 above. For discussion of background issues, see C A Gearty (2002) 118 LQR 248, (2003) 119 LQR 551, G Phillipson (2003) 119 LQR 183, and A Kavanagh (2004) 24 OJLS 259.

[105] See also *R (Anderson)* v *Home Secretary*, note 101 above (D Nicol [2004] PL 274 and A Kavanagh [2004] PL 537).

[106] *Wilson* v *First County Trust (No 2)* [2003] UKHL 40; [2004] 1 AC 816 (intervention by the Secretary of State for Trade and Industry).

[107] HL 151, 2006–7. App 6; see also *Ghaidan* v *Godin-Mendoza*, note 101 above (Appendix to Lord Steyn's speech) for an earlier account.

[108] See *R (Wright)* v *Health Secretary* [2009] UKHL 3, [2009] 1 AC 739 (Care Standards Act 2000, s 82(4) – royal assent shortly before the Human Rights Act was brought into force); and *A* v *Home Secretary* [2004] UKHL 56, [2005] 2 AC 68.

[109] See notably *Home Secretary* v *MB* [2007] UKHL 47, [2008] AC 440 (K D Ewing and J-C Tham [2008] PL 668).

[110] Note 101 above. See also *R* v *A*, note 98 above; *Wilson* v *First County Trust*, note 106 above; and *R (Nasseri)* v *Home Secretary* [2009] UKHL 23, [2010] 1 AC 1, at para [18].

[111] *R (Rusbridger)* v *Attorney-General* [2003] UKHL 38, [2004] 1 AC 357. See also *Doherty* v *Birmingham City Council* [2008] UKHL 57, [2009] 1 AC 367.

[112] HC Deb, 21 October 1998, col 1301.

[113] The government did, however, take its time in bringing forward amending legislation, and the detainees were not released from detention until three months had elapsed from the Lords decision.

order' for amending primary legislation so as to remove the incompatibility (s 10 and Sch 2). A remedial order may also be made after a decision by the Strasbourg court in proceedings against the United Kingdom has indicated that primary legislation is incompatible with the Convention (s 10(1)(b)), although again only if there are compelling reasons for doing so.[114] The stated purpose of this procedure (which has been criticised as being a new Henry VIII clause but which so far has not been widely used) is to enable incompatibility with a Convention right to be removed from the statute book more quickly than if an amending Act of Parliament were needed.[115]

The Human Rights Act and public authorities

Sections 6 and 7 of the Human Rights Act are particularly important for the enforcement of Convention rights in the courts. The Act makes it unlawful for public authorities (including courts and tribunals) to act in a way which is incompatible with Convention rights, unless primary legislation permits no other course of action (s 6). This also applies to acts of persons other than public authorities, where those acts are done in exercise of 'functions of a public nature' but not if the 'nature of the act' is private (s 6(3)(b), (5)). A distinction between public and private bodies arises in other aspects of public law, notably in determining whether a body is subject to judicial review, and whether a body is an 'emanation of the State' for the purposes of the vertical direct effect of EU law.[116] However, the House of Lords has counseled against relying on the jurisprudence under these different jurisdictions to guide the application of the Human Rights Act.[117] Although the case law on judicial review may be 'helpful', the EU jurisprudence is 'not', and the matter must be examined under the Human Rights Act 'in the light of the jurisprudence of the Strasbourg court as to those bodies which engage the responsibility of the State for the purposes of the Convention'.[118]

In the leading case on this question, it was acknowledged that s 6 applies to bodies 'whose nature is governmental in the broad sense of that expression, and would include government departments, local authorities, the police and the armed forces'.[119] But in addition to these 'core' public authorities, the Act is said to apply to 'hybrid' public authorities, that is to say non-governmental bodies carrying out governmental functions. Examples would include prisons run by private organisations, though there is no clear test to decide if a body is public or private for these purposes. It was held in the *Aston Cantlow* case, however, that a parochial church council (of the Church of England – the established church) was not a core public authority, by reference to the text of the Convention itself and jurisprudence relating to religious bodies. It was also held that the parochial church council was not a hybrid public authority either, though this was a matter that had to be dealt with on a case-by-case basis. In this case the council was seeking to enforce the duty of the respondents to pay for repairs to the church, which according to Lord Hope was effectively a 'civil debt', an obligation said to be private rather than public.

The main concern with the meaning of public authority, however, arises as a result of the growth of the private sector and voluntary agencies to provide public services, under contract with public authorities. Some alarm was caused by a developing body of case law in which the

---

[114] See SI 2001 No 3712 (Mental Health Act 1983 (Remedial) Order 2001; HL 57, HC 472 (2001–2)); SI 2004 No 66 (Naval Discipline Act 1957 (Remedial) Order 2004; HL 59, HC 477 (2003–4)); and SI 2007 No 438 (Marriage Act 1949 (Remedial) Order 2007; HL 248, HC 1627).

[115] For fuller details, see Ewing, note 79 above.

[116] See Chapters 31 and 8 D respectively.

[117] *Aston Cantlow and Wilmcote with Billesley Parochial Church Council v Wallbank* [2003] UKHL 37; [2004] 1 AC 546. See D Oliver [2000] PL 476, [2004] PL 329, and A W Bradley, in Supperstone, Goudie and Walker (eds), *Judicial Review*, ch 4.

[118] *Aston Cantlow*, para [52] (Lord Hope).

[119] Ibid, para [7] (Lord Nicholls).

Court of Appeal appeared to exclude the operation of the Act in such cases.[120] This line of authority was nevertheless confirmed in *YL v Birmingham City Council*,[121] a case concerned with a nursing home run by a large private company (Southern Cross), which cared for residents under a contract with a local authority. The issue arose when it was alleged that Southern Cross had violated the art 8 rights of an elderly resident by giving her 28 days' notice to quit following a disagreement with her family. The House of Lords held by a majority of 3:2 that even though most residents were placed in the company's nursing homes by local authorities under contract with the company, this did not make the company a public authority for the purposes of s 6. According to Lord Scott, Southern Cross was

> a company carrying on a socially useful business for profit. It is neither a charity nor a philanthropist. It enters into private law contracts with the residents in its care homes and with the local authorities with whom it does business. It receives no public funding, enjoys no special statutory powers, and is at liberty to accept or reject residents as it chooses (subject, of course, to anti-discrimination legislation which affects everyone who offers a service to the public) and to charge whatever fees in its commercial judgment it thinks suitable. It is operating in a commercial market with commercial competitors.[122]

This decision was a disappointment to the government, which had expressed concerns about the narrow construction of s 6, even before the *YL* decision was published.[123] It was also a disappointment to the JCHR which has twice reviewed the meaning of public authority, expressing criticism of the lower courts, and concern that the decisions would undermine the purpose of the Human Rights Act in 'bringing rights home'.[124] In both of these reports the JCHR explored a number of options to overcome the impact of the decisions, initially placing faith in litigation as a strategy in the hope that the House of Lords would reverse the Court of Appeal. But after *YL* that strategy was in disarray, though it would be possible to seek a decision of the Strasbourg court, which for reasons considered above would have a decisive effect in resolving the matter. In the meantime, legislation now provides that private nursing homes are to be treated as public authorities for the purposes of the Human Rights Act where they provide care on behalf of public bodies.[125] But this is a sticking plaster solution to the *YL* case, which may not produce a long-term settlement of the wider questions raised by the decision, and the earlier decisions of the Court of Appeal.[126]

The courts as public authorities

By virtue of s 7, an actual or potential victim of an unlawful act may bring proceedings in respect of the unlawful act or may rely on Convention rights as a defence in legal proceedings (for example, as a defence to a prosecution). In particular, the actual or potential victim may apply for judicial review of the public authority's decision (s 7(3), (4)). By restricting applications to victims or potential victims, the Act effectively bars some public interest groups and others with standing (a 'sufficient interest') in judicial review proceedings from bringing claims that public authorities

---

[120] See *Poplar Housing Association Ltd v Donoghue* [2001] EWCA Civ 595; [2002] QB 48; *R (Heather) v Leonard Cheshire Foundation* [2002] EWCA Civ 366; [2002] 2 All ER 936; *R (Johnson) v Havering London Borough Council* [2007] EWCA Civ 26, [2008] QB 1.

[121] [2007] UKHL 27, [2008] 1 AC 95.

[122] Ibid, para [26].

[123] HC Debs, 15 June 2007, col 1045 (Solicitor General).

[124] See HL 39, HC 382 (2003–04); HL 77, HC 410 (2006–07).

[125] Health and Social Care Act 2008, s 145.

[126] A private member's bill introduced by the Chairman of the JCHR in 2007 would have extended the scope of the Act by providing that 'a function of a public nature includes a function performed pursuant to a contract or other arrangement with a public authority which is under a duty to perform that function'. But the bill made no progress. See now *R (Weaver) v London and Quadrant Housing Trust* [2009] EWCA Civ 587; [2009] 4 All ER 865.

are violating Convention rights. A court or tribunal may provide 'such relief or remedy or make such order within its jurisdiction as it considers just and appropriate' (s 8(1)). However, damages for breach of Convention rights are available only in a civil court which otherwise has the power to award damages; and, in assessing damages, the civil court must take account of Strasbourg decisions awarding 'just satisfaction' under the Convention (s 8(2), (3)).[127] According to the House of Lords, 'the purpose of incorporating the Convention in domestic law through the 1998 Act was not to give victims better remedies at home than they could recover in Strasbourg but to give them the same remedies without the delay and expense of resort to Strasbourg'.[128]

Courts and tribunals are expressly stated to be public authorities. This means that courts and tribunals must conduct their affairs in a way which is consistent with Convention rights (such as the right to a fair trial (art 6) and the right to freedom of expression (art 10)). But it means much more, for it applies also to the remedies which a court may order. So it would not be possible for a court to issue an injunction if to do so would violate the Convention rights of the defendant; or to fail to issue an injunction if to do so would violate the Convention rights of the applicant. In this way the Act may have implications for the common law and indeed for litigation between private parties. So, although Convention rights are directly enforceable against only public authorities, it is impossible to rule out their enforcement indirectly by one private party against another.[129] This question – the so-called horizontal status of the Convention – has given rise to a great deal of analysis in the literature.[130] The better view appears to be that (i) Convention rights may not be directly enforced by one private party against another, but that (ii) Convention rights may be relied on in an established cause of action to extend the rights of either party.

An example would be where the applicant brings an action against the defendant for breach of confidence and relies in the course of these proceedings on the art 8 right to privacy in order to extend the boundaries of the protection which the common law otherwise provides,[131] though in this case the boundaries have been stretched by some distance.[132] In this way the values embodied in art 8 are made applicable 'in disputes between individuals or between an individual and a non-governmental organisation', as well as in disputes between 'individuals and a public authority'.[133] Convention rights will also be relevant in actions between private parties which are concerned with the application of statutory rights (such as the right of employees not to be unfairly dismissed), in view of the duty of the courts under s 3 of the Human Rights Act.[134] Concerns that the Act might be used to extend existing or develop new causes of action in litigation between private parties gave rise to special measures relating to freedom of expression. There was concern in particular from the newspaper industry and its self-regulators (the Press Complaints Commission) about the possible implications of the right to privacy in art 8. These and other concerns led to s 12 which applies where a court is considering whether to grant any relief which might affect the exercise of the Convention right to freedom of expression.

In these cases, s 12 limits the circumstances in which a court may make interim injunctions, though in view of the inclusion of the courts as public authorities it may be questioned whether these special measures are strictly necessary. Unless there are compelling circumstances, no interim injunction is to be granted without the respondent having been notified (s 12(2));

---

[127] See A R Mowbray [1997] PL 647.

[128] *R (Greenfield) v Home Secretary* [2005] UKHL 14; [2005] 1 WLR 673, at para [19] (Lord Bingham).

[129] Cf *RSPCA v Attorney-General* [2001] 3 All ER 530, at 547 (Lightman J).

[130] See M Hunt [1998] PL 423; G Phillipson (1999) 62 MLR 824; R Buxton (2000) 116 LQR 48; W Wade (2000) 116 LQR 217; A Young [2002] PL 232.

[131] *Douglas v Hello!* [2001] QB 967; *Venables v News Group Newspapers Ltd* [2001] Fam 430; *Campbell v MGN Ltd* [2004] UKHL 22; [2004] 2 AC 457. See ch 22 F.

[132] See *Mosley v NGN Ltd* [2008] EWHC 1777 QB; [2008] EMLR 20.

[133] *Campbell v MGN Ltd*, above, at para 17.

[134] *X v Y* [2004] EWCA Civ 662; [2004] ICR 1634; *Copsey v WWB Devon Clays Ltd* [2005] EWCA Civ 932; [2005] ICR 1789.

moreover, no interim relief is to be granted unless the court is satisfied that the applicant is likely to succeed at the full trial (s 12(3)).[135] Section 12(4) addresses in particular the threat to freedom of expression created by the right to privacy and is a remarkable testament to concerns about the latter. Thus a court is to have particular regard to the importance of the Convention right to freedom of expression and in proceedings relating to journalistic material to 'any relevant privacy code'. The idea here is that no injunction should be granted to restrain a publication on the ground that it violates the privacy of the applicant if the respondent can show that it complies with the Codes of Practice of the Press Complaints Commission or OFCOM respectively.[136] Section 13 contains special protection for religious bodies from the application of Convention rights which might undermine their doctrine and practices.[137]

D. Enhanced Parliamentary scrutiny

Although the courts are given significant powers by the Human Rights Act 1998, important questions also arise about the role of Parliament in scrutinising legislation on human rights grounds.[138] While lawyers tend to focus on the role of the courts, it is important that the contribution of Parliament is not overlooked, and it is a contribution that is formally encouraged by s 19 of the Human Rights Act. This provides that a minister in charge of a Bill must make a statement to the effect that the Bill is either (i) in his or her view compatible with Convention rights; or (ii) the government wishes the Bill to proceed even though he or she is unable to make a statement of compatibility.[139] In practice, Bills generally contain a statement of compatibility on their face, though it is not unknown for a Bill to declare that the minister is unable to make a statement that it is compatible, as in the case of the Communications Bill 2002, which the government was concerned might breach art 10 of the Convention because of the restrictions on political advertising on television.[140] In this case, however, the House of Lords subsequently held that the broadcasting ban was consistent with the right to freedom of expression.[141]

Also important in terms of parliamentary oversight is the creation of the Joint Committee on Human Rights, a select committee which came into operation in February 2001. This all-party committee has members drawn from both Houses of Parliament with terms of reference which include (i) an examination of ministerial statements of compatibility and (ii) remedial orders made under s 10. There is also a power to consider human rights issues generally, including human rights treaties other than the ECHR.[142] Initially, most of the Committee's time was spent examining bills

---

[135] This qualifies the normal rules relating to interim injunctions as set out in *American Cyanamid Ltd* v *Ethicon Co* [1975] AC 396 where the House of Lords held that in order to obtain interim relief the applicant need only show a serious issue to be tried and that the balance of convenience lies in favour of granting the injunction sought. The interim injunction holds the ring until the full trial of the action, which may not take place until some considerable time in the future. There is no need to show that a court is likely to grant the remedy sought at the trial of the action, with questions of legality being weighed against other factors in the balance of convenience. Such a procedure gives rise to interesting questions about the compatibility of procedural law with the principle of the rule of law, quite apart from its implication for human rights. Section 12(3) has been read by the House of Lords to mean that the applicant must show that he or she would probably (more likely than not) succeed at trial, in preference to the Court of Appeal's approach that the applicant need only show a real prospect of success: *Cream Holdings Ltd* v *Banerjee* [2004] UKHL 44; [2005] 1 AC 253.

[136] See further ch 23 B and C.

[137] See P Cumper [2000] PL 254.

[138] See M Ryle [1994] PL 192; Kinley, *The European Convention on Human Rights*; and K D Ewing, in Ziegler, Baranger and Bradley (eds), *Constitutionalism and the Role of Parliaments*, ch 14.

[139] Earlier versions of the *Ministerial Code* required ministers to consider the impact of the ECHR in preparing business for Cabinet.

[140] See HL 50, HC 397 (2002–03).

[141] *R (Animal Defenders' International)* v *Culture, Media and Sport Secretary* [2008] UKHL 15; [2008] 2 WLR 781.

[142] See HL 183, HC 1188 (2003–04); HL 99, HC 264 (2004–05).

(and occasionally statutory instruments) to determine whether they met Convention requirements, drawing to the attention of Parliament any concerns that it may have.[143] The Committee has been willing to challenge or to question ministers' claims that bills are compatible with the ECHR,[144] and it has been prepared to test proposed legislation for compatibility with other international instruments.[145] The Committee has been particularly vocal about legislation proposed by the government to deal with the problem of terrorism, and has produced powerful critiques of the control order regime introduced by the Prevention of Terrorism Act 2005.[146]

Although the JCHR thus scrutinises legislation to see if it is compatible with the ECHR, it is not always able to convince the government, which will have acted on legal advice of its own, legal advice which in all probability will have approved the government's proposed action. There are occasions, however, when a vigorous exchange takes place between the Committee and the government department concerned, and occasions too when the work of the Committee informs debates in the House. But unlike parliamentary committees in other jurisdictions, the JCHR has no power to delay the passage of a Bill because in its view the Bill appears to conflict with Convention obligations. Apart from its work in scrutinising legislation, the Committee has also conducted inquiries into topical issues and in this sense has operated like other select committees.[147] Among a number of notable reports are those dealing with (i) the rendition of terrorist suspects and the alleged complicity of British officials in the use of torture by foreign security and intelligence agencies;[148] and (ii) the extent to which British businesses are complying with international human rights obligations, an investigation that required consideration of a wide range of international human rights other than the ECHR, including instruments produced by the OECD and the International Labour Organization.[149]

E. Conclusion

The Human Rights Act appears to give the courts a great deal of scope 'to decide the limits of their own decision-making power'.[150] Apart from the uncertainties in ss 3, 4 and 6 to which we have already referred, there is also uncertainty about the content of the very broad Convention rights themselves, even if account is taken of the Strasbourg case law. In determining the manner and scope of operation of the Act, it is clear that different judges are approaching matters from quite different positions: between the cautious and the activist, the majority occupy a pragmatic position somewhere in the middle. There are, however, a number of factors which constrain the courts, not the least of which is the perception of the judges about where the Human Rights Act fits into the structure of the British constitution, an institution that is more frequently referred to in judicial opinions than at any time in the past. A matter of particular restraint is the principle of parliamentary supremacy which the courts widely acknowledge is built into the scheme of the Act, and which continues to be referred to as the 'prevailing constitutional doctrine'.[151] Indeed, in

---

[143] See J Hiebert (2005) 68 MLR 676; (2006) 69 MLR 7; (2006) 4 ICON 1. Also D Feldman [2002] PL 323.

[144] See HL 37, HC 372 (2001–02) (Anti-terrorism, Crime and Security Bill); HL 68, HC 334 (2004–05) (Prevention of Terrorism Bill); and HL 35, HC 283 (2004–5) (Identity Cards Bill).

[145] See HL 30, HC 314 (2001–02) (Homelessness Bill: consideration given to compatibility with International Convention on the Elimination of all Forms of Racial Discrimination, and International Covenant on Economic, Social and Cultural Rights); HL 96, HC 787 (2005–06) (Health Bill: consideration given to compatibility with the European Social Charter and the ICESCR).

[146] Ewing, *Bonfire of the Liberties*, ch 8.

[147] For background, see HL 239, HC 1575 (2006–07).

[148] HL152, HC 230 (2008–09).

[149] HL 5, HC 64 (2009–10).

[150] R (Pro-Life Alliance) v BBC [2003] UKHL 23; [2004] 1 AC 185, at para 76 (Lord Hoffmann).

[151] *Ghaidan v Godin-Mendoza*, note 101 above, para 64 (Lord Millett). See more recently, *Doherty v Birmingham City Council*, note 111 above.

one of the first cases to reach the Privy Council, Lord Bingham made clear that the courts will defer to 'the decisions of a representative legislature and a democratic government within the discretionary area of judgment accorded to these bodies'.[152] Lord Hope was to write in similar terms when he said that the courts should 'defer, on democratic grounds, to the considered opinion of the elected body as to where the balance is to be struck between the rights of the individual and the needs of society'.[153]

Although the courts at the highest level will thus defer to the decisions of Parliament in appropriate cases, there is now some unease about the use of the word deference. In *R (Pro-Life Alliance) v BBC*, Lord Hoffmann wished to give reassurance that 'its overtones of servility, or perhaps gracious concession, are inappropriate to describe what is happening'.[154] It is also striking that in more recent cases Lord Bingham has written about the need to ensure that 'the deliberate decisions of representative assemblies should be respected and given effect so long as they do not infringe rights guaranteed by the Convention'.[155] Respect has thus replaced deference, and is perhaps most marked in cases about social and economic policy concerned with the equitable distribution of public resources.[156] Lord Hoffmann has said that in a domestic system which is concerned with the separation of powers, 'such decisions are ordinarily recognised by the courts to be matters for the judgment of the elected representatives of the people'.[157] In *R (Carson) v Work and Pensions Secretary*,[158] it was said that the government did not have to justify to the courts why it treated pensioners resident overseas less favourably than those resident in the United Kingdom. It was enough for the Secretary of State to say that 'all things considered, Parliament considered the present system of payments to be a fair allocation of the resources available'.[159] Any suggestion that the House of Lords was unduly deferential or 'servile' was challenged by its decision in *A v Home Secretary*[160] which held that powers of detention without trial violated Convention rights because of their discriminatory impact. Nevertheless, there often remains an underlying caution on the part of the judges at the highest level.

---

[152] *Brown v Stott* [2003] 1 AC 681. See also *McIntosh Petitioner* 2001 SC (PC) 89, at 102.

[153] *R v DPP, ex p Kebeline*, note 96 above, at 381. See also *R (Alconbury Ltd v Environment Secretary* [2001] UKHL 23; [2003] 2 AC 295, para 60 (Lord Nolan).

[154] [2003] UKHL, [2004] 1 AC 185, at para 75. See J Jowell [2003] PL 592.

[155] *R (Kehoe) v Work and Pensions Secretary* [2005] UKHL 48; [2006] 1 AC 42.

[156] See *EM (Lebanon) v Home Secretary*, note 87 above, where it was acknowledged by Lord Hope (at para 9) that 'though many of the rights it contains have implications of a social or economic nature, the Convention is essentially directed at the protection of civil and political rights'.

[157] *R (Hooper) v Work and Pensions Secretary* [2005] UKHL 29; [2005] 1 WLR 1681 (denial of widow's benefit to widowers not a breach of article 14). See also *R (Wilkinson) v IRC* [2005] UKHL 30; [2005] 1 WLR 1718; *R (Williamson) v Education and Employment Secretary* [2005] UKHL 15; [2005] 2 AC 246; and *R (Carson) v Work and Pensions Secretary* [2005] UKHL 37; [2006] 1 AC 173. Similar views were expressed by Lord Millett in *Ghaidan v Godin-Mendoza* [2004] UKHL 30; [2004] 2 AC 557, at para 65 with regard to matters of social policy generally.

[158] [2005] UKHL 37; [2006] 1 AC 173.

[159] Ibid, para 36.

[160] [2004] UKHL 56; [2005] 2 AC 68. See ch 26 below.

CHAPTER 20

Nationality, immigration and extradition

A. Nationality

Nationality in international law

It is impossible to use a passport in travelling from one country to another without being aware of the significance of the national status which the passport gives to its holder. Both in international and national law, the nationality of an individual determines many aspects of the relationship which a person has with the state of which he or she is a national, and with other states. As has been said,

> To the extent to which individuals are not directly subjects of international law, nationality is the link between them and international law. It is through the medium of their nationality that individuals can normally enjoy benefits from international law.[1]

Customary international law recognises that it is primarily for each state to determine (through its own constitution and other laws) who are its nationals.[2] However, this power must be exercised with regard to principles of international law, indeterminate as these are, and must take account of treaty obligations that a state may have. In EU law, it is for each member state to decide who its citizens are and to afford mutual recognition to the decisions made by other states.[3] The fact that states enact their own rules on nationality may cause some persons to have dual or multiple nationality (although some states do not allow their people to have another nationality), or (more seriously) may cause others to have no nationality, i.e. to be stateless.[4]

Upon an individual's nationality depend other rights and duties that are largely determined by national law, as well as other matters that colour his or her relationship with the government of the state. The term citizenship has this broader meaning, and the nature and implications of British citizenship are currently being examined.[5] For some purposes the terms nationality and citizenship are inter-changeable: thus those who have British nationality are grouped in several categories of citizenship. The consequences of being a national of a state include such matters as liability to military service, the right to vote and hold political office, or even the right to own land or enter the civil service. However, in many states the ordinary civil and criminal law, including access to the legal system, applies to everyone within the state regardless of nationality. Under the European Convention on Human Rights, a state must respect the human rights of all persons within its jurisdiction.[6] One aspect of national law that depends crucially on nationality is the control of immigration into the country.

---

[1] Jennings and Watts, *Oppenheim's International Law*, p 849.

[2] Ibid, p 852; and Brownlie, *Principles of Public International Law*, ch 19, esp pp 383–7.

[3] Case C-369/90 *Micheletti* [1992] ECR I-4239; and see note 210 below.

[4] The UK is a party to the UN Convention on the Reduction of Statelessness, 1961. And see British Nationality Act 1981, sch 2.

[5] See Goldsmith, *Citizenship: our Common Bond* (2008).

[6] Ch 19 B. By customary international law, every state must observe minimum standards of treatment in respect of aliens in its territory: Jennings and Watts, p 903.

In general, and in the absence of treaty obligations to the contrary, a state is under no duty in international law to admit nationals of foreign states (aliens) to its territory. However, by the Geneva Convention on Refugees, art 33, a state must not expel or return refugees who manage to enter its territory if this would mean their going to a territory where their lives or freedom would be threatened through persecution.[7] A state's immigration law lays down admission procedures that apply to foreigners, regulates their status after entry and determines when they may be required to leave the country. A state's freedom to decide for itself which foreigners to accept is curtailed where it has entered into treaty obligations from which other states benefit. From its inception, the European Economic Community aimed to establish a common market in which the citizens of member states enjoy freedom of movement for economic purposes: freedom of movement and residence is now guaranteed as an aspect of EU citizenship, and this may extend to family members, without regard to their nationality.[8]

Immigration law does not usually regulate the admission and removal of a state's own citizens, for the obvious reason that the state has a duty in international law to admit to its territory such of its nationals as are removed from other states; and no other state is obliged to admit them.[9] The basic rules which determine who are citizens are often in the national constitution,[10] amplified if necessary by other legislation. In Britain, nationality developed from allegiance to the King owed by his subjects at common law, in return for which the sovereign had no power to expel his subjects from the realm. Only in the twentieth century were nationality and immigration control placed on a statutory basis.

Today these matters are governed primarily by the British Nationality Act 1981 and the Immigration Act 1971 (both as amended subsequently). One legacy of Britain's imperial past was that the categories of British subject under the British Nationality Act 1948 contained vastly more persons from Commonwealth countries and dependent territories than could be admitted to the United Kingdom. From 1962, immigration law was used to prevent certain classes of British subject from exercising their right at common law to enter the United Kingdom. To distinguish between British subjects who were permitted to live in the United Kingdom and those who were not, the Immigration Act 1971 created a statutory 'right of abode' and also the concept of 'patriality' to determine those who could be admitted.[11] The British Nationality Act of 1981 recast the law of nationality to take account of immigration policy, converting the criteria for patriality into criteria for nationality. This enabled patriality as such to disappear from immigration law.

At common law, a simple contrast was drawn between British subjects and aliens (foreigners), and the distinction appeared in legislation.[12] Today, other distinctions are often more significant, in particular (a) between persons who have the statutory right of abode in the United Kingdom, and those who do not; and (b) between citizens of EU countries (including the United Kingdom) and citizens from other countries (who are known in EU law as third-country nationals). The term 'alien' is used in this chapter in its common law meaning when it is appropriate to do so.

In the present section, we examine the main features of nationality law; section B outlines aspects of immigration control; and section C briefly outlines the law of extradition.

---

[7] This is the duty of *non-refoulement*; below, text to note 158.

[8] Council Directive 2004/38/EC; and Case C-127/08 *Metock* [2008] ECR I-6241.

[9] Jennings and Watts, p 857. For an ordinance that sought unlawfully to exclude the entire population of a British colony, see *R v Foreign Secretary, ex p Bancoult* [2001] QB 1067; and (the sequel) *R (Bancoult) v Foreign Secretary (No 2)* [2008] UKHL 61, [2009] 1 AC 453.

[10] See e.g. Constitution of the USA, 14th Amendment (1868), s 1: 'All persons born or naturalized in the US . . . are citizens of the US and of the State wherein they reside.'

[11] See section B.

[12] See e.g. Aliens Order 1953. The British Nationality Act 1981 defines 'alien' as 'a person who is neither a Commonwealth citizen nor a British protected person nor a citizen of the Republic of Ireland' (s 50(1)). The term alien is often used in international law: e.g. UN Declaration on the human rights of individuals who are not nationals of the country in which they live, 1985.

The legal rules in these areas are voluminous, complex, and frequently changed by legislation that is driven by controversial policies.[13] Technicalities abound and may have crucial significance for the individuals they affect. In the brief space of this chapter, the present account cannot be comprehensive and detailed exceptions are often not mentioned. The legislation on these matters invariably refers to 'the Secretary of State'. Although powers so conferred may be exercised by any Secretary of State, this chapter refers throughout to the Home Secretary, the minister responsible for this area of government.

The development of nationality law[14]

The development of nationality from the common law to the British Nationality Act 1981 has been shaped by the growth of the United Kingdom, by the transition from the Empire to today's Commonwealth,[15] and most recently by European integration. The subjects of the English king were those who owed allegiance to him. The primary means of becoming a subject was by the 'ius soli': a person born within the King's dominions became a subject regardless of the status of the parents.[16] As early as 1350, the English statute *De natis ultra mare* applied the 'ius sanguinis' (i.e. birth by descent, regardless of the place of birth) so that certain persons born abroad whose fathers (or in some cases both parents) were subjects would also be subjects. In *Calvin's case*,[17] those born in Scotland after James VI of Scotland had become James I of England were held not to be aliens in England, since they owed allegiance to the same king. In 1707, English and Scottish citizens became British subjects by reason of the Treaty of Union; they were joined by the Irish in 1800. Although citizenship was generally acquired on birth, it could be conferred by law, when individuals or defined classes were 'naturalised' by Parliament; from 1870, the power of naturalisation was exercised by the executive.[18]

In the high noon of Empire, the status of 'British subject' gave rise to a common nationality throughout the Empire. The British Nationality and Status of Aliens Act 1914 declared that all persons born within the King's dominions were British subjects.[19] Some territories (mainly in Africa and India) under British control were not possessions of the Crown, but were only in the protection of the Crown: persons born there were 'British protected persons', not British subjects.

At common law, those who were not British subjects were regarded as aliens. Aliens within the King's territory owed local allegiance to the monarch, and were entitled to protection of their person and property in the courts.[20] In the event of war being declared upon a foreign state, citizens of that state became enemy aliens; if in Britain, they lost their right to protection of the courts.[21] In 1698, Parliament declared that aliens were not to be permitted to vote,[22] but it was

---

[13] Two leading texts are Macdonald and Webber, *Immigration Law and Practice in the United Kingdom* and Jackson, Warr, et al., *Immigration Law and Practice*. Phelan and Gillespie, *Immigration Law Handbook* is an accessible collection edited to show the current state of the legislation.

[14] On the current law, see Fransman, *British Nationality Law*; Macdonald and Webber, ch 2. For the history, Dummett and Nicol, *Subjects, Citizens, Aliens and Others*; also Parry, *Nationality and Citizenship Laws of the Commonwealth*.

[15] Ch 15 C.

[16] An exception to the 'ius soli' was made for those born within the territory to a foreign envoy or to enemy aliens.

[17] (1608) 7 Co Rep 1a. And see *Stair Memorial Encyclopedia: the Laws of Scotland*, vol 14, pp 743–4.

[18] See Dummett and Nicol, pp 71–7.

[19] Subject to the exception of those born to foreign diplomats and to enemy aliens.

[20] A person who owes allegiance to the Crown is subject to the law of treason (*R v Casement* [1917] 1 KB 98; *Joyce v DPP* [1946] AC 347). The Crown's duty to provide protection in return for allegiance is not enforceable by judicial process: *China Navigation Co v A-G* [1932] 2 KB 197; *Mutasa v A-G* [1980] QB 114. Cf *R v Foreign Secretary, ex p Abbasi* [2002] EWCA Civ 1598.

[21] See text to notes 72–4 below.

[22] Dummett and Nicol, p 73.

not until 1905 that legislation restricted the entry of some aliens into the United Kingdom. In 1914, further measures for controlling the entry and presence of aliens were enacted.[23]

Until 1948 the status of British subject applied across the Empire. The entry of British subjects into the United Kingdom was not restricted by law, and the UK government had no power to regulate the admission of British subjects to the United Kingdom according to their place of origin. However, dominion and colonial legislatures commonly enacted immigration laws that restricted entry to their territories,[24] and this enabled each country to apply its own immigration policies, whether on racial or other grounds. British subjects did not have freedom to enter British territories across the world.

The British Nationality Acts 1948 and 1981

The desire of countries such as Canada and Australia to have their own nationality laws led to the British Nationality Act 1948.[25] The Act assumed that each independent state would provide its own scheme of nationality,[26] but it sought to create from this diverse group of nationalities a common class of all those who were nationals of a Commonwealth country, including the United Kingdom. Very confusingly, the Act used two interchangeable terms, *British subject* and *Commonwealth citizen*, to denote persons who were citizens of an independent state in the Commonwealth or of the United Kingdom (and its dependent territories).

For the United Kingdom and its dependencies, the 1948 Act created the single term *Citizen of the United Kingdom and Colonies* (CUKC). The Act did not change the common law right of all British subjects (both CUKCs and citizens of other Commonwealth states) to enter and reside in the United Kingdom; no distinction was made for this purpose between persons born and resident in the United Kingdom, those whose home was in a colony, and those who were citizens of other Commonwealth states.

After 1948, when a territory gained independence, the legislation conferring independence generally provided that its population would cease to be CUKCs and would become citizens of the new state. But they would continue to be 'Commonwealth citizens' under the 1948 Act, if the new state remained in the Commonwealth.[27] However, minority groups in the territory might be permitted to continue as CUKCs rather than become nationals of the new state, as were the Asian minorities in East Africa. It was the position of these minorities, many of whom were later forced to leave East Africa and wished to come to Britain, that led to the first legislation taking away the right of British subjects to enter the United Kingdom.[28]

The 1948 Act provided for a residual category of *British subjects without any other citizenship*, and it maintained the status of *British protected persons*. Irish citizens did not become Commonwealth citizens, since Ireland left the Commonwealth on becoming a republic in 1949. However, the Ireland Act 1949 declared that they were not aliens and that Ireland was not a foreign country; thus, while resident in the United Kingdom, Irish citizens may exercise political rights.

The British Nationality Act 1981 re-cast the law, creating new categories of citizenship that were narrower than under the 1948 Act and were meant to fit the United Kingdom's immigration policies. The Act also changed the old rule (ius soli) that conferred citizenship on all those born in the United Kingdom, to a more complex rule by which a child born in the United Kingdom

---

[23] British Nationality and Status of Aliens Act 1914; and see the Aliens Order 1953.

[24] Dummett and Nicol, pp 115–25.

[25] See Cmd 7326, 1948.

[26] Hence in the 1948 Act, s 32(7). And see *R v Foreign Secretary, ex p Ross-Clunis* [1991] 2 AC 439.

[27] However, they would owe allegiance to the British Crown only if their state recognised the Queen as head of state; today most Commonwealth states are republics: ch 15 C.

[28] See below, text to notes 86–8.

would become a British citizen only if the parents satisfy conditions as regards their immigration status.[29]

Categories of British citizenship

Under the 1981 Act, which came into effect on 1 January 1983 (and as modified subsequently),[30] there are six categories of British citizenship:

1 Those who before 1983 were citizens of the United Kingdom and Colonies (CUKCs) and had sufficient connection with the United Kingdom to be patrials under the Immigration Act 1971 became *British citizens*.[31]

2 Those who before 1983 were CUKCs because of their connection with a dependent territory but lacked sufficient connection with the United Kingdom to be patrials became *British Dependent Territories citizens*.[32] In 2002, this category was renamed *British Overseas Territory citizens* and, more significantly, nearly all its members received full British citizenship, carrying with it the right of abode in the United Kingdom.[33]

3 Those who before 1983 were CUKCs and did not come within the two previous categories formed a residual category, *British Overseas citizens*.[34]

4 Under the Hong Kong Act 1985, British Dependent Territories citizens whose connection was with Hong Kong could between 1987 and 1997 apply for registration as *British Nationals (Overseas)*.

5 The term *British subject* lost its former broad meaning: it now denotes those who under the 1948 Act were 'British subjects without citizenship' (including persons born in an independent Commonwealth country before 1949 who were neither citizens of that country nor CUKCs).[35]

6 *British protected persons* continued under the 1981 Act with no change from their status under the 1948 Act.[36]

For completeness, four other categories must be mentioned. (*a*) The term *Commonwealth citizen* retains the broad meaning that it had under the 1948 Act. It comprises citizens of some 53 Commonwealth states, including citizens of the United Kingdom (all persons in categories 1–5).[37] (*b*) *Citizens of the Republic of Ireland* as such have no British citizenship, but neither are they aliens. (*c*) The residual class of *alien* denotes persons who are outside all the foregoing categories.[38] (*d*) Under EU law, persons who are nationals of a member state have the status of *citizen of the*

---

[29] Under the Irish Constitution, the ius soli rule applies to births anywhere in Ireland but, following Case C-200/02 *Chen* [2004] ECR I-9925, the rule was amended to require at least one parent to be an Irish citizen.

[30] As well as Acts applying to the Falkland Islands and Hong Kong, the legislation includes British Overseas Territories Act 2002, Nationality, Immigration and Asylum Act 2002, Immigration, Asylum and Nationality Act 2006, and Borders, Citizenship and Immigration Act 2009. For a summary of the current rules, see Lord Goldsmith, *Citizenship: our Common Bond* (2008), annex C.

[31] See Immigration Act 1971, s 1(1) (section B below); British Nationality Act 1981, s 11.

[32] 1981 Act, s 23. Under the British Nationality (Falkland Islands) Act 1983, BDT citizens connected with the Falkland Islands were declared retrospectively to have become *British citizens* on 1 January 1981.

[33] British Overseas Territories Act 2002, s 3(1); British citizenship was not conferred on BOT citizens whose connection was with the Sovereign Base Areas in Cyprus (s 3(2)).

[34] 1981 Act, s 26.

[35] 1981 Act, ss 30–31.

[36] 1981 Act, ss 38 and 50(1).

[37] 1981 Act, s 37 and Sch 3.

[38] 1981 Act, s 50(1).

Union, and thus the rights conferred by the European treaties.[39] Except for Irish citizens, the citizens of all other EU states are aliens in United Kingdom law (unless as dual nationals they are also British citizens).

Acquisition of British citizenship after 1 January 1983

The following notes outline ways in which, under the 1981 Act, as amended, British citizenship (category (1) above) may be acquired where this did not occur by operation of law on 1 January 1983.

1 *Birth or adoption in the United Kingdom.* A person born or adopted in the United Kingdom (which for this purpose includes the Channel Islands and the Isle of Man)[40] on or after 1 January 1983 acquires British citizenship only if at least one parent is a British citizen, or is a member of the armed forces[41] or is settled in the United Kingdom. To be 'settled' in the United Kingdom, the parent must be 'ordinarily resident' there without being subject under the Immigration Act 1971 to any restriction on the period for which he or she may remain.[42] No one is 'ordinarily resident' who is in the United Kingdom 'in breach of the immigration laws'.[43] Since 2002, these rules of acquiring British citizenship by birth in the United Kingdom have applied also to births in a British overseas territory.[44]

2 *Citizenship by descent.* A person born outside the United Kingdom on or after 1 January 1983 acquires British citizenship by descent if at least one of the parents (*a*) is a British citizen otherwise than by descent;[45] or (*b*) is abroad in Crown service under the UK government or (on certain conditions) is working for the European Community or for certain public services.[46]

3 *Registration.* There are various grounds on which some who do not qualify under these rules may be registered by the Home Secretary as British citizens. For instance, registration is available to someone born in the United Kingdom who did not become a British citizen at birth if, while he or she is still a minor, one of the parents becomes a British citizen or is settled in the United Kingdom.[47] The Home Secretary also has a broad power to register a minor as a British citizen.[48] Registration as a British citizen is an entitlement for certain persons who meet requirements as to being settled or present in the United Kingdom.[49] But, as a general rule, registration may be granted only if the Home Secretary is satisfied that the individual is of good character.[50]

---

[39] These rights include the right to enter and reside in the territory of all member states, subject to certain limitations, and the right of those residing in a member state to vote and stand in local and European elections in that state: TFEU, arts 20–24. See ch 8 above and section B below.

[40] 1981 Act, s 50(1).

[41] Borders, Citizenship and Immigration Act 2009, s 42, amending 1981 Act, s 1.

[42] 1981 Act, s 50(2); see also s 50(3), (4); and section B.

[43] 1981 Act, s 50(5). And see Nationality, Immigration and Asylum Act 2002, s 11.

[44] British Overseas Territories Act 2002, Sch 1, para 1.

[45] For the meaning of British citizen by descent, see 1981 Act, s 14.

[46] Ibid, s 2. See also British Overseas Territories Act 2002, Sch 1, para 2.

[47] 1981 Act, s 1(3).

[48] Ibid, s 3(1). See also ibid, ss 4A–C, inserted in 2002.

[49] Ibid, s 4.

[50] Ibid, s 41A, inserted by Borders, Citizenship and Immigration Act 2009, s 47.

4 *Naturalisation*. The Home Secretary may grant naturalisation as a British citizen to any person who is of full age and capacity and satisfies requirements as to residence in the United Kingdom, character, language and future intentions,[51] and a more recent requirement of knowledge about life in the United Kingdom.[52] In 2009, a new policy of progress through several intermediate stages towards full citizenship was authorised.[53]

The departure made by the 1981 Act from the rule of 'ius soli' that birth in the United Kingdom qualifies for British citizenship has the effect that the citizenship of someone born since 1983 depends on the citizenship or immigration status of the parents, even though the exact nature of that status may not be known and may be difficult to determine. The complex rules as to registration could in practice mitigate some adverse effects of the departure from the former 'ius soli'.

Where the Home Secretary has discretion in registration or naturalisation, it must be exercised without regard to the race, colour or religion of persons affected.[54] The Act of 1981 initially excluded the giving of reasons for discretionary decisions and restricted judicial review, but these provisions did not override the Home Secretary's duty to act fairly.[55] The repeal of these provisions in 2002[56] brought UK law into conformity with the European Convention on Nationality 1997. Someone who claims the right to register as a British citizen may seek judicial review if registration is refused. However, since the relief obtained by judicial review is itself discretionary, the court may refuse relief on public policy grounds to an applicant guilty of criminal deception in obtaining citizenship.[57]

Termination of British citizenship

A British citizen may renounce that citizenship to acquire another nationality, but the renunciation does not take effect until it has been registered by the Home Secretary, who may on various grounds withhold registration.[58] More significantly, the Home Secretary may by order deprive a person of any citizenship status (except where this would make the individual stateless), if satisfied that the deprivation 'is conducive to the public good'.[59] And the Home Secretary may cancel any citizenship acquired through registration or naturalisation if this was obtained by fraud, false statements or concealment of material facts.[60] Before such an order is made, the reasons must be notified to the individual, who may appeal to a tribunal unless the decision was based on information which the Home Secretary certifies ought not to be made public in the interests of national security or international relations, or 'otherwise in the public interest'.[61]

---

[51] 1981 Act, s 6 and Sch 1. The requirements are less onerous where the applicant is married to a British citizen: s 6(2).

[52] Nationality, Immigration and Asylum Act 2002, s 1. For citizenship ceremonies, oaths and pledges, see Sch 1 to the Act.

[53] Borders, Citizenship and Immigration Act 2009, ss 39–41. These changes are not yet in force.

[54] 1981 Act, s 44(1).

[55] *R v Home Secretary, ex p Al-Fayed (No 1)* [1997] 1 All ER 228, applying *A-G v Ryan* [1980] AC 718.

[56] Nationality, Immigration and Asylum Act 2002, s 7.

[57] *R v Home Secretary, ex p Puttick* [1981] QB 767.

[58] The Home Secretary must be satisfied that the individual will acquire some other nationality and may refuse to register a renunciation in time of war: 1981 Act, s 12.

[59] 1981 Act, s 40 (2) (as amended in 2006). Cf the power to deport a non-British citizen where this is 'conducive to the public good': Immigration Act 1971, s 3 (5) inserted in 1999. On the former law, see *Home Secretary v Hicks* [2006] EWCA Civ 400 (British citizenship conferred on Australian detainee at Guantanomo Bay but simultaneously revoked).

[60] 1981 Act, s 40(3) (as amended in 2002).

[61] 1981 Act, s 40A (inserted in 2002).

Aliens

As we have seen, the class of aliens is defined by the British Nationality Act 1981.[62] Aliens present in the United Kingdom are subject to the general law and their rights are protected by the courts.[63] They are subject to common law and statutory rules affecting aliens except, in the case of European citizens, where those rules are inconsistent with EU law. Another exception applies to members of foreign armed forces visiting the United Kingdom.[64] Aliens are subject to some political disabilities: they have no right to vote (European citizens may vote in local and European elections);[65] they may not be members of the Privy Council or either House of Parliament;[66] and restrictions exist as to their appointment to civil or military office under the Crown.[67] Other restrictions affect their ownership of British ships and of aircraft registered in the United Kingdom.[68] Everyone within the jurisdiction of the United Kingdom benefits from the European Convention on Human Rights,[69] and from the Race Relations Act 1976, which outlaws discrimination on grounds (inter alia) of nationality and national origin.[70] In EU law, any discrimination against EU citizens on grounds of nationality is prohibited, 'within the scope of application of the Treaties' (for instance, in respect of working conditions and many state benefits).[71]

Should the United Kingdom declare war on another state, citizens of that state become enemy aliens; if in the country, they may be interned or expelled by the Crown.[72] However, in the absence of a formal declaration of war, Iraqi citizens in Britain did not become enemy aliens when the military occupation of Iraq began in 2003.[73] During the Gulf hostilities in 1991, the government detained Iraqi citizens in Britain relying on the power in the Immigration Act 1971 to detain foreigners with a view to deportation, but use of this power was not appropriate in the absence of an intention to deport.[74]

Freedom to travel

Under art 12(2) of the International Covenant on Civil and Political Rights, to which the United Kingdom is a party: 'Everyone shall be free to leave any country, including his own.' In Magna Carta, it was recognised that citizens ought to be free to enter and leave the realm, but the freedom of British citizens to travel abroad is not directly protected in law.[75] The old common law writ *ne exeat regno* originally enabled the Crown for reasons of state to prevent a subject from leaving the realm; it now merely prevents a wealthy defendant from leaving the jurisdiction to

---

[62] Note 12 above.

[63] See e.g. *Kuchenmeister v Home Office* [1958] 1 QB 496; *R v Home Secretary, ex p Cheblak* [1991] 2 All ER 319.

[64] See Visiting Forces Act 1952; ch 16 C.

[65] Ch 9 A.

[66] Act of Settlement, s 3. And see Electoral Administration Act 2006, s 18, amended by Constitutional Reform and Governance Act 2010, s 47.

[67] Aliens Employment Act 1955, s 1, modified by EC (Employment in the Civil Service) Order, SI 1991 No 1221. And see Armed Forces Act 2006, s 340.

[68] Status of Aliens Act 1914, s 17; UK (Air Navigation) Order 1980, SI 1980 No 1965.

[69] See e.g. *A v Home Secretary* [2004] UKHL 56, [2005] 2 AC 68 (indefinite detention of foreigners suspected of terrorism) and ch 26 G.

[70] The law was amended by SI 2003 No 1626 to give effect to Council Directive 2000/43/EC; ch 19 A.

[71] TFEU, art 18. And see *Case C-221/89, R v Transport Secretary, ex p Factortame Ltd (No 3)* [1992] QB 680.

[72] *Netz v Ede* [1946] Ch 244; *R v Bottrill, ex p Kuechenmeister* [1947] KB 41. And see Jennings and Watts, pp 904–10; McNair and Watts, *The Legal Effects of War*, chs 2 and 3.

[73] *Amin v Brown* [2005] EWHC 1670 (Ch).

[74] *R v Home Secretary, ex p Cheblak* [1991] 2 All ER 319; I Leigh [1991] PL 331 and F Hampson [1991] PL 507. Art 5(1)(f) ECHR permits a person to be detained 'to prevent his effecting an unauthorized entry into the country' or 'with a view to deportation or extradition'. For *Saadi v UK*, see note 129 below.

[75] The 4th Protocol to the ECHR dealing with freedom of movement has not been ratified by the United Kingdom and is outside the scope of the Human Rights Act 1998.

frustrate a lawful claim before the court.[76] Despite the necessity of having a passport to travel abroad, the issue of passports is a matter for the Crown, acting under the royal prerogative. Decisions to refuse or revoke a passport are subject to judicial review. While the government may lawfully have a policy to withhold passports in certain situations, reasons must be given for a refusal and the citizen must have a chance to show that an exception should be made to the policy.[77] Moreover, EU citizens have a right to leave their own member state

An individual's freedom to travel is subject to restraints imposed by Parliament in the interests of security, public order and the criminal law.[78] The Immigration (European Economic Area) Regulations 2006[79] sought to incorporate in national law free movement directives issued under the EC Treaty, but they did not deal with a British citizen's right under EU law to be issued with a travel document to facilitate movement within Europe. One aim of the Identity Cards Act 2006 was to link the recording of personal information required of those seeking passports with a new identity card scheme, but the Act did not place the issuing of passports on a statutory basis.[80] Since 2006, passports have been issued by the Identity and Passports Service.

B. Immigration and deportation[81]

Background to the Immigration Act 1971

In section A, we saw that under international law, and apart from treaty obligations, a state is entitled to control entry into its territory by nationals of other states. At common law, the Crown had power under the prerogative to prevent aliens from entering the United Kingdom.[82] In 1969, the position was summarised in this way:

> when an alien approaching this country is refused leave to land, he has no right capable of being infringed in such a way as to enable him to come to this court for the purpose of assistance . . . In such a situation the alien's desire to land can be rejected for good reason or bad, for sensible reason or fanciful or for no reason at all.[83]

At common law, although no definite authority existed, it was possible that the Crown had power to expel friendly aliens who had been admitted into the United Kingdom.[84] Such

---

[76] See *Felton v Callis* [1969] 1 QB 200 and *Al Nahkel for Contracting Ltd v Lowe* [1986] QB 235.

[77] *R v Foreign Secretary, ex p Everett* [1989] QB 811 (refusal to renew passport to someone abroad accused of serious crime in the UK). Passports are withheld in a few other situations including (*a*) to prevent a minor going abroad contrary to a court order or the wishes of the parent with custody; (*b*) until a citizen repays the cost of having been repatriated to the UK at public expense; and (*c*) rarely, to protect the public interest against travel by a person whose activities are demonstrably undesirable. And see HC Deb, 15 November 1974, col 265 (WA); HL Deb, 22 January 1981, col 558.

[78] For power to ban travel by football hooligans, drug traffickers and paedophiles, see respectively Football Spectators Act 1989; Criminal Justice and Police Act 2001, s 33; Sexual Offences Act 2003, s 114.

[79] SI 2006 No 1003.

[80] See pages 494–5, below.

[81] For the leading texts, see note 13 above.

[82] *Musgrove v Chun Teeong Toy* [1891] AC 272.

[83] *Schmidt v Home Secretary* [1969] 2 Ch 149, 172 (Widgery LJ). In 2001, despite humanitarian considerations, the Australian government prevented a ship laden with Afghans from landing in Australian territory: *Ruddock v Vadarlis* (2001) 183 ALR 1. Cf *R (European Roma Rights Centre) v Immigration Officer* [2004] UKHL 55, [2005] 2 AC 1 (UK immigration officers operated at Prague airport by agreement with Czech Republic, but could not discriminate against Roma in so doing).

[84] See Parry (ed.), *British Digest of International Law*, vol 6, pp 83–98; *A-G for Canada v Cain* [1906] AC 542, 547; Dicey, *Law of the Constitution*, pp 224–7; and C L Vincenzi [1985] PL 93.

prerogative powers of the Crown in respect of aliens have been expressly preserved,[85] but for virtually all purposes today, the executive relies on statutory powers for controlling the entry and presence of foreigners.

We have already seen that, by contrast with aliens, British subjects at common law could enter and remain in the United Kingdom without restriction. The right of British subjects (within the meaning of the 1948 Act) to enter the United Kingdom was severely restricted by the Commonwealth Immigrants Acts of 1962 and 1968. The 1962 Act, passed to check immigration from the Caribbean, India and Pakistan, subjected all British subjects to immigration control, except for those born in the United Kingdom and those who were citizens of the United Kingdom and Colonies (CUKCs) and held passports issued by the UK government.[86]

The Commonwealth Immigrants Act 1968 was passed in great haste to forestall what was feared might be a mass exodus to Britain from Kenya of persons of Asian origin who, when Kenya became independent in 1963, had chosen to continue as CUKCs rather than become Kenyan citizens. Since they held passports issued by the British government, they were not subject to the controls established by the 1962 Act.[87] The 1968 Act was notable because it took away from a non-resident CUKC the right of entry into the United Kingdom unless he or she, or at least one of his or her parents or grandparents, had a prior UK connection (for example, through having been born or naturalised in the United Kingdom). The 1968 Act thereby prevented other CUKCs from entering the United Kingdom, even though they were expelled from the state in which they had resided and were entitled to enter no other country. The government subsequently came under pressure to admit other UK citizens in similar circumstances and, despite the 1968 Act, did admit many of the Asians expelled from Uganda in 1972.[88]

The Immigration Act 1971 and after

The 1971 Act provided a new and extensive code for the control of immigration. When it came into operation in 1973, the distinction between aliens and Commonwealth citizens lost much of its significance in immigration law. Since it was in 1973 that the United Kingdom joined the European Communities, a new distinction arose between citizens of Community countries and those from non-Community countries.

Under the 1971 Act, the most important distinction was between those who had the new statutory right of abode in the United Kingdom and those who (whether coming from Europe or a Commonwealth country) were subject to immigration control and needed permission to enter the country. The 1971 Act created the concept of patriality to identify those British subjects who were considered to have a sufficient connection with the United Kingdom to entitle them to the right of abode. Patrials included (i) those who were CUKCs by reason of birth, naturalisation or registration in the United Kingdom or in the Islands (i.e. the Isle of Man and the Channel Islands); (ii) citizens of other Commonwealth countries who were born to a parent who at the time of the birth was a UK citizen by virtue of his or her birth in the United Kingdom or Islands; and (iii) women who were Commonwealth citizens and married to patrials. Those claiming to be patrial could prove their status by obtaining a certificate of patriality. In R v Home Secretary, ex p Phansopkar, the court ordered the Home Secretary to hear and determine an application for

---

[85] Immigration Act 1971, s 33(5), which ousts the principle in *A-G v De Keyser's Royal Hotel Ltd* [1920] AC 508 (ch 12 E).

[86] Passports issued by colonial governments did not entitle holders to enter the United Kingdom: *R v Home Secretary, ex p Bhurosah* [1968] 1 QB 266.

[87] For the controversy over the government's intentions towards the Kenyan Asians in 1963, see HC Deb, 27–28 February 1968; HL Deb, 29 February 1968; Steel, *No Entry*; Dummett and Nicol, ch 11.

[88] See *East African Asians v UK* (1973) 3 EHRR 76; A Lester [2002] PL 52. Cf *R v Home Secretary, ex p Thakrar* [1974] QB 684 (p 311 above).

such a certificate made by an Indian woman, married to a man who had become a UK citizen by registration; the woman's right to a certificate could not be withheld by arbitrary delay on the part of the Home Office.[89]

The concept of patriality was much criticised, primarily because patriality did not extend to persons who, like the East African Asians, were CUKCs but had no country to which they might go other than the United Kingdom. For this reason, the UK government could not ratify the Fourth Protocol to the European Convention on Human Rights, which declares that 'no one shall be denied the right to enter the territory of which he is a national'.[90] A second criticism was that patrials included citizens of Commonwealth countries if at least one of their parents or grandparents had been born in the United Kingdom: this rule plainly favoured those of British origin from countries such as Canada and Australia, exposing the 1971 Act to the charge that it was racially motivated.

Immigration law has been modified many times since 1971, with amending legislation being enacted every year or two,[91] especially in response to the increased volume of applications from many countries for admission that occurred in the 1990s. In 2007, the government recognised that the legislation was in urgent need of simplification and consolidation, and a draft Immigration Bill was published in 2009.[92] What follows is no more than a selective outline of aspects of a complex and imperfect body of legislation.

Immigration control

In broad terms, the following are the main categories for the purposes of immigration control. They mostly derive from the British Nationality Act 1981 and were explained in section A.

(*a*) *British citizens* (now including most British overseas territories citizens). They have the right of abode in the United Kingdom and do not need leave to enter or reside there.

(*b*) *British overseas citizens, British subjects and British protected persons.* In general, they do not have the right of abode, but they are entitled to be registered as British citizens if they have no other citizenship,[93] and thereby will acquire the right of abode.

(*c*) *Citizens of other Commonwealth countries.* In general, they do not have the right of abode in the United Kingdom, and are subject to immigration control, but some Commonwealth citizens, who as patrials under the 1971 Act had the right of abode in the United Kingdom, continue to have that right.[94]

(*d*) *Citizens of the Republic of Ireland.* They benefit from the 'common travel area' for immigration purposes formed by the United Kingdom, the Isle of Man, the Channel Islands and the Republic of Ireland. Travel within this area is not subject to immigration control.[95] Irish residents thus enter the United Kingdom from Ireland without passing through immigration control, but they

---

[89] [1976] QB 606. See now Immigration Act 1971, s 3(9) (b), as amended in 1988 (certificate of entitlement to right of abode). And cf *R v Home Secretary, ex p Mersin* [2000] INLR 511.

[90] See ch 19 B and cf *R v Home Secretary, ex p Thakrar* (above).

[91] The legislation includes: Immigration Act 1988, Asylum and Immigration Appeals Act 1993, Asylum and Immigration Act 1996, Immigration and Asylum Act 1999, Nationality, Immigration and Asylum Act 2002, Asylum and Immigration (Treatment of Claimants etc.) Act 2004, Immigration, Asylum and Nationality Act 2006, UK Borders Act 2007, Criminal Justice and Immigration Act 2008 (Part 10), Borders, Citizenship and Immigration Act 2009.

[92] See *Simplifying Immigration Law: the Draft Bill*, Cm 7330 and Cm 7666 (2009).

[93] British Nationality Act 1981, s 4B (inserted in 2002).

[94] 1971 Act, s 2(1) (b) and (2), as amended by British Nationality Act 1981.

[95] 1971 Act, s 1(3). And see s 9 and Sch 4. Provision for immigration checks at the border between Northern Ireland and the Republic of Ireland was made in the Borders, Citizenship and Immigration Bill, 2008–09, but was later withdrawn by the government.

are subject to deportation from the United Kingdom under the 1971 Act. Under the Terrorism Act 2000, port and border controls may be exercised on travel to and from Northern Ireland by police, immigration and customs officers.[96]

(*e*) *Nationals of other EU countries.* They enjoy the right to freedom of movement within the EU. When they are exercising an enforceable Community right to enter or remain in the United Kingdom, they do not require leave under the 1971 Act to do so.[97] To this category may be added the nationals of Iceland, Liechtenstein and Norway; these countries are outside the EU but are parties to the Agreement on the European Economic Area. The area comprises all EU states and the additional countries. The agreement ensures freedom of movement within the EEA for all qualified nationals of the states concerned.[98]

Other persons, in particular nationals of non-EEA countries, are in principle subject to immigration control. Within this large class, an important distinction is between visa nationals (i.e. those from countries requiring a visa to enter the United Kingdom, including many Commonwealth countries) and nationals of other countries.[99]

Under the 1971 Act, those who have the right of abode in the United Kingdom 'shall be free to live in, and to come and go into and from, the United Kingdom without let or hindrance', except such as may be required to enable their right to be established (s 1(1)). Those who are not British citizens and do not have the right of abode may not enter or remain in the United Kingdom unless leave is given to them in accordance with the Act: such leave may be given for a limited or an indefinite period (s 3(1)(a), (b)). Where a person is given a limited leave to enter or remain, conditions may be imposed that restrict employment or occupation in the United Kingdom, exclude recourse to public funds for maintaining the person and his or her dependants, require registration with the police or reporting to an immigration officer, or stipulate place of residence (s 3(1)(c)). Where indefinite leave to remain is given, no such conditions may be imposed (s 3(3)). Even if a non-British citizen has indefinite leave to remain, he may be deported if the Home Secretary deems that this would be 'conducive to the public good' or if another person to whose family he belongs is to be deported (s 3(5)).[100] A person's leave to enter or remain may lapse when he or she goes outside the Common Travel Area, and fresh leave will be needed on return (s 3(4)).

The 1971 Act exempts certain groups of non-British citizens from the need to get individual leave to enter and remain. These include non-British citizens who were settled in the United Kingdom on 1 January 1983; that is, they were 'ordinarily resident' in the country and were not subject under immigration laws to any restriction on the period for which they might remain.[101] Other groups exempted from the need to get individual leave to enter include crew members of a ship or aircraft coming temporarily to the United Kingdom, diplomats and others entitled to diplomatic privilege, and members of certain military forces.[102]

The 1971 Act, as amended, equips the Home Secretary, the UK Border Agency (created in 2007) and immigration officers with a very wide range of powers. These include power to grant or refuse leave for entry before an individual arrives in the United Kingdom; to examine persons arriving or leaving the country; to remove persons who are refused leave to enter, have entered unlawfully or have outstayed a limited leave to remain; and to detain persons pending examination or removal. Many powers of control on entry are vested directly in immigration officers.

---

[96] Ch 26 E.

[97] Immigration Act 1988, s 7; and text to notes 205–212 below.

[98] European Economic Area Act 1993; Directive 2004/38/EC of the European Parliament and Council; Immigration (European Economic Area) Regulations 2006, SI 2006 No 1003.

[99] Immigration (Leave to Enter and Remain) Order 2000, SI 2000 No 1161; also Immigration Rules, rr 24–30C and App 1.

[100] See pages 438–9 below.

[101] 1971 Act, ss 1(2) and 33(2A); *R v Home Secretary, ex p Mughal* [1974] QB 313.

[102] 1971 Act, s 8.

Other powers (for example, the decision to order deportation) are given to the Home Secretary. The legislation has sometimes required that certain powers must be exercised by the Home Secretary personally, but most powers may be exercised on his or her behalf by officials in the Home Office (including staff of the UK Border Agency).[103]

Part III of the Act, as extended by later Acts, created many criminal offences including illegal entry,[104] overstaying a limited leave to enter or remain, failure to observe a condition of a limited leave, assisting or harbouring illegal entrants, failure without reasonable excuse to submit to examination on arrival into the United Kingdom, securing or facilitating the entry of illegal entrants, trafficking people for exploitation,[105] and using deception to enter the United Kingdom. It is an offence to facilitate breaches of immigration law involving entry by non-citizens of the EU and to facilitate the arrival of asylum seekers.[106] Immigration authorities and police have wide powers of enforcement, including arrest, search and fingerprinting.[107] Detailed regulatory procedures exist when persons subject to immigration control seek to marry.[108] Onerous duties are laid on airlines and other carriers by Part II of the 1999 Act, which imposes penalties for carrying clandestine entrants.[109] Strict rules penalise the employment of immigrants who are not permitted to work.[110]

Immigration rules[111]

Authority for immigration policies derives from primary legislation, but the policies themselves are largely contained in immigration rules which the Home Secretary lays down as the practice to be followed in the administration of the Act (1971 Act, s 3(2)). Statements of the rules must be laid before Parliament. If such a statement is disapproved by resolution of either House passed within 40 days, the Home Secretary shall 'as soon as may be' make such changes in the rules as appear to him or her to be required.[112] In 2009, Lord Hoffmann said that the status of the rules is 'rather unusual'; they 'are not delegated legislation' but they create rights since they are binding on those who decide immigration appeals.[113] They are thus far from being mere circulars or guidance. They must be interpreted sensibly, according to the natural meaning of the words used,[114] and may be held ultra vires if they conflict with a statutory provision or on other grounds.[115] The present rules, dating from 1994 and often amended since,[116] are much fuller than earlier versions. Some passages merely refer to requirements in the legislation; some contain procedural rules;

---

[103] *R v Home Secretary, ex p Oladehinde* [1991] 1 AC 254, applying the so-called *Carltona* principle, ch 13 D above.

[104] See *R v Naillie* [1993] AC 674 and *R v Home Secretary, ex p Ku* [1995] QB 364.

[105] Asylum and Immigration (Treatment of Claimants etc.) Act 2004, s 4.

[106] Immigration Act 1971, ss 24A, 25(1). The latter offence does not apply to organisations which give free assistance to asylum seekers.

[107] Immigration and Asylum Act 1999, Part VII, as amended.

[108] Immigration and Asylum Act 1999, s 24; Asylum and Immigration (Treatment of Claimants etc.) Act 2004, ss 19–25. See *R (Baiai) v Home Secretary* [2008] UKHL 53, [2009] 1 AC 287.

[109] As amended in 2002, in response to *International Transport Roth GmbH v Home Secretary* [2002] EWCA Civ 158, [2003] QB 728.

[110] Immigration, Asylum and Nationality Act 2006, ss 15–26.

[111] Macdonald and Webber, pp 36–40; Legomsky, *Immigration and the Judiciary*, pp 50–72.

[112] New immigration rules were disapproved by the Commons on 22 November 1972 and 15 December 1982; in each case revised rules were later approved by the Commons. And see ch 28.

[113] *Odelola v Home Secretary* [2009] UKHL 25, [2009] 3 All ER 1061, [6]. Earlier judicial statements on the rules (including *R v Chief Immigration Officer, ex p Salamat Bibi* [1976] 3 All ER 843, 848) are reviewed by Buxton LJ in *Odelola v Home Secretary* [2008] EWCA Civ 308.

[114] *Alexander v IAT* [1982] 2 All ER 766.

[115] E.g. *R v IAT, ex p Begum* [1986] Imm AR 385.

[116] HC 395 (1994–5) (as amended). For the current rules, see works cited in note 13 above.

many state the policies to be applied or the factors to be taken into account in the exercise of discretion.

Under the rules, immigration control is to be exercised without regard to a person's race, colour or religion, and in compliance with the Human Rights Act 1998 (r 2). The rules do not apply to those who are entitled to enter the United Kingdom as EEA nationals (r 5). As far as entry is concerned, a person arriving in the United Kingdom must produce a valid passport 'or other document satisfactorily establishing his identity and nationality' (r 11) and also, if this is claimed, a passport or certificate establishing that he has the right of abode (r 12). Prior entry clearance is required of many persons wishing to enter, in the form of a visa or an entry certificate (rr 24–25A). Certain persons are admitted for short-term visits or other temporary purposes, for example as students (rr 57–87E). A person arriving for employment must normally hold a Home Office work permit (r 128), but work permits are not needed for certain occupations, including ministers of religion (rr 169–177G) and overseas journalists (rr 136–143). A Commonwealth citizen who can show that one grandparent was born in the United Kingdom does not need a work permit and may be admitted for five years (rr 186–93). Unmarried children born in the United Kingdom since 1983 who are not British citizens because of the status of their parents,[117] have left the country and later wish to return, will in general be given leave to return on the same basis as their parents (rr 304–9).

The Acts and the rules leave many difficult decisions of law, fact and discretion to be made by the immigration authorities. Important changes of policy can be made by altering the immigration rules, subject only to the parent legislation or (where applicable) to EU law. In this way, a 'points based system' for admitting non-EU citizens for employment or business purposes was introduced in 2008.[118] In addition to the rules, the Border Agency issues an 'operational enforcement manual' containing guidance and directions for its staff, that are often amended. Most of the manual is published.[119]

Immigration appeals[120]

Before 1969, there was no right of appeal against executive decisions refusing admission to the United Kingdom, the prevailing tradition being that those seeking admission had no right to be admitted. This tradition could not be maintained when immigration control was extended to Commonwealth immigrants.[121] A two-tier system of appeals operated under the Immigration Act 1971: immigration adjudicators heard appeals from decisions by immigration officials, and appeals from adjudicators were heard by the Immigration Appeal Tribunal. This system of appeals assumed great importance in the process of immigration control. Initially it was under the excessive influence of the Home Office, but from 1987 adjudicators were appointed by the Lord Chancellor and efforts were made to strengthen their independence. Decisions of the Appeal Tribunal were subject to judicial review in the High Court. In 1993 it became possible, with leave, to appeal from a final decision by the tribunal to the Court of Appeal; and asylum decisions were brought within the appeal system.

During the 1990s, the scheme came under great pressure caused by the rapid increase in asylum-related appeals and by weaknesses in initial decision making. The Human Rights Act 1998 created additional grounds for appealing and for seeking judicial review, but other legislation

---

[117] Section A above.

[118] See Immigration Rules, Part 6A and apps A–F.

[119] See www.ukba.homeoffice.gov.uk. A serious failure to publish the current policy on detaining foreign national prisoners pending deportation was revealed in *R (Abdi)* v *Home Secretary* [2008] EWHC 3166 (Admin), [2009] ACD 22. And see note 201 below.

[120] Macdonald and Webber, ch 18; Jackson and Warr, chs 26–29.

[121] See the Wilson report on immigration appeals (Cmnd 3387, 1967) and Immigration Appeals Act 1969.

sought to restrict the volume of appeals, for instance by excluding the right to appeal against certain decisions and by imposing strict time limits for appealing. In 2004, the two-tier structure was replaced by the single-tier Asylum and Immigration Tribunal.[122] This tribunal comprised a president (a High Court judge) and deputy presidents; its legally qualified members were known as immigration judges,[123] and appeals were heard by one or more members of the tribunal.[124] In 2010, the separate existence of the tribunal ended with the transfer of its jurisdiction to the tribunal system set up under the Tribunals, Courts and Enforcement Act 2007.[125] In this system, the First-tier Tribunal and the Upper Tribunal each include an Asylum and Immigration Chamber.

In broad but imprecise terms, the task of an immigration tribunal (now the First-tier Tribunal) is to hear appeals where these are permitted against 'immigration decisions', including refusal of leave to enter the United Kingdom, refusal of entry clearance, refusal to vary a limited leave to enter or remain, revocation of indefinite leave to remain, decisions to remove illegal entrants and overstayers from the country or to order deportation, and the refusal of certain asylum claims.[126] A detailed account of rights of appeal and the restrictions on those rights is outside the scope of this work. Thus, some decisions are subject to no right of appeal;[127] some appeals against a refusal of leave to enter the United Kingdom may be brought only from abroad;[128] some claims are subject to a 'fast-track' procedure in which time limits for appealing are very short;[129] and in some situations 'one-stop' rules apply to prevent the making of repeated appeals.

When an individual appeals against a decision, the tribunal must allow the appeal (i) if it considers that the decision 'was not in accordance with the law (including immigration rules');[130] or (ii) if it considers, where the decision involved the exercise of discretion, that the discretion 'should have been exercised differently'. In all other cases the appeal must be dismissed. No decision in accordance with the immigration rules is to be treated as having involved the exercise of discretion merely because the Home Secretary was asked to depart from the rules and refused to do so.[131] Decisions on appeal must comply with the individual's rights under the European Convention on Human Rights; the question of compatibility with the Convention (including the issue of proportionality, if this arises) must be decided by the tribunal for itself in the light of the facts that it has found, and it does not have a secondary, reviewing function.[132]

Given this framework of legislation, rules, rights of appeal and judicial review, those responsible for immigration control are called on to ensure that the system respects the requirements of law and the rights of individuals. One response to this by the Home Office has been to get Parliament to narrow the scope for judicial decisions. In 2004, legislation was used in a novel way to direct decision makers how to assess evidence relating to the credibility of individuals.[133]

---

[122] Asylum and Immigration (Treatment of Claimants etc.) Act 2004, s 26 and Sch 4.

[123] See SI 2005 No 227.

[124] On the operation of the two-tier system, see HC 211 (2003–04) (report by the Constitutional Affairs Committee).

[125] See ch 29 A.

[126] Nationality, Immigration and Asylum Act 2002, ss 82, 83 (substituted in 2004). See s 84 for the grounds for appeals under ss 82 and 83.

[127] Nationality, Immigration and Asylum Act 2002, ss 88–89, as substituted.

[128] Nationality, Immigration and Asylum Act 2002, s 92, as amended.

[129] See *R (Saadi) v Home Secretary* [2002] UKHL 41, [2002] 4 All ER 785 (policy of detention for this purpose held consistent with art 5(1)(f) ECHR, even for asylum seekers). At Strasbourg, the Grand Chamber upheld this decision by 11–6: *Saadi v UK*, 29 January 2008.

[130] Which includes the principles of administrative law: *Singh v IAT* [1986] 2 All ER 721, 728.

[131] Nationality, Immigration and Asylum Act 2002, s 86, as amended in 2004.

[132] *Huang v Home Secretary* [2007] UKHL 11, [2007] 2 AC 167.

[133] Asylum and Immigration (Treatment of Claimants etc.) Act 2004, s 8, considered in *JT (Cameroon) v Home Secretary* [2008] EWCA Civ 878, [2009] 2 All ER 1213.

Apart from the appeal process, the Home Secretary exercises a residual discretion[134] to permit individuals to enter or remain in the United Kingdom, which may (for instance) be exercised for humanitarian reasons or to provide redress for official errors. In 2003, the Home Secretary gave an extra-statutory 'amnesty' to families seeking asylum who had been in the United Kingdom for more than three years.[135]

Separate provision is made for some immigration appeals. Where the Home Secretary certifies that a decision (for instance, to order a deportation) has been taken wholly or partially in the interests of national security or of an international relationship of the United Kingdom, appeal lies to the Special Immigration Appeals Commission, and thence with leave by either party on a point of law to the Court of Appeal.[136] In hearing appeals, the Commission comprises a person who holds or has held high judicial office, an immigration judge, and someone with experience of national security. The Commission may for reasons of national security hear part of the appeal in closed session, during which the appellant is represented by a special advocate appointed by the Commission and both the appellant and his or her ordinary representative are excluded.[137]

The role of the superior courts in immigration decisions

The rights of appeal discussed above give effect to the principle that executive decisions that significantly affect an individual's immigration status ought to be subject to a right of appeal to an independent and impartial tribunal and (especially when difficult points of law are involved) to a further appeal or review. Where decisions are not subject to appeal, then in general judicial review is possible in the Administrative Court.[138] Judicial review is available except where it is excluded by legislation, but if there is a right of appeal, the individual must usually exercise that right rather than seek judicial review.[139] It is difficult to strike an acceptable balance between providing an unduly open door to the Administrative Court for every person affected by an immigration decision, and restricting access to the court so rigorously that unlawful and unfair decisions escape judicial supervision. There is a need for an efficient and speedy system of immigration control, but a system that respects the individual's rights and is fair cannot be achieved by excluding legal process. Rights under EU law carry with them the right to effective judicial protection.[140]

The value of judicial authority was shown in *M v Home Office*, concerning an asylum seeker who was removed to Zaire while his case was subject to judicial review, despite the judge's understanding that he would not be removed; the House of Lords held that the court had power to issue injunctions against the Home Office to prevent claimants being removed while litigation over their immigration status was ongoing. Breach of such an order would be contempt of court.[141]

---

[134] The legal basis for which is uncertain: C Vincenzi [1992] PL 300.

[135] The amnesty was considered in *AL (Serbia) v Home Secretary* [2008] UKHL 42, [2008] 4 All ER 1127.

[136] Special Immigration Appeals Commission Act 1997; Nationality, Immigration and Asylum Act 2002, ss 97, 97A; Special Immigration Appeals Commission (Procedure) Rules 2003, SI 2003 No 1034 (as amended in 2007) The former advisory procedure under the Immigration Act 1971 was held not to comply with a detainee's right under art 5(4) ECHR to have the lawfulness of detention decided by a court: *Chahal v UK* (1996) 23 EHRR 413. On the earlier right of appeal, see B A Hepple (1971) 34 MLR 501. On meaning of national security, see *Home Secretary v Rehman* [2001] UKHL 47, [2003] 1 AC 153 (UK's security affected even if R's activities targeted solely against foreign government).

[137] On the difficult questions of due process arising from this procedure, see *RB (Algeria) v Home Secretary* [2009] UKHL 10, [2009] 4 All ER 1045; *Home Secretary v AF (No 3)* [2009] UKHL 28, [2009] 3 All ER 643.

[138] See chs 30, 31 below.

[139] See p 716 below.

[140] See e.g. Case C-327/02 *Panayatove* [2004] ECR I-11055.

[141] [1994] 1 AC 377; and see p 711 below.

Richard Rawlings has referred to the area of immigration law in the 1990s as a 'gathering storm in the relations between the executive and the judiciary',[142] a reflection on the profound divergence that often exists between executive policies for regulating immigration and a 'rule of law' approach to individual rights. That divergence has sometimes caused ministers to accuse judges of obstructing their policies.[143] The changes made to the system of appeals in 2002 included substituting a summary procedure of statutory review in place of judicial review.[144] When a few months later the government wished to end the two-tier appeal structure, its Bill included an extreme 'ouster clause' that sought to abolish the right to seek judicial review of immigration decisions, including decisions by the Asylum and Immigration Tribunal, and substituted a very limited remedy that depended on a decision by the tribunal itself to refer a case to the court. Although the clause passed through the Commons, the storm of opposition that it provoked caused the government to abandon it before it was debated in the Lords.[145]

The legislation that emerged against this background produced an elaborate scheme for review and appeals regarding tribunal decisions.[146] Detailed provision for appeals on a point of law takes into account whether the tribunal's decision was made by a panel of three or more legally qualified members: if so, a party may seek leave to appeal on a point of law to the Court of Appeal.[147] When the decision has not been made by such a panel, the tribunal may, on the basis of a written procedure claiming error of law, be required by the Administrative Court to re-consider its decision.[148] After re-consideration by a different tribunal, a party may, with leave, appeal on a point of law to the Court of Appeal.[149] Although the legislation contains no general ouster clause of judicial review on the lines of that attempted in 2003, the scheme was intended to have the effect of reducing the availability of judicial review.[150] In 2009, provision was made to require some applications for judicial review of immigration and asylum decisions to be transferred from the Administrative Court to the Upper Tribunal of the unified tribunal system.[151]

We need not here explore the grounds on which judicial review of immigration decisions may be obtained,[152] nor what may constitute error of law under existing forms of statutory review and appeal. Grounds for review include acting contrary to statute or the Immigration Rules, error in interpreting the legislation or the Rules, improper or unfair procedure, and breach of an individual's legitimate expectations. Additional grounds for review arise both under EU law and the Human Rights Act 1998. The 1998 Act requires the superior courts to ensure that tribunal decisions observe the principles laid down by the Strasbourg Court when Convention rights are in issue.[153]

---

[142] R Rawlings (2005) 68 MLR 378, 380.

[143] Or of having 'taken leave of his senses', as Prime Minister Blair said of Sullivan J's decision in *R (S)* v *Home Secretary* [2006] EWHC 1111 Admin (case of the Afghani hijackers). The Court of Appeal described the judgment as 'impeccable': *S* v *Home Secretary* [2006] EWCA Civ 1157, [50].

[144] See R Thomas [2003] PL 479. And see *R (G)* v *IAT* [2004] EWCA Civ 1731, [2005] 2 All ER 165 (no judicial review where decision subject to statutory review under 2002 Act).

[145] Rawlings (note 142 above); A Le Sueur [2003] PL 225; Lord Woolf [2004] CLJ 317; and p 723 below.

[146] Nationality, Immigration and Asylum Act 2002, ss 103A–E (inserted in 2004).

[147] Ibid, s 103E.

[148] Ibid, s 103A.

[149] Ibid, s 103B.

[150] Cf *R (G)* v *IAT* [2004] EWCA Civ 1731, [2005] 2 All ER 165 (no judicial review available where decisions subject to statutory review by written procedure under the Act of 2002 as first enacted).

[151] Borders, Citizenship and Immigration Act 2009, s 53, amending Supreme Court Act 1981, s 31A, as inserted by Tribunals, Courts and Enforcement Act 2007, s 19.

[152] See ch 30.

[153] E.g. *Huang* v *Home Secretary* (note 132 above).

In addition to procedures of judicial review, statutory review and appeal, the ancient remedy of habeas corpus, that enables the legality of a person's detention to be determined, is sometimes used when detention occurs under immigration law.[154]

Refugees and asylum status

A difficult but important branch of national law is that which gives effect to international norms relating to refugees and asylum.[155] By customary international law, it was at one time up to each sovereign state to decide whether to admit any foreigner seeking refuge. The United Kingdom has a long history of admitting political and other refugees when this seemed justified in the national interest.[156] The migration of human beings in pursuit of survival or a more tolerable existence may occur for many reasons, including civil war and other disasters, whether natural or man-made. The Geneva Convention of 1951 defines a refugee rather narrowly, as being someone who:

> owing to well-founded fear of being persecuted *for reasons of race, religion, nationality, membership of a particular social group or political opinion*, is outside the country of his nationality and is unable, or owing to such fear, is unwilling to avail himself of the protection of that country.[157] (emphasis supplied)

The words italicised are often called 'the Convention reasons' for persecution. At the heart of the Convention is the duty of states under art 33 not to 'expel or return (*refouler*) a refugee in any manner whatsoever to the frontiers of territories where his life or freedom would be threatened' for a Convention reason.[158] Article 3 of the European Convention on Human Rights obliges states not to return someone to a country where there are substantial grounds for believing that he or she faces a real risk of being subjected to torture or to inhuman or degrading treatment or punishment A real risk of 'flagrant breaches' of other Convention rights may also prevent a removal.[159]

It was only in 1993 that the legislation gave some limited recognition to the United Kingdom's obligations under the Refugee Convention.[160] These duties are not breached if, instead of being returned to the country where they fear persecution, asylum seekers are sent to a 'safe third country', that is, one through which they passed in reaching the country in which asylum is sought and in which they had the first opportunity to claim asylum. Whether a third country can

---

[154] See *R v Governor of Durham Prison, ex p Hardial Singh* [1984] 1 All ER 983, approved in *R (SK) v Home Secretary* [2008] EWCA Civ 1204, [2009] 2 All ER 365. On availability of habeas corpus, see also *R v Home Secretary, ex p Muboyayi* [1992] QB 244; S Brown [2000] PL 31 and pp 726–9 below.

[155] The literature includes Goodwin-Gill, *The Refugee in International Law*; Hathaway, *The Law of Refugee Status*; Harvey, *Seeking Asylum in the UK*; Symes and Jorro, *Asylum Law and Practice*; Macdonald and Webber, ch 12.

[156] See Stevens, *UK Asylum Law and Policy*; Dummett and Nicol, ch 8.

[157] Geneva Convention on the Status of Refugees, 1951, art 1A(2) amended by the 1967 Protocol. The Convention is referred to in this section as the Refugee Convention.

[158] By Art 33(2), the duty does not apply where a refugee may on reasonable grounds be regarded as 'a danger to the security of the country' or who, having been convicted of a 'particularly serious crime' constitutes a danger to the community. Controversial legislation has sought to give a very broad meaning in the UK to Art 33(2): Nationality, Immigration and Asylum Act 2002, s 72. A statutory order purporting to specify 'particularly serious crimes' for this purpose was held *ultra vires* in *EN (Serbia) v Home Secretary* [2009] EWCA Civ 630.

[159] *Soering v UK* (1989) 11 EHRR 439; *Chahal v UK* (1996) 23 EHRR 413; *D v UK* (1997) 2 BHRC 273. On the relevance of other Convention rights, see *R (Ullah) v Special Adjudicator* [2004] UKHL 26, [2004] 2 AC 323. On subsidiary protection, see the EU Qualification Directive 2004/83/EC, 29 April 2004.

[160] Asylum and Immigration Appeals Act 1993, s 2 (nothing in immigration rules to lay down any practice contrary to the Geneva Convention). The Convention as a whole has not been incorporated in UK law: *R v Asfaw* [2008] UKHL 31, [2008] 3 All ER 775; *EN (Serbia) v Home Secretary* (above).

be regarded by the United Kingdom as 'safe' for this purpose must now be decided in accordance with legislation that classifies 'safe' countries in three lists.[161] The first list comprises the EU states, together with Norway and Iceland; the second list is of countries specified by the Home Secretary as safe both under the Refugee Convention and for human rights purposes; the third list is of countries specified as safe under the Refugee Convention. The inclusion of a country in one of these lists may, because of its record, be controversial; but it creates an irrebuttable presumption that the country is 'safe' for the purpose stated, and it restricts the appeal rights of the individuals concerned by preventing them bringing an appeal while in the United Kingdom.[162]

The Refugee Convention provides no judicial mechanism for supervising observance of the Convention, but states are expected to cooperate on Convention matters with the Office of the UN High Commissioner on Refugees.[163] Since interpretation of the Convention falls to national courts, divergent interpretations of the Convention may occur in the case law from different countries.[164] In one leading case, the issue was the meaning of the term 'membership of a particular social group'. The House of Lords held that two Pakistani women, forced to leave their homes after allegations of adultery and at risk of criminal proceedings if they returned, had a well-founded fear of persecution: women in Pakistan were a 'particular social group' for Convention purposes as they lived in a society which discriminated against them by denying them protection from violence which was afforded to men.[165] Such decisions by the House of Lords (now the Supreme Court) are binding only in the United Kingdom, but they are likely to influence decisions by courts in other countries.

The overriding approach of UK courts in asylum cases was indicated in 1988 by Lord Bridge:

> The most fundamental of all human rights is the individual's right to life and, when an administrative decision under challenge is said to be one which may put the applicant's life at risk, the basis of the decision must surely call for the most anxious scrutiny.[166]

The decision of whether there is a well-founded fear of persecution for a Convention reason involves both subjective and objective factors; the test is whether there is a real risk or likelihood of persecution if the applicant is returned,[167] not whether it is more probable than not that such persecution will occur. The fear must be well-founded at the time when the request for asylum is decided. A historic fear of persecution is not sufficient, but may support a present fear.[168]

Persecution for a Convention reason may arise where the home state is directly persecuting the refugees itself or fails to protect them against abusive treatment by others. When a Roma in Slovakia claimed to be at risk of attacks by neo-Nazi skinheads, it was held that 'persecution' implied a failure by the state to provide due protection against the attacks; protection under the

---

[161] Asylum and Immigration (Treatment of Claimants etc.) Act 2004, s 33 and Sch 3. See also EU Council Regulation 343/2003/EC.

[162] Nationality, Immigration and Asylum Act 2002, s 92, as affected by the Act of 2004, Sch 3, paras 5, 10, 15. On compatibility of the statutory lists with the ECHR, see *R (Nasseri)* v *Home Secretary* [2009] UKHL 23, [2009] 3 All ER 774.

[163] See UNHCR's *Handbook and Criteria for Determining Refugee Status* (1992), printed in Phelan and Gillespie (note 13 above).

[164] In *R* v *Home Secretary, ex p Adan* [2001] 2 AC 477, it was held that the authorities in Germany and France did not apply the 'true and autonomous meaning' of the Convention in regard to state responsibility for persecution by non-state agents. Cf Council Directive 2004/83/EC, art 6(c), and SI 2006, No 2525, regn 4.

[165] *R* v *IAT, ex p Shah* [1999] 2 AC 629. In *Fornah* v *Home Secretary* [2006] UKHL 46, [2007] 1 AC 412, a young woman from Sierra Leone at risk of genital mutilation was held to have a well-founded fear of persecution; Lord Bingham at [16] considered the meaning of Council Directive 2004/83/EC, art 10(1)(d).

[166] *R* v *Home Secretary, ex p Bugdaycay* [1987] AC 514, 531 (whether Ugandan at risk of being sent to Uganda if he were returned to Kenya).

[167] *R* v *Home Secretary, ex p Sivakumaran* [1988] AC 958.

[168] *Adan* v *Home Secretary* [1999] 1 AC 293. On the burden of proof in respect of past or present facts, see *Karanakaran* v *Home Secretary* [2000] 3 All ER 449.

Convention was said to be a surrogate for the protection that the home state should provide for vulnerable individuals.[169] But the evidence was held insufficient to show that the Roma was suffering from a 'sustained or systemic violation of basic human rights demonstrative of a failure of state protection'.[170]

Even if an applicant faces a real risk of persecution if returned, he or she is not protected by the Refugee Convention where there are serious reasons indicating that he or she has committed a crime against peace, a war crime, a crime against humanity, a serious non-political crime, or acts 'contrary to the purposes and principles of the United Nations'.[171]

This formulation implies that someone may be protected under the Refugee Convention who has committed a serious 'political crime'. In *T v Home Secretary*, an asylum seeker from Algeria had taken part in two terrorist incidents in which members of the public were killed. The majority in the House of Lords defined a crime as being a 'political crime' for purposes of the Convention if:

> (1) it is committed for a political purpose, i.e. with the object of overthrowing or subverting or changing the government of a state or inducing it to change its policy; and (2) there is a sufficiently close and direct link between the crime and the alleged political purpose. In determining whether such a link exists, the court will bear in mind the means used to achieve the political end and will have particular regard to whether the crime was aimed at a military or governmental target, on the one hand, or a civilian target, on the other, and in either event whether it was likely to involve the indiscriminate killing or injuring of members of the public.[172]

On the facts, the two crimes in Algeria were held to satisfy condition (1) but not condition (2), and the Home Secretary's decision to refuse asylum was upheld.

Difficult questions arise where the Home Secretary seeks for reasons of national security to remove someone from the United Kingdom, but the individual can show that he or she is at risk of persecution or of being treated in breach of art 3 ECHR, if returned to the home country. Under the Refugee Convention, a balancing exercise is necessary and return may be ordered if the public interest in national security is held to prevail.[173] But as a matter of European human rights law, the Strasbourg court has held that national security considerations must be excluded in applying art 3.[174] The result is that suspected terrorists whose claim for asylum fails may be protected by the Human Rights Act from removal.[175]

Under the Refugee Convention, the risk to security and liberty caused by a civil war is not enough to ground a claim to asylum, unless the individual can show fear of persecution for Convention reasons beyond the risks of civil war.[176] In such cases, 'subsidiary protection' may be justified, so that failure to gain asylum does not mean that the applicant will be removed from the United Kingdom (or that the claim was 'bogus'). During a civil war, and in other situations where

---

[169] *Horvath v Home Secretary* [2001] 1 AC 489.

[170] Ibid, at 498 (Lord Hope) quoting from Hathaway, above, pp 104–5.

[171] Geneva Convention, art 1 F. And see Immigration, Asylum and Nationality Act 2006, s 54 (declaring that certain acts relating to terrorism are contrary to UN purposes and principles). Also *MH (Syria) v Home Secretary* [2009] EWCA Civ 226, [2009] 3 All ER 564 and *R (JS)(Sri Lanka) v Home Secretary* [2009] EWCA Civ 364, [2009] 3 All ER 588.

[172] [1996] AC 742, 786–7. Lords Mustill and Slynn, concurring in the result, disagreed with condition (2), holding that acts of violence likely to cause indiscriminate injury to members of the public were outside the concept of 'political crime'. Cf Council Directive 2004/83/EC, art 12(2)(b).

[173] *R v Home Secretary, ex p Chahal* [1995] 1 All ER 658.

[174] *Chahal v UK* (1996) 23 EHRR 413; *Saadi v Italy* (2008) 24 BHRC 123; and Harris, O'Boyle and Warbrick, *Law of the ECHR*, 84–88.

[175] For one response to this, see Anti-terrorism, Crime and Security Act 2001, Part 4, and *A v Home Secretary* [2004] UKHL 56, [2005] 2 AC 68.

[176] *Adan v Home Secretary* [1999] 1 AC 293. On subsidiary protection, see Council Directive 2004/83/EC, ch 5; and Immigration Rules, rules 339-C–G. Also C-465/07 *Elgafaji* [2009] ECR I-00921, 17 February 2009.

it would be harsh or impracticable to compel individuals to return, the Home Secretary may permit them to remain on humanitarian grounds, or may grant temporary admission.[177]

Many asylum seekers cannot leave their countries without using false documents and on arrival in the country of destination are at risk of being treated as illegal entrants. Under the Refugee Convention, art 31, a state must not impose penalties for illegal entry on refugees who claim asylum without delay and show good cause for the entry. Remarkably, prosecutions in Britain were conducted without regard to art 31, until in 1999 it was held that asylum seekers had a legitimate expectation that executive authorities would observe the duties imposed by the Convention.[178] In 2004, it became a criminal offence, subject to certain defences, to attend an immigration or asylum interview without identity or travel documents.[179]

We have seen that the Refugee Convention does not provide a judicial mechanism for ensuring that states apply the Convention in a uniform way. Developments within the EU (outlined below) have brought about closer cooperation on asylum matters. The Treaty of Amsterdam in 1997 committed member states to developing minimum standards for asylum procedures and policies across the EU as a first step towards a common asylum system. The United Kingdom, Ireland and Denmark insisted that a measure in this area would not bind them unless they 'opted in' to accept it. The United Kingdom has since opted in to measures that include (a) a directive laying down minimum standards for the reception of asylum seekers, (b) the Dublin Regulation, stating criteria for determining which state is responsible for dealing with an asylum application, (c) a directive on minimum procedures for granting refugee status, and (d) a directive dealing with the recognition and status of third-country nationals or stateless persons as refugees.[180] This last directive seeks to promote a common approach to asylum claims but does not affect the obligations of states under the Refugee Convention. Effect has been given to the directive in the United Kingdom.[181]

Among difficulties arising from the increased number of asylum seekers during the 1990s was the cost of supporting them while they were in the United Kingdom and their claims were being considered. In 1996, the Court of Appeal declared unlawful social security regulations that deprived asylum seekers of the right to receive benefits if they had claimed asylum after entering the country and not at the port of entry, but the regulations were hastily validated by Parliament.[182] The 1999 Act authorised a national scheme of support for asylum seekers, enabling them to be dispersed to areas of Great Britain away from the south-east.

In 2002, by a last-minute addition to a Bill in Parliament, the Home Secretary was required to withhold all support from asylum seekers who were considered to be late in seeking refugee status after entering the United Kingdom, provided that this did not breach their rights under art 3, ECHR.[183] The inevitable tension between withholding support and protecting Convention

---

[177] Temporary admission may be for an indefinite period: *R (Khadir) v Home Secretary* [2005] UKHL 39, [2006] 1 AC 207.

[178] *R v Uxbridge Magistrates' Court, ex p Adimi* [2001] QB 667 (leading to s 31, Immigration and Asylum Act 1999). *Adimi* was approved in *R v Asfaw* [2008] UKHL 31, [2008] 3 All ER 775.

[179] Asylum and Immigration (Treatment of Claimants etc.) Act 2004, s 2 (s 2 is misleadingly entitled 'Entering United Kingdom without passport etc.'). And see *Thet v DPP* [2006] EWHC 2701 (Admin), [2007] 2 All ER 425 (duty to produce documents applies only to genuine travel documents).

[180] See (a) Council Directive 2003/9/EC, 27 January 2003 (Reception Directive); (b) Council Regulation (EC) 343/2003, 18 February 2003; (c) Council Directive 2005/85/EC, 1 December 2005 (Procedures Directive); (d) Council Directive 2004/83/EC, 29 April 2004 (Qualification Directive).

[181] Refugee or Person in Need of International Protection (Qualification) Regulations 2006, SI 2006 No 2525. And part 11 of the Immigration Rules (as amended).

[182] *R v Social Security Secretary, ex p JCWI* [1996] 4 All ER 385; Asylum and Immigration Act 1996, s 11. See C J Harvey [1997] PL 394. Cf *R v Wandsworth Borough Council, ex p O* [2000] 4 All ER 590, 599: 'If there are to be immigration beggars on our streets, then let them at least not be old, ill or disabled' (Simon Brown LJ).

[183] Nationality, Immigration and Asylum Act 2002, s 55.

rights led within days to over 150 claims for judicial review being made over the refusal of support. A decision by a senior judge (Collins J) that sought to resolve the difficulties caused the Home Secretary (Mr Blunkett) to attack the judge's independence and integrity.[184] The outcome was a decision by the House of Lords that the legislation did not justify deliberate action by the government if this would cause an imminent prospect for an asylum seeker of facing inhuman or degrading conditions in breach of art 3, ECHR.[185]

Deportation and removal from the United Kingdom[186]

The power to deport or to remove a person is a drastic power that must be subject to political and judicial safeguards. Before 1971, an alien could be deported *either* where a criminal court recommended deportation after his or her conviction for a crime punishable with imprisonment *or* if the Home Secretary deemed it 'conducive to the public good' that he or she should be deported. The latter power proved highly resistant to judicial review.[187] Deportation could at that time be used as 'disguised extradition' since, although the Home Secretary could not name the country to which the deportee must go, the same result could be achieved by placing him or her on a specified ship or aircraft.[188]

Today, there is no power to deport British citizens (although they may be extradited), and their right of abode in the United Kingdom may not be removed by executive decision.[189] Some Commonwealth citizens who have had the right of abode since before 1983 may be deprived of that right when the Home Secretary thinks that it would be 'conducive to the public good' for them to be excluded or removed.[190] In general, all non-British citizens are subject to powers of removal and deportation. Thus a non-British citizen who has or had limited leave to remain may be *removed* for having breached conditions of leave or overstayed, for having obtained leave to remain by deception or when a person to whose family he belongs is removed.[191] There are powers for the summary removal of illegal entrants and others refused leave to enter.[192] A non-British citizen may be *deported* if the Home Secretary considers that this would be 'conducive to the public good'; if 'another person to whose family he belongs' is being deported; or if he or she has been convicted of an offence punishable with imprisonment and is recommended for deportation by the trial court.[193] EU citizens are not exempt from deportation, but exercise of the power must have regard to their rights under Community law.[194]

The decision of whether an individual should be deported or removed is likely to involve the exercise of discretion, and an indication of the relevant factors is given in the immigration rules.[195] No-one may be deported or removed where this would involve a breach of the Refugee Convention or of the European Convention on Human Rights.[196] Since 2000, the courts have

---

[184] See A W Bradley [2003] PL 397, *R (Q) v Home Secretary* [2003] EWCA Civ 364, [2004] QB 36 and ch 18 C.

[185] *R (Limbuela) v Home Secretary* [2005] UKHL 66, [2006] 1 AC 396 (and S Palmer, [2006] CLJ 438). Legislation on asylum support includes Immigration and Asylum Act 1999, part 6 (as amended); Nationality, Immigration and Asylum Act 2002, part 3 and sch 3; and UK Borders Act 2007, s 17.

[186] Macdonald and Webber, chs 15, 16; Immigration Rules 1994, Part 13. And see C Phuong (2005) LS 117.

[187] See *R v Governor of Brixton Prison, ex p Soblen* [1963] 2 QB 243; P O'Higgins (1964) 27 MLR 521.

[188] *R v Home Secretary, ex p Chateau Thierry* [1917] 1 KB 922. And see section C below.

[189] Immigration Act 1971, s 2(1)(a).

[190] Immigration Act 1971, s 2A (inserted in 2006).

[191] Immigration and Asylum Act 1999, s 10.

[192] Immigration Act 1971, Sch 2, paras 8–11 (as amended).

[193] Immigration Act 1971, s 3(5), (6) (as amended).

[194] E.g. *R v Home Secretary, ex p Santillo* [1981] QB 778. See now Immigration (EEA) Regulations 2006, SI No 1003, part 4.

[195] Immigration Rules, part 13.

[196] Ibid, paras 380, 395D.

often had to consider whether a deportation or removal might breach the individual's Convention rights – particularly the right not to be subject to inhuman or degrading treatment (art 3, ECHR) and the right to respect for private and family life (art 8).[197] The complaint may be about the direct effects in the United Kingdom of the deportation or removal, or may (less commonly) be based on a real risk of what will happen to the individual in the country to which he or she is removed.[198]

In the exceptional case where the Home Secretary decides that a deportation is conducive to the public good in the interests of national security, the appeal is to the Special Immigration Appeals Commission.[199]

We have seen that non-British citizens are subject to deportation where the Home Secretary considers that this would be 'conducive to the public good' or where someone who is over 17 is convicted of an offence punishable with imprisonment and the court in sentencing him recommends deportation.[200] In 2006, it was discovered that the Home Office had failed to ensure that foreign national prisoners who had served their prison sentence were considered for deportation, even if their offences were serious and they had been recommended for deportation by the courts. The Home Secretary (Charles Clarke) resigned, and in a flurry of confused activity the Home Office applied a presumption that foreign prisoners who had completed their prison sentence would continue to be detained pending a decision on deportation.[201] In 2007, Parliament authorised what it called 'automatic deportation' for every 'foreign criminal' who (*a*) is not a British citizen, (*b*) is aged at least 18, and (*c*) is convicted in the United Kingdom for a 'serious offence' and imprisoned, or is sentenced to at least 12 months in prison.[202] The Home Secretary's duty to make a deportation order is, however, subject to exceptions that inevitably prevent deportation being automatic: in particular, deportation must not be ordered where removal would breach the deportee's rights under the ECHR or under EU law, or would breach the Refugee Convention.[203] For those 'foreign criminals' who may not be removed from the United Kingdom because of their Convention rights, Parliament went on to create a new 'special immigration status' which is subject to the imposition of arduous and intrusive conditions.[204]

Immigration law and the European Union

One aim of the Treaty of Rome 1957 in establishing the European Economic Community was to abolish 'obstacles to the free movement of persons, services and capital'.[205] This aim was to be achieved primarily through freedom of movement for workers, the right of establishment and the

---

[197] On the meaning of 'family life', see *Beoku-Betts* v *Home Secretary* [2008] UKHL 39, [2008] 4 All ER 1146. See also *EM (Lebanon)* v *Home Secretary* [2008] UKHL 64, [2009] 1 All ER 559.

[198] The distinction is drawn in *R (Ullah)* v *Special Adjudicator* [2004] UKHL 26, [2004] 2 AC 323, [7] and [9]; and see *R (Razgar)* v *Home Secretary* [2004] UKHL 27, [2004] 2 AC 368. See also *Huang* v *Home Secretary* (note 132 above), applied in *AG (Eritrea)* v *Home Secretary* [2007] EWCA Civ 801, [2008] 2 All ER 28 (circumstances in which interference with family life not justified by immigration control).

[199] See above, p 432.

[200] Immigration Act 1971, ss 3(5), (6) and 6 (as amended). See also s 7 (exemption from deportation for certain Irish and Commonwealth citizens ordinarily resident in the UK). On deportation of family members of deportee, see s 5(4) and Immigration Rules, paras 365–380.

[201] See *Abdi* v *Home Secretary* [2008] EWHC 3166 (Admin), [2009] ACD 22. Also reports by the Prisons Inspectorate: *Foreign national prisoners: a thematic report* (2006) and *Foreign national prisoners: a follow-up report* (2007). The detention of foreign nationals after serving their prison sentence is but one of many issues raised by current Home Office practice in detaining those whose immigration status is uncertain.

[202] UK Borders Act 2007, s 32.

[203] Ibid, s 33. Cf Immigration (EEA) Regulations (below, note 208), part 4.

[204] Criminal Justice and Immigration Act 2008, part 10.

[205] See Macdonald and Webber, ch 7; and Jackson and Warr, ch 4. For the history of EU law on asylum and immigration, see Stevens (note 156 above), ch 9. And generally Peers, *EU Justice and Home Affairs Law*.

freedom to supply services within member states.[206] Discrimination based on nationality between workers of member states as regards employment, remuneration and other conditions was prohibited. Treaty provisions, regulations and directives had direct effect in national law, modifying immigration powers which could otherwise be exercised under UK law.[207]

In this area, the original scope of Community law has been enlarged and transformed by subsequent treaties. As we saw in section A, all nationals of EU states are today citizens of the Union, having the right to move and reside freely within all member states, subject to limitations and conditions in the Treaty and in implementing measures.[208] The same freedom of movement extends beyond the EU to nationals of Iceland, Liechtenstein and Norway, being states within the European Economic Area. A national of a state within the European Economic Area must be admitted to the United Kingdom if he or she produces on arrival a valid national identity card or passport.[209]

The European treaties leave it to each member state to decide who are to be regarded as its nationals. In 1983, a declaration of the UK government recognised three categories of persons for this purpose: (*a*) British citizens; (*b*) British subjects with the right of abode in the United Kingdom; and (*c*) British dependent territory citizens from Gibraltar.[210] In 2002, the granting of British citizenship to virtually all British overseas territory citizens thereby gave them freedom of movement within Europe. The same freedom is not enjoyed by citizens of states from outside the EEA (third-country nationals), even if they are permitted to enter and obtain employment in an EU state.

The broad aim of creating an internal market was considered to give rise to the need for a common external frontier that would replace internal frontiers. In 1985, the Schengen Agreement was created (outside the framework of the European Treaties) with the aim of abolishing immigration controls between the participating European states. The United Kingdom and Ireland remained outside that Agreement.

In 1992, by the Treaty on European Union, member states agreed to cooperate (outside the Community structure) in matters of justice and home affairs (the 'Third Tier'), including policies on asylum immigration, and third-country nationals. The Treaty of Amsterdam 1997 brought these matters within the scope of the EC Treaty: the Council of Ministers was required to ensure not only free movement of persons in conjunction with measures on the external border, but also the observance of minimum standards relating to the reception of asylum seekers, the granting of refugee status, and temporary protection for displaced persons. At the same time, the Schengen Agreement, with related decisions and declarations (collectively referred to as 'the Schengen *acquis*') was brought within the EU framework; it was envisaged that closer cooperation on asylum and immigration policy would be established between the Schengen states.

In negotiations leading to the Amsterdam Treaty, the United Kingdom, Ireland and Denmark obtained recognition for their distinct positions on asylum and immigration policy. It was agreed that measures on asylum and immigration would not apply to those countries, unless a country notified the Council that it wished to accept a measure.[211] It was further agreed that the United

---

[206] See now arts 45, 49, 56 TFEU.

[207] See e.g. *Case 41/74, Van Duyn v Home Office* [1975] Ch 358 (exclusion of Dutch scientologist) and *Case C-370/90, R v IAT, ex p Home Secretary* [1992] 3 All ER 798. These situations would now be covered by, respectively, Immigration (EEA) Regulations (next note), regns 19–21 and 9.

[208] TFEU, arts 20(2)(a) and 21(1). See Regulation (EEC) No 1612/68 (as amended); and Parliament and Council Directive 2004/38/EC of 29 April 2004, implemented in Immigration (European Economic Area) Regulations 2006, SI 2006 No 1003. And see Wyatt and Dashwood, *European Union Law*, ch 17.

[209] Immigration (EEA) Regulations (above), regn 11(1). Family members who are third-county nationals must also be admitted.

[210] Cmnd 9062, 1983. The declaration was upheld in *Case C-192/99 R (Kaur) v Home Secretary* [2001] All ER (EC) 250. And see note 3 above.

[211] Art 69, EC Treaty and Protocol No 4 to the EC Treaty and the TEU, 1997.

Kingdom and Ireland would not be bound by the Schengen *acquis,* but could request to participate in some or all of the Schengen provisions. In fact, the United Kingdom has agreed to take part in a series of measures within the EU framework.[212]

Post-Lisbon, the Treaty on the Functioning of the EU provides that the Union shall (among other things) 'frame a common policy on asylum, immigration and external border control, based on solidarity between member states, which is fair towards third-country nationals'.[213] Although the United Kingdom still reserves the right to adopt its own policies and practices, it is certain that EU law will continue to exercise a dominant influence on the country's immigration law and policy.

C. Extradition[214]

The object of extradition is to ensure that those accused or convicted of serious crime do not escape from justice by crossing international boundaries. Extradition is the procedure by which a person present in state A may be arrested by the authorities of that state and handed over to state B, either because (i) he or she is wanted to stand trial for a criminal offence in state B or (ii) he or she has been convicted in state B of an offence and is wanted back to serve the lawful punishment. This procedure gives rise to questions both of international and national law. Requests for extradition may raise issues which are politically sensitive within a state or between states. Sometimes, an alternative to extradition may be for state A, in which the requested person is found, to place that person on trial in its own courts rather than return the fugitive to stand trial in state B. This is possible where the law of state A permits extra-territorial jurisdiction to be exercised over the alleged offences.[215]

The most notable extradition case in recent years was that of General Pinochet in 1998–2000. While the former president of Chile was in London for medical treatment, a Spanish prosecutor requested his extradition to Spain to stand trial for offences involving the international crime of torture. That crime became an offence in UK law on 29 September 1988, when the Criminal Justice Act 1988 implemented the UN Torture Convention of 1984. Although the House of Lords held that Pinochet, despite his status as a former head of state, was liable to be extradited for alleged torture occurring after September 1988,[216] the Home Secretary decided that he should not be extradited because of his medical condition.

Under the Extradition Act 1870, extradition occurred between the United Kingdom and states with whom extradition treaties had been concluded: the rules of extradition depended both on the Act of 1870 and on the Orders in Council that gave effect to the treaties. As between Commonwealth states, extradition was governed not by treaty but by the Fugitive Offenders Act 1967 (replacing an earlier Act of 1881). In the case of the Republic of Ireland, escaping wrongdoers were returned by a simple procedure authorised (within the United Kingdom) by the Backing of Warrants (Republic of Ireland) Act 1965.[217] Except in the case of Ireland, extradition procedures

---

[212] See measures listed in note 180 above.

[213] TFEU, art 67(2). See also arts 77 (management of external borders), 78 (common policy on asylum, subsidiary protection and temporary protection), 79 (development of common immigration policy).

[214] Jones and Doobay, *Extradition and Mutual Assistance*; Sambei and Evans, *Extradition Law Handbook*.

[215] See e.g. Criminal Justice Act 1988, s 134, incorporating the UN Torture Convention 1984 into UK law.

[216] *R v Bow Street Magistrate, ex p Pinochet Ugarte (No 3)* [2000] 1 AC 147. The majority's reasoning differed from that in *Pinochet Ugarte (No 1)* [2000] 1 AC 61. See Brody and Rainer (eds), *The Pinochet Papers*; Woodhouse (ed.), *The Pinochet Case*; Sands, *Lawless World*, ch 2.

[217] The UK case law included *Keane v Governor of Brixton Prison* [1972] AC 204 and *R v Governor of Winson Green Prison, ex p Littlejohn* [1975] 3 All ER 208. On the Irish case law, H Delany and G Hogan [1993] PL 93.

were characterised by a complex sequence of steps that included both judicial decisions (taken by designated magistrates, with review by habeas corpus in the High Court and thence on appeal to the House of Lords) dealing with whether an individual was in law liable to be extradited, and executive decisions (taken by the Home Secretary) concerned with the political question of whether someone who was so liable should in fact be extradited.

Subject to some changes made by the Criminal Justice Act 1988, the law of extradition was re-enacted in the Extradition Act 1989. This Act enabled the United Kingdom to ratify the European Convention on Extradition so that extradition to and from most European states could be governed by that Convention. In the Commonwealth, the Fugitive Offenders Act 1967 had operated by informal agreement of Commonwealth states. In 1990, an amended scheme for the Commonwealth was adopted and the Extradition Act 1989 was applied to it.[218]

As the Extradition Act 1989 had left much of the older law in place, extradition procedures in the United Kingdom continued to be cumbrous and lengthy, giving repeated opportunities to the individual to challenge a request for extradition in the courts.

After 1997, the government gave support to developing a structure for extradition in Europe that would provide a more effective response to the challenge of serious crime, in particular to creating a 'fast track' for extradition based on mutual recognition of judicial systems.[219] One week after the 9/11 attacks on the United States, the EC Commission issued a detailed proposal for European arrest warrants. On 13 June 2003, the EU Council adopted a 'framework decision' on the European arrest warrant and surrender procedures between member states.[220] With the aim of enabling the EU 'to become an area of freedom, security and justice', the scheme sought to replace extradition between European states 'by a system of surrender between judicial authorities' and to eliminate any place in the process for executive discretion.

The Extradition Act 2003 was enacted after extensive consultation and much discussion at Westminster.[221] It repealed the Extradition Act 1989 and the Backing of Warrants (Republic of Ireland) Act 1965. Part 1 of the Act created a new procedure for extradition to category 1 countries, based on the EU Council's framework decision. Part 2 of the Act set out the procedure for extradition to category 2 countries; aspects of this resemble the process under the 1989 Act,[222] but with modifications derived from the new scheme for Europe. Category 1 countries, designated by Order in Council, are in principle the EU member states; other countries may be added to this category by Order in Council, not including any country in which the death penalty exists under the general criminal law. Category 2 countries, again designated by Order in Council, are all other countries to which there may be extradition from the United Kingdom.[223]

It is not possible here to give more than a brief outline of the Act and the procedures used for Category 1 and Category 2 countries (the Act uses the term territory throughout). Some differences between the two schemes will be mentioned, as well as some of the principal cases. No reference will be made to many questions that arise under the Act, nor to Part 3 of the Act, which provides for extradition *to* the United Kingdom.

---

[218] Commonwealth Scheme for the Rendition of Fugitive Offenders, as amended in 1990.

[219] See proceedings of the Tampere EU Council in October 1999; and *The Law on Extradition: A Review* (Home Office, 2001).

[220] See 2002/584/JHA. The decision is binding on member states as to the result to be achieved, but leaves to member states the choice of form and methods.

[221] See reports by Home Affairs Committee (HC 138 (2002–03)); European Scrutiny Committee (HC 152 (2001–02)); Joint Committee on Human Rights (HC 1140, HL 158 (2001–02)); and European Union Committee (HL 34 and 89 (2001–02)).

[222] For the 1989 Act procedure, see the 13th edition of this work, pp 450–5.

[223] For the main designation orders, see SI 2003 Nos 3333 and 3334 (both as amended).

Extradition to Category 1 territories

Proceedings begin when the designated authority in the United Kingdom[224] receives an arrest warrant (termed in the Act a 'Part 1 warrant' but usually known as a European arrest warrant) issued by a judicial authority in a Category 1 territory. The warrant must name the person whose extradition is sought, stating whether he or she is accused of a specified offence, with a view to arrest and prosecution, or is unlawfully at large after conviction for a specified offence (s 2). A warrant in proper form may be executed in the United Kingdom by the police, and the individual who is arrested must be brought as soon as practicable before a senior District Judge designated by the Lord Chancellor (in Scotland, before the sheriff of Lothian and Borders (s 67)), hereafter referred to as the extradition judge.

At hearings before the extradition judge, the issues for decision include that of identifying the person arrested as the person named in the warrant (s 7), and whether the offence specified in the warrant is an 'extradition offence' (s 10(2)). In the simplest case (s 64(2)), it is an extradition offence if *(a)* the conduct occurred within the requesting state, and *(b)* the state certifies that the conduct is (1) within the 'European framework list' set out in the Framework Decision,[225] and (2) punishable in that state with three years or more in prison. If these conditions are satisfied, the judge need not consider whether the conduct would be a criminal offence if it occurred within the United Kingdom. However, a test of 'dual criminality' is relevant if the alleged offence is punishable in the requesting state by imprisonment for 12 months or more but for less than three years (s 64(3)). Extradition offences include international offences such as genocide, crimes against humanity and war crimes committed outside the United Kingdom (s 64(6), (7)).

Assuming that the warrant has specified an extradition offence, the extradition judge must not consider whether the evidence establishes a prima facie case to support the prosecution.[226] But he or she must decide whether extradition is barred on various grounds raising matters of principle. These grounds include:

(a) whether there has been such a lapse of time that extradition would be unjust or oppressive (s 14);[227]

(b) whether the warrant has been issued to prosecute or punish the individual 'on account of his race, religion, nationality, gender, sexual orientation or political opinions' (or whether extradition if granted might have this effect) (s 13);

(c) whether arrangements exist to ensure that the individual if extradited will be dealt with only for offences disclosed by the warrant (referred to in the Act as the rule of 'speciality', s 17);[228]

(d) whether extradition would be compatible with the individual's Convention rights (s 21);[229] and

(e) whether extradition would be unjust or oppressive by reason of the individual's physical or mental condition (s 25).

---

[224] This is the Serious Organised Crime Agency in England and Wales or (in Scotland) the Crown Office: SI 2003 No 3109 and SI 2006 No 594.

[225] The list is in Sch 2 to the Act. It includes such vague terms as participation in a criminal organisation, terrorism, computer-related crime, environmental crime, racism, xenophobia and swindling.

[226] Whether evidence of telephone intercepts was obtained unlawfully is a matter for the courts in the requesting state: *R (Hilali) v Governor of Whitemoor Prison* [2008] UKHL 3, [2008] AC 805.

[227] See *Kociukow v Polish Judicial Authority* [2006] EWHC 56 (Admin), [2006] 2 All ER 451.

[228] This rule was before 2003 known as the 'specialty rule'. Once someone has been extradited, UK courts have no jurisdiction to enforce the rule: *R (Hilali) v Westminster Magistrates' Court* [2008] EWHC 2892 (Admin), [2009] 1 All ER 834.

[229] Cf *Soering v UK* (1989) 11 EHRR 439.

Against the judge's decision of these matters, the individual or the requesting state may appeal on issues of law and fact to the High Court[230] (in Scotland, the High Court of Justiciary). In England and Wales, a further appeal lies to the Supreme Court, if the High Court certifies that a point of law of general importance is involved that ought to be considered by the Supreme Court (ss 32, 33). Apart from rights of appeal, a decision of the judge may not be questioned in legal proceedings (s 34), but in some situations not covered by the Act judicial review or an application for habeas corpus is possible.[231]

This procedure excludes any role for the Home Secretary to intervene. Either the criteria for extradition are held by the court to be satisfied (in which case extradition must occur), or they are not, and the individual must be released. The only situation in which a decision by the Home Secretary is needed in relation to a Part 1 warrant arises if the individual claims asylum while a decision on the extradition is pending, and the Home Secretary must then decide the asylum claim (ss 39–40).

Some critics of Part 1 have described it as being no more than a scheme for the backing of warrants, since they see it as falling far short of being a scheme of extradition on traditional lines. However, the House of Lords has held that the purposes of the Framework Decision will be frustrated as a matter of European law if national authorities try to enforce formalities additional to what is required by the decision.[232] It must be remembered that the scheme within Europe is intended to give effect to 'the principle of mutual recognition' which has been described as 'the cornerstone of judicial cooperation'.[233] The role of the UK courts in upholding this principle may seem to be unduly limited, given that judicial systems in Category 1 territories do not always deliver justice, but a return to old-style extradition within Europe would have very dubious benefits.

Extradition to Category 2 territories

The authority in international law for extradition to most territories in this category derives from a treaty with the state concerned. Part 2 of the Extradition Act 2003 contains a code of rules that may supersede existing treaty provisions,[234] dealing both with when extradition may occur as well as with procedure. The initial request for extradition is made to the Home Secretary, generally through diplomatic channels. If the request is valid, the Home Secretary must issue a certificate to this effect (s 70); this enables the extradition judge to issue an arrest warrant if satisfied that an extradition offence has been specified, supported by sufficient evidence to justify arrest (s 71). Certain countries may be designated as being required to produce not evidence but merely information to support the arrest (s 71(4)).[235]

At hearings held after the individual has been brought to court, the judge must order release if identity is not proved or if the documentation is incomplete (s 78). The judge's powers are more extensive than on a Part 1 extradition, one reason for this being that the dual criminality rule applies in all Part 2 cases.[236] In the simplest instance, it must be shown that (a) the alleged offence occurred in the Category 2 territory, (b) it was there punishable with at least 12 months in prison; and (c) it would, if it occurred in the United Kingdom, be an offence so punishable (s 137(2)). In addition to deciding whether extradition is barred by such matters as lapse of

---

[230] Extradition cases are heard by a Divisional Court of the Queen's Bench Division, usually comprising a Lord Justice of Appeal and a puisne judge.

[231] *Nikonovs v Governor of Brixton Prison* [2005] EWHC 2405 (Admin), [2006] 1 All ER 927; *R (Hilali) v Governor of Whitemoor Prison* (above).

[232] *Dabas v High Court of Justice, Madrid* [2007] UKHL 5, [2007] 2 AC 31.

[233] *Dabas*, [4]. Lord Bingham was quoting from the preamble to the Framework Decision.

[234] *R (Norris) v Home Secretary* [2006] EWHC 280 (Admin), [2006] 3 All ER 1011.

[235] See SI 2003 No 3334, art 3.

[236] As to which, in a case of alleged price-fixing, see *Norris v Govt of USA* [2008] UKHL 16, [2008] AC 920.

time,[237] physical or mental health of the individual, or breach of Convention rights (ss 79–83),[238] the judge must if necessary decide whether there is sufficient evidence to make a case requiring an answer at a summary trial (s 84).[239] If these issues are resolved in support of the extradition, it is then for the Home Secretary to decide whether extradition is excluded on certain other grounds.[240] By contrast with the law before 2003, the Home Secretary[241] *must* order extradition unless statutory reasons against this exist (s 101).

Part 2 of the Extradition Act contains a scheme , similar to that under Part 1, for appeals to the High Court against decisions that approve extradition or order the individual's release. These provisions are stated to be the only way by which decisions of the judge and the Home Secretary may be questioned in legal proceedings (s 116).

One controversial effect of Part 2 of the Act has been to enable extradition to occur from the United Kingdom to a country with which there is no reciprocity or mutuality, as was the traditional basis for extradition treaties. Thus, a British citizen resident in the United Kingdom was liable to be extradited to the USA for an alleged price-fixing conspiracy without evidence that he had committed any offence, since the Home Secretary had designated the USA as a country not required to satisfy the extradition judge that there was prima facie evidence of the offence; it was immaterial that residents in the USA still had the benefit of the prima facie evidence rule contained in the 1972 extradition treaty between the countries.[242] The extradition judge has inherent jurisdiction to hold that a foreign prosecutor is abusing the process of the court, but the US prosecutor was held not to act abusively as regards the 'NatWest three' by complying with the statutory requirements applicable to the USA;[243] nor in the case of the British computer hacker, Gary McKinnon, was the process of plea-bargaining held to be abusive.[244]

Another effect of the Act was to exclude from extradition law the exception for 'offences of a political character'. This exclusion had been part of the law since the nineteenth century but it had given rise to much difficult litigation.[245] In the case of *T* v *Home Secretary*, which we have seen in relation to asylum,[246] an Algerian alleged to have been involved in terrorist incidents claimed that he could not be extradited for what were 'political offences'. The House of Lords reviewed the case law and held that the definition of political offences should be the same in both asylum and extradition claims. Although the Extradition Act 2003 in effect abolished the exception for offences of a political character in the case of extradition to countries to which it still applied,[247] the individual may resist extradition (as we have seen) by showing that extradition is sought for the purpose of prosecuting or punishing him on account of grounds that include his race, religion, nationality and political opinions (ss 13, 81). These provisions broadly correspond to the test applied to asylum claims.

---

[237] See *Govt of USA* v *Tollman* [2008] EWHC 184 (Admin), [2008] 3 All ER 150; *Gomes* v *Govt of Trinidad and Tobago* [2009] UKHL 21, [2009] 3 All ER 549.

[238] See *R (Wellington)* v *Home Secretary* [2008] UKHL 72, [2009] 2 All ER 436 (mandatory life sentence without chance of parole held not to breach W's rights under Art 3 ECHR); *R (McKinnon)* v *Home Secretary* [2009] EWHC 2021 (Admin) (likely effect of extradition and imprisonment in USA on person with Asperger syndrome).

[239] The judge must not inquire into the evidence when a Category 2 country has been designated as being required to give information about the offences but not evidence (s 84(7)).

[240] These relate to the death penalty (s 94) and enforcement of the 'speciality rule' (s 95). As to the latter, see *R (Bermingham)* v *Director of Serious Fraud Office* [2006] EWHC 200 (Admin), [2007] QB 727.

[241] For Scotland, the decision will generally be taken by a member of the Scottish Executive (s 101(2)).

[242] *R (Norris)* v *Home Secretary* (note 234 above). And see case of the 'NatWest three', *R (Bermingham)* v *Director of Serious Fraud Office* (above).

[243] *R (Bermingham)* v *Director of Serious Fraud Office* (above).

[244] *McKinnon* v *USA* [2008] UKHL 59, [2008] 4 All ER 1012.

[245] See 13th edition of this work, pp 451–3.

[246] *T* v *Home Secretary* [1996] AC 742, summarised in the context of asylum law at p 436 above.

[247] The exception had already been removed from extradition within the EU after the 9/11 attacks by the EU Extradition Regulations, SI 2002 No 419 (authorised by Anti-terrorism, Crime and Security Act 2001, s 111).

Conclusion

In 1998, Lord Steyn, commenting on the law as it was then, referred to the 'transnational interest' in bringing to justice those accused of serious crimes and said that extradition treaties and statutes ought where possible to be given 'a broad and generous construction'.[248] On a first reading of the Extradition Act 2003, the processes now in place may appear complex, but in fact many obstacles to achieving transnational justice have been removed by the reforms, in particular by the effect given in Part 1 of the Act to the European arrest warrant. Despite the need for all courts in Europe to respect 'the principle of mutual recognition', it does not follow that the wishes of the requesting state ought always to prevail. Courts in the United Kingdom retain an important role in ensuring that core requirements of the Act are observed.

Notwithstanding the reforms made in the law of extradition in 2003, they are unlikely to have had any effect on the practice of certain countries (including the United States)[249] in resorting to self-help rather than extradition in seizing offenders or suspects who are present in other countries. Since 9/11 and the conflicts in Iraq and Afghanistan, there have been many reports of the practice of 'rendition' (not a term of art in international law) by which persons are detained and forcibly removed by state agents from country to country without any legal process; the term 'extraordinary rendition' may be used where removal takes place for purposes of detention and interrogation outside the normal legal system and where there is a real risk of torture or of cruel, inhuman or degrading treatment.[250] Such practices are contrary both to the protection of human rights in international law and to the 'rule of law' values that constitutional law seeks to uphold. As a matter of English law, in 1993 the House of Lords held that the High Court's power to stay a prosecution for abuse of process could be exercised where an accused person had been forcibly abducted to England from South Africa by an irregular procedure.[251] An instance of rendition from Zimbabwe to the United Kingdom by the UK's Secret Intelligence Service was in 2000 held unlawful by the Court of Appeal.[252] Under the European Convention on Human Rights, the lawful exercise of extradition is recognised, but not practices of abduction or 'rendition'.[253]

---

[248] *In re Ismail* [1999] 1 AC 320, 327.

[249] *US v Alvarez-Machain* 119 L Ed 2d 441 (1992).

[250] See Intelligence and Security Committee, *Rendition*, Cm 1771, 2007; and the All-Party Parliamentary Group on Extraordinary Rendition, *Extraordinary Rendition: Closing the Gap*, 2009.

[251] *R v Horseferry Road Magistrates' Court, ex p Bennett* [1994] 1 AC 42. Cf *Re Schmidt* [1995] 1 AC 339 (no discretion in English court under Extradition Act 1989 to stay extradition to Germany when ruse by police brought S to England from Ireland so that he could be arrested).

[252] *R v Mullen* [2000] QB 520, cited in *R (Binyam Mohamed) v Foreign Secretary* (revised judgment of Divisional Court, 31 July 2009, para 9(iii)).

[253] Art 5(1)(f) ECHR and e.g. *Bozano v France* (1987) 9 EHRR 297 (disguised extradition held to be unlawful deportation). And see the Marty Report, *Secret detentions and illegal transfers of detainees involving Council of Europe states* (2nd report of Special Rapporteur to Parliamentary Assembly, Council of Europe, 11 June 2007).

CHAPTER 21

The police and personal liberty

The preservation of law and order and the prevention and detection of crime are matters of great importance to the maintenance of organised government. But it is equally important that these concerns should not be used to justify equipping the police with more power than is absolutely necessary, for every power conferred on police officers inevitably means a corresponding reduction in the liberty of the individual. It is difficult to exaggerate the central importance of personal liberty in a free and democratic society. As the European Court of Human Rights reminded us, protection from arbitrary interference by the state with an individual's liberty is 'a fundamental human right' and as such it is protected by art 5 of the ECHR.[1] This is a measure which has assumed greater significance with the enactment of the Human Rights Act 1998, although it is by no means the only Convention right which will have a bearing on police conduct. As we shall see, arts 3 (inhuman and degrading treatment), 6 (fair trial) and 8 (respect for private life, home and correspondence) also have a role to play. There is thus a need to ensure that the police have adequate measures to protect the public without at the same time conferring powers that undermine the very freedom which the police are employed to defend.

A. Organisation of the police[2]

Local police forces

Under the Police Act 1996, England and Wales are divided into police areas, of which there are three kinds: the Metropolitan Police district, the City of London police, and those listed in Sch 1 to the Act. The Metropolitan Police was created in 1829 as the first modern British force: it is the only police force for which the Home Secretary was directly responsible as the police authority, though that responsibility has now passed to the Metropolitan Police Authority.[3] The chief officer of the Metropolitan Police is the Commissioner of Police for the Metropolis, appointed by the Crown on the advice of the Home Secretary, who must take into account the views of the Metropolitan Police Authority and the London Mayor. The City of London Police is a separate force; the chief officer, the Commissioner, is appointed by the police authority, the Court of Common Council, subject to the approval of the Home Secretary. Outside London there are 41 police areas listed in the Schedule to the 1996 Act, giving a total of 43. The 1996 Act also provides that for each police area there shall be a police authority (which in turn shall be a body corporate), but as a result of controversial measures introduced in 1994 and since, the composition of these authorities has changed, most notably by the reduction in the number of local authority councillors.

A police force is under the direction and control of the chief constable, though he or she must have regard to the local policing plan prepared by the police authority.[4] It is true that the police

---

[1] *Brogan v UK* (1989) 11 EHRR 117, at 134.

[2] For stimulating accounts of the issues, see Lustgarten, *The Governance of Police*, and Walker, *Policing in a Changing Constitutional Order*. For a perceptive account of organisational change in the police since 1954 (dealing with other issues besides), see T Newburn and R Reiner [2004] Crim LR 601.

[3] Greater London Authority Act 1999, s 319, amending Police Act 1996, s 101.

[4] For similar arrangements in London, see Greater London Authority Act 1999, s 314, inserting new Police Act 1996, s 59A.

authority has power to require the chief constable and any assistant chief constable to retire or resign in the interests of efficiency or effectiveness (ss 11, 12). In exercising this power, however, the police authority must act with the approval of the Home Secretary, who may take the initiative by requiring the police authority to retire or seek the resignation of the chief constable (s 42). The chief constable must be given an opportunity to make representations to the police authority or the Home Secretary before he or she can be required to retire or resign (ss 11, 42).[5] Chief constables are required to report annually to the police authority and (subject to a power of the chief constable with the support of the Home Secretary to withhold information which in the public interest ought not to be disclosed), the authority may require the chief constable to report on specific matters connected with the policing of the area (s 22). This is a power (previously contained in the Police Act 1964) to which Lord Scarman attached some importance in his inquiry into the Brixton riots in 1981. The breakdown of order in the social, and particularly racial, conditions of Brixton led Lord Scarman to make substantial criticisms of the police and their relations with the community.[6]

The Home Secretary

The Home Secretary has a statutory duty to exercise his or her powers in a manner 'best calculated to promote the efficiency and effectiveness of the police'.[7] He or she has a duty to determine 'strategic priorities' for policing in all areas of police authorities, though he or she must first consult the Association of Police Authorities and the Association of Chief Police Officers.[8] Where strategic priorities have been set in this way, the Home Secretary may direct police authorities to establish performance targets, the minister having a wide discretion to issue a direction to one or more or to all police authorities, and a power to impose different conditions on different authorities (s 38). He or she may also issue codes of practice relating to the discharge by police authorities of any of their functions (s 39), as well as codes of practice for chief officers (s 39A).[9] In cases where the Home Secretary is satisfied that a police force is failing to discharge any of its functions effectively, he or she may intervene and direct the authority to take 'specified measures' (s 40). Similar powers exist in relation to a failure by a police authority (s 40A).

In addition to these wide statutory powers, the Home Secretary exercises considerable financial control of a service the cost of which rose to £12 billion nationally.[10] Since 1856, a grant has been made from the exchequer towards the police expenses of local authorities. Payment of the grant, formerly 51 per cent of all approved expenses, is now determined annually by the Home Secretary with the approval of the Treasury. In determining how much an authority receives, the Home Secretary 'may exercise his discretion by applying such formulae or other rules as he considers appropriate' (s 46). Otherwise, the Home Secretary may prescribe by regulation the equipment to be used by police forces, as well as the 'particular procedures or practices' to be adopted by all police forces.[11] By s 50 of the 1996 Act, the Home Secretary may make regulations for the government, administration and conditions of service of police forces, in particular with respect to ranks, qualifications for appointment and promotion, probationary service, voluntary

---

[5] Cf *Ridge* v *Baldwin* [1964] AC 40, ch 30 B below, which concerned the dismissal of a chief constable under the pre-1964 legislation.

[6] Cmnd 8427, 1981.

[7] Police Act 1996, s 36. It is not a duty to promote the efficiency and effectiveness of the police.

[8] Ibid, s 37A (as inserted by the Police and Justice Act 2006).

[9] Inserted by Police Reform Act 2002, s 2.

[10] HC 353 (2006–7). According to the Home Affairs Committee, police expenditure in the UK (at 2.5% GDP) is the highest in the OECD: HC 364 (2007–08).

[11] Police Reform Act 2002, ss 6 and 7, amending Police Act 1996, s 53, and introducing s 53A. See also *R v Home Secretary, ex p Northumbria Police Authority* [1989] QB 28 (A W Bradley [1988] PL 298).

retirement, discipline, duties, pay, allowances, clothing and equipment. Her Majesty's Inspectors of Constabulary are appointed by and report to the Home Secretary, and may be directed by him or her to carry out an inspection of any force (s 54).

Centralisation of the police

The British system of policing was based on the principle of local police forces accountable to local communities. Indeed, in 1962 a royal commission on the police had rejected proposals for the creation of a national police force under the control of central government,[12] a position reaffirmed by the government in 2004. It is clear, however, that the principle of local policing is breaking down, reflecting not only a weakening of local government in the British constitution but also the growing political sensitivity about crime in the years since the royal commission reported in 1962.[13] So although we still do not have a national police force, we have one that is subject to greater centralised national control, as reflected most clearly in the 'national policing plan'. In the white paper *Building Communities, Beating Crime*, the government quite explicitly acknowledged that it has 'a clear role in setting the national direction and strategic framework for policing in England and Wales'.[14] In the same document it was also acknowledged that the Home Secretary has 'overall responsibility for ensuring the delivery of an efficient and effective police service',[15] and in recent years there has been great concern about better management of the police, improved standards in terms of the prevention and detection of crime, and greater consistency between police forces, as well as the need for greater community involvement in policing matters.

These powers of the Home Secretary in relation to local police forces have been accompanied by important organisational changes which have led to the creation of bodies with national responsibility for policing. The most important of these is the Serious Organised Crime Agency, with a Board and a Director General appointed by the Home Secretary. Its functions are to prevent and detect serious organised crime, and to contribute to the reduction of such crime.[16] Its other function is to gather, store, analyse and disseminate information relevant to the prevention, detection, investigation or prosecution of offences.[17] The Agency has the power to institute criminal proceedings, as well as to provide support to other police forces and law enforcement agencies. It is also provided that 'despite the references to serious organised crime in section 2(1), SOCA may carry on activities in relation to other crime if they are carried on for the purposes of any of the functions conferred on SOCA by section 2 or 3'.[18] The Agency must submit an annual report to the Home Secretary and the Scottish Ministers, which must be laid before Parliament and the Scottish Parliament.[19] The Home Secretary may determine the strategic priorities of the Agency, after first consulting the Scottish Ministers.[20] The Home Secretary also has other powers of direction and control,[21] and it is the Home Secretary who is responsible for funding the Agency.[22]

---

[12] Cmd 1728, 1962. See J Hart [1963] PL 283.

[13] See the white papers *Policing a New Century*, Cm 5326, 2001; *Building Communities, Beating Crime*, Cm 6360, 2004; and more recently *Protecting the Public: Supporting the Police to Succeed*, Cm 7749, 2009.

[14] Cm 6360, 2004, para 5.5.

[15] See also Police Act 1996, s 36.

[16] Serious Organised Crime and Police Act 2005, s 2.

[17] Ibid, s 3.

[18] Ibid, s 5(3).

[19] Ibid, s 7.

[20] Ibid, s 9.

[21] Ibid, ss 10–15.

[22] Ibid, ss 17–18.

B. Personal liberty and police powers

Police powers short of arrest

Most police powers affecting the individual's liberty depend on an arrest having been made. At common law, the pre-arrest powers of the police are very limited, a point illustrated by *Jackson* v *Stevenson*,[23] where it was held to be contrary to constitutional principle and illegal to search someone to establish whether there are grounds for an arrest.[24] Stop and search powers are now found in a number of statutes. By s 23 of the Misuse of Drugs Act 1971, a constable may search (and detain for the purpose of the search) anyone who is suspected on reasonable grounds to be in unlawful possession of a controlled drug.[25] Similar powers apply in relation to vehicles. Powers to stop and search are also found in Part I of the Police and Criminal Evidence Act 1984 (PACE).[26] Thus a constable may search a person or vehicle, or anything which is in the vehicle, for stolen or prohibited articles, a term defined to include an offensive weapon, an article used for the purpose of burglary or related crimes, or an article for destroying or causing damage to property.[27] The power may also be used where someone is suspected of carrying a knife,[28] or prohibited fireworks (s 1),[29] but may be so exercised only if the constable 'has reasonable grounds for suspecting that he will find stolen or prohibited articles' or any prohibited fireworks (s 1(3)), or that someone is carrying a knife or other sharp implement in a public place.[30]

The Home Office Code A (Code of Practice on the Exercise by Police Officers of Statutory Powers of Stop and Search),[31] gives some guidance as to reasonable grounds for suspicion, and emphasises that 'Reasonable suspicion cannot be based on generalisations or stereotypical images of certain groups or categories of people as more likely to be involved in criminal activity'.[32] If during a search a constable discovers articles to which the Act applies, they may be seized (s 1(6)). But before exercising these powers, a constable must (inter alia) inform the person to be searched of his or her name and police station and of the grounds for the search. The Act also requires a police officer to provide documentary evidence that he or she is a police officer if he or she is not in uniform (s 2). Details of the search must be recorded and if requested a copy must be supplied to the person searched (s 3). Failure to do so could render the action unlawful.[33] Reasonable force may be used by the police (s 117), but during any search made before an arrest a person may not be required to remove any clothing in public except for an outer coat, jacket or gloves (s 2(9)).[34]

---

[23] (1879) 2 Adam 255.

[24] See also *Kenlin* v *Gardner* [1967] QB 510 (no common law power to stop and question), and *R* v *Lemsatef* [1977] 2 All ER 835 (no common law power to detain a suspect to help the police with their inquiries).

[25] See *Wither* v *Reid* 1979 SLT 192 (on the distinction between (*a*) arrest and (*b*) detention for search).

[26] Note that they are powers of 'stop and search' not 'stop and question'. See Zander, *The Police and Criminal Evidence Act 1984*, p 11. However, a person acting in an anti-social manner may be required to give his or her name and address to a constable in uniform (Police Reform Act 2002, s 50), a power exercisable also by designated community support officers (ibid, Sch 4, para 3).

[27] See Criminal Justice Act 2003, s 1.

[28] Criminal Justice Act 1988, s 140.

[29] Serious Organised Crime and Police Act 2005, s 115.

[30] See Criminal Justice Act 1988, s 139.

[31] Issued under Police and Criminal Evidence Act 1984, ss 66, 67. There are in fact eight codes (A–H), each dealing with different aspects of police practice, several of which are referred to below.

[32] But compare paragraph 2.6: 'Where there is reliable information or intelligence that members of a group or gang who habitually carry knives unlawfully or weapons or controlled drugs, and wear a distinctive item of clothing or other means of identification to indicate their membership of the group or gang, that distinctive item of clothing or other means of identification may provide reasonable grounds to stop and search a person.'

[33] *Osman* v *DPP* (1999) 163 JP 725.

[34] See further Code A, paras 3.1–3.7. On the use of the s 1 power see Zander, above, pp 26–8.

Stop and search powers were extended in the Criminal Justice and Public Order Act 1994 (s 60) to prevent incidents of serious violence which it is reasonably anticipated may take place.

Under the Road Traffic Act 1988, s 163, a constable in uniform may require a person driving a vehicle or a cyclist to stop. Failure to do so is an offence. It has been held that in exercising this power the police may immobilise a vehicle by removing the keys. Where a police officer has required a vehicle to stop, he 'is entitled to take reasonable steps to detain it for such reasonable time as will enable him, if he suspects it to have been stolen, to effect an arrest and to explain to the driver the reason for the arrest'.[35] In some circumstances, a police officer can require the driver to produce his or her driving licence and his or her name, address and date of birth.[36] But otherwise the driver is under no duty to answer any questions which the police may ask: 'the right to silence in such a circumstance is predominant'.[37] In addition to powers conferred by the Road Traffic Act 1988, s 4 of PACE authorises the police to set up road checks when it is believed that there is or about to be in the locality during the period of the check someone who has committed or witnessed an indictable offence, someone who is intending to commit such an offence, or an escaped prisoner. This is a considerable power, though it can be used only for the purpose of determining whether the vehicle is carrying any of the categories of person referred to. It confers no power on the police to question the driver or occupants of a vehicle and imposes no duty on such people to respond to police questions.

Police powers of arrest

1 *Grounds for arrest.* Powers of arrest are not exclusive to the police and some may be exercised by any person. But today the very great majority of arrests are undertaken by the police. The significance of the act of arrest is that it is at that moment that an individual loses his or her liberty and, if the arrest is lawful, becomes subject to lawful detention. Arrests are of two kinds: (a) with a warrant and (b) without a warrant, and the latter may take place with statutory or common law authority. It is a precondition of a lawful arrest that it is executed in a lawful manner.

(*a*) *Arrest with a warrant.* Under the Magistrates' Courts Act 1980, s 1, criminal proceedings may be initiated either by the issue of a summons, requiring the accused to attend court on a certain day, or, in more serious cases, by a warrant of arrest, naming the accused and the offence with which he or she is charged. A warrant is obtained from a magistrate after a written application (information) has been substantiated on oath.[38] A warrant may be executed anywhere in England or Wales by a police constable.[39] If the warrant is to arrest a person charged with an offence, it may be executed even when a constable does not have it in his or her possession, but the warrant must be shown on demand to the arrested person as soon as possible.[40] Despite judicial dicta to the contrary,[41] a person arrested would seem entitled to know that he or she is being arrested under a warrant (for if not, how can he or she demand to see it?). Where a constable in good faith executes a warrant that seems valid on its face, he or she is protected from liability for the arrest by the Constables' Protection Act 1750 if it should turn out that the warrant was beyond the jurisdiction of the magistrate who issued it.[42] The requirement that the warrant be issued by a

---

[35] *Lodwick* v *Sanders* [1985] 1 All ER 577.

[36] Road Traffic Act 1988, s 163.

[37] *Lodwick* v *Sanders* [1985] 1 All ER 577, 581. But see later on the 'right to silence'.

[38] The exercise of the power may not be delegated: *R* v *Manchester Stipendiary Magistrate, ex p Hill* [1983] 1 AC 328.

[39] They may now be executed in Scotland: Criminal Justice and Public Order Act 1994, s 136. For the cross-border execution of warrants in the UK, see *R* v *Manchester Stipendiary Magistrate, ex p Granada Ltd* [2001] 1 AC 300 (C Walker [1997] 56 CLJ 114).

[40] Magistrates' Courts Act 1980, s 125D; and cf *R* v *Purdy* [1975] QB 288.

[41] *R* v *Kulynycz* [1971] 1 QB 367, 372.

[42] See also *McGrath* v *RUC* [2001] 2 AC 731.

magistrate is thus as much a safeguard for the police as it is for the person named on it. When an arrest warrant has been issued, a constable may enter and search premises to make the arrest, using such reasonable force as is necessary.[43]

(b) *Arrest without a warrant under PACE.* The law on arrest without a warrant was revised and amended by the Serious Organised Crime and Police Act 2005.[44] This abolished the distinction between arrestable and non-arrestable offences. As amended in 2005, s 24 of PACE now provides that a constable may arrest without a warrant (a) anyone who is about to commit an offence; (b) anyone who is in the act of committing an offence; (c) anyone whom he or she has reasonable grounds for suspecting to be about to commit an offence; and (d) anyone whom he or she has reasonable grounds for suspecting to be committing an offence. There are also powers of arrest where a constable suspects an offence has been committed, and where an offence has been committed. In the former case, a constable may arrest anyone whom he or she has reasonable grounds to suspect of being guilty of the offence. In the latter case, he or she may arrest anyone who is guilty of the offence or anyone whom he or she has reasonable grounds for suspecting to be guilty of it.[45] These powers of arrest contained in s 24(1)–(3) apply to any offence and not only to arrestable offences, as in the past. However, the powers are only exercisable if it is necessary to make the arrest because any of the reasons in s 24(5) exist, though in practice it may be difficult to see how significantly this will constrain the powers of the constable.[46] These reasons include the prompt and effective investigation of the offence, and the prevention of a prosecution from being hindered by the disappearance of the suspect.[47]

In addition to these powers of arrest by a constable, s 24A of PACE provides that a person other than a constable may arrest without a warrant anyone who is in the act of committing an indictable offence, and anyone whom he or she has reasonable grounds for suspecting to be committing an indictable offence. Moreover, where an indictable offence has been committed, a person other than a constable may arrest without a warrant anyone who is guilty of the offence or anyone whom he or she has reasonable grounds for suspecting to be guilty of it.[48] The fact that this universal power of summary arrest is confined to indictable offences is an important limitation, but most people will be unaware of which offences are indictable and which are not. Further limitations on this power (which may make its use unwise) are to be found in s 24A(3), which provides that it may only be exercised where the person making the arrest has reasonable grounds for believing that any of the reasons mentioned in s 24A(4) apply to make it necessary to arrest the person in question, and it is not reasonably practicable for a constable to make the arrest. Section 24A(4) provides in turn that the reasons justifying the summary arrest are to prevent the person arrested causing physical injury to himself or herself or another person, suffering physical injury, causing loss or damage to property, or making off before a constable can assume

---

[43] Police and Criminal Evidence Act 1984, ss 17, 117.

[44] For a fuller discussion, see R C Austin [2007] Crim Law Rev 459.

[45] On the meaning of reasonable grounds for suspicion, see *O'Hara v Chief Constable of the RUC* [1997] AC 286; *Buckley v Thames Valley Chief Officer* [2009] EWCA Civ 356. The latter emphasises that 'an arresting officer may rely on what he had been told by others who may be civilian informants, reliable or unreliable, or other officers, providing that the information thus assembled provides reasonable grounds for suspicion' (Hughes LJ, para [9]). Also *Metropolitan Police Commissioner v Raissi* [2008] EWCA Civ 1237.

[46] See also J R Spencer, NLJ, 1 April 2005.

[47] Before the necessity requirement introduced in 2005, the test adopted by the courts was the *Wednesbury* test (see ch 30 below) that the arrest (being the exercise of a discretionary power) had to be not unreasonable. But this was not a high threshold for the police to cross: see *Holgate-Mohammed v Duke* [1984] AC 437; *R v Chalkley* [1998] QB 848; *Cumming v Northumbria Chief Constable* [2003] EWCA Civ 1844. There will no doubt be shades of necessity, and the question now may be whether the constable had reasonable grounds to believe that the arrest was necessary for the reasons set out in s 24(5). Compare (*R(C) v 'A' Magistrates' Court* [2006] EWHC 2352 (Admin)).

[48] See *Walters v W H Smith & Son Ltd* [1914] 1 KB 595, and *R v Self* (1992) 95 Cr App R 42.

responsibility for him or her. These are seriously circumscribed powers, and in practice they may empower community support officers rather than citizens with no connection with the police.

2 *Common law powers of arrest without warrant.* Alongside the powers of arrest without a warrant under ss 24 and 24A of PACE, some residual common law powers continue in force. At common law, a police officer has a power to arrest without warrant anyone who commits a breach of the peace. But this power – the purpose of which is 'to deal with emergencies' – is one which 'belongs to the ordinary citizen as much as to the constable'.[49] The important decision in *R* v *Howell*[50] established that there is a power of arrest where a breach of the peace was committed in the presence of the person making the arrest; or if the person making the arrest reasonably believed that such a breach would be committed in the immediate future by the person arrested, even though at the time of the arrest he or she had not committed the breach; or if a breach of the peace has been committed and it is reasonably believed that a renewal of it is threatened. *Howell* also established that there can be no breach of the peace unless an act was done or threatened to be done which actually either harmed a person or his or her property, was likely to cause such harm, or put someone in fear of such harm being done.[51]

An apprehended breach of the peace is an essential ingredient in the power to arrest without a warrant for obstructing a police officer in the execution of his or her duty.

In *Wershof* v *Metropolitan Police Commissioner*[52] a young solicitor was telephoned by his brother and asked to come to the family jewellery shop where the brother was engaged in a dispute with a police officer about a ring which the officer thought had been stolen. When the solicitor arrived, he told the police officer that he could take the ring only if he gave a receipt for it. The officer refused to provide a receipt, the solicitor refused to let him have the ring, and after an argument the solicitor was arrested for obstructing a police officer in the execution of his duty. The police officer thereupon put a tight and painful grip on the solicitor's right arm and frog-marched him down the road. In a successful action by the solicitor for damages for assault, the court held that a police officer has power to arrest without a warrant a person who wilfully obstructs him in the execution of his duty only if the obstruction was such that an offender actually caused or was likely to cause a breach of the peace. In this case the solicitor would not have physically resisted a seizure of the ring by force and this should have been apparent to the police officer.

These common law powers were considered by the Court of Appeal in *Bibby* v *Chief Constable of Essex*[53] where they were said to be 'exceptional'. Referring to a number of decisions,[54] Schiemann LJ said that there were four preconditions which must be satisfied before the power can now be exercised. First, 'only a sufficiently real and present threat to the peace justified depriving a citizen, not at the time acting unlawfully, of his liberty'; second, the threat to the peace must come from the person to be arrested; third, the conduct must 'clearly interfere with the rights of others and its natural consequence must be "not wholly unreasonable violence" from a third party'; and finally, the conduct of the person to be arrested must be unreasonable. The Court of Appeal has also confirmed that (unlike in Scotland), breach of the peace is not an offence even though it provides grounds for summary arrest, and that anyone arrested should be released

---

[49] *McQuade* v *Chief Constable of Humberside* [2001] EWCA Civ 1330; [2002] 1 WLR 1347, at para [20].

[50] [1982] QB 416. See also *Albert* v *Lavin* [1982] AC 546, and *Foulkes* v *Merseyside Chief Constable* [1998] 3 All ER 705.

[51] A breach of the peace may occur in private premises: *McConnell* v *Chief Constable of Greater Manchester* [1990] 1 All ER 423.

[52] [1978] 3 All ER 540.

[53] *The Times*, 24 April 2000.

[54] *Foulkes* v *Chief Constable of Merseyside* [1998] 3 All ER 705, *Nicol* v *DPP* (1996) 160 JP 155, and *Redmond-Bate* v *DPP* [2000] HRLR 249.

when there is no longer a 'real danger' that the arrested person will commit another breach of the peace.[55]

3 *The manner of arrest*. Although the first ingredient of a proper arrest is the existence of lawful authority to make the arrest, it is not the only one. The arrest must also be executed in a proper manner, which means that the arrested person must be told of the fact of arrest (i.e. that he or she is under arrest) and also of the reasons for the arrest (PACE, s 28), measures 'laid down by Parliament to protect the individual against the excess or abuse of the power of arrest'.[56] The origin of the latter rule (requiring reasons to be given for the arrest) may be found in *Christie v Leachinsky*,[57] where the Liverpool police had purported to exercise a power of arrest contained in a local Act when they knew that the conditions for this were not met. When the officers concerned were later sued for wrongful arrest and false imprisonment, it was argued that the arrest was lawful because at the time they had information about Leachinsky which would have justified his arrest for another offence. The House of Lords held that the arrest was unlawful, since it was a condition of a lawful arrest that the person arrested should be entitled to know the reason for it. An actual charge need not be formulated at the time of arrest, but 'the arrested man is entitled to be told what is the act for which he is arrested'. Indeed, it has been said that 'giving the correct information of the reasons for an arrest was of the utmost constitutional significance'.[58]

This information must be given at the time of arrest or as soon as practicable thereafter.[59] Otherwise the arrest is unlawful (PACE, s 28(1), (3)) although there is nothing laid down in the Act specifying how the information should be communicated to an arrested person.[60] The issue was considered by the Court of Appeal in *Taylor v Thames Valley Chief Constable*[61] where it was said that the 'relevant principles remain those set out in *Christie*'s case'. In *Taylor*, a ten-year-old boy was arrested and was told that he had been arrested for violent disorder on 18 April at Hillgrove Farm (while he was attending an anti-vivisection protest with his mother). The arrest took place some six weeks later while the boy was taking part in another demonstration. It was held that the arrested person must be told 'in simple, non-technical language that he could understand, the essential legal and factual grounds for his arrest'.[62] It was also held that each case must depend on its own facts but that it has 'never been the law that an arrested person must be given detailed particulars of the case against him'.[63] In this case it was accepted that the information provided at the time of the arrest was sufficient, though it was also accepted that in some cases 'it will be necessary for the officer to give more facts than in others'.[64] Unlike the police stop and search powers, there is no statutory duty on police officers (even if not in uniform) to identify themselves as such to an arrested person.

---

[55] *Williamson v West Midlands Chief Constable* [2003] EWCA Civ 337; [2004] 1 WLR 14. For further treatment in the context of public assemblies, including discussion of *R (Laporte) v Gloucestershire Chief Constable* [2006] UKHL 55; [2007] 2 AC 105, see ch 24 below.

[56] *Hill v Chief Constable of South Yorkshire* [1990] 1 All ER 1046.

[57] [1947] AC 573, 593 (Lord Simonds). But note that the 1984 Act goes beyond the common law position: see *Hill v Chief Constable of South Yorkshire* (note 56 above). On the continuing importance of *Christie v Leachinsky*, see *O'Loughlin v Chief Constable of Essex* [1998] 1 WLR 374, *R v Chalkley* [1998] QB 848, and *Taylor v Thames Valley Chief Constable* [2004] EWCA Civ 858; [2004] 1 WLR 3155.

[58] *Edwards v DPP* (1993) 97 Cr App R 301.

[59] See *Dawes v DPP* [1995] 1 Cr App R 65.

[60] See *Nicholas v Parsonage* [1987] RTR 199.

[61] See note 57 above.

[62] Ibid, at para [24] (Clarke LJ), citing *Fox v UK* (1991) 13 EHRR 157.

[63] Ibid, at para [35].

[64] See *Murphy v Oxford* [1985] CA Transcript 56 (as cited in *Taylor*, above) where 'a person arrested for burglary was told that he was being arrested on suspicion of burglary in Newquay. As Lord Donaldson MR put it, no mention was made either of the fact that the premises in Newquay were a hotel or of the date on which the offence was committed' (ibid).

In relation to the requirements of s 28 of PACE, two interesting questions have arisen. First, what happens if the police are unable to inform the arrested person of the fact and reasons at the time of arrest and then fail to do so as soon as it becomes practicable? Does this subsequent failure mean that the earlier arrest is unlawful? In *DPP v Hawkins*,[65] the court's answer was no:

> When a police officer makes an arrest which he is lawfully entitled to make but is unable at the time to state the ground because it is impracticable to do so, . . . it is his duty to maintain the arrest until it is practicable to inform the arrested person of that ground. If, when it does become practicable, he fails to do so, then the arrest is unlawful, but that does not mean that acts, which were previously done and were, when done, done in the execution of duty, become, retrospectively, acts which were not done in the execution of duty.[66]

The second question relates to the position where the police have no reason to delay informing an arrested person of the fact and reasons for the arrest. Does this initial failure, rendering the arrest therefore unlawful, vitiate all the subsequent proceedings? Again, it seems not.

> In *Lewis v Chief Constable of South Wales*[67] two women were arrested for burglary but were not told why they were being arrested. They were then taken to a police station where they were informed of the reasons for the arrest, within (respectively) 10 minutes and 23 minutes after the time of arrest. Some five hours later both were released. They subsequently sued for wrongful arrest and false imprisonment and the question which arose was whether they were entitled to be compensated for 10 and 23 minutes respectively or for the entire five-hour period. The Court of Appeal agreed with the first instance decision that, although the initial arrest had been unlawful because the women had not been given the reasons for it, it ceased being unlawful when this was done. The court did not consider this result to be inconsistent with s 28(3) of PACE.

While a police officer may use reasonable force to make the arrest,[68] the use of unreasonable force does not necessarily make the arrest unlawful.[69]

C. Detention and questioning of suspects

Detention of suspects

An arrested person must be brought to a police station as soon as practicable after the arrest (s 30), although this may be delayed if his or her presence elsewhere is necessary for immediate investigation (s 30(10)). These provisions were amended by the Criminal Justice Act 2003, which introduced an exception to the duty under s 30(1) where the arrested person has been granted bail by a police officer at any time before arriving at a police station (so-called 'street bail' (s 30A)). At every police station that is designated for such detention,[70] there must be a custody officer who must be a police officer of the rank of sergeant or above (s 36).[71] It is the duty of the custody officer to authorise the detention of suspects if this is necessary to secure or preserve evidence relating to an offence or 'to obtain such evidence by questioning' the suspect (s 37). The custody officer is required to ensure that the detention is carried out in accordance with the 1984 Act and the Home Office Code of Practice on the Detention, Treatment and Questioning of Persons by

---

[65] [1988] 3 All ER 673.

[66] Ibid, at 674.

[67] [1991] 1 All ER 206.

[68] Police and Criminal Evidence Act 1984, s 117.

[69] *Simpson v Chief Constable of South Yorkshire Police*, The Times, 7 March 1991. Cf *Hill v Chief Constable of South Yorkshire*, note 56 above.

[70] See 1984 Act, s 35.

[71] On the limitations of this crucial measure designed 'to ensure that the welfare and interests of detained subjects are properly protected', see *Vince v Chief Constable of Dorset* [1993] 2 All ER 321.

Police Officers (Code C) (s 39), while a review officer is required by the Act to conduct regular reviews of detention.[72]

PACE now allows the police to detain people who have been arrested for up to 24 hours without being released or charged in the first instance (s 41). This may be extended to 36 hours by an officer of the rank of superintendent or above where the offence is an indictable offence (s 42), which includes murder, manslaughter, rape, kidnapping and much else besides. In the case of indictable offences, the period of 36 hours may be extended for up to 96 hours in total, if a magistrates' court (defined as a court of *two or more* justices of the peace, a potentially important safeguard) on application by the police is satisfied that further detention is justified to secure or preserve evidence by questioning the detainee (s 43). The detainee must be notified of the application to the magistrates and may be legally represented at the hearing. If the court does not authorise further detention, the detainee must be released or charged. Thus, from the time an arrested person reaches the police station, he or she may be detained for questioning by the police in connection with an indictable offence for up to 96 hours. A separate regime for the detention and questioning of terrorist suspects is to be found in the Terrorism Act 2000 (as amended).[73]

Securing and preserving evidence

The search of arrested or detained persons is authorised by s 54 of PACE which requires the custody officer to ascertain everything which the person has in his or her possession,[74] and empowers the custody officer to make a record of such items. Any item may be seized and retained except for clothing and personal effects, which may be seized only if the custody officer has reasonable grounds to believe the item is evidence relating to the offence; or believes that the arrested person may use the items in question to cause physical injury personally or to another, damage property, interfere with evidence, or assist him or her to escape. Under section 54A, an officer of the rank of inspector may authorise that a person detained in a police station be searched or examined to establish whether he or she has any mark that would tend to identify him or her as a person involved in the commission of an offence.[75] Section 55 authorises intimate searches, i.e. the physical examination of a person's body orifices other than the mouth.[76] But this may be done only if it has been authorised by an officer of the rank of inspector or above and there are reasonable grounds for believing that the person may have concealed on him or her either a Class A drug or an article which could be used to cause physical injury to himself or herself or others.

Section 61 of PACE allows fingerprints to be taken without consent with the authority of a police inspector in a wide range of circumstances,[77] while s 61A allows the police to take impressions of footwear.[78] By s 62, intimate samples may also be required in more limited circumstances, an intimate sample being defined to include various bodily fluids, including blood and swabs from

---

[72] Failure to conduct a review at the proper time could render detention unlawful: *Roberts* v *Chief Constable of Cheshire* [1999] 1 WLR 662. The review may be conducted by telephone if the appropriate officer is not present at the police station at the relevant time: 1984 Act, s 40A; also s 45A (video links), both provisions inserted by the Criminal Justice and Police Act 2001, s 73.

[73] See ch 26 below.

[74] For the position at common law, see *Lindley* v *Rutter* [1981] QB 128; *Brazil* v *Chief Constable of Surrey* [1983] 3 All ER 537.

[75] Introduced by the Anti-terrorism, Crime and Security Act 2001, s 90. The new section permits any such mark to be photographed without the consent of the detainee.

[76] See *R* v *Hughes* [1994] 1 WLR 876 (an intimate search requires physical intrusion, not visual examination).

[77] The circumstances in which prints may be taken and the nature of the prints which may be taken were extended by amendments introduced by the Criminal Justice and Police Act 2001, s 78. Fingerprints are defined to include palmprints.

[78] Serious Organised Crime and Police Act 2005, s 118.

intimate parts of the anatomy (s 65), but not now swabs taken from the mouth.[79] Unlike finger-prints, however, intimate samples may be taken only with the consent of the detainee. However, a refusal without good cause to give consent may lead a court to 'draw such inferences from the refusal as appear proper' (s 62(10)). A non-intimate sample (e.g. hair, a sample from under a nail, or a swab taken from the mouth) may, in contrast, be taken without consent, if authorised by an officer of the rank of inspector or above, if the offence for which the arrested person is being detained is a recordable offence (s 63). A non-intimate sample may also be taken without consent from a person who has been charged with or convicted of a recordable offence.[80] In some cases those in police detention may also be tested for drugs,[81] and arrested suspects (and others) may be photographed without their consent.[82]

Safeguards for suspects

The detention and questioning of suspects should be carried out in accordance with the safe-guards laid down in PACE and in Code C referred to above. The Act itself provides two safeguards. The first is the right not to be held incommunicado. A person who has been arrested and is held in custody in a police station is entitled on request to have a friend or relative (or some other person who is known to him or her) informed of the arrest, as soon as reasonably practi-cable (s 56).[83] The other safeguard provided by the Act is that arrested persons held in custody in a police station are entitled on request to consult a solicitor privately at any time (s 58).[84] It is for the person detained and not the police to decide who would be an appropriate solicitor for the purposes of giving advice.[85] In some cases the exercise of these rights may be delayed for up to 36 hours, where the arrest is for an indictable offence and where the delay has been authorised by an officer at least of the rank of inspector. This applies particularly where there is a risk of dan-ger to evidence or witnesses; or where the detained person has benefited from drug trafficking.[86] In other cases, both rights can be delayed for up to 48 hours and in some circumstances the right to consult a solicitor may be subject to the condition that it is conducted within 'the sight and hearing' of a uniformed officer.[87] There is no right to damages where the police act in breach of the duty to permit access to legal representatives,[88] though any evidence obtained from an accused person denied such representation may be inadmissible.[89]

---

[79] Criminal Justice and Public Order Act 1994, s 58, amending PACE, s 65. See now Serious Organised Crime and Police Act 2005, s 119.

[80] PACE, s 63(3A), (3B), inserted by Criminal Justice and Public Order Act 1994, s 55. See now Criminal Evidence (Amendment) Act 1997.

[81] 1984 Act, s 63B, inserted by Criminal Justice and Court Services Act 2000, s 57.

[82] PACE, s 64A (as amended by Serious Organised Crime and Police Act 2005, s 118).

[83] See R v Kerawalla [1991] Crim LR 451.

[84] See R v Samuel [1988] QB 615; R v Alladice (1988) 87 Cr App R 380. In R v South Wales Chief Constable, ex p Merrick [1994] 2 All ER 560 it was held that s 58 does not apply to give the accused the right of access to a solicitor where he is in custody in a magistrates' court following the denial of bail. But it was also held that there is a common law right to this effect 'which preceded the Act of 1984 and which [was] not abrogated by that Act' (p 572). This apparent common law right does not extend to having the solicitor present during police interviews: R v Chief Constable of the RUC, ex p Begley [1997] 1 WLR 1475. On the role of the solicitor, see R v Paris (1993) 97 Cr App R 99.

[85] R (Thompson) v Chief Constable of Northumbria [2001] 1 WLR 1342.

[86] Neither of the rights in ss 56 or 58 applies to persons arrested or detained under the Terrorism Act 2000, s 41 or Sch 8. The former gives a general arrest power without a warrant for offenders under the Act; and the latter deals with detention at ports and borders. Separate provision is made in the Terrorism Act 2000 for informing third parties and securing legal representation. See ch 26 below.

[87] Terrorism Act 2000, Sch 8, para 9.

[88] Cullen v Chief Constable of the RUC [2003] UKHL 39; [2003] 1 WLR 1763.

[89] R v Samuel, above, and see section E below.

So far as the right not to be held incommunicado is concerned, Code C referred to above provides that detained persons may receive visits at the custody officer's discretion and may speak on the telephone for a reasonable time to one person, although the call (other than to a solicitor) may be listened to and anything said used in evidence in any subsequent criminal proceedings (Code C, Part 5). As far as the right to legal advice is concerned, a person must be permitted to have his or her solicitor present while being interviewed by the police. The solicitor may be required to leave the interview only if his or her conduct is such that the interviewing officer is unable properly to put questions to the suspect (Part 6). The code also deals with such matters as the conditions of detention (Part 8), the giving of cautions to detained persons (Part 10), and the conduct of interviews (Part 11). Regarding cautions, a suspected person 'must be cautioned before any questions about [the suspected offence] . . . are put to [him]'. The effect of the Criminal Justice and Public Order Act 1994 is that the caution should be in the following terms: 'You do not have to say anything. But it may harm your defence if you do not mention when questioned something which you later rely on in court. Anything you do say may be given in evidence.' In conducting interviews, officers should neither try 'to obtain answers or elicit a statement by the use of oppression' nor 'indicate, except to answer a direct question, what action will be taken by the police if the person being questioned answers questions, makes a statement or refuses to do either' (Code C, Part 11).[90] Interviews should now be tape-recorded.[91]

The right to silence[92]

An important principle in criminal procedure is the right of a suspected or accused person to remain silent; it is for the police to obtain evidence of guilt, not for a suspect to clear himself or herself, strengthened now by art 6 of the ECHR which provides for the right to a fair trial.[93] The main control over abuse at the stage of questioning is exercised by the criminal courts.[94] It has long been established that a confession or statement by an accused person is not admissible in evidence at the trial unless it is voluntary, in the sense that it has not been obtained by fear of prejudice or hope of advantage, exercised or held out by a person in authority, or by oppression.[95] Although this principle was reinforced by the 1984 Act (excluding police evidence obtained oppressively), the right to silence has, however, been subject to erosion ever since, principally by measures that challenge the position accepted from time immemorial that the burden is on the police to obtain evidence of guilt, not on the suspect to prove innocence. Indeed, an early example of that erosion is to be found in the 1984 Act itself, which permits negative inferences to be drawn from an accused's failure to provide an intimate sample.

The drawing of negative inferences was extended by the Criminal Justice and Public Order Act 1994, which permits the court in criminal proceedings to draw such inferences as appear to it to be proper where the accused failed to mention 'any fact relied on in his defence in these proceedings' when questioned by the police or on being charged with an offence, where the fact was one which in the circumstances 'the accused could reasonably have been expected to

---

[90] In any period of 24 hours, a detained person normally should be allowed a continuous period of at least eight hours for rest, free from questioning, travel or other interruption arising out of the investigation (Part 12).

[91] See Code E (Code of Practice on Audio Recording Interviews with Suspects).

[92] On the different meanings of the right to silence, see *R v Director of Serious Fraud Office, ex p Smith* [1993] AC 1, per Lord Mustill. See generally Zander, pp 467–502. See also Cmnd 4991, 1972; and S Greer (1990) 53 MLR 709.

[93] Although 'not an absolute right', the right to silence is said by the European Court of Human Rights to lie 'at the heart of the notion of a fair procedure under article 6': see *Condron v UK* (2000) 31 EHRR 1, at 20. Also *Murray v UK* (1996) 22 EHRR 29.

[94] See *Lodwick v Sanders* [1985] 1 All ER 577, at 580–1 (Watkins LJ).

[95] *Ibrahim v R* [1914] AC 599. See now PACE 1984, ss 76, 78.

mention' (s 34).[96] The Act also permits a court or jury 'to draw such inferences as appear proper' from the failure of the accused to give evidence at his or her trial or without good cause to answer any question. The court or jury may, moreover, draw such inferences as appear proper in such circumstances in determining whether the accused is guilty of the offence charged. The accused is not, however, required to give evidence on his or her own behalf and is not guilty of contempt of court for failing to do so (s 35).[97] Subsequent amendments have confined the operation of these measures to situations where the accused has enjoyed the benefit of legal representation before remaining silent.[98] Although the drawing of adverse inferences is not itself a breach of the ECHR,[99] 'particular caution was required before a domestic court could invoke an accused's silence against him'.[100] There is no breach of art 6 when under the Road Traffic Act 1988 the owner of a vehicle is required to reveal the identity of its driver to a police officer.[101]

D. Police powers of entry, search and seizure[102]

Police powers of entry

'By the law of England', said Lord Camden in *Entick* v *Carrington*,[103] 'every invasion of private property, be it ever so minute, is a trespass. No man can set foot upon my ground without my licence, but he is liable to an action though the damage be nothing.'[104] There are, however, several circumstances in which the police may lawfully enter private property. One, as Lord Camden suggests, is with the consent of the owner or occupier.[105] Indeed, in *Robson* v *Hallett*[106] it was held that a police officer, like other members of the public coming to a house on lawful business, has an implied licence from the householder to walk to the front door and to ask whether he can come inside; and that he must be allowed a reasonable time to leave the premises before he becomes a trespasser. Otherwise, the police may have statutory authority to enter private property even without the consent of the owner. Under the Police and Criminal Evidence Act 1984, a police officer may enter private premises to execute a search warrant (s 8); and to execute an arrest warrant, arrest a person for an indictable offence,[107] arrest a person for certain public order or road traffic offences, recapture a person who is unlawfully at large,[108] save life and limb, or prevent serious damage to property (s 17).[109]

These powers under s 17 are generally exercisable only if the officer has reasonable grounds for believing that the person whom he or she is seeking is on the premises. There is a power to

---

[96] For background to the changes, see Royal Commission on Criminal Justice, Cm 2263, 1993, which argued in favour of the right to silence. The provisions have since been extended to post-charge questioning under the Counter-Terrorism Act 2008, s 22.

[97] See *R* v *Cowan* [1996] QB 373.

[98] Youth Justice and Criminal Evidence Act 1999, s 58; enacted in the light of *Murray* v *UK* (1996) 22 EHRR 29. But see *R* v *Ibrahim*, below.

[99] *Averill* v *UK* (2001) 31 EHRR 839, *Beckles* v *UK* (2003) 36 EHRR 162, and *R* v *Knight* [2003] EWCA Crim 1977; [2004] 1 WLR 340.

[100] *Beckles* v *UK*, note 99, above.

[101] *Brown* v *Stott* [2001] 1 AC 681.

[102] See Stone, *The Law of Entry, Search and Seizure*. Also Polyviou, *Entry, Search and Seizure: Constitutional and Common Law*.

[103] (1765) 19 St Tr 1030, 1066; ch 6.

[104] See also *Davis* v *Lisle* [1936] 2 KB 434.

[105] See Code of Practice for Searches of Premises by Police Officers (Code B) (2008 edn), Part 5.

[106] [1967] 2 QB 939. For fuller discussion, see Stone, above, ch 1.

[107] *Chapman* v *DPP* [1988] Crim LR 843.

[108] See *D'Souza* v *DPP* [1992] 4 All ER 545 (no right of entry unless *in pursuit* of someone unlawfully at large).

[109] The power of entry to save life and limb or to prevent serious damage to property may also be exercised by designated community support officers: Police Reform Act 2002, Sch 4, para 8.

search the premises entered, but only a search that is reasonably required for the purpose for which the power to enter was exercised. So if the officer enters premises under s 17 to arrest a person, he or she may search the premises to find that person, but may not under s 17 search for evidence relating to the offence. Other provisions of PACE confer this latter power.[110] Before exercising these powers of entry the police should normally inform the occupant of the reasons.[111] Additional powers of entry were conferred by the Police Act 1997, Part III, which enables senior police officers to authorise entry to and interference with property, mainly for the purposes of surveillance, as in the placing of listening devices. These controversial provisions were heavily amended as a result of opposition to the government's proposals in the House of Lords, so that in many instances (for example, in respect of domestic or office premises) the authorisation will not take effect until approved by a judicial commissioner.[112]

Apart from entry with consent or under statutory authority, a power of entry may arise from common law. Although PACE, s 17(5), abolishes all common law rules authorising the entry of private premises by the police, it is expressly provided that this does not affect any power of entry to deal with or prevent a breach of the peace. The existence of such a power appears to have been recognised in *Thomas* v *Sawkins*,[113] although the ratio of that case is controversial.[114] The application of the common law power was considered by the European Court of Human Rights in *McLeod* v *United Kingdom*.[115] In that case the complainant argued that by forcibly entering her house, ostensibly to prevent a breach of peace, the police had violated her right to respect for her home and private life in art 8 of the ECHR. The police had entered to help the complainant's former husband to recover property while the complainant was absent. The domestic courts held the entry to be lawful,[116] but the European Court of Human Rights upheld the complaint. The government argued that the entry could be justified under art 8(2). Although the Court accepted that the common law power was a power 'prescribed by law' for the purposes of art 8(2), it was held there that the exercise of the power could not be justified.

Police powers of search

1 *Search with a warrant.* The effect of decisions such as *Entick* v *Carrington* was that, except for the power to search for stolen goods, for which a warrant could be obtained at common law from a magistrate,[117] statutory powers were needed if the police were lawfully to search private premises. General powers for the granting of search warrants are to be found in s 8 of PACE.[118] A search warrant may be granted by a justice of the peace on an application by a police constable or designated investigating officer where there are reasonable grounds for believing that an indictable offence has been committed and that there is material on the premises which is likely to be of substantial value in the police investigation.[119] A search warrant may now take one of two forms. A 'specific premises' warrant is one which specifies the premises to be searched, while an 'all premises' warrant applies to any premises occupied or controlled by the person named in

---

[110] Police and Criminal Evidence Act 1984, s 32(2)(b). For an example of other powers of entry without a warrant, see *Whitelaw* v *Haining* 1992 SLT 956.

[111] *O'Loughlin* v *Chief Constable of Essex* [1998] 1 WLR 374.

[112] See further ch 22 C below.

[113] [1935] 2 KB 249; and see ch 24.

[114] See A L Goodhart (1936) 6 CLJ 22, and Ewing and Gearty, *The Struggle for Civil Liberties*, ch 6. The power is not confined to meetings. See *McLeod* v *Metropolitan Police Commissioner* [1994] 4 All ER 553.

[115] (1998) 27 EHRR 493.

[116] *McLeod* v *Metropolitan Police Commissioner* [1994] 4 All ER 553.

[117] See now Theft Act 1968, s 26.

[118] K W Lidstone (1989) 40 NILQ 333.

[119] See also the conditions set out in PACE 1984, s 8(3), considered in *Redknapp* v *City of London Police Commissioner* [2008] EWHC 1177.

the warrant.[120] The latter thus allows premises to be searched despite not being specified in the warrant, though these may be issued only where it is not reasonably practicable to specify all the premises of the person named in the warrant that may need to be searched. A warrant may now authorise multiple entries to the premises which it specifies.[121]

This power of magistrates to grant a warrant does not apply, however, to material which consists of or includes items subject to legal privilege, 'excluded material' or 'special procedure material'. Items subject to legal privilege include communications between a lawyer and his or her client (s 10),[122] while excluded material is defined to cover confidential personal records,[123] human tissue or tissue fluid taken for purposes of medical treatment and held in confidence, and journalistic material which is held in confidence (s 11).[124] Special procedure material refers to other forms of journalistic material,[125] and also other material that is held in confidence or subject to an obligation of secrecy and has been acquired in the course of any business, profession or other occupation (s 14). No warrant can be issued in relation to material subject to legal privilege, but orders may be issued by a judge under Sch 1, para 4,[126] following an *inter partes* hearing requiring excluded material or special procedure material to be delivered to a police constable or a designated investigating officer within seven days.[127] If this is not complied with, a judge may issue a warrant authorising a police officer or a designated investigating officer to enter and search premises and seize the material in question (Sch 1, para 12). A judge may issue both specific premises and all premises warrants for these purposes.

In some circumstances, a warrant may be secured under para 12 without first seeking an order under para 4. This practice was, however, strongly deprecated in *R v Maidstone Crown Court, ex p Waitt*,[128] where it was said: 'The special procedure under section 9 and schedule 1 is a serious inroad upon the liberty of the subject. The responsibility for ensuring that the procedure is not abused lies with circuit judges . . . The responsibility is greatest when the circuit judge is asked to issue a search warrant under paragraph 12. It is essential that the reason for authorising the seizure is made clear. The preferred method of obtaining material for a police investigation should always be by way of an *inter partes* order under paragraph 4, after notice of application has been served under paragraph 8. An *ex parte* application under paragraph 12 must never become a matter of common form and satisfaction as to the fulfilment of the conditions is an important matter of substance.'

Apart from thus extending the grounds for granting search warrants, the 1984 Act also introduced safeguards against misuse in the execution of a warrant.[129] These are found in ss 15 and 16 and they apply not only to search warrants issued under PACE, but also to warrants issued to a constable or a designated investigating officer 'under any enactment, including an enactment contained in an Act passed after this Act'.[130] An application, which is made ex parte, must be in

---

[120] PACE, s 8(1A), as inserted by the Serious Organised Crime and Police Act 2005, s 113.

[121] PACE, s 8(1C), as inserted by the Serious Organised Crime and Police Act 2005, s 114.

[122] Cf *R v Central Criminal Court, ex p Francis and Francis* [1989] AC 346. See *R v R* [1994] 4 All ER 260, and *R v Manchester Crown Court, ex p Rogers* [1999] 4 All ER 35.

[123] On confidential material, see Zuckerman [1990] Crim LR 472.

[124] Hospital records of patient admission and discharge are excluded material: see *R v Cardiff Crown Court, ex p Kellam*, The Times, 3 May 1993.

[125] On journalistic material, see s 13. Also *R v Bristol Crown Court, ex p Bristol Press Agency Ltd* (1987) 85 Cr App R 190; *R v Middlesex Crown Court, ex p Salinger* [1993] QB 564; *R v Manchester Stipendiary Magistrate, ex p Granada Television Ltd* [2001] 1 AC 300; and *R v Central Criminal Court, ex p Bright* [2001] 2 All ER 244.

[126] A judge for this purpose means a circuit judge, or a District Judge (Magistrates' Court): PACE 1984, Sch 1, para 17. As originally enacted, these powers were exercised only by circuit judges.

[127] The material may be surrendered voluntarily by the person who holds it without the consent of the person to whom it relates: *R v Singleton* [1995] 1 Cr App R 431.

[128] [1988] Crim LR 384. Also Zander, above, p 56.

[129] Further safeguards are in Code of Practice B above.

[130] Police and Criminal Evidence Act 1984, s 15(1).

writing and must explain the grounds for the application and the premises to be searched. The constable or designated investigating officer must answer on oath any question put by the justice of the peace or the judge. The warrant must specify the premises to be searched in the case of a specific premises warrant, and so far as this is reasonably practicable in the case of an all premises warrant.[131] A search warrant must be executed within three months from the date of its issue. Entry and search must be at a reasonable hour, and the police may be accompanied in the execution of a warrant by non-police officers who may be required to provide technical assistance.[132] Where the occupier of the premises is present, the police officers or designated investigating officers must identify themselves, produce the warrant, and supply a copy to the occupier.[133] When conducting a search, the police may detain individuals in one room while searching another room, and may use reasonable force to do so, if necessary.[134] If there is no person present, a copy of the warrant should be left in a prominent place on the premises. A search under the warrant does not authorise a general search of the premises, but only a search to the extent required for the purpose for which the warrant was issued (s 16).

> In *R v Longman*,[135] police officers with a search warrant effected entry to a house by deception, as a result of difficulties they had encountered in the past. A woman police officer in plain clothes pretended to deliver flowers. When the door was opened to her, other officers in plain clothes immediately entered the house, with one shouting 'Police, got a warrant' which he held in his hand. The Court of Appeal held that this procedure complied with ss 15 and 16 of PACE. The court rejected the contention that '*before entering* the premises a police officer must not only identify himself but must produce his warrant card and . . . also the search warrant and serve a copy of the search warrant on the householder'. It is enough that these things are done *after entry* to the premises. To hold otherwise, said Lord Lane CJ, would mean that the whole object of the more important type of search would be stultified.

2 *Search without a warrant.* Police powers to search without a warrant arise in three circumstances. The first is the power to search a person following arrest. Section 32 allows a constable (but no one else) to search an arrested person, at a place other than a police station, 'if the constable has reasonable grounds for believing that the arrested person may present a danger to himself or others'. A constable (but no one else) may search an arrested person for anything which might be used to escape from lawful custody, or for anything which might be evidence relating to an offence (s 32(2)), although in both these cases the power to search is a power to search only to the extent that is reasonably required for the purpose of discovering 'any such thing or any such evidence' (s 32(3)). Moreover, the power to search does not authorise the police to require a person to remove any clothing in public, except an outer coat, jacket or gloves (s 32(4)), but it does authorise the search of a person's mouth.[136] A police officer conducting such a search may seize any item which may cause physical injury, might assist in an escape from lawful custody, or is evidence relating to any offence (s 32(8)). The only items which may not be seized in this way are those which are subject to legal privilege (although no such exception applies to excluded material or to special procedure material) (s 32(9)).

The second power of search without a warrant is a power to search premises ancillary to arrest. The position is governed now also by PACE, s 32, whereby following the arrest of a person for an

---

[131] PACE, s 15(2A), as inserted by the Serious Organised Crime and Police Act 2005, s 113.

[132] Criminal Justice Act 2003, s 2, amending PACE, s 16. See *Lord Advocate's Reference (No 1 of 2002)* 2002 SLT 1017 for the position in Scotland.

[133] See *R v Chief Constable of Lancashire, ex p Parker* [1993] QB 577 (the warrant and any schedule must be shown; an uncertified photocopy is impermissible, rendering the search unlawful and requiring the return of any seized documents). See also *Redknapp v City of London Police Commissioner*, above (copy must be left).

[134] *DPP v Meaden* [2003] EWHC 3005 (Admin); [2004] 4 All ER 75.

[135] [1988] 1 WLR 619. See also *Linehan v DPP* [2000] Crim LR 861.

[136] Criminal Justice and Public Order Act 1994, s 59.

indictable offence, a constable (but no one else) may enter any premises in which the person was when arrested or immediately before he or she was arrested. The constable may search the premises for evidence relating to the offence for which the person was arrested (s 32(2)(b)). At common law, the power to search premises incidental to arrest was a power to search at the time of the arrest. So in *McLorie* v *Oxford*[137] it was held that after having arrested a suspect and detained him in custody, the police had no right to return to the house to search for the instruments of crime, even of serious crime; that is to say, no right to do so unless they could get a search warrant, although (as we have seen) that would not have been available in all circumstances where it might have been necessary. Yet although the police powers to secure search warrants are now much wider, so too are their powers of search ancillary to arrest without a warrant. Section 32 is at least open to the interpretation that the power to search the premises where the person was when arrested may be, but need not be, contemporaneous with the arrest.[138]

The third power of search without a warrant is a power to search the home of the arrested person, even though he or she was not arrested there and even though he or she was not there immediately before arrest. At common law, the courts seemed reluctant to recognise any such power, though there were suggestions that such a search might be permitted where the house search was concerned with securing evidence relating to the offence for which the person had been arrested.[139] Section 18 of PACE now permits a constable or a designated community support officer to enter and search any premises occupied or controlled by any person who is under arrest for an indictable offence if there are reasonable grounds to suspect that there is on the premises evidence (other than items subject to legal privilege) relating to that offence or to a related indictable offence. However, the power can be used only in relation to premises actually owned or controlled by the arrested person, and not premises the police reasonably believe to be so owned or controlled.[140] The exercise of the power should normally be authorised in writing by an inspector or an officer of a higher rank, although the power can be used without first taking a suspect to the police station and securing authorisation, if this is necessary for the effective investigation of the offence.

Police powers of seizure

The powers of search which we have discussed are generally also associated with a power of seizure. However, the nature of that power varies from case to case. In the case of entry to search for an escaped person or to make an arrest (s 17), there is no power to seize and retain property. In the case of search with a search warrant (s 8), there is a power only to seize and retain 'anything for which a search has been authorised'.[141] The same is true of the power to enter and search an arrested person's premises after arrest (s 18). In the case of a search of premises where the arrested person was at or immediately before the arrest (s 32), there is no power of seizure in the section itself, although in the case of a personal search there is a right to retain anything reasonably believed to be evidence of any offence, including an offence unrelated to the grounds for the arrest. What is the position if the police are on property for any of these purposes or if they are present with the consent of the owner or occupier and they stumble across something

---

[137] [1982] QB 1290.

[138] The power can be used only if the police officer has reasonable grounds for believing that there is evidence on the premises for which a search is permitted, and this must be the genuine reason for the entry: *R* v *Beckford* (1992) 94 Cr App R 43.

[139] *Jeffrey* v *Black* [1978] QB 490.

[140] *Khan* v *Metropolitan Police Commissioner* [2008] EWCA Civ 723; if there is any doubt, the police can always apply for a warrant.

[141] See *R* v *Chief Constable of Warwickshire, ex p Fitzpatrick* [1998] 1 All ER 65, and *R* v *Chesterfield JJ, ex p Bramley* [2000] 1 All ER 411.

which may suggest that an offence has been committed? In what circumstances, if any, can the police seize that evidence? Clearly, they can do so if they are present with a search warrant and the material relates to the offence for which the warrant was granted. But what if it relates to some wholly unconnected offence? Similarly, what is the position if the police enter under s 17 to make an arrest and stumble across incriminating evidence?

The power of seizure is governed at common law by the Court of Appeal decision in *Ghani* v *Jones*,[142] where it was held that before seizing private property in the course of an investigation, the police must have reasonable grounds for believing (*a*) that a serious crime has been committed; (*b*) that the article is the instrument by which the crime was committed or is material evidence to prove commission of the crime; and (*c*) that the person in possession of the article is implicated in the crime 'or at any rate his refusal (of consent to the police) must be quite unreasonable'; while (*d*) the police must not keep the article longer than is reasonably necessary; and (*e*) the lawfulness of the conduct of the police must be judged at the time and not (as in the earlier notorious decision of Horridge J in *Elias* v *Pasmore*) by what happens afterwards.[143] It was held in the latter case that the 'interests of the State' justified the police in seizing material that was relevant to the prosecution for any crime of any person, not only of the person who was arrested.

Additional powers of seizure and retention are in PACE, ss 19–22, and now the Criminal Justice and Police Act 2001, ss 50–70. These powers supplement but do not replace the common law powers (s 19(5)).[144] So to the extent that the statute is less extensive, the police may continue to rely on their common law powers as recognised by *Ghani* v *Jones*[145] and in subsequent cases.[146] The powers conferred by s 19 apply where a constable or a designated investigating officer is lawfully on any premises, whether by invitation, to make an arrest (in the case of a constable), or to conduct a search with or without a warrant. In such circumstances material may be seized where the constable or the designated investigating officer has reasonable grounds to believe *either* that it has been obtained as a result of the commission of any offence (s 19(2)); *or* that it is evidence in relation to an offence which he or she is investigating, or any other offence (s 19(3)). In either case, seizure is permitted only where this is necessary to prevent the items from being concealed, lost, damaged, altered or destroyed. The only restriction on what may be seized relates to items reasonably believed to be subject to legal privilege (s 19(6)). By s 21, a constable or a designated investigating officer who seizes anything is required, if requested, to provide a record of what is seized to the occupier of the premises or the person who had custody of it immediately before the seizure.

In addition, the person who had custody or control of the item seized has a right of access to it under the supervision of the police, although this may be refused if the officer in charge of the investigation reasonably believes that access would prejudice the investigation.[147] The effect of the changes introduced in 2001 is to enable the police to seize material so that it can be sifted elsewhere.[148]

---

[142] [1970] 1 QB 693.

[143] Cf *Frank Truman (Export) Ltd* v *Metropolitan Police Commissioner* [1977] QB 952; *Wershof* v *Metropolitan Police Commissioner* [1978] 3 All ER 540.

[144] On the continuing application of the common law, see *R (Rottman)* v *Metropolitan Police Commissioner* [2002] UKHL 20; [2002] 2 AC 692.

[145] [1970] 1 QB 693.

[146] See *Garfinkel* v *Metropolitan Police Commissioner* [1972] Crim LR 44.

[147] It has been said that these provisions 'vest in the police no title to the property seized but only a temporary right to retain property for the specified statutory purposes': *Costello* v *Chief Constable of Derbyshire* [2001] 1 WLR 1437 at 1441 (Lightman J).

[148] Criminal Justice and Police Act 2001, ss 50–70. For the position before the Act, see *R* v *Chesterfield JJ, ex p Bramley* [2000] QB 576.

E. Remedies for abuse of police powers

Self-defence[149]

At the time of interference with person or property, the citizen may have some right of self-defence and this can affect both civil and criminal liability. The point is acknowledged in the leading case, *Christie v Leachinsky*,[150] the ratio of which (as we have seen) forms the basis of what is now s 28 of PACE. There Lord Simonds said that 'it is the corollary of the right of every citizen to be thus free from arrest that he should be entitled to resist arrest unless that arrest is lawful'.[151] In *Abbassy v Metropolitan Police Commissioner*,[152] Woolf LJ acknowledged that one of the reasons for the rule that a person is to be told the reason for his arrest is so that, if what he is told is not a reason which justifies his arrest, he can exercise 'his right to resist arrest'.[153] On the other hand, under the Police Act 1996, s 89, it is an offence to assault, resist or wilfully obstruct a constable in the execution of his or her duty. There are therefore hazards in the way of a citizen who uses force to resist what he or she believes to be an unlawful arrest by police, whether of himself or herself or of a close relation.[154]

It has thus been pointed out that 'the law does not encourage the subject to resist the authority of one whom he knows to be an officer of the law'.[155] Although in *Kenlin v Gardiner* two boys were entitled to use reasonable force to escape from two constables who were seeking to question them,[156] in general it is inexpedient by self-defence to resist arrest by a police officer: if the arrest is lawful, the assault on the constable is aggravated because he or she is in execution of duty. But if a defendant 'applies force to a police or court officer which would be reasonable if that person were not a police or court officer, and the defendant believes that he is not, then even if his belief is unreasonable he has a good plea of self-defence'.[157] The offence of obstructing a constable in execution of his or her duty has been widely interpreted in English law;[158] the equivalent offence in Scotland has been interpreted as limited to some physical interference with the police.[159]

Habeas corpus[160]

If an individual is wrongfully deprived of liberty, it is not sufficient that he or she should be able to sue the gaoler for damages under the ordinary civil law. Whether detained by an official or by a private individual, it would be wrong that the detention should continue while the process of civil litigation takes its normal lengthy course. English law provides in the writ of habeas corpus a means by which a person detained without legal justification may secure prompt release. The person responsible for the detention is not thereby punished, but the person imprisoned is set free and may pursue such further remedies for compensation or punishment as may be

---

[149] See C Harlow [1974] Crim LR 528.

[150] [1947] AC 573.

[151] Ibid, at 591.

[152] [1990] 1 All ER 193.

[153] And see *Edwards v DPP* (1993) 97 Cr App R 301.

[154] *R v Fennell* [1971] QB 428.

[155] *Christie v Leachinsky* [1947] AC 573, 599 (Lord du Parcq).

[156] [1967] 2 QB 510. And see *Lindley v Rutter* [1981] QB 128; *Pedro v Diss* [1981] 2 All ER 59; and *Dawes v DPP* [1995] 1 Cr App R 65.

[157] *Blackburn v Bowering* [1994] 3 All ER 380, at 384.

[158] R C Austin [1982] CLP 187; Card, *Public Order Law*, ch 9.

[159] *Curlett v McKechnie* 1938 JC 176.

[160] And see ch 31 below.

available. Habeas corpus may be sought by convicted prisoners, those detained in custody pending trial, and those held by the police during criminal investigations;[161] those awaiting deportation or otherwise detained under the Immigration Act 1971; those awaiting extradition; and mental patients. We have seen that the Bill of Rights declared that excessive bail ought not to be required: legislation today encourages magistrates to give bail to persons awaiting trial whenever possible,[162] although this presumption has been seriously eroded by the Criminal Justice and Public Order Act 1994 in respect of serious offences (s 25) and offences committed while on bail (s 26).

Habeas corpus has often been described as 'the most important writ known to the constitutional law of England, affording as it does a swift and imperative remedy in all cases of illegal restraint or confinement'.[163] Its scope is potentially very wide. Suffice to say for present purposes that it is available to anyone who is illegally detained by the police. In 1981 Donaldson LJ pointed out that, 'all should know that the writ of habeas corpus has not fallen into disuse, but is . . . a real and available remedy'.[164] On that occasion, before the passing of PACE, the writ was issued in the case of a man who had been in police detention for two days without being charged or brought before magistrates. However, now that 'strict time limits apply to detention, with provision for magistrates' court warrants to extend detention periods, there should be very little scope for habeas corpus applications in relation to suspects in police custody'.[165] But an action would lie if someone were detained for more than 36 hours without a warrant or, as shown in *Re Gillen's Application*,[166] where there is evidence that the police are physically maltreating a suspect. An application for a writ of habeas corpus has 'virtually absolute priority over all other court business'.[167]

Legal proceedings against the police

A person who claims to be the victim of unlawful police conduct may be able to bring an action for damages against the chief constable, who is vicariously liable for the unlawful acts committed by his or her officers.[168] An action may be for assault, wrongful arrest, false imprisonment, trespass to property or goods,[169] or may take the form of an action for the return of property which has been improperly seized.[170] Similarly, it is possible to bring an action for malicious procurement of a search warrant; but it is necessary to show malice in order to succeed.[171] An action for malicious prosecution may be maintained by any person who is prosecuted for a criminal offence maliciously and without reasonable and probable cause; but it is difficult to win such an action

---

[161] See e.g. *R v Holmes, ex p Sherman* [1981] 2 All ER 612.

[162] Bail Act 1976.

[163] *Home Secretary v O'Brien* [1923] AC 603, 609 (Lord Birkenhead). And see ch 31.

[164] *R v Holmes, ex p Sherman* [1981] 2 All ER 612, 616.

[165] Robertson, *Freedom, the Individual and the Law*, p 43. But cf *Re Maychell, The Independent*, 26 February 1993 (territorial army officer detained under close arrest by military authorities for 75 days following a charge under the Official Secrets Act 1911, s 1. Habeas corpus refused because delay was not excessive in the circumstances).

[166] [1988] NILR 40.

[167] *R v Home Secretary, ex p Cheblak* [1991] 2 All ER 319, 322.

[168] Police Act 1996, s 88. See Lustgarten, pp 136–8. See also Clayton and Tomlinson, *Civil Actions against the Police*. On the liability of police civilian staff and the staff of private companies with police powers, see Police Reform Act 2002, s 42(7)–(10) (police authority a joint tortfeasor in the former case, the employer a joint tortfeasor in the latter case).

[169] See *O'Loughlin v Chief Constable of Essex* (note 111 above); and *Abraham v Metropolitan Police Commissioner* [2001] 1 WLR 1257.

[170] *Webb v Chief Constable of Merseyside Police* [2000] QB 427; *Costello v Chief Constable of Derbyshire* [2001] 1 WLR 1437. See now Criminal Justice and Police Act 2001, s 57.

[171] *Keegan v Merseyside Chief Constable* [2003] EWCA Civ 936; [2003] 1 WLR 2187.

against the police.[172] In principle, public officials are personally liable for their own wrongful acts. But special protection is given to some officials against certain liabilities,[173] while there are also severe limits on the ability of convicted persons to bring civil proceedings for trespass to the person, in which it must be shown – inter alia – that the conduct of the police was disproportionate.[174] Exemplary damages may be awarded against the police, even though there has been no oppressive behaviour or other aggravating circumstances.[175]

Civil liability may arise even where an arrest is lawful, for subsequent detention as well as the initial arrest must be in accordance with law.[176] In *Kirkham* v *Chief Constable of Greater Manchester*[177] it was held that the police owe a duty of care towards prisoners in their custody and that the widow of a man who had committed suicide while in police custody was entitled to damages in circumstances where there had been negligence by the police. And in *Treadaway* v *Chief Constable of West Midlands*,[178] damages of £50,000 (including £7,500 aggravated and £40,000 exemplary damages) were awarded to a claimant who had signed a confession 'only after he had been handcuffed behind his back and a succession of plastic bags had been placed over his head with the ends bunched up behind his neck causing him to struggle and pass out'. But there is no liability to someone who is injured while escaping from police custody after arrest, even if the attempted escape was foreseeable.[179] Many of the actions which are initiated against the police are settled before they reach the court. For example, in 2004 the Metropolitan Police paid £3,500 to each of 23 anti-monarchy protestors who claimed that they had been unlawfully arrested and falsely imprisoned on the day of the Queen's Golden Jubilee in June 2002.[180]

In 1997 concern about the size of damages awards in civil actions against the police led to the Court of Appeal issuing guidelines for juries on the level of exemplary damages in which an 'absolute maximum' of £50,000 should be awarded for particularly bad conduct by officers of at least the rank of superintendent.[181] This followed two cases in which awards of £302,000 and £220,000 respectively had been awarded to victims of police brutality.[182] Quite apart from civil proceedings, a criminal prosecution may be brought against a police force or individual police officers for unlawful conduct.[183] In England and Wales, the possibility of a private prosecution of a police officer is sometimes a valuable means of legal protection: in 1998 private prosecutions were brought against senior police officers for alleged manslaughter and neglect of duty following the Hillsborough football tragedy.[184] There are, however, serious difficulties in practice with private prosecutions or indeed any criminal prosecution against the police, even in cases following serious miscarriages of justice to which the actions of the police were alleged to contribute.[185] It

---

[172] See *Glinski* v *McIver* [1962] AC 726; *Wershof* v *Metropolitan Police Commissioner* [1978] 3 All ER 540. Cf *Hunter* v *Chief Constable of West Midlands Police* [1982] AC 529.

[173] See e.g. Constables' Protection Act 1750, s 6.

[174] Criminal Justice Act 2003, s 329; *Adorian* v *Metropolitan Police Commissioner* [2009] EWCA Civ 18.

[175] See also *Kuddus* v *Chief Constable of Leicestershire* [2001] UKHL 29; [2002] 2 AC 122; and ch 32 A.

[176] *Re Gillen's Application* [1988] NILR 40.

[177] [1990] 2 QB 283. See also *Reeves* v *Metropolitan Police Commissioner* [2001] 1 AC 360 – House of Lords reduced damages by half on account of contributory negligence. But compare *Orange* v *Chief Constable of West Yorkshire* [2001] EWCA Civ 611; [2002] QB 347.

[178] *The Times*, 25 October 1994.

[179] *Vellino* v *Chief Constable of Manchester* [2001] EWCA Civ 1249; [2002] 1 WLR 218.

[180] *The Guardian*, 5 February 2004.

[181] *Thompson* v *Metropolitan Police Commissioner* [1998] QB 498; and see ch 32 A.

[182] *The Guardian*, 20 February 1997.

[183] One of the most remarkable prosecutions occurred following the use of lethal force in 2005 against a young man (Jean Charles de Menenez) wrongly believed to be a terrorist suspect. He was shot dead by police officers at a tube station in south London. This led in 2007 to the conviction of the Metropolitan Police for breach of the Health and Safety at Work Act 1974. No proceedings were brought against individual officers in this case.

[184] See *R* v *DPP*, *ex p Duckenfield* [2000] 1 WLR 55.

[185] Cf *R* v *Bow Street Magistrates*, *ex p DPP* (1992) 95 Cr App R 9.

may be possible also to challenge some decisions of police officers in judicial review proceedings.[186] Indeed, in some cases this may be the only avenue, with the House of Lords having held that there may be no liability in damages against the police who deny suspects certain statutory rights.[187]

Complaints against the police

There have been a number of bodies which have dealt with claims about the misuse of police powers. Complaints may now be made to the Independent Police Complaints Commission, which was set up by the Police Reform Act 2002 to replace the Police Complaints Authority. The introduction of the new body appears to be due in part to political pressure for a wholly independent police complaints machinery,[188] and to concerns expressed by the Strasbourg Court about the independence of the previous Police Complaints Authority.[189] The Commission is an independent body appointed by the Home Secretary,[190] which came into operation on 1 April 2004 with jurisdiction over police authorities.[191] The aim of the new body is to enhance public confidence in the police complaints system, though the essence of the original procedure remains in place to the extent that in less serious cases it entails investigation of complaints by the police themselves. The first duty of the Commission is to ensure that there are suitable arrangements in place for the handling of complaints about the conduct of persons serving with the police, a term wide enough to include persons other than police constables,[192] but not the employees of private companies exercising police powers. Thereafter the Commission is under a duty to 'secure' that the arrangements are 'efficient and effective and contain and manifest an appropriate degree of independence', as well as a duty to 'secure' that public confidence is 'established and maintained' in these arrangements as well as in their operation.[193] The Commission also has a duty to record deaths and serious injuries in police custody.[194]

A complaint about the conduct of a person serving with the police may be made by a member of the public 'in relation to whom the conduct took place', as well as – in some circumstances – a member of the public who was adversely affected by or a witness to such conduct.[195] In addition to complaints, what are called 'conduct matters' and 'death or serious injury matters' may also be the subject of investigation. These are matters which are not the subject of a complaint but which (a) give rise to an indication that a person serving with the police may have committed a criminal offence or behaved in a way that would justify bringing disciplinary proceedings;[196] or (b) are matters which relate to the death or serious injury (referred to as DSI) of someone in police custody.[197] Both complaints, and conduct matters and DSI matters, may enter the system in one of three ways – by complaint or notice to the chief officer of police, the police authority, or the Commission.[198] (DSI matters must be referred to the Commission by the appropriate police authority for examination.) Once in the system, an issue which is proceeded with may be

---

[186] See *R (Thompson) v Chief Constable of Northumbria* [2001] EWCA Civ 211; [2001] 1 WLR 1342.

[187] *Cullen v Chief Constable of RUC* [2003] UKHL 39; [2003] 1 WLR 1763. And see ch 32 A.

[188] HC 258 (1997–8), and *The Stephen Lawrence Inquiry* (Report by Sir William McPherson), Cm 4262, 1999, Recommendation 58.

[189] *Khan v UK* (2000) 8 BHRC 310.

[190] Police Reform Act 2002, s 9.

[191] Ibid, s 10.

[192] Ibid.

[193] Ibid.

[194] Ibid.

[195] Ibid, s 12(1).

[196] Ibid, s 12(2).

[197] Ibid, s 12(2A)–2(D) (inserted by the Serious Organised Crime and Police Act 2005, s 160, Sch 12).

[198] Ibid, Sch 3.

dealt with in one of four ways: less serious cases may be dealt with by the police themselves by a process of 'local resolution', whereas more serious cases will be dealt with by the Commission. In between are cases which may be dealt with subject to Commission supervision or subject to Commission management. In the latter case the investigator is subject to Commission 'direction and control'.[199]

The Commission has no power to investigate complaints about the policy of a particular police force: it is a procedure designed only to deal with the conduct of people employed by the police.[200] Provision is made for appeals to the Commission against decisions by an appropriate police authority to investigate a complaint, and against the findings of an investigation by a police body. Where an investigation reveals that a criminal offence may have been committed, the matter must be referred to the DPP who must decide whether or not to institute criminal proceedings. Where criminal action is not taken, the Commission may direct a police authority to take disciplinary action against a police officer,[201] though no provision is made in the Act for the police officer to be heard in his or her defence before this instruction is given. The Commission has inevitably been drawn into a number of high profile incidents since it was formed, and concerns have been expressed about how effectively it has carried out its duties. Apart from sometimes appearing to take too narrow a view of its statutory powers,[202] the Commission was the subject of stinging criticism by the Home Affairs Committee which concluded that 'if the IPCC continues to fail to put complainants at the heart of the process we do not consider it can achieve its statutory duty of increasing public confidence in the police complaints system in England and Wales'.[203]

The admissibility of evidence

If the police act unlawfully by denying a citizen any rights provided by PACE; or if they secure evidence by unlawful means, as by an illegal search; or if they extract a confession from a suspect in breach of the code of practice, what is the position regarding the evidence which has been obtained in this way? Can it be used in legal proceedings against the accused? In the United States, unlawfully obtained evidence has been excluded by the Supreme Court, which has argued that constitutional rights to liberty and privacy should not be 'revocable at the whim of any police officer who, in the name of law enforcement itself, chooses to suspend [their] enjoyment'.[204] But in truth this is not an easy matter to resolve, for a difficult conflict of principle arises. On the one hand, there is a clear public interest in protecting the citizen against the unlawful invasion of his or her liberties by the police; on the other hand, there is an equally clear public interest in ensuring that those who commit serious criminal offences should not escape the consequences of their actions on what may be merely formal or technical grounds.[205] At common law in Scotland, it has long been the case that irregularity in the obtaining of evidence does not necessarily render it inadmissible, but it may do so; and whether unlawfully obtained evidence is admitted is a matter for the trial judge, who may deem it inadmissible if it has been obtained in circumstances of unfairness to the accused.[206]

---

[199] Ibid, Sch 3, para 18.

[200] Ibid, s 14.

[201] Ibid, Sch 3, para 27.

[202] R (Reynolds) v IPCC [2008] EWCA Civ 1160; see also R (Saunders) v IPCC [2009] EWCA Civ 187.

[203] HC 366 (2009–10).

[204] Mapp v Ohio, 367 US 643 (1961) (Justice Clark). See also Miranda v Arizona, 389 US 436 (1966).

[205] See Lawrie v Muir 1950 JC 19, 26 (Lord Cooper).

[206] HM Advocate v Turnbull 1951 JC 96. For a recent application of this principle, see HM Advocate v Purves 2009 SLT 969.

The position in England and Wales is now governed by ss 76 and 78 of PACE.[207] Section 76 provides that a confession made by an accused person may be given in evidence against him or her so far as it is relevant and is not excluded by the court exercising powers contained in s 76(2). This requires the court to exclude evidence obtained by oppression of the person who made it,[208] or 'in consequence of anything said or done which was likely, in the circumstances existing at the time, to render unreliable any confession which might be made in consequence thereof'.[209] Where a representation has been made to the court that a confession may have been secured in either of these ways, the onus is on the prosecution to establish otherwise (s 76(1)). The term oppression is defined 'to include torture, inhuman or degrading treatment, and the use or threat of violence (whether or not amounting to torture)' (s 76(8)).[210] In R v Fulling[211] the court said that otherwise 'oppression' should be given its ordinary meaning, that is to say, the exercise of authority or power in a burdensome, harsh or wrongful manner or giving rise to unjust or cruel treatment. In that case it was held that there was no oppression where a confession had been made by a woman after being told by police of her lover's affair with another woman.[212] But although oppressive conduct by the police is thus discouraged by s 76, much of the impact of this is lost by s 76(4), which provides that the exclusion of a confession does not affect the admissibility in evidence of any facts discovered as a result of the confession, or 'where the confession is relevant as showing that the accused speaks, writes or expresses himself in a particular way, of so much of the confession as is necessary to show that he does so'. The fruit of the poison tree thus appears to be edible in English law.

Section 78, introduced as a result of pressure in the Lords from Lord Scarman and others, provides that in any proceedings the court may refuse to allow evidence on which the prosecution proposes to rely 'if it appears to the court that, having regard to all the circumstances, including the circumstances in which the evidence was obtained, the admission of the evidence would have such an adverse effect on the fairness of the proceedings that the court ought not to admit it'.[213] Despite the lack of clarity in its drafting, there is evidence to suggest that, together with s 76, this provision has helped to induce the judges to take a more assertive approach when faced with improper police practice. Thus in R v Canale,[214] the Court of Appeal held that the trial judge should not have admitted evidence of interviews which had not been contemporaneously recorded by the police officers conducting the interviews: they had been written up afterwards.[215] These breaches of Code C, as it was then drafted, were described as 'flagrant', 'deliberate' and 'cynical'. In so holding, the Lord Chief Justice sharply observed:

> This case is the latest of a number of decisions emphasising the importance of the 1984 Act. If, which we find it hard to believe, police officers still do not appreciate the importance of that Act and the accompanying Codes, then it is time that they did.[216]

---

[207] For background, see Cmnd 8092, 1981, pp 112–18. Section 78 is qualified by the Criminal Procedure and Investigations Act 1996, Sch 1, para 26, in respect of proceedings before examining magistrates.

[208] On oppression, see R v Fulling [1987] QB 426. See also R v Ismail [1990] Crim LR 109. Cf R v Emmerson (1991) 92 Cr App R 284.

[209] On unreliability, see R v Goldenberg (1988) 88 Cr App R 285, R v Silcott, Braithwaite and Raghip, The Times, 9 December 1991 and R v Walker [1998] Crim LR 211.

[210] Confession evidence may also be excluded under s 78 (see below). See R v Mason [1987] 3 All ER 481.

[211] [1987] QB 426.

[212] For a disturbing example of oppression which 'horrified' the Court of Appeal, and in which the accused was 'bullied and hectored', see R v Paris (1993) 97 Cr App R 99. ('The officers . . . were not questioning him so much as shouting at him what they wanted him to say. Short of physical violence, it is difficult to conceive of a more hostile and intimidatory approach by officers to a suspect.')

[213] See K Grevling (1997) 113 LQR 667 for a full account.

[214] [1990] 2 All ER 187.

[215] See also R v Keenan [1990] 2 QB 54.

[216] [1990] 2 All ER 187, 190 (Lord Lane CJ).

Another area where s 78 has been invoked successfully by defendants relates to the denial of access to a solicitor,[217] though it has been said not to be possible 'to give general guidance as to how a judge should exercise his discretion under section 78' on the ground that 'each case had to be determined on its own facts'.[218]

It does not follow that evidence obtained in breach of the codes of practice or in breach of the defendant's statutory rights will always be held to be inadmissible. In more recent cases the courts have taken a more cautious approach to s 78 and the Court of Appeal in particular has been criticised for its willingness to admit improperly obtained evidence.[219] In R v Chalkley, the Court of Appeal emphasised that the test to be applied in determining whether to admit evidence is not whether the evidence has been obtained illegally or oppressively, but one of fairness: neither the 'labelling of conduct as unlawful' nor the 'application to it of the epithet oppressive' 'automatically overrides the fundamental test of fairness in admission of evidence'.[220] Particular difficulties have arisen with police undercover work, it having been held that obtaining evidence by entrapment, by an agent provocateur, or by a trick did not of itself require the judge to exclude it, although it may be excluded if the circumstances so require in the interests of fairness.[221] The House of Lords has held that evidence obtained by means of an illegally placed surveillance device is admissible:[222] the fact that the conduct of the police amounted to an apparent or probable breach of the ECHR, art 8, was simply 'a consideration which may be taken into account for what it is worth'.[223] Questions arise about the implications of art 6 of the ECHR for the admissibility of evidence, particularly since the Human Rights Act was enacted.[224] But the European Court of Human Rights has also held that irregularly obtained evidence may be admitted,[225] and the view of the English courts is that the requirements of s 78 of the 1984 Act and art 6 are the same in this respect.[226] As a result, there is no need to modify s 78 in the light of the jurisprudence of the Strasbourg Court.[227] It is also important to note, however, that English law is now much more flexible than in the past, particularly in relation to entrapment. Referring to it as 'State-created crime', the House of Lords has indicated that in appropriate cases evidence obtained in this way should be excluded under s 78 or proceedings should be stayed as an abuse of process.[228]

---

[217] R v Samuel [1988] QB 615; R v Absolam (1989) 88 Cr App R 332; R v Beylan [1990] Crim LR 185; R v Chung (1991) 92 Cr App R 314. But contrast R v Ibrahim [2008] EWCA Crim 880, [2009] 1 WLR 578.

[218] R v Smurthwaite [1994] 1 All ER 898.

[219] A Choo and S Nash [1999] Crim LR 929.

[220] [1998] QB 848, at 874 (Auld LJ). Also R v Smurthwaite (note 218 above) and R v Cooke [1995] 1 Cr App R 318.

[221] R v Smurthwaite (note 218 above). Also R v Sang [1980] AC 402, R v Christou [1992] QB 979, R v Latif [1996] 1 All ER 353 and Nottingham City Council v Amin [2000] 1 WLR 1071. For comment, see A J Ashworth (1998) 114 LQR 108. See now Regulation of Investigatory Powers Act 2000; ch 22 below.

[222] R v Khan [1997] AC 558. See now Police Act 1997, Part III. See ch 22 below. On the approach of the House of Lords to s 78, see also R v Southwark Crown Court, ex p Bowles [1998] AC 641, and R v P [2001] 2 All ER 58.

[223] At 582 (Lord Nolan). It has been argued that the courts should take a more robust attitude to the exclusion of evidence obtained in breach of Convention rights: see D Ormerod [2003] Crim LR 61.

[224] See for example R v Ibrahim, above.

[225] Schenck v Switzerland (1988) 13 EHRR 242. In Teixeira de Castro v Portugal (1998) 28 EHRR 101, the Court said that 'the admissibility of evidence is primarily a matter for regulation by national law and as a general rule it is for the national courts to assess the evidence before them. The Court's task under the Convention is not to give a ruling as to whether statements of witnesses were properly admitted as evidence, but rather to ascertain whether the proceedings as a whole, including the way in which evidence was taken, were fair' (at 114–15).

[226] See R v Looseley [2001] UKHL 53, [2001] 4 All ER 897, and Attorney General's Reference (No 3 of 1999) [2000] UKHL 63, [2001] 2 AC 91.

[227] Looseley, ibid.

[228] Ibid.

F. Accountability and control of the police[229]

Local police authorities

The police authority is responsible for ensuring an efficient and effective police force,[230] and for holding the chief constable to account.[231] In practice, however, the changes which started with the Police and Magistrates' Courts Act 1994 have gone some way to diminish further the already limited scope for local control of the police. Indeed, the current composition of police authorities raises questions about how effectively the police are subject to local democratic supervision, for it may well be that a police authority with a large 'independent' element will tend to shield rather than expose the police to community concerns.[232] A measure of the diminishing role of police authorities as agents of accountability is reflected in rather startling terms in the white paper, *Police Reform*, which preceded the changes introduced by the 1994 Act. There it was said that in future police authorities would 'act on behalf of local people as the "customer" of the service which the police force provides',[233] a role which not all will find beyond question. It is true that police authorities are now required to determine local policing objectives on an annual basis and that in doing so they must not only consult the chief constable and take into account any strategic priorities of the Home Office, but also consider any views obtained in accordance with arrangements made under s 96 of the 1996 Act.[234] This requires the police authority to make arrangements to obtain the views of the local population about local policing arrangements. The Act does not, however, prescribe what arrangements should be made for this purpose and so far as it gives any guidance, the white paper preceding it suggested that the duty might be discharged through the medium of local consultative groups (not necessarily elected) and by canvassing local views in a variety of ways, for example by public opinion surveys.[235]

The government has expressed concern about the value of existing arrangements for community involvement in local policing matters.[236] Additional concern about the 'widespread public ignorance of the existing police authorities'[237] led the government to question whether 'police authorities were sufficiently visible or accountable' to the communities they served.[238] The trend of recent policy development, however, will be to diminish the role of local authorities still further by making the police more directly 'responsive' to the communities they serve. In *Building Communities, Beating Crime*,[239] policing continues to be identified as a public service which should be responsive to 'customer' needs, the customers now being the people rather than the police authorities that represent them. In responding to these 'customers', the government has implemented a programme of neighbourhood policing which will lead to a number of other initiatives in its wake. These include the provision of more information to the public on an annual basis about policing arrangements in their locality, and (to continue the use of market metaphors) the introduction of 'contracts' (albeit of a non-enforceable nature) between police and communities

---

[229] On police accountability see Jefferson and Grimshaw, *Controlling the Constable*; Reiner, *The Politics of the Police*; Walker, *Policing in a Changing Constitutional Order*.

[230] Police Act 1996, s 6.

[231] Ibid, s 6(1)(b) (as inserted by the Police and Justice Act 2006).

[232] Following amendments made by the Police and Justice Act 2006, the composition of police authorities is set out in SI 2008 Nos 630 and 631.

[233] Cm 2281, 1994, p 20.

[234] Police Act 1996, s 6ZB (as inserted by the Police and Justice Act 2006).

[235] Cm 2281, 1994. By virtue of amendments to the 1996 Act introduced by the Police and Justice Act 2006, there is now Home Office supervision of these arrangements.

[236] Cm 6360, 2004, esp chs 1 and 2.

[237] HC 370 (2004–05).

[238] Cm 6600, 2005.

[239] Cm 6360, 2004, esp ch 1.

to build upon minimum standards set by national government. The Policing and Crime Act 2009 imposes another duty on local police authorities, this time to have regard to the views of people in the authority's area about policing in that area.[240]

Accountability to Parliament

It is both inevitable and desirable that there should be parliamentary interest in the work of the police. One problem which has often faced MPs wishing to raise police subjects in Parliament has been that there is no direct ministerial responsibility either for the acts of the police or for the decisions of police authorities. The position of London has always been exceptional, since it has long been recognised in the Commons that the Home Secretary accepts what has been described as an extremely wide and detailed responsibility for the Metropolitan Police.[241] The royal commission on the police in 1962 proposed additional powers for the central government which, the commission considered, would make the Home Secretary accountable to Parliament for the efficient policing of the whole country.[242] The Police Act 1964 did not go as far as the royal commission recommended, but the extent of ministerial responsibility for police outside London was undoubtedly widened by the Act, and has been widened by legislation ever since. Thus MPs who wish to raise a matter of local policing may now ask the Home Secretary whether he or she proposes to call for a report on the matter from the chief constable, institute an inquiry into the matter, to require the chief constable to resign in the interests of efficiency and so on. But the fact that such a question may be asked does not mean that as full an answer will be given as the MP would like. The Home Secretary will not give to Parliament details of police work which he or she considers should not be publicly disclosed. Nor does the jurisdiction of the Parliamentary Ombudsman include power to investigate complaints against the police.[243] On specific matters of great political concern, however, the Home Secretary may be willing to order an inquiry to be held,[244] or to lay before Parliament the report received from a chief officer of police.[245]

In view of the increasing powers of the Home Secretary for policing matters, there are also urgent questions about his or her accountability to Parliament for the way in which these powers are used. The Home Affairs Committee has examined a number of general policing matters,[246] and most recently has examined some of the recent reform initiatives relating to the structure and organisation of the police. However, the Committee was broadly supportive of these initiatives in a report which did not grapple with some of the wider constitutional issues which they raise. The Committee was satisfied that a 'performance culture' was becoming established in the police service, but was critical of the 'overall detection rates'. According to the Committee, 'it is right that the top priority should be crime reduction'.[247] But not only has the Committee failed to address some of the constitutional implications of recent changes, it has also proved to be ineffective in checking the increase in police powers. Its review of the Criminal Justice Bill in 2003 led it broadly to endorse the changes to PACE which the Bill proposed, with the exception of the power to expand the circumstances in which people could be detained for more than 24 hours without

---

[240] Policing and Crime Act 2009, s 1 (amending Police Act 1996, s 6).

[241] Marshall, *Police and Government.*

[242] Cmd 1728, 1962.

[243] See ch 29 D.

[244] See the reports by Lord Scarman into the Red Lion Square disorders, Cmnd 5919, 1975, and into the Brixton disorders, Cmnd 8427, 1981.

[245] E.g. HC 351 (1974), report from Metropolitan Police Commissioner on the Lennon case.

[246] E.g. Race relations and the 'sus' law (HC 559 (1979–80)); Deaths in police custody (HC 631 (1979–80)); Special Branch (HC 71 (1984–5)); Police funding (HC 553 (2006–07)); Policing in the twenty-first century (HC 364 (2007–08)); and the Serious Organised Crime Agency (HC 418 (2008–09)).

[247] HC 370 (2004–05). See also HC 612 (2001–02).

charge.[248] But here it was ignored by the government.[249] The Committee had nothing to say on the Serious Organised Crime and Police Bill in 2004–5, although the matter was thoroughly examined by the Joint Committee on Human Rights.

The role of the courts

Relying on the time-worn but seriously inaccurate sentiment that a police officer possesses few powers not enjoyed by the ordinary citizen and is only 'a person paid to perform, as a matter of duty, acts which if he were so minded he might have done voluntarily', the royal commission in 1962 came to an astonishing conclusion: 'The relation of the police to the courts is not . . . of any greater constitutional significance than the relation of any other citizen to the courts.'[250] The corrective was supplied in *R v Metropolitan Police Commissioner, ex p Blackburn*.[251]

> Under the Betting, Gaming and Lotteries Act 1963, certain forms of gaming were unlawful, and gaming clubs in London sought to avoid the Act. After legal difficulties in enforcing the Act had arisen, the Commissioner issued a secret circular to senior officers giving effect to a policy decision that no proceedings were to be taken against a gaming club for breach of the law, unless there were complaints of cheating or it had become the haunt of criminals. Blackburn sought an order of mandamus against the Commissioner which in effect ordered him to reverse that policy decision. The circular was withdrawn before the case was concluded, but the Court of Appeal held that every chief constable owed a duty to the public to enforce the law. That duty could if necessary be enforced by the courts. Although chief officers had a wide discretion with which the courts would not interfere, the courts would control a policy decision which amounted to a failure of duty to enforce the law. The court in this case left open whether Blackburn had a sufficient interest in the matter to ask for mandamus. In a later case brought by Blackburn to enforce the obscenity laws, the court held on the merits that the Commissioner was doing what he could to enforce the existing laws with the available resources and no more could reasonably be expected.[252]

Further consideration was given to the 'clear legal duty'[253] which the police owe to the public to enforce the law in *Hill v Chief Constable of West Yorkshire*, where it was held that the existence of a general duty in the police to suppress crime does not carry with it a liability to individuals for damage caused to them by criminals whom the police have failed to apprehend in circumstances when it was possible to do so.[254] The courts take the view that it would not be in the public interest for the police to be liable for negligence in the investigation of crime. In a controversial decision of the European Court of Human Rights, questions were raised about whether this exclusion of liability was compatible with the ECHR, art 6.[255] The Strasbourg Court has since made clear, however, that it misunderstood the position in English law.[256] Obvious difficulties are presented by the proposal that a court should direct a chief constable in the performance of his or her duties at the instance of a member of the public. It is one thing for a court to strike down instructions by a chief constable which are plainly illegal; it is another for the court to impose its own views on the priorities for the use of police resources.[257] Given that the courts must allow

---

[248] HC 138 (2002–03).

[249] Criminal Justice Act 2003, s 7.

[250] Cmnd 1728, p 34.

[251] [1968] 2 QB 118.

[252] *R v Metropolitan Police Commissioner, ex p Blackburn (No 3)* [1973] QB 241. See also *R v Chief Constable of Devon and Cornwall, ex p CEGB* [1982] QB 458, and *R v Oxford, ex p Levey*, The Times, 1 November 1986.

[253] *R v Metropolitan Police Commissioner, ex p Blackburn* [1968] 2 QB 118, at 138 (Salmon LJ).

[254] [1989] AC 53 (unsuccessful action in negligence brought by mother of a victim of the Yorkshire Ripper). Also *Brooks v Metropolitan Police Commissioner* [2005] UKHL 24; [2005] 2 All ER 289, and *Van Colle v Hertfordshire Chief Constable* [2008] UKHL 50, [2009] 1 AC 225. And see ch 32 A.

[255] *Osman v UK* (2000) 29 EHRR 245. See C A Gearty (2000) 64 MLR 179; T Weir [1999] CLJ 4.

[256] *Z v UK* (2002) 34 EHRR 97. See now *Van Colle v Hertfordshire Chief Constable*, above.

[257] See *R v Chief Constable of Sussex, ex p International Trader's Ferry Ltd* [1999] 2 AC 418.

the police discretion in carrying out their work, a capable chief constable with some appreciation of the law should have little difficulty in keeping within the permissible bounds.[258] Rather than relying to the extent that we have come to do on the autonomy and professional judgment of the chief officer to solve difficult questions of social policy for us and then looking to the courts to control their decisions, it might be better to reassess the proper scope for political direction and parliamentary discussion of police policies.

G. Conclusion

Whether in the field of maintaining public order or in the work of detecting and prosecuting crime, police decisions constantly involve the exercise of discretion, choice between alternative courses of action, and the setting of priorities for the use of limited resources. In a stable society it is easier for the police to seek to play an impartial and a non-political role, but even this role has latent political significance. In less stable conditions, issues of law and order acquire a more immediate political content. In the sometimes troubled 1980s, questions were often raised about the procedures for police accountability. Problems about police reaction to racial violence, to public demonstrations, and to the events surrounding the miners' strike in particular, all contributed to the concern, which persists to this day in a new context of policing designed to protect against terrorist activity. A complicating dimension is what some see as the movement towards greater centralisation of police work. There are many forms of cooperation between forces, but there is also now the potential for the development of common policies, through the activities of bodies such as the Association of Chief Police Officers (ACPO).[259] This emerging centralisation raises new questions about police accountability which the existing institutional structures may not be well suited to answer. But it should not be overlooked that police investigation of individual incidents can have national implications of the greatest significance. The circumstances surrounding the police response to the murder of the London teenager Stephen Lawrence raised a number of different questions of police conduct, and to a finding of institutional racism in aspects of the police service.[260] The policing of the G20 demonstration in 2009 raised different but also compelling concerns about the standards of behaviour expected of police officers individually and collectively.[261]

---

[258] See now *E v RUC Chief Constable* [2008] UKHL 66; [2008] WLR (D) 351.

[259] For statutory recognition of ACPO, see Police Act 1996, s 37A, and Police Reform Act 2002, s 96.

[260] *The Stephen Lawrence Inquiry*, Cm 4262, 1999.

[261] HC 418 (2008–09). See ch 24.

CHAPTER 22

The protection of privacy

Part of the trouble with privacy is that it is notoriously difficult to define. It is largely for this reason that the Younger Committee on Privacy recommended against the introduction of any such right as long ago as 1972, although the Committee was agreed that 'privacy requires additional protection'.[1] This was an influential report which was to structure the debate for almost a generation; until the Human Rights Act, there was no formal legal protection of privacy.[2] A second difficulty with the protection of privacy is in determining from whom the protection is needed. Many are agreed that the intrusive tendencies of the state – which for some has lurid Orwellian tendencies – ought to be contained. But many of the problems associated with the violation of privacy are perpetrated not by the state, but by other private parties – newspapers engaged in a never-ending circulation war, or employers checking on employees (in one famous case to monitor calls to a solicitor by an employee who was suing her employer for sex discrimination).[3] A third difficulty is that the invasion of personal privacy by a range of devices is now seen to be a necessary or expedient weapon in the fight against organised crime and other unlawful acts which threaten public safety and national security.[4] To this end, for example, a national DNA database has been established to hold information which can be checked by the police when investigating crime.[5]

A. The case for protection

Although these are persuasive concerns, they are not compelling. It is true that privacy is a concept of indeterminate scope and that it is closely related to concepts that might be encountered in the law of tort (trespass), equity (breach of confidence) or intellectual property (copyright). But it is important also for the public lawyer, at a time of growing anxiety about what is seen as the emergence of a 'surveillance society'.[6] Privacy is closely associated with liberty and with ideas about freedom from interference by the state.[7] As a principle, privacy is important also as a way of reinforcing other constitutional liberties – most notably the right to freedom of association and assembly. One of the principal means of violating the liberty of those individuals and organisations who support unpopular causes is to monitor them, to keep them under surveillance, to maintain records about their members, and to circulate information about them – to provide the fuel for oppression and discrimination.[8] It is true that the concept of privacy as protected by the

---

[1] Cmnd 5012, 1972, especially paras 651–2. See also for a valuable yet sceptical account, Wacks, *The Protection of Privacy*. Also, Wacks, *Personal Information*, especially ch 1.

[2] *Wainwright v Home Office* [2003] UKHL 53, [2004] AC 406.

[3] *Halford v UK* (1997) 24 EHRR 523.

[4] HC Deb, 6 March 2000, col 768 (Mr Jack Straw). These powers are now justified as being directed mainly at 'drug, terrorist, paedophilia and money-laundering crimes': ibid, col 834 (Mr Charles Clarke).

[5] For details, see *S and Marper v United Kingdom* [2009] 48 EHRR 50.

[6] See HC 58 (2007–08) (Home Affairs Committee); HL 18 (2008–09) (House of Lords Constitution Committee).

[7] See Lustgarten and Leigh, *In From the Cold*, p 40. See also D Feldman [2000] PL 61.

[8] For the surveillance of the Communist Party of Great Britain, see Ewing and Gearty, *The Struggle for Civil Liberties*, ch 3.

ECHR (art 8) and now the Human Rights Act 1998 extends some way beyond matters of this kind. But for the public lawyer the foregoing are core concerns which address fundamental issues about the political freedom of the individual in a democratic society.

New technologies which allow for even greater forms of surveillance make the case for some form of protection irresistible. But there can be no case for an unqualified or an unlimited right to privacy. Privacy is a restraint on freedom of expression and as such gives rise to concerns when relied on by public officials and politicians who have something to hide, and who wish to prevent the disclosure of information which may expose hypocrisy or worse. It is also a restraint on the activities of the police and other authorities in the criminal justice system who are engaged in legitimate activities in the public interest to detect the drug dealers and other traffickers in human misery. This is not to say, of course, that there should be no right to privacy: it is a case for balancing competing rights and interests. But where rights of privacy are restricted, there is a case for violations only where there is clear legal authority and only where there is a clear need for a legitimate purpose. And while it might be expected that the state would refrain from violating the privacy of the individual except where there is good cause to do so, equally it might be expected that the state would intervene to take steps to protect that privacy, particularly of the weak and vulnerable, from commercial exploitation and other forms of abuse by global media corporations and other powerful organisations.[9]

We have already encountered in chapter 21 one of the most invasive violations of privacy in the form of police entry and search of domestic premises. In this chapter we address other forms of infringement, as well as some of the different ways by which privacy is regulated and protected. We have identified privacy for the purposes of this chapter as being concerned with five principal matters. These are (i) surveillance in the sense of gathering of information about an individual; (ii) the interception of communications, an activity which is a particular form of surveillance, though it may be used also for other purposes, such as criminal investigation; (iii) the storage and use of information about the individual, a matter of acute concern in the computer era, though trade unionists and others will be aware of blacklisting from the earliest times;[10] and (iv) the creation of various databases by government departments and public bodies, on which information about individuals may be entered, to which they may or may not have access, and over the use of which they may or may not have any control. We also deal briefly (v) with aspects of interference with privacy by the press.

B. Surveillance: acquiring information

The first way in which the privacy of the individual may be undermined is by different techniques of surveillance in order to obtain information about him or her.[11] This may be done in a number of ways – by the state, by the press and by others: it may involve breaking into his or her home and rifling through personal effects, it may involve the use of bugging devices or it may involve the interception of communications of various kinds. As far as the common law is concerned, the placing of someone under surveillance is not in itself unlawful. But there are circumstances where various types of surveillance may be unlawful, although only where the surveillance involves an interference with existing rights already recognised by the law. The invasion of someone's privacy has not by itself given cause for the courts to intervene in the past.

---

[9] So much is required by the ECHR: see *Spencer v UK* (1998) 25 EHRR CD105; and by the Human Rights Act: see *Venables v News Group Newspapers Ltd* [2001] Fam 430.

[10] See *McKenzie v Iron Trades Employers' Insurance Association* 1910 SC 79. See now Data Protection Act 1998, Employment Relations Act 1999, s 3, and SI 2010 No 493.

[11] See *Robertson v Keith* 1936 SLT 9 and *Connor v HM Advocate* 2002 SLT 671.

Trespass

Perhaps the best known example of common law protection for privacy is *Entick* v *Carrington*,[12] where John Entick's home was the subject of an illegal entry and his possessions the subject of an illegal search. Although clearly a violation of his home and his private life, his action for damages succeeded because it was also a trespass to his property rights. In the memorable words of Lord Camden CJ, in one of the great judgments of the common law:

> No man can set his foot upon my ground without my licence, but he is liable for an action, though damage be nothing; . . . If he admits the fact, he is bound to show by way of justification, that some positive law has empowered or excused him.

In that case there was no power or excuse. It is true that the officers conducting the search were armed with a warrant issued by the Home Secretary. But this was no defence, because the Home Secretary had no legal authority to issue the warrant in the first place: such authority could be provided only by Parliament, save exceptionally in the case of warrants issued in relation to stolen goods.

The value of trespass as a means of protecting privacy in modern times was highlighted in *Morris* v *Beardmore*,[13] where the defendant was suspected of being involved in a road accident. He left the scene and was followed to his house by the police who entered with the permission of the defendant's son. Despite being told to leave the house, the police entered the bedroom of the defendant in order to take a breath specimen. He refused to provide the specimen and was arrested. It was held by the House of Lords that the requirement to undergo a breath test is unlawful if made as a result of a trespass to land committed against the person to whom the requirement is addressed. But an attempt to extend the law of trespass to cover surveillance by means of telephone tapping was made unsuccessfully in the *Malone* case.[14] In that case there were striking similarities with *Entick* v *Carrington*, in the sense that the interception was done under the authority of a warrant issued by the Home Secretary, who again had not been empowered by Parliament to issue such warrants. Nevertheless the application failed: the key difference with *Entick* v *Carrington* was that there was no violation of the applicant's property rights and no trespass. It was not necessary to enter the applicant's home to place the interception device, which in this case had been done at the telephone exchange.

Interference with property

The law of trespass took on a new role in relation to the use of listening devices by the police to record conversations involving people who were suspected of involvement in criminal activity.

> In *R* v *Khan*,[15] the accused was suspected of being involved in the importation of illegal drugs. The police placed a listening device on the outside of a house which he was visiting. This was done without any statutory authority, though in accordance with Home Office guidelines relating to the use of such devices. Nevertheless, it was accepted by the Crown that the conduct of the police involved both a trespass and damage to the property on which the device was placed. Khan was found guilty on charges relating to the importation of drugs, the evidence against him being found mainly in tape recordings acquired as a result of the listening device. He appealed against conviction and argued that the evidence should not have been admitted because it had been illegally obtained and had been obtained in breach of the ECHR, art 8. The appeal failed: in determining whether evidence should be admitted, the illegality of the means used is not decisive. The question was whether it was secured in circumstances which tainted the fairness of the proceedings. But although the House of Lords thought not, the case nevertheless exposed the illegality of this particular practice.[16]

---

[12] (1765) 19 St Tr 1030; and see ch 6 A.
[13] [1981] AC 446.
[14] *Malone* v *Metropolitan Police Commissioner* [1979] Ch 344.
[15] [1997] AC 558. See now *Khan* v *UK* (2001) 31 EHRR 1016.
[16] See also *R* v *Loveridge* [2001] 2 Cr App R 591 and *Teixeira de Castro* v *Portugal* (1998) 28 EHRR 101.

The 'lack of a statutory system regulating the use of surveillance devices' by the police led to an expression of astonishment from the bench.[17] It was all the more remarkable for the fact that similar activity by the security service required the authority of a warrant from the Home Secretary under the Security Service Act 1989. (The position relating to the security services is now governed by the Regulation of Investigatory Powers Act 2000, which is considered in section D.)

English law and practice relating to the use of listening devices by the police was found by the European Court of Human Rights to breach art 8 of the ECHR.[18] The use of bugging devices by the police is now governed by the Police Act 1997, Part III,[19] which proved to be extremely controversial at the time it was passed.[20] It provides that '[n]o entry on or interference with property or with wireless telegraphy shall be unlawful if it is authorised by an authorisation having effect under this Part' (s 92). Authorisation may be given to take action in respect of private property as may be specified in the authorisation, where the authorising officer believes that the action is necessary on the ground that it is likely to be of 'substantial value in the prevention or detection of serious crime'. It must also be shown that 'the taking of the action is proportionate to what the action seeks to achieve' (s 93).[21] For these purposes, conduct is to be regarded as serious crime only if (*a*) 'it involves the use of violence, results in substantial financial gain or is conducted by a large number of persons in pursuit of a common purpose', or (*b*) the offence is one for which a person over the age of 18 with no previous convictions could reasonably expect to be jailed for at least three years.[22]

Authorisation may be given by a chief constable; or by the Director General of the Serious Organised Crime Agency; or by any revenue and customs officer specially designated by the Commissioners for Revenue and Customs (s 93). Following subsequent amendments, authorisation may also be given by the chief constables of the Ministry of Defence Police and the British Transport Police, as well as the heads of the armed forces police (and the chairman of the Office of Fair Trading).[23] The authorisation should normally be given in writing, although in urgent cases it may be given orally (s 95).[24] In some cases, the authorisation will not take effect until approved by a surveillance commissioner appointed under s 91 of the Act.[25] Approval by a commissioner is required where any property specified in the authorisation is used as a dwelling or as a bedroom in a hotel or constitutes office premises. Approval is also required if it is likely to yield matters subject to legal privilege, confidential personal information or confidential journalistic material (s 97).[26] If approval is refused by a commissioner or if an authorisation is quashed, the authorising officer may appeal to the chief surveillance commissioner (s 104). The chief surveillance commissioner has a duty to keep the operation of these measures under review and to report annually to the Prime Minister (s 107).[27] Complaints by persons who are the subject of an authorisation under s 93 may be made to the Investigatory Powers Tribunal established under the Regulation of Investigatory Powers Act 2000, provided of course that they know that they are the subject of surveillance.

---

[17] [1997] AC 558, at 582 (Lord Nolan).

[18] *Khan v UK*, note 15 above.

[19] For a good account, see Fenwick, *Civil Rights: New Labour, Freedom and the Human Rights Act*, pp 372–7.

[20] See Ewing and Gearty, *A Law Too Far: Part III of the Police Bill 1997*.

[21] Police Act 1997, s 75(2)(b), as amended by the Regulation of Investigatory Powers Act 2000, s 75.

[22] As amended by the Criminal Justice and Court Services Act 2000, Sch 7.

[23] RIPA 2000, s 75.

[24] An oral authorisation lapses after 72 hours; written authorisations lapse after 3 months, although they may be renewed.

[25] This provides for the appointment of a chief commissioner and other commissioners by the Prime Minister. The persons appointed must be people who hold or have held senior judicial office.

[26] These terms are defined in ss 98–100.

[27] Police Act 1997, s 107(5A), as inserted by RIPA 2000, Sch 4(1).

Surveillance and undercover operations

Additional measures relating to surveillance are to be found in the Regulation of Investigatory Powers Act 2000, Part II.[28] This applies to surveillance activities not only by the police but by a large number of other agencies which now play a part in law enforcement, including the intelligence services, HM Revenue and Customs and local authorities. But the Act does not by any means apply to all surveillance.[29] Although the RIPA 2000 deals with a wider range of activities than the use of bugging devices, it applies to this form of surveillance as well, and thus adds what is at times a confusing layer of regulation on top of the Police Act 1997, Part III, which remains in place, subject to a number of amendments. The RIPA 2000 deals with what are referred to as *directed surveillance, intrusive surveillance* and *the conduct and use of covert human intelligence sources*.[30] Surveillance is *directed* if it is covert but not intrusive and undertaken for the purposes of a specific operation to obtain private information about a person.[31] Surveillance is *intrusive* if covert and (*a*) carried out in relation to anything taking place on any residential premises or in a private vehicle, and (*b*) involves the presence of an individual on the premises (such as a paid informer or someone who is concealed) or is carried out by means of a surveillance device. *Covert human intelligence sources* may be 'informants, agents [or] undercover officers'.[32]

These different forms of activity appear from time to time in the reported cases.[33] But until the RIPA 2000 they were conducted without formal legal authority (with the exception of intrusive surveillance conducted under the Police Act 1997). The 2000 Act is designed to ensure that practice in this area is brought into line with the ECHR by requiring that the different kinds of surveillance to which it applies are authorised in advance.[34] There is also a right to complain to the Investigatory Powers Tribunal established under the Act about any authorisation.[35] *Directed* surveillance may be authorised if necessary on one of several grounds specified in the Act (which include national security, the prevention or detection of crime, and the prevention of disorder) provided that the authorised surveillance is proportionate to the end to be achieved (s 28). A similar regime operates for the authorisation of *covert human intelligence sources* (s 29). In the case of *directed* surveillance, authorisation may be given by a designated person in one of a number of specified public authorities or types of public authority.[36] Predictably, these include the police and the intelligence services, but also various government departments, local authorities and other public bodies such as the Foods Standards Agency. In the case of surveillance by *covert human intelligence sources*, authorisation may be given by additional specified public authorities or types of public authority, including the Health and Safety Executive.

Intrusive surveillance is different. This may be authorised only on one of three grounds: where necessary in the interests of national security; for the purpose of preventing or detecting serious crime; or in the interests of the economic well-being of the United Kingdom. Again, the

---

[28] For a fuller treatment, see Fenwick, pp 377–85. For the comparable provisions in Scotland, see Regulation of Investigatory Powers (Scotland) Act 2000.

[29] See page 495 below.

[30] Regulation of Investigatory Powers Act 2000, s 26.

[31] Private information is defined to include any information relating to a person's private or family life: s 26(10). There will be circumstances where surveillance does not require authorisation: see Official Report, Standing Committee F, 30 March 2000, col 274.

[32] Official Report, Standing Committee F, 30 March 2000, col 274 (Mr Charles Clarke). See *Teixeira de Castro* v *Portugal* (1998) 28 EHRR 101.

[33] See *R* v *Smurthwaite* [1994] 1 All ER 898; *R* v *Latif* [1996] 1 WLR 104; *R* v *Khan* [1997] AC 558; and *Connor* v *HM Advocate* 2002 SLT 671.

[34] HC Deb, 6 March 2000, col 767 (Mr Jack Straw).

[35] Regulation of Investigatory Powers Act 2000, s 65, though the problem with this complaints procedure as well is that people will be unaware that they are or have been under surveillance; without that knowledge they will be in no position to make a complaint.

[36] SI 2003 No 3171.

authorisation must be proportionate to the end to be achieved by carrying it out (s 32). Authorising officers are chief constables, commissioners of police, provosts marshal, officers designated by HM Revenue and Customs, and the Director General of the Serious Organised Crime Agency (s 33). In the case of *intrusive* surveillance by the police and revenue and customs, an authorisation does not take effect unless approved by a surveillance commissioner (s 36). Provision is made for *intrusive* surveillance to begin in cases of urgency, without approval. An appeal lies to the chief surveillance commissioner by an authorising officer against any refusal by a surveillance commissioner to approve an authorisation. In the case of *intrusive* surveillance by the intelligence services, the Ministry of Defence and the armed forces, authorisation must be given by a Secretary of State, whose decision does not need to be approved and from whose decision there is no appeal by the person seeking the authorisation. A person who is the subject of a surveillance authorisation may make a complaint to the Investigatory Powers Tribunal. It has been held that *intrusive* surveillance can be used to eavesdrop on conversations between lawyers and their clients.[37]

Overlapping regimes

A great deal of the activity which is authorised by the Police Act 1997, Part III, would now fall within the definition of intrusive surveillance in the RIPA 2000 as well as the Regulation of Investigatory Powers (Scotland) Act 2000. So while the Police Act 1997 allows the use of surveillance devices in vehicles on the authorisation of the police alone, the RIPA 2000 would require such activity to be approved by a commissioner. In fact, the combined effect of the two regimes is that prior approval by a surveillance commissioner would normally be required for many forms of surveillance: in the case of dwellings, hotel bedrooms and offices it would be required by the Police Act; and in the case of vehicles it would be required by RIPA. Only exceptionally could bugging devices be used on the word of the police alone: one example would be the bugging of a known meeting place of suspected criminals (such as a warehouse or a pub). It should be emphasised, however, that other forms of police surveillance (such as watching someone (directed surveillance), or using informants or infiltrating organisations (covert human intelligence)) would not require the prior approval of a surveillance commissioner. The chief surveillance commissioner has been given additional duties to keep under review the operation of RIPA, Part II.[38]

C. Interception of communications

The interception of communications has been recognised by government as a 'patent invasion of individuals' privacy, and it should occur only when it is properly justified within the law'.[39] It involves the interception of both post and telephone communications and, as technology has advanced, now includes matters such as faxes, email and mobile phones. It has long been an offence to intercept the mail without the authority of a warrant granted by the Home Secretary.[40] In 1937, the practice was adopted whereby telephone calls would be intercepted under the authority of a warrant granted to the police or the security service by the Home Secretary.[41] But

---

[37] *McE v Northern Ireland Prison Service* [2009] UKHL 15; [2009] 1 AC 908.

[38] Regulation of Investigatory Powers Act 2000, s 62.

[39] HC Deb, 6 March 2000, col 771 (Mr Jack Straw).

[40] Post Office Act 1953, s 58. But see now Postal Services Act 2000, ss 83 and 84.

[41] Cmnd 283, 1957. Since 1966 it has been the practice of successive governments that the telephones of MPs are not to be tapped: HC Deb, 30 October 1997, col 861 (WA), a practice robustly defended by the House of Commons Home Affairs Committee: HC 58 (2007–8).

the legal basis for the practice remained obscure.[42] As we have seen, a legal challenge to the procedure in *Malone v Metropolitan Police Commissioner*[43] was unsuccessful on the ground that the interception of communications did not involve the violation of any of the rights of the applicant. There was no trespass, there was no breach of confidence, and he had no enforceable right to privacy in English law. The matter was said by Sir Robert Megarry V-C to be one which 'cries out for legislation'.[44] However, the practice was found to breach art 8 of the ECHR: although art 8(2) permits limitations on a person's art 8(1) rights, these must be prescribed by law, a requirement which was not met by the British practice of interception at the time.[45]

The statutory framework

The European Court of Human Rights did not comment on the substance of the procedures then in place for the granting of warrants by the Home Secretary to intercept communications. In effect, it merely invited the British government to introduce legislation to give these procedures statutory force. This is largely what happened, although the Interception of Communications Act 1985 also introduced a number of new safeguards to restrain any possible misuse of the new statutory procedures, addressing concerns that the practice of telephone tapping had been abused in the past.[46] But the 1985 Act has had to be substantially revised, for two reasons. The first is in response to another decision of the European Court of Human Rights, *Halford v United Kingdom*:[47] in that case it was held that the UK was in breach of art 8 for failing to regulate the interception of communications by employers. The second is in response to new technology and new means of communication. In particular, the 1985 Act did not apply to the use of cordless phones.[48] These and other issues have been addressed in the Regulation of Investigatory Powers Act 2000, Part I, although doubts were expressed shortly after its enactment about whether even these new provisions were sufficiently comprehensive.[49]

The RIPA 2000 repeals much of the 1985 Act, but the structure of the new regulatory framework remains largely the same.[50] This means that it is a criminal offence 'intentionally and without lawful authority' to intercept a communication transmitted by post or by means of a public telecommunication system (s 1(1)).[51] It is now also an offence intentionally and without lawful authority to intercept a communication being transmitted on a private communications system unless liability is excluded by s 1(6). Section 1(6) excludes criminal liability where the interception is conducted by the operator of a private telecommunications system with the express or implied consent of the person whose communication has been intercepted. Apart from criminal liability,

---

[42] Cmnd 283, 1957, p 15.

[43] [1979] Ch 344; C P Walker [1980] PL 184; V Bevan [1980] PL 431.

[44] [1979] Ch 344, at p 380.

[45] *Malone v UK* (1985) 7 EHRR 14.

[46] On which see *R v Home Secretary, ex p Ruddock* [1987] 2 All ER 518.

[47] (1997) 24 EHRR 523.

[48] *R v Effik* [1995] 1 AC 309.

[49] See Y Akdeniz, N Taylor and C Walker [2001] Crim LR 73.

[50] For a full account, see Fenwick, pp 345–70, and for a good critique, see D Ormerod and S McKay [2004] Crim LR 15.

[51] On the meaning of a public telecommunications system, see *Morgans v DPP* [2001] 1 AC 315 where it was held that call-logging devices were covered. But in *R v Effik* [1995] 1 AC 309 it was held that a cordless phone was not covered; and in *R v Taylor-Sabori* [1999] 1 WLR 858 it was held that pager messages were not covered. Both would be regarded as private communications. This means that under the 1985 Act any interception would not require a warrant and that evidence of the interceptions would be admissible in legal proceedings. A warrant is now required for the interception of private communications. The drafting of the RIPA 2000, s 1 is slightly different from the drafting of s 1 of the 1985 Act on which it is based. On the implications, see *R v Sargent* [2001] UKHL 54; [2003] 1 AC 347. On the meaning of interception, see *R v E* [2004] EWCA Crim 1243; [2004] 1 WLR 3279.

an innovation of the RIPA 2000 is the introduction of civil liability for employers and other operators of private telecommunications systems for interception which takes place without consent: in this case there is liability to either the sender or the recipient of the message or both.

Lawful authority

Lawful authority under the Regulation of Investigatory Powers Act 2000 will arise in one of a number of circumstances. The first is where both the sender and the recipient consent to the interception or where either has consented and the interception takes place by an undercover agent whose activities have been authorised under Part II of the Act (s 3).[52] The second is on one of the grounds specified in s 4 which gives statutory authority for interception without a warrant and without any additional formality. This applies to certain communications intercepted for certain business practices in accordance with rules made by the Secretary of State;[53] under prison rules;[54] in high-security psychiatric hospitals; and in state hospitals in Scotland. Third, authority may be provided by a warrant issued by the Secretary of State (s 5). There are now four grounds for the issuing of a warrant: the interests of national security, the prevention or detection of serious crime, safeguarding the economic well-being of the United Kingdom, and to give effect to an international mutual assistance agreement (s 5(3)).[55] The conduct authorised by the warrant must be proportionate to the end to be achieved, and before a warrant is granted consideration should be given to the possibility of the information being obtained by other means (s 5(4)).

There is no definition of national security in the Act, although it is now 'generally understood to refer to the survival and well-being of the state and community and includes such matters as threats to the security of the nation by terrorism, espionage and major subversive activity but is not confined to these matters'.[56] Serious crime is widely defined to mean either (a) a crime which could reasonably lead to imprisonment for at least three years if committed by someone over the age of 18 convicted of a first offence; or (b) conduct that 'involves the use of violence, results in substantial financial gain or is conduct by a large number of persons in pursuit of a common purpose' (s 81(3)). An application for a warrant may be made by one of a number of people specified in s 6(2): these include chief constables and the directors general of the Security Service and the Serious Organised Crime Agency, as well as the director of GCHQ, HM Revenue and Customs, and the Chief of Defence Intelligence. This represents an extension of the previous practice under the 1985 Act,[57] in relation to which it was reported that warrants were obtained only by NCIS (replaced by the Serious Organised Crime Agency), the Special Branch, Customs and Excise (replaced by HM Revenue and Customs), the RUC (now Police Service for Northern Ireland), the Scottish police, the security service, SIS and GCHQ, but 'no other agencies'.[58]

---

[52] The government gives the example of the situation where a kidnapper is telephoning the relatives of a hostage and the police wish to record the call in order to identify or trace the kidnapper. The operation will be authorised as surveillance rather than by means of an interception warrant: RIPA 2000, Explanatory Notes. See also *R v Rasool* [1997] 1 WLR 1092, which presumably would be decided differently today, for a number of reasons.

[53] SI 2000 No 2699. These have been controversial in a number of respects, not least because they allow interception without consent 'to investigate or detect the unauthorised use of telecommunications systems'. This would allow the monitoring of telephone calls and emails. But the Human Rights Act 1998 is lurking in the background and any exercise of power (at least by a public authority) would have to meet the standards set by art 8 of the ECHR.

[54] Cf *R v Owen* [1999] 1 WLR 949.

[55] According to the government the request 'would have to satisfy the law of the requesting country as well as UK interception law': HC Deb, 6 March 2000, col 832 (Mr Charles Clarke).

[56] Cm 4364, 1999, para 14. It has also been said that the 'normal object of a national security warrant is to assist in the build up of an intelligence picture, for example about a suspected terrorist or terrorist group' (ibid).

[57] Despite the government's concern that 'it should be used only by a narrow and tight range of agencies': HC Deb, 6 March 2000, col 831 (Mr Charles Clarke).

[58] Cm 4778, 2000. No warrant had ever been issued to anyone else: Cm 4364, 1999.

The application will be made to an appropriate minister, although the burden is carried mainly by the Home Secretary and the Scottish Ministers. Other ministers who sign warrants are the Foreign Secretary and the Secretary of State for Northern Ireland.[59] Applications are normally granted, although there are rare cases where, despite being 'reasonably and responsibly made', an application is refused because the minister has decided that it does not satisfy the statutory criteria. The fact that applications are normally but not always granted is not thought to be a problem: it shows that the Secretary of State is not a 'rubber stamp'.[60] There has been a sharp increase in the number of warrants issued, from a total of 519 by the Home Secretary and the Secretary of State for Scotland (now the Scottish Executive) in 1988 to 1,712 in 2008 (with a steady increase in between).[61] This substantial increase is not 'a cause for concern' and is due to the 'continuing incidence of serious and organised crime and an increased facility to counter it'.[62] These figures appear to relate only to warrants granted by the Home Secretary and the Scottish Executive for reasons of national security and the prevention and detection of crime. It is not known what the national security grounds cover, and the statistics do not include warrants issued by the Foreign Secretary or the Secretary of State for Northern Ireland, which are not made public on the ground that disclosure would be prejudicial to the public interest.[63]

Safeguards and supervision

The Regulation of Investigatory Powers Act 2000, Part I, contains a number of different safeguards designed to ensure that there is no abuse of the powers which it authorises. The Interception of Communications Commissioner was established under the Interception of Communications Act 1985 and the office is continued by virtue of s 57 of the RIPA. The Commissioner is a senior or former judicial figure and is appointed by the Prime Minister. The first holder of the office was Lord Justice Lloyd, who was succeeded in turn by Sir Thomas Bingham, Lord Nolan, Sir Swinton Thomas, and Sir Paul Kennedy. The Commissioner has a number of duties to review the operation of powers under the Act and he or she must report annually to the Prime Minister regarding the discharge of these duties. The report must then be laid before Parliament, although parts of it may be excluded in the public interest. The procedures adopted by the Commissioner are described in these reports. The practice of the Commissioner is to make twice-yearly visits to departments and agencies concerned with interception and to select a sample of warrants 'largely at random' for close inspection. In the course of these visits, the Commissioner seeks to satisfy himself that 'the warrants fully meet the requirements of RIPA, that proper procedures have been followed, and that the relevant safeguards and codes of practice have been followed'.[64] There has been no case of a warrant being unjustified, although a number of 'errors' are frequently acknowledged in the annual reports of the Commissioner.[65]

The second safeguard against abuse is the provision for a tribunal to deal with a wide range of complaints that may be made about the exercise of powers under the Act. Tribunals of this kind were previously established under the Interception of Communications Act 1985, the Security Service Act 1989 and the Intelligence Services Act 1994. These different tribunals are now combined into a single tribunal, the Investigatory Powers Tribunal, and Lord Justice Mummery became its first president in 2001. The tribunal has extended powers to reflect the wider range of

---

[59] HC 549 (2005–06), SE 2005/203, para 33.

[60] Cm 4001, 1998, paras 10, 11.

[61] HC 901 (2008–09), SG/2009/138.

[62] Cm 4778, 2000, para 14. In 1999 the numbers were even higher at 2,022.

[63] See HC 901 (2008–09), SG/2009/138, para 5.3. In 1994, the numbers were said to have declined in the former case (but from what to what?), but to have 'increased substantially' in the latter case: Cm 2522, 1994.

[64] HC 901 (2008–09), SG/2009/138, para 2.1.

[65] On which see Fenwick, p 354.

issues dealt with in RIPA 2000. However, the model for the new tribunal is that which was established in the 1985 Act, which authorised the Interception of Communications Tribunal to deal with complaints about the improper issuing of warrants under that Act. Although the Tribunal had a limited jurisdiction, it received a considerable number of applications. Between the time it was established in 1986 and 1999, it dealt with 712 complaints, not one of which was found to have breached the Act. As Lord Nolan pointed out in his 1997 report, the fact that not a single case succeeded 'led to a measure of suspicion as to the effectiveness of the Tribunal's work'.[66] But, as was pointed out, in only eight of the then 568 cases dealt with by the Tribunal was an interception carried out with the authority of a warrant and in each case the warrant had been properly issued.[67]

In many countries judicial intervention takes place at the point of granting the warrant: it is common practice for warrants to be granted by judges rather than by politicians.[68] The enactment of the RIPA provided an opportunity to consider adopting judicial authorisation rather than judicial supervision. But the Home Secretary expressed the view that 'it does not necessarily follow that, just because a judicial warrant is required, there is a greater safeguard for the individual'.[69] It is important to note, however, that the role of the Commissioner is not confined to safeguarding the rights of the individual. One reason for the increase in the number of Home Office and (what was then) Scottish Office warrants is the revocation in 1992 of the quota system which had been in operation for many years whereby a restriction was imposed on the number of warrants issued to the Customs and Excise on the one hand and the police on the other. The quota system was considered by the then Commissioner (Sir Thomas Bingham) who questioned whether 'the Secretary of State should circumscribe his discretion to authorise the issue of warrants by reference to an arithmetical norm'. There was 'much to be said for dealing with applications . . . very strictly on their merits and without reference to numerical constraints beyond those necessarily imposed by the existence of limited facilities'.[70]

The exclusion of the courts

Although senior judicial figures are thus involved as commissioners and as President of the Investigatory Powers Tribunal, there is little role for the courts in the operation of the Act. The tribunal is protected by a statutory provision which precludes judicial review of its decisions, including decisions as to jurisdiction.[71] Moreover, no evidence may be adduced in legal proceedings which tends to suggest that a warrant has been issued under the Act; or that an offence has been committed by a servant of the Crown, a police officer, a person providing a postal service or a public telecommunications operator (s 17).[72] This is designed to prevent 'the asking of

---

[66] Cm 4001, 1998, para 31.

[67] It is more difficult since RIPA to give details of interception complaints. The Commissioner gives details of the total number of complaints to the tribunal annually, without breaking them down according to category. So it is impossible to know how many of the 136 complaints received in 2008 related to interception and how many to the use of other forms of surveillance. Nor will the Commissioner say whether any of the three complaints upheld by the tribunal since it was established related to the interception of communications: HC 901 (2008–09), SG/2009/138, paras 6.1–6.3.

[68] For Opposition proposals for the same in this country, see HC Deb, 6 March 2000, col 688.

[69] Ibid, col 770.

[70] Cm 2173, 1993, paras 14–16. Other reasons for the increase is that there are more phones and more crime: HC Deb, 6 March 2000, col 830 (Mr Charles Clarke).

[71] Regulation of Investigatory Powers Act 2000, s 67(8).

[72] Interception evidence obtained by an unlawful interception is not admissible any more than interception evidence obtained by lawful interception. There would otherwise be 'a remarkable and unacceptable anomaly' (*Morgans v DPP* [2001] AC 315). See also *R v Sargent*, note 51 above. For consideration of some of the problems arising here, see *Attorney-General's Reference (No 5 of 2002)* [2004] UKHL 40; [2005] 1 AC 167.

questions suggesting that a warrant to intercept communications has been or is to be issued':[73] 'neither the existence of a telephone intercept under warrant nor the result thereof are to be disclosed in evidence'.[74] In this country, 'the content of interceptions may inform police investigations but may not form part of the evidence at any subsequent trial'.[75] The position compares with evidence obtained from listening devices and other forms of surveillance by the intelligence services and the police which may be disclosed not only for the purpose of preventing or detecting serious crime, but also for the purpose of criminal proceedings.[76] Although it might be thought that the total exclusion of interception evidence would normally benefit the defence, there may be circumstances where the accused is precluded from relying on evidence of the interception to rebut the case against him or her.[77] Proposals to relax the rules prohibiting the use of interception evidence in criminal prosecutions have been vigorously opposed by the Interception Commissioner.[78]

D. Storing and processing information

The storage and use of information about individuals is an issue which has assumed much greater significance as a result of the computer revolution and the greater capacity now to store and process personal information:

> One of the less welcome consequences of the information technology revolution has been the ease with which it has become possible to invade the privacy of the individual. No longer is it necessary to peep through keyholes or listen under the eaves. Instead, more reliable information can be obtained in greater comfort and safety by using the concealed surveillance camera, the telephoto lens, the hidden microphone and the telephone bug. No longer is it necessary to open letters, pry into files or conduct elaborate inquiries to discover the intimate details of a person's business or financial affairs, his health, family, leisure interests or dealings with central or local government. Vast amounts of information about everyone are stored on computers, capable of instant transmission anywhere in the world and accessible at the touch of a keyboard. The right to keep oneself to oneself, to tell other people that certain things are none of their business, is under technological threat.[79]

But we should not overlook the fact that the storage and use of personal information in different forms had occurred for many years before the invention of the computer. Obvious examples include the files maintained by the intelligence services about people deemed to be politically subversive;[80] the disclosure of medical information to insurance companies and employers;[81] and the blacklisting of trade unionists which was conducted by organisations sympathetic to employers. It goes without saying that the common law proved of little value to regulate much of this activity

---

[73] *R v Preston* [1994] 2 AC 130, at 144 (Lord Jauncey). There are, however, qualifications in s 18 whereby a trial judge may order material to be disclosed for exceptional purposes in exceptional circumstances. See generally, Standing Committee F, 28 March 2000, cols 228–39.

[74] *R v Preston*, ibid.

[75] *R v E*, note 51 above, at p 3289 (Hughes J).

[76] *R v Khan* [1997] AC 558, at 576 (Lord Nolan). See also *R v E*, note 51 above.

[77] *R v Preston* (note 73 above).

[78] Cm 7324, 2008 (proposals by a Committee of Privy Counsellors chaired by Sir John Chilcot), and HC 901 (2008–09), SG/2009/138, para 2.7 (response of the Interception Commissioner). See previously HC 315 (2006–07).

[79] *R v Brown* [1996] 1 AC 541, at 556 per Lord Hoffmann.

[80] See Lustgarten and Leigh, ch 5.

[81] See Access to Health Records Act 1990 by which the practice is now regulated, although in a manner which arguably permits access to too much information by employers and insurance companies, albeit with the 'consent' of the individual.

and indeed failed to develop any tools to deal with it. The use of this material did not attract liability for conspiracy to injure,[82] although there might be liability in defamation if the information were distributed – but only if it were untrue. The Security Service Act 1989 provided a limited opportunity for individuals to complain to the tribunal established by that Act about inquiries conducted about them by the security service, and about the disclosure of information 'for use in determining whether [they] should be employed'.[83] These complaints are now made to the Investigatory Powers Tribunal, and it is not known whether any of the only three complaints ever upheld by that tribunal relates to vetting or surveillance by the security service.

The Data Protection Act 1998

The important protection of this aspect of privacy is to be found in the Data Protection Act 1998. Designed to give effect to Council Directive 95/46/EC, this replaces the 1984 Act of the same name which applied only to computer-related data.[84] It has been held that the Directive does not violate Community obligations relating to freedom of expression, though member states are expected to have regard to freedom of expression considerations when implementing the Directive.[85] At the same time, however, the Act is to be construed in a purposive way to give effect to the Directive,[86] the primary objective of which is to protect individuals' fundamental rights, notably the right to privacy and accuracy of their personal data held by others.[87]

Data for the purposes of the 1998 Act are defined as 'information' which is recorded or processed by computer; as well as any other information which is recorded as part of a relevant filing system.[88] The Act also applies to certain health records, educational records, local authority records, and other information held by a public authority (s 1).[89] These terms have been narrowly construed by the Court of Appeal,[90] leading the Information Commissioner to conclude that 'it is likely that very few manual files will be covered by the provisions of the [1998 Act]. Most information about individuals held in manual form does not, therefore, fall within the data protection regime.'[91] Some data are described as being 'sensitive personal data', a subset, or a species, of 'personal data',[92] and defined to mean personal data consisting of any of the following information about the data subject: racial or ethnic origin, political opinions, religious belief, trade union status, physical or mental health or condition,[93] sexual life, the commission or alleged commission of an offence, and any criminal proceedings brought against him or her (s 2).[94] The other key concept

---

[82] *McKenzie v Iron Trades Employers' Insurance Association* 1910 SC 79.

[83] Security Service Act 1989, Sch 1(2) and (3): see Lustgarten and Leigh, pp 153–6.

[84] The following is a necessarily condensed account which highlights the main features of the Act.

[85] *Case C-101/01, Criminal Proceedings Against Lindqvist* [2004] QB 1014.

[86] *Campbell v MGN* [2002] EWCA Civ 1373; [2003] QB 633, Lord Phillips of Worth Matravers, at para 96. See also *Common Services Agency v Scottish Information Commissioner* [2008] UKHL 47, [2008] 1 WLR 1550, para 7 (Lord Hope), and *Johnson v Medical Defence Union* [2007] EWCA Civ 262, [2007] BMLR 99.

[87] *Durant v Financial Services Authority* [2003] EWCA Civ 1746, Auld LJ.

[88] A relevant filing system is defined to mean 'any set of information relating to individuals to the extent that, although the information is not processed by means of equipment operating automatically in response to instructions given for that purpose, the set is structured, either by reference to individuals or by reference to criteria relating to individuals, in such a way that specific information relating to a particular individual is readily accessible': Data Protection Act 1998, s 1(1).

[89] Public authority for this purpose has the same meaning as in the Freedom of Information Act 2000.

[90] *Durant v Financial Services Authority*, note 87 above.

[91] Information Commissioner, 'The *Durant* Case and its impact on the interpretation of the Data Protection Act 1998' (2004).

[92] *Common Services Agency v Scottish Information Commissioner*, above, para 37 (Lord Hope).

[93] On which see *Common Services Agency*, ibid.

[94] See *R (A) v Chief Constable of C* [2001] 1 WLR 461.

in the Act is 'the special purposes'. This is a term which is defined to mean journalism, artistic purposes or literary purposes (s 3).

Underpinning the Act are the eight data protection principles, with which data controllers must comply (s 4(4)). These are set out in Sch 1 as follows: (i) personal data shall be fairly and lawfully processed; (ii) they shall be obtained only for a specified and lawful purpose; (iii) they shall be 'adequate, relevant and not excessive' in relation to the purposes for which they are processed; (iv) they shall be accurate and kept up to date; (v) they shall not be kept longer than necessary for the purpose for which the data are processed; (vi) they shall be processed in accordance with the rights of the data subject; (vii) appropriate measures are to be taken against unauthorised or unlawful processing of personal data; and (viii) they shall not be transferred outside the European Economic Area.

These principles are subject to detailed interpretation in the Act itself and, in the case of the first, it is provided additionally that at least one of the six conditions in Sch 2 must be met. This provides that data are to be processed only if the data subject consents, or if the processing is necessary for one of a number of purposes which include the administration of justice and the exercise of any functions of the Crown, a minister of the Crown or a government department. The other conditions specified are that the processing is necessary for the purposes of a contract to which the data subject is a party; to comply with any legal obligation to which the data controller is subject; to protect the vital interests of the data subject; or for 'the purposes of legitimate interests pursued by the data controller or by the third party or parties to whom the data are disclosed'. Where the data are 'sensitive personal data', at least one of the eleven conditions in Sch 3 (as amended) must also be met.[95]

Data subjects and data controllers

The first of two key substantive aspects of the Act relate to the rights of the data subject, that is to say the person whose personal data are being stored and used by another. Under the Act the data subject is entitled on request and in writing to be (a) informed by any data controller whether any personal data are being processed by the data controller; (b) given a description of the personal data and the purposes for which they are being used, as well as the people to whom they may be disclosed; and (c) supplied with the information which is being processed and informed of the logic of any decision taken in relation to him or her (such as performance at work) which is based solely on the 'processing by automatic means of personal data' (s 7). This last is designed to protect people excluded credit because of their postal code or workers refused employment or promotion because of psychometric testing. There are a number of exceptions to the right of access (particularly where it would necessarily involve disclosing confidential information about another person), and provision is made as to the manner in which the information should be disclosed. In some circumstances, the data subject is entitled by giving notice in writing to require the data controller to stop processing his or her personal data, and an application

---

[95] These are (i) the data subject has given 'his explicit consent'; (ii) the processing is necessary for the purposes of exercising any right or duty of the data controller in connection with employment; (iii) the processing is necessary to protect the vital interests of the data subject; (iv) the processing is carried out in the course of the legitimate activities of a non-profit making association; (v) the information contained in the personal data has been made public as a result of steps deliberately taken by the data subject; (vi) the processing is necessary for purposes relating to legal proceedings; (vii) the processing is necessary for the administration of justice, the exercise of a statutory duty or the exercise of any functions of the Crown, a minister or a government department; (viii) the processing takes the form of the disclosure of sensitive personal data by an anti-fraud organisation and is necessary to prevent fraud; (ix) the processing is necessary for medical purposes and is undertaken by a health professional or another person who owes an equivalent duty of confidentiality; (x) the processing is undertaken for the purpose of ethnic monitoring; and (xi) any other circumstances specified in an order made by the Secretary of State.

may be made to court for an order to the data controller to correct or destroy any inaccurate personal data being stored or processed by the data controller.

The second of the two main substantive provisions of the Data Protection Act 1998 relates to the responsibilities of data controllers. Personal data are not to be processed unless the data controller has first registered with the Information Commissioner (s 17), a post which is created by the Act (s 6). Those applying for registration must describe the personal data to be processed, the purposes for which they are to be processed and the persons to whom the data controller intends to disclose the data (s 16). They must also provide a 'general description of measures to be taken for the purpose of complying with the seventh data protection principle' (s 18(2)(b)). There is in addition a duty to notify the Commissioner of any material changes to the practice of the data controller with regard to personal data (s 20). It is an offence to process data without being registered and to fail to notify any relevant changes (s 21). The Secretary of State is empowered to make regulations to provide for the appointment of data protection supervisors by data controllers: the role of the supervisor would be to monitor 'in an independent manner the data controller's compliance with the provisions of [the] Act' (s 23). An individual who suffers damage, as a result of a breach of the Act by a data controller is entitled to recover compensation from the latter; and in some cases it may be possible to recover also for distress suffered as a result of the breach (s 13).

Perhaps predictably there are a number of situations where the Act does not apply or where its application is diluted. There are at least ten such general categories of exempt data, the first of which are data where exemption is required for the purpose of safeguarding national security (s 28). These are exempt from all the data protection principles. A ministerial certificate stating that the exemption is required is enough for this purpose, though any person affected by the issuing of the certificate may appeal to the Administrative Appeals Chamber of the Upper Tribunal (previously the Information Tribunal National Security Appeals Panel) against the certificate (s 28(4)).

> In an important decision, the Information Tribunal – sitting to deal with national security appeals – overruled a blanket certificate of the Home Secretary exempting the Security Service from much of the Act. The Liberal Democrat MP Norman Baker wrote to the Service asking if it was processing personal data of his and if so what such data were. The Service could neither confirm nor deny. The decision of the Tribunal was confined to the duty of a data controller under s 7(1)(a) of the 1998 Act to inform people from whom a request is made whether or not their personal data are being processed. The Tribunal held that the ministerial certificate was too wide because it would 'exempt the Service from the obligation to respond positively to any request made to it under section 7(1)(a) of the Act, regardless of whether national security would be harmed by a positive response in a particular case'.[96] Following this decision the Home Secretary issued a fresh certificate under s 28 of the 1998 Act, which removed the blanket exemption of the Security Service.
>
> Individuals may now make an application to the Service which may be refused on the grounds of national security only on a case-by-case basis. The new certificate provides that 'no data shall be exempt from the provisions of section 7(1)(a) of the Data Protection Act 1998 if the Security Service, after considering any request by a data subject for access to relevant personal data, determines that adherence to the principle of neither confirming nor denying whether the Security Service holds data about an individual is not required for the purpose of safeguarding national security'. However, it has not proved to be any easier for individuals to determine whether the Security Service processes their personal data. In *Hitchens v Home Secretary*,[97] the Information Tribunal dismissed an appeal from a journalist who had asked the Security Service if it processed data about him and for access to the files he believed that it held on him about his time as

---

[96] *Baker v Home Secretary* [2001] UKHRR 1275.
[97] [2003] UKIT NSA 4.

'an extreme left-wing student' in the 1970s. The tribunal upheld the Security Service's decision not to confirm or deny whether such files existed.[98]

There is also an exemption from aspects of the first data protection principle for data processed for the prevention or detection of crime or for the assessment or collection of tax (s 29). There is then power vested in the Secretary of State to exempt by order from other aspects of the first data protection principle personal data relating to the physical or mental health of the data subject (s 30). Other exemptions relate to the activities of regulatory bodies (s 31), personal data which are processed with a view to publication as journalism, literature or art (s 32),[99] personal data which are processed for research purposes (including historical and statistical research) (s 33), manual data held by local authorities (s 33A), personal data which the data controller is obliged to make available to the public by statute (s 34), or otherwise disclose by virtue of any legal obligation or court order (s 35). An exemption is also made to avoid infringing parliamentary privilege (s 35A), for personal data processed for domestic purposes (s 36) and for other miscellaneous purposes (s 37).

The Information Commissioner

Enforcement of the Act is principally by means of the Information Commissioner and the First-tier Tribunal (Information Rights) (formerly the Information Tribunal) (s 6). The Commissioner is a continuation of the office of Data Protection Registrar under the Data Protection Act 1984, and is appointed by the government ('Her Majesty by Letters Patent' according to the statutory form) (s 6); but neither the Commissioner nor his or her staff are to be regarded as Crown servants. Appointments are for renewable fixed terms of up to five years each, though the same person may not hold office for more than two terms save in exceptional circumstances where the public interest so requires. But once appointed, a Commissioner can be removed within the term only after an address from both Houses of Parliament. The Tribunal in contrast is appointed by the Lord Chancellor, to include a legally qualified chairman and deputy chairmen, as well as persons to represent the interests of data subjects and data controllers respectively. The Tribunal is a tripartite body. National security cases are now heard by the Administrative Appeals Chamber of the Upper Tribunal, a superior court of record,[100] which consists of three judicial members for these purposes. This replaces the National Security Appeals Panel of the Information Tribunal. National security hearings will generally take place in private.[101]

The powers of the Commissioner have recently been enhanced following amendments made (curiously) by the Coroners and Justice Act 2009, which adds to the original powers of the Commissioner. The Commissioner may issue an enforcement notice to a data controller if satisfied that the data controller is breaching the data protection principles (s 40). The notice may require the data controller to take steps specified in the notice or to refrain from conduct specified in the notice. This might include the erasing of inaccurate data. The new provisions of s 41A enable the Commissioner effectively to initiate an investigation of government departments and other public authorities by way of an assessment notice, designed to enable the Commissioner to determine whether a data controller has complied or is complying with the data protection principles. An assessment notice under s 41A requires the data processor to permit the Commissioner to enter specified premises and to have access to and copies of specified documents. This is in addition to the original provisions of s 42 which permits any person directly affected by the processing of any data to seek an assessment from the Commissioner as to whether the processing

---

[98] See also *Hilton v Home Secretary* [2005] UKIT NSA 5.
[99] This exemption was widely construed by the Court of Appeal in *Campbell v MGN Ltd*, note 86 above.
[100] See ch 29 A below.
[101] SI 2009 No 2698 (L 15), esp regs 14(10) and 37(2A).

is being carried out in accordance with the Act. Where such a request has been made, the Commissioner may serve the data controller with an information notice requiring the data controller to furnish the Commissioner with specified information within a specified time (s 43).

Apart from the power to issue these and other notices (the duty to comply with which is underpinned by criminal sanctions), the Commissioner may also apply to a circuit judge or a district judge (magistrates' courts) for a warrant where there are reasonable grounds to suspect that a data controller is contravening the data protection principles or that an offence against the Act has been committed.[102] As amended in 2009, the Act provides that the warrant may authorise the entry and search of premises and the inspection, examination, operation and testing of any equipment which is found there, and which is used for the processing of personal data. The warrant also authorises the seizure of any material which may be evidence that the data principles have been violated or an offence committed. No warrant is to be issued in respect of any personal data processed for 'special purposes' except in limited circumstances. Except in cases of urgency or in order not to defeat the purpose of the entry, a warrant should normally be granted only if the data processor has refused access to the Commissioner. The Commissioner now has the power to impose monetary penalties on data controllers, where there is a serious and deliberate breach of the data protection principles (s 55A). The data controller must be given notice of intent in advance and an opportunity to make representations before the penalty is imposed (s 55B).

Data protection and the RIPA 2000

Provision is made in the RIPA 2000 to deal with the situation where it is deemed necessary for public authorities to secure access to communications data. Before the Act came into force, access to this information was governed by a voluntary regime set up under the Telecommunications Act 1984 and the Data Protection Act 1998. It was thought that this 'loosely regulated' regime was 'unacceptable in terms of human rights and because, in certain cases, it has led to unacceptably high demands on the public telecommunications operators'.[103] As a result, Chapter II of Part I of the RIPA introduces a statutory procedure whereby the law enforcement and other agencies can require service providers to supply communications data in defined circumstances.[104] These are that it is necessary to obtain the data in the interests of national security, for the purpose of preventing or detecting crime, or preventing disorder, in the interests of the economic well-being of the UK, in the interests of public safety, for the purpose of assessing or collecting taxes, in an emergency to prevent death or injury, or any other purpose specified in a ministerial order. Communications data are data about the use which the individual has made of a postal service or telecommunications system,[105] that is to say the 'who', 'when' and 'where' of a communication but not the content, not what was said or what was written.[106] Any request for such data must now be made by an authorised officer within a relevant public authority (such as a police force, the intelligence services, HM Revenue and Customs, or a local authority), and in the years ended 31 December 2008, public authorities as a whole are said to have made 504,073 requests for communications data to various service providers (including internet service providers).[107]

---

[102] Data Protection Act 1998, Sch 9.

[103] HC Deb, 6 March 2000, col 773 (Mr Jack Straw).

[104] RIPA 2000, s 22.

[105] Ibid, s 21(4) and (6). It has been said to cover 'billing data, subscriber data, details of numbers dialled or internet sites accessed by a given subscriber', but not 'for example, the content of voice calls': W Malcolm and D Barker, NLJ, 25 January 2002.

[106] HC 901, 2008–09, SG /2009/138, para 3.1.

[107] Ibid, para 3.8.

E. Government databases

The concerns expressed above about the storage and use of information have increased in intensity in recent years as a result of the expansion of databases held by various government departments and other public authorities. These include the NHS patients' database,[108] the DNA database, the National Identity Register, and the Police National Computer. Databases of these kinds are controversial not least because of a lack of confidence that they will be managed under properly secure conditions, undermining the need to protect the identity of the individual from misuse, one of the purposes of establishing some of these databases in the first place. Otherwise, there are concerns about (i) how and why some people appear on databases, particularly those where entry will carry a stigma or have potentially adverse consequences (such as the Police National Computer), (ii) what use is made of the personal information which may be recorded on databases maintained by government departments (with whom is the information shared and under what conditions?); and (iii) the right of access to the information by the individual whose information is recorded, if only to ensure that there are no mistakes and that any mistakes are corrected.

DNA database

One of the aims of the 1994 reforms to the Police and Criminal Evidence Act 1984 was to allow samples to be taken from arrested persons for DNA analysis, to be then stored on the National DNA database. DNA data are stored and kept on the database in perpetuity, regardless of whether the individual in question is subsequently charged or convicted of an offence. This means that the database inevitably holds the DNA data of the innocent as well as the guilty, reflecting the ambition of the Home Office that the United Kingdom should have the most comprehensive DNA database in the world, an ambition that appears to have been fulfilled by a database that includes information about more than 4 million people. Under the Police and Criminal Evidence Act 1984, the police are authorised to check information derived from samples obtained under the Act against other information or samples which are held by or on behalf of the police.[109] It is, however, a striking feature of the arrangements that there was no legislation establishing the database, no statutory body responsible for its management and supervision, and no statutory regulation of its use.

These arrangements were inevitably challenged as violating Convention rights. The leading case was brought by a child (S) who had been arrested charged with theft but found not guilty; and an adult (Marper) who was arrested (following a dispute with his wife) but not charged. In both cases samples were taken for DNA analysis and stored on the database, and in both cases it was argued that the retention of the data violated the Convention rights of the individuals concerned. In domestic legal proceedings, it was held by the House of Lords that the retention of fingerprints and samples of people who have not been charged or who have been charged and acquitted did not breach art 8(1) of the ECHR, and that if it did any such breach could be justified under art 8(2).[110] In an important decision of the Grand Chamber, the European Court of Human Rights disagreed strongly,[111] holding that the entry of the DNA of S and Marper onto the national DNA database was a breach of their Convention rights. The matter was subsequently addressed by the Crime and Security Act 2010 which allows for (i) the indefinite retention of the samples of people convicted of an offence; (ii) the retention for up to six years of the samples of adults who are arrested but not convicted; and (iii) the retention for up to three years of the

---

[108] See HC 153 (2008–09) (Public Accounts Committee).
[109] PACE, s 63A, amended by Criminal Justice and Police Act 2001, s 81.
[110] *R (S) v South Yorkshire Chief Constable* [2004] UKHL 39; [2004] 1 WLR 2196.
[111] *S and Marper v United Kingdom*, note 3 above.

samples of people under 18 who are arrested but not convicted.[112] The Act also provides that the Home Secretary must make arrangements for a National DNA Database Strategy Board to oversee the operation of the National DNA Database.[113]

Criminal record checks

A second prominent database maintained by the state is the Police National Computer. The Police Act 1997 established a procedure whereby some employers (particularly those whose activity involves employees working closely with children or vulnerable adults) could seek criminal record checks before making decisions to appoint people to certain positions. These checks are made on behalf of employers by the Criminal Records Bureau, an executive agency of the Home Office. As amended in 2005, the 1997 Act creates two different kinds of checks or certificates. The first are criminal record certificates (CRC) which list all the offences committed as well as cautions received by the individual in question which are recorded on central records (s 113A). If there are no such offences or cautions, this should be stated in the certificate. The second are enhanced criminal record certificates (ECRC) which should include the foregoing matters, but also any other relevant information about the individual held by the police which might be relevant and ought to be provided (though not if it would undermine the prevention or detection of crime) (s 113B).[114] In some cases the CRC or ECRC must also provide other information about the suitability of the individual, as provided by the Safeguarding Vulnerable Groups Act 2006.

These procedures have been introduced principally for reasons of public safety, with the need for effective procedures of this kind being highlighted by the notorious Soham school murders in which two schoolchildren were the victims of a school caretaker.[115] It has been noticed judicially, however, that use of these measures to obtain an ECRC 'has increased substantially since the scheme was first devised', and that the number of disclosures of information by means of ECRCs had reached 215,640 for 2007/2008 and 274,877 for 2008/2009. Moreover, 'not far short of ten per cent of these disclosures [had additional 'relevant information' on them] (17,560 for 2007/2008; 21,045 for 2008/2009)', with 'the release of sensitive information of this kind' in the context of increasing use of the procedure generally being said to be 'a cause of very real public concern'.[116] This is because of the impact on (i) employment opportunities, (ii) the opportunity to engage in unpaid work in the community, and (iii) the opportunity to 'establish and develop relations with others'. These problems are compounded where the data of innocent people are wrongly entered on the databases used by the CRB, or where the data are incorrect or exaggerated, there being uncertain opportunities for individuals to make corrections or changes.

Despite the serious purpose that this procedure is designed to address, it is nevertheless not surprising that questions should be raised here too under the Human Rights Act about the extent to which the disclosure of information can constitute a breach of art 8 of the ECHR. The matter has been considered by the Court of Appeal on a number of occasions, the procedures surviving judicial scrutiny. The matter was resolved conclusively by the Supreme Court in *R(L)* v *Metropolitan Police Commissioner*,[117] where the applicant had been offered employment as an assistant at a primary school which would involve close contact with children. Although she had no criminal convictions, ECRC revealed that her son had been placed on a child protection register because of neglect and disruptive behaviour at school. She was refused the job, and claimed that the disclosure of this information violated her art 8 right to private life. The Supreme Court

[112] Crime and Security Act 2010, s 14.
[113] Ibid, s 23.
[114] Police Act 1997, ss 113A, 113B
[115] See HC 653 (2003–04) (Bichard Report).
[116] *R(L)* v *Metropolitan Police Commissioner* [2009] UKSC 3, [2009] 3 WLR 1056, para 42 (Lord Hope).
[117] [2009] UKSC 3, [2009] 3 WLR 1056.

rejected the argument that art 8 was 'not engaged' in this case, and held that any disclosure would have to be justified under art 8(2). But this could be done within the framework of the existing legislation, which did not need to be declared incompatible with Convention rights, and on the facts there was no reason to challenge the decision to release the information about the appellant.

National Identity Register

The Identity Cards Act 2006 introduces a new concern about privacy, by establishing a National Identity Register and making provision for identity cards. These measures were justified by the government on a number of grounds, from the need to respond to terrorism, to the need to control access to public services by illegal migrants, and to the need to address the growing problem of identity theft. The 2006 Act imposes a duty on the Home Secretary to establish and maintain a National Identity Register (s 1), and a duty to enter on the register those people who apply and who are entitled to be entered on the register (s 2). Every individual over the age of 16 resident in the United Kingdom is entitled to be registered (s 2(2)), subject to a power of the Home Secretary to exclude some groups from the entitlement to be registered, including those with no right to remain in the country (s 2(3)). However, section 4 authorises the Home Secretary to 'designate' certain documents – such as passports – for the purposes of the Act. Where a document is designated, the Act provides that any applicant for such a document will also have to apply for entry to the National Identity Register and to have an ID card, unless they have already done so. An individual who applies to be registered may be required to allow fingerprints and other biometric information to be taken and recorded; to be photographed; and to provide any other information that may be required by the Home Secretary (s 5).

Those applying to be registered must be prepared to allow a considerable volume of personal information to be recorded on the register. The information in question is set out in Schedule 1 of the Act and runs to over three pages. Those registered will be given a National Identity Registration Number (s 2(3)), and must be issued with an identity card following a request for such a card to be issued (s 6). A person issued with an identity card will be required to notify the Secretary of State of any change of circumstances affecting the accuracy of the information held about him or her, with a failure to comply leading to the possibility of a civil penalty of up to £1,000 (s 10). This presumably applies to matters such as a change of address, the acquisition of a second home, or the driving licence number in the event of the individual passing his or her driving test. A crucial measure is section 13, whereby the provision of certain public services may be made conditional on an individual producing an ID card, though this does not apply to matters such as the payment of benefit or access to the NHS except in the case of those who are 'subject to compulsory registration' (s 13(2)) (on which see below). It is expressly provided that an individual should not be required to carry an ID card at all times, or to produce an ID card except when applying for public services (s 16).[118]

A major worry about the registration of so much personal data with the State relates to the way in which the data may be used. Under the Act, it will be possible for the information to be shared by the Home Secretary with other government agencies, in some circumstances without the consent of the individual concerned (s 17). It is true that otherwise it is an offence to pass on confidential information without lawful authority, a measure addressed principally to those who work with the register, ID cards, or with the National Identity Commissioner (s 27), who has been appointed to supervise the Register. Less certain, however, is the position of employees of a public

---

[118] As a matter of law, the police will have no right to require an individual to produce an ID card. But there is nothing to stop the police asking to see such a card, as when a person has been asked to 'stop and account', stopped and searched, or arrested under general police powers.

authority who, without permission, pass on to a third party information which has been lawfully released to them. It is far from clear whether there are adequate safeguards against such possible abuse in the Act, though one of the functions of the Commissioner is to review the arrangements 'for securing the confidentiality and integrity of information recorded in the Register' (s 22(3)). There are also unresolved questions about individual access to the register (in terms of inspecting or checking one's own entry), but disputes about this and other matters have been avoided so far by the government's failure fully to implement the 2006 Act in the wake of strong resistance from some sections of the public. The Act is being implemented very slowly, being applied very gradually and on a voluntary basis for British and EU nationals in the first instance.[119]

Protection of the individual

The *L* case considered above raised questions about the extent to which the police can release information about an individual, other than information about criminal convictions and cautions. But as we have seen, there are other issues which the individual may wish to challenge, including entry on some of these databases in the first place, the nature of the information that may be stored by the police, and the accuracy of the information that may be held. *R (Wright)* v *Secretary of State for Health*,[120] was concerned with the first of these questions, the Education Reform Act 1988 and Protection of Children Act 1999 having introduced a system for listing people deemed unsuitable for working with children, an initiative extended to vulnerable adults by the Care Standards Act 2000. The relevant law is now found in the Safeguarding Vulnerable Groups Act 2006, which establishes an Independent Safeguarding Authority, responsible for maintaining lists 'barring' people from various employments with children or vulnerable adults, on the basis of conduct which may not constitute a criminal offence, but may nevertheless raise questions about the suitability of an individual. According to *Wright* it would be a breach of Convention rights to bar someone provisionally without allowing the individual to make representations in advance, where this is done pending a proper resolution of the matter even though the individual may have a full hearing at the subsequent proceedings. This may provide some encouragement for those with other concerns.[121]

F. Privacy and the press

The emphasis in this chapter so far has been on state interference with privacy. But, as already pointed out, private parties may also be responsible for infringing the privacy of individuals. These private parties may include employers, insurance companies and newspaper proprietors.[122] It is true that some of the antics of the press will be caught by some of the measures already discussed, most notably telephone tapping or phone hacking,[123] which may be an offence unless there is consent under s 3 of the RIPA 2000. The use of surveillance devices by journalists will not require authorisation under the RIPA 2000 and may be unlawful if a trespass is involved. But a 'sting' operation – in a hotel bedroom, for example – may take place with the consent of the owner of the property.[124] And as far as data protection is concerned, we have seen that by s 32 the

---

[119] See Identity Commissioner, *Annual Report* (2009), para 5.2.

[120] [2009] UKHL 3, [2009] 2 WLR 267.

[121] But in *R (X)* v *West Midlands Chief Constable* [2004] EWCA Civ 1068, [2005] 1 WLR 65, it was held that the police are not under a duty to allow a person who is the subject of a criminal record check to make representations before the information is released.

[122] See *McGowan* v *Scottish Water* [2005] IRLR 167, and *Martin* v *McGuiness* 2003 SLT 1424.

[123] On which see HC 375 (2006–07), HC 362 (2009–10), paras 339–495 (dealing largely with the *News of the World*).

[124] *Grobbelaar* v *News Group Newspapers Ltd* [2001] 1 WLR 3024.

1998 Act expressly protects journalistic material. Yet the invasion of privacy by the press has given rise to great concern in recent years. Indeed, it is the infringement of privacy by the newspapers rather than by public authorities which has been primarily responsible for the growing demands for a legally enforceable right to privacy. There is a duty under the ECHR to take positive steps to ensure that Convention rights are observed, a duty which 'may involve the adoption of measures even in the sphere of relations between individuals'.[125] In this section we consider the evolution of such a right to protect individuals from what is in effect the violation of their privacy by unwanted publicity.[126]

Breach of confidence

The starting point is the equitable doctrine of breach of confidence.[127] The genesis of the modern action is *Prince Albert v Strange*,[128] which related to a number of etchings which the Prince had made of close members of his family. The defendant had obtained a copy of the etchings from an employee of a printer to whom they had been given by the Prince so that they could be reproduced. The Prince secured an injunction to restrain the defendant from exhibiting the etchings. In somewhat tendentious terms, the Lord Chancellor rejected the claim of the defendant that he was 'entitled to publish a catalogue of the etchings, that is to say, to publish a description or list of works or compositions of another, made and kept for the private use of that other, the publication of which was never authorised, and the possession of copies of which could only have been obtained by surreptitious and improper means'.[129] It was held that an injunction could lie in property, trust, confidence or contract. In *Argyll v Argyll*,[130] the court restrained the publication of confidential marital secrets and in doing so made clear that 'the court in the exercise of its equitable jurisdiction will restrain a breach of confidence independently of any right of law'. The publication of confidential information can thus be restrained, even though there is no breach of contract or any violation of property rights.[131]

Actions for breach of confidence have been brought on a number of occasions since *Argyll v Argyll* to restrain confidential information of a wide and varied kind.[132] In one case, it was held that an action could be brought where the defendant disclosed the existence of a sexual relationship between the applicant and another woman (a murder victim) which the applicant had told the defendant in confidence.[133] In another, it was held that a newspaper could be restrained from publishing a story to the effect that two unnamed doctors with AIDS were employed by a particular health authority and were continuing to practise despite their condition.[134] It has been held

---

[125] *Spencer v UK* (1998) 25 EHRR CD 105, at 112, citing *Plattform 'Ärtze für das Leben' v Austria* (1988) 13 EHRR 204.

[126] There are a number of miscellaneous statutory provisions which offer protection of the same kind. These are designed to prevent the publication of confidential or highly personal information which is disclosed in legal proceedings from being published. See Judicial Proceedings (Regulation of Reports) Act 1926 and the Children and Young Persons Act 1933, s 39. For an important discussion of the scope of the latter, see *Re S (a child)* [2004] UKHL 47; [2005] 1 AC 593.

[127] See Gurry, *Breach of Confidence*, H Fenwick and G Phillipson [1996] CLJ 447 and (2000) 63 MLR 660, and G Phillipson (2003) 66 MLR 726.

[128] (1849) 1 Mac&G 25. See also *Pollard v Photographic Co* (1888) 40 Ch D 345.

[129] Ibid, at p 42.

[130] [1967] Ch 302. The protection of confidentiality does not apply to sexual relationships outside marriage in the same way: *A v B plc* [2002] EWCA Civ 337; [2003] QB 195.

[131] The ingredients required to establish a breach of confidence are set out in *Coco v A N Clark Engineers Ltd* [1969] RPC 41, at p 47, and in *Attorney-General v Guardian Newspapers (No 2)* [1990] AC 109, at p 281.

[132] See *Saltman Engineering Co Ltd v Campbell Engineering Co Ltd* [1963] 3 All ER 413; *Fraser v Evans* [1969] 1 QB 349; *Lion Laboratories Ltd v Evans* [1985] QB 526.

[133] *Stephens v Avery* [1988] Ch 449. Also *Barrymore v News Group Newspapers Ltd* [1997] FSR 600.

[134] *X v Y* [1988] 2 All ER 648.

that there was a breach of confidence involved in the tapping of the applicant's telephone by a newspaper;[135] but that there was no breach of confidence when it was done by the police investigating criminal offences.[136] Thus although there is a public interest in protecting confidential information, there may be circumstances where a more compelling public interest favours disclosure.[137] As will be discussed below, liability for breach of confidence has evolved in recent recent years to encapsulate a wider liability for invasion of privacy, which is now likely often to be a feature of cases involving press disclosures of unwanted publicity. There remain circumstances, however, where an action to restrain a publication on the ground of breach of confidence alone may continue to be appropriate.[138]

Press Complaints Commission

Before addressing developments under the Human Rights Act, it is to be recognised that there are important self-regulatory measures designed to deal with privacy. Established and funded by newspaper publishers,[139] and subject to regular parliamentary scrutiny,[140] the Press Complaints Commission has produced a Code of Practice which deals with privacy, along with a number of other matters.[141] So far as privacy is concerned, the Code provides as follows:

> 3 Privacy
> (i) Everyone is entitled to respect for his or her private and family life, home, health and correspondence, including digital communications.
> (iii) Editors will be expected to justify intrusions into any individual's private life without consent. Account will be taken of the complainant's own public disclosures of information.
> (ii) It is unacceptable to photograph individuals in private places without their consent.

Private places are defined to mean 'public or private property where there is a reasonable expectation of privacy'. The PCC hears complaints about breaches of the Code of Practice and a newspaper is required to print any PCC adjudication to which it is a party 'in full and with due prominence'. But 'the PCC has no legal power to prevent publication of material, to enforce its rulings or to grant any legal remedy against the newspaper in favour of the victim'.[142]

Although the PCC is not a statutory body and its code of practice is not legally enforceable, there was concern during the enactment of the Human Rights Act 1998 that it might nevertheless be a public body for the purposes of that Act.[143] This means that it would be required to act in such a way as not to violate Convention rights and that it could be restrained in legal proceedings should it do so, either in the way in which it conducted its proceedings or in the adjudications which it gave. This would mean in particular that it would have to give due weight to the right to freedom of expression. Concerns expressed in Parliament by Lord Wakeham (then chairman of the PCC) led to an amendment to the Human Rights Bill and the introduction of what is now s 12 – a solution which emphasises that unlike in some countries, in this country freedom of expression is 'not in every case the ace of trumps' and must be qualified by other societal values, even though 'it is

---

[135] *Francome* v *Mirror Group Newspapers Ltd* [1984] 2 All ER 408.
[136] *Malone* v *Metropolitan Police Commissioner* [1979] Ch 344.
[137] *Attorney-General* v *Guardian Newspapers (No 2)*, note 131 above.
[138] *Napier* v *Pressdram Ltd* [2009] EWCA Civ 445.
[139] For background, see Cm 1102, 1990 (Calcutt report), and subsequently Cm 2135, 1993. The Commission has an independent chair as well as independent members and representatives of the national and regional press.
[140] See HC 294 (1992–93), HC 96 (1996–97), HC 375 (2006–07), HC 326 (2009–10).
[141] But with other matters as well, relating to various questions of journalistic ethics.
[142] *Spencer* v *UK* (1998) 25 EHRR CD 105.
[143] See HL Deb, 24 November 1997, col 772 (Lord Wakeham). On judicial review of the Commission, see *R (Ford)* v *Press Complaints Commission* [2001] EWHC 683 (Admin); [2002] EMLR 95.

a powerful card' to which the courts must always pay proper respect.[144] The amendment provides that courts are required to give due weight to freedom of expression (s 12(4)) – which they would surely be required to do anyway.[145] But it also provides that in proceedings which relate to journalistic, literary or artistic material, the court is to have regard – among other matters – to whether it would be in the public interest for the material to be published, as well as 'any relevant privacy code'.

What this seems designed to achieve is that if proceedings are brought to restrain a publication which relates to the private life of the applicant, the courts must take into account two questions: (i) is publication in the public interest, and (ii) has the newspaper complied with the PCC code? If the answer to both is 'yes', then the courts are less likely to restrain publication than if the answer is 'no'. In this way the PCC Code of Practice has an indirect legal effect: it is still not legally enforceable as such, but failure by a newspaper to comply with it could lead to a publication being restrained. In the words of Brooke LJ in *Douglas v Hello! Ltd*: 'A newspaper which flouts cl 3 of the code is likely in those circumstances to have its claim to an entitlement to freedom of expression trumped by article 10(2) considerations of privacy.'[146] Compliance with the code is, of course, not conclusive: the fact that a newspaper has complied with the code will not be a decisive factor if, for example, the courts take the view that the code or the way in which it is applied falls short of Convention rights as protected by art 8.[147] So in this way the PCC itself will need to ensure that its code is applied in a manner which reflects the requirements of art 8,[148] though it is clear that self-regulation (sometimes strongly criticised for its limited effectiveness) has not stopped the evolution of a legal right to privacy.

The Human Rights Act

Although the Human Rights Act does not permit an individual to sue a newspaper for a violation of privacy, the Act has nevertheless significantly advanced the cause of those who have argued that self-regulation of the newspaper industry is not a secure enough basis for the protection of privacy.[149] It is true that there is no duty on the part of the courts to 'create a free standing cause of action based on the Convention', but there is nevertheless a duty 'to act compatibly with convention rights in adjudicating upon existing common law causes of action',[150] leading to claims that the English courts should 'so far as possible, develop the common law in such a way as to give effect to Convention rights', and that 'in this way horizontal effect is given to the Convention'.[151] Since the Human Rights Act came into force, there have been a number of high profile cases brought by 'celebrities' and other people in the public eye challenging the publication of information about their private lives. In dealing with these cases the courts responded initially by absorbing Convention rights 'into the long established action for breach of confidence',[152] though with the passage of time it appears that a new tort of breach of privacy is emerging under the shadow of the Human Rights Act, which is related to and overlaps with (but is independent of) liability in equity for breach of confidence.[153]

---

[144] *Douglas v Hello! Ltd* [2001] QB 967, at p 982 (Brooke LJ).
[145] Cf *Douglas v Hello! Ltd*, ibid, at p 1004 (Sedley LJ).
[146] Ibid, at 994. See also *A v B plc* [2002] EWCA Civ 337; [2003] QB 195.
[147] See *Venables v News Group Newspapers Ltd* [2001] Fam 430.
[148] See also *Mosley v NGN Ltd (No 2)* [2008] EWHC 1777 (QB), para 16.
[149] For a good discussion, see HC 326 (2009–10).
[150] *Venables v News Group Newspapers Ltd* (note 147 above), at 446.
[151] *Associated Newspapers Ltd v Prince of Wales* [2006] EWCA Civ 1776, [2008] Ch 57, at para 25 (Lord Phillips).
[152] *A v B plc*, note 130 above, at para [4] (Woolf LCJ). See G Phillipson (2003) 66 MLR 726.
[153] For a discussion of this issue, see *Mosley*, above. See also R Buxton (2009) 29 OJLS 413.

Perhaps the landmark case in this process is the House of Lords decision in *Campbell v MGN Ltd*,[154] where a fashion model claimed successfully in part that her privacy had been violated by a newspaper which revealed details of her drug addiction. The House of Lords held that the newspaper had been entitled to disclose that the appellant was a drug addict who was receiving treatment, but not the details of the treatment she was receiving. The House of Lords also held that this conclusion was reinforced by clause 3(i) of the Press Complaints Commission's Code of Practice. In explaining the developing law of confidence, Lord Nicholls said:

> The continuing use of the phrase 'duty of confidence' and the description of the information as 'confidential' is not altogether comfortable. Information about a person's private life would not, in ordinary usage, be described as 'confidential'. The more natural description today is that the information is private. *The essence of the tort is better encapsulated now as misuse of private information.*[155]

Under the guidance of these developments, it was held that the private journals of the Prince of Wales commenting on the handover of Hong Kong to China were confidential and that the *Daily Mail* had acted unlawfully in publishing them. The journals in question had been leaked by a former employee of the Prince, and the Court of Appeal addressed the situation where publication 'involves a breach of a relationship of confidence, an interference with privacy or both', reinforcing the sense that privacy is emerging as a separate but overlapping cause of action.[156]

In *Associated Newspapers Ltd v Prince of Wales*,[157] the Court of Appeal also emphasised the importance of art 10, a matter given little consideration in the past in determining whether a publication should be restrained on public interest grounds. Where no breach of a confidential relationship is involved, a balance will have to be struck between art 8 and art 10 rights and 'will usually involve weighing the nature and consequences of the breach of privacy against the public interest, if any, in the disclosure of private information'.[158] Where, however, there is also a breach of confidence involved, this will tilt the balance more in the direction of restraining the publication, as in this case where it was said that 'those who engage employees, or who enter into other relationships that carry with them a duty of confidence, ought to be able to be confident that they can disclose, without risk of wider publication, information that it is legitimate for them to wish to keep confidential'.[159] The impact of the evolution of the law since *Campbell* is to be seen even more clearly in *Murray v Express Newspapers plc*,[160] where the child of a famous author (J K Rowling) succeeded in a claim that his art 8 rights had been violated by defendants who surreptitiously took photographs of him while in a public place being accompanied by his parents. It appears that injunctions may be obtained in such cases,[161] and that damages may be recoverable.[162]

---

[154] *Campbell v MGN Ltd* [2004] UKHL 22, [2004] 2 AC 457; and subsequently *Campbell v MGN Ltd (No 2)* [2005] UKHL 61; [2005] 1 WLR 3394.

[155] *Campbell v MGN Ltd* [2004] UKHL 22, [2004] 2 AC 457, at para 14. Emphasis added. In *Mosley* (above), it was explained that this cause of action applies 'even in circumstances where there is no pre-existing relationship giving rise of itself to an enforceable duty of confidence' (para 7).

[156] See also *Browne v Associated Newspapers Ltd* [2007] EWCA Civ 295; *Mosley v NGN Ltd*, above; and *Terry v Persons Unknown* [2010] EWHC 119 (QB).

[157] [2006] EWCA Civ 1776, [2008] Ch 57.

[158] Ibid, para 65.

[159] Ibid, para 67.

[160] [2008] EWCA Civ 446, [2008] WLR (D) 143.

[161] *Browne v Associated Newspapers Ltd*, above (subject to the requirements of the HRA, s 12(3) being met, on which see ch 19 above). See also *Terry v Persons Unknown* (above), and the controversial issue of 'super-injunctions', discussed at pp 525–6 below.

[162] *Mosley*, above. Damages may be aggravated but not exemplary.

G. Conclusion

By virtue of the Human Rights Act, art 8 is now enforceable in the domestic courts against public authorities.[163] This means that the exercise of different powers referred to in sections B and C of this chapter may now be challenged under the Human Rights Act and indeed that it may be possible to challenge some of the statutory provisions as being incompatible with Convention rights. But although none of the legislation can be presumed to be watertight, it is most unlikely that many challenges will succeed, though it is true that gaps continue to be exposed in the procedure for the interception of communications.[164] There are also unlikely to be many cases where the Human Rights Act will add much in practice to the legal armoury of the individual concerned that powers of surveillance and interception have been improperly exercised. By virtue of their different supervisory roles, senior and retired judges are now directly involved in the supervision and management of the different schemes, with the substance of which they seem broadly content, very rarely upholding complaints that the exercise of a power to infringe privacy has been improperly authorised.

Similarly, the legal powers of government relating to the storage and use of information about individuals in sections D and E above have been shown to be remarkably robust, and not easy to challenge. The same is true of other powers of public authorities, such as taking photographs of protestors,[165] the releasing of photographs of wanted suspects,[166] or advising the owners of caravan sites about the identity of convicted paedophiles.[167] Paradoxically, the weight of any right to privacy derived from the Human Rights Act is thus likely to be felt most acutely in the field of private law, to protect the individual's right to privacy from the exercise of private rather than state power, particularly that exercised by the press. It is true that the courts have emphasised the need in such cases to balance the interests of privacy against the wider interest in free speech. Newspaper proprietors and editors nevertheless complain that the balance is tilted too heavily in favour of the individual, though it is also the case that the conduct of some newspapers in the pursuit of profit in recent years has been disgraceful.[168] The emergence of a legal right to privacy is an indication of the failure of self-regulation under the Press Complaints Commission, whose procedures need to be overhauled.[169]

---

[163] See ch 19 C.

[164] *Liberty v United Kingdom* (2009) 48 EHRR 1 (in relation to the interception of up to 10,000 telephone calls coming from Dublin to London between 1990 and 1997).

[165] *Wood v Metropolitan Police Commissioner* [2009] EWCA Civ 414 (but unjustifiable retention and storage of photographs may breach Convention rights).

[166] *Hellewell v Derbyshire Chief Constable* [1995] 1 WLR 804 (pre HRA).

[167] *R v North Wales Police Chief Constable, ex p Thorpe* [1999] QB 396 (pre HRA, but ECHR considered).

[168] See HC 326 (2009–10).

[169] Ibid.

CHAPTER 23

Freedom of expression

The right to freedom of expression, in the words of art 10 of the European Convention on Human Rights, includes freedom to hold opinions 'and to receive and impart information and ideas without interference by public authority and regardless of frontiers'. This freedom is fundamental to the individual's life in a democratic society.[1] In the first place, it has a specific political content. The freedom to receive and express political opinions, both publicly and privately, is linked closely with the freedom to organise for political purposes and to take part in free elections:

> Without free elections the people cannot make a choice of policies. Without freedom of speech the appeal to reason which is the basis of democracy cannot be made. Without freedom of association, electors and elected representatives cannot bind themselves into parties for the formulation of common policies and the attainment of common ends.[2]

So does freedom of expression closely affect freedom of religion. Lawyers remember *Bushell's* case in 1670 as having established the right of the jury to acquit an accused 'against full and manifest evidence' and against the direction of the judge: they should also remember that Bushell was foreman of the jury which acquitted the Quakers William Penn and William Mead on charges of having preached to a large crowd in a London street contrary to the Conventicle Act.[3] Moreover, liberty of expression is an integral part of artistic, cultural and intellectual freedom – the freedom to publish books or produce works of art, however disconcerting they may be to the prevailing orthodoxy.[4]

A. The nature of legal protection

Rights and restraints

It has been said that freedom of expression is a 'sinew of the common law'.[5] Individuals are thus free to speak and write what they like, provided that what they say is not otherwise unlawful. In addition, protection is provided by the law of parliamentary privilege for proceedings in Parliament,[6] and there is a growing body of legislation which in different ways promotes and protects free speech in its widest sense. A statutory right to information is to be found in the Data Protection Act 1998 and the Freedom of Information Act 2000.[7] Both of these measures aid the work of the investigative journalist, whose role has been acknowledged judicially.[8] Also important is the Contempt of Court Act 1981, s 10, which protects the journalist from having to reveal his or her sources, although as discussed in chapter 18 above, this provision has been narrowly

---

[1] For a compelling statement, see *R v Shayler* [2002] UKHL 11; [2003] 1 AC 247, at para [21].

[2] Jennings, *Cabinet Government*, p 14. See also Laski, *A Grammar of Politics*, ch 3.

[3] *R v Penn and Mead* (1670) 6 St Tr 951.

[4] See also *R v Home Secretary, ex p Simms* [2000] 2 AC 115, at 126, per Lord Steyn. For a good account of some of the issues discussed in this chapter, see Barendt, *Freedom of Speech*.

[5] *R v Advertising Standards Authority, ex p Vernons* [1993] 2 All ER 202 (Laws J).

[6] See ch 11 A. But the protection of parliamentary privilege may be lost if comments in Parliament are repeated outside: *Buchanan v Jennings* [2004] UKPC 36; [2005] 1 AC 115. See further pp 522–3 below.

[7] See chs 22 E and 13 F respectively.

[8] *Loutchansky v Times Newspapers Ltd* [2001] EWCA Civ 536, [2002] QB 321.

construed against the journalists by the courts. It was also shown little respect by the Foreign Affairs Committee of the House of Commons in 2003 when it was interrogating the journalist Andrew Gilligan about the sources for his report that government documents relating to the Iraq war had been 'sexed up'.[9] In addition to the foregoing, the Public Interest Disclosure Act 1998 provides a limited protection for 'whistleblowers', that is to say workers who bring into the public domain serious concerns about the conduct of their employer's business.[10]

It remains the case nevertheless that freedom of expression is subject to a wide range of restrictions, many of which are long-standing. These restrictions are of two kinds: the first is censorship or prior restraint of material by state authorities before it is published or displayed; and the second is the imposition of penalties or the granting of redress in the case of someone specifically harmed by the material, after the event. Restrictions of the first kind have often been viewed with great suspicion, and have been strongly deprecated by the US Supreme Court in cases arising under the free speech guarantee in the First Amendment. Yet despite Blackstone's insistence that free speech meant 'laying no previous restraints upon publication',[11] there is still some censorship in Britain,[12] while the use of injunctions and so called 'super-injunctions' to restrain publications has seen something of a controversial revival in recent years. So far as restrictions of the second kind are concerned, there is a wide range of criminal offences which restrict free speech. These offences exist to protect public order; to protect public morality by punishing the publication of obscene material; and by virtue of the law on contempt of court, to maintain the authority and impartiality of the judiciary. Restrictions imposed by the law of defamation exist to protect the rights and reputations of others, while the developing law on breach of confidence may help to protect the privacy of individuals from unwanted intrusion.

The Human Rights Act

The right to freedom of expression has been formally strengthened by the Human Rights Act 1998, although even before the enactment and coming into force of this measure the right to freedom of expression was winning a new prominence in the case law, being supported by a number of powerful judicial dicta and extrajudicial statements.[13] It is true that the bold assertion of freedom of expression in art 10 of the ECHR is subject

> to such formalities, conditions, restrictions or penalties as are prescribed by law and are necessary in a democratic society, in the interests of national security, territorial integrity or public safety, for the prevention of disorder or crime, for the protection of health or morals, for the protection of the reputation or rights of others, for preventing the disclosure of information received in confidence, or for maintaining the authority and impartiality of the judiciary.

In this sense freedom of expression is the most heavily qualified of all the Convention rights, paradoxically perhaps in light of Lord Steyn's acknowledgement of freedom of expression as 'the lifeblood of democracy'.[14] Nevertheless, the Human Rights Act contains special protection in the sense that no remedy is to be granted which affects the exercise of the Convention right to freedom of expression without ensuring that the respondent has been notified of the proceedings and given an opportunity to reply (s 12(2)). This is particularly important in the context of an application for an interim injunction to restrain a publication. So too is the parallel requirement that interim

---

[9] HC 1044 (2002–03).

[10] See J Gobert and M Punch (2000) 63 MLR 25; and Hobby, *Whistleblowing and the Public Interest Disclosure Act 1998*.

[11] *Commentaries*, 9th edn, IV, p 151.

[12] The classic legal study of censorship is O'Higgins, *Censorship in Britain*.

[13] See *Reynolds v Times Newspapers Ltd* [2001] 2 AC 127, *McCartan Turkington Breen v Times Newspapers Ltd* [2001] 2 AC 277, *Loutchansky v Times Newspapers Ltd*, above, and *R v Shayler*, above.

[14] *R v Home Secretary, ex p Simms* [2000] 2 AC 115, at 126.

relief is not to be granted before a trial 'unless the court is satisfied that the applicant is likely to establish that publication should not be allowed' (s 12(3)). In all cases 'the court must have particular regard to the importance of the Convention right to freedom of expression' (s 12(4)).[15]

But the courts seem to have taken a cautious approach to these provisions, which are said not to require them 'to treat freedom of expression as paramount'.[16] In fact the Human Rights Act has made only a limited impact in the field of freedom of expression, despite the very robust judicial dicta in its defence to which we have already referred. Part of the reason for this limited impact is that 'the courts emphasised the importance of freedom of expression or speech long before the enactment of the 1998 Act'.[17] Indeed, a number of important decisions have been taken in recent years to extend the boundaries of free speech quite independently of the Human Rights Act (although clearly within its shadow),[18] but perhaps not as far as many would like. Another reason has been the willingness on the part of the courts to have the fullest regard for the rights and freedoms of others.[19] So we find that the rights of the press – and others – have been subordinated to the demands of copyright, defamation, 'public morality', national security, and confidentiality. Indeed, as discussed in chapter 22 the Act may have helped fashion a new restraint on press freedom by encouraging the development of an enforceable right to privacy on the back of the equitable doctrine of breach of confidence. These developments reflect an appreciation on the part of the judges that large newspapers can be engines of oppression and that newspaper proprietors, editors and journalists can trespass on the rights of others while exercising their own.

B. Prior restraint: censorship and ownership

Censorship

For many years dramatic and operatic performances in Great Britain were subject to the prior censorship of the Lord Chamberlain, an officer of the royal household. The Theatres Act 1968 abolished the requirement that plays should receive a licence before being performed (s 1).[20] Theatres are now licensed by local authorities, the licensing framework having been overhauled by the Licensing Act 2003. In place of censorship, rules against obscenity similar to those in the Obscene Publications Act 1959 are applied to the performance of plays (s 2), subject to a defence of public good (s 3). Other criminal restraints placed on theatrical performances are in respect of the use of threatening, abusive or insulting words or behaviour intended or likely to stir up racial hatred,[21] or occasion a breach of the peace.[22] Prosecutions for these various offences, including obscenity, require the consent of the Attorney General in England and Wales, though there are proposals to transfer this responsibility to the DPP or some other public official.[23] In addition, there may be no prosecution at common law for any offence the essence of which is that a performance of a play is 'obscene, indecent, offensive, disgusting or injurious to morality'; nor may there be prosecutions under various statutes relating to indecency (1968 Act, s 2(4)), an important safeguard against moral censorship.

[15] See ch 19 above.
[16] *Imutran Ltd* v *Uncaged Campaigns Ltd* [2001] 2 All ER 385, at 391.
[17] Ibid, at 391.
[18] For example, *Reynolds* v *Times Newspapers Ltd* [2001] AC 127.
[19] As illustrated by *R (Pro-Life Alliance)* v *BBC* [2003] UKHL 23; [2004] 1 AC 185.
[20] For the background, see HC 503 (1966–7). See also Findlater, *Banned!*
[21] Public Order Act 1986, s 20.
[22] Theatres Act 1968, s 6.
[23] See ch 18 above. Private prosecutions may be launched on other grounds, as in 2007 when a private prosecution for blasphemy was brought unsuccessfully by a Christian group in relation to 'Jerry Springer – the Opera'. Blasphemy has since been abolished. See below, p 509.

Censorship of films originated unintentionally with the Cinematograph Act 1909, which authorised local authorities to license cinemas in the interests of public safety, mainly against fire. In fact, with the approval of the courts,[24] local authorities extended the scope of licensing to other matters to include the approval of the films shown in licensed cinemas.[25] In the Cinematograph Act 1952, and more recently in the Cinemas Act 1985, Parliament confirmed the power of local authorities to license the films shown and required licensing authorities to impose conditions restricting children from seeing unsuitable films. The main work of censorship of films is undertaken by the British Board of Film Classification, a non-statutory body set up by the film industry, with the approval of central and local government. The board is responsible for the classification of films with special reference to the admission of young children and others under 18. Although a licensing authority normally allows the showing of films which have been classified by the board, the authority may not transfer its functions to the board and must retain power to review decisions of the board.[26] Thus it may refuse a local showing to a film classified by the board; it may vary the board's classification; or it may grant permission to a film refused a certificate by the board. Powers of local censorship are not popular with the film industry, but a case can be made for maintaining some local variation in issues of public morality.

The relationship between the system of film censorship and the law of obscenity and public indecency has caused many difficulties. By the Criminal Law Act 1977, s 53, the public showing of films was brought within the Obscene Publications Act, subject to a defence that showing a film is for the public good in the interests of drama, opera, ballet, or any other art, or of literature or learning. The consent of the DPP is required for a prosecution, and for the forfeiture of certain films. The Video Recordings Act 1984 established a scheme for the censorship of video recordings,[27] under which it is an offence to supply (whether or not for reward) any recording for which no classification certificate has been issued (s 9). Certain recordings are exempt from this requirement (such as those concerned with sport, religion or music and those designed to be educational) (s 2), and so are certain kinds of supply (s 4). A video work may not, however, be an exempted work if to any extent it depicts or is designed to encourage such matters as sexual or violent activity (s 2(2)).[28] Nor is it exempt if to any extent it depicts criminal activity which is likely to any significant extent to stimulate or encourage the commission of an offence (s 2(3)). Classification is conducted by the British Board of Film Classification, which may certify that a video work is suitable for general viewing, suitable only for persons over the age of 18,[29] or that it is to be supplied only in a licensed sex shop.[30]

Ownership and self-regulation

The historic freedom of the press means that, subject to the civil and criminal restraints on publication which will be considered later, any person or company may publish a newspaper or magazine without getting official approval in advance. For economic reasons, this liberty is unlikely to be exercised effectively on a national basis except by a very few newspaper publishers. Fears of a movement towards monopoly conditions in sectors of the press led to the enactment of provisions

---

[24] E.g. *LCC v Bermondsey Bioscope Ltd* [1911] 1 KB 445.

[25] See generally, Hunnings, *Film Censors and the Law*; Williams report on obscenity and film censorship, Cmnd 7772, 1979; Robertson, *Freedom, the Individual and the Law*, pp 238–41.

[26] *Ellis v Dubowski* [1921] 3 KB 621; *Mills v LCC* [1925] 1 KB 213.

[27] The Act was unusually repealed and revived in its entirety by the Video Recordings Act 2010 (without amendment), to comply with overlooked obligations under EU law.

[28] See *Kent CC v Multi Media Marketing*, The Times, 9 May 1995.

[29] On which see *Tesco Stores Ltd v Brent London Borough Council* [1993] 1 WLR 1037.

[30] For the procedures adopted by the Board, see *Wingrove v UK* (1996) 24 EHRR 1. For appeals to the Video Appeals Committee, see S Edwards [2001] Crim LR 305. On the implications of judicial review, see C Munro [2006] Crim Law Rev 957.

to ensure that newspaper mergers above a certain scale did not take place in a manner contrary to the public interest. This is not so much a restraint as a device to ensure diversity in opinion, and is a problem compounded now with the same global companies playing a large part in both the television and newspaper industries. It is important to ensure that there is not over-concentration of media ownership in a few hands, and important also to ensure that private media owners do not misuse the considerable power that ownership bestows. Britain has not, however, followed the route of some countries (notably Sweden) by subsidising newspaper owners in order more actively to promote diversity.

The current regime is now to be found in the Enterprise Act 2002, which was extended with modifications to media mergers by the Communications Act 2003. This replaced the procedure that operated under the Fair Trading Act 1973. Media mergers may involve advice, assessment and judgment by the Office of Communications (OFCOM), the Office of Fair Trading and the Competition Commission, and ultimately a merger may be blocked or modified by the Secretary of State on public interest grounds. These grounds relate to the need for accurate presentation of news in newspapers, free expression of opinion in newspapers, and a sufficient plurality of views in the newspaper market.[31] Yet despite these initiatives, the British newspaper industry remains heavily concentrated in the hands of a few proprietors, though the traditional press is now under intense competition from the internet and other media sources (particularly for advertising income).[32] Nevertheless, the political power of the press is not to be underestimated, and in 1995–96 the four principal newspaper publishers – News International, Mirror Group, United Newspapers, and Associated Newspapers – controlled between them 85 per cent of the national daily and 88.7 per cent of national Sunday circulation.[33]

Since 1953 newspaper proprietors have accepted a measure of self regulation to deal with abuse on the part of their editors and journalists. The Press Complaints Commission was created in 1991, to replace the Press Council, the Commission being funded by a voluntary levy of newspaper and magazine publishers. Apart from the independent chair, the Commission includes members with no press connections, as well as senior editors drawn from the national and regional newspapers and magazines. Its primary responsibilities include the handling of complaints of alleged violations of the Code of Practice which was published in 1991 (by the newspaper industry) to regulate its conduct on a range of matters dealing mainly with accuracy and privacy. The Code is kept under scrutiny and has been amended on a number of occasions since, as in 2004 when provisions were included to prohibit payments by newspapers to witnesses in criminal trials. Where there is a breach of the Code leading to a formal adjudication by the Commission, the publication concerned must publish the critical adjudication 'in full and with due prominence', but the Commission does not award compensation to successful complainants, nor does it have the power to impose financial penalties.

C. Regulation of television and radio[34]

The BBC

In the case of broadcasting, technical reasons have so far prevented access being open to all comers as in the case of the press. Even if all broadcasting were to be provided by privately owned companies, it would still be necessary for a regulatory agency to allocate channels and frequencies

---

[31] Enterprise Act 2002, s 58(2A) and (2B), as inserted by the Communications Act 2003.

[32] On the problems facing the local press in particular, see HC 43 (2009–10) (Culture, Media and Sport Committee).

[33] Williams, *Media Ownership and Democracy*, p 39. And see T Gibbons [1992] PL 279 and Gibbons, *Regulating the Media*, pp 207–11.

[34] Barendt, *Broadcasting Law*; Craufurd Smith, *Broadcasting Law and Fundamental Rights*.

to them. Until 1954, the British Broadcasting Corporation enjoyed a public monopoly of all broadcasting in the United Kingdom and it still provides a large share of broadcasting services. The BBC is a corporation set up by royal charter and it operates under the strategic direction of the BBC Trust and the Chairman of the BBC. The BBC's charter was renewed in 2006 for a period of ten years,[35] together with a new agreement between the corporation and the government whereby the broadcaster is subject to a number of duties.[36] These are similar in terms to those imposed on the commercial broadcasters by legislation. The charter is debated by both Houses of Parliament before it is granted by the Queen in Council, though it is open to question whether the BBC should be regulated by legislation rather than royal prerogative.[37] Although the BBC is mainly financed by a grant from the exchequer, equivalent to the net revenue of television licence fees, the structure of the BBC seeks generally to maintain its independence of the government of the day.

The BBC has a number of public purposes set out in the agreement with the government, under which it is still required to broadcast a daily account of the proceedings in Parliament. The regulatory provisions of the agreement mean that the BBC may not broadcast its own opinions about current affairs, being under a duty to do all it can to treat controversial subjects with due accuracy and impartiality, both in its news services and in other programmes dealing with matters of public policy or of political or industrial controversy. But 'due impartiality does not require absolute neutrality on every issue or detachment from fundamental democratic principles', the meaning of which is not specified. Under the general obligations of the BBC, the government in an emergency may request the corporation to broadcast certain specified material, and may also request that it does not broadcast other specified material, requests which under the terms of agreement must be met. Apart from these specific powers, the government may not control the BBC's programmes, although it may bring great pressure to bear, and disputes may erupt between the government and the BBC, as in 2003 when the government vigorously contested a claim by a BBC journalist that it had deliberately exaggerated Saddam Hussein's weapons capabilities in the run up to the invasion of Iraq in that year.[38]

Commercial television and radio

Television and radio services financed by advertising are now governed by the Broadcasting Acts 1990 and 1996, and by the Communications Act 2003. The Office of Communications (OFCOM) is the regulatory authority, replacing a number of bodies which previously performed a regulatory role, including the Independent Television Commission and the Broadcasting Standards Commission. As such, OFCOM is one of a growing number of regulators operating in British public life with what is by now a familiar mixture of roles and responsibilities, sometimes performing duties (such as the issuing and renewal of licences) that in the past were the responsibility of the Secretary of State. It is also the case that OFCOM's duties apply not only to broadcasting but also to telecommunications. So far as broadcasting is concerned, OFCOM is required to ensure the 'availability throughout the United Kingdom of a wide range of television and radio services which (taken as a whole) are both of high quality and calculated to appeal to a variety of tastes and interests'.[39] It is also required to ensure that there is a 'sufficient plurality of providers of different television and radio services', as well as the application of standards to protect the

---

[35] Cm 6925, 2006.
[36] Cm 6872, 2006.
[37] See HC 82 (2004–05) (Culture, Media and Sport Committee).
[38] See Lord Hutton, Report of the Inquiry into the Circumstances Surrounding the Death of Dr David Kelly, C.M.G. (2004).
[39] Communications Act 2003, s 3(2)(c).

public from the inclusion of 'offensive and harmful material' in broadcasting services.[40] These obligations are in addition to the duty to ensure that standards are in place to provide adequate protection to the public 'and all other persons' from both unfair treatment in programmes and unwarranted infringements of privacy by broadcasters.[41]

Curiously, OFCOM has no statutory duty to promote or uphold the right to freedom of expression, and indeed many of the foregoing duties are about restraints on free speech. But as a public authority, OFCOM is clearly bound by the obligations of the Human Rights Act and art 10 of the ECHR. OFCOM is, however, required to produce a code to promote certain statutory objectives dealing with broadcasting standards. There are 12 statutory objectives which cover both programme content and advertisements, and include a requirement of impartiality on matters of political or industrial controversy, a requirement that news is reported with 'due accuracy', and a requirement that the public are protected from harmful and offensive material.[42] The main restraint on advertising relates to political advertising. This is widely defined to mean (*a*) an advertisement which is inserted by or on behalf of a political organisation; (*b*) an advertisement which is directed towards a political end; or (*c*) an advertisement which has a connection with an industrial dispute.[43] Licence holders are required to comply with the standards code and OFCOM is required to establish procedures to deal with complaints that the standards have been breached.[44] OFCOM has also acquired the obligation to ensure that licence holders comply with the fairness code that was issued by the Broadcasting Standards Commission under the Broadcasting Act 1996,[45] this obligation having been transferred to OFCOM by the 2003 Act.[46] There is now a single code issued by OFCOM which deals with both standards and fairness issues.[47]

The Broadcasting Code

The Broadcasting Code – which applies in part to the BBC as well as the other broadcasters – is designed to balance the broadcasters' rights to freedom of expression with various rights of viewers and listeners (as well as programme participants and subjects). The code thus purports to set boundaries for the broadcaster, including those which relate to (*a*) standards, and (*b*) fairness. The standards' requirements amplify the matters specified in the legislation and give guidance on protecting young people, on protecting all members of the public from harmful and offensive material, and on ensuring that material likely to encourage disorder or crime is not included in broadcasts. The guidance also seeks to ensure that broadcasters exercise responsibility in dealing with religion, and it indicates what is needed to comply with obligations relating to due impartiality. A separate chapter on elections and referendums reminds the broadcasters about various legal obligations but also advises them that due weight must be given to 'the coverage of major parties during the election period'. The main parties for this purpose are the three national parties, extended in Scotland and Wales to include the principal nationalist parties. The broadcasters are also advised that they must consider giving 'appropriate coverage' to other parties and independent candidates 'with significant views and perspectives'.

So far as the fairness provisions are concerned, these emphasise the need to deal fairly with contributors to programmes and the need to obtain 'informed consent' from those who take part.

---

[40] Ibid, s 3(2)(d) and (e).

[41] Ibid, s 3(2)(f).

[42] Ibid, s 319.

[43] Ibid, s 321 (*R (Animal Defenders International)* v *Secretary of State for Culture, Media and Sport* [2008] UKHL 15, [2008] 2 WLR 781). On political advertising, see ch 9 D above.

[44] Communications Act 2003, s 325.

[45] Ibid, s 326.

[46] Ibid, Sch 1, para 14.

[47] OFCOM, *Broadcasting Code* (2009).

This means that contributors should be told 'the nature and purpose of the programme, what the programme is about and be given a clear explanation of why they were asked to contribute'. It is also provided that guarantees about confidentiality and anonymity 'should normally be honoured'. A related chapter of the Code on privacy provides that any breach of privacy must be warranted, and if the reason for breach of privacy is based on the public interest, the broadcaster must be able to demonstrate that the public interest outweighs the right to privacy. Special provisions deal with surreptitious filming and with people caught up in distressing events. Complaints about a breach of the fairness or privacy provisions of the Code may be made to OFCOM by someone affected or by someone authorised by him or her,[48] and OFCOM may refuse to entertain a fairness complaint relating to unjust or unfair treatment if the person making the complaint does not have a sufficient interest.[49] Other restrictions on complaints mean that they cannot be considered where the matter complained of is the subject of court proceedings, or if it appears to OFCOM that the person affected has a remedy by way of legal action in a court of law.[50]

The role of the courts

A few attempts have been made to challenge broadcasting content in the courts. A difficulty with the BBC, however, is that it was established under the prerogative and, at least until the *CCSU* case,[51] it was unclear to what extent those exercising power under the prerogative were subject to judicial review. As late as 1983, the High Court in Northern Ireland was unwilling to enforce the BBC's policy of political impartiality in an action brought by the Workers' Party contesting election broadcasting.[52] It is now well accepted, however, that the BBC is subject to judicial review.[53] So in *Houston* v *BBC*,[54] an interim interdict was granted to restrain the corporation from broadcasting in Scotland an extended interview with the Prime Minister three days before the local government elections. It was held that the pursuers had established a prima facie case that the broadcast would violate the BBC's duty, under the terms of its licence, to treat controversial subjects with due impartiality and that the balance of convenience favoured the granting of relief to prevent the programme being broadcast until after the close of the poll. The BBC is a public authority for the purposes of the Human Rights Act, which means that it not only enjoys Convention rights but that it must respect the Convention rights of others.

> In *R (Pro-Life Alliance)* v *BBC*[55] the broadcasting authorities refused to carry the pictures of a party election broadcast which had been submitted by the Alliance. The broadcast contained 'prolonged and deeply disturbing' images of an aborted foetus which the broadcasters believed to be contrary to their obligations to maintain taste and decency. It was argued for the Alliance in legal proceedings that this 'censorship' of the broadcast by the broadcasters violated art 10 of the ECHR. In reversing a decision of the Court of Appeal,

---

[48] A complaint may be made by a company alleging an infringment of its privacy: 'A company does have activities of a private nature which need protection from unwarranted intrusion.' See *R* v *Broadcasting Standards Commission, ex p BBC* [2001] QB 885.

[49] Broadcasting Act 1996, s 111. Cf *R* v *Broadcasting Complaints Commission, ex p Channel Four Television, The Times,* 6 January 1995 (the term 'direct interest' had to be broadly construed, even if it meant that 'too many complaints' would be made). But cf *R* v *Broadcasting Complaints Commission, ex p BBC, The Times,* 24 February 1995 (complaint by National Council for One Parent Families refused on the ground that it did not have a sufficiently direct interest in a *Panorama* programme which was said to build up a false picture of lone parents by using misleading and false information).

[50] Complaints may be made against the BBC: see Cm 6872, 2006.

[51] *Council of Civil Service Unions* v *Minister for the Civil Service* [1985] AC 374.

[52] *Lynch* v *BBC* [1983] NILR 193.

[53] *R (Pro-Life Alliance)* v *BBC* [2003] UKHL 23; [2004] 1 AC 185.

[54] 1995 SLT 1305. See also *R* v *BBC, ex p Referendum Party, The Times,* 29 April 1997.

[55] Note 53 above. For a critique, see E Barendt [2003] PL 580; J Jowell [2003] PL 592; and A Scott (2003) 66 MLR 224.

the House of Lords (by a majority) disagreed, with Lord Hoffmann in a robust speech expressing the view that it is not unreasonable to require political parties to comply with standards of taste and decency which are 'not particularly exacting'.

In contrast to the position of the BBC, there has never been much scope for disputing that – as statutory bodies – the commercial television and radio sector is subject to judicial review. This would be particularly true of the regulatory authorities such as OFCOM and its predecessor bodies such as the Independent Television Authority and the Independent Broadcasting Authority. But although the IBA like everyone else was required to observe the law, and although the IBA's decisions were subject to judicial review, the courts did not show a desire to assume the role of censor.[56] A similar restraint has been shown in the cases which have been brought to challenge party election broadcasts (more fully explained in chapter 9 D) and now the operation of the statutory restrictions on political advertising,[57] although there are exceptions to such restraint.[58] There are also cases where the television or radio company itself may be the subject of legal proceedings.

> In *R v Central Independent Television plc*[59] the respondents were due to broadcast a programme on the work of the obscene publications squad of Scotland Yard and in particular about the work of detectives engaged in tracing a man who was imprisoned on two charges of indecency. The man had previously been married to Mrs R who was the mother of his child and there was concern that the programme contained scenes which would identify the mother and the child, causing the latter distress. Invoking the parental jurisdiction of the court, the mother moved successfully to have the moving pictures of the father obscured, a decision reversed by the Court of Appeal which held that the press and broadcasters were entitled to publish the results of criminal proceedings, even though 'the families of those convicted had a heavy burden to bear and the effect of publicity on small children might be very serious'.

In a robust defence of freedom of expression, in a case where it was perhaps unnecessary, Hoffmann LJ said:

> Publication may cause needless pain, distress and damage to individuals or harm to other aspects of the public interest. But a freedom which is restricted to what judges think to be responsible or in the public interest is no freedom. Freedom means the right to publish things which government and judges, however well motivated, think should not be published. It means the right to say things which 'right-thinking people' regard as dangerous or irresponsible. This freedom is subject only to clearly defined exceptions laid down by common law or statute.

It is to a consideration of some of these exceptions that we now turn.

D. Offences against public order

Changing nature of criminal law

By section 73, the Criminal Justice and Coroners Act 2009 abolished the common law offences of seditious libel and blasphemous libel, offences which were covered in earlier editions of this book. The former made it an offence to create political discontent and disaffection (and as such was a handy tool against the pioneering socialists in the late nineteenth and early twentieth

---

[56] *Attorney-General, ex rel McWhirter v IBA* [1973] QB 629.

[57] *R v Radio Authority, ex p Bull* [1997] 2 All ER 561; *R (Animal Defenders International) v Secretary of State for Culture, Media and Sport*, note 43 above.

[58] *Wilson v Independent Broadcasting Authority* 1979 SLT 279. Cf *Wilson v Independent Broadcasting Authority* 1988 SLT 276. Also C Munro NLJ, 4 October 1996, p 1433, and NLJ, 11 April 1997, p 528.

[59] [1994] Fam 192.

centuries),[60] while the latter made it an offence to outrage and insult a Christian's feelings (and as such was a handy tool to be used against those who linked Jesus Christ to homosexuality).[61] The abolition of both offences was long overdue, with neither being used directly in modern times, though blasphemy was used by the British Board of Film Classification when it refused to issue a classification certificate under the Video Recordings Act 1984 for a film entitled *Visions of Ecstasy* which included an 'intense erotic' moment between St Teresa and Jesus Christ. The decision was taken on the ground that the film was blasphemous, and the decision was upheld by the Video Appeals Committee.[62] Nevertheless, these offences were increasingly anomalous at a time of greater political plurality and vigour in public debate, and at a time when cultural diversity made it inappropriate to single out one religion (albeit that of the established church) for special treatment.

The abolition of these offences should not be taken as a retreat of the criminal law as a source of restraint on free speech. There are two reasons for this, the first being that many other chapters in this book reveal a wide range of criminal constraints on freedom of expression. These include contempt of court restricting the publication of material calculated to prejudice a fair trial or interfere with the administration of justice (chapter 18), and official secrecy and associated common law offences (misconduct in a public office) which deal with the disclosure and reporting of material dealing with certain kinds of government information (chapter 25). Secondly, however, it is important to emphasise that while sedition and blasphemy have been abolished, there remains on the statute book legislation that addresses in more modern form the kind of mischief to which both of these offences were principally addressed. Thus it might be argued that statutory measures dealing with incitement to religious hatred are a more wide-ranging restriction on free speech than that imposed in modern times by blasphemy, while the offence of inducing terrorism is a more precise and targeted way of addressing the concerns of sedition in a contemporary context (there being significant overlap between this statutory offence introduced in 2008 and the common law offence abolished in 2009).

So far as restraints on free speech in the interests of public order are concerned, these restrictions tend to be responses to particular problems at particular times, and the issues considered here overlap with those considered in chapters 24 and 26 in particular. If, however, sedition was a crime of the eighteenth and nineteenth centuries in particular, incitement to disaffection is a restriction introduced to deal with the activities of the Communist party in the 1930s as it tried to encourage soldiers and sailors to disaffect. Similarly, the law relating to the incitement to racial hatred is a restriction introduced to deal with the menace of far-right parties with racist views at a time of growing ethnic diversity. Finally, the offence of inducing terrorism is a response to the activities of some supporters of terrorist organisations (widely defined) and their willingness publicly to express that support. In other words the legal restrictions are symptoms of temporal problems which – at least in the case of incitement to disaffection – are allowed to remain on the statute book long after the mischief to which they were directed has gone.

Incitement to disaffection[63]

Parliament has on several occasions legislated to prevent the spread of disaffection, mainly to protect members of the armed forces, who might otherwise be exposed to attempts to persuade them to disobey their orders. The Incitement to Mutiny Act 1797, passed following the Nore

---

[60] *R v Burns* (1886) 16 Cox CC 355, *R v Aldred* (1909) 22 Cox CC 1. More recently, see *R v Chief Metropolitan Stipendiary Magistrate, ex p Choudhury* [1991] QB 429. And see Williams, *Keeping the Peace*, ch 8, and E C S Wade (1948) 64 LQR 203.

[61] *R v Lemon* [1979] AC 617. And see *Gay News Ltd v UK* (1982) 5 EHRR 123.

[62] See *Wingrove v United Kingdom*, above.

[63] Bunyan, *The Political Police in Britain*, pp 28–36; Ewing and Gearty, *The Struggle for Civil Liberties*, chs 2–5.

mutiny, made it a felony maliciously and advisedly to endeavour to seduce members of the armed forces from their duty and allegiance to the Crown or to incite members to commit any act of mutiny. Although the 1797 Act has been repealed (and although seditious libel has been abolished), the Aliens Restriction (Amendment) Act 1919, s 3, still prohibits an alien from causing sedition or disaffection among the civil population as well as among the armed forces; and it is an offence for any alien to promote or interfere in an industrial dispute in any industry in which he or she has not been bona fide engaged in the United Kingdom for at least two years preceding an alleged offence. The Police Act 1996, s 91, replacing legislation first passed in 1919 at a time of serious unrest within the police, prohibits acts calculated to cause disaffection among police officers or to induce them to withhold their services or commit breaches of discipline. Under the Incitement to Disaffection Act 1934, which passed through Parliament against severe criticism from a variety of quarters, it is an offence maliciously and advisedly to endeavour to seduce a member of the armed forces from his or her duty or allegiance.

The 1934 Act contains stringent provisions for the prevention and detection of the offence, including wide powers of search on reasonable suspicion, but a warrant may be issued only by a High Court judge. Moreover, it is an offence for any person, with intent to commit or to aid, counsel or procure commission of the main offence, to have in his or her possession or under his or her control any document of such a nature that the distribution of copies among members of the forces would constitute that offence. Notwithstanding the safeguards in the Act, it does restrain certain forms of political propaganda; and it could be used to suppress or interfere with the distribution of pacifist literature. Prosecutions under the Act in England require the consent of the Director of Public Prosecutions. This consent was given between 1973 and 1975 for prosecution of members of a campaign for the withdrawal of British troops from Northern Ireland in respect of leaflets which they had prepared. One conviction was upheld by the Court of Appeal.[64] The accused has a right to jury trial: it would be a matter for the jury to decide whether a leaflet which gave information to a soldier about procedures for leaving the army and his or her rights as a soldier was an attempt to seduce him or her from duty or allegiance to the Crown.

Incitement to racial hatred

It has long been recognised that the preservation of public order justifies the imposition of criminal sanctions on those who utter threats, abuse or insults in public places which are likely to give rise to a breach of the peace.[65] In 1965, when Parliament first created machinery to deal with racial discrimination,[66] an offence of incitement to racial hatred was created which was not dependent on proof of an immediate threat to public order. The reason for this was the belief that racial hatred itself contains the seeds of violence.[67] The position is now governed by the Public Order Act 1986, which deals specifically with 'racial hatred', taken to mean 'hatred against a group of persons defined by reference to colour, race, nationality (including citizenship) or ethnic or national origins' (s 17). This replaces measures enacted in the Race Relations Act 1976 and previously in the Race Relations Act 1965.[68] By s 18 of the 1986 Act, it is an offence for a person to use threatening, abusive or insulting words or behaviour or to display any material which is threatening, abusive or insulting if he or she does so with intent to stir up racial hatred or if in

---

[64] *R v Arrowsmith* [1975] QB 678; and see *Arrowsmith v UK* (1978) 3 EHRR 218 (no infringement of European Convention on Human Rights).

[65] Ch 24.

[66] Ch 19 A.

[67] See D G T Williams [1966] Crim LR 320; Lester and Bindman, *Race and Law*, ch 10; and P M Leopold [1977] PL 389.

[68] *R v Britton* [1967] 2 QB 51; *R v Malik* [1968] 1 All ER 582. See also A Dickey [1968] Crim LR 48.

the circumstances racial hatred is likely to be stirred up.[69] The Act applies to publicising or distributing such material (s 19), theatrical performances (s 20), the distribution, showing or playing of a recording of visual images or sounds (s 21), and television and radio broadcasts (s 22).

The offence in s 23 of the Act relates to the possession of material which if published or displayed would amount to an offence under the Act. Where there are reasonable grounds for suspecting that a person has possession of such material, a justice of the peace may grant a warrant to a police constable authorising the entry and search of premises for the material in question. It is not an offence to publish a fair and accurate report of proceedings in Parliament (or the Scottish Parliament or the Welsh Assembly), or of proceedings publicly heard before a tribunal or court where the report is published contemporaneously with the proceedings (s 26). No prosecution in England and Wales may occur without the consent of the Attorney General (s 27). Although these are wide-ranging restrictions, they are justifiable primarily because a serious threat to personal security and dignity, not to mention public order, is inherent in certain forms of political and social expression. Nevertheless, controversy was sparked when in 2006 these provisions were extended to apply also to incitement to religious hatred, this being 'hatred against a group of persons defined by reference to religious belief or lack of religious belief'.[70] The law was later extended to cover incitement to hatred on grounds of sexual orientation.[71]

Incitement to terrorism

A third public order restriction on free speech was introduced by the Terrorism Act 2006. By section 1, this applies to a statement that is likely to be understood by some or all of the members of the public to whom it is published as 'a direct or indirect encouragement or other inducement to them to the commission, preparation or instigation of acts of terrorism'. For this (and other purposes in the Act) 'public' is defined to mean 'the public of any part of the United Kingdom or of a country or territory outside the United Kingdom, or any section of the public' (s 20(3)(a)).[72] It is an offence to publish a statement to which the foregoing applies if at the time the statement is published the accused intends members of the public to be directly or indirectly encouraged to commit acts of terrorism, or is reckless as to whether they will be so encouraged or induced (s 1(2)). It is then provided that statements are likely to be understood as indirectly encouraging the commission of acts of terrorism if they glorify the commission or preparation of acts of terrorism, provided it can reasonably be inferred that what is being glorified is 'being glorified as conduct that should be emulated' (s 1(3)). Other provisions in the Act define glorification to include 'any form of praise or celebration' (s 20(2)). This is an offence that carries a penalty of up to seven years' imprisonment if convicted on indictment.

Related to the above, section 2 creates a separate offence in relation to terrorist publications. Section 2 applies to various forms of dissemination of such publications, which begs three questions, First, what is meant by *terrorist* for these purposes (a question which also arises in relation to section 1 as well). The answer lies in section 1 of the Terrorism Act 2000 where terrorism is defined widely to mean action or the threat of action involving serious violence or serious damage to property, which is designed to influence the government or intimidate the public or a

---

[69] It is not now necessary, as it was under the 1965 Act, to prove that the accused intended to stir up racial hatred: in practice, such proof had been too stringent a requirement for the law to be an effective restraint on racist propaganda. See also W J Wolffe [1987] PL 85 and S Poulter [1991] PL 371.

[70] Racial and Religious Hatred Act 2006, s 1, inserting new ss 29A–29N into Public Order Act 1986.

[71] Criminal Justice and Immigration Act 2008, s 74, Sch 16; amending Public Order Act 1986.

[72] It also applies to public meetings, whether entry is on payment of a fee or not (s 20(3)(b)).

section of the public, and is undertaken to advance an ideological cause.[73] For these purposes the government to be influenced need not be the United Kingdom government, but could be a foreign government, and the activity being planned could be planned to be undertaken overseas. This leads to the second question of what is meant by a *publication* for these purposes. Here s 2(13) defines it to mean an article or record of any description that contains matter to be read, listened to, or looked at or watched, which means that it covers traditional printed material (such as leaflets and pamphlets) as well as more sophisticated internet-based material (in relation to which new powers are given to the police by s 3 to require people to remove terrorism related material from internet sites).

Having thus defined *terrorist* and *publication*, the third task involves putting both together: what is a *terrorist publication*? Here s 2(3) provides that it applies to publications likely to be understood by those or some of those to whom it becomes available to be 'a direct or indirect encouragement or other inducement to them to the commission, preparation or instigation of acts of terrorism', or to be 'useful' in the commission or preparation of such acts. For these purposes as well, 'matter that is likely to be understood by a person as indirectly encouraging the commission or preparation of acts of terrorism includes any matter which [glorifies terrorism]' (s 2(4)). The section 2 offence is committed only if the dissemination (for example by circulation, sale or loan) takes place with the intention that the dissemination will have the effect of directly or indirectly encouraging or inducing the commission, preparation or instigation of acts of terrorism (s 2(1)). This is, thus, a complicated offence which requires an intention to encourage or induce acts of terrorism by the dissemination of a publication which encourages or induces acts of terrorism. Like section 1, it is also an offence that carries a penalty of up to seven years' imprisonment if convicted on indictment (s 2(11)). It was also very controversial, and attracted a great deal of opposition from both sides in Parliament.[74]

E. Obscene publications

Before the Act of 1959

It resulted from the development of the law concerning the printing of books that, as with seditious, blasphemous and other libels, it became an offence punishable by the common law courts to publish obscene material. This jurisdiction was exercised for the first time in *Curl's* case when the court held that it was an offence to publish a book which tended to corrupt morals and was against the King's peace.[75] The flourishing business of pornography in the Victorian underworld led to the Obscene Publications Act 1857. This Act gave the police power to search premises, seize obscene publications kept for sale, and bring them before a magistrates' court for destruction. The Act did not define 'obscene' but its sponsor, Lord Campbell, stated that it was to apply 'exclusively to works written for the single purpose of corrupting the morals of youth, and of a nature calculated to shock the common feelings of decency in any well regulated mind'.[76] In 1868, in *R v Hicklin*, Cockburn CJ declared the test for obscenity to be:

---

[73] This is a definition which overlaps with the now abolished offence of seditious libel, which also emphasised (i) an intention to change the constitution, by (ii) violent means. See *R v Burns*, note 60 above and *R v Aldred*, note 60 above. The common law offence was probably wider and more elastic in principle, though it had probably become unusable in practice, having been designed for a different age.

[74] For guidance, see *R v Rahman* [2008] EWCA Crim 1465; [2008] 4 All ER 661.

[75] (1727) 17 St Tr 153; Robertson, *Obscenity*, ch 2.

[76] HL Deb, 25 June 1857, col 329.

whether the tendency of the matter charged as obscenity is to deprave and corrupt those whose minds are open to such immoral influences and into whose hands a publication of this sort may fall.[77]

This test came to dominate the English law of obscenity. It required account to be taken of the circumstances of publication: in *Hicklin's* case, Cockburn CJ said that immunity for a medical treatise depended on the circumstances, since the publication of some medical details would not be fit for boys and girls to see. But the test did not permit the author's intention to be taken into account. Although the tendency to deprave and corrupt was often assumed from the character of a book, who might the potential readers be? In 1954, in *R v Reiter*, the Court of Criminal Appeal took the view that a jury should direct their attention to the result of a book falling into the hands of young people.[78] But a few months later, in *R v Martin Secker Warburg Ltd*, Stable J asked: 'Are we to take our literary standards as being the level of something that is suitable for the decently brought up young female aged 14?'.[79] Other difficulties in the law included the use of the 1857 Act against serious literature; the failure of the 1857 Act to enable a publisher or author to defend a work against destruction; and the tendency of prosecutors to take selected passages of a book out of context. A lengthy campaign by publishers and authors led to the Obscene Publications Act 1959.[80]

The Obscene Publications Acts 1959 and 1964

The 1959 Act, which does not apply to Scotland, sought both to provide for the protection of literature and to strengthen the law against pornography. For the purposes of the 1959 Act (but not of other Acts in which the word 'obscene' is used):[81]

an article shall be deemed to be obscene if its effect or (where the article comprises two or more distinct items) the effect of any one of its items is, if taken as a whole, such as to tend to deprave and corrupt persons who are likely, having regard to all relevant circumstances, to read, see or hear the matter contained or embodied in it (s 1(1)).[82]

A wide definition of 'article' (s 1(2)) includes books, pictures, films, records and such things as film negatives used in producing obscene articles,[83] and video cassettes.[84] It is an offence to publish an obscene article, whether for gain or not, or to have obscene articles in one's possession, ownership or control for the purpose of publication for gain or with a view to such publication,[85] whether for sale within Britain or abroad.[86] The definition of 'publishing' includes distributing, circulating, selling, hiring and, for example, showing pictures or playing records; since 1991 it includes television and sound broadcasting,[87] and since 1994 it has included the transmitting of electronically stored data.[88] It is a defence to prove that publication of an obscene article is

[77] (1868) LR 3 QB 360, 371.
[78] [1954] 2 QB 16.
[79] [1954] 2 All ER 683, 686 (Kauffman's *The Philanderer*).
[80] See HC 123 (1957–58); and Robertson, *Obscenity*, pp 40–4.
[81] *R v Anderson* [1972] 1 QB 304, 317 (*Oz, School Kids Issue*).
[82] On the item by item test, see *R v Anderson*, ibid, at 312.
[83] 1964 Act, s 2, the sequel to *Straker v DPP* [1963] 1 QB 926.
[84] *A-G's Reference (No 5 of 1980)* [1980] 3 All ER 816.
[85] 1959 Act, s 2(1), as amended in 1964. See *R v Taylor* [1995] 1 Cr App R 131 (publication where films depicting obscene acts are developed, printed and returned to the owner).
[86] *Gold Star Publications Ltd v DPP* [1981] 2 All ER 257; and see (1983) 5 EHRR 591.
[87] Broadcasting Act 1990, s 162, amending 1959 Act, by inserting s 1(4)–(6).
[88] Criminal Justice and Public Order Act 1994, s 168(1). See *R v Perrin* [2002] EWCA (Crim) 747.

justified 'as being for the public good on the ground that it is in the interests of science, literature, art or learning or other objects of general concern'. Expert evidence on the literary, artistic, scientific or other merits of an article is admissible to establish or negative the defence of public good.[89]

The 1959 Act, s 3, confers search, seizure and forfeiture powers similar to those in the 1857 Act. A warrant may be obtained by a constable (or the DPP) from a magistrate for the search of specified premises, stalls or vehicles, where there is reasonable suspicion that obscene articles are kept for publication for gain. When a search is made, articles believed to be obscene and also documents relating to a trade or business may be seized. The seized articles must be brought before a magistrate. When notice has been given to the occupier of the premises to show cause why the articles should not be forfeited, the magistrates' court may order forfeiture if satisfied that the articles are obscene and were kept for publication for gain. The owner, author or maker of the articles may also appear to defend them against forfeiture. The defence that publication is for the public good is available and expert evidence relating to the merits of the articles may be called. In these proceedings there is no right to the decision of a jury, but there are rights of appeal to the Crown Court or the High Court. Because of certain defects in the 1959 Act, the Act of 1964 was passed to strengthen the law against publishing obscene matter. Inter alia, the Act made it an offence to have an obscene article for publication for the purposes of gain,[90] and authorised a forfeiture order to be made following a conviction under the 1959 Act.

One difficulty is the 1959 Act's definition of obscenity as 'a tendency to deprave and corrupt'. The definition makes it impossible to rely on such synonyms as 'repulsive', 'filthy', 'loathsome' or 'lewd'[91] and requires the jury to consider whether the effect of a book is to tend to deprave and corrupt a significant proportion of those likely to read it. 'What is a significant proportion is entirely for the jury to decide.'[92] In cases relating to the internet in particular, however, it may not be appropriate for 'the task of the jury [to] be complicated by a direction that the effect of the article must be such as to tend to deprave and corrupt a significant proportion, or more than a negligible number of likely viewers'.[93] Lord Wilberforce has said: 'An article cannot be considered as obscene in itself: it can only be so in relation to its likely readers.'[94] Experienced police officers may for practical purposes not be susceptible to being depraved and corrupted,[95] but it seems that a man may be corrupted more than once.[96] Although the circumstances in which articles are sold are relevant, it is no defence for booksellers to prove that most of their sales are made to middle-aged men who are already addicted to pornography; articles may 'deprave and corrupt' the mind without any overt sexual activity by the reader resulting.[97] Obscenity is not confined to sexual matters: a book dealing with the effects of drug taking may be obscene,[98] as may cards depicting violence when sold to children.[99]

---

[89] 1959 Act, s 4.

[90] Cf *Mella v Monahan* [1961] Crim LR 175.

[91] *R v Anderson* [1972] 1 QB 304; cf the perceptive analysis by Windeyer J in *Crowe v Grahame* (1968) 41 AJLR 402, 409.

[92] *R v Calder & Boyars Ltd* [1969] 1 QB 151, 168. But it is 'more than a negligible number' (*R v O'Sullivan* [1995] 1 Cr App R 455).

[93] *R v Perrin* [2002] EWCA (Crim) 747. According to the court 'such a direction is all too likely to give rise to a request for further assistance as to what proportion is significant, or what number is negligible'.

[94] *DPP v Whyte* [1972] AC 849, 860.

[95] *R v Clayton and Halsey* [1963] 1 QB 163.

[96] *Shaw v DPP* [1962] AC 220, 228 (CCA).

[97] *DPP v Whyte* [1972] AC 849, 867.

[98] *Calder (Publications) Ltd v Powell* [1965] 1 QB 509; *R v Skirving* [1985] QB 819.

[99] *DPP v A & BC Chewing Gum Ltd* [1968] 1 QB 159.

Common law offences

In *Shaw* v *DPP*,[100] the appellant had published the *Ladies' Directory*, an illustrated magazine containing names, addresses and other details of prostitutes and their services. The House of Lords upheld Shaw's conviction for the offence of conspiracy to corrupt public morals. Lord Simonds accepted that the law must be related to the changing standards of life, having regard to fundamental human values and the purposes of society; he said that 'there remains in the courts of law a residual power to enforce the supreme and fundamental purpose of the law, to conserve not only the safety and order but also the moral welfare of the State'.[101] It was the jury which provided a safeguard against the launching of prosecutions to suppress unpopular or unorthodox views. Lord Reid, dissenting, rejected the view that the court was guardian of public morals. This controversial decision derived in part from the supposed offence of conspiracy to effect a public mischief, which was later held not to be part of criminal law.[102] Although Shaw was also convicted for having published an obscene book, contrary to the 1959 Act, *Shaw's* case enabled prosecutions to be brought at common law for conspiracy rather than for breaches of the 1959 Act. Thereafter the Law Officers assured the House of Commons that a conspiracy to corrupt public morals would not be charged so as to circumvent the 'public good' defence in the 1959 Act.[103]

In *Knuller Ltd* v *DPP*,[104] however, the House of Lords reaffirmed the decision in *Shaw*, in a case in which the appellants had published a magazine containing advertisements by male homosexuals seeking to meet other homosexuals. The Lords upheld a conviction of the appellants for conspiracy to corrupt public morals, rejecting a defence based on the Sexual Offences Act 1967 by which homosexual acts between adult males in private had ceased to be an offence. A second conviction for conspiracy 'to outrage public decency' was quashed on the ground of misdirection, but a majority of the House held that at common law it was an offence to outrage public decency and also to conspire to outrage public decency; and that such a conspiracy could take the form of an agreement to insert outrageously indecent matter on the inside pages of a magazine sold in public.[105] Lords Reid and Diplock did not agree that 'outraging public decency' was an offence; Lord Reid said, 'To recognise this new crime would go contrary to the whole trend of public policy followed by Parliament in recent times.'[106] Nevertheless, the abolition of common law conspiracy with the introduction of new statutory offences in the Criminal Law Act 1977 was stated expressly not to affect a conspiracy that involves an agreement to engage in conduct which tends to corrupt public morals or outrages public decency.[107]

Although the common law offence has thus been recognised and preserved by statute,[108] prosecutions for conspiracy to corrupt public morals or to outrage public decency are very unusual. One such case, however, is *R* v *Gibson*,[109] in which both the owner of an art gallery and an artist were convicted for exhibiting a model's head to the ears of which were attached earrings made out of a freeze-dried human foetus of three or four months' gestation. The case raised the question whether a prosecution at common law to outrage public decency was precluded by s 2(4) of the Obscene Publications Act 1959, whereby common law proceedings are not to be brought where 'it is of the essence of the offence that the matter is obscene'. The Court of Appeal held

---

[100] [1962] AC 220.
[101] Ibid, p 268. See D Seaborne Davies (1962) 6 JSPTL 104, J E Hall Williams (1961) 24 MLR 626 and Robertson, *Obscenity*, ch 8.
[102] *DPP* v *Withers* [1975] AC 842.
[103] HC Deb, 3 June 1964, col 1212.
[104] [1973] AC 435.
[105] See now *R* v *Walker* [1996] 1 Cr App R 111.
[106] *Knuller Ltd* v *DPP* [1973] AC 435, 459.
[107] Criminal Law Act 1977, s 5(3); cf s 53(3).
[108] See also Theatres Act 1968, s 2(4).
[109] [1990] 2 QB 619; M Childs [1991] PL 20.

that there are two broad types of offence involving obscenity and that the 1959 Act applied only in respect of one (those involving the corruption of public morals) but not the other (those which involve an outrage on public decency, whether or not public morals are involved). This decision may make it easier for the Crown to bring prosecutions at common law, thereby circumventing the defences which would otherwise be available in a prosecution brought under the Act. Of these, the most important is undoubtedly the public good defence in s 4. However, the offence can only be committed in public and only if seen by others.[110]

Reform of the law

The law of obscenity and indecency was reviewed by a highly regarded Home Office committee (chairman, Professor Bernard Williams) which reported in 1979.[111] The committee analysed the purposes for which regulation of obscenity was justified. It considered that the existing law should be scrapped and a fresh start made with a comprehensive new statute. In particular, terms such as 'obscene', 'indecency', 'deprave and corrupt' should be abandoned as having outlived their usefulness.[112] The government did not accept these recommendations; nor it seems did the courts, with the Court of Appeal expressing concern about the 'evil' of 'pornography' within three years of the publication of the Williams Report.[113] Since 1979, Parliament has generally added fresh layers of restrictive legislation, with an example to be found in the Criminal Justice and Immigration Act 2008. This not only increases the penalties under the Obscene Publications Act 1959 (to five years), but also introduces a new offence of possessing extreme pornographic images. The latter is expressed to (i) relate to defined activities listed in the Act, and (ii) to be 'grossly offensive, disgusting or otherwise of an obscene character', though there is no definition of obscene (or 'disgusting') for these purposes (s 63). The Human Rights Act has yet to have an impact here.[114]

One of the main challenges in this area at the present time relates to the internet, where there is a real concern about child pornography and the sexual solicitation of children, as well as problems of access by children to unsuitable material. Unlike other forms of electronic media there is no statutory regulation of the internet to regulate access to sexually explicit or other material (although internet service providers and internet users will be subject to ordinary civil and criminal liabilities, such as defamation and incitement to racial hatred).[115] In the United Kingdom, the matter is addressed by a further example of self-regulation, in the form of the Internet Watch Foundation which was established in 1996 by UK internet service providers to advise internet users about how best to restrict access to harmful or offensive content on the internet generally.[116] The Foundation is independent of government and, although it works very closely with government, has no statutory powers. Internet users report material to the Foundation which they believe to be criminal: this can be for any reason, although complaints are overwhelmingly about child

---

[110] *R v Hamilton* [2007] EWCA Crim 2062, [2008] 2 WLR 107.

[111] Cmnd 7772, 1979. See Simpson, *Pornography and Politics – the Williams Report in Retrospect*.

[112] *R v O'Sullivan*, note 92 above. It seems that there is little to be said for the existing law, which is routinely criticised in academic literature: see P Kearns [2007] Crim Law Rev 667; C McGlynn and E Rackley [2007] Crim Law Rev 677. However, the current provisions are flexible and allow prosecution policy to move with the times: what was obscene in 1960 will not be regarded as obscene in 2010 as the basis for a prosecution. See CPS, *Code for Crown Prosecutors* (2010).

[113] *R v Holloway* (1982) 4 Cr App R (S) 128. According to the court 'the only way of stamping out this filthy trade is by imposing sentences of imprisonment on first offenders and all connected with the commercial exploitation of pornography'.

[114] Cf *Belfast City Council v Miss Behavin' Ltd* [2007] UKHL 19.

[115] See *Godfrey v Demon Internet Ltd* [2001] QB 201 (defamation), and *R v Perrin* [2002] EWCA Crim 747 (obscene publications). See generally on this hugely controversial issue, Akdeniz, Walker and Wall (eds), *The Internet, Law and Society*.

[116] See www.iwf.org.uk.

pornography. If on investigation the material is thought to be criminal, the internet service provider will be asked to remove it and the information will be passed to the police.

F. Defamation

The nature of liability

In an impressive report on *Press Standards, Privacy and Libel*, the Culture, Media and Sport Committee of the House of Commons warmly welcomed the abolition of criminal libel by the Coroners and Justice Act 2009.[117] However, defamation continues to give rise to civil liability, the law being designed to protect the reputation of the claimant from improper attack.[118] In principle, the law provides a remedy for false statements which expose a person to 'hatred, ridicule or contempt', or which tend to lower him or her 'in the estimation of right-thinking members of society generally'.[119] For this purpose words are to be given 'the natural and ordinary meaning [they] would have conveyed to the ordinary reasonable reader'.[120] Defamation takes two main forms: (*a*) slander (defamation in a transitory form by spoken word or gesture) and (*b*) libel (defamation in a permanent form such as the written or printed word). By statute, words used in the course of broadcasting and of public performances in a theatre are treated as publication in permanent form.[121] In the interest of free speech, neither local authorities (and by inference central government departments) nor political parties may bring an action in defamation.[122] It is thus an anomaly of English law that corporations may sue in libel (all the more anomalous for the fact that trade unions may not).[123]

Actions for defamation are one of the few surviving forms of civil action where either party has a right to insist on trial by jury.[124] When the judge rules that a statement is capable of being regarded as defamatory, it is the jury which decides whether the applicant has been defamed and if so the damages that he or she should recover. There is a presumption that defamatory words cause harm, and substantial damages may be awarded for injury to reputation and may include exemplary damages[125] – designed 'to prevent a newspaper profiting from the libel by increasing

---

[117] HC 362 (2009–10), para 235.

[118] See *Reynolds v Times Newspapers Ltd* [2001] 2 AC 127, at 201 (Lord Nicholls) and *Kearns v Bar Council* [2003] EWCA Civ 331; [2003] 1 WLR 1357, at p 1373 (Simon Brown LJ). For fuller accounts of the law of defamation, see textbooks on the law of tort and also Robertson, *Freedom, the Individual and the Law*, ch 7 and Mitchell, *The Making of the Modern Law of Defamation*.

[119] *Sim v Stretch* (1936) 52 TLR 669, 671 (Lord Atkin). For an action to succeed, the publication must be read as a whole, rather than one or more isolated passages. See *Charleston v News Group Newspapers Ltd* [1995] 2 AC 65.

[120] *Bonnick v Morris* [2002] UKPC 31; [2003] 1 AC 300.

[121] Broadcasting Act 1990, s 166; and Theatres Act 1968, s 4.

[122] See respectively *Derbyshire County Council v Times Newspapers Ltd* [1993] AC 534 and *Goldsmith v Bhoyrul* [1998] QB 459; E Barendt [1993] PL 449. Public servants may sue for libel: *Gough v Local Sunday Newspapers (North) Ltd* [2003] EWCA Civ 297; [2003] 1 WLR 1836 (borough solicitor accused of incompetence).

[123] *Steel v McDonald's Corporation* [1999] EWCA Civ 1144; *Tesco Stores Ltd v Guardian* [2008] EWHC 14 (QB); *Jameel v Wall Street Journal* [2006] UKHL 44, [2007] 1 AC 359. For a discussion of defamation and companies, see HC 362 (2009–10), paras 164–178 where the case for reforming the existing law is considered. The position is even more anomalous for the fact that the litigation costs of a UK company are most likely to be tax deductible, which means that they will be paid for indirectly by the taxpayer in a situation where legal aid is not available.

[124] Senior Courts Act 1981, s 69. See *Alexander v Arts Council of Wales* [2001] EWCA Civ 514; [2001] 1 WLR 1840. There are exceptions, for example where the court is of the opinion that the trial will require a prolonged examination of documents.

[125] *Broome v Cassell & Co Ltd* [1972] AC 1027; *Riches v News Group Newspapers Ltd* [1986] QB 256; and *John v Mirror Group Newspapers* [1997] QB 586.

its circulation'.[126] In *John* v *Mirror Group Newspapers*,[127] however, it was proposed that judges give greater guidance to libel juries about damages, this following the decision of the European Court of Human Rights in the *Tolstoy* case in which it was held that a libel award of £1.5 million in favour of Lord Aldington was a violation of the applicant's right to freedom of expression under art 10 of the ECHR.[128] But juries are not bound by this guidance and the appeal court can interfere only if the jury has substantially exceeded what a reasonable jury could consider appropriate.[129] Nevertheless, damages have been very much reduced, with an award of £200,000 for a serious allegation of child sex abuse being thought to have been the highest in recent years.[130]

Fair comment and privilege

The defendant in a libel action may seek to justify the defamatory statement, by proving at the trial that what he or she said was true. Not every detail of the statement need be shown to be literally true, provided that the defendant shows it to be true in substance.[131] In addition, the defence of 'fair comment' protects expressions of opinion on matters of public interest. The comment itself can be quite outspoken, and even unfair, provided that the comment could have been made by an honest person holding strong, exaggerated or even prejudiced views. It is also important that the comment does not contain any incorrect allegations of fact,[132] that the subject of the comment is a matter of public interest, and that malice on the part of the defendant is not shown.[133] The policies and acts of politicians are clearly of public interest. In *Silkin* v *Beaverbrook Newspapers Ltd*, described by Diplock J as an important case since it concerned 'the right to discuss and criticise the utterances and actions of public men', a former Cabinet minister sued the *Sunday Express* over remarks by a political columnist which pointed to inconsistencies between the plaintiff's speeches in Parliament and his business interests: the jury decided that the defence of fair comment had been established.[134]

Publication of statements that would otherwise be defamatory may be protected if made in circumstances of absolute or qualified privilege. Many, though not all, of the common law categories of privilege are now the subject of statutory privilege, though as the House of Lords has pointed out, the categories of privilege at common law are not closed.[135] So far as the Defamation Act 1996 is concerned, absolute privilege applies to, inter alia, (*a*) statements made during parliamentary proceedings and statements in the official reports of debates or in other papers published by order of either House of Parliament;[136] (*b*) statements made by one officer of state to another in the course of his or her official duty, a privilege which in absolute form applies only to certain communications at a high level;[137] (*c*) reports by and statements to the Parliamentary Ombudsman;[138] (*d*) the internal documents of a foreign embassy;[139] and (*e*) the fair

---

[126] *Thompson* v *Metropolitan Police Commissioner* [1998] QB 498, at p 512.

[127] [1997] QB 586.

[128] *Tolstoy Miloslavsky* v *UK* (1995) 20 EHRR 442.

[129] *Kiam* v *MGN Ltd* [2002] EWCA Civ 43; [2003] QB 281.

[130] HC 362 (2009–10), para 122. See also *Galloway* v *Daily Telegraph* [2006] EWCA Civ 17, [2006] EMLR 221 (£150,000).

[131] See *Polly Peck (Holdings) plc* v *Trelford* [1986] QB 1000; *Prager* v *Times Newspapers* [1988] 1 All ER 300; *Bookbinder* v *Tebbit* [1989] 1 All ER 1169; and *Cruise* v *Express Newspapers plc* [1999] QB 931.

[132] See Defamation Act 1952, s 6.

[133] See *Telnikoff* v *Matusevitch* [1992] 2 AC 343 and *Branson* v *Bower* [2002] QB 737.

[134] [1958] 2 All ER 516, discussed in *Reynolds* v *Times Newspapers Ltd* [1998] 3 WLR 862 (CA).

[135] *Reynolds* v *Times Newspapers Ltd* [2001] 2 AC 127, at 197 (Lord Nicholls).

[136] Ch 11 A.

[137] E.g. *Chatterton* v *Secretary of State of India* [1895] 2 QB 189.

[138] Parliamentary Commissioner Act 1967, s 10(5); ch 29 D.

[139] *Al-Fayed* v *Al-Tajir* [1988] QB 712.

and accurate report of proceedings in public before a court in the United Kingdom if published contemporaneously with the proceedings. For this purpose a court includes any tribunal or body exercising the judicial power of the state.[140] Absolute privilege also applies to the fair and accurate report of public proceedings of the European Court of Justice and the European Court of Human Rights.[141]

Qualified privilege, unlike absolute privilege, is destroyed as a defence if the plaintiff proves malice on the part of the defendant.[142] Under the Defamation Act 1996, Sch 1, such privilege arises in two types of case. The first comprises reports privileged without 'explanation or contradiction'.

> This first category applies to the fair and accurate report of public proceedings of a legislature or international organisation anywhere in the world;[143] a court anywhere in the world;[144] or a person appointed to hold a public inquiry by a government or legislature anywhere in the world.[145] It also applies to the fair and accurate report of any public document and of any material published by or on the authority of a government or legislature anywhere in the world,[146] as well as to any matter published anywhere in the world by an international organisation or conference.[147]

The second category comprises reports privileged subject to explanation or contradiction, in the sense that there is no defence if the plaintiff shows that the defendant failed following a request, 'to publish in a suitable manner a reasonable letter or statement by way of explanation or contradiction'.[148]

> This second category includes 'a notice or other matter issued for the information of the public' by the legislature, government or any authority carrying out governmental functions (expressly defined to include police functions) of any member state of the EU; and a fair and accurate report of proceedings at any public meeting in the UK of (a) a local authority or local authority committee; (b) a justice of the peace acting otherwise than as a court exercising judicial functions; (c) a commission or tribunal; (d) a local authority inquiry; or (e) any other statutory tribunal, board or inquiry. The second category also includes the fair and accurate reports or copies of (a) public meetings,[149] (b) a general meeting of a UK public company, (c) documents circulated to members of UK public companies, (d) the findings of one of a number of regulatory bodies of a voluntary nature, and (e) any adjudication or report by a body or person designated by the Lord Chancellor.[150]

---

[140] Defamation Act 1996, s 14(3)(a). And see *Trapp* v *Mackie* [1979] 1 All ER 489, and *Mahon* v *Rahn (No 2)* [2000] 1 WLR 2150.

[141] Defamation Act 1996, s 14(3)(b)–(d).

[142] Ibid, s 15(1). But carelessness, impulsiveness or irrationality do not amount to malice: *Horrocks* v *Lowe* [1975] AC 135, though any of these may 'cost a journalist dear' in an action against the press – *Loutchansky* v *Times Newspapers (Nos 2–5)* [2001] EWCA Civ 536; [2002] QB 321. See also on qualified privilege, *Kearns* v *Bar Council* [2003] EWCA Civ 331; [2003] 1 WLR 1357.

[143] See also ch 11 A.

[144] See also ch 18 D and *Webb* v *Times Publishing Co* [1960] 2 QB 535.

[145] See *Tsikata* v *Newspaper Publishing plc* [1997] 1 All ER 655 (report need not be a contemporary report).

[146] See *Curistan* v *Times Newspapers Ltd* [2008] EWCA Civ 432; [2008] 3 All ER 923 (privilege not lost because of the publication in the same article of extraneous material not privileged).

[147] Defamation Act 1996, Sch 1, Part 1.

[148] Ibid, s 15(2)(a).

[149] A press conference has been held to be a public meeting the reporting of which attracts qualified privilege, and this extends to written press releases distributed but not necessarily read out at the meeting: *McCartan Turkington Breen* v *Times Newspapers Ltd* [2001] 2 AC 277.

[150] Defamation Act 1996, Sch 1, Part II. The protection does not apply to the publication of a matter which is not of public concern or the publication of which is not for the public benefit (s 15(3)): see *Kingshott* v *Associated Kent Newspapers* [1991] 1 QB 88.

Responsible journalism

The position of the press is very different in the United States, where the effect of Supreme Court decisions on the freedom of the press has been to create a new law of libel concerning matters of public or general interest under which the press has much greater freedom to publish information and comment than under English law.[151] In an action brought by a public figure, the applicant must prove that the publication was false and that it was published either with knowledge of its falsity or with serious doubts as to its truth. It has been said in the High Court of Australia that the great virtue of the American approach is that 'it offers some protection to the reputation of the individual who is defamed and at the same time offers a large measure of protection to the publisher'.[152] This is an issue which has given rise to a lively body of jurisprudence in a number of Commonwealth countries in recent years, with the courts in Australia, New Zealand and South Africa moving in different ways to allow a greater degree of latitude to the press in the interests of freedom of expression and democratic accountability of politicians.[153]

The adoption of a somewhat similar approach was rejected by the House of Lords in *Reynolds v Times Newspapers Ltd*,[154] where the newspaper sought 'the incremental development of the common law' by the recognition of a new category of qualified privilege for a defamatory statement of fact. This was the category of 'political information', broadly defined to mean 'information, opinion and arguments concerning government and political matters that affect the people of the United Kingdom'. It was argued that 'malice apart', the publication of such information should be privileged 'regardless of the status and source of the material and the circumstances of publication'. Although very sensitive of the need to protect freedom of expression, the House of Lords nevertheless concluded that this approach did not go far enough to protect the reputation of the individual from being besmirched without foundation; it was also thought to be 'unsound in principle to distinguish political discussion from discussion of other matters of serious public concern'. The House of Lords preferred a solution that 'enables freedom of speech to be confined to what is necessary in the circumstances of the case', and one in which 'having regard to the admitted or proved facts', the question whether the publication was subject to qualified privilege 'is a matter for the judge'.[155]

In so holding, the House of Lords accepted that there was a duty or interest on the part of the press to impart information for the benefit of the democratic process and that there was an interest on the part of electors in receiving such information to enable them to make informed political choices. In determining whether qualified privilege applies to any particular publication, Lord Nicholls said that the court should have regard to a non-exhaustive list of ten factors. These were: the seriousness of the allegation; the nature of the information; the source of the information; steps taken to verify the information; the status of the information; the urgency of the matter; whether comment was sought from the claimant; whether the article contained the gist of the claimant's side of the story; the tone of the article; and the circumstances and timing of the article. In the *Reynolds* case, there was no qualified privilege where the newspaper had failed to carry an account of the claimant's side of the story.[156] In developing these principles, Lord Nicholls said that 'the common law does not seek to set a higher standard than that of responsible

---

[151] *New York Times v Sullivan*, 376 US 254 (1964). See Lewis, *Make No Law*, where it is argued that without this decision it is questionable whether the press could have done as much as it has to penetrate the power and secrecy of modern government or to inform the public of the reality of policy issues.

[152] *Theophanos v Herald and Weekly Times* (1994) 68 ALJR 713 (I Loveland [1996] PL 126).

[153] See respectively *Lange v Australian Broadcasting Corp* (1997) 145 ALR 96; *Lange v Atkinson* [1998] 3 NZLR 424, [2000] 3 NZLR 385; and *National Media Ltd v Bogoshi* 1998 (4) SA 1196.

[154] [2001] 2 AC 127.

[155] For a full discussion expressing disappointment at the approach, see I Loveland [2000] PL 351. And for a general review of this area of the law, see Loveland, *Political Libels*. See also Barendt, *Freedom of Speech*, pp 220–2.

[156] See also *Galloway v Daily Telegraph*, note 130 above; Cf *Bonnick v Morris* (above, note 120).

journalism, a standard the media themselves espouse'.[157] These principles have now become well established, and with judges now encouraged not to apply them rigidly,[158] the *Reynolds* defence is thought to provide a firm basis for investigative journalism.

Defamation and parliamentary privilege

A rather paradoxical and unanticipated protection for the press emerged as a result of the operation of art 9 of the Bill of Rights of 1689, which precludes any court from impeaching or questioning the freedom of speech and debates or proceedings in Parliament. In the decision of the Privy Council in *Prebble v Television New Zealand Ltd*,[159] the plaintiff was a Cabinet minister in the New Zealand government who claimed that he had been defamed by the television company. The defendant wished to demonstrate the truth of the allegations by relying on things said or done in Parliament, but was confronted by the Bill of Rights. In upholding the lower courts on the first point to arise, the Privy Council held that: 'Parties to litigation, by whomsoever commenced, cannot bring into question anything said or done in the House (whether by direct evidence, cross-examination, inference or submission) that the actions or words were inspired by improper motives or were untrue or misleading.' But on a second point, the Privy Council reversed a decision of the lower court to stay the proceedings in the light of the disability under which the defendant laboured, on the ground that although there 'may be cases in which the exclusion of material on the grounds of parliamentary privilege makes it quite impossible fairly to determine the issues between the parties', on the facts this was not one of them. Where, however, 'the whole subject matter of the alleged libel relates to the plaintiff's conduct in the House so that the effect of parliamentary privilege is to exclude virtually all the evidence necessary to justify the libel', the proceedings should be stayed not only to prevent an injustice to the defendant, but also to avoid the 'real danger' that 'the media would be forced to abstain from the truthful disclosure of a member's misbehaviour in Parliament'.

> Although the plaintiff was permitted to proceed with his action on the facts, the impact of the *Prebble* decision was immediately felt in this country by two Conservative members of Parliament. In the case of Rupert Allason,[160] an action against *Today* newspaper was stayed, the defendant seeking to show that which was prohibited, namely that 'early day motions were at least inspired by improper motives'. To enforce parliamentary privilege but to refuse a stay would be unjust to the defendant, who would be deprived of their only defence 'while allowing the plaintiff to continue on an unsatisfactory and unfair basis'. In the view of Owen J, MPs 'had to take the ill consequences together with the good consequences' of parliamentary privilege. In the case of Neil Hamilton, it was claimed by the plaintiff that he had been libelled by the *Guardian* which alleged that he had received money from a businessman in return for asking ministers questions which were intended to further that businessman's interests. On this basis it was ruled by May J that the case could not proceed as the evidence directly involved proceedings in Parliament.[161]

The *Prebble* case and its progeny were thought to create a real injustice and in the House of Lords an amendment to the Defamation Bill was introduced by Lord Hoffmann.[162] It was pointed out, however, that it would be unfortunate if the amendment 'were seen in some way to be especially for the protection of the rights of Mr Hamilton or any other MP currently engaged in legal proceedings'. The issue was therefore dealt with as a 'matter of principle'; it was enacted that any person might waive the protection of any rule of law which prevented proceedings in Parliament

---

[157] [2001] 2 AC 127, at p 202.

[158] *Jameel v Wall Street Journal Europe* [2006] UKHL 44, [2007] 1 AC 359. And see *Roberts v Gable* [2007] EWCA Civ 721, [2008] QB 502; *Charman v Orion Publishing Group Ltd* [2007] EWCA Civ 972, [2008] 1 All ER 750.

[159] [1995] 1 AC 321. G Marshall [1994] PL 509, M Harris (1996) 8 *Auckland UL Rev* 45.

[160] *Allason v Haines, The Times*, 25 July 1995.

[161] For details, see HL Deb, 7 May 1996, cols 24–5. See also cols 42–3 (regarding Mr Ian Greer).

[162] Ibid, col 24.

being impeached or questioned in any court or place out of Parliament. This allows the individual to overcome the problem presented by art 9 of the Bill of Rights in the following way: a claimant may bring an action in defamation to vindicate his or her reputation provided he or she is willing to permit the defence to refer to proceedings in Parliament in order to justify what it had written. On the other hand, if the claimant is not prepared to waive the protection of art 9 then *Prebble* will continue to apply and the action may be stayed, on the ground that the newspaper must be allowed in defamation proceedings to prove that what it said was true. Newspapers would otherwise be 'extremely reluctant to criticise what anyone said in Parliament if it meant that they could be sued while they had to stand with their hands tied behind their backs'.[163] But although s 13 'deals specifically with the circumstances raised by Mr Hamilton's case against the *Guardian*',[164] Mr Hamilton dropped his action against the newspaper. He was subsequently found by the House of Commons Committee on Standards and Privileges to have received money from Mr Al Fayed for lobbying services. In a second libel case, this time against Mr Al Fayed about allegations made by him on television, Mr Hamilton invoked s 13 of the 1996 Act to waive parliamentary privilege. This enabled his parliamentary conduct to be challenged and was found by the House of Lords to provide a complete answer to the attempt by the defence to have the action stayed because of parliamentary privilege.[165] The libel action failed.

G. Breach of confidence

In the law of defamation, the courts are reluctant to ban publication of a book or article before trial of the action; in particular, the courts do not restrain publication of a work, even though it is defamatory, when the defendant intends to plead justification or fair comment on a matter of public interest and it is not manifest that such a defence is bound to fail.[166] According to Griffiths LJ in *Herbage* v *Pressdram Ltd*, this is because of 'the value the court has placed on freedom of speech and . . . also on freedom of the press, when balancing it against the reputation of a single individual, who . . . can be compensated in damages'.[167] In actions for breach of confidence, however, damages may be recovered but emphasis is laid on the power of the court by an injunction to prohibit publication which would be in breach of confidence. We have already seen in chapter 22 how the action for breach of confidence has provided the basis for the emerging right to privacy. But the law relating to confidentiality does not apply only to protect information relating to the private life of the individual. The same action was invoked in 1975 by the Attorney General in his attempt to restrain publication of the Crossman diaries. While in that case an injunction was not granted, Lord Widgery CJ ruled that publication of information received by a Cabinet minister prejudicial to the collective responsibility of the Cabinet would be restrained if the public interest clearly required this.[168] It must be emphasised that the label of 'confidential' applied to a document, whether by a public authority or not, does not mean that the court will restrain publication of it should a copy reach a newspaper. In *Fraser* v *Evans*, the court refused to ban publication of a confidential report which Fraser, a public relations consultant, had prepared for the Greek government, when the *Sunday Times* had obtained a copy of it from Greek sources: Fraser's contract with the Greek government required him but not the government to keep it confidential.[169]

---

[163] Ibid, col 251.
[164] *Hamilton* v *Al Fayed* [2001] 1 AC 395, Lord Browne-Wilkinson. See A Sharland and I Loveland [1997] PL 113, and K Williams (1997) 60 MLR 388.
[165] *Hamilton* v *Al Fayed*, ibid. See A W Bradley [2000] PL 556.
[166] *Fraser* v *Evans* [1969] 1 QB 349.
[167] [1984] 2 All ER 769, 771.
[168] *A-G* v *Jonathan Cape Ltd* [1976] QB 752. See also *Commonwealth of Australia* v *John Fairfax and Sons Ltd* (1980) 147 CLR 39.
[169] [1969] 1 QB 349.

Spycatcher and national security

It is nevertheless clear that an action for breach of confidence may be brought to restrain the publication of government secrets. In this respect, the action acquired considerable prominence as a tool for restraining the disclosure of secret information by disaffected members of the security services. Because of this context, severe difficulties are encountered in defining the relationship between a private duty of confidence, the public interest in the protection of confidence, and the public interest in information being made known.[170] The most sensational case to raise these difficulties was the *Spycatcher* case.

> Mr Peter Wright, a retired security service officer, wrote a book, *Spycatcher*, in which he claimed to reveal secrets relating to activities of the British security service. The book was due to be published initially in Australia, which the British government sought an injunction to restrain. Two British newspapers (the *Guardian* and the *Observer*) carried accounts of what the book was said to contain, at which point the Attorney General moved for an injunction to restrain the newspapers from carrying any such reports. An interim injunction was granted on the ground that publication would be a breach of confidence. Legal proceedings to restrain publication in Australia failed,[171] and the book was also published in the United States. When copies of the book began freely to enter the United Kingdom, the *Guardian* and the *Observer* moved to have the interim injunctions discharged, on the ground that there was now no public interest in maintaining the injunctions in view of the fact that the contents of the book were widely known and freely available throughout the world. The House of Lords (by a majority of three to two) refused the application on the ground that the restrictions remained necessary in the public interest (for reasons that were neither clear nor convincing).[172]
>
> However, the Attorney General's application for permanent injunctions against the newspapers failed.[173] The House of Lords agreed that security service personnel owe a lifelong duty of confidence and that they may be restrained by injunction from disclosing any information which they obtain in the service of the Crown, as may any third party to whom such information is improperly conveyed. However, the availability of the book in the United States fatally undermined the government's claim that the maintenance of the injunctions was necessary in the public interest. In the opinion of Lord Keith, 'general publication in this country would not bring about any significant damage to the public interest beyond what has already been done. All such secrets as the book may contain have been revealed to any intelligence service whose interests are opposed to those of the United Kingdom.'[174] But although the actions for permanent injunctions failed, the conviction of several newspapers for contempt of court was subsequently upheld by the House of Lords. The appellants had published material which breached the terms of the injunctions against the *Observer* and the *Guardian*, and it was held that in their conduct they had interfered with the administration of justice.[175]

It was subsequently held by the European Court of Human Rights that the refusal of the House of Lords in 1987 to discharge the injunctions violated art 10 of the European Convention on Human Rights on the ground that, after publication of the book in the United States, the material in question was no longer confidential.[176] Breach of confidence has nevertheless become an established basis for regulating the publication of material about the security service,[177] and this continues to be the position, notwithstanding the Human Rights Act.

---

[170] *X v Y* [1988] 2 All ER 648. Other difficult cases include *Schering Chemicals v Falkman Ltd* [1982] QB 1. And see Cripps, *The Legal Implications of Disclosure in the Public Interest*.

[171] (1987) 8 NSWLR 341 (Powell J); (1987) 75 ALR 353 (NSW Court of Appeal); (1988) 78 ALR 449 (High Court of Australia). See Turnbull, *The Spycatcher Trial*.

[172] *A-G v Guardian Newspapers Ltd* [1987] 3 All ER 316.

[173] *A-G v Guardian Newspapers Ltd (No 2)* [1990] 1 AC 109.

[174] For a fuller treatment of this intricate affair, see Ewing and Gearty, *Freedom under Thatcher*, pp 152–69. See also D G T Williams (1989) 12 Dalhousie LJ 209; and A W Bradley [1988] All ER Rev 55.

[175] *A-G v Times Newspapers Ltd* [1992] 1 AC 191.

[176] *The Observer v UK* (1992) 14 EHRR 153. And see I Leigh [1992] PL 200.

[177] See *Lord Advocate v Scotsman Publications Ltd* [1990] 1 AC 812; N Walker [1990] PL 354.

In *Attorney-General* v *Times Newspapers Ltd*[178] the newspaper gave an undertaking to the Attorney General not to publish information about the secret service (SIS) which had been given to them by Richard Tomlinson, a former agent. When his book was subsequently published in Russia, *The Times* successfully applied to the court to have the undertaking varied, to allow them to publish any of Tomlinson's material which was 'generally accessible to the public at large'. The Attorney General thought that this variation was too wide, but the Court of Appeal overruled his objections and also rejected his claim that any publication should be approved in advance either by himself or by the court. Having regard to the Human Rights Act the court did not think it right that the newspaper 'should seek confirmation from the Attorney General or the court that facts that they intend to republish have been sufficiently brought into the public domain by prior publication so as to remove from them the cloak of confidentiality'. But the court emphasised that the newspaper was bound by confidentiality, the effect of the decision being that the newspaper alone should be responsible for determining when it thought the boundaries had been reached. Should it break the obligation, it would be 'subject to the sanctions that exist for contempt of court'.

So although Times Newspapers succeeded in having the undertaking varied, the result was hardly a ringing endorsement of freedom of expression, despite the Human Rights Act. The court also stated: 'It is desirable that there should usually be consultation between a newspaper and representatives of SIS before the newspaper published information that may include matters capable of damaging the service or endangering those who serve in it.' Such consultation does, in fact, take place. Where a publication is made in breach of confidence, the agent may be required to account for his or her profits.[179]

'Super-injunctions' and parliamentary privilege

As we have seen in chapter 22, liability for breach of confidence has developed under the Human Rights Act, which has not led to an unequivocal vindication of free speech in this area. This is partly because Convention rights include the right to respect for one's private life, a provision which has to be balanced against the Convention right to freedom of expression. Breach of confidence continues to provide a basis of restraint of information which has political implications, as well as information that deals with personal or commercial secrets. One such example discussed in chapter 22 relates to the journals of the Prince of Wales in which there was criticism of Chinese government officials at the time of the hand over of Hong Kong from the United Kingdom.[180] Another is provided by the Trafigura affair, which raises questions also about the use of so-called 'super-injunctions' to prevent discussion of matters of public interest. The issue arose when Paul Farrelly MP tabled a parliamentary question about Trafigura which had obtained an injunction preventing the disclosure of an internal document relating to 'the alleged dumping of toxic waste in the Ivory Coast'.[181] The problem arose because a month earlier an injunction had been granted against the *Guardian* (and 'persons unknown') preventing it from publishing details of the report.

The latter injunction also prohibited the fact that the injunction had been obtained, stating in terms that the respondent must not communicate or disclose 'the information that the Applicants have obtained an injunction'. A 'third level of secrecy was granted by the judge in that Trafigura and subsidiary's identities as claimants were replaced by the random initials "RJW" and "SJW" '.[182] The gravity of this matter was increased still further when Trafigura informed the *Guardian* that it would be in breach of the injunction if it reported Mr Farrelly's question, which led the

---

[178] [2001] 1 WLR 885.
[179] *Attorney-General* v *Blake* [2001] AC 268.
[180] *Associated Newspapers Ltd* v *Prince of Wales* [2006] EWCA Civ 1776, [2008] QB 57.
[181] HC 362 (2009–10), para 94.
[182] Ibid, para 95.

newspaper to report on its front page that it was unable to report a parliamentary question.[183] On this occasion, the Lord Chief Justice issued an unprecedented statement a week later doubting whether the injunction could prevent discussion of the matter in Parliament,[184] a view supported by the Speaker who resisted calls on behalf of the company for a debate on libel to be halted on sub judice grounds.[185] In the course of that debate, the Parliamentary Under-Secretary of State for Justice agreed that reporting of any such matter in Parliament was protected by the Parliamentary Papers Act 1840, s 3, and that the *Guardian* was free to report Mr Farrelly's question.[186] The injunction was eventually withdrawn, and the position of the *Guardian* was thus vindicated.

H. Conclusion

The Trafigura affair highlights the different potential threats to freedom of expression, with attempts to use the law of confidence directly to prevent the publication of a report, the identity of applicants for an injunction, and the existence of an injunction; and indirectly to prevent the press reporting of a parliamentary question, and a debate in Parliament. While the drama also reveals the continuing importance of parliamentary privilege as a means of protecting freedom of expression, the conclusion of the affair leaves a number of outstanding questions unresolved, not least the use of 'super-injunctions' to restrain publicity, as a new form of prior restraint.[187] In the meantime, although much has been done to remove redundant laws by statute (seditious, blasphemous, obscene and criminal libel), in some cases these laws have been replaced by legislation which occupies much the same territory. And although much has been done by statute and judicial decision to contain the scope of libel law, other restraints have been fashioned by the courts to protect the privacy of individuals. These contrasts and contradictions are a reminder that there will always be those who wish to impose restraints on the speech of others, with the result that freedom of expression will never be unlimited. It is the responsibility of each generation to ensure that the desire for restraint is strongly resisted and applied no further than is absolutely necessary in defence of what ought to be compelling countervailing interests.

---

[183] *The Guardian*, 13 October, 2009.
[184] HC 362 (2009–10), para 97.
[185] Ibid, paras 98, 102.
[186] See ch 11 above.
[187] See also *Terry v Persons Unknown* [2010] EWHC 119 (QB).

CHAPTER 24

Freedom of association and assembly

This chapter examines the principal features of the law relating to freedom of association and assembly.[1] These freedoms traditionally were protected in the same way as other freedoms in English law; that is to say, people are free to associate and assemble to the extent that their conduct is not otherwise unlawful. The principle is best illustrated in the context of freedom of assembly by the seminal decision in *Beatty* v *Gillbanks*:[2]

> Members of the Salvation Army insisted on marching through the streets of Weston-super-Mare despite violent opposition from the 'Skeleton Army' and despite an order from the magistrates that they should not march. In an attempt to stop the Salvationist marches, the police sought to have their leaders bound over to keep the peace on the ground that they had committed an unlawful assembly. If the Salvationists had not marched there would clearly have been no disturbance of the peace. As previous processions had led to disorder, the Salvationists knew that similar consequences were likely to ensue. The Divisional Court held that the acts of the Salvation Army were lawful and that it was not a necessary and natural consequence of these acts that disorder should have occurred. The court did not accept that a man might be punished for acting lawfully if he knew that his doing so might lead another man to act unlawfully.

Although historically the common law might thus offer some protection, cases in which freedom of assembly triumphed nevertheless tended in practice to be unusual, in view of the wide range of statutory (and common law) 'exceptions' to the legal principle. Protection for freedom of assembly has, however, now been enhanced by the Human Rights Act, with the right to freedom of association and assembly now being expressly protected by art 11 of the ECHR. But as in the case of the common law, these Convention rights are subject to significant qualifications and permitted limitations, provided they are 'prescribed by law' and 'necessary in a democratic society'. There thus continues to be a tension between freedom and restraint, and it is this tension that will be explored in the following pages.

A. Freedom of association[3]

The law generally imposes no restrictions on the freedom of individuals to associate together for political purposes. People are free to form themselves into political parties, pressure groups, community associations and so on, without any official approval. People are also free to determine with whom they will associate: organisations ought not to be required to accept into membership or to retain individuals who for one reason of another have beliefs which collide with those of the organisation.[4] Trade unions, for example, cannot normally be required to take into membership

---

[1] See Ewing and Gearty, *The Struggle for Civil Liberties*, chs 5 and 6; Ewing and Gearty, *Freedom under Thatcher*, ch 4; and Ewing, *Bonfire of the Liberties*, ch 4. Also Feldman, *Civil Liberties and Human Rights*, ch 18; C A Gearty, in McCrudden and Chambers (eds), *Individual Rights and the Law in Britain*, ch 2; Fenwick, *Civil Rights*, ch 4. Further, Morgan, *Conflict and Order*, and Townshend, *Making the Peace*. For Scotland, see Ewing and Dale-Risk, *Human Rights in Scotland*, ch 9.

[2] (1882) 9 QBD 308. And see Hart and Honoré, *Causation in the Law*, pp 333–5. Cf *Deakin* v *Milne* 1882 10 R (J) 22 and *Hutton* v *Main* 1891 19 R (J) 5.

[3] See K D Ewing, in McCrudden and Chambers (eds), *Individual Rights and the Law in Britain*, ch 8.

[4] See *RSPCA* v *Attorney-General* [2001] 3 All ER 530.

people (such as members of the British National Party), whose beliefs and conduct are thought to be contrary to the principles of the union.[5] Freedom of association thus swings both ways: it is a right of the individual, but simultaneously a right of individuals in association, and sometimes the exercise of both rights gives rise to an irreconcilable conflict in which only one can prevail.

The first exception to the right to freedom of association relates to the need to promote a politically neutral public service. As we saw above, there continue to be restrictions on the political activities of civil servants, these depending to a great extent on the seniority of the official in question and the nature of the work in which he or she is engaged. Although these restrictions relate mainly to political activities rather than membership of political or other organisations, it would surely be unusual for senior civil servants to align themselves formally with a political party.[6] Similarly, local government officers in politically restricted posts may not actively engage in party politics, although there does not appear to be a restriction on membership of a political party,[7] while police officers may not take any active part in politics,[8] a rule designed 'to prevent a police officer doing anything which affects his impartiality or his appearance of impartiality'.[9] Concerns about external security led to the controversial banning of trade union membership at Government Communications Headquarters (GCHQ) in 1984, a ban which was not revoked until 1997.[10]

A second exception to the right to freedom of association lies in the banning of certain forms of association, even by people who are not otherwise restricted in their political activities. Under the Public Order Act 1936, s 1, it is an offence for any person in a public place or at a public meeting to wear a uniform signifying association with a political organisation or with the promotion of any political object.[11] Passed in response to the conduct of fascists in the 1930s, s 2 of the same Act makes it an offence (a) to organise or train the members or supporters of any association for the purpose of enabling them to be used in usurping the functions of the police or the armed forces, or (b) to organise and train (or equip) them, either for enabling them to be employed for the use or display of physical force in promoting any political object, 'or in such manner as to arouse reasonable apprehension that they are organised and either trained or equipped for that purpose'.[12]

More recently, the Terrorism Act 2000 re-enacted wide-ranging restrictions on membership and participation in the activities of terrorist organisations.[13] This Act contains what appears to be the only example of British legislation which makes it an offence simply to be a member of a specific organisation;[14] the proscribed organisations include Al Qaida and Hamas, as well as proscribed 'Irish Groups'. There are, in fact, 14 proscribed organisations listed in the Terrorism Act 2000, Sch 2; the Act contains a power for more to be added (s 3), as a result of which another 46 have been proscribed.[15]

---

[5] Employment Act 2008, s 19, implementing *ASLEF* v *United Kingdom* [2007] IRLR 361; K D Ewing (2007) 36 ILJ 425; (2009) 38 ILJ 50.

[6] See ch 13 E.

[7] Local Government and Housing Act 1989, ss 1, 2 (as amended most recently by the Local Democracy, Economic Development and Construction Act 2009); SI 1990 No 851. These arrangements have been found not to violate the ECHR, art 10: *Ahmed* v *UK* (2000) 29 EHRR 1. See G Morris [1998] PL 25; [1999] PL 211.

[8] SI 2003 No 527, reg 6 and Sch 1. See also Police Act 1996, s 64(1), restrictions on freedom of police officers to join trade unions.

[9] *Champion* v *Chief Constable of Gwent* [1990] 1 All ER 116.

[10] See ch 25 below. Also, Fredman and Morris, *The State as Employer*.

[11] See *O'Moran* v *DPP* [1975] QB 864. See now Terrorism Act 2000, s 13.

[12] *R* v *Jordan and Tyndall* [1963] Crim LR 124; D G T Williams [1970] CLJ 96, 102–4.

[13] Terrorism Act 2000. Part II.

[14] K D Ewing, note 3 above.

[15] See ch 26 below.

B. The right of public meeting

Public meetings may be held in the open air in places to which the public have free access. However, it is usually necessary to get the prior consent of the owners of the land. Many local authorities have made by-laws governing the use of parks for various purposes, including public meetings; breach of these by-laws is a criminal offence, unless the court is prepared to hold the by-law to be ultra vires,[16] and a civil remedy may also be available to restrain persistent breach of the law.[17] Otherwise, it may be possible to hold an assembly on the highway without the need for prior consent.[18] But the scope of this right is very limited: the assembly must be 'reasonable and non-obstructive, taking into account its size, duration and the nature of the highway'. It must, moreover, be 'not inconsistent with the primary right of the public to pass and repass'.[19] As we shall see in the pages that follow, it may be very difficult to hold an assembly on the highway without inadvertently acting unlawfully.

In the case of Trafalgar Square in London, statutory regulations have been made under which approval is required from the Greater London Authority and the Mayor acting on its behalf.[20] Similarly, in the case of Hyde Park, no meetings may be held as of right:[21] although Speaker's Corner is available for any who wish to speak, the law is applied there 'as fully as anywhere else'.[22] More recently, concerns about demonstrations near Parliament have seen the introduction of an offence to organise, take part in or carry on a demonstration in the vicinity of Parliament without the prior approval of the Metropolitan Police Commissioner, which may be withheld on a number of grounds.[23] These restrictions were held to apply to demonstrations that had started before the Act was passed (such as the protest by Brian Haw opposite an entrance to the House of Commons),[24] while it was also held that the responsibilities of the Metropolitan Police Commissioner under the Act could be delegated to junior officers.[25]

For meetings, rallies or assemblies which are not held in the open air, a major practical restriction is the need to find premises for them, to say nothing of the cost of hiring a hall and dealing with security.[26] The organisers of an unpopular cause may find it difficult to hire suitable halls, whether these are owned by private individuals or by public authorities such as a local council. However, candidates at local, parliamentary and assembly elections are entitled to the use of schools and other public rooms for the purpose of holding election meetings.[27] Otherwise local authorities appear to have a wide discretion in deciding to whom to let their halls, although this discretion is subject to law and may now be open to challenge on the ground of illegality under the Human Rights Act 1998.[28] But not even the Human Rights Act has fully met the

---

[16] *De Morgan* v *Metropolitan Board of Works* (1880) 5 QBD 155; *Aldred* v *Miller* 1925 JC 21; *Aldred* v *Langmuir* 1932 JC 22. And see *R* v *Barnet Council, ex p Johnson* (1990) 89 LGR 581 (condition excluding 'political activity' at community festival held invalid).

[17] Cf *Llandudno UDC* v *Woods* [1899] 2 Ch 705.

[18] *DPP* v *Jones* [1999] 2 AC 240. See p 533 below.

[19] Ibid, per Lord Irvine (Lord Chancellor).

[20] Greater London Authority Act 1999, s 383.

[21] *Bailey* v *Williamson* (1873) 8 QBD 118; Royal Parks and Other Open Spaces Regulations 1997, SI 1997 No 1639 (as amended by SI 2004 No 1308).

[22] *Redmond-Bate* v *DPP* [2000] HRLR 249.

[23] Serious Organised Crime and Police Act 2005, s 132.

[24] *R(Haw)* v *Home Secretary* [2006] EWCA Civ 532, [2006] QB 780.

[25] *DPP* v *Haw* [2007] EWHC 1931 (Admin), [2008] 1 WLR 379.

[26] Under the Criminal Justice and Public Order Act 1994, s 170, the security costs of political party conferences may be met by the Treasury.

[27] Representation of the People Act 1983, ss 95, 96. See *Webster* v *Southwark Council* [1983] QB 698; *Ettridge* v *Morrell* (1986) 85 LGR 100.

[28] Such decisions may also be open to challenge if the refusal to let a hall is unreasonable in the *Wednesbury* sense: *Wheeler* v *Leicester City Council* [1985] AC 1054. Cf *Verrall* v *Great Yarmouth BC* [1981] QB 202.

argument that local authorities in particular should be under a general duty to make their halls available to all groups, whether popular or unpopular, without discriminating between them on political or other grounds.[29]

Such a duty applies to universities and higher and further education institutions under the Education (No 2) Act 1986. By s 43, the governing bodies of such establishments must 'take such steps as are reasonably practicable to ensure that freedom of speech within the law is secured for members, students and employees of the establishment and for visiting speakers'. This includes an obligation 'to ensure, so far as is reasonably practicable, that the use of any premises of the establishment is not denied to any individual or body of persons on any ground connected with (a) the beliefs or views of that individual or of any member of that body; or (b) the policy or objectives of that body'. Governing bodies must issue and keep up to date a code of practice to facilitate the discharge of these duties.

In *R* v *University of Liverpool, ex p Caesar-Gordon*,[30] the university authorities refused permission for a meeting at the university to be addressed by two first secretaries from the South African Embassy. This was done because of fear that in the event of the meeting taking place public violence would erupt in Toxteth, the residential area adjacent to the university. On an application for judicial review by the chairman of the student Conservative Association, the Divisional Court held that, on a true construction of s 43(1), the duty imposed on the university is local to the members of the university and its premises. Its duty is to ensure, so far as is reasonably practical, that those whom it may control, that is to say its members, students and employees, do not prevent the exercise of freedom of speech within the law by other members, students and employees and by visiting speakers in places under its control. But under s 43(1), the university was not entitled to take into account threats of 'public disorder' outside the confines of the university by persons not within its control. A declaration was granted that the university acted ultra vires in denying permission to hold the meeting. The court suggested, however, that had the university authorities confined their reasons when refusing permission 'to the risk of disorder on university premises and among university members', then no objection could have been taken to their decisions.

C. Public processions and assemblies

Public processions

By contrast with static meetings on the highway, at common law a procession in the streets is prima facie lawful, being no more than the collective exercise of the public right to use the highway for its primary purpose.[31] This does not mean that it would be a reasonable use of the highway for a dozen demonstrators to link arms and proceed down a street so as to interfere with the right of others to use the highway or for a large group of demonstrators to decide to obstruct a street: a procession would become a nuisance 'if the right was exercised unreasonably or with reckless regard of the rights of others'.[32] It might also be held to be an obstruction of the highway.

But because processions were prima facie lawful, statutory powers were needed if the police were to control them. General powers were contained in the Public Order Act 1936, passed at a time when fascist marches in the East End of London were a serious threat to order. These powers were extended by the Public Order Act 1986. The first major change was the introduction of a requirement that the organisers of a public procession should give advance notice to the police (s 11). The duty applies in respect of processions designed (a) to demonstrate support for or opposition to the views or actions of any person or body of persons; (b) to publicise a cause or

---

[29] Street, *Freedom, the Individual and the Law* (5th edn), p 56.

[30] See E Barendt [1987] PL 344.

[31] A Goodhart (1937) 6 CLJ 161, 169.

[32] *Lowdens* v *Keaveney* [1903] 2 IR 82, 90 (Gibson J); and see *R* v *Clark (No 2)* [1964] 2 QB 315.

campaign; or (c) to mark or commemorate an event. There are a few exclusions from the duty to notify,[33] but most processions for political purposes will be caught by these requirements. The notice, which must specify the proposed time, date and route, must be delivered to a police station (in the area where the procession is to start) at least six clear days in advance.

In addition to this notice requirement, the 1986 Act extends the grounds for which conditions can be imposed on public processions, as well as the circumstances whereby such processions may be banned. So in addition to the original ground of 'serious public disorder' in the 1936 Act, a senior police officer may impose conditions where he or she reasonably believes that the procession may result in serious damage to property or serious disruption to the life of the community. He or she may also impose conditions where the purpose of the organisers of the procession is to intimidate others (s 12). The conditions may be such as appear necessary to prevent disorder, damage, disruption or intimidation, including conditions prescribing the route and prohibiting entry to a specified public place. Unlike the 1936 Act, there is no restriction on the giving of directions relating to the display of flags, banners or emblems. If these powers to impose conditions are not enough to prevent serious public disorder, the chief officer of police may apply to the local authority (or in London the metropolitan police commissioner) for a banning order under what is now s 13 of the 1986 Act. The power to issue a banning order is restricted to serious public disorder; the section does not permit an order to be made on the wider grounds on which conditions may be imposed.

Similar powers in Scotland are in the Civic Government (Scotland) Act 1982[34] By s 62, the organisers of a public procession must notify (at least 28 days in advance) both the police and the local authority in whose area the procession is to be held. After consulting the chief constable, the local authority may then prohibit the holding of the procession or impose conditions upon it. This may be done having regard to the likely effect of the procession in relation to public safety, public order, damage to property, and disruption to the life of the community, while the local authority should also have regard to any 'excessive burden on the police'.[35] It thus appears not only that a local authority in Scotland could ban a specific march (whereas in England and Wales the ban must be on the holding of all public processions or of any class of public processions specified in the order), but that the grounds for imposing a ban (or conditions) are both different and wider.

Another important difference between Scots law and the 1986 Act is the appeal procedure in s 64 of the Civic Government (Scotland) Act 1982. Thus, a person who has given notice of a procession under s 62 may appeal within 14 days to the sheriff against an order prohibiting or imposing conditions on the procession. The grounds of appeal are limited by the statute to error of law, mistake of fact, unreasonable exercise of discretion or that the local authority have 'otherwise acted beyond their powers'. There is no comparable provision in the Public Order Act 1986. It is true that the organiser of a procession could seek judicial review of a banning order or of an order to impose conditions.[36] But, unlike in Scotland, this would be review and not an appeal, and it would be in the High Court under the judicial review procedure and not in the local sheriff court. In any event, as the Court of Appeal has made clear in a case involving a banning order

---

[33] By s 11(2), there is no duty to notify where 'the procession is one commonly or customarily held in the police area (or areas) in which it is proposed to be held or is a funeral procession organised by a funeral director acting in the normal course of his business'. A monthly cycle ride by large numbers of cyclists through the streets of London which did not follow any particular route was held to fall within s 11(2): *Kay* v *Metropolitan Police Commissioner* [2008] UKHL 69, [2009] 2 All ER 935.

[34] See Ewing and Dale-Risk, note 1 above, ch 9. See also W Finnie, in Finnie, Himsworth and Walker (eds), *Edinburgh Essays in Public Law*, pp 251–77.

[35] Police, Public Order and Criminal Justice (Scotland) Act 2006, s 71, amending Civic Government (Scotland) Act 1982, s 63.

[36] Judicial review was also available in principle to challenge banning orders under s 3(2) of the Public Order Act 1936. See *Kent* v *Metropolitan Police Commissioner*, *The Times*, 15 May 1981. For the position under the European Convention on Human Rights, see *Plattform 'Ärzte für das Leben'* v *Austria* (1988) 13 EHRR 204.

under s 3(2) of the 1936 Act, it is not willing to encourage such applications.[37] There is also the practical problem of securing judicial review in enough time before the procession is due to be held. There is no duty on the police to give notice of the conditions 'as early as possible', as there is on the local authority in Scotland.[38] If the police exercise their powers unreasonably, it may be possible for anyone arrested for violating the conditions to challenge their legality as a defence in criminal proceedings. But this will not restore their right to participate in the procession, or the right to conduct the procession as initially conceived.

Public assemblies

Police powers specifically to regulate public assemblies were introduced in the Public Order Act 1986 (s 14). The senior police officer present at an assembly (or the chief constable in the case of an assembly intended to be held) may impose conditions as to its location and duration, as well as the number of people who may be present. These conditions may be issued where it is reasonably believed (a) that the assembly may result in serious public disorder, serious damage to property, or serious disruption to the life of the community; or (b) that the purpose of organising the assembly is to intimidate others. A public assembly is defined to mean an assembly of two or more people in a public place which is wholly or partly open to the air (s 16).[39]

There is no procedure in the Act for challenging instructions issued under this power, although if they are issued long enough in advance, judicial review is available in principle. The only other means of challenging any directions would be collaterally, as a defence in criminal proceedings for violating a direction given under the Act. It could be argued that the police had exceeded their powers, for example, because the purpose of an assembly was to cause inconvenience and embarrassment to third parties, rather than to intimidate them.[40] Nevertheless, the section gives the police wide powers to control public assemblies, and by the power to issue directions, to frustrate the purpose of the assembly. In a report on the G20 protests in 2009 (at which a bystander died after an incident with a police officer), the House of Commons Home Affairs Committee noted concerns about the way in which this power is now being used, drawing attention in particular to an alleged failure of the police properly to communicate their use of section 14, so that to 'the protesters being dispersed it seemed as if the police, without warning had began to use force to clear a peaceful protest'.[41]

The Criminal Justice and Public Order Act 1994 added new powers in respect of public assemblies, corresponding to the powers relating to public processions in s 13 of the 1986 Act.[42] These powers apply to 'trespassory assemblies', that is to say an assembly 'on land to which the public has no right of access or only a limited right of access', a definition wide enough to include the public highway. The power of the police – in what is now Public Order Act 1986, s 14A – is activated where a chief officer 'reasonably believes' that such an assembly of 20 or more people (a) is likely to be held without the permission of the occupier of the land, and (b) may result in serious disruption to the life of the community or significant damage to land, a building or monument of historical, architectural, archaeological or scientific importance.

If these conditions are met, the chief officer of police may apply to the local authority for an order prohibiting all 'trespassory assemblies' in the district or part of it, for a specified period of

---

[37] *Kent v Metropolitan Police Commissioner* (note 36 above).

[38] Civic Government (Scotland) Act 1982, s 63.

[39] As amended by the Anti-social Behaviour Act 2003, s 57. Before then a public assembly for this purpose was defined as meaning an assembly of at least 20 people.

[40] *Police v Lorna Reid* [1987] Crim LR 702.

[41] HC 418 (2009–10), para 27. The same report also expressed concerns about the use of section 14 against journalists covering protests.

[42] On the 1994 Act, see M J Allen and S Cooper (1995) 59 MLR 364.

up to four days in an area within five miles' radius of a specified centre. The order, which may be varied or revoked before it expires, may be made after consulting the Secretary of State (who must give consent before an order may be made), and the order may be made as requested, or with modifications. In Scotland there is no need for ministerial approval to the making of the order (or in granting it with varied terms), while in London the order may be issued by the Metropolitan Police Commissioner with the consent of the Home Secretary. It is an offence to organise or take part in an assembly which is known to be prohibited and a constable in uniform may stop any person reasonably believed to be on the way to an assembly 'likely to be an assembly which is prohibited', and 'direct him [or her] not to proceed in the direction of the assembly'. It is an offence to fail to comply with a direction.

> In DPP v Jones[43] an order had been made prohibiting the holding of assemblies within a four-mile radius of Stonehenge from 29 May to 1 June 1995. While the order was in force, a peaceful assembly was held within the area covered by the order. When those present refused to disperse, they were arrested and convicted of trespassory assembly. The conviction was overturned by the Crown Court, and on an appeal by way of case stated it was held that conduct could constitute a trespassory assembly even though the conduct complained of was peaceful and did not obstruct the highway. On a further appeal to the House of Lords, the question was whether the assembly exceeded the public's right of access to the highway for the purposes of the definition of a 'trespassory assembly': if the public had the right to use the highway in this way, there would be no 'trespass' under the 1986 Act as amended. The House of Lords (dividing 3:2) reinstated the decision of the Crown Court. The Lord Chancellor said that the right to use the highway was not limited to passage and repassage: 'the public highway is a public place which the public may enjoy for any reasonable purpose, provided the activity in question does not amount to a public or private nuisance and does not obstruct the highway by unreasonably impeding the primary right of the public to pass and repass: within these qualifications there is a public right of peaceful assembly on the highway'.[44]

D. Freedom of assembly and private property rights

Picketing

The purpose of picketing is to enable pickets to impart information to those entering or leaving premises, or in some cases to seek to persuade them not to enter in the first place. It has been said that the Human Rights Act 'arguably has created a "right to picket" to the extent that the right to peaceful assembly has been guaranteed by Article 11 of the [ECHR]'.[45] However, those who picket may be subject to directions issued by the police under s 14 of the Public Order Act 1986. The police may also issue directions to prevent a breach of the peace; failure to comply with such directions may lead to an arrest for obstructing a police officer.[46] But even if a picket is perfectly peaceful and is not subject to regulation by the police in these ways, those who participate may in law be committing offences for which they can be arrested without a warrant.

1 *Criminal and civil liability.* The offence most obviously committed by those engaged in peaceful picketing is obstruction of the highway under the Highways Act 1980, s 137, for the purposes of which the highway includes the pavement as well as the road. A picket is no more a lawful or unlawful use of the highway than is any other kind of assembly.[47] Under the Trade Union and Labour Relations (Consolidation) Act 1992, s 241 (a measure originally contained in the Conspiracy

---

[43] [1999] 2 AC 240; G Clayton (2000) 63 MLR 252.

[44] Ibid, at 257.

[45] *Gate Gourmet London Ltd v TGWU* [2005] EWHC 1889 (QB), [2005] IRLR 881, para 22 (Fulford J).

[46] See pp 546–8 below.

[47] See *Broome v DPP* [1974] AC 587; *Kavanagh v Hiscock* [1974] QB 600; and *Hirst v Chief Constable of West Yorkshire* (1987) 85 Cr App R 143.

and Protection of Property Act 1875, s 7), it is an offence for a person 'wrongfully and without legal authority' to 'watch and beset' premises where a person works or happens to be with a view to compelling him or her to abstain from doing something which he or she is entitled to do. This is an offence introduced to deal with the workplace, but there is no reason why its application should be so limited. Having apparently fallen into disuse, what is now s 241 was revived during the miners' strike of 1984/85 as one of the weapons in the police armoury for dealing with the large-scale picketing which then took place.[48]

Apart from possible criminal liability, those who organise a picket may also face civil liability. There is authority for the view that picketing premises may constitute a private nuisance against the owner or occupier of these premises. At least the law is sufficiently unclear that an interlocutory injunction may be granted in an application by such an applicant.

> In *Hubbard* v *Pitt*, a community action group organised a peaceful picket outside the offices of estate agents in Islington, distributing leaflets and displaying placards to protest against the firm's part in improving property at the expense of working-class residents. On the issue of whether an interim injunction should be issued to the firm against the pickets, Forbes J held that the picketing was unlawful since it was not in contemplation or furtherance of a trade dispute (on the significance of which, see below) and was inconsistent with the public right to use the highway for passage and repassage. But in the Court of Appeal, the majority upheld the interim injunction on quite different grounds, holding only that the plaintiffs had a real prospect of establishing at the eventual trial that the protesters were committing a private nuisance against them and that the balance of convenience lay in favour of the picketing being stopped until the main hearing of the action. Lord Denning MR dissented, holding that the use of the highway for the picket was not unreasonable and did not constitute a nuisance at common law; he considered that picketing other than for trade disputes was lawful so long as it was done merely to obtain or communicate information or for peaceful persuasion.[49]

During the miners' strike of 1984/85 an attempt was made – successfully in the short term – to extend the tort of private nuisance. So in *Thomas* v *NUM (South Wales Area)*,[50] Scott J held that pickets would be liable not only to the owner or occupier of the premises being picketed, but also to workers (and presumably others) who were 'unreasonably harassed' in entering the premises. This extension of tortious liability was subsequently disapproved by Stuart-Smith J, in relation to an industrial dispute at Wapping in 1985/86.[51]

2 *Special rules for trade disputes.* Special rules govern picketing in the case of trade disputes. As now provided by the Trade Union and Labour Relations (Consolidation) Act 1992, s 220:

> It shall be lawful for a person in contemplation or furtherance of a trade dispute[52] to attend
> (*a*) at or near his own place of work; or
> (*b*) if he is an official of a trade union, at or near the place of work of a member of that union whom he is accompanying and whom he represents
> for the purpose only of peacefully obtaining or communicating information or peacefully persuading any person to work or abstain from working.[53]

---

[48] See P Wallington (1985) 14 ILJ 145.

[49] [1976] QB 142. See P Wallington [1976] CLJ 82. But picketing is not necessarily a nuisance: see K Miller and C Woolfson (1994) 23 ILJ 209, at pp 216–17.

[50] [1986] Ch 20. See K D Ewing [1985] CLJ 374. See now Protection from Harassment Act 1997, and *Hunter* v *Canary Wharf* [1997] AC 655.

[51] *News Group Newspapers Ltd* v *SOGAT 1982 (No 2)* [1987] ICR 181.

[52] For the meaning of the term 'trade dispute', see Trade Union and Labour Relations (Consolidation) Act 1992, s 244.

[53] See also the Code of Practice on Picketing issued under the 1992 Act (note 56 below).

This provision, unlike its predecessors, restricts the freedom to picket in a trade dispute to one's own place of work. Secondary picketing – the picketing of other workplaces – is thus excluded.[54] There is no restriction in the Act on the number of people who may picket in this way, but a Code of Practice on Picketing issued by the then Department of Employment (with parliamentary approval)[55] recommends no more than six people at any particular site, although this could be reduced if the police are of the view that, to prevent a breach of the peace, a smaller number is necessary.[56]

Even if these requirements are met, there is no right on the part of pickets to stop vehicles and to compel drivers and their occupants to listen to what they have to say. In *Broome v DPP*,[57] the House of Lords refused to read such a right into a statutory predecessor of the current law on the ground that it would involve reading into the Act words which would seriously diminish the liberty of the subject. Everyone has the right to use the highway free from the risk of being compulsorily stopped by any private citizen and compelled to listen to what he or she does not want to hear.[58] Pickets thus have a right to seek to communicate information or to seek peacefully to persuade, but not to stop persons or vehicles.

The purpose of the special provisions relating to picketing in trade disputes is to give workers and trade union officials a limited protection from both criminal and civil liability. So far as the criminal law is concerned, those who picket peacefully for the permitted purposes will not be liable under either the Highways Act 1980, s 137, or the Trade Union and Labour Relations (Consolidation) Act 1992, s 241. This is because the latter, by s 220 (providing that picketing 'shall be lawful'), gives legal authority to obstruct the highway and to watch and beset. If, however, the purpose of the picket is deemed to be the causing of an obstruction rather than the peaceful communication of information, then s 220 of the 1992 Act will not prevent those involved from being arrested and convicted.

So far as civil liability is concerned, s 220 provides an immunity from liability for private nuisance where the pickets are acting peacefully.[59] But it does not provide immunity where the purpose of the picket is adjudged to be to harass others, as in *Thomas v NUM (South Wales Area)*.[60] Together with s 219 of the 1992 Act, s 220 also gives pickets immunity in tort for conspiracy, inducing breach of contract, and intimidation.[61] In this case, however, the protection is of qualified value, for it applies only where the increasingly tight restrictions on the conduct of industrial action have been complied with, including the holding of a secret ballot and the giving of appropriate notice to employers.

There may be circumstances where picketing in the course of a trade dispute does not involve the commission of a tort and where as a result the immunity is unnecessary. Although such cases are rare, they are not unknown.

---

[54] As to secondary action under the old law, see *Duport Steels Ltd v Sirs* [1980] 1 All ER 529.

[55] SI 1992 No 476. Failure to comply with the code does not render any person liable to proceedings, but it may be taken into account by a court or tribunal. See e.g. *Thomas v NUM (South Wales Area)* (note 50 above).

[56] Code of Practice on Picketing, para 51. These restrictions do not, however, prevent strikers and their supporters from attending demonstrations near rather than at the workplace: see *Gate Gourmet London Ltd v TGWU*, above (200 people demonstrating at a site some 500 metres from the workplace).

[57] [1974] AC 587. Also *Kavanagh v Hiscock* [1974] QB 600.

[58] [1974] AC 587, 603.

[59] *Hubbard v Pitt* [1976] QB 142.

[60] [1986] Ch 20.

[61] For full consideration of these questions, reference should be made to the labour law texts, e.g. Collins, Ewing and McColgan, *Labour Law: Text and Materials*; Deakin and Morris, *Labour Law*; and Smith and Thomas, *Employment Law*.

In *Middlebrook Mushrooms Ltd* v *Transport and General Workers' Union*[62] the plaintiff employers were in dispute with some of their employees who went on strike and were subsequently dismissed. The employees then organised a campaign to distribute leaflets outside supermarkets to persuade shoppers not to buy the plaintiff's mushrooms. An injunction was granted at first instance to restrain the defendants from directly interfering with the employer's contracts, but was discharged on appeal. Neither party relied on the 1992 Act and it was held that in order for the defendants' action to be tortious, the persuasion had to be directed at one of the parties to the contracts allegedly interfered with (in this case between the supermarket and the employers). Here the 'suggested influence was exerted, if at all, through the actions or the anticipated actions of third parties who were free to make up their own minds'. The leaflets were directed at customers and contained no message which was directed at the supermarket managers.

Sit-ins, squatting and forcible entry

In recent years the expression of protest has often taken the form of entry onto private land, most notably by animal rights protesters and environmental activists, the former protesting about field sports and vivisection, the latter about the building of new motorways, power stations or airports, which in the process spoil or destroy the natural or built environment. Other groups to engage in this type of activity are workers protesting about the threat of job losses, and peace campaigners anxious about nuclear weapons or the role of British troops in Afghanistan or Iraq.

1 *Criminal liability.* There is no right to enter private property for these purposes,[63] and this form of protest action may fall foul of some of the measures already discussed, although there are other provisions which may be relevant. So in *Chandler* v *DPP*,[64] an attempt by nuclear disarmers to enter and sit down outside an RAF base was held to be a conspiracy to commit a breach of the Official Secrets Act 1911, s 1(1), which makes it an offence for any purpose prejudicial to the safety of the state to approach or enter 'any prohibited place'. In *Galt* v *Philp*,[65] a sit-in at a hospital laboratory by scientific officers was held to be a breach of s 7 of the Conspiracy and Protection of Property Act 1875 (now s 241 of the Trade Union and Labour Relations (Consolidation) Act 1992).

Action of this type is also governed to some extent by the Criminal Law Act 1977, which extensively reformed the law following the recommendation of the Law Commission.[66] Part I creates a statutory offence of conspiracy, which was charged in *R* v *Jones*[67] where the accused entered an RAF base with the intent to cause criminal damage to military equipment at the time of the Iraq war. It was no defence that the events in Iraq were unlawful under international law, the court rejecting a claim to this effect based on the Criminal Damage Act 1971. Part II of the 1977 Act created various offences relating to entering and remaining on property. These include (*a*) without lawful authority, to use or threaten violence for the purpose of securing entry into any premises on which another person is present and against the will of that person (s 6); (*b*) to remain on residential premises as a trespasser after being required to leave by or on behalf of a displaced residential occupier of the premises (s 7); (*c*) without lawful authority, to have offensive weapons on premises after having entered them as a trespasser (s 8); (*d*) to enter as a trespasser any foreign embassies and other diplomatic premises (s 9); and (*e*) to resist or obstruct a sheriff or bailiff seeking to enforce a court order for possession (s 10). Additional measures directed at trespassing on

---

[62] [1993] ICR 612.

[63] *Appleby* v *United Kingdom* (2003) 37 EHRR 38 (exclusion of protestors from a shopping centre not a breach of the ECHR). See J Rowbottom [2005] EHRLR 186.

[64] [1964] AC 763. There may also be liability for breach of regulations made under the Military Lands Act 1892: *Francis* v *Cardle* 1988 SLT 578.

[65] [1984] IRLR 156. See K Miller (1984) 13 ILJ 111. For the offence under the 1992 Act, see p 534 above.

[66] HC 176 (1975–6). Cf *Kamara* v *DPP* [1974] AC 104.

[67] [2006] UKHL 16; [2007] 1 AC 136.

private land 'with the common purpose of residing there for any period' were introduced by the Public Order Act 1986.[68]

Yet further restrictions were introduced by the Criminal Justice and Public Order Act 1994. Indeed, Part V of the Act is entitled 'Public Order: Collective Trespass or Nuisance on Land', but deals with a wide range of different issues, not all of which are concerned with freedom of assembly. This part of the Act deals, for example, with people trespassing on land, 'with the common purpose of residing there for any period' (s 61),[69] gatherings on land in the open air of 20 or more persons (whether or not trespassers) at which amplified music is played during the night (so-called raves) (s 63),[70] the removal of squatters (ss 75–6) and unauthorised campers residing on land, without the consent of the occupier (s 77). The Act does, however, deal expressly with questions of freedom of assembly and public protest, not least in the provision which it makes for 'trespassory assemblies', the terms of which we have already encountered.

Otherwise s 68 deals with what are referred to as 'disruptive trespassers', the main targets being animal rights' activists who trespassed on land to disrupt fox-hunting events. But s 68 is not confined to such activity, the government declining to accept an Opposition amendment to limit its scope to country sports, on the ground that there is no reason why events such as church fêtes, public race meetings or open-air political meetings 'should suffer the invasion of others who intend to intimidate, obstruct or disrupt these proceedings'.[71] Thus it is an offence (of aggravated trespass) for any person to trespass on land to intimidate persons taking part in lawful activities or to obstruct or disrupt such activity.[72] The senior police officer present at the scene is empowered to require anyone committing or participating in aggravated trespass to leave the land in question; failure to do so is an offence.[73]

More recent concerns about demonstrations at or near royal palaces led to the introduction of a new criminal offence making it an offence to enter or be on any designated site as a trespasser.[74] A designated site is one designated by the Secretary of State and may include any Crown land, any land owned privately by the Queen or the Prince of Wales, and any land designated in the interests of national security.

2 Civil liability and injunctions. As in the case of picketing,[75] liability in civil law has an important role to play here too.

In *Department of Transport* v *Williams*,[76] an application was made for injunctions to restrain protesters from action designed to disrupt the building of the M3 extension over Twyford Down. Interim injunctions were granted by Alliott J to restrain the defendants from (i) entering upon land specified in the order, (ii) interfering with the use of the highway specified in the order, and (iii) interfering with the carrying on of work authorised by the M3 Motorway Scheme (SI 1990 No 463). In the case of the first injunctions, it was held that these could be granted on the ground of trespass, but that the second should be set aside because they added nothing to the first. The third required there to be a basis in law for holding that it was tortious to

---

[68] See *Krumpa* v *DPP* [1989] Crim LR 295.

[69] See *R (Fuller)* v *Dorset Chief Constable* [2002] EWHC Admin 1057; [2003] QB 480.

[70] As amended by the Anti-social Behaviour Act 2003, s 58.

[71] Official Report, Standing Committee B, 8 February 1994, col 614.

[72] See *Winder* v *DPP*, The Times, 14 August 1996 (Schiemann LJ); *DPP* v *Barnard*, The Times, 9 November 1999 (Laws LJ); *DPP* v *Tilly* [2002] Crim LR 128; and *McAdam* v *Urquhart* 2004 SLT 790. It is no defence to a charge under s 68 that the activities being disrupted were unlawful under international law: *R* v *Jones* [2006] UKHL 16; [2007] 1 AC 136.

[73] It is no defence to a charge under s 68 that the accused (in this case protestors against genetically modified crops who disrupted the drilling of maize) had an honest and genuine belief about the dangers of such crops: *DPP* v *Bayer* [2003] EWHC 2567 (Admin); [2004] 1 WLR 2856 (DC).

[74] Serious Organised Crime and Police Act 2005, s 128.

[75] *Hubbard* v *Pitt* [1976] QB 142 (p 534 above).

[76] The Times, 7 December 1993.

prevent or interfere with the department's carrying out of works under the authorisation in the statutory instrument. It was held that in such a case an injunction could be grounded in the tort of wrongful interference with business; the unlawful means for the purposes of establishing this was found in the Highways Act 1980, which provides by s 303 that it is an offence wilfully to obstruct any person carrying out his lawful duties under the Act.[77]

The risk of civil liability is particularly serious in view of the principle in *American Cyanamid Co v Ethicon Ltd*[78] that an interim injunction may be granted on the ground that there is a serious issue to be tried and that the balance of convenience is in favour of relief, pending the trial of the action.[79] The defendant thus need not be acting unlawfully to be restrained, it being possible and indeed likely that the balance of convenience will lie in favour of the plaintiff where disorder is threatened. On the other hand, it has been held that *American Cyanamid Co* does not deal with the situation where the granting or otherwise of the interim injunction is likely to dispose finally of the matter,[80] as in the case of a protest, the cause of which may well have passed before the matter comes to trial. In these cases, it has been held that 'the degree of likelihood the plaintiff would have succeeded in establishing his right to an injunction if the action had gone to trial, is a factor to be brought into the balance'.[81]

Applications for injunctions to restrain assemblies of various kinds are likely to encounter claims based on the Human Rights Act 1998 to the extent that the injunction will undermine the right to freedom of assembly. In these circumstances the courts are likely to give more weight to the respondent's defence than might otherwise have been the case.[82]

E. Public order offences

Riot and violent disorder

As well as the rules relating to assemblies and processions, there are several ways in which breaches of public order constitute offences. Such offences were initially developed through the common law, but following Law Commission recommendations in 1983[83] these common law offences were abolished and replaced with new offences in the Public Order Act 1986.[84]

The first of these is *riot*, defined by s 1 of the 1986 Act to apply where 12 or more persons who are present together use or threaten unlawful violence for a common purpose in circumstances where their conduct 'would cause a person of reasonable firmness present at the scene to fear for his personal safety'.[85] The scope of the offence is widened considerably, since no person of reasonable firmness need actually be present at the scene and since, unlike at common law, a riot may be committed in private as well as in a public place.[86] Although charges of riot are unusual

---

[77] See also *CIN Properties Ltd v Rawlins*, The Times, 9 February 1995; and *Phestos Shipping Co Ltd v Kurmiawan* 1983 SLT 388.

[78] [1975] AC 396.

[79] For the similar position in Scotland, see *McIntyre v Sheridan* 1993 SLT 412.

[80] *NWL Ltd v Woods* [1979] ICR 867 (a trade dispute case, where the *American Cyanamid Co* rule was modified by statute).

[81] Ibid, at 881 (Lord Diplock).

[82] See *Gate Gourmet London Ltd*, note 45 above. Where the case raises freedom of expression issues, see Human Rights Act 1998, s 12, discussed in ch 19 C above.

[83] Criminal Law: Offences Relating to Public Order (Law Commission 123).

[84] 1986 Act, Part I. For the background to the 1986 Act, see Cmnd 7891, 1980; HC 756 (1978–80); Cmnd 9510, 1985. Also Law Commission, Criminal Law: Offences Relating to Public Order (above).

[85] For the common law definition, see *Field v Metropolitan Police Receiver* [1907] 2 KB 853. At common law riot could be committed by three or more people. For a general account of the law in practice, see Vogler, *Reading the Riot Act*.

[86] Public Order Act 1986, s 1(5).

today,[87] they were brought during the miners' strike of 1984/85, although many of the prosecutions collapsed in controversial circumstances.[88]

When a riot is in progress, the police and other citizens may use such force as is reasonable in the circumstances to suppress it.[89] Anyone convicted of riot is liable to imprisonment of up to ten years or a fine, or both,[90] while anyone who suffers property damage in a riot may bring a claim for compensation against the police authority under the Riot (Damages) Act 1886.[91] Compensation has been paid for damage done by those celebrating the end of the First World War,[92] and by football fans seeking to climb into Stamford Bridge football ground to watch Chelsea play Moscow Dynamo during their famous post-war British tour.[93]

Section 2 of the Public Order Act 1986 replaces the old common law offence of unlawful assembly with an offence of *violent disorder*. The history of unlawful assembly is an important part of the history of the law of public order. After the lapse of the Seditious Meetings Act 1817, it fell to the courts to develop the definition of an unlawful assembly, upon which depended the powers of the police to control and disperse such assemblies.[94] The statutory offence clears up some of the confusion of the old law.[95] Violent disorder is committed where three or more persons who are present together use or threaten unlawful violence and their conduct (taken together) is such as would cause a person of reasonable firmness present at the scene to fear for his or her personal safety. As with riot, no person of reasonable firmness need actually be present, and the offence may be committed in private as well as in public places.

As with the old common law rules, a meeting which begins as a lawful gathering may become an unlawful assembly if disorder takes place, weapons are produced, or if language inciting an offence is used by speakers. But unlike the common law, under the statutory offence, when this transformation occurs persons present who do not share the unlawful purpose are not guilty of violent disorder. A person is guilty of violent disorder only if he or she intends to use or threaten violence or is aware that his or her conduct may be violent or threaten violence.[96] Such a person is liable on conviction on indictment to imprisonment for up to five years and on summary conviction to imprisonment for up to six months.[97] In both cases a fine may be imposed rather than or as well as imprisonment. At common law when an unlawful assembly was in progress, it was the duty of every citizen to assist in restoring order, for example by dispersing or by going to the assistance of the police.[98] Presumably the duty survives the abolition of the common law offence and its replacement with violent disorder.[99]

---

[87] Charges of mobbing and rioting were unsuccessfully brought in Scotland during the miners' strike in 1972, when strikers used force to prevent supplies of coal reaching a power station. See P Wallington (1972) 1 ILJ 219.

[88] See McCabe and Wallington, *The Police, Public Order and Civil Liberties*, p 163.

[89] Criminal Law Act 1967, s 3. The Riot Act 1714 has now been repealed, both for England and Wales, and Scotland.

[90] Public Order Act 1986, s 1(6).

[91] *Field v Metropolitan Police Receiver*, note 85 above; *Munday v Metropolitan Police Receiver* [1949] 1 All ER 337. For a detailed examination of the Act, see *Yarl's Wood Immigration Ltd v Bedfordshire Police Authority* [2009] 2 All ER 886 (Beatson J). In Scotland, compensation is payable under the Riotous Assemblies (Scotland) Act 1822, s 10 (as amended by the Local Government etc. (Scotland) Act 1994). The government drew these provisions to the attention of local residents worried about the risk of riots during the G8 summit at Gleneagles in 2005.

[92] *Ford v Metropolitan Police Receiver* [1921] 2 KB 344.

[93] *Munday v Metropolitan Police Receiver*, above.

[94] Leading cases included *R v Vincent* (1839) 9 C & P 91, and *R v Fursey* (1833) 6 C & P 80. See also Hawkins, *Pleas of the Crown*, c 63, s 9.

[95] See *R v Chief Constable of Devon and Cornwall, ex p CEGB* [1982] QB 458. See also HC 85 (1983–4), p 38.

[96] Public Order Act 1986, s 6(2). The same is true for riot, see s 6(1).

[97] Ibid, s 2(5).

[98] Charge to the Bristol Grand Jury (1832) 5 C & P 261; *R v Brown* (1841) Car & M 314. And see *Devlin v Armstrong* [1971] NILR 13.

[99] Cf *A-G for Northern Ireland's Reference (No 1 of 1975)* [1977] AC 105.

Prosecutions for unlawful assembly and violent disorder are not unknown in modern times. When serious disorder occurred at a demonstration protesting against a Greek dinner at the Garden House Hotel in Cambridge (at a time when the Greek government was unpopular in radical circles) students in the forefront of the disorder were convicted of riot and unlawful assembly.[100] In *Kamara v DPP*,[101] students from Sierra Leone occupied the Sierra Leone High Commission in London, locking the staff in a room and threatening them with an imitation gun. Their conviction for, inter alia, unlawful assembly was upheld by the House of Lords, which ruled that it was not necessary to show that an unlawful assembly had occurred in a public place. As we have seen, this ruling has been given statutory force for the purposes of violent disorder.[102]

Unlawful assembly charges were brought during the miners' strike of 1984/85, reflecting 'a specific prosecution policy intended to have a deterrent effect even before charges were proved and sentence pronounced'. However, many charges were dropped before the first hearing and, of those which did proceed, only 'a few indictments for unlawful assembly resulted in conviction'.[103] A few charges of *affray* were also brought during the strike. This ancient offence consists of unlawful fighting or a display of force by one or more persons in a public place or on private premises, involving a degree of violence calculated to terrify persons present who are of reasonably firm character.[104] The Public Order Act 1986 placed this offence on a statutory footing (s 3).[105]

Threatening, abusive and insulting behaviour

Apart from riot, violent disorder and affray, the other category of offences dealt with by the Public Order Act 1986 relates to threatening, abusive and insulting behaviour. This offence – which appears to correspond to the Scottish common law offence of breach of the peace – was originally enacted in the Public Order Act 1936, s 5. This provided that it was an offence to use threatening, abusive or insulting words or behaviour with intent to provoke a breach of the peace or whereby a breach of the peace was likely to be occasioned. If the purpose of ss 1–4 of the 1936 Act was to regulate the conduct of fascist demonstrators in the 1930s, the purpose of s 5 was, it seems, to deal with communist counter-demonstrators who would disrupt fascist rallies.

Section 5 of the 1936 Act has been replaced by ss 4 and 5 of the Public Order Act 1986. By s 4:

A person is guilty of an offence if he –
(*a*) uses towards another person threatening, abusive or insulting words or behaviour, or
(*b*) distributes or displays to another person any writing, sign or other visible representation which is threatening, abusive or insulting,
with intent to cause that person to believe that immediate unlawful violence will be used against him or another by any person, or to provoke the immediate use of unlawful violence by that person or another, or whereby that person is likely to believe that such violence will be used or it is likely that such violence will be provoked.

---

[100] *R v Caird* (1970) 54 Cr App R 499. And see *The Listener*, 8 October (S Sedley) and 26 November 1970 (A W Bradley).

[101] [1974] AC 104. For unlawful assembly during an industrial dispute, see *R v Jones* (1974) 59 Cr App R 120.

[102] Public Order Act 1986, s 2(4).

[103] McCabe and Wallington, pp 99–100.

[104] *Button v DPP* [1966] AC 591; *Taylor v DPP* [1973] AC 964.

[105] By s 3 of the 1986 Act, a person is guilty of *affray* if he uses or threatens unlawful violence towards another and his conduct is such as would cause a person of reasonable firmness present at the scene to fear for his personal safety. Where two or more persons use or threaten the unlawful violence, it is their conduct taken together that must be considered. See *I v DPP* [2001] UKHL 10; [2002] AC 285 (brandishing petrol bombs constitutes an offence; but it must be directed towards a person or persons present at the scene).

This provision of the 1986 Act was supplemented by a new s 4A inserted by the Criminal Justice and Public Order Act 1994. This provides that it is an offence for a person with intent to cause another person harassment, alarm or distress to (a) use 'threatening, abusive or insulting words or behaviour, or disorderly behaviour'; or (b) display any writing, sign or other visible representation which is threatening, abusive or insulting, thereby causing that person or another person (who need not be the intended target of the conduct) 'harassment, alarm or distress'. This complements s 5 of the 1986 Act by which it is an offence for any person to use the words or behaviour in s 4 (a) or display material referred to in s 4 (b) within the hearing of any person 'likely to be caused harassment, alarm or distress thereby'.[106]

All three offences may be committed in a public or private place, although no offence is committed in a private place where the words or behaviour are used by a person within a dwelling and the person harassed, alarmed or distressed is also inside the dwelling. It is a defence under ss 4A and 5 that the accused's conduct took place inside a dwelling and that he or she had no reason to believe that it would be seen or heard outside. It is also a defence under ss 4A and 5 that the accused's conduct was reasonable,[107] and additionally under s 5 that he or she had no reason to believe that there was any person within hearing or sight who was likely to be caused harassment, alarm or distress.[108] Moreover, a person is guilty of an offence under ss 4 and 5 only if he or she intends or is aware that the conduct is threatening, abusive, insulting or disorderly.[109]

As with s 5 of the 1936 Act, the crucial words 'threatening, abusive or insulting' are not defined.[110] Decisions under s 5 of the 1936 Act may thus be helpful in the construction of ss 4, 4A and 5 of the 1986 Act. On what is meant by insulting, the leading case is *Brutus v Cozens*.[111]

> During a Wimbledon tennis match, Brutus and other anti-apartheid protesters went on to the court, distributed leaflets and sat down. The spectators strongly resented the interruption of play. Brutus was prosecuted for using insulting behaviour whereby a breach of the peace was likely to be occasioned. The justices dismissed the charge, finding that the conduct was not insulting. On appeal by the prosecutor, the Divisional Court directed the justices that behaviour was insulting if it affronted other people and evidenced a disrespect or contempt for their rights, and thereby was likely to cause the resentment which the spectators had expressed at Wimbledon. The House of Lords unanimously allowed an appeal by Brutus against this direction, holding that 'insulting' was to be given its ordinary meaning and that the question of whether certain behaviour had been insulting was one of fact for the justices to determine. Lord Reid pointed out that s 5 of the 1936 Act did not prohibit *all* speech or conduct likely to occasion a breach of the peace. Vigorous, distasteful and unmannerly speech was not prohibited. There could be no definition of insult: 'an ordinary sensible man knows an insult when he sees or hears it.'

---

[106] The threat of violence is not a requirement of s 5 (nor indeed of s 4A), and 'a police officer can be a person who is likely to be caused harassment and so on' (*DPP v Orum* [1988] 3 All ER 449).

[107] On which see *DPP v Percy* [2002] Crim LR 835 which considers the relationship between the reasonableness defence and Convention rights, notably art 10. In that case a conviction for desecrating the American flag in the presence of American soldiers was overturned because the district judge had not given adequate weight to Convention rights. But it seems clear that had he more fully considered this defence, he could quite properly have convicted. See *Hammond v DPP* [2004] Crim LR 851.

[108] See *Morrow, Geach and Thomas v DPP* [1994] Crim LR 58 (defence not made out in a case of a protest outside an abortion clinic – 'shouting slogans, waving banners, and preventing staff and patients from entering' thereby causing distress to patients).

[109] See *DPP v Clarke* (1992) 94 Cr App R 359 (defendants displaying pictures outside an abortion clinic: even though the defendants must have been aware that pictures might cause alarm or distress, it did not follow that they intended them to be threatening, abusive or insulting or were aware that they might be so). On the other hand, it is not necessary that anyone has suffered harassment, alarm or distress: *Norwood v DPP* [2003] Crim LR 888 (poster displayed from flat window with words 'Islam out of Britain').

[110] [1973] AC 854.

[111] Ibid. Cf *Coleman v Power* (2004) 209 ALR 182 (High Ct of Australia).

It is not enough that the accused's conduct is insulting. Under the Act it must, for example in the case of s 4, be likely to provoke violence. This corresponds with the requirement in s 5 of the 1936 Act that the accused's conduct be likely to provoke a breach of the peace. In *Jordan v Burgoyne*,[112] the accused was convicted under s 5 because a speech he made in Trafalgar Square was provocative 'beyond endurance' to Jews, blacks and ex-servicemen in the crowd. It was held that the words used were insulting, and the Divisional Court rejected the interpretation of the court below that the words used by the defendant were not likely to lead ordinary, reasonable persons to commit breaches of the peace. In the view of the court the defendant must 'take his audience as he finds them, and if those words to that audience or that part of the audience are likely to provoke a breach of the peace, then the speaker is guilty of an offence'.[113] A similar conclusion would be reached under the 1986 Act.

An important issue under s 4 of the 1986 Act relates to the question of how soon after insulting conduct must the violence be likely to take place. Section 5 of the 1936 Act 'did not require that the breach of the peace which was either intended or likely to be occasioned should follow immediately upon the actions of the defendant'. The question whether such a requirement now exists was considered in *R v Horseferry Road Magistrate, ex p Siadatan*.[114]

> The applicant laid an information against Penguin Books and Mr Salman Rushdie, the publishers and author of *The Satanic Verses*, which many devout Muslims found offensive. It was alleged that the respondents had distributed copies contrary to s 4(1) of the 1986 Act on the ground that the book contained abusive and insulting writing whereby it was likely that unlawful violence would be provoked. On a strict construction of the Act, the Divisional Court held that the magistrate was correct in refusing to issue a summons. In the view of the court, the requirement in the Act that the insulted person should be 'likely to believe that such violence will be used' means that the insulted person is likely to believe that the violence will be used immediately. Watkins LJ observed: 'A consequence of construing the words "such violence" in s 4(1) as meaning "immediate unlawful violence" will be that leaders of an extremist movement who prepare pamphlets or banners to be distributed or carried in public places by adherents to that movement will not be committing any offence under s 4(1) albeit that they intend the words in the pamphlet or on the banners to be threatening, abusive and insulting and it is likely that unlawful violence will be provoked by the words in the pamphlet or on the banner.'[115]

Although s 4 of the 1986 Act thus appears to be narrower than the corresponding provisions of the 1936 Act, the police have other powers which may go some way towards closing any 'gap in the law which did not exist under the 1936 Act'.[116] These include the powers conferred by the Police Act 1996, s 89(2), which is discussed below. It is a separate offence if any of the foregoing offences under ss 4, 4A or 5 of the 1986 Act are racially or religiously aggravated,[117] a provision widely construed by the House of Lords.[118]

Other offences

1 *Obstruction of the highway.* As already pointed out, it is an offence under the Highways Act 1980, s 137 if 'a person without lawful authority or excuse in any way wilfully obstructs the free

---

[112] [1963] 2 QB 744.
[113] Ibid, at 749.
[114] [1991] 1 QB 260.
[115] Compare *DPP v Ramos* [2000] Crim LR 768.
[116] [1991] 1 QB 260, at 266.
[117] Crime and Disorder Act 1998, s 31, as amended by Anti-terrorism, Crime and Security Act 2001, s 39. On the meaning of racially or religiously aggravated: s 28, considered in *Norwood v DPP*, above, and *DPP v M* [2004] EWHC 1453 (Admin); [2004] 1 WLR 2758. Indecent or racialist chanting at designated football matches is also an offence: Football (Offences and Disorder) Act 1999, s 9.
[118] *R v Rogers* [2007] UKHL 8, [2007] 2 All ER 433.

passage along a highway'. An obstruction in this sense is caused when a meeting or assembly is held on the highway (which for this purpose includes the pavement as well as the road). It is no defence that the obstruction affected only part of the highway leaving the other part clear.[119] Nor is it a defence that the arrested person was only one of a number of people causing the obstruction,[120] or that the defendant believed that she was entitled to hold meetings at the place in question or that other meetings had been held there.[121]

The offence thus gives wide powers to the police to disperse what may be a peaceful assembly and it has been widely used. Following *DPP v Jones*,[122] however, it is now recognised that the highway may be lawfully used for some political purposes where this does not interfere with the primary purpose of the highway which is passage and repassage. Such use will provide a lawful excuse to any charge of obstruction. This is a conclusion which had been reached already in *Hirst v Chief Constable of West Yorkshire*[123] by the Divisional Court in relation to the Highways Act 1980, a decision which was expressly approved in *Jones*.

> A group of animal rights supporters were demonstrating outside a furrier's shop, and handing out leaflets. They were convicted of obstruction of the highway, contrary to the Highways Act 1980, s 137. In reversing the convictions Glidewell LJ said that the question whether someone was causing an obstruction without lawful excuse was to be answered by deciding whether the activity in which the defendant was engaged was or was not a reasonable user of the highway. This would be for the magistrates to decide, but it was clearly anticipated that the distribution of handbills could be a reasonable user.

In 2002, Westminster City Council was unable to obtain an injunction to stop an anti-war protest by a single individual (Brian Haw), who maintained a vigil over many years in Parliament Square.[124] Apart from the Highways Act 1980, obstruction of the highway is a public nuisance, which may be prosecuted as an indictable offence at common law.[125] The view of the CPS, however, is that this is an offence to be used sparingly, and not to be used where there is legislation covering the same ground (as would be the case in the event of an obstruction of the highway).[126]

2 *Protection from harassment.* Closely associated with the Public Order Act 1986, ss 4, 4A and 5 is the Protection from Harassment Act 1997, which has been said to be concerned with 'serious and persistent' forms of harassment.[127] The Act is considered briefly in this chapter because it has been used against protestors (particularly animal rights but also environmental protestors), and as a way of regulating the exercise of the right to freedom of assembly.

It is unlawful to pursue a course of conduct which amounts to the harassment of another and which the person pursuing the conduct knows or ought to know amounts to harassment (s 1(1)). This has been extended so that a person must not pursue a course of conduct which involves (*a*) knowingly harassing two or more persons, with (*b*) intent to persuade another person 'not to do something that he is entitled or required to do', or 'to do something that he is not under any obligation to do' (s 1(1A)).[128] It is a defence that the course of conduct was reasonable in the circumstances (s 1(3)).[129]

---

[119] *Homer v Cadman* (1886) 16 Cox CC 51.
[120] *Arrowsmith v Jenkins* [1963] 2 QB 561.
[121] Ibid. Cf *Cambs CC v Rust* [1972] 2 QB 426.
[122] [1999] AC 240; p 533 above.
[123] (1987) 85 Cr App R 143. See S Bailey [1987] PL 495.
[124] *The Guardian*, 5 October 2002. See now Serious Organised Crime and Police Act 2005, ss 132–8.
[125] *R v Clark (No 2)* [1964] 2 QB 315. See also *News Group Newspapers Ltd v SOGAT 82 (No 2)* [1987] ICR 181. On public nuisance and the ECHR, see *R v Rimmington* [2005] UKHL 63, [2006] 1 AC 459.
[126] CPS, Legal Guidance (2010), And see *R v Rimmington* (above).
[127] *Ferguson v British Gas* [2009] EWCA Civ 46, [2009] 3 All ER 304, at para [53] (Sedley LJ); also Fenwick, *Civil Rights*, p 162.
[128] As inserted by Serious Organised Crime and Police Act 2005, s 125. See also s 126 (similar provisions in relation to harassment of a person in his or her home).
[129] See *DPP v Selvanayagam*, *The Times*, 23 June 1999 (conduct cannot be reasonable if in breach of a court injunction).

Apart from being an offence to pursue a course of conduct in breach of ss 1 or 1(A) (s 2), civil proceedings may be brought by a victim for an injunction to restrain an unlawful course of conduct and for damages suffered as a result (s 3).[130] An injunction may also be sought where there is a breach of s 1A (s 3A), on this occasion by either the target of the harassment or the persons who are being persuaded to do or not to do something as an instrument of the harassment. It is, moreover, an offence under s 4 to engage in a course of conduct which causes another person to fear on at least two occasions that violence will be used against him or her.

Where a person has been convicted of an offence, a court may issue a restraining order against the person concerned, prohibiting the defendant from doing anything specified in the order which amounts to harassment or which will cause a fear of violence (s 5). A similar power has been introduced in relation to people who have been acquitted (s 5A). Breach of an order is an offence under the Act,[131] which has been adapted for application to Scotland (s 8).

> The scope of the powers under the 1997 Act (as amended) is illustrated by the well publicised decision in *Oxford University v Broughton*,[132] where the university obtained injunctions under the Act against a number of leading animal rights activists and animal rights organisations. The conduct of the defendants was jeopardising the completion of new laboratories where it was believed experiments would be conducted on animals. The order prohibited protestors from harassing protected persons and from entering an exclusion zone around the construction site except once a week at a time approved in the injunction. The most controversial feature of the injunction was the definition of 'protected persons'. This extended to the members and employees of the university and their families, the employees and shareholders of the contractor, as well as their families, servants or agents, and any person seeking to visit the laboratory or any premises or home belonging to or occupied by a protected person. The High Court rejected a claim that these restraints amounted to an unjustifiable restriction on Convention rights.

Additional restraints on demonstrating outside someone's home were introduced by the Criminal Justice and Police Act 2001 – as amended in 2005[133] – in response to the activities of animal rights protestors who picketed the homes of directors and employees of companies said to be engaged in vivisection.[134] Still further restraints on animal rights groups are to be found in the Serious Organised Crime and Police Act 2005, s 145. These have the effect of making it an offence to interfere with commercial relationships in a manner designed to harm animal research.

3 *Breach of the peace.* In English law there is no offence of breach of the peace, though the apprehension of a breach of the peace is important in the law of arrest (on which see ch 21), and for the exercise of police powers under the Police Act 1996, s 89(3) (on which see below).[135] The position is different in Scotland, where the long established common law offence of breach of the peace applies broadly to include the use of violent and threatening language in public, and breaches of public order and decorum.

In a leading case to which reference is still made, it was said that the offence involves conduct which 'will reasonably produce alarm in the minds of the lieges, not necessarily in the sense of

---

[130] See *Huntingdon Life Sciences Ltd v Curtin*, The Times, 11 December 1997; *Thomas v News Group Newspapers Ltd* [2002] EMLR 78; *Daiichi Pharmaceuticals UK Ltd v Stop Huntingdon Animal Cruelty* [2003] EWHC 2337 (QB); [2004] 1 WLR 1503; and *Oxford University v Broughton* [2004] EWHC 2543 (QB).

[131] See *R v Evans* [2004] EWCA Crim 3102; [2005] 1 WLR 1435.

[132] [2004] EWHC 2543 (QB).

[133] Serious Organised Crime and Police Act 2005, ss 126, 127.

[134] Criminal Justice and Police Act 2001, s 42. The same Act also permits directors of such companies not to publish their home addresses.

[135] See also *Lansbury v Riley* [1914] 3 KB 229 (power of magistrates to bind over to keep the peace when it is apprehended that someone may breach the peace; but power not exercisable unless a breach of the peace is anticipated: *Percy v DPP* [1995] 3 All ER 124 (a non-violent peace protest). This is a useful restraint to be used against those engaged in on-going and persistent campaigns.

personal fear, but alarm lest if what is going on is allowed to continue it will lead to the breaking up of the social peace'.[136] The broad nature of this offence probably explains why, on facts very similar to those in *Beatty* v *Gillbanks*, the Scottish courts convicted the local leaders of a Salvation Army procession of breach of the peace.[137] Breach of the peace is commonly used by the police in public order situations. During the miners' strike of 1984/85, of the 1,046 charges brought in Scotland, no fewer than 678 of these were for breach of the peace.[138]

Although used to deal with a wide range of anti-social behaviour, this offence may serve as a flexible and adaptable restraint on different forms of political activity and public protest. It is used not only against pickets in trade disputes, but also in response to (i) the selling of a National Front newspaper outside a football ground (Tynecastle Park),[139] (ii) the provocative conduct of participants in an Orange march,[140] (iii) the activities of environmental protestors (sitting in a tree to prevent it being felled by motorway contractors),[141] (iv) the actions of peace movement activists at the Faslane naval base,[142] and (v) a noisy demonstration in the Scottish Parliament.[143]

The incorporation of Convention rights provided an opportunity to argue before the Scottish courts that the indeterminacy of the offence of breach of the peace violates art 7 of the ECHR. But the argument failed,[144] as have other challenges to breach of the peace convictions based on arts 10 and 11 of the Convention. In *Jones* v *Carnegie*,[145] the High Court of Justiciary rejected an attempt to restrict the scope of the offence to cases where there was 'evidence of actual alarm or annoyance'. It is enough that the conduct is 'genuinely alarming and disturbing to any reasonable person'. Although the substance of the offence has been narrowed in scope in recent decisions (it is no longer enough to show that the conduct of the accused is annoying, and the offence can no longer be committed in private without any 'public' element),[146] the courts have emphasised that the test of whether a breach of the peace has taken place is an objective one and that it is not necessary to show that anyone has actually been alarmed or disturbed.[147]

F. Preventive powers of the police

Entry into meetings

In a public place like Trafalgar Square, there can be no doubt of the power of the police to be present and to deal with outbreaks of disorder if they occur. Where a public meeting is held on private premises, the power of the police to attend is less certain. At one time the official view of the Home Office was that except when the promoters of a meeting asked the police to be present in the meeting, they could not go in, unless they had reason to believe that an actual breach of the peace was being committed in the meeting.[148] This view was stated after disorder occurred at a

---

[136] *Ferguson* v *Carnochan* (1889) 2 White 278.

[137] *Deakin* v *Milne* (1882) 10 R(J) 22.

[138] McCabe and Wallington, p 164.

[139] *Alexander* v *Smith* 1984 SLT 176.

[140] *McAvoy* v *Jessop* 1989 SCCR 301.

[141] *Colhoun* v *Friel* 1996 SCCR 497.

[142] *Smith* v *Donnelly* 2001 SLT 1007; *Jones* v *Carnegie* 2004 SLT 609.

[143] *Jones* v *Carnegie*, ibid.

[144] *Smith* v *Donnelly*, above.

[145] Note 142 above. The court approved *Alexander* v *Smith*, above, and *McAvoy* v *Jessop*, above, though also said that 'peaceful protest, in which the accused did no more than hand out leaflets and hold up a banner and where that did not involve any provocation . . . would be unlikely to justify a conviction for breach of the peace' (p 616). For discussion of the wider issues, see P Ferguson (2001) 5 *Edin Law Rev* 145.

[146] See *Harris* v *H M Advocate* [2009] HCJAC 80.

[147] *Jones* v *Carnegie*, above.

[148] HC Deb, 14 June 1934, col 1968.

fascist meeting at Olympia in London, when the stewards inflicted physical violence on dissentients in the audience. No police were stationed on the premises, although large numbers had been assembled in nearby streets. Within a year, the court disapproved of the Home Office view of the law.

> In *Thomas* v *Sawkins*[149] a meeting had been advertised in a Welsh town (a) to protest against the Incitement to Disaffection Bill which was then before Parliament, and (b) to demand the dismissal of the Chief Constable of Glamorgan. The meeting was open to the public without payment, and the police arranged for some of their number to attend. The promoter requested the police officers to leave.
>
> A constable committed a technical assault on the promoter thinking that the promoter was on the point of employing force to remove a police officer from the room. There was no allegation that any criminal offence had been committed at the meeting or that any breach of the peace had occurred. When the promoter prosecuted the constable for assault, the magistrates' court found that the police had reasonable grounds for believing that if they were not present there would be seditious speeches and other incitement to violence, and that breaches of the peace would occur; that the police were entitled to enter and remain in the hall throughout the meeting; and that consequently the constable did not unlawfully assault the promoter.
>
> In the Divisional Court these findings were upheld. Lord Hewart CJ was of opinion that the police have powers to enter and to remain on private premises when they have reasonable grounds for believing that an offence is imminent or likely to be committed; nor did he limit this statement to offences involving a breach of the peace. In the opinion of Avory J, 'the justices had before them material on which they could probably hold that the police officers in question had reasonable grounds for believing that, if they were not present, seditious speeches would be made and/or that a breach of the peace would take place. To prevent any such offence or a breach of the peace the police were entitled to enter and remain on the premises.'[150]

Although the second objective of the meeting in *Thomas* v *Sawkins* was admittedly provocative to the local police, it did not suggest an incitement to violence, which was a necessary element in the offence of sedition. Nor does protest against a Bill involve a breach of the peace. It is unclear whether Lord Hewart's opinion is confined to public meetings on private premises or whether it also applies to private meetings and other activities on private premises. May the police enter any private premises if they reasonably believe that any offence is imminent or is likely to be committed? The judgments in the case gave scant consideration to the argument that as soon as the promoter asked the police to withdraw from the premises, this rescinded the open invitation given to the public (including the police) to attend. Did this not make the officers trespassers on private premises from that point onwards?[151] It may be that it is in the public interest that the police should be entitled to enter and remain in any public meeting: but why should a similar right apply to private meetings? Doubts as to the width of *Thomas* v *Sawkins* are resolved by the Police and Criminal Evidence Act 1984, which preserves the power of the police to enter premises to deal with or prevent a breach of the peace, but otherwise abolishes all common law powers of the police to enter premises without a warrant.[152]

Obstruction of the police

The statutory offence of obstructing the police in the execution of their duty has already been considered in relation to the law of arrest.[153] It is no less important in the law of public order. The

---

[149] [1935] 2 KB 249. See Ewing and Gearty, *The Struggle for Civil Liberties*, ch 6.
[150] [1935] 2 KB 249, at 256.
[151] *Davis* v *Lisle* [1936] 2 KB 434; *Robson* v *Hallett* [1967] 2 QB 939.
[152] 1984 Act, s 17(5), (6); ch 21 D.
[153] Police Act 1996, s 89(2). See ch 21 B.

leading case is *Duncan* v *Jones*[154] in 1936, which gave rise to fears about the uses to which the offence could be put.

Mrs Duncan was forbidden by Jones, a police officer, to hold a street meeting at a place opposite a training centre for the unemployed. She refused to hold the meeting in another street 175 yards away. Fourteen months previously, Mrs Duncan had held a meeting at the same spot, which had been followed by a disturbance in the centre attributed by the superintendent of the centre to the meeting. Mrs Duncan mounted a box on the highway to start the meeting but was arrested and charged with obstructing a police officer in the execution of his duty. There was no allegation of obstruction of the highway or of inciting any breach of the peace. The lower court found (a) that Mrs Duncan must have known of the probable consequences of her holding the meeting, viz, a disturbance and possibly a breach of the peace, and was not unwilling that such consequences should ensue, (b) that Jones reasonably apprehended a breach of the peace, (c) that in law it therefore became his duty to prevent the holding of the meeting, (d) that by attempting to hold the meeting Mrs Duncan obstructed Jones when in the execution of his duty. The Divisional Court upheld the conviction. Humphreys J remarked that on the facts as found, Jones reasonably apprehended a breach of the peace: it then became his duty 'to prevent anything which in his view would cause that breach of the peace'.

The decision has been strongly criticised on several grounds. First, for reasons of principle. Goodhart remarked:

At first sight it may seem unreasonable to say that a police officer cannot take steps to prevent an act which, when committed becomes a punishable offence. But it is on this distinction between prevention and punishment that freedom of speech, freedom of public meeting and freedom of the press are founded.[155]

Second, the decision gave rise to concern about the nature of the power extended to police officers. On one view, it would give a police officer power to prevent the holding of a lawful meeting if he or she suspected not that the meeting itself might be disorderly but that breaches of the peace might occur as a result of the meeting, whether committed by supporters or opponents of the speakers at the meeting. The reasoning of Humphreys J brings forward in time and widens the preventive powers of the police to a degree that could lead to intolerable restrictions on the liberty of meeting. On this basis the police could forbid a meeting in the students' union of a college from taking place merely because a 'disturbance' had previously occurred in the college after a similar meeting.

Yet despite this criticism and concern, the offence of obstructing a police officer is now an important weapon in the armoury of police powers for controlling public protest. Although *Duncan* v *Jones* illustrates the power to issue directions as to location where this is considered necessary to maintain the peace, other cases illustrate that the power may be used to issue directions as to numbers. In *Piddington* v *Bates*,[156] a police officer gave instructions that during a trade dispute at a factory in North London only two pickets would be permitted outside each entrance. When the appellant insisted on joining the pickets, despite a police officer's instructions not to do so, he was arrested for obstruction. The Divisional Court dismissed his appeal against the conviction, in which it was argued that a restriction to two pickets was arbitrary and unlawful. In the view of Lord Parker CJ, 'a police officer charged with the duty of preserving the Queen's peace must be left to take such steps as, on the evidence before him, he thinks are proper'.[157]

But apart from this wide power to give directions as to how a demonstration or picket is conducted, more recent developments indicate that the power permits the police to give directions not only to disperse a demonstration but effectively to ban or to prevent one from being held in

---

[154] [1936] 1 KB 218; Ewing and Gearty, ch 5.
[155] (1937) 6 CLJ 22, 30. See also E C S Wade (1937) 6 CLJ 175, and T C Daintith [1966] PL 248.
[156] [1960] 3 All ER 660.
[157] Ibid, at 663.

the first place. In *Moss v McLachlan*[158] the defendants were stopped at a motorway exit by police officers who suspected that they were travelling to attend a picket line at one of a number of collieries several miles away. When they refused to turn back, they were arrested for obstructing a police officer in the execution of his duty. Their appeals against conviction were dismissed, with Skinner J observing that 'The situation has to be assessed by the senior police officers present. Provided they honestly and reasonably form the opinion that there is a real risk of a breach of the peace in the sense that it is in close proximity both in place and time, then the conditions exist for reasonable preventive action including, if necessary, the measures taken in this case.'[159]

> The exercise of this power was considered by the House of Lords for the first time in *R (Laporte) v Gloucester Chief Constable*,[160] where a coach carrying demonstrators was travelling to RAF Fairford. The coach was stopped by the police some three miles short of its destination, and its occupants prevented by the police from travelling to the site of the demonstration. These steps had been taken because the police suspected that there were a number of hard-line protestors on the coach, which was returned to London along with its occupants under police escort. It was held that the action taken against the applicant Laporte was unlawful and could not be justified; there was no evidence that a breach of the peace was 'imminent', though the position may have been different if the police had intervened at a later stage in the journey, provided the evidence on the ground would have justified such intervention.[161] In the course of its decision, the House of Lords rejected the existence of a wider common law power claimed by the police that they could do whatever was reasonable to prevent a breach of the peace.[162]

Containment or 'kettling' of demonstrators

A practice of containment by the police which has emerged in recent years is sometimes referred to as 'kettling'. This involves detaining protestors in large groups for long periods of time until any risk of violence perceived to exist by the police has passed. Apart from the fact that people are being detained against their wishes in this way, there are the additional problems of people being detained for long periods of time in adverse weather conditions, in situations of great discomfort, and without access to food, medicines and other facilities. There is also the problem that passers-by with no interest in the demonstration may be unwittingly swept up in the police containment. It is unclear how long this routine has been used as a standard practice by the police, but its use as a policing tool shot to prominence during May day protests in 2001, and again at the G20 protests in the City of London eight years later. The use of the practice at the 2001 event led to legal proceedings on the part of two of those who were 'kettled', the question arising whether the police conduct could be justified as an application of the power to take steps to prevent a breach of the peace, and if so whether it violated the Convention rights of the individuals concerned.

These issues were raised in *Austin v Metropolitan Police Commissioner*,[163] where the House of Lords held that the police did not act unlawfully when on May day 2001 they detained a large number of protestors for up to seven hours in Oxford Circus, London, without sufficient toilet facilities or food and drink. In proceedings against the police for false imprisonment and violation of ECHR article 5, one applicant complained that she was refused permission to leave the scene to pick up her child, while another was refused permission to leave despite not being a protestor

---

[158] [1985] IRLR 76. See G S Morris (1983) 14 ILJ 109. Also *O'Kelly v Harvey* (1883) 15 Cox CC 435.

[159] [1985] IRLR 76, at 78. For evidence of the practice being adopted by the Scottish police (although inevitably on a different legal base, possibly breach of the peace), see Miller and Woolfson, note 49 above, at pp 220–1.

[160] [2006] UKHL 55, [2007] 2 AC 105.

[161] On which see *Albert v Lavin* [1982] AC 546.

[162] The case was said to be very different from *Moss v McLachlan* (above), a decision approved though said to have 'carried the notion of imminence to extreme limits'.

[163] [2009] UKHL 5, [2009] 3 All ER 455. (H Fenwick [2009] PL 737).

yet caught up in the police response. Following a detailed analysis of the speeches in the *Laporte* case (above), the Court of Appeal held that the conduct of the police was justified as being necessary to prevent a breach of the peace which they believed to be imminent.[164] So far as the detention of people who were not protestors is concerned, the Court of Appeal held that 'where (and only where) there is a reasonable belief that there are no other means whatsoever whereby a breach or imminent breach of the peace can be obviated, the lawful exercise by third parties of their rights may be curtailed by the police'. This was said to be 'a test of necessity' which 'can only be justified in truly extreme and exceptional circumstances', and the action taken in such circumstances 'must be both reasonably necessary and proportionate.'

The decision of the Court of Appeal was upheld by the House of Lords which considered whether the conduct of the police violated the article 5 rights of those who had been 'kettled'. But although it was noted that art 5 (on the right to liberty) is a Convention right which is not qualified in any way, it was held that there was no breach, Lord Neuberger taking the view that it was unrealistic to contend that art 5 came into play at all. This is despite the fact that in the *Laporte* case, it had been held by the Divisional Court that there had been a breach of art 5 when the police had returned to London the demonstrators they had intercepted on their way to the demonstration.[165] The demonstrators had been returned to London on the coach which had brought them, being accompanied along the M4 motorway by a full police escort, without any opportunity to stop until they had reached their destination. The decision of the House of Lords is, however, subject to a requirement that the police conduct is proportionate and reasonable, though clearly there will be scope for debate about when that boundary is reached, especially as it was held that a seven-hour detention in cold weather did not violate that standard. A more critical view of police practice was adopted by the Home Affairs Committee in the aftermath of the G20 protests in 2009, where it was said that kettling should only be used 'sparingly' and in 'clearly defined circumstances' which should be 'codified'.[166]

G. Freedom of assembly and the Human Rights Act 1998

In recent years there has been a growing recognition on the part of the courts of the importance of freedom of assembly,[167] and there have been a number of cases which have made bold claims about its value.[168] These cases reflect a significant change in judicial attitude which previously had been concerned in a rather one-dimensional way with public order to the neglect of other considerations. The developments in the English courts are reflected to some extent by developments in the European Court of Human Rights,[169] but it appears that the growing liberalisation has arisen quite independently of the Human Rights Act 1998,[170] although obviously within its shadow. It is perhaps premature to draw too many conclusions about emerging trends, especially as we continue to be reminded that 'in a democratic society the protection of public order lies at the heart of good government'.[171] But the recognition of the importance of freedom of assembly parallels the growing appreciation of freedom of expression which is to be found in some of the contemporary case law,[172] and may be explained to some extent by the willingness

---

[164] [2007] EWCA Civ 989. [2008] QB 660.
[165] [2004] EWHC 253 (Admin), [2004] All ER (D) 313.
[166] HC 418 (2008–09).
[167] On which see the valuable article by H Fenwick (1999) 62 MLR 491, esp pp 492–5.
[168] *Redmond-Bate* v *DPP* [2000] HRLR 249 and *DPP* v *Jones* [1999] 2 AC 240.
[169] *Steel* v *UK* (1998) 28 EHRR 603; *Hashman* v *UK* (1999) 30 EHRR 241.
[170] See esp *DPP* v *Jones* [1999] 2 AC 240.
[171] *R (McCann)* v *Manchester Crown Court* [2002] UKHL 39, [2003] 1 AC 787, at para [41] (Lord Hope).
[172] See ch 23.

on the part of some judges to see freedom of assembly as, in effect, an instrument of freedom of expression.[173] It is particularly significant that, in the leading case on freedom of assembly, the then Lord Chancellor should consider the 'public's rights of access to the public highway' as 'an issue of fundamental constitutional importance'.[174]

Changing judicial attitudes are demonstrated in a number of ways. In the first place, there is now a recognition that passage and repassage are not the only lawful uses of the highway. As we have seen, it was acknowledged in *DPP* v *Jones* that 'the holding of a public assembly on a highway can constitute a reasonable user of the highway and accordingly will not constitute a trespass', even if it did not follow that 'a peaceful and non-obstructive public assembly on a highway is always a reasonable user and is therefore not a trespass'.[175] This recognition at the highest level of the right of lawful assembly on the highway is accompanied by an emerging preparedness on the part of the courts to read down legislation which is being used to impose an unwarranted restraint on freedom of assembly:

> In *Huntingdon Life Sciences Ltd* v *Curtin*[176] the court allowed the British Union for the Abolition of Vivisection to be removed from an injunction (granted ex parte) to restrain three defendants from harassing the plaintiffs, a company which undertook research on animals and which had complained of a sustained and menacing campaign against it and its employees. The injunction had been issued under the Protection from Harassment Act 1997. In granting the request to vary the injunction, Eady J said that the 1997 Act 'was clearly not intended by Parliament to be used to clamp down on the discussion of matters of public interest or upon the rights of political protest and public demonstration which was so much part of our democratic tradition'. He had 'little doubt that the courts would resist any wide interpretation of the Act as and when the occasion arose' and thought it 'unfortunate that the terms in which the provisions of the Act were couched were seen to sanction any such restrictions'.[177]

There also appears to be a greater willingness on the part of at least some judges to challenge the exercise of discretion by police officers who take steps, including arrest, to disperse an assembly in order to prevent a breach of the peace. In the *Redmond-Bate* case, it was said:

> Free speech includes not only the inoffensive but the irritating, the contentious, the eccentric, the heretical, the unwelcome and the provocative provided it does not tend to provoke violence. Freedom only to speak inoffensively is not worth having.[178]

But it should not be overlooked that this last passage is from a case concerned with individuals who had been arrested for refusing to stop preaching on the steps of Wakefield Cathedral when instructed to do so by the police. The same vigorous approach to freedom of assembly has not always been adopted in other cases – such as those involving noisy anti-globalisation or angry anti-war protestors. In these cases Convention rights have yielded to other concerns, notably the need to maintain public order under common law rules created long before the enactment of the Human Rights Act 1998.[179] Together with a continuing flow of legislation restricting freedom of assembly,[180] such cases tend to suggest that the main impact of Convention rights in this area will

---

[173] For a valuable account of the link between these two different freedoms, with a full analysis of *DPP* v *Jones*, see H Fenwick and G Phillipson [2000] PL 627.

[174] *DPP* v *Jones*, note 43 above, at 251.

[175] Ibid, per Lord Hutton, at 293.

[176] *The Times*, 11 December 1997. See also *Gate Gourmet London Ltd* v *TGWU*, note 45 above. But cf *Oxford University* v *Broughton*, note 132 above.

[177] But see *DPP* v *Selvanayagam*, *The Times*, 23 June 1999.

[178] *Redmond-Bate* v *DPP*, note 168 above (Sedley LJ).

[179] *R (Laporte)* v *Chief Constable of Gloucestershire Constabulary*, note 160 above, and *Austin* v *Metropolitan Police Commissioner*, note 33 above.

[180] Such as the Serious Organised Crime and Police Act 2005.

not be to call into question the substantive law, but to constrain the manner of its exercise.[181] This means that the public authorities – local authorities and the police – will be bound to have regard to arts 10 and 11 when exercising discretionary powers, such as the power to arrest in the case of the police. The severe criticism of the policing of the G20 protests in 2009 suggests that the Act is only slowly having an effect and that there is some way to go before it can be said to have led to practical change on the ground.[182]

---

[181] For a very sober account of the practical impact of the Human Rights Act on freedom of assembly, see A Geddis [2004] PL 853.

[182] See HC 418 (2008–09). (Home Affairs Committee on the G20 protests); and see also HL 47, HC 360 (2008–09) (detailed examination of right of public protest by JCHR).

CHAPTER 25

State security and official secrets

The maintenance of the security of the state is a primary duty of the government. But in performing this duty, it is important that governments do so without trespassing on individual liberty any more than is necessary. Today state security, or more commonly national security, is mentioned in a large number of statutes which make special provision for matters relating to national security. Thus the Parliamentary Ombudsman may not investigate action with the authority of the Secretary of State for the purposes of protecting the security of the state,[1] and rights under the Data Protection Act 1998 may be excluded for the purpose of safeguarding national security.[2] The right of journalists to protect their sources may have to yield to the interests of national security,[3] as may the right of access to official information under the Freedom of Information Act 2000.[4]

Although common law may at first sight appear to take little account of state necessity,[5] national security is a matter to which the courts nevertheless attach considerable importance.[6] But this does not mean that the judges should abstain at the mere mention of national security: to do so would seriously compromise the rule of law.[7] The terrorist attacks in the United States in September 2001 appeared initially to have induced British judges to move further into the background when national security is raised.[8] But in more recent cases the House of Lords has made it clear that the 'war on terror' will not be accepted as an excuse for the discriminatory violation of Convention rights or the breach of basic common law rules prohibiting the use of evidence obtained by torture.[9]

Security and intelligence

There are three principal security and intelligence agencies operating in the United Kingdom, with overlapping responsibilities. These are the security service, the Secret Intelligence Service, and GCHQ; the Defence Intelligence Staff also has intelligence functions. Formal machinery for these agencies to bring intelligence to the attention of government is provided by the Joint Intelligence Committee, which was established in 1936 as a sub-committee of the Committee of Imperial Defence.[10] Part of the Cabinet Office since 1957, the JIC meets frequently, its main function being to provide ministers and senior officials with 'coordinated intelligence assessments on a range of issues of immediate and long term importance to national interests, primarily in the

---

[1] Parliamentary Commissioner Act 1967, Sch 3(5).

[2] See ch 22 E.

[3] Contempt of Court Act 1981, s 10; *Secretary of State for Defence* v *Guardian Newspapers Ltd* [1985] AC 339.

[4] See ch 13 F.

[5] *Entick* v *Carrington* (1765) 19 St Tr 1030.

[6] E.g. *Conway* v *Rimmer* [1968] AC 910, at 955, 993; *A-G* v *Jonathan Cape Ltd* [1976] QB 752, 768.

[7] For a powerful statement of the judicial role in national security cases, see A Barak (2002) 116 Harv L Rev 19.

[8] *Home Secretary* v *Rehman* [2001] UKHL 47; [2003] 1 AC 153. A Tomkins (2002) 118 LQR 200.

[9] *A* v *Home Secretary* [2004] UKHL 56, [2005] 2 AC 68 (ch 26 E); and *A* v *Home Secretary (No 2)* [2005] UKHL 71; [2006] 1 All ER 575 (ch 19 A). See also Lord Bingham (2003) 52 ICLQ 841, Lord Steyn (2004) 53 ICLQ 1, and Lord Hope (2004) 53 ICLQ 807. But compare *Home Secretary* v *Rehman* (note 8 above), esp per Lord Hoffmann.

[10] Lord Butler (Chair), Review of Intelligence on Weapons of Mass Destruction: Report of a Committee of Privy Counsellors, HC 898 (2003–04), para 41.

fields of security, defence and foreign affairs'.[11] As well as the intelligence agencies (the 'producers'), the Committee includes various intelligence 'users', notably the Ministry of Defence and the Foreign Office, the Treasury, the Department of Business, Innovation and Skills, and the Home Office. Other departments may also attend when relevant, as also may representatives of the intelligence agencies of the United States, Canada and Australia. The JIC is a committee of officials whose chairman is responsible for supervising its work and for ensuring that its 'warning and monitoring role is discharged effectively'.[12] According to the Butler Committee in 2004,

> The JIC thus brings together in regular meetings the most senior people responsible for intelligence collection, for intelligence assessment and for the use of intelligence in the main departments for which it is collected, in order to construct and issue assessments on the subjects of greatest current concern. The process is robust, and the assessments that result are respected and used at all levels of government.[13]

The collection of this information at home and abroad gives rise to serious questions about effective political accountability for security measures. There has, however, been in recent years a welcome lifting of the veil of secrecy which has for so long surrounded the security and intelligence services. This is reflected in part by the open discussion of the JIC and its intelligence assessments in the Butler inquiry, appointed in 2004 to investigate the intelligence coverage available in respect of weapons of mass destruction. It is reflected more notably in the greater role of legislation in regulating the affairs of the security services, and in particular by the extension of the principle of judicial oversight and with it the publication of annual reports by the judicial commissioners. It is reflected further in the slightly greater degree of openness and accountability in terms of the financing of the security and intelligence services. Although there is still some way to go,[14] since 1994 the government has brought forward in a single published vote the aggregate expenditure of all three agencies, this being 'fully open to scrutiny by the Comptroller and Auditor-General, apart from limited restrictions to protect the identities of certain sources of information and the details of particularly sensitive operations'.[15]

Many of the reforms which have taken place in recent years have been driven by the European Convention on Human Rights and, more recently, by the requirements thought likely to arise under the Human Rights Act 1998. As we have seen,[16] many of the provisions of the Convention allow for exceptions and these generally include national security, provided that the restriction can be shown to be prescribed by law and necessary in a democratic society. This is true, for example, of arts 8, 9, 10 and 11. One of the difficulties with the procedures and practices operating in this country was their relative informality and the lack of clear legal rules setting out the functions and powers of the security and intelligence services.[17] So to the extent that the activities of the security services violate the private life of the individual, it could not be said until recently

---

[11] Ibid, para 43.

[12] http://www.cabinetoffice.gov.uk/security_and_intelligence/community/central_intelligence_machinery/joint_intelligence_committee.aspx.

[13] Butler, above, para 43.

[14] For a stark example of the lack of transparency in the existing arrangements, see the heavily redacted report of the Intelligence and Security Committee, Cm 6510, 2005.

[15] HC Deb, 24 November 1993, col 52 (WA). In the Appropriation (No 2) Act 2005, £489,312,000 was voted from the Consolidated Fund to the security and intelligence services for 2005–06; and in the Appropriation (No 3) Act 2005, a further £646,646,000 was voted. By the time of the Appropriation (No 2) Act 2009, the resources allocated to the security and intelligence services for administration and operations had risen to £1,857,861,000. This will rise to £2,354 million in 2010–11 (Cm 7844, 2010, para 16). The government will not say how this budget is allocated to the different services.

[16] See ch 19.

[17] *Malone* v *UK* (1984) 7 EHRR 14; *Hewitt and Harman* v *UK* (1992) 14 EHRR 657; and *Khan* v *UK* (2001) 31 EHRR 1016.

that the restrictions were prescribed by law. But, of course, it is not enough that there should be legal authority for such restrictions. Also important is the nature and quality of the law: to satisfy the Convention any restriction on Convention rights must be proportionate to the objective which it is sought to be achieved, and this is as true of national security as it is of the other grounds for limiting convention rights.

The security service

The security service was created in the War Office in 1909 to deal with the fears about German espionage in the period immediately before the First World War. The unit was called MO5, and later MI5. In 1935, MI5 was amalgamated with the section of the Metropolitan Police dealing with counter-subversion and in that year it changed its name to the security service.[18] The domestic security service is, however, still referred to as MI5. A remarkable feature of these developments is that they took place without statutory authority. The service was set up by executive decision (presumably under the royal prerogative) with functions determined by the executive and accountable only to the executive. In his report on the security service following the Profumo scandal in 1963, Lord Denning wrote:

> The Security Service in this country is not established by Statute nor is it recognised by Common Law. Even the Official Secrets Acts do not acknowledge its existence. The members of the Service are, in the eye of the law, ordinary citizens with no powers greater than anyone else. They have no special powers of arrest such as the police have. No special powers of search are given to them. They cannot enter premises without the consent of the householder, even though they may suspect a spy is there. If a spy is fleeing the country, they cannot tap him on the shoulder and say he is not to go. They have, in short, no executive powers. They have managed very well without them. We would rather have it so, than have anything in the nature of a 'secret police'.[19]

According to Lord Denning, this absence of legal powers was made up for by the close cooperation between the security service and the police, particularly the Special Branch.[20] The security service would make all the initial investigations relying on its technical resources and specialised field force. But as soon as an arrest was possible, the police were called into consultation and from that point onwards both forces worked as a team. Because of the lack of executive power of the security service, an arrest would be made by the police and if a search warrant were sought, this too would be done by the police.[21]

Before the Security Service Act 1989 (on which see below), the operation of the service was governed by a directive issued by the Home Secretary in 1952 (Sir David Maxwell Fyffe) to the Director General.[22] This provided that, although the security service was not a part of the Home Office, the Director General would be responsible to the Home Secretary personally, with a right on appropriate occasions of direct access to the Prime Minister. The directive also stated that the service 'is part of the Defence Forces of the country', and that 'its task is the Defence of the Realm as a whole, from external and internal dangers arising from attempts at espionage and sabotage, or from actions of persons and organisations whether directed from within or without the country, which may be judged to be subversive of the State'. The work of the service was to be strictly limited to what is necessary for these purposes and was expressly required to be kept absolutely free from any political bias or influence. Questions of the political responsibilities of the service

---

[18] For a full account of its origins from non-official histories, see Andrew, *Secret Service*. See also West, *MI5: British Security Service Operations 1909–45*; and *A Matter of Trust: MI5, 1945–72*. For further analyses, see Ewing and Gearty, *The Struggle for Civil Liberties*, ch 2; Gill, *Policing Politics*; Lustgarten and Leigh, *In from the Cold*; Williams, *Not in the Public Interest*, part 2; and Bunyan, *The Political Police in Britain*, chs 3, 4.

[19] Cmnd 2152, 1963.

[20] See p 562 below.

[21] Cmnd 2152, 1963, para 273.

[22] Reproduced in *R v Home Secretary, ex p Hosenball* [1977] 3 All ER 452 in the judgment of Lord Denning MR.

were clarified by Lord Denning in his 1963 report.[23] Although the function of the service is the defence of the realm, political responsibility did not (and does not) lie with the Secretary of State for Defence, but with the Home Secretary and the Prime Minister, who is advised on security matters by the Cabinet Secretary.[24] However, it has been an open question for many years just what degree of political responsibility has existed, particularly in view of the convention that ministers 'do not concern themselves with the detailed information which may be obtained by the Security Services in particular cases, but are furnished with such information only as may be necessary for the determination of any issue on which guidance is sought'.[25]

Since 1989 the work of the service has changed in response to the new and evolving international position, and the so-called 'war on terror' in particular. During the Cold War the service was concerned to a large extent with counter-subversion and counter-espionage. So far as the former is concerned, it was reported in 1995 that the threat from subversive organisations had decreased to the point where it was assessed as being 'low'. The Communist Party of Great Britain (CPGB) no longer existed, while the main surviving organisation (the Communist Party of Britain) was assessed to be only about 1,100 strong, compared to 25,000–30,000 in the CPGB in the 1970s and 56,000 at its peak in 1942.[26] According to the Security Commission, it had been agreed inter-departmentally that the investigation of subversive organisations should be reduced,[27] and in 1992 the service assumed a new responsibility in the form of 'Irish republican terrorism', which was transferred from the Special Branch. Although this step seems clearly to have been inspired by the need to fill the gap in the work of the service caused by the end of the Cold War, it was explained in Parliament that the service already had responsibility for Irish loyalist and international terrorism and for Irish republican terrorism overseas.[28] Indeed, it was only the accident of history which had given the police the leading responsibility for Irish republican terrorism, a decision which had been taken in 1883 when the Special Irish Branch was formed to track down Fenians who at the time were placing bombs in London. The security service is now greatly concerned with international terrorism, though it also continues to be troubled by the risk of Northern Irish terrorist activity (mainly by dissident groups). Otherwise espionage from Russian and Chinese agents continues to be a concern, with the security service reporting that the number of Russian agents has not fallen since the Soviet days.

The Secret Intelligence Service, GCHQ and the Defence Intelligence Staff

The existence of the Secret Intelligence Service (SIS or MI6 as it is more commonly known) was first officially acknowledged in May 1992, although it was founded in 1909, albeit not in its modern form. Despite the ending of the Cold War, the government is nevertheless of the view that there is a role for the security and intelligence services 'alongside the armed services and diplomatic services in protecting and furthering the interests of Britain and its citizens at home and abroad'.[29] The threats which are said to make the continued existence of these agencies necessary 'include nuclear, chemical, biological and conventional proliferation of weapons', as well as 'terrorism and the threat to our armed forces in times of conflict, serious crime, espionage and sabotage'.[30] According to the SIS website,[31] the Service collects intelligence subject to requirements and priorities established by the JIC and approved by ministers. It uses 'human and technical' sources for these purposes, and works with a wide range of foreign intelligence and security

---

[23] See also Wilson, *The Labour Government 1964–70*, p 481.
[24] Cmnd 2152, 1963, para 238.
[25] Ibid.
[26] Pelling, *The British Communist Party*, p 192.
[27] Cm 2930, 1995.
[28] HC Deb, 8 May 1992, cols 297–306.
[29] HC Deb, 22 February 1994, col 155 (Mr Douglas Hurd).
[30] Ibid (giving examples of the work of MI6 in the contemporary world).
[31] http://www.sis.gov.uk/output/what-we-do.html.

services, as well as other British agencies such as GCHQ, the security service (MI5), the armed forces, the Foreign Office, the Home Office, the Ministry of Defence, and HM Revenue and Customs. The service gathers intelligence and operates overseas, though based in London.

Although it had been operating at least since 1947, Government Communications' Headquarters (GCHQ) was not publicly acknowledged to exist until the trial of Geoffrey Prime, an official who was convicted under s 1 of the Official Secrets Act 1911 in 1982 for passing information to the Soviet Union. This was followed by a report of the Security Commission which not only revealed the existence of the centre but also gave an account of the security procedures in operation there, including those for physical and document security.[32] It came more prominently to the fore in 1984 when controversially the government announced a trade union ban,[33] one irony of which is that as a result GCHQ 'has become as well known in political circles as MI5 and MI6'.[34] Officially, the centre 'provides government with information' to 'support policy-making and operations in the fields of national security, military operations, law enforcement and economic well being'. The intelligence is said to lie 'at the heart of the struggle against terrorism', and contributes to the prevention and detection of serious crime. GCHQ also 'supplies crucial intelligence to the UK armed forces, wherever they may be deployed'.[35] The Director of GCHQ, like the Chief of SIS, is personally responsible to the Foreign Secretary, subject to the overall responsibility of the Prime Minister for security and intelligence matters. Both GCHQ and SIS have been placed on a statutory footing by the Intelligence Services Act 1994 (on which see below).

Established in 1964, the Defence Intelligence Staff is run by the Chief of Defence Intelligence. The work of DIS includes intelligence collection, and like the other agencies it contributes to the work of the JIC.[36] An 'integral part' of the Ministry of Defence,[37] DIS provides intelligence for the armed forces and other government departments, and analyses information from a wide variety of sources, both overt and covert. The Chief of Defence Intelligence is responsible to the Secretary of State for Defence, subject to the overall responsibility of the Prime Minister, and both the secretary of state and members of the Defence Intelligence Staff are subject to a degree of statutory supervision and accountability in the manner in which at least some of their powers are exercised. Under the Regulation of Investigatory Powers Act 2000, the DIS may apply for an interception warrant and the DIS may use the various forms of surveillance authorised by that Act.[38] But the DIS does not fall within the definition of the intelligence services in the Act (which is confined to the security service, the Secret Intelligence Service and GCHQ). Nor is the DIS the only part of the Ministry of Defence intelligence activity, which includes 'intelligence elements throughout the armed forces and within the single Service Commands'.[39] It is funded from the Defence Votes.[40]

The Security Service Act 1989[41]

The security service is now governed to some extent by the Security Service Act 1989.[42] In providing for the continuation of the service, the Act defines its function to be 'the protection of

---

[32] Cmnd 8876, 1983.

[33] See p 564 below.

[34] Official Report, Standing Committee E, 15 March 1994, col 115.

[35] http://www.sis.gov.uk/output/what-we-do.html.

[36] See also HC 115 (1995–6) (Scott Report), para C 2.26.

[37] http://www.mod.uk/DefenceInternet/AboutDefence/WhatWeDo/SecurityandIntelligence/DIS.

[38] Regulation of Investigatory Powers Act 2000, s 6, 41.

[39] Statement on the Defence Estimates 1994, Cm 2550, 1994, p 41.

[40] See now http://www.cabinetoffice.gov.uk/security_and_intelligence/community/agencies/defence_intelligence_staff.aspx.

[41] See I Leigh and L Lustgarten (1989) 52 MLR 801; also Ewing and Gearty, *Freedom under Thatcher*, pp 175–88.

[42] For arrangements in other countries, see S Farson [1992] PL 377 (Canada), and Lee, Hanks and Morabito, *In the Name of National Security* (Australia). See also Lustgarten and Leigh, note 18 above, which is strong on Australian and Canadian developments.

national security and, in particular, its protection against threats from espionage, terrorism and sabotage, from the activities of agents of foreign powers and from actions intended to overthrow or undermine parliamentary democracy by political, industrial or violent means' (s 1(2)). The term 'national security' is not defined, although it has been said to be wider than the particular heads specified in the Act.[43] The service also has the task of safeguarding the economic well-being of the country against threats posed by the actions or intentions of persons outside the United Kingdom (s 1(3)). By an amendment to the 1989 Act introduced by the Security Service Act 1996, it is also the function of the service to act in support of the activities of police forces and other law enforcement agencies in the prevention and detection of serious crime. According to the government, this last provision reflects 'the firm intention' that the service 'should be deployed against organised crime' and that the 'drug traffickers, the money launderers and the racketeers' are to become the service's new targets. The role of the service is to be 'a supporting one' in this capacity, the legislation reflecting fully 'the principle that the public and the law enforcement agencies will retain the primary responsibility'.[44] Nevertheless, these provisions were extremely controversial and gave rise to concern in Parliament and elsewhere. There is no definition of 'serious crime' and no guarantee that the work of the service will be confined to organised crime, the search for a definition of which was dismissed, as it would 'distract us from our task', and could create 'loopholes that could be exploited by unscrupulous defence lawyers to challenge the legality of the security service's involvement in a case'.[45] Admittedly, the executive powers of the service are restricted by a definition of serious crime which restrains the circumstances in which a warrant may be issued to interfere with property, but even this is extremely wide, as was pointed out during the committee stage in the House of Lords.[46] Apart from the absence of effective legal boundaries, concerns were also expressed about the lack of accountability of the service when performing its function in assisting the police: there will be no accountability to local police authorities and no supervision by the Independent Police Complaints Commission.[47]

In exercising these wide powers, the service continues to be under the operational control of the Director General, who is appointed by the Home Secretary (s 2(4)). The duties of the Director General, who must make an annual report to the Prime Minister and the Home Secretary (s 2), include taking steps to ensure that the service does not take any action to further the interests of any political party (s 2(2)(b)). This is narrower than the rule contained in the Maxwell Fyffe directive which required the service to be kept free from 'any political bias or influence', a rule which allegedly did not prevent the surveillance of the Campaign for Nuclear Disarmament or trade unions involved in pay disputes.[48] The 1989 Act also conferred a new power on the service. This was the power to apply to the Home Secretary for a warrant authorising 'entry on or interference with property' (s 3).[49] Hitherto there was no power to grant any warrant, but it appears that the service may not have been unduly impeded in the absence of such a power. Indeed, in *Attorney-General v Guardian Newspapers (No 2)* Lord Donaldson MR appeared willing to turn a blind eye to

[43] Cm 1480, 1991. Although not 'easily defined', it 'includes the defence of the realm and the government's defence and foreign policies involving the protection of vital national interests at home and abroad'. What is a vital national interest is 'a question of fact and degree', more 'easily recognised when being considered than defined in advance'.

[44] HL Deb, 14 May 1996, cols 398–9 (Baroness Blatch). The meaning of detection for these purposes is widely defined: s 1(5), as inserted by the Regulation of Investigatory Powers Act 2000, s 82(1).

[45] HL Deb, 14 May 1996, cols 398–9 (Baroness Blatch).

[46] HL Deb, 10 June 1996, col 1495 (Lord Williams of Mostyn).

[47] This point is considered in some detail at HL Deb, 10 June 1996, cols 1500–20. For a particularly powerful critique, see the *The Guardian*, 10 June 1996 (editorial).

[48] Allegations to this effect were made by a retired MI5 officer, Cathy Massiter, in a Channel 4 television programme. For the unsuccessful challenge to the legality of this activity, see *R v Home Secretary, ex p Ruddock* [1987] 2 All ER 518.

[49] On the way this power is exercised, see Cm 1480, 1991, para 3.

the unauthorised entry of private property by the security services, referring to it as a 'covert invasion of privacy' which might be considered excusable in the defence of the realm.[50] Section 3 was replaced by ss 5 and 6 of the Intelligence Services Act 1994 (on which see below).[51]

The 1989 Act is significant also for having introduced new procedures for the supervision of the service. These are modelled on procedures introduced in the Interception of Communications Act 1985, which were discussed in chapter 22. The 1989 Act made provision for the appointment of a Security Service Commissioner, being someone who holds or has held high judicial office (s 4); and also a Security Service Tribunal to hear complaints against the service (s 5). The Commissioner was required to keep under review the power of the Home Secretary to issue warrants to the service. The office of Commissioner was held from its inception by Lord Justice Stuart-Smith. But unlike the Commissioner appointed under the Interception of Communications Act 1985, the Security Service Commissioner did not provide details of the number of warrants issued under s 3 in any one year, explaining that this was because of the 'comparatively small number of warrants issued under the 1989 Act and the fact that the purpose for which they can be granted is more restricted than under the 1985 Act'.[52] The practice of the Commissioner was to review all the warrants issued, reviewed and cancelled,[53] and in some cases the products obtained by the operation.[54] He always found the procedures in good order and warrants to have been properly issued. An exception was in 1999 when in one case an application was said to be 'thin and lacking in particularity'. After interviewing the responsible officers, he was able to conclude that the application had been properly made and the officers in question were asked to make a supplementary written statement to the Secretary of State to clarify the position. Notwithstanding this apparent irregularity, the Commissioner was nevertheless able to report that the 'Secretaries of State have been properly advised' and that they 'have exercised their powers under the Act correctly'.[55]

The office of Security Service Commissioner was abolished by the Regulation of Investigatory Powers Act 2000, with a new Intelligence Services Commissioner now having oversight for all the intelligence services (including in some cases those attached to the Ministry of Defence).[56] The Intelligence Services Commissioner is required to keep under review the way in which both ministers and members of the intelligence services exercise their powers under Parts II and III of the Regulation of Investigatory Powers Act 2000, in so far as these powers relate to the intelligence services. These include powers connected with surveillance. In addition to oversight by the Commissioner (who must report annually to the Prime Minister), the Regulation of Investigatory Powers Act 2000 provides that the investigatory powers tribunal established by s 65 of the Act may hear complaints against any of the intelligence services,[57] this replacing the jurisdiction of the tribunal created by the 1989 Act. The investigatory powers tribunal is the appropriate forum for dealing with such complaints concerned with conduct by the intelligence services which relates to the complainant, his or her property, or his or her communications. This means that the tribunal is not confined to bugging or telephone tapping, but could conceivably cover all forms of conduct targeted at an individual, including security vetting. In the unlikely event of a complaint

---

[50] [1990] AC 109, at 190. Cf *Entick* v *Carrington* (1765) 19 St Tr 1030.

[51] See Cm 3253, 1996.

[52] Cm 1480, 1991. And see Cm 3253, 1996.

[53] Cm 4002, 1998, para 5; Cm 4365, 1999, para 7; and Cm 4779, 2000, para 15.

[54] Cm 4365, 1999, para 7.

[55] Cm 4779, 2000, paras 16 and 17.

[56] Regulation of Investigatory Powers Act 2000, s 59(2).

[57] On the jurisdiction of the tribunal, see *A* v *B* [2009] UKSC 12. A total of 338 complaints were made to the 1989 Act tribunal between 1989 and 1999: Cm 4779, 2000, para 37. In 42 of these cases it appears that the complainant was the subject of a personal file kept by the security service.

being upheld (and only three ever have been),[58] the tribunal may make an award of compensation or other order as it thinks fit, including the cancelling of any warrant or authorisation and the destruction of any records held about the complainant.[59] The Secretary of State is empowered to make regulations providing for an appeal from a tribunal's decision.

The Intelligence Services Act 1994

So far as the Secret Intelligence Service is concerned, its activities are governed by the Intelligence Services Act 1994, which also applies to GCHQ. The functions of SIS are stated by s 1(1) to be (*a*) the obtaining and providing of information relating to the actions or intentions of persons outside the British Islands, and (*b*) the performing of 'other tasks relating to the actions or intentions of such persons'. These extraordinarily wide provisions are constrained by s 1(2) which provides that the statutory functions are exercisable only (*a*) in the interests of national security (with 'particular reference to the defence and foreign policies of Her Majesty's Government'), (*b*) in the interests of the economic well-being of the United Kingdom, or (*c*) in support of the prevention or detection of serious crime.[60] The 'interests of national security' are not otherwise defined, nor (more surprisingly) is what constitutes 'serious crime'.[61] And although 'a well-worn provision', it was acknowledged that a power to take action 'in the interests of the economic well-being' of the UK 'sometimes causes puzzlement as to what it can mean'.[62] It was explained, however, that the power 'might be useful' where 'substantial British economic interests were at stake or where there was a crisis or a huge difficulty about the continued supply of a commodity on which our economy depended'.[63] Under the Act the agencies are not permitted to become involved in domestic economic, commercial or financial affairs, although they may acquire information that has a bearing on domestic issues.[64]

The Act also places GCHQ on a statutory footing, under the authority of the Foreign Secretary. By virtue of s 3, its functions are twofold: the first being 'to monitor or interfere with electromagnetic, acoustic and other emissions and any equipment producing such emissions' (and 'to obtain and provide information derived from or related to such emissions or equipment'). The second duty is to provide advice and assistance about language and cryptology to the armed forces, government departments or any other organisation approved by the Prime Minister. As in the case of SIS these functions are exercisable only in the interests of national security (with particular reference to the defence and foreign policies of the government); or the interests of the economic well-being of the United Kingdom 'in relation to the actions or intentions of persons outside the British Islands; or in support of the prevention and detection of serious crime'. These measures were strongly criticised in standing committee as providing a mandate which is 'wide

---

[58] HC 902 (2008–09), SG / 2009/139, para 46. According to the Commissioner, the Investigatory Powers Tribunal Rules 2000 prohibit him on the grounds of confidentiality from disclosing specific details about these complaints, though he did say rather elliptically that 'the conduct complained of was not authorised in accordance with the relevant provisions of RIPA nor was it a complaint against any of the agencies or persons whose conduct [he had] been responsible for reviewing' (ibid).

[59] In two of the three cases referred to above (both decided in 2008), the Commissioner reported that in the first case 'the Tribunal ordered payment of an award of compensation to the complainant, [but] the respondents were not required to destroy the relevant records'. In the second case, 'no award of compensation was made but the respondents were ordered to destroy the evidence of the unauthorised conduct' (ibid).

[60] The meaning of detection and prevention for these purposes is widely defined: s 11(1A), as inserted by the Regulation of Investigatory Powers Act 2000, s 82.

[61] See Cm 3288, 1996, para 8.

[62] HC Deb, 22 February 1994, col 157 (Mr Hurd).

[63] Ibid.

[64] See HC 115 (1995–6) (Scott Report).

and sweeping', inadequately constrained by the 'partial stricture' that it be exercised in the interests of national security.[65] It was pointed out in reply, however, that there were a number of safeguards in the Act to prevent the abuse of power (according to the minister there were 11 in total). So far as the duty of GCHQ to assist in the prevention and detection of crime is concerned, this was said not to be new, but had been going on for 'decades'. It appears that GCHQ intervenes when criminals use 'sophisticated communications devices to commit a crime' and assists in the deciphering of diaries and notebooks kept by criminals in sophisticated codes.[66]

The Act authorises 'entry on or interference with property or with wireless telegraphy' by each of the three security and intelligence agencies, provided that any such action is taken with the authority of a warrant issued by the Secretary of State (or in some cases the Scottish Ministers);[67] otherwise the action is 'unlawful', although unlike the unauthorised interception of communications it is not an offence. A warrant may be issued only if the Secretary of State 'thinks it necessary' for the purpose of assisting the agency making the application in carrying out any of its functions, provided that the taking of the action is proportionate to what the action seeks to achieve (s 5). A warrant issued on the application of either the SIS or GCHQ may not relate to British property, unlike warrants issued to the security service which may be issued for two such purposes. The first relates to the traditional functions of the service, as defined in s 1(2) and (3) of the Security Service Act 1989, in which case it may relate to property in Britain, without further qualification. The second relates to the function of the service added by the Security Service Act 1996, namely to act in support of the police and law enforcement agencies in the prevention and detection of serious crime. In this case the warrant may authorise action in respect of property in Britain, but only if the action is to be taken in relation to offences that involve violence, result in substantial financial gain, or constitute conduct by a large number of persons in pursuit of a common purpose, or if the offence is one which carries a term of three years' imprisonment on conviction for the first time.[68] Warrants are normally to be issued by a Secretary of State (or in some cases a member of the Scottish Executive)[69] and are valid for up to six months, although they may (but need not) be cancelled before the period of six months expires (s 6).

Apart from the power to interfere with property (albeit with the authority of a warrant), the 1994 Act also contains a remarkable power for the Secretary of State to authorise a person to commit an act 'outside the British Islands' which would be unlawful 'under the criminal or civil law of any part of the United Kingdom' (s 7). The effect of an authorisation under this so-called 'James Bond clause'[70] is to give the individual committing an offence (or other unlawful act) immunity from legal liability in this country (but not in the country in which the crime or unlawful act may be committed), although authorisation should only be given where the acts to be done by the authorisation are 'necessary for the proper discharge of a function of the Intelligence Service or GCHQ'. Understandably, these powers gave rise to some concern in Parliament, with one Opposition member pointing out that they grant 'the Secretary of State complete power to authorise activities that violate the law of other states as well as that of the United Kingdom. There is no limit on what can be authorised. In extreme cases the use of lethal force will be allowed.'[71] Ministers were, however, rather coy about the way in which these powers would be used, and appeared to think it enough to reassure the House that 'certain actions can be undertaken by

---

[65] Official Report, Standing Committee E, 15 March 1994, col 117.

[66] Ibid, col 132.

[67] See SI 1999 No 1750.

[68] 1994 Act, s 5, as amended by Security Service Act 1996.

[69] SI 1999 No 1750.

[70] HL Paper 152, HC 230 (2008–09), para 53. The government will not reveal the number of occasions on which this power has been used.

[71] Official Report, Standing Committee E, 17 March 1994, col 174.

the agencies under the specific authority of ministers only,'[72] and were unwilling to contemplate even an obligation to report annually to the Intelligence and Security Committee (on which see below) on the number and general description of all acts authorised under this section, on the ground that provision was made for the appointment of a judicial commissioner to ensure that the ministers' powers were exercised properly.[73]

Political responsibility for the agencies was said to be 'primarily' that of the Foreign Secretary 'under the Prime Minister'.[74] Under the Act, however, the operations of the SIS continue to be under the control of the Chief of the Intelligence Service (s 2), while the operations of GCHQ continue to be under the control of its Director (s 4). Each is responsible for ensuring the efficiency of the respective services, and that no information is obtained by their organisations except so far as is necessary for the proper discharge of their functions. They must also ensure that information is not disclosed by their organisations except 'so far as necessary' for the proper discharge of their functions, and that the respective agencies do not take 'any action to further the interests of any United Kingdom political party' (ss 2(2)(b), 4(2)(b)). By a strange quirk of drafting (although it may not be unintended) either service may disclose information even though it is not necessary for it to do so in 'the proper discharge of its functions'. Thus the SIS may disclose material (without violating the duty of the Chief of the Intelligence Service) on the additional (but not necessarily consequential) ground that it is in the interests of national security, for the prevention or detection of serious crime, or for the purpose of any criminal proceedings (s 2(2)(a)). GCHQ may disclose information falling into the last of these three categories, even though, again, disclosure is not necessary for the proper discharge of its functions, a much narrower incidental power than that possessed by SIS. Both the Chief of Intelligence Service and the Director of GCHQ are required to make an annual report to the Prime Minister and the Foreign Secretary, and they may report to either 'at any time' on any matter relating to the work of their respective services (ss 2(4) and 4(4)).

Following the precedents established in 1985 and 1989, the 1994 Act made provision for the creation of an Intelligence Services Commissioner (appointed by the Prime Minister and being a person who holds or has held high judicial office) and a tribunal for the investigation of complaints about the SIS or GCHQ. The decisions of both the Commissioner and the tribunal (including decisions as to jurisdiction) were not subject to appeal and were not liable to be questioned in any court of law. The jurisdictions of the Intelligence Services Commissioner and the Security Service Commissioner were merged by the Regulation of Investigatory Powers Act 2000, and the jurisdiction of the security and intelligence tribunal was transferred to the investigatory powers tribunal. From 2000 to 2006, the office of Intelligence Services Commissioner was held by Lord Brown of Eaton-under-Heywood (a Lord of Appeal in Ordinary since 2004) who as Simon Brown LJ was the first President of the tribunal appointed under the 1994 Act above. Lord Brown was replaced as Commissioner by Sir Peter Gibson, a retired member of the Court of Appeal, who like his predecessor appears generally to have been satisfied with the operation of the procedures under the Act.[75] In common with his predecessor, however, Sir Peter Gibson is unwilling to reveal how many warrants are issued or authorisations granted under the 1994 Act. So far as complaints to the investigatory powers tribunal are concerned, the nature of its jurisdiction is such that it is not possible to say precisely how many complaints are made specifically in relation to the security and intelligence services. However, no fewer than 799 complaints were made to the tribunal between its creation in 2000 and the end of 2008 in relation to all of its jurisdictions. As we have seen, the

---

[72] HC Deb, 22 February 1994, col 160.

[73] Official Report, Standing Committee E, 17 March 1994, col 175.

[74] HC Deb, 22 February 1994, col 154.

[75] HC 902 (2008–09), SG/2009/139, para 31. The Commissioners have, however, drawn attention to a number of 'errors' where no valid warrant or authorisation had been issued in relation to covert activity. In 2008, for example, there were 18 such cases: ibid, 47.

tribunal upheld only three of these complaints, though we are not permitted to know the reasons why.[76]

Special Branch and Counter-Terrorism Command[77]

Another agency engaged in work related to state security has emerged from what was previously the police Special Branch, which as we have seen was formed in 1883 in response to a Fenian bombing campaign in London. After three years the word 'Irish' was dropped from the Branch's title and it was expanded to deal with other security problems. After 1945 provincial police forces established their own permanent Special Branch, 'primarily to acquire intelligence, to assess its potential operational value, and to contribute more generally to its interpretation'.[78] In this way the Special Branch assists both the security service and the Secret Intelligence Service in carrying out their statutory duties. Home Office guidelines emphasised that the acquisition of high-grade intelligence is vital to the work of the Special Branch and explained the different ways by which intelligence is gathered: 'the handling of covert human intelligence sources, intelligence gathering, field enquiries, intelligence passed on from other parts of the police service, and surveillance by conventional and technical means'.[79] Although terrorism is the 'key priority' for the Special Branch,[80] there is also an acknowledgement that Special Branches in most forces have responsibility for gathering intelligence on threats to public order and community safety from individuals 'motivated by racial hatred or political conviction'. In addition, the Special Branch gathers intelligence on 'political and animal rights extremist activity, anti-globalisation and environmental extremism'.[81]

Following the London bombings in 2005, the Metropolitan Police Special Branch was merged with the Anti-Terrorist Branch to form the Counter-Terrorism Command (also known as SO 19), which combines the intelligence-gathering role of the former with the investigation role of the latter.[82] The Counter-Terrorism Command (CTC) is said now to be 'the primary police resource for countering terrorism', and is a 'very large and complex command', with a headcount of approximately 1,500 which was 'still growing'.[83] As such the CTC has a number of responsibilities, which include 'bringing to justice' people engaged in terrorism, domestic extremist and related offences; providing a 'proactive and reactive' response to such activity, to include its prevention and disruption; gathering and exploiting intelligence on terrorism and extremism in London; and assisting the security and intelligence services in carrying out their statutory functions.[84] In fact, the CTC stands at the apex of a complex National Counter-Terrorism Network of police units of various kinds, explained as follows:

> The sort of coalface of countering terrorism is essentially every police force because all officers and staff have a role to be aware and to make contributions to a national effort. Then you have the local force special branches in each force, then the next level up is the counter-terrorism intelligence units, the next level up is the counter-terrorism units, the five larger ones, and at the top, I guess, is the Counter-Terrorism Command in London.[85]

---

[76] HC 1244 (2001–02); HC 1048 (2002–3); HC 884 (2003–04); HC 548 (2004–05); HC 314 (2006–07); HC 253 (2007–08); HC 948 (2007–08); and HC 902 (2008–09).

[77] See Bunyan (note 18 above), and Allason, *The Branch: A History of the Metropolitan Police Special Branch 1883–1983.*

[78] *Home Office Guidelines on Special Branch Work in the United Kingdom* (2004), para 18.

[79] Ibid, para 19.

[80] Ibid, para 20.

[81] Ibid, para 27.

[82] *The Times*, 3 October 2006.

[83] HC 212 (2008–09), Minutes of Evidence, 12 February 2009, Q 97 (Mr Bob Quick QPM).

[84] http://www.met.police.uk/so/counter_terrorism.htm.

[85] HC 212 (2008–09), Minutes of Evidence, 12 February 2009, Q 98.

Special Branches thus continue to play an important part as local intelligence gatherers.[86] It is important to emphasise, however, that Special Branch officers are police officers with no additional powers.

Security procedures in the civil service[87]

Since 1948 procedures have been in place to seek to exclude from sensitive positions in the civil service those who are perceived to be a threat to national security. The first of these, the so-called purge procedure, was thought to have been introduced (in 1948) as a result of American pressure following major spy scandals in the immediate post-war period. The aim was to ensure that 'no one who is known to be a member of the Communist Party, or to be associated with it in such a way as to raise legitimate doubts about his or her reliability, is employed in connection with work, the nature of which is vital to the security of the State'.[88] This was followed by the introduction of positive vetting in 1952, which had been on the agenda at least since the arrest and conviction of Klaus Fuchs in 1950 for communicating atomic secrets to the Soviet Union, for which he was sentenced to 14 years' imprisonment. Its implementation was a direct consequence of the defection of Donald MacLean and Guy Burgess to Moscow, in the aftermath of which the Foreign Secretary set up a committee under the chairmanship of Sir Alexander Cadogan to examine all aspects of the security arrangements in the Foreign Office. The committee reported in November 1951, approving plans for positive vetting which had already been prepared, and recommending that it should apply widely within the Foreign Service. The committee proposed that vetting should cover not only 'political unreliability' but also 'the problem of character defects, which might lay an officer open to blackmail, or otherwise undermine his loyalty and sense of responsibility'. The practice of positive vetting was thus introduced as a 'regular system' at the beginning of 1952, but without recourse to legislation, or without even informing or seeking the approval of Parliament.[89] It has since been extended well beyond the Foreign Service.

The procedures were revised in 1985, again in 1990 and, most recently, in 1994. In a statement on vetting policy,[90] it was announced that, '[in] the interests of national security, safeguarding Parliamentary democracy and maintaining the proper security of the Government's essential activities, it is the policy of HMG that no one should be employed in connection with work the nature of which is vital to the interests of the State', if they fall within one of five categories. The first of these relates to those who are or who have been involved in or associated with espionage, terrorism, sabotage or actions intended to overthrow or undermine parliamentary democracy by political, industrial or violent means. The second category applies to anyone who is or has recently been a member of an organisation which has advocated such activities or associated with any such organisation or its members 'in such a way as to raise reasonable doubts about his or her reliability'. The third and fourth categories apply to those who are 'susceptible to pressure or improper influence', and to those who have shown 'dishonesty or lack of integrity which throws doubt upon their reliability', while the fifth applies in respect of those who have 'demonstrated behaviour' or are 'subject to circumstances which may otherwise indicate unreliability'. Less rigorous inquiries are made in the case of those who have frequent and uncontrolled access to

---

[86] Ibid.

[87] See Fredman and Morris, *The State as Employer*, pp 232–6; Robertson, *Freedom, the Individual and the Law*, pp 148–52.

[88] HC Deb, 25 March 1948, cols 3417–26. See M L Joelson [1963] PL 51. The procedure was applied also to fascists, although communists were the real target.

[89] 'Not surprisingly the purge procedure has been regarded as of dwindling importance since Positive Vetting has been applied to new entrants to sensitive posts in the civil service for more than thirty years': Lustgarten and Leigh, p 131.

[90] HC Deb, 15 December 1994, col 765 (WA).

SECRET information than in the case of those who deal with TOP SECRET information. In the former case individuals are subjected to a security check, whereas in the latter case the level of clearance to which the person is submitted is known as developed vetting and will involve inquiries being made of people familiar with the person concerned. Counter-terrorist checks (CTC) are also made in respect of a number of sensitive posts. A major change in recent years has been the relaxation of the rule whereby homosexuality was an automatic bar to security clearance for posts involving access to highly classified information. But the susceptibility of the subject to blackmail or pressure by a foreign intelligence service continues to be a factor in the vetting of all candidates for such positions.[91]

These non-statutory procedures are complemented by an extra-statutory appeals mechanism which was announced in 1997.[92] The Security Vetting Appeals Panel (chaired by a High Court judge) now hears appeals against the refusal or withdrawal of security clearance. The Panel has no jurisdiction in cases involving new recruits, nor does it apply to members of the security and intelligence services, but is otherwise available to 'all those . . . in the public and private sectors and in the armed forces' who are subject to security vetting, have 'exhausted existing appeals mechanisms within their own organisations and remain dissatisfied with the result'.[93] Members of the security and intelligence services who have a grievance about their security clearance could complain to the Investigatory Powers Tribunal, as indeed could anyone else who believes that a refusal to grant them clearance was as a result of the actions of one of these services. Persons refused clearance are usually given reasons by the department in question, unless national security requires otherwise. A complaint may be made in writing to the Panel setting out the reasons; the respondent department will reply in writing; and an oral hearing may then be held. Proceedings of the Panel are in principle subject to judicial review.[94] Apart from complaints to the SVAP, a refusal or withdrawal of security clearance could be challenged in statutory proceedings, for example in an employment tribunal where there is an allegation of race, religious or sex discrimination.[95]

The security service and employment law

Staff employed by the security and intelligence services were traditionally denied the rights normally extended to other workers.[96] The Trade Union and Labour Relations (Consolidation) Act 1992 gives rights in relation to trade union membership, among other things; the Employment Rights Act 1996 covers a larger area, including rights relating to unfair dismissal. Both of these statutes apply to Crown servants,[97] but in both cases an exception was made for those in Crown employment in respect of whom there was a ministerial certificate exempting the employment from the protection of the legislation 'for the purpose of safeguarding national security'.[98] Certificates were issued excluding the members of the security services and subsequently the staff at GCHQ, where rights in respect of trade union membership were unilaterally withdrawn in

---

[91] HC Deb, 23 July 1991, col 476 (WA). Also HC Deb, 12 January 2000, col 287 et seq.

[92] For an account of the procedures operating before then, see Lustgarten and Leigh, pp 139–49; Fredman and Morris, p 233.

[93] HC Deb, 19 June 1997, col 243 (WA).

[94] *R v Director of GCHQ, ex p Hodges*, The Times, 26 July 1988. See also *R v Home Secretary, ex p Hosenball* [1977] 3 All ER 452, 460.

[95] *Tariq v Home Office*, UKEAT/0168/09/DA, [2009] All ER (D) 100. See now [2010] EWCA Civ 462.

[96] For a full account of public service employment law generally, including the position of civil servants, see Fredman and Morris, note 87 above.

[97] Trade Union and Labour Relations (Consolidation) Act 1992, s 273; Employment Rights Act 1996, s 191. And see ch 32 B.

[98] Trade Union and Labour Relations (Consolidation) Act 1992, s 275; Employment Rights Act 1996, s 193.

controversial circumstances in 1984.[99] This rather foolish decision did more than anything to draw attention to GCHQ and the work which it does, as well as generating international criticism for breaching the freedom of association guarantees in International Labour Organization Convention 87, an international treaty to which the United Kingdom is a party.[100] Trade union rights at GCHQ were substantially (but not wholly) restored in 1997.[101]

The position under the Employment Relations Act 1999 is that almost all employment rights now apply to members of the security services, with a number of exceptions and qualifications.[102] It is expressly provided that the protections for whistleblowing extended by the Public Interest Disclosure Act 1998 do not apply in relation to employment in the security service, SIS or GCHQ. There are, however, procedures introduced after the *Spycatcher* affair designed to enable members of the security services to raise concerns internally.[103] But the right of workers to be accompanied by a trade union official in grievance or disciplinary matters at the workplace does not apply to the members of the intelligence services.[104] It is also provided that in some circumstances an employment-related complaint must be dismissed by the employment tribunal where it is shown that the action complained of was taken for the purpose of safeguarding national security. This applies specifically to cases where the complainant is alleging that he or she has been subjected to a detriment because of trade union membership or activities; or that he or she has been unfairly dismissed.[105] But it is not only where an individual has been dismissed for reasons of national security that sensitive security matters may be raised in tribunal proceedings. There is a fear that security matters could be ventilated in a hearing where someone has been dismissed because of misconduct, or alleges that he or she has been discriminated against on grounds of race or sex.

The Employment Relations Act 1999 introduced a number of procedural changes to address such concerns, although the changes were mildly controversial and led to criticism of the government by the Intelligence and Security Committee (paradoxically for not going far enough to protect the officials).[106] These changes related first to the tripartite structure of the tribunal, with the Secretary of State empowered to make regulations to alter the normal composition of the employment tribunal (i) in cases relating to Crown employment proceedings, where (ii) it is expedient to do so in the interests of national security. Further, they relate to the procedure adopted by the tribunal, with the Secretary of State again empowered to make regulations authorising him or her to issue directions to an employment tribunal in Crown employment proceedings where it is expedient in the interests of national security to do so. The directions may require a tribunal to sit in private, to exclude the applicant or his or her representative from all or part of the proceedings, to take steps to conceal the identity of a particular witness, or to keep the reasons for its decision secret. If either of the last two directions is given, it is an offence to publish anything likely to lead to the identification of the witness, or the reasons for the tribunal's decision.[107] Regulations made under these powers – which also allow for the appointment of a

---

[99] See *Council of Civil Service Unions* v *Minister for the Civil Service* [1985] AC 374; G S Morris [1985] PL 177.

[100] But it did not breach the ECHR, art 11: *CCSU* v *UK* (1988) 10 EHRR 269; S Fredman and G S Morris (1988) 17 ILJ 105.

[101] For a fuller account, see 12th edition of this work, pp 647–8; also Ewing, *Britain and the ILO*.

[102] See Employment Relations Act 1999, Sch 8, amending the 1992 and 1996 Acts respectively.

[103] See *R* v *Shayler* [2002] UKHL 11; [2003] 1 AC 247. See also Rimington, *Open Secret*, pp 176–7.

[104] Employment Relations Act 1999, s 15. See HL Deb, 8 July 1999, col 1101. The government claimed that 'the security and intelligence services already have good grievance and disciplinary procedures in place' (col 1101).

[105] Employment Tribunals Act 1996, s 10(1), as inserted by the Employment Relations Act 1999, Sch 8. But see *B* v *BAA plc* [2005] IRLR 927 for the narrowing of the operation of this provision.

[106] Cm 4532, 1999. Also Cm 4777, 2000.

[107] Employment Tribunals Act 1996, s 10B, as inserted by the Employment Relations Act 1999, Sch 8.

special advocate to represent the interests of someone (including an applicant) excluded from any proceedings – have been held to be consistent with Convention rights.[108]

The Official Secrets Acts 1911–89[109]

The Official Secrets Acts 1911–89 serve two distinct but related purposes:

(a) to protect the interests of the state against espionage and other activities which might be useful to an enemy and therefore injurious to state security;

(b) to guard against the unauthorised disclosure of information which is held by servants of the state in their official capacity, whether or not the information has any direct reference to state security as such.

The legal sanctions under (b) help to support the sanctions against espionage, since it may in a particular case be possible to prove unauthorised disclosure of information without being able to prove elements of espionage. But they may also serve to protect the corridors of power against disclosure of information and publicity which a government might find politically embarrassing or inconvenient. The Official Secrets Act 1911, on which later Acts have been built, was passed rapidly through Parliament in circumstances in which ministers emphasised purpose (a) as the primary object of the Act, and did not mention purpose (b). In 1972, the Franks committee on s 2 of the 1911 Act commented that new legislation should be introduced to separate the espionage laws from the general protection of official information.[110]

Section 1(1) of the 1911 Act creates a group of offences, mainly connected with espionage. It is an offence, punishable with 14 years' imprisonment:

> if any person for any purpose prejudicial to the safety or interests of the State –
> (a) approaches, inspects, passes over or is in the neighbourhood of, or enters any prohibited place within the meaning of this Act; or
> (b) makes any sketch, plan, model, or note which . . . might be or is intended to be directly or indirectly useful to an enemy; or
> (c) obtains, collects, records, or publishes or communicates to any other person any secret official code word, or pass word, or any sketch, plan, model, article, or note, or other document or information which . . . might be or is intended to be directly or indirectly useful to an enemy.

The italicised phrase caused difficulties when charges under s 1 were brought following a non-violent political demonstration against an RAF base, in *Chandler v DPP*.[111]

> Anti-nuclear demonstrators sought to immobilise an RAF bomber base by sitting down on the runway. They were arrested as they approached the base and charged with conspiring to enter a prohibited place for a purpose prejudicial to the safety or interests of the state, contrary to s 1 of the 1911 Act. The trial judge refused to allow the accused to bring evidence to show that it would be beneficial to the United Kingdom if the government's nuclear policy were abandoned. For a variety of interlocking reasons, the House of Lords unanimously upheld the conviction. The demonstrators admittedly wished to obstruct the use of the airbase and it was immaterial that they believed that such obstruction would ultimately benefit the country. The offences created by the 1911 Act, s 1 were not confined to spying but included sabotage and other acts of physical interference.

---

[108] See *Tariq v Home Office*, above. For the relevant regulations, see SI 2004 No 1861, esp Sch 2. It should be emphasised, however, that the provisions of the Regulations meet Convention obligations only if construed consistently with these obligations. See *Tariq*, above, and *AB v Ministry of Defence*, UKEAT 0101_09_2407.

[109] Ewing and Gearty, *The Struggle for Civil Liberties*, ch 2; Bailey and Taylor, *Civil Liberties: Cases and Materials*, ch 8; Andrew, *Secret Service*; Williams, *Not in the Public Interest*, part 1.

[110] Cmnd 5104, 1972.

[111] [1964] AC 763.

This decision was criticised,[112] but it seems impossible to argue that Parliament intended a spy who had passed military secrets to a foreign power to be able to establish as a defence that his or her purpose in so doing was to force the British government to change its policies. The outcome in *Chandler*'s case would have been different if the demonstrators' intention had merely been to hold a protest meeting on the road outside the airbase, since the prosecution would have had to establish that to protest about nuclear policy was itself an act prejudicial to the interests of the state. In *Chandler*'s case, Lord Devlin alone stressed that it was for the jury to decide all questions of fact, including the issue of the accused's purpose and its likely effect on the interests of the state. During an official secrets trial in 1978, Mars-Jones J indicated that the use of s 1 in situations that fell short of spying and sabotage could be oppressive.[113] Cases since then have been concerned mainly with spying, including the convictions of Geoffrey Prime in 1983,[114] Michael Bettaney in 1984,[115] and Michael Smith in 1993,[116] all of whom had communicated secret information to the USSR. The other celebrated s 1 prosecution in the 1980s was that of eight signals intelligence officers based in Cyprus.[117] But unlike the cases of Prime, Bettaney and Smith, the prosecution failed. A subsequent inquiry by David Calcutt QC revealed that the accused had been unlawfully and oppressively detained while investigations were being conducted by the police and security service.[118]

Section 2 of the 1911 Act created a plethora of over 2,000 different offences related to the misuse of official information.[119] In particular, by s 2(1) it was an offence punishable by two years' imprisonment

> if any person having in his possession or control . . . any document or information . . . which has been entrusted in confidence to him by any person holding office under Her Majesty . . . communicates the . . . document or information to any person, other than a person to whom he is authorised to communicate it or a person to whom it is in the interests of the State his duty to communicate it.[120]

Other offences included the unauthorised retention of documents and failure to take reasonable care of documents. Section 2 plainly extended to the disclosure of information which bore no relation to national security.[121] An offence could be committed even though the information was not secret,[122] and even though it was disclosed in order to promote rather than undermine British interests abroad.[123] The scope of the section – well described as a 'catch all'[124] – was, however, mitigated in two ways. First, as with all offences under the Official Secrets Acts, the consent of the Attorney General in England (or the Lord Advocate in Scotland) was necessary before any prosecution could be brought.[125] Second, the authorisation which prevented disclosure of information being an offence could be wholly informal and could be implicit in the circumstances of disclosure. Ministers and many senior civil servants, by what was known as the practice of

---

[112] D Thompson [1963] PL 201.

[113] A Nicol [1979] Crim LR 284; Aubrey, *Who's Watching You?*

[114] *R v Prime* (1983) 5 Cr App R (S) 127.

[115] *R v Bettaney* [1985] Crim LR 104.

[116] Cm 2903, 1995.

[117] See A W Bradley [1986] PL 363. See also Cmnd 9923, 1986.

[118] Cmnd 9781, 1986.

[119] Cmnd 5104, 1972, para 16.

[120] In *R v Ponting* [1985] Crim LR 318 the trial judge, McCowan J, directed the jury that the interests of the state are the interests of state as determined by the government of the day.

[121] See *Loat v James* [1986] Crim LR 744.

[122] *R v Crisp* (1919) 83 JP 121.

[123] *R v Fell* [1963] Crim LR 207.

[124] Cmnd 5104, 1972, para 17.

[125] Official Secrets Act 1911, s 8.

self-authorisation, were able to decide for themselves how much information to disclose, at least in matters relating to their own duties.[126] Thus, if an off-the-record briefing was given to a journalist (for example, to enable him to 'leak' the contents of a Bill before it is published in Parliament) no breach of the Official Secrets Acts would have occurred. More than once it had been stressed that s 2 of the 1911 Act was not to be blamed for secrecy in government, since at any time ministers could adopt a more open approach.[127] Nonetheless, the form of the 1911 Act often presented journalists with a real difficulty in knowing what they might safely publish.

Other provisions of the Official Secrets Acts include s 7 of the 1920 Act, under which it is an offence to attempt to commit any offence under the Acts or to endeavour to persuade another person to commit such an offence, or to aid and abet or to do *any act preparatory* to the commission of such an offence. Under the 1920 Act, s 8, a court may exclude the public from the trial of an offence under the Acts if the prosecution applies for this on the ground that the publication of evidence would be prejudicial to national safety. This measure, which is employed in s 1 prosecutions[128] and which has also been employed in s 2 cases,[129] is an important departure from the general rule of 'the English system of administering justice' that 'it be done in public'.[130] For if 'the way the courts behave cannot be hidden from the public ear and eye this provides a safeguard against judicial arbitrariness or idiosyncrasy and maintains the public confidence in the administration of justice'.[131] Even if a prosecution is held behind closed doors, the accused and his or her lawyer may not be excluded and sentence must be delivered in open court.[132] Section 6 of the 1920 Act effectively removes a suspect's right of silence in a case brought under s 1 of the 1911 Act by providing that a Secretary of State may authorise the police to call a prospective witness for questioning about a s 1 offence, and in this event refusal to attend or to give information constitutes an offence.[133] Moreover, s 9 of the 1911 Act confers wide powers of search and seizure, authorising a magistrate to grant a search warrant permitting the police to enter and search premises 'and every person found therein', and to seize anything which is evidence of an offence under the Act 'having been or being about to be committed'. In cases of 'great emergency' where in the interests of the state immediate action is necessary, written authority for such a search may be granted by a superintendent of police.

> In January 1987 it was reported that the BBC had decided not to broadcast a programme about the Zircon spy satellite in the interests of national security. In so doing the Corporation denied that there had been any government pressure. Two days later, an injunction was obtained by the Attorney General restraining the journalist responsible for the programme, Duncan Campbell, from talking or writing about the contents of the film. He could not be found, however, to be served with the injunction, whereupon the *New Statesman* published details about the contents of the film. This was followed by a Special Branch raid of the *New Statesman*'s offices, and subsequently of the BBC's premises in Glasgow. The latter raid – which lasted for 28 hours – was conducted under the authority of a warrant granted under s 9 of the 1911 Act.[134] The police filled several police vans with documents, discarded film clips and over 200 containers of film. It was never entirely clear what the police were looking for, and no prosecutions followed. The episode illustrates the extent to which the 1911 Act may be used oppressively, even without a prosecution taking place.[135]

---

[126] Cmnd 5104, 1972, para 18.

[127] E.g. Cmnd 4089, 1969, p 11; Cmnd 5104, 1972, ch 5.

[128] E.g. in the cases of *Bettaney*, note 115 above, and the Cyprus intelligence personnel, p 567 above.

[129] E.g. in the *Ponting* case, note 120 below.

[130] *A-G v Leveller Magazine Ltd* [1979] AC 440, at 449–50.

[131] Ibid, at 450.

[132] Official Secrets Act 1920, s 8(2).

[133] Before the Official Secrets Act 1939 amended the 1920 Act, s 6, refusal on demand by a police inspector to disclose the source of information obtained in breach of the Acts was itself an offence (*Lewis v Cattle* [1938] 2 KB 454).

[134] The warrant was arguably unlawful, having been issued by a sheriff, not by a justice of the peace: R Black (1987) *J of the Law Society of Scotland* 138.

[135] For fuller details, see Ewing and Gearty, *Freedom under Thatcher*, pp 147–52. See also A W Bradley [1987] PL 1, 488.

The Official Secrets Act 1989

The operation of the Official Secrets Act 1911, s 2, was examined closely by a committee chaired by Lord Franks which reported in 1972.[136] The committee had been appointed after an unsuccessful prosecution of the *Sunday Telegraph* for publishing Foreign Office documents relating to the Labour government's policy towards the Nigerian civil war.[137] The committee reported that the law then in force was unsatisfactory and that there should be a new Official Information Act, to protect only certain forms of information, namely:

(*a*) classified information relating to defence or internal security, or to foreign relations, or to the currency or to the reserves, the unauthorised disclosure of which would cause serious injury to the interests of the nation;

(*b*) information likely to assist criminal activities or to impede law enforcement;

(*c*) Cabinet documents (in the interests of collective responsibility);[138]

(*d*) information which has been entrusted to the government by a private individual or concern (for example, for tax or social security purposes or in a census).

The requirement that information of the kind specified in (*a*) must be classified would make necessary a new system of classifying documents which, unlike the existing system, would have legal consequences. Offences under the proposed new Act were recommended to include the communication by a Crown servant, contrary to his or her official duty, of information subject to the Act; the communication by any person of information of the kinds set out in (*a*), (*b*) and (*c*) which he or she reasonably believed had reached him or her as a result of a breach of the Act; and the use of official information of any kind for purposes of private gain.

The Franks committee therefore recommended that protection of official information by criminal sanctions should continue only where the public interest clearly required this. But no reform of the Official Secrets Acts was forthcoming at that time, although other weaknesses in the law became evident during the so-called ABC trial in 1978.[139] In 1979 the Conservative government introduced not a Freedom of Information Bill but a Protection of Official Information Bill. This sought to give absolute protection to information regarding security and intelligence, regardless of whether that information was already available to the public.[140] But the Bill was abandoned by the government because of the severe political reaction to the disclosure that Anthony Blunt had been a Russian spy, a disclosure which could have been criminal if the Bill had been enacted. Pressure for reform was maintained in the 1980s, with interest fuelled by some controversial prosecutions. These included the cases of Sarah Tisdall, a Foreign Office clerk, who leaked to the *Guardian* a secret document relating to the delivery of cruise missiles to Greenham Common,[141] and Clive Ponting, a senior official in the Ministry of Defence, who leaked to an MP documents relating to the sinking of the Argentinian vessel, the *General Belgrano*, during the Falklands War.[142] Tisdall was convicted but Ponting was found not guilty, a verdict which ran counter to McCowan J's direction to the jury.[143]

The pressure for reform culminated in the Official Secrets Act 1989, which many would argue does not go far enough.[144] While repealing s 2 of the 1911 Act, the 1989 Act introduced new

---

[136] Cmnd 5104, 1972.

[137] See Aitken, *Officially Secret*.

[138] Cf ch 13 B.

[139] A Nicol [1979] Crim LR 284.

[140] HL Deb, 5 November 1979, col 612; cf Cmnd 7285, 1978, para 31.

[141] For the circumstances, see *Secretary of State for Defence v Guardian Newspapers Ltd* [1985] AC 339.

[142] See Ponting, *The Right to Know: The Inside Story of the Belgrano Affair*. Also R Thomas [1986] Crim LR 318.

[143] *R v Ponting* [1985] Crim LR 318.

[144] For background, see Cm 408, 1988. For analyses, see S Palmer [1990] PL 243; Birkinshaw, *Reforming the Secret State*.

restrictions on the unauthorised disclosure of an admittedly narrower range of information. One category of information protected from disclosure relates to security and intelligence, in that s 1 of the Act distinguishes between disclosures without lawful authority by security and intelligence staff, on the one hand, and civil servants and government contractors, on the other.[145] So far as the former are concerned, it is an offence for any such person to disclose any information obtained in the course of employment in the service; in the case of the latter, the unauthorised disclosure is unlawful only if 'damaging' to the work of the security and intelligence services. Sections 2 and 3 make it an offence for a civil servant or government contractor, without lawful authority, to disclose any information relating to defence or international affairs if the disclosure is damaging. In the case of defence, disclosure is defined as being damaging if it damages the capability of the armed forces to carry out their tasks, while in both cases disclosure is damaging if it endangers the interests of the United Kingdom abroad or endangers the safety of British citizens abroad (s 2(2)).[146] It is an offence by s 4 for a civil servant or a government contractor to disclose without lawful authority any information if this results in the commission of an offence, facilitates an escape from legal custody, or impedes the prevention or detection of offences or the apprehension or prosecution of suspects. Section 4 further provides that it is an offence to disclose information 'relating to the obtaining of information' (as well as any information obtained) as a result of warrants issued under the Interception of Communications Act 1985 or the Regulation of Investigatory Powers Act 2000, s 5 (phone tapping), the Security Services Act 1989 (interference with private property) or the Intelligence Services Act 1994 (interference with property or unlawful acts done outside the UK). It is thus not an offence under s 4 to disclose information obtained unlawfully without a warrant, although it might be an offence under s 1.

The offences under the Act are committed only where disclosure is made without lawful authority. This corresponds to the former s 2 of the 1911 Act, whereby the offence was committed only if the disclosure was unauthorised. The question of when a Crown servant was authorised to disclose information is, as we have seen, one which gave rise to considerable difficulty, particularly in the case of Cabinet ministers and senior officials.[147] By s 7 of the 1989 Act, a disclosure is authorised if it is made in accordance with the official duty of the minister or civil servant concerned, though any refusal of a request by a member of the security services to disclose protected information is (in principle) subject to judicial review.[148] An offence may be committed not only by the official disclosing the information, but also by a third party, such as a newspaper, which reports it. Although it is no longer an offence to receive information protected against disclosure (as it was under s 2 of the 1911 Act), it is an offence for the recipient to disclose the information without lawful authority, knowing or having reasonable cause to believe that it is protected from disclosure (s 5). In effect, it is an offence for a newspaper to publish protected information which has been leaked without authority. Controversially, there is no public interest defence available in this or indeed in other cases, the government having rejected such a measure.[149] However, in these circumstances, a newspaper is liable only if the disclosure is damaging and is made knowing or having reasonable cause to believe that it is damaging.

---

[145] See s 12 on the scope of the Act.

[146] Section 3 was used successfully against David Keogh, an official in the Whitehall communications centre, who leaked a document setting out the details of a meeting between George Bush and Tony Blair in 2004 about the war in Iraq dealing in particular with the US assault on the Iraqi city of Fallujah. Keogh passed the document to Leo O'Connor, an assistant to a Labour MP. O'Connor was charged and convicted under section 5 of the Act (see below). Thr trials took place in 2007, and both Keogh and O'Connor received jail sentences. See Ewing, *Bonfire of the Liberties*, pp 154–8.

[147] See Cmnd 5104, 1972, para 18.

[148] See *R v Shayler* [2002] UKHL 11; [2003] 1 AC 247.

[149] Cm 408, 1988.

Official secrets and human rights

Many of the offences under the Official Secrets Acts are associated with the publication of information. Many prosecutions have been for the same reason. The question which now arises is whether these measures are consistent with the guarantees of free speech in the ECHR and whether the Human Rights Act provides a defence to anyone prosecuted under the Official Secrets Acts 1911–89. This is a question which has become more urgent in recent years following another spate of unauthorised disclosures by a number of former members of the security and intelligence services in the late 1990s. These include Richard Tomlinson, who published a book in Russia and also material on the internet identifying individuals who recruited for the security and intelligence services. They also include David Shayler, who fled to France after a number of high-profile revelations about the activities of the security service. On his return from France, Mr Shayler was charged, convicted and imprisoned under the Official Secrets Act 1989. In some of the preliminary litigation, the House of Lords held that although Mr Shayler was entitled to the protection of freedom of expression under the Human Rights Act, the Official Secrets Act was designed to protect national security and the restriction which it imposed on freedom of expression was justified.[150] No proceedings were brought against a former director of M15 who published her memoirs in 2001 in a blaze of publicity, the book also being serialised in the *Guardian* newspaper in the same year.

The question whether the Official Secrets Acts are compatible with the Human Rights Act was raised in *Attorney-General* v *Blake*[151] where it was held that the Attorney General was entitled to an account of profits earned by a former member of the security and intelligence services for a publication which was made in breach of a contractual obligation not to disclose material obtained as a result of his employment. In the course of the case it was argued that s 1 of the Official Secrets Act 1989 is 'drawn too widely' because it criminalises disclosure of information when no damage results, by focusing on the 'status of the individual who makes the disclosure, rather than on the nature of the information itself'. But although the House of Lords preferred not to deal with this point, Lord Nicholls drew attention to another factor which appears to be decisive in an action where the Human Rights Act is relied on by a member of the security and intelligence services. This was the undertaking not to disclose information which Blake had voluntarily given when he joined the service. According to Lord Nicholls, neither Blake nor any other member of the service should have an incentive to break this undertaking. He continued:

> It is of paramount importance that members of the service should have complete confidence in all their dealings with each other, and that those recruited as informers should have the like confidence. Undermining the willingness of prospective informers to co-operate with the services, or undermining the morale and trust between members of the services when engaged on secret and dangerous operations, would jeopardise the effectiveness of the service. An absolute rule against disclosure, visible to all, makes good sense.[152]

It is unclear when – if ever – the prosecution of a disclosure in breach of the Official Secrets Act 1989 would be regarded as a disproportionate protection of national security. But in the *Shayler* case, the House of Lords seemed satisfied that there were adequate internal safeguards to enable a member of the security service to bring wrongdoing to the attention of the authorities without the need for unauthorised public disclosure in the press. Although the Human Rights Act thus may not present a serious obstacle to prosecutions under the Official Secrets Act 1989, political circumstances may make it difficult to proceed with such a charge. The point is

---

[150] *R v Shayler*, above. The affair has generated a body of case law. See also *Attorney-General* v *Punch* [2002] UKHL 50; [2003] 1 AC 1046 and *R (Bright)* v *Central Criminal Court* [2001] 2 All ER 244.

[151] [2001] 1 AC 268.

[152] Ibid, at 287.

highlighted by the case of Kathryn Gun, a GCHQ official who was charged under the 1989 Act for allegedly leaking an email from US spies to their British counterparts. It was claimed that the email – sent on 31 January 2003 and published by the *Observer* – tended to show that the Americans wanted British support to find out the voting intentions and negotiating positions of some UN Security Council member states on the forthcoming resolutions about Iraq. The charges were subsequently withdrawn, in the face of Ms Gun's defence that she leaked the email 'to save lives from being lost in a war'. According to the BBC, the government was concerned that this 'could persuade a jury and would lead to the reputation of the Official Secrets Act being damaged'. It was also explained that 'the government had made a political calculation that a random selection of a dozen jurors would be likely to be so instinctively anti-war that an acquittal would be likely'.[153]

Defence advisory notices

The Official Secrets Acts impose important restrictions on press freedom in the sense that they effectively control the information which might be made available. And as we saw in chapter 23 G, the action in equity for breach of confidence has the capacity to do much the same. Indeed, it was this which formed the basis for controlling the press during the so-called *Spycatcher* affair in 1987. But there are other restrictions and fetters on press freedom which have been introduced in the interests of national security. One of these is the system of 'DA' notices (known previously as 'D' notices),[154] a form of extra-legal censorship in which the press cooperates with the government. It is to be emphasised, however, that the system is voluntary and is not legally binding, with the broadcasters and publishers determining whether or not to comply. A DA notice is a means of providing advice and guidance to the media about defence and counter-terrorist information, the publication of which would be damaging to national security. DA notices are issued by the Defence, Press and Broadcasting Advisory Committee (DPBAC), an advisory body composed of senior civil servants and editors from national and regional newspapers, periodicals, news agencies, television and radio. The committee is chaired by a Permanent Under-Secretary of State in the Ministry of Defence and although membership may be varied by agreement, in 2009 there were four members representing government departments (Home Office, Ministry of Defence, Foreign Office and Cabinet Office (the Security Intelligence Coordinator)) and 15 members nominated by the media (with Google now being represented). The committee normally meets twice a year to review the contents of existing notices and the advice and guidance given by its secretary over the course of the year.

The system was overhauled in 1993 (following a review by the committee itself) in the light of international changes (in particular the break-up of the Soviet Union and Warsaw Pact), and the increased emphasis on openness in government. As a result, the number of standing notices was reduced from eight to six, and their content and style revised to make them more relevant and user-friendly. It was as a result of this review that the name of the notices was changed from D to DA notices and that of the committee to Defence, Press and Broadcasting Advisory Committee, 'better to reflect the voluntary and advisory nature of the system'.[155] Further revision in May 2000 led to a reduction in the number of notices from six to five (although from time to time it may be found necessary to issue a DA notice on a particular subject). The five DA notices are now published on the committee's website,[156] and deal respectively with Military Operations, Plans and Capabilities (DA Notice 1); Nuclear and Non-Nuclear Weapons and Equipment (DA Notice 2); Ciphers and Secure Communications (DA Notice 3); Sensitive Installations and Home

---

[153] http://news.bbc.co.uk (26 February 2004).
[154] D Fairley (1990) 10 OJLS 430; Williams, *Not in the Public Interest*, ch 4.
[155] HC Deb, 23 July 1993, col 454 (WA).
[156] www.dnotice.org.uk.

Addresses (DA Notice 4); and United Kingdom Security and Intelligence Services and Special Forces (DA Notice 5). Each of the notices gives details of the kind of information which editors are requested not to publish, usually information which relates to defence or anti-terrorist capabilities, or to individuals who might be a terrorist target. The notices also include a 'rationale' explaining their purpose.

The secretary of the committee plays a key role in advising the media on the interpretation of notices. Recent incumbents have included a retired rear-admiral and more recently a former RAF officer. The secretary 'is available at all times to Government departments and the media to give advice on the system', and in September 2001 he advised the media to minimise speculation about imminent military action in Afghanistan for fear of helping the 'enemy'.[157] It is a problem that DA notices are inevitably drafted in general terms, although it is the application of a DA notice to a particular set of circumstances on which the secretary is expected to give guidance, after consultation with government departments as appropriate. The committee makes clear, however, that the secretary is not 'invested with the authority to give rulings nor to advise on considerations other than national security'; and, on the other hand, that the 'notices have no legal standing and advice offered within their framework may be accepted or rejected partly or wholly'. Compliance with the DA notice system does not relieve the editor of responsibilities under the Official Secrets Acts; nor indeed will it necessarily prevent legal proceedings being brought to restrain any publication or broadcast.[158] The importance of the secretary's role was shown in 1967 when the *Daily Express* published a report that copies of private cables and telegrams sent overseas from the United Kingdom were regularly made available to the security authorities, a practice authorised by the Official Secrets Act 1920, s 4. The Prime Minister, Mr Wilson, claimed that this article was a breach of a 'D' notice. An investigation by three privy counsellors established that this was not the case but that there had been misunderstandings to which the secretary of the committee had contributed.[159] The Defence Committee of the House of Commons reviewed the 'D' notice system in 1980 and concluded (with reservations) that 'D' notices should be maintained, despite sharp divisions within the press about the value of the scheme which, judged in legal terms, is manifestly imperfect and imprecise.[160]

The Security Commission[161]

An initiative taken in 1964 as a result of the Profumo affair was designed to respond to breaches of security as they arise. The creation of the Security Commission was announced by the Prime Minister, Sir Alec Douglas-Home, on 23 January 1964 with the following terms of reference:

> If so requested by the Prime Minister, to investigate and report upon the circumstances in which a breach of security is known to have occurred in the public service, and upon any related failure of departmental security arrangements or neglect of duty; and, in the light of any such investigation, to advise whether any change in security arrangements is desirable.

---

[157] *The Independent*, 27 September 2001. In April 2009 it was reported that the Committee contacted the media about photographs which had been taken of a senior police officer as he entered No 10 Downing Street. The photographs showed in some detail the contents of a document the police officer had been carrying, revealing information about a sensitive police undercover operation in a terrorist investigation: *Daily Telegraph*, 9 April 2009.

[158] See *A-G v BBC*, *The Times*, 18 December 1987 regarding the broadcast by the BBC of a radio series (*My Country Right or Wrong*) about the security service.

[159] Cmnd 3309 and 3312, 1967; Hedley and Aynsley, *The D-notice Affair*. In 1967 Prime Minister Wilson rejected the finding that no breach of a 'D' notice had occurred but he later admitted that his handling of the affair was wrong: *The Labour Government 1964–70*, pp 478–82, 530–4.

[160] HC 773 (1979–80); J Jaconelli [1982] PL 37.

[161] For a full account, see Lustgarten and Leigh, pp 476–92.

The Prime Minister also stated that before asking the Security Commission to investigate a particular case, he would consult the Leader of the Opposition.[162] Normally the Commission sits in private and it is left to the Commission to determine whether legal representation of witnesses is necessary for the protection of their interests. The chairman of the Security Commission is a senior judge and it may also include members of the civil service, the armed forces and the diplomatic service. Recent chairmen have included Lord Diplock, Lord Bridge, Lord Griffiths, Lord Lloyd, Dame Elizabeth Butler-Sloss, and Sir Charles Mantell.[163]

The Commission may be called upon to investigate in a wide range of circumstances. So, for example, after two ministers (Earl Jellicoe and Lord Lambton) resigned in 1973 because of sexual impropriety, the Commission considered whether security had been endangered by their conduct.[164] In 1982, the Commission completed a full review of security procedures in the civil service,[165] and in 1983 it reported on the security implications of the conviction for spying of Geoffrey Prime, a member of staff at GCHQ.[166] Since then the Commission has reported on the security implications of the conviction under s 1 of the Official Secrets Act 1911 of Michael Bettaney, a member of the security services;[167] on security in signals intelligence following the (unsuccessful) prosecution of the 'Cyprus 8';[168] and the security implications of the case of Michael Smith, convicted (in 1993) under s 1 of the 1911 Act.[169] The last-mentioned report gives a remarkable and disarmingly frank assessment of the work of the security service, it being reported that 'Michael John Smith first came to the notice of the Security Service in November 1971 when a Michael Smith living in Birmingham applied to join the Communist Party of Great Britain (CPGB). Efforts were made at that stage by the Security Service and the police, at the former's request, to identify Smith but without result.' The Security Commission 'is not an oversight body, an inspectorate, or an appeal tribunal. It does not sit continuously, is not pro-active, has no links with any department or ministry, and has no adjudicative function'. By the same token, it 'may venture on any terrain where security may be said to be involved', and it may go wherever the Prime Minister directs.[170] But it is no substitute for effective parliamentary oversight of the security and intelligence services, and it is now largely overshadowed by the Intelligence and Security Committee established in 1994, although it continues to be asked by the Prime Minister to inquire into sensitive matters, as in 1999 following the conviction of a naval officer under the Official Secrets Act 1911, s 1, and in 2004 following concerns about security procedures at Buckingham Palace.[171]

Parliamentary scrutiny

1 *The Home Affairs Committee.* In 1999 the Home Affairs Committee of the House of Commons concluded that 'the accountability of the security and intelligence services to Parliament ought to be a fundamental principle in a democracy'.[172] Yet there is some way to go before this principle is fully realised, with successive governments resisting the possibility of full parliamentary

---

[162] HC Deb, 23 January 1964, cols 1271–5. The terms of reference were subsequently modified. The chairman of the Commission's view is also considered before any matter is referred to it.

[163] For details of composition and procedure, see Lustgarten and Leigh, pp 476–87.

[164] Cmnd 5367, 1973.

[165] Cmnd 8540, 1982.

[166] Cmnd 8876, 1983.

[167] Cmnd 9514, 1985.

[168] Cmnd 9923, 1986.

[169] Cm 2930, 1995.

[170] Lustgarten and Leigh, p 477.

[171] Cm 6177, 2004.

[172] HC 291 (1998–9), para 48.

scrutiny of the security and intelligence services.[173] In 1992 the Home Affairs Committee invited the Director General of the Security Service to appear before them, possibly in private. In a series of remarkable exchanges, the invitation was declined after consultation with the Home Secretary, who later said that he would consider whether the committee might meet her informally, 'perhaps over lunch'. This stance was adopted following the convention 'under which information on matters of security and intelligence is not placed before Parliament', which the Home Secretary regarded 'as binding in relation to Departmental Select Committees no less than in relation to Parliament itself'. In his view, the security service was not to be regarded as falling within the ambit of any select committee, although this need not 'prevent the Director General from having a meeting with [the Chairman of the Committee] and one or two senior members on an informal basis to discuss the work of the Security Service in general terms providing that the Government's position is understood'. Mrs Rimington (the then Director General) was said to share this view and would 'accordingly be in touch with [the Chairman] to invite [him] and a couple of [his] senior colleagues to lunch'. As the committee said, however, an informal lunch with Mrs Rimington (who was 'permitted to lunch with the press'), 'while a welcome move towards openness', was 'no substitute for formal parliamentary scrutiny of the Security Service'.

The Home Affairs Committee was of the view that the service fell within its terms of reference and that 'the value-for-money of the Security Service and its general policy are proper subjects for parliamentary scrutiny as long as such scrutiny does not damage the effectiveness of the Service'. The committee then reviewed the various options for enhanced accountability of the service by means of parliamentary scrutiny which in its view would meet 'an important public interest and help to protect against any possible future abuse of power'.[174] For its part, however, the government responded by saying that in 1989 Parliament had considered very carefully the question of oversight.[175] It had concluded in favour of preserving the existing approach to accountability, by which the Director General of the Security Service is responsible to the Home Secretary of the day, who is himself accountable to Parliament for the work of the security service. (It is, however, a strange kind of accountability which labours under a convention which prevents matters relating to security and intelligence from being placed before Parliament.) The government also referred to the procedures for judicial oversight of the service by means of a commissioner and a tribunal under the Security Service Act 1989. In the government's view, this system had worked well in the three and a half years since the 1989 Act had come into force, although, once again, it is a strange kind of oversight which examines only the exercise of specific statutory powers rather than the work of the service as a whole, and more importantly which has no base in Parliament itself. The government accepted that the position should be examined afresh and an opportunity to do so was provided by the Intelligence Services Act 1994, where important concessions in the direction of democratic accountability were made, although it is open to question whether they go far enough. In 1998 the then Home Secretary (Mr Jack Straw) refused a request from the Home Affairs Committee to take evidence from the Director General of the Security Service in a public session, offering instead a briefing from the Director General.[176]

2 *The Intelligence and Security Committee.* [177] One of the reasons given by Mr Straw for refusing the Home Affairs Committee's request was that Parliament had given responsibility for overseeing the security service to the Intelligence and Security Committee. Under the Intelligence Services Act 1994, this committee of parliamentarians (it is not a parliamentary committee) is

---

[173] HC Deb, 16 December 1989, col 36; also HC 773 (1979–80); HC 242 (1982–3); HC Deb, 12 May 1983, col 444 (WA).

[174] HC 265 (1992–3).

[175] Cm 2197, 1993.

[176] HC 291 (1998–9), app 1.

[177] See M Supperstone [1994] PL 329.

charged with the responsibility of examining 'the expenditure, administration and policy' of the security service, the intelligence service and GCHQ (s 10(1)). It consists of nine members drawn from both the House of Commons and the House of Lords (although none may be a minister of the Crown) and is appointed by the Prime Minister after consulting the Leader of the Opposition. In 2009 the committee was chaired by a former Cabinet minister and included among its other eight members one member of the House of Lords, as well as MPs from the three major political parties. The secretariat of the committee is drawn from the Cabinet Office, not from Parliament. Under the Act the committee is required to make an annual report on the discharge of its functions to the Prime Minister, which must then be laid before Parliament, although parts of the report may be held back, after consultation with the committee, if it appears to the Prime Minister that the publication of any matter would be prejudicial to any of the agencies. Some of the reports are badly disfigured by redaction.[178]

In its first report, the committee commented that because of the nature of its work 'it must have access to national security information', with the result that committee members 'have all been notified under the Official Secrets Act 1989'. The constitutional position was that the committee was 'now operating within the "ring of secrecy"', reporting directly to the Prime Minister on its work and, through him, to Parliament. An important development reported in 1999 was the appointment of an investigator by the committee to enable it more fully to examine different aspects of agencies' activities.[179] The committee's annual reports reveal that it has examined a wide range of issues. These include the priorities and plans of the agencies, their financing, and personnel management issues. An interesting issue raised in the annual reports for 1997–98 and 1998–99 respectively relates to the destruction of security service files. It was noted in 1998 that 110,000 files had been destroyed since 1992, the vast majority of which related to subversion, on targets about whom the service was no longer conducting any investigations. Following concerns that the service was solely responsible for the review and destruction of files and that some form of 'independent check should be built into the process', it was agreed that Public Record Office officials should be involved in the examination of files identified by the security service for destruction.[180]

The committee has also issued specific reports on a number of contentious issues, including most notably the publication of the so-called Mitrokhin Archive. This consisted of material held by the KGB which Mr Mitrokhin had removed from Russia and which identified a number of British citizens as Soviet agents. A number of these individuals were subsequently named in public, although none was prosecuted, their identities having been known to or suspected by the authorities in this country for many years. The report of the Intelligence and Security Committee in fact provides a fascinating insight into the working of the intelligence services at a number of levels. It was revealed, for example, that the security service had failed to consult the Law Officers about whether one of the alleged spies should be prosecuted, taking the view that prosecution would not be in the public interest, a decision which it ought to have been for the Attorney General to make. More recent international events have led the committee to investigate the adequacy and assessment of the evidence relating to 'weapons of mass destruction' claimed to have been held by Iraq in the period before the invasion of that country in 2003.[181] In a separate report, some light was cast on the role of British agents in the detention of British nationals by the United States in Afghanistan and Guantanamo Bay, as well as Iraq, though there were obvious constraints

---

[178] See Cm 4309, 1999 (Sierra Leone).

[179] Cm 4532, 1999; and see Cm 4073, 1998; also HC 291 (1998–9), para 14.

[180] Cm 4073, 1998, and Cm 4532, 1999. For more recent annual reports giving an account of other concerns (such as security vetting, the Official Secrets Act, relationships with the media, the use of interception evidence in legal proceedings, document security, torture and rendition, and cyber security) see Cm 5542, 2002; Cm 5837, 2003; Cm 6240, 2004; Cm 6510, 2005; Cm 7299, 2008; Cm 7542, 2009; Cm 7807, 2010; and Cm 7844, 2010.

[181] Cm 5972, 2003.

on the ability of the committee to conduct a meaningful investigation. Nevertheless, the committee found evidence of some concerns being expressed by British intelligence officers, and also revealed that intelligence officers had interviewed detainees without the knowledge of ministers.[182]

Conclusion

Arguments about the accountability of the security and intelligence services have intensified in recent years, partly as a result of allegations about their role in the mistreatment of terrorist suspects by foreign governments.[183] A number of allegations have been made of British complicity in the torture of such suspects, and the matter has been the subject of investigation by the JCHR in a powerful report that asked some searching questions about the conduct of British officials. Yet although the Director General of the Security Service gave a private briefing to the Home Affairs Committee in 2007 about the government's Counter-Terrorism proposals (after he had addressed the Society of Editors on the same subject),[184] it appears that the services still do not recognise select committees as bodies to whom they are formally accountable.[185] It is true that scrutiny is undertaken by the Intelligence and Security Committee, which has sometimes been critical of the security service (notably in the context of Rendition).[186] But doubts have been raised about the adequacy of the Committee as an instrument of proper ministerial accountability of the security and intelligence services to Parliament.[187] The annual reports of the Committee are late in publication (the report for 2007–08 was published in March 2009);[188] they are very heavily redacted (to the point of futility on some issues); and there are claims that the Committee is not supplied with all relevant information by the services it scrutinises.[189] In the light of evidence emerging in the course of recent legal proceedings (notably in the *Binyam Mohamed* case discussed in chapter 32 C below), the case for greater and more intense parliamentary scrutiny of the operational activities of the security and intelligence services appears irresistible.

---

[182] Cm 6469, 2005.

[183] See ch 32, p 760 below (the case of Binyam Mohamed). See also Cm 7807, 2010.

[184] HC 43 (2007–08). The content of this briefing is not reported as evidence by the committee, and although it is acknowledged that the briefing 'informed' the committee's report, it is not clear how.

[185] See J Evans, 'Defending the Realm', Speech by Director General of the Security Service, 15 October 2009, see also HL Paper 152, HC 230 (2008–09), paras 55–56.

[186] Cm 7171, 2007. And see ch 20 C.

[187] HL Paper 152, HC 230 (2008–09), para 65. The same report also highlights the unwillingness of ministers to account to Parliament for the work of the security services: see ch 10 D above.

[188] Cm 1542, 2009.

[189] *Guardian*, 6 March 2009 (Richard Norton-Taylor). See also Cm 7807, 2010, paras 159–61 (on overlooked documents).

CHAPTER 26

Emergency powers and terrorism

In times of grave national emergency, normal constitutional principles may have to give way to the overriding need to deal with the emergency. In Lord Pearce's words, 'the flame of individual right and justice must burn more palely when it is ringed by the more dramatic light of bombed buildings'.[1] Thus, the European Convention on Human Rights, art 15, permits a member state to take measures derogating from its obligations under the Convention 'in time of war or other public emergency threatening the life of the nation'. The United Kingdom government has exercised the right of derogation in respect of events in Northern Ireland and more recently in response to international terrorism in the aftermath of events in the United States on 11 September 2001.[2]

But even under such circumstances no derogation is permitted from art 2 (which protects the right to life) except in the case of deaths resulting from lawful acts of war, art 3 (which prohibits the use of torture), art 4(1) (which prohibits slavery) and art 7 (which bars retrospective criminal laws). Thus even in grave emergencies there are limits beyond which a state may not go, and it is open to question whether and how far 'the desirability of an effective remedy for judicial review must yield to the higher interests of the State'.[3] This chapter examines the role of the armed forces and the use of statutory emergency powers during war and peace and includes an account of recent anti-terrorist legislation. Emphasis will be both on the increased powers of the state in emergencies and on the continuing limits on state action.

EMERGENCY POWERS

The provisions discussed in this part entail the use of special or emergency powers to deal with very exceptional circumstances. They are rarely invoked, and when they are invoked it is typically for a short period (though the use of troops in Northern Ireland lasted for the best part of a generation). Here we are concerned with three forms of such intervention of varying levels of seriousness and intrusion into standard practice, beginning with (i) the use of troops to assist the civil authorities (as was the case in Northern Ireland from 1969 to 2007),[4] progressing in severity to (ii) the use of emergency powers (as for example in war time or to deal with other threats to the life or needs of the community), concluding most severely with (iii) the introduction of martial law (a matter which in recent times has been of historical interest only in Great Britain). It should be said, however, that the nature of the emergencies which governments face has changed over the course of the last 100 years or so, and so has the nature of the response. The main concern now is not world war or large-scale industrial disputes but international terrorism, leading to emergency laws of a permanent nature, constantly in operation, as discussed later in this chapter.

---

[1] *Conway v Rimmer* [1968] AC 910, 982.

[2] See ch 19 B.

[3] *R v Home Secretary, ex p Adams* [1995] All ER (EC) 177, at 185 (Steyn LJ). See *R v Home Secretary, ex p Cheblak* [1991] 2 All ER 319 where judicial review yielded rather too easily. Compare the thoughtful discussion of this issue by Sedley J in *R v Home Secretary, ex p McQuillan* [1995] 4 All ER 400, at 420–1. See now *A v Home Secretary* [2004] UKHL 56; [2005] 2 AC 68 (p 597 below).

[4] For details, see 14th edn of this book, pp 628–9.

A. Use of troops in assisting the police

Legal authority

In chapter 24 we examined the main powers available to the police in maintaining public order. For the last 100 years or so, the police, with greater or less difficulty depending on the circumstances, have been able to control and contain public protest in Great Britain, though not in Northern Ireland. Apart from unrest in Glasgow in 1919, it has not been necessary to deploy troops for peace-keeping activities in Great Britain on any occasion since the First World War.[5] They have been required, however, to maintain essential services during strikes (for example, the firefighters' strike in 2003),[6] and on occasion to deal with extreme terrorist action (for example, the occupation of the Iranian embassy in London in May 1980), as well as to assist with the disposal of carcasses during the foot and mouth epidemic on British farms in 2001.[7] But in the nineteenth century and earlier, when there was less political freedom and police forces were weaker, the local magistrates were expected to call in detachments of soldiers to restore order when necessary. By contrast with nineteenth-century practice, the 'civil power' that may call in the armed forces today appears no longer to be the local magistracy, but the Home Secretary, acting on a request from a chief officer of police.[8] It is then for the Secretary of State for Defence to respond to the call.

A decision to call in the troops to restore order was, in the past at least, a decision enabling firearms to be used to repress the disturbances. This use of the troops may be illustrated by a rather late example, the Featherstone riots in 1893.[9] When the police were engaged elsewhere, a small detachment of soldiers was summoned to protect a colliery against a riotous crowd which broke windows and set buildings on fire. As darkness was falling, a magistrate called on the crowd to disperse and he read the proclamation from the Riot Act. When the crowd did not disperse, the magistrate authorised the soldiers to fire and their officer decided that the only way to protect the colliery was to fire on the crowd. Two members of the crowd were killed. A committee of inquiry held that the action of the troops was justified in law. Matters would now have to be exceptionally grave before the armed forces were called upon to restore and maintain order, as emphasised by events such as the miners' strike of 1984/85 and the fuel protests of September 2000.[10] Despite large-scale public disturbances, national coordination of policing, together with new training and operational methods, meant that it was unnecessary to deploy the army in either of these situations for peace-keeping purposes.[11]

When troops are thus used, what is the basis of their authority? Whatever may be the rules today that govern the decision that the armed forces should be called in,[12] their legal authority to act in a situation of riot seems to rest on no statutory or prerogative powers of the Crown, but simply on the duty of all citizens to aid in the suppression of riot and on the duty of the armed forces to come to the aid of the civil authorities.[13] In place of the common law rules on the use of force in the prevention of crime, s 3 of the Criminal Law Act 1967 now provides:

---

[5] See Williams, *Keeping the Peace*, pp 32–5.

[6] Cm 3223, 1996, pp 27–8.

[7] The armed forces provide assistance to other departments in a number of ways: apart from counter-drug activities, it includes fishing protection and assistance in natural emergencies: Cm 5109, 2001, p 3. See also Cm 6041, 2003, para 1.6.

[8] HC Deb, 8 April 1976, col 617. See also E Bramall (1980) 128 *Jl of Royal Society of Arts* 480; S C Greer [1983] PL 573; and Evelegh, *Peace Keeping in a Democratic Society*, pp 11–21, 91–4.

[9] Report of the Committee on the Disturbances at Featherstone, C 7234, 1893. And see HC 236 (1908).

[10] On which see H Fenwick and G Phillipson (2001) 21 LS 535.

[11] See McCabe and Wallington, *The Police, Public Order and Civil Liberties*, pp 49–50.

[12] See authorities cited in note 8 above.

[13] *Charge to Bristol Grand Jury* (1832) 5 C & P 261.

A person may use such force as is reasonable in the circumstances in the prevention of crime, or in effecting or assisting in the lawful arrest of offenders or suspected offenders or of persons unlawfully at large.

Thus, the use of firearms must be justified by the necessity of the situation and does not become legal by reason of the decision to call in the troops. Indeed, the use of excessive force or the premature use of firearms would render the officer in command and the individual soldiers personally responsible for death or injuries caused. Issues of liability are decided by the criminal or civil courts after the event,[14] and may give rise to court-martial proceedings.[15]

In modern conditions, the proposition that to call in the troops makes possible the use of firearms needs to be qualified in two ways. First, the police have already had to train and equip themselves with firearms 'to deal with armed criminals and political terrorists not posing any extraordinary problem or capable of posing a limited threat'.[16] The occasions on which firearms may be carried are governed by police rules, and this may involve the use of lethal force, as was tragically revealed by the death of Jean-Charles de Menezes in the aftermath of the London terrorist bombings in July 2005. An error of judgement on the part of a police officer could lead to criminal proceedings against him or her, and any use of lethal force must now be examined by the Independent Police Complaints Commission,[17] with art 2 of the ECHR requiring any death at the hands of the police (and other state officials) to be effectively investigated.[18] Second, it is no longer correct, as was said in 1893, that a soldier can act only by using deadly weapons.[19] To call in the army to deal with civil unrest would indeed be of incalculable political significance. But the British army's experience in Northern Ireland suggests that there are many other ways of dealing with hostile crowds which are more effective and less deadly than firing into them – batons, riot shields, water cannon, rubber bullets and even CS gas – and the armed forces do not have a monopoly on the use of CS gas.[20]

Legal liability

The use of the troops to assist the civil authorities has arisen most recently in relation to events in Northern Ireland. These events have also tested the legal authority of the soldier when deployed in such circumstances, and it has been suggested that the legal position of the soldier called to assist the civil authorities in Northern Ireland to contain terrorist or political violence may not be the same as that of his or her counterpart called to assist the civil authorities elsewhere for other purposes:

> There is little authority in English law concerning the rights and duties of a member of the armed forces of the Crown when acting in aid of the civil power; and what little authority there is relates almost entirely to the duties of soldiers when troops are called upon to assist in controlling a riotous assembly. Where used for such temporary purposes it may not be inaccurate to describe the legal rights and duties of a soldier as being no more than those of an ordinary citizen in uniform. But such a description is in my view misleading in the circumstances in which the army is currently employed in aid of the civil power in Northern Ireland . . . In theory it may be the duty of every citizen when an arrestable offence is about to be committed in his presence to take whatever reasonable measures are available to him to prevent the commission of the crime; but the duty is

---

[14] See *R v Clegg* [1995] 1 AC 482, and *Bici v Ministry of Defence* [2004] EWHC 786 (QB).

[15] See ch 16 above.

[16] Cmnd 6496, 1976, p 95.

[17] See ch 21 E above.

[18] See *McKerr v UK* (2002) 34 EHRR 20; *Jordan v UK* (2003) 37 EHRR 2; and *Finucane v UK* (2004) 37 EHRR 656. See also *In re McKerr* [2004] UKHL 12; [2004] 1 WLR 807.

[19] C 7234, 1893, pp 10, 12.

[20] On the power to make it available to the police, see ch 12 E above.

one of imperfect obligation and does not place him under any obligation to do anything by which he would expose himself to the risk of personal injury . . . In contrast to this a soldier who is employed in aid of the civil power in Northern Ireland is under a duty, enforceable under military law, to search for criminals if so ordered by his superior officer and to risk his own life should this be necessary in preventing terrorist acts. For the performance of this duty he is armed with a firearm, a self-loading rifle, from which a bullet, if it hits the human body, is almost certain to cause serious injury if not death.[21]

It has been said by the government, however, that 'service personnel are given certain specific powers under the law (for example, to make arrests and carry out searches) in order to enable them to carry out effective support to the RUC [now the Police Service of Northern Ireland]. In exercising these powers and in seeking to uphold the law, service personnel remain accountable to the law at all times. They have no immunity, nor do they receive special treatment. If service personnel breach the law, they are liable to arrest and prosecution under the law. This applies equally to the use of force, including lethal force.'[22]

Considerable controversy has, nevertheless, arisen from time to time as a result of the use of firearms by the military, most notably on 30 January 1972 when 13 civilians were killed 'when the army opened fire during a demonstration in Derry'.[23] Between 1969 and 1994 the security forces are said to have been responsible for 357 deaths in Northern Ireland, of which 141 were republican 'military activists', 13 were loyalist equivalents and 194 were civilians. Eighteen of these deaths led to criminal charges, with a total of six convictions being secured, one for attempted murder, one for manslaughter and four for murder.[24]

> In *Attorney-General for Northern Ireland's Reference (No 1 of 1975)*[25] the accused was a soldier on foot patrol who shot and killed a young man in an open field in a country area in daylight. The shot had not been preceded by a warning shot and the rifle was fired after the deceased ran off after having been told to halt. The area was one in which troops had been attacked and killed by the IRA and where a surprise attack was a real threat. When the accused fired, he believed that he was dealing with a member of the IRA, but he had no belief at all as to whether the deceased had been involved or was likely to be involved in any act of terrorism. In fact, the deceased was an 'entirely innocent person who was in no way involved in terrorist activity'. After the soldier's acquittal for murder, the House of Lords held that the stated circumstances (where 'he fires to kill or seriously wound an unarmed person because he honestly and reasonably believes that person is a member of a proscribed organisation [in this case the Provisional IRA] who is seeking to run away, and the soldier's shot kills that person') raised an issue for the tribunal of fact as to whether the Crown had established beyond reasonable doubt that the shooting constituted unreasonable force. According to Lord Diplock (at p 138), 'there is material upon which a jury might take the view that the accused had reasonable grounds for apprehension of imminent danger to himself and other members of the patrol if the deceased were allowed to get away . . . , and that the time available to the accused to make up his mind was so short that even a reasonable man could only act intuitively'.

On the other hand, in *R v Clegg*[26] it was held that a soldier who used excessive force in self-defence leading to the death of the victim was guilty of murder rather than manslaughter.

---

[21] *A-G for Northern Ireland's Reference (No 1 of 1975)* [1977] AC 105, at 136–7 (Lord Diplock).

[22] Statement on the Defence Estimates 1994, p 36.

[23] C A Gearty (1994) 47 CLP 19, at p 33. See HC 220 (1971–2) (Widgery Report). In 1998 a second inquiry into these events was appointed, but had not reported by December 2009. See *R v Lord Saville of Newdigate, ex p A* [1999] 4 All ER 860.

[24] Gearty and Kimbell, *Terrorism and the Rule of Law*, pp 57–8.

[25] [1977] AC 105. See also *Farrell v Defence Secretary* [1980] 1 All ER 166; *R v Bohan and Temperley* (1979) (5) BNIL; *R v Robinson* (1984) (4) BNIL 34; *R v McAuley* (1985) (10) BNIL 14. See also R J Spjut [1986] PL 38 and [1987] PL 35.

[26] [1995] 1 AC 482.

The use of firearms by the authorities in Northern Ireland gave rise to allegations of a shoot-to-kill policy, these being directed at both the RUC and the armed forces.[27] The allegations were sufficiently serious that an inquiry was appointed under the chairmanship of Mr John Stalker, the Deputy Chief Constable of Greater Manchester.[28] Following Mr Stalker's removal from the inquiry in controversial circumstances, it was completed by the Chief Constable of West Yorkshire. No evidence was published to substantiate the allegations,[29] although the controversy was revived following the decision of the European Court of Human Rights in *McCann v United Kingdom*,[30] which concerned the fatal shooting of three IRA activists in Gibraltar in 1987.

> Three known IRA personnel were shot by four SAS officers while it was thought that they were about to detonate a bomb, to the danger of life on Gibraltar. It transpired that this belief was erroneous and that the suspects were not only unarmed, but that they also were not in possession of bomb equipment at the time of their deaths. They were nevertheless shot 29 times (one suspect being shot 16 times) in highly controversial circumstances. By a majority of 10 to 9, the Court held that there had been a breach of art 2 which in protecting the right to life was said to rank as 'one of the most fundamental provisions in the Convention'.[31] There was no evidence of 'an execution plot at the highest level of command in the Ministry of Defence or in the Government'; although 'all four soldiers shot to kill', on the facts and in the circumstances the actions of the soldiers did not in themselves give rise to a violation of art 2. But it was held that the operation as a whole was controlled and organised in a manner which failed to respect art 2, and that the information and instructions given to the soldiers rendered inevitable the use of lethal force in a manner which failed to take adequately into consideration the right to life of the three suspects. Having regard 'to the decision not to prevent the suspects from travelling into Gibraltar, to the failure of the authorities to make sufficient allowances for the possibility that their intelligence assessments might in some respects, at least, be erroneous, and to the automatic recourse to lethal force when the soldiers opened fire', the Court was not persuaded that 'the killing of the three terrorists constituted the force which was no more than absolutely necessary in defence of persons from unlawful violence'.[32]

Allegations of a shoot-to-kill policy of the security forces in Northern Ireland gave rise to litigation – in the European Court of Human Rights and in the domestic courts under the Human Rights Act – at the instance of bereaved families concerned that adequate steps have not been taken to investigate the deaths of people allegedly killed by the RUC.[33] That litigation continues.[34]

B. Emergency powers in war and peace

Emergency powers in time of war

Before the mid-nineteenth century it was the practice in times of national danger to pass what were often known as Habeas Corpus Suspension Acts.[35] Such Acts took various forms. Some

---

[27] For suggestions that such an alleged policy conflicts with the ECHR, see *Farrell v UK* (1983) 5 EHRR 466. See also *McCann v UK* (1995) 21 EHRR 97.

[28] See Stalker, *Stalker*.

[29] See HC Deb, 25 January 1988, cols 21–35.

[30] (1995) 21 EHRR 97.

[31] Art 2(1) provides that 'Everyone's life shall be protected by law', while art 2(2) provides by way of qualification that 'Deprivation of life shall not be regarded as inflicted in contravention of this Article when it results from the use of force which is no more than absolutely necessary: (a) in defence of any person from unlawful violence . . .'

[32] The political reaction to the decision was very critical of the Court: see e.g. HL Deb, 29 January 1996, col 1225. Compare C Gearty, 'After Gibraltar', *London Review of Books*, 16 November 1995.

[33] See cases referred to in note 18 above.

[34] *Jordan v Lord Chancellor* [2007] UKHL 14, [2007] 2 WLR 754.

[35] Dicey, *The Law of the Constitution*, pp 229–37.

prevented the use of habeas corpus for securing speedy trial or the right to bail in the case of persons charged with treason or other offences. Others conferred wide powers of arrest and detention which would not normally have been acceptable. After the danger was over, it was often the practice to pass an Indemnity Act to protect officials retrospectively from liability for illegal acts which they might have committed. During the two world wars, habeas corpus was not suspended but extremely wide powers were conferred on the executive. The Defence of the Realm Acts 1914–15 empowered the Crown to make regulations by Order in Council for securing public safety or for the defence of the realm.[36] In R v Halliday, ex p Zadig the House of Lords held that this general power was wide enough to support a regulation authorising the Secretary of State to detain persons without trial on the grounds of their hostile origins or associations.[37] In a powerful and memorable dissent, Lord Shaw of Dunfermline declined to infer from the delegation of a general power to make regulations for public safety and defence the right to authorise the detention of a man without trial and without being accused of any offence.

Although the powers of the executive were wide, it was still possible to challenge defence regulations in the courts.

> In *Attorney-General v Wilts United Dairies Ltd*[38] an attempt by the Food Controller to impose a charge of two pence a gallon as a condition of issuing licences for the supply of milk was held invalid, on the ground that the Food Controller's power under defence regulations to regulate the supply of milk did not confer power to impose charges upon the subject. Doubt was also expressed whether a regulation conferring such a power would have been within the general power to make regulations for the public safety or the defence of the realm. In *Chester v Bateson*[39] a defence regulation empowered the Minister of Munitions to declare an area in which munitions were manufactured to be a special area. The intended effect of such a declaration was to prevent any person without the consent of the minister from taking proceedings to recover possession of any dwelling-house in the area, if a munitions worker was living in it and duly paying rent. It was held that Parliament had not deliberately deprived the citizen of access to the courts and that the regulation was invalid, since it could not be shown to be a necessary or even reasonable way of securing the public safety or the defence of the realm.

Such decisions explain the passing after the war of the wide Indemnity Act 1920 and a separate Act relating to illegal charges, the War Charges Validity Act 1925.

When war was declared in 1939 the Emergency Powers (Defence) Act 1939 empowered the making of regulations by Order in Council which appeared necessary or expedient for the public safety, the defence of the realm, the maintenance of public order, the efficient prosecution of any war in which His Majesty might be engaged and the maintenance of supplies and services essential for the life of the community. There followed a list of particular purposes for which regulations could be made, including the detention of persons in the interests of public safety or the defence of the realm. To avoid another *Wilts United Dairies* case, the Treasury was empowered to impose charges in connection with any scheme of control under Defence Regulations. Treasury regulations imposing charges required confirmation by an affirmative resolution of the House of Commons. Other regulations had to be laid before Parliament after they were made and could be annulled by negative resolution within 28 days.[40] Compulsory military service was imposed by separate National Service Acts and compulsory direction of labour to essential war work was authorised by the Emergency Powers (Defence) (No 2) Act 1940. Although access to the courts was not barred, the scope for judicial review of executive action was limited. Thus the courts could not consider whether a particular regulation was necessary or expedient for the purposes

---

[36] For a fascinating account of these powers and their operation, see Rubin, *Private Property, Government Requisition and the Constitution, 1914–1927*. See also Ewing and Gearty, *The Struggle for Civil Liberties*, ch 2.

[37] [1917] AC 260. See D Foxton (2003) 119 LQR 455.

[38] (1921) 37 TLR 884.

[39] [1920] 1 KB 829.

[40] Ch 28.

of the Act which authorised it.[41] The courts could, however, hold an act to be illegal as being not authorised by the regulation relied on to justify it.[42]

Special problems of judicial control arose in relation to the power of the executive to authorise detention without trial in the interests of public safety or the defence of the realm. Under Defence Regulation 18 B, the Home Secretary was empowered to detain those whom he had reasonable cause to believe came within specified categories (including persons of hostile origin or association) and over whom it was necessary to exercise control. Persons detained could make objections to an advisory committee appointed by the Home Secretary. The Home Secretary had to report monthly to Parliament on the number of persons detained and the number of cases in which he had not followed the advice of the committee. It was open to a detainee to apply for habeas corpus, but such applications had little chance of success in view of the decision of the House of Lords in *Liversidge v Anderson*.[43] In spite of a powerful dissenting judgment by Lord Atkin, the House took the view that the power to detain could not be controlled by the courts, if only because considerations of security forbade proof of the evidence on which detention was ordered. The words 'had reasonable cause to believe' only meant that the Home Secretary must have a belief which in his mind was reasonable. The courts would not inquire into the grounds for his belief, although apparently they might examine positive evidence of mala fides or mistaken identity.[44] Stress was laid on the responsibility of the Home Secretary to Parliament. In only one case did a person who had been detained under the regulation secure his release by habeas corpus proceedings. His detention having been ordered on the ground that he was connected with a fascist organisation, he was wrongly informed that the order had been made on the ground of his being of hostile origins and association. The Divisional Court ordered his release, but the Home Secretary thereupon made a new order for his detention.[45]

Civil Contingencies Act 2004

A distinguishing feature of the war-time powers described above is that they were ad hoc measures which were repealed shortly after the wars ended. Emergencies of different kinds may arise in peacetime. Until quite recently the concern of governments was with the consequences of large-scale industrial action organised by trade unions which might disrupt the supply of essential services. It was for this reason that provision was made in the Emergency Powers Act 1920 for declarations of a state of emergency and the making of emergency regulations.[46] These powers applied where there were events of such a nature as to deprive the community or a substantial part of the community of the essentials of life. Although designed principally to deal with industrial action, these powers were also capable of being used where an emergency was caused in other ways, such as natural disaster or a serious nuclear accident.[47] In practice, however, the Act was used only in response to strikes by coalminers, dockers and power workers, and was last used in 1974. In all it was used on 12 occasions,[48] and it has now been repealed with new emergency

---

[41] *R v Comptroller-General of Patents, ex p Bayer Products* [1941] 2 KB 306. See also *Pollok School v Glasgow Town Clerk* 1946 SC 373.

[42] E.g. *Fowler & Co (Leeds) Ltd v Duncan* [1941] Ch 450.

[43] [1942] AC 206; and see C K Allen (1942) 58 LQR 232 and R F V Heuston (1970) 86 LQR 33.

[44] Lord Wright at 261. The majority decision in *Liversidge v Anderson* cannot now be relied on as an authority, either on the point of construction or in its declaration of legal principle: *R v Home Secretary, ex p Khawaja* [1984] AC 74, at 110 (Lord Scarman), and see e.g. *Ridge v Baldwin* [1964] AC 40, at 73 (Lord Reid).

[45] *R v Home Secretary, ex p Budd* [1942] 2 KB 14; *The Times*, 28 May 1941. On Regulation 18 B generally, see Simpson, *In the Highest Degree Odious*.

[46] See Ewing and Gearty, *The Struggle for Civil Liberties*, chs 2 and 4.

[47] See HC Deb, 14 February 1996, col 629 (WA).

[48] For a full account, see Morris, *Strikes in Essential Services*; also G S Morris [1980] PL 317 and C Whelan (1979) 8 ILJ 222.

powers to be found in Part II of the Civil Contingencies Act 2004. This is designed to extend the circumstances in which such powers may be used.

An emergency is now defined to mean an event or situation which threatens human welfare, the environment, or the security of the United Kingdom (s 19). These terms are widely defined to include matters such as loss of life and damage to property; contamination of land, water or air and flooding; and war and terrorism. As a result, it ought not to be necessary for governments to take additional ad hoc powers to deal with war should such an event arise, though equally the taking of such powers would hardly be a surprise. Unlike the 1920 Act, these emergency powers can be invoked without a state of emergency being declared and without the need to invoke the Act being considered by Parliament. There will, however, be an opportunity for Parliament to consider the emergency regulations which are made by the government to deal with the emergency (s 20). These regulations may be made by the Queen in Council (s 20(1)), but in some circumstances it may be possible for the regulations to be made by a senior minister, defined to include the Prime Minister, Foreign Secretary, Home Secretary and Chancellor of the Exchequer (s 20(2)). Regulations may be made where it is necessary to prevent, control or mitigate the effect of the emergency, provided the measures in question are in 'due proportion' to the situation they are designed to address (s 21).

The emergency regulations may be made for a wide range of purposes, such as protecting human life, health and safety, and protecting or restoring property (s 22). There are in fact no fewer than 12 purposes for which the regulations may be made. In addressing these purposes, extensive powers may be taken in the regulations. These include the requisition or destruction of property (with or without compensation), and prohibiting freedom of movement or freedom of assembly (s 22(3)). Some of the powers are vague and open ended, such as the power to prohibit 'other specified activities' (s 22(3)(h)),[49] and the power to confer jurisdiction on a court or tribunal (including a court or tribunal established by the regulations) (s 22(3)(n)). Other powers relate to the deployment of the armed forces (s 22(3)(l)). But emergency regulations may not impose military conscription or prohibit strikes or other industrial action (s 23(3)). There are also limits on the power to create criminal offences by emergency regulations, on the penalties that may be imposed for such offences, and on the ability to alter criminal procedure (s 23(4)). All such offences must be tried in the magistrates' court in England and Wales or in the Sheriff Court in Scotland (s 23(4)).

The emergency regulations may apply without parliamentary approval for up to seven days, but lapse thereafter if such approval is not forthcoming (s 27). They may be amended by Parliament (s 27(3)). Once approved, the regulations are valid for 30 days unless revoked (s 26), but they may be renewed for further periods of up to 30 days (s 27(4)). The emergency regulations will not apply to Scotland or Wales unless the First Minister or the National Assembly for Wales respectively have been consulted (s 29). Once made, the regulations may be subject to judicial review, including review under the Human Rights Act. The government had originally proposed that emergency regulations should have the status of primary legislation in what appeared as an attempt to limit the scope for judicial review. But this proposal was strongly criticised in Parliament by the Joint Committee which had been established to consider the draft Bill,[50] as well as by the House of Commons Defence Committee and the House of Lords Constitution Committee.[51] According to the Joint Committee there was no need to exclude human rights protection in this way, given that the judges are not overly activist in dealing with challenges to emergency powers, and are unlikely to prevent government taking action to protect public safety.[52] The

---

[49] Defined in turn to mean 'specified by, or to be specified in accordance with, the regulations': s 22(4).

[50] HL 184, HC 1074 (2002–03), paras 144–56.

[51] HC 557 (2002–03), paras 67–8; HL 184, HC 1074 (2002–03), Appendix. See also JCHR: HC 1005, HL 149 (2002–03), para 3.11.

[52] HL 184, HC 1074 (2002–03), para 149.

government accepted these criticisms and the Bill was amended so that emergency regulations are to be treated as what they are, namely secondary legislation for the purposes of the Human Rights Act.

C. Martial law

The meaning of martial law

The term martial law may be given a variety of meanings. In former times martial law included what is now called military law.[53] In international law, martial law refers to the powers exercised by a military commander in occupation of foreign territory. In the present context, martial law refers to an emergency amounting to a state of war when the military may impose restrictions and regulations on citizens in their own country.[54] In such a situation of civil war or insurrection, the ordinary functioning of the courts gives way before the tasks of the military in restoring the conditions which make normal government possible. Unlike the use of armed force for restoring order during riots, when the military are subject to direction by the civil authorities and to control by the courts if excessive force is used, under martial law the military authorities are (for the time being) the sole judges of the steps that should be taken. These steps might involve taking drastic measures against civilians, for example, the removal of life, liberty or property without due process of law, but possibly accompanied by the creation of military tribunals to administer summary justice. Such tribunals are not to be confused with the courts-martial which regularly administer military law.

It would be wrong to state the principal aspects of martial law as if they were part of present-day law, if only for the reason that within Great Britain occasions for the exercise of martial law have not arisen since at least 1800. Moreover, the Petition of Right 1628 contains a prohibition against the issue by the Crown of commissions of martial law giving the army powers over civilians, at least in peacetime, and the meaning of this prohibition is far from clear today.[55] In times of national emergency today, Parliament prefers to give the civil and military authorities wide powers of governing by means of temporary legislation. It is submitted, therefore, that any discussion of the possible operation of martial law in Great Britain must assume that Parliament itself is prevented by the urgency of events from giving the necessary powers to the military authorities. If Parliament is sitting but refuses to pass emergency legislation, there would seem to be great difficulty, from a constitutional standpoint, in accepting that extraordinary powers of the military arise by process of common law.[56] Moreover, short of a military coup or an extreme emergency in which human survival becomes the only criterion, it must be assumed that the government continues to control the armed forces and to be responsible for their use to Parliament. In Northern Ireland since 1969, at no time did the British government invoke the doctrine of martial law as a justification for exempting the actions of the forces from scrutiny in the courts; instead there was reliance on statutory powers or on the use of common law powers falling far short of a martial law situation.

An attempt to describe the doctrine of martial law must be based on case law arising out of the Boer War, the civil war in Ireland early in the 1920s, and incidents in the earlier history of British colonies. But it would take an alarming deterioration in political stability for it to be necessary to determine whether this mingled case law is applicable in Great Britain.[57] During the two world wars, the civil and criminal courts continued to function in Great Britain although

---

[53] Ch 16 B.

[54] Keir and Lawson, *Cases in Constitutional Law*, ch III C; Heuston, *Essays in Constitutional Law*, pp 150–62.

[55] Cf *Marais v General Officer Commanding* [1902] AC 109, 115.

[56] Cf *Egan v Macready* [1921] 1 IR 265, 274.

[57] Cf the argument in Dicey, *The Law of the Constitution*, ch 8, that martial law is unknown to the law of England.

their operation was subject to statutory restrictions. No state of martial law was declared. The Defence of the Realm Act 1914 authorised for a few months the trial of civilians by court-martial for offences against defence regulations. The Emergency Powers (Defence) (No 2) Act 1940, passed under the threat of imminent invasion, gave authority for special war zone courts to exercise criminal jurisdiction if, on account of military action, criminal justice had to be more speedily administered than in the ordinary courts. Such courts were never required to sit. In Northern Ireland since 1969, the ordinary civil and criminal courts continued to function, although in dealing with terrorist offences the powers and procedures of the criminal courts were much amended.[58]

Position of the courts during martial law

If, in a state of civil war or insurrection, the administration of justice breaks down because the courts are unable to function, it follows as a matter of fact that the acts of the military in seeking to restore order cannot be called into question in the courts so long as this situation lasts. As the English Law Officers said in 1838 in relation to the power of the governor of Lower Canada to proclaim martial law, martial law 'can only be tolerated because, by reason of open rebellion, the enforcing of any other law has become impossible'.[59] If in such a situation the executive proclaims martial law, the proclamation does not increase the powers of the military but merely gives notice to the people of the course which the government must adopt to restore order. In 1838 the Law Officers considered that, when the regular courts were in operation, any persons arrested by the military must be delivered to the courts to be dealt with according to law: 'there is not, as we conceive, any right in the Crown to adopt any other course of proceeding'.[60]

In 1902, in the *Marais* case, the Privy Council significantly extended the doctrine of martial law by holding that a situation of martial law might exist although the civil courts were still sitting. During the Boer War martial law had been proclaimed over certain areas of Cape Colony: Marais, a civilian, sought in the Supreme Court at Cape Town to challenge the legality of his arrest and detention for breach of military rules in an area subject to martial law. Lord Halsbury, on behalf of the Judicial Committee, declared that where war actually exists, the ordinary courts have no jurisdiction over the military authorities, although there might often be doubt as to whether a situation of war existed, as opposed to a mere riot or other disturbance.[61] Once a war situation had been recognised to exist, the military would presumably be able to deal with the inhabitants of an area under martial law on the same footing as the population of a foreign territory occupied during a war between states, subject only to the possibility of being called to account for their acts in civil courts after the resumption of normal government at a later date.

Advantage of the *Marais* case was taken by the United Kingdom government during the serious disturbances in Ireland in 1920–21. Early in 1920 the Westminster Parliament passed the Restoration of Order in Ireland Act, which gave exceptional powers to the executive, created new offences, provided for civilians to be tried and sentenced by properly convened courts-martial and prescribed the maximum penalties that could be imposed. Yet, in December 1920, martial law was proclaimed in areas of Ireland and the general officer commanding the army declared inter alia that any unauthorised person found in possession of arms would be subject to the death penalty. The general also established informal military courts for administering summary justice to those alleged to have committed the prohibited acts. In *R v Allen*, the King's Bench Division in Ireland refused to intervene in the case of a death sentence imposed by such a military court on a civilian for possession of arms. The court held that a state of war existed in the area in question; that

---

[58] Terrorism Act 2000, Part 7. See section E below.
[59] Opinion of J Campbell and R M Rolfe, 16 January 1838; Keir and Lawson, p 231.
[60] Ibid.
[61] *Marais v General Officer Commanding* [1902] AC 109. And see *Tilonko v A-G of Natal* [1907] AC 93.

military acts could not therefore be questioned in the civil courts even though the latter were still operating; and that the army authorities could take the lives of civilians if they deemed it to be absolutely essential. It was immaterial that Parliament had not authorised the death penalty for unauthorised possession of arms.[62]

The decisions of other Irish courts were not all so favourable to the army. In *Egan v Macready*, O'Connor MR distinguished the *Marais* case, holding that the Restoration of Order in Ireland Act 1920 created a complete code for military control of the situation which excluded the power of the army to impose the death penalty where Parliament had not granted this; he ordered the prisoner to be released by issuing habeas corpus.[63] In *R (Garde) v Strickland*, the court in strong terms asserted its power and duty to decide whether or not a state of war existed which justified the application of martial law, holding also that, as long as that state existed, no court had jurisdiction to inquire into the conduct of the army commander in repressing rebellion.[64] In *Higgins v Willis*, in which an action was brought for wrongful destruction of a civilian's house, the court declared that the plaintiff had a right to have his case against the military decided by the courts as soon as the state of war had ceased.[65] In the only decision by the House of Lords, *Re Clifford and O'Sullivan*, on facts similar to those in *R v Allen* it was held that the courts could not, by issuing a writ of prohibition, review the proceedings of a military tribunal set up under a proclamation of martial law.[66] This decision turned on the technical scope of the writ of prohibition, at that time considered to be available only against inferior bodies exercising judicial functions.[67] The House of Lords regarded the military tribunal in question, which was not a regularly constituted court-martial, as merely an advisory committee of officers to assist the commander in chief; moreover its duties had already been completed. The House expressly refrained from discussing the merits of other remedies that might be available, for example, a writ of habeas corpus. It followed that the army's decision to take the life of a citizen did not become subject to judicial control merely because an informal hearing had been given to the civilian by a military tribunal.

Position of the courts after martial law ends

After termination of the state of martial law, the courts have jurisdiction to review the legality of acts committed during the period of martial law. It is not possible to state with any certainty what standards will be applied by the courts in respect either of criminal or civil liability. First, there is no doubt that at common law many acts of the army which are necessary for dealing with civil war and insurrection will be justified; nor would there be liability at common law for damage to person or property inflicted accidentally in the course of actual fighting.[68] But what is not clear is whether the test should be that of strict necessity or merely bona fide belief in the necessity of the action, whether a stricter standard may be required in the case of some acts than others or where the burden of proof should lie. Second, there is some uncertainty as to the legal effect of superior orders.[69] Third, in the past it was usual after martial law for an Act of Indemnity to be passed giving retrospective protection to the armed forces. On the basis of *Wright v Fitzgerald*[70] it would seem that in interpreting an Indemnity Act, the courts presume that Parliament does not

---

[62] [1921] 2 IR 241. See Campbell, *Emergency Law in Ireland 1918–1925*. For Cabinet discussion of martial law in Ireland, see Jones, *Whitehall Diary*, vol 3, part I.

[63] [1921] 1 IR 265, criticised in Heuston, p 158.

[64] [1921] 2 IR 317.

[65] [1921] 2 IR 386.

[66] [1921] 2 AC 570.

[67] Ch 31.

[68] *Burmah Oil Co v Lord Advocate* [1965] AC 75; and ch 12 D.

[69] Ch 16.

[70] (1798) 27 St Tr 765, discussed by P O'Higgins (1962) 25 MLR 413.

intend to indemnify a defendant for merely wanton or cruel acts not justified by the necessities of the situation, but the extent of protection depends on the terms of the Indemnity Act, which may be both explicit and very wide.[71]

LEGAL RESPONSES TO TERRORISM

Special legislation dealing with terrorism was first introduced in Britain in 1974, following the Birmingham pub bombings in that year.[72] Although said by its author to be 'drastic',[73] the Prevention of Terrorism (Temporary Provisions) Act 1974 was at least subject to the formality of annual renewal by Parliament, while subsequent Prevention of Terrorism (Temporary Provisions) Acts expired after five years: hence the reference to temporary provisions in their short titles. But perhaps inevitably, these temporary provisions became permanent, with the Terrorism Act 2000 being designed to implement the recommendations of an *Inquiry into Legislation Against Terrorism* conducted by Lord Lloyd of Berwick in 1996.[74] Passed just after the Belfast Agreement in 1999, and just before the 9/11 attacks in New York and Washington in 2001, the 2000 Act has become a cornerstone in the government's response to international as well as domestic terrorism.

D. Definition of terrorism

The first question to ask in examining any body of law conferring special restrictions on the individual or in conferring special powers on the state is simply this: to what activity do the restrictions apply?

Here, one of the most controversial features of the Terrorism Act 2000 is the wide definition of terrorism in s 1 to mean action or the threat of action (including action outside the United Kingdom) which (*a*) falls within s 1(2); (*b*) is designed to influence a government (or an international governmental organisation), or to intimidate the public or a section of the public; and (*c*) is made for the purpose of advancing a political, religious, racial or ideological cause. Much of the concern relates to the wide scope of the action falling within s 1(2), which applies not only to serious violence, serious damage to property and the endangering of human life, but also to creating 'a serious risk to the health or safety of the public or a section of the public', as well as seriously interfering with or seriously disrupting an electronic system.

Section 1 also makes it clear that the Act applies to terrorist activity overseas, as well as that directed at the British government. The action to which the section applies may be action outside the United Kingdom and the government which it is designed to influence may be the government of the United Kingdom (or a part thereof), or of a country other than the United Kingdom.[75] This wide definition gave rise to a great deal of comment and a number of difficult questions were raised as the Bill was passing through Parliament. A good example is the following:

---

[71] See the notorious example in *Phillips v Eyre* (1870) LR 6 QB 1 and cf Indemnity Act 1920.

[72] Special powers to deal with threats to security in Northern Ireland are, however, almost as old as the Province itself. See Civil Authorities (Special Powers) Act 1922, replaced by Northern Ireland (Emergency Provisions) Act 1973, amended in 1975 and 1977 and re-enacted in 1978, 1987, 1991 and 1996. On the 1922 Act, see Calvert, *Constitutional Law in Northern Ireland*, ch 20; Campbell, *Emergency Law in Ireland 1918–1925*; and Ewing and Gearty, *The Struggle for Civil Liberties*, ch 7. The 1973 Act was preceded by the Diplock Report, Cmnd 5185, 1972.

[73] Jenkins, *A Life at the Centre*, p 394.

[74] Cm 3420, 1996. See also the important report by Gearty and Kimbell, *Terrorism and the Rule of Law*.

[75] See *R v F* [2007] EWCA (Crim) 243, [2007] 2 All ER 193.

If someone decided to break into a mink farm in order to release the mink from their cages, or to break into a research station and destroy the animals' cages, that would clearly be an act of serious violence. It would be a criminal act – and one that I deplore. But why should such organisations be classified as terrorist under [section] 1?[76]

The Home Secretary conceded that this conduct might well fall under s 1, but felt that the answer to the potentially wide scope of the legislation lay in the self-restraint of the prosecuting authorities.[77]

The Home Secretary also drew attention to the Human Rights Act 1998 and to arts 5 and 6 of the ECHR as a 'profound safeguard against the disproportionate use of the powers' in the Act.[78] There was nevertheless still concern about the application of the definition to international terrorism. One recurring question was whether British-based support for the anti-apartheid activities of the ANC in South Africa before the end of apartheid would have been caught by the Act. Other concerns related to 'international campaigns, such as those that support, for example, the actions of the Kurds resisting being driven from their lands by the building of dams, the resistance of the Ogoni in Nigeria to the theft and pollution of their lands, and the resistance of the Amazon Indians to the destruction of their rainforests. All those campaigns of resistance have involved incidents of violent collision with those who would destroy people's livelihoods and lives.'[79] Although the government expressed the view that support for such international causes 'will not even remotely come under the [Act]', it has since been held that 'the terrorist legislation applies to countries which are governed by tyrants and dictators'.[80]

E. Terrorist organisations and terrorist funds

Terrorist organisations

Part II of the Terrorism Act 2000 restricts freedom of association in the United Kingdom by proscribing specified organisations. This is a procedure that has a long history,[81] and there are 14 bodies listed in Sch 2, all connected with events in Northern Ireland. But the Secretary of State also has power to add to the list by order (s 3), a power which was expanded in 2006 (to cover organisations which glorify terrorism),[82] and which has been exercised in respect of another 46 organisations which are said to be involved in terrorist activities in different parts of the world but which are thought to operate in or from this country.[83] Before an organisation may be added to the list, the Secretary of State must believe that it is 'concerned in terrorism' (s 3(4)),

---

[76] HC Deb, 14 Dec 1999, col 155 (Mr Douglas Hogg). There was also the case of the women who attacked the Hawk aircraft with hammers, as well as the case of the Trident Ploughshares 2000 organisation, which attacked the Trident submarine – ibid, col 200.

[77] Thus, 'I believe that we must have some confidence in the law enforcement agencies and the courts. If we look back at the past 25 years, we can see that the powers have been used proportionately in the face of an horrific threat from terrorism in Ireland and from international terrorism' (HC Deb, 14 Dec 1999, col 155). See also at col 165 (independence of the police, the DPP and the Attorney General). The consent of the DPP is necessary before any prosecution (s 117).

[78] Ibid, col 160. It was also claimed by a former minister from the Opposition benches that 'the integrity of Ministers is often bolstered by the knowledge of the existence of judicial review' (HC Deb, 14 Dec 1999, Mr Tom King).

[79] HC Deb, 14 December 1999, col 160 (Mr Alan Simpson).

[80] R v F [2007] EWCA (Crim) 243, [2007] 2 All ER 193. In the same case it was said that 'there is no exemption from criminal liability for terrorist activities which are motivated or said to be morally justified by the alleged nobility of the terrorist cause'.

[81] See R v Z [2005] UKHL 35; [2005] 2 AC 645, paras [3]–[8].

[82] Terrorism Act 2006, s 21, amending 2000 Act, s 3.

[83] See http://security.homeoffice.gov.uk/terrorist-threat/proscribed-terrorist-orgs/proscribed-terrorist-groups/. Of these 46, 44 were banned under the original powers in the 2000 Act, and the other two as a result of the 2006 amendments.

which means not only that it commits or prepares acts of terrorism, but that it promotes or encourages terrorism or is 'otherwise concerned in terrorism' (s 3(5)).

The Secretary of State also has the power to remove an organisation by order from the proscribed list, following an application by the organisation or any person affected by the organisation's proscription (s 4). Given that it is an offence to be a member of a proscribed organisation (on which see later), this could be a bold move, particularly if the application is refused. If the Secretary of State refuses the application, an appeal may be made to the Proscribed Organisations Appeal Commission, which is required to apply the principles of judicial review (s 5), with a right of appeal from the Commission on a point of law to the Court of Appeal, Court of Session or Court of Appeal in Northern Ireland, as appropriate (s 6).[84] In general a decision to proscribe an organisation is not subject to judicial review, with a proscribed organisation being expected by the courts to use the statutory de-proscription procedure,[85] where it may be represented by a special advocate appointed by one of the government's law officers.[86]

> In *R v Z*[87] the question was whether the Real IRA was a proscribed organisation. The proscribed organisations in the Schedule include the IRA but not the Real IRA, a newly formed splinter group that did not accept the peace process. Reading the legislation very widely, the House of Lords held that the term IRA applied to an organisation 'whatever relationship (if any) it has to any other organisation of the same name'. Although there was a risk that 'a group within the extended IRA family would be proscribed which was currently non-violent', Lord Bingham concluded that 'it might well have been thought unlikely that a body bearing the name IRA or any variant of it would be at all friendly to parliamentary democracy'.[88]

It is an offence to be a member (or to profess membership) of a proscribed organisation (s 11), a measure said to be of 'extraordinary breadth'.[89] It is a defence under s 11(2) if the defendant can prove that the organisation was not proscribed while he or she was a member, a burden read down by the House of Lords to be evidential rather than legal. This is despite the fact that Parliament had clearly intended otherwise when enacting the 2000 Act, providing a nice example of how the Human Rights Act, s 3 is binding on future or subsequently enacted legislation.[90] It is an offence to invite support for such an organisation (s 12), or to organise a meeting (whether in public or private) in support of such an organisation. Breach of these provisions could lead to imprisonment of up to ten years or to a fine or both, after a conviction on indictment (s 12(6)).

In addition to the foregoing, it is an offence under s 13 for a person in a public place to wear an item of clothing or wear, carry or display an article 'in such a way or in such circumstances as to arouse reasonable apprehension that he is a member or supporter of a proscribed organisation' (s 13(1)). Conduct violating s 13 may also be unlawful under s 1 of the Public Order Act 1936, which makes it an offence to wear a political uniform in public. Although the 1936 Act was designed initially for use against Oswald Mosley's fascists, this measure was used successfully in 1975 against IRA members who led funeral processions in England, dressed in dark pullovers, dark berets and dark glasses.[91] The restrictions in the Terrorism Act 2000 (and the 1989 Act which preceded it) are wider, there being no need to show that the demonstration of support amounts to the wearing of a uniform as such: a small emblem such as a ring would be enough.

---

[84] See *Lord Alton of Liverpool* v *Home Secretary* [2008] EWCA Civ 443, [2008] WLR (D) 141, which together with the decision of the POAC which the Court of Appeal upholds, gives a good insight into the proscription procedure in the Home Office.

[85] *R (Kurdistan Workers' Party)* v *Home Secretary* [2002] EWHC (Admin) 644.

[86] 2000 Act, Sch 3, para 7.

[87] See note 81 above.

[88] Ibid, para [20].

[89] *Attorney-General's Reference No 4 of 2002* [2004] UKHL 43; [2005] 1 AC 264, para [47] (Lord Bingham).

[90] Ibid.

[91] *O'Moran* v *DPP* [1975] QB 864.

Terrorist funds

Part III of the Terrorism Act 2000 (as amended by the Anti-terrorism, Crime and Security Act 2001) deals with terrorist property, defined to mean both money and property likely to be used for the purposes of terrorism, including any resources of a proscribed organisation (s 14). It is an offence to solicit, receive or give money or property for terrorist purposes (s 15). The Act contains additional measures which were first introduced in 1989 'to strike at the financial roots of terrorism',[92] at a time when it was thought that the IRA (then the main target) had an annual income of £3–4 million, generated not only by robbery and extortion, but also by apparently legitimate business activity which gave the organisation 'an assured income and a firmer base'.[93] So, apart from the direct financing of terrorism, it is an offence to use or possess money or property for terrorist purposes (s 16). Although property for this purpose includes magazines and other literature, it has been held that s 16 does not violate art 10 of the ECHR, since it falls well within art 10(2).[94]

It is also an offence to be involved in 'an arrangement' whereby money or property is made available for terrorist purposes (s 17). This is intended to cover banking transactions involving payments to a customer's order and also an arrangement whereby money or other property is made available to a lawful business and either that money, or the profits of that activity, is 'intended to be used for terrorist purposes'. Section 18 contains the so-called laundering offence, making it unlawful to enter into an arrangement 'which facilitates the retention or control by or on behalf of another person of terrorist property', by concealment, removal from the jurisdiction, transfer to nominees or 'in any other way'. As pointed out by Lord Carlile, this is an extremely wide provision, explaining that 'an estate agent collecting rent from office premises might be totally unaware that the ultimate beneficiaries of the profits are a company operating for the benefit of a terrorist organisation'. However, as Lord Carlile also stated, 'if charged, the statutory defence made available under section 18(2) would place a reverse burden upon him to show "that he did not know and had no reasonable cause to suspect that the arrangement related to terrorist property"'.[95]

Where someone suspects that another person has committed an offence under ss 15–18, it is an offence not to inform the police as soon as reasonably practicable (s 19).[96] There is an exception for employees who have informed their employer in accordance with any procedure for reporting concerns of this kind (although if the employer has no procedure there would be no defence for failing to notify the police). There is also an exception for lawyers in relation to information obtained from a client in connection with the provision of legal advice. But there is no exception for journalists,[97] although there is a general defence of reasonableness from which journalists might benefit.[98] Section 21 deals with the position of police informers, so that it is not an offence for a person to withhold information under ss 15–18 if acting with the express consent of the police; nor is it an offence to be involved in a money-laundering arrangement after informing the police that the money or other property in question is terrorist property.

The latter provision would protect the bank or other body which is the medium for the unlawful action and also give the police access to information about the arrangement. Additional measures introduced by the Anti-terrorism, Crime and Security Act 2001 – ss 21A and 21B – impose duties of disclosure on the financial services industry. Where a person is convicted of an offence under

---

[92] HC Deb, 6 Dec 1988, col 212 (Mr Douglas Hurd).

[93] Ibid, col 213.

[94] *O'Driscoll v Home Secretary* [2002] EWHC 2477 (Admin).

[95] Lord Carlile, *Report on the Operation in 2004 of the Terrorism Act 2000* (2005), para 42. Lord Carlile is the government's independent reviewer of the terrorism legislation, who carries out his reviews under statutory authority.

[96] Amended by the Counter-Terrorism Act 2008, s 77.

[97] A point which was raised in Parliament at Second Reading in the Commons: HC Deb, 14 Dec 1999, col 181 (Fiona Mactaggart). See also J J Rowe [2001] Crim LR 527, at pp 537–8.

[98] HL Deb, 23 May 2000, col 653 (Lord Bassam).

ss 15–18, a court may make an order for the forfeiture of money or property destined for terrorist use or which was the subject of an arrangement for handling or laundering terrorist funds (s 23). There are powers for the seizure, detention and forfeiture in civil proceedings of cash intended to be used for terrorist purposes, as well as cash which represents the resources of a proscribed organisation or property obtained through terrorism. The powers of forfeiture may be exercised even though no criminal proceedings have previously been brought in connection with the cash.[99]

F. Terrorist investigations and counter-terrorist powers

Terrorist investigations

A 'terrorist investigation' is defined to mean an investigation of one of five matters: the commission, preparation or instigation of acts of terrorism; an act which appears to have been done for the purposes of terrorism; the resources of a proscribed organisation; the possibility of making a proscription order under s 3; and the commission, preparation or instigation of an offence under the Terrorism Act 2000 itself, or the Terrorism Act 2006, Part 1 (s 32).

Sections 33–36 empower the police to impose *cordons* for up to 28 days in the course of terrorist investigations and to order people to leave the area, to leave premises in the cordoned area and to remove vehicles from the area. An order designating a cordoned area, may be made by a police officer of the rank of superintendent or above, although it may also be made by an officer of lesser rank where necessary 'by reason of urgency' (s 34(2)). There are few formalities associated with the exercise of this power: if made orally, the designation is to be confirmed in writing as soon as reasonably practicable; and it can only be made for 14 days in the first instance, to be renewed as necessary. There is no reporting to the Home Secretary or to anyone else on the exercise of this power and not even an annual reporting obligation on the number of times the power is exercised.[100]

There are extensive powers conferred on the police to obtain *information for the purposes of a terrorist investigation*. By virtue of s 37 and Sch 5, a justice of the peace may issue a search warrant (all premises or specific premises), if there are reasonable grounds for believing that there is material on the premises to which the application relates which is likely to be of substantial value to the investigation (Sch 5, para 1(5)), and does not consist of items subject to legal privilege or excluded or special procedure material (as defined by PACE) (para 4).[101] In the case of excluded or special procedure material, a constable may apply to a circuit judge or a district judge (magistrates' court) for an order requiring the person in possession to produce it for the constable to take away or have access to it (paras 5–10). For these purposes, documents may be taken away and examined to determine if they should be seized, provisions which do not apply to items subject to legal privilege.[102] There is no provision in the Terrorism Act 2000 requiring the application for an order to be made *inter partes*.[103]

Where an order is not complied with or where access to the material is needed more immediately, the constable may apply to a circuit judge or a district judge (magistrates' court) for a warrant

---

[99] Anti-terrorism, Crime and Security Act 2001, s 1 and Sch 1.

[100] These powers may also be exercised in some circumstances by the British Transport Police and by the Ministry of Defence Police following amendments introduced by the 2001 Act.

[101] Separate provisions deal with police access to confidential customer information held by banks, extended in 2001 to include a police power to monitor bank accounts (with the authority of a circuit judge or sheriff) and to freeze accounts. See Terrorism Act 2000, Sch 6 and Anti-terrorism, Crime and Security Act 2001, ss 4–16, and Schs 2 and 3.

[102] Counter-Terrorism Act 2008, ss 1–9. The same applies to the search powers under the 2000 Act, s 43. See below.

[103] Compare the procedures under PACE 1984: see ch 21 D. For the procedure to be followed in such cases see *R v Middlesex Guildhall Crown Court, ex p Salinger* [1993] QB 564.

to search the premises (again specific premises or all premises) for the excluded or special procedure material (paras 11 and 12). A circuit judge or a district judge (magistrates' court) may also issue an order requiring a person to provide an explanation of any material which has been produced or seized under the foregoing provisions (para 13). In cases 'of great emergency', a police officer of the rank of superintendent or above may by written order authorise conduct which would otherwise require a judicial warrant (para 15).[104] Amendments introduced in 2001 make it an offence to fail to provide information to the police if the person in question 'knows or believes' that the information 'might be of material assistance' in preventing the commission by another person of an act of terrorism.[105]

Police powers

Police powers of arrest, search, and stop and search are dealt with in Part V of the Terrorism Act 2000. They apply to someone who is a terrorist, defined to mean not only someone who has committed an offence under the Act, but also someone who has been 'concerned in the commission, preparation or instigation of acts of terrorism'. For this purpose terrorism carries the meaning set out in s 1 (s 40).

Section 41 gives a power to a constable to *arrest without a warrant* a person whom 'he reasonably suspects to be a terrorist'.[106] A person so arrested may be detained for up to 48 hours, in contrast to the normal 24 or 36 hours. A lawful arrest is a precondition of any such detention.[107] Further detention must be authorised by a warrant issued by a judicial authority (a district judge (magistrates' courts) in England and Wales; a sheriff in Scotland; or a county court judge or resident magistrate in Northern Ireland).[108] A person should not be detained for more than 14 days in total from the time of arrest,[109] though by virtue of controversial amendments introduced in 2006, the period of 14 days may be extended to 28 days with appropriate judicial authority, where this is necessary for the purpose of an investigation.[110] Provision is made in Sch 8 for the treatment of persons detained under these powers.[111]

In addition to powers of arrest, a police officer may apply to a justice of the peace for a warrant to *enter and search* any premises on reasonable suspicion that a person concerned with the commission, preparation or instigation of acts of terrorism will be found there (s 42). There are also powers under the Terrorism Act 2006 authorising a police constable to apply to a justice of the peace for a warrant to enter and search premises for terrorist publications of the kind prohibited by section 2 of the same Act (that is to say, publications that encourage or glorify terrorism). In addition, a police officer has the power to *stop and search* a person whom 'he reasonably suspects to be a terrorist', in order 'to discover whether he has in his possession anything which may constitute evidence that he is a terrorist' (s 43(1)). A police officer may also *search* a person

---

[104] In cases of great emergency, such a police officer may also require a person to provide an explanation of any material seized in pursuance of an order under para 15 (para 16).

[105] Anti-terrorism, Crime and Security Act 2001, s 117, inserting a new s 38 B into the Terrorism Act 2000.

[106] See *O'Hara v Chief Constable of the RUC* [1997] 1 All ER 129. Section 41 does not appear to meet the objections raised about its predecessors, namely that they permitted the police to arrest and detain someone who has not and is not suspected of having committed an offence. This remains the case and doubt has been raised about whether this power is consistent with art 5 of the ECHR. See J J Rowe [2001] Crim LR 527, esp pp 532–3 where the author refers to concerns raised in Parliament by Lord Lloyd as the Bill was being enacted.

[107] *Forbes v HM Advocate* 1990 SCR 69.

[108] The detained person may be excluded from the proceedings in which such an application is made: see *Ward v Police Service of Northern Ireland* [2007] UKHL 50.

[109] As originally enacted the period of detention was seven days; the increase to 14 days was made by the Criminal Justice Act 2003, s 306.

[110] Terrorism Act 2006, s 24.

[111] See also *Re Gillen's Application* [1988] NILR 40 (habeas corpus in the event of unlawful detention).

arrested under s 41 'to discover whether he has in his possession anything which may constitute evidence that he is a terrorist' (s 43(2)).

Other – highly controversial – *stop and search powers* are contained in s 44,[112] which are much wider than the more limited powers in s 43. Thus, s 44 enables a senior police officer to grant an 'authorisation' for renewable periods of 28 days which in turn 'authorises' a constable in uniform in the area or place specified in the authorisation to stop and search vehicles and pedestrians. An authorisation – which ceases to have effect within 48 hours unless approved by the Secretary of State (s 46(4)) – may only be given if 'expedient for the prevention of acts of terrorism'; but once given the power of stop and search may be exercised 'whether or not the constable has grounds for suspecting the presence' of articles of a kind which could be used in connection with terrorism.[113] The over-use of these powers by the police has been widely criticised, with 8,000–10,000 uses each month in 2008 being said by the government's independent reviewer of terrorist legislation to be 'alarming'.[114]

> In the case of *Gillan*, the House of Lords held that the exercise of this power against a student and a journalist at an arms fair in East London did not breach their Convention rights.[115] This was despite the fact that the Metropolitan Police have turned what were enacted as temporary powers into permanent powers, with each 28 day authorisation being renewed on its expiry, so that there was a rolling series of authorisations. The European Court of Human Rights took a different view, holding that the s 44 powers violated the right to private life in art 8 of the ECHR, and that the arbitrary nature of the powers were such that they could not be said to be in accordance with law for the purposes of justification under art 8(2).[116] In the House of Lords in contrast, Lord Bingham had doubted whether 'an ordinary superficial search of the person can be said to show a lack of respect for private life'.

Terrorist offences

Part VI of the 2000 Act contains a number of new terrorist offences. Section 54 provides that it is an offence to provide or receive instruction or training in the making or use of firearms, radioactive material, explosives, or chemical, biological or nuclear weapons. It is also an offence to direct the activities of an organisation which is concerned in the commission of acts of terrorism (s 56), and to possess any article for a purpose connected with the commission, preparation or instigation of acts of terrorism (s 57). It is a defence to prove that the article was not in the possession of the individual for a terrorist purpose, and while the burden of proof is on the defendant (s 57(2)), it has been said that this is 'evidential rather than persuasive or legal'.[117] Sufficient evidence of possession may be established where the accused and the article in question are both present on the premises (s 57(3)).[118]

Section 58 makes it an offence for a person to collect or record any information of a kind likely to be useful to a person committing or preparing an act of terrorism. Particularly controversial in operation is s 58A (introduced by the Counter-Terrorism Act 2008). Designed to protect conspicuous potential targets of terrorist activity and thus apparently unexceptionable, this applies to

---

[112] This provision has its origins in Prevention of Terrorism (Temporary Provisions) Act 1989, s 13A (inserted by the Criminal Justice and Public Order Act 1994, s 81); and s 13B (inserted by the Prevention of Terrorism (Additional Powers) Act 1996).

[113] On the extension of these powers to the British Transport Police and the Ministry of Defence Police, see Anti-terrorism, Crime and Security Act 2001, Sch 7.

[114] Lord Carlile, *Report on the Operation in 2008 of the Terrorism Act 2000 and of Part 1 of the Terrorism Act 2006* (2009), para 147.

[115] *R (Gillan) v Metropolitan Police Commissioner* [2006] UKHL 12; [2006] 2 AC 307.

[116] *Gillan and Quinton v United Kingdom* [2009] ECHR 28.

[117] See HL Deb, 23 May 2000, col 754 (Lord Bassam).

[118] Compare *R v DPP, ex p Kebeline* [2000] 2 AC 326.

conduct which elicits or attempts to elicit information about an individual who is or who has been a member of the armed forces, the intelligence services or the police. The offence is committed in respect of information of a kind likely to be useful to someone committing or preparing an act of terrorism. It is also an offence to publish or communicate such information. By virtue of s 59 it is an offence to incite terrorism overseas, a measure designed to 'deter those who use the United Kingdom as a base from which to promote terrorist acts abroad'.[119]

The problem with s 58A is that it has emerged perhaps unwittingly as a serious threat to free speech, with journalists and photographers claiming that it is being used by the police to prevent them from taking photographs of police officers in particular. It would be unfortunate if the press were to be prevented by this or any other measure from photographing police officers while performing their duties, for example with excessive force. Admittedly, section 58A (2) does provide that it is a 'defence for a person charged with an offence under this section to prove that they had a reasonable excuse for their action'. Nevertheless, this is a matter which attracted the attention of the government's independent reviewer of terrorist legislation, who expressed concern that the legislation should be used in this way:

> It should be emphasised that photography of the police by the media or amateurs remains as legitimate as before, unless the photograph is *likely* to be of use to a terrorist. This is a high bar. It is inexcusable for police officers ever to use this provision to interfere with the rights of individuals to take photographs. The police must adjust to the undoubted fact that the scrutiny of them by members of the public is at least proportional to any increase in police powers – given the ubiquity of photograph and video enabled mobile phones.[120]

G. Detention without trial, control orders and secret justice

As we have seen, much of the Terrorism Act 2000 applies to international terrorism. The definition of terrorism includes conduct designed to influence the government, and for this purpose government is defined to mean the government of the United Kingdom or a part of the United Kingdom, or 'of a country other than the United Kingdom'.[121] It is also an offence under the 2000 Act to incite terrorism overseas,[122] and under the Criminal Law Act 1977 (as amended in 1998)[123] to be part of a conspiracy to commit offences outside the United Kingdom. Nevertheless, the attacks on the United States on 11 September 2001 led to the introduction of additional powers addressed specifically to international terrorism, though many of these powers – contained in the Anti-terrorism, Crime and Security Act 2001 – were to prove even more contentious than the provisions of the Terrorism Act 2000 which they complement.[124] Provisions relating to the indefinite detention without trial of foreign nationals in particular were the subject of withering criticism in Parliament and from the courts,[125] as well as from a committee of Privy Counsellors chaired by Lord Newton which had been appointed to review the Act as a whole.[126]

---

[119] HC Deb, 14 Dec 1999, col 162.

[120] Lord Carlile, *Report on the Operation in 2008 of the Terrorism Act 2000 and of Part 1 of the Terrorism Act 2006* (2009), para 197.

[121] Terrorism Act 2000, s 1(4)(d).

[122] Ibid, ss 59–61.

[123] Criminal Justice (Terrorism and Conspiracy) Act 1998, s 5.

[124] See A Tomkins [2002] PL 205 and H Fenwick (2002) 65 MLR 724.

[125] For concerns expressed in Parliament, see HL 38, HC 381 (2003–04) (Joint Committee on Human Rights). For the position of the courts, see *A v Home Secretary* [2004] UKHL 56; [2005] 2 AC 68, esp Lords Scott and Hoffmann.

[126] Lord Newton's committee had been appointed under 2001 Act, s 122. See Privy Counsellors' Committee, *Anti-terrorism, Crime and Security Act 2001 Review: Report* (HC 100 (2003–04)).

Detention without trial

One of the most symbolically important provisions of the Terrorism Act 2000 was the repeal of the provisions in the Northern Ireland (Emergency Provisions) Act 1996 dealing with the detention without trial – or internment – of terrorist suspects. Although the power to intern was retained until the commencement of the 2000 Act,[127] it was in practice discontinued in 1975, having proved to be not only highly controversial but also of questionable effect.[128] In *Ireland v United Kingdom*,[129] the European Court of Human Rights held that these procedures violated art 5 of the ECHR, but that derogation could be justified under art 15.[130] A fresh derogation was made to authorise new powers of detention without trial contained in Part 4 of the Anti-terrorism, Crime and Security Act 2001. These highly contentious measures provided that the Secretary of State could issue a certificate in respect of an individual whose presence in the United Kingdom was reasonably believed to present a risk to national security and who was reasonably suspected of being a terrorist (s 21(1)). A terrorist for this purpose was defined with reference to international terrorism (s 21(2)), and terrorism carried the same meaning for this Act as it did for the Terrorism Act 2000.

Where a certificate was issued that someone was a suspected international terrorist, the individual could be refused leave to enter or remain in the United Kingdom, or deported or removed in accordance with immigration law (s 22).[131] But there might be circumstances where removal or deportation was prevented by 'a point of law which wholly or partly relates to an international agreement' or to 'a practical consideration' (s 23). An example of the former would be art 3 of the ECHR which – as construed by the Strasbourg Court – prevents the deportation of individuals to countries where they might suffer inhuman or degrading treatment or punishment.[132] In these cases the 2001 Act provided that the suspected international terrorist could be detained indefinitely without trial (s 23). An appeal lay to the Special Immigration Appeals Commission by someone who had been certified as a suspected international terrorist (s 25) and the Commission was required to cancel a certificate if it concluded that there were no reasonable grounds for the suspicion. The Commission was required to review any certificate after six months and at three-monthly intervals thereafter. A review could also be conducted at the request of the certified individual if the Commission considered that the review should be held because of a change of circumstances (s 26). There was an appeal on a point of law to the Court of Appeal or the Court of Session (s 27).[133]

In *A v Home Secretary*[134] these provisions relating to detention were dealt a fatal blow by the House of Lords. Proceedings were brought by nine foreign nationals who were being or who had been detained indefinitely without trial.[135] The Special Immigration Appeal Commission upheld the government's decision to derogate from the Convention but also granted a declaration that the legislation was incompatible with art 14 of the ECHR to the extent that it discriminated against foreign nationals. The government's appeal on this latter

---

[127] See HC Deb, 9 January 1996, col 37. Cf Cm 2706, 1995, p 33.

[128] For background, see Cm 1115, 1990. A full account of the procedures is given in *Ireland v UK* (1978) 2 EHRR 25.

[129] (1978) 2 EHRR 25.

[130] It was also held, however, that the techniques employed to interrogate interned suspects violated art 3 as inhuman and degrading treatment.

[131] See ch 20.

[132] See e.g. *Chahal v UK* (1996) 23 EHRR 413.

[133] By virtue of an amendment made by the 2001 Act, the Special Immigration Appeals Commission is now a superior court of record (s 27). See ch 20.

[134] [2004] UKHL 56; [2005] 2 AC 68. See A Tomkins [2005] PL 259; T Hickman (2005) 68 MLR 655; M Arden (2005) 121 LQR 604; M Elliott (2010) 8 *Int Jo of Const Law* 131.

[135] Two exercised their right to leave the country, one had been released on bail, one had been released without conditions, and one had been transferred to Broadmoor Hospital on grounds of mental illness.

point was upheld by the Court of Appeal, but the declaration was reinstated by the House of Lords in a majority decision of 8:1. The House of Lords agreed that there was a public emergency threatening the life of the nation, thereby justifying the derogation from art 5 of the Convention. But the House of Lords also concluded that the steps taken against foreign nationals were disproportionate and discriminatory. As a result, the derogation order was quashed.[136] Moreover, a declaration was issued under the Human Rights Act 1998 that s 23 of the 2001 Act was incompatible with art 5 and 14 of the ECHR, 'in so far as it is disproportionate and permits detention of suspected international terrorists in a way that discriminates on the ground of nationality or immigration status'.

Sections 21–32 of the 2001 Act were repealed by the Prevention of Terrorism Act 2005, and in subsequent proceedings in the European Court of Human Rights some of the detainees were awarded compensation for the violation of their Convention rights.[137]

Control orders

In removing the power of indefinite detention (albeit in a 'prison with three walls' – in the sense that the detainees were always free to leave the United Kingdom), the Prevention of Terrorism Act 2005 introduced new powers of executive restraint.[138] These are control orders, with a control order being defined as 'an order against an individual that imposes obligations on him for purposes connected with protecting members of the public from a risk of terrorism' (s 1(1)). Control orders may be of two kinds: (i) non-derogating control orders may be made by the Home Secretary and must not impose obligations inconsistent with the individual's right to liberty under ECHR, art 5; and (ii) derogating control orders may be made only by a court on an application by the Home Secretary. Before the power to make derogating control orders can be invoked, procedures set out in the 2005 Act, s 6 must first be complied with. Until that has been done, only non-derogating control orders may be made. This, however, is not a significant constraint, as there is wide scope for non-derogating control orders, where 'necessary for purposes connected with preventing or restricting involvement by that individual in terrorism-related activity' (s 1(3)).

The conditions that may be imposed require careful reading. By virtue of s 1(4), they are as follows:

- a prohibition or restriction on his possession or use of specified articles or substances;
- a prohibition or restriction on his use of specified services or specified facilities, or on his carrying on specified activities;
- a restriction in respect of his work or other occupation, or in respect of his business;
- a restriction on his association or communications with specified persons or with other persons generally;
- a restriction in respect of his place of residence or on the persons to whom he gives access to his place of residence;
- a prohibition on his being at specified places or within a specified area at specified times or on specified days;
- a prohibition or restriction on his movements to, from or within the United Kingdom, a specified part of the United Kingdom or a specified place or area within the United Kingdom;

---

[136] See subsequently SI 2005 No 1071.
[137] *A v United Kingdom* [2009] ECHR 301.
[138] The Bill was bitterly contested in Parliament and the government had to make a number of concessions to secure its passage. See J Hiebert (2005) 68 MLR 676.

- a requirement on him to comply with such other prohibitions or restrictions on his movements as may be imposed, for a period not exceeding 24 hours, by directions given to him in the specified manner, by a specified person and for the purpose of securing compliance with other obligations imposed by or under the order;

- a requirement on him to surrender his passport, or anything in his possession to which a prohibition or restriction imposed by the order relates, to a specified person for a period not exceeding the period for which the order remains in force;

- a requirement on him to give access to specified persons to his place of residence or to other premises to which he has power to grant access;

- a requirement on him to allow specified persons to search that place or any such premises for the purpose of ascertaining whether obligations imposed by or under the order have been, are being or are about to be contravened;

- a requirement on him to allow specified persons, either for that purpose or for the purpose of securing that the order is complied with, to remove anything found in that place or on any such premises and to subject it to tests or to retain it for a period not exceeding the period for which the order remains in force;

- a requirement on him to allow himself to be photographed;

- a requirement on him to co-operate with specified arrangements for enabling his movements, communications or other activities to be monitored by electronic or other means;

- a requirement on him to comply with a demand made in the specified manner to provide information to a specified person in accordance with the demand;

- a requirement on him to report to a specified person at specified times and places.

These provisions have been used to impose what has been described as a form of house arrest, with Lord Bingham saying on one occasion that an 'analogy with detention in an open prison was apt'.[139] People were detained at home for periods of up to 18 hours every day,[140] with little access to the outside world, and subject to frequent visits by the police and the companies responsible for the electronic monitors placed in the homes of people under a control order.[141] Questions were raised whether the tight conditions imposed on controlled persons under ostensibly non-derogating control orders were consistent with Convention obligations,[142] a matter on which the House of Lords disagreed sharply, with Lord Brown occupying the middle ground in holding that a control order imposing detention at home for up to 16 hours a day is the maximum that could be imposed consistently with the right to liberty under art 5 of the ECHR.[143] Although the control order regime is perhaps less restrictive of liberty than detention in prison, more people have been subject to control orders than were ever detained under the 2001 Act, and control orders apply equally to British nationals as to the nationals of other countries.[144] Additional powers in relation to controlled persons were taken in the Counter-Terrorism Act 2008, these allowing

---

[139] *Home Secretary v JJ* [2007] UKHL 45, [2007] 3 WLR 642, at para [24].

[140] See *Home Secretary v JJ* [2006] EWCA Civ 1141, [2007] 1 QB 146, para [4] (Lord Phillips).

[141] For details (drawn from evidence to the JCHR), see K D Ewing and J-C Tham [2008] PL 668.

[142] For a sceptical view of whether the constraints on liberty under non-derogating orders are compatible with art 5, see HL122, HC 915 (2005–06) (Joint Committee on Human Rights).

[143] *Home Secretary v JJ* [2007] UKHL 45, [2008] AC 385.

[144] A total of 18 orders had been made in the first year of the scheme's operation. Of these, 11 were made against people who had been detained under the 2001 Act, but nine of these were removed after five and a half months when the individuals in question were served with notice of intention to deport. By the end of 2009, a total of 45 people had been the subject of a control order. For details, see Carlile, *Fifth Report of the Independent Reviewer Pursuant to Section 14(3) of the Prevention of Terrorism Act 2005* (2010), para 17.

for the taking of fingerprints and other samples (without consent) from a person subject to a control order.[145]

Special advocates and secret trials

Non-derogating control orders are of two kinds and are made by the Home Secretary with the permission of a High Court judge, which must be granted before the control order is made (s 3(1)(a)). In urgent cases or in the case of the people who had been detained under the repealed provisions of the 2001 Act, prior approval of a High Court judge is not required before a control order is made, though all such orders must be referred immediately to the High Court for confirmation (s 3(1)(b),(c)). Confirmation may be refused where the Home Secretary's decision to make a control order has been 'obviously flawed' (s 3(3)(b)). Although the government was thus required by political pressure to provide for judicial involvement in the control order system, the proceedings are nevertheless conducted largely in secret, in order to prevent the disclosure of evidence which would be contrary to the public interest. Much of the evidence against an individual who is the subject of a control order will be based on intelligence reports, the releasing of which (even to the subject of the control order) might reveal details about the work of the security and intelligence services or the identity of informers that the government would rather keep quiet.

Under the Civil Procedure Rules governing control order cases (and the same was the case in proceedings relating to detention without trial), the subject of a control order may (i) be excluded from part of the proceedings; (ii) be denied access to all the evidence being used against him or her; and (iii) not be given the full decision of the Court if the public interest so requires.[146] It is true that a Special Advocate may be appointed to represent his or her interests before the court, but this is a person who is not chosen by the person subject to a control order, and in any event there are restrictions in the procedural rules on the ability of the Special Advocate to communicate with the controlled person or his or her legal representative.[147] This procedure was nevertheless upheld by the House of Lords (again divided) in a challenge claiming that it violated ECHR, art 6, with Baroness Hale taking the view that it would be possible for the courts to provide the controlled person with sufficient procedural protection.[148] Following the decision of the Strasbourg court in the *A* case (above, p 598),[149] the House of Lords (sitting as a bench of nine) subsequently held that the Civil Procedure Rules were to be read in such a way as to ensure that the controlled person has 'sufficient information about the allegations against him to give effective instructions to the Special Advocate'.[150]

H. Conclusion: terrorism and human rights

The response to terrorism has been at a considerable cost to traditional liberties formally protected by the common law, the ECHR, and the Human Rights Act. We have seen measures which compromise in varying degrees of severity the right to liberty (art 5), the right to privacy (art 8), the right to freedom of expression (art 10), and the right to freedom of association (art 11), as well

---

[145] 2008 Act, s 10 (amending PACE, ss 61, 64). Similar provision is made in ss 11, 12 for Scotland and Northern Ireland. For powers of retention and use of samples, see 2008 Act, ss 14–18. See also Crime and Security Act 2010, s 56 (police powers of personal search and seizure of controlled persons).

[146] For a discussion, see Ewing, *Bonfire of the Liberties*, ch 7.

[147] On the rise and spread of the special advocate, see J Ip [2008] PL 717.

[148] *MB and AF v Home Secretary* [2007] UKHL 46, [2007] 3 WLR 681. See K D Ewing and J-C Tham, above.

[149] *A v United Kingdom* [2009] ECHR 301.

[150] *Home Secretary v AF* [2009] UKHL 28, [2009] 3 All ER 643, at para 81 (Lord Hope).

as the right to private property (First Protocol, art 1). It has also led to permanent changes to the criminal justice system, for although the special provisions of the Terrorism Act 2000 (Part VII) relating to Northern Ireland have lapsed,[151] key provisions have been re-enacted in another form, albeit with modifications. This is true for example of the restrictions on trial by jury, no longer to be found in the Terrorism Act 2000, but re-enacted in the Justice and Security (Northern Ireland) Act 2007.

Yet the foregoing measures by no means exhaust the restraints that have been introduced since 9/11 in particular, with further restrictions on freedom of expression discussed in chapter 23,[152] and the additional restraints on private property (in terms of the freezing of personal property) being considered in chapters 17 and 28).[153] Other departures from standard practice include the provisions authorising the post-charge questioning of terrorist suspects,[154] and the requirement that those convicted of a terrorist offence register with the police (under notification procedures),[155] and are thereby subject to foreign travel restriction orders, which do exactly as their name suggests.[156] While attempts can doubtless be made to justify all of this as being a necessary response to particular circumstances, there are concerns that many of the restrictions are over-broad and that terrorist activity has been used as a cover to take powers which bear little relationship to the public emergency which induced them.

It is incumbent on both Parliament and the courts to ensure that the case for such powers is fully established and that the powers in question go no further than the circumstances require. Although the drift of legislation is inexorably in the direction of greater executive intervention, there are signs that both Parliament and the courts are growing increasingly uneasy about the impact of such legislation on human rights.[157] Parliament inflicted a major defeat on the government in 2005 by rejecting proposals for 90-day detention before charge,[158] while in 2004 – in the *A* case considered above[159] – the House of Lords found its voice to declare detention without trial to be incompatible with Convention rights. Even though it was accepted that there was a 'public emergency threatening the life of the nation', in that case the House of Lords gave notice that the measures taken to deal with it must be proportionate and non-discriminatory.[160] There may be a need for that voice to be heard more often.

---

[151] See the 14th edition of this book, pp 646–9, for an account of these measures.
[152] Introduced by the Terrorism Act 2006 (encouraging terrorism).
[153] See also Counter-Terrorism Act 2008, ss 62–73.
[154] Terrorism Act 2006, s 22.
[155] Counter-Terrorism Act 2006, ss 40–61.
[156] Ibid, s 58.
[157] For a powerful account of the role of the courts in these circumstances, see A Barak (2002) 116 Harv L Rev 19.
[158] HC Deb, 9 November 2005, cols 382–6.
[159] [2004] UKHL 56; [2005] 2 AC 68; above p 597.
[160] Compare *Home Secretary* v *Rehman* [2001] UKHL 47; [2003] 1 AC 153.

Part IV

ADMINISTRATIVE LAW

CHAPTER 27

Administrative law – an introduction

The role of the courts in securing judicial review of the decisions of public authorities is a feature of government in the United Kingdom of great constitutional significance. This significance has increased during the last 25 years, both because of the number of cases coming to the courts[1] and the content of the leading cases. This may be why judicial review is sometimes thought to be the only part of administrative law that lawyers need to know. But this is no more correct than to say that employment lawyers need study only the law of unfair dismissal or tort lawyers the law of negligence. Certainly, the law of judicial review, outlined in chapters 30 and 31, is a vital part of administrative law, but the part must not be mistaken for the whole.

A formal definition of administrative law is that it is a branch of public law concerned with the composition, procedures, powers, duties, rights and liabilities of the various organs of government that are engaged in administering public policies. These policies are either laid down by Parliament in legislation or developed by the government and other authorities in the exercise of their executive powers. On this broad definition, administrative law includes at one extreme the principles and institutions of constitutional law outlined in earlier chapters; and at the other the detailed rules in statutes and ministerial regulations that govern the provision of complex social services (such as social security and education), the regulation of economic activities (such as financial services), the control of immigration, and environmental law.

It will be evident that there is no 'bright line' demarcating constitutional and administrative law. Building on the account of constitutional principles already given, this part of the book deals with aspects of administrative law relevant to all areas of government. These are the powers of the executive to make secondary, or delegated, legislation; the system of administrative justice whereby tribunals and inquiries and the Parliamentary Ombudsman make decisions or provide redress for individual grievances; judicial review; and the liability of public authorities, notably central government, to be sued for damages. The aim will be to identify the key rules and processes that help to ensure that lawful and just standards of public administration are observed.[2]

Functions of administrative law

One important function of administrative law is to enable the tasks of government to be performed, by creating administrative agencies and equipping them with powers to act on behalf of the state and of the community at large. A second function is to govern the relations between public bodies, for example, between the Secretary of State and a local authority or between two local authorities.[3] A third function is to govern the relations between a public agency and the

---

[1] In 1981, 533 applications for judicial review were made, of which 376 were allowed; in 1994, 3,208 were made and 1,260 allowed: Bridges, Meszaros and Sunkin, *Judicial Review in Perspective*, app 1. In 2008, 7,169 applications were made and leave was granted in 914 cases (*Judicial and Court Statistics 2008*).

[2] For fuller accounts, see the textbooks on administrative law by (respectively) Cane, Craig, Endicott, and Wade and Forsyth. Also Richardson and Genn (eds), *Administrative Law and Government Action*; Harlow and Rawlings, *Law and Administration*; Taggart (ed.), *The Province of Administrative Law*; and Beatson, Matthews and Elliott, *Administrative Law: Text and Materials*.

[3] See respectively *R (Shrewsbury Council) v Communities and Local Government Secretary* [2008] EWCA Civ 148, [2008] 3 All ER 548; *Bromley BC v Greater London Council* [1983] AC 768.

individuals or private bodies over whose affairs the agency exercises power.[4] We have seen that at the heart of the 'rule of law' is the principle of government according to law.[5] Since every public agency needs legal powers to perform its tasks, it necessarily follows that the agency must not go outside its powers. The content and extent of powers granted will reflect the social, economic and political values recognised in society. The granting of powers is subject both to express conditions or limitations, and also to implied requirements, such as the duty to exercise powers in good faith and not corruptly.

Individuals are affected by administrative powers in many ways, sometimes to their benefit and sometimes to their detriment. An individual's rights are seldom absolute: thus a landowner whose farm is required for a new reservoir does not have an absolute right to prevent acquisition of the land for a lawful purpose that is considered to be in the public interest. Nor, to take a very difficult example, do parents with a seriously ill child have an absolute right to medical treatment for him or her in the NHS when this is not recommended on clinical grounds.[6] Conversely, the powers of public authorities should not themselves be regarded as absolute. Private individuals, local communities and minority groups, all have a right to legal protection when confronted with the coercive powers of the state. Since there are few absolutes, the law has to determine the form and extent of that protection and the basis on which disputes may be resolved. The more fundamental the rights of the individual affected, the greater ought to be the degree of protection.[7]

The constitutional background to administrative law

Earlier chapters described the structure of central government; the responsibility of ministers to Parliament; the use of public bodies to regulate public utilities; and the effect of public powers on the individual's rights and liberties. The legislative supremacy of Parliament is relevant to administrative law, since (except where a conflict with Community law arises) no court can hold that the powers of an agency created by Act of Parliament are invalid or inoperative, although the Human Rights Act 1998 permits a statute to be declared incompatible with Convention rights. Whether or not the judicial review of executive acts is founded directly on the supremacy of Parliament,[8] there is no doubt that Parliament may, as it did in the Human Rights Act, modify the judicial approach to the interpretation of legislation and extend the courts' powers in supervising the acts and decisions of public authorities.[9] Where an agency's powers do not come from an Act of Parliament, but from other legislative measures (such as legislation enacted in Northern Ireland, Scotland or Wales, or ministerial regulations) the courts may review the legality of the agency's powers, as well as the decisions taken in reliance on those powers.

In a modern legal system, the way that disputes arising out of administration are handled is of constitutional significance. Where, as in Germany, there are separate superior courts, one entrusted with interpreting the constitution and one dealing with disputes between the citizen and the administration, a distinction between constitutional and administrative law can be based on the actual work done by the two courts. In the United Kingdom such a distinction cannot be drawn:[10] although the section of the High Court in England and Wales dealing with judicial review was in 2000 re-named the Administrative Court, appeals from the court go along with other civil cases to the Court of Appeal and thence the Supreme Court. Issues of constitutional significance may

---

[4] E.g. R (Roberts) v Parole Board [2005] UKHL 45, [2005] 2 AC 738.

[5] Ch 6.

[6] R v Cambridge Health Authority, ex p B [1995] 2 All ER 129.

[7] This principle was expressly approved in respect of judicial review in R v Ministry of Defence, ex p Smith [1996] QB 517, 554.

[8] See Forsyth (ed.), Judicial Review and the Constitution; and p 670 below.

[9] Ch 19 C.

[10] And see Craig, Public Law and Democracy, ch 1.

arise from civil cases brought against public officials[11] as well as from cases involving criminal justice[12] and judicial review.[13] As is shown by many cases against public authorities today,[14] the fact that the Human Rights Act makes it unlawful for public authorities to act inconsistently with the Convention rights is another reason why administrative and constitutional cases cannot be separated. The criminal law as such falls outside administrative law, but the operations of the police and the penal system often give rise to disputes about the exercise of powers (for example, over the rights of convicted prisoners against the prison authorities).[15] The procedures of Parliament fall outside administrative law, but the rules of public audit affect the working of government departments,[16] and parliamentary procedures for the scrutiny of delegated legislation may be relevant in cases of judicial review.[17]

Historical origins of administrative law

One result of the seventeenth-century constitutional conflicts was to limit the power of the Privy Council in London to supervise the justices of the peace for the counties, who met quarterly to dispense criminal justice and also to deal with administrative matters. Although there was little central control over the justices, their powers in such matters as the poor law, licensing and highways, came from Acts of Parliament; if it was claimed that they were exceeding their powers, their decisions could be challenged in the Court of King's Bench on grounds of legality by means of the prerogative writs.[18] Particularly during the nineteenth century, Parliament established new local bodies such as the poor law guardians, public health boards and school boards; eventually elected local authorities were created and new departments of central government emerged. In his lectures in 1887–88, the historian Maitland was aware that public law must extend to these new organs of government:

> Year by year the subordinate government of England is becoming more and more important. The new movement set in with the Reform Bill of 1832: it has gone far already and assuredly it will go further. We are becoming a much governed nation, governed by all manner of councils and boards and officers, central and local, high and low, exercising the powers which have been committed to them by modern statutes.[19]

The Court of King's Bench extended its controlling jurisdiction to include these bodies. Since they exercised statutory powers, disputes about the limits of their power could be settled by means of the prerogative writs. These procedures for judicial control over inferior courts were used to review the exercise of powers by local authorities and, in the twentieth century, by ministers of the Crown.[20] Given the scale of government in the twenty-first century, the need for judicial review of executive decisions to be available is undiminished.

Inevitably, the supervisory role of the courts has developed as patterns of government have changed. Judicial review of decisions by ministers is complementary to, not a substitute for,

---

[11] E.g. *Austin v Metropolitan Police Commissioner* [2009] UKHL 5, [2009] 3 All ER 455.

[12] E.g. *Boddington v British Transport Police* [1999] 2 AC 143.

[13] E.g. *R (Purdy) v DPP* [2009] UKHL 45, [2009] 4 All ER 1147.

[14] E.g. *Austin v Metropolitan Police Commissioner* (above).

[15] E.g. *R (Daly) v Home Secretary* [2001] 2 AC 532; and see *Roberts v Parole Board* (above).

[16] See Turpin, *Government Procurement and Contracts* and ch 17 D.

[17] Ch 28; and see *HM Treasury v Mohammed Jabar Ahmed* [2010] UKSC 2.

[18] See Henderson, *Foundations of English Administrative Law*; Woolf, Jowell and Le Sueur, *De Smith's Judicial Review of Administrative Action*, ch 15.

[19] Maitland, *Constitutional History*, p 501.

[20] See e.g. *R v Glamorganshire Inhabitants* (1700) 1 Ld Raym 580 (review of rates levied by county justices to pay for repairs to bridge), *Board of Education v Rice* [1911] AC 179 and *Local Government Board v Arlidge* [1915] AC 120, on which see Dicey, *The Law of the Constitution*, app 2.

ministerial responsibility to Parliament. Remarkably, in the three legal systems of the United Kingdom, the grounds of judicial control have never been defined in legislation. However, by the common law doctrine of precedent, principles have developed both for policing the limits of powers and for reviewing the use of discretionary powers. In 1992, an eminent New Zealand judge summarised administrative law in this way: 'The administrator must act fairly, reasonably and according to law. That is the essence and the rest is mainly machinery.'[21] And in 2010, Lord Bingham, the leading judge of our time, declared this principle as being at the heart of the rule of law.

> Ministers and public officers at all levels must exercise the powers conferred on them in good faith, fairly, for the purposes for which the powers were conferred, without exceeding the limits of such powers and not unreasonably.

This principle applies whenever public power is exercised, regardless of whether it is derived from legislation or, as a matter of common law, from the royal prerogative.[22] It is the detailed application of this general principle that we will examine in chapters 30 and 31.

In Scotland, the detailed history is different but the general form of the development has been similar. After the abolition of the Privy Council for Scotland, following the Union with England in 1707, the Court of Session adopted a supervisory role comparable to that of the Court of King's Bench in England. Since the prerogative writs were never part of Scots law, and since a separate court of equity was never created, the remedies for controlling inferior tribunals and administrative agencies were obtained from the Court of Session by the procedures used for civil litigation between private parties. But the principles upon which judicial control was founded were remarkably similar to those developed in English law.[23] The sheriff court exercised an important role in enabling many local administrative disputes to be settled judicially.[24] Since 1900, much of the development in government has been by statute law applying both in England and Scotland; the response of the Scottish courts has been similar to that of the English courts.

In Scotland, as well as Northern Ireland and Wales, there is now a layer of devolved government to which administrative law applies. Apart from questions as to the extent of the devolved powers, which must be decided in accordance with the devolution legislation,[25] decisions by the devolved governments are subject to the same process of judicial review as are decisions of other public bodies.

Dicey's misconception

The study of administrative law in Britain was formerly impeded by a misleading comparison which the constitutional writer, A V Dicey, drew over a hundred years ago between the law in France (*droit administratif*), under which separate administrative courts (headed by the Conseil d'Etat) determined disputes concerning the exercise of administrative power, and the common law in England.[26] Dicey contrasted what he saw as the disadvantages in the French system of administrative courts with the advantages enjoyed in Britain where the common law, as Dicey saw it, subjected executive actions to control by the same courts and on the same principles as governed relationships between private citizens. Dicey believed that the common law gave

---

[21] Sir Robin Cooke, quoted in *R v Devon CC, ex p Baker* [1995] 1 All ER 73, 88.

[22] E.g. *CCSU v Minister for Civil Service* [1985] AC 374; *R (Bancoult) v Foreign Secretary (No 2)* [2008] UKHL 61, [2009] 1 AC 453.

[23] See e.g. *Moss Empires Ltd v Glasgow Assessor* 1917 SC (HL) 1. Also *Stair Memorial Encyclopaedia, The Laws of Scotland*, vol 1, title Administrative Law (reissue 2000); Clyde and Edwards, *Judicial Review*.

[24] *Brown v Hamilton DC* 1983 SC (HL) 1.

[25] Ch 3 B.

[26] *The Law of the Constitution*, ch 12 and app 2. For critiques of Dicey's approach, see F H Lawson (1959) 7 *Political Studies* 109, 207; and H W Arthurs (1979) 17 *Osgoode Hall LJ* 1. See also Brown and Bell, *French Administrative Law* and, for a recent appraisal of the French system, J-M Sauvé [2008] PL 531.

the citizen better protection against the executive than the French system. Unfortunately, he overlooked the weaknesses of the archaic law that then protected the Crown and government departments from being sued.[27] Moreover, his denial that *droit administratif* existed in England led many to suppose that there was no such thing as administrative law in the United Kingdom. We shall examine in the next section some notable steps in the history of administrative law in Britain in the twentieth century. It was in the landmark decision of *Ridge* v *Baldwin* in 1964 that Lord Reid said: 'We do not have a developed system of administrative law – perhaps because until fairly recently we did not need it'.[28] Old beliefs died hard,[29] but it could not be denied today that the United Kingdom has a developed system of administrative law. Lord Diplock described the rapid development of 'a rational and comprehensive system of administrative law' as having been 'the greatest achievement of the English courts' in his judicial lifetime.[30] Another judge has written that in this area of common law, 'the judges have in the last 30 years changed the face of the United Kingdom's constitution'.[31]

Administrative law in Europe is today a fertile ground for comparative research and analysis.[32] Despite many developments on both sides of the English channel that have occurred since Dicey wrote, the French system of *le contentieux administratif* is based on the use of separate administrative courts, whereas the British system relies heavily on the superior civil courts. In both systems, the essential principles of judicial control are judge-made and do not derive from codes or statutes. In France, the price paid for a separate administrative jurisdiction is a complex body of law at the divide between the civil and administrative courts; and conflicts between the two systems of courts must (if necessary) be settled by the *Tribunal des conflits* or by legislation. But the French system has developed rules of procedure (for example, regarding the obtaining of evidence from government departments) and rules of substantive liability (for example, regarding liability for harm caused by official acts) which take account of the public setting of the disputes. The latter rules often impose special duties upon public authorities (for example, liability without fault in some circumstances),[33] not merely immunities.

By contrast, the British approach (as we shall see in chapter 32) has been to apply the same general principles of liability in contract and tort to public bodies as well as to private citizens.[34] The position is different regarding judicial review of official decisions, since this jurisdiction has no direct counterpart in private law. We consider later in this chapter the extent to which a distinction between public and private law now exists. While procedures can always be improved, the Administrative Court is able to provide a fair and effective decision when the legality of official acts is challenged, and in case of urgency it may act very quickly indeed.

Milestones in development of administrative law

The explosion of government in the twentieth century did not wait for lawyers and academic writers in Britain to acquire an understanding of administrative law. The first books on the

---

[27] These defects were very evident after the First World War: see Cmd 2842, 1927, discussed by J Jacob [1992] PL 452; and ch 32 A.

[28] [1964] AC 40, 72.

[29] When the Immigration Bill 1971 was being debated, the Home Secretary (Mr Maudling) said: 'I have never seen the sense of administrative law in our country, because it merely means someone else taking the Government's decisions for them' (Standing Committee B, 25 May 1971, col 1508).

[30] *Re Racal Communications Ltd* [1981] AC 374, 382; and *R v Inland Revenue Commissioners, ex p National Federation of Self-Employed* [1982] AC 617, 641. And see Lord Diplock [1974] CLJ 233; Lord Scarman [1990] PL 490.

[31] S Sedley, in Richardson and Genn (note 2 above), p 36.

[32] See e.g. Schwarze, *European Administrative Law*.

[33] R Errera [1986] CLP 157.

[34] *Dorset Yacht Co v Home Office* [1970] AC 1004; ch 32 A. And see Fairgrieve, Andenas and Bell (eds), *Tort Liability of Public Authorities in Comparative Perspective*.

subject by that name appeared in the late 1920s.[35] At that time a narrow approach was taken to the subject, confining it to delegated legislation and the exercise of judicial powers by administrative bodies. The hesitant development of administrative law between the wars may be shown by reference to the Committee on Ministers' Powers, appointed in 1929 at a time when a storm of criticism was directed against departments by some judges, barristers, MPs and academic lawyers at Oxford. The critics were led by the Lord Chief Justice (Hewart), whose outspoken book, *The New Despotism*,[36] argued that Britain was experiencing administrative lawlessness rather than the rule of law. The Committee on Ministers' Powers was required to examine the powers of ministers exercised by means of delegated legislation or 'judicial or quasi-judicial decision', and to consider what safeguards were needed to secure 'the sovereignty of Parliament and the supremacy of the law'.

The committee rejected the charge of bureaucratic tyranny that Hewart and other critics had made against Whitehall, and went on to analyse in terms of constitutional principle the legislative and judicial powers of ministers. It made many recommendations to improve delegated legislation and administrative justice.[37] These recommendations were not adopted, and it was only in 1944 that the House of Commons established a committee to scrutinise delegated legislation.[38]

In 1955, when the government machine was again under attack from sections of political opinion,[39] the Committee on Administrative Tribunals and Inquiries was appointed to review (a) the constitution and working of statutory tribunals appointed in connection with the functions of ministers and (b) the operation of administrative procedures that included the holding of public inquiries or hearings on behalf of ministers, especially in relation to the compulsory purchase of land. This committee (the Franks committee) reported in 1957.[40] In examining the post-war use of tribunals and inquiries, Franks adopted a more pragmatic approach than the Ministers' Powers report had done, finding it difficult to distinguish conceptually between the 'judicial' and 'administrative' decisions of ministers. The report made a detailed appraisal of existing tribunals and inquiries, arguing that they should be marked by the qualities of openness, fairness and impartiality. The committee also concluded that judicial control, whether by appeal to the courts or by use of the prerogative orders, should be maintained and if necessary extended. This influential report led to the Tribunals and Inquiries Act 1958 which, in setting up the Council on Tribunals and in other ways, laid foundations for the evolution of tribunals and inquiries over the next 50 years.[41]

The Franks report dealt solely with areas of government where recourse to a tribunal or a public inquiry was already available. But in many areas of governmental power neither safeguard existed, and the law provided no systematic redress for individuals suffering from maladministration. These two matters were examined in 1961 by a non-governmental committee appointed by Justice.[42] The resulting report (the Whyatt report), *The Citizen and the Administration*, made two far-reaching recommendations: (a) except where there are overriding policy considerations that prevent it, a citizen should be entitled to appeal from a discretionary decision made by a department to an impartial tribunal; to avoid the creation of many new tribunals, there should be a general tribunal to hear appeals against discretionary decisions; and (b) a Parliamentary Commissioner

---

[35] Robson, *Justice and Administrative Law*, and Port, *Administrative Law*. And see G Drewry, in Supperstone, Goudie and Walker (eds), *Judicial Review*, ch 2. For a different approach, see Willis, *The parliamentary powers of English government departments*.

[36] Described by Lord Bingham as 'a powerful and very readable polemic' that made a 'corruscating attack' on practices of the day: see Bingham, *The Rule of Law*, p 48. And see Allen, *Bureaucracy Triumphant*.

[37] Cmd 4060, 1932 (MPR).

[38] This was the forerunner of today's parliamentary committees on delegated legislation: see ch 28.

[39] The attack was intensified by the Crichel Down affair: ch 7 above.

[40] Cmnd 218, 1957.

[41] Ch 29 A and B, and see J A G Griffith (1959) 22 MLR 125.

[42] For comment, see I M Pedersen [1962] PL 15; J D B Mitchell [1962] PL 82; A W Bradley [1962] CLJ 82.

(Ombudsman) should be appointed to investigate complaints of maladministration. The first recommendation was not accepted, but the office of Parliamentary Ombudsman was created in 1967, a constitutional reform that has stood the test of time.

Although these reports dealt with major aspects of public administration, the judicial review of government decisions was marked during the middle years of the twentieth century by what has been called the 'great depression' or the 'long sleep'[43] – when the judiciary appeared to acquiesce in an unjustified diminution of their role. When in the late 1960s the senior judges became willing to make greater use of their powers, attention concentrated on the archaic and highly technical processes by which judicial review had to be obtained. In 1976, the English Law Commission recommended major procedural reforms;[44] these were implemented between 1977 and 1981, creating the procedure of application for judicial review.[45] A similar but not identical procedure was introduced into Scots law in 1985.[46]

In 1979, the refusal by successive governments to make a general inquiry into administrative law led to the formation of a non-governmental committee, jointly by Justice and All Souls College Oxford, to review administrative law in the United Kingdom. Despite a protracted inquiry, none of the committee's recommendations were adopted,[47] but two of the most important, dealing with the duty to give reasons for decisions and the need for victims of unlawful administrative action to have a right to compensation, remained on the reform agenda in 2009.[48]

In the last twenty years, the Law Commission for England and Wales has inquired into several aspects of administrative law. In 1994, having examined the mechanisms of judicial review and statutory appeals to the High Court,[49] it proposed some modest changes in procedure and nomenclature. In 2000, some changes made to the process of judicial review included the re-labelling of historic remedies and the naming of the Administrative Court.[50] At the same time, the Human Rights Act 1998 came into effect with far-reaching implications for administrative law, since it introduced new rules of statutory interpretation, required public authorities to act consistently with Convention rights and thereby created new grounds of judicial review.[51] While initially it could be claimed that the effect of the Human Rights Act was merely to reinforce existing rules of the common law, in reality the House of Lords (and since 2009 the Supreme Court) has given much attention to claims that would have failed apart from the Act.[52]

Law and the administrative process

The principle that government must be conducted according to law means that for every act performed in the course of government there must be legal authority.[53] That authority is usually

---

[43] See respectively Wade and Forsyth, *Administrative Law*, p 14; S Sedley in Andenas and Fairgrieve (eds), *Tom Bingham and the transformation of the law*, p 183.

[44] Cmnd 6407, 1976; cf Scottish Law Commission, *Remedies in Administrative Law*, 1971.

[45] Ch 31.

[46] See works cited in note 23. Also T Mullen, K Pick and T Prosser [1995] PL 52; and CMG Himsworth in Supperstone, Goudie and Walker (eds), *Judicial Review*, ch 21.

[47] *Administrative Justice: Some Necessary Reforms*; see P McAuslan [1988] PL 402, C T Emery [1988] PL 495.

[48] The English Law Commission was in 2009 engaged in examining the redress that should be available to individuals affected by sub-standard administration: see Law Com, Consultation Paper no. 187, 2008; and T Cornford [2009] PL 70.

[49] Law Com No. 226; HC 669 (1993–4). See also Lord Woolf [1992] PL 221; R Gordon [1995] PL 11; C T Emery [1995] PL 450.

[50] See *Review of the Crown Office List* (Bowman report), 2000; Civil Procedure Rules, Part 54.

[51] See chs 19 C, 30 A. Also A W Bradley, in Supperstone, Goudie and Walker (eds), *Judicial Review*, ch 4.

[52] S Shah and T Poole [2009] PL 347.

[53] The contrary view, expressed in *Malone* v *Metropolitan Police Commissioner* [1979] Ch 344, was disapproved in *R* v *Somerset CC, ex p Fewings* [1995] 3 All ER 20, and would conflict with the ECHR. See Harris, O'Boyle and Warbrick, *Law of the ECHR*, pp 344–8, 399–407.

derived expressly or by implication from statute or sometimes from the royal prerogative. Moreover, the Crown has at common law the same capacity as any other person to make contracts, own property etc.[54] A public body must be able to show that it is acting in accordance with legal authority when its action (for example, the levying of a tax) adversely affects the rights or interests of a private individual. Exceptionally, the public interest may require the government to satisfy a court that its decisions are lawful even if no private individuals are affected except as members of the public at large.[55]

It is not possible to describe the administrative process in terms of law alone. There are many tasks (for example, budgeting and co-ordination) to which law is not of primary relevance. The creation of executive agencies, like many developments within the civil service, has not been authorised by legislation, being regarded as essentially a form of departmental management. Many politicians and administrators are likely to view law instrumentally as a means of achieving social or economic policies. In areas of government such as taxation, the detailed rules are found in statutes or in judicial decisions interpreting the statutes. Even so, those rules may not provide the complete picture since from time to time the revenue authorities exercise an extra-statutory discretion not to enforce payment of tax in a situation which neither Parliament nor the government can have foreseen. But the practice of granting extra-statutory concessions would defeat the whole purpose of imposing taxes by law if it became widespread; by the nature of a tax concession, it may escape challenge in a court of law.[56]

By contrast with taxation, in many areas of government the nature of the legal framework is deliberately skeletonic, to allow for a flexible discretion on the part of the department concerned in promoting policies that are nowhere laid down in statutory rules. Thus the department responsible for promoting international development has a broad power to provide economic or humanitarian assistance to overseas countries,[57] that can be used to promote widely differing policies. Wide discretion is found in many areas of government, such as the control of immigration or the granting of permission for the development of land. In principle, the exercise of discretion is subject to control by the courts if it is exercised unlawfully. In practice, the use of discretion is often closely controlled through policy decisions taken by ministers or departmental rules which lay down how officials should exercise their powers.[58] At one time, such policies and rules were often protected from publication outside Whitehall, but today's more open approach to government requires disclosure of all policies and rules that are relevant to decision-making in individual cases.

Many officials are therefore concerned with administering government policies rather than with administering the law as such. It is often difficult to separate administration of an existing policy from the making of a new policy. When a department is exercising discretionary powers and a case arises that raises new features, a decision on the facts will serve as a precedent for future decisions of a similar kind. Thus the process gives rise to the formulation of a more detailed policy than had previously existed. If a large department is not efficiently organised, officials may have difficulty in discovering what the current policy on a matter actually is.[59]

---

[54] B V Harris (1992) 108 LQR 626, and (2007) 123 LQR 225. The Crown's power to make payments without statutory authority may not be used when this would contradict the clear intention of Parliament: *R (Wilkinson) v IRC* [2005] UKHL 30, [2006] 1 All ER 529.

[55] See e.g. *R v Foreign Secretary, ex p Rees-Mogg* [1994] QB 552; *R v Foreign Secretary, ex p World Development Movement* [1995] 1 All ER 611; and ch 31.

[56] But not judicial criticism: *Vestey v IRC* [1980] AC 1148. Cf *R v IRC, ex p National Federation of Self-Employed* [1982] AC 617; and see below page 637.

[57] International Development Act 2002. And see *R v Foreign Secretary, ex p World Development Movement* (above).

[58] On departmental rules and 'quasi-legislation', see ch 28. For the relevance of policies in planning decisions, see *R (Alconbury Developments Ltd) v Environment Secretary* [2001] UKHL 23, [2003] 2 AC 295.

[59] See *R (Abdi) v Home Secretary* [2008] EWHC 3166 (Admin), [2009] ACD 22 (notes 119, 201, above, in ch 20).

Decision making within a department is very different from the process by which a court settles a dispute. A civil case, for example, is decided by the judge after hearing evidence and legal arguments brought before the court by the parties in an adversary procedure.[60] Oral proceedings take place in public before the judge, in the presence of the parties and their lawyers. A reasoned decision is announced in open court; when made it can be challenged only by appeal to a higher court. By contrast, departmental decisions are typically taken in secret, without an adversary procedure. Often it is not known at what level in the department the decision has been taken. Political pressure may be brought to bear both before and after the decision. Except where a statute so requires, or where it would be unfair for reasons to be withheld, reasons for the decision are not in law required to be given.

Although the two processes of administrative and judicial decision-making are different, we should not assume that one method is superior to the other or suppose that a department should always try to adopt the methods of a court. Much depends on the type and number of decisions to be made and on the results which it is desired to achieve from a particular scheme. Where such decisions directly affect an individual's civil rights and obligations, as in the case of decisions granting or refusing planning permission, the right to a fair hearing under art 6(1) ECHR arises, but this does not prevent ministers deciding such questions after a hearing or public inquiry, provided that the decisions are themselves subject to a sufficient level of judicial review.[61] Decisions made on the basis of general rules and after a procedure that enables the facts to be ascertained and competing considerations to be assessed are likely to be fairer than if made without such aids to decision-making.[62] Thus many classes of decisions that are taken by civil servants at first instance (in such areas as taxation, social security and immigration) are subject to an appeal to independent tribunals, which apply a modified form of judicial procedure in making decisions. In other cases, a stage of the administrative process is exposed to view in the form of a public inquiry, while leaving the final decision in the hands of the minister or department.[63]

Powers, duties and discretion

A recurring feature in administrative law is the interplay between powers, duties and discretion. If someone satisfies the legal rules that govern who may vote in parliamentary elections, then he or she has a right to be entered on the electoral register and a right to vote in the area where he or she is registered. The relevant officials are under a correlative duty to give effect to these rights. Many situations that arise in the course of public administration are less clear-cut. Thus a minister may be under a duty to achieve certain broad policy objectives without in law being required to take action of any particular kind. Clearly, steps taken in the performance of such a duty involve the exercise of discretion. As Lord Diplock said:

> The very concept of administrative discretion involves a right to choose more than one possible course of action on which there is room for reasonable people to hold differing opinions as to which is to be preferred.[64]

Where an Act confers authority to administer a branch of government, it may confer a broad duty on the minister and other public authorities to fulfil certain policy objectives. It may impose specific duties on the minister to act when certain conditions exist and it will probably confer

---

[60] Cf art 6(1), ECHR (ch 19 B) by which everyone has a right to a fair and public hearing 'in the determination of his civil rights and obligations'.

[61] R (Alconbury Developments Ltd) v Environment Secretary (above).

[62] See J Jowell in Jowell and Oliver (eds), The Changing Constitution, 6th edn, ch 1.

[63] Ch 29 A and B.

[64] Secretary of State for Education v Tameside MB [1977] AC 1014, at 1064. And see Davis, Discretionary Justice, and Galligan, Discretionary Powers.

powers on the authorities concerned. In administrative law, 'power' has two meanings, which are not always distinguished: (*a*) the capacity to act in a certain way (for example, power to provide a library service or to purchase land by agreement for a sports field); and (*b*) authority to restrict or take away the rights of others (for example, power to regulate the mini-cab trade in a city or to buy land compulsorily that is needed for a public purpose). Since it is inherent in the nature of a power that it may be exercised in various ways, use of a power invariably requires the exercise of discretion. Often there is a duty to exercise a discretion. When an official decides to perform a duty or to exercise a power or discretion in a certain way, the decision may delight some persons and disappoint others. Within a democracy, important choices of this kind should be made by those who have political responsibility for them, not by judges.[65] Those whose rights or interests are adversely affected by an administrative decision may wish to challenge it, whether by taking any political action to get it changed that is still possible, by using any rights of appeal that exist, or by seeking judicial review.

A difficult question arises when, under severe constraints on expenditure, a public authority takes its resources into account in deciding whether it can provide a certain benefit to an individual or must, for example, close down valuable community services. Here the legal answer may depend on the exact terms of the legislation under which the service or benefit is provided.[66] The statute may impose a duty which must be performed in any event or confer a qualified duty or a discretion, the exercise of which may depend on the individual's situation and other matters. In such cases, the reviewing court is not concerned with the political merits of the authority's policy, but it must protect individual rights where these are granted by statute. Questions often arise as to where the dividing line comes between matters that a public authority should decide and those that should be decided by the judges.[67] The Human Rights Act 1998 has made it more likely that such questions will arise, for instance when a court must decide whether action taken in the public interest that limits enjoyment of a Convention right passes the test of proportionality.[68]

These matters will be considered more fully in later chapters. We now consider two other general matters, namely classification of powers and the distinction between public and private law.

Classification of powers

Under a written constitution founded on a formal separation of powers, it may be necessary for a court to decide whether legislative or executive action has improperly infringed the judicial power.[69] Although this is not the case in the United Kingdom, there are several purposes in administrative law for which it may be needed to classify the powers of government as being legislative, administrative or judicial in character. Under the Statutory Instruments Act 1946 in its application to earlier statutes, a distinction was drawn between instruments that were *legislative* and those that were *executive* in character.[70] The jurisdiction of the Parliamentary Ombudsman applies to 'action taken in the exercise of *administrative* functions' by a government department, which may mean that it does not extend to the functions of departments which are legislative in character.[71] Under the Crown Proceedings Act 1947, s 2(5), the Crown is not liable for the acts of

---

[65] See the *Alconbury* case (above), esp paras [48] (Lord Slynn), [70] (Lord Hoffmann), [139–141] (Lord Clyde).

[66] *R v Gloucestershire CC, ex p Barry* [1997] AC 584; cf *R v Cambridge Health Authority, ex p B* [1995] 2 All ER 129 and *R v Sefton Council, ex p Help the Aged* [1997] 4 All ER 532.

[67] E.g. *Bromley BC v Greater London Council* [1983] AC 768 and the *Alconbury* case (above); and ch 30. Also Lord Devlin (1978) 41 MLR 501 and Lord Irvine [1996] PL 59.

[68] See ch 30 A.

[69] *Liyanage v R* [1967] 1 AC 259; *Independent Jamaica Council for Human Rights (1998) Ltd v Marshall-Burnett* [2005] UKPC 3, [2005] 2 AC 356. And ch 5.

[70] SI 1948 No 1, reg 2(1); ch 28.

[71] Parliamentary Commissioner Act 1967, s 5(1); ch 29 D.

any person who is discharging responsibilities of a *judicial* nature.[72] This absolute rule of non-liability has now been altered by the Human Rights Act 1998, s 9, under which the Crown must in some circumstances compensate those who have lost their liberty by reason of a judicial act.[73]

In some other contests it may be necessary to decide whether a particular procedure may be described as judicial. Thus, absolute privilege at common law protects a witness who gives evidence at a statutory inquiry into a teacher's dismissal.[74] The law of contempt of court extends to employment tribunals and mental health tribunals[75] but not to a local valuation court which decides disputes about the valuation of property under the rating system.[76] And the effect of the Human Rights Act, giving effect to Article 6(1) ECHR, is that it may be necessary to decide whether someone's 'civil rights and obligations' have been determined after a fair and public hearing 'by an independent and impartial tribunal'.[77]

While many powers may be described without difficulty as legislative (in particular, a power to make regulations), administrative (for instance, power to decide where a government office should be located) or judicial (for example, power to decide the meaning of a disputed statute), other powers are so classifiable, if at all, only with difficulty. Laws are not always general in application: legislative form may be used to give effect to the government's decision of an individual case.[78] Government departments exercise both formal and informal powers of rulemaking: is the delegation of executive powers to be regarded as a legislative act?[79] How should we classify, for instance, the decision to build a motorway?[80] Does a decision change its character from being judicial to administrative if it is transferred from a court to a government department?[81]

There were formerly two linked reasons in administrative law why the classification of functions was emphasised. First, it was supposed that the ancient writs of prohibition and certiorari, which had long been available to control inferior courts and tribunals, could be used against administrative bodies only if those bodies were obliged to 'act judicially'. Second, it was believed that administrative bodies had to observe the rules of natural justice only when they were performing 'judicial' functions.[82] So long as these beliefs survived, writers on public law were much concerned with the nature of administrative and judicial functions.[83] The term 'quasi-judicial' came into vogue to describe a function which could not easily be classified as either judicial or administrative.[84]

The heresy that a public authority's powers had to be described as 'judicial' before its decisions could be subject to judicial review was dispelled by the House of Lords in *Ridge* v *Baldwin*, the decision which opened the way to the subsequent rise of judicial review. It was there held that where officials had power to make decisions affecting the rights of individuals, the duty to act judicially was readily inferred from the nature of the power; it was not necessary to look for any express elements, such as the duty to give a formal hearing.[85] Today, administrative functions are

---

[72] Ch 32 A. See *Quinland* v *Governor of Swaleside Prison* [2002] EWCA Civ 174 [2003] QB 306.

[73] The 'judicial act of a court' includes 'an act done on the instructions, or on behalf, of a judge' (Human Rights Act 1998, s 9(5)).

[74] *Trapp* v *Mackie* [1979] 1 All ER 489.

[75] *Peach Grey & Co* v *Sommers* [1995] 2 All ER 513; *P* v *Liverpool Daily Post plc* [1991] 2 AC 370.

[76] *AG* v *BBC* [1981] AC 303; ch 18 D.

[77] See *Runa Begum* v *Tower Hamlets Council* [2003] UKHL 5, [2003] 2 AC 430; and P Craig [2003] PL 753.

[78] *Hoffmann-La Roche & Co* v *Trade Secretary* [1975] AC 295.

[79] Cf *Blackpool Corpn* v *Locker* [1948] 1 KB 349.

[80] *Bushell* v *Environment Secretary* [1981] AC 75.

[81] Cf *Local Government Board* v *Arlidge* [1915] AC 120.

[82] Ch 30 B.

[83] See D M Gordon (1933) 49 LQR 94, 419; Robson, *Justice and Administrative Law*, ch 1; Jennings, *Law and the Constitution*, app 1.

[84] See e.g. *Errington* v *Minister of Health* [1935] 1 KB 249; *Franklin* v *Minister of Town Planning* [1948] AC 87; and ch 30 B. See also Wade and Forsyth, *Administrative Law*, pp 405–415.

[85] [1964] AC 40; ch 30 B.

subject to judicial review without it being necessary for a court first to apply a classificatory label.[86] Public authorities are under a general duty to act fairly, even though the precise content of 'fairness' varies according to the context.[87] And, as we have seen above, public authorities are required by the Human Rights Act to exercise their functions consistently with rights under the ECHR; this obligation has specific consequences in the case of decisions that are subject to the right of due process guaranteed by art 6(1).[88]

Public and private law

A different classification problem comes from the tendency that the courts adopted after 1980 of resolving questions about jurisdiction, liability and procedure by asking whether the matter was one of private or public law. This formal distinction is reflected in the structure of many European legal systems. Thus in France many public law disputes are decided by the administrative courts; private law is a matter for the civil courts. By contrast, in Britain the superior civil courts exercise an undivided jurisdiction over all justiciable disputes, whether they concern private citizens or public authorities.[89]

Lord Woolf has described public law as 'the system which enforces the proper performance by public bodies of the duties which they owe to the public'; and private law as 'the system which protects the private rights of private individuals or the private rights of public bodies'.[90] On this basis, the emphasis in public law is on holding public authorities to account for their conduct, and in private law on safeguarding individual rights. This analysis may help to explain some essential differences between applying for judicial review (a matter of 'public law') and bringing an action in tort ('private law'). But the distinction is deceptively simple. For one thing, Lord Woolf's two systems overlap to a significant extent. In the common law tradition, the system which protects the private rights of individuals *is* to an important extent the system which enforces the performance by public bodies of the duties which they owe to the public, at least if the public is regarded as comprising all private individuals.[91] Personal liberty, for example, is protected both by the law of habeas corpus[92] and by the law of tort (action for false imprisonment): does habeas corpus come within public law (as the aim is to get the court to order the detainee's release if the detention is unlawful) and the tort remedy within private law (as it may lead to damages being paid to the wrongly detained person)? Similarly, a landowner may take action to protect his property against trespass, whether the trespasser is a government department or a neighbouring owner. Comparable questions arise under the Human Rights Act, which protects the individual's Convention rights as well as imposing a duty on public authorities not to infringe those rights.[93] When someone seeks to protect her Convention right to privacy against a public authority, should the proceedings be classed as being a matter of public or private law? Could the answer depend on whether the individual is seeking the (private law) remedy of damages, or the (public

---

[86] The language of judicial, quasi-judicial and administrative functions is rarely heard today but in *R v Army Board, ex p Anderson* [1992] QB 169, the Board's power to decide on a soldier's complaint of racial discrimination was held to be judicial; cf *R v Department of Health, ex p Gandhi* [1991] 4 All ER 547.

[87] See ch 30 B.

[88] See note 60 above. For the application of art 6(1) to planning decisions, see *R (Alconbury Developments Ltd) v Environment Secretary* [2001] UKHL 23, [2003] 2 AC 295. Also A W Bradley, in Supperstone, Goudie and Walker (eds) *Judicial Review*, pp 55–62.

[89] Cf J D B Mitchell [1965] PL 95, advocating the creation of a new public law jurisdiction.

[90] [1986] PL 220, 221. Also Lord Woolf [1995] PL 57, 60–5.

[91] E.g. *Entick v Carrington* (1765) 19 St Tr 1030; *Cooper v Wandsworth Board of Works* (1863) 14 CB (NS) 180; and see ch 6. Also Allison, *A Continental Distinction in the Common Law.*

[92] See chs 21 E and 31.

[93] Human Rights Act 1998, s 6.

law) remedy of quashing the authority's decision? In either event, the claimant may want to restrain further breaches of privacy by the authority, a remedy that is available both in 'public' and 'private' proceedings.

Very often when a private claimant (C) is in dispute with a public authority (P), P's position is founded on a power or duty that has been conferred on it by Parliament. This form of legal justification is not usually available to a private person. In this situation, to overcome P's reliance on statutory authority, C may seek to show that P has (for instance) acted outside the statute or has not followed the correct procedure.[94] This requires the court to review the validity of P's defence, but this is in essence the same task as when a judge must decide in a case against the police whether they had lawful authority for entering and searching private property or making an arrest. What the common law tradition stresses is that, even if there were always a clear-cut demarcation between public bodies and private persons,[95] the acts of public officials are (apart from the effects of statute) in principle subject to the ordinary law that applies to private persons.[96]

The courts have two broad tasks in administrative law. The first (which we may call 'judicial review') arises when an individual challenges the legality of a decision taken by a public authority and the court must, in exercising a supervisory jurisdiction, decide whether to uphold or set aside the decision. This task has no exact equivalent in private law, although in areas such as trusts, company and trade union law, disputes may arise as to the validity of decisions by trustees, company directors and trade union committees, and supervisory principles may be applied in the process of review.[97] The second broad task (which we may call 'governmental liability') arises when individuals seek compensation or damages for loss caused by a public authority's unlawful acts. This task has much in common with the general law of tort, contract and restitution, which applies to public and private entities alike.

An extreme form of separation between public and private law arises where (as in France) 'judicial review' and 'governmental liability' questions are not decided by the ordinary civil courts but are reserved to administrative courts, composed of different judges and applying distinct rules of substance and procedure. A lesser form of separation occurs in Germany and Italy, where 'judicial review' is entrusted to the administrative courts, but 'liability' questions are decided by the civil courts. In the United Kingdom, by contrast, 'governmental liability' cases are decided by the ordinary civil courts and 'judicial review' in the Administrative Court (which has no separate judiciary, the court being composed of High Court judges designated for the purpose). It is now possible for a claim for damages to be made at the same time as a claim for judicial review, but this then gives rise to a two-stage process in which the claim for damages is dealt with after a successful claim for judicial review; and damages will be awarded only if liability in tort is established.[98] Judicial review procedure in the Administrative Court differs in several ways from that of ordinary civil litigation. But the same appellate courts hear appeals in both liability and judicial review cases.

Certainly, some cases of governmental liability must be decided by rules that do not apply to ordinary actions in tort or contract between private individuals. However, as we shall see in chapter 32, the liability of a public body, such as a social services authority, to compensate an

---

[94] This was the situation in the iconic *Cooper* v *Wandsworth Board of Works* (p 692 below).

[95] And see *YL* v *Birmingham Council* (below).

[96] See ch 32 A and B. Sir William Wade's argument in (1985) 101 LQR 180, 195–7, that *CCSU* v *Minister for the Civil Service* [1985] AC 374 concerned private law issues has received no support.

[97] See Oliver, *Common Values and the Public–Private Divide*; and Craig, in Taggart (ed.), *The Province of Administrative Law*, ch 10.

[98] See ch 32 A.

individual for injury that she has suffered from neglect by the authority, depends in part on statutory rules that determine the authority's powers, but also on the test of whether a duty of care existed at common law and, if so, on whether reasonable care was exercised by the authority in using its powers.[99]

Much discussion about the public law/private law distinction arose from the decision of the House of Lords in *O'Reilly v Mackman*,[100] in which it was held that the procedure of applying for judicial review *must* be used to challenge disciplinary decisions made in prisons, and that it was an abuse of process to seek a remedy equivalent to judicial review by means of an ordinary writ-action. The decision gave rise to the so-called exclusivity rule, that led to much complex and costly litigation concerning the procedural choices made by litigants. Eventually, a more flexible approach to these matters was adopted.[101]

One question that arose in these cases concerned the choice of procedure when the same dispute raised questions of private law rights and public law duties. In *Davy v Spelthorne Council*, the House of Lords held that an action for negligence against a local council was 'an ordinary action for tort' which did not raise 'any issue of public law as a live issue'.[102] Lord Wilberforce urged caution in using the public/private law distinction:

> Before the expression 'public law' can be used to deny a subject a right of action in the court of his choice it must be related to a positive prescription of law, by statute or by statutory rules. We have not yet reached the point at which mere characterisation of a claim as a claim in public law is sufficient to exclude it from consideration by the ordinary courts.[103]

As we have seen, the Human Rights Act 1998 makes it no easier for a clear distinction to be drawn between private and public law. The scheme of the Act (by s 6(1)) is to impose a duty to act compatibly with Convention rights in relation to *all* the functions of a 'core' public authority (such as a local council or a government department), whether the nature of a specific act is public or private. And by s 6(5) of the Act, bodies that are not public authorities for all purposes ('hybrid' bodies, with a mixture of public and private functions) have duties under the Act only in respect of acts that are public in their nature. The courts found it difficult to determine whether private companies that are paid by public authorities to provide services (such as care of the elderly) are themselves to be regarded as 'public authorities'; and the leading decision on this question has been reversed by Parliament.[104] The importance of identifying public authorities under the 1998 Act is to an extent offset by the rule that courts and tribunals are themselves public authorities for the purposes of the Act; they thus have a duty to act consistently with Convention rights in adjudicating on disputes that arise between private parties.[105]

We have seen that the broad purposes served by judicial review are the same in both English law and the law of Scotland. However, the law in Scotland has escaped the difficulties discussed

---

[99] *X (Minors)* v *Bedfordshire CC* [1995] 2 AC 633; *Barrett* v *Enfield Council* [2001] 2 AC 550; and ch 32 A.

[100] [1983] 2 AC 237.

[101] See pages 716–18 below.

[102] [1984] AC 262; and see P Cane [1984] PL 16.

[103] [1984] AC at 276. And see *Mercury Communications Ltd* v *Director General of Telecommunications* [1996] 1 All ER 575, 581 (Lord Slynn).

[104] See *YL* v *Birmingham Council* [2007] UKHL 27, [2008] AC 95 (and J Landau [2007] PL 630). Earlier cases included *Poplar Housing Association Ltd* v *Donoghue* [2001] EWCA Civ 595, [2002] QB 48 and *R (Heather)* v *Leonard Cheshire Foundation* [2002] EWCA Civ 366, [2002] 2 All ER 936. See D Oliver [2000] PL 476 and [2004] PL 329, M Sunkin [2004] PL 643, H Quane [2006] PL 106. For the sequel to the *YL* case, see Health and Social Care Act 2008, s 145. And see ch 19 C.

[105] Ch 19 C. And see e.g. *Campbell* v *MGN Ltd* [2004] UKHL 22, [2004] 2 AC 457. Also H W R Wade (2000) 116 LQR 217; M Hunt [1998] PL 423.

in this section almost entirely, since the supervisory jurisdiction of the Court of Session does not depend on the private law/public law distinction.[106]

Local government – a note

The emphasis in this book is on the constitutional structures that underlie the democratic government of the United Kingdom. In the context of administrative law, we are concerned with how public bodies provide services, exercise regulatory powers and so on. At a national level, the government's tasks include oversight of the economy, control of the physical environment, provision or oversight of services such as health and education, management of the state's revenues, promotion of 'law and order' and maintenance of the judicial system. As the case of the police shows, it is neither necessary nor desirable that all public services should be provided directly from Whitehall. Moreover, given privatisation of the public utilities and the involvement of private companies in many sectors of government, not all public services are provided directly by public authorities.

In the history of public administration in the United Kingdom, local authorities have played an important role, second in importance only to central government, and they have featured prominently in the evolution of administrative law. Since the nineteenth century, local councils have been affected by such doctrines of public law as the *ultra vires* rule, whereby a council, with power to levy local taxes and impose charges for services, and receiving grants from central government, may incur expenditure only for purposes authorised by statute.[107] More recently, local government has been subjected to a bewildering quantity of legislative changes (including reorganisation of areas, new forms of local taxation and novel methods of management within councils).[108] The elected councils continue to promote local democracy, as well as providing or enabling social services and administering regulatory systems and licensing at a local level. But an outline of the structure and operation of local government is outside the scope of this book.

In view of the conflicting demands made on local authorities and their limited fund-raising powers, they are often involved in the contentious side of administrative law, whether seeking judicial review against central government[109] or other local authorities,[110] defending claims for judicial review brought by individuals,[111] regulatory agencies[112] or central government[113] or resisting actions for damages in tort resulting from alleged failures of duty.[114] Local councils have never had the privileges and immunities that government departments enjoy as agents of the Crown.[115] Local administrators are not civil servants and management methods are often very different from those in central government.[116] Councillors operate in a political context and the

---

[106] *West v Secretary of State for Scotland* 1992 SLT 636; and see CMG Himsworth in Goudie, Supperstone and Walker (eds), *Judicial Review*, ch 21.

[107] Ch 30 A.

[108] See Bailey (ed.), *Cross on Local Government Law* and Himsworth, *Local Government in Scotland*. See also Loughlin, *Local Government in the Modern State*; and (the same) *Legality and Locality: the Role of Law in Central–Local Government Relations*.

[109] E.g. *R v Environment Secretary, ex p Hammersmith BC* [1991] 1 AC 521.

[110] E.g. *Bromley Council v GLC* [1983] 1 AC 768.

[111] E.g. *R v Gloucestershire CC, ex p Barry* [1997] AC 584; *Miss Behavin' Ltd v Belfast Council* [2007] UKHL 19, [2007] 3 All ER 1007. On the use of judicial review against local authorities, see M Sunkin et al. [2007] PL 545.

[112] E.g. *R v Birmingham Council, ex p EOC* [1989] AC 1155.

[113] E.g. *Lord Advocate v Dumbarton DC* [1990] 2 AC 580.

[114] *X (Minors) v Bedfordshire CC* [1995] 2 AC 633; *Barrett v Enfield Council* [2001] 2 AC 550.

[115] E.g. *Mersey Docks Trustees v Gibbs* (1866) LR 1 HL 93; ch 32 A.

[116] The principle in *Carltona Ltd v Commissioners of Works* [1943] 2 All ER 560 (p 115 above) does not apply in local government.

legality of party groups has been recognised,[117] but they are subject to mechanisms for securing public accountability and proper standards of conduct.

Finally, local councils are 'public authorities' for purposes of the Human Rights Act 1998. Every local authority must exercise its functions in a way that is compatible with the Convention rights, except where, as a result of primary legislation, it is unable to act differently or has acted to give effect to primary legislation that could not be read in a manner compatible with the Convention rights.[118]

---

[117] *R v Waltham Forest BC, ex p Baxter* [1988] QB 419; and see I Leigh [1988] PL 304.
[118] Human Rights Act 1998, s 6(1), (2)(a). And see *YL v Birmingham Council* (above, note 104).

CHAPTER 28

Delegated legislation

We saw in chapter 27 that during the twentieth century it came to be realised that the operation of government is carried on to a large extent not directly through laws made by Parliament, but by means of rules made by members of the executive under powers delegated to them by Parliament. This vast body of rules is known as delegated legislation, but it may also be described as secondary (or subordinate) legislation, by comparison with the primary legislation found in Acts of Parliament. In a few areas (especially in the conduct of foreign policy) government still relies not on statutory powers, but on the royal prerogative, that is, the common law powers that are exclusive to the Crown. However, so far as the power to legislate is concerned, it was held long ago in the *Case of Proclamations*[1] that the Crown had no residual power to legislate so as to impose obligations or restrictions on the people. Over 300 years later it was held that this funda-mental principle did not prevent the Crown having power under the prerogative to confer financial benefits on the victims of criminal violence.[2]

The term statute law covers both Acts of Parliament and delegated legislation. The main distinction between the two levels of statute law is that delegated legislation, unlike an Act of Parliament, is not the work of a supreme Parliament and is subject to judicial review. Nevertheless, the combined effect of the two levels is to set up public bodies to perform the tasks of govern-ment, and to equip them with the detailed powers needed for operating public services. It is very rare for an Act to contain all the provisions which are essential if a complex service is to be provided. An Act frequently does no more than outline the main features of the scheme, leaving many details to be filled in by subordinate legislation. In complex areas of government such as education, planning and immigration, there are often publications which bring together primary and subordinate legislation, along with codes of practice, ministerial circulars and some-times a digest of the case law. The bulk of statutory instruments is formidable. In 2006, there were enacted 55 Public General Acts which in total ran to nearly 5,400 pages. In the same year over 3,500 statutory instruments were issued; although many of these were local in effect, the twelve published volumes of general instruments amounted to over 11,400 pages.

Historical development

The formal process by which a Bill becomes an Act has never been the sole method of legislation. In the earliest years of Parliament, it was difficult to distinguish between enactment by the King in Parliament and legislation by the King in Council. Even when legislation by Parliament had become a distinct process, broad power to legislate by proclamation remained with the Crown. In 1539, by Henry VIII's Statute of Proclamations, royal power to issue proclamations 'for the good order and governance' of the country was recognised to exist and such proclamations were to be enforced as if made by Act of Parliament. One reason given for the Act was that sudden occasions might arise when speedy remedies were needed which could not wait for the meeting

---

[1] (1611) 12 Co Rep 74, p 50 above; and ch 12 D. The Crown retains prerogative power to legislate for certain over-seas possessions, but subject to judicial review: *R (Bancoult) v Foreign Secretary (No 2)* [2008] UKHL 61, [2009] 1 AC 453; and ch 15 C.

[2] *R v Criminal Injuries Compensation Board, ex p Lain* [1967] 2 QB 864.

of Parliament; the Act contained saving words to protect the common law, life and property. The repeal of the statute in 1547 made little difference to the Tudor use of proclamations and Henry VIII's name remains associated with the controversial practice of delegating power to the executive to amend Acts of Parliament.

The practice of Parliament delegating power to make laws is of long standing. An instance of delegation to the Commissioners of Sewers in respect of rivers and land drainage dates back to 1531. After 1689, the annual Mutiny Acts delegated power to the Crown to make regulations for the better government of the army, but it was not until the nineteenth century that delegation of wide legislative power became common. The first modern Factories Act in 1833 conferred power on the inspectors appointed under the Act to make orders and regulations, breaches of which were punishable under the criminal law.[3] A very wide power that remained law for over a century was the power, first vested in the Poor Law Commissioners, 'to make and issue all such rules, orders and regulations for the management of the poor . . . and for carrying this Act into execution . . . as they shall think proper'.[4]

The late nineteenth century saw a great increase in the delegation of legislative power to government departments and other bodies, granted piecemeal as need arose. The Rules Publication Act 1893 sought to introduce order into the proliferation of powers in Whitehall, by creating a generic term, 'statutory rules and orders', and requiring that such measures be published. During both world wars, Parliament granted power in very wide terms to the government to make regulations for the conduct of the war.[5]

After 1918, some lawyers and politicians became concerned at the wide legislative powers of government departments. The inquiry by the Committee on Ministers' Powers[6] concluded that unless Parliament was willing to delegate law-making powers, it would be unable to pass the kind or quantity of legislation which modern public opinion required. The committee drew attention to certain dangers in delegated legislation and proposed greater safeguards against abuse. In 1946, the Statutory Instruments Act replaced the Rules Publication Act 1893 and promoted a greater uniformity of procedure. Since 1944, a scrutinising committee has been regularly appointed by Parliament, first by the Commons and today by the Commons and Lords jointly. The practice of delegated legislation has been reviewed by many parliamentary committees,[7] but the flood of subordinate legislation shows no sign of abating. Between 1981 and 1996 the number of instruments subject to parliamentary procedure increased by around 50 per cent, that is, from under 1,000 a year to around 1,500 a year; of these the number subject to the negative procedure in Parliament almost doubled, from some 700 in the early 1980s to around 1,300 in the period 1994–99.[8] During this period, the contents of instruments may have changed. As one committee said in 1986, 'Instead of simply implementing the "nuts and bolts" of Government policy, statutory instruments have increasingly been used to change policy, sometimes in ways that were not envisaged when the enabling primary legislation was passed.'[9]

In 1996, another committee concluded that 'there is . . . too great a readiness in Parliament to delegate wide legislative powers to Ministers, and no lack of enthusiasm on their part to take

---

[3] Labour of Children etc. in Factories Act 1833. See now Health and Safety At Work etc. Act 1974, ss 15 and 80.

[4] Poor Law Amendment Act 1834, s 15.

[5] Ch 26 B. Defence of the Realm Act 1914; Emergency Powers (Defence) Act 1939. See Carr, *Concerning English Administrative Law*; Allen, *Law and Orders*; and (written from a different standpoint) Ewing and Gearty, *The Struggle for Civil Liberties*.

[6] Ch 27.

[7] HC 310 (1952–3); HL 184, HC 475 (1971–2); HL 204, HC 468 (1972–3); HC 588–1 (1977–8), ch 3; HC 152 (1995–6); and HC 48 (1999–2000).

[8] HC 152 (1995–6), para 10 and HC 48 (1999–2000), para 25. For the negative procedure, see p 630 below.

[9] HC 31–xxxvii (1985–6), p 2.

such powers'.[10] Such committees have criticised the way in which Parliament gives 'second-rate' consideration to secondary legislation.[11]

The need for delegated legislation

Most constitutions today recognise the need for legislation to exist at several levels within the legal system. Sometimes the need arises from the desire to devolve powers from the centre to the regions or to elected councils within local government areas. Even if the Scottish Parliament and the Welsh Assembly make laws for Scotland and Wales respectively, the cities in those countries need some local laws that differ from those in rural areas.

A more general reason for delegated legislation is that the time available to Parliament for legislature is limited. If Parliament attempted to enact all new statutory rules itself, the legislative machine would clog up, unless the procedure for considering Bills was streamlined to a point at which detailed scrutiny by the legislators would be impossible. Even if the United Kingdom recognised a strict doctrine of separation of powers,[12] this would not create a bright line to distinguish between the laws that *should* be contained in primary legislation and the more detailed or technical rules that can properly be entrusted to the section of government that is administering a public service. Power to make detailed regulations on, for instance, road traffic or social security may be entrusted to the relevant government department, provided that there are procedures to ensure that some oversight is exercised by Parliament over the use made of the power.[13]

Another factor is that much delegated legislation deals with technical matters that are best regulated by a process in which the experience of relevant experts, professional bodies and commercial interests can be fully utilised. The greater the technicality involved in the content of such rules, the less suitable they are for consideration by the usual legislative process and the less likely they are to generate enough political interest to be included in the government's legislative programme.

An important justification for the existence of secondary legislation is that in many areas of government, especially when new services or schemes are established, it is not possible to foresee every difficulty that may arise in practice and detailed rules may be needed to accompany the parent Act.[14] Delegated legislation makes it possible to amend such rules as it is discovered how they are operating. There are also practical reasons why many new Acts should not come into effect as soon as the royal assent is given. It is common today for an Act to delegate power to a minister to make commencement orders, bringing into operation all or successive parts of the Act. There is no duty on the minister to exercise a commencement power, but the minister must not act so as to defeat Parliament's expectation that the Act will come into operation.[15]

---

[10] HC 152 (1995–6), para 14, endorsed in HC 48 (1999–2000), para 26.

[11] P Tudor (2000) 21 *Statute Law Review* 149, 150.

[12] See ch 6.

[13] In 2008–9, the House of Commons spent $12^{1}/_{2}$ hours in all (just over 1 per cent of its time) debating statutory instruments subject to affirmative resolution, and just over 7 hours on those subject to negative procedure (*Sessional Returns*). These figures do not include the time spent on statutory instruments by committees of the Commons and Lords.

[14] When the community charge, or poll tax, was brought in by the Local Government Finance Act 1988, no fewer than 47 sets of regulations were made in the years 1989–91.

[15] *R v Home Secretary, ex p Fire Brigades Union* [1995] 2 AC 513. It is customary for commencement orders not to be subject to any parliamentary process, in either the positive or negative forms. Cf *R (Haw)* v *Home Secretary* [2006] EWCA Civ 532, [2006] QB 780.

Delegated legislation may also be needed in times of emergency when a government has to take action quickly and in excess of its normal powers. Many written constitutions include provision in emergency for suspending formal guarantees of individual liberty. In the United Kingdom, the Civil Contingencies Act 2004 (replacing the Emergency Powers Act 1920) makes permanent provision enabling the executive to legislate subject to parliamentary safeguards in certain emergencies.[16] Under the little-known United Nations Act 1946, by Orders in Council the government may make such provision as appears necessary to give effect to decisions by the UN Security Council calling for sanctions (but not the use of armed force) to preserve international peace and security.[17]

Exceptional types of delegated legislation

While much delegated legislation is essential, governments are often tempted to obtain from Parliament greater powers than they should be given. Criticism centres on particular types of delegated legislation.

Matters of principle

There is a clear threat to parliamentary government if power is delegated to legislate on matters of general policy or if so wide a discretion is conferred that it is impossible to be sure what limit the legislature intended to impose. In practice Acts of Parliament frequently confer legislative powers in wide terms. One reason for this is that if powers are phrased more narrowly, this will make it more likely that the department will need to seek increased powers from Parliament in future. A proposal that Parliament should adopt a policy of passing framework legislation, with all details left to delegated legislation, was rightly rejected by the House of Commons Committee on Procedure in 1978, on the ground that this would further weaken parliamentary control.[18] Nonetheless, governments sometimes propose Bills that have been described as 'skeleton Bills', Bills that are 'little more than a licence to legislate'.[19] Such Bills can operate only when extensive regulations are made and MPs may ask to see the proposed regulations before approving a Bill in this form. But there are few absolutes in this area and legislative practice is often a compromise between different attitudes to delegation.

Delegation of taxing power

We have seen how vital to the development of parliamentary government was the insistence that Parliament alone could authorise taxation.[20] This insistence survives in an attenuated form, but modern pressures, particularly associated with the economy, require Parliament to delegate some powers in relation to taxation. In particular, the working of a system of customs duties combined with the development of the European Union has made necessary the delegation of power to

---

[16] Ch 26 B.

[17] In *Her Majesty's Treasury* v *Mohammed Jabar Ahmed* [2010] UKSC 2, the Supreme Court quashed as *ultra vires* of the 1946 Act Orders in Council that froze the assets of persons suspected of being involved in international terrorism. The Orders were retrospectively validated by the Terrorist Asset-Freezing (Temporary Provisions) Act 2010.

[18] HC 588-I (1977–8), ch 2.

[19] See Tudor (note 11 above), p 152: in the period 1992–9 four Bills were described by the House of Lords Delegated Powers Committee as skeletal, two as near skeletal: HL Paper 112 (1998–9), para 23. The lack of flesh may apply only to one or two limbs of a Bill: ibid, para 28. The Committee requires full justification to be given for use of skeleton Bills: HL 110 (2004–5), paras 25–9.

[20] Ch 4 A.

give exemptions and reliefs from such duties.[21] The government also has power to vary certain classes of indirect taxation by order of the Treasury.[22] These powers are subject to parliamentary control in that orders imposing import duties or varying indirect taxation cease to have effect unless they are confirmed by a resolution of the House of Commons within a limited time.

Sub-delegation

When a statute delegates legislative power to a minister, exercisable by statutory instrument, it may be assumed that Parliament intends the statutory instrument itself to contain the rules. Is it a proper use of such powers for the instrument to sub-delegate legislative power, by authorising rules to be made by another body or by another procedure? The legal maxim, *delegatus non potest delegare*, means that a delegate may not sub-delegate his or her power, but the parent Act may always override this by authorising sub-delegation, as did the Emergency Powers (Defence) Act 1939. Without express authority in the parent Act, it is doubtful whether sub-delegation of legislative powers is valid. However, emergency regulations under the Civil Contingencies Act 2004 may 'make provision of any kind that could be made by Act of Parliament' (s 22(3)), and the breadth of this power may authorise sub-delegation. Where sub-delegation occurs, control by Parliament becomes more difficult. In 1978, the Joint Committee on Statutory Instruments criticised the recurring tendency of departments to seek to bypass Parliament by omitting necessary detail from statutory instruments and vesting a wide discretion in ministers to vary the rules without making further statutory instruments.[23] Under the European Communities Act 1972, sub-delegation is prohibited except for rules of procedure for courts or tribunals.[24]

Retrospective operation

It follows from the supremacy of Parliament that Acts may have retrospective operation.[25] If on occasion retrospective legislation is considered necessary, this must either be done in express words by Parliament itself or, if done through delegated legislation, only on the express authority of a statute.[26] By reason of art 7, ECHR, applied by the Human Rights Act 1998, delegated legislation may not retrospectively create new offences or impose additional penalties.

Exclusion of the jurisdiction of the courts

The power of the courts in reviewing delegated legislation is confined to declaring it *ultra vires*, whether on grounds of substance or procedure,[27] a power that is now subject to the court's duty where possible of protecting rights under the Human Rights Act. While control over the merits of delegated legislation is a matter for ministers and for Parliament, the possibility of control by the courts should not be excluded. It should never be for a minister to determine the limits of his or her own powers.[28]

---

[21] European Communities Act 1972, s 5; Customs and Excise Duties (General Reliefs) Act 1979.

[22] Excise Duties (Surcharges or Rebates) Act 1979.

[23] HL 51, HC 579 (1977–8), p 10; and see *Customs and Excise Commissioners v J H Corbitt (Numismatists) Ltd* [1981] AC 22.

[24] European Communities Act 1972, s 2(2) and Sch 2.

[25] Ch 4 B.

[26] See e.g. *R (Stellato) v Home Secretary* [2007] UKHL 5, [2007] 2 AC 70. Cf the unsatisfactory decision in *R v Social Security Secretary, ex p Britnell* [1991] 2 All ER 726 (upholding 'transitional provisions' that had a retrospective effect).

[27] See pp 634–6 below.

[28] Yet under the Counter-Inflation Act 1973, Sch 3, para 1, an order made under part II of the Act could 'define any expressions used in the provisions under which it is made'. And see *Jackson v Hall* [1980] AC 854.

Authority to modify an Act of Parliament

However undesirable this might appear in principle, Parliament has for long been known to delegate to ministers power to amend Acts of Parliament.[29] The term 'Henry VIII clause' is given to such provisions and numerous examples are found in the Scotland Act 1998 and the Government of Wales Act 2006.[30] When the power in a new Act is restricted to amending earlier Acts that are directly affected by the new reforms, the power is less objectionable than when it extends to amending the very Act that contains the power.[31] Yet some Acts dealing with schemes of social and industrial control empower a minister to broaden or narrow the scope of the schemes in the light of experience.[32] Moreover, some statutes confer on ministers power to modify not merely existing but also future Acts.[33]

Three instances of delegated power to modify Acts of Parliament may be given. The European Communities Act 1972, by s 2(2), authorises the making of Orders in Council and ministerial regulations to implement Community obligations of the United Kingdom, to enable rights under the European treaties to be exercised and 'for the purpose of dealing with matters arising out of or related to any such obligations or rights'. Schedule 2 to the Act excludes certain matters from the general power, including the imposition of taxes, retroactive legislation and the sub-delegation of legislative power (other than power to make rules of procedure for any court or tribunal). Subject to these limitations, measures made under s 2(2) may make 'any such provision (of any such extent) as might be made by Act of Parliament' (s 2(4)). The intention in using such wide language must have been to exclude the possibility of judicial review on grounds of vires in the case of instruments made under s 2(2).[34]

An unusual power to amend primary legislation was created by the Human Rights Act 1998, s 10.[35] This authorises ministers or the Queen in Council to make remedial orders when a superior court has declared primary legislation incompatible with a Convention right or the European Court of Human Rights has made a similar finding. The aim of a remedial order is to amend the offending legislation so as to remove the incompatibility. As with orders under the Legislative and Regulatory Reform Act (below), the making of an order is subject to an unusually full form of parliamentary supervision.[36]

The third instance of power to amend primary legislation is found in the Legislative and Regulatory Reform Act 2006. Replacing an earlier Act of 2001, this enables ministers to amend or repeal existing Acts with the aim of removing or reducing any burden resulting from that legislation, in respect of such matters as financial cost, administrative inconvenience and obstacles to efficiency (s 1). This power is subject to many conditions and qualifications: thus the new provision must not impose, abolish or vary any tax (s 5(1)), may not create new offences punishable with imprisonment for more than two years (s 6(1)), must not authorise any forcible entry, search

---

[29] MPR, pp 36–8; Carr, *Concerning English Administrative Law*, pp 41–7.

[30] See in the Scotland Act 1998, ss 30(2), 79, 89, 104–8, 113(5), 114, 124 and Sch 7. These powers were considered necessary to enable ministers to implement devolution (see HL 101, 124, 146 (1997–8)). They are not to be confused with the power of the Scottish Parliament to make laws for Scotland, that necessarily includes power to amend Westminster Acts on devolved matters.

[31] See e.g. Freedom of Information Act 2000, s 75 (Secretary of State may by order repeal or amend any statutory provision which appears to him to be capable of preventing the disclosure of information).

[32] Health and Safety at Work etc. Act 1974, ss 15 and 80; Sex Discrimination Act 1975, s 80, esp sub-s (3).

[33] See N W Barber and A L Young [2003] PL 112. Also Delegated Powers and Regulatory Reform Committee, *Guidance for Departments* (2007), para 16.

[34] See HL Deb, 17 February 1976, cols 399–417, and HL 51, HC 169 (1977–8), pp 17–18. Cf *R v HM Treasury, ex p Smedley* [1985] QB 657. And see ch 8 E.

[35] See ch 19 C.

[36] See below page 633.

or seizure (s 7(1)), and may not amend the Human Rights Act 1998 (s 8).[37] A power such as this provides an alternative to legislation by Bill, and new procedures within Parliament have become necessary for preventing their misuse.[38]

Nomenclature

Despite the Statutory Instruments Act 1946, terminology is often confusing. The term 'statutory instrument' is a comprehensive expression to describe all forms of subordinate legislation subject to the 1946 Act.[39] Within the scope of the Act are many powers conferred on ministers by Acts dating back from before the 1946 Act. As regards Acts passed thereafter, there are two categories of statutory instrument: (a) legislative powers conferred on the Queen in Council and stated in the parent Act to be exercisable by Order in Council; (b) legislative powers conferred on a minister of the Crown and stated to be exercisable by statutory instrument. The first of these, the statutory Order in Council, must be distinguished from prerogative Orders in Council, which are not statutory instruments at all, though some of these are published in the annual volumes of statutory instruments. One reason why some powers are vested in the Queen in Council is that the more prestigious formality of an Order in Council may seem appropriate to some classes of legislation.[40] In the past powers were occasionally vested in a named minister, but today powers are generally vested in 'the Secretary of State'; this means that the powers may in law be exercised by any holder of the office of Secretary of State. Many statutory instruments apply only in one locality, but the term does not include local by-laws or such matters as the confirmation of compulsory purchase orders. Confusingly, some kinds of rule made under statutory authority are not statutory instruments, for example immigration rules under the Immigration Act 1971 and regulations made by the Electoral Commission under the Political Parties, Elections and Referendums Act 2000.

Although statutory instrument is the generic term, various names are applied to the schemes of rules made by statutory instrument: orders, regulations, warrants, schemes, directions and so on. Several of these terms may be used in a single Act to distinguish different procedures for different purposes. In practice, the term 'regulation' is used mainly for matters of wide general importance. Where the legislation deals with procedure, rules are generally enacted, for example, the Civil Procedure Rules. With the term 'order' there is less uniformity; thus a commencement order may bring into effect all or part of an Act of Parliament and in town planning law a general development order contains detailed rules for the control of development.

To add to the scope for confusion, statutes may authorise the making of codes of practice, guidance and other forms of rules and provide sanctions of various kinds if they are not followed.[41] These measures must be distinguished from informal administrative rules (guidelines,

---

[37] While the new measure must 'make the law more accessible or more easily understood' (s 3(4)), it is puzzling that it must not 'remove any necessary protection', nor must it be 'of constitutional significance' (s 3(2), (d) and (f)).

[38] On earlier legislation preceding the 2006 Act, see [1995] PL 21 (M Freedland) and 34 (C M G Himsworth). On how the government's Bill for the 2006 Act was cut down in Parliament, see P Davis, [2007] PL 677. It originally included a remarkably broad power that would have enabled the government to abolish long-established rules of the common law (Davis, at 685). The mammoth Company Law Reform Bill, 2005–06, included a super-affirmative clause (later abandoned), the avowed intention of which was to make it unnecessary for any future reforms of company law to be made by Parliament!

[39] The official abbreviation for statutory instruments is SI followed by the year and number, e.g. SI 2004 No 252 (or SI 2004/252).

[40] No discussion of an Order takes place in the Privy Council when it is made: and ministers have the same responsibility to Parliament for Orders in Council as for other statutory instruments.

[41] For an official definition of codes of practice, see p 637 below.

circulars, etc.), which are made without express statutory authority; they are considered later in this chapter.

The Human Rights Act 1998 draws a distinction between what it defines as 'primary legislation' and 'subordinate legislation'.[42] The reason for the distinction is to protect Acts of Parliament from being set aside or invalidated by the courts for inconsistency with Convention rights. But the demarcation line drawn is unsatisfactory in that the Act includes in 'primary legislation' various measures that are not Acts of Parliament. These include measures of the Church Assembly, instruments made under primary legislation that amend Acts of Parliament and Orders in Council made under the Crown's prerogative.[43] There is no good reason why, if a minister uses a Henry VIII clause to amend a statute, and thereby creates inconsistency with a Convention right, the minister's action should be treated as if it were an Act of Parliament.

If delegated legislation is a necessary phenomenon in the modern state, then it is essential (1) that the process by which it is made should include the consultation of interests; (2) that Parliament should retain the ability to oversee and supervise the use of delegated powers; (3) that delegated legislation should be published; and (4) that it is subject to challenge in the courts should reasons for this arise.

Consultation of interests

Unlike the process of primary legislation, which (at least in democratic theory) makes possible public debate of the purpose and contents of a Bill as it passes through both Houses, most delegated legislation comes into force as soon as it is made public, either at once or after a short interval stated in the document itself. Since there is no general requirement of prior publicity, an ordinary person has little chance of getting to know about proposed statutory instruments. But the department proposing to make a new instrument frequently embarks on consultation with interests affected by the proposal. Some Acts make this obligatory. Many social security regulations must be submitted in draft to the Social Security Advisory Committee, whose disagreements, if any, with the Secretary of State must be reported to Parliament along with the regulations.[44] So too, the Administrative Justice and Tribunals Council must be consulted before rules of procedure for many tribunals and inquiries are made.[45] Several Acts do not specify the bodies to be consulted, leaving it to the minister to consult with such associations and bodies as appear to him or her to be affected.[46] Where there is a duty to consult, either because of a statutory duty or a consistent practice of consultation,[47] the courts have laid down the criteria for proper consultation: it must be undertaken when the proposal is at a formative stage; sufficient reasons must be given for the proposal to enable an informed response to be given; adequate time must be allowed for the response to the proposals; and the product of consultation must be conscientiously taken into account when the ultimate decision is made.[48] Where there is a duty to consult, fairness may require disclosure to an interested person of the scientific advice on which the minister is

---

[42] Human Rights Act 1998, ss 3(2), 4, 21 (1). And see ch 19 C.

[43] See P Billings and B Pontin [2001] PL 21.

[44] Social Security Administration Act 1992, ss 170, 172–4. See *Howker v Work and Pensions Secretary* [2002] EWCA Civ 1623, [2003] ICR 405 (regulations invalid where department misled advisory committee).

[45] Tribunals, Courts and Enforcement Act 2007, sch 7, part 3; Tribunals and Inquiries Act 1992, s 9 (as amended).

[46] For the effect of failure to consult, see *Agricultural Training Board v Aylesbury Mushrooms Ltd* [1972] 1 All ER 280; also *R v Social Services Secretary, ex p Association of Metropolitan Authorities* [1986] 1 All ER 164.

[47] See *Council of Civil Service Unions v Minister for the Civil Service* [1985] AC 374.

[48] *R v North Devon Health Authority, ex p Coughlan* [2001] QB 213, at [108]. Cf the government's *Code of Practice on consultation* (2008).

proposing to rely.[49] Even where there is no duty to consult before delegated legislation is made, departments often consult interests likely to be affected, since this consultation may bring about access to specialised knowledge that exists outside government and help to promote consensus.

Control and supervision by Parliament

To what extent does Parliament control or supervise the making of delegated legislation? An answer to this difficult question must deal with the following matters: (*a*) the powers conferred; (*b*) procedures for making statutory instruments; (*c*) the role of the House of Lords; (*d*) technical scrutiny of statutory instruments; and (*e*) considering the merits of statutory instruments.

The conferment of powers

Since all delegated legislative powers stem from statute, there is always, at least in theory, an opportunity at the committee stage of a Bill to examine clauses that seek to delegate legislative powers. As long ago as 1931, the Ministers' Powers Committee recommended that Bills conferring such powers should be referred to a standing committee in each House to report whether there were any objections of principle to them.[50] It was only in 1992 that the House of Lords appointed a committee (on the lines of a committee of the Australian Senate) to consider clauses in Bills proposing to delegate legislative powers and to receive for each Bill a government memorandum justifying the proposals. By reporting promptly on such proposals, the committee (now named the Committee on Delegated Powers and Regulatory Reform) aims to discourage the granting of excessive powers and to ensure that an appropriate level of scrutiny is included in the parent legislation. Its reports receive no media attention, but it has often persuaded the government to accept its views on such questions as the choice of procedure for parliamentary scrutiny in relation to a specific Bill.[51]

Procedures for making statutory instruments

In delegating legislative powers to government, Parliament typically provides for some parliamentary control or oversight to be built into the use of specific powers. However, two basic reasons for delegating legislative power are pressure on Parliament's time and the technical nature of the subject-matter; the very object of delegation would be frustrated if Parliament had to approve each instrument in detail. The procedure through which a statutory instrument must pass depends on the terms of the parent Act. The principal procedures are the following:

(*a*) laying of draft instrument before Parliament, and requiring affirmative resolution before instrument can be 'made';

(*b*) laying of instrument after it has been made, to come into effect only when approved by affirmative resolution;

(*c*) laying of instrument that takes immediate effect, but requires approval by affirmative resolution within a stated period as a condition of continuance;

---

[49] *R v Health Secretary, ex p US Tobacco International Inc* [1992] QB 353.

[50] MPR, pp 67–8. Cf HC 310 (1952–3).

[51] See C M G Himsworth [1995] PL 34, P Tudor (2000) 21 *Statute Law Review* 149, HL 112 (1998–9) and HL Paper 110 (2004–5), ch 2. The Committee's *Guidance for Departments* (2007), outlines criteria for deciding whether proposals for delegation and proposed levels of parliamentary supervision are 'appropriate'. See e.g. HL Paper 113 (2006–07) (delegation concerning biometric identification in UK Borders Bill) and HL Paper 41 (2009–10) (power of minister to amend Copyright, Designs and Patents Act 1988).

(*d*) laying of instrument that takes immediate effect, subject to annulment by resolution of either House;

(*e*) laying in draft, subject to resolution that no further proceedings be taken – in effect a direction to the minister not to 'make' the instrument;

(*f*) laying before Parliament, with no further provision for control.[52]

In a few instances a 'super-affirmative' procedure has been created to deal with exceptional forms of delegated legislation;[53] at the other extreme, some statutory instruments are not required to be laid before Parliament at all (as will be the case if the parent Act is silent on laying before Parliament).

In cases (*a*)–(*c*) (*positive procedure*), an affirmative resolution of each House (or in the case of financial instruments, of the Commons alone) is needed if the instrument is to come into force or to remain in operation. In cases (*d*) and (*e*) (*negative procedure*), no action need be taken in either House unless there is some opposition to the instrument.

Of these procedures, by far the most common is case (*d*) (subject to annulment); the most common of the positive procedures is case (*a*). Under the positive procedure, the government must secure an affirmative resolution in each House and, if necessary, it must allot time in the Commons for such a resolution; current practice in the Commons is for the instrument to be debated, however briefly, in a 'delegated legislation committee'.[54] Under the negative procedure, any member who so wishes may 'pray' that the instrument be annulled. It was formerly impossible for time to be found to debate all prayers for annulment which had been tabled.[55] The situation has been eased by the use of delegated legislation committees and by changes in the timetabling of Commons business,[56] but it would be a very rare event indeed for the House to adopt a motion to annul a statutory instrument.

A novel provision made by the European Communities Act 1972 was that a statutory instrument made under s 2(2) should be subject to annulment by a resolution of either House unless a draft of the instrument had been approved by each House before the instrument was made.[57] Thus the government may choose whether the negative or positive procedure should be used. Both Labour and Conservative governments were criticised for choosing the negative procedure for important measures modifying Acts of Parliament.[58]

One feature common to these procedures is that neither House may amend a statutory instrument, except for very rare instances where amendment is expressly authorised by the parent Act.[59] If it is clear that a House is not satisfied with an instrument as it stands, the minister must withdraw it and make a fresh instrument.

An Act that delegates legislative powers will specify the parliamentary procedures that are to apply. In addition, the Statutory Instruments Acts 1946 contains some general requirements. By s 4, where an instrument must be laid in Parliament after being made, it must in general be laid before it comes into operation; the heading of such an instrument must state three dates, showing (i) when it was made, (ii) when it was laid in Parliament and (iii) when it came into operation.

---

[52] It is customary for commencement orders to be subject to no parliamentary control; and see *R (Stellato)* v *Home Secretary* (note 26 above). In such cases, there could be a motion to 'take note' of the instrument: see HC SO 118(4)(b).

[53] Page 633, below.

[54] See HC SO 118.

[55] A Beith (1981) 34 *Parliamentary Affairs* 165; Griffith and Ryle (eds), *Parliament*, pp 345–52.

[56] See HC SO 17 and 118.

[57] European Communities Act 1972, Sch 2, para 2.

[58] HL 51, HC 169 (1977–8), para 36; HC 15–viii (1981–2); and see Cmnd 8600, 1982.

[59] Census Act 1920, s 1(2); Civil Contingencies Act 2004, s 27(3).

What constitutes laying before Parliament is governed by the practice of each House[60] and an instrument may be laid when Parliament is not sitting. The rule that an instrument must be laid before it comes into operation is clear, subject to statutory provision for immediate operation in cases of urgency. Although there is no binding judicial authority on the matter, it is submitted that failure to lay an instrument prevents it from coming into operation.[61] But the position may be doubtful in the case of such delegated legislation as is outside the 1946 Act. While under the 1946 Act an interval of one day between laying and operation is in law sufficient, departments are urged to ensure that the interval is not less than 21 days.[62]

By s 5 of the 1946 Act, where an instrument is subject to annulment, as in procedure (*d*) above, there is a uniform period of 40 days during which a prayer for annulment may be moved, exclusive of any time during which Parliament is adjourned for more than four days or is prorogued or dissolved. Where, as in procedure (*e*), an instrument is laid in draft but subject to the negative procedure, the same period of 40 days applies. In the case of instruments which need an affirmative resolution before they can come into operation (procedure (*b*)), no set period is provided as the government in each case must decide how urgently the instrument is needed. Under procedure (*c*) the period for obtaining the affirmative resolution is stated in the parent Act.

The role of the House of Lords

Because of its majority in the Commons, the government can expect to win any vote taken on a statutory instrument. The position is different in the Lords: and in 2000 the royal commission on House of Lords reform considered that a reformed upper house should make a strong contribution to enhanced scrutiny of secondary legislation.[63]

Although a parent Act may expressly confine control of statutory instruments to the Commons, the House of Lords is usually granted the same powers of control as the Commons. Moreover, the procedure under the Parliament Acts 1911 and 1949 for by-passing the Lords applies to Bills and not to statutory instruments. But it is extremely rare for the House of Lords to exercise its veto over subordinate legislation. When on 18 June 1968 the House rejected an order containing sanctions against the Rhodesian government made under the Southern Rhodesia Act 1965,[64] this caused the Labour government to propose (unsuccessfully) to abolish the power of the Lords to veto statutory instruments.[65] In 1994 the House declared that it had an 'unfettered freedom to vote on any subordinate legislation submitted for its consideration'.[66] In 2000, the House exercised this freedom, rejecting the Greater London Election Rules because of a disagreement over granting candidates a free postal delivery.[67] The Lords thus have the power to veto all instruments, except financial instruments that are laid only in the Commons. They sometimes adopt a resolution disapproving of an instrument without rejecting it, to induce the government to think again. In 2006, after a full examination of this issue, a joint committee of both Houses found that while the upper House should not regularly reject statutory instruments,

---

[60] Laying of Documents before Parliament (Interpretation) Act 1948. See HL SO 71, HC SO 159. Also *R v Immigration Appeal Tribunal, ex p Joyles* [1972] 3 All ER 213.

[61] Cf A I L Campbell [1983] PL 43. The point was assumed but not decided in *R v Social Services Secretary, ex p Camden BC* [1987] 2 All ER 560 (A I L Campbell [1987] PL 328).

[62] HL 51, HC 169 (1977–8), pp 11–12; and *Statutory Instrument Practice* (Cabinet Office, 2006), 4.13.

[63] Cm 4534, 2000, ch 7. See also Russell, *Reforming the House of Lords*, pp 269–70; Shell, *The House of Lords*, ch 8.

[64] A month later, on 18 July 1968, an identical order was approved by the Lords.

[65] Cmnd 3799, 1969, pp 22–3; Parliament (No 2) Bill 1969, clauses 13–15. And see ch 10 B.

[66] HL Deb, 20 October 1994, col 356.

[67] HL Deb, 22 February 2000, cols 136 and 182. Equivalent rules were later approved: HL Deb, 6 March 2000, col 849.

'in exceptional circumstances it may be appropriate for it to do so'. This conclusion was accepted by the government.[68]

The technical scrutiny of statutory instruments

In the oversight of subordinate legislation, both Houses depend on the work of committees advised by qualified persons. All general statutory instruments laid before Parliament, as well as other statutory orders, come under scrutiny by the Joint Committee on Statutory Instruments, consisting of seven members appointed from each House. The members from the Commons meet separately to scrutinise those instruments which are laid only in the Commons. The joint committee is advised by the Speaker's Counsel and by Counsel to the Lord Chairman of committees.

The committee must consider whether the attention of the Houses should be drawn to an instrument on various legal and procedural grounds. In summary, these are:

(*a*) that an instrument imposes a charge on public revenues or requires payments to be made to any government department or public authority or prescribes the amount of such charge or payments;

(*b*) that it has been made under an Act that excludes it from challenge in the courts;

(*c*) that it purports to have retrospective effect where the parent Act does not authorise this;

(*d*) that there has been unjustifiable delay by the department (in publishing it, laying it in Parliament or in giving notice that it has come into operation before being laid);

(*e*) that there is doubt as to whether it is intra vires or that it makes unusual or unexpected use of the delegated powers;

(*f*) that for any reason its form or purport need to be elucidated;

(*g*) that its drafting is defective; or

(*h*) 'on any other ground which does not impinge on its merits or on the policy behind it'.[69]

Around 1,500 instruments are examined by the committee each year, but relatively few instruments are reported to the two Houses.[70] Before such a report is made, the department concerned will have sent to the committee an explanation of the position. An adverse report does not in itself have any effect on the instrument; in particular, if the committee expresses doubts about the vires of an instrument, that is a question that only the courts may decide.

Considering the merits of statutory instruments

The Joint Committee on Statutory Instruments does not examine the merits or policy of an instrument. Occasionally, these matters may be discussed by the whole House of Commons on an affirmative resolution or on a prayer for annulment, but in general such debates are held in delegated legislation committees. Several such committees are regularly appointed, on the lines of the Public Bill committees used for the committee stage of Bills.[71] In the committee, one and a half hours are allowed for considering each instrument.[72] After this consideration, a vote on the

---

[68] See HL Paper 265, HC 1212 (2005–06), ch 6; and the government response, Cm 6997, 2006, paras 36–47.

[69] HC SO 151; HL SO 74.

[70] In 2008, 59 instruments out of 1,486 were drawn to the attention of the Houses, 45 of these for defective drafting, 8 for failure to observe proper practice: HL Paper 136, HC 884 (2008–09).

[71] Ch 10 A.

[72] HC SO 118. Those relating to Northern Ireland may be debated in the Northern Ireland Committee for two-and-a-half hours: HC SO 115(2).

instrument may be taken in the whole House without further debate. The committee debate enables important issues to be ventilated, but many such debates are no more than a formality.

Certain delegated measures that require the particularly close attention of Parliament form the new category of 'super-affirmative' instruments that has been created to legitimise the exercise of new 'Henry VIII' powers by ministers to amend primary legislation. Two instances of these instruments may be mentioned.

One, under the Human Rights Act 1998, s 10, is the 'remedial order' by which the government amends primary legislation to remove an inconsistency with a Convention right. The other, under the Legislative and Regulatory Reform Act 2006, amends primary legislation for such purposes as to ease the burden of a regulatory scheme.[73] The procedure laid down by these two Acts provides for greater scrutiny than is usual and requires each House to accept that the statutory conditions for making the order are satisfied; and the period for parliamentary action is 60 days rather than the usual 40. In the former case, the Joint Committee on Human Rights has the primary task of scrutinising remedial orders.[74] Under the 2006 Act, this is entrusted to the Regulatory Reform Committee (Commons)[75] and the Delegated Powers and Regulatory Reform Committee (Lords).

In order that each House may inform itself about EC secondary legislation, committees of the two Houses exercise functions comparable with those of the committees which deal with statutory instruments.[76]

This account of secondary legislation is confined to the Westminster Parliament and does not deal with procedures in Edinburgh, Cardiff and Belfast for dealing with measures that are subordinate to the legislation adopted by the devolved Parliament or Assembly.[77]

Publication of statutory instruments

Although it is desirable that all legislation should be publicised before it takes effect, there are some matters, for example changes in indirect taxation, where the object of the legislation might be defeated if it had to be made known to the public in advance. The Statutory Instruments Act allows that for essential reasons a statutory instrument may come into operation even before it is laid before Parliament, with the safeguard that the Lord Chancellor and the Speaker must be provided with an immediate explanation. More generally, it provides a uniform procedure for numbering, printing and publishing statutory instruments.[78] An instrument classified as local by reason of its subject matter and certain classes of general instrument may be exempted from the requirements of printing and sale. Each year is published a collected edition of all general instruments made during the year which are still operative. It is a defence in proceedings for breach of a statutory instrument to prove that it had not been issued by the Stationery Office at the date of the alleged breach, unless it is shown by the prosecutor that reasonable steps had been taken to bring the purport of the instrument to the notice of the public, or of persons likely to be affected by it, or of the person charged.[79] Thus ignorance of a statutory instrument is no defence, but in certain circumstances failure to issue an instrument may be. Where regulations impose

---

[73] And see above page 626.

[74] For the procedure, see Human Rights Act 1998, sch 2; and also HC SO 152B.

[75] See HC SO 14.

[76] Ch 8 C.

[77] See e.g. Scotland Act 1998, ss 52, 117, 118, and Sch 4, para 11; Standing Orders of the Scottish Parliament, ch 10.

[78] Statutory Instruments Act 1946, s 2, amended by the Statutory Instruments (Production and Sale) Act 1996.

[79] Statutory Instruments Act 1946, s 3(2); R v *Sheer Metalcraft Ltd* [1954] 1 QB 586. For the argument that at common law delegated legislation must be published before it can come into force, see D J Lanham (1974) 37 MLR 510 and [1983] PL 395; cf A I L Campbell [1982] PL 569.

restrictions on Convention rights, there is a strong argument that they must be published before the restrictions can be said to be 'prescribed by law'.[80]

Challenge in the courts

If made in accordance with the prescribed procedure, and within the powers conferred by the parent Act, a statutory instrument is as much part of the law as the statute itself. The essential difference between statute and statutory instrument is that, unlike Parliament, a minister's powers are limited. Consequently, if a department attempts to enforce a statutory instrument against an individual, the individual may as a defence question the validity of the instrument. The courts have power to decide this question even though the instrument has been approved by resolution of each House of Parliament.[81]

The validity of a statutory instrument may be challenged on two main grounds: (*a*) that the content or substance of the instrument is ultra vires the parent Act; (*b*) that the correct procedure has not been followed in making the instrument. The chances of success in such a challenge depend essentially on the terms of the parent Act, as interpreted by the court.[82] The duty under the Human Rights Act 1998, s 3(1), to interpret legislation consistently with Convention rights where this is possible, significantly widens the scope for challenging the validity of delegated legislation. To summarise a complex matter, except where the parent Act expressly or by necessary implication authorises regulations to be made that infringe Convention rights, a general power to make regulations on a given subject must be interpreted as *excluding* power to make regulations that infringe Convention rights.[83] The Human Rights Act thus requires the courts to strike down a secondary instrument where it is not possible to interpret it as being consistent with Convention rights, even though apart from the 1998 Act the regulation would have been valid. But the court may not strike down secondary legislation where primary legislation prevents the secondary legislation being made in any other terms.[84] In the latter case, the court may, under the 1998 Act, s 4, declare that the regulation is incompatible with a Convention right. Moreover, the interpretation and enforcement of delegated legislation may be subject to the requirements of EU law.[85]

Quite apart from human rights and EU law, there is a long-established presumption of interpretation that Parliament does not intend delegated powers to be exercised for certain purposes unless by express words or by necessary implication it has clearly authorised them. The principles that no one should be deprived of access to the courts except by clear words of Parliament and that there is no power to levy a tax without clear authority are illustrated in cases arising out of defence regulations made during the First World War.[86] The former principle was applied in 1997 when an order by the Lord Chancellor increasing the court fees payable for litigation and requiring them to be paid by someone on income support was held to deprive that person of the constitutional right of access to the courts.[87] That basic principles can cut down the width of such

---

[80] See e.g. *Silver v UK* (1983) 5 EHRR 347; and A W Bradley, in Supperstone, Goudie and Walker (eds), *Judicial Review*, pp 62–5.

[81] *Hoffmann-La Roche v Trade Secretary* [1975] AC 295.

[82] See *R v Environment Secretary, ex p Spath Holme Ltd* [2001] 2 AC 349.

[83] See A W Bradley, R Allen and P Sales [2000] PL 358; D Squires [2000] EHRLR 116; and Bradley, in Supperstone, Goudie and Walker (eds), *Judicial Review*, pp 43–5.

[84] Human Rights Act 1998, s 3(2). And ch 19 C.

[85] See e.g. *R (Barker) v Bromley Council* [2006] UKHL 52, [2007] 1 AC 470 (failure of planning regulations properly to implement a European directive).

[86] *A-G v Wilts United Dairies Ltd* and *Chester v Bateson*, discussed in ch 26 B.

[87] *R v Lord Chancellor, ex p Witham* [1998] QB 575. Executive policies are subject to review on similar grounds: *R (Daly) v Home Secretary*, [2001] UKHL 26, [2001] 2 AC 532.

expressions as 'power to make such regulations as seem to the minister to be necessary' was illustrated in *Commissioners of Customs and Excise* v *Cure and Deeley Ltd*.

> The Finance (No 2) Act 1940 empowered the Commissioners to make regulations providing for any matter for which provision appeared to them to be necessary for giving effect to the statutory provisions relating to purchase tax. Regulations were made under which, if proper tax returns were not submitted by manufacturers, the Commissioners might determine the amount of tax due, 'which amount shall be deemed to be the proper tax due', unless within seven days the taxpayer satisfied the Commissioners that some other sum was due. *Held* that the regulation was invalid in that it purported to prevent the taxpayer proving in a court the amount of tax actually due, and substituted for the tax authorised by Parliament some other sum arbitrarily determined by the Commissioners.[88]

By similar reasoning a court might declare invalid a statutory instrument which purported to have retrospective effect in the absence of clear authority from Parliament. In Scotland, the Court of Session quashed a regulation made by the Secretary of State which removed from qualified teachers the right to continue teaching without first registering with a statutory Teaching Council.[89] The Home Secretary's power to make rules for the management of prisons did not permit him to make rules fettering a prisoner's right of access to the courts.[90] But in *McEldowney* v *Forde*, which concerned freedom of association in Northern Ireland, the House of Lords by 3–2 upheld a remarkably phrased ban on republican clubs imposed by the Northern Ireland Minister for Home Affairs,[91] a decision that would be indefensible under the Human Rights Act today. In 1990, by-laws made by the Defence Secretary barring access to Greenham Common, then a nuclear missile base, were held ultra vires because they ignored the provision in the Military Lands Act 1892 that such by-laws must not prejudicially affect the rights of the commoners.[92] Social security regulations which deprived certain asylum seekers of benefits while their appeals for asylum were pending were unlawful because their effect was to prevent the right to appeal from being exercised.[93] In 2010, the Supreme Court quashed Orders in Council (made under the United Nations Act 1946) that permitted the freezing of assets of persons suspected of involvement in international terrorism, since the orders went beyond the scope of the Act.[94]

The courts do not lightly strike down a statutory instrument, but if necessary they apply a test of unreasonableness where a regulation is so unreasonable that Parliament cannot be taken as having authorised it to be made under the Act in question.[95] However, where an order by the Environment Secretary 'capping' local councils' expenditure was subject to approval by resolution of the Commons, the House of Lords held that if the order came within the 'four corners' of the parent statute it was subject to review for unreasonableness only on the extreme grounds of bad faith, improper motive or manifest absurdity.[96]

A serious procedural error by the department concerned could lead to an instrument being set aside. Where there was a duty to consult interested organisations before regulations were made, it was held that the mere sending of a letter to an organisation did not amount to consultation;[97]

---

[88] [1962] 1 QB 340. See also *R* v *IRC, ex p Woolwich Building Society* [1991] 4 All ER 92.

[89] *Malloch* v *Aberdeen Corpn* 1974 SLT 253; and see Education (Scotland) Act 1973.

[90] *Raymond* v *Honey* [1983] AC 1 and *R* v *Home Secretary, ex p Leech* [1994] QB 198.

[91] [1971] AC 632. And see D N MacCormick (1970) 86 LQR 171.

[92] *DPP* v *Hutchinson* [1990] 2 AC 783. And see note 104 below.

[93] *R* v *Social Security Secretary, ex p Joint Council for Welfare of Immigrants* [1996] 4 All ER 385.

[94] *HM Treasury* v *Mohammed Jabar Ahmed* [2010] UKSC 2.

[95] *Maynard* v *Osmond* [1977] QB 240; *Cinnamond* v *British Airports Authority* [1980] 2 All ER 368; *R* v *Home Secretary, ex p Javed* [2001] EWCA 789, [2002] QB 129.

[96] *R* v *Environment Secretary, ex p Hammersmith BC* [1991] 1 AC 521, applying *Notts CC* v *Environment Secretary* [1986] AC 240 (C M G Himsworth [1986] PL 374, [1991] PL 76).

[97] The *Aylesbury Mushrooms* case, note 46 above.

and no effective consultation occurred when a department failed to allow sufficient time for this.[98] But not every procedural error vitiates the statutory instrument, and if there has been substantial compliance with a prescribed procedure, minor irregularities may be overlooked.[99]

Where because of its content or procedure an instrument is to an extent defective, this does not necessarily mean that the whole instrument is a nullity; it may still be operative to its lawful extent or bind persons not affected by the defect of procedure.[100] To decide when such 'severance' is permissible may involve a textual, or 'blue pencil' test (does deletion of the offending phrase or sentence leave a grammatical and coherent text?) and also a test of whether, after deletion of the unlawful part, the substance of the provision remains essentially unchanged in purpose and effect from what had been intended.[101]

Early in the twentieth century it was supposed that if the parent Act provided that regulations when made should have effect 'as if enacted in this Act', the courts could not inquire into the validity of the regulations; the correct view has long been that this expression in the parent Act adds nothing to the binding effect of a properly made instrument.[102] Where a tribunal must adjudicate on the rights of an individual and the extent of those rights is directly affected by a regulation, the tribunal must if necessary decide whether the regulation is valid;[103] its decision on this issue will be subject to appeal or review. And if someone is prosecuted for breach of a regulation or by-law, it is always a good defence in law for the defendant to show that the instrument in question is invalid.[104]

By-laws are a form of delegated legislation that generally applies only in a particular locality or certain public places (for example, airports). They are usually made by a local council or a statutory undertaking and are subject to ministerial confirmation before they take effect. The courts formerly exercised greater control over by-laws than over departmental regulations.[105]

Administrative rule-making

Legislation by statutory instrument is more flexible than primary legislation, since the law can be changed without the need for a Bill to pass through Parliament. Nonetheless, statutory instrument procedures are complex and the instruments are expressed in formal language. In government today, many less formal methods of rule-making are used. Such methods are sometimes directly authorised by Act of Parliament, but rules so made may have an uncertain legal status (for example, immigration rules made under the Immigration Act 1971).[106] Two forms of rule-making that are often authorised by statute are codes of practice and administrative guidelines or notes of guidance.[107] In 2003, the Cabinet Office defined codes of practice in the following way.

---

[98] *R v Social Services Secretary, ex p Association of Metropolitan Authorities* [1986] 1 All ER 164. See also *Howker v Work and Pensions Secretary* (note 44 above).

[99] See Woolf, Jowell and Le Sueur, *De Smith's Judicial Review*, pp 251–8; and ch 30 B.

[100] *Dunkley v Evans* [1981] 3 All ER 285; the *Aylesbury Mushrooms* case, note 46 above.

[101] *DPP v Hutchinson* [1990] 2 AC 783 (A W Bradley [1990] PL 293); and *R v IRC, ex p Woolwich Building Society* [1991] 4 All ER 92. Cf *R (Confederation of Passenger Transport) v Humber Bridge Board* [2003] EWCA 842, [2004] QB 310 (power of court to remedy evident mistake in statutory instrument).

[102] *Minister of Health v R* [1931] AC 494.

[103] *Chief Adjudication Officer v Foster* [1993] AC 754 (D Feldman (1992) 108 LQR 45; A W Bradley [1992] PL 185).

[104] E.g. *R v Reading Crown Court, ex p Hutchinson* [1988] QB 384; *Boddington v British Transport Police* [1999] 2 AC 143.

[105] See *Kruse v Johnson* [1898] 2 QB 91; *Cinnamond v British Airports Authority* [1980] 2 All ER 368.

[106] See ch 20 B.

[107] See e.g. Police and Criminal Evidence Act 1984, Part VI; Freedom of Information Act 2000, ss 45 and 46.

A code of practice is an authoritative statement of practice to be followed in some field. It typically differs from legislation in that it offers guidance rather than imposing requirements: its prescriptions are not hard and fast rules but guidelines which may allow considerable latitude in their practical application and may be departed from in appropriate circumstances. The provisions of a code are not directly enforceable by legal proceedings, which is not to say that they may not have significant legal effects. A code of practice, unlike a legislative text, may also contain explanatory material and argument.[108]

Such codes of practice are often met in branches of law such as that on the use of police powers and employment disputes. Although codes of practice and guidance do not have the force of delegated legislation and generally do not have a mandatory effect,[109] the issuing department may be expected either to observe them or take steps to change them.[110] A local authority or a body such as an NHS trust must follow statutory guidance from central government except where it can state good reasons for not doing so.[111]

Depending on the parent Act, these rules may totally evade the procedures for parliamentary control described earlier. In fact, many administrative rules are issued without direct statutory authority. This phenomenon was once described as 'administrative quasi-legislation',[112] when it was related to the practice of issuing the official interpretation of doubtful points in statutes and of stating concessions that would be made in individual cases. The practice has continued, for the revenue authorities often choose to waive the application of over-harsh laws rather than seek changes in the legislation. In 1979, the then Inland Revenue's use of executive discretion rather than a statutory basis for assessing tax was described by the House of Lords as unconstitutional.[113] As Walton J had said: 'One should be taxed by law, and not be untaxed by concession.'[114]

In many areas of government, such as town planning, education and health, ministerial statements of policy and circulars to local authorities have a practical effect which falls little short of declaring or modifying the law. On matters of general policy where controversial issues are involved, government by circular is not a satisfactory substitute for legislation. Nor can such circulars require the performance of unlawful acts.[115]

Informal rule-making is frequently adopted by departments in order that wide discretion vested in public authorities may be exercised by officials in a reasonably uniform and consistent manner.[116] In the past, many authorities were reluctant to publish such rules. This defensive attitude caused problems when a person affected by the rules wished to know the reasons for a decision. In the past, secrecy was maintained when changes had been made in published rules or policies and the government wished to avoid the changes becoming known. This occurred

---

[108] *Guide to Legislative Procedures* (Cabinet Office, 2003), app C, para 2.1. This appendix does not appear in the website version of this Guide available in 2009.

[109] See e.g. *Laker Airways v Department of Trade* [1977] QB 643.

[110] *R v Home Secretary, ex p Khan* [1985] 1 All ER 40 (A R Mowbray [1985] PL 558).

[111] *R v Islington Council, ex p Rixon* [1997] ELR 66; *R (Munjaz) v Ashworth Hospital Authority* [2005] UKHL 58, [2006] 2 AC 148 (hospital's policy on detention of mental patients upheld despite departing from code of practice). Also *R (Daniel Thwaites plc) v Wirral Magistrates* [2008] EWHC 838 (Admin), [2009] 1 All ER 239 (duty of licensing authority to 'have regard to' guidance from Secretary of State).

[112] R E Megarry (1944) 60 LQR 125; Ganz, *Quasi-Legislation*; R Baldwin and J Houghton [1986] PL 239. Informal administrative rules may be termed 'tertiary rules' (Baldwin, *Rules and Government*, ch 4) or, in the European context, 'soft law': K Wellens and G Borchardt (1989) 14 EL Rev 267. Also Craig, *Administrative Law*, pp 750–6.

[113] *Vestey v IRC (No 2)* [1980] AC 1148.

[114] *Vestey v IRC* [1979] Ch 177, 197. See *R (Wilkinson) v IRC* [2005] UKHL 30, [2006] 1 All ER 529 (extra-statutory concession could not be made to grant widowers a tax allowance that Parliament had granted only to widows).

[115] *Royal College of Nursing v DHSS* [1981] AC 800; *Gillick v West Norfolk Health Authority* [1986] AC 112.

[116] E.g. Local Authority Social Services Act 1970, s 7 (guidance of Secretary of State) and s 7A (directions by Secretary of State) (added by NHS and Community Care Act 1990, s 50).

notably with the changed policies on the export of defence-related equipment to Iraq, which caused ministers repeatedly to give misleading answers to MPs.[117]

Like any large organisation, a public authority may wish to give instructions to its staff on purely internal matters without publishing them. But rules which directly affect the individual should be published, one reason for this being to enable someone outside the organisation to check whether the rules have been sensibly applied. Problems arising out of the use of departmental rules have frequently come before the Parliamentary Ombudsman, most notably in the Sachsenhausen case[118] and are also likely to arise in the context of European Convention rights.[119] Now that the policy of greater openness in government is established, the case for publishing departmental rules and other explanatory material on which official decisions are based cannot be resisted, except where publication might prejudice vital aspects of national security, crime detection or prevention, protection of children and so on.

These matters are governed by the Freedom of Information Act 2000 (and its Scottish equivalent), which gives a right to information held by public authorities covered by the Act, subject to exemptions for particular categories of information. Every public authority must adopt and maintain a publication scheme approved by the Information Commissioner.[120] The scheme must specify the classes of information to be published, and this may include the policies and procedures of the public authority in question.[121]

---

[117] See HC 115 (1995–6) (Scott Report) esp vol IV, para K.
[118] Ch 29 D, and see A R Mowbray [1987] PL 570.
[119] See e.g. *Silver* v *UK* (1983) 5 EHRR 347.
[120] Freedom of Information Act 2000, ss 19–20. For the pre-Act position on publication of departmental rules, in-house manuals and the like, see *Code of Practice on Access to Government Information* (2nd edn, 1997), para 3 (ii).
[121] See further ch 13 F.

CHAPTER 29

Administrative justice

The title of this chapter may seem a contradiction in terms: there are such marked differences between the way in which decisions are made by civil servants and ministers on the one hand, and by the courts on the other, that the two systems, administration and justice, should be kept quite separate. However, as we will see in relation to judicial review, there is a strong tendency in administrative law for principles derived from the courts, such as the doctrine of natural justice,[1] to be applied to official decisions. The same tendency applies to developing institutions within government. In his seminal book, *Justice and Administrative Law*, first published in 1928, Robson described the extent to which 'trial by Whitehall' had developed in the British constitution. He argued that the judicial powers given to administrative bodies promoted the welfare of society and that administrative justice could become 'as well-founded and broad-based as any other kind of justice now known to us and embodied in human institutions'.[2] Today, the influence of administrative justice is seen in decisions of the European Court of Human Rights interpreting art 6 of the European Convention.[3]

In this chapter, we examine various institutions and procedures that are located within a broad territory somewhere between the world of government departments on one hand and that of the law courts on the other. This territory is liable to be the site of diverse struggles for possession between competing interests from the administrative and legal worlds. In one sector of the territory that was formerly under strong departmental influence, namely administrative tribunals, the judicial model of decision-making now holds undoubted sway. Indeed, the British system of tribunals must no longer be referred to with the adjective 'administrative'. The system will be outlined in section A of this chapter, but in a future edition it could well be included in chapter 18, as a vital element in the machinery of justice alongside the ordinary courts.

In another sector, that of public inquiries (section B), government departments exercise the dominant influence over the decision-making, but key aspects of the procedures exist to promote the fairness and openness of the process. Section C deals with inquiries appointed under the Inquiries Act 2005 (which replaced older legislation). This Act provides a formal process of impartial fact-finding for discovering what happened when things have gone seriously wrong in government or major scandals and disasters have occurred. Section D is concerned with the Parliamentary Ombudsman. The function of this office is to investigate individual complaints about government action and to discover whether injustice has been caused by official errors: the Ombudsman carries out this function by investigatory means which owe little to court procedures, and the Ombudsman's powers fall short of requiring a remedy to be provided, although an acceptable remedy is usually the result when the Ombudsman decides that injustice has occurred.

---

[1] Ch 31 B.

[2] Robson, *Justice and Administrative Law*, p 515. The remit of the Administrative Justice and Tribunals Council (page 646 below) includes a definition of 'administrative justice' (Tribunals, Courts and Enforcement Act 2007, sch 7, para 13 (4)). But in the scheme of the Act this appears separately from the Council's functions concerning tribunals and inquiries, which are an integral part of 'administrative justice' in a broader sense.

[3] See e.g. C Harlow in Alston (ed.), *The EU and Human Rights*, ch 7; A W Bradley, in Supperstone, Goudie and Walker (eds), *Judicial Review*, pp 55–62. Also Harris and Partington (eds), *Administrative Justice in the 21st Century*, pt 5 and Adler (ed.), *Administrative Justice in Context*.

A. Tribunals[4]

Reasons for creation of tribunals

For many centuries Britain has had specialised courts in addition to the courts of general jurisdiction. Medieval merchants had their courts of pie poudre; the tin miners of Devon and Cornwall had their courts of Stannaries.[5] From the early nineteenth century until they were abolished in 2009, the General Commissioners of Income Tax provided a local court for resolving disputes about the amount of tax that an individual should pay. The growth of the modern state led to the creation of many new procedures for settling the disputes that arose from the impact of public powers and duties on the rights and interests of private persons. The National Insurance Act 1911, in creating the first British social insurance scheme, provided for individual disputes that arose to be decided on appeal by an independent panel. Indeed, the history of social security appeals is central to the history of tribunals in the twentieth century: after 1945, the structure of appeals became a notable feature of the welfare state.[6]

When Parliament creates new public services or regulatory schemes, questions and disputes will inevitably arise from operation of the legislation. There are three main means of enabling such questions and disputes to be settled: (*a*) by conferring new jurisdiction on the ordinary courts; (*b*) by creating new machinery in the form of a tribunal, sometimes with the right of appeal to a higher tribunal or to the courts; or (*c*) by leaving decisions to be made by the administrative bodies responsible for the scheme. Possible variants in solution (*c*) include (i) allowing an individual to seek review at a higher level within the same public body of a decision that he or she does not accept; (ii) providing for an appeal to another administrative body (for example, from a local council to central government), or (iii) requiring a hearing or public inquiry to be held before certain decisions are made. Whether or not any provision of these kinds is made, the procedure of judicial review is potentially available to supervise the legality of decisions. But judicial review, which should be an exceptional remedy, does not provide a right of appeal and is unable to ensure the quality of numerous decisions at first instance.

One achievement of the Franks committee on tribunals and inquiries, which reported in 1957,[7] was to make clear that tribunals and inquiries differed in their constitutional status and functions. No tribunal ought to be seen as part of the structure of a government department, for tribunals exercised functions which were essentially judicial in character, although of a specialised nature. As the Franks committee stated in words of great significance:

> We consider that tribunals should properly be regarded as machinery provided by Parliament for adjudication rather than as part of the machinery of administration. The essential point is that in all these cases Parliament has deliberately provided for a decision outside and independent of the Department concerned.[8]

On the other hand, the public inquiry, while it granted those affected by official proposals with some safeguards against ill-informed and hasty decisions, was essentially a step in a complex process leading to a departmental decision for which a minister was responsible to Parliament.

---

[4] See report of the Franks committee, Cmnd 218, 1957, parts II and III; Farmer, *Tribunals and Government*; Richardson and Genn (eds), *Administrative Law and Government Action*, part II; Harlow and Rawlings, *Law and Administration*, ch 11; and Leggatt, *Tribunals for Users*.

[5] See *R v East Powder Justices, ex p Lampshire* [1979] QB 616.

[6] On these tribunals, see Baldwin, Wikeley and Young, *Judging Social Security*; Fullbrook, *Administrative Justice and the Unemployed*; Adler and Bradley (eds), *Justice, Discretion and Poverty*; cf R Sainsbury, in Harris and Partington (eds), *Administrative Justice in the 21st Century*, ch 22.

[7] See page 610 above.

[8] Cmnd 218, 1957, p 9; ch 27.

The constitutional logic of the view that tribunals are 'machinery provided by Parliament for adjudication' reached its culmination fifty years after the Franks report, in the Tribunals, Courts and Enforcement Act 2007. We shall see that this Act deals with tribunals as a vital part of the machinery of justice, operating alongside the ordinary civil courts.

Court and tribunals – some comparisons

Although there is today no doubt about the judicial role of tribunals, the existence of tribunals was sometimes in the past thought to weaken the judiciary and the authority of the ordinary courts.[9] In fact, the machinery of the courts is not suited for settling all disputes arising out of the work of government. One reason for this is the need for specialised knowledge (in areas such as taxation, social security or immigration) if disputes are to be settled expeditiously and consistently. Another reason is the large volume of appeals that arise from first-instance decisions in such areas. Further, while policy decisions and oversight of a department's work are entrusted to ministers, the efficient administration of many areas of government depends on there being a body of rules which officials can apply without constant recourse to a minister.[10] The right of appeal against an official's decision at first instance is a better remedy for the aggrieved individual than the principle of ministerial responsibility, since it provides a means of discovering whether the rules have been correctly applied or whether a decision has been made that is contrary to the department's professed policies.

In many areas of government (such as taxation or social security), the rules applicable are laid down in statutes or statutory instruments. The rules are first applied by officials, and the individual may then appeal to a tribunal that must also apply the rules. If the rules produce an unsatisfactory outcome, the minister can change the outcome of future decisions only by amending the statutory rules. Thus the relationship between minister and tribunal is similar to that which exists between the government and the judges in the courts. Tribunals exist not because they exercise a discretion which it would be improper to confer on judges, but because they undertake the adjudication required more efficiently than the courts.[11] As was said in relation to claims for social security, 'For these cases we do not want a Rolls-Royce system of justice.'[12]

Factors favouring the use of tribunals have included the need for procedure which avoids the formality of the courts; the need, if a new social policy is introduced, for the speedy, cheap and decentralised decision of many cases; and the need for expert knowledge in the tribunal, whose members may include both lawyers and also other professionals or lay persons. Another factor has been that the legal profession has no monopoly of the right to represent parties to tribunal proceedings: there is a value in enabling the individual affected to be heard in person by the tribunal.[13] In 1957, when the status of tribunals had not been clearly established, the Franks committee reflected a traditional preference for courts rather than tribunals in expressing the view that 'a decision should be entrusted to a court rather than to a tribunal in the absence of special considerations which make a tribunal more suitable'.[14] There have been so many changes since then in the procedures of both tribunals and courts that this now seems a very dated viewpoint. Certainly, most tribunals are concerned with disputes between a private individual and a public authority (these may be termed, disputes between *citizen and the state*). This does not apply to

[9] See e.g. Lord Scarman, *English Law – the New Dimension*, part III. For a historical critique, see Arthurs, *Without the Law: Administrative Justice and Legal Pluralism in the 19th Century.*

[10] This fact underlies the present use in Whitehall of executive agencies: see ch 13 D.

[11] Cf the distinction between 'policy-oriented' and 'court-substitute' tribunals: Farmer, ch 8, and H Genn, in Richardson and Genn (eds), ch 11 (note 4 above).

[12] Street, *Justice in the Welfare State*, p 3.

[13] See G Richardson and H Genn [2007] PL 116, re-assessing the right to an oral hearing.

[14] Cmnd 218, 1957, p 9.

employment tribunals, which deal with disputes between the parties to the employment relationship. However, even with this exception there is a striking overlap in the decisions made by courts and tribunals. For instance, in hearing claims for unlawful discrimination brought against employers, employment tribunals make decisions that other legal systems entrust to a labour court; and cases alleging unlawful discrimination against bodies other than employers are brought in the county court.

The essentials of good adjudication apply to both tribunals and courts. The right under art 6(1) ECHR to a fair hearing before an independent and impartial court or tribunal does not depend on the label applied to the decision-maker. It is fundamental that neither judges nor tribunal members should be subject to dismissal when a government department is dissatisfied with their decisions. Procedure in a tribunal is often said to be informal. But informality is difficult to reconcile with the need for legal precision[15] and tribunal procedures are not always less formal than procedures in a comparable court. When a county court is dealing with a small claim through arbitration, its procedure is very informal.

Although some tribunals do exercise jurisdiction at first instance (this is true of employment tribunals), the right to go to a tribunal usually arises only where a public body or official has first made a decision that the individual disputes. The need for individuals to appeal will depend to a large extent on whether the public body in question has taken reasonable steps to ensure that they 'get decisions right first time'.[16]

A safeguard common to all tribunals is that it should be possible to challenge their decisions on points of law, whether by appeal to a higher court or tribunal or by judicial review. In 1957, the Franks committee considered that the ideal appeal structure took the form of a general appeal from the tribunal of first instance to an appellate tribunal, and that all tribunal decisions should be subject to review by the courts on points of law. That ideal structure has often been absent. Until the reform of the tribunal system made in 2007, the confusing lack of system in relation to tribunals extended to the piecemeal provision made for appeals.[17] Where no right of appeal is provided in the legislation, the decisions and procedures of a tribunal are subject to judicial review.[18]

In 1957, many tribunals provided 'second-class justice', using procedures that lacked openness and impartiality, and sometimes displaying the prejudices of the government department which ran them. Since then, standards and expectations have risen. Today, it is impossible to describe the functions of tribunals except in terms that also apply to courts.[19]

The background to the Tribunals, Courts and Enforcement Act 2007

We have seen that the Franks committee in 1957 concluded that tribunals should be regarded as machinery for adjudication and that their operation should be marked by fairness, openness and impartiality. Some general reforms to strengthen the position of tribunals vis-à-vis their 'parent' departments were made by the Tribunals and Inquiries Act 1958 (re-enacted in 1971 and again in 1992). They included the need to ensure that tribunal members were protected against interference or arbitrary removal by the parent department, and they required the Lord Chancellor to be involved both in the appointment of tribunal members and in their removal.[20] The 1958 Act also

---

[15] See Genn, note 11 above.

[16] *Transforming Public Services* (note 25 below), para 3.9.

[17] See Lord Woolf (1988) 7 CJQ 44; Law Commission, *Administrative Law: Judicial Review and Statutory Appeals* (HC 669, 1993–4), part XII.

[18] See chs 30, 31.

[19] A very different distinction is drawn in Australia between 'administrative tribunals' and the courts: see P Cane [2009] PL 479 and (same author) *Administrative Tribunals and Adjudication*.

[20] See Tribunals and Inquiries Act 1992, ss 6, 7.

provided a right to appeal on points of law from certain tribunals to the High Court (in Scotland, to the Court of Session) and required all tribunals, if requested on or before the giving or notification of a decision, to give reasons for the decision.[21] Another reform in 1958 was the creation of the Council on Tribunals,[22] the predecessor of the present Administrative Justice and Tribunals Council. The council's functions were advisory and it had no executive powers.

Despite the post-Franks reforms, the numerous tribunals that came to exist did not form a single system. Countless variations in tribunal procedures and rights of appeal existed. While the Council on Tribunals sought to develop general standards that should apply to all tribunals,[23] it could not require departments to adopt these standards. The Council had no power to prevent new tribunals being created, nor to require a tribunal to be abolished that had ceased to serve a useful purpose.

The Leggatt review of tribunals

In 2001, for the first time since the Franks report of 1957, a review of all tribunals was conducted. It was undertaken for the Lord Chancellor by a retired Court of Appeal judge, Sir Andrew Leggatt, assisted by an expert panel.[24] He found that, leaving regulatory bodies to one side, there were some 70 different tribunals in England and Wales, between them disposing of nearly a million cases each year. But of the 70 tribunals, only 20 heard more than 500 cases a year: many of the tribunals were defunct and some had never had any cases to decide. Leggatt criticised the lack of system in tribunals, commenting that tribunals had grown up in a haphazard way, created piecemeal by legislation and separately administered by government departments with wide variations of approach, in a way that (in his view) took more account of departmental needs than the convenience of tribunal users. He proposed the creation of what would indeed be a system of administrative justice, 'a single, overarching structure' that would give the individual improved access to all tribunals. Although this would involve reorganising the structure and servicing of tribunals, many tribunals, particularly those with large caseloads, would continue to function with little practical change in their decision-making being necessary.

There was certainly no need for as many as 70 separate tribunals. The Leggatt review proposed that there should be a single tribunal system, administered by an integrated tribunal service, and operating in divisions according to subject matter. The divisions proposed by Leggatt would have brought together existing tribunals under nine headings: (*a*) education; (*b*) employment; (*c*) finance and revenue; (*d*) health and care; (*e*) immigration and asylum; (*f*) property, land and valuation; (*g*) social security, pensions and criminal injury compensation; (*h*) transport; and (*i*) aspects of trade, competition, patents and copyright. Leggatt also proposed the creation of a general tribunal to hear appeals from the first tier of tribunal decisions, since the 'tribunal maze' extended to a bewildering variety in the rights of appeal.

The government's response to the Leggatt review

The Leggatt review has led to a far-reaching transformation in the position of tribunals. In 2004, a government white paper, *Transforming Public Services: Complaints, Redress and Tribunals*,[25] set out

---

[21] Ibid, ss 10,11.

[22] For accounts of the Council, see earlier editions of the present work. Also D G T Williams [1984] PL 73 and (1990) 9 CJQ 27; Harlow and Rawlings, *Law and Administration*, pp 505–9; D L Foulkes (1993) *Eur Rev of Public Law* (special issue) 262.

[23] See e.g. the Council's report, *Tribunals – their Organisation and Independence* (Cm 3744, 1997) and the Council's *Guide to Drafting Tribunal Rules* (2005).

[24] See Leggatt, *Tribunals for Users*, and comment by A W Bradley [2002] PL 200.

[25] Cm 6243, 2004.

a broad perspective for reform that would not only create a unified tribunal system, able to pro-vide 'formal hearings and authoritative rulings where these are needed', but (going beyond Leggatt) would also have a mission of enabling disputes to be resolved 'fairly and informally' in conjunc-tion with other agencies.[26] The reforms included bringing tribunals together into a new general purpose tribunal, and forming a unified Tribunals Service, to make possible the flexible use of tribunal personnel and accommodation, and the development of common procedures.

The white paper also wished to change the approach to resolving disputes and providing redress for grievances; it argued that decision-taking by tribunals is only one process by which administrative justice can meet the needs of the individual and the public service. In the govern-ment's view, the existence of a right to a tribunal decision was compatible with the use of other processes (for instance, an ombudsman) to redress individual grievances.[27]

Tribunals, Courts and Enforcement Act 2007

A main aim of the Act was to carry through the complex reform of tribunals initiated by the Leggatt review.[28] Part 1 of the Act set up two new general tribunals, with the function of replac-ing the great majority of the former first-instance and appellate tribunals: the First-tier Tribunal to make first-instance decisions, and the Upper Tribunal to hear appeals from the First-tier Tribunal (s 3). The Act created the office of Senior President of Tribunals, appointed by the Queen on the advice of the Lord Chancellor (s 2). The first Senior President is Sir Robert Carnwath, Lord Justice of Appeal, and the Act envisages that his successors will also be drawn from the Court of Appeal or from the appellate courts in Scotland and Northern Ireland.[29] In a statement of principle that reinforces the assimilation of tribunals to the courts, the guarantee of judicial independence given in the Constitutional Reform Act 2005[30] for judges in the civil and criminal courts was extended to those holding judicial office in the new tribunals (s 1).

The Senior President must take account of the need for tribunals to be accessible, for their proceedings to be fair, quick and efficient, for tribunals to have available suitable expertise to deal with specialised areas of law, and for the development of new informal methods of resolving disputes (s 2). The Senior President reports each year to the Lord Chancellor on matters relevant to cases coming before the First-tier and Upper Tribunals (s 43), has authority to make repre-sentations to Parliament, and is required to represent the views of all tribunal members (sch 1, paras 13, 14). The two tribunals comprise persons who are legally qualified and are known as judges, as well as non-legal members who may have professional qualifications (for instance, in medicine or valuation) or be lay persons with relevant experience.

The First-tier Tribunal is organised in a system of chambers, each headed by a judge as president. The Lord Chancellor has power by order to transfer the functions of many tribunals to the appropriate chamber, whereupon the former tribunals are abolished. In February 2010, the First-tier Tribunal comprised six divisions: (*a*) the War Pensions and Armed Forces Compensation Chamber; (*b*) the Social Entitlement Chamber (dealing with social security, child support, asylum support and criminal injuries compensation); (*c*) the Health, Education and Social Care Chamber (mental health review, special educational needs and disability, and care standards); (*d*) the General Regulatory Chamber (whose multifarious functions include consumer credit and

---

[26] Ibid, para 4.21.

[27] *Transforming Public Services*, chs 3 and 4. The value of proportionate dispute resolution (including conciliation, early neutral evaluation and mediation) was advanced. And see M Adler (2006) 69 MLR 958; M Supperstone, D Stilitz and C Sheldon [2006] PL 299; S Boyron [2006] PL 320.

[28] See R Carnwath [2009] PL 48.

[29] If it is not possible to appoint a judge at appellate level, the Judicial Appointments Commission will operate a selection process: sch 1, parts 1 and 2.

[30] See ch 18 C.

estate agent appeals, charity appeals, information disputes, and driving standards agency appeals): (*e*) the Tax Chamber (income tax, VAT and duties); and (*f*) the Immigration and Asylum Chamber.[31] Also projected was a seventh chamber, the Land, Property and Housing Chamber (to take over from such bodies as the agricultural lands tribunal and the leasehold valuation tribunal).[32] Members of the First-tier Tribunal may sit in more than one chamber. Employment tribunals are outside this structure, but like the First-tier Tribunal chambers they are administered by the general Tribunals Service.

The Upper Tribunal is organised in a smaller number of chambers: (1) the Administrative Appeals Chamber; (2) the Tax and Chancery Chamber; (3) the Lands Chamber (this has taken over the work of the Lands Tribunal); and (4) the Immigration and Asylum Chamber. The president of each chamber (except for the Lands Chamber) is a High Court judge. In outline, each chamber hears appeals from one or more chambers of the First-tier Tribunal. However, the First-tier Tribunal has power to review its own decisions (exercisable once only in any case) and it may then take a fresh decision, may refer the case to the Upper Tribunal or may decide that no action is needed.[33] The purpose of this review is to deal rapidly with decisions that are considered to be clearly wrong, so avoiding the need for an appeal. The parties to a decision by the First-tier Tribunal have a right of appeal to the Upper Tribunal, but only on a point of law and only with the leave of either Tribunal. A novel feature of the scheme is that the Upper Tribunal may in specified classes of case exercise a so-called 'judicial review' jurisdiction, closely modelled on judicial review proceedings in the Administrative Court; and certain proceedings may be transferred from the Administrative Court to the Upper Tribunal, and vice versa (ss 15–21). From the Upper Tribunal, there is a right of appeal with leave to the Court of Appeal (in Scotland, to the Inner House of the Court of Session) (ss 13–14).[34]

One valuable result of the two-tier structure is to rationalise the diverging procedures that separate tribunals had used. This task has been carried out by the Tribunal Procedure Committee, chaired by a Court of Appeal judge. The aims of the procedure rules include that of ensuring that in tribunal proceedings 'justice is done'; that the tribunal system is 'accessible and fair'; that proceedings are 'handled quickly and efficiently'; and that the rules are 'both simple and clearly expressed'.[35]

All appointments to the First-tier and Upper Tribunals are made by the Judicial Appointments Commission. The 2007 Act contains rules of eligibility for appointment to the Tribunals that may encourage greater diversity in their membership.[36] The flexible and wide-ranging jurisdiction of the two Tribunals should mean that no other tribunals need be created in future: if as a result of legislation new decisions are to be made that require a right of appeal, power to decide the appeals can be conferred on the First-tier Tribunal, and then assigned to an appropriate chamber.

Some tribunals continue to exist outside the two-tier scheme created by the Act of 2007. They include the Investigatory Powers Tribunal, created by the Regulation of Investigatory Powers Act 2000, and the Proscribed Organisations Appeal Commission, created under the Terrorism Act 2000. There are also decisions for which there is no right of appeal to a tribunal, but which are subject to statutory procedures for administrative review. This applies to discretionary payments

---

[31] The functions of the former Asylum and Immigration Tribunal have been divided between this chamber of the First-tier Tribunal and the related chamber in the Upper Tribunal. And see ch 20.

[32] See 2007 Act, sch 6 (tribunals replaced); and sch 8 (General Commissioners of Income Tax abolished). And see the Senior President's First Annual Report, *Tribunals Transformed* (2010).

[33] 2007 Act, s 9. The Upper Tribunal has a similar power (s 10).

[34] On the meaning attached to errors of law at this level, see Carnwath (note 28 above) at 61–64.

[35] 2007 Act, s 22(4). The rules take account of the specialist needs of each chamber. All the procedure rules are listed on the Tribunals.gov.uk website. They include the Tribunal Procedure (Upper Tribunal) Rules 2008, SI No 2698 of 2008 (as amended).

[36] 2007 Act, schs 2, 3; Qualifications for Appointment of Members to the First-tier Tribunal and Upper Tribunal Order 2008 (SI No 2692 of 2008), as amended.

from the Social Fund, intended to be a residual way of meeting acute hardship, and to many decisions made by local councils. Although outside the two-tier tribunal structure, these decisions plainly come within the 'administrative justice' element of the Administrative Justice and Tribunals Council.[37] Tribunals that are now outside the two-tier tribunal structure may be brought within the scheme, provided that they exist under statutory authority. This means that private and domestic tribunals must remain outside the scheme, but bodies that hear appeals from decisions made by local councils may in future be added to it.

Administrative support for the two Tribunals, including staffing and premises, is provided by the Tribunals Service, an executive agency within the Ministry of Justice.

Administrative Justice and Tribunals Council

We have seen that the Tribunals and Inquiries Act 1958 created the Council on Tribunals, an advisory body with a duty to keep under review the working of a large number of tribunals and procedures that involved a statutory inquiry or hearing in areas such as town planning and compulsory purchase. Throughout the half-century of its existence, the council emphasised the qualities of fairness, openness and impartiality which the Franks report in 1957 stressed that tribunals should possess.

Despite the council's efforts, it could not resist the proliferation of tribunals. In 2001, Sir Andrew Leggatt was critical of the council's record, but he favoured its continued existence, 'to act as the hub of the wheel of administrative justice, or at any rate tribunal justice'.[38] Responding to these and other criticisms of the council, the government decided to provide the council with an extended remit and a new name, the Administrative Justice and Tribunals Council.[39] References to 'the council' hereafter are to this body.

The re-named council, which has Scottish and Welsh committees, consists of between 10 and 15 members appointed by an interlocking variety of processes to which the Lord Chancellor, the Scottish ministers and the Welsh ministers all contribute to a varying extent. The Parliamentary Ombudsman is a member of the council by reason of holding that office. The council reports annually to the Lord Chancellor and the Scottish and Welsh ministers. The council's principal functions are (a) to keep the administrative justice system under review, (b) to keep under review the constitution and working of specified tribunals, and (c) to keep under review the working of statutory inquiries.[40] The fact that the remit of the council, compared with the former Council on Tribunals, has been broadened by the inclusion of 'administrative justice' is to be welcomed. 'The administrative justice system' is defined for this purpose as

the overall system by which decisions of an administrative or executive nature are made in relation to particular persons, including

(a) the procedures for making such decisions,

(b) the law under which such decisions are made, and

(c) the systems for resolving disputes and airing grievances in relation to such decisions.[41]

However, the structure of the council's remit does not make clear that tribunals and inquiries are themselves important features in the landscape of administrative justice.[42] And the mention of an 'overall system' refers to what is desirable, not to what now exists.

---

[37] Below, note 41.
[38] Leggatt, *Tribunals for Users*, para 7.49.
[39] 2007 Act, ss 44–45 and sch 7. And see the council's report for 2008–9.
[40] Functions (b) and (c) were formerly vested in the Council on Tribunals.
[41] 2007 Act, sch 7, para 13(4).
[42] And see note 2 above.

The council's functions concerning administrative justice include considering ways in which the system may be made 'accessible, fair and efficient', and the council may advise ministers on developing the system and may make proposals for research.[43] The council has examined ways in which initial decision-making within government departments can be improved.[44] The council is studying the scope for developing the use of proportionate dispute resolution (including mediation), and it has examined the availability of advice and legal services in areas such as asylum claims and mental health.

The former Council on Tribunals had to be consulted by departments before rules of procedure were made for tribunals under its oversight. Consultation of this kind is not required in respect of the First-tier and Upper Tribunals, but the council appoints a member to serve on the Tribunals Procedure Committee. But the council must be consulted before rules of procedure are made as regards other tribunals that are within its oversight.[45] In 2009, these included the Traffic Commissioners, valuation tribunals, residential property tribunals, parking and traffic appeals, school admission and exclusion appeal panels, and schools adjudicators.[46]

The Council on Tribunals was created long before devolution, although it always had a Scottish committee. The Scotland Act 1998 had a complex impact on this position, and the Scottish Parliament has power to create a separate body with oversight of all tribunals and inquiries in Scotland that come within its devolved powers. A related question is what the impact of devolution should be on the tribunals in Scotland (such as those dealing with taxation, social security, immigration and employment), that operate under legislation that is not devolved to Edinburgh. In 2009, active consideration was being given both in Scotland and in Wales to the future oversight of tribunals and of administrative justice in those countries.[47]

Conclusion

The constitutional position of tribunals has been transformed by the reforms initiated by the Leggatt review and given effect by Parliament in 2007.[48] Most issues over tribunals that arose between 1957 and 2007 are now of historical interest alone. The legislative changes have had to be matched by an extensive re-deployment of administrative and judicial resources. The full benefits of having a system of tribunals that is assimilated to the system of courts are yet to be felt, but the allocation of decision-making to the First-tier and Upper Tribunals should make possible a flexible and effective interface between these tribunals, and the Administrative Court and Court of Appeal. The tribunals comply fully with the standards of judicial decision-making required by Art 6(1) ECHR. It is unlikely (unless Parliament were to go back on the Act of 2007) that tribunals could come under covert political influence or control. To take one example, the creation of the Immigration and Asylum chambers within the two-tier structure should prove to last longer than other attempts to structure decision-making in this controversial area. Finally, the commitment of the Administrative Justice and Tribunals Council to the wider landscape of administrative justice, including the principle of proportionate dispute resolution, should ensure that tribunal procedures are not raised to a level of formality that prevents decisions being made in a manner that is accessible, effective and understood by the public.

---

[43] Act of 2007, sch 7, para 13(1).

[44] The council's report for 2008–9 mentions initial decision-making in the Pension, Disability and Carers Service, the UK Borders Agency (asylum decisions) and criminal injuries compensation.

[45] Act of 2007, sch 7, para 24.

[46] See the council's report for 2008–9, pp 19–23.

[47] See annual reports of the Scottish and Welsh committees for 2008–09.

[48] As has been convincingly argued by Carnwath LJ in his first annual report as Senior President of Tribunals (note 32 above).

B. Public inquiries

As we have seen in section A, the status of tribunals in the United Kingdom is now largely assimilated to that of the courts: the legally qualified members of the First-tier and Upper Tribunals are termed judges, and the Tribunals have a close relationship with the Administrative Court and Court of Appeal. The nature of public inquiries is different. The public inquiry is an administrative process that became widespread during the twentieth century as government departments acquired power to intervene in matters of local government such as housing, public health, compulsory purchase and town planning. The issues that caused central government to become involved often arose out of a conflict between a local authority's policies and the rights and interests of individuals. Public inquiries of this kind (conducted locally by an official of central government, most commonly designated an 'inspector')[49] should not be confused with inquiries investigating matters of national concern, that may be held under the Inquiries Act 2005; these are considered in section C below.

Two views on the nature of inquiries have often been expressed. As seen by the Franks committee in 1957, the 'administrative' view was to regard the inquiry as a step leading to a ministerial decision in the exercise of discretion, for which the minister was responsible only to Parliament. By contrast, on the 'judicial' view, the inquiry appeared 'to take on something of the nature of a trial and the inspector to assume the guise of a judge', so that the ensuing decision must be based directly on the evidence presented at the inquiry.[50]

The Franks committee rejected these two extreme interpretations. In the committee's view, the objects of the inquiry procedure were (a) to protect the interests of the citizens most directly affected by a governmental proposal by granting them a right to be heard in support of their objections; and (b) to ensure that thereby the minister would be better informed of the whole facts of the case before the final decision was made.[51] To ensure a balance between the conflicting interests, Franks recommended (1) that individuals should know in good time before the inquiry the case they would have to meet; (2) that any relevant lines of policy laid down by the government should be disclosed at the inquiry; (3) that the inspectors who conduct inquiries should be under the control of the Lord Chancellor, not of the minister directly concerned with the subject matter of their work; (4) that the inspector's report should be published together with the letter from the minister announcing the final decision; (5) that the decision letter should contain full reasons for the decision, including reasons to explain why the minister had not accepted recommendations of the inspector; (6) that it should be possible to challenge a decision made after a public inquiry in the High Court, on the grounds of jurisdiction and procedure.[52]

With one exception, the Franks recommendations were accepted and their effect can still be seen in the procedure of public inquiries today. The exception was the recommendation that inspectors be transferred to the Lord Chancellor's department. This was not adopted, but the status of inspectors has changed since 1957, when they worked in the department responsible for planning. In 2009, over 350 full-time and around 100 part-time inspectors formed the Planning Inspectorate, an executive agency created in 1992 and serving England and Wales. The Inspectorate reports to the Secretary of State for Communities and Local Government (whose responsibilities included local government, housing and town planning) and to the Welsh Assembly Government. The inspectors decide appeals on such matters as the refusal of planning permission and

---

[49] In Scotland, the commonly used term is that of 'reporter'.

[50] Cmnd 218, 1957, p 58.

[51] 'The purpose of an inquiry is two-fold: it is both to reach a rational planning decision and to allow the various parties to have their concerns heard': HC 364 (1999–2000), para 34 (Committee on Environment, Transport and Regional Affairs).

[52] Cmnd 218, 1957, part IV.

enforcement action taken by local councils; they may also conduct inquiries before major planning decisions are made by ministers, and into local development plan documents.[53]

From its creation in 1958 and until 2007, the Council on Tribunals had power to consider and report on matters arising out of the conduct of statutory inquiries. This power has now passed to the Administrative Justice and Tribunals Council.[54] In this context, 'statutory inquiry' includes both an inquiry or hearing held by or on behalf of a minister in pursuance of a duty imposed by any statutory provision, and also what is known as a discretionary inquiry, that is, an inquiry initiated by a minister in exercise of a statutory discretion, where such an inquiry is designated for this purpose by statutory instrument.[55]

The inquiries examined by the Franks committee mostly concerned such matters as the compulsory purchase of land for public purposes (such as a new town, a power station or a motorway), and disputes under planning law about the use and development of land. Inquiries and similar procedures serve many other purposes, for example to inquire into electoral boundaries[56] or to investigate the failure by a local authority to maintain proper standards of care in relation to children.[57]

Rules of procedure for public inquiries

Under the Tribunals and Inquiries Act 1992, s 9, as amended, the Lord Chancellor may, after consulting the Administrative Justice and Tribunals Council, make rules regulating the procedure at statutory inquiries. Rules have been made in respect of inquiries held for many purposes, including inquiries into compulsory purchase orders, appeals against the refusal of planning permission; and inquiries into development plans and major infrastructure projects. By way of illustration, on a compulsory purchase of land by a public authority other than a minister,[58] if an inquiry is to be held the Secretary of State must give notice to the acquiring authority and those entitled to object, and may cause a pre-inquiry meeting to be held to discuss procedural matters. Due notice of the inquiry must be given to the public authority and to every owner of an interest in the land affected who has objected to the making of the compulsory purchase order. At least 28 days before the inquiry, the public authority must send to every objector and to central departments a full statement of the reasons for the order. Both objectors and the public authority have a right to appear at the inquiry and to be represented, whether by a lawyer or another person. In advance of the inquiry, a written statement of evidence may be required from any person entitled to appear at the inquiry. Objectors must be informed of the views of any government departments which support the order, and their representatives are required to attend the inquiry to give evidence about departmental policy. However, the inspector may disallow a question put to such a representative if in the inspector's opinion it is 'directed to the merits of government policy'.

Subject to the rules, procedure at the inquiry is determined by the inspector. The degree of formality depends on the circumstances of the inquiry, particularly the extent of legal representation. The inspector may visit the land alone before or during the inquiry, but if he or she makes a formal visit during or after the inquiry, notice must be given to the public authority and to the objectors, who have the right to be present. The inspector's report must include his or her

---

[53] For an assessment of the Inspectorate, see HC 364 (1999–2000) and, in response, Cm 4891, 2000.

[54] Page 646 above.

[55] Tribunals and Inquiries Act 1992, s 16(2). And see Tribunals and Inquiries (Discretionary Inquiries) Order 1975, SI 1975 No 1379 (as frequently amended).

[56] Ch 9 B.

[57] See Justice/All Souls report, *Administrative Justice*, pp 312–27; S Sedley (1989) 52 MLR 469; L Blom-Cooper [1993] CLP 204 and e.g. the (Laming) report of inquiry into the death of Victoria Climbié, Cm 5730, 2003. Also SOLACE, *Getting it Right: guidance on the conduct of effective and fair ad hoc inquiries* (2002). And section C below.

[58] See Compulsory Purchase by Non-Ministerial Authorities (Inquiries) Procedure Rules 1990, SI 1990 No 512.

conclusions and recommendations, if any; it will be sent to the parties when the minister's decision is notified to them.

One important rule deals with the situation where the minister, after considering the inspector's report, either differs from the inspector on a finding of fact or, after the close of the inquiry, 'takes into consideration any new evidence or new matter of fact (not being a matter of government policy)'. In such a case, if the minister proposes not to follow the inspector's recommendation because of this new material, the public authority and objectors must be informed and they have the right to require the inquiry to be reopened. The background to this lies in what was known as the chalk-pit affair:[59] after an inquiry into a controversial application to extract chalk in the Essex countryside, the department that conducted the inquiry consulted privately with the Ministry of Agriculture about the harm that the chalk working would cause to neighbouring property. This secret consultation was defended at the time, but today it would breach the inquiry rules.

The aim of the procedure rules is to protect the fairness and openness of the inquiry process: the rules are enforceable in the courts, and the requirement to observe them exists alongside duties at common law derived from the principle of natural justice.[60] If a particular inquiry is not governed by statutory rules of procedure, there is in any event a duty to observe common law rules of natural justice or fairness.[61] Although the procedure rules define those who are entitled to notice of an inquiry and to take part, they give the inspector a discretion to allow other persons to appear at the inquiry. In practice, community associations and other interest groups are permitted to take part and thereby they acquire a right to come to the Administrative Court if it is alleged that the procedure rules have not been observed.[62]

In its earliest years, the former Council on Tribunals took an active part in shaping the inquiry rules and in seeking to secure the award of costs to those taking part in inquiries, at least for owners who successfully object to the compulsory purchase of their land. More recently, the conduct of public inquiries has raised fewer questions, and the Administrative Justice and Tribunals Council today gives relatively little time to them. If there has been a departure from proper procedure, the Administrative Court (unlike the council) may give an effective remedy to those aggrieved by setting aside the inquiry. Alternatively, where someone is adversely affected by the improper conduct of an inquiry, or by acts of the department related to the inquiry, he or she may take the complaint to the Parliamentary Ombudsman, who can make a full investigation into the matter and may recommend the department to provide a remedy.[63]

The changing use of public inquiries

The public inquiry continues to be a part of the process by which certain decisions are made, especially those concerning use of land for developments of environmental significance, but its role has diminished. One consequence of the Franks report was the greater legalisation of inquiries. Increased involvement of the legal profession in inquiries put pressure on the planning process, and led to delays and over-centralisation of decision-making on many local issues. Many steps have been taken to restrict the use of the public inquiry and to encourage the use of speedier procedures. For instance, the Planning and Compulsory Purchase Act 2004, ss 100–1, authorised the use in connection with compulsory purchase of a *written representations* procedure that has long been available for planning appeals, but only if the objectors consent to this; if consent is not given, then either a public inquiry must be held or they must be given a *hearing*, in each case

---

[59] See J A G Griffith (1961) 39 *Public Administration* 369; and *Buxton v Minister of Housing* [1961] 1 QB 278.
[60] Ch 30 B.
[61] *Fairmount Investments Ltd v Environment Secretary* [1976] 2 All ER 865; *Bushell's case*, note 74 below.
[62] *Turner v Environment Secretary* (1973) 72 LGR 380.
[63] Section D below.

before a member of the Planning Inspectorate. Another variant of the full-scale inquiry is the *examination in public*, first used for examining amendments to structure plans under the Town and Country Planning Act 1990, and later used to consider 'regional spatial strategies', prepared by regional planning bodies.[64] In the case of an examination in public, anyone may make written representations about the proposed plan, but no one has the right to be heard at the examination, which is limited to specified topics.[65]

As regards the control of development, delay has been reduced by transferring the power to decide planning appeals from the Secretary of State to the inspectorate. All appeals regarding applications for planning permission and all appeals against enforcement notices may be decided by an inspector;[66] however, the Secretary of State retains power to decide certain appeals and may 'call in' applications for decision.[67] An inspector's decision is subject to review in the courts, but the Secretary of State is not responsible to Parliament for it. In their decision-making, inspectors must take account of published planning policies, at the national, regional or local level, as well as all other material considerations and views of the parties. In 2008–9, the inspectorate made over 21,000 planning decisions:[68] 79 per cent were decided on the basis of written representations exchanged between the parties;[69] 16 per cent after a hearing in private given to the parties;[70] only 5 per cent of appeals were decided after a public inquiry.[71] In 2008, the Secretary of State was given power (to be exercised through the Planning Inspectorate) to decide whether a planning appeal should be decided by a local inquiry, a hearing before the inspector, or on the basis of representations in writing.[72]

The transfer of power to the inspectors to decide planning appeals was possible because in most cases only local issues arose, but the role of the inquiry in matters of national importance has often been controversial. During the 1970s, government policy in promoting motorways led to stormy scenes at inquiries, as objectors realised that proceedings at an inquiry might have little effect where the Department of Transport had already decided that a new motorway was needed. In 1978, a review of highway procedures made detailed proposals for improving the assessment of need for new trunk roads and for restoring public confidence in the inquiry system.[73] So far as the courts were concerned, the history of motorway inquiries culminated in *Bushell v Environment Secretary*.[74]

> During a lengthy inquiry held concerning the M40 extension near Birmingham, the inspector allowed objectors to bring evidence challenging estimates of future traffic growth, but refused to allow civil servants to be cross-examined on these. After the inquiry and before the minister made a decision, the department revised its traffic estimates, but the minister did not allow the inquiry to be reopened to examine the new estimates. The objectors claimed that natural justice entitled them (*a*) to cross-examine officials on the traffic predictions and (*b*) to a re-opening of the inquiry. The House of Lords upheld the motorway orders, holding that

---

[64] Planning and Compulsory Purchase Act 2004, part 1.

[65] Ibid, ss 7–9. See ss 20, 23 for a similar procedure for independent examination of local development plan documents by an inspector; the examination may be based on written representations, but a hearing may be held before the inspector if this is requested.

[66] 1990 Act, Sch 6 and SI 1997 No 420 (as amended).

[67] 1990 Act, ss 77–79. And see the *Alconbury* case (note 76 below).

[68] Planning Inspectorate Statistical Report, 2008–9.

[69] See Town and Country Planning (Appeals) (Written Representations Procedure) (England) Regulations 2009, SI 2009 No 452.

[70] See Town and Country Planning (Hearings Procedure) (England) Rules 2000, SI 2000 No 1626.

[71] See Town and Country Planning (Appeals) (Determination by Inspectors) (Inquiries Procedure) (England) Rules 2000, SI 2000 No 1625.

[72] Planning Act 2008, s 196, inserting s 319A into Town and Country Planning Act 1990.

[73] Cmnd 7133, 1978; Council on Tribunals, report for 1977–78, p 25 and app C; P H Levin (1979) 57 *Public Administration* 21.

[74] [1981] AC 75. And see *R v Transport Secretary, ex p Gwent CC* [1988] QB 429.

natural justice had not been infringed. The judges stressed that an inquiry was quite unlike civil litigation. An inspector had wide discretion to disallow cross-examination if it would serve no relevant purpose. The methods of predicting future traffic growth were an essential element in national policy for motorways, and were not suitable for investigation at local inquiries. Lord Edmund-Davies, dissenting, held that the objectors had been denied 'a fair crack of the whip'.[75]

This decision was a reminder that a public inquiry into a controversial proposal put forward by a government department is only part of a political process in which the minister cannot be expected to assume a cloak of judicial impartiality. A similar reminder was given in R (Alconbury Developments Ltd) v Environment Secretary.[76]

A Human Rights Act challenge was made to the minister's power to determine planning appeals which, instead of being decided by an inspector, had been 'called in' for the minister to decide. Similar challenges were made to the minister's power to approve a compulsory purchase order under the Highways Act 1980 and a new rail link under the Transport and Works Act 1992. The claimants argued that (1) the decisions affected their civil rights; (2) by art 6(1) ECHR, such questions must be determined by an independent and impartial tribunal, failing which a decision must be subject to review by a court with full jurisdiction to consider its legality; (3) the Secretary of State was not such a tribunal; and (4) there was insufficient judicial control of the decisions to satisfy art 6(1) ECHR, since the statutory appeals available did not provide for a rehearing on the merits. The House of Lords broadly approved points (1)–(3), but rejected point (4), holding that art 6(1) ECHR did not require a court to rehear the merits of the decisions; the statutory appeals to the High Court provided sufficient review of their legality. Lord Clyde said: 'We are concerned with an administrative process and an administrative decision. Planning is a matter for the formation and application of policy. The policy is not a matter for the courts but for the executive' (para 139).

Earlier, in Bryan v United Kingdom,[77] the Strasbourg Court had held that no breach of art 6(1) ECHR occurred where an inspector's decision on a planning appeal was subject to an appeal to the High Court that extended to all grounds of judicial review; such control by the national court overcame the fact that the position of the inspector was not an independent court or tribunal for the purposes of art 6(1). Because of Bryan v United Kingdom, the challenge in Alconbury focused on the fact that the decisions were made by the minister, not by an inspector.

The strain placed upon the inquiry in relation to proposals of national importance was evident in the inquiry conducted (exceptionally) by a High Court judge into the proposal by British Nuclear Fuels Ltd to establish a nuclear fuel reprocessing plant at Windscale,[78] the marathon inquiry conducted into the proposal by the Central Electricity Generating Board to build a PWR nuclear power station in Suffolk[79] and the even longer inquiry into the fifth air terminal at Heathrow,[80] from which even a consortium of local authorities around Heathrow had to withdraw because of the cost of representation. Such lengthy procedures are a means of scrutinising in public the technical and environmental aspects of controversial proposals, but a government department is unlikely to be deflected from its chosen policy by a critical report from a planning inspector.[81]

---

[75] [1981] AC at 118.

[76] [2001] UKHL 23, [2003] 2 AC 295. See D Elvin and J Maurici [2001] Jl of Planning Law 883.

[77] (1995) 21 EHRR 342, applying Albert and Le Compte v Belgium (1983) 5 EHRR 533.

[78] See P McAuslan (1979) 2 Urban Law and Policy 25.

[79] See M Purdue et al. [1985] PL 475, [1987] PL 162; O'Riordan, Kemp and Purdue, Sizewell B: An Anatomy of the Inquiry.

[80] Report by R Vandermeer QC on the Heathrow Terminal Five inquiry (2001), and see HC Deb, 20 November 2001, col 177.

[81] After a long inquiry into a projected accommodation centre near Oxford for asylum seekers, the inspector reported against the scheme, but the Secretary of State approved it. The local council's legal challenge failed: R (Cherwell DC) v First Secretary of State [2004] EWCA Civ 1420, [2005] 1 WLR 1128. But the scheme was abandoned by the Home Office a few months later.

New powers of authorising transport projects and schemes affecting harbours and canals were given to ministers by the Transport and Works Act 1992, which aimed to reduce the need for special powers to be obtained by private Acts.[82] For schemes of national significance, before the Secretary of State could make an order for a scheme, each House of Parliament must first have resolved to approve the proposal. The Secretary of State might hold a public inquiry or grant a hearing into objections to a scheme, but these proceedings would be limited by the parliamentary approval that had been given.

Difficulties have continued to be experienced in relation to the handling of major infrastructure projects dealing with such matters as energy, water and transport.[83] The Planning and Compulsory Purchase Act 2004, s 44, gave power to the Secretary of State to deal with infrastructure projects of national or regional importance. The minister could appoint an inspector as 'lead inspector', to conduct a public inquiry into aspects of the project, with power to set a timetable for the inquiry and to appoint additional inspectors to conduct concurrent sessions of the inquiry into specific matters.

Following reviews of the planning system and of the handling of major transport proposals,[84] further changes were made by the Planning Act 2008. This introduced a new system for major infrastructure projects, to exclude altogether any future public inquiry like those into the Sizewell B power station and the fifth terminal at Heathrow. Instead, the Act created an Infrastructure Planning Commission to examine applications for consent to nationally significant projects in fields of energy, transport, water and waste (s 1). National policy statements that affect the projects may be adopted by the Secretary of State, subject to prior consultation and publicity; the statements must be laid before Parliament and are subject to scrutiny in each House (s 9). Where such statements have been adopted, the Commission decides whether to approve the project, but must do so in accordance with the policy statement. Members of the Commission, sitting singly or as a panel, are appointed to examine particular applications and to decide whether there was adequate consultation before the application was made.

The public examination of such a project is in principle to be dealt with by written representations (s 90). But a hearing may be held on specific issues (s 91), and a hearing must be held if the proposal involves compulsory acquisition and an owner asks to be heard (s 92). The Act does not authorise a public inquiry at any stage, but an 'open-floor hearing' may be held at which any interested persons may make representations (s 93). All hearings must be in public, but time limits may be imposed, and cross-examination of witnesses is strictly limited. Nevertheless, the inspector may allow oral questioning if necessary to ensure that representations are adequately tested, or that an individual has a 'fair chance' to put his or her case (s 94 (7)). Significantly, 'representations relating to the merits of a policy set out in a national policy statement' are excluded (s 98(4)). If there is a national policy statement applying to the project, the Commission must decide whether to grant the application for the development; if there is no national policy statement, the decision will be made by the Secretary of State. An order to permit the development may be challenged by judicial review but, in keeping with the desire to reduce delay, the period for challenge is restricted to six weeks from publication of the order or (if later) from publication of the reasons for the order (s 118).[85]

---

[82] See HL 97 (1987–8) and Cm 1110, 1990. Also Council on Tribunals, report for 1989–90, pp 42–5, and report for 1991–2, pp 44–7. And see p 192 above.

[83] On the government proposal in 2001 that parliamentary approval for certain major projects should be obtained in advance of a public inquiry, see HC Deb, 20 July 2001, col 521W; J Popham and M Purdue [2002] *JI of Planning Law* 137.

[84] See K Barker, *Review of Land Use Planning*, 2006 and R Eddington, *Transport Study*, 2006, which were followed by the white paper, *Planning for a Sustainable Future*, Cm 7120, 2007.

[85] In general, judicial review must be sought within three months of the decision challenged. Statutory review of planning and similar decisions must be sought within six weeks. See p 719 below.

One problem under this process is that campaigners against particular projects will find it difficult to accept that the issues can be fairly examined by the Commission, if the Commission is bound by a national policy statement made by the Secretary of State, especially if this is site-specific as to a new reservoir, wind farm or power station. For this and other reasons, objectors are likely to seek judicial review of proceedings under the 2008 Act,[86] even if the disputed issues are essentially policy questions which (the framers of the Act would argue) should be decided by Parliament.

This account of the changing use of public inquiries may suggest that we need to differentiate between two broad categories (while recognising that an intermediate 'grey' category exists between them): (*a*) decisions (such as the approval of major wind farms, high-speed rail links or power stations) that have a high content of national policy, are controversial, environmentally sensitive and cannot be decided by adjudication, but only by a governmental decision for which there must be political accountability; and (*b*) more routine matters, such as small-scale planning applications, which are decided in accordance with national, regional and local policies, initially by local authorities but with a right of appeal to the Planning Inspectorate. In this second category, discretion must still be exercised by the decision-makers, although sometimes the outcome depends on application of rules. When a planning inspector deals with this second category of questions, then this function is arguably comparable with that of the tribunals that we considered in section A – which cannot be said of the duties of ministers in deciding whether, for instance, nuclear power is in the national interest.

C. The Inquiries Act 2005

Both tribunals and inquiries form part of the regular structure of administrative justice and numerous decisions are made each year by these procedures. This section deals with something different – the legal provision for enabling a national disaster or major scandal to be the subject of investigation, with a view to finding out the reasons for the event, whether individuals or public authorities were responsible for it, and the lessons to be learned. When such inquiries are held, it is essential that they are conducted impartially and with full regard to the evidence given to them. For this reason, serving judges have in the past been appointed to conduct such inquiries, but today retired judges are preferred. The government nearly always has a direct interest in these inquiries, since the ministers and civil servants concerned may thereby come under close public scrutiny. MPs have a strong interest in inquiries as a means of allaying concern and establishing accountability; and the inquiries are paid for by the taxpayer. Some inquiries are concerned with questions of human rights, especially where deaths have occurred.[87] Many inquiries are held without statutory authority; others are conducted under legislation specific to the subject matter (whether, for instance, it concerns policing, rail accidents, or failures in the NHS). We deal first with the inquiries which, until its repeal in 2005, were held under the Tribunals of Inquiry (Evidence) Act 1921.

The Tribunals of Inquiry (Evidence) Act 1921

In the nineteenth century, parliamentary committees were occasionally appointed to inquire into matters of concern, such as alleged corruption in government. Use of these committees was

---

[86] J Maurici [2009] *Jl of Planning Law* 446.

[87] Under art 2, ECHR, the state must investigate unnatural deaths, including deaths in which the state may be implicated. See *Jordan* v *UK* (2003) 37 EHRR 2; also HL 26, HC 224 (2004–5), ch 2. This duty has increased the significance of inquests and (in Scotland) fatal accident inquiries. See also *R (Hurst)* v *North London Coroner* [2007] UKHL 13, [2007] 2 AC 189; *R (JL)* v *Justice Secretary* [2008] UKHL 68, [2009] 2 All ER 521. And M Requa and G Anthony [2008] PL 443.

discredited in 1913 when a Commons committee investigated the conduct of members of the Liberal government in the Marconi affair and the committee produced three conflicting reports.[88] The 1921 Act provided a more reliable way of securing an impartial investigation into major events. When the government had decided that a formal inquiry was necessary with powers of obtaining evidence, the two Houses would resolve that a 'tribunal of inquiry' be appointed to inquire into a matter of 'urgent public importance'; this enabled the tribunal to be appointed by the government. The tribunal would be granted all the powers of the High Court (in Scotland, of the Court of Session) to examine witnesses and require production of documents. When a person summoned as a witness failed to attend or refused to answer questions which the tribunal had power to ask, the chairman of the tribunal could report the matter to the High Court or Court of Session for inquiry and punishment as a contempt of court.[89]

In more than 80 years, only 24 tribunals of inquiry were appointed. Serious allegations of corrupt or improper conduct in the public service that were inquired into included a leakage of Budget secrets (1936), alleged bribery of ministers and civil servants (1948), premature disclosure of information relating to the raising of the bank rate (1957) and the disastrous financial operations of the Crown Agents (1978).[90] Other matters of public anxiety were the tragic Aberfan disaster (1966), the 'Bloody Sunday' shootings in Londonderry (1972), the Dunblane shootings (1996) and abuse of children in care in North Wales (1999).[91] In 1998, Lord Saville, together with two judges from Canada and Australia, was appointed to make a second inquiry into the 'Bloody Sunday' events, but the progress of this inquiry has been unusually costly and protracted.[92]

Such tribunals of inquiry usually consisted of a senior judge, assisted by one or two additional members or expert assessors. The tribunal would hear witnesses in public, called to the inquiry by counsel instructed by the Treasury Solicitor. Witnesses were entitled to be legally represented and their costs could be met from public funds. They would be cross-examined by lawyers appearing at the tribunal and questioned by the tribunal. Because of the inquisitorial proceedings, steps might be needed to protect witnesses from being inculpated in giving evidence on charges which had not been formulated in advance and which they had no chance of contesting.[93] The Attorney General could assure witnesses that no criminal charges would be brought against them in respect of their evidence.

In 1966, a royal commission (chaired by Salmon LJ) concluded that tribunals of inquiry should be appointed only in cases of vital public importance, but that the possibility of an inquisitorial procedure must be retained.[94] The commission recommended six 'cardinal principles' to protect persons whose reputations might be affected; for example, a witness should be told beforehand of allegations against him or her, and should be entitled to legal representation, to cross-examine others giving evidence and to call witnesses. In 1969, a departmental committee, also chaired by Salmon LJ, examined the rules of contempt of court in relation to these inquiries, in particular operation of the sub judice rule.[95] When the law on contempt of court was reformed in 1981,

---

[88] See Donaldson, *The Marconi Scandal*.

[89] See *A-G v Mulholland and Foster* [1963] 2 QB 477 (imprisonment of journalists for refusing to disclose their sources); and ch 18 D.

[90] See Cmd 5184, 1936; Cmd 7616, 1948; Cmnd 350, 1957; HC 364 (1981–2). See Keeton, *Trial by Tribunal*; and Z Segal [1984] PL 206.

[91] HC 553 (1966–7); HC 220 (1971–2); Cm 3386, 1996; and HC 201 (1999–2000).

[92] The inquiry was subject more than once to judicial review: see *R v Lord Saville of Newdigate, ex p A* [1999] 4 All ER 860; B Hadfield [1999] PL 663. At the end of 2009, the report was still awaited.

[93] This criticism was made of the tribunal which investigated the collapse of the Vehicle and General Insurance Company: HC 133 (1971–2).

[94] Cmnd 3121, 1966.

[95] Cmnd 4078, 1969. And see Cmnd 5313, 1973.

many of the changes were applied to tribunals of inquiry; its proceedings were deemed to be 'active' from the time of its appointment until its report was presented to Parliament.[96]

Other forms of inquiry

The public procedures of a tribunal of inquiry were not considered suitable for a review of events leading to the Falklands Islands hostilities that involved access to secret diplomatic and intelligence documents; instead, Lord Franks was appointed to chair a committee of privy counsellors. A similar method was adopted for the Butler review of intelligence on weapons of mass destruction in Iraq.[97] In 2009, Sir John Chilcot and other privy counsellors were appointed by the Prime Minister, after consulting opposition parties, to examine British involvement in Iraq from 2001 until July 2009. Chilcot's broad terms of reference were to establish as accurately as possible the way government decisions were made before and during the conflict, and to identify the lessons to be learned. The committee decided to hear as much evidence as possible in public; witnesses were questioned by the committee, and lawyers were absent from the public proceedings.

Other inquiries have been held under subject-specific legislation, for example into the conduct of the police or health authorities, or rail accidents.[98] Other inquiries have been conducted less formally and without statutory powers (including Lord Denning's dramatic inquiry into the Profumo affair in 1963).[99] As well as the Franks, Butler and Chilcot inquiries already mentioned, other non-statutory inquiries have included Sir Richard Scott's inquiry (1992–96) into the export of arms to Iraq,[100] and Lord Hutton's inquiry into the death of Dr David Kelly.[101] Such inquiries are 'judicial' in that they are conducted by a judge, although similar inquiries are conducted by other persons (for instance, the Bichard inquiry into the background to the Soham murders).[102] Their procedure is investigative and they have no power to compel witnesses to attend. Since they are not protected by the law of contempt of court, the subject matter can be discussed freely in the media. In the arms for Iraq inquiry, Sir Richard Scott was told that if he needed them, powers under the 1921 Act would be granted; he was eventually satisfied that he had full access to all official witnesses and papers.[103] In that inquiry, the inquisitorial procedure for taking evidence in public was criticised for its effect on witnesses, who were permitted legal assistance but not representation.[104] In Scott's view, however, the Salmon 'principles' mentioned earlier did not apply fully to an investigatory inquiry.[105] Thereafter, in a report on inquiry procedures, the Council on Tribunals stressed that the Salmon 'principles' were recommendations, not rules of law, and that it was 'wholly impracticable' to devise a single set of rules to govern every inquiry.[106]

---

[96] Contempt of Court Act 1981, s 20; and see ch 18 D.

[97] See the Butler report, HC 898 (2003–4).

[98] See respectively the (Macpherson) inquiry into the killing of Stephen Lawrence, Cm 4262, 1998; the (Kennedy) inquiry into the Bristol Royal Infirmary, Cm 5207, 2001; and the (Cullen) inquiry into the Paddington rail disaster (*The Ladbroke Grove Rail Inquiry, Parts 1 & 2*, Health and Safety Executive, 2001).

[99] Cmnd 2152, 1963; and Cmnd 3121, 1966, pp 19–21.

[100] See HC 115 (1995–6); and ch 7 above, note 90. Also I Leigh and L Lustgarten (1996) 59 MLR 695; and A W Bradley, in Manson and Mullan (eds), *Commissions of Inquiry*, ch 2.

[101] HC 247 (2003–4). For his reply to media criticism of the report, see Lord Hutton [2006] PL 807.

[102] The Bichard inquiry report, HC 653 (2003–4).

[103] Scott report, section A, ch 1.

[104] See Lord Howe [1996] PL 445; and Scott report, app A, part D. Also B K Winetrobe [1997] PL 18; L Blom-Cooper [1993] CLP 204 and [1994] PL 1; C Clothier [1996] PL 384; M C Harris [1996] PL 508; Leigh and Lustgarten (note 100 above), pp 694–701; and H Grant [2001] PL 377.

[105] Scott report, sections B and K, ch 1; and R Scott (1995) 111 LQR 596.

[106] Report of Council on Tribunals for 1995–96, app A.

The Inquiries Act 2005

Against this background, the Inquiries Act 2005 provides a new legal framework for inquiries, but it does not affect the power of a government to appoint non-statutory inquiries. The Act repealed the 1921 Act and the legislation for subject-specific inquiries of the kind already mentioned.[107] The immediate background to the Act included commitments by the government to hold inquiries into several prominent deaths that had occurred in Northern Ireland as to which there were allegations of police or official collusion, and a desire to avoid the costs and delay of another inquiry under the 1921 Act. There was an understandable view that it was time to look again at the legal basis for inquiries in general.[108]

In outline, the Act empowers any minister in the UK government[109] to appoint an inquiry when 'particular events' have caused or may cause public concern, or 'there is public concern that particular events may have occurred' (s 1(1)). Such an inquiry may not determine a person's civil or criminal liability, but may find facts from which it is likely that liability may be inferred (s 2). The minister appoints the chairman of the inquiry, either to act alone, or with other members appointed by the minister after consulting the chairman (ss 3, 4). In making appointments, the minister must take into account the expertise of the panel, the need for balance and the services of assessors (ss 8, 11). The inquiry's terms of reference are settled and may be amended by the minister, after consulting the chairman or proposed chairman (s 5(3), (4)). Parliament must be informed of the inquiry, but is not required to approve the minister's decision (s 6). No member of the inquiry panel may have a direct interest in the subject matter or a close association with an interested party, except where this could not reasonably be regarded as affecting the impartiality of the panel (s 9). If the minister proposes to appoint a judge to serve on an inquiry, he or she must consult the president of the court concerned; for judges in England and Wales, this will be the Lord Chief Justice; in Scotland, the Lord President of the Court of Session; and for the Supreme Court, the president of the court (s 10, as amended). But the Act does not prevent the minister from appointing a judge who is willing to be appointed, even if the president does not consent to the appointment. In some circumstances, the minister may suspend an inquiry, but only after consulting the chairman, and notice of the suspension with reasons must be laid before Parliament (s 13); the minister may even bring the inquiry to an end before it has reported, subject to consulting the chairman and notifying Parliament (s 14).

The procedure and conduct of an inquiry are to be as directed by the chairman, subject to fairness and the need to avoid unnecessary costs (s 17). The chairman must take reasonable steps to ensure public access to the inquiry and the evidence, but restrictions on access may be imposed by the minister or the chairman, for instance for the purpose of reducing 'harm or damage' that would otherwise be caused (ss 18, 19). The 'harm or damage' includes damage to national security or international relations, damage to economic interests of the United Kingdom and damage caused by disclosure of commercially sensitive information (s 19(5)).[110] The chairman may require witnesses to attend the inquiry and produce relevant documents (s 21), subject to the exclusion of privileged information (s 22).[111] The inquiry report must be sent to the minister (s 24). It is for the minister, or in some circumstances the chairman, to arrange for publication of the full report, subject to the omission of material that might cause 'harm or damage' of the kind mentioned (s 25). Reports when published are laid before Parliament (s 26).

The Act makes it an offence (s 35) to fail to comply with notices from the chairman under s 21, and such notices may be enforced in the High Court (in Scotland, the Court of Session) as if they

---

[107] For the repealed statutes, see Sched 3.

[108] See the report of the Commons Public Administration Committee, *Government by Inquiry* (HC 51, 2004–5). However, by 2010 no inquiries under the 2005 Act had been appointed.

[109] The Act confers similar powers on the devolved authorities in Scotland, Wales and Northern Ireland.

[110] See also s 23 (risk of damage to the economy).

[111] The law of public interest immunity in civil proceedings (see ch 32 C) applies to inquiries: s 22(2).

had been issued in civil proceedings (s 36). Anyone who wishes to challenge decisions of the minister in relation to the inquiry or decisions by the panel has only 14 days from becoming aware of a decision in which to seek judicial review (although the court may extend the period) (s 38). The costs of the inquiry are to be borne by the minister, but the minister may notify the panel if it is going outside the terms of reference and the minister need not bear future costs if the panel ignores this warning (s 39). Rules of procedure and evidence may be made by the Lord Chancellor (s 41).

While there was certainly a good case to be made for further general legislation on inquiries,[112] aspects of the Act are controversial.[113] By eliminating altogether the need for Parliament to approve proposed inquiries, as required by the 1921 Act, the Act is open to the criticism that while inquiries often involve the acts and decisions of government departments, it is ministers who decide to hold an inquiry, appoint the chairman and panel members, settle and enforce the terms of reference, restrict public access to the inquiry and impose restrictions on publication. It is difficult to understand why a minister should be able to deploy a judge for this purpose against the wishes of the president of the court concerned, particularly as not all matters of public concern imposing political pressure on the government justify the use of judges. It will be important for parliamentary and public opinion to uphold the highest standards of integrity in the recourse made by governments to the Inquiries Act. The use of public resources for inquiries cannot be justified unless the findings made by inquiries are likely to allay public concern.[114] Despite enactment of the Inquiries Act in 2005, governments will probably continue to appoint non-statutory inquiries, knowing that such an inquiry can if necessary be converted into a statutory inquiry at short notice.[115]

D. The Parliamentary Ombudsman

This section focuses on the Parliamentary Ombudsman, an office created in 1967 to provide for the redress of individual grievances against government. Although the idea derived from the Ombudsman in Scandinavian countries and New Zealand,[116] the British model was designed to fit alongside other means of remedying citizens' grievances, such as challenge in the courts (in the 1960s judicial review was a little used remedy), appeal to tribunals, the right to be heard at a public inquiry, and parliamentary means, such as an MP's letter or question to the minister concerned. Although each remedy may be effective in the appropriate situation, each has its particular limitations.[117] By comparison with those remedies, the value of the ombudsman model is that it provides an accessible, cheap (from the viewpoint of someone with a complaint against officialdom), non-legalistic and general-purpose remedy, by which an individual can get his or her grievance examined by an independent and impartial person, experienced in the ways of government and able to distinguish good from bad administration.

After more than forty years of the Parliamentary Ombudsman, we can see that its success, admittedly within a structure that now seems overly rigid, led to similar initiatives in Britain in local government, the NHS and other areas of the public sector. The use of ombudsman-type procedures has also taken root in the private sector. Commitment to the ombudsman concept within a large organisation (whether governmental or commercial) is to accept the principle that

---

[112] See note 108 above.

[113] See the report of the Joint Committee on Human Rights cited in note 87 above.

[114] This is a factor that the Act rightly refers to in two places: ss 19(4)(a) and 25(5)(a).

[115] See *R (D) v SSHD* [2006] EWCA Civ 143, [2006] 3 All ER 946, [43]–[46].

[116] On comparative aspects, the earlier literature includes Rowat (ed.), *The Ombudsman*; Gellhorn, *Ombudsmen and Others*; Hill, *The Model Ombudsman*; Stacey, *Ombudsmen Compared*.

[117] Cf *The Citizen and the Administration* (the Whyatt report), p 610 above; and Cmnd 2767, 1965.

individuals need effective redress against the mistakes, inefficiencies and other failings that occur in corporate conduct.

When the office of 'Parliamentary Commissioner for Administration' was created in 1967, it was indicative of the caution with which this was done that the word 'ombudsman' was not allowed to appear in the legislation. The statutory title just stated has always been cumbrous and in 1994 the government agreed that 'at the first opportunity' of legislation it would be changed to 'Parliamentary Ombudsman'.[118] No such opportunity had arisen by 2010! In fact, the present holder of the office, Ms Ann Abraham, describes herself as 'Parliamentary Ombudsman'.[119] While the Parliamentary Ombudsman has close links with the executive, the office was designed as an extension of Parliament; and it has virtually no links with the judicial system. As Sir Cecil Clothier, then the Ombudsman, said in 1984:

> The office . . . stands curiously poised between the legislative and the executive, while discharging an almost judicial function in the citizen's dispute with his government; and yet it forms no part of the judiciary.[120]

It may not matter that it is difficult to locate the Ombudsman within a formal separation of powers, but it is important that the Ombudsman should be recognised as having a constitutional role that can help to maintain the electorate's faith in democracy and strengthen the principle of accountable government: yet this dimension is often absent from discussion of constitutional reform.[121] On one view, the essence of the ombudsman idea for the ordinary person is accessibility, flexibility, informality and humanity. On another view, the Ombudsman provides an authoritative means of 'judging' the conduct of faceless officials and bureaucracies, thus helping to develop *systems* of administration that are both humane and effective. In the British version of the Ombudsman, both aspects of the role are seen at work.

Status and jurisdiction[122]

The Parliamentary Ombudsman is appointed by the Crown and in future will hold office for not more than seven years, without the possibility of reappointment; she may be removed by the Crown for misbehaviour, following addresses by both Houses (s 1, as amended).[123] Originally, the appointment was solely a matter for the government, but the chairman of the Commons committee on the Ombudsman (currently the Public Administration Committee) is now consulted before an appointment is made.[124] The Ombudsman's salary is charged on the Consolidated Fund (s 2). She appoints the staff of the office, subject to Treasury consent as to numbers and conditions of service (s 3). Of the seven Ombudsmen who served between 1967 and 2002, five came to the post after civil service careers and two were Queen's Counsel; the present Ombudsman (Ms Ann Abraham) came from a different background, having worked in public sector housing and citizens' advice.

---

[118] See HC 619 (1993–4).

[119] Or, as in her annual reports, 'Parliamentary and Health Service Ombudsman'.

[120] Report for 1983 (HC 322 (1983–4)), p 1.

[121] See the valuable series of articles by Ann Abraham in (2008) 61 *Parliamentary Affairs* at 206, 370, 535, 681 and in [2008] PL 1. Also R Kirkham, B Thompson and T Buck, (2009) 62 *Parliamentary Affairs* 600.

[122] References in the text are to the Parliamentary Commissioner Act 1967, as amended. The literature includes Gregory and Hutchesson, *The Parliamentary Ombudsman*; Seneviratne, *Ombudsmen: Public Services and Administrative Justice*; Harlow and Rawlings, *Law and Administration*, ch 12; A W Bradley [1980] CLJ 304; C Clothier [1986] PL 204; G Drewry and C Harlow (1990) 53 MLR 745; N O'Brien [2009] PL 466.

[123] 1967 Act, amended by Employment Equality (Age) Regulations 2006, SI 2006 No 1031.

[124] Cmnd 6764, 1977. See HC 619 (1993–4) for the government's agreement to amend the law to provide for appointment following an address by the Commons moved after consultation with the Opposition: the law has not been amended.

The formal task of the Ombudsman is to investigate complaints by private persons that they have suffered injustice in consequence of maladministration by government departments and many non-departmental public bodies, in the exercise of their administrative functions (s 5). The area of jurisdiction is defined by the 1967 Act, Sch 2 of which lists the departments and other bodies subject to investigation. This list may be amended by Order in Council (s 4), and this is done whenever bodies are abolished or created. Section 4 restricts the bodies which may be entered in Sch 2 to (a) government departments; (b) bodies exercising functions on behalf of the Crown; (c) bodies established under the prerogative, an Act of Parliament or Order in Council, or by a minister, that fulfil certain criteria as to the source of their income and the power of appointment to them.[125]

The Ombudsman has no jurisdiction over the devolved authorities in Scotland or Wales, nor over bodies which are outside central government, for example, local authorities, the police and universities, although she may investigate complaints about the way in which central departments have discharged their functions in these fields. Many matters are excluded from investigation for which ministers are or may be responsible to Parliament (s 5(3) and Sch 3). Thus the Ombudsman may not investigate:

(a) action taken in matters certified by a Secretary of State to affect relations between the UK government and other governments, or international organisations;

(b) action taken outside the UK by any officer representing or acting under the authority of the Crown;[126]

(c) administration of dependent territories outside the UK;

(d) action taken by a Secretary of State under the Extradition Acts;

(e) action taken by or with the authority of a Secretary of State for investigating crime or protecting the security of the state, including action so taken with respect to passports;

(f) (1) the commencement or conduct of civil or criminal proceedings before any UK court, court martial or international court; (2) action taken by persons appointed by the Lord Chancellor as administrative staff of courts or tribunals, being action taken on the authority of persons acting in a judicial capacity;[127]

(g) an exercise of the prerogative of mercy;

(h) action taken on behalf of central government by authorities in the NHS;

(i) matters relating to contractual or other commercial transactions on the part of central government;[128]

(j) appointments, discipline and other personnel matters in relation to the civil service and the armed forces, and decisions of ministers and departments in respect of other branches of the public service;

(k) the grant of honours, awards or privileges within the gift of the Crown.

It was these restrictions that led to criticism that the 1967 Act sought to carve up areas of possible grievances in an arbitrary way.[129] The exclusion of the NHS was later put right by the

---

[125] The numerous bodies within jurisdiction include the Arts Council, Charity Commission, English Nature, National Gallery, Sport England, OFSTED and utility regulators such as OFCOM.

[126] The acts of British consuls abroad, other than honorary consuls, are within jurisdiction, if the complainant is resident or has a right of abode in the United Kingdom: 1967 Act, s 6(5).

[127] And see note 135 below.

[128] This is subject to an exception for transactions relating to land bought compulsorily or under threat of compulsory powers. But for this exception, a latter-day Crichel Down affair (ch 7) would be outside the Ombudman's jurisdiction.

[129] HC Deb, 18 October 1966, col 67 (Quintin Hogg MP). Cf report by Justice, *Our Fettered Ombudsman*, 1977.

creation of an Ombudsman for the Health Service, a post that for England has always been held by the Parliamentary Ombudsman. The restrictions which have been most criticised are in (*i*) and (*j*) above. The government may by Order in Council revoke any of these restrictions (s 5(4)), but despite frequent recommendations from the Commons committee mentioned above, successive governments have refused to revoke the restriction on personnel matters in (*j*).[130]

A limitation of a different kind is that the Ombudsman may not normally investigate any action in respect of which the complainant has or had a right of recourse to a tribunal or a remedy in a court of law, although she may do so if in a particular case the citizen could not reasonably be expected to exercise the right (s 5(2)). Thus, if an individual wishes to challenge a decision about tax or social security, he or she should appeal to the relevant tribunal. But the Ombudsman often accepts that a complainant cannot be reasonably expected to embark on the hazardous course of litigation.[131]

The complainant need not be a British citizen, but in general must be resident in the United Kingdom or have been present in the United Kingdom when the offending action occurred, or the action concerned must relate to rights or obligations arising in the United Kingdom (s 6(4)).

There is a time bar: the Ombudsman may investigate a complaint only if it is made to an MP within 12 months from the date when the citizen first had notice of the matter complained of, except where circumstances justify the Ombudsman in accepting a complaint made later than this (s 6(3)).

It is for the Ombudsman to determine whether a complaint is duly made under the Act; in practice, many complaints identify the injustice that has been suffered more closely than the maladministration that caused it.[132] The Ombudsman has an express discretion to decide whether to investigate a complaint.[133] Her decisions are in principle subject to judicial review, if grounds for the Administrative Court to intervene can be shown. Thus, if she were to investigate a complaint that is outside her jurisdiction, the decision could be quashed;[134] and no one could be liable for refusing to supply information to her (s 9). However, it would be unsatisfactory if the acts of someone charged to promote the resolution of grievances were to generate a mass of satellite litigation. The extent of the Ombudsman's powers may involve difficult legal issues.[135] Where the Ombudsman has to exercise a discretion under the 1967 Act, the court will not intervene except where it is satisfied that the discretion has been exercised unlawfully.[136]

Procedure

One important feature of the ombudsman idea is that the Ombudsman should be accessible to the individual. But in Britain the citizen has no right to present a complaint to the Parliamentary Ombudsman. A complaint must first be addressed to an MP by the person who claims to have suffered injustice (s 5(1)). It is for the MP to decide whether to refer the complaint to the

---

[130] See e.g. HC 615 (1977–8); and Cmnd 7449, 1979.

[131] Cf *R v Commissioner for Local Administration, ex p Croydon BC* [1989] 1 All ER 1033, 1044–5. See HC 735 (2005–6), paras 18–20 on use of this discretion.

[132] Cf *R v Local Commissioner for Administration, ex p Bradford Council* [1979] QB 287, 313.

[133] 1967 Act, s 5(5). And see *Re Fletcher's Application* [1970] 2 All ER 527.

[134] See *R (Cavanagh) v Health Service Commissioner* [2005] EWCA Civ 1578, [2006] 3 All ER 543 (Health Service Ombudsman 'has no power of investigation at large').

[135] See Courts and Legal Services Act 1990, s 110 (extending jurisdiction to certain staff of courts and tribunals, but not if acting on judicial authority), and the Parliamentary Commissioner Act 1994.

[136] *R v Parliamentary Commissioner for Administration, ex p Dyer* [1994] 1 All ER 375. In *R v PCA, ex p Balchin* [1998] 1 PLR 1 (Sedley J) and (*the same*) *No 2* [2000] 2 LGR 87 (Dyson J), decisions by successive Ombudsmen rejecting a complaint against the Department of Transport were quashed; see P Giddings [2000] PL 201 and, for the sequel, note 166 below. See also *R (Attwood) v Health Service Commissioner* [2008] EWHC 2315 (Admin), [2009] 1 All ER 415.

Ombudsman. Usually complainants will take their complaint to their constituency MP, but the Act does not require this. Very many inquiries and complaints are received directly by the Ombudsman, whose staff advise the individual what action may be open, including the advice that a complaint within the Ombudsman's remit cannot be considered unless it is forwarded by an MP.[137] In 1993 retention of the 'MP filter' was supported by a Commons committee, but many MPs (including the present successor to that committee) now wish the filter to be abolished.[138]

The 1967 Act lays down a formal procedure by which the Ombudsman first decides whether a complaint received via an MP falls within jurisdiction. If it does, she must decide whether a full investigation would be justified, and there may be practical factors that make this unnecessary (if for instance it is unlikely that an investigation will lead to a worthwhile outcome, or if it is likely that an informal intervention with the relevant department will resolve the complaint).[139] If she decides to make a full investigation, the department and persons named in the complaint must have an opportunity to comment (s 7(1)). The investigation, carried out in private, will generally involve examining departmental records. The Ombudsman may compel witnesses to give evidence and produce documents (s 8). Investigations are not restricted by public interest immunity (s 8(3)),[140] but she may not see documents which are certified by the Secretary of the Cabinet, with the Prime Minister's approval, as relating to proceedings of the Cabinet or a Cabinet committee (s 8(4)). When a formal investigation is completed, the Ombudsman sends the MP concerned a report on the investigation (s 10(1)). If it appears that injustice was caused through maladministration and has not been remedied, she may lay a special report before Parliament (s 10(3)). Reports relating to an investigation are absolutely privileged in the law of defamation (s 10(5)). A minister may not veto an investigation, but may require the Ombudsman to omit from a report information that would prejudice the safety of the state or be against the public interest (s 11(3)).

These powers of investigation give the Ombudsman a formidable instrument for scrutinising departmental action should it be necessary, but there is little value in a prolonged scrutiny of cases in which it is rapidly apparent (and accepted by the department) that mistakes were made in handling the individual's affairs. The present Ombudsman has developed the use of flexible procedures that are more focused on the needs of the complainant than in the past.[141] Her aim is to find the most effective way of resolving the complaint, if possible by informal means; her staff maintain a dialogue with the complainant, and encourage departments to provide an appropriate outcome without delay when this is justified.

Despite her power to investigate and report on complaints, the Ombudsman has no power to enforce provision of a remedy. Thus she cannot alter a departmental decision or award compensation to a citizen, although she may suggest an outcome that she would regard as acceptable. In the very great majority of cases, departments agree to such an outcome, but in exceptional cases a department may refuse and may argue that the Ombudsman's conclusions are mistaken.

In *R (Bradley)* v *Work and Pensions Secretary*,[142] the Department of Work and Pensions refused to accept certain findings by the Ombudsman of maladministration regarding information given to members of certain final salary pension schemes that later collapsed. When several affected persons sought judicial review of the refusal, the court examined the Ombudsman's findings in great detail. The Court of Appeal held that the minister was not bound to accept the Ombudsman's findings of maladministration and might come to its

---

[137] Cf Report of PCA for 1978 (HC 205 (1978–9)), p 4.

[138] See HC 33–I (1993–4), pp xv–xx; M Elliot [2006] PL 84, 90–2; and now, HC 107 (2009–10).

[139] See the Ombudsman's report for 2008–9 (HC 786, 2008–9), pp 8–9.

[140] See ch 32 C.

[141] See her report for 2004–5, HC 348 (2005–6), pp 36–41; and for 2008–9 (above), pp 9–10.

[142] [2008] EWCA Civ 36, [2008] 3 All ER 1116. And see R Kirkham, B Thompson and T Buck [2008] PL 510; JNE Varuhas (2009) 72 MLR 102. After the Court of Appeal's decision, the Secretary of State proposed a modified form of compensation that the Ombudsman considered acceptable.

own conclusion about what had occurred. However, the minister's decision could be set aside if it was irrational, in the sense that it was not supported by 'cogent reasons' for rejecting the Ombudsman's conclusions. In a later case, the Divisional Court held that the government's reasons for rejecting several findings by the Ombudsman concerning the Equitable Life affair lacked cogency and reasoning.[143]

A minister is usually under a strong obligation to accept the Ombudsman's findings, but a report may have such political implications that a minister could come under pressure not to do so;[144] and if there has been a systemic failure affecting hundreds or thousands of persons, the costs of providing a remedy may be large. To support the Ombudsman in this situation, and to oversee the office, the Public Administration Committee in the Commons examines her reports and takes evidence from departments that she has criticised. The committee has made valuable studies of such matters as the powers and remit of the Ombudsman, the meaning of maladministration, remedies and the need for reform of the various public sector ombudsmen.[145]

The Ombudsman's casework

What is meant by the phrase, 'injustice to the person aggrieved in consequence of maladministration' (s 10(3))? No definition and no illustrations of maladministration and injustice are given in the Act. Maladministration includes such defects as 'neglect, inattention, delay, incompetence, ineptitude, perversity, and arbitrariness'.[146] Many examples of maladministration are found in the Ombudsman's reports. They include failure to give effect to assurances given to a citizen;[147] incorrect advice and delay in dealing with a benefit claim;[148] failure to treat someone with respect;[149] failure to give proper effect to a department's policy guidance;[150] dilatory enforcement of regulations against asbestosis;[151] failure to make departmental policy known in the press;[152] and even the making of misleading statements by a minister in Parliament.[153]

Even if maladministration has occurred, this does not mean that injustice has thereby been caused to the individual. Conversely, injustice or hardship may exist, caused not by maladministration but by legislation or a judicial decision. Injustice for this purpose means not merely injury of a kind that a court may remedy, but includes 'the sense of outrage aroused by unfair or incompetent administration, even where the complainant has suffered no actual loss'.[154]

One cause of difficulty has been the relation between maladministration and discretionary decisions. Unlike the New Zealand Ombudsman, who may find that such a decision was wrong, the Ombudsman may not question the merits of a discretionary decision taken without maladministration (s 12(3)). Where errors have been made in the procedures leading to a discretionary decision, she can report accordingly. But what if a discretionary decision has caused manifest hardship to the individual, but no identifiable defect has occurred in the procedures leading up to

---

[143] *R (Equitable Members Action Group) v HM Treasury* [2009] EWHC 2495 (Admin).

[144] In 1975, the government was supported by the Commons in rejecting the Ombudsman's finding that the government had some responsibility for holidaymakers' losses arising from collapse of the Court Line group: HC Deb, 6 August 1975, col 532.

[145] See HC 33–I (1993–4); HC 619 (1993–4); HC 112 and 316 (1994–5); HC 612 (1999–2000); HC 448 (2002–3).

[146] HC Deb, 18 October 1966, col 51 (R H S Crossman MP).

[147] See A W Bradley [1981] CLP 1, 8–11.

[148] See e.g. HC 348 (2005–6), pp 26–7.

[149] Ibid, p 25.

[150] A R Mowbray [1987] PL 570. See also A R Mowbray [1990] PL 68 and P Brown, in Richardson and Genn (note 4 above), ch 13 (remedies for misinformation).

[151] HC 259 (1975–6), p 189. On the Ombudsman's response to official delay, see S N McMurtrie [1997] PL 159.

[152] HC 680 (1974–5).

[153] HC 498 (1974–5).

[154] Both judgments in *R v PCA, ex p Balchin*, note 136 above, approved this quotation from Mr Crossman's speech to Parliament in 1966.

it? In such a case, the Ombudsman may infer an element of maladministration from the very decision itself or may inquire into harsh decisions based on the over-rigorous application of departmental policies.[155] An account of maladministration prepared in 1993 by Sir William Reid, then Ombudsman, included 'unwillingness to treat the complainant as a person with rights' and 'failure to mitigate the effects of rigid adherence to the letter of the law where that produces manifestly inequitable treatment'.[156]

Three leading examples of the Ombudsman's investigations may be given. The Sachsenhausen case was the first occasion on which a department was found to be seriously at fault.[157]

> Under the Anglo-German Agreement of 1964, the German government provided £1 million for compensating UK citizens who suffered from Nazi persecution during World War Two. Distribution of this money was left to the discretion of the UK government. In 1964, the Foreign Secretary (Mr Butler) approved rules for distributing it. Later the Foreign Office withheld compensation from 12 persons who claimed under the rules because they had been detained within the Sachsenhausen concentration camp. Pressure from many MPs failed to get this decision reversed and a complaint was referred to the Ombudsman. By this time the whole of the £1 million had been distributed to other claimants. After an extensive investigation, the Ombudsman reported that there were defects in the procedure by which the Foreign Office reached its decisions and subsequently defended them, and that this maladministration had damaged the reputation of the claimants. When this report was debated in the Commons, the Foreign Secretary (Mr George Brown) assumed personal responsibility for the decisions, which he maintained were correct. He nonetheless made available an additional £25,000 in order that the claimants might receive the same rate of compensation as successful claimants on the fund.[158]

At that time, the prevailing view was that the 'Butler rules' were not enforceable in law since they conferred no rights on the claimants, but on similar facts today the claimants could seek judicial review of the Foreign Office decisions, based on the legitimate expectations created by the rules.[159]

The most extensive investigation that by 1989 had been undertaken by the Ombudsman was into the Barlow Clowes affair, referred to him by no fewer than 159 MPs.[160]

> In 1988, the Barlow Clowes investment business collapsed, leaving millions of pounds owing to investors, many of whom were older persons of modest means. The Department of Trade and Industry had licensed the business under the Prevention of Fraud (Investments) Act 1958 (later replaced by the more rigorous Financial Services Act 1986), though there were indications that the business was not properly conducted. The Ombudsman found that there had been maladministration by civil servants in five respects. As a result, the losses to investors exceeded what they would have been had the department exercised its regulatory powers with a 'sufficiently rigorous and enquiring approach'.[161]

The government took the unusual course of rejecting the findings of maladministration, but nonetheless undertook *ex gratia* to provide £150 million to compensate investors for up to 90 per cent of their loss. Had the investors attempted to sue the DTI in negligence, they would almost certainly have failed to establish in law that the department owed them a duty of care.[162]

The third example has striking resemblances to the Sachsenhausen case above.

---

[155] HC 9 (1968–9); HC 350 (1967–8), and see G Marshall [1973] PL 32.

[156] Report of PCA for 1993, HC 290 (1993–4), p 4.

[157] HC 54 (1967–8); HC 258 (1967–8); G K Fry [1970] PL 336; Gregory and Hutchesson (note 122), ch 11.

[158] HC Deb, 5 February 1968, cols 105–17.

[159] Ch 30 C.

[160] See PCA, HC 76 (1989–90); HC 671 (1987–8) (the Le Quesne report); HC 99 (1989–90); and R Gregory and G Drewry [1991] PL 192, 408.

[161] HC 76 (1989–90), para 8.12.

[162] *Yuen-Kun Yeu v A-G of Hong Kong* [1988] AC 175 and *Davis v Radcliffe* [1990] 2 All ER 536; ch 31 A.

In 2000, the Ministry of Defence announced an *ex gratia* scheme for compensating British military and civilian persons interned by the Japanese during World War Two. Professor Hayward, a British citizen who had been interned as a boy, was refused payment because neither he, his parents nor grandparents had been born in the United Kingdom. The Ombudsman (Ann Abraham) found that the MoD embarked on the scheme before it had worked out the rules of eligibility; it had developed new criteria after payments had begun without checking that they were compatible with those already used; and it could not show that the scheme had been administered correctly. She recommended that the government should apologise to those affected, review operation of the scheme and reconsider the claims of Hayward and others so placed. The MoD agreed to apologise, but refused to review the scheme or to reconsider. It was only when the Commons Committee on Public Administration called the Minister for Veterans from the MoD to give evidence that the MoD began a review – having just 'discovered' that inconsistent criteria had been used.[163] Three months later, the MoD widened the scheme to include British citizens with 20 years' residence in the United Kingdom.

At one time, the services of the Ombudsman had little publicity and were under-used. During the 1990s, the number of complaints made rose from 801 in 1991 to a record figure of 1,933 in 1996 before falling back slightly. In 2000–1, 1,721 new complaints were received and the Ombudsman disposed of 1,787 cases.[164] Since then, the level of complaints has risen, although recent statistics are difficult to compare with earlier years. In 2008–9, the Parliamentary Ombudsman received over 7,600 inquiries, relating to nearly 8,000 complaints against government departments and other public bodies. These included nearly 2,700 (34% of the total) against the Department for Work and Pensions, nearly 2,200 (27%) against Revenue and Customs, over 800 (10%) against the Home Office and nearly 750 (9%) against the Ministry of Justice. The great majority of these complaints were rejected as being not properly made, 'out of remit' or premature, and others were concluded by means of an informal intervention with the department. Only 210 were accepted for investigation (much fewer than in 2007–08): these included 76 against Work and Pensions, 66 against the Home Office, 24 against Revenue and Customs, and 18 against the Ministry of Justice. Of the investigations reported during the year, 60% of complaints were fully or partially upheld, but this percentage ranged from the Home Office (96% of 25 reports), Work and Pensions (75% of 80 reports), and Justice (63% of 19 reports) to Revenue and Customs (40% of 113 reports).[165]

When there has been maladministration causing loss or other harm to the individual, the department will often pay *ex gratia* compensation, as in the Barlow Clowes affair. For instance, someone who loses social security benefits because of incorrect advice from an official should receive the amount of benefit lost, together with interest. In a case in 2005, which the Ombudsman investigated jointly with the Local Government Ombudsman, the Department of Transport and a county council were both held to have been at fault: it was recommended that each authority should pay compensation of £100,000 to the complainants.[166]

As we have seen, the Ombudsman may not compel a department to provide a remedy; but where injustice caused by maladministration has not been remedied, she may lay a report before Parliament (s 10(3)). The first such report in 1978 led to a government decision to introduce legislation enabling the injustice to be remedied.[167] In 1995, a second report resulted from the government's refusal to accept that the Department of Transport had acted wrongly over the

---

[163] See *A Debt of Honour*, HC 324 (2005–6); and HC 735 (2005–6). See also *R (Association of British Civilian Internees in the Far East) v Defence Secretary* [2003] EWCA Civ 473, [2003] QB 1397; R Kirkham (2006) 69 MLR 792.

[164] Report of PCA for 2000–1 (HC 5 (2001–2)).

[165] Figures derived from the report of the Parliamentary and Health Service Ombudsman for 2008–9. Health service figures have been omitted.

[166] See HC 475 (2005–6). This followed the judicial review of earlier reports by the Ombudsman: see note 136 above.

[167] HC 598 (1977–8); Local Government, Planning and Land Act 1980, s 113; [1982] PL at pp 61–3.

planned Channel Tunnel rail link and the blight this caused to properties in Kent.[168] In 1997, the department adopted a scheme for compensating certain owners which the Ombudsman considered acceptable.

More recently, three such reports have been issued, dealing respectively with the 'debt of honour' owed to British citizens held in detention by the Japanese during the Second World War,[169] the failure to remedy the injustice caused to many pensioners in the Equitable Life affair,[170] and the failure to remedy injustice caused to small farmers by the Rural Benefits Agency's poor administration of the Single Payment Scheme 2005.[171] The 1967 Act plainly left decisions as to provision of a remedy to the political process, but it would be cause for concern if it became frequent for governments to refuse to give effect to the Ombudsman's reports.

Other special reports are issued to Parliament by the Ombudsman from time to time to deal with matters with important implications for many individuals that have been referred to her by many MPs.[172] Reports such as these demonstrate the contribution that the Ombudsman's work on complaints of poor administration can make to the encouragement of good administration.[173]

Other Ombudsmen in the public sector[174]

The ombudsman model has been applied in other areas of government. Although complaints about the NHS were excluded from the remit of the Parliamentary Ombudsman, a scheme of Health Service Ombudsmen for England, Wales and Scotland was later introduced.[175] Complaints about health authorities, NHS trusts and other bodies may be referred directly to the Ombudsman by a member of the public. There is no 'MP filter', but complaints must be first raised with the appropriate NHS body. In 1996, the scope of NHS complaints was enlarged to include complaints in respect of primary health functions such as general medical and dental services, and by the removal of a statutory bar which had prevented the Ombudsman from investigating complaints about clinical judgement.[176] From 2004 to 2009, complainants who were not satisfied with the initial answer that they received had to notify them for review to the Healthcare Commission. In April 2009, this body was abolished and complaints by way of review now come to the Health Service Ombudsman. The Parliamentary Ombudsman was formerly appointed Health Service Ombudsman in Scotland and Wales as well as in England. Today, as the health service is devolved in Scotland and Wales, NHS complaints in those countries are handled by the Scottish and Welsh Ombudsmen respectively. Although the legislation remains separate, the present Ombudsman organises her resources as a single office, producing a composite annual report.[177] As Health Service Ombudsman, she has published special reports dealing with the problems of NHS funding for long-term care of elderly and disabled people.[178]

---

[168] HC 193 (1994–5); report of PCA for 1995, HC 296 (1995–6), pp 42–5. Also HC 270 and 819 (1994–5) and HC 453 (1996–7); R James and D Longley [1996] PL 38.

[169] See note 163 above.

[170] See the Ombudsman's reports, HC 324 (2005–6) and HC 435 (2008–9). Also earlier reports HC 809 (2002–3) and HC 413 (2004–5). On the use of special reports, see R Kirkham [2005] PL 740.

[171] See HC 81 (2009–10).

[172] See e.g. the report on the UK Border Agency (*Fast and Fair?*), HC 329, 2009–10.

[173] See the Ombudsman's *Principles of Good Administration, Principles of Good Complaint Handling*, and *Principles for Remedy* (revised, 2009).

[174] See Seneviratne, *Ombudsmen: Public Services and Administrative Justice*.

[175] See the consolidating Health Service Commissioners Act 1993.

[176] Health Service Commissioners (Amendment) Act 1996.

[177] HC 348 (2005–6).

[178] See HC 399 (2002–3) and HC 144 (2004–5).

As far as local government is concerned, there is a Commission for Local Administration in England (of which the Parliamentary Ombudsman is an *ex officio* member).[179] The scheme resembles the Parliamentary Ombudsman model, but with differences. Individuals may complain to one of the three Local Government Ombudsmen regarding maladministration by local authorities, joint boards, police authorities and other bodies, and (since 2008) concerning failures in service and failures to provide a service. Since 1988, it has been possible to complain either directly to an Ombudsman or by referring the matter to a member of the body in question; but before the Ombudsman may investigate, the complaint must have been brought to the notice of the authority in question. The complainant must specify the conduct which he or she considers to be maladministration, or at least identify the matter giving rise to complaint.[180] Certain matters are excluded from investigation, for instance complaints about action which affects all or most of the inhabitants in the local area. As with the Parliamentary Ombudsman, the local Ombudsman has no means of compelling the provision of a remedy, but a council has power to pay compensation where the Ombudsman reports in favour of a complaint.[181] If no satisfactory response is made by the council to the Ombudsman's first report, he or she may issue a second report that recommends the action to be taken, including measures to remedy a matter and to prevent its recurrence in the future, and (where relevant) to provide a remedy for injustice caused; the report may require local publicity to be given to the affair.[182] A strong case may be made for imposing a legal obligation on a council to provide a remedy in such circumstances.[183]

Although the ability of the various Ombudsmen to cooperate with one another has been enlarged,[184] it would take an exceptional person in England to know how and to whom complaints against officialdom may be referred. Devolution to Scotland and Wales has made possible the creation of an integrated office of Ombudsman in each country.[185] The Scottish Public Services Ombudsman provides a 'one stop shop' to receive complaints regarding the Scottish executive, the NHS, higher and further education institutions, local government and many other public bodies.[186] He or she is appointed for a term of five years, with the possibility of reappointment, and reports to the Scottish Parliament. For Wales, the Westminster Parliament created the office of Public Services Ombudsman for Wales, with jurisdiction broadly corresponding to that of the Scottish Ombudsman, but subject to the many differences in the two schemes of devolution.[187] The Ombudsman for Wales is appointed for a term of seven years, with no reappointment. When a body, such as a local authority, refuses to accept the Ombudsman's recommendation for a remedy, the Ombudsman may certify to the High Court that the authority has failed to take action on the report without lawful excuse, and the Court may then consider what action to take.[188] In both Wales and Scotland, the Parliamentary Ombudsman retains powers in relation to areas of government (such as immigration, taxation and social security) that are not devolved.

---

[179] Local Government Act 1973, Part III, as amended. On the many changes made by the Local Government and Public Involvement in Health Act 2007, see M Seneviratne [2008] PL 627.

[180] *R v Local Commissioner, ex p Bradford Council* [1979] QB 287.

[181] Local Government Act 1974, s 31(3), as amended.

[182] Ibid, s 31(1)–(2H), as amended by the Local Government and Housing Act 1989.

[183] Cf Commissioner for Complaints Act 1969 (Northern Ireland), s 7 (power of county court to award damages). See also HC 448 (1985–6), C M G Himsworth [1986] PL 546 and Justice/All Souls Committee report, *Administrative Justice – Some Necessary Reforms*, ch 5.

[184] See in particular the Regulatory Reform (Collaboration etc between Ombudsmen) Order 2007, SI 2007 No 1889.

[185] See M Elliot [2006] PL 84.

[186] The office was created by the Scottish Public Services Ombudsman Act 2002 (Scotland). Complaints about cross-border public authorities that relate to devolved matters may be investigated.

[187] M Seneviratne [2006] PL 6; Public Services Ombudsman (Wales) Act 2005.

[188] Ibid, s 20.

In April 2000, a Cabinet Office review of public sector ombudsmen in England[189] concluded that the legislation needed a radical overhaul: integrated arrangements for complaints of maladministration should be made for central and local government, the NHS and other bodies. Individuals should have a common right of access to the new-style Ombudsmen. The review was welcomed by the select committee on public administration,[190] but a consultation paper was issued only in August 2005.[191] Instead of primary legislation, for which no time could be found, the outcome was an order under the Regulatory Reform Act 2001.[192] This enabled the various ombudsmen to collaborate fully in investigations, to delegate functions to each other's staff, to issue advice and guidance on good administrative practice, and to resolve complaints informally.[193]

The desire for joined-up Ombudsmen is not easy to satisfy in a simple way, given the increasing complexity of levels of government and forms of public administration. In response to the Citizen's Charter initiative in 1991,[194] some departments appointed so-called 'lay adjudicators' to deal promptly with grievances that had not been dealt with satisfactorily by the officials concerned. Thus the Inland Revenue appointed a Revenue Adjudicator;[195] and the Home Office appointed a Prisons Ombudsman for England and Wales,[196] whose onerous tasks include dealing with the complaints of prisoners and immigration detainees, and investigating the deaths of persons in detention. Further, the European Parliament appoints an Ombudsman to hear complaints from EU citizens of maladministration on the part of European institutions, except for the Court of Justice and the Court of First Instance acting in their judicial role.[197]

Although the ombudsman concept originated as a safeguard against abuses in government, it has spread in a variety of forms to the private sector, with banks, building societies, insurance companies and many others appointing ombudsmen to deal with complaints from dissatisfied customers; their position is generally founded upon contract, but in the case of the legal profession, the Legal Services Ombudsman was created by statute.[198] These processes are outside the scope of this book, but their success will have an impact on the ombudsman model in the public sector, encouraging further progress being made towards prompt, accessible and cost-effective remedies. An important subject which deserves much attention in coming years is the extent to which ombudsmen in the United Kingdom should become a means for ensuring that public authorities respect the human rights of the individuals whose lives they are affecting.[199]

---

[189] Cabinet Office, *Review of Public Sector Ombudsmen in England* (2000) (the Collcutt review).

[190] See HC 612 (1999–2000).

[191] Cabinet Office, *Reform of Public Sector Ombudsmen Services in England* (2005). See M Elliot [2006] PL 84.

[192] See p 626 above; and note 184 above.

[193] See e.g. the valuable report, *Six lives: the provision of public services to people with learning disabilities* (HC 203, 2008–9) by the Parliamentary and Local Government Ombudsmen.

[194] See Cm 1599, 1991; HC 158 (1991–2). Also A W Bradley [1992] PL 353; A Barron and C Scott (1992) 55 MLR 526.

[195] See P Morris [1996] PL 309.

[196] The title is inappropriate, because of potential confusion with the Parliamentary Ombudsman: see HC 33–I (1993–4), p x. See also *R (D) v Home Secretary* [2006] EWCA Civ 143, [2006] 3 All ER 946 and note 87 above.

[197] For the work of the EU Ombudsman, see HL 117 (2005–6). See also EU Charter of Fundamental Rights (2000), art 43 and TFEU, art 228.

[198] Courts and Legal Services Act 1990, ss 21–6. And cf the Judicial Appointments and Conduct Ombudsman, created by the Constitutional Reform Act 2005, s 62.

[199] See N O'Brien [2009] PL 466 for a perceptive discussion of this question.

CHAPTER 30

Judicial review of administrative action – I

Judicial review of executive action is an essential process in a constitutional democracy founded upon the rule of law. Whatever statutory provision is made for appealing against official decisions, it is salutary that all decision makers exercising public power should know that the courts exercise jurisdiction over the *legality* of their decisions, on such matters as the extent of their powers and the proper observance of procedure. Certainly, judicial review is no substitute for administrative or political control of the *merits, expediency* or *efficiency* of decisions; and matters such as the level of expenditure that should be permitted to local councils are not inherently suitable for decision by a court.[1] But the courts can ensure that decisions made by public authorities conform to the law and that standards of fair procedure are observed.

In exercising this jurisdiction, the courts take account of both the legislation that applies to the subject of the dispute and the principles of administrative law that have developed from judicial decisions. The role of the judiciary is first to determine the legal rules that apply and then to decide on the facts whether the rules have been breached. While the background of common law rules does not change overnight, 'Parliament, understandably and indeed inevitably, tends to lay down different rules for different situations'; the judges 'are continually being faced with the need to study, interpret and apply new versions of the rules'.[2]

The legislation that applies to public authorities is made up of many separate Acts, varying widely in the powers conferred, the agencies in whom powers are vested and the extent of protection for private interests. Because of this, judicial review always has a tendency to fragment into disparate branches of law, such as education, housing and immigration law. Yet general principles have emerged from numerous judicial decisions affecting public authorities, and awareness of those principles is essential when specific statutes are before the court.

Judicial review of administrative action involves the judges in developing legal principles against a complex and often changing legislative background. In this dynamic branch of the law, precedents must be used with care. Lord Diplock warned in 1981 that 'judicial statements on matters of public law if made before 1950' were likely to be a misleading guide to the current law;[3] since 1981 changes in the law have continued to occur, as the coverage of government by judicial review has spread and the depth of review has intensified. It was formerly said that judicial review of administrative action 'is inevitably sporadic and peripheral' when set against the entire administrative process.[4] But the general principles which emerge from the judicial process should not be haphazard, incoherent or contradictory.[5]

The legal solution to many administrative disputes inevitably involves the reviewing court in choosing between the merits of the opposing arguments,[6] and the outcome is often unpredictable. Even if the relevant principles are clear, their application to particular facts is seldom clear-cut. Since the court's decision may have a political impact when it concerns the cherished

---

[1] *R v Environment Secretary, ex p Hammersmith Council* [1991] 1 AC 521, 662.
[2] Ibid, at 561 (Lord Donaldson MR).
[3] *R v IRC, ex p National Federation of Self-Employed* [1982] AC 617, 640.
[4] Woolf, Jowell and Le Sueur, *De Smith's Judicial Review*, p 5.
[5] For a perceptive critique of the underlying theories, see D J Galligan (1982) 2 OJLS 257.
[6] See e.g. the acute difference of judicial opinion in the controversial decision of the Law Lords by 3–2 in *R (Bancoult) v Foreign Secretary (No 2)*, p 50 above; and M Elliott and A Perreau-Saussine [2009] PL 697.

policy of a minister or local authority, this may lead to criticism of the judges for political bias.[7] A prominent instance of this occurred in 1981, when the cheap fares policy for London of the (Labour) Greater London Council (GLC) was challenged in the courts by the (Conservative) Bromley Council. Some extravagant language was used by two judges in the Court of Appeal (Lord Denning MR and Watkins LJ) in condemning the actions of the GLC, but that court's decision was upheld in more restrained terms by a unanimous House of Lords.[8] Many cases of judicial review (for instance, in relation to immigration policy or anti-terrorist measures) give rise to political controversy, but it is fundamental that the judges should decide such cases on legal grounds, not for reasons relating to their own political views. Unjustified charges that the judges have their own covert agenda for obstructing government policies have sometimes been made by ministers whose decisions have been set aside. The landmark decision in M v *Home Office*[9] that the Home Secretary (Kenneth Baker) was in contempt of court over the removal from Britain of a Zairean asylum seeker may indeed have had an impact on Mr Baker's political standing: but the decision owed nothing to party politics and everything to what the judges considered should be the proper relationship between the executive, the courts and the individual.

This chapter outlines the grounds on which courts exercise the function of judicial review.[10] Some are of long standing in the common law, such as the rule against bias and the right to a fair hearing; others, such as proportionality and legitimate expectations, are still developing. Before we consider these grounds, three preliminary matters must be mentioned.

First, the foundations of judicial review have been the subject of vigorous scholarly debate.[11] In the background to the debate is the historical growth of public law in an unwritten constitution. The theoretical base for the system of judicial review is difficult to find, given the questions raised by the interface between the supremacy of Parliament and the rule of law.[12] One approach (styled the 'ultra vires' theory) emphasises that the ultra vires doctrine is fundamental to the principles of judicial review; since these principles have developed through statutory interpretation, they depend for their legitimacy on the intention of Parliament. Since Parliament has not prohibited the evolution of judicial review, its intention must have been to authorise it.

By contrast, the 'common law' theory stresses the common law foundations of judicial review. It does not dispute the authority of legislation by Parliament, but argues that the grounds of review are judge-made, have never the subject of comprehensive legislation, and include principles of fair and just administration far beyond anything that Parliament has intended. Further, judicial review extends to non-statutory powers. It is not founded on a fiction of parliamentary intent but is an aspect of the rule of law, a principle that is of coordinate authority with the supremacy of Parliament. In response to this 'common law' theory, a 'modified ultra vires theory' has been advanced.[13] Instead of relying on the direct and specific intent of Parliament, this view attributes to Parliament a generalised and indirect intent that the rule of law should be upheld; thus judicial review may be said to accord with the intent of Parliament.

Underlying this debate are concerns about the supremacy of Parliament, and about the authority of the judiciary should a political crisis develop regarding judicial review. All sides accept that Parliament has authority to legislate on the scope of judicial review, whether to enlarge it or to restrict it in specific ways;[14] but some 'common law' theorists are probably less

---

[7] E.g. Griffith, *The Politics of the Judiciary*, chs 3–7.

[8] *Bromley Council v Greater London Council* [1983] AC 768; and see the sequel *R v London Transport Executive, ex p GLC* [1983] QB 484. Also J Dignan (1983) 99 LQR 605; H Sales [1991] PL 499.

[9] *M v Home Office* [1994] 1 AC 377.

[10] For the procedure of judicial review, see ch 31.

[11] See the valuable collection of articles in Forsyth (ed.), *Judicial Review and the Constitution*. Also P A Joseph [2001] PL 354 and J Laws, in Supperstone, Goudie and Walker (eds), *Judicial Review*, ch 6.

[12] Chs 4 and 5.

[13] See Elliott, *The Constitutional Foundations of Judicial Review*, reviewed by P Craig and N Bamforth [2001] PL 763.

[14] See pp 719–23 below.

willing than the 'ultra vires' adherents to accept that Parliament has absolute authority to exclude judicial review.[15]

The second matter relates to classification of the grounds of judicial review. In the GCHQ case in 1984, Lord Diplock classified the grounds on which administrative action is subject to judicial control under three heads, namely illegality, irrationality and procedural impropriety; he accepted that further grounds (for example, proportionality) might be added as the law developed.[16] In 1986, the President of the New Zealand Court of Appeal commented that 'the substantive principles of judicial review are simply that the decision-maker must act in accordance with law, fairly and reasonably'.[17] This is an admirable summary of the policy behind the law, but a great deal needs to be known about the meaning attached to each of its three strands if it is to serve as a guide to decision making.

The third matter is the remarkable impact of the Human Rights Act 1998 upon judicial review.[18] In brief, by s 3, the Act requires every court, where it is possible to do so, to apply and interpret legislation compatibly with Convention rights. By s 6(1), it is unlawful for public authorities (except where they are required to do so by primary legislation) to act in a way which is incompatible with Convention rights. And by ss 6–7, judicial review is the residual procedure for protecting Convention rights if there are no other proceedings in which the issue of human rights may be raised. Accordingly, the 1998 Act extended the existing grounds of judicial review by a requirement of great breadth and complexity, namely that all public authorities must act consistently with Convention rights.

A. Judicial review on substantive grounds

This section is concerned with grounds of review relating to the substance or content of the official decision or action that is under review; grounds relating to the procedure by which a decision was made are considered in the following section. Although the emphasis is on English law, the principles of judicial review in the law of Scotland are very similar.[19]

The ultra vires rule (excess of powers)

When a public authority is intending to exercise a power vested in it by legislation, it must do so in accordance with the legislation, both as regards the limits of the power and as regards any detailed conditions that must be observed when the power is used. If a public authority acts beyond the limits of the power, its acts are to that extent invalid as being ultra vires. The ultra vires doctrine cannot be used to question the validity of an Act of Parliament; but provides the foundation enabling the court to intervene when a public authority has departed from the legislation. (The ultra vires doctrine also applies to the rare cases in which a government department may be seeking to exercise a power stemming from the royal prerogative at common law.)[20] The simplest instance of the rule is where a local council, whose capacity to act and to regulate private activities is derived from statute, acts outside the scope of that authority. Two examples may be given.

---

[15] See *obiter dicta* by three judges (Steyn, Hope and Hale) in *R (Jackson) v Attorney General* (p 65 above).

[16] *CCSU v Minister for Civil Service* [1985] AC 374, 410; cf 414 (Lord Roskill).

[17] Sir Robin Cooke, in Taggart (ed.), *Judicial Review of Administrative Action in the 1980s*, p 5.

[18] See pages 680–2, 685–6 below. Also ch 19 C, and A W Bradley, in Supperstone, Goudie and Walker (eds), *Judicial Review*, ch 4.

[19] See *Stair Memorial Encyclopedia of the Laws of Scotland*, vol 1, Administrative Law (reissue, 2000); Clyde and Edwards, *Judicial Review*; C Himsworth in Supperstone, Goudie and Walker (eds), *Judicial Review*, ch 21.

[20] See *R (Bancoult) v Foreign Secretary (No 2)*, note 6 above. And see ch 12 E.

In *R* v *Richmond Council, ex p McCarthy and Stone Ltd*, a local planning authority began charging a fee of £25 for informal consultations between its planning officers and developers intending to seek planning permission for new development. The council was required by law to determine all applications for planning permission that were made, whether or not such informal consultations had been held. *Held*, by the House of Lords, while it was conducive or incidental to the council's planning functions that its officers should have informal consultations with intending developers, the fee of £25 was not lawful, since making such a charge was not incidental to those functions. The House applied the principle that no charge on the public can be levied by a public body without clear statutory authority.[21]

In *Hazell* v *Hammersmith Council*, the local authority (as other councils had done) in 1983 established a fund for conducting transactions in the capital money market, by which the council could benefit from future movements in interest rates. These transactions included interest rate swaps, options to make such swaps, forward rate agreements and so on. If interest rates fell, the council would benefit; in fact, rates went up and large capital losses were made by the council. In a second stage of the policy, the council made further swaps, but solely to limit the extent of its losses while extricating itself from the market. The district auditor applied for a declaration that all the transactions were unlawful. *Held*, the council had no power to enter into interest swap transactions, which by their nature involved speculation in future interest rates, since they were inconsistent with the statutory borrowing powers of the council and were not 'conducive or incidental to' those powers.[22]

As these cases illustrate, the powers of an authority include not only those expressly conferred by statute but also those which are reasonably incidental to those expressly conferred.[23] The courts are often required to decide whether a general power to do X includes by implication or interpretation a specific power to do Y.[24] A local council's implied powers do not include what on other grounds is objectionable.

In *Crédit Suisse* v *Allerdale Council*, the council set up a company to provide a leisure pool complex (which was plainly within the council's powers) together with time-share accommodation (which eventually was held not to be); since the council was restricted from itself borrowing the necessary capital, it guaranteed repayment of a loan of £6 million made by the plaintiff bank to the company. The company did not earn enough from selling time-shares to repay the loan. *Held*, the guarantee was void and unenforceable, as the legislation had provided a comprehensive code of borrowing powers. The project was 'an ingenious scheme designed to circumvent the no doubt irksome controls imposed by central government'.[25]

Decisions such as these created much uncertainty relating to the private funding of new developments by local councils. In 1997, Parliament widened the power of councils to enter into contracts for provision of assets, services, goods and associated finance, and authorised councils to certify certain contracts as being within their powers.[26] The rule requiring statutes to be observed applies to all public authorities, but its application in any case necessarily depends on the powers vested in the public body. Government departments benefit from the rule that the Crown as a legal person is not created by statute and has capacity at common law to own property, enter into

---

[21] [1992] 2 AC 48.

[22] [1992] 2 AC 1; and see M Loughlin [1990] PL 372, [1991] PL 568.

[23] As regards local authorities, see Local Government Act 1972, s 111 (as amended). Similar provision is often made for other bodies e.g. Parole Board (Criminal Justice Act 1991, sch 5, para 1(2)(b); and see *R (Roberts)* v *Parole Board*, note 176 below (Board's implied power to withhold sensitive information from prisoner and appoint special advocate to act for him).

[24] See e.g. *R (W)* v *Metropolitan Police Commissioner* [2006] EWCA Civ 458, [2007] QB 399 (whether statutory power at night to 'remove' a person under 16 from a dispersal area to his home included power to use coercion).

[25] [1997] QB 306 (Neill LJ); and see *Crédit Suisse* v *Waltham Forest Council* [1997] QB 362.

[26] Local Government (Contracts) Act 1997: certification does not protect a contract from judicial review, but the court may for certain reasons determine that a certified contract that would otherwise be ultra vires should have effect in law. See also Local Government Act 2000, s 2; J Howell [2004] JR 72.

contracts, employ staff etc.[27] However, a department that is exercising statutory powers of regulation may not use them so as to conflict with other statutes or exceed its powers in other ways.

> In *R v Social Security Secretary, ex p Joint Council for the Welfare of Immigrants*[28] the minister had power under the Social Security Contributions and Benefits Act 1992 to make regulations regarding eligibility for income support. To discourage asylum seekers from coming to the United Kingdom, the minister made regulations that barred certain asylum seekers from receiving income support, although they were entitled to remain in the country while their appeals under the Asylum and Immigration Appeals Act 1993 were determined. The Court of Appeal held, by 2–1, that the regulations would, for some asylum seekers, render nugatory their appeal rights; as they conflicted with the 1993 Act, the regulations were ultra vires.

Nor may a department incur expenditure which does not meet the relevant conditions imposed by Parliament.[29] When a public body's conduct is challenged as ultra vires or contrary to statute, the court's attention focuses on the Act which is claimed to be the source of its authority. But the process of judicial review is far from being a narrow exercise in statutory interpretation. One reason for this is that acts taken under the prerogative or from another non-statutory source may themselves be subject to judicial review.[30] A second reason is that many statutes confer broad discretion on public authorities; judicial control of such discretion, to which we now turn, goes well beyond statutory interpretation.[31]

Unlawful use of discretionary powers[32]

We have already seen that the concept of a discretion involves the possibility of choosing between several decisions or courses of action, each of which may be lawful.[33] However, in exercising a discretion, an official or public body may (intentionally or inadvertently) make a decision or embark on action which the court considers to be unlawful. For centuries, the courts have supervised such decisions.[34] While the court will not substitute its own decision for the decision made by the official or body to whom the law entrusts the discretion, it may intervene where a discretion appears not to have been lawfully exercised. Even if the language of a statute seems to confer an absolute discretion, the courts will be very reluctant to hold that their power to review the action taken is excluded. As was said in a leading Canadian case on the improper cancellation of a liquor licence, 'In public regulation of this sort there is no such thing as absolute or untrammeled "discretion" [by which] . . . action can be taken on any ground or for any reason that be suggested to the mind of the administrator'.[35] The attitude of the courts to claims that a minister has unlimited discretion is shown in *Padfield v Minister of Agriculture*.

---

[27] See *B v Harris* (1992) 108 LQR 626 and (2007) 123 LQR 225; A Lester and M Weait [2003] PL 415. Also *R v Health Secretary, ex p C* [2000] 1 FCR 471 and *R (Shrewsbury Council) v Communities and Local Government Secretary* [2008] EWCA Civ 148, [2008] 3 All ER 548.

[28] [1996] 4 All ER 385. And see *R (BAPIO) v Home Secretary* [2008] UKHL 27, [2008] AC 1003: NHS guidance restricting employment of foreign doctors held unlawful (by Lords Bingham and Carswell) as aim could be achieved only by amending Immigration Rules.

[29] *R v Foreign Secretary, ex p World Development Movement* [1995] 1 All ER 611.

[30] See *CCSU v Minister for the Civil Service* [1985] AC 374; *R v Panel on Take-overs, ex p Datafin plc* [1987] QB 815. And note 20 above.

[31] J Jowell and A Lester [1987] PL 368.

[32] See Woolf, Jowell and Le Sueur, *De Smith's Judicial Review*, chs 9, 11; Wade and Forsyth, *Administrative Law*, chs 10, 11; Craig, *Administrative Law*, chs 16, 17, 19. And see Galligan, *Discretionary Powers*.

[33] See ch 27, text at notes 64–8.

[34] See e.g. *Rooke's case* (1598) 5 Co Rep 99b: '"Discretion" means . . . that something is to be done according to the rules of reason and justice, not according to private opinion.'

[35] Rand J in *Roncarelli v Duplessis* (1959) 16 DLR (2d) 689, 705.

Under the Agricultural Marketing Act 1958, the milk marketing scheme included a complaints procedure by which a committee of investigation examined any complaint made about the operation of the scheme 'if the Minister in any case so directs'. Padfield, a farmer in south-east England, complained about the prices paid to farmers in that region by the Milk Marketing Board. The minister refused to direct that the complaint be referred to the committee of investigation, and claimed that he had an unfettered discretion in deciding whether or not to refer such complaints. *Held*, the minister would be directed to deal with the complaint according to law. The reasons given by the minister for his refusal were not good reasons in law and showed that he had not exercised his discretion in a manner which promoted the intention and objects of the Act. Lord Reid said: 'the policy and objects of the Act must be determined by construing the Act as a whole, and construction is always a matter of law for the court.'[36]

This decision was also significant in that the judges, after examining the reasons given by the minister to see whether they conformed to the Act, were prepared to assume that he had no better reasons for his decision. The willingness of the judges to impose limits upon the minister's discretion in *Padfield* matches the way in which they have frequently cut down the width of local authority discretions. Thus a local planning authority may grant planning permission 'subject to such conditions as they think fit', but the courts have severely limited the apparent width of this power.[37]

The distrust of excessive discretion explains why even the Home Secretary's power to refuse naturalisation to an alien without giving reasons was subject to a procedural requirement of fairness;[38] and why a power to grant what would otherwise be a 'conclusive' certificate may be reviewed if the power is inconsistent with Community law.[39] In the past the courts were readier to accept that executive discretion was immune from judicial review than they are today. A notorious instance of the courts' refusal to review executive discretion arose during the Second World War: in *Liversidge* v *Anderson*,[40] the House of Lords, Lord Atkin dissenting, held that the power of the Home Secretary to detain anyone whom he had reasonable cause to consider to be of hostile origin or association was a matter for executive discretion and that the courts must accept a statement by the Home Secretary that he believed he had cause to order the detention. This is an example of extreme judicial deference to executive decision-making, best explained by the context of wartime, and it has no authority today.

We now consider various grounds on which the exercise of discretion may be reviewed by the courts. In practice, these grounds overlap and a poorly reasoned decision may be defective on several grounds.

1 Irrelevant considerations. Powers are not lawfully exercised if the decision-maker takes into account factors that in law are irrelevant or leaves out of account relevant matters. Thus the Home Secretary acted unlawfully when, in deciding whether it was justified to release from prison two young men who as children had been convicted of murder, he took into account an irrelevant matter (public petitions demanding that the murderers be imprisoned for life) and refused to take account of a relevant matter (their progress and development in detention).[41] A decision to award a council house to a councillor, enabling her to go in front of others on the housing list, was unlawful, having been influenced by the view of the chairman of the housing committee that it would help her to be re-elected.[42] Where rates of over £50,000 had been

---

[36] [1968] AC 997, 1030 (Lord Reid). In *R* v *Environment Secretary, ex p Spath Holme Ltd* [2001] 2 AC 349, 396, Lord Nicholls said: 'The discretion given by Parliament is never absolute or unfettered.'

[37] E.g. *R* v *Hillingdon Council, ex p Royco Homes Ltd* [1974] QB 720.

[38] *R* v *Home Secretary, ex p Fayed* [1997] 1 All ER 228.

[39] E.g. *Case C-222/84, Johnston* v *Chief Constable, RUC* [1987] QB 129.

[40] [1942] AC 206. See R F V Heuston (1970) 86 LQR 33, (1971) 87 LQR 161; Simpson, *In the Highest Degree Odious*.

[41] See e.g. *R* v *Home Secretary, ex p Venables* [1998] AC 407.

[42] *R* v *Port Talbot Council, ex p Jones* [1988] 2 All ER 207.

overpaid to a council on an unoccupied warehouse, the council did not lawfully exercise its statutory discretion to refund overpaid rates when it refused to do so for reasons which disregarded the statutory purpose of the discretion.[43]

The court's power to rule that certain considerations are irrelevant may severely limit the scope of general words in a statute,[44] but the courts do not always interpret statutory discretion narrowly.[45] The converse of the proposition that an authority must not take into account irrelevant considerations is that it must take into account relevant considerations. However, to invalidate a decision it is not enough that considerations have been ignored which *could* have been taken into account: it is only when the statute 'expressly or impliedly identifies considerations *required to be taken into account* by the authority as a matter of legal obligation' that a decision will be invalid because relevant considerations were ignored.[46] Thus there are factors which the decision-maker *may* take into account, but need not do so.[47] While it is for the court to rule whether particular factors are relevant or irrelevant and whether they were taken into consideration, it is generally for the decision-maker to decide what weight to give to a relevant consideration that is taken into account.[48] However, if undue weight is given to one factor, this may cause the decision to be reviewed on grounds of reasonableness or proportionality.[49]

2 *Improper purposes.* The exercise of a power for an improper purpose is invalid. Improper purposes include malice or personal dishonesty on the part of the officials making the decision, but examples of this kind are rare. Most instances of improper purpose have arisen out of a mistaken interpretation by a public authority of its powers, sometimes contributed to by an excess of zeal in the public interest. Thus a city council which was empowered to buy land compulsorily for the purpose of extending streets or improving the city could not validly buy land for the purpose of taking advantage of an anticipated increase in value of the land.[50] In *Congreve v Home Office*, where the Home Office had threatened certain holders of television licences that their licences would be revoked by the Home Secretary if they did not each pay an extra £6, the Court of Appeal held that it was an improper exercise of the Home Secretary's power of revocation 'to use a threat to exercise that power as a means of extracting money which Parliament had given the Executive no mandate to demand'.[51] In *Porter v Magill*,[52] it was unlawful for the Conservative majority on the Westminster council to adopt a policy of selling council houses in certain parts of the city in the belief that home owners were more likely than council tenants to vote Conservative. The House of Lords accepted that councillors are elected and in due course may stand for re-election, but stressed that a council's powers must be used for the purposes for which they were conferred, not to promote the electoral advantage of a political party.

Difficulty arose in an earlier case from Westminster when the council was motivated both by lawful and unlawful purposes.

---

[43] *R v Tower Hamlets Council, ex p Chetnik Developments Ltd* [1988] AC 858.

[44] See e.g. *Mixnam's Properties Ltd v Chertsey UDC* [1965] AC 735 (G Ganz (1964) 27 MLR 611).

[45] E.g. *Roberton v Environment Secretary* [1976] 1 All ER 689 (risk of assassination of Prime Minister relevant to diversion of footpath on Chequers Estate); *R v Westminster Council, ex p Monahan* [1990] 1 QB 87 (relevant to permission for office development near Covent Garden that profits would fund improvements in opera house).

[46] *CREEDNZ Inc v Governor-General* [1981] 1 NZLR 172, 183 (Cooke J) (emphasis supplied), approved in *Re Findlay* [1985] AC 318, 333.

[47] See *R v Somerset CC, ex p Fewings* [1995] 3 All ER 20, at 32 (Simon Brown LJ). (By 2–1, ban on hunting deer on council's land held unlawful as council had not based ban on its powers of land management; but belief that deer hunting was cruel was not necessarily irrelevant.)

[48] *Tesco Stores v Environment Secretary* [1995] 2 All ER 636; *R v Cambridge Health Authority, ex p B* [1995] 2 All ER 129.

[49] See pp 679–82 below.

[50] *Municipal Council of Sydney v Campbell* [1925] AC 338. In *Crédit Suisse v Allerdale Council* (above), the scheme was designed to evade a statutory borrowing restriction.

[51] [1976] QB 629, 662 (Geoffrey Lane LJ).

[52] [2001] UKHL 67, [2002] 2 AC 357. See also *R v Lewisham Council, ex p Shell UK Ltd* [1988] 1 All ER 938.

> The Westminster Corporation was empowered to provide public conveniences but not pedestrian subways. Underground conveniences were designed so that the subway leading to them provided a means of crossing a busy street. It was sought to stop the scheme on the ground that the real object was the provision of a crossing and not public conveniences. The court refused to intervene. 'It is not enough to show that the corporation contemplated that the public might use the subway as a means of crossing the street. In order to make out a case of bad faith, it must be shown that the corporation constructed the subway as a means of crossing the street under colour and pretence of providing public conveniences not really wanted.'[53]

In such cases a distinction has sometimes been drawn between purpose and motive, so that where an exercise of power fulfils the purposes for which the power was given, it matters not that those exercising it were influenced by an extraneous motive. But the motive–purpose distinction is difficult to maintain and several other tests have been applied, including the test of what was the dominant purpose or the rather stricter rule, already outlined, that the presence of any extraneous or irrelevant considerations invalidates the decision.[54]

3 Error of law. An authority which is entrusted with a discretion must direct itself properly on the law or its decision may be declared invalid.

> In *R v Home Secretary, ex p Venables*, the Home Secretary increased from 10 to 15 years the 'tariff period' which two young murderers would have to serve before being considered for release. The Home Secretary stated that young offenders sentenced to detention during Her Majesty's pleasure would be dealt with on the same basis as adult offenders on whom mandatory life sentences had been imposed. *Held*, by 3–2, the Home Secretary by this statement misdirected himself in law. 'His legal premise was wrong: the two sentences are different. A sentence of detention during Her Majesty's pleasure requires the Home Secretary to decide from time to time ... whether detention is still justified. The Home Secretary misunderstood his duty. This misdirection by itself renders his decision unlawful.'[55]

So too, when a county council decided to ban deer hunting over its land, but without considering the extent of its powers, the policy was quashed.[56] Decisions such as these illustrate Lord Diplock's statement that 'the decision-maker must understand correctly the law that regulates his decision-making power and must give effect to it'.[57]

The notion of error of law goes wider than a mere mistake of statutory interpretation. A minister commits an error of law if (inter alia) he or she acts when there is no evidence to support the action or comes to a conclusion to which, on the evidence, he or she could not reasonably have come.[58] These principles were highlighted in 1976 when a Labour Secretary of State and a Conservative council clashed over the re-organisation of secondary education.

> Under a power now contained in s 496 of the Education Act 1996, if the Secretary of State was satisfied that an education authority was proposing to act unreasonably, he or she could issue such directions to the authority as appeared expedient. When in May 1976 the newly elected Tameside council proposed, contrary to an earlier plan, to continue selection for entry to five grammar schools in the coming September, the Secretary of State directed the council to adhere to the earlier plan. The House of Lords refused to enforce this direction, holding that it was valid only if the Secretary of State had been satisfied that no reasonable authority could act as the council was proposing to. 'Unreasonable' in s 68 did not mean conduct which the Secretary of State thought was wrong. On the facts, there was no material on which the Secretary of State

---

[53] *Westminster Corpn v London and North Western Railway Co* [1905] AC 426, 432 (Lord Macnaghten); cf *Webb v Minister of Housing* [1965] 2 All ER 193.

[54] Woolf, Jowell and Le Sueur, *De Smith's Judicial Review*, pp 276–80.

[55] *R v Home Secretary, ex p Venables* [1998] AC 407, 518–19 (Lord Steyn).

[56] *R v Somerset CC, ex p Fewings* [1995] 3 All ER 20.

[57] *Council of Civil Service Unions v Minister for the Civil Service* [1985] AC 374, 408.

[58] *Edwards v Bairstow* [1956] AC 14; applied to ministers' decisions in *Coleen Properties Ltd v Minister of Housing* [1971] 1 All ER 1049. On error of law generally, see J Beatson (1984) 4 OJLS 22. See also note 130 below.

could have been satisfied that the council was acting unreasonably. He must therefore have misdirected himself as to the grounds on which he could act.[59]

Reliance on error of law as a ground for controlling discretion places the courts in a position of strength vis-à-vis the administration since it is peculiarly for the courts to identify errors of law. As the *Tameside* case indicated, error of law is a sufficiently pliable concept to enable the judges, if they feel it is necessary, to make a very close scrutiny of the reasons for a decision and the facts on which it was based. Moreover, as we shall see later in this chapter, there is now a general rule that a tribunal which makes an error of law in reaching a decision must be held to be exceeding its jurisdiction.

4 Unauthorised delegation. A body to which the exercise of discretion has been entrusted by statute may not delegate the exercise of that discretion to another person or body unless the statute can be read as having authorised such delegation. In general, a statute that authorises one level of delegation does not thereby authorise further delegation. In *Barnard* v *National Dock Labour Board*, the national board lawfully delegated disciplinary functions over registered dockers to local boards; a local board acted unlawfully when it sub-delegated the power to suspend dockers to the port manager.[60]

The rule against unauthorised delegation of powers might seem to require all powers vested in a minister to be exercised by him or her personally. However, in the case of central government the courts have accepted that powers and duties conferred on a minister may properly be exercised by officials for whom the minister is responsible to Parliament or by a junior minister.[61] Accordingly, information available to officials advising a minister is deemed to be information taken into account by the minister.[62] But where a statutory duty is vested in one minister, he or she may not adopt a policy by which the decision is effectively made by another minister.[63] And, where a discretion is vested in a subordinate officer, it may not be taken away by orders from a superior.[64] Similar principles apply to statutory agencies. Thus the Police Complaints Board could not adopt a rule of taking no action on complaints which the Director of Public Prosecutions had decided should not lead to criminal proceedings;[65] but the Commission for Racial Equality could delegate to its staff the task of conducting formal investigations into alleged discrimination.[66] In local government, there is now wide authority for councils to delegate their functions to committees, sub-committees and officers.[67]

5 Discretion may not be fettered. The powers of public bodies typically include making discretionary decisions, whether in granting a benefit sought by an individual – be it planning permission, a licence, or admission to a school – or imposing a penalty (such as revoking a licence or excluding a pupil for misconduct). In law, the decision-maker must consider the matter 'on its merits', taking into account all relevant circumstances. It is impossible to assess the merits of an

---

[59] *Education Secretary* v *Tameside Council* [1977] AC 1014 (D Bull (1987) 50 MLR 307).

[60] [1953] 2 QB 18. And e.g. *Young* v *Fife Regional Council* 1986 SLT 331.

[61] *Carltona Ltd* v *Commissioners of Works* [1943] 2 All ER 560; *Re Golden Chemical Products* [1976] Ch 300. See also *R v Home Secretary, ex p Oladehinde* [1991] 1 AC 254; D Lanham (1984) 100 LQR 587; *R v Home Secretary, ex p Doody* [1994] 1 AC 531, 566 (power of Home Secretary to determine penal element of life sentence for murder); and ch 13 D.

[62] *National Association of Health Stores* v *Health Secretary* [2003] EWHC Admin 3133.

[63] *Lavender & Son Ltd* v *Minister of Housing* [1970] 3 All ER 871, distinguished in *Audit Commission* v *Ealing Council* [2005] EWCA Civ 556; J Braier [2005] JR 216.

[64] *Simms Motor Units Ltd* v *Minister of Labour* [1946] 2 All ER 201.

[65] *R v Police Complaints Board, ex p Madden* [1983] 2 All ER 353.

[66] *R v Commission for Racial Equality, ex p Cottrell & Rothon* [1980] 3 All ER 265. Cf *Financial Ombudsman Service* v *Heather Moor and Edgecomb Ltd* [2008] EWCA Civ 643, [2009] 1 All ER 328.

[67] Local Government Act 1972, s 101.

individual case without considering general matters, such as relevant standards, current policies and decisions made in other cases. Legislation may indeed prevent the decision-maker from exercising any discretion,[68] but if the law provides for the exercise of discretion, this must not be prejudged or fettered by a binding rule. The decision-maker may adopt a general policy and indicate that it will be applied in the absence of exceptional circumstances,[69] but may not have a rule that certain applications will always be refused.[70]

These principles apply to the exercise of discretionary powers vested in government departments, but departments cannot function effectively unless they formulate policies as to how a particular discretion will be exercised. Such policies may not be treated as binding rules.

> Under a scheme for discretionary investment grants to industry, the Board of Trade applied a rule that grants could not be paid in respect of items costing less than £25 and refused to pay a grant to a firm which had spent over £4 million on gas cylinders costing £20 each: the House of Lords accepted that the department was entitled to make such a rule or policy, provided that it was prepared to listen to arguments for the exercise of individual discretion.[71]

In such a case, individuals may find it very difficult to persuade officials that they should receive preferential treatment. Their right might be more realistically described as a right to ask that the general policy should be changed.[72] Good administration would seem to require that public authorities should be able to adopt definite policies without this interfering with the proper exercise of discretion.[73] Where, for instance, a discretionary scheme of making educational awards is subject to financial constraints, it may be very difficult for the decision-maker to treat all individual applications fairly and keep within budget.[74] Public authorities that have adopted policies must take steps to see that they are applied consistently, and must bring them to the notice of the actual decision makers.[75] A government department that is unable to make known a policy to guide its staff in decision-making cannot be working efficiently.[76]

6 *Breach of a local authority's financial duties.* One ground of review in local government law that has caused much controversy is that councils are expected to observe standards of financial responsibility to local taxpayers. In *Roberts* v *Hopwood*, the House of Lords held invalid a decision by the Poplar council in 1923 to pay a minimum wage of £4 per week to all adult employees, regardless of the work which they did, their sex and the falling cost of living; the judges considered that the council had exceeded its power to pay such wages as it saw fit, by making gifts or gratuities to its staff.[77] Sixty years later, the principle that local authorities owe a fiduciary duty to their ratepayers in financial management was prominent in *Bromley Council* v *Greater London Council*.[78] The House of Lords held that the GLC must exercise its powers in relation to London

---

[68] As in *Security Industry Authority* v *Stewart* [2007] EWHC 2338 (Admin), [2008] 2 All ER 1003.

[69] See e.g. *R* v *Home Secretary, ex p P and Q* [2001] 2 FLR 383 (policy of allowing mothers in prison to keep babies with them under the age of 18 months).

[70] *R* v *Port of London Authority, ex p Kynoch* [1919] 1 KB 176, 184 (dictum of Bankes LJ). See D J Galligan [1976] PL 332. Also *R* v *Home Secretary, ex p Venables* [1998] AC 407 (discretion fettered by rigid policy of ignoring child's development in prison) and *R* v *Home Secretary, ex p Hindley* [2001] 1 AC 410 (Home Secretary prepared to reconsider decision on whole life tariff at any time).

[71] *British Oxygen Co* v *Board of Trade* [1971] AC 610.

[72] Ibid, at 631 (Lord Dilhorne).

[73] Cf *A-G ex rel Tilley* v *Wandsworth BC* [1981] 1 All ER 1162 and *R* v *Rochdale BC, ex p Cromer Ring Mill Ltd* [1982] 3 All ER 761.

[74] *R* v *Warwick CC, ex p Collymore* [1995] ELR 217; *R* v *London Borough of Bexley, ex p Jones* [1995] ELR 42. The cases are reviewed by C Hilson [2002] PL 111.

[75] *R (Rashid)* v *Home Secretary* [2005] EWCA Civ 744; and see M Elliott [2005] JR 281.

[76] See *R (Abdi)* v *Home Secretary* [2008] EWHC 3166 (Admin), [2009] ACD 22.

[77] [1925] AC 578. And see *Prescott* v *Birmingham Corpn* [1955] Ch 210.

[78] [1983] AC 768.

transport with due regard to business principles; the GLC's decision to cut fares by 25 per cent had caused a big increase in the subsidy payable by ratepayers and a sharp loss in rate support grant paid from central government. The council was thus in breach of the fiduciary duty which it owed to London ratepayers. However, a modified scheme of subsidy for London fares later survived legal challenge.[79] In *Pickwell* v *Camden Council* the court accepted as lawful a local pay settlement made by the council during national strikes which was more favourable to workers in Camden than was the national settlement.[80]

7 Unreasonableness (irrationality). A judge may not on judicial review set aside an official decision merely because he or she considers that the matter should have been decided differently. Judicial review does not provide a right to appeal on the merits of the decision. However, in exceptional circumstances a decision may be set aside for unreasonableness and if this ground for review is raised the court will have the difficult task of considering whether a decision that is otherwise within the powers of the authority may be said to be 'unreasonable'.

> *Associated Provincial Picture Houses Ltd* v *Wednesbury Corporation*[81] concerned the Sunday Entertainments Act 1932, that gave a local council power to permit cinemas to open on Sundays, 'subject to such conditions as the [council] think fit to impose'. The Wednesbury council allowed cinemas to show films on Sundays, on condition that no children under 15 should be admitted to the performances, with or without an adult. Very many councils permitted children to go to the cinema on a Sunday if they were accompanied by an adult. The condition in Wednesbury was challenged by one of the cinemas. *Held*, the condition was neither ultra vires nor unreasonable.

In his much-quoted judgment, Lord Greene MR set out what is now termed the *Wednesbury* test, namely that a court may set aside a decision for unreasonableness only when the authority has come to a conclusion 'so unreasonable that no reasonable authority could ever have come to it'.[82] The judgment emphasised that unreasonableness is closely related to other grounds of review, such as irrelevant considerations, improper purposes and error of law.

The meaning of 'unreasonable' was central to the *Tameside* case, as we have seen. Lord Diplock said there that 'unreasonable' denotes 'conduct which no sensible authority acting with due appreciation of its responsibilities would have decided to adopt'.[83] In the GCHQ case, the same judge made the test more exacting by calling the test one of irrationality: it meant 'a decision which is so outrageous in its defiance of logic or of accepted moral standards that no sensible person who had applied his mind to the question to be decided could have arrived at it'.[84] In 1998, Lord Cooke regretted that some *Wednesbury* phrases had become 'established incantations'; he preferred 'the simple test' of whether the decision under review 'was one which a reasonable authority could reach'.[85]

What can now be seen is that the test of unreasonableness does not apply uniformly to all kinds of decision. There are some decisions (for instance, allocating financial resources to local councils) where the court would intervene for unreasonableness only in exceptional circumstances.[86] By contrast, if fundamental human rights are in issue, as where the life of an asylum

---

[79] *R* v *London Transport Executive, ex p GLC* [1983] QB 484.

[80] [1983] QB 962 (and C Crawford [1983] PL 248). Cf *Allsop* v *North Tyneside Council* (1992) 90 LGR 462.

[81] [1948] 1 KB 223.

[82] On the principles of *Wednesbury* review, see P Walker [1995] PL 556, Lord Irvine of Lairg [1996] PL 59, R Carnwath [1996] PL 245, J Laws in Forsyth and Hare (eds), *The Golden Metwand and the Crooked Cord*, pp 185–201, A Le Sueur [2005] JR 32 and P Walker, in Supperstone, Goudie and Walker (eds), *Judicial Review*, ch 8.

[83] *Education Secretary* v *Tameside Council* [1977] AC 1014, at 1064.

[84] *Council of Civil Service Unions* v *Minister for the Civil Service* [1985] AC 374, 410.

[85] *R* v *Chief Constable of Sussex, ex p International Trader's Ferry Ltd* [1999] 2 AC 418, 452.

[86] *R* v *Environment Secretary, ex p Nottinghamshire CC* [1986] AC 240.

seeker may be at risk, 'the basis of the decision must surely call for the most anxious scrutiny'.[87] In 1996, the Court of Appeal held that an unreasonable decision was

> one beyond the range of responses open to a reasonable decision-maker. But in judging whether the decision-maker has exceeded this margin of appreciation the human rights context is important. The more substantial the interference with human rights, the more the court will require by way of justification before it is satisfied that the decision is reasonable in the sense outlined above.[88]

Despite this significant development, the court upheld the government's policy that banned homosexuals from serving in the armed forces. However, the policy later failed the test of proportionality in European human rights law, because of its effect on the claimants' right to respect for their private lives.[89]

The *Wednesbury* test has often been said to present too high a hurdle in the way of a challenge to official action, and critics have argued that the European test of proportionality provided a better approach to the control of discretion. In 1991, an attempt to get British courts to adopt the test of proportionality was made in *R v Home Secretary, ex p Brind*.[90] The House of Lords held that, without incorporation of the European Convention on Human Rights (and except when rights in Community law were affected),[91] British courts could not review executive decisions on the basis of proportionality. Applying the *Wednesbury* test, the House upheld a government ban on the broadcasting of direct statements by representatives of proscribed organisations in Northern Ireland.

In 2001, Lord Cooke described the *Wednesbury* case as 'an unfortunately retrogressive decision' in that it 'suggested that there are degrees of unreasonableness and that only a very extreme degree can bring an administrative decision within the legitimate scope of judicial invalidation'.[92] Yet decisions have continued to be based on the *Wednesbury* test. The Home Secretary's decision to include Pakistan in a 'white list' of countries in which persecution of individuals was unlikely to occur was held irrational.[93] By contrast, a scheme for compensating British civilians interned by the Japanese during the Second World War was upheld: it was considered reasonable for British citizens who claimed to be required to show that they had a close link with the United Kingdom.[94]

The position of proportionality altered dramatically when the Human Rights Act 1998 came into effect.

8 Proportionality. In varying forms, the concept of proportionality is found in the constitutional law of countries such as Germany and Canada,[95] as well as in Community law and in European human rights law.[96] In outline, if action to achieve a lawful objective is taken in a situation where

---

[87] *R v Home Secretary, ex p Bugdaycay* [1987] AC 514, 531.

[88] *R v Ministry of Defence, ex p Smith* [1996] QB 517, 554 (Sir Thomas Bingham MR).

[89] *Lustig-Prean v UK* (1999) 29 EHRR 548.

[90] [1991] 1 AC 696.

[91] As in the *International Trader's Ferry* case.

[92] *R (Daly) v Home Secretary* [2001] UKHL 26, [2001] 2 AC 532, para [32].

[93] *R v Home Secretary, ex p Javed* [2001] EWCA Civ 789, [2002] QB 129.

[94] *R (ABCIFER) v Defence Secretary* [2002] EWCA Civ 473, [2003] QB 1397. In a later decision, the scheme was held to be indirectly discriminatory under the Race Relations Act 1976: [2006] EWCA Civ 1293, [2006] 1 WLR 3213 (and see p 665 above).

[95] See *R v Oakes* (1986) 26 DLR (4th) 200. For instances from the Caribbean, see *De Freitas v Permanent Secretary of Ministry of Agriculture* [1999] 1 AC 69 and *Thomas v Baptiste* [2000] 2 AC 1.

[96] See M Fordham and T de la Mare, in Jowell and Cooper (eds), *Understanding Human Rights Principles*, pp 27–89; Ellis (ed.), *The Principle of Proportionality in the Laws of Europe*; Schwarze, *European Administrative Law*, ch 5; P Walker, in Supperstone, Goudie and Walker (eds), *Judicial Review*, pp 214–32. For a valuable survey, see T Hickman [2008] PL 694.

it will restrict a fundamental right, the effect on the right must not be disproportionate to the public purpose sought to be achieved. The test applies in respect of European Convention rights, many of which (for instance, the right to freedom of expression) are subject to such restrictions 'as are prescribed by law and are necessary in a democratic society' for specified public purposes.[97] A restriction cannot be regarded as 'necessary in a democratic society' unless it is proportionate to the legitimate aim pursued.[98] If in a given situation there is a need for public action to restrict the right, the restriction 'must be necessary and proportionate to the damage which the restriction is designed to prevent'.[99] Any further restriction is unjustifiable.

One striking effect of the Human Rights Act has been to require the courts to apply the test of proportionality in almost every case when a claim for judicial review is based on an infringement or restriction of a Convention right. The test may be applied in challenges to Acts of Parliament or to the exercise of discretion,[100] and whether the remedy is sought by judicial review or by appeal.[101] In *R (Daly) v Home Secretary*,[102] a prison policy that barred a prisoner in a closed prison from being present while his cell was searched, even when letters between him and his solicitor were examined, was held by the House of Lords to be unlawful on common law grounds. It was also held to infringe Daly's right under art 8(1) ECHR to respect for his correspondence to a greater extent than was necessary. Lord Steyn commented that proportionality was likely to mean a greater intensity of review than the *Wednesbury* test or even the heightened scrutiny test applied in *R v Ministry of Defence, ex p Smith*,[103] but he denied that this meant there had been a shift to 'merits review'.

The fact that proportionality is now a key mechanism in the protection of Convention rights raises difficult questions about the extent to which the courts may substitute their views for decisions taken by ministers, Parliament or, for instance, the broadcasting authorities.[104] Must the courts decide every human rights case by applying their view of what they regard as correct? Certainly the court is required by the Human Rights Act to decide whether there has actually been a violation of the Convention, and must not find that there has been a breach merely because the decision-maker has not used words that refer to the ECHR.[105] But this does not mean that a considered assessment of the implications by a responsible decision-maker must be ignored by the court. In its case law, the Strasbourg Court accepts that states exercise a 'domestic margin of appreciation' at national level. A different formula is needed in national law for defining what has been called the 'discretionary area of judgment'[106] by public authorities that the courts should respect. The notion of 'judicial deference' has been much discussed in judgments[107] and articles.[108] Depending on the context, issues of constitutional respect and institutional competence may arise. When in 2004 the Law Lords held indefinite detention for suspected terrorists to be incompatible with the Convention right to liberty,[109] the decision cannot be said to have been deferential to

---

[97] Art 10(2) ECHR. See *Sunday Times v UK* (1979) 2 EHRR 245; and ch 19 C.

[98] As in *Dudgeon v UK* (1981) 4 EHRR 149.

[99] *R v Home Secretary, ex p Brind* [1991] 1 AC 696, 751 (Lord Templeman).

[100] See, respectively, *A v Home Secretary* [2004] UKHL 56, [2005] 2 AC 68; *R (Farrakhan) v Home Secretary* [2002] EWCA Civ 606, [2002] QB 1391.

[101] On recourse by way of appeal, see *Huang v Home Secretary* [2007] UKHL 11, [2007] 2 AC 167.

[102] [2001] UKHL 26, [2001] 2 AC 532.

[103] See text at note 88.

[104] As in *R (Pro-Life Alliance) v BBC* [2003] UKHL 23, [2004] 1 AC 185.

[105] See *R (Begum) v Denbigh High School* [2006] UKHL 15, [2007] 1 AC 100; *Belfast Council v Miss Behavin' Ltd* [2007] UKHL 19, [2007] 3 All ER 1007.

[106] See Lester and Pannick (eds), *Human Rights Law and Practice*, pp 122–9.

[107] See Lord Hoffmann's criticism of deference in *R (Pro-Life Alliance) v BBC* above, paras [74–7].

[108] Including R Clayton [2004] PL 33, R Edwards (2002) 65 MLR 859, J Jowell [2000] PL 671, [2003] PL 592 and ch 4 in Craig and Rawlings (eds) *Law and Administration in Europe*; I Leigh [2002] PL 265; Lord Steyn [2005] PL 346.

[109] *A v Home Secretary*, note 100 above.

Parliament or the government, even though the context of national security might have called for this.[110]

Failure to perform a statutory duty

We have so far been considering judicial review when a public authority exceeds its powers or misuses a discretion. An authority may also act unlawfully if it fails to perform a duty imposed upon it by statute as, for instance, when a local authority decided not to fund the provision required by children with special educational needs, and left this to be paid for by the governors of the children's school.[111] In that case, a specific statutory duty was enforced, but many duties are more general in character and may not be so clearly enforceable. Thus the Education Act 1996, s 9, obliges both the Secretary of State and local education authorities to pay regard 'to the general principle that pupils are to be educated in accordance with the wishes of their parents, so far as that is compatible with the provision of efficient instruction . . . and the avoidance of unreasonable public expenditure'. This duty was held to require local authorities to take parental wishes into account, but it did not oblige the authorities to give effect to them.[112]

By contrast, under the Education Act 1944, s 8, education authorities had a duty 'to secure that there shall be available for their areas sufficient schools . . . for providing full time education . . .'. In *Meade* v *Haringey BC*, a local authority was faced with strike action by caretakers and ancillary staff and decided that all schools should close until further notice. The Court of Appeal held that parents who suffered as a result of this decision had a remedy in court, and that the council would be in breach of its duty if it closed the schools in sympathy with a trade union's claims at a time when the closure could reasonably have been avoided.[113] However, later decisions have referred to the duty in issue in *Meade* as a 'target duty': 'The metaphor recognises that the statute requires the relevant public authority to aim to make the prescribed provision but does not regard failure to achieve it without more as a breach.'[114] Several recent statutes include statements that express policy aspirations but are framed in terms of legal duty. When charities supporting persons living in fuel poverty claimed that the government was failing in its duty under the Warm Homes and Energy Conservation Act 2000 to adopt a strategy for measures that would end fuel poverty 'as far as reasonably practicable', it was held that the legal duty must be understood in terms of effort or endeavour; and budgetary resources could properly be taken into account in considering what was 'reasonably practicable'.[115] But where a council was bound to provide accommodation for a homeless family that would give them a 'reasonable opportunity' of finding a home elsewhere, the duty did not permit account to be taken of the council's financial resources.[116]

In these cases, judicial review enables the court to give an authoritative ruling as to the nature and extent of the duty in question. The words used in an Act of Parliament may leave it in doubt

---

[110] Cf *Home Secretary* v *Rehman* [2001] UKHL 47, [2003] 1 AC 153, [62] (Lord Hoffmann). And see A Kavanagh [2009] PL 287.

[111] *R* v *Hillingdon Council, ex p Queensmead School* [1997] ELR 331.

[112] *Watt* v *Kesteven CC* [1955] 1 QB 408, applied in *Cumings* v *Birkenhead Corpn* [1972] Ch 12. In 1980, local authorities came under an enforceable duty to respect parental preferences regarding school admissions (and see School Standards and Framework Act 1998, s 86).

[113] [1979] 2 All ER 1016. The duty is now found in the Education Act 1996, s 14.

[114] *R* v *London Borough of Islington, ex p Rixon* [1997] ELR 66, citing *R* v *ILEA, ex p Ali* (1990) 2 Admin LR 822. And see *R (G)* v *Barnet Council* [2003] UKHL 57, [2004] 2 AC 208 (general duty of social service authorities under Children Act 1989, s 17 held not enforceable).

[115] *R (Friends of the Earth)* v *Energy Secretary* [2009] EWCA Civ 810.

[116] *R (Conville)* v *Richmond Council* [2006] EWCA Civ 718, [2006] 4 All ER 917. Also *R (M)* v *Gatehead Council* [2006] EWCA Civ 221, [2007] 1 All ER 1262 (duty to provide secure accommodation for juvenile on request by police).

whether a public authority has a duty or a discretion. Sometimes the word 'may' used in legislation is equivalent to 'must'.[117]

Even if an individual succeeds in claiming judicial review (as a public law remedy), it does not follow that she also has the right (in private law) to damages based on the breach of duty. Thus prison governors must observe the statutory rules made for the conduct of the prisons, but a prisoner affected by a breach of the rules has no right to sue for damages.[118]

The concept of jurisdiction[119]

Our discussion so far of the grounds of review has been phrased in terms of powers, discretion and duties. In many cases, however, use is made of the language of jurisdiction. For historical reasons, as we saw in chapter 27, the concepts of vires (powers) and jurisdiction are closely linked. Often it makes no difference which terminology is used, except that the language of jurisdiction is more appropriate when used in relation to an inferior court or tribunal. Decisions of such bodies were subject to control by higher courts, whether by way of an appeal (if there was one) or by the remedies that preceded judicial review today. Supervision by the higher courts did not provide a fresh decision on the merits, but sought to ensure that the body in question had observed the rules upon which its power to make decisions depended. According to a famous dictum in *R v Nat Bell Liquors*:

> That supervision goes to two points: one is the area of the inferior judgment and the qualifications and conditions of its exercise; the other is the observance of the law in the course of its exercise.[120]

This approach distinguished between the rules that limited the powers of the lower court or tribunal, and the rules that it had to observe in deciding a matter within its powers. Thus a tribunal could be dealing with a matter that was 'within its jurisdiction' but while doing so could make an error of law. For procedural reasons, many older cases were concerned with the elusive distinction between (*a*) an error made by a tribunal on a point of jurisdiction and (*b*) an error of law made by a tribunal 'within jurisdiction'.

Today, the law has fortunately developed to a point at which we need no longer struggle with the concept of an 'error of law within jurisdiction', for the reason that all errors of law made by a tribunal now give rise to judicial review. The recent pages of this history begin with a House of Lords decision that illustrates the difficulties of distinguishing between jurisdictional and non-jurisdictional matters, *Anisminic Ltd v Foreign Compensation Commission*.[121]

> The Foreign Compensation Commission was a tribunal created by the Foreign Compensation Act 1950. It had rejected a claim made by a British company (Anisminic) under a scheme for compensating British subjects who had lost property in Egypt during the Suez affair in 1956. The reason for rejection was that, on the commission's interpretation of the relevant Order in Council, it was fatal to the claim that Anisminic's assets in Egypt had after 1956 been acquired by an Egyptian company, since the order required that any 'successor in title' to the British claimant had to be of British nationality. In the absence of any right to appeal, Anisminic had to establish not only that the commission's interpretation of the order was erroneous, but also that the commission's decision rejecting the claim was a nullity, since the 1950 Act excluded the power of the High Court to review errors of law made within the jurisdiction of the commission. *Held*, by a majority in the House of Lords, the commission's interpretation of the Order in Council was wrong (since the Egyptian company was not Anisminic's 'successor in title'); this error had caused the commission to take into account a factor (nationality of the Egyptian company) which was irrelevant to Anisminic's claim. Thus the commission had exceeded the limits of its jurisdiction and the decision rejecting the claim was a nullity.

---

[117] *Padfield v Minister of Agriculture* [1968] AC 997.

[118] *R v Deputy Governor of Parkhurst Prison, ex p Hague* [1992] 1 AC 58. And see ch 32 A.

[119] Woolf, Jowell and Le Sueur, *De Smith's Judicial Review*, ch 4; Wade and Forsyth, *Administrative Law*, ch 8; and Craig, *Administrative Law*, ch 14.

[120] [1922] 2 AC 128, 156.

[121] [1969] 2 AC 147; and see H W R Wade (1969) 85 LQR 198, B C Gould [1970] PL 358, L H Leigh [1980] PL 34.

The main issue for present purposes is whether *Anisminic* established the rule that *all* errors of law made by a tribunal cause the tribunal to exceed its jurisdiction. On a reading of the speeches in *Anisminic*, this does not seem to have been intended, but in *Pearlman* v *Keepers and Governors of Harrow School*, Lord Denning MR said that the distinction between an error which entails absence of jurisdiction and an error made within the jurisdiction should be abandoned, and that the new rule should be that 'no court or tribunal has any jurisdiction to make an error of law on which the decision of the case depends'.[122]

This position was confirmed when, in *R* v *Hull University Visitor, ex p Page*, the House of Lords held unanimously that *Anisminic* had established that all errors of law made by a tribunal were subject to judicial review 'by extending the doctrine of ultra vires'. Parliament must be taken to have conferred power on a tribunal subject to it being exercised 'on the correct legal basis'; a misdirection in law in making the decision rendered the decision ultra vires.[123]

An important proposition that is not affected by the *Anisminic* and *Hull University* cases is that no tribunal or other decision-maker has power conclusively to determine the limits of its own jurisdiction.[124] Lord Mustill has said that the question of jurisdiction is 'a hard-edged question. There is no room for legitimate disagreement.'[125] What has been called the doctrine of jurisdictional fact arises when a decision-maker's jurisdiction depends on a 'precedent fact' which must if necessary be established by the court and not by the decision-maker.[126] To take the example of the Home Secretary's power to deport an alien when this would be conducive to the public good: if X is detained under this power with a view to deportation and claims that she is not subject to deportation as she is a British citizen, the court must examine the relevant evidence and must decide the matter for itself; on this issue the court is not confined to a supervisory role.

This fundamental principle was re-established by the House of Lords in *R* v *Home Secretary, ex p Khawaja*.[127] The case concerned the power of the Home Secretary to remove from the United Kingdom those who were 'illegal entrants' under the Immigration Act 1971. The House applied the principle that (in Lord Scarman's words) 'where the exercise of an executive power depends upon the precedent establishment of an objective fact, it is for the court, if there be a challenge by way of judicial review, to decide whether the precedent requirement has been satisfied'.[128] On this test, it was not sufficient that the immigration officers reasonably believed Khawaja to be an illegal entrant; his status as an illegal entrant had to be established by evidence before the power to remove him could be exercised. This strict test is particularly suitable when someone's liberty is at stake.[129]

Mistake of fact

Apart from the jurisdictional fact doctrine mentioned above, an attempt to seek judicial review of a decision based on the claim that the decision-maker made an error of fact will generally be met

---

[122] [1979] QB 56, 70. This was supported by Lord Diplock in *Re Racal Communications Ltd* [1981] AC 374, 383.

[123] [1993] AC 682, 701.

[124] The word to be emphasised here is 'conclusively'. When a new claim comes to a tribunal, the tribunal may at the outset have a duty to decide whether it is within its jurisdiction: such a decision may, depending on the legislation, be challenged by exercising a right of appeal (if there is one) and/or by judicial review. For the difficulties of appealing when a tribunal has a very restricted jurisdiction, see *BBC* v *Sugar* [2009] UKHL 9, [2009] 4 All ER 111.

[125] *R* v *Monopolies and Mergers Commission, ex p South Yorkshire Transport Ltd* [1993] 1 All ER 289, 293. Lord Mustill accepted that a criterion on which a body's jurisdiction depends may be 'broad enough to call for the exercise of judgment'.

[126] See R Williams [2007] PL 793 for a re-assessment of jurisdictional review of errors of law and fact.

[127] [1984] AC 74, reversing *R* v *Home Secretary, ex p Zamir* [1980] AC 930.

[128] [1984] AC at 108.

[129] *Khawaja* was applied in *Tan Te Lam* v *Superintendent of Tai A Chau Detention Centre* [1997] AC 97.

by the reply that judicial review does not provide a right of appeal. This is the more likely if there was some evidence for and some against the disputed finding, since the claimant is, in effect, asking the court to substitute itself for the decision-maker in deciding an issue of fact. But suppose that there has been an evident mistake in a finding of fact that is directly material to the decision – for example, a decision based on a statement that is clearly incorrect (such as a planning decision to refuse development on land that is said to be in the green belt, when this has never been the case). Here, a claim for review may well succeed on other grounds – such as taking into account an irrelevant consideration (the false description of the land), coming to a conclusion for which there is no evidence (which is an error of law),[130] unfairness (if the claimant had no opportunity to deal with the issue) or *Wednesbury* unreasonableness. However, in *R v Criminal Injuries Compensation Board, ex p A*,[131] four members of the House of Lords accepted that a decision could be quashed for a material error of fact. Thereafter it was held that a mistake of fact giving rise to unfairness is a separate head of challenge where there is an appeal on a point of law.[132] Related to this is the consideration that if, for the purposes of art 6(1) ECHR, an official decision affects an individual's civil rights, a reviewing court must be able to control essential findings of fact, although it is not required to provide a rehearing on every evidentiary issue.[133]

Acting incompatibly with Convention rights

The Human Rights Act 1998, s 6(1), provides: 'It is unlawful for a public authority to act in a way which is incompatible with a Convention right.' An act for this purpose includes a failure to act – but not a failure to make any primary legislation (s 6(6)). And the act of a public authority is not unlawful if, as a result of primary legislation, the authority could not have acted differently or if it gives effect to legislation that cannot be read in a way compatible with Convention rights.[134]

While issues as to the lawfulness of a public authority's act under s 6(1) may be raised in any court or tribunal proceedings to which they are relevant (s 7(1)), the scheme of the Act extends the scope of judicial review into the broad expanse of all Convention rights, including the right to life (art 2), the right to a fair hearing (art 6(1)), the right to respect for private and family life (art 8) and freedom of expression (art 10). It follows that decisions of public authorities are subject to judicial review and may be held unlawful, even if apart from the Act no such claim could have been made. In practice, applicants for judicial review may seek to rely both on Convention rights and on the grounds for review that are available at common law. In some cases, the human rights claims do not affect the outcome; in others, as we have seen in respect of proportionality, they may be decisive in the claimant's favour.[135]

Judges in the United Kingdom dealing with judicial review must (because of the Human Rights Act, s 2) be prepared to apply case law from Strasbourg even if they consider that case law to be

---

[130] On the law/fact distinction, see W A Wilson (1963) 26 MLR 609, (1969) 32 MLR 361; and E Mureinik (1982) 98 LQR 587. And see text at note 58 above; and *Edwards* v *Bairstow* [1956] AC 14.

[131] [1999] 2 AC 330 (on a matter of 'crucial importance' to A's claim for compensation, Board proceeded on basis of inaccurate police evidence about a medical examination). See T H Jones [1990] PL 507 on the earlier authorities.

[132] *E v Home Secretary* [2004] EWCA Civ 49, [2004] QB 1044. See P Craig [2004] PL 788, and R Williams (note 126 above) who examines the effects of different forms of error of fact.

[133] And see *R (Alconbury Developments Ltd) v Environment Secretary* (p 652 above), esp Lord Slynn at [53] and Lord Nolan at [61].

[134] On the meaning of 'public authority', *R (YL) v Birmingham Council* [2007] UKHL 27, [2008] 1 AC 95 has been reversed: see p 412 above. On the Convention rights, see ch 19 B.

[135] E.g. *R (Wood) v Metropolitan Police Commissioner* [2009] EWCA Civ 414, [2009] 4 All ER 951 (police retaining photographs of demonstrators in breach of art 8 ECHR); *R (JL) v Justice Secretary* [2008] UKHL 68, [2009] 2 All ER 521 (full inquiry into young offender's suicide attempt required by art 2 ECHR).

unsatisfactory.[136] When decisions by a public authority are under review, it does not matter that the authority did not expressly deal with Convention issues in making its decision,[137] for the task of the reviewing court is to decide whether the actual outcome on the facts was a breach of Convention rights. However, a public authority that ignores its obligations under the Act must obviously be at greater risk of its decisions being challenged as unlawful.

Since the Human Rights Act has had such a broad impact on the potential scope of judicial review, a question that arises is whether it is possible or desirable to maintain a clear distinction between judicial review on human rights grounds, and the 'traditional' grounds of review described in this chapter, or whether it is inevitable that Convention rights 'must be woven into the fabric of public law'.[138] In the following section, this question will arise as to the relationship between the right to a fair hearing at common law, and the right to a fair hearing under art 6(1) ECHR.

B. Review on procedural grounds

Although the content of a public body's decision may be within the powers of the body taking it, exercise of the power may be lawful only if the proper procedure for making the decision has been observed.[139] If there is a failure to observe essential procedural requirements, then the decision will be invalid. These requirements are often found in the legislation which confers the power in question. Others are derived from the common law doctrine of natural justice or, as it is now widely known, the doctrine of fairness.

Statutory requirements

Where statute authorises a decision to be made after a certain procedure has been followed, failure to observe the procedure may result in the purported decision being declared a nullity.

> In *Ridge* v *Baldwin*, the Brighton police committee summarily dismissed their chief constable following his trial at the Central Criminal Court on charges of conspiracy; his acquittal had been accompanied by serious criticism of his conduct by the trial judge. Disciplinary regulations under the Police Act 1919 required a formal inquiry to be held into charges brought against a chief constable before he could be dismissed. The committee contended that this procedure did not apply to a power of dismissal authorised by an earlier Act. The House of Lords *held* that the disciplinary regulations applied to the dismissal: 'inasmuch as the decision was arrived at in complete disregard of the regulations it must be regarded as void and of no effect'.[140]

But not every procedural error invalidates administrative action. The courts have often distinguished between procedural requirements which are mandatory (breach invalidates) and those which are directory (breach does not invalidate). This seemingly clear distinction takes no account of whether there has been a total or partial failure to observe the procedure; nor of whether the procedural defect caused actual prejudice to anyone.[141]

In 1979, Lord Hailsham suggested that the courts in this area are faced with 'not so much a stark choice of alternatives but a spectrum of possibilities'. He continued: 'The jurisdiction is

---

[136] See *Home Secretary* v *AF (no 3)* [2009] UKHL 28, [2009] 3 All ER 643, applying *A* v *UK* (2009) 26 BHRC 1 (use of special advocates); see esp speeches of Lords Hoffmann and Rodger ([98]: 'Even though we are dealing with a UK statute, in reality, we have no choice').

[137] See cases cited in note 105 above.

[138] See e.g. Lord Walker's view in *Doherty* v *Birmingham Council* [2008] UKHL, [2009] 1 AC 367, [108–9].

[139] A point made in the quotation from the *Nat Bell Liquors* case, already cited (note 120 above).

[140] [1964] AC 40, 117 (Lord Morris of Borth-y-Gest); and see p 693 below.

[141] Compare *Coney* v *Choyce* [1975] 1 All ER 979 (no prejudice from failure to notify school closure at school entrance) with *Bradbury* v *London Borough of Enfield* [1967] 3 All ER 434 (complete failure to notify proposed changes in composition of schools).

inherently discretionary, and the court is frequently in the presence of differences of degree which merge almost imperceptibly into differences of kind.'[142] In that case, a planning authority failed to notify landowners of their right of appeal to the Secretary of State against a decision that adversely affected them: this failure invalidated the decision. In a later case, the Court of Appeal held that where a required procedure had not been observed, to ask if the requirement was mandatory or directory was no more than a 'first step' leading to such questions as whether there was substantial compliance; whether the non-compliance was capable of being waived; and what was the position if it had not been or could not be waived.[143] In 2005, the Privy Council held in *R v Soneji* that the mandatory/directory distinction was not useful: the emphasis ought to be on examining the effects of non-compliance and on appraising the intention of the legislature in laying down the procedures to be followed.[144] In several cases thereafter, the judges took a more relaxed view of incorrect procedure, so much so that doubts were raised about the value of having rules that need not be observed. Where a fundamental rule of criminal procedure had not been observed, Lord Bingham emphasised that the effect of the 'sea change wrought by *Soneji*' had been exaggerated and did not warrant 'a wholesale jettisoning of all rules affecting procedure'.[145] The reasons why procedural rules exist are so diverse that contrasting decisions are inevitable,[146] but good administration will not be encouraged if statutory procedures can be lightly set aside.

Natural justice

The origin of natural justice is to be found in certain assumptions made in the past by judges about the procedures that should be followed if justice is to be done; those assumptions have led to the emergence of rules, and such rules continue to evolve today. Many aspects of natural justice at common law are reinforced under the Human Rights Act 1998 by the right to a fair hearing under art 6(1) ECHR:

> In the determination of his civil rights and obligations or of any criminal charge against him, everyone shall be entitled to a fair and public hearing within a reasonable time by an independent and impartial tribunal established by law.

The common law rules are generally consistent with the Convention right to a fair hearing, but the two systems are far from identical. On the one hand, common law rules are at the mercy of legislation by Parliament, which may lay down procedures that on any showing are unfair; but under the Human Rights Act, such legislation may be declared incompatible with art 6(1).[147] Also, art 6(1) requires the hearing to be before an 'independent and impartial tribunal', and this enables issues to be raised about guarantees for judicial independence that are outside the scope of natural justice.[148] On the other hand, the European meaning of 'civil rights and obligations' in art 6(1) does not include important areas of public law, such as taxation and immigration, even though natural justice applies to them as a matter of national law.[149]

---

[142] *London and Clydeside Estates Ltd* v *Aberdeen DC* [1979] 3 All ER 876, 883.

[143] *R v Immigration Appeal Tribunal, ex p Jeyeanthan* [1999] 3 All ER 231, applied in *Attorney-General's Reference (No 3 of 1999)* [2001] 2 AC 91.

[144] [2005] UKHL 49, [2006] 1 AC 340.

[145] *R v Clarke* [2008] UKHL 8, [2008] 2 All E 665, [20].

[146] See e.g. *Seal v Chief Constable of South Wales* [2007] UKHL 31, [2007] 4 All ER 177; and *Adorian v Metropolitan Police Commissioner* [2009] EWCA Civ 18, [2009] 4 All ER 227.

[147] E.g. *R (Wright) v Health Secretary* [2009] UKHL 3, [2009] 2 All ER 129 (statute authorising suspension of nurse's right to work but without a prior right to be heard).

[148] See e.g. *Starrs v Ruxton* 2000 JC 208; (1999) 8 BHRC 1.

[149] See e.g. *R (Smith and West) v Parole Board* [2005] UKHL 1, [2005] 1 All ER 755. On the interaction of art 6(1) and fairness, see M Westgate [2006] JR 57; P Craig [2003] PL 753; and A W Bradley, in Supperstone, Goudie and Walker (eds), *Judicial Review*, pp 55–62.

As an unwritten principle, natural justice evolved through the control exercised by the central courts over inferior bodies, such as local justices and the governing bodies of corporations.[150] The rules of natural justice were applied to arbitrators, and to the disciplinary functions of professional bodies and voluntary associations. With the growth of governmental powers affecting an individual's property or livelihood, natural justice supplemented the shortcomings of legislation. Public authorities had to observe natural justice in some of their functions and it was for the courts to decide when this obligation arose. Before considering natural justice as a principle of administrative law, the two main rules of natural justice can be illustrated with examples of how they apply to the ordinary courts.

1 *The rule against bias.* The essence of a fair judicial decision is that it has been made by an impartial judge. This has been the subject of many decisions at common law, to which can now be added decisions of the European Court of Human Rights, interpreting the right under art 6(1) ECHR to a determination by an 'independent and impartial tribunal'.[151] The main rule against bias[152] is that a judge may be disqualified from acting in a case on two grounds, the first being where he or she has a direct pecuniary interest, however small, in the subject matter of the case; thus a judge who is a shareholder in a company appearing as a litigant must decline to hear the case, except with consent of the parties.[153] The automatic disqualification of a judge also applies where there is no financial interest, but the decision of the case between the parties would affect the promotion of a cause by one party with which the judge is closely involved.[154] This situation arose when, as one of five Law Lords who heard an appeal concerning General Pinochet's extradition, Lord Hoffmann was director of a charity associated with Amnesty International, that had argued at the appeal in support of the extradition and was thus in the position of being a party to the case. The judge's involvement with the charity was not disclosed during the hearing. It was held that the decision could not stand and the appeal was heard again by a different panel of Law Lords.[155]

Secondly, apart from a pecuniary interest or identification with one of the parties, a judge is disqualified when (in Lord Hope's words) *'the fair-minded and informed observer, having considered the facts* [relating to an allegation of bias], *would conclude that there was a real possibility that the tribunal was biased'.*[156] Under this form of the test, approved by the House of Lords in 2001, disqualification is not automatic but depends on whether an informed observer would conclude there was a 'real possibility of bias' once the facts had been ascertained.

Three comments may be made on the italicised test. First, where bias is alleged, the reviewing court does not have to decide whether the judge was in fact biased, since 'bias operates in such an insidious manner that the person alleged to be biased may be quite unconscious of its effect'.[157] Second, the test acknowledges that 'in any case where the impartiality of a judge is in question the appearance of the matter is just as important as the reality'.[158] Lord Hewart's dictum, that it is 'of fundamental importance that justice should not only be done but should manifestly and undoubtedly be seen to be done', comes from *R v Sussex Justices, ex p McCarthy*:

---

[150] Ch 27; and Supperstone, Goudie and Walker (eds), *Judicial Review*, chs 10, 11.

[151] The leading Convention cases on judicial bias were reviewed in *Hoekstra v HM Advocate* 2001 SLT 28. And see D Williams [2000] PL 45 and K Malleson [2002] 22 LS 53.

[152] *R v Rand* (1866) LR 1 QB 230; and *Wildridge v Anderson* (1897) 25 R (J) 27.

[153] *Dimes v Grand Junction Canal (Proprietors of)* (1852) 3 HLC 759. And see R Cranston [1979] PL 237. Cf *R v Mulvihill* [1990] 1 WLR 438.

[154] *R v Bow Street Magistrate, ex p Pinochet Ugarte (No 2)* [2000] 1 AC 119. For comment on 'automatic disqualification', see A Olowofoyeku [2000] PL 456.

[155] See p 312 above.

[156] *Porter v Magill* [2001] UKHL 67, [2002] 2 AC 357, at [103] (Lord Hope).

[157] *R v Gough* [1993] AC 646, 672 (Lord Woolf).

[158] *Ex p Pinochet Ugarte (No 2)*, at 139 (Lord Nolan).

The acting clerk to the justices was a member of a firm of solicitors who were to represent the plaintiff in civil proceedings as a result of a collision in connection with which the applicant was summoned for a road traffic offence. The acting clerk retired with the bench, but was not asked to advise the justices on their decision to convict the applicant. *Held*, that, as the clerk's firm was connected with the case in the civil action, he ought not to advise the justices in the criminal matter and therefore could not properly discharge his duties as clerk. The conviction was quashed, despite the fact that he had taken no part in the decision.[159]

Third, the test for judicial bias approved in *Porter v Magill* resolves long-standing uncertainty as to whether in establishing bias it was enough that an observer had a 'reasonable suspicion' that a tribunal might be biased, or whether it must beyond this be shown that in fact there was a 'real likelihood' or 'real danger' of bias. On this issue there had been divergence between the English and Scottish courts. An earlier formula adopted by the House of Lords, that sought to lay down a single test for all purposes,[160] was not followed in some Commonwealth decisions.[161] Nor was it consistent with the Strasbourg case law on art 6(1) ECHR, which favours an objective test of the risk of bias in the light of all factors known to the court.[162]

The possibility of bias may arise not only where a judge has an interest in the subject matter or a relationship with one of the parties, but also from matters that mean that he or she is not coming to the case with an open mind, including improper procedure occurring before a decision is made.

In *Locabail (UK) Ltd v Bayfield Properties Ltd*,[163] the Court of Appeal dealt with five cases in which bias was alleged in respect of such matters as a judge's opinions, social relationships and former professional activities. The court stressed the importance of full disclosure. A judge 'would be as wrong to yield to a tenuous or frivolous objection as he would to ignore an objection of substance'; but 'if in any case there is real ground for doubt, that doubt should be resolved in favour of recusal'.[164] There was, however, no room for doubt in a Scottish case, when a senior judge who had just retired but was still sitting as an appeal judge, published a colourful newspaper article in which he referred to the ECHR as offering 'a field day for crackpots, a pain in the neck for judges and legislators, and a goldmine for lawyers'. It was held that the article would create an apprehension that the judge would be biased in presiding over a criminal appeal in which the appellants (convicted of drug-smuggling) were relying on their Convention rights.[165] Questions often arise about the impartiality of members of courts and tribunals, and juries.[166] Situations in which there was held to be a 'real possibility of bias' include the following:

(*a*) a Scottish judge heard a case brought by a prisoner that challenged the interpretation placed on a statute by the government, when the judge had earlier (while sitting in Parliament as a minister) upheld that interpretation as being the correct view;[167]

(*b*) during a lengthy hearing in the Restrictive Practices Court, the economist member of the court asked economic consultants, who were giving expert evidence for one party in the case, about the prospects of obtaining employment with them;[168]

---

[159] [1924] 1 KB 256.

[160] *R v Gough* [1993] AC 646.

[161] E.g. *Webb v R* (1994) 181 CLR 41.

[162] *Piersack v Belgium* (1982) 5 EHRR 169 and decisions cited by Lord Hope in *Porter v Magill*, [99]–[102].

[163] [2000] QB 451. Cf *R v Inner West London Coroner, ex p Dallaglio* [1994] 4 All ER 139 (refusal to resume inquest into *Marchioness* disaster).

[164] *Locabail*, at [21] and [25].

[165] *Hoekstra v HMA* (note 151 above).

[166] *R v Abdroikov* [2007] UKHL 37, [2008] 1 All ER 315; *R v Khan* [2008] EWCA Crim 531, [2008] 3 All ER 502 (circumstances in which police officers, prosecuting solicitors and prison officers may not sit as jurors).

[167] *Davidson v Scottish Ministers* [2004] UKHL 34, [2004] UKHRR 1079. Cf *R (Al-Hasan) v Home Secretary* [2005] UKHL 13, [2005] 1 WLR 688.

[168] *In re Medicaments and Related Classes of Goods* [2001] 1 WLR 700.

(c) shortly before hearing a long commercial case, a High Court judge realised that a principal witness for one side was planned to be a friend whom he had known for 30 years, but he decided to hear the case after ascertaining that his friend would not in fact be called; the Court of Appeal required the judge to recuse himself, even though this would delay the hearing.[169]

But there was held to be no 'real possibility of bias' when

(i) it was claimed that the medically qualified member of a disability tribunal, who had long experience of providing medical reports to the Department of Work and Pensions, would be unconsciously biased because of this;[170] and

(ii) a Scottish judge refused to withdraw from an immigration case concerning a Palestinian asylum-seeker, formerly active in the Palestine Liberation Organisation, who claimed that the judge could not be impartial because of her membership of the International Association of Jewish Lawyers. [171]

In exceptional circumstances of necessity, a judge may have to deal with a case where the law makes no provision for any other person to do so.[172]

2 The right to a fair hearing. It is fundamental to a just decision that each party should have the opportunity of knowing the case against him or her and of replying to this. Both parties must have the chance to present their version of the facts and to make submissions on the relevant rules of law. Each side must be able to comment on all material considered by the judge, and neither side must communicate with the judge behind the other's back. Although the court's rules of procedure embody these principles, the unwritten right to a hearing may operate even in the courts. Thus the High Court could not order a solicitor personally to bear costs caused by his misconduct without giving him an opportunity to deal with the complaint.[173] However, the requirements of natural justice are not invariable: although a party to civil proceedings is normally entitled to know all the material considered by the judge, there may be exceptional circumstances, particularly regarding the welfare of children, when a court may take into account material that has not been seen by all the parties.[174] In a controversial decision, the House of Lords held by 3–2 that the Parole Board (which in some cases must give an oral hearing to a prisoner whose release on licence has been revoked)[175] need not disclose to a prisoner or his lawyer sensitive material directly affecting his release on licence, but could make it available to a special advocate on condition that it was not disclosed to the prisoner or his lawyer.[176] This decision, upholding a practice by the Board that was contrary to the general principles of justice, was the more remarkable in that the Board had no express power to adopt it.

Natural justice and administrative authorities

The rules of natural justice have been applied to many decisions made outside the courts. From those rules has developed what is now a universal rule that public authorities must act fairly in

---

[169] *AWG Group Ltd* v *Morrison* [2006] EWCA 6, [2006] 1 All ER 967. Cf *Taylor* v *Lawrence* [2002] EWCA Civ 90, [2003] QB 528.

[170] *Gillies* v *Work and Pensions Secretary* [2006] UKHL 2, [2006] 1 All ER 731.

[171] *Helow* v *Home Secretary* [2008] UKHL 62, [2009] 2 All ER 1031 (no evidence that the judge endorsed some views expressed in the Association's publications). And see L Blom-Cooper [2009] PL 199.

[172] *Jeffs* v *New Zealand Dairy Board* [1967] 1 AC 551. But cf *Kingsley* v *UK* (2001) 33 EHRR 288; and I Leigh [2002] PL 407.

[173] *Abraham* v *Jutsun* [1963] 2 All ER 402.

[174] See *Re K (Infants)* [1965] AC 201. Contrast *McMichael* v *UK* (1995) 20 EHRR 205.

[175] *R (West)* v *Parole Board* [2005] UKHL 1, [2005] 1 All ER 755.

[176] *R (Roberts)* v *Parole Board* [2005] UKHL 45, [2005] 2 AC 738 (note the powerful dissenting speeches by Lords Bingham and Steyn). On the use of special advocates, see *A* v *UK* (2009) 26 BHRC 1, adopted in *Home Secretary* v *AF (no 3)* [2009] UKHL 28, [2009] 3 All ER 643.

making decisions, and this has contributed to a greater openness in government. Before that rule developed, a court would ask whether in relation to a particular decision there was a duty to observe natural justice (a duty to 'act judicially'). If the power to decide affected a person's rights, property or character, it was more likely to be subject to natural justice; so was a decision made by a procedure involving a choice between two opposing views, in a manner resembling litigation.[177] The essential rules of natural justice (including the individual's right to know the charges against him, and a right to reply to them) applied to the use of disciplinary powers, including such penalties as expulsion, by bodies such as universities[178] and trade unions.[179] The same rules were applied in a classic nineteenth-century decision to action by a local authority directed against an individual's property.

> In *Cooper v Wandsworth Board of Works*, the plaintiff sued the board for damages in trespass for demolishing his partly built house. He had failed to notify his intention to build the house to the board, which thereupon had a statutory power to demolish the building. *Held*, that the board should have given a hearing to the plaintiff before exercising their statutory power of demolition. 'Although there are no positive words in a statute requiring that the party shall be heard, yet the justice of the common law shall supply the omission of the legislature.'[180]

The rule against bias has also been applied to local authorities. When the Barnsley markets committee revoked a stallholder's licence for a trivial and isolated misdemeanour, that decision was quashed. Not only did the committee hear the evidence of the market manager (who was in the position of a prosecutor) in the absence of the stallholder, but the manager was present throughout the committee's deliberations.[181] When the grant of permission for a superstore was challenged by an environmental group because of the private interests of members of the planning authority (only some of which had been declared), it was held that the rules of bias arising from personal interest were not limited to judicial bodies but applied generally in public law, albeit with adjustments for the statutory context in question.[182]

Natural justice and ministers' powers

The older instances of natural justice pre-date the development of modern government, as is evident from *Cooper v Wandsworth Board of Works*. From the late nineteenth century onwards, powers were increasingly granted to government departments, headed by a minister but staffed by civil servants; the powers might sometimes be accompanied by some statutory safeguards against arbitrary action. To what extent can judge-made rules of fair procedure supplement the legislation?[183] And is the rule that no person may be judge in their own cause relevant when the power to decide disputes arising from official policies is entrusted to the minister whose department is responsible for those policies?[184] To illustrate the chequered history of the extent to which the courts could apply natural justice to ministers' powers, we may look briefly at some key decisions from earlier years, before judicial review took the form it has today. In 1915, the House of Lords in *Local Government Board v Arlidge* held that natural justice required little more than the carrying out in good faith of a department's own procedures.

---

[177] See R B Cooke [1954] CLJ 14. Cf *Durayappah v Fernando* [1967] 2 AC 337, 349.

[178] *Dr Bentley's* case (1723) 1 Stra 557; cf *Ceylon University v Fernando* [1960] 1 All ER 631.

[179] *Annamunthodo v Oilfield Workers' TU* [1961] AC 945; cf *Breen v AEU* [1971] 2 QB 175.

[180] (1863) 14 CB (NS) 180, 194 (Byles J).

[181] *R v Barnsley Council, ex p Hook* [1976] 3 All ER 452.

[182] *R v Environment Secretary, ex p Kirkstall Valley Campaign Ltd* [1996] 3 All ER 304. And see Local Government Act 2000, part III , requiring councils to adopt a code of conduct for councillors.

[183] Cf *Wiseman v Borneman* [1971] AC 297, 308 (Lord Reid); *Lloyd v McMahon* (note 211 below).

[184] In the context of the Human Rights Act 1998, this question was raised in the *Alconbury Developments* case: note 133 above.

Under legislation dealing with slum housing, Arlidge, who owned a house that had been declared unfit for habitation, appealed against the decision. The Local Government Board held a local inquiry into the appeal, in which Arlidge took part. His appeal failed. Arlidge then came to court, arguing that he was entitled to see the inspector's report on the inquiry, and to have an oral hearing before whoever it was in the Board had made the final decision. *Held*, that Parliament, having entrusted decision of the appeal to the board, must have intended the board to follow its usual procedures. So long as officials dealt with the question referred to them without bias, and gave the parties an adequate opportunity of dealing with the issues, the board's procedures need not resemble those of a court of law.[185]

Similarly, in *Board of Education v Rice* it was held that in disposing of an appeal the Board of Education must act in good faith and listen fairly to both sides, since that was a duty which lay on every decision-maker. The board could obtain information in any way it wished, but it must give a fair opportunity to the parties to correct or contradict any relevant statement prejudicial to them.[186]

These decisions, particularly *Arlidge*, made it clear that departments need not adopt court-like procedures in deciding questions 'which were more or less of a judicial character'.[187] In cases from the 1930s concerning slum clearance and compulsory purchase, most attempts to apply natural justice to the powers of ministers were unsuccessful. Exceptionally, in *Errington v Minister of Health*, the court quashed a slum clearance order where, after a public inquiry into the order, councillors discussed the issues with the ministry and a civil servant visited the houses without notice being given to the owner.[188] In such cases, the courts accepted that the final decision of the minister could be based on matters of policy, but asserted that the department exercised judicial or quasi-judicial functions at the public inquiry stage.[189]

This approach was called into question in *Franklin v Minister of Town and Country Planning* where, under the New Towns Act 1946, a public inquiry had been held into objections to an unpopular order that the minister had made, designating Stevenage as the first post-war new town. Rejecting the argument that the minister was biased in confirming his own order, the House of Lords held that there was no evidence that the minister had not genuinely considered the inspector's report on the inquiry. The House said that at no stage was a judicial or quasi-judicial duty imposed on the minister: his duty to consider the inspector's report was purely administrative.[190] The decision in *Franklin* was later followed by the Franks report on tribunals and inquiries,[191] which did not attempt to resolve the difficulties involved in classifying functions as 'administrative', 'quasi-judicial' or 'judicial', and instead commended the qualities of fairness, openness and impartiality.

Today, most public inquiries are governed by procedural rules which require high standards of openness and fairness, and which the courts enforce.[192] But such rules have not been applied to all inquiries; and common law rules of natural justice may still be relevant.[193] In *Bushell v Secretary of State for the Environment*, concerning a controversial motorway inquiry, the judges, as they had done in *Franklin*, stressed the administrative character of the minister's decision and protected crucial aspects of the official process from full investigation at the inquiry.[194] A somewhat similar

---

[185] [1915] AC 120.
[186] [1911] AC 179.
[187] See Dicey, *Law and the Constitution*, app 2 (reprinting his influential article in (1915) 31 LQR 148).
[188] [1935] 1 KB 249.
[189] This followed the analysis made in the MPR, 1932; see ch 27.
[190] [1948] AC 87 (criticised by H W R Wade (1949) 10 CLJ 216).
[191] See ch 27, and ch 29A and B.
[192] See ch 29 B.
[193] *Fairmount Investments Ltd v Environment Secretary* [1976] 2 All ER 865.
[194] [1981] AC 75; ch 29 B.

approach was taken when decisions concerning the control and ownership of land were scrutinised for compliance with the right to a fair hearing under art 6(1) ECHR.[195]

The present scope of natural justice

The importance of natural justice in judicial review of administrative action has not been in doubt since the landmark decision of the House of Lords in *Ridge* v *Baldwin*, the facts of which we have already seen in relation to statutory procedures.

> The power of the Brighton police committee under an Act of 1882 was to dismiss 'any constable whom they think negligent in the exercise of his duty or otherwise unfit for the same'. Claiming to act under this power, they dismissed the chief constable without giving him a hearing. The Court of Appeal held that in dismissing the chief constable, 'the defendants were acting in an administrative or executive capacity just as they did when they appointed him'.[196] The House of Lords overruled this view: quite apart from the procedure laid down by the discipline regulations, natural justice required that a hearing should have been given before the committee exercised its power. The failure to give a hearing invalidated the dismissal, and the subsequent hearing given to Ridge's solicitor did not cure the earlier defect.[197]

This decision could have been regarded narrowly as one based on an interpretation of specific legislation. In fact, *Ridge* v *Baldwin* was the first of a group of House of Lords decisions during the 1960s that began to lay the foundations for judicial review today. Especially important was the holding in *Ridge* that the duty to observe natural justice was not confined to powers classified as 'judicial' or 'quasi-judicial'. This enabled the courts to apply natural justice in a very wide variety of situations. In 1970, Megarry J remarked that the courts were tending to apply natural justice to all powers of decision unless the circumstances indicated to the contrary.[198] The benefits of *Ridge* v *Baldwin* spread to many persons, including students,[199] police officers,[200] school teachers,[201] market stallholders,[202] residents of local authority homes at risk of closure,[203] those affected by decisions of self-regulatory bodies[204] and, most notably, convicted prisoners in respect of prison discipline and the parole system.[205] In 1980, on an appeal from the Bahamas concerning refusal of an individual's constitutional right to citizenship, the Judicial Committee held that natural justice must be observed by any person with authority to determine questions affecting the rights of individuals.[206] But natural justice, now more commonly referred to as fairness, is not limited to situations in which private rights are affected, and the courts protect a wide variety of individual interests against unfair action by public bodies.[207]

---

[195] See *Bryan* v *UK* (1995) 21 EHRR 342; and the *Alconbury Developments* case (note 133 above).

[196] [1963] 1 QB 539, 576 (Harman LJ).

[197] [1964] AC 40; and see A W Bradley [1964] CLJ 83.

[198] *Gaiman* v *National Association for Mental Health* [1971] Ch 317, 333 (power to expel members of company limited by guarantee) In *Bates* v *Lord Hailsham* [1972] 3 All ER 1019, the same judge held (in an extempore response to an ex parte application) that a general duty of fairness does not arise in respect of delegated legislation. This is too absolute a proposition to be acceptable today.

[199] E.g. *R* v *Aston University Senate, ex p Roffey* [1969] 2 QB 538; and *Glynn* v *Keele University* [1971] 2 All ER 89.

[200] *R* v *Kent Police Authority, ex p Godden* [1971] 2 QB 662; *Chief Constable of North Wales* v *Evans* [1982] 3 All ER 141.

[201] *Hannam* v *Bradford Corpn* [1970] 2 All ER 690; *Malloch* v *Aberdeen Corpn* [1971] 2 All ER 1278.

[202] *R* v *Barnsley Council, ex p Hook* [1976] 3 All ER 452; *R* v *Wear Valley Council, ex p Binks* [1985] 2 All ER 699.

[203] *R* v *Devon CC, ex p Baker* [1995] 1 All ER 73.

[204] *R* v *LAUTRO, ex p Ross* [1993] QB 17.

[205] E.g. *R* v *Hull Prison Visitors, ex p St Germain* [1979] QB 425 and (the same) *(No 2)* [1979] 3 All ER 545; *Leech* v *Deputy Governor of Parkhurst Prison* [1988] AC 533; *R* v *Home Secretary, ex p Doody* [1994] 1 AC 531.

[206] *A-G* v *Ryan* [1980] AC 718.

[207] Cf *O'Reilly* v *Mackman* [1983] 2 AC 237, 275, 283 (Lord Diplock). For the protection of new social interests, see e.g. *R* v *Norfolk CC Social Services Dept, ex p M* [1989] QB 619.

Fairness and natural justice

The scope of natural justice is best understood against the broad perception that it is the duty of the courts to ensure that *all* administrative powers are exercised fairly, that is, in accordance with principles of fair procedure. It has never been possible to describe the contents of natural justice except in general terms. Today, the essence of natural justice may be explained simply in terms of fairness. In 1994, a challenge by mandatory life prisoners to the procedure for making parole decisions led to the following analysis by Lord Mustill, who derived six principles from the authorities in answer to the question, 'What does fairness require in the present case?':

> (1) Where an Act of Parliament confers an administrative power there is a presumption that it will be exercised in a manner which is fair in all the circumstances. (2) The standards of fairness are not immutable. They may change with the passage of time, both in the general and in their application to decisions of a particular type. (3) The principles of fairness are not to be applied by rote identically in every situation. What fairness demands is dependent on the context of the decision, and this is to be taken into account in all its aspects. (4) An essential feature of the context is the statute which creates the discretion, as regards both its language and the shape of the legal and administrative system within which the decision is taken. (5) Fairness will very often require that a person who may be adversely affected by the decision will have an opportunity to make representations on his own behalf, either before the decision is taken, with a view to producing a favourable result; or after it is taken, with a view to procuring its modification; or both. (6) Since the person affected usually cannot make worthwhile representations without knowing what factors may weigh against his interests fairness will very often require that he is informed of the gist of the case which he has to answer.[208]

The procedural effects of natural justice and fairness

On the basis that a public authority must act fairly in making its decisions, and remembering that fairness is concerned with procedural matters, not with the substance of a decision, what in practical terms must the public authority do? Much depends on the nature of the decision. In a situation where a public office or other benefit is being withdrawn for reasons of misconduct or incompetence, the 'irreducible minimum' at the core of natural justice is (*a*) the right to a decision by an unbiased tribunal; (*b*) the right to have notice of the charges against the individual; and (*c*) the right to be heard in answer to those charges.[209]

In cases where no misconduct is alleged (for example, in the case of school or residential home closures, where parents or residents must in fairness be consulted by the local authority), then (*a*) consultation must take place at a time when the proposals are at a formative stage; (*b*) sufficient reasons must be given for the proposal to permit intelligent consideration and response; (*c*) adequate time must be allowed; and (*d*) the product of consultation must be conscientiously taken into account when the ultimate decision is taken.[210]

Many detailed procedural questions arise to which there are no general answers. In some contexts individuals do not have the right of an oral hearing,[211] but if the body in question has to decide questions as to someone's conduct or competence, the individual is entitled to know what evidence is given against him or her and must have a fair opportunity to rebut it.[212] Regulatory

---

[208] *R v Home Secretary, ex p Doody* [1994] 1 AC 531, 557 (establishing the right of prisoners to be informed of relevant material and reasons for decisions affecting their release on parole).

[209] Lord Hodson in *Ridge v Baldwin* [1964] AC 40, at 132.

[210] *R v North Devon Health Authority, ex p Coughlan* [2001] QB 213, at [108] (Lord Woolf MR). And see *R v Devon CC, ex p Baker* [1995] 1 All ER 73.

[211] *Lloyd v McMahon* [1987] AC 625. Also *R (Smith) v Parole Board (No 2)* [2005] UKHL 1, [2005] 1 All ER 755 (Board need not give oral hearing in every case, but must do so in some cases); *R (Hammond) v Home Secretary* [2005] UKHL 69, [2006] 1 AC 603.

[212] *Chief Constable of North Wales v Evans* [1982] 3 All ER 141.

bodies that expect officials to do preliminary work for them must nonetheless be in a position to come to their own decisions.[213] Where a soldier claimed that he had been subject to racial harassment, members of the Army Board could not decide on the complaint judicially without meeting to consider the matter; and the soldier was entitled to see all the material on which the board reached its decision, other than documents for which public interest immunity was properly claimed.[214] An individual has no universal right to be legally represented regardless of the nature of the proceedings in question,[215] but in some circumstances a body with power to permit legal representation may not reasonably refuse it.[216] No breach of natural justice occurs when the opportunity of being heard is lost through the fault of a party's lawyer.[217]

There is no absolute rule that natural justice does not apply in the case of preliminary investigations, inspections or suspensions pending a final decision,[218] but the right to a hearing is often excluded because of the need for urgent action or because the individual's rights will be observed at a later stage.[219]

Many aspects of procedure raise issues of fairness: thus it may be unfair for a tribunal to refuse adjournment of a hearing.[220] The manner in which evidence is obtained by tribunals is subject to constraints of natural justice,[221] but hearsay evidence is usually permitted.[222] An individual may be entitled to cross-examine those giving evidence against him or her[223] or obtain the names of potential witnesses from the other side.[224] But it is sometimes sufficient that only the gist of allegations against an individual is made known.[225] It was held contrary to natural justice for a commission with investigative powers to make findings of fact that individuals had been guilty of serious misconduct, when the findings were supported by no evidence of probative value and there had been no opportunity to rebut them.[226]

Considerations of national security may seriously reduce the scope for natural justice.[227] The current practice of appointing 'special advocates' to deal with sensitive matters affecting national security enables allegations and evidence to be withheld from the individual. The use of special advocates 'is an attempt to resolve the tension between due process and national security'[228] and this limited way of protecting the right to fair procedure is arguably better than nothing; but the special advocate cannot in the ordinary sense of the word be said to be 'representing' the individual.[229]

Three matters may be mentioned briefly. First, if fairness or natural justice would entitle someone to be heard, a court should be slow to brush aside that right on the ground that a hearing

---

213 *R v Commission for Racial Equality, ex p Cottrell and Rothon* [1980] 3 All ER 265.

214 *R v Army Board of Defence Council, ex p Anderson* [1992] QB 169. And see ch 32 C.

215 *R v Maze Prison Visitors, ex p Hone* [1988] AC 379.

216 *R v Home Secretary, ex p Tarrant* [1985] QB 251.

217 *R v Home Secretary, ex p Al-Mehdawi* [1990] 1 AC 876 (J Herberg [1990] PL 467).

218 *Rees v Crane* [1994] 2 AC 173 (Trinidad judge entitled to notice of complaints against him at initial stage of dismissal procedure).

219 *Wiseman v Borneman* [1971] AC 297; *Furnell v Whangarei High Schools Board* [1973] AC 660; *Norwest Holst Ltd v Trade Secretary* [1978] Ch 201.

220 *R v Cheshire CC, ex p C* [1998] ELR 66.

221 *R v Deputy Industrial Injuries Commissioner, ex p Moore* [1965] 1 QB 456; *Crompton v General Medical Council* [1982] 1 All ER 35.

222 *T A Miller Ltd v Minister of Housing* [1968] 2 All ER 633.

223 *R v Board of Visitors, ex p St Germain (No 2)* [1979] 3 All ER 545. Cf *R v Commission for Racial Equality, ex p Cottrell and Rothon* (note 213).

224 *R v Blundeston Board of Visitors, ex p Fox-Taylor* [1982] 1 All ER 646.

225 *R v Gaming Board, ex p Benaim and Khaida* [1970] 2 QB 417; *Maxwell v Dept of Trade* [1974] QB 523.

226 *Mahon v Air New Zealand Ltd* [1984] AC 808.

227 *R v Home Secretary, ex p Hosenball* [1977] 3 All ER 452; *R v Home Secretary, ex p Cheblak* [1991] 2 All ER 319.

228 J Ip, [2008] PL 717, 741.

229 See note 176 above; also p 600 above.

would make no difference to the outcome.[230] The second matter is whether the failure by an authority to give a hearing to which the individual is entitled is cured by a full and fair hearing given later by an appellate body. No absolute rule applies: sometimes the appeal proceedings may take the form of a full rehearing and this may cure the earlier defect, but in other situations the individual may be entitled to a fair hearing at both stages. In intermediate cases, the court must decide 'whether, at the end of the day, there has been a fair result, reached by fair methods'.[231]

The third matter concerns the legal effect, if any, of a decision reached in breach of natural justice. When a breach of natural justice is established, then on the authority of *Ridge* v *Baldwin* the decision in question is void and a nullity.[232] However, until such a decision is declared to be void by a court, it is capable of having some effect in law and it may be the basis of an appeal to a higher body.[233]

Does fairness require reasons to be given?

Although the giving of reasons 'is one of the fundamentals of good administration',[234] at common law there is no general duty to give reasons for decisions.[235] In many situations, legislation requires reasons to be given, whether only if requested[236] or in all cases (for instance, whenever planning permission is refused). Despite the absence of a general duty to give reasons, the courts do often require reasons to be given. Thus, reasons must be stated for a discretionary decision, if a right of appeal is valueless without this.[237] Fairness may require the giving of reasons, because of the impact of the decision on the individual.[238] Thus a prisoner sentenced to a mandatory life sentence was entitled to know the reasons for the Home Secretary's decision as to the minimum period that he must serve. In the leading case, Lord Mustill said:

> The giving of reasons may be inconvenient, but I can see no grounds at all why it should be against the public interest: indeed, rather the reverse. That being so, I would ask simply: Is refusal to give reasons fair? I would answer without hesitation that it is not.[239]

This approach applies to many decisions that closely affect the individual. Moreover, reasons must be given if a decision in the absence of explanation may appear arbitrary, harsh, mistaken or unreasonable:[240]

> if all other known facts and circumstances appear to point overwhelmingly in favour of a different decision, the decision-maker who has given no reasons cannot complain if the court draws the inference that he had no rational reason for his decision.[241]

Even when a statute excluded the giving of reasons for the refusal of naturalisation, the Home Secretary's duty to act fairly was held to mean that he must give sufficient information on the

---

[230] *John* v *Rees* [1970] Ch 345, 402; and *R* v *Chief Constable, Thames Valley, ex p Cotton* [1990] IRLR 344, 352. And see Lord Bingham [1991] PL 64.

[231] *Calvin* v *Carr* [1980] AC 574, discussed by M Elliott (1980) 43 MLR 66.

[232] The holding in *Durayappah* v *Fernando* [1967] 2 AC 337 that failure to give a hearing made the decision voidable and not void was contrary to legal principle: see H W R Wade (1967) 83 LQR 499 and (1968) 84 LQR 95.

[233] *Calvin* v *Carr* (above). And see S Sedley [1989] PL 32.

[234] *Breen* v *AEU* [1971] 2 QB 175, 191 (Lord Denning MR). See also G Richardson [1986] PL 437; P Neill, in Forsyth and Hare (eds), *The Golden Metwand and the Crooked Cord*, pp 161–84; P P Craig [1994] CLJ 282.

[235] *R* v *Trade Secretary, ex p Lonrho plc* [1989] 2 All ER 609; *R* v *Higher Education Funding Council, ex p Institute of Dental Surgery* [1994] 1 All ER 651; *Hasan* v *Trade and Industry Secretary* [2008] EWCA Civ 1311, [2009] 3 All ER 539.

[236] E.g. Tribunals and Inquiries Act 1992, s 10 (certain tribunals must on request supply reasons); ch 29 A.

[237] *Minister of National Revenue* v *Wright's Canadian Ropes* [1947] AC 109.

[238] *R* v *Home Secretary, ex p Doody* [1994] 1 AC 531.

[239] Ibid, at 564–5.

[240] *R* v *Civil Service Board, ex p Cunningham* [1991] 1 All ER 310 (J Herberg [1991] PL 340).

[241] *R* v *Trade Secretary, ex p Lonrho plc* [1989] 2 All ER 609, 620 (Lord Keith).

matters that concerned him to enable the applicants to make such representations as they could on those matters.[242]

Although the courts indirectly require the giving of reasons in many situations, they have not held that reasons should be given for all decisions.[243] A general ruling to this effect is overdue, even if it were accompanied by an exception for situations in which public interest considerations had to prevail over the general rule.

As it is, the procedure of judicial review supports the giving of reasons. If an individual receives no reasons for a decision and obtains permission for judicial review, the decision-maker will be expected to disclose relevant information so that the court can properly decide the claim for review.[244] A court is likely to hold that there must have been some operative reasons at the time the decision was made and will wish to discover what these were; little weight may be attached to reasons created after the decision was made.[245] The court may sometimes accept evidence as to the reasoning of the decision-maker even if it was not explained at the time, but breach of a statutory duty to give reasons with the decision may cause the court to quash the decision for error of law.[246] Where there is a duty to give reasons, 'proper and adequate reasons must be given' which are intelligible and deal with the substantial points in issue.[247] Concise reasons may be enough, but a general formula that does not deal with the disputed issues in a case is unlikely to be acceptable.

European law requires that reasons be given when this is necessary to secure effective protection of a Community right.[248] Where art 6(1) ECHR entitles the individual to a fair hearing before an independent and impartial court or tribunal, the court or tribunal is expected to give reasons for its decision, so that the parties and the public may understand the basis for it.[249]

Space does not permit this chapter to include an account of the extensive case law of the European Court of Human Rights on the right to a fair trial under art 6(1) ECHR.[250] If judicial review of a public authority's decision is sought on grounds of fairness, both the common law and art 6(1) may well be relevant but it must be remembered that the scope of art 6(1) is both wider and narrower than the common law of fairness.[251]

C. Legitimate expectations

A ground of judicial review linked with fairness that has undergone rapid development since the 1980s is that of legitimate expectations.[252] This principle exists in other systems of law (including those of Canada, Germany and the EU)[253] and is an aspect of legal certainty. In their dealings with public agencies, private persons need to know if they can rely on statements by officials or on

---

[242] *R v Home Secretary, ex p Al Fayed* [1997] 1 All ER 228.

[243] See *Stefan v General Medical Council* [1999] 1 WLR 1293. And see Lord Bingham's summary of the law in *R v Ministry of Defence, ex p Murray* [1998] COD 134.

[244] Cf *R v Lancashire CC, ex p Huddleston* [1986] 2 All ER 941 (and A W Bradley [1986] PL 508).

[245] See A Schaeffer [2004] JR 151.

[246] *R v Westminster City Council, ex p Ermakov* [1996] 2 All ER 302. See also *R (Richardson) v North Yorkshire CC* [2003] EWCA Civ 1869, [2004] 2 All ER 31, [31]–[42].

[247] *Re Poyser and Mills' Arbitration* [1964] 2 QB 467, 478. On the adequacy of reasons for a planning decision, see *South Bucks DC v Porter (No 2)* [2004] UKHL 33, [2004] 4 All ER 775.

[248] See e.g. *Case 222/86, UNECTEF v Heylens* [1989] 1 CMLR 901.

[249] *Hadjianastassiou v Greece* (1992) 16 EHRR 219.

[250] See e.g. Harris, O'Boyle and Warbrick, *Law of the ECHR*, ch 6.

[251] See text at notes 147–9 above.

[252] See R Baldwin and D Horne (1986) 49 MLR 685; C F Forsyth [1988] CLJ 238; P P Craig (1992) 108 LQR 79. For an account of the law today, see Moules, *Actions against Public Officials*, chs 2, 3.

[253] Schwarze, *European Administrative Law*, ch 6; Schönberg, *Legitimate Expectations in Administrative Law*; Moules, ch 3.

decisions that have been notified to them. In business and commercial affairs, an individual may hold others to their word when a *contract* has been concluded between them. But decisions like the issue of a licence or the grant of a permission do not usually take a contractual form, nor does a statement of government policy or an indication of future action. When is a private individual entitled to hold a public authority to its word? Is the authority free to change its mind or to disavow an official who has given an assurance that a certain decision would be made? And when a government policy is in place, and private persons have relied on that policy continuing, can it be changed and replaced by a new policy from which they derive less benefit?

Revocation of an existing decision

We deal first with the situation in which a public body has made a *decision* conferring a benefit upon an individual that it later tries to revoke and replace with a fresh decision that is less favourable to her. If the agency took the first decision properly and told her of it, without qualifying it as 'provisional' or 'subject to review', a court will hold that the agency has exercised its discretion and may not alter the decision to the individual's disadvantage.[254] This position is subject to express statutory provision. Thus the social security statutes permit earlier decisions to be reviewed, for example when fresh information is available.[255] Planning permission that has been granted may be revoked, but only on payment of compensation.[256] Apart from legislation, an authority that has conferred a continuing benefit on someone under a mistake of fact may revoke the benefit for the future when it discovers the true position.[257] And when the original benefit was based on a mistake of law, the authority may make a fresh decision based on a correct view of the law.[258]

In a situation not unlike the revocation of an earlier decision, Lord Denning MR in 1969 distinguished between foreign nationals who had to leave Britain when their leave to remain expired, and those whose leave to remain was terminated prematurely by the Home Office: the latter, but not the former, had a 'legitimate expectation, of which it would not be fair to deprive [them] without hearing what [they have] to say'.[259]

When official assurances are binding

The principle of legitimate expectation came into play when the Hong Kong government gave a public *assurance* to illegal entrants into the colony who had come from Macao that they would be interviewed and their merits considered before it would be decided whether to deport them. The Judicial Committee explained why this assurance should be enforced:

> When a public authority has promised to follow a certain procedure, it is in the interest of good administration that it should act fairly and implement its promise, so long as implementation does not interfere with its statutory duty.[260]

For similar reasons, an assurance that confers a benefit on an individual may be enforced, even though the legislation does not provide for this. Where a Nigerian woman (without permanent leave to remain in the United Kingdom) wished to return to her home for Christmas and was given a firm assurance by the Home Office (confirmed in her passport) that she would be

---

[254] *Re 56 Denton Road Twickenham* [1953] Ch 51. Cf *R v Home Secretary, ex p Consuelo* (CA, 3 May 2002).

[255] E.g. Social Security Administration Act 1992, ss 25, 30.

[256] Town and Country Planning Act 1990, ss 97, 107.

[257] *Rootkin v Kent CC* [1981] 2 All ER 227.

[258] *Cheung v Herts CC, The Times,* 4 April 1986; C Lewis [1987] PL 21.

[259] *Schmidt v Home Secretary* [1969] 2 Ch 149.

[260] *A-G of Hong Kong v Ng Yuen Shiu* [1983] AC 629, 638 (Lord Fraser). And see *R v Liverpool Corporation, ex p Liverpool Taxis Association* [1972] 2 QB 299.

readmitted if she came back by 31 January, the immigration officer could not refuse to admit her when she returned before that date.[261]

For an assurance of this kind to be enforceable, the official statement must have been 'clear, unambiguous and devoid of relevant qualification'.[262] In 1985, it was held that when tax officials have given a definite and unqualified assurance to a taxpayer as to what the tax consequences of a transaction will be, the Revenue are bound by it if the assurance would between private persons create a contractual duty or an estoppel.[263] But the ability of the court to enforce such an assurance may be affected by other factors affecting the public interest. In a similar case, where tax officials had told taxpayers that an element in proposed dealings would be treated as capital and not as income, but later dealt with it as income, Bingham LJ said:

> If a public authority so conducts itself as to create a legitimate expectation that a certain course will be followed it would often be unfair if the authority were permitted to follow a different course to the detriment of one who entertained the expectation . . . But fairness is not a one-way street. It imports the notion of equitableness, of fair and open dealing, to which the authority is as much entitled as the citizen. The Revenue's discretion . . . is limited. Fairness requires that its exercise should be on a basis of full disclosure.[264]

Thus, for the Revenue's assurance to be enforced, the taxpayer must have 'put all his cards face upwards on the table'.[265] And the individual's claim to a legitimate expectation may yield to a broader notion of fairness, taking account of the public interest and the principle of legality.[266]

When consistent practice may create a legitimate expectation

A legitimate expectation may arise even in the absence of an assurance, where a public agency has followed a *consistent practice* of acting in a certain way, and then suddenly changes the practice without any warning. In the GCHQ case,[267] the invariable practice of the government had been to consult with civil service unions before changing terms of employment for civil servants; because of this, the unions had a legitimate expectation of being consulted before the Thatcher government withdrew from staff at GCHQ the right to join a union. However, there was some evidence from the Cabinet Secretary that the government decided against consultation for reasons of national security; this factor was held to prevail over the unions' legitimate expectation. In another case, for 25 years the Revenue had accepted tax refund claims without taking any notice of a statutory time limit: it was held that the Revenue could not without notice begin to refuse refunds on the basis that the claims were late.[268]

When a change of policy may be affected by a legitimate expectation

It is common practice for a public authority to make known the policy that it intends to follow on a given subject: while that policy is in place, individuals may reasonably expect that the policy will be applied to them and will not be simply ignored.[269] If there is a *change of policy*, especially

---

[261] *R v Home Secretary, ex p Oloniluyi* [1989] Imm AR 135. Also *R v Home Secretary, ex p Khan* [1985] 1 All ER 40 (A R Mowbray [1985] PL 558).

[262] *R v IRC, ex p MFK Ltd* [1990] 1 All ER 91, 110.

[263] *R v IRC, ex p Preston* [1985] AC 835. The comparison with private law may not now be apt: *R (Reprotech (Pebsham) Ltd) v East Sussex CC* (note 295 below).

[264] *R v IRC, ex p MFK Ltd*, 110–1. Also *R v Jockey Club, ex p RAM Racecourses Ltd* [1993] 2 All ER 225, 236 (Stuart-Smith LJ).

[265] See *R v IRC, ex p MFK Ltd* above.

[266] See the estoppel cases mentioned at notes 289–95 below.

[267] *Council of Civil Service Unions v Minister for the Civil Service* [1985] AC 375.

[268] *R v IRC, ex p Unilever plc* [1996] STC 681.

[269] As it was in *R (Rashid) v Home Secretary* [2005] EWCA Civ 744.

if this is done without any warning or publicity, individuals may be disappointed not to receive the benefit that they had expected. All public authorities must be able to change their policies from time to time, and the courts have held that while individuals may hope to get the benefit of an existing policy or legal rule, they do not have a legitimate expectation that the policy or rule will not be changed.[270] In a case in which the policy for granting parole to long-term prisoners had been tightened up, so that they had to spend longer in prison before they could be considered for parole, Lord Scarman said:

> Given the substance and purpose of the legislative provisions governing parole, the most that a convicted prisoner can legitimately expect is that his case will be examined individually in the light of whatever policy the Secretary of State sees fit to adopt . . .[271]

Some complaints about a change of policy are complaints about procedure, for instance when the only company making oral snuff claimed that it should have been consulted before a decision was made to ban the sale of that product.[272] But a legitimate expectation arising from an existing policy may sometimes go much further than a complaint about procedure.

> In *R v Ministry of Agriculture, ex p Hamble Fisheries Ltd*, a policy regulating the catching of fish permitted the practice of obtaining a licence for a larger trawler by exchanging this for licences from other boats. After a company bought two small trawlers for this purpose, but before it applied for the new licence, the ministry brought in a stricter policy to accord with European decisions. The new policy included transitional provision that took care of licence applications that had been sent in but not yet decided. The company was refused a licence under the new policy. *Held* (Sedley J), a legitimate expectation could give rise to a substantive claim for the benefit sought, and could (if fairness required this) oblige the ministry to make an exception to its policy. In fact, the new policy allowed claims already submitted to be decided under the old policy, and fairness did not require a further exception to be made to the new policy.[273]

When a legitimate expectation may lead to a substantive remedy

This judgment broke new ground in two ways, by holding (*a*) that a legitimate expectation might lead to the award of a substantive benefit (and not merely a procedural remedy, such as the right to be consulted); and (*b*) that the court must conduct a balancing exercise in considering whether the effect of a changed policy was 'fair', or amounted to an abuse of power, not merely whether the policy met the *Wednesbury* test of unreasonableness. The *Hamble Fisheries* judgment (initially described by the Court of Appeal as heresy),[274] was approved in *R v North Devon Health Authority, ex p Coughlan*.[275]

> In 1993, a health authority moved seriously disabled patients into a new facility after assuring them that they could live there for as long as they chose. In 1998, the authority decided to close the facility and transfer the patients to local authority care. *Held*, the decision to terminate care in the NHS was based on a mistaken view of the legislation. The promise to the patients had created a legitimate expectation of a substantive benefit, the frustration of which would be so unfair as to amount to an abuse of power. There was no 'overriding public interest' to justify departure from the promise.

The court's reasoning in *Coughlan* raised difficult questions as to what criteria should be applied by the court in appraising the new policy and assessing the implications for the public

---

[270] See *Re Findlay* [1985] AC 318; and *Hughes v DHSS* [1985] AC 776 (civil servants hoping for benefit of favourable retirement age, but age raised before they could retire).

[271] *Re Findlay*, at 338. Also *R v Home Secretary, ex p Hargreaves* [1997] 1 All ER 397 (minimum eligibility of prisoners for home leave postponed). See T R S Allan [1997] CLJ 246, S Foster (1997) 60 MLR 727.

[272] As in *R v Health Secretary, ex p US Tobacco International Inc* [1992] QB 353.

[273] [1995] 2 All ER 714.

[274] *R v Home Secretary, ex p Hargreaves*, above.

[275] [2001] QB 213, distinguishing *Hargreaves*.

authority in granting a substantive remedy.[276] One result of *Coughlan* was a surge in the number of cases in which claims based on legitimate expectations were made, seldom with the success that was achieved in *Coughlan*. In *R (Bibi) v Newham Council*, the court made a valuable analysis of what such a claim involves:

> In all legitimate expectation cases, whether substantive or procedural, three practical questions arise. The first question is to what has the public authority, whether by practice or by promise, committed itself; the second is whether the authority has acted or proposed to act unlawfully in relation to its commitment; the third is what the court should do.[277]

It is particularly difficult for the court to grant a substantive remedy when an assurance has been given to the claimant about the granting of something from a limited stock of resources (e.g. housing) on which there are many competing claims.[278]

Other aspects

It is not possible to establish a claim based on a legitimate expectation where the effect of this would be contrary to statutory provision, and where the representation or assurance given to the claimant must be regarded as ultra vires.[279] But, as we have seen, legitimate expectations may arise in relation to the making or revision of departmental policies, as for instance when the government tightened up immigration policies on which groups of skilled immigrants had already relied in coming to the United Kingdom.[280] Where a government white paper promised 'the fullest public consultation' before any decision to support new nuclear power plants was made, there was held to be no good reason for this promise to be broken.[281] Contrasting with these cases, the decision to withdraw a discretionary scheme for compensating victims of miscarriage of justice was not affected by a legitimate expectation.[282] In many cases of legitimate expectation, claimants can show that they have relied to their detriment upon the policy or statement under review, and this may strengthen their case for a substantive remedy, but proof of such reliance is not an invariable requirement.[283]

In a developing area of public law, the views of judges are likely to differ about the pace of change and the direction in which the law should move. When in 2008 the House of Lords was dealing with the judicial review of prerogative Orders in Council, one branch of the case concerned legitimate expectations. The law in this area was not in dispute, but the court divided 3–2 in its assessment of whether the statement relied on by the claimant was 'clear, unambiguous and devoid of relevant qualification'. The statement had been made in 2000 by the Foreign Secretary, the late Robin Cook, responding to a decision by the court that the Chagos islanders had been

---

[276] See P Craig and S Schønberg [2000] PL 684, 698–700; cf M Elliott [2000] JR 27, arguing that *Wednesbury* provides the proper standard of review.

[277] [2001] EWCA Civ 607, [2002] 1 WLR 237. On the implications of this approach, see I Steele (2005) 121 LQR 300; also P Sales and K Steyn [2004] PL 564. On the use of proportionality in cases of legitimate expectation, see *R (Nadarajah) v Home Secretary* [2005] EWCA Civ 1363 (Laws LJ).

[278] As in *R (Bibi) v Newham Council* (above).

[279] *R v Education Secretary, ex p Begbie* [2000] 1 WLR 1115. For contrary suggestions, see *Rowland v Environment Agency* [2003] EWCA Civ 1885, [2005] Ch 1, criticised by S Hannett and L Busch [2005] PL 729. On whether legitimate expectations may arise from an unincorporated treaty, see ch 15 B.

[280] *R (BAPIO Action) Ltd v Health Secretary* [2008] UKHL 27, [2008] AC 1003 (Lords Rodger and Mance: changed guidance on employment of overseas trained doctors in NHS breached legitimate expectations of those who had already come to the UK); see CJS Knight [2009] PL 15. Also *R (HSMP Forum Ltd) v Home Secretary* [2009] EWHC 711 (Admin).

[281] *R (Greenpeace Ltd) v Trade and Industry Secretary* [2007] EWHC 311 (Admin).

[282] *R (Bhatt Murphy) v Independent Assessor* [2008] EWCA Civ 755; and see CJS Knight (above).

[283] See *R (Bibi) v Newham Council* (above).

excluded from their home islands by an unlawful ordinance.[284] The Foreign Secretary said that the government accepted the decision and would not appeal against it, and that a new ordinance would be made permitting the islanders to return (as was done). In 2004, without any consultation with the islanders, the government made Orders in Council which set aside their right to return. On judicial review of these orders, the majority (Lords Hoffmann, Rodger and Carswell) held that Robin Cook's statement had not been a 'clear and unambiguous promise' from which a legitimate expectation arose.[285] The minority (Lords Bingham and Mance) disagreed, taking the same view as a unanimous Court of Appeal had done. Lord Bingham said that the islanders

> were clearly intended to think, and did, that for the foreseeable future their right to return was assured. The government could not lawfully resile from its representation without compelling reason, which was not shown.[286]

Reaching the same conclusion, Lord Mance delivered a powerful analysis of the rise of legitimate expectations in public law, that ought to be studied by every reader of this chapter.[287]

Estoppel and government action

This discussion has focused on the concept of legitimate expectations. At an earlier time, a public authority's promise as to how it would exercise a statutory function was usually ignored since it was thought that it could have no legal effect.[288] At that period, the courts invoked the doctrine of estoppel in easing the plight of someone who had relied on an assurance from an official only to find that it was not binding. In a notable decision, *Robertson v Minister of Pensions*,[289] Denning J applied this principle:

> Whenever government officers, in their dealings with a subject, take on themselves to assume authority in a matter with which the subject is concerned, he is entitled to rely on their having the authority which they assume. He does not know and cannot be expected to know the limits of their authority, and he ought not to suffer if they exceed it.

This valuable principle was rejected by a conservative House of Lords,[290] because it was thought to allow officials to play fast and loose with legal rules, whether relating to criminal law[291] or to the limits of a public authority's powers, duties or jurisdiction.[292] Thus estoppel could not affect the obligation to perform a statutory duty. But even though an estoppel (which is a rule of evidence) could not prevail over a rule of law, there were good reasons why public authorities, including the Crown, should be subject to the operation of estoppel in administrative matters. It was said in 1962 that estoppel could not hinder the exercise of a statutory discretion,[293] but some scope was found for estoppel where informal assurances given by planning officials had been relied on by individuals.[294]

---

[284] *R (Bancoult) v Foreign Secretary* [2001] QB 1067.

[285] *R (Bancoult) v Foreign Secretary (No 2)* [2008] UKHL 61, [2009] 1 AC 453.

[286] Ibid, [77].

[287] Ibid, [173–185].

[288] Cf *ex p Coughlan* (note 275 above), at [55].

[289] [1949] 1 KB 227.

[290] *Howell v Falmouth Boat Construction Co* [1951] AC 837.

[291] Cf *R v Arrowsmith* [1975] QB 678 and authorities there cited.

[292] *Maritime Electric Co v General Dairies Ltd* [1937] AC 610; *Rhyl UDC v Rhyl Amusements Ltd* [1959] 1 All ER 257; *Essex Congregational Union v Essex CC* [1963] AC 808.

[293] *Southend Corporation v Hodgson (Wickford) Ltd* [1962] 1 QB 416. But a prior assurance may be a factor that must be taken into account in the exercise of discretion: *R (Bibi) v Newham Council* (note 277 above).

[294] *Lever Finance Ltd v Westminster Council* [1971] 1 QB 222, criticised in *Western Fish Ltd v Penwith DC* [1981] 2 All ER 204. Also A W Bradley [1981] CLP 1.

In 2002, these planning cases were considered by the House of Lords. A recycling company claimed that an informal opinion given in 1991 by a local official that planning permission was not required for a certain use of land should be treated as a binding decision by the local authority acting under statutory powers. The House rejected this argument, since the planning legislation required a formal application to be made for such a decision and imposed other procedural requirements. Even if the local council had been a private party, there was no material for an estoppel. Referring to the concept of legitimate expectation and to the difficulties of applying estoppel to planning decisions, Lord Hoffmann said:

> It seems to me that in this area, public law has already absorbed what is useful from the moral values which underlie the private law concept of estoppel and the time has come for [public law] to stand upon its own two feet.[295]

The implications of this decision are not confined to planning law. Future decisions concerning the effect of informal procedures are likely to turn on arguments of legitimate expectation rather than estoppel.

Legitimate expectations, compensation and the Ombudsman

We have seen that the concept of legitimate expectations may be invoked by those who, on judicial review, either claim that an authority's decision should be quashed or seek a substantive benefit that has been denied to them (as in *Coughlan*). In the next chapter, we will see that judicial review does not typically lead to the award of damages or compensation as a remedy. By contrast, decisions of the Parliamentary Ombudsman often lead to compensation when individuals have suffered injustice through maladministration.[296] In many cases in which a claimant has suffered loss arising from breach of a legitimate expectation by a public authority, it is likely that the same facts would found a complaint of maladministration that could be referred to the Ombudsman.

---

[295] *R (Reprotech (Pebsham) Ltd)* v *East Sussex CC* [2002] UKHL 8, [2002] 4 All ER 58. A W Bradley [2002] PL 597 and M Elliott [2003] JR 71.
[296] See ch 29 D.

CHAPTER 31

Judicial review of administrative action – II

In chapter 30 we considered the principles which the courts apply to the exercise of administrative powers by public authorities. We now examine the procedures by which the courts exercise their supervisory jurisdiction.[1] Review may take place indirectly, when an issue as to the validity of administrative action is decided in the course of ordinary civil or criminal proceedings.[2] So too, the validity of action by a public authority may be relevant to a private law action in contract or tort (chapter 32). But here we are mainly concerned with the procedures by which the acts and decisions of public authorities are subject to direct review by the courts.

The primary procedure in English law[3] is that of an application (or claim) for judicial review, often referred to in short as 'judicial review'. It was created by reforms between 1977 and 1982 which, like many procedural reforms of the common law, did not seek to change the jurisdiction of the High Court in reviewing the legality of the work of public authorities. In particular, the sphere of application of the new procedure was not defined. Since then, judicial review has derived benefits from reforms in the general procedure of civil litigation, but there are still reasons for maintaining a distinctive procedure for judicial review.[4] Here we first look briefly at the earlier position in English law before we deal with the procedure for judicial review itself. Thereafter the chapter will deal with statutory remedies created for the review of certain decisions, the exclusion of judicial review and the system of remedies in Scots law. The chapter concludes with a brief account of habeas corpus, a remedy against executive action which takes away individual liberty.

Forms of relief

When the action or decision of a public authority or official is challenged by judicial review, the claimant may ask the court to provide one or more of the following forms of relief against the defendant:

(*a*) to quash, or set aside as a nullity, a decision that is ultra vires or otherwise unlawful;

(*b*) to restrain the defendant from acting ultra vires or otherwise unlawfully;

(*c*) to order the defendant to perform its lawful duties;

(*d*) to declare the rights and duties of the parties;

(*e*) to order the defendant to pay compensation for loss or injury suffered; and

(*f*) to secure temporary relief, pending the outcome of the proceedings.

The main defect in English law used to be that while procedures existed for all these forms of relief to be obtained, there was no single procedure for doing so. Often the procedures for obtaining one or more of these reliefs were mutually incompatible and the law was fragmented into the

---

[1] A very informative book dealing with the topics in this chapter is Lewis, *Judicial Remedies in Public Law*. See also Supperstone, Goudie and Walker (eds), *Judicial Review* and works on administrative law that have already been cited.

[2] See pp 716–18 below.

[3] A similar but not identical procedure was created in Scotland in 1985; p 724 below. For Northern Ireland, see P Maguire, in Hadfield (ed.), *Judicial Review, A Thematic Approach*, app.

[4] For arguments to the contrary, see D Oliver [2002] PL 91.

law of different remedies. Today, there is a comprehensive procedure for securing whatever relief is appropriate. The main effect of the reforms was that certain remedies which had long been available – namely the prerogative orders (mandamus, prohibition and certiorari), injunctions and declarations – became *forms of relief*[5] obtainable by the single procedure of application for judicial review. These changes in procedure were accompanied by a reorganisation of the business of the Queen's Bench Division of the High Court that led to the unpublicised creation of an administrative court,[6] which in 2000 was given the formal name of the Administrative Court.[7] In 2004, more re-naming took place when the prerogative orders lost their historic names: they are now known as mandatory orders, prohibiting orders and quashing orders.[8] In this chapter references to the present procedure will wherever possible use this terminology.

The prerogative orders

The prerogative writs of mandamus, prohibition and certiorari (later restyled orders)[9] were the principal means by which the former Court of King's Bench exercised jurisdiction over local justices and other bodies.[10] Although the writs issued on the application of private persons, the word 'prerogative' was apt because they had sprung from the right of the Crown to ensure that justice was done by inferior courts and tribunals. The Crown as such played no part in the proceedings, and orders could be sought by or against a minister or a government department. Since the prerogative orders upheld the public interest in the administration of justice, aspects of the procedure (in particular, the need for leave from the court, the summary procedure and the discretionary remedies) were significantly different from litigation that protected an individual's private rights.

A *mandatory order* is an order from the High Court commanding a public authority or official to perform a public duty, in the performance of which the applicant has a sufficient legal interest. The order does not lie against the Crown as such. However, it may enforce performance of a duty imposed by statute on a minister or on a department or on named civil servants, provided that the duty is one which is owed to the applicant and not merely to the Crown.[11] Today the order is used to enforce performance of duties which directly affect the claimant.[12]

A mandatory order will not lie if the authority has complete discretion whether to act or not. But there may be a duty to exercise a discretion or to make a decision, such as the duty of a tribunal to hear and determine a case within its jurisdiction. Thus the Home Secretary was required by mandamus to determine an application by the wife of a UK citizen for a certificate to which she was entitled, and which would enable her to enter the United Kingdom.[13] So too the statutory duty of a tribunal to give reasons for its decisions may be enforced in this way. Where a minister may in the exercise of default powers give directions to a local authority, such a direction may be enforced by a mandatory order, provided that the direction is lawful.[14] Failure to comply is a contempt of court and is punishable accordingly.

---

[5] Senior Courts Act 1981, s 31(1). This Act was enacted as the Supreme Court Act 1981 but (confusingly) it was re-named by the Constitutional Reform Act 2005, which created the present Supreme Court.

[6] L Blom-Cooper [1982] PL 250, 260.

[7] Practice Note (Administrative Court: Establishment) [2000] 4 All ER 1071.

[8] See SI 2004 No 1033, amending ss 29 and 31, Senior Courts Act 1981.

[9] Administration of Justice (Miscellaneous Provisions) Acts 1933, s 5, and 1938, s 7.

[10] Woolf, Jowell and Le Sueur (eds), *De Smith's Judicial Review*, ch 15; Henderson, *Foundations of English Administrative Law*.

[11] *R v Special Commissioners for Income Tax* (1888) 21 QBD 313, 317. Cf *R v Lords of the Treasury* (1872) LR 7 QB 387. And see Harding, *Public Duties and Public Law*, pp 87–96.

[12] E.g. *Padfield v Ministry of Agriculture* [1968] AC 997.

[13] *R v Home Secretary, ex p Phansopkar* [1976] QB 606.

[14] *Education Secretary v Tameside Council* [1977] AC 1014.

A *prohibiting order* is an order issued to prevent an inferior court or tribunal from exceeding its jurisdiction, or acting contrary to the rules of natural justice, where something remains to be done which can be prohibited. A *quashing order* (formerly certiorari) is today a means of quashing decisions by inferior courts, tribunals and public authorities where one or more grounds for judicial review exist. By setting aside a defective decision, a quashing order enables a fresh decision to be taken.

As means of jurisdictional control, prohibition and certiorari formerly covered much the same ground. The main difference was that certiorari quashed a decision already given, and prohibition prevented a decision being made which if made would be subject to certiorari. Both orders may be sought in the same proceedings when a decision in excess of jurisdiction has already been made and other similar decisions have yet to be made.[15] Likewise quashing and mandatory orders may be sought in the same proceedings, the first to quash a decision in excess of jurisdiction and the second to compel the tribunal to hear and determine the case according to law.[16]

Although both certiorari and prohibition originated as means of supervising inferior courts and tribunals, they have long been available against ministers, departments, local authorities and other administrative bodies. It is not necessary now to examine the steps by which this broadening in the application of the remedies took place during the twentieth century.[17] Without this enlargement, the remedies could not have provided the basis for an effective system of administrative law. It is salutary to remember that it was only in 1979 that the Court of Appeal held that prison visitors exercising disciplinary powers over prisoners were subject to review by certiorari, after argument which included debate as to the scope of the remedy.[18] In 1988, the House of Lords held that the governor of a prison was also subject to judicial review and Lord Bridge spoke in terms that made clear how much the language of debate had changed, even since 1979:

> The principle is now as well established as any principle can be in the developing field of public law that where any person or body exercises a power conferred by statute which affects the rights or legitimate expectations of citizens and is of a kind which the law requires to be exercised in accordance with natural justice, the court has jurisdiction to review the exercise of that power.[19]

In other words, if the power to make such decisions existed, no separate issue arose as to the availability of a remedy. These decisions concerned the exercise of statutory powers, but the supervisory jurisdiction extended also to prerogative powers and to certain regulatory powers, even if they did not derive from statute.[20]

Another necessary development concerned the individual's standing (or *locus standi*) to seek review of a decision. English law has never recognised a 'popular action' (*actio popularis*), whereby anyone may challenge the conduct of a public authority regardless of whether he or she is affected by it. Formerly, the rules on what right or interest must be shown by an applicant for a prerogative order might vary with the particular remedy being sought.[21] This is no longer the case, and the law of standing to sue causes few difficulties today.[22]

---

[15] *R v Paddington Rent Tribunal, ex p Bell Properties Ltd* [1949] 1 KB 666.

[16] E.g. *R v Hammersmith Coroner, ex p Peach* [1980] QB 211.

[17] Leading judgments are in *R v Electricity Commissioners, ex p London Electricity Joint Committee* [1924] 1 KB 171 (Atkin LJ); *Ridge v Baldwin* [1964] AC 40 (Lord Reid); *R v Criminal Injuries Compensation Board, ex p Lain* [1967] 2 QB 864 (Lord Parker CJ); and *O'Reilly v Mackman* [1983] 2 AC 237 (Lord Diplock).

[18] *R v Board of Visitors of Hull Prison, ex p St Germain* [1979] QB 425.

[19] *Leech v Deputy Governor of Parkhurst Prison* [1988] AC 533, 561.

[20] Respectively *R v Criminal Injuries Compensation Board, ex p Lain* (note 17); and *R v Panel on Take-overs, ex p Datafin plc* [1987] QB 815.

[21] See Thio, *Locus Standi and Judicial Review*.

[22] See p 714 below.

Injunctions[23]

While the prerogative orders enabled the courts to exercise a supervisory jurisdiction over inferior tribunals and public authorities, the injunction is an equitable remedy available in all branches of law, public and private, to protect a person's rights against unlawful infringement. Since English law was not founded upon a distinction between public and private law, injunctions were available in what is now regarded as the public law field, to restrain unlawful interference with private rights by a public authority[24] or to stop ultra vires expenditure by a local authority.[25] One result of the legal history is that today, in matters subject to judicial review, there is a complete overlap in scope between injunctions and prohibiting orders. In matters of private law that do not involve public authorities at all, the claimant must seek an injunction by ordinary civil process.

Certain aspects of the law on injunctions may be noted. First, injunctions are not available against 'the Crown' as a legal entity, and they are not available in private law proceedings brought directly against the Crown.[26] In place of an injunction in private law proceedings against the Crown, the court may make an order declaring the rights of the parties, and if necessary the court may grant an interim declaration, which the Crown would be expected to observe.[27] However, Community law may require injunctive relief to be available against the Crown.[28] In 1994, the House of Lords cut down the immunity of the Crown as an entity by holding that an injunction may be issued in judicial review proceedings against government departments, ministers and civil servants.[29]

A second matter concerns the historic procedure known as the 'relator action'. This name was given to an action by a private person seeking an injunction on a matter of public right (such as a public nuisance caused by obstruction of a highway) in which he or she did not have a personal right or interest sufficient to sue in his or her name.[30] This difficulty was overcome by the Attorney General, as guardian of the public interest, consenting to his name being used as nominal plaintiff. Relator actions are now very rare indeed, mainly for the reason that judicial review will nearly always be available (by the usual procedure) whenever a claimant wishes to restrain unlawful action by a public authority. Relator actions have occasionally been used in a different way to enforce the criminal law, when existing penalties are inadequate to deter breaches of the law, for example when planning controls or fire precautions are ignored by those who find it profitable to break the law.[31] Another reason for the rarity of relator actions is that a local authority may under the Local Government Act 1972, s 222, institute proceedings in its own name when it considers it expedient to do so for promoting the interests of local inhabitants.[32] Such proceedings may make it necessary for the court to rule on the extent of the local authority's powers and duties.[33]

---

[23] Woolf, Jowell and Le Sueur (eds), *De Smith's Judicial Review*, pp 800–5, 888–93, 897–9; Wade and Forsyth, *Administrative Law*, pp 474–480.

[24] E.g. *Pride of Derby Angling Association v British Celanese Ltd* [1953] Ch 149.

[25] *A-G v Aspinall* (1837) 2 My & Cr 406.

[26] Crown Proceedings Act 1947, s 21; ch 32 C.

[27] Civil Procedure Rules, 25.1(1). For the former position, see *R v IRC, ex p Rossminster Ltd* [1980] AC 952.

[28] *R v Transport Secretary, ex p Factortame Ltd* [1990] 2 AC 85; *(The same) (No 2)* [1991] 1 AC 603. See also the Public Supply Contracts Regulations 1991, SI 1991 No 2679, reg 26, authorising injunctive relief against the Crown for breach of the regulations.

[29] *M v Home Office* [1994] 1 AC 377; and note 65 below.

[30] See *Benjamin v Storr* (1874) LR 9 CP 400; *Boyce v Paddington BC* [1903] 1 Ch 109; *Barrs v Bethell* [1982] Ch 294.

[31] *A-G v Bastow* [1957] 1 QB 514; *A-G v Harris* [1961] 1 QB 74; *A-G v Chaudry* [1971] 3 All ER 938.

[32] *Stoke-on-Trent Council v B & Q (Retail) Ltd* [1984] AC 754; *Kirklees Council v Wickes Building Supplies Ltd* [1993] AC 227. And see B Hough [1992] PL 130.

[33] See *Re Z (local authority: duty)* [2004] EWHC 2817 (Fam), [2005] 3 All ER 280 (social services authority under no duty to prevent vulnerable adult being taken to Switzerland for assisted suicide).

The Attorney General retains power to act in the public interest to uphold the law and this might be exercised on the relation of someone who lacked sufficient interest to sue in his or her own name. In such a case, the Attorney General would have absolute discretion in deciding whether to consent. The Attorney General is nominally accountable to Parliament for such decisions, but they need not be justified in the courts nor may the courts overrule them.[34] It does not follow, however, that all discretionary decisions by the Attorney General are immune from judicial review since, like a chameleon, the various functions of the office acquire colour from the context in which they are exercised.[35] Significantly, there is no recorded instance of a relator action against a government department.

Finally, the High Court may grant an injunction to restrain a person from acting in an office to which he or she is not entitled and may declare the office to be vacant. This procedure takes the place of the ancient process of an information in the nature of a writ of *quo warranto*.[36]

Declaratory judgments[37]

A declaratory judgment is one which merely declares the legal relationship of the parties and is not accompanied by any sanction or means of enforcement. The authority of a court's ruling on law is such that a declaratory judgment will normally be enough to restrain both the Crown and public authorities from illegal conduct. By the Civil Procedure Rules, 40.20: 'The courts may make binding declarations whether or not any other remedy is claimed.'

It is convenient in some public law disputes for the law to be determined in relation to particular facts without a need to seek a coercive remedy. An early example arose in *Dyson* v *Attorney-General*, where a taxpayer obtained a declaration against the Crown that the tax authorities had no power to request certain information from him on pain of a £50 penalty for disobedience.[38] The jurisdiction to grant declarations is as wide as the law itself, except that the judges may as a matter of discretion impose limits on its use. Thus an action for a declaratory judgment must be based on a concrete case which has arisen. The courts are reluctant to grant a bare declaration that can have no legal consequences[39] and will not give answers to hypothetical questions that have been raised in the absence of any genuine dispute about the subject matter.[40] However, courts have reviewed the legality of advisory guidance that in itself has no legal effect.[41]

The court will not give a declaratory opinion in civil proceedings as to a matter that is in issue in concurrent criminal proceedings[42] and, even at the request of the Attorney General, will not grant a declaration that conduct would be criminal except in a very clear case.[43] Where a statute both creates a duty and provides the procedure for enforcing it, this may exclude declaratory

---

[34] *Gouriet* v *Union of Post Office Workers* [1978] AC 435; and see P P Mercer [1979] PL 214, B Hough (1988) 8 LS 189, and Edwards, *The Attorney-General, Politics and the Public Interest*, pp 120–58.

[35] Two recent reports on the office of Attorney General are HL Paper 93, 2007–8 (Committee on the Constitution) and HC 306, 2006–7 (Constitutional Affairs Committee).

[36] Senior Courts Act 1981, s 30; cf Local Government Act 1972, s 92.

[37] Woolf, Jowell and Le Sueur (eds), *De Smith's Judicial Review*, pp 805–11; Zamir and Woolf, *The Declaratory Judgment*.

[38] [1912] 1 Ch 158.

[39] *Maxwell* v *Dept of Trade* [1974] QB 523.

[40] *R (Rusbridger)* v *A-G* [2003] UKHL 38, [2004] 1 AC 357.

[41] E.g. *Gillick* v *West Norfolk Health Authority* [1986] AC 112. In 1994, the Law Commission recommended that the High Court be authorised in its judicial review jurisdiction to make advisory declarations on points of general importance: Law Com No 226, pp 74–6. And see J Laws (1994) 57 MLR 213.

[42] *Imperial Tobacco Ltd* v *A-G* [1981] AC 718.

[43] *A-G* v *Able* [1984] QB 795. Special considerations arise in medical cases where a patient cannot consent to treatment: e.g. *F (Mental Patient: Sterilisation)* [1990] 2 AC 1; *Airedale NHS Trust* v *Bland* [1993] AC 789; cf *R (Pretty)* v *DPP* [2001] UKHL 61, [2002] 1 AC 800.

proceedings.[44] But the existence of a statutory procedure for obtaining a decision on whether planning permission was needed did not prevent a landowner from coming to court for a declaration as to the extent of existing development rights.[45]

Actions for a declaration formerly had some procedural advantages over the prerogative orders and were brought for this reason. Thus, instead of being quashed by certiorari, the decision of a tribunal could be declared invalid as being in excess of jurisdiction or in breach of natural justice,[46] but the court could not by a declaration decide afresh a question entrusted by statute to a minister or tribunal.[47] The use of the declaration in this way was greatly restricted when the procedure of application for judicial review was created.[48]

The Human Rights Act 1998, by enlarging the jurisdiction of the courts in protecting European Convention rights, has necessarily broadened the potential scope of declaratory judgments. A special feature of the Act is the power that it gives to a superior court to declare that a statutory provision that cannot be interpreted in a way that is consistent with a Convention right is incompatible with the right. A 'declaration of incompatibility' of this kind has distinctive features that do not apply to the declaratory judgments discussed above. In particular, unlike the more usual form of declaratory judgment, a declaration of incompatibility does not affect the validity, operation or enforcement of the statutory provision to which it relates, and it 'is not binding on the parties to the proceedings in which it is made'.[49] These unusual limitations do not apply when the court gives a declaratory judgment in customary form regarding the powers of a public authority, in a case that does not require the court to rule on the compatibility of primary legislation with Convention rights.

The creation of applications for judicial review

We turn now to examine the procedure by which the remedies considered above may be obtained. The procedure today presents a remarkable contrast with the position in the 1970s, when there was an urgent need for reform in the remedies available in administrative law. The procedural difficulties were such that the success of a case often depended on the choice of remedy, and there were many procedural differences between the prerogative orders on the one hand, and declarations and injunctions on the other. These matters provided serious obstacles to a court's ability to deal with the substantive issues of public law that might arise.[50] In 1977, a new Rule of the Supreme Court (Order 53), created the procedure of 'application for judicial review' and this reform was confirmed by Parliament in 1981. The business of the High Court was reorganised: in place of a divisional court of two or three judges (this was retained for criminal cases), some Queen's Bench judges were designated to decide judicial review cases in civil matters, and a 'Crown Office list' was created, to cover judicial review, statutory appeals and similar matters. In 2000, after a review by Sir Jeffery Bowman of the conduct of the heavy case load in the Crown Office list, Order 53 was replaced by Part 54 of the Civil Procedure Rules; and the court in which sit the High Court judges designated to hear claims for judicial review and related cases was named the Administrative Court.[51]

---

[44] *Barraclough* v *Brown* [1897] AC 615.

[45] *Pyx Granite Co Ltd* v *Ministry of Housing* [1960] AC 260.

[46] *Anisminic Ltd* v *Foreign Compensation Commission* [1969] 2 AC 147; *Ridge* v *Baldwin* [1964] AC 40.

[47] *Healey* v *Minister of Health* [1955] 1 QB 221; *Argosam Finance Ltd* v *Oxby* [1965] Ch 390.

[48] See the discussion of *O'Reilly* v *Mackman* [1983] 2 AC 286 (p 716 below).

[49] Human Rights Act 1998, s 4(5).

[50] Report on Remedies in Administrative Law, Cmnd 6407, 1976.

[51] CPR, Part 54 and Part 54 Practice Direction; also *Practice Direction (Administrative Court: Establishment)* [2000] 4 All ER 1071. See Bowman, *Review of the Crown Office List*, March 2000.

Applications for judicial review: the procedure

By s 31 of the Senior Courts Act 1981, as amended, applications to the High Court for mandatory, prohibiting and quashing orders[52] (and for an injunction restraining a person from acting in a public office to which he or she is not entitled) *must* be made, in accordance with rules of court, by an application for judicial review. The High Court also has power (1981 Act, s 31(2)) to make a declaration or grant an injunction whenever an application for judicial review has been made seeking that relief, if it would be 'just and convenient' to do so. In exercising this discretion the court must have regard among other things to the nature of the matters in respect of which the prerogative orders apply, the nature of the persons and bodies against whom the orders lie and all the circumstances. Thus, if account is taken of the scope of the prerogative orders, declarations and injunctions *may* be granted on an application for judicial review. The Act does not state whether within this field an application for judicial review is to be the sole means of obtaining an injunction or declaration.

Permission of the court is needed for every application for judicial review (s 31(3)). By this rule, derived from earlier procedure for the prerogative orders, a two-stage process exists: (*a*) the court decides whether to permit an application for review to proceed and, if so, (*b*) a substantive hearing of the application takes place.

The first step in the procedure before any claim is filed with the court is that a prospective claimant should if possible comply with the pre-action protocol.[53] In outline, this involves a letter to the public authority or official whose act or decision is in question containing sufficient information to enable a reasoned reply to be given, in the hope that the issues may be identified and litigation avoided. If it cannot be avoided, the claimant must file a claim form with the Administrative Court in London,[54] stating the act or decision to be reviewed, the relevant facts and grounds, and the remedy sought. Notice is given to the defendant and other interested parties; who must within 21 days state whether they intend to contest the claim and, if so, must give a summary of the grounds they will rely on. The granting of permission is generally decided on the papers by a single judge,[55] but the judge may request a short hearing in open court. A hearing is held if interim relief is sought. If permission is refused or granted subject to conditions, the claimant may ask for a hearing. If permission is still withheld, the claimant may appeal to the Court of Appeal.[56] In the past, the 'filter' stage operated very unevenly, but it is a safeguard against a flood of 'hopeless' cases and vexatious challenges.[57] Once permission has been granted, further evidence may be filed and the substantive hearing takes place before a single judge or a divisional court (that usually consists of a Lord Justice of Appeal, sitting with a High Court judge).

Claims for judicial review must be made promptly and 'in any event not later than three months after the grounds to make the claim first arose', but the period may be shorter for a particular claim if legislation so provides.[58] If the court considers that the case is one which requires

---

[52] These orders may for convenience be referred to as 'the prerogative orders'. The change of names in 2004 did not affect the jurisdiction of the High Court to make them.

[53] As well as Part 54, CPR and the pre-action protocol, helpful information is given in the Administrative Court's *Notes of Guidance on Applying for Judicial Review*.

[54] Certain claims for judicial review may now be filed in Birmingham, Cardiff, Leeds or Manchester, and it is intended that some claims will be heard and decided within the relevant region. See Practice Direction 54D (and S Nason [2009] PL 440).

[55] In 2010, over 40 High Court judges were designated to sit in the Administrative Court.

[56] CPR 52.15. If the Court of Appeal also refuses leave, the House of Lords has no jurisdiction to grant leave. And see *R (Burkett) v Hammersmith LBC* [2002] UKHL 23, [2002] 3 All ER 97 (HL has jurisdiction if CA grants leave but rejects claim on its merits).

[57] See A Le Sueur and M Sunkin [1992] PL 102; Bridges, Meszaros and Sunkin, *Judicial Review in Perspective*, chs 7, 8 and (same authors) [2000] PL 651.

[58] CPR 54.5. For the operation of these rules, see *R (Burkett) v Hammersmith LBC* (above). Also *Lam v UK* (ECtHR, 5 July 2001) and M J Beloff, in Forsyth and Hare (eds), *The Golden Metwand and the Crooked Cord*, pp 267–95.

urgent action (for instance, a challenge to school admission decisions), it may refuse permission for a claim that is not made promptly, even within the three-month period. The court may extend time if there is a good reason to do so, but the parties may not agree to extend time.[59]

Under the Senior Courts Act 1981, s 31(6), the court may refuse to grant leave for an application or may refuse relief sought by the claimant if it considers that the granting of the relief 'would be likely to cause substantial hardship to, or substantially prejudice the rights of, any person or would be detrimental to good administration'. Despite some difficulty arising from the interaction of this provision with the procedure rules, it is now established that where permission has been granted for judicial review, the court at the substantive hearing may not set aside that permission on the ground that there had been unjustified delay in the claim being made; however, delay may be a reason for withholding relief that would otherwise be justified.[60]

If permission to proceed with a claim for judicial review is given, the court may order a stay of proceedings to which the claim relates.[61] The court may grant other interim relief, including mandatory orders and interim declarations,[62] applying the test of balance of convenience that is appropriate in civil proceedings generally,[63] but with regard to special considerations applicable to public law litigation.[64]

The 1981 Act did not expressly provide for interim relief against the Crown, but in *M v Home Office*[65] it was held that the language of s 31 enabled coercive orders (including interim injunctions) to be made against ministers and officers of the Crown in judicial review proceedings.

On an application for judicial review, the court may award damages, restitution or the recovery of money if such an award has been claimed and the court is satisfied that it could have been obtained by an action brought for the purpose.[66] But the 1981 Act did not alter the substantive rules of liability in damages and the fact that the claimant has suffered financial loss because of a decision that is quashed as invalid in itself gives rise to no liability.[67] Thus even successful applicants for judicial review are seldom able to obtain damages: however, under the Human Rights Act 1998, s 8, the court may grant compensation if it is satisfied that this is 'necessary to afford just satisfaction' to the person whose Convention rights have been infringed.[68]

A claim for judicial review must be supported by such written evidence as is available and a witness statement confirming the truth of the facts relied on; the defendant may file evidence in reply. The claimant owes a duty to the court to disclose all relevant material of which he or she is aware, even if it weakens the claim; the defendant has a similar 'duty of candour' to disclose relevant material the existence of which may be unknown to the claimant.[69] The court may order disclosure of specific documents, further information and cross-examination of witnesses, except where the defendant establishes that certain evidence is protected by public interest immunity.[70]

---

[59] CPR 3.1(2)(a); 54.5(2).

[60] See *R v Criminal Injuries Compensation Board, ex p A* [1999] 2 AC 330; *R v Dairy Produce Tribunal, ex p Caswell* [1990] 2 AC 738 (and A Lindsay [1995] PL 417).

[61] CPR 54.10. Under the former RSC Order 53, r 10, 'stay of proceedings' was interpreted broadly in *R v Education Secretary, ex p Avon Council* [1991] 1 QB 558.

[62] CPR 25.1(1). This power was not formerly available: *R v IRC, ex p Rossminster Ltd* [1980] AC 952.

[63] *American Cyanamid Co v Ethicon Ltd* [1975] AC 396.

[64] See e.g. *R v Kensington and Chelsea BC, ex p Hammell* [1989] QB 518 and *R v Inspectorate of Pollution, ex p Greenpeace Ltd* [1994] 4 All ER 321.

[65] [1994] 1 AC 377 (H W R Wade (1991) 107 LQR 4; M Gould [1993] PL 368). For the Crown Proceedings Act 1947, s 21, see ch 32 C.

[66] Senior Courts Act 1981, s 31(4) as amended by SI 2004 No 1033.

[67] Ch 32 A; e.g. *Dunlop v Woollahra Council* [1982] AC 158.

[68] And see page 742 below.

[69] See O Sanders [2008] JR 244, discussing effect of *Tweed v Parades Commission for Northern Ireland* [2006] UKHL 53, [2007] 1 AC 650.

[70] See ch 32 C.

In practice, many cases turn on the documents that record the decision-making process. It is often said that a claim for judicial review is unsuitable for resolving disputes of fact. However, the court must decide issues of fact that are essential to a claim (such as whether a decision-maker was biased, or whether proper consultation took place); and questions requiring disclosure may well arise on issues of proportionality on a claim under the Human Rights Act.[71]

Where the court decides to quash the decision under review, it generally remits the matter to the decision maker, with an appropriate direction, but if there is no purpose in remitting it the court may take the decision itself.[72] The Civil Procedure Rules permit claims begun by ordinary procedure to be transferred, with permission of the court, into a claim for judicial review and, conversely, a claim for judicial review may be transferred into an ordinary claim.[73]

We now consider a group of issues which have arisen in relation to judicial review, namely (a) the scope and extent of review, (b) standing to apply for review, (c) the effect of alternative remedies, (d) whether judicial review is exclusive (e) the discretion of the court in granting review, (f) statutory machinery for review, and (g) statutory exclusion of judicial review.

Scope and extent of judicial review

Much greater use is made of the procedure for judicial review than was formerly made of the prerogative orders. If an application for review concerns decisions of a public authority or official, the courts readily accept jurisdiction in judicial review, except if a reason to the contrary is shown.[74] Thus, decisions taken under prerogative powers are subject to review, unless the court considers their subject matter to be non-justiciable.[75] Also reviewable are decisions by local authorities in controlling access to public property, initiating legal proceedings and matters preliminary to the award of contracts.[76] Two broad exceptions to the availability of judicial review exist. First, some decisions are subject to statutory appeals and similar procedures which, to a greater or lesser extent, exclude judicial review.[77] Second, public authorities are in general subject to the ordinary law of contract, tort and property. Since *O'Reilly v Mackman*,[78] such branches of law are said to fall within private law, to distinguish them from the rules of public law applied on judicial review. A claim for judicial review may not be used in place of an ordinary action in contract or tort, just because the defendant is a public authority.

Thus, when such an authority dismisses an employee, the employee's primary remedy is a claim for unfair dismissal or a claim under the contract of employment.[79] However, depending on the circumstances, decisions by public authorities as employers may stem from or involve issues of public law.[80] Public sector employees such as NHS hospital staff[81] and civil servants[82] must generally use procedures open to them in employment law rather than seek judicial review.

---

[71] And see *Tweed v Parades Commission* (above), [32], [38–40] (Lord Carswell); [56–7] (Lord Brown).

[72] Senior Courts Act 1981, s 31(5); and CPR 54.19.

[73] CPR, Part 30 and 54.20. For effect of this on the 'exclusive remedy' issue, see p 718 below.

[74] See Woolf, Jowell and Le Sueur (eds), *De Smith's Judicial Review*, ch 3; Lewis, *Judicial Remedies in Public Law*, chs 2, 4.

[75] See the *CCSU* case, below; *R v Ministry of Defence, ex p Smith* [1996] QB 517; *R (Bancoult) v Foreign Secretary (No 2)* [2008] UKHL 61, [2009] 1 AC 453. Cf *Reckley v Minister of Public Safety (No 2)* [1996] AC 527.

[76] Respectively *Wheeler v Leicester City Council* [1985] AC 1054; *Avon CC v Buscott* [1988] QB 656; and *R v Enfield Council, ex p TF Unwin (Roydon) Ltd* [1989] 1 Admin LR 51.

[77] See pp 719–22 below.

[78] [1983] 2 AC 237, p 716 below.

[79] *R v BBC, ex p Lavelle* [1983] 1 All ER 241.

[80] E.g. *CCSU v Minister for Civil Service* [1985] AC 374; cf H W R Wade (1985) 101 LQR 180, 190–6.

[81] *R v East Berks Health Authority, ex p Walsh* [1985] QB 152, and p 751 below.

[82] *R v Lord Chancellor's Department, ex p Nangle* [1992] 1 All ER 897.

This does not necessarily apply to holders of public office such as police and prison officers[83] whose position is based on statute. Judicial review may be available if an employment dispute raises issues as to the powers of the public authority or other matters suitable for redress by judicial review.[84]

A difficult question is what constitutes a 'public law dispute' for judicial review purposes. The prerogative orders were not, and judicial review is not, available against bodies such as trade unions or commercial companies.[85] Membership of a trade union is based on contract. If a trade unionist complains that her expulsion from the union was in breach of union rules or infringed natural justice, she may sue the union for damages and an injunction. Bodies such as the National Greyhound Racing Club and the Jockey Club are not subject to judicial review, even if they regulate major areas of sport, but contractual remedies will often be available.[86] Nor are decisions by religious bodies subject to judicial review.[87] The position of the universities is more complex. In older colleges and universities that have a visitor, academic staff or students with grievances against the institution had to refer them to the visitor, whose decisions are subject to judicial review, but only on certain grounds.[88] Legislation has now excluded from the visitor's jurisdiction employment disputes involving academic staff, and complaints by students and former students.[89] Many of the newer universities and colleges have no visitor and their decisions are subject to judicial review on the usual grounds.[90]

The most difficult case is that of regulatory bodies which derive their powers neither directly from statute[91] nor from contract. Despite having no formal legal status, the City Panel on Takeovers and Mergers is subject to judicial review, since its functions 'de facto' are in the nature of public law powers and are indirectly supported by statutory sanctions.[92] The effect of privatisation and 'market testing' of public services has produced some conflicting decisions.[93] Publicly owned undertakings are subject to judicial review in respect of some of their functions.[94]

Inferior courts, such as magistrates' courts and county courts, are subject to judicial review. So is the Crown Court, 'other than its jurisdiction in matters relating to trial on indictment'.[95] This limitation expresses an important principle that makes it necessary to distinguish between those

---

[83] *R v Home Secretary, ex p Benwell* [1985] QB 554. By the Criminal Justice and Public Order Act 1994, s 126, prison officers acquired the same employment rights as other civil servants: G S Morris [1994] PL 535. See also *R (Tucker) v National Crime Squad* [2003] EWCA Civ 2, [2003] ICR 599 (no judicial review of decision to end police secondment).

[84] See *McLaren v Home Office* [1990] ICR 824. Also S Fredman and G Morris [1988] PL 58, [1991] PL 484, (1991) 107 LQR 298.

[85] *R (West) v Lloyd's of London* [2004] EWCA 506, [2004] 3 All ER 251 (Lloyd's underwriting syndicates not within public law).

[86] *Law v National Greyhound Racing Club Ltd* [1983] 3 All ER 300; *R v Disciplinary Committee of the Jockey Club, ex p Aga Khan* [1993] 2 All ER 853. And see M Beloff [1989] PL 95; N Bamforth [1993] PL 239. Cf *Finnigan v New Zealand Rugby Football Union Inc* [1985] 2 NZLR 159 (private association exercising function of major national importance).

[87] *R v Chief Rabbi, ex p Wachmann* [1993] 2 All ER 249.

[88] *R v Hull University Visitor, ex p Page* [1993] AC 682.

[89] See respectively Education Reform Act 1988, s 206 and Higher Education Act 2004, s 20.

[90] See *R v Metropolitan University of Manchester, ex p Nolan* [1994] ELR 380 and cf *Clark v University of Lincolnshire* [2000] 3 All ER 752.

[91] Unlike the Law Society; see e.g. *Swain v Law Society* [1983] 1 AC 598.

[92] *R v Panel on Take-overs and Mergers, ex p Datafin plc* [1987] QB 817 (C F Forsyth [1987] PL 356; D Oliver [1987] PL 543); *R v Advertising Standards Agency, ex p Insurance Service plc* (1990) 2 Admin LR 77.

[93] Compare *R v Lord Chancellor, ex p Hibbit & Saunders* [1993] COD 326 (D Oliver [1993] PL 214) and *R v Legal Aid Board, ex p Donn & Co* [1996] 3 All ER 1.

[94] *R v British Coal Corpn, ex p Vardy* [1993] ICR 720. See ch 14 D.

[95] Supreme Court Act 1981, s 29(3); R Ward [1990] PL 50; *In re Ashton* [1994] 1 AC 9 and *R v Manchester Crown Court, ex p DPP* [1993] 4 All ER 928. See also *R v DPP, ex p Kebeline* [2000] 2 AC 326 (decision to prosecute subject to criminal process, not to judicial review).

decisions of the Crown Court that are subject to judicial review and others which can be challenged only by appeal after a trial. A somewhat similar situation arises when the legislation setting up a particular tribunal indicates that judicial review is available in respect of some but not all decisions by the tribunal.[96]

This discussion has not yet taken account of the effects of the Human Rights Act 1998. As we have seen,[97] the Act obliges public authorities (and bodies that exercise functions both of a public nature and of a private nature) to act consistently with Convention rights. The defining of public authorities under the 1998 Act has given rise to difficult decisions.[98] It has been observed that the case law on the scope of judicial review is not determinative of whether a body is a public authority for the purposes of the Act,[99] but the two bodies of case law must influence each other. Although the Act indicates that judicial review is the residual remedy for enforcing Convention rights, it does not alter the position of public sector employees, whose remedy for unfair dismissal still lies in the employment tribunal.

Standing to apply for judicial review

At the stage when leave is sought for an application for judicial review, the court must not grant leave 'unless it considers that the applicant has a sufficient interest in the matter to which the application relates'.[100] The test of 'sufficient interest' was first proposed by the Law Commission in 1976 as a formula which would replace the various tests of standing for the prerogative orders and other remedies and would allow for further development in the law. It plainly allows the court discretion to decide what may constitute 'sufficient interest'. To what extent did it alter existing rules of *locus standi*?

> In *R v Inland Revenue Commissioners, ex p National Federation of Self-employed*, a body of taxpayers challenged arrangements made by the Commissioners for levying tax on wages paid to casual employees on Fleet Street newspapers. For many years the employees had given fictitious names to evade tax, but the Commissioners agreed with the employers and unions on a scheme for collecting tax in future and for two previous years, in return for an undertaking by the Commissioners not to investigate any earlier years. The Federation, complaining that their members were never treated so favourably, applied for a declaration that the arrangement was unlawful, and a mandamus ordering the Commissioners to collect tax as required by law. The Court of Appeal held, assuming the agreement to be unlawful, that the Federation had sufficient interest in the matter for their application to be heard. The House of Lords *held* that the question of sufficient interest was not merely a preliminary issue to be decided when leave was being sought on an application for judicial review, but had to be resolved in relation to what was known by the court of the matter under review. On the evidence, the tax agreement was a lawful exercise of the Commissioners' discretion. In general, unlike local ratepayers,[101] a taxpayer did not have an interest in challenging decisions concerning other taxpayers. In the circumstances, the Federation did not have sufficient interest to challenge the Commissioners' decisions.[102]

The speeches in this case contain a wide diversity of opinions about the test of 'sufficient interest'. The above account is based on the views of three judges (Lords Wilberforce, Fraser and

---

[96] See *R (Cart) v Upper Tribunal* [2009] EWHC 3052 (Admin), [2010] 1 All ER 908.

[97] See ch 19 C.

[98] Including *Poplar Housing Association Ltd v Donohue* [2001] EWCA Civ 595, [2002] QB 48; *Aston Cantlow PCC v Wallbank* [2003] UKHL 37, [2004] 1 AC 546; *YL v Birmingham Council* [2007] UKHL 27, [2008] AC 95. The articles include D Oliver [2000] PL 476, [2004] PL 329; M Sunkin [2004] PL 643; C Donnelly [2005] PL 785; J Landau [2007] PL 630.

[99] *Aston Cantlow PCC v Wallbank* (above), [52] (Lord Hope).

[100] Senior Courts Act 1981, s 31(3).

[101] *Arsenal FC v Ende* [1979] AC 1.

[102] [1982] AC 617. And see Woolf, Jowell and Le Sueur, *De Smith's Judicial Review*, ch 2.

Roskill), although Lord Fraser also stressed that the test of 'sufficient interest' was a logically prior question which had to be answered before any question of the merits arose. Lord Scarman paid lip-service to the existence of a test of standing separate from the merits, but his conclusion (that the Federation had no sufficient interest *because* they had not shown that the tax authorities had failed in their duties) virtually eliminated any prior test of standing separate from the merits. Lord Diplock, emphasising the utility of the then new procedure of application for judicial review, argued for a very broad test of standing; he was alone in holding that the Federation had sufficient interest to seek review, but that the case for review failed on its merits.

What emerges from the case is that at the permission stage, the court has a discretion to turn away those without a legitimate concern ('in other words a busybody'),[103] but at the substantive hearing other questions of standing may be raised. A court should not refuse permission for lack of sufficient interest unless it knows enough of the legal and factual context to be sure that this is justified; in advance of examining the merits, the court may be unable to make a surgical separation between 'sufficient interest' and the essence of the case.

In most claims for judicial review, the question of sufficient interest presents no problems, although for the parties not to raise the issue does not confer on the court jurisdiction that is otherwise absent.[104] An ordinary taxpayer had interest to challenge the government's proposal to designate as a 'Community treaty' a treaty providing extra funds to the Community.[105] The Equal Opportunities Commission had standing to challenge statutory provisions which discriminated against women employees in breach of their Community rights.[106] Trade unions acting in their members' interests and environmental groups have standing to challenge decisions on relevant issues,[107] but difficulties may arise when a claimant is not personally affected by a decision and is acting in the public interest.[108] Thus a non-profit-making company formed to protect the site of a Shakespearian theatre had no standing to review a minister's decision refusing to schedule the site as a historic monument.[109] Relatives of a child who was killed by two young boys had no standing to seek review of a decision by the Lord Chief Justice as to the minimum period in detention that the two youths should serve.[110]

A different test of standing was created by the Human Rights Act 1998, s 7: a claim that a public authority acted incompatibly with a Convention right (in breach of s 6) may be brought only by someone who is a 'victim' of the act within the meaning of art 34 ECHR. Strasbourg case law does not permit cases to be brought by representative bodies and pressure groups unless they themselves are victims of a breach of their Convention rights.[111] Such bodies must thus ensure that one or more 'victims' are claimants for judicial review in order to rely on s 6 of the 1998 Act. There is no victim test for persons who wish to rely on other provisions of the Act, such as the requirement by s 3 that legislation must be interpreted consistently with the Convention, wherever this is possible.

---

[103] *R v Somerset CC, ex p Dixon* [1998] Env LR 111. And see *R (Edwards) v Environment Agency* [2003] EWHC 736 (Admin), [2004] 3 All ER 21. In the Fleet Street case, above, Lord Scarman referred to the exclusion of 'busy-bodies, cranks and mischief-makers' but it may not always be obvious whether a claimant is a mischief-maker or a champion of liberty.

[104] *R v Social Services Secretary, ex p CPAG* [1990] 2 QB 540.

[105] *R v HM Treasury, ex p Smedley* [1985] QB 657; *R v Foreign Secretary, ex p Rees-Mogg* [1994] QB 552. See also *R v Felixstowe Justices, ex p Leigh* [1987] QB 582.

[106] *R v Employment Secretary, ex p EOC* [1995] 1 AC 1.

[107] *R v Inspectorate of Pollution, ex p Greenpeace Ltd (No 2)* [1994] 4 All ER 329; *R v Home Secretary, ex p Fire Brigades Union* [1995] 2 AC 513; *R v Foreign Secretary, ex p World Development Movement* [1995] 1 All ER 611. And P Cane [1995] PL 276.

[108] See Law Com No 226, pp 41–4 and report by Justice, *A Matter of Public Interest* (1996).

[109] *R v Environment Secretary, ex p Rose Theatre Trust Co* [1990] 1 QB 504. See K Schiemann [1990] PL 342 and P Cane [1990] PL 307.

[110] *R (Bulger) v Home Secretary* [2001] EWHC 119 (Admin). The claim was also rejected on its merits.

[111] See Harris, O'Boyle and Warbrick, *Law of the ECHR*, 790–99.

Alternative remedies[112]

Another issue considered at the permission stage stems from the principle that the prerogative orders are a residual remedy. In a leading nineteenth-century case, mandamus was refused where a statute created both a duty and a specific remedy for enforcing it (complaint to central government).[113] Today, an individual must use an express right of appeal if this will meet the substance of the complaint.[114] Tribunals exist for deciding claims to social security, disputes over tax, immigration claims and so on. Judicial review is not an optional substitute for an appeal to a tribunal with relevant jurisdiction.[115] The existence of an alternative remedy does not deprive the Administrative Court of jurisdiction, but requires the court to exercise its discretion: whether leave for judicial review to proceed is granted will depend on whether the statutory remedy is a satisfactory and effective alternative to review.[116] Thus, the default powers of ministers concerning social service complaints may deal with the factual issues raised by a complaint, but do not enable important points of law to be resolved.[117] Sometimes the reason for withholding permission is merely that the application for judicial review is premature, as, for instance, where a right of appeal is open to the individual. In other cases, a judicial remedy may be justified, if the decision at first instance is manifestly ultra vires[118] or there has been abuse of statutory procedure by the authority.[119] But where to protect consumers the sale of an unsafe product was banned by a local authority, the manufacturer was required to appeal to the magistrates' court and could not seek judicial review.[120] In such cases, the court considers such matters as the comparative speed, expense and finality of the alternative processes, the need for fact-finding and the desirability of an authoritative ruling on points of law.[121]

Does judicial review provide an exclusive procedure?[122]

Although the House of Lords failed to sound a clear note in the *National Federation* case, the House in two later cases was unanimous in holding that litigants who wished to challenge official decisions must do so by applying for judicial review (under the then Order 53). The question arose because the Senior Courts Act 1981 did not expressly exclude someone from suing in public law cases for an injunction or declaration, or for damages for breach of statutory duty. The issue had arisen in numerous cases concerning immigrants, prisoners, homeless persons and others.

> In *O'Reilly v Mackman*, convicted prisoners who had lost remission of sentence in disciplinary proceedings after riots at Hull prison sued for a declaration that the decisions were null and void because of breaches of natural justice.[123] The defendants applied to have the action struck out on the ground that the decisions in

---

[112] See C Lewis [1992] CLJ 138 and (same author) *Judicial Remedies in Public Law*, ch 11 G.

[113] *Pasmore v Oswaldtwistle Council* [1898] AC 387. And see *Barraclough v Brown* [1897] AC 615 (declarations).

[114] *R v Paddington Valuation Officer, ex p Peachey Property Co* [1966] 1 QB 380; *R (Davies) v Financial Services Authority* [2003] EWCA Civ 1128, [2003] 4 All ER 1196.

[115] *R (G) v Immigration Appeal Tribunal* [2004] EWCA Civ 1731, [2005] 2 All ER 165.

[116] *Leech v Deputy Governor of Parkhurst Prison* [1988] AC 533. If an appeal against an immigration decision can be brought only from outside the United Kingdom, this may not be a satisfactory alternative to judicial review; cf *Chikwamba v Home Secretary* [2008] UKHL 40, [2009] 1 All ER 363.

[117] *R v Devon CC, ex p Baker* [1995] 1 All ER 73. Cf *R (Cowl) v Plymouth Council* (below, note 145).

[118] *R v Hillingdon Council, ex p Royco Homes Ltd* [1974] 1 QB 720.

[119] *R v Chief Constable, Merseyside, ex p Calveley* [1986] QB 424.

[120] *R v Birmingham Council, ex p Ferrero Ltd* [1993] 1 All ER 530.

[121] *R v Falmouth Port Health Authority, ex p South West Water Ltd* [2001] QB 445.

[122] See Woolf, Jowell and Le Sueur, *De Smith's Judicial Review*, pp 164–68; Wade and Forsyth, *Administrative Law*, pp 566–81; Craig, *Administrative Law*, ch 26.

[123] See *R v Board of Visitors of Hull Prison, ex p St Germain* [1979] QB 425.

question could be challenged only by an application for judicial review. *Held* (House of Lords) while the court had jurisdiction to grant the declarations sought, the prisoners' case was based solely on rights and obligations arising under public law. Order 53, by its requirement of leave from the court and by its time limit, protected public authorities against groundless or delayed attacks. It would 'as a general rule be contrary to public policy, and as such an abuse of the process of the court, to permit a person seeking to establish that a decision of a public authority infringed rights to which he was entitled to protection under public law to proceed by way of ordinary action and by this means to evade the provision of Order 53 for the protection of such authorities' (Lord Diplock).[124] And in *Cocks v Thanet DC*, the House held that a homeless person who challenged a decision by a local authority that he was not entitled to permanent accommodation must do so under Order 53, not by suing in the county court for a declaration and damages for breach of statutory duty.[125]

Although Parliament in 1981 had not provided that judicial review should be an exclusive remedy, these two decisions left no doubt that the Law Lords wished to carry further than Parliament had done the issue of exclusivity. The step taken in *O'Reilly* was justified on practical grounds, namely that litigants could be required to use the judicial review procedure as the former defects in the prerogative orders had been cured. But in seeking to protect public authorities from a flood of litigation,[126] *O'Reilly* relied heavily on the public law/private law distinction, despite the difficulties that this presents in English law.[127]

One consequence of *O'Reilly* was that much expensive litigation ensued in testing the procedural choices made by litigants, rather than in deciding the merits of their grievances. Sir William Wade's view in 2000 was dramatic: 'The need for law reform is clearly greater now than it was before 1977.'[128] This view seriously understated the general benefits that resulted from the reforms in 1977–82. Moreover, several decisions by the Lords after *O'Reilly* showed that there is no absolute rule of procedural exclusivity.[129] In *O'Reilly*, Lord Diplock had stated that an exception to the rule might exist where the invalidity of an official decision arose 'as a collateral issue in a claim for infringement of a right of the plaintiff arising under private law'.[130] The converse of this situation arose when a local council sued one of its tenants for non-payment of rent and the tenant raised the defence that rent increases made by the council were ultra vires. Although the tenant could have sought judicial review of the increases (and had not done so), the defence was held to be a proper defence of the tenant's private rights.[131]

In 1992, Lord Diplock's suggested exception was applied directly in *Roy v Kensington Family Practitioner Committee*. An NHS committee, acting under statutory powers, had deducted 20 per cent from money due to Dr Roy for providing medical services to the NHS. Dr Roy sued by ordinary action for the full amount. He was granted a declaration that the deduction had not been properly made, and judicial review of the deduction was not required.[132] This decision by the Lords was a significant step in reassessing the limits of the exclusivity rule. Lords Bridge and Lowry favoured restricting the *O'Reilly* rule to situations in which the individual's *sole* aim was to challenge a public law act or decision; thus the rule would not apply when an action to vindicate private rights *might* involve some questions as to the validity of a public law decision.[133] In 1995,

---

[124] [1983] 2 AC 237, 285. And see C F Forsyth [1985] CLJ 415; and Justice/All Souls Report, *Administrative Justice*, ch 6.

[125] [1983] 2 AC 286. In *O'Rourke v Camden Council* [1998] AC 188, the decision in *Cocks* was applied but other aspects of the case were disapproved.

[126] See Woolf, *Protection of the Public – A New Challenge*, ch 1; and (the same) [1986] PL 220; [1992] PL 221, 231.

[127] Ch 27.

[128] Wade and Forsyth, *Administrative Law* (8th edn, 2000), p 653.

[129] *Davy v Spelthorne Council* [1984] AC 262 (action in negligence relating to disputed enforcement notice).

[130] [1983] 2 AC 237, 285.

[131] *Wandsworth Council v Winder* [1985] AC 461.

[132] [1992] 1 AC 624 (P Cane [1992] PL 193).

[133] [1992] 1 AC 624, at 629 and 653 respectively.

the Lords further limited the effect of *O'Reilly*, holding that a regulatory decision interpreting a statutory licence might be questioned by proceedings in the Commercial Court.[134] Subsequent decisions reinforced the trend towards greater procedural flexibility and discouraged reliance on procedural defences.[135]

A relevant factor in this trend is that the Civil Procedure Rules permit transfer into and out of judicial review proceedings: a transfer in either direction will be decided by a judge designated to sit in the Administrative Court, who will consider if the claim raises issues of public law to which Part 54 CPR should apply.[136] Since the time limit that applies to judicial review is much shorter than for most civil claims,[137] a case that begins as a claim for judicial review is unlikely to strike a problem of limitation if it is transferred into ordinary procedure. In the converse situation, where the judicial review time-limit has not been observed even though the claim is solely concerned with public law issues, the judge may refuse to transfer the claim *into* judicial review procedure and this may cause the claim to fail for abuse of process.[138]

We have seen that in *O'Reilly*, Lord Diplock said that an exception to the rule of exclusivity could exist where the invalidity of an official decision arose 'as a collateral issue in a claim for infringement of a right of the plaintiff arising under private law'.[139] One form of collateral review occurs when tribunals whose task it is to decide whether a particular benefit should be paid to an individual under a statutory scheme are able to decide on the validity of the relevant regulations.[140] The issue of procedural exclusivity was raised when individuals sought to defend themselves against enforcement action by public authorities. It is now settled that an individual prosecuted for breach of subordinate legislation such as by-laws can as a defence plead that the legislation is invalid, and is not barred from doing so by failure to seek judicial review.[141] But under certain statutory schemes (for instance, the licensing of sex shops or the enforcement of planning control),[142] someone adversely affected by a public authority's decision may have no choice but to seek judicial review if he or she wishes to raise issues that will be outside the scope of a criminal court to determine.

Judicial discretion in judicial review proceedings

It has been said that judicial discretion is at the heart of administrative law.[143] Certainly, a judge has discretion to exercise at the permission stage, for instance relating to an issue of delay or alternative remedy. A study of how this discretion is exercised has shown that, especially since 2000, when permission became generally a matter to be decided on the papers (which may include the defendant's response), there has been a decline in the percentage of claims for which permission

---

[134] *Mercury Communications Ltd v Director General of Telecommunications* [1996] 1 All ER 575.

[135] See *Rye (Dennis) Pension Fund v Sheffield Council* [1997] 4 All ER 747 (county court action to secure payment of housing grant); *Steed v Home Secretary* [2000] 3 All ER 226 (HL); *Clark v University of Lincolnshire* [2000] 3 All ER 752; *D v Home Office* [2005] EWCA Civ 38, [2006] 1 All ER 183 (detained immigrants entitled to sue for damages on basis that their detention unlawful and not bound to seek judicial review); *Bunney v Burns Anderson* [2007] EWHC 1240 (Ch), [2007] 4 All ER 246.

[136] CPR, part 30; CPR rule 54.20 (and related practice direction).

[137] See page 710 above.

[138] And see *Clark v University of Lincolnshire* (above).

[139] Page 717 above.

[140] *Chief Adjudication Officer v Foster* [1993] 1 All ER 705 (D Feldman (1992) 108 LQR 45 and A W Bradley [1992] PL 185).

[141] *Boddington v British Transport Police* [1999] 2 AC 143 (C Forsyth [1998] PL 364).

[142] Respectively *Quietlynn Ltd v Plymouth Council* [1988] QB 114; *R v Wicks* [1998] AC 92. And see A W Bradley [1997] PL 365.

[143] See Lord Cooke, in Forsyth and Hare (eds), *The Golden Metwand and the Crooked Cord*, pp 203–20. Also Lewis, *Judicial Remedies in Public Law*, ch 11.

is granted.[144] In *R (Cowl)* v *Plymouth Council*,[145] the Court of Appeal drew attention to the importance of avoiding litigation whenever possible, and held that in the early stages of a claim for judicial review the parties and (if necessary at the permission stage) the judge, should actively consider alternative ways of resolving the dispute, whether by use of alternative procedures such as a statutory complaints procedure, or of other means such as mediation that are available under the Civil Procedure Rules.[146]

At the substantive hearing, the court exercises further discretion in deciding whether to grant relief even if grounds for review have been established. Although a judge may be reluctant to withhold relief in such a case,[147] relief has been denied for reasons such as the applicant's conduct and motives[148] and the public inconvenience that a remedy might entail.[149] Relief was withheld where planning permission had been granted on the basis of a factual error, but the court was satisfied that it would have been granted apart from this.[150] Similar flexibility was shown when, in reviewing decisions of the City's Take-over Panel, the Court of Appeal stated that in that context the court would see its role as 'historic rather than contemporaneous', i.e. that the court would seek to guide the panel in its future conduct of affairs, not to intervene in ongoing takeover battles.[151] But it is one thing to hold that the findings of the court speak for themselves and that no declaration is needed, but it is much less justifiable, when a claimant has made out his or her case, for the court in its discretion to discover reasons for withholding relief.

Statutory machinery for challenge

The technicalities of the prerogative remedies in their unreformed state often led in the past to legislation providing a simpler procedure for securing judicial review. Such legislation always related to specific powers of government and usually included provisions excluding other forms of judicial review.

An important example is provided by the standard procedure for the compulsory purchase of land. After a compulsory purchase order has been made by the local authority and, if objections have been raised, an inquiry has been held into the order, the minister must decide whether to confirm the order. If it is confirmed, there is a period of six weeks from the confirmation during which any person aggrieved by the purchase order may challenge the validity of the order in the High Court[152] on two grounds: (1) that the order is not within the powers of the enabling Act; or (2) that the requirements of the Act have not been complied with and that the objector's interests have been substantially prejudiced thereby.[153] These grounds have been interpreted as covering all grounds upon which judicial review may be sought, including in (1) matters affecting vires, abuse of discretion and natural justice, and in (2) observance of all relevant statutory procedures.[154]

---

[144] V Bondy and M Sunkin [2008] PL 647. In 2006, the success rate in non-immigration civil cases of judicial review was 35% and in asylum and immigration cases, 14%. Overall it was 22%.

[145] [2001] EWCA Civ 1935, [2002] 1 WLR 803.

[146] On the use of alternative dispute resolution in administrative law, see M Supperstone, D Stilitz and C Sheldon [2006] PL 299 and S Boyron [2006] PL 247. On the increasing likelihood that claims for judicial review will be settled by consent, not by adjudication, see V Bondy and M Sunkin [2009] PL 237.

[147] See T Bingham [1991] PL 64. Also S Sedley [1989] PL 32 (criticising the use of discretion in *R* v *Chief Constable of North Wales* [1982] 3 All ER 141).

[148] E.g. *R* v *Commissioners of Customs and Excise, ex p Cooke* [1970] 1 All ER 1068.

[149] *R* v *Social Services Secretary, ex p Association of Metropolitan Authorities* [1986] 1 All ER 164.

[150] *R* v *North Somerset Council, ex p Cadbury Garden Centre Ltd, The Times*, 22 November 2000.

[151] *R* v *Panel on Take-overs and Mergers, ex p Datafin plc* [1987] QB 815. And see C Lewis [1988] PL 78.

[152] Or in Scotland in the Court of Session. On when the six weeks begin to run, see *Griffiths* v *Environment Secretary* [1983] 2 AC 51.

[153] Acquisition of Land Act 1981, s 23 (consolidating earlier Acts).

[154] *Ashbridge Investments Ltd* v *Minister of Housing* [1965] 3 All ER 371; *Coleen Properties Ltd* v *Minister of Housing* [1971] 1 All ER 1049.

When an aggrieved person makes an application to the High Court, the court may make an interim order suspending the purchase order, either generally or so far as it affects the applicant's property. If the order is not challenged in the High Court during the six-week period, the order is statutorily protected from challenge; any other form of judicial review of the order is excluded, before or after the confirmation of the order.[155]

This method of challenge, which first appeared in the Housing Act 1930, was a distinct improvement on legislative attempts to exclude judicial review of ministers' actions altogether and the remedy it provided was much more effective than reliance on the prerogative orders at common law. Today, it provides a statutory form of review in respect of many decisions relating to the control of land.[156] Use of this remedy has enabled the High Court to give its entire attention to the principles of judicial review in issue, uncomplicated by procedural or jurisdictional questions. The time limit on the right of challenge is necessary in order that, if no objection is taken promptly, the authorities concerned can put the decision into effect. Other statutory remedies include the right to appeal to the High Court on matters of law from many tribunals[157] and on points of law in respect of planning decisions.[158] Although these remedies are not applications for judicial review within the meaning of the Senior Courts Act 1981, s 31, they are heard in the Administrative Court.[159] By enabling there to be judicial review of executive decisions, they help to satisfy the requirements of art 6 ECHR.[160]

An applicant to the court must, however, come within the scope of the procedure and the question of who may do so depends on the statutory provisions. The six-week right to challenge compulsory purchase orders and planning decisions is given to 'any person aggrieved'. This clearly includes owners who object to their land being compulsorily purchased, but in 1961 it was held not to include neighbouring owners who had objected at a public inquiry to proposed new development; they were considered to have no legal interest that would render them aggrieved persons in law.[161] In 1973, a more generous interpretation was given to the phrase 'person aggrieved', including within it the officers of an amenity association who had opposed new development at a public inquiry.[162] Today, there are many reasons why the term 'person aggrieved' should be given a meaning consistent with the broad test of 'sufficient interest' that applies to judicial review in general.

Given the reforms in the procedure for judicial review that we have examined in this chapter, is there still a need for a separate statutory form of challenge to certain decisions? The Planning Act 2008 created the Infrastructure Planning Commission for granting development consent to major projects.[163] By s 118, a legal challenge to an order of the Commission that grants such consent may be made in the Administrative Court (in Scotland, in the Court of Session) only if (a) proceedings are brought by way of a claim for judicial review and (b) the claim is filed within six weeks of the publication of the order, or the reasons for it (if this is later). This is a welcome development, since the challenge may be decided on the basis of the general rules of judicial review. The time-limit is not generous, but in such cases, as with compulsory purchase orders and the like, those affected will almost always have been involved in proceedings prior to the making of the development order.

---

[155] Acquisition of Land Act 1981, s 23; and see p 721 below.
[156] E.g. Town and Country Planning Act 1990, ss 284–8; Planning and Compulsory Purchase Act 2004, s 113.
[157] Tribunals and Inquiries Act 1992, s 11.
[158] Town and Country Planning Act 1990, ss 289, 290.
[159] See CPR, Part 52 (esp 52.17, 18 and section III).
[160] See R (Alconbury Developments Ltd) v Environment Secretary [2001] UKHL 23, [2003] 2 AC 295 and Bryan v UK (1995) 21 EHRR 342.
[161] Buxton v Minister of Housing [1961] 1 QB 278; cf Maurice v London CC [1964] 2 QB 362.
[162] Turner v Environment Secretary (1973) 72 LGR 380.
[163] See ch 29 B.

Statutory exclusion of judicial control[164]

When judges are interpreting legislation, they apply a strong presumption that the legislature does not intend access to the courts to be denied. Where Parliament has appointed a specific tribunal for the enforcement of new rights and duties, it is necessary to have recourse to that tribunal in the first instance. In principle, the tribunal's decisions will be subject to judicial review. But many statutes have contained words intended to oust the jurisdiction of the courts. Such provisions have long been interpreted by the judges so as to leave, if possible, their supervisory powers intact.[165] One frequent clause was that a particular decision 'shall be final', but this does not exclude judicial review.[166] Such a clause means simply that there is no right of appeal from the decision. Another clause which does not deprive the courts of supervisory jurisdiction is where a statutory order when made shall have effect 'as if enacted in the Act' which authorised it; the court may nonetheless hold the order to be invalid if it conflicts with provisions of the Act.[167] The fact that a tribunal is described by statute as a 'superior court of record' is not sufficient to exclude the supervisory jurisdiction of the High Court.[168]

It is then only by an exceptionally strong formula that Parliament can deprive the High Court or the Court of Session of supervisory jurisdiction over inferior tribunals and public authorities. As we have seen, exclusion clauses frequently accompany the granting of an express right to challenge the validity of an order or decision during a limited time. Thus, subject to the possibility of challenge to the order within six weeks of its confirmation, a compulsory purchase order 'shall not, either before or after it has been confirmed, made or given, be questioned in any legal proceedings whatsoever . . . .'.[169]

> In *Smith* v *East Elloe Council* the plaintiff, whose land had been taken compulsorily for the building of council houses nearly six years previously, alleged that the making of the order had been caused by wrongful action and bad faith on the part of the council and its clerk. She submitted that the exclusion clause did not exclude the court's power in cases of fraud and bad faith. The House of Lords held by 3–2 that the effect of the Act was to protect compulsory purchase orders from judicial review except by statutory challenge during the six-week period. Although the validity of the order could no longer be challenged, the action against the clerk of the council for damages could proceed.[170]

A very different attitude towards an exclusion clause was taken by the House of Lords in 1968 in a decision which we have already considered in relation to jurisdictional control.

> In *Anisminic Ltd* v *Foreign Compensation Commission*, the Foreign Compensation Act 1950, s 4(4), provided that the determination by the commission of any application made under the Act 'shall not be called in question in any court of law'. The commission was a judicial body responsible for distributing funds supplied by foreign governments as compensation to British subjects. It rejected a claim made by Anisminic, for a reason which the company submitted was erroneous in law and exceeded the commission's jurisdiction. *Held*, by a majority, s 4(4) did not debar a court from inquiring whether the commission had made in law a correct decision on the question of eligibility to claim. 'Determination' meant a real determination, not a purported determination. By taking into account a factor which in the view of the majority was irrelevant to the scheme, the commission's decision was a nullity. Lord Wilberforce said, 'What would be the purpose of

---

[164] Woolf, Jowell and Le Sueur, *De Smith's Judicial Review*, pp 184–205; Wade and Forsyth, *Administrative Law*, pp 610–34; Craig, *Administrative Law*, ch 27.

[165] E.g. *Colonial Bank of Australasia* v *Willan* (1874) 5 PC 417 (express exclusion of certiorari not effective where manifest defect of jurisdiction).

[166] *R* v *Medical Appeal Tribunal, ex p Gilmore* [1957] 1 QB 574.

[167] *Minister of Health* v *R* [1931] AC 494.

[168] *R (Cart)* v *Upper Tribunal* [2009] EWHC 3052 (Admin), [2010] 1 All ER 908 (but note the distinction in respect of judicial review drawn between the Special Immigration Appeals Commission and the Upper Tribunal).

[169] Acquisition of Land Act 1981, s 25.

[170] [1956] AC 736.

defining by statute the limits of a tribunal's powers, if by means of a clause inserted in the instrument of definition, those limits could safely be passed?'[171]

The decision is a striking example of the ability of the courts to interpret privative clauses in such a way as to maintain the possibility of judicial review. Although the authority of *Smith v East Elloe Council* was questioned in the *Anisminic* case, it was not overruled: indeed, the issues involved in considering the finality of a compulsory purchase order are different from those involved in considering whether an award of compensation should be subject to review. A further distinction is between a statute that seeks to exclude the jurisdiction of the courts entirely (as in *Anisminic*) and a statute that confers a right to apply to the courts for review within a stated time (as in the case of a compulsory purchase order) but excludes judicial review thereafter. In 1976, the statutory bar on attempts to challenge the validity of a purchase order after the six-week period was held to be absolute: an aggrieved owner could not bring such a challenge some months later, even though he alleged that the order had been vitiated by a breach of natural justice and good faith which he had only discovered after the six-week period.[172] Even if the purchase order must stand, this should not prevent the owner from seeking compensation from those responsible for alleged acts of bad faith.

Parliamentary authority to exclude judicial review

We have seen that in the debate about the foundations of judicial review even those who denied that parliamentary intent was the basis of judicial review accepted that Parliament could restrict or exclude judicial review in specific instances.[173] Today, an attempt by Parliament to do so might conflict with European law. Thus a certificate issued by the Secretary of State for Northern Ireland that purported to be 'conclusive evidence' that a police decision was taken for reasons of national security was held to be contrary to the principle of effective judicial control in European Community law.[174] When a similar certificate prevented a Roman Catholic company from pursuing a complaint of religious discrimination in the award of contracts, the 'conclusive evidence' rule was held to be a disproportionate restriction on the right of access to a court and thus it breached art 6(1) ECHR.[175] Where a matter concerns 'civil rights and obligations', as in that case, exclusion of access to a court will violate art 6(1).[176] According to the Strasbourg case law, a national legislature may impose reasonable time limits on access to a court, but such restrictions must not impair the essence of the right.[177] The rule that judicial review must be sought promptly and in any event within three months would be likely to comply with art 6; so in most cases would the six-week rule on challenges to planning and compulsory purchase decisions. But an absolute exclusion of review after six weeks might be disproportionate in a case where relevant information is concealed by officials until after the right of access to a court has lapsed. No issues as to art 6 of the ECHR are raised by the exclusion of judicial review on matters that do not involve an individual's 'civil rights and obligations', such as the validity of an Act of the Scottish Parliament[178] or a Speaker's certificate under the Parliament Act 1911.[179]

---

[171] [1969] 2 AC 147, 208 (and ch 30 A above). For the legislative sequel, see Foreign Compensation Act 1969, s 3.

[172] *R v Environment Secretary, ex p Ostler* [1977] QB 122 (N P Gravells (1978) 41 MLR 383 and J E Alder (1980) 43 MLR 670). Also *R v Cornwall CC, ex p Huntington* [1994] 1 All ER 694.

[173] Ch 30, at p 727.

[174] *Case 222/84 Johnston v Chief Constable RUC* [1987] QB 129.

[175] *Tinnelly & Sons Ltd v UK* (1998) 27 EHRR 249.

[176] See e.g. *Zander v Sweden* (1993) 18 EHRR 175 and *Fayed v UK* (1994) 18 EHRR 393.

[177] *Stubbings v UK* (1996) 23 EHRR 213.

[178] Scotland Act 1998, s 28(5).

[179] Parliament Act 1911, s 3.

Parliament has an uneven record in relation to the exclusion of the courts. The Franks committee in 1957 recommended that no statute should oust the prerogative orders. In response, the Tribunals and Inquiries Act 1958 (re-enacted in 1992, s 12) provided that:

(*a*) any provision in an Act passed before 1 August 1958 that any order or determination shall not be called into question in any court; or

(*b*) any provision in such an Act which by similar words excludes any of the powers of the High Court

shall not prevent the remedies of certiorari or mandamus (now quashing and mandatory orders) from being available. A more general provision protects the supervisory jurisdiction of the Court of Session. These provisions do not apply: (i) to an order or determination of a court of law, or (ii) where an Act makes provision for application to the High Court within a stated time (for example, the power to challenge a purchase order within six weeks, as in *Smith* v *East Elloe Council*).[180]

For several reasons, s 12 of the 1992 Act is far from being a sufficient response to the problem of ouster clauses. First, for the constitutional reason that Parliament is not able to bind what a future Parliament may do, it has had no application to any legislation enacted since August 1958.[181] Second, the protection given in English law to what are now quashing and mandatory orders should be replaced by broader protection (as in Scotland) for judicial review in general. Third, s 12 has been held not to apply to 'conclusive evidence' clauses.[182] Given the developments in relation to judicial review in European law, there is a case to be made for a statute that would create a strong rule of interpretation to preserve the possibility of judicial review that would apply to all legislation, whenever enacted, on the lines of the Human Rights Act 1998, s 3. Such a rule would not block a determined attempt by the executive to remove judicial review from one or more areas of government. But if such an attempt were made in Parliament, it might help to ensure that the two Houses would rigorously scrutinise the government's proposals and motivation.[183]

The need for such scrutiny was tested by a remarkable ouster clause in the Asylum and Immigration (Treatment of Claimants etc.) Bill 2004. The government sought to remove the right to judicial review of decisions by the proposed Asylum and Immigration Tribunal, and of deportation and removal decisions made by the Home Secretary and officials. The clause expressly excluded a court from considering proceedings to determine whether a purported determination or decision was a nullity by reason of lack of jurisdiction, irregularity, error of law, breach of natural justice or any other matter; limited provision was made for review in case of bad faith or if Convention rights were affected.[184] The clause passed through a complaisant House of Commons but was withdrawn by the government before it was debated in the Lords. It raised fundamental questions about the authority of Parliament to dispense with an independent and impartial scheme of judicial review.

---

[180] *Hamilton* v *Secretary of State for Scotland* 1972 SLT 233.

[181] See e.g. Intelligence Services Act 1994, s 9(4); Police Act 1997, s 91(10). By the Regulation of Investigatory Powers Act 2000, s 67(8), decisions by the tribunal set up by the Act '(including decisions as to whether they have jurisdiction) shall not be subject to appeal or be liable to be questioned in any court'.

[182] *R* v *Registrar of Companies, ex p Central Bank of India* [1986] QB 1114. A different view of 'conclusive evidence' clauses might be taken in other contexts.

[183] For consideration of legislation that removed or substantially impaired the role of the High Court in judicial review, see Lord Woolf [1995] PL 57, 68; cf the comments of Lord Irvine [1996] PL 59, 75–8.

[184] The text of the clause is at [2004] JR 97, with related articles and parliamentary materials. See also Lord Woolf [2004] CLJ 317; A Le Sueur [2004] PL 225; and ch 20 B.

Remedies in Scots administrative law[185]

The prerogative orders were never part of Scots law, except to the extent that they were introduced into Scotland by legislation for the purposes of revenue law, nor did a separate court of equity develop in Scotland. Apart from statutory remedies like the six-week right to challenge a compulsory purchase order, which apply both in Scotland and England, administrative law remedies in Scotland are essentially the same remedies as are available in private law to enforce matters of civil obligation. The most important of these remedies (which are now available subject to procedural changes made in 1985 and subsequently) are (a) the ancient remedy of *reduction*, by which any document (including decisions of tribunals, local by-laws, the dismissal of public servants and disciplinary decisions) may be quashed as being in excess of jurisdiction, in breach of natural justice or in other ways contrary to law;[186] (b) the no less ancient remedy of *declarator*, from which the English declaration of right was derived; (c) the remedies of *suspension* and *interdict*, which together serve broadly the same purposes as prohibition and injunction in English law; (d) the action for damages for breach of civil obligation; and (e) a summary remedy to enforce performance of statutory duties, comparable with but not identical to mandamus.[187] By contrast with the former English law, all relevant forms of relief may be sought in the same proceedings.[188]

Several differences from English law may be noted. First, it was established in *Watt* v *Lord Advocate* that while the remedy of reduction may be used to quash decisions of tribunals which are in excess of their jurisdiction, it is not available to review errors of law made by a tribunal within jurisdiction.[189] However, the Court of Session also held that the error of law in question had led the tribunal to exceed its jurisdiction, since it had caused a statutory entitlement to unemployment benefit to be withheld on an extraneous consideration. This decision applied to Scots law the principle in *Anisminic Ltd* v *Foreign Compensation Commission*.[190]

Second, in Scots law there is no direct equivalent to relator proceedings. However, the rules on title and interest to sue enable individuals to sue directly to enforce many public rights.[191] In *Wilson* v *Independent Broadcasting Authority*, members of a group campaigning in the 1979 referendum on devolution had title and interest to sue for an interdict to restrain a series of political broadcasts which did not maintain a balance between the two sides. The judge, Lord Ross, could see 'no reason in principle why an individual should not sue in order to prevent a breach by a public body of a duty owed by that public body to the public'.[192] This welcome statement of principle departed from some earlier decisions.[193] In 1987, the organisation Age Concern Scotland was held to have title but no interest to challenge as ultra vires official guidance that limited the making of supplementary payments to old people for severe weather conditions.[194] Although a teachers' association had title and interest to challenge a university's unlawful action where its

---

[185] *Stair Encyclopedia of the Laws of Scotland*, vol I, reissue, part 4; C M G Himsworth, in Supperstone, Goudie and Walker (eds), *Judicial Review*, ch 21; Clyde and Edwards, *Judicial Review*, part 5.

[186] See e.g. *Malloch* v *Aberdeen Corpn* [1971] 2 All ER 1278; *Barrs* v *British Wool Marketing Board* 1957 SC 72.

[187] Court of Session Act 1988, s 45(b); *T Docherty Ltd* v *Burgh of Monifieth* 1971 SLT 12. Other remedies include an order *ad factum praestandum* (for performance of a specific duty) and a decree of repetition (that could for instance issue to recover money paid over in response to an ultra vires demand).

[188] E.g. *Macbeth* v *Ashley* (1874) LR 2 HL (Sc) 352.

[189] 1979 SC 120.

[190] Note 171 above. Also *Stair Encyclopedia*, paras 45, 47–50; Clyde and Edwards, pp 597–603.

[191] *Duke of Atholl* v *Torrie* (1852) I Macq 65; *Ogston* v *Aberdeen Tramways Co* (1896) 24 R 8. Also *Stair Encyclopedia*, paras 122–38; Clyde and Edwards, ch 10.

[192] 1979 SC 351.

[193] *D & J Nicol* v *Dundee Harbour Trustees* 1915 SC (HL) 7; *Simpson* v *Edinburgh Corp* 1960 SC 313.

[194] *Scottish Old People's Welfare Council, Petitioners* 1987 SLT 179. Clyde and Edwards suggest that prematurity was the reason why there was no interest (p 377). In *PTOA Ltd* v *Renfrew Council* 1997 SLT 1112, the taxi drivers' association lacked title to sue in challenging the council's licensing policy.

members could not be expected to do so individually,[195] the test of standing in Scotland is applied more strictly than the test of 'sufficient interest' in English law.[196]

Third, difficult situations brought about by official failures may sometimes be resolved by the power of the Court of Session to exercise an extraordinary equitable jurisdiction in the form of the *nobile officium* of the court.[197]

Since 1985 Scotland has had a procedure of application for judicial review, which shares a name with but is different from the English model. It was introduced later in Scotland than in English law, because the acute difficulties relating to the prerogative orders and other remedies did not exist in Scots law. However, the ordinary procedures of civil litigation were realised to be unsuitable for the prompt resolution of disputes arising in areas such as housing and immigration.[198]

In 1985, rules of court[199] established a procedure of petition, known as an application for judicial review, which *must* be used whenever an application is made to the supervisory jurisdiction of the Court of Session for one or more of the remedies mentioned earlier. The rules are intended to provide for the rapid handling of every application, with the main steps being under the control of individual judges designated for the purpose.[200] The leave of the court is not required for an application, but an application without any merits may sometimes be briskly rejected. Although the rules impose no time limit on petitions for judicial review, under general principles of Scots law a petition may fail on a plea of *mora* (delay), taciturnity and acquiescence.[201]

One problem that has arisen is that the 'supervisory jurisdiction' of the Court of Session is not defined in legislation, though it has often been described in judgments.[202] It cannot be defined by reference to the remedies that may be granted on a successful application for judicial review since those remedies are available throughout the civil law. Some judgments after 1985 drew for this purpose upon the private law/public law distinction in English law,[203] but in 1992 the Court of Session in *West v Secretary of State for Scotland*[204] robustly rejected that distinction. It held that the court has power under its supervisory jurisdiction 'to regulate the process by which decisions are taken by any person or body to whom a jurisdiction, power or authority has been delegated or entrusted by statute, agreement or any other instrument', in particular where there was a 'tripartite relationship' between the decision maker, the individual affected and the person or body from whom the power to decide was derived. In *West*, a prison officer was seeking judicial review of a decision by the Scottish Office that his removal expenses should not be paid after he had been transferred from one prison to another. This dispute was seen as one arising from a contract of employment, with no features bringing the dispute within the 'supervisory jurisdiction'.[205] The

---

[195] *Educational Institute of Scotland v Robert Gordon University*, The Times, 1 July 1996.

[196] See Lord Hope [2001] PL 294, discussing *Rape Crisis Centre and Brindley, Petitioners* 2000 SCLR 807 (petitioners had no title to review Home Secretary's decision to admit an American boxer and convicted rapist to fight in Glasgow). Cf *Uprichard v Fife Council* 2000 SCLR 949.

[197] *Ferguson, Petitioners* 1965 SC 16.

[198] See *Brown v Hamilton* 1983 SLT 397, 418 (Lord Fraser); *Stair Encyclopedia*, p 191; and A W Bradley [1987] PL 313.

[199] See now Rules of the Court of Session, ch 58.

[200] But this does not always ensure that petitions are dealt with quickly – see the drawn-out procedural complexities that led to *Somerville v Scottish Ministers* [2007] UKHL 44, [2007] 1 WLR 2734.

[201] *Stair Encyclopedia*, para 121; see *Hanlon v Traffic Commissioners* 1988 SLT 802; *Uprichard v Fife Council* 2000 SCLR 949; and *Somerville v Scottish Ministers* [2006] CSIH 52, 2007 SLT 96, [90]–[94].

[202] E.g. *Moss Empires Ltd v Glasgow Assessor* 1917 SC (HL) 1.

[203] Including *Tehrani v Argyll Health Board (No 2)* 1990 SLT 118 and *Watt v Strathclyde Council* 1992 SLT 324. See Himsworth (note 185) and Lord Clyde, in Finnie, Himsworth and Walker (eds), *Edinburgh Essays in Public Law*, pp 281–93.

[204] 1992 SLT 636. See W J Wolffe [1992] PL 625; *Stair Encyclopedia*, para 115; Clyde and Edwards, *Judicial Review*, pp 344–7.

[205] See also *Naik v Stirling University* 1994 SLT 449 and *Blair v Lochaber Council* 1995 SLT 407.

court's approach to jurisdiction was based on an analysis of the process of decision-making and its review. Later judgments have doubted whether a 'tripartite relationship' is always essential.[206] Since there is no divergence between the substantive grounds of judicial review in English and Scots law, *West* may enable the Scottish courts to apply supervisory jurisdiction to regulatory and similar powers of private organisations, when in English law this would be impeded by the private/public distinction.

In 2009, the report of the (Gill) Civil Courts Review in Scotland examined the increased workload caused by judicial review and found that the procedure was in need of reform. In particular, (*a*) the complex two-part rule of title and interest to sue should be replaced by a rule of 'sufficient interest'; (*b*) a time limit of three months for seeking judicial review should be introduced, similar to the English model; (*c*) a petitioner for review should have to obtain leave to proceed from a judge after the respondent has had a chance to oppose the granting of leave: the granting of leave would depend on whether the petition had a reasonable prospect of success. If adopted, these changes would bring the Scottish procedure for judicial review significantly closer to that in English law.

Habeas corpus[207]

The prerogative writ of habeas corpus is in English law an important remedy in respect of public or private action which takes away individual liberty. It was formerly used as the means of securing judicial control of executive acts in extradition law,[208] and it is still used to a lesser extent in other areas involving detention, such as immigration control,[209] mental health,[210] child care[211] and criminal procedure.[212] Unlike the prerogative orders, the writ has not been the subject of recent legislative reform. The writ originally enabled a court of common law to summon persons whose presence was necessary for pending proceedings. In the fifteenth and sixteenth centuries, King's Bench and Common Pleas used habeas corpus to assert their authority over rival courts and to release persons imprisoned by such courts in excess of their jurisdiction. In the seventeenth century, the writ was used to check arbitrary arrest by order of the King or the King's Council.[213]

It was of the essence of habeas corpus that it was a procedure by which the court could determine the legality of an individual's detention, effectively and without delay. Habeas Corpus Acts were enacted in 1679, 1816 and 1862,[214] not to widen the jurisdiction of the courts but to enhance the effectiveness of the writ and to ensure that applications were dealt with promptly. Thus the 1679 Act prohibited evasion of habeas corpus by transfer of prisoners detained for 'any criminal or supposed criminal matter' to places outside the jurisdiction of the English courts on pain of heavy penalties. The 1816 Act gave the judge power in civil cases to inquire summarily into the truth of the facts stated in the gaoler's return to the writ, even though the return was 'good and

---

[206] See *Naik v Stirling University* above; *McIntosh v Aberdeenshire Council* 1999 SLT 93, 97; and cf *Blair v Lochaber Council* 1995 SLT 407.

[207] See Sharpe, *The Law of Habeas Corpus*; Clark and McCoy, *The Most Fundamental Legal Right*; Lewis, *Judicial Remedies in Public Law*, ch 12. On the history, HEL IX 108–25 and Forsyth, *Cases and Opinions on Constitutional Law*, ch 16. See also S Brown [2000] PL 31; and ch 21 E.

[208] Ch 20 C. On the exclusion of habeas corpus by the Extradition Act 2003, see *R (Hilali) v Governor of Whitemoor Prison* [2008] UKHL 3, [2008] AC 805.

[209] E.g. *R v Durham Prison (Governor), ex p Hardial Singh* [1984] 1 All ER 983; and *Tan Te Lam v Superintendent of Tai A Chau Detention Centre* [1997] AC 97.

[210] E.g. *Re S-C (mental patient)* [1996] QB 599; *GD v Edgware Community Hospital* [2008] EWHC 3572 (Admin).

[211] *LM v Essex CC* (1999) 1 FLR 988.

[212] *R (Bentham) v Governor of Wandsworth Prison* [2006] EWHC 121 (QB).

[213] For *Darnel's* case and the Petition of Right, see ch 12 D.

[214] For the detail, see Taswell-Langmead, *English Constitutional History*, pp 432–6.

sufficient in law'.[215] The 1862 Act provided that the writ was not to issue from a court in England into any colony or foreign dominion of the Crown where there were courts having authority to grant habeas corpus. Detention within Northern Ireland and Scotland is a matter for the courts in those jurisdictions.[216]

Habeas corpus is described as a writ of right which is granted *ex debito justitiae*. This means that a prima facie case must be shown before it is issued but, unlike the prerogative orders, it is not a discretionary remedy and it may not be refused merely because an alternative remedy exists.[217] Habeas corpus is a remedy against *unlawful* detention: thus it enabled the court to decide whether a profoundly retarded and autistic person incapable of giving consent could be detained under the Mental Health Act 1983 without an order being made for compulsory detention.[218] This decision concerned the limits of a hospital trust's statutory powers of detention. It is more difficult to know whether habeas corpus is a remedy for correcting every error made by a body with power to detain.

Certainly, the writ does not provide a right of appeal for those detained by order of a court or tribunal. It might be supposed that habeas corpus lies whenever there are grounds for judicial review of a decision to detain someone, but the position is much less clear-cut than this.[219] Indeed, the reforms in judicial review procedure that we have considered in this chapter did not apply to habeas corpus, and the two procedures remain separate. In *Rutty's* case,[220] the High Court, acting under the Habeas Corpus Act 1816 to examine the truth of the facts stated in the return, held that there had been no evidence before the magistrate eight years earlier to justify an order that an 18-year-old woman with learning difficulties be detained. But in a line of immigration cases during the 1970s, the courts were most reluctant to make effective use of habeas corpus as a means of reviewing executive decisions, for example in the case of someone about to be removed from the country as an illegal entrant.[221] We have seen that in *Khawaja's* case the House of Lords reversed this trend.[222]

During the 1990s, the Court of Appeal distinguished between the scope of habeas corpus and the grounds of judicial review, holding that habeas corpus could mount a challenge to the jurisdiction or vires of a detention decision, but not if the decision was 'within the powers' of the decision-maker yet was defective for reasons such as procedural error, mistake of law, or unreasonableness. The reason given for this limitation on habeas corpus was that, in the latter class of cases, the decision was lawful until it had been quashed by an order of certiorari.[223] However, this approach seems deeply flawed: it is based on an outdated distinction (between 'errors as to jurisdiction' and 'errors within jurisdiction') which has ceased to apply in judicial review generally. It is now settled that breaches of natural justice, errors of law and so on cause a decision to be ultra vires:[224] how then can such a decision be held to be 'within powers' in the law of habeas corpus? When individual liberty is at stake, it would be unjust for the court to refuse habeas corpus to

---

[215] See e.g. *R v Board of Control, ex p Rutty* [1956] 2 QB 109.

[216] *Re Keenan* [1972] 1 QB 533; *Re McElduff* [1972] NILR 1; *R v Cowle* (1759) 2 Burr 834, 856.

[217] *R v Governor of Pentonville Prison, ex p Azam* [1974] AC 18, 31 (CA).

[218] *R v Bournewood NHS Trust, ex p L* [1999] 1 AC 458.

[219] Woolf, Jowell and Le Sueur, *De Smith's Judicial Review*, pp 195, 868; Rubinstein, *Jurisdiction and Illegality*, pp 105–16, 176–86.

[220] Note 215 above.

[221] The decisions include *R v Home Secretary, ex p Mughal* [1974] 1 QB 313 and *R v Home Secretary, ex p Zamir* [1980] AC 930. And see C Newdick [1982] PL 89.

[222] *R v Home Secretary, ex p Khawaja* [1984] AC 74 and ch 30 A.

[223] *R v Home Secretary, ex p Cheblak* [1991] 2 All ER 319; *R v Home Secretary, ex p Muboyayi* [1992] 1 QB 244. In *Muboyayi*, habeas corpus was issued urgently to stop removal of an individual pending decision of his application for judicial review; the court could now issue an interim injunction against removal: *M v Home Office* (note 65 above).

[224] See *Ridge v Baldwin* [1964] AC 40; *Anisminic Ltd v Foreign Compensation Commission* [1969] 2 AC 147; *R v Hull University Visitor, ex p Page* [1993] AC 682.

someone who had shown that the decision to detain him or her was ultra vires but first required to be quashed by certiorari: to avoid the injustice, the court would need to grant the detainee permission to apply for judicial review and to quash the decision concerned forthwith. Although this approach has been authoritatively criticised for eroding habeas corpus,[225] it was applied in 1996 where young persons had been wrongly imprisoned for non-payment of fines, and the court held that their detention could be challenged by judicial review, but not by habeas corpus.[226]

This uncertainty affecting habeas corpus is reflected in case law at Strasbourg: the European Court of Human Rights held in the case of a mental patient that habeas corpus did not enable the English court to determine both the substantive and formal legality of the detention,[227] but reached the opposite conclusion in the case of persons suspected of terrorist offences.[228] By art 5(4) ECHR, every person who is detained is entitled to take proceedings by which the lawfulness of the detention is decided speedily by a court, and release is ordered if the detention is unlawful. This is one of the most fundamental of all human rights and art 5(4) is known in Europe as 'the habeas corpus provision'.[229] The awkward interface that has developed in English law between habeas corpus and judicial review needs to be resolved.[230] One possible reform would be to amend the Senior Courts Act 1981, s 31, to add an order of habeas corpus to the forms of relief that may be granted on judicial review, and this would leave intact the law on the writ of habeas corpus. In practice, it is already possible for an applicant to apply both for habeas corpus and, in the alternative, by judicial review for a mandatory order directing release on conditions.[231]

Normally the applicant for habeas corpus will be the person detained, but a relative or other person may apply on his or her behalf if the detainee cannot do so. Application is made to the High Court *ex parte* (that is, without the other side being heard) supported by an affidavit or statement of fact.[232] If prima facie grounds are shown, the court ordinarily directs that notice of motion be given to the person having control of the person detained (for example, a prison governor) but notice may also be served on a minister (for example, the Home Secretary) who is responsible for the detention and who may file evidence in reply. On the day named, the merits of the application will be argued. If the court decides that the writ should issue, it orders the prisoner's release forthwith. Under this practice the respondent need not produce the prisoner in court at the hearing: exceptionally, an applicant may be allowed to present his or her case in person.[233] No return to the writ is made as the writ itself has not been issued. In exceptional cases the court may order the issue of the writ on the *ex parte* application if, for example, the detainee is at risk of being taken outside the jurisdiction. Disobedience to the writ is punishable by fine or imprisonment for contempt of court, and there may be penalties under the Act of 1679. Officers of the Crown are subject to the writ.[234] An appeal from the High Court's decision in a civil matter may go via the Court of Appeal to the House of Lords, and in a criminal matter (for example, in extradition proceedings) from the Divisional Court to the Lords, with leave.[235]

---

[225] Law Commission, Law Com No 226, part XI; H W R Wade (1997) 113 LQR 55. Also A Le Sueur [1992] PL 13; M Shrimpton [1993] PL 24.

[226] R v *Oldham Justices, ex p Cawley* [1997] QB 1. And see S Brown [2000] PL 31. Cf *Re S-C (mental patient)* [1996] QB 599 (habeas corpus granted when social worker's application for S-C's detention was untruthful).

[227] *X v UK* (1981) 4 EHRR 188.

[228] *Brogan v UK* (1988) 11 EHRR 117.

[229] Harris, O'Boyle and Warbrick, *Law of the ECHR*, pp 182–96.

[230] See e.g. *B v Barking, Havering and Brentwood NHS Trust* (1999) 1 FLR 106; *Sheikh v Home Secretary* [2001] ACD 93; and O Davies [1997] JR 11.

[231] See *R (A and others) v Home Secretary* [2007] EWHC 142 (Admin).

[232] RSC, Ord 54 (kept in being by the Civil Procedure Rules).

[233] *Re Wring* [1960] 1 All ER 536. And see *M v Home Office* [1994] 1 AC 377.

[234] *Re Thompson* (1889) 5 TLR 565; *Secretary of State v O'Brien* [1923] AC 603.

[235] Detailed provision for appeals is in the Administration of Justice Act 1960 (ss 5, 14, 15) as amended by the Access to Justice Act 1999. On the civil/criminal distinction, see e.g. *Amand v Home Secretary* [1943] AC 147, 156.

The writ of habeas corpus has no exact counterpart in Scots law, but ever since the Scottish Parliament's Act in 1701 for preventing Wrongous Imprisonment there have been strict provisions restricting the length of time within which a person committed for trial may be held in custody.[236] As regards civil detention, the Court of Session may order the release of any person who is unlawfully detained. If no more convenient remedy is available (for example, by a suspension and interdict), the detained person may petition the Inner House of the Court of Session for release in the exercise of the *nobile officium* of the court.

---

[236] On the '80 day' and '110 day' rules, see the Criminal Procedure (Scotland) Act 1995, s 65.

CHAPTER 32

Liability of public authorities and the Crown

In chapters 30 and 31, we examined the law that enables the courts to review the decisions of public authorities on grounds such as ultra vires, error of law and breach of natural justice. We now consider the position of public authorities in relation to civil liability.[1] In principle, public authorities in English law are subject to the same rules of liability in tort and contract as apply to private individuals. There is no separate law of administrative liability for wrongful acts.[2] However, to maintain public services and perform regulatory functions, public authorities require powers which are not available to private individuals. Many public works, such as motorways and power stations, could not be created unless there was power in the public interest to override private rights that might be affected. Parliament legislates to enable public authorities to intervene in private economic activities through regulation or licensing, and in private and family life in the interests of protecting children, the mentally ill and other vulnerable persons. Such powers are often accompanied by statutory protection against liability.

At several points in this chapter, the position of the Crown will be examined. In the past, important distinctions were drawn between (a) the Crown, including departments of central government, and (b) other public bodies, such as local authorities and statutory corporations. While many of these distinctions have been removed, notably by the Crown Proceedings Act 1947, others remain in being. This chapter deals, in section A, with the liability of public authorities and the Crown in tort and, in section B, with contractual liability. Section C deals with other aspects of the law relating to the Crown, including procedural immunities and privileges and the rules on non-disclosure of evidence in the public interest.

As with many aspects of public law, the liability of public authorities has been much affected by European law. The liability of EU organs under art 240 TFEU to compensate for serious breaches of EU law that they commit is paralleled by the duty of member states 'to make good loss and damage caused to individuals by breaches of Community law for which they can be held responsible',[3] for example by failure to implement a Community directive. We have already seen the impact of Community law on the supremacy of Parliament that was manifest in the *Factortame* litigation concerning the Merchant Shipping Act 1988, enacted to protect British fishing interests.[4] Later in the same affair, the House of Lords held, after analysing the decision-making that lay behind the 1988 Act, that the Act was a 'sufficiently serious infringement' of Community law to justify the award of compensatory damages.[5] The criteria which led to this decision were derived from Community law, which requires, for a finding that a breach is 'sufficiently serious', that a member state has 'manifestly and gravely disregarded the limits on the exercise of its discretion'. But the procedural aspects of such a claim in damages may be governed by national law, provided

---

[1] Wade and Forsyth, *Administrative Law*, chs 20, 21; Craig, *Administrative Law*, chs 28, 29; Hogg and Monahan, *Liability of the Crown*; Harlow, *State Liability – Tort Law and Beyond*; Fairgrieve, *State Liability in Tort*; Fairgrieve, Andenas and Bell (eds), *Tort Liability of Public Authorities in Comparative Perspective*; Kneebone, *Tort Liability of Public Authorities*; Cornford, *Towards a Public Law of Tort*; Lewis, *Judicial Remedies in Public Law*, ch 14.

[2] As was stressed in Dicey's account of the 'rule of law': ch 6.

[3] *Cases C-6/90 and C-9/90, Francovitch v Italy* [1991] I-ECR 5357, para 37. Also *Cases C-46/93, Brasserie du Pêcheur SA v Germany* and *C-48/93, R v Transport Secretary, ex p Factortame Ltd* [1996] ECR I-1029; P Craig (1993) 109 LQR 595 and (1997) 113 LQR 67; and C Lewis, in Forsyth and Hare (eds), *The Golden Metwand and the Crooked Cord*, p 319.

[4] See ch 4 C and ch 8.

[5] *R v Transport Secretary, ex p Factortame Ltd (No 5)* [2000] 1 AC 524.

that this does not discriminate against EU law and does not prevent individuals from enforcing their European rights.[6] State liability may arise under EU law even for decisions of the highest national courts.[7]

In respect of human rights, by art 41 ECHR, where a Convention right has been violated and national law does not allow full reparation to be made, the Strasbourg Court 'shall, if necessary, afford just satisfaction to the injured party', by requiring the state to pay compensation. We will consider below the manner in which the Human Rights Act 1998 makes it possible to obtain such compensation in national courts.

The impact of the new rules in EU and human rights law is being felt at a time when key principles of the liability of public authorities in the United Kingdom are in a volatile state. In 2004, Lord Steyn made comments on the law on negligence and statutory duties that apply generally to the law of state liability:

> This is a subject of great complexity and very much an evolving area of law. No single decision is capable of providing a comprehensive analysis. It is a subject on which an intense focus on the particular facts and on the particular statutory background, seen in the context of the contours of our social welfare state, is necessary. On the one hand, the courts must not contribute to the creation of a society bent on litigation, which is premised on the illusion that for every misfortune there is a remedy. On the other hand, there are cases where the courts must recognise on principled grounds the compelling demands of corrective justice . . .[8]

The evolving nature of the law is seen in decisions by the House of Lords, including four that Lord Steyn described as 'milestone' decisions.[9] No more than an outline of the main aspects of the law can be given here.

Relevant aspects of the law in Scotland will be mentioned briefly in each section. Although the common law in Scotland regarding the position of the Crown differed from that in England, the same broad approach to the liability of public authorities has been followed in both legal systems, especially since the Crown Proceedings Act 1947.

A. Liability of public authorities and the Crown in tort

Individual liability

In the absence of statutory immunity, every person is liable for wrongful acts that he or she commits and for omissions that give rise to actions in tort at common law or for breach of statutory duty. This applies even if an officer representing the Crown claims to be acting out of executive necessity.

> In *Entick v Carrington*[10] the King's Messengers were held liable in an action of trespass for breaking and entering the plaintiff's house and seizing his papers, even though they were acting in obedience to a warrant issued by the Secretary of State. This was in law no defence as the Secretary had no legal authority to issue such a warrant.

Obedience to orders is not normally a defence whether the orders are those of the Crown, a local authority,[11] a company or an individual employer.[12] The principle that superior orders are

---

[6] See e.g. rejection of the Community law claim in *Three Rivers DC v Bank of England (No 3)* [2001] UKHL 16, [2003] 2 AC 1.

[7] See e.g. *Case C-224/01, Köbler v Austrian Republic* [2004] QB 848.

[8] *Gorringe v Calderdale Council* [2004] UKHL 15, [2004] 2 All ER 326, para [2].

[9] *X v Bedfordshire CC* [1995] 2 AC 633; *Stovin v Wise* [1996] AC 923; *Barrett v Enfield Council* [2001] 2 AC 550; and *Phelps v Hillingdon Council* [2001] 2 AC 619.

[10] (1765) 19 St Tr 1030; ch 6 A.

[11] *Mill v Hawker* (1875) LR 10 Ex 92.

[12] For the position of the armed forces, see ch 16.

no defence to an action in tort would, if unqualified, have placed too heavy a burden on many subordinate officials. At common law an officer of the court, such as a sheriff, who executes an order of the court is protected from personal liability unless the order is on its face clearly outside the jurisdiction of the court.[13] Moreover, it has been found necessary to provide protection for certain classes of official. Thus some statutes exempt officials from being sued in respect of acts done bona fide in the course of duty.[14] The Constables Protection Act 1750 protects constables who act in obedience to the warrant of a magistrate, though the magistrate acted without jurisdiction in issuing the warrant. The Mental Health Act 1983, s 139, affords constables and hospital staff protection against civil and criminal liability in respect of acts such as the compulsory detention of a mental patient, unless the act was done in bad faith or without reasonable care.[15] The liability of individual officials will therefore turn both on the powers which they may exercise and on their privileges and immunities. But no general immunity is enjoyed by officers or servants of the Crown.[16]

Vicarious liability of public authorities

The individual liability of public officials was historically important in establishing that public authorities were themselves subject to the law, but individual liability is not today a sufficient basis for the liability of large organisations, whether in the private or public sectors. It is now essential to be able to sue an individual's employer, if only because the employer is a more substantial defendant: a successful claimant wants the certainty of knowing that any damages and costs awarded will in fact be paid.

In cases not involving the Crown, it has long been the law that a public authority is, like any other employer, liable for the wrongful acts of its servants or agents committed in the course of their employment. It was established in 1866 that the liability of a public body whose servants negligently execute their duties is identical with that of a private trading company.

> In *Mersey Docks and Harbour Board Trustees v Gibbs*,[17] a ship and its cargo were damaged on entering a dock by reason of a mud bank left negligently at the entrance. The trustees were held liable and appealed to the House of Lords on the ground that they were not a company deriving benefit from the traffic, but a public body of trustees constituted by Parliament for the purpose of maintaining the docks. That purpose involved authority to collect tolls for maintenance and repair of the docks, for paying off capital charges and ultimately for reducing the tolls for the benefit of the public. It was held that these public purposes did not absolve the trustees from the duty to take reasonable care that the docks were in such a state that those who navigated them might do so without danger.

In spite of the argument that a corporation should not be liable for a wrongful act, since a wrongful act must be beyond its powers, a corporation is, like any other employer, liable for the torts of its employees acting in the course of their employment. Thus hospital authorities are liable for negligence in the performance of their professional duties by physicians and surgeons whom they employ.[18] Under general principles of vicarious liability, a public authority is not liable for acts committed by an employee who is acting outside the course of employment 'on a frolic

---

[13] *The Case of the Marshalsea* (1613) 10 Co Rep 76a.

[14] E.g. National Health Service Act 1977, s 125; Financial Services Act 1986, s 187.

[15] On the earlier law, see *R v Bracknell Justices, ex p Griffiths* [1976] AC 314; and *Ashingdane* v *UK* (1985) 7 EHRR 528. On s 139 of the 1983 Act, see *Seal* v *Chief Constable of South Wales* [2007] UKHL 31, [2007] 4 All ER 177. Cf *Adorian* v *Metropolitan Police Commissioner* [2009] EWCA Civ 18, [2009] 3 All ER 227.

[16] The suggestion to the contrary in *R v Transport Secretary, ex p Factortame Ltd* [1990] 2 AC 85, 145 was rightly disapproved in *M* v *Home Office* [1994] 1 AC 377. And see *D* v *Home Office* [2005] EWCA Civ 38, [2006] 1 All ER 183.

[17] (1866) LR 1 HL 93 (discussed in Kneebone (note 1 above), ch 2).

[18] *Cassidy* v *Minister of Health* [1951] 2 KB 343. For the vicarious liability of education and social service authorities, see *Barrett* v *Enfield Council* and *Phelps* v *Hillingdon Council* (above, note 9).

of his own'. But where a prisoner is ill-treated by prison officers, the Home Office may be vicariously liable even if those acts amount to misfeasance in public office, when the ill-treatment is a misguided or unauthorised method of performing their duties;[19] and the owners of a school were liable for sexual abuse of boys by a house warden, the abuse being very closely connected with his employment.[20] An exception to vicarious liability may arise when an official, although appointed and employed by a local authority, carries out functions under the control of a central authority or in the exercise of a distinct public duty imposed by the law.[21] There was formerly no vicarious liability in respect of police officers, but the chief constable is now liable for their acts committed in the performance of their functions,[22] and the vicarious liability extends to acts of racial discrimination.[23]

Tort liability of the Crown

There were two main rules which until 1948 governed the liability of the Crown: (*a*) the rule of substantive law that the King could do no wrong; (*b*) the procedural rule derived from feudal principles that the King could not be sued in his own courts. The survival of these rules into modern times meant that before 1948 the Crown could be sued neither in respect of wrongs that had been expressly authorised nor in respect of wrongs such as negligence committed by Crown servants in the course of their employment.[24] Nor were government ministers vicariously liable for the staff in their departments, since in law ministers and civil servants are alike servants of the Crown.[25] It was anomalous that this immunity of the Crown applied to central government. The rigour of the immunity was eased before 1948 by concession. Acting through the Treasury Solicitor, departments would often defend an action against a subordinate official and pay damages if he or she were found personally liable for a wrongful act. From this there developed the practice by which the Crown might nominate a defendant on whom a writ could be served. In 1946, this practice was disapproved by the House of Lords,[26] and it became urgently necessary for the law to be changed to permit the Crown to be sued in tort. In 1927 a draft Bill had been proposed by a government committee, but opposition from within Whitehall prevented reform of the law.[27] The law was at last placed on a new basis by the Crown Proceedings Act 1947.

With important exceptions, this Act (which applies only to proceedings by and against the Crown 'in right of Her Majesty's Government in the United Kingdom')[28] established the principle that the Crown is subject to the same liabilities in tort as if it were a private person of full age and capacity in respect of (*a*) torts committed by its servants or agents, (*b*) the duties which an employer at common law owes to his or her servants or agents, and (*c*) any breach of the common law duties of an owner or occupier of property (s 2(1)). The Crown is thus vicariously

---

[19] *Racz v Home Office* [1994] 2 AC 45; and p 742 below.

[20] *Lister v Hesley Hall Ltd* [2001] UKHL 22, [2002] 1 AC 215.

[21] *Stanbury v Exeter Corpn* [1905] 2 KB 838.

[22] Police Act 1996, s 88; see also Police Reform Act 2002, s 47 (civilian staff); and ch 21 E.

[23] Race Relations (Amendment) Act 2000, s 4, reversing *Farah v Metropolitan Police Commissioner* [1997] 1 All ER 289.

[24] See e.g. *Viscount Canterbury v A-G* (1842) 1 Ph 306 (negligence of Crown servants causing Houses of Parliament to burn down).

[25] *Raleigh v Goschen* [1898] 1 Ch 73; *Bainbridge v Postmaster-General* [1906] 1 KB 178. And see *M v Home Office* [1994] 1 AC 377, 408–9.

[26] *Adams v Naylor* [1946] AC 543.

[27] Cmd 2842, 1927. See J Jacob [1992] PL 452 and Jacob, *The Republican Crown*, ch 2. Also *Matthews v Ministry of Defence* [2003] UKHL 4, [2003] 1 AC 1163 (Lord Bingham).

[28] S 40(2)(b), (c). See *Tito v Waddell (No 2)* [1977] Ch 106; *Mutasa v A-G* [1980] QB 114; *R v Foreign Secretary, ex p Indian Assn of Alberta* [1982] QB 892; and *R (Quark Fishing Ltd) v Foreign Secretary* [2005] UKHL 57, [2006] 1 AC 529.

liable for the torts of its servants or agents, for example, negligent driving by a government driver while in the course of her employment.

The Crown is also liable for breach of a statutory duty, provided that the statute is one which binds the Crown as well as private persons (s 2(2)), such as the Occupiers' Liability Act 1984. The Act of 1947 imposes no liability enforceable by action in the case of statutory duties which bind only the Crown or its officers.

The 1947 Act elaborates the principle of Crown liability in some detail. Thus the Crown's vicarious liability is restricted to the torts of its officers as defined (s 2(6)). This definition requires that the officer shall be (a) appointed directly or indirectly by the Crown and (b) paid in respect of his duties as an officer of the Crown at the material time wholly out of the Consolidated Fund,[29] moneys provided by Parliament or a fund certified by the Treasury. This excludes, for example, the police. There is no vicarious liability for officers acting in a judicial capacity or in execution of judicial process (s 2(5)),[30] or for acts or omissions of a Crown servant unless apart from the Act the servant would have been personally liable in tort (s 2(1)). The general law relating to indemnity and contribution applies to the Crown as if it were a private person (s 4). The Act does not authorise proceedings against the Sovereign in her personal capacity (s 40(1)) and does not abolish any prerogative or statutory powers of the Crown, in particular those relating to defence of the realm and the armed forces (s 11(1)).

Under the 1947 Act, there were formerly two exceptions from liability in tort. The first related to the armed forces. By s 10, neither the Crown nor a member of the armed forces was liable in tort in respect of acts causing death or personal injury which were committed by a member of the armed forces while on duty, where (a) the victim was a member of the armed forces on duty at the time or, if not on duty as such, was on any land, premises, ship, aircraft or vehicle being used for purposes of the armed forces and (b) the injury was certified by the Secretary of State as attributable to service for purposes of pension entitlement. This certificate did not guarantee an award of a pension unless the conditions for entitlement were fulfilled.[31] There certainly must be a public scheme for compensating members of the armed forces who suffer injury or death during their service. But should this exclude the right to sue for common law damages? In 1987, Parliament legislated to put into suspense s 10 of the 1947 Act.[32] Section 10 can be revived if it appears to the Secretary of State necessary or expedient to do so, for example by reason of imminent national danger or for warlike operations outside the United Kingdom. Until it is so revived, and it was not as regards operations in Iraq and Afghanistan, members of the armed forces (and in the event of death, their dependants) may sue fellow members (and the Crown vicariously) in respect of injuries or death arising out of their service. When a soldier sued for personal injury caused during the Gulf operations in 1991 (for which s 10 was not revived), the Court of Appeal held that no duty of care was owed to him by his fellow soldiers during battle conditions.[33]

The second exception from liability for tort formerly applied to the Post Office when it was a government department, for acts or omissions in relation to postal packets or telephonic communications (s 9). Nor was there any liability in contract.[34] When the Post Office became a

---

[29] Ch 17.

[30] See *Jones v Department of Employment* [1989] QB 1 and *Welsh v Chief Constable of Merseyside* [1993] 1 All ER 692. For the position under the Human Rights Act 1998, s 9, see p 744 below. Also I Olowofoyeku [1998] PL 444. Cf the different approach in Community law: *Köbler v Austrian Republic* (above, note 7).

[31] *Adams v War Office* [1955] 3 All ER 245. On s 10, see also *Pearce v Defence Secretary* [1988] AC 755.

[32] Crown Proceedings (Armed Forces) Act 1987; see F C Boyd [1989] PL 237. The 1987 Act was not retrospective: *Matthews v Ministry of Defence* [2003] UKHL 4, [2003] 1 AC 1163 (Crown's former immunity compatible with art 6(1) ECHR). See also National Audit Office, *Ministry of Defence Compensation Claims* (HC 957, 2002–3).

[33] *Mulcahy v Ministry of Defence* [1996] QB 732; and ch 16. On liability for off-duty activities, see *Ministry of Defence v Radclyffe* [2009] EWCA Civ 635.

[34] *Triefus & Co Ltd v Post Office* [1957] 2 QB 352.

public corporation, the existing limitations on liability for postal and telephone services were continued.[35]

Subject to these exceptions, the Crown Proceedings Act assimilated the tortious liabilities of the Crown to those of a private person. However, in many situations involving the potential liability of the government, the analogy of private liability is not directly helpful. Some claims against the Crown have been held to be non-justiciable,[36] but in general the courts seek to apply to governmental action rules derived from, for example, the common law of negligence.[37]

In Scotland, the position of the monarch in respect of Crown proceedings was not identical with that in English law, the Court of Session being less willing than the English courts to grant the King immunity from being sued.[38] However, it was held in 1921 that the Crown was not vicariously liable for the wrongful acts of Crown servants.[39] Section 2 of the 1947 Act established such liability in Scotland, although the terminology is modified. Thus 'tort' in the Act's application to Scotland means 'any wrongful or negligent act or omission giving rise to liability in reparation'.[40]

The Crown Proceedings Act thus enabled the Crown to be sued in English law in tort and, in Scotland, in the law of delict or reparation. We will now consider aspects of the substantive law governing the liability in tort of public authorities in general.

Statutory authority as a defence

Where acts of a public body interfere with an individual's rights (whether these concern property, contract or liberty), those acts will be unlawful unless legal authority for them exists. Such authority may be found in legislation or in common law. Where Parliament expressly authorises something to be done, it cannot be wrongful to act in accordance with that authority. It will depend on the legislation whether compensation is payable for the rights which Parliament has authorised to be taken away. The construction of many public works affecting private rights of property (for example, nuclear installations or motorways) is subject to detailed rules of compensation in the relevant legislation.[41] But express provision for compensation is not always made. It is then for the court in interpreting the legislation to decide what powers are authorised and whether any compensation is payable. In the process of interpretation, the court will assume that, when discretionary power is given to a public body, there is no intention to interfere with private rights, unless the power is expressed in such a way as to make interference inevitable.

In *Metropolitan Asylum District* v *Hill*, hospital trustees were empowered by statute to build hospitals in London. A smallpox hospital was built at Hampstead in such a way as to be a nuisance at common law. *Held*, in the absence of express words or necessary implication in the statute authorising the trustees to commit a nuisance, building of the hospital was unlawful. 'Where the terms of the statute are not imperative, but permissive, when it is left to the discretion of the persons empowered to determine whether the general powers committed to them shall be put into execution or not, ... the fair inference is that the Legislature intended that discretion to be exercised in strict conformity with private rights and did not intend to confer licence to commit nuisance in any place which might be selected for the purpose.'[42]

---

[35] Post Office Act 1969, ss 6(5), 29, 30; British Telecommunications Act 1981, s 70. And see Postal Services Act 2000, s 90.
[36] E.g. *Tito* v *Waddell (No 2)* and *Mutasa* v *A-G* (note 28 above).
[37] See below, pp 738–41.
[38] See J D B Mitchell [1957] PL 304.
[39] *MacGregor* v *Lord Advocate* 1921 SC 847.
[40] Crown Proceedings Act 1947, s 43(b).
[41] See e.g. Nuclear Installations Acts 1965 and 1969 (as amended by Energy Act 1983, Part II).
[42] (1881) 6 App Cas 193, 212–13 (Lord Watson).

If, however, the exercise of a statutory power or duty necessarily involves injury to private rights, there is no remedy unless the statute provides compensation.[43]

> In *Allen v Gulf Oil Refining Ltd*, the House of Lords held that a local Act which envisaged the building of an oil refinery at Milford Haven, though it gave the company no express power to construct the refinery and did not define the site, did give authority for construction and use of the refinery. Such authority protected the company against liability for nuisance to neighbouring owners which was the inevitable result of the construction of the refinery, though the Act gave the owners no compensation for the loss of their rights.[44]

The courts have sometimes placed a heavy onus on the defendant to show that a nuisance that has occurred is an inevitable consequence of the statute. But in *Marcic v Thames Water Utilities Ltd*,[45] where a house in London suffered repeated flooding by overflowing sewage, the statutory undertaking responsible for sewerage was not liable to the owner for this serious nuisance. The duties of the defendant were held to be enforceable only by the regulator under the Water Industry Act 1991: despite the malfunctioning of the statutory scheme, the right to sue *in nuisance* had been taken away by the Act.[46]

Even where, as in the cases of *Allen* and *Marcic*, the right to sue in nuisance is taken away, this does not relieve a body exercising statutory powers of the duty to use reasonable care to avoid causing unnecessary injury. As an old dictum of Lord Blackburn put it,

> . . . no action will lie for doing that which the legislature has authorised, if it be done without negligence, although it does occasion damage to anyone; but an action does lie for doing that which the legislature has authorised, if it be done negligently.[47]

This statement must be read in context: it applies only where a statute authorises an act to be done which will necessarily cause some injury to private rights, and where the act is performed carelessly so causing unnecessary injury to those rights.[48] Such additional injury is outside the protection given by the statute. However, if a public authority which merely has a power to act, and not a duty, decides to take action but acts inefficiently, it is not liable unless the inefficiency causes extra damage to an individual: this was so held in the difficult case of *East Suffolk Catchment Board v Kent*, when the use by a river board of an ineffective method of removing flood water from a farmer's land was held to create no liability towards the farmer.[49]

Statutory duties[50]

It was at one time the view that anyone harmed by failure to perform a statutory duty could bring an action for damages against the person or body liable to perform it.[51] This has long since ceased to be the law, since the enormous variety of duties imposed by statute means that there can be no single method of enforcing public duties. Some duties, for example the duty of the Secretary of State for Children, Schools and Families to promote the education of the people of England

---

[43] *Hammersmith Rly Co v Brand* (1869) LR 4 HL 171.
[44] [1981] AC 1001.
[45] [2003] UKHL 66, [2004] 2 AC 42. The statutory scheme was held to comply with the ECHR.
[46] But the Act did not protect Thames Water from being sued for negligence: *Dobson v Thames Water Utilities* [2009] EWCA Civ 28, [2009] 3 All ER 319.
[47] *Geddis v Proprietors of Bann Reservoir* (1878) 3 App Cas 430, 455–6.
[48] *X v Bedfordshire CC* [1995] 2 AC 633, 733.
[49] [1941] AC 74. And see M J Bowman and S H Bailey [1984] PL 277. Cf *Fellowes v Rother DC* [1983] 1 All ER 513, 522 and *Stovin v Wise* (note 73 below).
[50] Stanton et al., *Statutory Torts*, ch 2; Harding, *Public Duties and Public Law*, ch 7.
[51] See *Atkinson v Newcastle Waterworks Co* (1877) 2 Ex D 441.

and Wales,[52] are effectively unenforceable by legal proceedings of any kind.[53] Some duties are enforceable only by recourse to statutory compensation.[54] Very many duties may, as we have seen, be enforced by a mandatory order obtained by judicial review.[55] Some statutes provide for a criminal penalty in the event of a breach of duty. Where the statute that creates a duty provides a specific sanction for breach (for example, prosecution) or a remedy for those affected to use, the courts may hold that no other means of enforcing the duty exists.[56]

In some situations, particularly where the statutory duty closely parallels a common law duty (for example, to use care not to cause personal injury) the breach of statutory duty gives rise to a private right of action for damages; such an action is akin to an action for negligence, except that liability depends on breach of the duty itself, not on there being a lack of care.[57] An action for breach exists if it can be shown by interpreting the statute that the duty was imposed for the protection of a certain class and that the legislature intended to confer on members of that class the benefit of a right of action.[58] It is notoriously difficult to evaluate all the factors that are relevant when a court is deciding whether a statutory duty is enforceable by an action for damages and the statute is silent on the point.[59] Where a public authority fails to perform a statutory duty imposed upon it, an individual who is adversely affected may in principle seek judicial review. Laying emphasis on the use of judicial review, recent judicial decisions have limited the availability of damages as a remedy for breach of public duties.

> In *X (minors)* v *Bedfordshire Council*,[60] the House of Lords considered a group of claims for damages arising from the defective performance by local councils of duties relating to the education and welfare of children. The alleged breaches included the failure of a social service authority to take children into care who were badly in need of protection against abuse; a converse error by social workers in taking a child into care believed to be at risk of sexual abuse, when the identity of her abuser was mistaken; and failures by education authorities to identify the special educational needs of children and to provide appropriate schooling. The councils applied to have these claims struck out as disclosing no cause of action. *Held*, so far as the actions were based on breach of statutory duty, they were disallowed. The duties in question gave rise to no private rights of action; nor were the councils under a duty of care in performing them. The education cases were allowed to proceed so far as they were based on the councils' vicarious liability for the professional negligence of teachers and educational psychologists; there was no such vicarious liability for social workers and psychiatrists reporting to the councils on alleged child abuse.

The House of Lords later confirmed that there was no claim for breach of statutory duty against an education authority for failure to diagnose a child's special needs, but that the authority was liable vicariously for the failure of its employee (an educational psychologist) to show the professional skill that could reasonably have been expected.[61] In a similar welfare context, a homeless person denied temporary housing by a local authority in breach of its duty could enforce the statute by judicial review, but could not recover damages for the breach.[62] In a very different

---

[52] Education Act 1996, s 10.

[53] Ch 30 A, p 682 above.

[54] Note 41 above.

[55] Ch 31.

[56] See *Cutler* v *Wandsworth Stadium Ltd* [1949] AC 398; *Lonrho Ltd* v *Shell Petroleum Co Ltd* [1982] AC 173, 185; *Scally* v *Southern Health Board* [1992] 1 AC 294. Cf *Marcic* v *Thames Water Utilities Ltd* (above, note 45) (duties enforceable only by regulator).

[57] E.g. *Reffell* v *Surrey CC* [1964] 1 All ER 743.

[58] See *X* v *Bedfordshire CC* [1995] 2 AC 633, 731.

[59] See Bennion, *Statutory Interpretation*, Code, s 14 (pp 67–85).

[60] [1995] 2 AC 633; see P Cane (1996) 112 LQR 13; L Edwards (1996) 1 Edin LR 115.

[61] *Phelps* v *Hillingdon Council* [2001] 2 AC 619.

[62] *O'Rourke* v *Camden Council* [1998] AC 188. And see R Carnwath [1998] PL 407.

context, a prisoner adversely affected by a breach of prison rules had no action in damages arising from the breach. Lord Jauncey said:

> The fact that a particular provision was intended to protect certain individuals is not of itself sufficient to confer private law rights upon them, something more is required to show that the legislature intended such conferment.[63]

The same approach was applied by the House of Lords on facts which, had the Human Rights Act applied, might have led to a different outcome.

> In *Cullen v Chief Constable of the RUC*, the main issue was whether anti-terrorism legislation granting a detained person the right to consult a solicitor conferred a right to sue for damages when the police wrongly prevented a detainee from having access to a solicitor, even though he suffered no direct injury or harm because of this. The Lords held by 3–2 that the aim of the legislation was to create a 'quasi-constitutional' right for the benefit of the public at large, not for the protection of a particular class of individuals: the appropriate remedy was judicial review. In a strong dissenting judgment, Lords Bingham and Steyn were in no doubt that Parliament had intended to create 'a new and remedial provision for the conferment on detainees of a statutory right of access to solicitors'; the statutory language was 'entirely apt to create private law rights'.[64]

It is evident from these and many other decisions[65] that different policy considerations apply to (*a*) the public law remedies obtainable by judicial review, and (*b*) the private law remedy of damages. The interaction between public law concepts and the common law of negligence has caused continuing difficulties in regard to the liability of public authorities, some of which are outlined in the next section.

Public authorities and liability for negligence

Although the Crown Proceedings Act 1947 assimilated the tort liability of the Crown to that of a private person, the duties of government give rise to issues of liability which are not easily resolved by applying legal principles that mainly govern the acts of private persons. Most actions by public authorities stem from legislation. And many disputes as to liability turn directly on the relationship between (*a*) common law rules on the duty of care; (*b*) the legislation, which broadly will confer either a duty or a power to act; and (*c*) the rules of administrative law that apply when judicial review is sought.

> In *Dorset Yacht Co v Home Office*,[66] the Home Office was sued for the value of a yacht which had been damaged when seven Borstal boys absconded at night from a Borstal summer camp on an island in Poole harbour. The plaintiffs alleged that the boys were able to abscond because of the negligence of their officers. The Home Office argued that the system of open Borstals would be jeopardised if any liability was imposed on the government for the wrongful acts of those who absconded. The House of Lords held, Lord Dilhorne dissenting, that the Home Office was liable for the negligence of the officers; in the circumstances the officers owed a duty of care to the yacht owners, the damage to the yacht being reasonably foreseeable as the direct consequence of a failure by the officers to take reasonable care.

This decision had broad consequences for the developing law of negligence, but it was based on the finding of negligence by the officers, and it did not extend to the situation in which it was claimed that an executive discretion (for example, to transfer someone to an open prison) had

---

[63] *R v Deputy Governor of Parkhurst Prison, ex p Hague* [1992] 1 AC 58, 171 (Lord Jauncey); see also *Calveley v Chief Constable, Merseyside Police* [1989] AC 1228.

[64] [2003] UKHL 39, [2004] 2 All ER 237.

[65] See e.g. *Hill v Chief Constable of West Yorkshire* [1989] AC 53; *Elguzouli-Daf v Commissioner of Metropolitan Police* [1995] QB 335; and *Stovin v Wise* [1996] AC 923.

[66] [1970] AC 1004. And see Booth and Squires, *The Negligence Liability of Public Authorities*.

been improperly exercised. Lord Diplock in *Dorset Yacht* suggested that questions of liability for the exercise of discretion were to be settled by applying the public law concept of ultra vires rather than the civil law concept of negligence.[67] This influential suggestion led to an immense amount of litigation, in particular concerning the exercise of discretion by a public authority in deciding whether to use its regulatory powers. One approach taken was to distinguish between (*a*) decisions that involved policy questions (for instance, use of an authority's resources) and were likely to be unsuitable for judicial determination, and (*b*) the operational tasks performed by the authority once it decided to use its regulatory powers, a task which would be more suitable for judicial appraisal.[68] But this distinction between policy questions and operational tasks proved an elusive way of deciding whether a public authority was liable for a particular misfortune.

In 1990, in *Caparo Industries plc v Dickman*,[69] which concerned the duty of care owed by company auditors to potential investors in the company, the Lords adopted a three-part test applying to new situations in which it was sought to establish liability for negligence: (1) whether the harm to the claimant was foreseeable; (2) whether the parties were in a relationship of proximity; and (3) whether it was 'fair, just and reasonable' that the defendant should owe a duty of care to the claimant. This decision confirmed[70] that 'novel categories of negligence' would develop 'incrementally and by analogy with established categories, rather than by a massive extension of a prima facie duty of care', restrained only by indefinable policy considerations seeking to limit the scope of the duty of care. When criterion (3) is applied to novel claims brought against a public body, judges exercise a broad discretion in assessing the consequences for public policy of holding the body liable.

The courts have restricted the imposition of liability in several contexts, particularly as regards claims for economic loss arising out of regulatory functions[71] and claims seeking to impose a private law duty of care on the public functions of the police.[72] Inevitably, the outcome of judicial policy-making is uncertain.

> In *Stovin v Wise*, a county council as highway authority had statutory power to remove an earth bank that it knew restricted visibility at a dangerous road junction, but it failed to do so. When an accident occurred at the junction, was the council liable for failure to exercise its power? The House of Lords held (by 3–2) that a duty of care to users of the highway to remove the bank arose only if (*a*) it was 'irrational' (in the public law sense) for the power *not* to be used and (*b*) there were exceptional factors indicating that the policy of the legislation was to confer a right to sue on a person injured when the power was not exercised. The majority held that neither condition was satisfied, adding that it was 'important, before extending the duty of care owed by public authorities, to consider the cost to the community of the defensive measures which they are likely to take to avoid liability'.[73] The dissenting judges held that, being aware of the danger, the council was under a common law duty of care towards road users to use its powers to remove the cause of the danger.

As can be seen in the judgments in *Stovin v Wise*, one difficulty in applying the three-part test in *Caparo Industries* was the presumed need in cases against public authorities to reconcile this with the rules of ultra vires. Must the court, when concerned with the careless exercise of statutory functions, decide first that the acts in question were ultra vires, for instance on the

---

[67] [1970] AC 1004, at 1067.

[68] The application of this principle in *Anns v Merton Council* [1978] AC 728 was for wider reasons held to be wrong in *Murphy v Brentwood Council* [1991] 1 AC 398.

[69] [1990] 2 AC 605.

[70] Quoting from *Sutherland Shire Council v Heyman* (1985) 60 ALR 1, 43–4 (Brennan J).

[71] *Yuen Kun-yeu v A-G of Hong Kong* [1988] AC 175; *Davis v Radcliffe* [1990] 2 All ER 536. And see H McLean (1988) 8 OJLS 442.

[72] *Hill v Chief Constable of West Yorkshire* [1989] AC 53; *Calveley v Chief Constable, Merseyside* [1989] AC 1228. But cf *Swinney v Chief Constable of Northumbria* [1997] QB 464 and *Waters v Commissioner of Metropolitan Police* [2000] 4 All ER 934. And see discussion below of the *Osman* litigation.

[73] [1996] AC 923, 958 (Lord Hoffmann). And see S H Bailey and M J Bowman [2000] CLJ 85, 101–19.

ground of *Wednesbury* unreasonableness?[74] In *X v Bedfordshire Council*,[75] on a claim that a public authority had been negligent in exercising a statutory discretion, it was held that the first requirement was to show that its decision was 'outside the ambit of the discretion altogether': if it was not outside that ambit, the public authority could not be in breach of any duty of care owed to the claimant.

In later decisions, the Lords have taken a different view. *Barrett v Enfield Council* concerned a claim that a social services authority had breached a common law duty of care that it owed to the claimant while he had been in its care as a child. Lord Slynn stated that acts done pursuant to the lawful exercise of discretion may be subject to a duty of care, even if some element of discretion is involved.[76] Lord Hutton said that, in a case involving personal injuries but not policy issues that the courts were ill-equipped to decide, it was preferable for the court to proceed 'by applying directly the common law concept of negligence than by applying as a preliminary test the public law concept of *Wednesbury* unreasonableness . . .'.[77] In 2004, when the failure of a highway authority to use its powers was again before the Lords, Lord Steyn commented that the analysis made by Lord Hoffmann in *Stovin* had been qualified by the intervening decisions of the House.[78]

Judicial reluctance to impose duties of care on public authorities has caused some claimants to have recourse to Strasbourg. In *Osman v Ferguson*, despite strong facts, the Court of Appeal struck out a claim against the police for negligently failing to prevent a fatal attack, holding that the claim was 'doomed to failure';[79] the court applied the ruling in *Hill v Chief Constable of West Yorkshire*[80] that it would be against public policy for the police to be under any liability to the victims of crimes committed by those whom the police failed to apprehend. The Strasbourg Court held in 1998 that this decision to strike out *Osman v Ferguson* was in breach of art 6(1) ECHR, since the effect was to give the police a blanket immunity from being sued in respect of their acts and omissions relating to criminal offences.[81]

This decision at Strasbourg was criticised for having transformed the right to a fair hearing under art 6(1) into an evaluation of the substantive rights that should exist in national law.[82] Three years later, in *Z v UK*,[83] a sequel to the Lords' decision in *X v Bedfordshire Council*, the Strasbourg court changed its position, holding by 12–5 that for an English court to strike out an action did not breach art 6(1) since there would have been a full and fair hearing, argued in law on the basis that all facts were as claimed by the claimants. However, on the evidence in *Z v UK* the court held that for young children to have been left by the local authority to live with cruel and abusive parents for over four years breached their right under art 3 ECHR to be protected against inhuman or degrading treatment; further, the claimants' right under art 13 ECHR to an effective remedy had been breached by the English legal system. In this serious case, the court ordered the UK government to pay substantial compensation to the claimants.

Despite the Strasbourg court's volte-face in *Z v UK*, the influence of European human rights law has contributed to a reluctance by the judges to grant public authorities a 'blanket immunity'

---

[74] See ch 30 A.

[75] Note 60 above.

[76] [2001] 2 AC 550, 571. This point was confirmed in *Phelps v Hillingdon Council* [2001] 2 AC 619, 653.

[77] [2001] 2 AC 550 at 586.

[78] *Gorringe v Calderdale Council* [2004] UKHL 14, [2004] 2 All ER 326.

[79] [1993] 4 All ER 344, 354. A 15-year-old boy and his family for months suffered extreme harassment from the boy's former teacher, culminating when he fired at them, severely injuring the boy and killing his father. The police knew of the harassment and of threats by the assailant before the fatal attack occurred.

[80] [1989] AC 53 (a case brought by the family of the last victim of the 'Yorkshire Ripper').

[81] *Osman v UK* (1998) 29 EHRR 245.

[82] See e.g. C A Gearty (2001) 64 MLR 159.

[83] (2001) 34 EHRR 3; see C A Gearty (2002) 65 MLR 87. The applicant children complained that the council had delayed for four years before taking them into care, despite extreme circumstances, and that this had caused them serious physical and emotional harm.

by ruling in an absolute manner that claims against a public authority must be struck out in the absence of any duty of care. In *D v East Berkshire NHS Trust*,[84] the Lords held that where doctors suspected that children had been abused by their parents, it would not be fair, just and reasonable to impose on the doctors a common law duty of care towards the parents, although they owed such a duty to the children (just as local authorities owed a duty to the children in performing their statutory duties of protection); but it was accepted that there might be exceptional circumstances in which a different conclusion might be justified.[85] In *Brooks v Metropolitan Police Commissioner*,[86] where a public inquiry had established that a police investigation into serious racist crimes had been badly conducted, the Lords upheld the rule that in exercising functions of crime prevention and detection, the police owed no duty of care to the victims and witnesses of crime. In a very different context, no duty of care was owed to the owners of a nursing home by a health authority in obtaining a magistrate's order to close down the home without notice, even though it was established later that the closure was wholly unjustified.[87]

By contrast with the judges' reluctance to impose a new duty of care on a public body in discharging its statutory functions, some aspects of negligence are readily applied in the public sector. Thus, under *Hedley Byrne & Co v Heller*,[88] someone who relies to his or her detriment on inaccurate statements made by an official in the course of the latter's duties may have a remedy in negligence for loss suffered: and a local authority was liable when an environmental health officer, acting in an advisory role, negligently required expensive and unnecessary alterations to be made to a farm guesthouse.[89] When a county council was excessively slow to use statutory powers of taking over management of a school that was suffering acute dissension within its governing body, the council was held liable for having caused personal injury (through extreme stress) to the headteacher because of the delay: the council's common law duty of care to the headteacher was held to 'march together with' the proper discharge of its statutory functions.[90]

Misfeasance in public office

It is a fundamental assumption of the law that those who exercise public functions should do so in good faith and without malicious or spiteful motives. Bad faith must not, of course, be assumed merely because a public body has made a decision that is corrected by judicial review. But where it is shown that a body or official was not acting in good faith, liability in tort may exist.[91] Instances of the tort do not often occur, and claimants have what may be the difficult task of proving that named individuals within a public authority acted in bad faith and were not motivated by acceptable reasons.[92] Unusually, in *Bourgoin SA v Ministry of Agriculture*, it was

[84] [2005] UKHL 23, [2005] 2 All ER 443; S H Bailey (2006) 26 LS 155.

[85] Ibid, at [91] (Lord Nicholls). Lord Bingham, dissenting, refused to strike out the claim without fuller inquiry into the facts. See also *Carty v Croydon Council* [2005] EWCA Civ 19, [2005] 2 All ER 517.

[86] [2005] UKHL 24, [2005] 2 All ER 489 (a sequel to the killing of Stephen Lawrence). In *Brooks*, doubts were expressed about aspects of *Hill v Chief Constable of West Yorkshire* (note 72 above), but *Hill* was applied in *Van Colle v Chief Constable of Hertfordshire* [2008] UKHL 50, [2009] 1 AC 225.

[87] *Jain v Trent Health Authority* [2009] UKHL 4, [2009] 1 AC 853.

[88] [1964] AC 465.

[89] *Welton v North Cornwall DC* [1997] 1 WLR 570. See also *Harris v Wyre Forest DC* [1990] 1 AC 831 and *T (minor) v Surrey CC* [1994] 4 All ER 577.

[90] *Connor v Surrey Council* [2010] EWCA Civ 286. The judgment of Laws LJ contains a valuable review of the extensive case law since *Dorset Yacht*.

[91] See *Roncarelli v Duplessis* (1959) 16 DLR (2d) 689; *David v Abdul Cader* [1963] 3 All ER 579 (malicious refusal of licence) (A W Bradley [1964] CLJ 4); *Micosta SA v Shetland Islands Council* 1986 SLT 193. Also J McBride [1979] CLJ 323, and Moules, *Actions against Public Officials*, ch 5.

[92] See *Weir v Transport Secretary* [2005] EWHC 2192 (Ch) (claim by shareholders arising from minister's decision to send Railtrack into liquidation).

conceded that the minister knew that he did not have the powers that he purported to exercise: it was held that liability for misfeasance would arise.[93]

The tort arises only from the conduct of a public officer in relation to his or her official functions. Liability depends on the state of mind of the officer and takes two forms:

> First there is the case of targeted malice by a public officer, i.e. conduct specifically intended to injure a person or persons. This type of case involves bad faith in the sense of the exercise of public power for an improper or ulterior motive. The second form is where a public officer acts knowing that there is no power to do the act complained of (or reckless as to whether there is) and that the act will probably injure the plaintiff. It involves bad faith inasmuch as the public officer does not have the honest belief that his act is lawful.[94]

The tort is founded upon the dishonest conduct of the official and is one of the intentional torts: an omission to act is not sufficient, unless this arose from a dishonest decision not to act. The tort is not actionable unless the claimant can prove that he or she has suffered material damage, including financial loss and physical or mental injury, and it is not enough to show distress, injured feelings or annoyance.[95] As regards the first form of the tort, targeted malice, it makes no difference whether the official exceeds his or her power or complies with the letter of the power.[96] It appears that local councillors could be liable for misfeasance if, intending to damage the interests of a particular lessee, they voted for a resolution requiring the council's rights as owner of property to be exercised against the lessee.[97] Misfeasance in public office was committed when the corporate officer of the House of Commons breached the rules that governed the placing of a contract to provide the windows of a costly new building for the House.[98] Vicarious liability may arise for misfeasance in office where this is an improper way of performing an officer's duties or is very closely connected with the performance of those duties.[99] Exemplary damages may be payable for misfeasance in public office.[100]

Tort liability, compensation and the Human Rights Act

It is outside the scope of this book to enumerate all the duties, both positive and negative, deriving from the ECHR that the Human Rights Act (HRA) imposes on public authorities. But in outline we may consider whether the ECHR will strengthen the protection that the law of torts gives to individuals against arbitrary, careless or oppressive acts by public authorities.[101]

By the HRA, s 6, a public authority must act consistently with Convention rights, except where primary legislation makes this impossible.[102] As we saw in chapter 31A, public authorities that use

---

[93] [1986] QB 716.

[94] *Three Rivers Council v Bank of England (No 3)* [2001] UKHL 16, [2003] 2 AC 1 (Lord Steyn). For a review of the case law, see Clarke J in this case [1996] 3 All ER 558 (and C Hadjiemmanuil [1997] PL 32). The Lords refused by 3–2 to strike out the case: [2003] 2 AC 1, 237. After a prolonged trial, the case collapsed, there being no evidence of dishonesty: [2006] EWHC 816 (Comm).

[95] *Watkins v Home Secretary* [2006] UKHL 17, [2006] 2 All ER 353 (bad faith of prison officers in opening prisoner's confidential legal correspondence: no material damage). A prisoner removed from an open to a secure prison suffers material damage thereby: *Karagozlu v Metropolitan Police Commissioner* [2006] EWCA Civ 1691, [2007] 2 All ER 1055.

[96] *Three Rivers Council v Bank of England (No 3)* [2003] 2 AC 1, 235 (Lord Millett, citing *Jones v Swansea Council* [1989] 3 All ER 162).

[97] *Jones v Swansea Council* [1990] 3 All ER 737.

[98] *Harmon CFEM Facades (UK) Ltd v Corporate Officer of the House of Commons* (2000) 67 Con LR 1.

[99] *Racz v Home Office* [1994] 2 AC 45. See also *Lister v Hesley Hall Ltd* (note 20 above).

[100] *Kuddus v Chief Constable of Leicestershire* [2001] UKHL 29, [2002] 2 AC 122; and see note 112 below.

[101] See Dame Mary Arden [2010] PL 140.

[102] See ch 19 B.

their powers in a way that infringes Convention rights are acting unlawfully; if they do, their actions are subject to judicial review. Is there also a remedy in tort?

Under art 41 ECHR, the Strasbourg court shall 'if necessary' afford 'just satisfaction' to someone whose rights have been infringed where full reparation has not been paid at the national level.[103] Under the HRA s 8, a civil court or tribunal with power to award damages has a similar power to award damages to someone whose Convention rights have been infringed if this would be 'just and appropriate' and is necessary to afford 'just satisfaction'; and the court must take account of the practice of the Strasbourg court. Those who hoped that this would open the door to many new claims for compensation have been disappointed. *Anufrijeva v Southwark Council*[104] concerned breaches of art 8 (right to respect for private and family life) occurring through inefficiency and delay by local authorities and the Home Office. The Court of Appeal held that damages were not recoverable as of right, even where a Convention right had been breached: a balance had to be struck between the interests of the claimant and the public as a whole; claimants should seek any damages that might be payable by attaching the request to a claim for judicial review. Even so, the judges were concerned that a claim for compensation if brought by adversary proceedings would probably cost more than the amount of any award.

In *R (Greenfield) v Home Secretary*,[105] a convicted prisoner had been required to serve extra days for a drug offence within the prison, and he had not had a fair hearing under art 6(1) ECHR. The House of Lords rejected his claim for compensation, holding there to be no right under the 1998 Act to compensation for every infringement of Convention rights; the power to order compensation was not central to protection of human rights; procedural faults of the kind in Greenfield's case would not attract compensation unless the claimant could show a causal link between the procedure and the actual outcome; and the courts must not follow national scales of damages. Lord Bingham said, 'the 1998 Act is not a tort statute. Its objects are different and broader'; he warned of the 'risk of error if Strasbourg decisions given in relation to one article of the Convention are read across as applicable to another'.[106]

Accordingly, a claimant who alleges that her Convention rights have been infringed by a public authority (and nothing more than this) may not sue in tort but must proceed under s 7 HRA; it is then for the court to decide whether a payment by way of 'just satisfaction' should be made. However, the restrictive principles in *Greenfield* will not arise where there has been a breach of Convention rights (for instance, of art 3 ECHR (prohibition of torture) or of art 5 (right to liberty)) and on the same facts it can be shown that the authority has committed torts in relation to the torture or false imprisonment. In these instances, damages in tort may be recovered and compensation under the 1998 Act is unlikely to be unnecessary.

When it is claimed that a public authority, either through positive action or an omission to act, has infringed an individual's Convention rights, and where it is not disputed that a duty of care arises in national law, then the courts may be willing to decide the extent of that duty of care by reference to case law under the Convention.[107] By contrast, where a duty of care of relevant scope is not clearly recognised in national law and where it is uncertain whether the claimant's case would be protected at Strasbourg, a claim may be allowed to proceed in the law of tort and not under the Convention.[108] Another decision by the Lords has been said to be 'an example of a

---

[103] See A R Mowbray [1997] PL 647; Law Commission, *Damages under the Human Rights Act 1998* (Cm 4853); J Hartshorne [2004] EHRLR 660; T R Hickman, in Fairgrieve, Andenas and Bell (eds) (above, note 1), ch 2; D Fairgrieve, (the same), ch 4.

[104] [2003] EWCA Civ 1406, [2004] QB 1124.

[105] [2005] UKHL 14, [2005] 2 All ER 240. And see R Clayton [2005] PL 429.

[106] *R (Greenfield) v Home Secretary* (above), paras [19], [7].

[107] See *Savage v South Essex Partnership NHS Trust* [2008] UKHL 74, [2009] 1 All ER 1053 (failure by psychiatric hospital to take reasonable operational measures to prevent suicide of patient where a real and immediate risk of that event).

[108] *Mitchell v Glasgow Council* [2009] UKHL 11, [2009] 3 All ER 205.

situation in which the court has used a Convention right as a launch pad for a possible development in the future'.[109]

When the breach of a Convention right results from a judicial act, an award of damages may be made under the HRA, s 9, only (*a*) if the act is not done in good faith, or (*b*) if an award is necessary under art 5(5) ECHR to compensate for unlawful detention. Any award will be made against the Crown, not against the judge.

Other aspects of governmental liability

Two other aspects of the liability of public authorities may be briefly mentioned.

First, ever since the general warrant cases in the 1760s in which exemplary damages were awarded for unlawful search and seizure, the courts have had power to award exemplary damages for oppressive, arbitrary or unconstitutional acts in the exercise of public power.[110] It was formerly considered that the power was limited to certain torts for which exemplary damages had been awarded before 1964,[111] but in 2001, in a case of alleged misfeasance in public office by a police officer, the House of Lords held that this limitation was not justified and that such a rigid rule would limit the future development of the law.[112] Juries considering the award of exemplary damages against the police must be directed by the trial judge as to the permissible range of such awards.[113]

Second, the law of restitution was applied by the House of Lords in resolving a fundamental question as to the obligations of public authorities in *Woolwich Building Society* v *Inland Revenue Commissioners (No 2)*.[114] Nearly £57 million in tax had been paid under protest by the society under regulations which were held to be ultra vires.[115] The House held by 3–2 that there was a general restitutionary principle by which money paid pursuant to an ultra vires demand by a public authority was recoverable as of right, not at the discretion of the authority. This, said the majority, was required both by common justice and by the principle in the Bill of Rights that taxes should not be levied without the authority of Parliament.[116] Among the questions left open by Lord Goff's speech was whether the same principle applies if taxes are levied wrongly because the tax inspector misconstrued a statute or regulation. On this point Lord Goff commented that 'it would be strange if the right of the citizen to recover overpaid charges were to be more restricted under domestic law than it is under Community law'.[117] A claim for restitution may now be included in a claim for judicial review.[118]

Tort liability and judicial review

In an era when the use of judicial review has expanded dramatically, as has liability for breach of duties owed in European Community law, the United Kingdom courts have resisted an equivalent expansion in the liability of public bodies to be sued for damages. We have seen that in France

---

[109] Arden (note 101 above) at p 152, referring to the speech of Lord Scott in *Ashley* v *Chief Constable of Sussex* [2008] UKHL 25, [2008] 1 AC 962.

[110] *Wilkes* v *Wood* (1763) Lofft 1; *Rookes* v *Barnard* [1964] AC 1129, 1226. And see *Lancashire CC* v *Municipal Mutual Insurance Ltd* [1997] QB 897.

[111] *AB* v *South West Water Services Ltd* [1993] QB 507, applying *Broome* v *Cassell and Co Ltd* [1972] AC 1027.

[112] *Kuddus* v *Chief Constable of Leicestershire* (above, note 100) overruling *AB* v *South West Water Services Ltd*.

[113] *Thompson* v *Metropolitan Police Commissioner* [1998] QB 498.

[114] [1993] AC 70. See P B H Birks [1980] CLP 191, [1992] PL 580; J Beatson (1993) 109 LQR 401.

[115] *R* v *IRC, ex p Woolwich Building Society* [1991] 4 All ER 92.

[116] See chs 2 A and 17.

[117] [1993] AC 70, at 177. Also *Deutsche Morgan Grenfell plc* v *Inland Revenue Commissioners* [2006] UKHL 49, [2007] 1 AC 558; and Goff and Jones, *The Law of Restitution*, ch 27.

[118] Supreme Court Act 1981, s 31(4), amended by SI 2004 No 1033.

both the judicial review of decisions and the power to award compensation for wrongful acts committed by public authorities are entrusted to the administrative courts.[119] Under the French system, rules of public liability have developed which differ from the rules of liability in civil law. In English law, by contrast, public authorities and officials are in principle subject to the same law of civil liability as private persons. Thus a claim in damages against a public authority must be based on an existing tort (including negligence, nuisance, trespass to the person, false imprisonment[120] and misfeasance in public office) or on a specific right of action created by statute. Yet the existing categories of tort do not include all instances in which a public body may cause loss to an individual through acts or omissions that as a matter of public law are in some way wrongful.

In particular, English law does not accept that an individual has a right to be indemnified for loss caused by invalid or ultra vires administrative action.[121] Although a claimant for judicial review may seek damages or restitution together with quashing, mandatory, declaratory and restraining orders, this has not changed the substantive rules of liability.[122] Thus a prisoner may seek judicial review of a decision to put him in solitary confinement for 28 days, but has no right to sue the governor or the Home Office for damages, whether for breach of prison rules or for false imprisonment.[123]

When a trader's licence for a market stall is cancelled in breach of natural justice, he or she may by judicial review recover the licence[124] but has no right to compensation for the intervening loss of income unless, exceptionally, the market authority acted with malice.[125] It is well established that a public authority's decision may be invalid, in the sense of being ultra vires, without this giving rise to a right to damages.[126]

In *Rowling* v *Takaro Properties Ltd*, a New Zealand Cabinet minister had acted ultra vires in refusing consent to the proposed development of a luxury hotel; this had caused Japanese investors to lose interest in the project. When the minister was sued for damages by the developer, the Judicial Committee held that, even assuming that a duty of care was owed by the minister to the developer, he was not in breach of that duty: his decision had been based on a tenable view of his powers and was neither unreasonable nor negligent.[127]

In *Jain* v *Trent Health Authority*,[128] the claimants' nursing home was suddenly closed down when, without giving notice to the owners, the registration authority obtained a closing order from a magistrate. Five months later, a tribunal upheld the owners' appeal and found that the immediate closure of the home was not justified. But by then the business had been ruined. The owners sued the health authority for economic damage caused by negligence. *Held*, the health authority's powers of registration and inspection were intended to protect the interests of the residents of the homes. The fact that the statutory procedures were insufficient to prevent damage to the owners did not mean that the health authority owed them a duty of care.

In 1986, the Court of Appeal rejected a claim for damages brought by French turkey farmers who had been adversely affected by a ban on importing turkeys into Britain that had been imposed in breach of the EC Treaty by the Ministry of Agriculture; the majority held that it was a sufficient remedy for the French farmers that they could have sought judicial review of the

---

[119] Ch 27. Brown and Bell, *French Administrative Law*, ch 8. Also Markesinis et al., *Tortious Liability of Statutory Bodies* (comparing English, French and German law).

[120] See *R v Governor of Brockhill Prison (No 2)* [2001] 2 AC 19 (damages for detention beyond lawful date of release).

[121] *Hoffmann-La Roche* v *Secretary of State for Trade* [1975] AC 295, 358 (Lord Wilberforce).

[122] See ch 31; and see e.g. *Page Motors Ltd* v *Epsom and Ewell BC* (1982) 80 LGR 337, and P Cane [1983] PL 202; *Davy* v *Spelthorne BC* [1984] AC 262.

[123] *R v Deputy Governor of Parkhurst Prison, ex p Hague* [1992] 1 AC 58.

[124] *R v Barnsley Council, ex p Hook* [1976] 3 All ER 452.

[125] See p 741 above.

[126] See e.g. *Dunlop v Woolahra Council* [1982] AC 158.

[127] [1988] AC 473.

[128] [2009] UKHL 4, [2009] 1 All ER 957.

ban.[129] It has since become clear that, as Oliver LJ held in dissent, the protection of rights under Community law requires the payment of compensation to cover the period between imposition of the ban and its revocation.[130]

It is unfortunate that the events in *Jain* above occurred before the Human Rights Act came into effect, since the owners of the nursing home could in that event have based their claim for compensation not on the common law but on their Convention rights, including the right to a hearing (art 6(1)), and right to peaceful enjoyment of their property (art 1, First Protocol). This recourse may also be available in cases in which the UK courts hold that the police owe no duty of care to potential victims of serious crime.

In matters not covered by EU law or the HRA, those who suffer loss caused by unlawful, unfair or unreasonable decisions by a public authority have a genuine complaint about the state of the law. In some circumstances, where maladministration by central or local government has caused individuals to suffer injustice, they may be able to obtain compensation by complaining to the appropriate Ombudsman; but the authority is not at risk of being sued for damages.[131] In 1988, the Justice/All Souls committee on administrative law recommended that the law should provide for compensation to be paid to one who sustains loss as a result of acts or decisions that are wrongful or contrary to law or are a result of excessive delay.[132] Not surprisingly, no government since 1988 has endorsed this proposal.

In 2008, the Law Commission issued a consultation paper, *Administrative Redress: Public Bodies and the Citizen*.[133] This reviewed the range of remedies available when substandard administration occurs, and argued that radical reform was needed in respect of the remedies obtainable through the courts, since negligence actions against public bodies were 'uncertain and unprincipled' and the torts of misfeasance in public office and breach of statutory duty were unsuitable 'in the modern era'. The particular reform suggested would involve defining the 'truly public' functions of public authorities; these would not be subject to the law of negligence and would give rise to compensation only for 'serious fault' and on a discretionary basis. This confusing proposal is not at all likely to be adopted.[134] A more practical step would be a limited reform enabling the Administrative Court on judicial review to grant compensation to an individual who has suffered serious economic loss from an invalid administrative act.[135]

B. Contractual liability[136]

The making of contracts is the means whereby an infinite number of transactions occur in a market economy, and many contracts are made by public authorities. Legislation is the primary means of creating duties and rights in public law, such as the duty to pay taxes or the right to receive free medical services. Often government has a choice to make in deciding whether to rely on legislative commands or contract to achieve a certain goal: thus, to recruit the armed forces,

---

[129] *Bourgoin SA v Ministry of Agriculture* [1986] QB 716. The claim of misfeasance in public office against the Minister of Agriculture was allowed to proceed.

[130] See e.g. the *Francovitch* and *Factortame (No 5)* cases, at notes 3 and 5 above.

[131] Ch 29 D; and *R v Knowsley BC, ex p Maguire* (1992) 90 LGR 653. And see M Amos [2000] PL 21.

[132] *Administrative Justice, Some Necessary Reforms*, ch 11.

[133] Earlier publications by the Commission were a discussion paper *Monetary Remedies in Public Law* (2004) and a scoping paper, *Remedies against Public Bodies* (2006). See R Bagshaw (2006) 26 LS 4.

[134] See M Fordham [2009] PL 1 and T Cornford [2009] PL 70.

[135] Cf Harlow, *State Liability – Tort Law and Beyond*, pp 115–16: proposal for the Administrative Court to have an equitable power to award compensation for administrative fault when abnormal loss or a gross violation of human rights has occurred.

[136] Street, *Governmental Liability*, ch 3; Mitchell, *The Contracts of Public Authorities*; Turpin, *Government Procurement and Contracts*; Hogg, *Liability of the Crown*, ch 9.

the policy may be to employ a wholly professional army based on recruiting volunteers in return for pay or to compel all persons of a certain age to serve alongside a nucleus of regular soldiers. Legislation is needed both to authorise conscription and to levy taxation to pay for the armed forces, but a significant distinction may be drawn in achieving certain ends between (*a*) reliance on legislative commands (*imperium*) and (*b*) use of government's economic resources (*dominium*).[137]

The government, formerly the monarch, has long met many of its needs by exercising *dominium* and making contracts.[138] Trends in public policy since 1979 have expanded the purposes for which contracts are used, from the procurement of labour, goods and other assets to the contracts placed by the Home Office for companies to manage prisons and detention centres;[139] the authority given by Parliament for 'contracting out' statutory functions;[140] and the privatisation of public utilities.[141] Sometimes the shell of a contract is used, without legal content, as with the creation of the 'internal market' in the NHS in 1990[142] and the use of 'framework agreements' to govern executive agencies.[143] The 'private finance initiative' and public–private partnerships enable new projects to be financed and managed, to a greater or lesser extent, jointly by the public and private sectors.[144] One commentator has written: 'The techniques of public administration have been refashioned in the mould of the private commercial sector . . . Contract has replaced command and control as the paradigm of regulation.'[145] A French lawyer has remarked on the tendency 'in all major industrialised countries' to 'a growing contractualisation of relations between administrative bodies and society, as well as among administrative bodies themselves'.[146]

In English law, the contracts of public authorities are in principle subject to the same law that governs contracts between private persons. There is no separate jurisdiction governing administrative contracts, as there is in France.[147] Nevertheless, these generalisations must be qualified. First, contracts made on behalf of the Crown are subject to some exceptional rules, which were modified but not necessarily abolished by the Crown Proceedings Act 1947 (below). Apart from these rules, it might appear that the Crown has unlimited power at common law to enter into contracts,[148] but this is subject to statute: where the Crown or ministers have statutory power to take certain action (for instance, managing the prison system) through officials acting under direction from ministers, legislation is needed if power is to be conferred on a private company and exercised by its employees.

Secondly, we have seen that statutory bodies such as local authorities are subject to legal control exercised through the rules of ultra vires, as regards the substance of action that they may take and the procedure by which decisions are made. Thus a contract which it is beyond the power of a local authority to make is void and unenforceable;[149] but effect has now been given by

---

[137] This distinction is developed by T C Daintith [1979] CLP 41 and (same author) in Jowell and Oliver (eds), *The Changing Constitution* (1994), ch 8.

[138] See e.g. *The Bankers' case* (1695) Skin 601. A later monarch, George IV, rented jewels to display in his crown that he could not afford to buy.

[139] Criminal Justice Act 1991, ss 84–91, Sch 10; Criminal Justice and Public Order Act 1994, ss 7–15.

[140] Deregulation and Contracting Out Act 1994, Part II.

[141] See ch 14.

[142] See D Longley [1990] PL 527 and J Jacob [1991] PL 255.

[143] On the role of contracts in government generally, see Harden, *The Contracting State*; Craig, *Administrative Law*, ch 5; Harlow and Rawlings, *Law and Administration*, chs 8, 9.

[144] See M Freedland [1994] PL 86, [1998] PL 288.

[145] M Hunt, in Taggart (ed.), *The Province of Administrative Law*, p 21.

[146] J-B Auby [2007] PL 40, 42.

[147] Mitchell, *Contracts of Public Authorities*, ch 4; Brown and Bell, *French Administrative Law*, pp 202–11.

[148] See BV Harris (1992) 108 LQR 626, (2007) 123 LQR 225.

[149] *Rhyl UDC v Rhyl Amusements Ltd* [1959] 1 All ER 257; *Hazell v Hammersmith Council* [1992] 2 AC 1; *Crédit Suisse v Allerdale Council* [1997] QB 306; and ch 30 A.

legislation to some contracts that would otherwise fail under this rule.[150] Also, a contract made by a public authority may be held void on the ground that it seeks to fetter the future use of the authority's discretionary powers.[151] Thus, where a planning authority in Cheshire agreed with Manchester University to discourage new development within the vicinity of the Jodrell Bank radio telescope, the purported agreement was without legal effect.[152] And the fact that a local authority has contracted with a company for certain services does not prevent the authority from using a statutory power to make by-laws, even if the by-laws make the future performance of the contract impossible or unprofitable for the contractor.[153] A full account of the making of contracts in local government would examine the effect of a council's standing orders on awarding contracts, public audit, and statutes that impose objectives such as 'best value' in the placing of contracts.[154]

An underlying question of great difficulty concerns the use of judicial review as a remedy regarding the contractual decisions of public authorities. It is often uncertain whether there is a 'sufficient public law element' in a dispute to justify use of judicial review. Judicial review should not be used when it is merely claimed that a public body is in breach of contract.[155] But contractual situations may well involve issues as to the abuse of public power, so that judicial review would be appropriate.[156]

The economic importance of public procurement contracts has long been recognised in EU law and the European directives on this matter are implemented by delegated legislation within the United Kingdom, creating rights and duties enforceable in the ordinary courts.[157] The public procurement rules require authorities that enter into certain contracts to follow open procedures for the tendering process for contracts above a stated value, to observe certain criteria in awarding the contract, to specify lawful policy objectives, and to state reasons for choosing a particular contractor. If these duties are breached, a company whose tender has not succeeded may sue the authority for damages.[158]

Contractual liability of the Crown

In English law before 1948, the Crown's immunity from being sued directly in the courts was not confined to liability in tort and extended to all other aspects of civil liability. But it had long been regarded as essential that an individual should be able to obtain judicial redress under a contract made with the Crown or government department. The petition of right was originally a remedy for recovering property from the Crown, but it became available to enforce contractual obligations. The practice was simplified by the Petitions of Right Act 1860. A petition of right lay in respect of any claim arising out of contracts by which the Crown could be bound, but not in respect of claims in tort. It lay also for the recovery of real property, for damages for breach

---

[150] Local Government (Contracts) Act 1997; ch 30 A.

[151] *Ayr Harbour Trustees* v *Oswald* (1883) 8 App Cas 623; *Triggs* v *Staines UDC* [1969] 1 Ch 10; *Dowty Boulton Paul Ltd* v *Wolverhampton Corpn (No 2)* [1973] Ch 94.

[152] *Stringer* v *Minister of Housing* [1971] 1 All ER 65.

[153] *William Cory & Son Ltd* v *City of London* [1951] 2 KB 476. And see text to notes 169–72 below.

[154] See respectively *R* v *Enfield Council, ex p Unwin (Roydon) Ltd* (1989) 1 Admin LR 51; *Porter* v *Magill* [2001] UKHL 67, [2002] 2 AC 357; and the Local Government Act 1999.

[155] See p 713 above.

[156] See S H Bailey [2007] PL 444.

[157] See Directives 2004/17/EC and 2004/18/EC of the European Parliament and Council; Public Contracts Regulations 2006 (SI 2006 No 5) and Utilities Contracts Regulations 2006 (SI 2006/6). And see Arrowsmith, *The Law of Public and Utilities Procurement*.

[158] In *Harmon CFEM Facades (UK) Ltd* v *Corporate Officer, House of Commons* (2000) 67 Con LR 1, 72 Con LR 21, the claimant submitted the lowest tender but was not awarded the contract; it won substantial damages for breaches of duty (including failure to state relevant criteria and unlawful post-tender negotiations) and breach of implied contract.

of contract[159] and to recover compensation under a statute.[160] Before a petition could be heard by the court, it had to be endorsed with the words *fiat justitia* (let right be done) by the Crown, acting on the opinion of the Attorney General. When a petition of right was successful, the judgment took the form of a declaration of the petitioner's rights and, being observed by the Crown, was as effective as a judgment in an ordinary action.

By s 1 of the Crown Proceedings Act 1947, in all cases where a petition of right was formerly required, it is possible to sue the appropriate government department or, where no department is named for the purpose, the Attorney General, by ordinary process either in the High Court or in a county court.

While the Petitions of Right Act 1860 was repealed by the Crown Proceedings Act 1947, it appears to have been kept in being for proceedings in matters of contract or property against the Sovereign personally.[161] The 1947 Act applies only to proceedings against the Crown in right of the government of the United Kingdom, not in claims that arise in respect of the Crown's overseas territories.[162]

In Scotland the petition of right procedure had never existed, since it was always possible to sue the Crown in the Court of Session on contractual claims or for the recovery of property.[163] Accordingly, s 1 of the 1947 Act does not apply to Scotland.

In general the ordinary rules of contract apply to the Crown: thus an agent need have only ostensible authority to bind the Crown and there is no rule requiring the actual authority of the Crown.[164] Those who make contracts on behalf of the Crown, as its agents, are in accordance with the general rule not liable personally.[165] Statutory authority is not needed before the Crown can make a contract, but payments due under the Crown's contracts come from money provided by Parliament; if Parliament exceptionally provides that no money is payable to a certain contractor, payments that would otherwise be due may not be enforced.[166] If a contract expressly provides that payments are to be conditional on Parliament appropriating the money, the Crown is not liable if Parliament does not do so. But, in general, 'the prior provision of funds by Parliament is not a condition preliminary to the obligation of the contract'.[167] Payments due under contract are made out of the general appropriation for the class of service to which the contract relates and not from funds specifically appropriated to a particular contract. It is usually accepted that the Crown has full contractual capacity as a matter of common law,[168] but this cannot entitle the Crown to make contracts which are contrary to statute. Moreover, there is a rule of law, the exact extent of which it is not easy to determine, that the Crown cannot bind itself so as to fetter its future executive action.

In *Rederiaktiebolaget Amphitrite* v *R*, a Swedish shipping company, Sweden being a neutral in the First World War, was aware that neutral ships were liable to be detained in British ports. They obtained an undertaking from the British government that a particular ship, if sent to this country with certain cargo, would not be detained. Accordingly the ship was sent with such a cargo, but the government withdrew the undertaking and

---

[159] *Thomas* v *R* (1874) LR 10 QB 31.

[160] *A-G* v *De Keyser's Royal Hotel* [1920] AC 508.

[161] Crown Proceedings Act 1947, s 40(1); *Franklin* v *A-G* [1974] QB 185, 194.

[162] Before Rhodesia achieved lawful independence as Zimbabwe, difficulties as to Crown proceedings arose over the non-payment of interest to holders of Rhodesian government stock; see *Franklin* v *A-G* [1974] QB 185; *Franklin* v *R* [1974] QB 202.

[163] Mitchell, *Constitutional Law*, p 304.

[164] See *A-G for Ceylon* v *Silva* [1953] AC 461 on the difficulties of establishing ostensible authority in relation to the Crown. Cf *Re Selectmove Ltd* [1995] 2 All ER 531.

[165] *Macbeath* v *Haldimand* (1786) 1 TR 172; and see *Town Investments Ltd* v *Department of the Environment*, note 199 below.

[166] *Churchward* v *R* (1865) LR 1 QB 173.

[167] *New South Wales* v *Bardolph* (1934) 52 CLR 455, 510 (Dixon J); Street, *Governmental Liability*, pp 84–92.

[168] See B V Harris (1992) 108 LQR 626; cf M Freedland [1994] PL 86, 91–5.

refused clearance for the ship. On trial of a petition of right, *held*, the undertaking of the government was not enforceable as the Crown was not competent to make a contract which would have the effect of limiting its power of executive action in the future.[169]

It has been suggested that the defence of executive necessity only 'avails the Crown where there is an implied term to that effect or that is the true meaning of the contract';[170] or again that the defence has no application to ordinary commercial contracts. A preferable view is that the *Amphitrite* case illustrates a general principle that the Crown, or any public authority, cannot be prevented by an existing contract from exercising powers which are vested in it either by statute or common law for the protection of the public interest.[171]

> In *Commissioners of Crown Lands v Page*, the Crown sued for arrears of rent due under a lease of Crown land that had been assigned to the defendant. The defence was that the land had been requisitioned by a government department and that this constituted eviction by the Crown as landlord. The Court of Appeal held that the arrears were payable. Devlin LJ said: 'When the Crown, in dealing with one of its subjects, is dealing as if it too were a private person, and is granting leases or buying and selling as ordinary persons do, it is absurd to suppose that it is making any promise about the way in which it will conduct the affairs of the nation.'[172]

As we have seen, some problems arise in relation to the contracts of public authorities to which English law provides no certain answer, for instance concerning the power of a public body to decide with whom to contract and whom to remove from its list of approved contractors.[173] This power was used by the Labour government in 1975–78 to require companies who were granted contracts to observe a non-statutory pay policy.[174] This is an outstanding example of a government's ability to achieve public goals without recourse to legislation.[175]

We have also seen that where European rules on public procurement apply, the pre-contractual procedures observed by public authorities are controlled, with recourse to the courts if the rules are breached. Where these rules do not apply, the legal regime is uncertain. In one case, the Lord Chancellor's Department was held to have acted unfairly in awarding a contract, but the process was held not to be subject to judicial review.[176] The courts should, however, uphold fairness and legitimate expectations in this situation. Thus, the National Lottery Commission acted unlawfully in deciding not to award the next licence for the Lottery to the existing licensee (Camelot) but to enter into negotiations with the rival bidder (the People's Lottery).[177] In Northern Ireland, the right not to be discriminated against on religious grounds was held by the Strasbourg Court to apply to public procurement decisions.[178] Control over government contracts is exercised by the Comptroller and Auditor General. Much government practice in placing and administering contracts derives from rulings of the Public Accounts Committee.[179] In view of the numerous government contracts awarded each year, remarkably few disputes arising from them reach the courts. Disputes are resolved by various forms of consultation, negotiation or arbitration. The Review Board for Government Contracts, established in 1969 under an agreement between the government and the Confederation of British Industry, regularly reviews the profit formula for non-competitive government contracts and it may also examine in relation

---

[169] [1921] 3 KB 500.
[170] *Robertson v Minister of Pensions* [1949] 1 KB 227, 237 (Denning J).
[171] Street, *Governmental Liability*, pp 98–9; Mitchell, *Contracts of Public Authorities*, pp 27–32, 52–65.
[172] [1960] 2 QB 274, 292; see also *William Cory & Son Ltd v City of London* (above, note 153).
[173] Turpin, *Government Procurement and Contracts*, ch 4. And see text to notes 155–6 above.
[174] G Ganz [1978] PL 333.
[175] T C Daintith [1979] CLP 41.
[176] *R v Lord Chancellor, ex p Hibbit & Saunders* [1993] COD 326 (D Oliver [1993] PL 214). Cf *R v Legal Aid Board, ex p Donn & Co* [1996] 3 All ER 1. Also S Arrowsmith (1990) 106 LQR 277; A Davies (2006) 122 LQR 98.
[177] *R v National Lottery Commission, ex p Camelot Group plc* [2001] EMLR 43.
[178] *Tinnelly & Sons Ltd v UK* (1998) 27 EHRR 249.
[179] Ch 17.

to a particular contract a complaint that the price paid is not 'fair and reasonable'. Government contracts are excluded from the jurisdiction of the Parliamentary Ombudsman.[180]

Service under the Crown

Service under the Crown has long been an instance of the special contractual position of the Crown; it is generally held to be part of the prerogative that the Crown employs its servants at its pleasure, whether in the civil service or the armed forces.[181] The Crown formerly claimed that its freedom to dismiss its servants at will was necessary in the public interest and this claim was accepted in the older case law. Thus, in the absence of statutory provision,[182] no Crown servant had a remedy for wrongful dismissal. Even when a colonial servant had been engaged for three years certain, only for the appointment to be terminated prematurely, the court reasoned that it was 'essential for the public good that it should be capable of being determined at the pleasure of the Crown'.[183]

While at common law civil servants lacked tenure of office, in practice they enjoyed a high degree of security. This security depended on convention rather than law, and the collective agreements on conditions of service which were applied to civil servants did not give rise to contractual rights.[184] Indeed, it was for long uncertain whether Crown service was a contractual relationship at all, and it was doubtful whether civil servants could even sue for arrears of pay.[185] Today, most provisions of the Employment Rights Act 1996 apply to civil servants, and they are protected against unfair dismissal.[186] They are also protected against discrimination in relation to their employment.[187]

In 1991, a newer look was given to the common law when it was held that civil servants are employed by the Crown under contracts of employment, since the incidents of a contract are present and the civil service pay and conditions code deal in detail with the relationship. Although the code states that the relationship is governed by the prerogative and that civil servants may be dismissed at pleasure, neither the Crown nor civil servants intend the contents of the code to be merely voluntary.[188] However, the same court held that an aggrieved civil servant could not seek judicial review of a dismissal or other action.[189]

The law on Crown service is thus more contractual than it once was. However, some limitations on employment rights are likely to bear more heavily on civil servants than on other employees, such as the rule that employment tribunals may not consider a complaint of unfair dismissal where dismissal was for reasons related to national security. Moreover, in cases involving Crown employees, special procedures may be adopted by the tribunals in dealing with issues affecting national security.[190]

In 2010, by part 1 of the Constitutional Reform and Governance Act, the employment and management of the civil and diplomatic service was placed on a statutory basis, but this will not necessarily have an immediate impact on the matters discussed in this section.

---

[180] Ch 29 D.

[181] See *CCSU v Minister for the Civil Service* [1985] AC 374 and cf Sir William Wade (1985) 101 LQR 180.

[182] E.g. the rule that judges hold office during good behaviour (ch 18 C), *Gould v Stuart* [1896] AC 575 and *Reilly v R* [1934] AC 176.

[183] *Dunn v R* [1896] 1 QB 116; G Nettheim [1975] CLJ 253. Cf *Dunn v MacDonald* [1897] 1 QB 401.

[184] *Rodwell v Thomas* [1944] KB 596; cf *CCSU v Minister for the Civil Service* (above).

[185] *Kodeeswaran v A-G of Ceylon* [1970] AC 1111; cf *Cameron v Lord Advocate* 1952 SC 165.

[186] Employment Rights Act 1996, s 191.

[187] Sex Discrimination Act 1975, s 85; Race Relations Act 1976, s 75 (as amended); Disability Discrimination Act 1995, s 64. And see SI 2003 No 1660, reg 36 and SI 2003 No 1661, reg 36. Ch 19 A.

[188] *R v Lord Chancellor's Department, ex p Nangle* [1992] 1 All ER 897 (see S Fredman and G Morris [1991] PL 485 and (1991) 107 LQR 298).

[189] For which see text to notes 155–6 above.

[190] Employment Rights Act 1996, ss 10, 193; Employment Relations Act 1999, Sch 8. See *Balfour v Foreign and Commonwealth Office* [1994] 2 All ER 588.

Members of the armed forces have less protection in law than civil servants, and the system of command and discipline stands in the way of assimilating military service to civilian employment. Some statutory employment rights apply to the armed forces.[191] In respect of discrimination on grounds of race, sex, sexual orientation and religion or belief, a member of the forces has a right of recourse to an employment tribunal but only after having pursued a complaint by means of the internal redress of complaints procedure.[192] Members of the armed forces, like all other persons, may seek protection for their Convention rights under the Human Rights Act 1998,[193] although the extent of their rights may be affected by their duties.

C. The Crown in litigation: privileges and immunities

As we have already seen,[194] 'the Crown' is a convenient term in law for the collectivity that now comprises the monarch in her governmental capacity, ministers, civil servants and the armed forces. Lord Templeman said in 1993: 'The expression "the Crown" has two meanings, namely the monarch and the executive.'[195] When the monarch governed in person, royal officials properly benefited from the monarch's immunities and privileges. But despite the ending of personal government, the institutions of central government continued to benefit from Crown status. The shield of the Crown extended to what was described as the general government of the country or 'the province of government',[196] but not to local authorities or to other public corporations. Notwithstanding the Crown Proceedings Act 1947, for several reasons it may be necessary to know whether a public authority has Crown status.[197] It is very common for an Act which creates a new public body to state whether and to what extent it should enjoy Crown status,[198] but this does not always happen. Whether because of express legislation or judicial interpretation, a public agency may be regarded as having Crown status for some purposes, but not for others.

In regard to central government, the concept of 'the Crown' has various consequences. Contracts are generally concluded in the name of individual departments and ministers, acting expressly or impliedly for the Crown.

In *Town Investments Ltd* v *Department of the Environment*, the issue was whether a rent freeze imposed by counter-inflation legislation applied to two office blocks in London, of which the Secretary of State for the Environment was the lessee 'for and on behalf of Her Majesty'; the offices were occupied by a variety of departments, and in part by the US Navy. The House of Lords *held* (Lord Morris dissenting) that the Crown was the tenant and that the premises were occupied for the purpose of a business carried on by the Crown; the leases were therefore subject to the rent freeze. Lord Diplock stated that it was public law that governed the relationships between the Queen in her political capacity, government departments, ministers and civil servants: executive acts of government done by any of them 'are acts done by "the Crown" in the fictional sense in which that expression is now used in English public law'.[199]

---

[191] Employment Rights Act 1996, s 192, amended by Armed Forces Act 1996, s 26.

[192] Armed Forces Act 1996, ss 21–3. See also SI 2003 Nos 1660 (regn 36) and 1661 (regn 36); and p 334 above.

[193] Cf *R* v *Ministry of Defence, ex p Smith* [1996] QB 517; and *Smith* v *UK* (2000) 29 EHRR 728.

[194] Ch 12, text at notes 3–7. And see in Sunkin and Payne (eds), *The Nature of the Crown*, ch 2 (Sir W Wade) and ch 3 (M Loughlin).

[195] *M* v *Home Office* [1994] 1 AC 377, 395.

[196] *Mersey Docks Trustees* v *Cameron* (1861) 11 HLC 443, 508; *BBC* v *Johns* [1965] Ch 32.

[197] E.g. liability to taxation and the criminal law; whether staff are Crown servants (*R* v *Barrett* [1976] 3 All ER 895). And see ch 14.

[198] See e.g. Parliamentary Standards Act 2009, Sch 1, para 9 (Independent Parliamentary Standards Authority not to be regarded as servant or agent of Crown).

[199] [1978] AC 359, 381 (and see C Harlow (1977) 40 MLR 728).

This decision revealed a striking anomaly, namely that the Crown as tenant could take the benefit of the rent freeze, whereas the Crown as landlord was not barred from increasing the rents which its tenants had to pay. The legal reasons for this inequity will be mentioned in the next paragraph. Although in 1991 the Court of Appeal considered 'the Crown' not to be a legal person, the House of Lords later held that 'at least for some purposes' the Crown has legal personality.[200] Whether the Crown may be described as a corporation sole or a corporation aggregate[201] is a question of no importance: the long-standing practice of Parliament has been to legislate on the basis that the Crown is a continuing legal entity.

Application of statutes to Crown[202]

As we have seen, under the 1947 Act the Crown may be sued for breach of statutory duty. But nothing in the Act affects 'any presumption relating to the extent to which the Crown is bound by an Act of Parliament' (s 40(2)(f)). The rule that Acts do not bind the Crown, that is, that the Crown's rights and interests are not prejudiced by legislation unless a statute so enacts by express words or by necessary implication, significantly limits governmental liability for breach of statutory duty. It is by this rule, for example, that Crown property is in law exempt from taxation and much environmental legislation. This immunity of central government from regulation that applies to private persons goes much further than is justifiable, and Parliament has begun to remove the immunity piecemeal.[203] In 1947, the Privy Council took a strict view of the test of 'necessary implication', holding that in the absence of express words the Crown is bound by a statute only if the purpose of the statute would be 'wholly frustrated' if the Crown were not bound.[204] In 1989, as we saw in chapter 12, in *Lord Advocate* v *Dumbarton Council*, the House of Lords for the first time considered the legal basis of Crown immunity. The Court of Session had held that in some instances (for example, where its property was not affected) the Crown could be bound by town planning and highways legislation. Reversing this decision, the House held that the Crown is not bound by any statutory provision 'unless there can somehow be gathered from the terms of the relevant Act an intention to that effect'.[205] For an Act to bind the Crown it is sufficient for it to be shown that if the Act did not do so its purpose would be frustrated in a material respect, not that its purpose would be wholly frustrated. It is good legislative practice for new Acts to state expressly whether and to what extent they apply to the Crown.[206] Where an Act does not apply to the Crown or its servants acting in the course of duty, a Crown servant is not liable criminally if he or she disregards the statute.[207] But these rules do not prevent the Crown deriving benefits from legislation. Even though the Crown is not named in an Act, the Crown may take advantage of rights conferred by the Act, as in the *Town Investments* case.[208]

---

[200] *M* v *Home Office* [1992] QB 270, [1994] 1 AC 377, 424.

[201] E.g. *Re Mason* [1928] Ch 385.

[202] *Street, Governmental Liability*, ch 6; Hogg and Monahan, *Liability of the Crown*, ch 11; Bennion, *Statutory Interpretation*, pp 206–12.

[203] E.g. National Health Service and Community Care Act 1990, s 60. But cf *R (Cherwell DC)* v *First Secretary of State* [2004] EWCA Civ 1420, [2005] 1 WLR 1128.

[204] *Province of Bombay* v *Municipal Corpn of Bombay* [1947] AC 58 and *Madras Electric Supply Co Ltd* v *Boarland* [1955] AC 667.

[205] [1990] 2 AC 580, 604 (ch 12 D and J Wolffe [1990] PL 14). Contrast *Bropho* v *State of Western Australia* (1990) 171 CLR 1 (and S Kneebone [1991] PL 361).

[206] E.g. Race Relations Act 1976, s 75, considered in *Home Office* v *CRE* [1982] QB 385, and amended by Race Relations (Amendment) Act 2000. The Human Rights Act 1998 binds the Crown: s 22(5).

[207] *Cooper* v *Hawkins* [1904] 2 KB 164. See now Road Traffic Regulation Act 1984, s 130. On the Crown's 'axiomatic' immunity in criminal law, M Sunkin [2003] PL 716; M Andenas and D Fairgrieve [2003] PL 730.

[208] Crown Proceedings Act 1947, s 31; and note 199 above.

Procedure

Where the Act of 1947 enables proceedings to be brought against the Crown in English courts, whether in tort or contract or for the recovery of property, in principle the normal procedure of litigation applies. The action is brought against the appropriate department, the Minister for the Civil Service being responsible for publishing a list of departments and naming the solicitor for each department to accept process on its behalf; in cases not covered by the list, the Attorney General may be made defendant. The trial follows that of an ordinary civil action, but differences arise in respect of remedies and enforcement. The most important is that in place of an injunction or a decree of specific performance, the court makes an order declaring the rights of the parties (s 21(1)); and no injunction may be granted against an officer of the Crown if the effect 'would be to give any relief against the Crown which could not have been obtained in proceedings against the Crown' (s 21(2)). Although at common law an injunction lay against an officer of the Crown who was threatening to commit a wrong such as a tort,[209] for many years after 1947 s 21 was interpreted broadly so as to deprive the court of power to grant such relief.[210] The inability of the court to grant injunctions excluded the power to grant interim injunctions, and at that time English law did not allow an interim declaration to be made.[211]

It is now clear that the powers of the court in respect of the executive are not so limited as was previously believed. First, the court may grant injunctive relief where necessary to protect rights under Community law.[212] Second, the House of Lords held in *M v Home Office*, applying ss 23(2) and 38(2) of the 1947 Act, that the restrictions on injunctive relief do not apply to applications for judicial review, which are not 'proceedings against the Crown' for the purposes of the 1947 Act.[213] Third, it was also held in *M v Home Office* that s 21(2) of the 1947 Act does not prevent injunctive relief being granted against officers of the Crown (including ministers) who have personally committed or authorised a tort and applies only in respect of duties laid on the Crown itself. As Lord Woolf said, 'it is only in those situations where prior to the Act no injunctive relief could be obtained that s 21 prevents an injunction being granted'.[214] But he added that declaratory relief against officers of the Crown should normally be the appropriate remedy.

Other provisions maintaining the special position of the Crown include the rule that judgment against a department cannot be enforced by the ordinary methods of levying execution or attachment; the department is required by the Act to pay the amount certified to be due as damages and costs (s 25);[215] and that there can be no order for restitution of property, but the court may declare the claimant entitled as against the Crown (s 21(1)).

An action for a declaration may be brought against the Crown without claiming other relief, for example where a wrong is threatened,[216] but not to determine hypothetical questions which may never arise, for example, as to whether there is a contingent liability to a tax.[217]

In civil litigation, when the claimant seeks an interim injunction against the defendant to maintain the status quo pending the final decision, the court grants such a request only if the claimant gives an undertaking as to damages, so that the defendant's loss may be made good if the action

---

[209] *Tamaki v Baker* [1901] AC 561.
[210] *Merricks v Heathcoat-Amory* [1955] Ch 567.
[211] See *R v IRC, ex p Rossminster Ltd* [1980] AC 952. See now Civil Procedure Rules, r 25.1(1)(b).
[212] *Case C-213/89, R v Transport Secretary, ex p Factortame Ltd (No 2)* [1991] 1 AC 603; ch 8 D.
[213] [1994] 1 AC 377; S Sedley, in Forsyth and Hare (eds), *The Golden Metwand and the Crooked Cord*, pp 253–66; T Cornford, in Sunkin and Payne (eds), *The Nature of the Crown*, ch 9.
[214] [1994] 1 AC 377, 413, disapproving *Merricks v Heathcoat-Amory* above (note 210); and see H W R Wade (1991) 107 LQR 4.
[215] Cf *Gairy v A-G of Grenada* [2001] UKPC 30, [2002] 1 AC 167 (rule of no coercive relief against Crown yields to G's constitutional right not to be deprived of property without compensation).
[216] *Dyson v A-G* [1912] 1 Ch 158.
[217] *Argosam Finance Co v Oxby* [1965] Ch 390.

ultimately fails. When the Crown is seeking to assert rights of property or contract, the Crown may be expected to give such an undertaking. But when the Crown takes proceedings to enforce the law, an undertaking as to damages is generally not appropriate.[218]

In Scotland, which has a distinct system of civil procedure, actions in respect of British or United Kingdom departments (like the Ministry of Defence or HM Revenue and Customs) may be brought against the Advocate General for Scotland, an office created by the Scotland Act 1998; in respect of departments of the devolved Scottish Administration, actions are brought against the Lord Advocate.[219] Actions may be raised by and against the Crown in either the Court of Session or the sheriff court. So far as remedies against the Crown are concerned, the decision in *M v Home Office* did not in terms extend to Scotland, given that separate provision applying to Scottish civil procedure had been made in the Crown Proceedings Act 1947. In *Davidson v Scottish Ministers*[220] the House of Lords had to decide whether the Court of Session had power to grant interim or final interdicts against the Crown in cases brought by way of judicial review, or whether s 21(1)(a) of the 1947 Act, which appeared to rule this out, applied only to proceedings against the Crown to enforce private rights. Overruling earlier Scottish authority to the contrary, the Lords held that the 1947 Act had never been intended to prevent the Scottish courts granting interim or final interdicts against the Crown in proceedings (analogous to judicial review) that invoked the 'supervisory jurisdiction'[221] in relation to acts of the Crown or its officers. In broad terms, this confirmed that the benefit of the principle in *M v Home Office* could extend to Scotland. When the devolved prison service in Scotland broke an undertaking it had given to the court not to open certain mail being received by a prisoner, the Lords held that in relation to contempt of court, ministers and civil servants in the Scottish government are in the same position as their counterparts in Whitehall.[222]

Non-disclosure of evidence: public interest immunity

Disclosure of documents in civil litigation (formerly termed discovery) is a procedure by which a party may inspect all documents in the possession or control of an opponent which relate to the matters in dispute. By s 28 of the 1947 Act, the court may order discovery against the Crown and may require the Crown to answer interrogatories, that is, written questions to obtain information from the other party on material facts. But the Act expressly preserves the existing rule of law (formerly known as 'Crown privilege') that the Crown may refuse to disclose any document or to answer any question on the ground that this would be injurious to the public interest; the Act even protects the Crown from disclosing the mere existence of a document on the same ground. Public interest immunity (which became known as PII in the wake of the Matrix Churchill trial in 1992 discussed below) is not restricted to proceedings in which the Crown is a party and may apply also to civil proceedings between private individuals. Although PII is important for the police, its main function is as a means of keeping secret information held by central government. Vital defence and security interests must be protected against the harmful exposure of information in judicial proceedings. But who should decide in a particular situation what must not be disclosed? It is not surprising that ministers and officials may be tempted to exaggerate the harm that would be done by disclosing information they wish to keep secret. But even if they were always to resist the temptation,[223] they are not in a position to assess the harm to the system of justice if the court is barred from seeing relevant information. That being so, the courts have a

---

[218] *Hoffmann-La Roche & Co v Trade Secretary* [1975] AC 295 (enforcement of price control for drugs). And see *Kirklees Council v Wickes Building Supplies Ltd* [1993] AC 227.

[219] Crown Suits (Scotland) Act 1857 as amended by the Scotland Act 1998, Sch 8, para 2.

[220] [2005] UKHL 74, 2005 SLT 110, overruling *McDonald v Secretary of State for Scotland* 1994 SLT 692.

[221] See p 725 above.

[222] See *Beggs v Scottish Ministers* [2007] UKHL 3, [2007] 1 WLR 455.

[223] And they do not – see below *R (Binyam Mohamed) v Foreign Secretary* [2010] EWCA Civ 65.

vital role to play in balancing the need for secrecy against the demands made by the law makes. This role of the courts saw a remarkable development over the second half of the twentieth century, and the challenge to the system of justice continues today.

1 **The leading cases.** We can start at the height of the Second World War with the decision in *Duncan* v *Cammell Laird & Co.*[224]

> Early in 1939 a new submarine sank while on trial with the loss of 99 lives, including civilian workmen. Many families of those who died brought actions in negligence against the company which had built the submarine under contract with the Admiralty. In a test action, the company objected to producing documents relating to the design of the submarine. The First Lord of the Admiralty directed the company not to produce the documents on the ground of Crown privilege, since disclosure would be injurious to national defence. *Held* (House of Lords) the documents should not be disclosed. Although a validly taken objection to disclosure was conclusive, and should be taken by the minister himself, the decision ruling out such documents was that of the judge. In deciding whether it was his duty to object, a minister should withhold production only where the public interest would be harmed, for example, where disclosure would be injurious to national defence or to good diplomatic relations, 'or where the practice of keeping a class of documents secret is necessary for the proper functioning of the public service'.[225]

On this basis, documents might be withheld either because the *contents* of those documents must be kept secret (as in *Duncan*'s case itself) or on the much wider ground that they belonged to a *class* of document which must be treated as confidential, for example civil service memoranda and minutes, to guarantee candour of communication on public matters within government. Thereafter, the practice developed of withholding documents simply on the minister's assertion that they belonged to a class of documents which it was necessary to withhold 'in the public interest for the proper functioning of the public service'.[226] It seemed that the courts could not overrule the minister's objection if taken in correct form.

Concern at these wide claims was to an extent eased when in 1956 privilege ceased to be claimed for factual reports about accidents involving government employees and certain medical reports. From 1962, statements made to the police during criminal investigations were not withheld where the police were sued for malicious prosecution or wrongful arrest, and might at the discretion of the judge be disclosed in other civil proceedings, provided that police informers were not identified.[227] But despite these concessions, it was still considered that in English law a minister's decision to withhold documents was conclusive.[228] By contrast, in Scots law a court was obliged to take account of the minister's decision but could in exceptional circumstances overrule it if the interests of justice so required: justifying this position, Lord Radcliffe said: 'The interests of government, for which the Minister should speak with full authority, do not exhaust the public interest'.[229]

In 1968, in a landmark decision, the Lords overruled an objection by the Home Secretary to production of certain police reports.

> In *Conway* v *Rimmer*[230] a former probationary constable, C, sued a police superintendent for malicious prosecution after an incident of a missing electric torch had led to C being acquitted of theft and then dismissed from the police. The Home Secretary claimed privilege for (a) probationary reports on C and (b) the

---

[224] [1942] AC 624. For the subsequent history, see J Jacob [1993] PL 121.

[225] [1942] AC at 642.

[226] See *Ellis* v *Home Office* [1953] 2 QB 135 and *Broome* v *Broome* [1955] P 190 for the harsh operation of the rule; and J E S Simon [1955] CLJ 62.

[227] See HL Deb, 6 June 1956, cols 741–8 and 8 March 1962, col 1191.

[228] Foe decisions questioning this, see *Merricks* v *Nott-Bower* [1965] 1 QB 57 and *Re Grosvenor Hotel London (No 2)* [1965] Ch 1210; D H Clark (1967) 30 MLR 489.

[229] *Glasgow Corpn* v *Central Land Board* 1956 SC (HL) 1, 19. And see *Whitehall* v *Whitehall* 1957 SC 30.

[230] [1968] AC 910; D H Clark (1969) 32 MLR 142.

defendant's report on the investigation into the incident. He certified that these were confidential reports within a class of documents production of which would be injurious to the public interest. *Held,* the court has jurisdiction to order the production of documents for which immunity is claimed. The court will give full weight to a minister's view, but this need not prevail if the relevant considerations are such that the judges have the experience to weigh them.

The House of Lords thus established that it is for the courts to hold the balance in the contest between secrecy and disclosure. *Conway* v *Rimmer* enabled English law on this matter to be brought broadly into line with Scots law. It opened the way for further decisions on issues that included (*a*) the use as evidence of material which is subject to constraints of confidentiality; (*b*) disclosure of documents relating to the formulation of government policy; (*c*) the grounds which must be shown before the court will inspect documents; and (*d*) the use of public interest immunity in criminal proceedings.

In *Rogers* v *Home Secretary,*[231] the Lords refused to order production of a secret police report to the Gaming Board about an applicant for a gaming licence, holding that the report fell into a class of documents which should not be disclosed. It was emphasised that the power to withhold evidence on grounds of public interest should not be described as a privilege of the Crown.

The fact that documents are regarded as confidential by their authors is no reason why they should as a class be immune from disclosure on grounds of public interest. Where a government department holds material supplied in confidence by companies regarding commercial activities, the court's decision on disclosure will depend on an assessment of factors such as the reasons for disclosure and the harm that disclosure might cause to the public interest.[232]

In *D* v *National Society for Prevention of Cruelty to Children,* the House of Lords held that public interest as a ground for non-disclosure of confidential material was not confined to the efficient functioning of government departments.[233] The Court of Appeal had ordered the NSPCC to reveal the identity of someone who had informed it of a suspected case of child abuse. The NSPCC, established by royal charter, had a statutory responsibility to take proceedings for the care of children. The Lords held, by analogy with the rule protecting the identity of police informers, that the names of informants to the society should not be disclosed.

In *Science Research Council* v *Nassé,*[234] the House of Lords held that on an employee's complaint of unlawful discrimination, no question of public interest immunity (PII) could arise in respect of confidential reports on other employees held by the employer. Lord Scarman stated that PII was restricted 'to what must be kept secret for the protection of government at the highest levels and in the truly sensitive areas of executive responsibility'.[235] However, the language of PII was used in *Campbell* v *Tameside Council,* where a teacher had been assaulted by an 11-year-old pupil and wished to see psychologists' reports held by the council; the Court of Appeal ordered discovery after inspecting the reports, since the public interest in the administration of justice outweighed any harm to the public service resulting from production of the reports.[236]

In *Conway* v *Rimmer,* which concerned low-level police reports, Lord Reid had said that Cabinet minutes and documents concerned with policy-making were protected against disclosure, as the inner working of government should not be exposed to ill-informed and biased criticism.[237] In *Burmah Oil Co Ltd* v *Bank of England,*[238] the issue arose of whether such high-level documents were always protected from disclosure.

---

[231] [1973] AC 388.

[232] Compare *Crompton Amusement Machines Ltd* v *Commissioners of Customs and Excise* [1974] AC 405 and *Norwich Pharmacal Co* v *Commissioners of Customs and Excise* [1974] AC 133.

[233] [1978] AC 171.

[234] [1980] AC 1028.

[235] Ibid, at 1088.

[236] [1982] QB 1065.

[237] [1968] AC 910, 952; see also Lord Upjohn at 993.

[238] [1980] AC 1090; D G T Williams [1980] CLJ 1.

In 1975 Burmah Oil had with government approval agreed to sell its holdings in BP stock to the Bank of England as part of an arrangement protecting the company from liquidation. Later the company sued to have the sale set aside as unconscionable and inequitable. It wished to see documents held by the bank, including (a) minutes of meetings attended by ministers and (b) communications between senior civil servants on policy matters. The Crown contended that it was 'necessary for the proper functioning of the public service' that the documents be withheld. The House of Lords *held* that the Crown's claim of immunity was not conclusive. If it was likely (or reasonably probable) that the documents contained matter that was material to the issues in the case, the court might inspect them to determine where the balance lay between the competing public interests. Having inspected the documents, the Lords ordered that they be not produced since they did not contain material necessary for disposing fairly of the case.

In *Burmah Oil*, the judges had moved far beyond the position in *Conway* v *Rimmer*, accepting that there might be circumstances in which a high-level governmental interest must give way before the interests of justice. Even Cabinet papers are not immune from disclosure in an exceptional case where the interests of justice so require.[239]

Did *Burmah Oil* mean that the judges should regularly inspect and if necessary order production of documents relating to policy-making within government? In *Air Canada* v *Trade Secretary*[240] the House of Lords upheld the Secretary of State's claim for immunity and refused to inspect the documents. In civil litigation, as the rules then stood, one party might inspect relevant documents held by the other side if discovery was *necessary* either for disposing fairly of the action or for saving costs.[241] In *Air Canada*, the House applied to a judicial review case stricter rules than would apply to litigation between private parties where public interest immunity was not claimed. The majority (Lords Fraser, Wilberforce and Edmund-Davies) held that for a court to exercise the power of inspection, it was not sufficient that the documents *might* contain information relevant to the issues in dispute; the party seeking access to the documents must show that it was *reasonably probable* that the documents were likely to help his or her case. A speculative belief to this effect was not enough. This decision was a reminder that even in judicial review proceedings, the court does not have a power at will to inspect all relevant documents held within government. We shall see below that the Human Rights Act has made it somewhat easier for an order of disclosure to be obtained in judicial review proceedings.[242]

In *R* v *Chief Constable of West Midlands Police, ex p Wiley*,[243] the House of Lords held, overruling decisions by the Court of Appeal,[244] that confidential statements made during investigation of complaints against the police were not as a class immune from disclosure in civil litigation. 'The recognition of a new class-based public interest immunity requires clear and compelling evidence that it is necessary', said Lord Woolf; no sufficient case had been made to justify a general immunity for such statements held by the police. But a statement need not be disclosed if it identified the identity of a police informer.

Although PII arose in the context of civil litigation, immunity from disclosure extends to criminal proceedings, albeit in a different form.[245] Plainly the public interest in keeping material secret can be damaged by disclosure wherever it occurs, but the public interest in the administration of

---

[239] As in the Australian case of *Sankey* v *Whitlam* (1978) 21 ALR 505. See also *Air Canada* v *Trade Secretary* [1983] 2 AC 394, 432 (Lord Fraser); I G Eagles [1980] PL 263. And cf *US* v *Nixon* 418 US 683 (1974), when the interests of criminal justice led to disclosure of the Watergate tapes.

[240] [1983] 2 AC 394; Lord Mackay (1983) 2 CJQ 337 and T R S Allan (1985) 101 LQR 200.

[241] RSC Ord 24. See now Civil Procedure Rules, part 31, esp r 31.19.1.

[242] See *Tweed* v *Parades Commission for Northern Ireland* (below). In ch 31, see text to notes 69–71.

[243] [1995] 1 AC 274.

[244] Including *Makanjuola* v *Metropolitan Police Commissioner* [1992] 3 All ER 617.

[245] *R* v *Ward* [1993] 2 All ER 577, *R* v *Davis* [1993] 2 All ER 643. And see *Rowe* v *UK* (2000) 8 BHRC 325. The present rules on disclosure in criminal procedure are outside the scope of this work; but see *R* v *H* [2004] UKHL 3, [2004] 2 AC 134.

justice is at its strongest when, if evidence is withheld from production in a criminal trial, this may prevent the accused from establishing a defence.[246]

In November 1992, the trial of three Matrix Churchill executives for the unlawful export of arms to Iraq brought these issues to public notice. Before the trial, four ministers had signed PII certificates withholding documents that concerned whether the defendants' purpose in exporting machinery to Iraq was known to the security services and thus to the government. PII was claimed on 'class' grounds that included protecting the functioning of government and maintaining the secrecy of intelligence operations. Having inspected the documents, the trial judge ordered disclosure, and the trial collapsed.[247] Sir Richard Scott's inquiry into 'arms for Iraq' made a penetrating study of the use of PII certificates in the case.[248] Among his criticisms were that 'class' claims for PII had been made which ought to have had no place in a criminal trial, that the claims extended to documents 'of which no more could be said than that they were confidential', and that inadequate and misleading advice had been given to ministers when they were asked to sign PII certificates.[249] This included advice that in effect left ministers with no option but to claim immunity on a class basis, even if the public interest did not require such a claim to be made. This view of the law was corrected in *R v Chief Constable of West Midlands Police, ex p Wiley*, where the Lords held that documents which are relevant to litigation *should* be produced unless disclosure would cause substantial harm. 'A rubber stamp approach to public interest immunity by the holder of a document is neither necessary nor appropriate.'[250]

In response to the Scott report, the Attorney General in 1996 reviewed the use of PII for government documents in England and Wales, and stated that the government would no longer rely on the former division into 'class' and 'contents' claims. Ministers would in future claim PII 'only when it is believed that disclosure of a document would cause real harm to the public interest'. PII certificates would identify in more detail the contents of a document and the damage which disclosure would do, and this would 'allow even closer scrutiny of claims by the court, which is always the final arbiter'.[251] It is now settled that when ministers have claimed PII for evidence in civil litigation, it is for the judge to whom such a claim is made to study the evidence and decide whether the public interest in keeping the material secret is outweighed by the interests of justice.[252]

2 Public interest immunity today. The law has thus come a very long way since *Duncan v Cammell Laird* distinguished between 'contents' and 'class' as a basis for withholding documents in the public interest. The government's decision in 1996 not to withhold documents on 'class' grounds probably contributed to an immediate reduction in the number of reported cases concerning PII in civil litigation. But the potential for tension between executive secrecy and open justice has intensified since 9/11, as the effects of the 'war against terror' have impinged upon basic human rights.

One indication of this is the increasing use of procedure whereby the executive appoints special advocates to 'represent' an individual when the court is dealing with secret material that cannot be disclosed to the individual. Special advocates were authorised by the Special Immigration

---

[246] Non-disclosure by the prosecution, with the judge's approval, of relevant evidence by reason of PII may cause a trial to be unfair in breach of art 6(1) ECHR: see *Edwards and Lewis v UK* (2003) 15 BHRC 189 (evidence re entrapment), distinguishing *Jasper v UK* (2000) 30 EHRR 441.

[247] See A W Bradley [1992] PL 514, A T H Smith [1993] CLJ 1, I Leigh [1993] PL 630. On the Scott report, see [1996] PL 357–507; also I Leigh and L Lustgarten (1996) 59 MLR 695.

[248] In the Scott report (HC 115, 1995–6), see on PII vol III, chs G.10–15 and G.18; vol IV, ch K.6. Also R Scott [1996] PL 427; Tomkins, *The Constitution after Scott*, ch 5; I Leigh, in Thompson and Ridley (eds), *Under the Scott-light*, pp 55–70.

[249] Scott report, para G18.104.

[250] [1995] 1 AC 274, 281 (Lord Templeman). And see *Savage v Chief Constable of Hampshire* [1997] 2 All ER 631.

[251] HC Deb, 18 December 1996, cols 949–50. And see M Supperstone [1997] PL 211.

[252] In *Somerville v Scottish Ministers* [2007] 1 UKHL 44, [2007] 1 WLR 2734, the Lords reminded the Scottish courts that this was the duty of the judge at first instance.

Appeals Commission Act 1997 for certain immigration appeals, but the model was applied without statutory authority by the Parole Board.[253] In exceptional cases, the criminal courts accept the use of specially appointed advocates to make submissions to the judge about the material to be protected, on condition that no information is passed to the defendant or the defendant's representatives.[254] The issue of a PII certificate in judicial review proceedings is not in itself a reason for the appointment of a special advocate to deal with material that cannot be disclosed to the claimant, since it is primarily for the judge to decide where the balance of interests may lie.[255] The use of special advocates does not ensure that the individual has a fair hearing that satisfies Art 6(1) ECHR.[256]

Another repercussion of the 'war on terror' on the protection of human rights is seen in *R (Binyam Mohamed) v Foreign Secretary*.[257]

> A former detainee at Guantanomo Bay sought judicial review of a refusal by the Foreign Secretary to provide information relevant to his trial on terrorist charges in the USA. After protracted hearings over material withheld by the Foreign Secretary, and after dealing with much of this material in closed proceedings, the Divisional Court decided to include in its published judgment seven brief paragraphs confirming that the claimant had suffered, at the least, cruel, inhuman and degrading treatment at the hands of the US authorities. The Foreign Secretary argued that publication of the court's conclusions would prejudice co-operation between the British and US security services. The Court of Appeal held that the claim to PII was not justified in the context of the litigation: the paragraphs did not reveal information that would be of interest to a terrorist or harmful to national security, and the information was already in the public domain. The argument to censor the published judgment engaged 'concepts of democratic accountability and, ultimately, the rule of law itself'.[258]

Finally, one effect of the Human Rights Act 1998 is that many claims for judicial review now turn on whether acts of a public authority that restrict a Convention right satisfy the test of proportionality. For this reason, in *Tweed v Parades Commission of Northern Ireland*,[259] where the commission's decision regarding a proposed parade was challenged, the House of Lords held that the court should adopt a more flexible and less restrictive approach to disclosure on judicial review, and should deal with the request for disclosure in the light of all the circumstances. If the applicant requested disclosure of a complete document rather than the defendant's summary of it, it should be inspected by the judge to decide whether disclosure could affect the outcome of the challenge. If so, the judge would need at that point to decide any claim to PII that the defendant had made.

---

[253] *R (Roberts) v Parole Board* [2005] UKHL 45, [2005] 2 AC 738; and see pp 600, 690 above.

[254] See *R v H* [2004] UKHL 3, [2004] 2 AC 134, paras [10]–[39]. The 'closed material' procedure requiring a special advocate may be used on a civil claim for damages: *Bisher Al Rawi v Security Service* [2009] EWHC 2959 (QBD).

[255] *Murungaru v Home Secretary* [2008] EWCA Civ 1015; *Home Secretary v AHK* [2009] EWCA Civ 287, [2009] 1 WLR 2049.

[256] *Home Secretary v AF (No 3)* [2009] UKHL 28, [2009] 3 WLR 74, applying *A v UK* (2009) 26 BHRC 1.

[257] [2010] EWCA Civ 65, on appeal from the Divisional Court at [2009] EWHC 2549.

[258] Ibid, [56]. For stringent judicial criticism of failings by the Ministry of Defence in regard to PII certificates, see *Khuder Al-Sweady v Defence Secretary* [2009] EWHC 1687 (Admin).

[259] [2006] UKHL 53, [2007] 1 AC 650. And see O Saunders [2008] JR 244.

BIBLIOGRAPHY

ADLER, M (ed.), *Adminstrative Justice in Context*, 2010

ADLER, M, & BRADLEY, A W (eds), *Justice, Discretion and Poverty*, 1976

AITKEN, J, *Officially Secret*, 1971

AKDENIZ, Y, WALKER, C, & WALL, D (eds), *The Internet, Law and Society*, 2000

ALDERMAN, R K, & CROSS, J A, *The Tactics of Resignation*, 1967

ALEXANDER, L (ed.), *Constitutionalism: Philosophical Foundations*, 1998

ALLAN, T R S, *Constitutional Justice: A Liberal Theory of the Rule of Law*, 2001

ALLAN, T R S, *Law, Liberty and Justice: The Legal Foundations of British Constitutionalism*, 1993

ALLASON, R, *The Branch: A History of the Metropolitan Police Special Branch 1883–1983*, 1988

ALLEN, C K, *Law and Orders*, 3rd edn, 1965

ALLEN, C K, *Bureaucracy Triumphant*, 1931

ALLISON, J W F, *A Continental Distinction in the Common Law: A Historical and Comparative Perspective on English Public Law*, rev edn, 2000

ALLISON, J W F, *The English Historical Constitution: Continuity, Change and European Effects*, 2007

ALSTON, P (ed.), *The EU and Human Rights*, 1999

AMERY, L S, *Thoughts on the Constitution*, 2nd edn, 1953

AMOS, M, *Human Rights Law*, 2006

ANDENAS, M, & FAIRGRIEVE, D (eds), *Tom Bingham and the Transformation of the Law*, 2009

ANDREW, C, *Secret Service: The Making of the British Intelligence Community*, 1985

ANDREWS, J A (ed.), *Welsh Studies in Public Law*, 1970

ANSON, W R, *The Law and Custom of the Constitution*, vol. I, *Parliament* (ed. M L Gwyer), 5th edn, 1922; vol. II, *The Crown* (ed. A B Keith), 4th edn, 1935

ARNULL, A, *The European Union and its Court of Justice*, 2nd edn, 2006

ARNSTEIN, W L, *The Bradlaugh Case*, 1965

ARROWSMITH, S, *The Law of Public and Utilities Procurement*, 2nd edn, 2005

ARTHURS, H W, *Without the Law: Administrative Justice and Legal Pluralism in the 19th Century*, 1985

AUBREY, C, *Who's Watching You?*, 1981

AUST, A, *Modern Treaty Law and Practice*, 2000

AUSTIN, J, *The Province of Jurisprudence Determined* (ed. H L A Hart), 1954

BAGEHOT, W, *The English Constitution* (introduction R H S Crossman), 1963

BAILEY, S H (ed.), *Cross on Local Government Law*, looseleaf, 1991

BAILEY, S H, HARRIS, D, & JONES, T, *Civil Liberties: Cases and Materials* (6th edn by S H Bailey and N Taylor), 2009

BALDWIN, J R, WIKELEY, N, & YOUNG, R, *Judging Social Security: The Adjudication of Claims for Benefit in Britain*, 1992

BALDWIN, R, *Rules and Government*, 1995

BARENDT, E, *Broadcasting Law: A Comparative Study*, 1993

BARENDT, E, *Freedom of Speech*, 2nd edn, 2005

BARNETT, A (ed.), *Power and the Throne: the Monarchy Debate*, 1994

BARNETT, A, *This Time: Our Constitutional Revolution*, 1997

BARNETT, J, *Inside the Treasury*, 1982

BASSETT, R G, *1931: Political Crisis*, 1958

BEATSON, J, & CRIPPS, Y (eds), *Freedom of Expression and Freedom of Information*, 2000

BEATSON, J, MATTHEWS, M H, & ELLIOTT, M, *Administrative Law: Text and Materials*, 3rd edn, 2005

BEER, S H, *Modern British Politics*, 1965

BEER, S H, *Treasury Control*, 2nd edn, 1957

BELL, J S, *French Constitutional Law*, 1992

BELLAMY, R, *Political Constitutionalism: A Republican Defence of the Constitutionality of Democracy*, 2007

BENNION, F, *Statutory Interpretation: A Code*, 5th edn, 2008

BENTHAM, J, *Handbook of Political Fallacies* (ed. H A Larrabee), 1962

BERCUSSON, B, *European Labour Law*, 2nd edn, 2009

BERGER, R, *Impeachment*, 1973

BERKELEY, H, *The Power of the Prime Minister*, 1968

BETTEN, L, & GRIEF, N, *EU Law and Human Rights*, 1998

BINGHAM, T, *The Rule of Law*, 2010

BIRKINSHAW, P, *Freedom of Information*, 3rd edn, 2001

BIRKINSHAW, P, *Reforming the Secret State*, 1991

BIRRELL, D, & MURIE, A, *Policy and Government in Northern Ireland: Lessons of Devolution*, 1980

BLACKBURN, R, *The Electoral System in Britain*, 1995

BLACKBURN, R, *King and Country: Monarchy and the Future King Charles III*, 2006

BLACKBURN, R, *The Meeting of Parliament*, 1990

BLACKBURN, R & PLANT, R (eds), *Constitutional Reform: The Labour Government's Constitutional Reform Agenda*, 1999

BLACKBURN, R, & POLAKIEWICZ, J (eds), *Fundamental Rights in Europe: The European Convention on Human Rights and its Member States 1950–2000*, 2001

BLACKSTONE, *Commentaries on the Laws of England*, 10th edn, 1787; 14th edn, 1803

BLOM-COOPER, L, DREWRY G, & DICKSON, B (eds), *The Judicial House of Lords, 1876–2009*, 2009

BLOM-COOPER, L J, & DREWRY, G, *Final Appeal*, 1972

BOGDANOR, V, *Devolution in the United Kingdom*, 1999

BOGDANOR, V, *Politics and the Constitution*, 1996

BOGDANOR, V, *The Monarchy and the Constitution*, 1995

BOGDANOR, V, *Multi-party Politics and the Constitution*, 1983

BOGDANOR, V, *The New British Constitution*, 2009

BOGDANOR, V, *The People and the Party System*, 1981

BOGDANOR, V (ed.), *The British Constitution in the Twentieth Century*, 2003

BOLINGBROKE, H ST J, *Political Writings* (ed. D Armitage), 1997

BOOTH, C, & SQUIRES, D, *The Negligence Liability of Public Authorities*, 2006

BRAGG, B, *A Genuine Expression of the Will of the People*, 2001

BRAZIER, R, *Constitutional Practice*, 3rd edn, 1999

BRAZIER, R, *Constitutional Reform: Re-shaping the British Political System*, 3rd edn, 2008

BRAZIER, R, *Ministers of the Crown*, 1997

BREWER-CARIAS, A R, *Judicial Review in Comparative Law*, 1989

BRIDGES, LORD, *The Treasury*, 2nd edn, 1966

BRIDGES, L, MESZAROS, G, & SUNKIN, M, *Judicial Review in Perspective*, 2nd edn, 1995

BRODY, R, & RATNER, M (eds), *The Pinochet Papers*, 2004

BROMHEAD, P A, *Private Members' Bills in the British Parliament*, 1956

BROWN, L N, & BELL, J S, *French Administrative Law*, 5th edn, 1998

BROWN, L N, & KENNEDY, T, *The Court of Justice of the European Communities*, 5th edn, 2000

BROWNLIE, I, *Principles of Public International Law*, 7th edn, 2008

BROWNLIE, I, & GOODWIN-GILL, G S, *Basic Documents on Human Rights*, 6th edn, 2010

BRYCE, J, *Studies in History and Jurisprudence*, 1901

BUCKLAND, P, *The Factory of Grievances*, 1979

BUNYAN, T, *The Political Police in Britain*, 1976

BURROWS, N, *Devolution*, 2000

BUTLER, D, *Governing without a Majority: Dilemmas for Hung Parliaments in Britain*, 1983

BUTLER, D (ed.), *Coalitions in British Politics*, 1978

BUTLER, D E, *The Electoral System in Britain since 1918*, 2nd edn, 1963

CALVERT, H, *Constitutional Law in Northern Ireland*, 1968

CAMPBELL, C, *Emergency Law in Ireland 1918–1925*, 1994

CAMPBELL, T D, EWING, K D, & TOMKINS, A (eds), *Sceptical Essays on Human Rights*, 2001

CANE, P, *Administrative Law*, 4th edn, 2004

CANE, P, *Administrative Tribunals and Adjudication*, 2009

CARD, R, *Public Order Law*, 2000

CARMICHAEL, P, & DICKSON, B, *The House of Lords*, 1999

CARNALL, G, & NICHOLSON, C (eds), *The Impeachment of Warren Hastings*, 1989

CARR, C, *Concerning English Administrative Law*, 1941

CARTWRIGHT, T J, *Royal Commissions and Departmental Committees in Britain*, 1975

CHESTER, D N, *The Nationalization of British Industry, 1945–51*, 1975

CHESTER, D N, & BOWRING, N, *Questions in Parliament*, 1962

CHITTY, J, *Prerogatives of the Crown*, 1820

CLARK, D, & MCCOY, G, *The Most Fundamental Legal Right: Habeas Corpus in the Commonwealth*, 2000

CLARKE, R, *New Trends in Government*, 1971

CLAYTON, R, & TOMLINSON, H, *Civil Actions Against the Police*, 3rd edn, 2003

CLAYTON, R, & TOMLINSON, H, *The Law of Human Rights*, 2nd edn, 2009

CLYDE, LORD, & EDWARDS, D J, *Judicial Review*, 2000

COLLINS, H, EWING, K D, & MCCOLGAN, A, *Labour Law*, 2nd edn, 2005

CONVERY, J, *The Governance of Scotland*, 2000

COOK, R, *The Point of Departure*, 2003

COOMBES, D, *The Member of Parliament and the Administration*, 1966

CORNFORD, T, *Towards a Public Law of Tort*, 2008

COSGROVE, R A, *The Rule of Law: Albert Venn Dicey, Victorian Jurist*, 1980

COWLEY, P (ed.), *Conscience and Parliament*, 1998

COWLEY, P, *The Rebels: How Blair Mislaid his Majority*, 2005

CRAIES, W F, *On Legislation* (ed. D Greenberg) 9th edn, 2008

CRAIG, P P, *Administrative Law*, 6th edn, 2008

CRAIG, P P, *Public Law and Democracy in the UK and the USA*, 1991

CRAIG, P P, & DE BURCA, G, *EU Law: Text, Cases and Materials*, 4th edn, 2007

CRAIG P P, & RAWLINGS, R W, *Law and Administration in Europe: Essays in Honour of Carol Harlow*, 2003

CRAUFURD SMITH, R, *Broadcasting Law and Fundamental Rights*, 1997

CRICK, B, *The Reform of Parliament*, 2nd edn, 1968

CRIPPS, Y, *The Legal Implications of Disclosure in the Public Interest*, 2nd edn, 1994

CROSS, R, & TAPPER, C, *Evidence* (ed. C Tapper), 11th edn, 2007

CROSS, R, *Precedent in English Law* (eds R Cross & J W Harris), 4th edn, 1991

CROSS, R, *Statutory Interpretation* (eds J Bell & G Engle), 1995

CYGAN, A J, *The United Kingdom Parliament and European Union Legislation*, 1998

DAINTITH, T C, & PAGE, A C, *The Executive in the Constitution: Structure, Autonomy and Internal Control*, 1999

DALE, W, *The Modern Commonwealth*, 1983

DALYELL, T, *Devolution, the End of Britain?*, 1977

DAVIES, P L, & FREEDLAND, M R, *Labour Legislation and Public Policy: A Contemporary History*, 1993

DAVIS, K C, *Discretionary Justice*, 1969

D'ENTREVES, A P, *The Notion of the State*, 1967

DE SMITH, S A, *The New Commonwealth and its Constitutions*, 1964

DEAKIN, S, & MORRIS, G S, *Labour Law*, 5th edn, 2009

DEVINE, T M, *The Scottish Nation 1700–2000*, 1999

DICEY, A V, *The Law of the Constitution* (ed. E C S Wade), 10th edn, 1959

DICEY, A V, & RAIT, R S, *Thoughts on the Union between England and Scotland*, 1920

DONALDSON, A G, *Some Comparative Aspects of Irish Law*, 1957

DONALDSON, F, *The Marconi Scandal*, 1962

DONALDSON, G, *Edinburgh History of Scotland*, vol. 3, *James V–James VII*, 1965

DOUGLAS-SCOTT, S, *The Constitutional Law of the European Union*, 2002

DREWRY, G (ed.), *The New Select Committees*, 2nd edn, 1989

DRUCKER, H (ed.), *Scottish Government Yearbook 1980*, 1980

DUMMETT, A, & NICOL, A, *Subjects, Citizens, Aliens and Others: Nationality and Immigration Law*, 1990

DWORKIN, R, *Taking Rights Seriously*, 1977

EDWARDS, J LI J, *The Attorney-General, Politics and the Public Interest*, 1984

EDWARDS, J LI J, *The Law Officers of the Crown*, 1964

ELLIOTT, M, *The Constitutional Foundations of Judicial Review*, 2001

ELLIS, E, *The Principle of Proportionality in the Laws of Europe*, 1999

ELTON, G R, *Studies in Tudor and Stuart Politics and Government* (2 vols), 1974

ENDICOTT, T, *Administrative Law*, 2009

ENGLEFIELD, D (ed.), *Commons Select Committees*, 1984

ERSKINE MAY, *Parliamentary Practice (The Law, Privileges, Proceedings and Usage of Parliament)* (ed. W R McKay), 23rd edn, 2004

EVANS, G (ed.), *Labor and the Constitution, 1972–1975*, 1977

EVATT, H V, *The King and His Dominion Governors*, 1936

EVELEGH, R, *Peace Keeping in a Democratic Society*, 1978

EWING, K D, *Britain and the ILO*, 2nd edn, 1994

EWING, K D, *The Funding of Political Parties in Britain*, 1987

EWING, K D, *Trade Unions, the Labour Party and the Law*, 1983

EWING, K D (ed.), *The Funding of Political Parties: Europe and Beyond*, 1999

EWING, K D, *The Cost of Democracy: Party Funding in Modern British Politics*, 2007

EWING, K D, *Bonfire of the Liberties: New Labour, Human Rights and the Rule of Law*, 2010

EWING, K D, & DALE-RISK, K, *Human Rights in Scotland – Text, Cases and Materials*, 2004

EWING, K D, & GEARTY, C A, *The Struggle for Civil Liberties: Political Freedom and the Rule of Law in Britain 1914–1945*, 2000

EWING, K D, & GEARTY, C A, *Freedom Under Thatcher: Civil Liberties in Modern Britain*, 1990

EWING, K D, & ISSACHAROFF, S (eds), *Party Funding and Campaign Financing in International Perspective*, 2006

FAIRGRIEVE, D, *State Liability in Tort*, 2003

FAIRGRIEVE, D, ANDENAS, M, & BELL, J (eds), *Tort Liability of Public Authorities in Comparative Perspective*, 2002

FAIRHURST, J, *Law of the European Union*, 7th edn, 2009

FARMER, J A, *Tribunals and Government*, 1974

FAWCETT, J E S, *The British Commonwealth in International Law*, 1963

FELDMAN, D J, *Civil Liberties and Human Rights in England and Wales*, 2nd edn, 2002

FELDMAN, D J (ed.), *English Public Law*, 2nd edn, 2009

FENWICK, H, *Civil Rights: New Labour, Freedom and the Human Rights Act*, 2000

FENWICK, H M, PHILLIPSON, G, & MASTERMAN, R M W (eds), *Judicial Reasoning under the UK Human Rights Act*, 2007

FERGUSON, W, *Edinburgh History of Scotland*, vol. 4, *1689 to the Present*, 1968

FFORDE, J S, *The Bank of England and Public Policy 1941–1958*, 1992

FINDLATER, R, *Banned!*, 1967

FINNIE, W, HIMSWORTH, C, & WALKER, N (eds), *Edinburgh Essays in Public Law*, 1991

FISHER, J, *British Political Parties*, 1996

FLINDERS, M, GAMBLE, A, HAY, C, & KENNY, C (eds), *The Oxford Handbook of British Politics*, 2009

FOLEY, M, *The Politics of the British Constitution*, 1999

FOLEY, M, *The Rise of the British Presidency*, 1993

FOLEY, M, *The Silence of Constitutions: Gaps, 'Abeyances' and Political Temperament in the Maintenance of Government*, 1989

FORD, P, & G (ed.), *Luke Graves Hansard's Diary, 1814–1841*, 1962

FORSEY, E A, *The Royal Power of Dissolution of Parliament in the British Commonwealth*, 1943

FORSYTH, C (ed.), *Judicial Review and the Constitution*, 2000

FORSYTH, C, & HARE, I (eds), *The Golden Metwand and the Crooked Cord: Essays in Honour of Sir William Wade*, 1998

FORSYTH, W, *Cases and Opinions on Constitutional Law*, 1869

FOSTER, C D, *British Government in Crisis*, 2005

FOX, H, *The Law of State Immunity*, 2003

FRANKLIN, M N, & NORTON, P (eds), *Parliamentary Questions*, 1993

FRANSMAN, L, *British Nationality Law*, 3rd edn, 2005

FREDMAN, S, & MORRIS, G S, *The State as Employer: Labour Law in the Public Services*, 1989

FREEMAN, E A, *The Growth of the English Constitution*, 1872

FRIEDMANN, W G, & GARNER, J F (eds), *Government Enterprise*, 1970

FRYDE, E B, & MILLER, E (eds), *Historical Studies of the English Parliament 1399–1603*, 1970

FULBROOK, J, *Administrative Justice and the Unemployed*, 1978

FULLER, L L, *The Morality of Law*, 1964

GALLIGAN, D J, *Discretionary Powers: A Legal Study of Official Discretion*, 1987

GANZ, G, *Quasi-Legislation: Recent Developments in Secondary Legislation*, 1987

GEARTY, C A, *Principles of Human Rights Adjudication*, 2004

GEARTY, C A (ed.), *European Civil Liberties and the European Convention on Human Rights*, 1997

GEARTY, C, *Civil Liberties*, 2007

GEARTY, C A, & KIMBELL, J A, *Terrorism and the Rule of Law*, 1995

GELLHORN, W, *Ombudsmen and Others*, 1966

GERHARDT, M J, *The Federal Impeachment Process: A Constitutional and Historical Analysis*, 2nd edn, 2000

GIBBONS, T, *Regulating the Media*, 2nd edn, 1997

GIDDINGS, P J (ed.), *Parliamentary Accountability: A Study of Parliament and Executive Agencies*, 1995

GILL, P, *Policing Politics*, 1994

GOFF, LORD & JONES, G H, *The Law of Restitution*, 7th edn, 2007

GOLDSWORTHY, J, *The Sovereignty of Parliament: History and Philosophy*, 1999

GOODWIN-GILL, G, *The Refugee in International Law*, 3rd edn, 2007

GOUGH, J W, *Fundamental Law in English Constitutional History*, 1955

GRAHAM, C, *Regulating Public Utilities*, 2000

GRAHAM, C, & PROSSER, T (eds), *Waiving the Rules: The Constitution under Thatcherism*, 1988

GRANT, W, & MARSH, D, *The Confederation of British Industry*, 1977

GRAYLING, A C, *Towards the Light: The Struggle for Liberty and Right that Made the Modern State*, 2007

GREGORY, R, & HUTCHESSON, P G, *The Parliamentary Ombudsman*, 1975

GREY, Earl, *Parliamentary Government*, 1864

GRIFFITH, J A G, *The Politics of the Judiciary*, 5th edn, 1997

GRIFFITH, J A G, *Parliamentary Scrutiny of Government Bills*, 1974

GRIFFITH, J A G, & RYLE, M, *Parliament* (eds R Blackburn and A Kennon), 2nd edn, 2002

GURRY, F, *Breach of Confidence*, 1984

HADDEN, T, & BOYLE, K, *The Anglo-Irish Agreement*, 1989

HADFIELD, B, *The Constitution of Northern Ireland*, 1989

HADFIELD, B (ed.), *Judicial Review, A Thematic Approach*, 1995

HADFIELD, B (ed.), *Northern Ireland: Politics and the Constitution*, 1992

HAILSHAM, LORD, *The Dilemma of Democracy*, 1978

HAILSHAM, LORD, *On the Constitution*, 1992

HALLIDAY, S, *Judicial Review and Compliance with Administrative Law*, 2004

HANHAM, H J, *The Nineteenth Century Constitution, 1815–1914*, 1969

HARDEN, I, *The Contracting State*, 1992

HARDING, A J, *Public Duties and Public Law*, 1989

HARLOW, C, *State Liability – Tort Law and Beyond*, 2004

HARLOW, C, & RAWLINGS, R, *Law and Administration*, 3rd edn, 2009

HARRIS, D, & DARCY, J, *The European Social Charter*, 2nd edn, 2001

HARRIS, D J, O'BOYLE, M, & WARBRICK, C, *Law of the European Convention on Human Rights*, 2nd edn, 2009

HARRIS, M, & PARTINGTON, M (eds), *Administrative Justice in the 21st Century*, 1999

HARRISON, A J, *The Control of Public Expenditure, 1979–1989*, 1989

HART, H L A, *The Concept of Law*, 1961

HART, H L A, & HONORE, A M, *Causation in the Law*, 1959

HARTLEY, T C, *The Foundations of European Community Law*, 6th edn, 2007

HARVEY, C, *Seeking Asylum in the UK: Problems and Prospects*, 2000

HATHAWAY, J, *The Law of Refugee Status*, 1991

HAWKINS, W, *Pleas of the Crown*, 6th edn (by T Leach), 2 vols, 1787

HAYEK, F A, *The Constitution of Liberty*, 1963

HAZELL, R (ed.), *The English Question*, 2006

HAZELL, R (ed.), *The State of the Nations 2003: The Third Year of Devolution in the United Kingdom*, 2003

HAZELL, R (ed.), *The State and the Nations: The First Year of Devolution in the United Kingdom*, 2000

HAZELL, R, & RAWLINGS, R W, *Devolution, Law Making and the Constitution*, 2005

HEALEY, D, *The Time of My Life*, 1989

HEARD, A, *Canadian Constitutional Conventions: The Marriage of Law and Politics*, 1991

HEARN, W E, *The Government of England*, 1867

HECLO, H, & WILDAVSKY, A, *The Private Government of Public Money*, 1974

HEDLEY, P, & AYNSLEY, C, *The D-Notice Affair*, 1967

HENDERSON, E G, *Foundations of English Administrative Law*, 1963

HENNESSY, P, *The Prime Minister: The Office and its Holders Since 1945*, 2000

HENNESSY, P, *Whitehall*, rev edn, 1990

HENNESSY, P, *Cabinet*, 1986

HEUSTON, R F V, *Essays in Constitutional Law*, 2nd edn, 1964

HEWART, LORD, *The New Despotism*, 1929

HILL, L B, *The Model Ombudsman*, 1976

HIMSWORTH, C M G, *Local Government Law in Scotland*, 1995

HIMSWORTH, C M G, & MUNRO, C R, *The Scotland Act 1998*, 2nd edn, 2000

HIMSWORTH, C M G, & O'NEILL, C M, *Scotland's Constitution: Law and Practice*, 2nd edn, 2009

HOBBY, C, *Whistleblowing and the Public Interest Disclosure Act 1998*, 2001

HOGG, P W, *Constitutional Law of Canada*, 4th edn, 1997

HOGG, P W, & MONAHAN, P, *Liability of the Crown*, 3rd edn, 2000

HOLDSWORTH, W, *A History of English Law* (14 vols), 1923–64

HOLT, J C, *Magna Carta*, 2nd edn, 1992

HOOD PHILLIPS, O, *Reform of the Constitution*, 1970

HOOD PHILLIPS, O, & JACKSON, P, *Constitutional and Administrative Law*, 8th edn (by P Jackson and P Leonard), 2001

HUNNINGS, N M, *Film Censors and the Law*, 1967

HUNT, M, *Using Human Rights Law in English Courts*, 1997

INGMAN, T, *The English Legal Process*, 12th edn, 2008

JACKSON, D, & WARR, G, *Immigration Law and Practice*, 4th edn, 2008

JACOB, J M, *The Republican Crown: Lawyers and the Making of the State in 20th Century Britain*, 1996

JACOBS, F G, & WHITE, R C A, *The European Convention on Human Rights* (eds C Overy and R C A White), 4th edn, 2006

JAMES, S, *British Cabinet Government*, 1992

JANIS, M, KAY, R, & BRADLEY, A W, *European Human Rights Law: Text and Materials*, 3rd edn, 2008

JEFFERSON, T, & GRIMSHAW, R, *Controlling the Constable: Police Accountability in England and Wales*, 1984

JENKINS, R, *A Life at the Centre*, 1991

JENKINS, R, *Mr Balfour's Poodle*, 1954

JENNINGS, I, *Cabinet Government*, 3rd edn, 1959

JENNINGS, I, *The Law and the Constitution*, 5th edn, 1959

JENNINGS, I, *Parliament*, 2nd edn, 1957

JENNINGS, R, & WATTS, A, *Oppenheim's International Law: The Law of Peace*, 9th edn, 1992

JOHNSTON, A, *The Inland Revenue*, 1965

JONES, A, & DOOBAY, A, *Extradition and Mutual Assistance*, 3rd edn, 2005

JONES, T, *Whitehall Diary*, vol. 3 (ed. R K Middlemas), 1971

JOSEPH, P A, *Constitutional and Administrative Law in New Zealand*, 3rd edn, 2007

JOWELL, J, & COOPER, J (eds), *Understanding Human Rights Principles*, 2001

JOWELL, J L, & OLIVER, D H (eds), *The Changing Constitution*, 3rd edn, 1994; 4th edn, 2000; 5th edn, 2004; 6th edn, 2007

JUSTICE, All Souls Committee, *Administrative Justice: Some Necessary Reforms*, 1988

KAVANAGH, A, *Constitutional Review under the UK Human Rights Act 1998*, 2009

KEATING, M J, & MIDWINTER, A, *The Government of Scotland*, 1983

KEETON, G W, *Trial by Tribunal*, 1960

KEIR, D L, & LAWSON, F H, *Cases in Constitutional Law*, 6th edn, 1979

KENNY, A (ed.), *The Oxford History of Western Philosophy*, 2000

KERR, J, *Matters for Judgment*, 1979

KING, A, *The British Constitution*, 2007

KING, A, *Does the United Kingdom still have a Constitution?*, 2001

KINLEY, D, *The European Convention on Human Rights: Compliance Without Incorporation*, 1993

KNEEBONE, S, *Tort Liability of Public Authorities*, 1998

KOSTAL, R W, *A Jurisprudence of Power: Victorian Empire and the Rule of Law*, 2005

LASKI, H J, *A Grammar of Politics*, 5th edn, 1967

LATHAM, R T E, *The Law and the Commonwealth*, 1949

LAUNDY, P, *The Office of Speaker*, 1964

LAWRENCE, R J, *The Government of Northern Ireland*, 1965

LAWSON, N, *The View from No. 11*, 1993

LEE, H P, HANKS, P, & MORABITO, V, *In the Name of National Security: The Legal Dimensions*, 1995

LEGOMSKY, S H, *Immigration and the Judiciary: Law and Politics in Britain and America*, 1987

LEIGH, I, & MASTERMAN, R, *Making Rights Real: The Human Rights Act in its First Decade*, 2008

LESTER, A, & BINDMAN, G, *Race and Law*, 1972

LESTER, A, PANNICK, D, & HERBERG, J (eds), *Human Rights Law and Practice*, 3rd edn, 2009

LE SUEUR, A (ed.), *Building the United Kingdom's Supreme Court – National and Comparative Perspectives*, 2003

LEWIS, A, *Make No Law*, 1991

LEWIS, C B, *Judicial Remedies in Public Law*, 4th edn, 2009

LIKIERMAN, J A, *Cash Limits and External Financing Limits*, 1981

LINKLATER, M, & LEIGH, D, *Not Without Honour*, 1986

LOCKE, J, *Two Treatises of Government* (ed. P Laslett), rev edn, 1988

LOUGHLIN, M, *Legality and Locality: The Role of Law in Central–Local Government Relations*, 1996

LOUGHLIN, M, *Public Law and Political Theory*, 1992

LOUGHLIN, M, *Local Government in the Modern State*, 1986

LOVELAND, I, *Political Libels: A Comparative Study*, 2000

LOVELAND, I, *By Due Process of Law? Racial Discrimination and the Right to Vote in South Africa 1850–1960*, 1999

LOVELAND, I D, *Constitutional Law, A Critical Introduction*, 5th edn, 2009

LOWELL, A L, *The Government of England*, 1912 edn

LUMB, R D, & MOENS, G A, *The Constitution of the Commonwealth of Australia* (7th edn by G Moens and J Trone), 2007

LUSTGARTEN, L, *The Governance of the Police*, 1986

LUSTGARTEN, L, & LEIGH, I, *In From the Cold: National Security and Parliamentary Democracy*, 1994

MACCORMICK, N, *Questioning Sovereignty: Law, State, and Nation in the European Commonwealth*, 1999

MACDONALD, I A, & WEBBER, J, *Immigration Law and Practice in the United Kingdom*, 6th edn, 2005

MCCABE, S, & WALLINGTON, P, *The Police, Public Order and Civil Liberties: Legacies of the Miners' Strike*, 1988

MCCRUDDEN, C (ed.), *Regulation and Deregulation: Policy and Practice in the Utilities and Financial Services Industries*, 1999

MCCRUDDEN, C, & CHAMBERS, G (eds), *Individual Rights and the Law in Britain*, 1993

MCILWAIN, C H, *Constitutionalism, Ancient and Modern*, 1947

MACKINTOSH, J P, *The British Cabinet*, 3rd edn, 1977

MACKINTOSH, J P, *Specialist Committees in the House of Commons – have they failed?* (rev), 1980

MCNAIR, LORD, *Law of Treaties*, 2nd edn, 1961

MCNAIR, LORD, & WATTS, A D, *The Legal Effects of War*, 4th edn, 1966

MAITLAND, F W, *The Constitutional History of England*, 1908

MAJOR, J, *The Autobiography*, 1999

MANN, F A, *Foreign Affairs in English Courts*, 1986

MANSON, A, & MULLAN, D (eds), *Commissions of Inquiry: Praise or Reappraise?*, 2003

MARGACH, J, *The Abuse of Power*, 1978

MARKESINIS, B S, *The Theory and Practice of Dissolution of Parliament*, 1972

MARKESINIS, B S, AUBY, J-B, COESTER-WALTJEN, D, & DEAKIN, S F, *Tortious Liability of Statutory Bodies: A Comparative and Economic Analysis of Five English Cases*, 1999

MARSHALL, G, *Constitutional Conventions*, 1984

MARSHALL, G, *Constitutional Theory*, 1971

MARSHALL, G, *Parliamentary Sovereignty and the Commonwealth*, 1957

MARSHALL, G, *Police and Government*, 1965

MARSHALL, G, & MOODIE, G C, *Some Problems of the Constitution*, 5th edn, 1971

MATHIJSEN, P S R F, *A Guide to European Union Law*, 8th rev edn, 2004

MIDDLEMAS, K, & BARNES, J, *Baldwin*, 1969

MILIBAND, R, *Capitalist Democracy in Britain*, 1982

MILL, J S, *Representative Government*, 1861

MILLETT, J D, *The Unemployment Assistance Board*, 1940

MILNE, D, *The Scottish Office*, 1957

MITCHELL, J D B, *Constitutional Law*, 2nd edn, 1968

MITCHELL, J D B, *The Contracts of Public Authorities*, 1954

MITCHELL, P, *The Making of the Modern Law of Defamation*, 2005

MONTESQUIEU, *The Spirit of the Laws* (eds A M Cohler, B C Miller & H S Stone), 1989

MOORE, W H, *Act of State in English Law*, 1906

MORE, J S, *Lectures on the Law of Scotland* (ed. J McLaren), 1864

MORGAN, J, *Conflict and Order: The Police and Labour Disputes in England and Wales 1900–39*, 1987

MORISON, J, & LIVINGSTONE, S, *Reshaping Public Power: Northern Ireland and the British Constitutional Crisis*, 1995

MORRIS, A (ed.), *The Growth of Parliamentary Scrutiny by Committee*, 1970

MORRIS, G S, *Strikes in Essential Services*, 1986

MORRIS, H F, & READ, J S, *Indirect Rule and the Search for Justice*, 1972

MORRISON, H, *Government and Parliament*, 3rd edn, 1964

MOSLEY, R K, *The Story of the Cabinet Office*, 1969

MOULES, R, *Actions against Public Officials: Legitimate Expectations, Misstatements and Misconduct*, 2009

MOUNT, F, *The British Constitution Now: Recovery or Decline?*, 1992

MOWBRAY, A R, *Cases and Materials on the European Convention on Human Rights*, 2nd edn, 2007

MOWBRAY, A R, *The Development of Positive Obligations under the ECHR by the European Court of Human Rights*, 2004

MUNRO, C R, *Studies in Constitutional Law*, 2nd edn, 1999

MUNRO, J, *Public Law in Scotland*, 2003

NAVOTS, S, *The Constitutional Law of Israel*, 2007

NICOL, D, *EC Membership and Judicialization of British Politics*, 2001

NICOLSON, I F, *The Mystery of Crichel Down*, 1986

NICOLSON, H, *King George V*, 1952

NOBLES, R, & SCHIFF, D, *Understanding Miscarriages of Justice*, 2000

NOLAN, LORD, & SEDLEY, S, *The Making and Remaking of the British Constitution*, 1997

NORMANTON, E L, *The Accountability and Audit of Governments*, 1966

NORTON, P, *Parliament in British Politics*, 2nd edn, 2005

NORTON, P, *The Commons in Perspective*, 1981

NORTON, P, *Dissension in the House of Commons 1945–1974*, 1975; *1974–1979*, 1980

O'CONNELL, D P, & RIORDAN, A, *Opinions on Imperial Constitutional Law*, 1971

O'HIGGINS, P, *Censorship in Britain*, 1972

OLIVER, D, *Constitutional Reform in the UK*, 2004

OLIVER, D, *Common Values and the Public-Private Divide*, 1999

OLIVER, D, & DREWRY, G (eds), *The Law and Parliament*, 1998

OLIVER, P C, *The Constitution of Independence: The Development of Constitutional Theory in Australia, Canada and New Zealand*, 2005

OLOWOFOYEKU, A, *Suing Judges: A Study of Judicial Immunity*, 1993

O'RIORDAN, T, KEMP, R, & PURDUE, M, *Sizewell B: An Anatomy of an Inquiry*, 1988

PAGE, A, REID, C, & ROSS, A, *A Guide to the Scotland Act 1998*, 1999

PAINE, T, *Rights of Man* (ed. B Kucklick), 1989

PANNICK, D, *Judicial Review of the Death Penalty*, 1982

PARRIS, H, *Constitutional Bureaucracy*, 1969

PARRY, C, *Nationality and Citizenship Laws of the Commonwealth*, 2 vols, 1957–60

PARTINGTON, M, *Introduction to the English Legal System*, 4th edn, 2008

PATERSON, A, *The Law Lords*, 1982

PEERS, S, *EU Justice and Home Affairs Law*, 2nd edn, 2006

PEERS, S, & WARD, A (eds), *The EU Charter of Fundamental Rights: Politics, Law and Policy*, 2004

PELLING, H, *The British Communist Party: A Historical Profile*, 1975

PHELAN, M, & GILLESPIE, J, *Immigration Law Handbook*, 6th edn, 2009

PIMLOTT, B, *The Queen: A Biography of Elizabeth II*, 1996

PINTO-DUSCHINSKY, M, *British Political Finance 1830–1980*, 1981

POLLOCK, F, & MAITLAND, F W, *History of English Law*, vol. 1, 1898

POLYVIOU, P G, *Entry, Search and Seizure: Constitutional and Common Law*, 1982

PONTING, C, *The Right to Know: The Inside Story of the Belgrano Affair*, 1985

PORT, F J, *Administrative Law*, 1929

PRECHAL, S, *Directives in EC Law*, 2nd edn, 2005

PRICE, R, DE SILVA, N, & CLAYTON, R, *Parker's Law and Conduct of Elections*, 1996

PROSSER, T, *Laws and the Regulators*, 1997

PROSSER, T, *Nationalised Industries and Public Control: Legal, Constitutional and Political Issues*, 1986

RANT, J W, *Court Martial and Service Law* (3rd edn by J Blackett), 2009

RAWLINGS, H F, *The Law and the Electoral Process*, 1988

RAWLINGS, R W, *Delineating Wales: Constitutional, Legal and Administrative Aspects of National Devolution*, 2003

RAZ, J, *Ethics in the Public Domain: Essays in the Morality of Law and Politics*, 1994

REID, G, *The Politics of Financial Control*, 1966

REINER, R, *The Politics of the Police*, 3rd edn, 2000

RENTON, R W, & BROWN, H H, *Criminal Procedure in Scotland*, 6th edn (by G H Gordon & C H W Gane) 1996

RICHARD, I, & WELFARE, D, *Unfinished Business: Reforming the House of Lords*, 1999

RICHARDS, P G, *Parliament and Conscience*, 1970

RICHARDS, P G, *Patronage in British Government*, 1963

RICHARDSON, G, & GENN, H (eds), *Administrative Law and Government Action: The Courts and Alternative Mechanisms of Review*, 1994

RILEY, P W J, *The Union of England and Scotland*, 1978

RIMINGTON, S, *Open Secret: The Autobiography of the Former Director-General of MI5*, 2001

ROBERTS, C, *The Growth of Responsible Government in Stuart England*, 1966

ROBERTS-WRAY, K, *Commonwealth and Colonial Law*, 1966

ROBERTSON, G, *Freedom, the Individual and the Law*, 7th edn, 1993

ROBERTSON, G, *Obscenity*, 1979

ROBSON, W A, *Justice and Administrative Law*, 3rd edn, 1951

ROBSON, W A, *Nationalised Industries and Public Ownership*, 2nd edn, 1962

ROGERS, S (ed.), *The Hutton Inquiry and its Impact*, 2004

ROSEVEARE, H, *The Treasury*, 1969

ROWAT, D C, *The Ombudsman*, 2nd edn, 1968

ROWBOTTOM, J, *Democracy Distorted: Wealth, Influence and Democratic Politics*, 2010

ROWE, P, *Defence: The Legal Implications*, 1987

ROWE, P (ed.), *The Gulf War 1990–91 in International and English Law*, 1993

ROWE, P, *The Impact of Human Rights Law on Armed Forces*, 2006

RUBIN, G R, *Private Property, Government Requisition and the Constitution 1914–1927*, 1994

RUBINSTEIN, A, *Jurisdiction and Illegality*, 1965

RUNCIMAN, W G, *Hutton and Butler: Lifting the Lid on the Workings of Power*, 2004

RUSSELL, M, *Reforming the House of Lords: Lessons from Overseas*, 2000

RYLE, M, & RICHARDS, P G (eds), *The Commons under Scrutiny*, 3rd edn, 1988

SAJO, A, *Limiting Government: An Introduction to Constitutionalism*, 1999

SAMBEI, A, & JONES, J, *Extradition Law Handbook*, 2005

SAMPFORD, C J H, *Retrospectivity and the Rule of Law*, 2006

SANDS, P, *Lawless World* (rev edn), 2006

SANDS, P, *Torture Team: Uncovering War Crimes in the Land of the Free* (rev edn), 2009

SAWER, G, *Federation under Strain*, 1977

SCARMAN, LORD, *English Law – The New Dimension*, 1974

SCHØNBERG, S, *Legitimate Expectations in Administrative Law*, 2000

SCHWARZE, J, *European Administrative Law*, rev edn, 2006

SENEVIRATNE, M, *Ombudsmen: Public Services and Administrative Justice*, 2002

SHARPE, R J, *The Law of Habeas Corpus*, 2nd edn, 1989

SHAW, J, *The Transformation of Citizenship in the European Union: Electoral Rights and the Restructuring of Political Space*, 2007

SHAW, M N, *International Law*, 6th edn, 2008

SHELL, D, *The House of Lords*, 2nd edn, 1992

SIBLEY, T, & JEFFRIES, J, *The Shameful Deportation of a Trade Union Leader*, 2008

SIMPSON, A W B, *Human Rights and the End of Empire: Britain and the Genesis of the European Convention*, 2001

SIMPSON, A W B, *In the Highest Degree Odious*, 1992

SIMPSON, A W B, *Pornography and Politics – the Williams Report in Retrospect*, 1983

SINGER, P, *Democracy and Disobedience*, 1973

SMITH, I T, & THOMAS, G H, *Employment Law*, 9th edn, 2007

SMITH, J C, & HOGAN, B, *Criminal Law* (ed. D Ormerod), 12th edn, 2008

SMITH, T B (ed.), *The Laws of Scotland: Stair Memorial Encyclopedia*, vols 1 & 5, 1987

SORENSEN, M (ed.), *Manual of Public International Law*, 1968

SPENCER, J R, *Jackson's Machinery of Justice*, 8th edn, 1989

STACEY, F, *Ombudsmen Compared*, 1978

STALKER, J, *Stalker*, 1988

STANTON, K, SKIDMORE, P, HARRIS, M, & WRIGHT, J, *Statutory Torts*, 2003

STEEL, D, *A House Divided; the Lib-Lab Pact and the Future of British Politics*, 1980

STEEL, D, *No Entry*, 1969

STEPHEN, J F, *Digest of Criminal Law*, 1877

STEPHEN, J F, *History of the Criminal Law of England* (3 vols), 1883

STEVENS, D, *UK Asylum Law and Policy: Historical and Contemporary Perspectives*, 2003

STEVENS, R, *Law and Politics: The House of Lords as a Judicial Body, 1800–1976*, 1979

STEVENS, R B, *The Independence of the Judiciary, The View from the Lord Chancellor's Office*, 1993

STEWART, J D, *British Pressure Groups*, 1958

STONE, R, *The Law of Entry, Search and Seizure*, 4th edn, 2005

STREET, H, *Freedom, the Individual and the Law*, 5th edn, 1982

STREET, H, *Governmental Liability*, 1953

STREET, H, *Justice in the Welfare State*, 2nd edn, 1975

SUNKIN, M, & PAYNE, S (eds), *The Nature of the Crown: A Legal and Political Analysis*, 1999

SUPPERSTONE, M, GOUDIE, J, & WALKER, P (eds), *Judicial Review*, 3rd edn, 2005

SWINFEN, D B, *Imperial Appeal: The Debate on the Appeal to the Privy Council, 1833–1986*, 1987

SWINFEN, D B, *Imperial Control of Colonial Legislation 1813–1865*, 1965

SYMES, M, & JORRO, P, *Asylum Law and Practice*, 2003

TAGGART, M (ed.), *The Province of Administrative Law*, 1997

TAGGART, M (ed.), *Judicial Review of Administrative Action in the 1980s*, 1987

TASWELL-LANGMEAD, T P, *English Constitutional History* (ed. T F T Plucknett), 11th edn, 1960

TERRY, C S, *The Scottish Parliament 1603–1707*, 1905

THAIN, C, & WRIGHT, M, *The Treasury and Whitehall*, 1995

THIO, S M, *Locus Standi and Judicial Review*, 1971

THOMPSON, B, & RIDLEY, F F (eds), *Under the Scott-light: British Government seen through the Scott Report*, 1997

THOMPSON, E P, *Whigs and Hunters: The Origin of the Black Act*, 1975

THOMPSON, E P, *Writing by Candlelight*, 1980

TILEY, J, *Revenue Law*, 6th rev edn, 2008

TOMKINS, A, *Our Republican Constitution*, 2005

TOMKINS, A, *The Constitution after Scott: Government Unwrapped*, 1998

TOWNSHEND, C, *Making the Peace: Public Order and Public Security in Modern Britain*, 1993

TRENCH, A (ed.), *The Dynamics of Devolution: The State of the Nations 2005*, 2005

TRENCH, A (ed.), *Has Devolution made a Difference? The State of the Nations 2004*, 2004

TRENCH, A (ed.), *The State of the Nations 2001: The Second Year of Devolution in the United Kingdom*, 2001

TRENCH, A (ed.), *The State of the Nations 2008*, 2008

TRIBE, L, *Constitutional Choices*, 1985

TRIDIMAS, T, *The General Principles of EU Law*, 2nd edn, 2006

TURNBULL, M, *The Spycatcher Trial*, 1989

TURPIN, C C, *Government Procurement and Contracts*, 1989

TUSHNET, M, *The Constitution of the USA: A Contextual Analysis*, 2009

VILE, M J C, *Constitutionalism and the Separation of Powers*, 1967

VOGLER, R, *Reading the Riot Act: The Magistracy, the Police and the Army in Civil Disorder*, 1991

WACKS, R, *Personal Information*, 1989

WACKS, R, *The Protection of Privacy*, 1980

WADE, H W R, *Constitutional Fundamentals*, 1980

WADE, H W R, & FORSYTH, C F, *Administrative Law*, 10th edn, 2009

WALKER, J, *The Queen has been Pleased*, 1986

WALKER, N, *Policing in a Changing Constitutional Order*, 1998

WALKER, P GORDON, *The Cabinet*, rev 1972

WALKER, S, *In Defense of American Liberties*, 1990

WALKER, C P, & STARMER, K, *Justice in Error*, 1993

WALKLAND, S A (ed.), *The House of Commons in the Twentieth Century*, 1979

WATT, B, *UK Election Law: A Critical Examination*, 2006

WEATHERILL, S, & BEAUMONT, P R, *EC Law*, 3rd edn, 1999

WEBB, P, *The Modern British Party System*, 2000

WEILER, J H H, *The Constitution of Europe: 'Do the new clothes have an emperor?' and Other Essays on European Integration*, 1999

WEIR, S, *Unequal Britain*, 2006

WEIR, S, & BEETHAM, D, *Political Power and Democratic Control in Britain*, 1999

WEST, N, *A Matter of Trust: MI5, 1945–72*, 1982

WEST, N, *MI5: British Security Service Operations 1909–45*, 1983

WHEARE, K C, *Modern Constitutions*, 2nd edn, 1966

WHEARE, K C, *The Constitutional Structure of the Commonwealth*, 1960

WHEARE, K C, *The Statute of Westminster and Dominion Status*, 5th edn, 1953

WHEELER-BENNETT, J, *King George VI*, 1958

WHITE, F, & HOLLINGSWORTH, K, *Audit, Accountability and Government*, 1999

WHITE, R M, & WILLOCK, I D, *The Scottish Legal System*, 4th edn, 2008

WHITLAM, G, *The Truth of the Matter*, 1979

WHITTINGTON, K E, *Constitutional Construction: Divided Powers and Constitutional Meaning*, 1999

WHITTY, N, MURPHY, T, & LIVINGSTONE, S, *Civil Liberties Law: The Human Rights Act Era*, 2001

WICKS, E, *The Evolution of a Constitution: Eight Key Moments in British Constitutional History*, 2006

WILLIAMS, E N, *The 18th Century Constitution, 1688–1815*, 1960

WILLIAMS, D G T, *Keeping the Peace*, 1967

WILLIAMS, D G T, *Not in the Public Interest*, 1965

WILLIAMS, G, *Media Ownership and Democracy*, 2nd edn, 1996

WILLIAMS, O C, *History of Private Bill Procedure*, 2 vols, 1949

WILLIS, J, *The Parliamentary Powers of English Government Departments*, 1933

WILSON, H, *The Governance of Britain*, 1976

WILSON, H, *The Labour Government, 1964–70*, 1974

WILSON, S S, *The Cabinet Office to 1945*, 1975

WINETROBE, B K, *Realising the Vision: A Parliament with a Purpose*, 2001

WOLFE, J N (ed.), *Government and Nationalism in Scotland*, 1969

WOODHOUSE, D, *The Office of Lord Chancellor*, 2001

WOODHOUSE, D, *Ministers and Parliament: Accountability in Theory and Practice*, 1994

WOODHOUSE, D (ed.), *The Pinochet Case: A Legal and Constitutional Analysis*, 2000

WOOLF, SIR H, *Protection of the Public – A New Challenge*, 1990

WOOLF, LORD, JOWELL, J & LE SUEUR, A, *De Smith's Judicial Review*, 6th edn, 2007

WYATT, D, & DASHWOOD, A, *European Union Law* (eds A Arnull, A Dashwood, M Ross and D Wyatt), 5th edn, 2006

YOUNG, A, *Parliamentary Sovereignty and the Human Rights Act*, 2009

YOUNG, H, *The Crossman Affair*, 1976

ZAMIR, I, WOOLF, LORD, & WOOLF, J, *The Declaratory Judgment*, 3rd edn, 2002

ZANDER, M, *Cases and Materials on the English Legal System*, 10th edn, 2007

ZANDER, M, *The Police and Criminal Evidence Act 1984*, 5th edn, 2005

ZIEGLER, K, BARANGER, D, & BRADLEY, A W, *Constitutionalism and the Role of Parliaments*, 2007

INDEX